DICTIONARY OF
Philosophy
AND Religion

DISCARD

DICTIONARY OF
Philosophy
AND Religion

Eastern and Western Thought

NEW AND ENLARGED EDITION

WILLIAM L. REESE

HUMANITIES PRESS
NEW JERSEY

First edition published 1980 by Humanities Press International, Inc.
165 First Avenue, Atlantic Highlands, New Jersey 07716

New and Enlarged edition first published in 1996

4/21/97 PH 25⁰⁰

© 1980, 1996 by William L. Reese

Library of Congress Cataloging-in-Publication Data
Reese, William L.
   Dictionary of philosophy and religion / William L. Reese. — New
and enlarged ed.
      p. cm.
   ISBN 0–391–03864–8. — ISBN 0–391–03865–6 (pbk.)
   1. Philosophy—Dictionaries. 2. Religion—Dictionaries.
   I. Title.
   B41.R43 1996
   103—dc20   95–52148
                                                       CIP

Printed in the United States of America

10 9 8 7 6 5 4 3 2 1

To L.F.R.
whose voice is still heard

CONTENTS

PREFACE

The present volume, although termed a *Dictionary of Philosophy and Religion*, has many encyclopedic features including analyses of the thought of virtually all major philosophers and religious leaders. It is a dictionary in the sense that its major emphasis is on explication of terms, while its encyclopedic aspect is a recognition that the key terms of philosophy and religion are best explored in the context of the conceptual systems of those who have introduced and developed them. One of the key features of the volume is the extent of its cross-references. The analysis of each thinker is presented in a numbered sequence of ideas, and references are made from concepts or topical headings to the location where the concept is treated in the entry of the individual thinker. For example, turning to the topic, "Universals," brings one to a discussion containing cross-references to the positions of 43 philosophers on the topic, constituting a comprehensive history of that concept in philosophy. Among the entries the reader will note that the mention of Plato is followed by "(*q.v.* 1)," directing one to the first point under the entry, "Plato," for further elucidation of his view of absolute realism in the context of his general philosophy. The mention of "Aristotle (*q.v.* 7)" similarly directs the reader to point number 7 in the Aristotle entry for elucidation of his view of moderate realism. "Ockham (*q.v.* 6)" refers to the sixth numbered point in the Ockham discussion for further information on his position of nominalism, and "Locke (*q.v.* 4)" refers one to the fourth point of the Locke entry for his view of conceptualism.

Cross-references run from philosophical movements as well as topics, to the positions of individual philosophers. By following out such references it should be possible to gain a "fix" on any important philosophical topic. The treatment of philosophical and religious ideas in their relations to individuals and movements is designed to encourage a process of orientation through conceptual triangulation, beginning from any term, person, or movement, and proceeding to the other two. General terms used in the sketches of individual philosophers will usually be found to have been treated in their own right, and lead to other individuals who have used the term in the same, or in a related, sense. In the case of most philosophers it has been possible to relate them to a movement, likewise treated, so that readers may refer from philosopher to school or movement, and thus to other philosophers with similar orientation. The reader is thus encouraged to engage in personal exploration of the themes, movements, and thinkers important in philosophy and religion.

It has been our goal to provide reliable, but not exhaustive, information on the topics treated. In this regard, in addition to the firmament of works of individual authors, every item of the dictionary has been checked against the following compendia: *Encyclopedia of Philosophy*, ed. Paul Edwards, 8 vols. (New York: Macmillan Company), 1967; *Diccionario de Filosofía*, ed. José Ferrater Mora, 4th edition, Editorial Sudamericana, 1958; the so-called philosophers' edition of the *Encyclopedia Britannica*, 11th edition, 30 vols., 1910; André Lalande, *Vocabulaire Technique et Critique de la Philosophie*, Neuvième Ed., 1962; *The Great Ideas: A Syntopicon* (Great Books of the Western World, ed.-in-chief, R.M. Hutchins), vols. 1 & 2; *Dictionary of Philosophy and Psychology*, ed. James Mark Baldwin, 3 vols., 1960; *The Concise Encyclopedia of Western Philosophy and Philosophers*, ed. J.O. Urmson (New York: Hawthorne Books, Inc.), 1960; John Passmore, *A Hundred Years of Philosophy* (London: Gerald Duckworth & Co., Ltd.), 1957; *Dictionary of Scholastic Philosophy*, ed. B. Wuellner, (Milwaukee: Bruce Publishing Co.), 1956; *The Encyclopedia of Religion*, ed.-in-chief, M. Eliade, 16 vols. (New York: Macmillan Publishing Co.), 1987; *Encyclopedia of Indian Philosophies*, ed. K. Potter and S. Bhattacharyya, 6 vols. (Princeton: Princeton University Press), 1978–92; *Abingdon Dictionary of Living Religions*, ed. by K. Crim (Nashville: Abingdon), 1981; *An Encyclopedia of Religion*, ed. Vergilius Ferm (New York: The Philosophical Library), 1945; *Encyclopedia of Religion and Religions*, ed. E. Royston Pike (New York: Meridian Books), 1959; *A Source Book in Indian Philosophy*, ed. S. Radhakrishnan and C.A. Moore (Princeton: Princeton University Press), 1957; *A Source Book in Chinese Philosophy*, trans. and comp. Wing-Tsit Chan (Princeton: Princeton University Press), 1963; Chandradhar Sharma, *Indian Philosophy: A Critical Survey* (New York: Barnes and Noble), 1962; and *Philosophers Speak of God*, ed. Hartshorne and Reese (Chicago: University of Chicago Press), 1953. In addition, substantial use has been made of the *Encyclopaedia of Religion and Ethics*, ed. James Hastings, 13 vols., (New York: Charles Scribner's Sons), 1908–26; W.C. and Martha Kneale, *The Development of Logic* (Oxford: Clarendon Press), 1962; and the Italian *Enciclopedia Filosofica*, 6 vols. (Firenze: G.C. Sansoni), 1967.

For more extensive analyses than we have provided, the reader should turn to the multi-volumed encyclopedias; *i.e.*, the sets edited by Edwards, Hastings, Ferrater Mora, Eliade, Potter, and the Italian encyclopedia. Finally, of course, the reader will consult the writings of the individuals themselves; the treatment of each individual includes a list of principal writings. One point of importance in the conceptual triangulation mentioned above is the desirability of moving from term and movement to bibliographies of the individual thinkers presented in the dictionary. If no writings are given, it is because none or only fragments have survived.

In addition to topics, individuals, and movements, the volume likewise contains sketches, both historical and analytical, of the fields of philosophy. Here the reader may gain initial orientation to the areas of ethics, aesthetics, value theory, epistemology, logic and philosophy of science—once again with cross-references to individual thinkers—as well as a discussion of the variety of ways in which philosophy, as a discipline, has been understood through the centuries. With respect to logic the dictionary contains an extensive list of informal fallacies with definitions and examples, discussions of immediate inference, syllogisms, the antilogism, the construction of truth tables, the propositional calculus, quantification theory, and the logic of relations.

The initial sentence of this Preface promised analyses of virtually all major philosophers and religious leaders. The limitation denotes those major figures whose work is so dependent on the statements of their colleagues in continuing dialogue that any free standing position is rare, and its summary statement both difficult to frame and provisional, because calendric. Nonetheless, for incontestably major figures of this kind we have provided such provisional summaries. In other cases we await further closure and disclosure.

The decision to compose a single dictionary of philosophy and religion derived from the observation that dictionaries of philosophy and dictionaries of religion necessarily make extensive reference to the other area. The inclusion of both in a single volume is thus natural, and makes possible a fuller appreciation of the similarities and differences of the two areas. The weighting of the dictionary in terms of Western philosophy, noted by some reviewers of the first edition, was more inevitable than deliberate. Our point in promising religion as well as philosophy, and East as well as West, is that religion is essential in understanding philosophy and, in a burgeoning world culture, inattention to Asian philosophy would be unthinkable. The second edition expands the openings into religion and Asian philosophy.

It was editor Richard Huett who in 1961 conceived the idea of the dictionary and enlisted my energies for its writing; he too whose encouragement at every stage made possible the project's continuing; and who in the situation of a serious derailment of plans helped the manuscript to its home in Humanities Press, one of the most distinguished imprints in philosophy. My gratitude to him is immense; it extends to Simon Silverman and Keith Ashfield as well. This second edition is dedicated to the memory of Lillian F. Reese, 1894–1945. The importance to this edition of W.L.R. III's contributions as Editorial and Research Assistant is here gratefully acknowledged.

William L. Reese
Slingerlands, New York

KEY

The abbreviations used in this volume include *q.v.* (refer to), *fl.* (flourished), *c.* (*circa*), arr. (arranged), ed. (edited), comp. (compiled), *cf.* (compare), as well as the language notations listed below.

The entries of the dictionary are liberally cross-referenced. When the reader comes upon a term or name followed by "*q.v.*" and a number, *e.g.*, Aristotle (*q.v.* 6), this means that the numbered point in the entry given (in our example, the 6th point of the Aristotle entry) contains additional information pertinent to the topic under discussion. One objective of the dictionary is maximum comprehensiveness. For this reason virtually every person or term mentioned anywhere in the text will have its own entry to which the reader may refer. In the case of the few individuals mentioned with no separate entry, their names, where mentioned, are generally accompanied by dates or major publications.

Apart from unusual cases, noted below, all titles of books listed in the dictionary are rendered in English. It is to be assumed in each case, however, unless contrary notice is given, that the writing was done in the language appropriate to the nationality of the speaker. During the Middle Ages that language was Latin for all of Europe. Where an author has written in several languages, the language of a given book is indicated by an appropriate notation ("E" for English, "F" for French, "G" for German, "Gr" for Greek, "H" for Hungarian, "L" for Latin, "S" for Swedish, "Skt." for Sanskrit, etc.). In some cases it was more convenient to provide information covering the languages of authorship in the text preceding the listed titles. Where the book has been translated into English, this fact is indicated by a capital "T" following the title. In general, translators' titles follow their originals very closely. In cases where a translator has departed widely from the author's title, we have provided our own close translation of the original title, followed by the translator's title. In all such cases the date given is that of the original publication, and not the publication date of the translation.

xiii

The only instance where titles are given in a foreign language are those where the translated volume has retained a non-English title, as in the case of Thomas Aquinas' *Summa Theologica*, or where translation provides no gain to the reader in terms of information, *e.g.*, Duns Scotus' *Quaestiones Quodlibetales*.

Of the problems involved in transliterating Sanskrit into the Roman alphabet, the three of most importance to us can be seen in the transliterated names "Kṛṣna" and "Śiva," which appear in widespread convention, the former with dots under the "r" and the "s," the latter with an "acute accent" mark over the "Ś." The phonetic representation of the first 2 examples is "Krishna," with an "i" appearing after the "r" and an "h" after the "s," and of the 3rd example "Shiva" with an "h" after the "S." To approximate this usage we have given the Romanized Sanskrit spellings in double form. In entry headings both forms are used. Since the "sh" and "ri" forms are closer to English pronunciation, that spelling is used ordinarily in the text. Exceptions to this occur when the transliterated Sanskrit is represented, *e.g.*, in the first line of an entry or within parentheses following the English usage of the transliterated Sanskrit term. With respect to Sanskrit titles the "s," "ś," and "r" forms are invariably used.

A

AARON BEN SAMUEL.
Q.v. Cabala (3a).

ABARBANEL.
Q.v. Leon Hebreo.

ABBOT, FRANCES ELLINGWOOD. 1836–1903.
American philosopher of religion. Born in Boston. Studied at Harvard and Meadville Theological Seminary (Chicago). Minister of Unitarian congregations in New Hampshire and Ohio. Editor of *The Index* (1870–80), which later became *The Monist*. Taught at Harvard (1888), filling in for Josiah Royce.

Main philosophical writings: *Scientific Theism*, 1885; *The Way Out of Agnosticism*, 1890; *The Syllogistic Philosophy* (2 vols.), 1906.

(1) Combining Darwin with Kant, and a criticism of Hegel, Abbot produced what he called "scientific realism," holding that relations are objective, and that existence and knowledge are in "dynamic correlation," both within ourselves and in nature. So understood scientific realism implies a scientific theism.

(2) Adding in Kantian ethics Abbot presented in his final work what he called "a unitary and universal system" uniting being, knowing, and doing.

ABDUCTION.
From the Latin *ab* ("away") and *ducere* ("to lead").

(1) In Aristotle abduction refers to those types of syllogistic inference which fail to carry certainty with them, whether due to a weak connection between the major and middle terms, or the middle and minor terms.

(2) For C. S. Peirce (*q.v.* 8), abduction is one of three basic forms of inference, along with induction and deduction.

Abduction is the means whereby hypotheses are generated, moving from a particular case to a possible explanation of the case. As in Aristotle, so for Peirce abduction is a mode of probable inference. For Peirce the inference has the following form: The surprisng fact, F, is observed. If H were true F would be commonplace. Therefore, H is (possibly) true.

ABE, MASAO.
Q.v. Emptiness.

ABELARD, PETER. 1079–1142.
French philosopher and theologian. Studied with Roscelin, and William of Champeaux. Among the disputations in which he was involved the one with William of Champeaux on the problem of universals (*q.v.*) turned out to be most constructive. Opened several schools of philosophy and theology, especially in Paris where, 1113, the celebrated, yet unfortunate, Heloise- Abelard story began. His book, *On the Divine Unity and Trinity*, was condemned as heretical and burned in 1121. Abbot of St. Gildas, 1125. He lectured at Ste. Genevieve, Paris, from 1136–49. Accused of heresy by St. Bernard and condemned by the Council of Sens, 1141. An appeal to Pope Innocent II led to a prohibition against his continuing to teach. Withdrew to Cluny where he remained until his death. His passionate faith in reason stirred all of Europe, and helped shape a new intellectual climate for the schools.

Principal writings: *Yes and No*, 1122; *Christian Theology* (T), 1124; *Theology of the "Supreme Good"* (T), and *Know Thyself* (T), between 1125–38; as well as four treatises on logic.

(1) Having studied under two teachers, Roscelin and William of Champeaux,

1

who stood at opposite poles on the question of universals, Abelard sought a middle way. This assertion oversimplifies the story but only in not being sufficiently tentative. Roscelin was, at least, widely understood to be an out and out nominalist, believing that individual things alone exist, and that the universal is a mere word (*flatus vocis*). Roscelin's student, William of Champeaux, held that each species of things has an essential nature, and this nature is in each individual thing belonging to that species, entirely and wholly present. The individual members of each species, then, differ from each other only accidentally.

(2) Abelard moved to his own position by means of a disputation with William of Champeaux. On William's view, Abelard contended, any one thing can really be said to be at the same time in different places: Socrates is really Plato, and occupies two places simultaneously. In addition, what we say of any two members of a species can also be said of God. God, too, is a substance, and is hence on this view identical with all that is, so that one consequence of the doctrine is pantheism. In countering such criticism William of Champeaux changed his view to hold that the essences or natures of any two things of the same species are numerically different, although alike in resulting in the same properties.

(3) Abelard's position would seem to be not very different from the position to which he forced William of Champeaux although Abelard approaches the problem in the manner of Roscelin. His doctrine includes at least the following points: (a) We predicate names of things; and there are both universal and particular names. (b) It is not the word as *flatus vocis* that we predicate of things, but the name or word in its logical content which we predicate, that is, the word as *sermo*. (c) This logical content is "common to all" to which it applies while "proper to none." It is the result of abstraction freed from the individuating circumstances of the individual thing. He also calls this content "a common and confused image of many things." The content of the universal words, or concepts, then may be said to be derived from the things, but not to be in them quite as we conceive that content. At the same time, however, he holds that the exemplars or divine ideas are in the mind of God; hence, his view fits both realism and conceptualism.

(4) Next in order of importance to his view of universals is the attitude expressed in his *Sic et Non*, or *Yes and No*, in which are collected contradictory opinions of the Fathers on the leading issues of theology and philosophy. He felt the individual thinker should be at liberty to judge among these alternatives, not forced to believe. Against most of the intellectuals of his day he believed in the primacy of inquiry over faith: "By doubting we are led to inquire, by inquiry we perceive the truth."

(5) In the *Scito Te Ipsum* or *Know Thyself* he developed the view that sin implies both knowledge and intent to do evil. This view places the ethical center of gravity in the will, and forces some adjustment in the doctrine of original sin.

(6) He made significant contributions to the development of logic. These are discussed under Logic (6).

ABHIDHAMMA (in Pali) AND ABHIDHARMA (in Sanskrit).

From *abhi* ("higher" or "special") and *dhamma* or *dharma* ("doctrine"). The terms refer to collections of Buddhist texts containing summaries of Buddhist doctrine, and are used in connection with the further term *pitaka*, meaning "collection" (literally, "basket"). The two major special doctrine collections are the Pali *Abhidhamma Pitaka* of the Theravada (*q.v.*) school, and the Sanskrit *Abhidharma Pitaka* of the Sarvastivada (*q.v.*) school, now extant only in Chinese, and only partially extant.

(1) The summaries, explanations, and analyses of these collections work from source material accepted as going back to Buddha himself. The initial *Dhamma* or *Dharma* ("doctrine") of Buddha's teaching makes up the five *Nikayas* (*nikaya*, Pali meaning "collection") or *Agamas* (Sanskrit meaning "tradition"), preserved under the collective name of the *Sutta Pitaka* (Sanskrit, "basket of sermons"). The disciplinary rules of Buddhist monasticism form a second early source, called the *Vinayas* (*vinaya*, Sanskrit for "discipline"), collected as the *Vinaya Pitaka* ("basket of discipline"). The *Dhamma* and the *Vinaya*, as

they were called, were not only committed to memory but studied and expounded, these studies formed the basis of the third collection, called the *Abhidhamma* or *Abhidharma Pitaka*.

(2) The canon of Buddhist scriptures was thus tripartite, a *Tripitaka* (*tipitaka* in Pali), or "three basket cannon." Both the Theravadan and Sarvastivadan schools worked from *Tripitakas*; and this seems to have been the case for each of the eighteen to twenty schools into which early Buddhism had divided. While these bodies of literature remained in agreement with respect to the first two baskets, the *Sutta* and *Vinaya Pitakas*, their third baskets differed radically. The reason is that the interpretations of the special doctrine baskets, despite their objective of providing insight into, and guidance for, Buddhist life and thought, while diminishing the possibility of further schisms, were made in separate schools, divided from each other both administratively and geographically. For this reason, while the *Abhidharma* and *Abhidhamma* collections consist of seven books dealing with a wide range of common topics, including problems of ethics, cosmology, consciousness, and the self, the material is quite different. The same must have been the case with each of the 18 to 20 "third basket" collections.

(3) The *Abhidharma Kośa* (*kośa* meaning "treasure" in Sanskrit) is a Nepalese collection, existing only in Tibetan and two Chinese versions. This material provides the basis of much Chinese and Japanese Buddhism.

(4) The canons are further augmented by numerous commentaries and other post-canonical works.

ABHINIVEŚA (ABHINIVESHA).
Sanskrit term signifying persistent attachment to multiplicity. One of the five kinds of delusive attachment of the Yoga system (*q.v.* Yoga 3).

ABORTION.
Q.v. Dworkin (4).

ABRAHAM BEN SAMUEL ABULIAFA.
Spanish cabalist. *Q.v.* Cabala (3c).

ABSOLUTE.
From the Latin *absolutus*, meaning "the perfect" or "completed." The term stands opposed to the *relative*, and frequently means simply the negation of the relative, *i.e.*, as that which is independent of relation. The term carries the sense of the fixed, the independent, the unqualified, the completed. Its principal use in philosophy has been in systems of metaphysics. It has also had use in value theory and in natural philosophy. At various times the term has been applied to *e.g.*, time, space, value, truth, and God. No easy classification of the uses of the term is possible. Descartes applied the term to the self-evident principles and demonstrated propositions capable of use in deducing solutions to further problems. Fichte applied the term to the ego as the initiating power of knowledge and reality. The Absolute, a noun standing for the name of God, was introduced in the East by Gaudapada (*q.v.* 1, 3) as early as the 6th century A.D.; and in the West (some 800 years later) by Nicholas of Cusa (*q.v.*), who regarded God as both Absolute Maximum and Absolute Minimum. The term was utilized by Fichte (*q.v.* 8), and Schelling (*q.v.* 1). Hegel uses the term (*q.v.* 3, 18, 22) as the name for the capstone entity of his system, the Absolute Spirit, which has dimensions of absolute truth and beauty. In this usage the term entered the vocabulary of 19th-century idealism, and continued to characterize representatives of this school into the 20th century. In most of its usages by idealist philosophers the term is employed in the original Latin sense, indicating a posited wholeness, unity, and completeness of reality, which yet somehow lies beyond the world of our experience. The Russian philosopher, Soloviev (*q.v.* 3) equated the Absolute with reality, which he regarded as a living organism. It has been used in the East in recent years (*q.v.* Sri Aurobindo 1) as an alternate term for Brahman.

ABSOLUTE EGO.
Q.v. Fichte (3).

ABSOLUTE IDEALISM.
Q.v. Idealism (3); Hegel (8–22).

ABSOLUTE PRAGMATISM.
Q.v. Royce (8).

ABSOLUTE REALISM.
Q.v. Realism (1); Universals (2, 4, 8, 12).

ABSOLUTE SUCHNESS.

Ashvaghosha's name for reality. *Q.v.* Aśvaghoṣa (1, 2, 5).

ABSOLUTION.

Q.v. Penance (2).

ABSTRACTION.

From the Latin *abstractus*, past participle of the verb *abstrahere* ("to draw from").

(1) In Aristotelian and Scholastic philosophy (*q.v.* Aristotle 3 and Thomas Aquinas 5) abstraction is the process whereby universal ideas come to be appropriated by the mind. Abstraction is possible because of the *hylomorphic* nature of substance, *i.e.*, that substance is composed of matter and form. The mind receives a sense datum or phantasm and draws out the form, thereby providing a universal for intellectual use.

(2) For Locke (*q.v.* 4) abstraction takes place by drawing out what is common to a group of individual things, on the basis of a comparison of their similarities and differences.

(3) In contemporary logic and mathematics abstraction is the name of that operation upon a variable which produces a function.

ABYSS.

Q.v. Valentinus; Jacob Boehme.

ACADEMY, PLATONIC.

Q.v. Plato's Academy.

ACCIDENT.

From the Latin *accidens*, present participle of *accidere*, "to happen."

In Aristotelian and Scholastic philosophy, that mode of being which inheres in some other being, such as the mode of existence of the redness in an apple. To be contrasted with substantial being, such as the mode of existence of the apple itself. Not only a quality such as redness, however, but any of the nine Aristotelian categories (*q.v.* Aristotle 4, 6) other than substance itself.

ACCIDENTAL FORM.

Q.v. Form (5c).

ACHILLES PARADOX.

Q.v. Zeno of Elea (5).

ACOSMISM.

From the Greek *a* ("not") and *kosmos* ("world"). The term was coined by Hegel to refer to the doctrine that the world is unreal and that only God exists. Hegel applied the term to the philosophy of Spinoza, but that may be a misapplication. The term fits more exactly the Acosmic Pantheism of Shankara. *Q.v.* Pantheism 9, 15.

ACQUAINTANCE, KNOWLEDGE BY.

Q.v. Russell (6).

ACT.

A Latin term derived from *agere* ("to do"). The Greek term is *energeia*.

(1) Aristotle (*q.v.* 7–8) contrasted act (*energeia*) with potency (*dynamis*), associating the former with form and the latter with matter.

(2) The same contrast in Scholastic philosophy is between *actus* and *potentia*. A distinction is made between first and second act. By "first act" is meant the form of a thing, and by "second act" the operation of the thing. "Act" suggests in this terminology both actuality and activity. In contrast to other beings, God is regarded as *actus purus*.

(3) Gentile (*q.v.* 1) spoke of his philosophy as a philosophy of the pure act. What he meant, however, was that action—in his sense, human activity—was to be given primary ontological status.

(4) Mead (*q.v.* 4) regarded the act, beginning with the gesture, as the central category of all analysis and meaning.

ACTION, PHILOSOPHY OF.

Q.v. Blondel (1).

ACTIONISM.

Q.v. Rudolf Eucken.

ACTUAL ENTITY.

Q.v. Whitehead (9).

ACTUALISM.

Q.v. Giovanni Gentile (1).

ACTUALITY.

Q.v. Aristotle (8); Weiss.

ACTUAL OCCASION.

Q.v. Whitehead (9).

ACTUS PURUS.

A Latin term meaning "pure act" or "pure actuality." This is the appropriate name for God in Scholastic philosophy. As purely actual, God is the one being without potentiality; hence the highest, or only complete, Being. *Q.v.* Aquinas (4); Act.

ACT UTILITARIANISM.

Q.v. Utilitarianism; Brandt (1).

ADAM KADMON.

The hermaphroditic, primordial man of the Cabala (*q.v.* 1f).

ADDITION.

Q.v. Propositional Calculus (11).

ADELARD OF BATH. 12th cent. A.D.

English philosopher. Taught in Paris and Laon. He translated Euclid from Arabic into Latin. In the medieval dispute over universals Adelard advanced a "doctrine of indifference" to the effect that, depending upon the way it is viewed, an object of the understanding can be regarded either as an individual or a universal. Nonetheless, he likewise held that the Platonic perspective represents the superior point of view.

Principal writings: *On the Things of Nature*; *On Questions of Nature*.

ADEQUATION.

From the Latin *ad* ("to") and *aequare* ("make equal"). Aquinas used the Latin *adequatio* in defining truth (*q.v.* 11) as the adequation of thought to thing.

AD HOC.

The Latin phrase, meaning "to this," suggests the directional character of the *ad hoc*. In the logic of explanation an *ad hoc* hypothesis (*q.v.* 7, 10) is one formed to explain a given phenomenon, but differing from powerful hypotheses in not being derivable from other phenomena or yielding other testable consequences. The value of such an hypothesis, applying only to the phenomenon from which it was derived, is hence open to considerable doubt.

ADIAPHORA.

Q.v. Melanchthon (1).

ADICKES, ERICH. 1866–1928.

German philosopher. Born near Bremen. Studied in Berlin. Taught at Münster and Tübingen. A representative of neo-Kantianism (*q.v.* 7) retaining the influence of his teacher Friedrich Paulsen (*q.v.*), Adickes came to the Kantian position after phases of voluntaristic pantheism and spiritual pluralism.

ADI GRANTH.

From the Sanskrit *adi* ("first") and *granth* ("book"). The sacred scriptures of the Sikhs (*q.v.* Sikhism), dating from 1604 A.D., dictated by the fifth guru, Arjun, in a succession of ten. The compilation consists of hymns and verses principally by Nanak (*q.v.*), the first guru, and founder of the religion, Amar Das the third guru, and Arjun, the fifth, although it also includes material from the ninth guru, hymns of pre-Nanak saints, and the verses of early Sikh poets. The final compilation of material, the *Dasam Granth* ("tenth book") was compiled in 1704 by the tenth guru, Govind Singh. Thereafter the title of guru was bestowed on the *Dasam Granth*, itself, as the "true emperor."

ADLER, FELIX.

Q.v. Ethical Culture.

ADOPTIONISM.

The theological doctrine that Christ, born as a mortal being, became the Son of God by adoption. The doctrine, appearing in several forms in the first three centuries A.D., led to the Adoptionist Controversy in 8th-century Spain, and was condemned in the Charlemagne-sponsored synods of 792, 794, and 799.

ADORNO, THEODOR W. 1903–1969.

Born in Frankfurt, Germany. Educated at the University of Frankfurt. Co-director of the Institute For Social Research (1955–58), and director (1958–69), of this organized center of the Frankfurt School (*q.v.*).

Principal writings: *Dialectic of Enlightenment* (with M. Horkheimer) (T), 1944 (initially titled *Philosophical Fragments*); *Philosophy of Modern Music* (T), 1949; *The Authoritarian Personality* (with other members of the Frankfurt School) (T), 1950; *Minima Moralia: Reflections From Damaged Life* (T), 1951; *Prisms* (T), 1955.

(1) Although Adorno agreed with, and contributed to, the thrust of the Frankfurt School in its criticism of positivism and industrial society, and its rethinking

of Marxism (for these aspects of his work (*q.v.* Frankfurt School 2–4), his special contribution came from his "negative dialectics." On the surface this suggests that he retained of Marxism no more than its critique of bourgeois class-consciousness. His special point of view, however, can be seen to have its source in Marx.

(2) The point of the negative dialectics is that a single principle applies to all social and philosophical theories: "The whole is the false," and truth resides only in discrepant details which are aphoristic in form. "Every thought which is not idle," he tells us, has "branded on it the impossibility of its full legitimation." Every totalizing synthesis falsifies its own content and becomes pretentious.

(3) What is true in philosophy is also true of music. Composers introduce fresh musical qualities out of their own subjective freedom, *e.g.*, tonality in Beethoven's case. But these qualities must be made part of a rational whole. When organized, the subjectivity and freedom are lost. Indeed, "the new ordering of twelve-tone technique virtually extinguishes the subject."

(4) Life itself "describes a wavering, deviating line, disappointing by comparison with its promises." Something positive, however, remains. The one thing the negative critique accomplishes is keeping open the promise that things might be better in some alternative approach to knowledge and society even though such a promise, actualized, would also fail. The promise is a far cry from the Marxist vision of a classless society, yet it is derived from that source.

(5) Adorno's opposition to totalization and his sense of damaged life originated in his work on aesthetics. His Frankfurt School predecessor in aesthetics was Walter Benjamin (*q.v.* Frankfurt School, The. A.), in whose studies on Brecht (*Understanding Brecht* (T), posthum. 1966), and Baudelaire (*Charles Baudelaire* (T) published in sections 1939–1968 and *The Arcades Work* in *Collected Works*, 1955), the argument was made that the fetishism of commodities (*q.v.* Marx 10) had fragmented modern experience. From Benjamin's standpoint, Baudelaire's poetry and Proust's prose reflected, while trying to overcome, such fragmentation. This is the fragmentation treated by Adorno.

From this standpoint it can be seen that Adorno's position comes from Marx through Benjamin.

AD QUEM.
From the Latin *ad* ("to") and *quem* ("which"). The phrase, along with *ad quod* ("to what") is used in referring to the end point, tendency, or goal of an argument or chain of reasoning. To be contrasted with *a quo*, referring to the corresponding beginning point.

AD QUOD.
Q.v. Ad Quem.

ADṚṢṬA (ADRISHTA).
Q.v. Vaiśeṣika (5).

ADVAITA.
Sanskrit term meaning "nonduality." The term refers to the central idea of the Vedantic philosophy that one's self (the *atman*), and the soul of all things (the Brahman) are identical. The school of Indian thought stressing nonduality is known as *Advaita Vedanta* (*q.v.* Vedanta 2). The religio-philosophical task of human life is to dispel our mistaken beliefs in duality, including, of course, the belief in our separateness from Brahman. The chief representatives of the school are Gaudapada (*q.v.*) and Shankara (*q.v.* 1–4).

ADVENTITIOUS IDEAS.
One of Descartes' three classes of ideas, along with "factitious" and "innate" (*q.v.* Descartes 4). Adventitious ideas come from experience, entering the mind through sensation.

AELIUS THEON.
Q.v. Rhetoric (10).

AENESIDEMUS. 1st century B.C.
Greek philosopher. Born in Crete. Taught in Alexandria. Reviving Pyrrhonism (*q.v.*) and systematizing its arguments, Aenesidemus set its form of extreme skepticism against both Stoicism and the moderate skepticism of the Academy (*q.v.* Plato's Academy).

Principal writings: *Pyrrhonic Discourses*, 8 volumes; only references remain.

(1) Following Pyrrho (*q.v.*) with respect both to suspending judgment on all matters, as well as the development of *ataraxia*, or imperturbability, Aenesidemus

developed the tropes, or headings, which require the suspension of judgment.

(2) He organized his tropes into a list of ten. Judgment must be suspended due to: (a) the variety of species among living forms manifesting different modes of perception; (b) the variety of classes of men manifesting individual differences; (c) differences in the data given by different senses; (d) differences in perception due to different states of every organism; (e) the differences following the variety of positions one can take up with respect to an observed object including distance; (f) differences in the medium through which perception occurs; (g) differences in the states of the objects themselves; (h) the impossibility of eliminating the contradictions and discriminating between the multiplicity of factors involved in judgment; (i) differences due to frequency of occurrence, the rare occurrence seeming wondrous due to infrequency alone; (j) and differences due to customs, habits, beliefs, and states of development of different peoples.

(3) He argued against causality on the ground that, *e.g.*, if cause precedes effect there must be a moment when the particular cause has caused and the effect not yet begun, and this moment reveals the incoherence of the idea.

AEON.

Among Valentinian Gnostics, especially, the name given to the semi-divine, spiritual intermediaries emanating from God and bridging between God and the material world, which meant—in their view—bridging between good and evil. *Q.v.* Valentinus.

AESTHETICISM.

Q.v. Walter Pater (1).

AESTHETICS.

From the Greek *aisthesis* ("sensation"). This term has come to designate not the whole domain of the sensible, but only that portion to which the term "beauty" may apply. The term was introduced by Baumgarten (*q.v.* 1, 3) who defined the term broadly, although theory of beauty made up part of the study. Herbart (*q.v.* 1, 4) also used the term in a broad sense. It was really Hegel who canonized the more limited reference of the term by using it to refer to his writings on art.

Theories concerning the nature of the beautiful in art or in art and nature, however, begin at least with Socrates, and have engaged the energies of philosophers ever since. Among significant theories the following may be cited:

(1) A number of Indian philosophers, scattered through the ages, associated for example, with the Sankhya and Vedanta systems, find the blissful goal of life to be aesthetic in nature, and related to equanimity, a kind of inner harmony. Sankhya thinkers relate it to reason, Advaitan Vedantas to the *atman* (*q.v.*). Among the paths to God for some is the cultivation of one's aesthetic sense. The sound "Brahman," considered to be the origin of speech, is also the origin of music. Music, then, can serve as a path to God, and becomes a kind of Yoga (*q.v.*).

(2) Plato (*q.v.* 1, 5g) held to an imitation theory of art, believing art to be an imitation of some aspect of the space-time world which was for him an imitation of an imitation. Beauty, on the other hand, referred to the symmetry and proportion of form; and was to be found primarily in the abstract ideas after which the world is patterned, in his view.

(3) Aristotle (*q.v.* 13) modifying Plato's imitation theory so that art became an imitation not of an actual, but of a possible thing, produced a theory in which beauty depends on organic unity, a unity in which every part contributes to the quality of the whole.

(4) A somewhat similar point of view has been expressed in this century by DeWitt Parker, who held that the master principle of form is organic unity; and that this supposes the organization of all the elements of the experience into a single, inclusive whole.

(5) Plotinus (*q.v.* 8) associated the beautiful with a radiance or splendor, resulting from the quality of unity in the object. For Plotinus the One was a divine principle, more or less completely reflected in the world.

(6) Thomas Aquinas (*q.v.* 10) combines principles from his predecessors, while developing the concept at the same time. Beauty is that which gives pleasure on sight, and is hence related to the cognitive faculties. Beautiful objects must have integrity or perfection, proportion or harmony, and brightness or clarity.

(7) In the 20th century Jacques Maritain (*q.v.* 3) continued this tradition, holding that the view of beauty as a transcendental, of art as a concrete embodiment of beauty pleasing to the intellect, and a sign of something more divine, can be illuminating to the modern mind.

(8) Shaftesbury (*q.v.* 1–2) and Hutcheson (*q.v.* 2) interpret beauty in terms of a special inner sense sensitive to harmony.

(9) Immanuel Kant (*q.v.* 9) turned our attention to the aesthetic judgment, finding beauty in whatever produced a sense of harmony in the relations between the faculties of the will and the understanding.

(10) Friedrich Schiller (*q.v.* 1) believed the aesthetic to be the basic category of life, stemming from a play impulse, and allowing morality and feeling to coexist in unity.

(11) Hegel (*q.v.* 18–19) finds beauty to be the presentation of truth in sensuous form. Put otherwise, it is the Absolute shining through appearance.

(12) Bosanquet (*q.v.* 4) is a follower of Hegelian idealism in aesthetic terms, utilizing Hegel's notion of the "concrete universal," and the importance of imagination.

(13) Croce (*q.v.* 2) likewise followed the idealistic tradition, finding beauty in the specific act of the imagination which produces a novel and complete intuition. Secondarily, it is found in the successful expression of such acts.

(14) For Schopenhauer (*q.v.* 5), the aesthetic moment comes in an appreciation of an idea apart from its particularity by a knower who has escaped the conditions of his individual existence. It is just as true to say that the aesthetic involves the appreciation of the throbbing will in things by an awareness liberated for the moment from the conditions of particular existence.

(15) Nietzsche (*q.v.* 1) follows Schopenhauer in holding that emotion in art represents the underlying dynamism of the universe, and is for that reason attractive to us. At the same time, however, the highest art—as in tragedy—combines Apollonian rationality with Dionysiac passion.

(16) Tolstoy (*q.v.* 3), indeed, defines art to be an expression of emotion, and the work of art to be its vehicle. At the same time an ethical interest enters his discus-

sion; he holds that aesthetic satisfaction centers in artistic embodiment of the highest and best feelings to which humanity has risen.

(17) For Lessing (*q.v.* 1) the arts stand to each other in a nonreductive fashion, each having its own function and principles.

(18) Santayana (*q.v.* 9) defines the aesthetic quality as "objectified pleasure."

(19) Collingwood (*q.v.* 3) finds art, along with religion, science, history, and philosophy, to be mutually supportive forms of human experience. Taken together, one approaches the concrete reality of things in their historicity.

(20) Edward Bullough contributed to aesthetics the concept of "psychical distance." An object is viewed aesthetically when we put it out of gear with our practical selves, and interpret even our feelings in this experience as characteristics of the object.

(21) Theodor Lipps (*q.v.*) finds *Einfühlung*, or empathy, to be the core concept of the aesthetic experience. This occurs when we feel ourselves into objects and experiences outside ourselves, projecting our feelings and activities into the object unintentionally, while remaining contemplative and free from practical compulsion.

(22) H.S. Langfeld defines aesthetics as "the science of beauty and ugliness." The two are relative to each other, and at opposite ends of the scale of values. His view combines the emphases of Bullough on psychical distance, and Lipps on empathy, while adding to Lipps' analysis the claim that there is "tentative" activity within the self in this experience.

(23) In relation to Freud (*q.v.* 4) what is aesthetically compelling relates to the inner drama of man, rooted in the great drives of life and death, sex and guilt. The artistic consciousness works through repression and sublimation of this material. When it is well-done we are captivated by the transformed material.

(24) A somewhat different approach to art occurs in the writings of Jung (*q.v.* 1). The aesthetic material to which we respond is the archetypal deposit within the unconscious of every individual. The artist works in terms of this material, however, unknowingly, and to this we respond.

(25) If one thinks in terms of quality, one thinks of the work of D.W. Prall for whom the object of aesthetic experience is the intuited surface of the world. In sensation we receive the structural and qualitative relations of that surface.

(26) Dewey (*q.v.* 6) finds art in experience. Dividing experience into instrumental and consummatory phases, art becomes experience in its consummatory phase. Hence, art is to be found not only in the fine arts, but characterizes experience wherever it moves toward consummation.

(27) Stephen C. Pepper (*q.v.* 2) works with a combination of the two preceding approaches, finding aesthetic quality to be a function of contextual relations so arranged that the eye or ear is held by the qualities, and led back and forth without being permitted to wander from them in order that their richness and intensity may be educed.

(28) Clive Bell understands each instance of beauty to be, at the same time, an instance of significant form, suggesting a variety of ways of signifying and communicating apart from ordinary discourse.

(29) Roger Fry shares, at least in part, the view of Bell. He sometimes speaks of the "aesthetic emotion," for example. But he also holds that the aesthetic experience involves the apprehension of certain kinds of relations presented to us in the sense-data of experience.

(30) Susanne Langer (*q.v.*) in her earlier work identified the arts with the presentation of "unconsummated symbols" to our awareness. These bear intentionality, yet lack dictionary definition. In her later work an entire world is presented whose categories are not actual but "virtual" time, space, etc.

(31) Ortega y Gasset (*q.v.* 4) suggests that contemporary art is seeking a new basis through dehumanization. Traditionally, at least classically, art has sought to glorify the human form and human attributes. The dehumanization of the arts is thus a constructive quest for a new standing ground.

(32) Thomas Munro (*q.v.*) argues for a scientific aesthetics, empirical in tone and research oriented, studying works of art and their development much as biology studies the organic world.

(33) I.A. Richards may be taken as a representative of emotivism in art, as well as of linguistic analysis. Distinguishing emotive from descriptive meaning, he holds that the arts express emotional-volitional attitudes rather than insights that might relate to descriptive propositions.

(34) Georg Lukács (*q.v.*) in his later Marxist works held that form is determined by content, that abstract art is therefore degenerate, and that social realism is the only valid approach to the aesthetic. Social relations become the basis of aesthetics, refuting his early neo-Kantian stand.

(35) William Empson (*q.v.*) discussed the role of ambiguity in poetry.

(36) Beginning with Cassirer's (*q.v.* 2) theory of symbols, as had Langer (30 above), Goodman (*q.v.* 5) argued that aesthetic symbols have greater density, repleteness, exemplification, and more complex reference than other symbols. This affects the nature of the "cognition in and for itself" which is the purpose of art.

(37) For Beardsley (*q.v.* 1, 3) the aesthetic is a unique experience, having intrinsic value, triggered by the qualities of intensity, unity, and complexity in the aesthetic object. For the Beardsley-Wimsatt Intentional and Affective Fallacies in literary criticism, *q.v.* New Criticism.

AETIOLOGY.
　　Q.v. Etiology.

AEVUM.
　　Q.v. Time (8).

AFFECT.
　　A term used in the rational psychology of Spinoza (*q.v.* 4) to name the variety of feelings, purposes, and drives which motivate us. Since the affects are internal their influence upon us would seem to allow a kind of self-determination.

AFFECTIVE FALLACY.
　　Q.v. New Criticism.

AFFIRMATIVE PROPOSITIONS.
　　The A and I propositions of syllogistic logic (*q.v.* Syllogism 1–5).

AFFIRMING THE ANTECEDENT.
　　Q.v. Syllogism (9).

AFFIRMING THE CONSEQUENT.
Q.v. Fallacies (27).

A FORTIORI.
A Latin phrase meaning "all the more" or "with the greater force." A type of argument in which two cases are compared, a lesser and a greater. The argument runs from the lesser to the greater case. If from the lesser case one is able to gain a certain consequence how much more certain one should be able to expect this consequence, or a stronger result, in the greater case; *e.g.*, if a householder will give a stranger who is in need a loaf of bread rather than a stone, how much more certainly, *a fortiori* we can expect our heavenly father to care for us.

AGAMAS.
Q.v. Vaiṣnavism (3e, 4).

AGÁPE.
Greek term meaning "selfless love." The term is derived from the *agápe* or "love feast" of the early Christians, a common meal to promote "Christian fellowship" frequently associated with the sacrament. *Q.v.* Love (6); Nygren.

AGAPISM.
Q.v. Peirce (13).

AGNI.
A Sanskrit term meaning "fire." One of the most important of the Vedic gods, Agni was god of the altar fire; and also represented the trinity of earthly fire, lightning and sun. In this extended sense he was the mediator between the gods and man.

AGNOSTICISM.
From the Greek *a* ("not") and *gignoskein* ("to know"). A term coined by T.H. Huxley (*q.v.*) to express a position of suspended belief. Huxley used the term to apply to any proposition for which the evidence was insufficient for belief. It is usually, however, applied principally to suspension of belief with respect to God. Protagoras (*q.v.* 5), holding that with respect to the gods he has no way of knowing that they exist or do not exist, would exemplify the ordinary sense of the term, agnosticism. Also *q.v.* Spencer (4), who relates the term to the Unknowable, and Stephen (*q.v.*) who helped to popularize

the term. Also *q.v.* Westermarck (3).

AGREEMENT, METHOD OF.
Q.v. Mill, John S. (4).

AGREEMENT AND DIFFERENCE, JOINT METHOD OF.
Q.v. Mill, John S. (4).

AGRIPPA. c. 2nd or 3rd century A.D.
Greek philosopher. A skeptical philosopher in the manner of Aenesidemus (*q.v.*) and Pyrrho (*q.v.*), Agrippa summarized in five tropes, or headings, the arguments supporting the skeptical suspension of judgment.

(1) The first trope supporting suspension of judgment is the disagreement among philosophers concerning what, if anything, can be known. There is no criterion by which we can evaluate the claims of the philosophers, some supporting sense, some supporting reason; others supporting sense and reason together.

(2) The second trope relates to the fact that every proof requires premises which in turn must be proved, and so on back in an infinite regress.

(3) Thirdly, all data is relative: sensation to the sentient being, reason to the intelligent being. The relativity of data prevents us from knowing what a thing is in itself.

(4) Fourthly, although we try to avoid regress by positing hypotheses, the truth of the hypotheses has not been determined. Therefore, we cannot accept as true the conclusions following from them.

(5) Fifthly, there is a vicious circle in attempting to establish the sensible by reason, since reason itself needs to be established on the basis of sense.

AGRIPPA VON NETTESHEIM, HENRY CORNELIUS. 1486–1535.
German philosopher and cabalist. Born in Cologne. Studied at the University of Cologne. During a stormy and unsettled life he served four heads of state, including Charles V, and was for a time physician to the Queen Mother of Francis I. His lectures at universities and his published work were invariably controversial, arousing the antagonism of the Inquisition. His interest in cabalism was an outrage to many, yet his major work disowned such an enterprise along with the sciences and the arts. Finding epis-

temological uncertainty and vanity everywhere, he urged a return to primitive Christianity and devotion to the Scriptures. His works were written in Latin.

Principal writings: *On the Occult Philosophy*, (written 1510, published 1531–33); *On the Uncertainty and Vanity of the Sciences and the Arts* (T), 1530.

AHANKARA.
Q.v. Sankhya (5c).

AHIMSA.
A Sanskrit term meaning non-injury. Basic to the practice of Hinduism, Buddhism, and Jainism. Because each living thing is in process of working out its salvation, one must be careful not to interfere in any way. The prohibition has religious force. *Q.v.* Jainism (3); Yoga (4); Gandhi (2).

AHRIMAN.
Also known as Angra Mainyu. The malevolent deity of the Zoroastrian religion, locked in combat with Ahura Mazda, or Ormazd, the benevolent deity of the religion (*q.v.* Zoroaster 1–3, 5–6).

AHURA MAZDA.
Also known as Ormazd. The benevolent deity of the Zoroastrian religion, locked in combat with Ahriman, or Angra Mainyu, the evil spirit (*q.v.* Zoroaster 1–3, 5–6).

AI.
From the Chinese, meaning "love." For Mo Tzu (*q.v.* 3) and Han Yu, key term in achieving the good and right.

AI.
Q.v. Artificial Intelligence (3).

AIMS OF LIFE (HINDU).
Q.v. Puruṣarthas.

AIR, THE.
For Putnam (*q.v.* 6), the Absolutely Inconsistent Rule ("Infer every statement from every premise and from every set of premises, including the empty set"). Rationality requires the rule's rejection, leading to the one *a priori* truth: "Not every statement is true."

AJATIVADA.
Sanskrit term meaning "no-origination." A doctrine of Gaudapada (*q.v.* 1), hold-

ing the sole reality to be the Absolute.

AJITANATHA.
Q.v. Vardhamana.

AJIVA.
Q.v. Jainism (1).

AJIVIKAS.
From Sanskrit *ajivat* ("vows"). A heterodox Indian sect lasting from the sixth-century B.C. to the fifteenth century A.D. Founded by Makkhali Gosala from a group of wandering ascetics in the Ganges plain, the order of Ajivikas rivaled the Buddhists and the Jains for a considerable period (until the 2nd century B.C.).

(1) The philosophical position they held in contrast to their rivals, is that free will is an illusion, *niyat* ("fate," "destiny") exercising complete control through 8,400,000 cycles of time until the "End of Sorrow." No human action has any effect on *Karma*, lessening or increasing it. The rigid order of *niyat* holds firm until the end.

(2) In southern India the doctrine was further elaborated: (a) for only a few is release permanent at the end of the millions of cycles. The rest are fated to return to earth for another round of cycles. (b) In apparent contradiction to (a), there appeared among southern Ajivikas a Parmenidean-like doctrine of time as illusion and reality as "unmoving permanence." (c) The soul is atomic (as are all things), and in its disembodied state is immense (500 leagues in size). (d) Gosala becomes a divinity occasionally visiting the earth to increase faith among his followers.

AKIBA, BEN JOSEPH.
Q.v. Bar Kokhba.

AKṢARA (AKSHARA).
From Sanskrit, meaning "imperishable." Used in the *Upanishads* as an alternative name for Brahman.

ALBERINI, CORIOLANO.
Q.v. Latin American Philosophy (9).

ALBERTISTS.
The name given to the followers of Albertus Magnus (*q.v.*). Originally, the name for all Thomists since Albertus

Magnus was the teacher of Thomas Aquinas.

ALBERTUS MAGNUS, ST. 1206–1280.

Born in Bavaria. Studied in Padua and Bologna, joined the Dominican order, 1223. Taught at University of Paris (1245–48), where Thomas Aquinas was among his students, and at Cologne. Part of his time was taken up by administrative tasks for the Dominicans; and he was Bishop of Ratisbon from 1260 to 1262. Interested in the physical sciences, as well as in philosophy and theology, he insisted on the importance of observation and experiment. Not only called "The Great," but also "Doctor Universalis."

Principal writings: *Commentary on the Sentences of Peter Lombard*, 1240–49; *Handbook on Creatures*, 1240–43; *Commentary on the Pseudo-Dionysius*, 1248–54; *On the Unity of the Intellect*: and an unfinished *Handbook of Theology* 1270–80, whose authorship is possibly multiple, and in any case, questioned.

(1) Immersing himself in the translations of and about Aristotle from Greek and Arabic manuscripts, Albertus Magnus performed the much needed function of interpreting Aristotle to the European mind. The result of his commentaries is, in fact, however, a fusion of Aristotelianism and Neoplatonism since he was no more able than his predecessors to separate Aristotle from his interpreters.

(2) He views God as the necessary being in whom essence and existence are identical. He proves God's existence from motion and the impossibility of an infinite chain of principles, in Aristotle's fashion. He finds God's nature to be intelligent, omnipotent, living, free, and unitary.

(3) At the same time in the manner of the Pseudo-Dionysius he finds that we know not what God is; but what God is not.

(4) And in the manner of the Neoplatonists he finds reality flowing from God in a series of emanations in which the intelligences and their spheres are produced, leading down to things of this earth.

(5) He denied that angels and human souls were composed of matter and form, while not presenting a very clear alternative.

(6) He believed in the value of philosophy, and distinguished it from theology, holding that philosophic reason cannot demonstrate the creation of the world in time. On the other hand he believed that the immortality of the soul can be so demonstrated. Metaphysics treats of God as the first Being, while theology treats of God as revealed by faith. The philosopher uses the general light of reason where the theologian utilizes the supernatural light of faith.

(7) He displayed an interestingly empirical temper of mind, which must have helped establish his interest in Aristotle's work. He worked in the fields of both botany and zoology. Concerning method in the physical sciences he remarked that experience alone can give certainty; and he found it necessary on occasion to criticize Aristotle for being insufficiently empirical in some matters.

(8) His great contribution, however, lay in systematizing the material in the Latin translations of Aristotle's works.

ALBIGENSIANS.

Named after the town of Albi in southern France. A branch of the Cathari, the Albigensians (or Albigenses) existed between the 11th and 13th centuries. Ascetic in manner the group was anti-clerical, and held to the Manichaean (*q.v.* Manichaeism) equation of evil with matter, and light with good. Also *q.v.* Paulicians.

ALBINUS. 2nd cent. A.D.

Greek philosopher. A member of the School of Gaius (*q.v.*) and associated with the Fourth Academy (*q.v.* Plato's Academy 4), Albinus systematized the doctrines of his teacher. Combining the thought of Plato and Aristotle with that of Stoicism he emerged with a point of view Neoplatonic in tone where knowledge is a means to religious insight, and three-fold divisions are prominent: *e.g.* the division of reality into pure form, ideas, and matter; the division of God into an unmoved mover with two hypostases.

Principal writings: *Prologue* and *Epitome*.

ALCMAEON. 5th cent. B.C.

Greek philosopher. Regarded by Aristotle as a disciple of Pythagoras, Alcmaeon believed in a law of universal harmony applying to both the natural and social worlds. As a physician he believed health to require a balance of opposites in the body. He believed the soul to be immortal and identified it with perfect circular motion, finding instances of such motion both in the psyche and in the stars. To the Pythagorean table of opposites he is alleged to have added the secondary and relative qualities of sweet-bitter, black-white, and large-small.

ALCOTT, BRONSON.

Q.v. Personalism (1); The Transcendent (4).

ALCUIN. 735–804.

English Churchman and educator, studied at the cathedral school of York. On Charlemagne's invitation he became, in 781, a member of Charlemagne's court, commissioned to establish schools and spread Latin culture among the Franks.

Established at court a palace academy and library; included among the scholars were Charlemagne, the members of his family, and the palace clerics. In 790 he returned to England, but was called back several times on special commissions. He spent his last years in charge of the Abbey of St. Martin at Tours, where he made the abbey school a model of excellence.

Principal writings: Letters and poems, manuals of grammar, rhetoric, dialectic; commentaries on the Bible; a theological treatise, *On the Trinity*, sent to Charlemagne in 802.

ALEMBERT, JEAN LE ROND D'. 1717–1783.

French philosopher and mathematician. Born in Paris. Studied in the Jansenist College of Mazarin. Largely self taught, he made contributions to both mathematics and physics, but his work was uneven. Co-editor of the great *Encyclopedia* (with Diderot), and author of its introductory essay.

Principal writings: *Treatise on Dynamics*, 1743; *Preliminary Discourse of the Encyclopedia*, 1751; *Mélange of Literature, History, and Philosophy*, 5 vols., 1752; *Essays on the Elements of Philosophy*, 1759; *Mathematical Opuscules*, 1761–80.

(1) Adopting an empirical view of the origin of all knowledge he correlated the various scientific and humane disciplines with the human faculties responsible for them: history with memory, science and philosophy with reason, and the arts with imagination.

(2) In D'Alembert's view mathematics is likewise empirical, dealing with the more general characteristics of things. Although interested in the newly developing probability theory, his contributions to the discipline were largely erroneous: *i.e.*, that the probability of an event happening is initially one-half since it can either happen or not happen, that every throw of heads makes it more likely that the next throw will be tails, and that the probability of heads once in two times is two-thirds (where everyone else had held it to be three-fourths).

(3) Philosophy does not in his view relate to anything transcendent, but is to be composed, and used, as a guide to the world which is the object of scientific study. He gradually moved toward atheism and materialism.

(4) He passionately supported the ideals of the Enlightenment, and the role of education in bringing them about.

ALEPH-NULL.

Q.v. Cantor (4–8).

ALEXANDER OF HALES. 1185–1245.

English philosopher and theologian. Born in Shropshire. Studied and taught at the University of Paris throughout his life. St. Bonaventure (*q.v.*) was one of his students and disciples.

Principal writings: *Commentary on the Sentences of Peter Lombard; Glosses on the Sentences of Peter Lombard; Disputed Questions; The Summa Theologica of the Irrefragable Doctor, Alexander of Hales* (jointly), 4 vols.

(1) An early Scholastic, among his contributions was the introduction of the *Sentences* of Peter Lombard (*q.v.*) into the theological curriculum of the university. Although the *Summa*, attributed to him under the name, "Doctor irrefragabilis," was a joint work completed after his death, it provides a clear precedent for the Scholastic method of stating the problem, indicating objections, responses to the objections, solution to the problem, and justification of the solution. Exactly this method was standard in later *Summae*.

(2) Becoming a Franciscan in 1237, he was part of the Augustinian movement of the 13th century, and was subject to Neoplatonic influences including, according to some, the influence of Avicebron (*q.v.*). Although he had available to him virtually all of the works of Aristotle, the *Summa* to which he contributed is directed toward the justification of the Augustinian tradition.

ALEXANDER, SAMUEL. 1859–1938.

British philosopher. Born in Sidney Australia. Studied at Oxford. Professor, University of Manchester, 1893–1923.

Principal writings: *Moral Order and Progress*, 1889; *Locke*, 1908; *Space, Time, and Deity*, 2 vols., 1920; *Spinoza and Time*, 1921; *Art and Instinct*, 1927; *Beauty and Other Forms of Value*, 1933; *Philosophical and Literary Pieces* (ed. J. Laird), 1939.

(1) Epistemologically a realist, Alexander explained error as the misplacing of a real object—placing the illusionary image in the world rather than in our mind, for example. On the other hand, he also held that truth is relative, grows obsolete, and may turn to falsehood; and that not even logical relations are eternal.

(2) The framework of Alexander's metaphysics is supplied by the doctrine of emergent evolution. Beginning with the thought that a thing is a complexus of motions, he identities space-time as pure motion, and views space-time as the source or origin of existing things.

(3) Motion is one among a number of properties of space-time. These properties Alexander terms the categories. These primordial properties of space-time will also characterize whatever emerges from space-time. Besides motion his categories are substance, quantity, number, existence, universality, relation, and order.

(4) The emergents have in order physical, chemical, physiological, and mental qualities. The movement is toward complexity. Evolution has a *nisus* ("a striving"), toward ever higher levels.

(5) The concept of God is treated in these terms. We can mean by God the entire space-time world in *nisus* toward the next emergent. Or we can mean by God the characteristic of transcendence which the next emergent has to what exists. He terms this characteristic "deity." From the standpoint of the dog, humanity is deity. From the standpoint of all existence the next emergent is deity. Since the process of evolution has no end, the quality of deity remains in a sense always transcendent.

ALEXANDRIAN SCHOOL. 310 B.C.-642 A.D.

(1) In the broad sense the term "Alexandrian School" refers to any one of the intellectual traditions associated with Alexandria between 310 B.C. when Ptolemy Soter founded a school and library in Alexandria, and 642 A.D. when Alexandria was captured by the Muslims. The library became famous, and the number of schools expanded, including Neo-pythagoreanism and Neoplatonism, as well as Christian and Jewish scholars— the former represented by Pantaenus, Clement (*q.v.*) and Origen (*q.v.*), the latter represented by Philo Judaeus (*q.v.*). When the library was burned it contained 700,000 volumes.

(2) In the narrow sense "Alexandrian School" is taken to refer to the school of Neoplatonic thought in Alexandria, counterpart to the School of Athens (*q.v.*) with which it had many relations. The dates of the Neoplatonic school were from around 430 to 642 A.D. The first head of the Alexandrian School of Neoplatonism was Hierocles (*q.v.*), who had studied with Plutarch, founder of the School of Athens. He was followed by Hermias who had studied with Syrianus (*q.v.*), in his time likewise head of the School of Athens. Hermias was followed by Ammonius who had among his students both Asclepius (*q.v.*) and Olimpiodorus (*q.v.*), as well as John Philoponus (*q.v.*) who held to a doctrine of "tritheism."

AL-FARABI. 10th century A.D.

Islamic philosopher. Died around 950 A.D. Continued the attempts of the Baghdad School to reconcile Platonic and Aristotelian ideas.

Principal writings: *On the Principles of the Views of the Inhabitants of the Excellent State or The Ideal City; Commentary on Aristotle; Philosophy of Plato and Aristotle; Short Commentary on Aristotle's Prior Analytics* (T); *The Fusul al-Madani; Aphorisms of the Statesman of al-Farabi* (T).

(1) God is the One in Whom essence and existence are identical, and from God

proceeded the intelligence, world soul, and cosmos. The world, having emanated from God, is eternal. Man's highest goal is identification with the One. Such identification has theological and philosophical aspects.

(2) An Aristotelian influence can be seen in his marshaling of arguments for God. He used three arguments: (a) Because things are naturally passive their motion must be explained, and this requires a first mover. (b) Because things must have efficient causes, there must be a first cause. (c) Because the things of this world are contingent, they must have received their existence from a necessary being (*q.v.* Aquinas 6).

(3) In philosophy, logic is the introductory study; and its mastery has not only philosophical but also religious importance, intellectual perfection being part of our religious goal.

(4) Philosophy has two main divisions: theoretical philosophy and practical philosophy. Theoretical philosophy includes physics (all of the separate sciences) and metaphysics. Practical philosophy is what we know as ethics.

ALGEBRA, BOOLEAN.
Q.v. Boole, George.

ALGEBRA OF LOGIC.
The name applied in the 19th century to that development, influenced by mathematics, beyond traditional logic. Contributing significantly to this development were Boole, De Morgan. Jevons, Peirce, Venn, and Schröder, each of which *q.v.*

AL-GHAZZALI. 1058–1111.
Islamic philosopher, associated with Baghdad. The movement of his thought was from an initial position of skepticism into mysticism and orthodoxy. From this vantage point he first clearly described, and then vigorously attacked, Al-Farabi and Avicenna in his principal writings. Some later philosophers, knowing only the first book, classed him with the men he opposed. In fact he helped establish the mystical tradition of Sufism, founding a school in this tradition.

Principal writings: *The Intentions of Philosophers; Self-Destruction of the Philosophers* (*q.v.* Averroës); *Revival of the Religious Sciences; Incoherence of the Philosophers*

(T); *Deliverance from Error* (T); *The Beginning of Guidance* (T); *The Incoherence of the Incoherence* (T).

(1) Opposing the views of Al-Farabi and Avicenna concerning both the eternity of the universe and its (logical) relationship as an emanation of God, Al-Ghazzali stoutly defended the creation of the universe as occurring in time and out of nothing.

(2) His emphasis on the divine sovereignty led him to a doctrine of causality, identical to the doctrine of Occasionalism (*q.v.*). Effects do not flow from causes. God produces the cause. Later he produces what we call the "effect."

(3) Furthermore, since reason is limited to the exploration of phenomena, we must rely upon some other means of coming in contact with reality.

(4) One such means is the Qur'an which contains revealed truth.

(5) Another means is mystical intuition which is available to any man who conforms to the appropriate ascetic discipline. Through prayers, fasting, and the avoidance of sensuality the final intuition of God can be attained.

ALGORITHM.
Derived from Al-Khwarizmi or Al-Korisimi, the surname of the author of a famous 9th-century Arabic work on arithmetic, replacing the abacus with 10-digit computation. The work was translated into Latin, and all such books came to be called *Algorismus*, and so the term came to mean the operations of arithmetic in Arabic notation. It now refers to any sort of logical or mathematical operation with any sort of notation, but especially one whose series of steps contains built-in repetition. The term is widely used in computer science where the logical triad of assumption, proof, conclusion becomes input data, algorithm, output data. D.E. Knuth (*Fundamental Algorithms*, 1973) cites 5 properties of algorithms: finiteness, definiteness, input, output, effectiveness.

ALIENATION.
(1) Marx's first view of alienation is described in his *Economic and Philosophical Manuscripts of 1844* (*q.v.* Marx 1). It is a process of the concretization of man's inner nature which then becomes property, and separates one person from

another. His later writings contain at least four forms of alienation (*q.v.* Marx 8, 9).

(2) The alienated individual is a theme often treated in Existentialism (*q.v.*), perhaps most clearly in the concept of inauthenticity.

AL-KINDI. c. 813–873.

Islamic philosopher. Early member of the Baghdad School. Of the tribe of Kindah he lived in Basra and Baghdad where he died. The first of the great Arabian followers of Aristotle, he initiated the encyclopedic form of philosophical treatise developed more than a century later by Avicenna (*q.v.*). It was Al-Kindi's translation of Books 4–6 of Plotinus' *Enneads* which was wrongly attributed to Aristotle, perhaps through the translator's error, and which circulated until the 13th century as the *Theology of Aristotle*.

Principal writings: The earliest metaphysical work in Arabic, *The Metaphysics*, as well as works on geometry, astronomy, astrology, arithmetic, music (developed on arithmetical principles), physics, medicine, psychology, meteorology, and politics.

(1) Following Aristotle he distinguished the active from the passive intellect, and held the latter to be actualized by the former.

(2) Discursive reasoning and demonstration are the achievements of a third and fourth intellect, respectively.

(3) In ontology he hypostatizes the categories. He names five categories—matter, form, motion, place, and time—and regards them as primary substances.

ALLAH.

Arabic contraction of *al-ilah* (the god), as in the monotheistic Islamic chant *la ilaha illa allah*, ("There is no God but the God," *i.e.*, "There is no God but Allah.") *Q.v.* Mohammed; Islam.

ALLEGORICAL INTERPRETATION OF SCRIPTURES.

Q.v. Thomas Woolston.

ALLEGORY.

Q.v. Myth (1, 3, 4); Philo Judaeus (1); Origen; St. Augustine (11); Thomas Woolston.

ALONSO DE LA VERACRUZ. 1507–1584.

Mexican philosopher. Born in Toledo.

Centering his interests in logic and natural philosophy, he opposed nominalism, followed the Thomistic interpretation of Aristotle, and especially the *Summulae logicales* of Peter of Spain (*q.v.*). Also *q.v.* Latin American Philosophy.

ALS OB.

From German, meaning "as if." *Q.v.* Vaihinger, Hans (1). A key term in his view of the way experience is controlled through the construction of fictional entities.

ALTERATION.

For Aristotle (*q.v.* 8), one of three basic types of change, namely "change of quality," to be distinguished from growth and diminution which is "change of quantity," and locomotion, which is "change of place."

ALTERITY.

Q.v. Levinas (1).

ALTHUSSER, LOUIS. 1918–1990.

Born in Algeria. French political philosopher. Educated and taught at École Normale Supérior. Joined the French Communist party in 1948.

Principal writings: *For Marx* (T), 1965; *Reading Capital* (T), 2 vols., 1965; *Lenin and Philosophy and Other Essays* (T), 1971; *Essays on Ideology*, 1971, 1976; *Politics and History* (T), 1972; *Essays in Self-Criticism* (T), 1974; *That Which Cannot Endure in the Communist Party*, 1978; *The Future Lasts Forever: a Memoir* (T), 1992.

(1) Determined to rescue Marx from ideological (*i.e.*, humanistic) interpretations (for example, *q.v.* the Frankfurt School 5, 6, 10; Lukács; Sartre 8) Althusser called for a strict reading of Marx in terms of Marx alone. Even though a student of Bachelard (*q.v.*), and oriented toward de Saussure, Lévi-Strauss, Lacan and Freud, he denies being a structuralist, and calls Structuralism (*q.v.*) "structuralist ideology."

(2) His structuralist vocabulary is, however, unmistakable. Marxism is described as a "science of structural relations," society is viewed as a decentered, structured whole with an interplay of "difference" among its four basic levels; the economic, political, ideological, and theoretical. Causality is also structural, taking place through the contradictions within and among the four levels. The motive force of history is the working

out of these structural contradictions. And revolution is possible when a synchrony of contradictions on various levels are simultaneously present.

(3) In place of the strict economic determinism found in many versions of Marxism, the economic basis has only indirect dominance. Each of the four levels is granted its own relative autonomy; and the economic level plays a "last instance" role effecting, indirectly and incompletely, the "structure in dominance" of the synchronic whole.

(4) While science is objective, the rest of society, including the four levels, is engulfed in ideology. What ideology does is intermix imaginary relations with the conditions of existence, so that their beliefs are false representations. The "apparatuses" of the state are ideological, including family, education, religion, trade unions, and pre-Marxist philosophies. They all reflect bourgeois ideology projected in mythical thinking.

(5) Marxism is not ideological, because Marx was able to work through his ideological beginnings, reaching the objective viewpoint expressed in his mature writings (1857–83). The endpoint was the science of historical materialism, an epoch-making "scientific theory of theoretical practice." The "epistemological break" necessary for this achievement was transition from the bourgeois to the proletarian point of view. The science thus represents in theory the people's class struggle. This is also the only standpoint from which society can be viewed objectively. From this standpoint philosophy is understood to be the weapon of revolution which is to change the world.

ALTIZER, THOMAS.
    Q.v. Death of God Theologians; Theology (20).

ALTRUISM.
    From Latin *alter* meaning "other." Coined by the French philosopher, Auguste Comte (*q.v.*). The term implies regard for and devotion to the interests of others, even to the sacrifice of personal interests.

AMBIGUITY.
    A word, term, or expression is said to be ambiguous, or to have the property, "ambiguity," when it is capable of hav-

ing more than a single sense. Ambiguity can lead to the fallacy of Equivocation (*q.v.* Fallacies 3). Also *q.v.* Vagueness; William Empson.

AMBIGUOUS MIDDLE TERM, FALLACY OF.
    Q.v. Fallacies (24).

AMBROSE, ST.
    Q.v. Virtue (6).

AMELIUS. 3rd century A.D.
    Hellenic-Roman philosopher. Born in Etruria. Joined Plotinus in Rome in 246, and was thereafter one of his disciples (*q.v.* Neoplatonism 7).
    Principal writings: *On the Difference Between the Opinions of Plotinus and those of Numenius*; also *Commentaries* on Plato's *Republic* and *Timaeus*.

AMITABHA.
    The Savior of the Pure Land sect of Mahayana Buddhism (*q.v.* 7); also the reincarnated Panchen Lama of Lamaism (*q.v.* 1–2).

AMMONIUS SACCAS. c. 175–242.
    Hellenic philosopher. Born a Christian he was converted to Hellenism, and became a member of the Alexandrian School (*q.v.*). An illustrious teacher, Plotinus (*q.v.*) studied with him for eleven years; Longinus (*q.v.*) studied with him; Origen the Neoplatonist (*q.v.*); and many more. Sometimes credited with the role of founder of Neoplatonism (*q.v.* 5) before Plotinus (also *q.v.* Numenius for a similar claim). The claim is difficult to assess since his disciples were sworn to secrecy concerning the content of his philosophy. He seems to have been interested, at least, in reconciling the philosophies of Plato and Aristotle.

AMPHIBOLY.
    Q.v. Fallacies (1).

AMPLIATIVE.
    From Latin *ampliare* meaning "to make wider."
    "Ampliative judgment" and "synthetic judgment" are identical in meaning, referring to judgments whose predicates are not implicit in the meanings of their subject terms. "Synthetic judgment" contrasts with "analytic judgment" as "ampliative

judgment" contrasts with "explicative judgment."

"Ampliative inference" on the other hand is the type of inference in which something predicated in the conclusion is not found in the premises, *i.e.,* that form of induction in which by analogy one affirms of the whole what was found to be true of a part of the whole.

ANABAPTISTS.

From the Greek *ana* ("again") and *baptizo* ("dip"). A movement denying the validity of infant baptism which arose in 1521, originally against Luther's reforms as having retained an unscriptural Romish mode of baptism. Luther interviewed the leaders of the group, rejecting them and their ideas. The movement, denied the cities, flourished in the country. When the Peasants' War broke out in 1527 Thomas Münzer, leader of the Anabaptists, was found to be also one of the leaders of the insurrection. This connection probably explains the vehemence of Luther's (*q.v.* 7) injunction to the German princes, urging them to put down the revolt. The insurgents were defeated and Münzer, among others, was executed. The movement, claiming that social and religious reform must occur together, continued to spread but without cohesion. The term, "Anabaptist," came to be used loosely to designate any person or group carrying to excess the reform principles of Protestantism.

ANAGOGICAL INTERPRETATION.

From the Greek *ana* ("up") and *agoge* ("a leading"). The term refers to interpretations, usually of Scripture, leading one "upward," *i.e.,* toward the spiritual or mystical. The anagogical is thus a type of allegorical interpretation.

ANALOGIA ENTIS.

A Latin term meaning "analogy of being." *Q.v.* Analogy (2).

ANALOGIES OF EXPERIENCE.

For Kant (*q.v* 3) the *a priori* principles making possible the unity of human experience. The three principles, deriving from the category of Relation, are substance, causality, and reciprocity. For Kant the principles are derived from the basic types of propositions, and imply the orderings of substance, cause, and community according to which we interpret experience.

ANALOGY.

From Greek *ana* ("according to") and *logos* ("ratio, proportion").

(1) A relation of similarity between two or more things allowing the drawing of probable or necessary conclusions depending on the kind of relation in question. In general, finding similarities in some respects we reason by analogy that there will be similarities in other respects. If the cases are not sufficiently similar to support the reasoning we have a *false analogy*. (*Q.v.* Fallacies 17.)

(2) In the *analogia entis* or Analogy of Being of the Scholastics the assumption of grades of excellence provides a means of arguing from one case to another on differing levels of being, and finally to perfect being. For the analogy of attribution, *q.v.* Cajetan (2); for the analogy of proportionality, *q.v.* Cajetan (2), and Aquinas (4). Przywara (*q.v.*) provides an instance of a modern philosopher who centers his thought around the analogy of being.

(3) For the view that there is no analogy of being, since the concept of being is univocal *q.v.* William of Ockham (9).

(4) The most famous theological argument from analogy is that of William Paley (*q.v.* 2).

(5) For Barth (*q.v.* 3) the *analogia entis* was replaced by an *analogia fidei*, an analogy of faith, since religious truth is God-given.

ANALYSIS, INTENTIONAL.

A type of analysis introduced by Husserl (*q.v.* 5–8) taking the intentional aspect of experience to be fundamental, and exhibiting the development of all philosophy from this starting point.

ANALYSIS, PHILOSOPHICAL.

According to Ayer (*q.v.* 6, 7) analysis is the function of philosophy, and consists of translating sentences needing clarification into other sentences which contain neither the key words of the original sentences, nor synonyms for them.

ANALYTIC.

From Greek *analytikos*, derived from the verb *analyein*, "to resolve into its elements."

(1) Aristotle (*q.v.* 5–6) used the term

to name his logical treatises: the *Prior Analytics* containing his analysis of the syllogism, the *Posterior Analytics* containing analyses of the conditions of demonstrable knowledge.

(2) Kant (*q.v.* 1–3) in the section of his first critique, called "Transcendental Analytic," analyzed the functions of reason within experience, especially with respect to its contribution to the structured phenomena of our experience. The main burden of the Transcendental Analytic concerns the deduction of the categories present in experience.

ANALYTIC JUDGMENT, STATEMENT, OR PROPOSITION.

A judgment, statement, or proposition having the properties of necessity and universality by virtue of the fact that the predicate of the judgment is a result of analysis of the subject term.

(1) The language we have used is that of Immanuel Kant who distinguished analytic from synthetic judgments, as well as holding to the possibility of a *synthetic a priori* judgment (*q.v.* Immanuel Kant 1).

(2) The Kantian view derived, in fact, from his predecessor, Leibniz (*q.v.* 10–11), who distinguished truths of reason from truths of fact, finding the former to rest on the principle of identity, and their negations to be contradictions.

(3) Hume (*q.v.* 5) also utilized the distinction between truths of reason and truths of fact.

(4) Since the 18th century there have been many studies of the analytic. C.I. Lewis (*q.v.* 3) held it to derive from linguistic convention, having to do with the relation between our criteria of classification and the meanings of the expression in use.

(5) In recent times the logical empiricists (*q.v.* Schlick 3) have stressed the importance of the distinction between analytic and synthetic statements; and it is often held that logic and mathematics rest on analytic statements.

(6) Quine (*q.v.* 6), objecting to the rigidity of the distinction between analytic and synthetic statements, as drawn by the logical empiricists, argues that an analytic statement is merely one of the parts of the conceptual scheme remote from the experiential periphery.

ANALYTIC PHILOSOPHY.
Q.v. Philosophy (45).

ANALYTIC PSYCHOLOGY.
Q.v. Psychology (11); Jung.

ANALYTICITY.
The study of the nature of, and conditions necessary for, analytic judgments. *Q.v.* Carnap (9, 11); Quine (4).

ANAMNESIS.
A Greek term meaning "to recall to memory." Plato's (*q.v.* 1) doctrine of knowledge as recollection of the ideas known to the soul in a previous existence, and forgotten in the trauma of birth.

ANANDA.
Q.v. Sat (1); Hinduism (5b).

ANARCHISM.
From the Greek *an* ("without") plus *archos* ("head"). As applied to a political and philosophical doctrine this term became current only in the 19th century. First used in this sense by Proudhon, it was taken up by Bakunin and has since been used to designate a variety of doctrines centering on the belief that the organized state is the cause of human injustice and should be eliminated. The means of its elimination varies with the anarchist; the points of view include evolutionists and revolutionists, those committed to violence and those committed to non-violence.

(1) William Godwin (*q.v.*), an English political writer, expected anarchism to arrive through man's gradual moral progress.

(2) Max Stirner (*q.v.*), a German philosopher, believed that its advent must be by means of individual rebellion rather than revolution; and that such rebellion must follow the cultivation of individualism.

(3) Joseph Proudhon (*q.v.*), a French philosopher, supported the gradual growth of mutualism, an increased human social sense. This spread of voluntary cooperation is to replace the state.

(4) Mikhail Bakunin (*q.v.*), Russian political writer and activist, adhered to a doctrine of revolutionary collectivist anarchism leading to the destruction of the state.

(5) Leo Tolstoy (*q.v.* 1–2), Russian

novelist and social philosopher, advocated non-violent moral revolution leading to the abolition of the state. He represented a position of religious anarchism.

(6) Peter Kropotkin (*q.v.*), Russian author and social philosopher, argued that Darwinian theory has overstressed competition in evolution; and that mutual aid is equally important. Anarchism is the movement back to a natural society.

ANASTIKAYA.

Sanskrit term meaning "nonphysical." Used in Jainism (*q.v.* 1) in the phrase *anastikaya dravya* ("nonphysical substance").

ANATMAN.

From the Sanskrit *an* ("not") and *atman* ("soul") (*anatta* in Pali). One of the three principal doctrines of Theravada Buddhism (*q.v.* 1, 4).

ANAXAGORAS. 499–422 B.C.

Greek philosopher. Born in Ionia, he gained his fame in Athens as one of the Periclean circle of gifted men. Having written that sun and moon are made of earth and rock he drew the anger of the people who preferred to think of these bodies as divine. Thrown in jail he managed to escape, returning to Ionia. Like Empedocles (*q.v.*) he recognized a limited truth in each side of the Parmenidean-Heraclitean impasse between being and becoming, and this required a pluralistic approach to the problem.

Principal writings: *On Nature*, existing only in quoted fragments.

(1) Using the maxims "there is a portion of everything in everything" and "there is always a smaller," Anaxagoras reached the conception of a world composed of infinitely small particles (seeds, he called them), qualitative in nature, whose mixture produces the gross qualities of our experience.

(2) Generation and destruction, as well as change in quality, occur through spatial rearrangement of these particles. All distinctions except spatial ones are due to preponderances in the mixture of qualitative particles.

(3) Mind alone, or *Nous* avoids intermixture, yet mind too is a collection of particles. Mind particles are of all particles the smallest and purest, and the only ones which are self-moving.

(4) All processes of change, including the origins of world-systems, are due to the action of mental particles on the other particles, setting up whirling motions capable of producing worlds.

(5) Hence, worlds evolve from natural causes, and so do all forms of life.

(6) It is due to their whirling motions that heavenly bodies become incandescent.

(7) Eclipses are due to the interpositions of the earth.

(8) The earth is flat in shape and floats on the air; earthquakes are to be explained by a rocking of the earth on the air beneath when the air above strikes the air below. Thunder and lightning are explained similarly.

(9) According to Anaxagoras, we perceive through contrast. Since there is a portion of everything in everything, qualities in the world are picked up by contrasting qualities within the perceiver.

ANAXIMANDER. 610–547 B.C.

Greek philosopher. Born in Miletus. Member of a noble family. Led Milesian emigrants to found a new colony. Allegedly invented the sun dial and geographical mapping.

Principal writings: *On the Nature of Things.*

(1) The things of the world gain their determinate natures out of a "boundless indeterminacy or *apeiron* into which they also return at last. The idea of the indefinite "boundless" provides a standard reference point for the explanation of change.

(2) The destruction of anything, as it goes out of being, satisfies a principle of cosmic justice: "And from what source things arise to that they return of necessity when they are destroyed; for they suffer punishment and make reparation to one another for their injustice according to the order of time."

(3) The "boundless" is eternal and uncreated, and characterized by an eternal motion and restlessness.

(4) Space, with which the "boundless" may be partly identified, extends indefinitely outward and it hence becomes natural to believe in a plurality of world systems.

(5) The world is formed by a separation of opposite qualities, such as warm and cold, from out of the "boundless."

(6) Sun, moon, and stars derived from the break-up of a sphere of flame which initially enclosed the earth.

(7) Eclipses were explained, in his system, by claiming that we see heavenly bodies through something like "breathing holes" which sometimes become stopped up.

(8) This earth bears the shape of a cylinder, its depth being one-third its breadth, and floats freely in space since "it is the same distance from all things" in its world system.

(9) A propounder of evolutionary theory, he believed that life had its origin in moisture, that all animal forms evolved, and that the ancestry of man led back to the fish.

ANAXIMENES. 588–524 B.C.

Greek philosopher. Born in Miletus. Son of Eurystratos, younger contemporary of Anaximander whose pupil or friend he is said to have been.

(1) All things come from, and go back to, air, a basic principle which he seems to have understood in a somewhat psychic sense, identifying air and the breath of life. Air holds the world together, and also human life. It is a divine principle and the key to change.

(2) Change occurs in terms of a second principle, condensation-rarefaction. The series runs from stone through earth, water, cloud, wind, and fire, the earlier members of the series representing attenuated modifications of the basic substance.

(3) Earth and sun, moon, and stars (not earthly but fiery substances) rest on air; but the heavenly bodies are not pictured as going under the earth, but around it, "as a cap is moved about the head," and the sun is hidden in its passage back to its morning starting point by some of the "higher parts of the earth."

(4) Since he believed stars to be something like fixed nailheads in a crystalline vault, he made a distinction between stars and planets.

(5) The rainbow is produced by the sun's rays falling on "thick condensed air."

(6) Earthquakes are due to dryness and moisture in the earth.

ANDERSON, ALAN R.

Q.v. Deontic Logic.

ANDRONICUS OF RHODES. 1st cent. B.C.

Hellenic Philosopher. Head of a resurgent Aristotelian movement in Alexandria, Andronicus recovered the writings of Aristotle which had passed through numerous vicissitudes, having rested for a vast amount of time—some say a century—hidden in a basement, and then having been seized as a prize of war. Having gained possession of the writings, Andronicus began the work of codifying them. It was in this labor that he invented the term "Metaphysics" (q.v.) to apply to an untitled treatise of Aristotle. The book is apparently named in terms of its position in the corpus of Aristotle's work.

He ordered and commented on the work of Theophrastus as well as that of Aristotle, while conducting his own investigations into logic.

ANGELL, J. R.

Q.v. Psychology (5).

ANGLICAN COMMUNION.

Q.v. Church of England.

ANGRA MAINYU.

Q.v. Ahriman, Zoroaster (1).

ANGST.

German term meaning "dread." A basic fact of human nature, according to existentialist philosophy, *Angst* is a nameless fear which has no object. Q.v. Kierkegaard (5); Heidegger (3); Unamuno (2); Bultmann (2); Sartre (5).

ANIMA.

Q.v. Jung (4).

ANIMISM.

From the Latin *anima* meaning "soul." The doctrine that all things are ensouled or at least possess a vital principle akin to the life-principle. (1) The view presented by E.B. Tylor held that all religion has arisen from a primitive belief in animism, and that this is attested to by the nature of early religious and magical rites and ceremonies. (2) In philosophy, *hylozoism* (q.v.) may be a formalized equivalent of this point of view.

ANIMISTIC MATERIALISM.

Q.v. Montague (2).

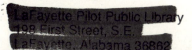

ANIMUS.

Q.v. Jung (4).

ANITYA.

From Sanskrit, "impermanence," (*anicia* in Pali). One of the three principal doctrines of Theravada Buddhism (*q.v.* 1, 3).

ANNIKERIS. 3rd cent. B.C.

Greek philosopher. A leader of the Cyrenaic School (*q.v.* Cyrenaicism), Annikeris was much closer to the views of Aristippus (*q.v.*) than those of Hegesias (*q.v.*), his contemporary. He differed from Aristippus, however, in finding value not only in individual acts of pleasure, but in pleasures deriving from social relationships; thus, he recommends that we should be willing to suffer pain in order to gain pleasures of friendship, parental respect, the gratitude of others, and patriotism.

ANOMALOUS MONISM.

Q.v. Davidson (1–4).

ANSCOMBE, GERTRUDE. 1919– .

British philosopher. Born in London. Educated at Oxford and Cambridge. Taught at Cambridge. An enthusiastic student of Wittgenstein, Anscombe has been translator and editor of his posthumous publications. Her book, *Intention*, is written in the style of the later Wittgenstein. Proceeding through numerous examples, Anscombe shows us that intentions are a form of description of events which are actions. The character of being intentional pertains to actions whose descriptions match an appropriate combination of the following: they are voluntary, pertain to the future, answer the special question "why," and naturally utilize phrases such as "in order to" or "because" (in some sense). Suppose yourself to be lying on a bed, and someone asks: "What are you doing?" To answer "lying on a bed" would not, while "resting" would, be an expression of intention.

Principal writings: *Intention*, 1957; *An Introduction to Wittgenstein's "Tractatus"*, 1959; *Three Philosophers* (with P. Geach), 1961; *The Collected Philosophical Papers of G.E.M. Anscombe*, 1981; *Ethics, Religion and Politics*, 1981; *From Parmenides to Wittgenstein*, 1981; *Metaphysics and the Philosophy of Mind*, 1981.

ANSELM, SAINT. 1033–1109.

Medieval philosopher. Born in Aosta, Italy. Joining the Benedictine order, Anselm held positions of responsibility both in France and England. Advancing from prior to abbot to archbishop, he became Archbishop of Canterbury in 1093. Augustinian in orientation and approach, Anselm is best known for his formulation of a distinctive and celebrated argument for God, the Ontological Argument. This argument is presented in the *Proslogion*, his most cited work.

Principal writings: *Proslogion* (T); *Monologion* (T); *De Grammatico* (T); *On Truth: Why the God-Man?*

(1) Anselm puts the ontological argument in two different ways: (a) God is "that than which nothing greater can be conceived." This conception carries the implication that its object exists, for not only does it carry the sense of combining in itself all perfections, but if we try to understand God as nothing more than an idea in the understanding, the understanding at once formulates the idea of a greater being, namely one existing not only in the understanding but also in reality. (b) God is that which cannot be conceived not to exist. Although it seems that Anselm got to this formulation from his first way of putting it, this is the stronger formulation. It allows one to maintain the absolute inconceivability of the divine non-existence. It allows one to urge that the phrase "the non-existence of the divine" contains a contradiction, and that the conclusion "God exists" is a necessary truth.

(2) The first way of putting the argument was criticized in Anselm's time by Gaunilo, claiming that on the same ground it can be argued that a perfect island exists, since if it did not exist then any other island, really existing, would be more perfect than the perfect island in our understanding, and this would be a contradiction. Anselm answers by repeating the argument in its strict form, that is, (b) above; and hence this would seem to be his true position. The first way of putting the argument was also criticized by Kant (*q.v.* 5c). "Existence," he said, "is not a predicate." Nothing is added to the value of any entity by saying that it exists; there is not a penny more in

one hundred real, than in one hundred possible, dollars. Judging from his answer to Gaunilo, Anselm would probably have answered Kant that while Kant's analysis fits the case of all contingently existing beings it does not fit the case of the divine being whose essence and existence are inseparably connected.

(3) God being that which cannot be conceived not to exist, if we can so much as conceive of God, we must assert that He exists, and He must exist. And if we are conceiving, by our admission, a being which may exist in our understanding alone, we are not conceiving of God. In this unique case existence follows from conceivability. Since among the criteria of conceivability is consistency, the issue shifts for Anselm from God's existence to the problem of His nature.

(4) In the rest of the *Proslogion* God is said to be self-existent, creator, sensible though not a body, omnipotent, all-knowing, supremely just, passionless, supremely compassionate, omnipresent but not existing in space and time, eternal, and unitary. The consistency of these ideas, and especially those which seem most paradoxical such as God's relation to space and time, are further explored in the *Monologion*.

(5) But the *Monologion*, further, contains Anselm's reflections on the Trinity whose image is the rational mind. A certain natural consonance, then, unites man and God. And man's soul being immortal, eternal blessedness is his goal.

(6) In *Cur Deus Homo?* or *Why the God-Man?* Anselm examines the scheme of redemption, beginning with man's fall, God becoming man in Christ, and dying for man's sins, providing a satisfaction proportionate to man's guilt, a gift of Himself which demands for truth's sake a proportionate reward, this reward being man's salvation.

(7) With respect to the problem of universals Anselm followed the Augustinian tradition, holding to the reality of abstract, intelligible objects. It was, indeed, Anselm who accused Roscelin (*q.v.*) of holding that the universal is a mere *flatus vocis* (*q.v.*). In arguing against Roscelin, Anselm seems to have held that there is but one substance or nature in all men.

(8) Lest Anselm be viewed as a rationalist, it should also be noted that he adopted the principle of St. Augustine (*q.v.* 11), "*Credo ut intelligam*" ("I believe in order to understand"). Faith thus is expected to precede and pave the way for reason.

AN SICH.

(1) In the Kantian philosophy (*q.v.* Kant 2) a thing or event independent of experience. The *ding an sich* (thing-in-itself) is to be contrasted with the experienced, and hence phenomenal, thing.

(2) In Hegel the term is also used, but there the *an sich* is not only separate from consciousness but therefore in large measure potential, latent, undeveloped, or impoverished.

(3) The term is also used by Sartre (*q.v.* 5), the French phrase being *en soi*. Sartre distinguishes between the *en soi*, or "in itself," and the *pour soi*, or "for itself." The former is applied to that which is without, and the latter to that which possesses, awareness.

ANTECEDENT.

In sentences, or propositions, of the form "if A, then B" A is called the antecedent, and B the consequent (*q.v.* Proposition 2).

ANTHONY THE HERMIT, ST.

Q.v. Monasticism.

ANTHROPOCENTRISM.

From the Greek *anthropos* ("man") and *kentron* ("center"). The view that man is, or must look upon himself as, the center of reality. Not a philosophical concept in itself, the term has analogies to the view of Protagoras (*q.v.* 1) that "man is the measure of all things." Protagoras' view has two interpretations: individual man is the measure, and man (taken generically) is the measure. The second interpretation of Protagoras' position fits the meaning of "anthropocentrism" exactly. The theory, reflected through a large part of the history of philosophy that man is a microcosm of the macrocosm (*q.v.*), a reflection of the whole of reality, has some analogy to this term, as do the various schools of Idealism (*q.v.*), holding that reality is of the nature of mind.

ANTHROPOLOGY, PHILOSOPHICAL.

The term, literally meaning "philosophical knowledge of man," applies to those studies which treat man as a "whole being," attempting to avoid or go beyond approaches in which man is regarded merely as a scientific object. The movements of Phenomenology, Existentialism, and Personalism are frequently cited as exemplifying the attitude of Philosophical Anthropology; and Scheler, Cassirer, Teilhard de Chardin, and Polanyi are often cited among its representative thinkers.

ANTHROPOMORPHISM.

From the Greek *anthropomorphos* ("of human form"). The attribution of human qualities to the divine; thus, the conceiving of God or the gods in human form.

ANTHROPOPATHISM.

From the Greek *anthropos* ("man") and *pathein* ("suffering"). A term coined by the writer and critic John Ruskin (1819–1900) to designate the state of mind leading to what he called the "pathetic fallacy," *i.e.*, emotional strain or grief leading the poet to ascribe to nature the emotions of sympathy or cruelty. In the works of Tennyson and Shelley he pointed out numerous instances of the pathetic fallacy, endowing nature with human feelings.

ANTHROPOSOPHY.

Q.v. Steiner.

ANTICHRIST.

In I John 2:18, 22; 4:3; and II John 7 where, alone in the New Testament the term is used, it simply means one who denies Christ. In extension, however, the term signifies a great force, filling the world with evil, whose defeat will lead to the Second Coming. In the extended sense the Antichrist has been taken to be, at different times, the Roman Empire, specific emperors (*e.g.* Nero), Mohammed, and the popes themselves (by Wycliffe and Luther).

ANTICIPATIONS OF PERCEPTION.

Kant's doctrine that all sensations have some intensive magnitude or degree. According to Kant we can know this in advance of experience, although we cannot know in advance what the quality or degree will be.

ANTI-FEDERALISTS.

Q.v. Federalist Papers (1–3).

ANTILOGISM.

From the Greek *antilogismos* meaning "a countercharge." The term refers to a method of checking on the validity of a syllogism. The discovery was made by Mrs. Christine Ladd Franklin, a student of the American philosopher, Charles Peirce (*q.v.*). The method also demonstrates the unity of structure in syllogisms of different moods and figures (*q.v.* Syllogism 3 and 4).

(1) The antilogism, also called the "inconsistent triad," is formed by negating the conclusion of a syllogism. If the syllogism is valid, then it will be seen that three things are true of the resulting inconsistent triad: (a) it will be composed of two universal propositions, and one particular proposition; (b) the two universal propositions will have a common term; (c) the other two terms (apart from the common term) will make up the particular proposition. If you negate the conclusion of a syllogism and find the resulting antilogism has these three properties, then the original syllogism was valid.

(2) If we take as our syllogism

All humans are mortal

All patriarchs are human

Therefore, all patriarchs are mortal, and contradict the conclusion

All humans are mortal

All patriarchs are human

Therefore, some patriarchs are not mortal,

the resulting antilogism has the desired three characteristics: the first two premises are in this case the universal ones, the conclusion is particular; "human" is a term common to the two universal propositions; and "patriarch" and "mortal" are contained in the particular proposition. Hence, the original syllogism was valid.

And since this will be true of any other valid syllogism, the antilogism provides a powerful check on the validity of syllogistic reasoning.

(3) The three properties stand out more graphically if we work with a more abstract scheme. The terms of the syllogism with which we worked (using M for

middle term, S for subject term, and P for predicate term) have the following structure:

MP

SM

SP (*Q.v.* Syllogism 3)

To say "All M is P" is the same as saying "the M that is not P is equal to 0." To say "All S is M" is the same as "the S that is not M is equal to 0" etc. Using a bar (—) over a letter to stand for "not" the syllogism might be written:

$$M\bar{P} = O$$
$$S\bar{M} = O$$
$$\therefore S\bar{P} = O$$

Now we form our antilogism merely by placing a slash over the "=" sign. This will now read "the S that is not P is not equal to zero," which will have the same meaning as "Some S is not P" (*e.g.*, "Some patriarchs are not mortal.")

$$M\bar{P} = O$$
$$S\bar{M} = O$$
$$\therefore S\bar{P} \neq O$$

Inspection will show that our schematic antilogism has the necessary three properties.

The "No S is P" proposition is written "SP = O."

The "Some S is P" proposition is written "SP ≠ O."

With this information any syllogism can be put into schematic form, and its validity tested.

ANTINOMIANISM.

From the Greek *anti* ("against") and *nomos* ("law"). The name of a recurrent tendency in Christian history to reject the law—Mosaic, ecclesiastical, or even moral—as no longer binding, and to substitute faith alone. The problem of the relation of the Mosaic law to the Gospel is treated in the writings of the Apostle Paul (*q.v.*). Among the groups with antinomian tendencies one might mention the Gnostics (*q.v.*), the Marcionites (*q.v.* Marcion), and the Manichaeans (*q.v.*). A recrudescence of the tendency occurred in the 16th and 17th centuries with Familists, Davidists, and Adamists. Luther (*q.v.*) and Melanchthon (*q.v.*) were involved in one such controversy, settled by the Formula of Concord.

ANTINOMY.

Also from the Greek *anti* ("against") and *nomos* ("law"). In one sense the term merely means the opposition to each other (or contradiction) of two conclusions. More specifically, the term is sometimes taken to refer to two opposing conclusions, each beginning from plausible premises, and issuing from valid steps of inference. An instance of this usage is to be seen in Immanuel Kant's *Critique of Pure Reason* where, in the section on the "Antinomies of Pure Reason" four examples of this kind of opposition are advanced (*q.v.* Immanuel Kant 4). A more elaborate listing is to be found in the fourteen antinomies of the Buddhist philosopher, Nagarjuna (*q.v.* 8).

ANTIOCHUS OF ASCALON. 1st cent. B.C.

Greek philosopher. A disciple of Philo of Larissa whom he succeeded as head of the Fourth Academy (*q.v.* Plato's Academy 4), holding this position from around 88 B.C. until his death in 68 B.C. The skepticism of the Second and Third Academies had by now dissipated, and Antiochus argued against skepticism that the intellect had in itself a sufficient test of truth. Antiochus related Plato and Aristotle in the manner of the middle Stoics (*q.v.* Stoicism 2), Panaetius (*q.v.*) and Posidonius (*q.v.*), and was called by Cicero an eclectic Stoic.

ANTIPHON.

Q.v. Sophists (8).

ANTI-REALISM.

Q.v. Dummet (3–5).

ANTISTHENES. c. 444–366 B.C.

Greek philosopher. A follower of Socrates. Regarded by later Stoics as founder of the School of Cynics. This seems to have been an effort on their part to gain prestige by tracing the antecedents of their own movement back to Socrates along the line Zeno-Crates-Diogenes-Antisthenes-Socrates. In fact, however, Diogenes (*q.v.*) should be regarded as the founder of Cynicism. The school of Antisthenes, whose members are sometimes referred to (as by Aristotle) as Antistheneans, is more fairly regarded as Socratic.

Principal writings: Although only isolated fragments have survived, numerous references to his voluminous writings in ethics, logic, politics, and metaphysics are scattered through the works of the ancients.

(1) Among the points on which he agreed most closely with Socrates are: (a) there is one true God who cannot be known from an image; (b) the use of myth is appropriate in ethics and philosophical discourse; (c) one of the important goals of philosophy is definition.

(2) Apparently he supported a neo-Eleatic logic which held the principle of contradiction to lack validity. Aristotle opposed him on this point. At the same time he held that universals are merely names.

(3) His disagreement with the later Cynics may be seen in that he rejected luxury as superfluous but prized education, believed in self-improvement and helpfulness to others, sought wisdom but did not regard himself as wise, accepted pleasure as a good while prizing especially the pleasures which come as a result of physical labor. The Cynics on the other hand rejected luxury as vicious, rejected education while regarding themselves as wise, and regarded all pleasure as evil.

ANTISYLLOGISM.
Q.v. Logic (15).

ANTITHESIS.
From the Greek *anti* ("against") and *tithenai* ("to set"). Etymologically, the term is comparable in meaning to "antinomy" and "contradiction." (1) In Kant's "Antinomies of Pure Reason" the "antithesis" is the negative member of the antinomy, the one opposing the thesis (q.v. Kant 4). (2) In Fichte (q.v. 3) and in Hegel (q.v. 3–9) "antithesis" is the middle member of the triad, opposing the thesis; the opposition of thesis and antithesis is resolved by the synthesis, the third member of the triad.

ANUBHAVA.
Q.v. Intuition (12).

APAGOGE.
From the Greek *apo* ("from") and *agein* ("to lead").

(1) In Aristotelian logic an abductive syllogism (q.v. Abduction 1).

(2) The method of indirect demonstration whereby one demonstrates the ab-

surdity of the conclusion contradictory to one which is to be established (q.v. Reductio Ad Absurdum.)

APATHIA.
A Latin term from the Greek *apatheia*, derived from *a* ("not") and *pathos* ("suffering"). This Greek virtue of utter tranquility served as the most important value for the Stoics (q.v. Marcus Aurelius 1). It is to be compared to the state of *ataraxia* (q.v.) stressed among the Epicureans (q.v. Epicurus 10).

APEIRON.
A Greek term meaning "boundless, indeterminate, infinite." (1) In Anaximander (q.v. 1) that from which all determinate being comes, and into which it goes. (2) For the Pythagoreans (q.v. Pythagoras 6–7) one of two principles: the Unlimited (*apeiron*) which opposes the Limit (*peras*).

APHASIA.
Q.v. Pyrrho (2).

APHRODITE-ADONIS.
Q.v. Mystery Religions (2).

APHTHONIUS.
Q.v. Rhetoric (10).

APOCALYPSE.
From the Greek *apokaluptein* ("to uncover or disclose"). The doctrine that the world is soon to be destroyed by fire, purified from evil, and that the righteous would be resurrected to live in a purified order of things. Popular in the last centuries before Christ, the doctrine generated a body of apocalyptic literature. Daniel, Revelation, and a number of the books of the Apocrypha (q.v.) belong to this literature.

APOCATASTASIS.
From the Greek *apokatastasis* meaning "complete restoration." A concept of universal salvation held by Origen the theologian (q.v. 4).

APOCRYPHA.
From the Greek *apokruphos* ("secret"). The fourteen books of Scriptural style and of late composition which were excluded from the canon of the Old Testament. This is a Protestant usage, Catholics terming the same books "deuterocanonical." In addition to history and doctrine, there

is an emphasis on the apocalypse (*q.v.*) in many of these books. Also *q.v.* Toland (2).

APODICTIC or APODEICTIC.

From the Greek *apo* ("from") and *deiknynai* ("to show"). In logic and metaphysics the term applies to propositions or judgments. Apodictic propositions and judgments are necessary, that is without alternative. They are to be contrasted with problematic (*q.v.*) propositions which deal with possibilities, and assertoric (*q.v.*) propositions which make contingent factual assertions. We are dealing with the last of the propositional modes: possibility, actuality, and necessity. The treatment of these modalities in logic is termed Modal Logic (*q.v.*). Also *q.v.* Logic (25). Kant (*q.v.* 3) distinguishes these as the three modes of judgment. *Q.v.* Modality.

APODOSIS.

A Greek term meaning "a giving back," the term refers to the "then" clause of an if-then statement, of any conditional statement. The conditional clause is the *protasis*.

APOLLINARIANISM.

The Christological doctrine that in Jesus the *Logos* (a perfect divine nature) assumed a human body, exercising the functions ordinarily performed by the human mind. The view was advanced by Apollinaris (310–390 A.D.), Bishop of Laodicea, in opposition to the doctrine of Arianism (*q.v.*). Both doctrines, in fact, were held to be unorthodox.

APOLLINARIS.

Q.v. Apollinarianism.

APOLLO.

One of the most important of the Olympian gods, the son of Zeus and Leto, Apollo became identified with manly youth and beauty, poetry, music, healing, and oracular wisdom. God of the oracle at Delphi, as Phoebus Apollo he was a divinity of radiance and light. The first Greek god to be admitted into the Roman religion.

APOLLONIAN.

One of the two elements in Nietzsche's explanation of the nature of Greek tragedy. (*Q.v.* Nietzsche 1.) The Apollonian element represents measure, order, and harmony. It stands in contrast to a Dionysian element stressing passion, and non-rational properties generally.

APOLLONIUS OF TYANA. 1st cent. A.D.

Greek philosopher. Along with his contemporary, Moderatus of Gades (*q.v.*), one of the neo-Pythagoreans. After extensive travels he is said to have established a school of philosophy in Ephesus. Presenting the Pythagorean teachings as a philosophy of life in which man is a citizen of the universe, Apollonius held that there is a supreme God above all other gods, beyond the reach of reason and not requiring sacrifices.

Principal writings: *Life of Pythagoras; Concerning Sacrifice*.

APOLOGISTS, THE.

Principally 2nd century A.D. The name given to those Church Fathers whose principal role lay in defending Christianity against paganism, against the state, and against Greek philosophy.

(1) The earliest Apologies on record are from the early 2nd century. *The Preaching of Peter*, author unknown, assumed the first of the above-mentioned roles. The work was widely circulated, widely used, and indeed became part of the book of Aristides (*q.v.* 2 below). Another book, *Quadratus*, took up the second of these roles. The book was presented to Hadrian and argued for better treatment of Christians by the state.

(2) Aristides (*q.v.*) continued the defense of Christianity against paganism, arguing for the superiority of the Christian "race" over all others. This book, too, was apparently directed toward the Emperor Hadrian.

(3) Justin Martyr (*q.v.*) directed his *Apology* both to Hadrian and to Marcus Aurelius (*q.v.*), taking the position that Greek philosophy is by itself incomplete, and that Christianity is in fact the true philosophy.

(4) Athenagoras (*q.v.*) combined all three roles, directing an appeal to Marcus Aurelius to ameliorate the unfair treatment received by Christians in the Roman judicial process, and presenting arguments for the resurrection of the dead.

(5) Tatian (*q.v.*), a disciple of Justin, was considerably more antagonistic toward

the Greek tradition than was his mentor.

(6) Theophilus of Antioch (*q.v.*) followed Tatian in this attitude.

(7) Minucius Felix (*q.v.*) on the other hand attempted to show not only that Christians are philosophers but that philosophers, when they do their work properly, are Christians.

(8) The Apologist most diametrically opposed to this blending of traditions is Tertullian (*q.v.*). He held that reason and revelation are contradictory, vigorously attacking the Greek tradition in philosophy, as well as Gnosticism, and paganism generally.

(9) Irenaeus (*q.v.*) and his disciple Hippolytus (*q.v.*) made their defense of Christianity by vigorous attacks on the false knowledge of the Gnostics who were powerful in that age.

(10) Arnobius (*q.v.*) refuted Platonic preexistence, while supporting a Christian notion of the creation of the soul by God.

(11) Lactantius (*q.v.*) and Eusebius (*q.v.*) of Caeserea continued the Apologetic tradition in the 3rd and 4th centuries A.D.

APOLOGY.

A form of discourse in defense of one's position. Among the most famous instances of such discourse one may cite Plato's *Apology*, giving Socrates' defense of his philosophic life and mission (*q.v.* Socrates 1), the entire movement of early Christian apologists (*q.v.*), and Cardinal Newman's *Apologia pro Vita Sua*, where he defends his philosophical and religious development, including his leaving the Anglican Church for Catholicism (*q.v.* Newman 3).

APOPHANTIC JUDGMENT.

From the Greek *apophantikos* ("proposition"). The subject-predicate form of judgment thought by Aristotle to be basic. The term has been used by William Hamilton and Husserl, among others.

APOSTASY.

From the Greek *apostasia* ("a defection"). In Roman Catholicism a total desertion of, or departure from, one's faith or from holy orders or from the monastic state. A formal apostate is subject to excommunication.

A POSTERIORI.

From the Latin *a* ("from") and *posteriori* ("the later"). The term designates a kind of knowledge which can be gained only from experience; hence, it can be formulated only after observation or experiment. Opposed to *a priori* (*q.v.*). Among those making analyses of the opposed terms and their combinations is Immanuel Kant (*q.v.* 1).

APOSTLES' CREED.

Its origin was not apostolic but derived from catechetical statements which gradually became accepted. The creed is now almost universally recognized by Western Catholics. It begins: "I believe in God the Father almighty, creator of heaven and earth."

APOTHEOSIS.

From the Greek *apo* ("from") and *theoun* ("to deify"). The elevation of a mortal to the rank of a god. Virtually all cultures show evidence of the transformation of heroes and rulers into divinities. With the decline of republican convictions the custom entered the Roman Empire. The persecution of Christians stemmed in large part from their refusal to acknowledge the emperor as divine.

APPEARANCE.

In the history of philosophy the term stands in contrast to reality. At times the relation is that of illusion or falsity to truth. Most often, however, at least in Western philosophy, the relation is that of opinion—that which may or not be true—to truth.

(1) For Parmenides (*q.v.* 1, 2) the world as we interpret it is almost complete illusion.

(2) It was Plato (*q.v.* 1) whose twice-divided line set the standard view identifying appearance and opinion.

(3) The Eastern tradition of Advaita (*q.v.*) Vedanta held to the stronger interpretation, and Shankara (*q.v.* 3) remains its outstanding representative.

(4) Something like the Platonic view was presented by Immanuel Kant (*q.v.* 2, 3) who termed the appearances *phenomena* and the reality *noumena*.

(5) T.H. Green (*q.v.* 1) regarded the distinction between appearance and reality as a distinction between mind as limited and mind as absolute.

(6) F.H. Bradley (*q.v.* 2, 3) represents a virtual return to Parmenides. Even the style of argumentation is the same.

APPERCEPTION.

(1) In Leibniz (*q.v.* 1) the term referred to the inner state's awareness of itself where perception referred to its awareness of external things.

(2) For Kant (*q.v.* 11d) the term denotes the unity of self-consciousness either in its empirical or its transcendental form.

APPETITES.

From the Latin *appetere* ("to strive after, long for"). The term applies to the dynamic, striving aspect of human nature.

(1) In Aristotle (*q.v.* 11) the appetites constitute the irrational part of the soul. The development of moral will involves bringing the appetites under the control of reason.

(2) Aquinas (*q.v.* 7) accepted this analysis, and carried it further, partly on the basis of the work of John of Damascus. The view of Aquinas, and that of other Scholastics, distinguished concupiscible, irascible, and rational appetites.

APPETITION.

(1) The term is sometimes used to apply to the process of satisfying the appetites (*q.v.*) discussed in the preceding section.

(2) In Spinoza (*q.v.* 4) the term applies to the sense of *conatus*, or striving, which is in his analysis central to human life.

(3) In Leibniz (*q.v.* 1) the scope of appetition is extended throughout reality, and refers to the manner of action of the extensionless monads which constitute the world.

(4) Whitehead (*q.v.* 20) followed Leibniz in accepting appetition as a universal category describing the activity of the most basic ontological units.

APPROPRIATION.

The subjective approach to truth favored by Kierkegaard (*q.v.* 1). He contrasted his view with the objective approach of science, which he called "endless approximation," and which he opposed.

A PRIORI.

From the Latin *a* ("from") and *priori* ("the preceding"). Used in contrast to *a posteriori* (*q.v.*) to refer to those conclusions which we derive from what has already been laid down, and not from experience. Thus, it refers to what we can derive from our definitions and what is implicit in the meanings of ideas already accepted. (*Q.v.* Hume 5).

(1) Kant (*q.v.* 1) develops both the general notion of the *a priori* and the more specialized notion of the *synthetic a priori* (*q.v.*). (2) The *a priori* is more widely discussed today under the headings Analytic (*q.v.*), Analytic Judgment (*q.v.*), and Tautology (*q.v.*). (3) For a view of the *a priori* as related to transcendent truth *q.v.* Maréchal (2).

"A" PROPOSITION.

Q.v. Proposition (1); Syllogism (3, 6a).

AQUINAS, ST. THOMAS. 1225–1274.

Medieval philosopher-theologian. Born in the vicinity of Naples, Italy. After studying under both Benedictines and Dominicans, he joined the Dominican order in 1243. Beginning in 1245 he studied with Albertus Magnus in Paris. These studies were continued in Cologne from 1248–52. From 1252–59 he was again in Paris where he taught theology at the University of Paris. From 1259–68 he was advisor to the papal court in Rome. From 1269–72 he was again in Paris, and from 1272–74 in Naples. He was canonized in 1323. Centering his philosophic activity around the determination, interpretation, and defense of Aristotle's system of thought while adapting it to the needs of the 13th century (more dramatically termed "the baptism of Aristotle"), Thomas Aquinas achieved a system of thought which has shown itself to have enduring worth. In 1879 Thomist philosophy was given official sanction by Pope Leo XIII.

Principal writings: *On Being and Essence* (T), 1242–43; *On Truth* (T), 1256–59; *On Potency* (T), 1259–63; *Summa Contra Gentiles* (T), 1260; *On the Divine Names* (T), 1261; *On Evil* (T), 1263–68; *Summa Theologica* (T), 1265–72; *On the Eternity of the World* (T), 1270; *On Separate Substances* (T), 1271; in addition, minor works.

(1) Accepting the task of bringing Aristotelian philosophy into the framework of the Christian faith, Aquinas held that

philosophy and religion complement each other. In the appropriate relationship man begins with the exercise of his reason. Depending upon his strength of intellect much or little can be achieved by reason; but at some point one must pass beyond reason to faith. The line where the transition occurs moves up or down depending on the individual; and what one man can achieve by reason another will have to take on faith. Knowledge of the existence of God, for example, might be the product of reason for one person, and an article of faith for someone else; but the articles of faith, properly speaking, *i.e.*, the Incarnation, the Trinity, etc., are beyond the reach of reason for everyone, and yet as revealed and sacred doctrine, they represent the highest wisdom. They must necessarily be approached by means of faith. Miracles are in the same case. They are beyond the reach of our reason, contradicting the order known to us, yet expressing a higher order known to God.

(2) Knowledge of God is available through a negative way, the *via negationis* and a positive way, the *via eminentiae*. We can know that God is not like us; and we can know that the perfections of existence, taken in a more eminent way, will apply to God.

(3) But we can know this only if the idea of God is required by human reason, and this means that the idea of God must be required in explaining the world of our experience. Aquinas advances five ways, the *quinque viae*, in which the idea of God is required in explaining the world: (a) There is motion in the world; and whatever is moved is moved by another. But if all of the links in the chain of motions were intermediate links, we should have no complete explanation of motion. Hence, at the origin of each series of moved movers there must be an initial mover, which is unmoved. This unmoved mover men call God. (b) There are efficient causes in the world. I may explain a given happening by mentioning its cause; but then the cause in turn must be explained; and the task of explanation will not have been completed so long as my references are to intermediate causes. Hence there must be included in my explanation reference to a first cause. And to this cause everyone

gives the name, God. (c) The world contains contingent beings coming to be and passing away. If all beings are contingent, and if the series of past times is an infinite series (an assumption I think Aquinas meant to apply to this argument), then there should have been a time in which these contingent beings would have passed away simultaneously, leaving nothing at all. (If all things are contingent it is surely at least possible that they should perish simultaneously. And it is a property of an infinite series that everything possible for the series is actually in it.) But in this case, since one cannot get something from nothing, there should now be nothing. But this is not the case; and hence not everything is contingent; and there must exist a necessary being; we speak of this being as God. (d) In experience we recognize degrees of truth, goodness, nobility and the like. In order for our judgments of this sort to make sense there must exist in a supreme manner truth, goodness, and nobility. But, siding with Aristotle against Plato, only beings exist. Hence there must be a Supreme Being who is truth, goodness and nobility. (e) All things, both animate and inanimate, are goal directed, acting to achieve ends. But inanimate objects cannot direct themselves to these ends; hence, as the arrow is directed by the archer, the world must be directed by an intelligent being. This being men call God.

(4) Since the term, "Being," is used in many ways, we have to use a principle of analogy in fixing the appropriate import of our terms. And since there are certain "transcendental" terms which go beyond any genus, and apply to everything that is, they are attributes of everything. The transcendentals are *ens, res, unum, aliquid, verum, bonum*, (being, thing, unity, distinction, true, good). All beings are things with unity, distinguished from what is not themselves. All beings are what they are, hence in relation to knowledge, are true. And all beings tend toward their ends or goals and so fit the Aristotelian-Thomistic definition of goodness.

When we join the transcendentals to the principles of analogy, we begin to be able to discern, within limits, God's nature. The analogy we have in mind is called the analogy of proportionality, which can be expressed:

The properties of x   The properties of y
_____ are to _____ as _____ are to _____
x's being   y's being

From this we would be led to expect that in measure as God's being exceeds ours so will the properties of his being. The five ways establish certain of these properties, leading us to conceive of a being of a certain kind. In relating this Being to the transcendentals we gain other properties. From all of this emerges the classical idea of a perfect being synthesizing Platonic, Aristotelian, and Augustinian ideas. God is perfect and unchanging, utterly simple and unitary, hence indestructible, absolute truth and goodness, not related to the world, yet everything in the world is related to Him. And yet, since the divine mind contains the archetypes of all existence, simply in knowing Himself He is able to know at once all that is, was, or will be. In His self-awareness all time is concentrated in an eternal moment, in a *totum simul*. Aquinas argued that while God is the primary cause of all things, among secondary causes some are necessary and others contingent. Thus free will is compatible with God's foreknowledge and God's causation of all things. Furthermore, using the Aristotelian terminology, but in a typically Aquinian manner, to express the status of a necessary being, God's essence and existence are identical, hence He cannot fail to exist. In comparison to all other things God is pure actuality (*actus purus*) with no admixture of potentiality; thus, too, His being is from Himself and not another. He has *aseitas* (a "from" *se* "self") in contrast with those beings derived from another. These conceptions relate to Aquinas' development of Aristotelian metaphysics, to which we must now turn.

(5) The world of Aquinas, like that of Aristotle, is made up of individual substances, composed of prime matter and substantial form, interacting— affecting each other—in various ways. Instances of formed matter are differentiated by differences among the forms, and these differences allow us a vertical dimension of levels of reality, depending on the dignity of the form involved.

Reality can be viewed, in fact, as an hierarchical pyramid of beings, whose lowest level is unformed matter, prime matter, and whose highest level is pure form without material entanglement, *i.e.*, God. God is to be regarded as pure actuality; prime matter, correspondingly, is to be viewed as pure, unmixed potentiality. Between these two extremes are to be found various levels of instances of formed matter, the order of nature; and both form and matter are abstract metaphysical elements of the concrete individual substance. Prime matter cannot exist by itself, and is hence something like an abstraction when so conceived. Pure form can exist by itself, and indeed cannot avoid existing.

What we have thus far set down is common to the accounts of both Aristotle and Aquinas. The latter, like Aristotle, thought of truth as correspondence. "*Veritas*" he said, "*est adaequatio rei et intellectus.*" (Truth is the adequation of thing and intellect.) Also like Aristotle he treated perception and abstract thought as involving a separation of the form of a thing from its material conditions. The position in this respect, is that of moderate realism. Aquinas tells us that the universal has a foundation in the individual essence of the thing; and the abstractive act of intellect consists in forming a universal essence from the numerically distinct but alike essences of individual things. Metaphysically, at least, Aquinas adds to Aristotle's account an additional principle.

(6) This principle, "the double composition of essence and existence," enables Aquinas to discriminate prime matter, ordinary contingent things made of form and matter, ranks of angels (each one being the only member of its class) contingent and yet composed of form without matter, and God the necessary being without composition whose essence is his existence. To the earlier account has been added, it will be noticed, a type of immaterial finite being. This is accomplished in the following manner: Instead of saying that formed matter yields an individual substance, one holds that formed matter yields the essence of the individual thing to which existence must still be added. There is first, then, a composition of form and matter

followed by a second composition of essence and existence. Thus Aquinas can interpose between ordinary substances and God the immaterial angels who are pure forms, yet not necessary beings, since, in addition to their essential forms, existence must be added. Sensible substance, on the other hand, consists of "signate matter" ordered to three dimensions. The view of Aquinas is hence more complex than that of Aristotle who held matter to be the principle of individuation and form to be that which ordered a thing to its species.

(7) Regarding the soul as man's substantial form, Aquinas distinguished intellectual, volitional, and appetitive functions therein. When turning to goods satisfying to the senses, the appetite is said to be *concupiscible*, and the passions related to this function include love, desire, delight, hate, aversion, and sorrow. When turning to goods satisfying to the intellect, this is called the *rational* appetite (or will); a second form of love relates to this aspect of the soul. The movement of protecting one's satisfactions, present and future, in either of these senses is called the irascible appetite, and the passions related to this function are fear, daring, hope, despair, and anger. The function of the intellect is to understand, and this includes apprehension, judgment, and reasoning. The intellect abstracts universal meanings from sense experience by means of phantasms standing for the species of perceived things; for Aquinas this required a division into two functions: the passive intellect (*intellectus possibilis*) which receives the phantasm, and the agent or active intellect (*intellectus agens*) which grasps the abstracted meaning. Even though he interpreted psychic activity in functional terms the universality of the functions of intellect and will provided Aquinas with an argument for the soul's immateriality; and thus, too, for its creation by God out of nothing (*q.v.* 6 above).

(8) Following Aristotle quite closely in his ethical theory, Aquinas treated happiness as the end of life, while identifying it with divine beatitude. So far as the term "good" is concerned, it is clear from the preceding section that the idea of good can be derived from the goods naturally satisfying to the appetites. But the virtues which one gains by an Aristotelian analysis must be complemented by the "theological" virtues of faith, hope, and love, justifying grace being their foundation. It is usually said that Aquinas follows a natural law ethic; it might also be called an ethic of the natural reason. His basic principle is that good is to be done and evil avoided. His understanding of law is "an ordinance of reason promulgated for the common good." His view of right action is an action which "proceeds to its end in accord with the order of reason and of eternal law." Thus the notion of "right" emerges from the notion of "good" through the medium of order and law. Ethics rests on principles of the practical reason where science rests on principles of theoretical reason. Prudence, *i.e.* right reason about things to be done, likewise rests on the practical reason.

(9) It is the same kind of law that directs man with respect to right and wrong in daily life as directs him to the political common good in society. And this is the natural law or *jus naturale*. Just as there are laws implanted in physical nature, which are natural laws, so are there laws implanted by the creator in human nature and discernible by man's reason. The only difference is that man has the power to disobey the laws of his nature.

Aquinas distinguishes four interrelated types of law: the divine or eternal law; natural law; the law of nations; and positive or civil law. For Aquinas the basis of all lawfulness is the *jus divinum* or eternal law in the mind of God. This law is given to man in part through divine revelations; but another part is implanted in man, as we have seen, and is available to man through the use of his reason. This is the natural law or *jus naturale*. The natural law is further specified in terms of two further types of law: civil law or *jus civile* and the law of nations or *jus gentium*. Civil law is, of course, the set of laws governing a given society. Aquinas finds that since societies differ, and are in different situations, the precepts of natural law must be particularized to fit the contingent circumstances of each society. This process of particular determination is similar to the artistic process where general forms are particularized in details. The law of nations is the set of laws on which all societies agree. It would be the body of international law. This set of laws is likewise drawn from natural law; but its determination is by way of deduction, as conclusions are drawn from premises.

(10) Aquinas defines art as "right reason in making things." He defines the beautiful as that which gives pleasure when perceived. In his view three factors are closely associated with the beautiful: *consonantia* or harmony; *integritas* or perfection; *claritas* or brilliance. To associate the beautiful with harmony and unity is reminiscent of Aristotle; to relate the unity of a thing to its radiance or brilliance is reminiscent of Plotinus. In addition to physical beauty, there is a spiritual beauty which derives from the due ordering of spiritual goods.

A QUO.

From the Latin *a* ("from") and *quo* ("which"). The phrase, part of the vocabulary of Scholastic philosophy, refers to the point of origin of an argument, that is, to the principles, assumption, and definitions from which it is derived. To be contrasted with *ad quem* (*q.v.*).

ARABIC PHILOSOPHY.

Q.v. Alexandrian School; Islamic Philosophy.

ARANYAKAS.

Q.v. Vedas (3).

ARBOR PORPHYRII.

The Tree of Porphyry, a manner of illustrating the relations of genus, species, and individuals, widely influential throughout the Middle Ages. *Q.v.* Porphyry (1).

ARCESILAUS. 315–241 B.C.

Greek philosopher. Born in Aeolia. Head of the Platonic Academy following Crates (*q.v.* 1). Founder of the Second, or Middle, Academy. A moderate skeptic, he attacked the Stoic claim of the possibility of universal knowledge. On the other hand, however, his doctrine of the *eulogon* held that the guide to life must be probability, and that this required adoption of the alternatives supported by sets of mutually supporting reasons.

Principal writings: Discussed by Cicero and Sextus Empiricus. No writings survive.

ARCHELAUS. 5th cent. B.C.

Greek philosopher. Born in Athens or Miletus. Disciple of Anaxagoras. Is said to have succeeded his teacher as head of the latter's school. Like Anaxagoras (*q.v.*) he utilized *nous* (mind) as a principle of motion. Adhered to a scheme of evolution, and to a geocentric theory of the universe. He made a distinction between nature and convention, anticipating the Sophists (*q.v.*) in adhering to the conventionality of all political and social judgments.

ARCHE.

A Greek term signifying "that which was in the beginning."

(1) Among the Ionian philosophers (*q.v.* Anaximander 1) the first substance or primal element.

(2) For the Pythagoreans the term referred to the origin of the number series (*q.v.* Pythagoras 4, 6–8).

(3) For Plato's usage *q.v.* Archetype (1).

(4) In Aristotle (*q.v.* 2, 9) the term refers both to principles of action in a causal sense, and to principles of demonstration.

(5) In the Gospel of John, the beginning which is identified with the Word or *Logos*.

ARCHETYPE.

From the Greek *arche* ("primal") plus *typos* ("figure" or "pattern"). (1) For Plato (*q.v.* 1, 9) the original forms or ideas in which things participate and of which they are copies. (2) In Scholasticism (*q.v.* Aquinas 4) the archetypes have as their location the divine mind. (3) In Locke (*q.v.* 8) the term shifts in meaning to signify things in the world, the originals of our ideas. (4) With Jung (*q.v.* 2, 4–7) another shift occurs, and the term refers to the primordial forms of the collective unconscious.

ARCHITECTONIC.

The term has been used to describe a philosophical system constructed according to a consistent plan. (1) The Kantian philosophy is said to be architectonic in that its plan, as exemplified in the categories, is derived from the basic distinctions of formal logic (*q.v.* Kant 3). (2) On the other hand Charles Peirce (*q.v.* 2), likewise claiming that philosophy should be architectonic, derived his pattern from a phenomenological examination of immediate experience, as well as a survey of all of the fields of human knowledge.

ARCHYTAS. 4th century B.C.

Greek philosopher. Lived in Tarentum. A second generation Pythagorean, a student of Philolaus (*q.v.*) and friend of Plato, who separated the school's number theory from its mystical and religious setting, thus making possible important advances both in the theoretical development of arithmetic and geometry, and their application to the universe in scientific terms. To those who held that space was finite he issued the challenge that they explain to him why, were he taken to its edge, he could not reach beyond.

ARDIGÓ, ROBERTO. 1828–1920.

Italian philosopher. Born in Cremona. Professor in the University of Padua. The leading Italian positivist, Ardigó argued strongly in its defense against the rising tide of Italian idealism in the latter part of the 19th century.

Selected writings: *Psychology as a Positive Science; Positivism and the Unknowable of H. Spencer; Empiricism and Science; Philosophy and Positivism;* all in his *Works,* 12 vols., 1882–1918.

(1) Philosophy is made up of the disciplines concerned with the phenomena of thought; logic, epistemology aesthetics, sociology, ethics, law, and economics. (2) In addition, philosophy includes the general realm of the Indistinct. The Indistinct is the source of that which is now distinct; it now includes that which will be distinct tomorrow. It is the infinite in progressive development. (3) The difference between self and things is nothing more than the difference between an "autosynthesis" and a "heterosynthesis" of neutral elements. (4) Freedom is possible because chance exists in the world. Although individual causal series are determined, the causal intersections of these series are undetermined, and hence unpredictable.

ARETE.

The Greek term for virtue. It is a fulfillment term. For Aristotle (*q.v.* 11) who may be taken to represent the Greeks in this respect, *arete* is the fulfillment of the function of being human.

ARETE THE CYRENAIC.

Q.v. Cyrenaicism (2).

ARGUMENT.

Q.v. Peirce (16).

ARGUMENTS FOR GOD.

Q.v. God (B.); Ontological Argument; Teleological Argument; Cosmological Argument.

ARGUMENTUM AD BACULUM.

Q.v. Fallacies (8).

ARGUMENTUM AD HOMINEM.

Q.v. Fallacies (9).

ARGUMENTUM AD IGNORANTIAM.

Q.v. Fallacies (14).

ARGUMENTUM AD JUDICIUM.

An argument relying on the judicious sense or common sense of humankind.

ARGUMENTUM AD MISERICORDIAM.

Q.v. Fallacies (10).

ARGUMENTUM AD POPULUM.

Q.v. Fallacies (6).

ARGUMENTUM AD REM.

An argument which adheres to the point, hence avoiding the fallacies which involve moving away from the point at issue in one of a great variety of ways.

ARGUMENTUM AD VERECUNDIAM.

Q.v. Fallacies (11).

ARGUMENTUM A FORTIORI.

Q.v. A Fortiori.

ARGUMENTUM EX CONCESSO.

An argument taking as its basis the propositions conceded to be true by one's opponent.

ARHAT.

From the Sanskrit root *arh* ("worthy," "deserving"). The highest state of spiritual development in Theravada Buddhism (*q.v.* 1, 6), in Pali *arahant.*

ARIANISM. 4th cent. A.D.

The name of a dispute which wracked the early church, continued from 318 to 381 A.D., required 18 councils before it was ended, beginning with the famous Council of Nicaea in 325 A.D., and ending with the Council of Constantinople in 381 A.D. The subject of the dispute was the meaning of the incarnation in relation to the Christian premise of monotheism. Praxeas, Sabellius, and others had viewed Christ as virtually a transient manifestation of God; Arius thought he detected this view in a charge to his clergy on the part of Alexander, Bishop of Alexandria. Arius, a presbyter of Alexandria, in stating his own view distinguished sharply between the Father and the Son subordinating the latter to the former. This set the stage for the controversy. The subtle distinction between *homoousian* and *homoiousian* became important. Is the Son *homoousias* with the Father (*i.e.*, of the same essence or substance), or *homoiousias* (of similar essence or substance)? The Nicene formula, holding the Son to be *homoousias* with the Father became the orthodox position. *Q.v.* Christology (1–2).

ARIŞTANEMI (ARISHTANEMI).

Q.v. Vardhamana.

ARISTARCHUS.

Q.v. Crates (2).

ARISTIDES. 2nd century A.D.

Christian Apologist. Apparently born and lived in Athens. His *Apology* was addressed to the Emperor Hadrian and was perhaps read to him on the occasion of the latter's visit to Athens. Aristides regarded the Christians as alone possessing the truth about God, and indeed as constituting a special race originating with Christ. Having the truth, Christians are able to live holy and righteous lives. Chaldeans, Greeks, and Egyptians have all erred. The Jews are praiseworthy in their adherence to monotheism, but a superstition with respect to rites and ceremonies remains. *Q.v.* Apologists (2).

Principal writings: *Apology.*

ARISTIPPUS. 435–356 B.C.

Greek philosopher. Born and lived in Cyrene. One of the disciples of Socrates who, after the latter's death, began his own school of philosophy. Named the Cyrenaic School (*q.v.* Cyrenaicism) after its location, it is counted as one of the three major Socratic Schools (*q.v.*). Aristippus held the position of hedonism (*q.v.*), that good and evil are reducible to pleasure and pain. The end of life is self-gratification, and philosophy is the study of the best means of living pleasantly. Although the emphasis is on immediate pleasure, his point of view does include a measure of rational control. Like Antisthenes (*q.v.* 2) he believed that universals were merely names.

ARISTIPPUS THE YOUNGER.

Q.v. Cyrenaicism (2).

ARISTOCRACY.

From the Greek *aristos* ("best") and *kratein* ("to rule"). One of the perennially formulated types of ideal government, aristocracy means rule by the best in the interests of the whole society but without the participation of the governed.

(1) For Plato (*q.v.* 5f) aristocracy was the ideal social structure, standing in contrast to four degenerate forms of government.

(2) For Aristotle (*q.v.* 12), on the other hand, aristocracy was one of three desirable forms of government, sharing Aristotle's commendation with monarchy and polity.

(3) For Hobbes (*q.v.* 8) it simply meant that form of government where the sovereign power is in the hands of the few.

(4) Jefferson (*q.v.* 4–5) believed there is among humans a natural aristocracy of virtue and talent which must replace the false aristocracy of birth and wealth.

ARISTON OF ALEXANDRIA. 1st cent. B.C.

Hellenic philosopher. Initially a member of the Academy (*q.v.* Plato's Academy) under Antiochus (*q.v.*) he later joined the newly renascent Aristotelian school in Alexandria. Andronicus of Rhodes (*q.v.*) was its head at the time.

Principal writings: a commentary on the *Categories.*

ARISTON OF CHIOS. 3rd cent. B.C.

Greek philosopher. A member of the Lyceum (*q.v.*), he followed Lycon (*q.v.*) as its head around 228 B.C.

ARISTOTELIANISM.

The philosophy of those who follow Aristotle (*q.v.*) is not entirely uniform. The Stagirite has been variously interpreted in different ages. In designating the followers of Aristotle we shall use the neutral term "Aristotelian" rather than the more colorful term "Peripatetic" (*q.v.*), the reason being that the latter term mistakenly suggests that Aristotle's method of teaching was that of conversation during a stroll.

(1) Aristotle founded a school, the Lyceum (*q.v.*), which existed without interruption from the date of its founding in 339 B.C. until around 200 B.C. The school began as a center for scientific investigation. This remained a central theme throughout its history, although in some periods polemic with other schools of philosophy and monographs on the history of philosophy outweighed the attention paid to science. The school was in decline from the middle of the 3rd century on.

(2) A vigorous resurgence of Aristotelianism occurred in Alexandria in the 1st century B.C. The movement centered around Andronicus of Rhodes (*q.v.*) who had recovered the writings of Aristotle after a century-long disappearance. Others important to the Aristotelian school of Alexandria are Ariston of Alexandria (*q.v.*) and Nicholas of Damascus (*q.v.*). In a general sense Ptolemy (*q.v.*), whose astronomy was accepted for 1400 years and Galen (*q.v.*), whose medical analyses endured at least as long, were members of the school.

(3) Between the 4th and 7th centuries A.D. the schools of Neoplatonism in Athens and Alexandria frequently studied Aristotle along with Plato, and indeed often held that the two systems of thought were compatible (*q.v.* Neoplatonism 8, 9). Outside these schools were other philosophers, such as Themistius (*q.v.*) who held a similar point of view. Themistius lived principally in Constantinople although he spent one period of his life in Rome. Boethius (*q.v.*), whose life was lived principally in Rome, provides another instance. Aristotelianism and Neoplatonism tended to merge during this period. The identification of the two strands was intensified by the mistaken identification with Aristotle of two Neoplatonic treatises in fact translated from the work of Proclus and Plotinus (*q.v.*. Neoplatonism 11–12).

(4) The great period of Islamic philosophy (*q.v.*) lies between the 9th and 13th centuries, centering on the interpretation of Aristotle. As indicated above, there were mistaken reasons for the Platonized versions of Aristotle which emerged from the analyses. But the great names of Al-Kindi (*q.v.*), Al-Farabi (*q.v.*), Avicenna (*q.v.*), and Al-Ghazzali (*q.v.*) kept alive an Aristotelian heritage, making possible the medieval synthesis of the 13th century.

(5) Among the many Jewish philosophers whose work on Aristotle held great importance for the medieval synthesis the names of Avicebron (*q.v.*) and Maimonides (*q.v.*) must be cited.

(6) The medieval synthesis itself (*q.v.* Medieval Philosophy 8–15) might well be viewed as the philosophy of Aristotle modified by the implications of commitment to the Christian faith. There was likewise a component of Platonism or Neoplatonism, but the mistaken identifications referred to in (3) above had been discovered.

(7) The school of Thomism (*q.v.*) emerged from the Middle Ages in strength, and continues to the present day. But the view of Thomas Aquinas was not the only form of Aristotelianism to emerge from the Middle Ages. Scotism (*q.v.*), the philosophy of Duns Scotus, likewise survived. Somewhat more indirectly the philosophy of Suarez (*q.v.*), initiated in the 16th century, and developed from a Thomistic base, preserves an Aristotelian core.

ARISTOTLE. 384–322 B.C.

Greek philosopher. Born in Stagyra, Macedonia. Son of Nicomachus, physician to the king. At 18 entered Plato's Academy, and studied there nearly 20 years. Upon Plato's death a rival was named head of Plato's Academy, and Aristotle left Athens. Circa 342, became tutor to Alexander, son of King Phillip of Macedon. In 335 he returned to Athens, founding his own school, the Lyceum. Upon Alexander's accession to power Aristotle received support, financially and otherwise, from the young ruler. Upon Alexander's death in 323, in the face of a surge of anti-Macedonian feeling, Aristotle went voluntarily into exile "lest," he is reported to have said, "Athens sin twice against philosophy." Died in exile the following year.

Principal writings: (a) In Logic, the *Organon*, including among others, the *Categories* (T), *Topics* (T), *On Sophistical Refutations* (T); (b) in Physical Science, the *Physics* (T), *On the Heavens* (T), *On Generation and Corruption* (T), *Meteorology* (T); (c) in Biology, the *History of Animals* (T), *On the Parts of Animals* (T), *On the Movement of Animals* (T), *On the Progression of Animals* (T); (d) in Psychology, *On the Soul* (T), *Parva Naturalia* (T); (e) In Metaphysics, *The Metaphysics* (T); (f) in Ethics and Social Philosophy, *Nicomachean Ethics* (T), *Magna Moralia* (T), *Eudemian Ethics* (T), the *Politics* (T) and *Constitution of Athens* (T); (g) in Aesthetics, the *Rhetoric* (T) and the *Poetics* (T).

(1) Aristotle was the first philosopher to have a fairly clear grasp of the many facets implicit in the production of knowledge. Not only was he able to discern the role of definition, induction, and deduction, in the development of science, he was also able to see differences in the sciences, distinguishing them into theoretical sciences which aim at truth (*theoria*), practical sciences aiming at action (*praxis*), and productive sciences aimed at making (*poiesia*). Truth is correspondence, saying "of what is that it is and of what is not that it is not." The activity of making or producing is called *poiesia*; and the knowledge relating to this kind of production, poietic knowledge. The components of knowledge relate differently in these different disciplines, and the more abstract disciplines, such as mathematics and metaphysics, are more completely ordered to changelessness and necessity; and it seems clear that for Aristotle not only metaphysics but also mathematics as the most abstract disciplines, bear a special relationship to the other fields, such as physics, astronomy, psychology, and biology.

(2) The inner relations of the field of knowledge can be set forth in some clarity if one asks for the role of intuition in the production of knowledge. Intuition has two principal roles: (a) We intuit particulars of sense directly; and

reasoning about whether we have intuited them is simply inappropriate. Aristotle would have been neither disturbed nor grieved by the claim of the skeptic that the existence of an external world cannot be proved. Aristotle would agree, since the world is to be experienced, providing a basis for deductions, but not itself deduced. He did argue, however, that the presence of sensation implies the existence of the sensible; and that sensation is an act common to the sensible and the sentient. Even so, the basic attitude is that of acceptance of the sensible world as given. From sense particulars we form definitions, make inductions, provide the premises for deductions. (b) At the other pole of our experience, we also intuit the most general principles of explanation, including logical principles themselves. And between these poles the basic structuring of theories goes on. There is a family of terms, including definition (*q.v.* 4 below), axiom, postulate, and hypothesis, operating in the forms of explanation. Axioms are the indemonstrable primary premises of demonstration, notions commonly held to be true; postulates relate to the subject whose attributes are to be examined. Unlike axioms they are demonstrable, but used in the given inquiry without demonstration. Hypotheses are like postulates in that they are capable of proof, but accepted for the purpose of the examination without proof. They differ from postulates in ranging more widely, and including more than the primary premises of the demonstration.

(3) For instance, we make inductions from the particulars of sense, providing generalizations and abstractions. Aristotle's sense of induction reflects a confidence in an intuition, or direct seeing, of the nature of what is before one, which is foreign to contemporary inductive theory. Indeed, in the comparison of any two sense data, one can generalize about their nature, seeing what they have in common, and how they differ. In *On Memory and Recollection* (Ch. II, par. 6–11) he advanced the associative principles of similarity, contrast, and contiguity to apply to this process. Induction separates the sense datum from some of the conditions of its existence in the world,

making generalization possible. Abstraction is the same process carried further. When done correctly we are both thinking the form in, and abstracting the form from, the images or *phantasmata* of sense. Mathematics represents a high level of abstraction, an abstraction from the existence of things in the world.

(4) The role of definition will serve to illustrate not only how closely Aristotle thought it possible for our ideas to parallel the world, but also the predicables of Aristotle's logic. Aristotle believed in real definitions. Definitions were true, or not true, of the thing defined. And a true definition would express the essence of the thing defined. To do so, it is necessary to relate the term being defined to the large class of which it is a member, that is, its genus, and at the same time one must state how the sub-class of the thing in question (the species) differs from other members of the genus class. When "man" is defined as "rational animal," this is a definition by genus and difference, the genus being "animal" and the *differentia* being "rationality."

The description of definition has given us three of the five predicables: species, genus, and difference. The other two predicables are "property" and "accident." While the definition is expected to state the essence of a thing, a "property," while not stating the essence, yet belongs only to that thing. For example, to be capable of learning grammar is a property of man, and yet this capacity is not part of the definition of "man." An "accident," on the other hand, is a predicate with only a contingent relation to its subject. It just happens to characterize the subject in question. The brown of the table is an accident in that the table might have been some other color, and might be another color tomorrow.

(5) Because Aristotle believed that the advance of knowledge depended on the discovery of "middle terms," it is clear that deduction must be regarded as an important aspect of his thought. Indeed, since he means by science "demonstrated knowledge of the causes of things," science in his view is a matter of syllogistic deduction from certain premises. Aristotle's logic was a logic predicating terms of subjects, and

although there exist some differences between the ideas of predication and of class membership, the theory of the syllogism can be expressed more simply, certainly more graphically, in the vocabulary of classes. The tradition of syllogistic logic deriving from Aristotle became a class logic. The reader may turn to the entry, Syllogism, for a discussion of syllogistic logic as a logic of classes. Similarly the three laws of thought derive from Aristotle. He says of the principle of contradiction that "the firmest of all principles is that it is impossible for the same thing to belong and not to belong to the same thing at the same time in the same respect." And he says of the principle of excluded middle: "It is not possible that there should be anything between the two parts of a contradiction, but it is necessary either to affirm or deny one thing of any one thing." He nowhere states the principle of identity (*q.v.*), although it is presupposed. When one's premises are not certain but only probable, a transition from science to dialectic has occurred. There is a further shift to eristic where one's goal is no longer knowledge but merely victory in disputation.

(6) It is convenient to note that the linguistic distinctions of Aristotle's subject-predicate logic are paralleled by an ontology made up of individual substances interacting in various ways, characterized by properties of various sorts. When Aristotle lists his Categories, a list of the basic classifications into which whatever can be named will fit, substance is listed first as the basic category; and the remainder of the list is composed of the attributes of substance, or the ways in which substance exists: in a certain quantity, of a certain quality, with certain relations, in a certain place (the inner boundary of the containing body), at a certain time, in a certain position, in a certain state, in a certain condition of action, or of being acted upon (called "passion" or "affection"). For Aristotle existence is basically the existence of a substance; and the meaning of existence is different—more dependent, derivative—for quantities, relations, and the other categories.

(7) Aristotle selected "substance" as his basic category because "substance" is his

basic ontological unit and substance in its primary sense, "that which is," defines the order of nature (*q.v.* 3), involving form, matter, and an internal principle of movement. Substance in its primary sense, termed *ousia prote* or "first substance," includes the key terms "form" and "matter" which explicate its components. They express the idea of structure, and that which is structured. For example, he defined the soul as the form of the body. There is a sense in which form and matter are relative terms. What is in one sense formed matter (say a block of marble) is in another sense just matter (for the statue to be formed). Aristotle also thinks of the less determined as matter and the more determined as form; so he tends to think of the genus as matter, and the species as form. When the idea of the structured is pressed beyond such relativities we arrive at Aristotle's doctrine of "prime matter," the utterly formless potentiality for becoming "this" or "that." Prime matter, however, cannot exist by itself, and hence is in one sense an abstraction. The idea of form likewise cannot exist apart from matter, and is an abstraction, except in the case of the pure form which is God, and certain lesser forms designed to bolster his somewhat inadequate astronomy. Together, form and matter make an individual substance; and it is the accidents of matter which make the substance this particular chair.

(8) The idea of potentiality belongs to matter, and the idea of actuality to form. Of course, the idea of actuality belongs preeminently to God, the pure form; and while it belongs to form in any case where form is compared to matter, we must remember that ordinarily forms cannot exist without matter; and that in the clearest sense it is not form, but substance, that is actual. The absence of a potentiality in a thing is called a privation. To the complete fulfillment of a thing on the other hand, Aristotle applies the terms "entelechy" and "*energeia*, "the former referring to the state of completion and the latter to the power of that state. One of Aristotle's chief contributions to philosophy was the concept of potentiality. It has many applications in his philosophy. For example, his most recurrent interpretation of infinity is that of "potential

infinity." Potential infinity is the statement of a capacity; it applies to that which can be infinitely divided, augmented, or diminished. But the infinitely divisible is not actually divided into an infinite series. According to Aristotle one of the mistakes of Zeno (*q.v.*) in his elaboration of the paradoxes of time and motion is that he did not distinguish between actual and potential infinities. Aristotle's definition of continuity also requires the idea of potential infinity. The "continuous" is that subdivision of the contiguous whose limits are one and the same, and contained in each other. This implies that the parts of the continuous are infinitely divisible; or as Aristotle says "divisible into divisibles that are infinitely divisible" (Physics 231b). The potentiality-actuality contrast allowed him to develop a dynamic reality, which he yet constrained within rather narrow limits. He is able to express dynamically the sense in which an acorn is potentially an oak, but he is not able to express the sense in which an entire species might have developed from a potentiality. Indeed, in his view species are fixed and immutable. Potentiality is also limited by the fact that of the three basic types of change— "alteration" or change of quality, "growth and diminution" or change of quantity, and "locomotion" or change of place— Aristotle believes that the last is primary in the sensible world. In any change which occurs in the sensible world, change of place must occur, preceding any other type of change, and the transmission of force thus occurs only through contact.

(9) The ideas of form and matter, potentiality and actuality, play a significant role in Aristotle's analysis of causation. In arriving at his point of view Aristotle, canvassing the opinions of others, found four types of cause which he called efficient, final, material, and formal. *Efficient cause* is very close to our ordinary notion of cause. It denotes the manner in which substances act upon one another through locomotion and contact. *Final cause* in its ordinary sense designates the end stage of a process, forming a natural unity, like the growth of an individual organism from seed to maturity, this end stage exercising an attraction on the earlier stages due to its

relatively greater perfection. When he holds that chance exists at the intersection of independent causal chains he seems to be thinking of both efficient and final cause. In its supreme sense final cause designates the eternal being controlling the universe by means of the attraction inherent in its own perfections. *Material* and *formal cause* are the constituents—matter and form—within substance; and, in addition, as with final cause, there is a supreme example of the eternal or divine Form, the form of forms, and final cause of final causes.

In the coming to be of a statue the efficient cause would be found in the blows of the chisel upon the marble block; the final cause would be the reason why the sculptor was at work in the making of the statue; the material cause would be the marble out of which the statue was made; and the formal cause would be the form, or structure, or abstract proportionality exemplified in the final product. All four causes are to be found in all that is, although in natural objects the final and formal causes coincide since it is the final cause of the acorn to become an oak, and since this is also the form to be realized.

(10) It is now possible to bring together the modal relations of propositions and of beings. In terms of propositions these relations can be expressed in terms of truth and falsity. The actual is the true. The necessary is that which cannot be false. The impossible is the contrary of the necessary. The possible is that which is true or may be true, and whose contrary is not necessarily false. In terms of beings one speaks of existence and non-existence. The two categories of existent beings are those which are contingent, having the possibility of not existing, and those which are necessary. God is the necessary and fully actual being who directs the world as its final cause and form of forms. Aristotle believes that God's existence can be proven. The proof begins from his analysis of time. Time can have no beginning because every "now" implies a "before"; and since time is the numbering of motion with respect to before and after, motion must also be eternal; hence reality has always been and there was no creation. Now if there has always been change there must also be an eternal cause of change. And Aristotle believes what is required here is an unmoved or prime mover on the ground that the natural first term of a series of moved movers will be a cause imparting motion without itself being moved, and this leads directly to Aristotle's conception of a supreme being as absolutely perfect who moves the world by being loved. His mental content is, in Aristotle's famous phrase, a "thinking on thinking"; and self-sufficient and self-aware, he knows his own being, but not the world. Aristotelian theism, developed most completely in his *Metaphysics*, occupies a consistent position, since God's absolutism is not contravened by any relativity toward the world. The account is to be compared with that of Thomas Aquinas (*q.v.* 4) whose deity is presumed absolute, and yet possesses knowledge of the world.

(11) Aristotle presented the world an account of value in which happiness (*eudaimonia*) is presumed to be the goal of life, while pleasure is merely the concomitant of successful functioning. Happiness is properly pursued when it has a strong rational component. Since it is the ability to reason which separates man from other creatures, man's happiness by nature must include the development of his reason. And moral virtue involves the rational control of desires. He stresses the importance both of dianoetic and moral virtues, the former relating to reason and the latter to rational control of the sensitive and appetitive life. For Aristotle the soul has a rational as well as an irrational part. The rational part is the seat of intellect, and may be divided into an active and a passive part. One way of interpreting Aristotle is that the active intellect (which makes all things) survives the body and is immortal. The passive intellect, which becomes all things and is the seat of individuality, does not. The irrational part is the seat of appetites and desire. While one part of man's rational nature has no relation to desire, another part can exercise a controlling influence on desire. This occurs through the development of habits, and leads to a moral will. Development of man's rational nature leads to the intellectual virtues of wisdom and insight. *Sophia* (speculative wisdom), combining

intuitive reason and rigorous knowledge of first causes and principles, is best exemplified by the discipline of Metaphysics. The appropriate development of man's affective nature leads to the moral virtues implying norms of conduct. The stress on development allows one to view Aristotle as an early spokesman of self-realization as the end of life.

In terms of action, then, a virtuous life means doing the right thing in the right way to the right person to the right degree; that is, it involves the ability to determine the golden mean, and this is the mean between extremes. The development of *phronesis* (practical wisdom) helps in discovery of the mean. The mean lies between the extreme of deficiency and the extreme of excess. Aristotle remarks that the mean most often lies nearer excess than deficiency. Courage, a virtuous state, lies between the deficiency of cowardice and the excess of foolhardiness, but closer to the latter. Temperance lies between insensibility and gluttony; friendship between obsequiousness and contentiousness; justice lies between the deficiency of allowing one's rights to be trampled, and the excess of trampling over the rights of others. Following the mean in all things allows a life of maximum value satisfaction.

(12) Man is a political animal; and virtue must be exercised as a citizen. Aristotle regarded the family as the basic unit of the state, and the state as a creation of nature, since in isolation man is not self-sufficient. There are gradations of ability separating free men, women, and slaves. Free men have the capacity to reason; women lack this capacity, but can understand when the reasoning is explained; natural slaves are those who can obey commands but lack both reason and understanding. He distinguished three kinds of acceptable government: monarchy, aristocracy, and polity. The third, somewhat akin to constitutional democracy, he preferred, criticizing communism, and stressing the importance of the family and of a prosperous middle class. Three unacceptable forms of government are tyranny, oligarchy, and popular democracy. These are deformations of the acceptable forms.

(13) In the general sense, art is a branch of knowledge different from both theoretical science and practical wisdom. It is concerned with the application of theoretical principle to beautiful or useful objects. Works of fine art have their treatment in the *Poetics*. In the *Poetics* Aristotle advanced the idea that a work of art is an imitation of the possible or probable, not of something actual only, thus expanding Plato's doctrine of imitation. Poetry differs from history in that history deals with the particular, and poetry—in this respect like philosophy—deals with the universal. Aristotle's expansion of the criterion for beauty in fact stressed unity in variety, an organic unity with no inessential features. His canons of tragedy (*q.v.* 1)—designed to provide a catharsis of the emotions of terror and pity, the action occurring within a single day, etc.—have had great historical importance.

(14) In the *Rhetoric* Aristotle searches for the rules of persuasion through analysis of examples of effective oratory. Rhetoric is not a science but an art. It is not an art of persuasion but rather the art of being able to discern in each case the available means of persuasion. It is the counterpart of dialectic since both deal with probabilities and commonly held opinions. But the end of persuasion entails that the popular syllogism or enthymeme (*q.v.*) will be central to the analysis and practice of this art. The *Rhetoric* contains a distinction between types of law. Aristotle distinguishes between the written law and the universal law, permanent and changeless. He also calls this the natural law. His advice is that one should appeal to the universal law if the written law goes against one's case: if not, one's appeal should be to the written law.

ARISTOTLE'S DICTUM.
Q.v. Dictum De Omni Et Nullo.

ARISTOXENOS. 4th cent. B.C.
Greek philosopher. Born in Tarentum. Disciple of Aristotle and member of the Lyceum (*q.v.*). He applied the Pythagorean doctrine of harmony to the relation between soul and body, as well as to problems of musical form.

Principal writings: *The Characteristics of Rhythm.*

ARITHMETIC, FOUNDATIONS OF.

(1) Peano (*q.v.*) demonstrated that all of the natural numbers and their relations can be deduced from five postulates. (2) Dedekind (*q.v.*) discovered how to define real numbers in terms of rational numbers. (3) Frege (*q.v.*) demonstrated the possibility of defining rational numbers in terms of logical entities. (4) Russell (*q.v.* 2–4) and Whitehead (*q.v.* 1–2) developed this program in their *Principia Mathematica*, thus basing arithmetic on logic. *Q.v.* Mathematics 5–13.

ARIUS. 256–336.

Presbyter of Alexandria, whose challenge to Bishop Alexander of Alexandria initiated the Arian controversy. *Q.v.* Arianism.

ARJUNA.

Q.v. Vaiṣnavism (2a).

ARMINIUS, JACOBUS. 1560–1609.

Dutch theologian. Born in Oudewater, South Holland. Studied at the University of Leiden, then at Geneva. Ordained in 1588. Professor at Leiden, 1603 until his death. Founder of the Arminian theology. He believed, against Calvin, in human freedom in the state of grace, that the divine decree is contingent upon the individual's repentance or its absence, that believers may be certain of their salvation, and that the regenerate can live without sin. The Remonstrant Church of the Reformed Theology is rooted in his teachings.

Principal writings: *Works*, 3 vols., 1629.

ARMSTRONG, D.M.

Q.v. Materialism (21); Identity Theory (2).

ARNAULD, ANTOINE. 1612–1694.

French theologian and philosopher. Born in Paris. Studied at the Sorbonne where he taught from 1613 until his expulsion in 1656. The separation was due to the Jansenist views which he shared with Pascal (*q.v.* Jansenism). Between 1668 and 1678 he enjoyed a decade without persecution, being received even by Louis XIV. At the end of this period renewed persecution made it necessary for him to leave France, settling in Brussels, where he continued his defense of Jansenism and of the Cartesian philosophy until his death.

Principal philosophical writings: *The Art of Thinking* (with Pierre Nicole) (T), also known as the *Port Royal Logic*, 1662; *Concerning True and False Ideas* (T), 1683.

(1) Arnauld developed a non-Aristotelian logic following the Cartesian method of dividing a problem into its parts and moving from simple to complex (*q.v.* Descartes 10). In the spirit of Descartes he developed eight rules of method (*q.v.* Logic 16).

(2) He likewise contributed the fourth set of objections to Descartes' *Meditations*, pointing out the circularity in his reasoning: the idea of God depends on the clarity and distinctness of our perception of Him, and that clear and distinct perception's are true depends on God's existence (*q.v.* Descartes 3–6).

(3) Against the view of Malebranche (*q.v.* 1–2) that the ideas we think are in God, and that we are directly aware of them, Arnauld defended the more usual view that ideas are in us and represent the world when true.

ARNOBIUS. 3rd–4th cent. A.D.

Christian thinker. Like Minucius Felix (*q.v.*) he held a somewhat low opinion of philosophy and of human reason. He refuted Platonic pre-existence by presenting the case of a man isolated from birth. Such a person, he claimed, would show no signs of intellect. Principal writings: *Adversus Gentes*.

ARNOLD, MATTHEW. 1822–1888.

English poet and literary critic. Born at Laleham. Educated at Oxford where he eventually also taught. Inspector general of schools for thirty-five years, he urged the idea of culture throughout his life.

Principal writings: *Essays in Criticism*, 1865; *Culture and Anarchy*, 1869; *Literature and Dogma*, 1873; *God and the Bible*, 1875; *Mixed Essays*, 1879; *Discourses in America*, 1885; *Essays in Criticism*, 2nd series, 1888.

(1) Defining culture as a pursuit of our "total perfection" through knowledge of the best thought and sayings, Arnold held the function of culture to be criticism and refinement of traditional notions and habits. Elsewhere he defined culture as "the passion for sweetness and light, and what is more the passion for making them prevail."

(2) He regarded literature as one of the chief agents in achieving culture. He found the essential part of the Bible to be the Christian ethic, which alone can stand against any criticism, and which also reflects the spirit of culture.

(3) Labeling the upper, middle, and lower classes the "Barbarians," the "Philistines," and the "Populace" respectively, he found in each class a saving remnant standing for the spirit of culture. It is the increase of this group through education which he took to be the chief task of human culture.

ARROW, KENNETH.
  Q.v. Decision Theory.

ARS COMBINATORIA.
  A Latin phrase meaning the "combinatory art." The phrase was used by Leibniz (*q.v.* 11–12) to signify the general program of building complex concepts from simple ones according to rule. In 1666 Leibniz wrote *De Arte Combinatoria,* containing his program for (1) a universal language (called a "universal characteristic") for investigators, and (2) a universal mathematics (*mathesis universalis*). Although the goal has not been achieved, the program has attracted an increasing amount of attention.

ARS DISSERENDI.
  Q.v. Ramus (1).

ARS MAGNA.
  The great art of Raymond Lull (*q.v.*) was a method of exhausting the possible alternatives for any subject-predicate relationship. The method was mechanical and utilized rotating circles. Lull's goal anticipated the *Ars combinatoria* (*q.v.*) of Leibniz. *Q.v.* Logic (11).

ART.
  From the Latin *ars* signifying any purposeful making or doing.
  (1) in Plato (*q.v.* 1) art is the activity or object of any making or doing controlled by the movement down from theory to practice, and contrasting with the upward movement toward theory. But in the 10th book of the *Republic* (*q.v.* Plato 5g) the fine arts are regarded as an "imitation of an imitation."
  (2) In Aristotle (*q.v.* 13) art is one of three branches of knowledge. Contrasting

with theoretical science and practical wisdom, art is a branch of knowledge concerned with the principles relevant to the production of beautiful or useful objects.

(3) Aquinas (*q.v.* 10) follows both of his predecessors, defining art as right reason in making things.

(4) Lessing (*q.v.*) held that each art has its own governing principles.

(5) Hegel (*q.v.* 19) distinguished between three kinds of art, which are also stages in its development: Symbolic, Classical, and Romantic.

(6) Schopenhauer (*q.v.* 5) regarded music as the highest of the arts.

(7) For the view that art encompasses a blend of Apollonian and Dionysian elements, *q.v.* Nietzsche (1).

(8) Dewey (*q.v.* 6) viewed art as experience in its consummatory phases.

For standard interpretations of the fine arts *q.v.* Aesthetics.

ARTHA.
  Sanskrit term for "aim." *Q.v. Puruṣarthas.*

ARTHAŚASTRA (ARTHASHASTRA), THE.
  Q.v. Kautilya.

ARTICLES OF FAITH.
  Propositions concerning the interpretation of a religion which are to be taken on faith. In Christianity (*q.v.*) the articles of faith were determined at crucial points through Councils. The articles of faith include the interpretation to be given the Trinity and the Incarnation. The Thirty-Nine Articles of the Church of England, and the twenty-four articles of Methodism are also cases in point. For the Swedenborgian Articles of Faith *q.v.* Swedenborg (7).

ARTIFICIAL FORMS.
  Q.v. Form (5g).

ARTIFICIAL INTELLIGENCE.
  A term coined in 1955 by mathematician and computer expert John McCarthy to describe computer programs designed to simulate functions of the human brain, while substituting electronic for neurological networks. As computer simulations of symbolic reasoning become increasingly sophisticated the question of how to interpret them has provided a spectrum of answers.

(1) In 1950 Alan Turing (*q.v.*), "Computing Machinery and Intelligence," argued that if machines can be constructed to function in such a manner that their feedback cannot be distinguished from intelligent human responses, there would be no point in denying to them the attribute of thought. The question is whether computers and their programs have or can approach that level of indiscernibility.

(2) In 1975 K.M. Colby (*Artificial Paranoia*) produced a computer program whose interactive responses could not be distinguished by psychiatrists from those of a person with severe paranoia. He argued that this passed Turings's challenge in the limited area of paranoid thought.

(3) Searle (*q.v.* 5 and *Mind, Brains and Science*, ch. 2, 1984) places computer scientists generally in the position he calls "strong AI" ("strong artificial intelligence"): Mind is to brain as software program is to computer hardware. In this position "The brain is just a digital computer and the mind is just a computer program." As advocates of strong AI he specifically mentions Herbert Simon ("Computers do think."), Alan Nevell, Freeman Dyson, Marvin Minsky, and John McCarthy himself ("Machines as simple as thermostats can be said to have beliefs.")

(4) Rhetoric to one side, these and other computer scientists are producing increasingly sophisticated programs. McCarthy's LISP ("List Processing"), as well as programs designed to adapt mathematical logic to common-sense reasoning, set the pattern for research in the field for 25 years. Now, to oversimplify, the formalistic, top down approach of McCarthy is complemented by a more empirical bottom up approach in Connectionism and Neo-connectionism whose programs involve networks of computers acting in parallel and for whom the brain involves the parallel functioning of vast numbers of neurons. With respect to this history the more representative position is expressed by David Waltz ("The Prospect for Building Truly Intelligent Machines," 1988) that it will be possible "to build hardware with brain level power within thirty years."

(5) If strong AI identifies brains with digital computers and minds with software programs, weak AI would find these relations to be analogical. As for the manner of bridging between intentionality (*q.v.*) and the non-intentional level, Dennett (*q.v.* 2–5) utilizes a series of sublevels of successively more stupid armies of homunculi (*q.v.*) whose final level is characterized by such abysmal stupidity that they can be "replaced by a machine."

(6) Searle (*q.v.* 3–5) finds no problem here. Intentionality pertains to the macrolevel, which we identify with mind, and is caused by the micro-level of brain processes. Minds are not computer programs. If one could build a computer capable of thought, it would need all the important powers of, and be equivalent to, a human brain.

ARYAN SUPREMACY.
Q.v. Gobineau.

ASANA.
From the Sanskrit, meaning "sitting." In Yoga (*q.v.* 4) and other systems of Indian philosophy, the emphasis on posture as one of the conditions of spiritual progress.

ASANGA. 4th or 5th cent. A.D.
Indian philosopher. Founder of the Yogachara (Way of Yoga) or Consciousness-Only School. In the founding of the school he was assisted by his younger brother, Vasubandhu (*q.v.*) who was known as the systematizer of the position.

Principal writings: *Mahayanabhidharmasangiti-śastra; Mahayanasam-parigraha-śastra; Mahayanasutralankara-śastra.*

(1) Like certain of his predecessors in Mahayana Buddhism he held that reality is devoid of plurality, and that all phenomena are subjective in character. His addition was to hold that the nature of the real is pure consciousness.

(2) Surrounded by illusion—which includes even the empirical ego—the way of liberation requires the destruction of this illusion. One will first realize the imaginary nature of external objects; then the imaginary character of the individual mind. Third, one will grasp the nondual nature of pure consciousness as neither existence nor nonexistence, neither affirmation nor negation, neither identity nor difference. At last even this state will be transcended and the state of liberation, wherein all categories are merged, will be reached.

ASAT.

From the Sanskrit meaning "non-being." The opposite of "*Sat*" (*q.v.*) meaning "being." A theory of the origin of being from non-being dating back to Vedic times.

ASCETICISM.

From the Greek *askesis* meaning "self-denial." The view, which has been an important theme of both Eastern and Western religion and has played a minor role in philosophy, that the body is to be denied, possibly mortified, in order to make possible the purification of the soul in its progress toward salvation.

(1) The point can be exemplified very widely in religion. In Hinduism (*q.v.* 3) the third and fourth stages of life are expected to embody renunciation, separation from family, and a mendicant life as a means to purification. Although Buddha sought a middle path, asceticism remained a powerful force among his followers (*q.v.* Buddha 3). In Yoga, which had its roots in Buddhism, the techniques for disciplining the body are often quite rigorous. In *Hatha-yoga* such techniques are central to the discipline (*q.v.* Yoga 5). In early Christianity (*q.v.* 3) the churches faced a continuing problem of overemphasis on the ascetic life. Monasticism was one solution to the problem; but the medieval movement of the Flagellants (*q.v.*) is a reminder that the attraction of self-denial continued as a vital force in the movement of Christianity.

(2) In philosophy the ascetic life can be observed in those philosophies such as Pythagoreanism (*q.v.* Pythagoras) and Neoplatonism (*q.v.* Plotinus) where philosophy is interpreted as a means to salvation, as well as in Cynicism (*q.v.*) which involves a rejection of the most widely accepted human values.

ASCLEPIADES. 1st or 2nd cent. B.C.

Greek philosopher. Born in Prusa or Chios (Bythinia). A disciple of Epicurus (*q.v.*), Asclepiades adopted from the Academician Heraclides (*q.v.*) his cosmology of atoms and the void, while asserting the presence of only quantitative differences among the atoms rather than the qualitative differences present in Heraclides' view. Typically Epicurean, he emphasized the role of observation in inference.

ASCLEPIUS OF ALEXANDRIA. fl. around 450 A.D.

Hellenic philosopher. Studied with Proclus (*q.v.*) and with Ammonius of Alexandria. A member of the Alexandrian School of Neoplatonism.

Principal writings: A commentary on Plato's *Timaeus*.

ASEITAS.

From the Latin *a se* ("being for oneself"). Applied in the Scholastic philosophy to the Being of God in contrast with *ab alio* (being from another), the kind of being possessed by other things (*q.v.* Aquinas 4). Identical in meaning to "self-caused" and "uncaused."

ASHTORETH.

Q.v. Baal (2).

AS IF, PHILOSOPHY OF.

Q.v. Hans Vaihinger (1–3).

ASMITA.

A Sanskrit term meaning "I am-ness." A false egoism which confuses the sensible self with the true self, or *purusha* (*q.v.*). One of the five kinds of suffering to be overcome in the Yoga system (*q.v.* Yoga 3).

ASPARŚAYOGA (ASPARSHAYOGA).

Q.v. Guadapada (3); Yoga (6).

AŚRAMAS (ASHRAMAS), THE FOUR.

From a Sanskrit root meaning "to exert oneself." Thus, "the four exertions" or duties.

(1) The four exertions in Hindu life developed only gradually from three functions which had existed side by side and in partial opposition: the study of the *Vedas*, the responsibilities of raising a family (especially having sons in order that the "thread" of race be not broken), and the effort to gain religious enlightenment.

(2) The three functions turned into four stages, or duties, confronting every twice-born male, that is, every *Brahmin*, and later for every male of the three superior castes (*q.v.*): the *Brahmins*, *Kshatriyas*, and *Vaishyas* (excluding only the *Shudras*, although the *Upanishads* taught their inclusion). The instruction varied for each caste, different responsibilities attaching to differences of position in life.

The four *ashramas* moved from the duties of the student (the *Brahmacarin*, "wandering about in Brahman"), the householder (*Gṛhastha*), the forest-dweller (*Vanaprastha*), and the renouncer (*Sannyasin*). The last two stages constitute a division of the effort at enlightenment, the forest-dweller practising austerities to break worldly attachments, the renouncer or *Sannyasin* living without attachment or desire, remaining open to increasing knowledge of the *Atman-Brahman* identity (*q.v.* Hinduism 5b) and final emancipation (*q.v.* Hinduism 3).

(3) All four of the stages were religiously motivated. The object of the twelve student years was to gain knowledge of the *Vedas* whose rituals were necessary for every aspect of life. Since this knowledge was in possession of the *Brahmins*, the student age males of the superior castes would study in the home of a *Brahmin* guru. The duty of the householder was not only to have sons and satisfy social responsibilities, but to continue in private the study of the *Vedas*, follow the religious rituals, and give alms. At the approach of old age, having satisfied his social obligations and having seen his grandsons, the aged man enters the final two stages, addressing himself to his own final liberation. The fourth stage emerges as the final *ashrama* in the later *Upanishads*, the *Sannyasin* making the supreme experiment in practical religion.

(4) The four *ashramas* have a loose connection with the *Puruṣarthas* (*q.v.*), or aims of life, whose final stage is *Moksha*, release from the wheel of *Samsara* (*q.v.*).

ASSENT, NOTIONAL AND REAL.

Q.v. Newman (7–8).

ASSERTION SIGN.

The mark "⊢" introduced by Frege (*q.v.* 3) to distinguish between the mere stating or naming of a proposition, and holding it to be true. Adopted by Russell (*q.v.*) and Whitehead (*q.v.*) in *Principia Mathematica*.

ASSERTORIC JUDGMENT.

One of the three modes of judgment distinguished by Kant (*q.v.* 3), that one asserting that something is (or is not). The other two modes are those of the Problematic judgment (*q.v.*) and the

Apodeictic (*q.v.*) judgment. The analysis of modality goes back at least to Aristotle. For something of its history *q.v.* Modality. Also *q.v.* Logic (25).

ASSISI, FRANCIS OF.

Q.v. Francis.

ASSOCIATION, MUTUAL PROTECTION.

Q.v. Nozick (2).

ASSOCIATIONAL PSYCHOLOGY.

Q.v. Psychology (3, 9, 16).

ASSOCIATION OF IDEAS.

A term introduced into philosophy by John Locke. The view that complex mental phenomena are derived from the joining together of simple elements according to a small set of principles. Although the great popularity of the concept derives from the British empiricists, its origin goes back to Greek philosophy.

(1) Plato (*q.v.* 12) utilized the principles of contiguity and similarity in explaining how ideas unite with each other.

(2) Aristotle (*q.v.* 3) invoked the principles of similarity, contrast, and contiguity.

(3) Hobbes (*q.v.* 4) used principles of association to explain mental functioning, distinguishing between chance and controlled associations.

(4) Locke (*q.v.* 4) utilized all of the principles of his followers, set forth below, without making a catalogue of these principles. Some of these connections seemed to him natural, while others were a result of chance or custom.

(5) Berkeley (*q.v.* 2) names similarity, causality, and co-existence or contiguity as his principles.

(6) Hume (*q.v.* 2) names resemblance, contiguity in time or place, and cause and effect. But causality reduces to constant conjunction, a type of contiguity, and contrast reduces to causality plus resemblance.

(7) Hartley (*q.v.*) developed an associationist psychology out of Locke's ideas from the principle of contiguity alone.

(8) Condillac (*q.v.* 3–4) followed Locke, making these principles available to the French public. The list now remains essentially unchanged.

(9) Both James Mill (*q.v.*) and his son,

John Stuart Mill (*q.v.* 1), followed out the line of the British empiricists developed by Hartley, applying the associationalist principles widely.

(10) Bain (*q.v.*), influenced by J.S. Mill, continued the tradition, applying the principles of associationalism to the analysis of mental states.

ASSOCIATIVE LAW.

Q.v. Propositional Calculus (15).

ASSUMPTION.

From the Latin *ad* ("to") and *sumere* ("take"). The taking for granted of the truth of a proposition for the sake of the argument which follows.

(1) From Boethius (*q.v.*) on, the earlier Latin logicians used this term as a technical name for the minor premise of a syllogism.

(2) In his *Logic* Mill (*q.v.*) used the term in a double sense: to designate the mathematical truths serving as the point of departure in a proof, and to designate the starting point of any deduction in abstraction from the question of the truth or falsity of the statement. It is the latter sense of the term which is commonly taken, and this is the sense closest to the Latin transliteration.

(3) Assumption, then, is usually accepted as having the least specific meaning in the family of terms likewise including Axiom (*q.v.*), Hypothesis (*q.v.*), and Postulate (*q.v.*).

ASSUMPTION OF THE BLESSED VIRGIN MARY.

A doctrine of the Roman Catholic Church promulgated by Pope Pius XII in 1950 to the effect that the mother of Jesus was at the moment of her death "assumed" body and soul into heaven.

AṢṬANGAYOGA (ASHTANGAYOGA).

The eightfold path of discipline. *Q.v.* Yoga (4).

ASTIKA.

Sanskrit term meaning "orthodox." Any system of thought accepting the authority of the *Vedas* (*q.v.* 4). To be contrasted to the *Nastika* systems which do not accept their authority.

ASTIKAYA.

Sanskrit term meaning "physical." Used in Jainism (*q.v.* 1) in the phrase *astikaya dravya* or "physical substance." The term applied to matter, motion, rest, and space.

ASU.

Sanskrit, "breath of life." *Q.v.* The *Vedas* (1).

AŚVAGHOṢA (ASHVAGHOSHA). 1st cent. A.D.

Indian philosopher. The chief expounder of Mahayana Buddhism. Claiming that after Buddha's death there were many errors of interpretation among those who sought to understand his teachings, Ashvaghosha set out to explain the fundamental teachings of the Buddha.

Principal writings: *The Awakening of the Faith in the Mahayana.*

(1) Ashvaghosha holds that reality is "Absolute Suchness," that which it is, beyond the categories of human understanding.

(2) But the "Absolute Suchness," tainted by ignorance, appears as "Conditional Suchness," *i.e.,* as the manifold phenomenal world, including the apparent plurality of finite selves. In fact, as the calm water of the ocean, whipped by wind, appears as waves, so does consciousness, as the result of ignorance, appear as finite minds.

(3) The relative phenomenal world cannot be sublated by reason since this, too, is relative or relational. We must get beyond intellect and approach reality directly, and Buddha utilized words and definitions to lead the seeker beyond words and definitions.

(4) Following Buddha's example the *bodhisattvas*, those on the way to enlightenment, defer Nirvana in order to enable others to overcome their ignorance, and so end their suffering.

(5) In the state of enlightenment we are aware of our Absolute Suchness and identify with the self-existent immortal reality.

ASYMMETRICAL RELATIONS.

Q.v. The Logic of Relations (11).

ATARAXIA.

From the Greek *a* ("not") and *taraktos* ("disturbed"). The state of serene, untroubled pleasure. *Ataraxia* was held to be the ideal state of mind and feeling by Democritus (*q.v.* 11), Epicurus (*q.v.* 10),

Pyrrho (*q.v.* 3), Lucretius (*q.v.* 9), and their followers. It should be compared to the somewhat different ideal state, *apathia* (*q.v.*), recommended by the Stoics.

THE ATHANASIAN CREED.

Not by Athanasius (*q.v.*), but attributed to him in the 7th century. By the 13th century it was equal in importance to the Nicene (*q.v.*) and Apostles' (*q.v.*) creeds. The creed begins, after an introductory comment that those who fail to accept it will be excluded from salvation: "And the Catholic faith is this: that we worship our God in Trinity and Trinity in unity; neither confounding the persons, nor dividing the substance."

ATHANASIUS. c. 300–373.

Christian theologian and Churchman. The most redoubtable opponent of Arianism (*q.v.*) in the 4th century, it was Athanasius who pressed the *homoousian* interpretation of the relation between the Father and the Son, not only at the Council of Nicea (325), but throughout his life. This interpretation, that the Father and the Son are "of the same essence" or "of the same substance," stood in contrast with the Arian view which subordinated the Son to the Father.

A deacon in the church at Alexandria he became bishop following Alexander in 328 A.D. He won all of Egypt to his interpretation but in the process spent many years in exile. Although formally deposed much of the time between 335 and 364, he nonetheless continued to maintain relations with his church by means of pastoral letters. His stormy life ended just eight years before the Council of Constantinople which finally adjudicated the dispute, agreeing finally to the position he had pressed throughout his life.

Principal writings: *Against the Gentiles* (T); *On the Incarnation*; *Orations against the Arians* (T); *Apology against the Arians* (T); *On Doctrine* (T).

ATHARVAVEDA.

One of the four collections of hymns used in the Vedic sacrifices. *Q.v. Vedas* (1d).

ATHEISM.

From the Greek *a* ("not") plus *theos* ("God"). The doctrine of disbelief in a supreme being.

(1) The term has frequently been applied to those who disbelieve in the popular gods. This was the case with Anaxagoras (*q.v.* 6) who held that the sun was a stone rather than a god. At about the same time Buddha (*q.v.* God 68) held the impermanence of all things to be incompatible with the permanent, unchanging nature attributed to divine beings. Socrates (*q.v.* 1) was charged with disbelieving in the gods of the state (although he seems to have been a monotheist), Theodorus the atheist (*q.v.*) was exiled from his city because of his disbelief in anything divine, and Spinoza (*q.v.* 2, 3), whose God was ultimately identical with the world, was charged with being a pantheist (*q.v.*). Pantheists have often been classed with atheists, due to the "strangeness" of their views of the divine.

(2) From the other side, there exists a long tradition of those who have believed that religion rests on superstition. Here the tradition extends from Heraclitus (*q.v.* 7) and Xenophanes (*q.v.* 1) through Meslier (*q.v.* 1), Feuerbach (*q.v.* 1, 2), and Marx (*q.v.* 5) to Freud (*q.v.* 6) who finds the source of religion in group neurosis. Meslier expresses the view that religion is a tool to control the masses, and a similar point is implicit in Marxist thought.

(3) Apart from the emotional charge and countercharge of the preceding, there is the fact that the philosophy of Materialism (*q.v.*) does not require a god, and this tradition has had a long history within philosophy both East and West. The extensive list of philosophers discussed under that heading fits equally well here.

(4) In one strand of voluntaristic and existentialist philosophy including Schopenhauer (*q.v.* 3, 4), Nietzsche (*q.v.* 4), and Sartre (*q.v.* 3) the atheistic alternative is present. Some find this alternative even in Tillich (*q.v.* 1, 3) who views God as the power of Being Itself, but perhaps this may be viewed as a doctrine close to the Pantheism mentioned in (1) above. The recent Death of God theologians derive from the philosophers in this group.

(5) Sidney Hook (*q.v.* 3) affirmed an "open-minded atheism" joined to a guaranteed freedom of religious belief.

ATHEISMUSSTREIT.

A German controversy over atheism in the University of Jena. The dispute revolved around the views of Fichte (*q.v.*) and led to his dismissal from the university.

ATHENAGORAS. Late 2nd cent. A.D.

Christian Apologist. Apparently born and lived in Athens. His apology was presented to Marcus Aurelius. In it he defends Christian practices and attacks the pagan religions, especially their penchant for polytheism. He quotes Greek poets and philosophers in favor of monotheism and presents an *a priori* argument for God. In his work on the resurrection of the dead he combines religious and philosophical considerations in his arguments. A strong influence of Platonism is evident in his orientation (*q.v.* Apologists 4).

Principal writings: *Apology*; *Embassy for the Christians* (T); *On the Resurrection of the Dead* (T).

ATHENS, SCHOOL OF.

Q.v. School of Athens.

ATMAN.

Sanskrit term meaning "self" or "soul." In the *Upanishads* (*q.v. Vedas* 4) and in the Vedanta (*q.v.*) philosophy, *Atman* as the individual soul and Brahman (*q.v.*), are to be held identical. Shankara (*q.v.* 2, 4–5) gives one of the standard analyses of this identity. *Q.v.* Hinduism (5b).

ATOMISM.

From the Greek *a* ("not") and *tomos* ("cut"). The concept is, then, of a primary constituent of reality which cannot be further divided. The theory of the atom was developed quite early both in the East and the West. Since the theory is sometimes, but not always, associated with Materialism, the reader should also refer to that heading.

(1) The earliest theory of atomism is to be found in the Indian philosophy of Jainism (*q.v.* 1) which arose some time after 800 B.C.

(2) In the Western world the 5th-century B.C. theory of Leucippus and Democritus (*q.v.*) held the ultimate constituents of things to be spatial entities not further divisible; the objects of ordinary life are thus compounds formed of such entities.

(3) Epicurus (*q.v.* 2) continued the development of the theory in the West in the 4th century B.C. as did Heraclides (*q.v.*) although the latter held to qualitative differences among the atoms.

(4) Strato (*q.v.* 1) in the 3rd century, held the view that the atoms are infinitely divisible, and respond to heat and cold.

(5) In the Eastern world the tradition was continued in the 4th century by two of the Orthodox systems of Indian philosophy, Nyaya (*q.v.*) and Vaisheshika (*q.v.*), as well as by some of the northern Buddhists.

(6) In the 1st century B.C. in the Western world, Lucretius (*q.v.*) followed Democritus and Epicurus, while further endowing the atoms with a voluntary power to swerve, thus setting up vortices and initiating worlds.

(7) The final developments of atomic theory occurred in the West. Galileo (*q.v.* 3) found atomism to be consistent with his experimental studies. The 17th-century development of corpuscular theory among the philosophers began from the theories of Democritus and Epicurus. Pierre Gassendi (*q.v.*) followed Epicurus specifically, as did Berigard (*q.v.*) and Maignan (*q.v.*) while Descartes (*q.v.* 8) developed an original point of view identifying matter and extension.

(8) Since the 17th century atomism has been the accepted scientific interpretation.

ATON.

Q.v. Monotheism.

ATONEMENT.

From the Middle English *at* ("at") and *on* ("one") meaning "to be at one with." The term and concept refer particularly to a Western manner of viewing the relation of man to God.

(1) In the Old Testament an annual ceremony designed to cleanse the temple, priesthood, and people of their sins while renewing their special relationship with God. The ritual included fasting and sacrifice. The ceremony continues to be observed within Judaism (*q.v.*), stressing confession and repentance of sins, on Yom Kippur, a day set aside as the holiest day of the year.

(2) The Christian view of the Atonement is that Christ, sacrificing Himself for mankind, did in His death on the

cross make reparation for man's sins against God, thus reconciling man and God, and opening to man again the possibility of eternal life. The idea that Christ's death has a redeeming power, providing a vicarious atonement, is present in the writings of the Apostle Paul (*q.v.* 3) as well as in the Church Fathers (*q.v.* Irenaeus 1–2). The view is developed in the claim of Anselm (*q.v.* 6) that the God-Man substituted Himself for the totality of human sins, thus making human salvation possible. This view was standard throughout the Middle Ages, until challenged by the view of Grotius (*q.v.* 6) that the Atonement was an object lesson to humanity, contributing to the divine government of the world.

(3) The closest Eastern correlate to the Christian concept of the Atonement is to be found in the redeeming power of the bodhisattvas (*q.v.*) in Mahayana Buddhism (*q.v.* 1–2). Correlative to the general conception of gaining unity with the divine are the concepts of *moksha* (*q.v.*) and *satori* (*q.v.*). This may require coming to terms with *karma* (*q.v.*). But one very important view is that the necessary change must occur in our awareness, since in fact we have always been one with God (*q.v.* Atman).

ATTICUS. 2nd cent. A.D.
A Platonic philosopher who made a sharp separation between Plato's thought and that of Aristotle, mixing the former so completely with Stoic doctrines that he is often regarded as a Stoic. Against Aristotle he held that the world was created, that the ideas exist as thoughts in the mind of God, that the soul is immortal and hence separable from the body, and that God is not an unmoved mover but capable of intervention in the world. For likeminded philosophers of this period *q.v.* Nicostratus and Celsus.

ATTRACTION AND REPULSION, PRINCIPLE OF.
Q.v. Empedocles (3).

ATTRIBUTE.
From the Latin *ad* ("to") and *tribuere* ("ascribe"). Hence, that which is ascribed to a thing.
(1) For Aristotle (*q.v.* 6) the world divides into individual substances and attributes of those substances. In one sense the attributes are all of the characteristics predicable of substance under the categories of time, place, relation, etc. In a logical sense the attributes are the predicables themselves. For this distinction *q.v.* Aristotle (4).

(2) For Aquinas, and in Scholastic metaphysics generally, the above-mentioned distinctions apply. In addition, for the Scholastics the transcendentals—*e.g.*, the one, the true, and the good—are said to be attributes of everything (*q.v.* Aquinas 4).

(3) For Descartes (*q.v.* 8) thought and extension are the two mutually opposed attributes of reality.

(4) Spinoza (*q.v.* 2, 6) broadened the Cartesian conception, holding attributes to be those characteristics constituting the essence of substance, holding their number to be infinite, although the two known to us are thought and extension.

(5) In theology the term "attribute" is used to refer to the essential characteristics of the divine. The attributes of God differ, of course, in different conceptions of the divine (*q.v.* God A). In Classical Theism, the traditional Western conception of God (*q.v.* Theism 3), these attributes include unity, simplicity, incorporeality, eternity, omnipotence, and omniscience.

ATTRITION.
Q.v. Penance (3).

AUFKLÄRUNG.
German term meaning "enlightenment." The term applies to the 18th-century movements of emancipation from prejudice through knowledge, arising not only in Germany, but also in France and England. *Q.v.* Enlightenment (B).

AUGSBURG CONFESSION.
A statement of Lutheran doctrine in 21 articles plus 7 on ecclesiastical abuses, which has become the foundation of the Lutheran faith. Written by Melanchthon (*q.v.*), it was agreed to by Luther, and presented to Emperor Charles V at the Diet of Augsburg in 1530 (*q.v.* Luther 12, 16).

AUGUSTINE, SAINT. 354–430.
Born in Thagaste, North Africa, he became Bishop of Hippo in 396. Between

these two events he lived out his *Confessions*, the most influential autobiography of all time, culminating in his conversion to Christianity. From an apparently innocent childhood, marred on one occasion by pear-stealing, he graduated in turn to frivolity, mistress-keeping, Manichaeism, Neoplatonism, and the profession of rhetoric, leading him by his 32nd year to a conversion marked by the hearing of a voice, "Take up and read," and the turning to a Scripture passage from St. Paul. Among the influences, leading to conversion, were the sermons of Ambrose, Bishop of Milan.

Principal writings: *On Free Will* (T); *Concerning the Teacher* (T); *The Confessions* (T); *On Christian Doctrine*; *The Enchiridion on Faith, Hope and Love* (T); *On the Trinity* (T); *The City of God* (T).

(1) The path to happiness, true contentment, or salvation is the path of self-knowledge. The same path is marked out by man's quest for beauty, truth, and goodness. Augustine testifies that the terminus of this quest, when we know ourselves, and our situation, is inevitably God, our hearts being restless until they rest in Him.

(2) But also, and incidentally, it turns out that the only intellectually valid position to hold is Christian theism; hence, part of the movement into self-knowledge is concerned with one's capacity for philosophic truth (although there are other paths); and St. Augustine found himself incapable of understanding Christian theism until he had learned to appreciate Platonism, discovering a basis for holding immaterial entities (that is, ideas) to exist. Finally, of course, the eternal ideas, or *rationes aeternas*, exist in the mind of God.

(3) The importance of philosophic defensibility can be seen in Augustine's eagerness either to refute philosophical positions or to assimilate them to Christianity. Skepticism would be an instance of the first tendency, and Platonism of the second.

(4) His refutation of skepticism reflects again the inwardness of the path of self-knowledge, anticipating Descartes. One cannot avoid the idea of truth. If I doubt, I am sure of the truth that I doubt. If I am deceived, then at least I must exist in order to be deceived ("*Si fallor, sum*").

(5) As one cannot avoid the idea of truth, so also one cannot avoid the ideas of beauty and goodness. In all three cases St. Augustine makes use of the Platonic point that norms are implicit in the judgments we make, and these norms require one to grant the existence of Truth, Beauty, and Goodness. And our awareness of these norms is in some sense our awareness of God, since God is our true Good, the true Beauty, and Truth itself.

(6) For St. Augustine the discovery of God through Truth, Beauty, and Goodness marks an inward path. The tenth book of the *Confessions* traces that path from sights and sounds through imageless ideas to the Being sensed through, yet above, the mind, and often termed by St. Augustine, in an apparent metaphor, "the inexhaustible light" or "the intelligible light." There is a sense, indeed, derived from his Neoplatonic background, in which the intelligible light is original, and physical light is derivative, the former causing the latter. In another sense, since God is not merely "the intelligible light," a metaphorical element is unmistakable and ineradicable. Even so, St. Augustine points toward the possibility of inner experience as the sanction (partial in his case) of religion, "the light" of one's intellect encountering an inner intelligible light not one's own. This inwardness was to have its own career.

(7) He also believed that the order of nature provided evidence or "traces" of God; here he argued from the teleological perspective that combined design and motion; but outward signs carried for him nothing like the evidential power of inner experience.

(8) Just as the conception of God as a corporeal being had been a stumbling block lying in the path of his conversion, so had been his youthful conception of evil as physical in nature. Both doctrines came from his attachment to Manichaeism; and both were overcome by his discovery of Platonism. St. Augustine adopted the Neoplatonic notions that evil is a privation, and nothing positive. Anything, then, insofar as it is, is good; but as blindness is a privation of sight, so evil is in general the lack of a positive good. And yet this description is not quite accurate since St. Augustine also treats evil as comparable to the dark shadows of a painting,

which, taken by themselves, are unattractive, but which contribute to the beauty of the total experience. We have, then, two interpretations of evil: it is a result of privation, and it is a result of limited perspective.

(9) Accepting on faith the recognized tenets of Christianity, St. Augustine was nonetheless willing to go to great lengths in arguing for these doctrines. Interpreting the persons of the Trinity as exemplifying Being, Knowledge, and Love, he found many signs pointing to the validity of the conception and his interpretation. He was most pleased with an image of the Trinity within the self. "We are, and we know that we are, and we love to be and to know that we are." This image stands even against the skeptics, for even if he is mistaken he is, in order to be mistaken; and therefore correctly knows that he is, and loves this being and knowledge.

(10) As for God's nature, Augustine affirms God's perfection, eternity, infinity, and incomprehensibility, His simplicity and unity, His essentiality without accidents, creator of the world out of nothing, a being so different from all others that apparently contradictory statements can be true of Him simultaneously—i.e., He can be interior and exterior to all things, unmoving cause of all, eternal, yet contain all time and in knowing His own nature He can know the total future without depriving man of the freedom to choose. The claim would be that these assertions are contradictory only when God is regarded as a being in the class of other beings, thus underlining, once again, the need for our understanding to gain a subtlety adequate, at least in part, to its object. Augustine's conception of an infinite Being was the standard for more than a thousand years beyond his time.

(11) But this entire delineation, stressing his intellectual development, drops from sight the vital fact that for Augustine belief is held properly to precede, and to pave the way for, understanding. The motto, "*Credo ut intelligam*" ("I believe in order to understand"), expresses Augustine's adherence to this doctrine, despite the extent of his interest in reason. His faith in Scripture would seem to illustrate the motto, also; and yet any scriptural interpretation offensive to the reason can be replaced by one which does not offend. He found allegorical interpretations in all parts of the Scriptures; the story of the Good Samaritan contained the entire scheme of human redemption which is initiated by God's grace. And the succession of his experiences clearly illustrates the development of human understanding to the point where it can accommodate the affirmations of faith. Miracles, for example, can be understood rationally inasmuch as both miracles and nature are expressions of the will of God. Philosophy and theology thus interpenetrate in this tradition.

(12) His interpretation of man carries out these dual themes. Man is so completely burdened by original sin, passing it along the generations through conception, that no one deserves salvation. That God predestines some to this end is a great and unmerited gift of grace, while the assignment of others to perdition is what all deserve. At the same time he views ethical questions from the standpoint of the happiness principle, or *eudaimonism*, which he joins to God's ideal perfection as its norm, and to the centrality of love. Indeed, virtue is defined as the, *ordo amoris* ("order of love", or better, "rightly ordered love"). As further evidence of this duality of pattern, it was Augustine who first held man's free will to be consistent with God's foreknowledge and foreordination, partly because freedom in its ultimate sense means doing what one ought to do and is thus identified with the good. Finally, man's relation to God is the relation of creature to creator and goal. Man's temporality contrasts with God's eternity; and time is itself present in and measured by the soul of man. Whatever else time may be, it is much less clear than God's eternity. Man, a union of soul and body, has a significance which extends beyond this life, his soul continuing to exist after death although it did not pre-exist.

(13) And, indeed, man is attracted in this life by two loves—the love of God and the love of self—and history results from their tension. By choice each man is a citizen of one of the two cities, the City of God or the City of Man, Jerusalem or Rome. These things are presented in

The City of God, where St. Augustine develops a philosophy of history while defending Christianity against the charge that there existed a significant correlation between the rise of Christianity and the fall of Rome. The occasion for the analysis was the sack of Rome in 410 by Alaric, the Goth. While the City of God is exempt from breakdown, the City of Man is not. In the City of Man all of the risks of contingent being are present. Between these two alternatives, however, there is a third—Rome as shaped by Jerusalem, the state shaped by the values of the City of God. To some extent, this is a relevant ideal, and was partially shaped by Augustine. But his clearest view is that the values of the City of God, held by the Church, are superior to those of civil society; the Church then is superior to the state, and its voice should be heard in the state. He usually divides human history into four periods: paradise before the fall, the world after the fall, the period of the law, and the period in which we now exist—after the first coming of Christ—a period of grace. At times he divides the four periods into seven to match the seven days of creation.

AUM.
Q.v. Om.

AUROBINDO, SRI (AUROBINDO GHOSE). 1872–1950.
Indian philosopher. A leader of the Advaita Vedanta (*q.v.*) philosophy in modern India, Aurobindo considered the illusionism of Shankara (*q.v.*) a misinterpretation of the *Upanishads* (*q.v.*).

Principal writings: *Essays on the Gita* (E), 1926–44, 1950; *The Life Divine* (E), 2 vols., 1947; *The Synthesis of Yoga* (E), 1948; *The Supramental Manifestation upon Earth* (E), 1952.

(1) Reality exists in a graded series which begins in matter, and mounts to the Absolute itself, or Brahman. The essential power of Brahman requires his descent into the finite.

(2) That same power requires the finite to struggle toward the infinite. On one level this struggle is the evolution of lower into higher forms. On another level man seeks, and must seek, identity with the Absolute by passing beyond the level of the mental into the divine life.

(3) The means of this passage is called "integral *yoga*," providing a transformation of mind, life, and body.

AUSSERSEIN.
Q.v. Meinong (1).

AUSTIN, JOHN L. 1911–1960.
English philosopher. Studied at Oxford, becoming a fellow there in 1933. He taught at Oxford throughout his professional life. His early death was due to throat cancer.

Principal writings: *Philosophical Papers*, 1961; *How to Do Things with Words*, 1962; *Sense and Sensibilia*, 1962.

(1) Convinced of a lack of thoroughness in the investigation of the resources and problems of language both on the part of philosophers and linguists generally, Austin philosophized by means of a detailed and exhaustive examination of the words and sentences appropriate to the problem under consideration.

(2) In expressing his conclusions, Austin proposed that: An utterance following the conventions of grammar is a *phatic* act, and its utterance a *pheme*. A *pheme* with sense and reference is a *rhetic* act, and its utterance a *rheme*. In this context he distinguished between locutionary, illocutionary, and perlocutionary speech acts. The expression of any proper sentence is a *locutionary act*. But the matter does not end here. The locutionary act contains an *illocutionary act*; that is to say, the locution is of a certain kind with a certain intention, and this can often be determined only by the context within which the locution occurs. The locution has the force of affirming or denying, promising, consenting, vowing, suggesting, thanking, appointing, diagnosing, etc. The list of illocutionary acts related to the locutionary act could be extended considerably. The two language acts we have identified lead to a third language act. The *perlocutionary act* is the act you in fact succeed in performing by means of the two preceding language acts. If my locutionary act is the sentence, "The book is damaged," the related illocutionary act might be a simple affirmation, or report; on the other hand it might contain a suggestion, a request, or a demand, for example, that the book be repaired, replaced, or the purchase price refunded;

and the perlocutionary act might be simply agreement to what had been affirmed, or an action to repair the book, replace it, or refund the purchase price, depending upon the situation in which the locution is made.

(3) Austin's analysis called attention to the importance and extent of the role of performative utterances in speech. Truth and falsity characterize a relatively small set of human utterances which he called "constative." A far larger set is made up of *performative* utterances; that is, the utterance is itself the performance of the language act in question, and not a report of that performance. The utterance of the minister, "I pronounce you man and wife," spoken in the marriage ceremony, is performative. Promising, consenting, appointing, guaranteeing, vetoing, are instances of performative utterances.

(4) In *Sense and Sensibilia* he applies his methods of analysis to problems of perception. The positions which fall by the way are those holding that we do not directly perceive objects, and especially the sense-datum theory that objects are inferred from sense-data. He seems to defend a Common Sense Realism (*q.v.*) and the sophistication of the ordinary person with respect to problems of perception.

AUTHENTICITY.

From the Greek *authentes* ("one who acts with authority, or what is done by one's own hand"). Anticipated in fiction by Goethe (*q.v.* 1), the term has come into philosophic use with the existentialists, for whom it is an important value term.

(1) Jaspers (*q.v.* 1) held that the purpose of philosophy is to awaken men to authenticity.

(2) Heidegger (*q.v.* 2-5) identified the achievement of authenticity and the path to pure Being.

(3) For the view that the achievement of authenticity is the end of life, *q.v.* Ortega y Gasset (3).

(4) Bultmann (*q.v.* 2) believed authenticity to be possible only through the Word as revealed in Christ.

(5) For Sartre (*q.v.* 3-4) authenticity stems from any active involvement which avoids bad faith.

AUTOLOGICAL.

Q.v. Paradox (4).

AUTONOMY.

From the Greek *autos* ("self") and *nomos* ("law"). Hence, the reference is to that which gives law to itself, or is its own law. (1) Politically, autonomy refers to the power or right of self-government on the part of a city, state, or nation. (2) Immanuel Kant (*q.v.* 6-7) held that the human will is autonomous when it acts from its own inner principle, and heteronomous (*q.v.*) when it accepts a principle from outside itself. (3) Tillich (*q.v.* 2) discusses the autonomous reason, distinguishing it from the heteronomous and theonomous reason.

Also *q.v.* Putnam (10).

AUTOSYNTHESIS.

Q.v. Ardigó (3).

AVALOKITEŚVARA. (AVALOKITESHVARA).

The reincarnated Dalai Lama of Lamaism (*q.v.* 1-2) whose *mantra* is *Om mani padme hum* (*q.v.* 1).

AVATAR.

From the Sanskrit *avatara* ("descent"). The term refers to the descent of a deity to earth and its incarnation in human, or animal. In Hinduism the term applies mainly to Vishnu (*q.v.*). Nine avatars of the god have already appeared, and a tenth is expected.

AVEMPACE. End of 11th cent.–1138 A.D.

Arabic philosopher. Born in Spain where he spent most of his life, although he died in Morocco, apparently a victim of poisoning. Combining the ideas of the active intellect and mystical ascent, Avempace held man's goal to be a state of reality with no opposition of matter and form, or thought and being.

Selected writings: *Regimen of the Solitary* (T in part).

AVENARIUS, RICHARD. 1843–1896.

German philosopher. Born in Paris. Studied at Leipzig. Professor at the University of Zurich. His doctrine of *Empiriocriticism* (*q.v.*) influenced William James, and was specifically attacked by Lenin (*q.v.* 2) as reactionary. His view is very close to that of Mach (*q.v.*) who was attacked on the same grounds.

Principal writings: *Philosophy as a Thinking of the World in Accordance with the Principle of Least Energy*, 1876; *Critique of Pure Experience*, 2 vols., 1888–90; *The Human Concept of the World*, 1891.

(1) *Empiriocriticism* is an approach to the world through pure experience, and pure experience is simply the given, devoid of assumptions. Following the principle of least energy, one systematically excludes from one's mental content all elements not specifically given in direct experience.

(2) The result is an avoidance of dualism, since self and environment, as well as mental and physical processes, will be viewed as contrasting values of a single experience.

(3) Logical relations, and categories of thought, are constructed, not given. And these constructions are made in terms of the problems we sense: (a) A problem appears as a sense of strain. (b) We exert effort to solve it. (c) The solution appears as a sense of release from strain.

(4) The series of experiences has behind it a bodily series on which consciousness depends. The series mentioned in (3) has a somewhat different form in the bodily series, *i.e.*: (a) A departure from balance in the system. (b) Continuation of this imbalance. (c) Return of the system to balance.

(5) The error of going beyond experience to posit substantial objects as opposed to the self, mind as opposed to body, etc. is termed by Avenarius *introjection*. To avoid introjection one must follow the procedures of *Empiriocriticism*.

AVERROËS. 1126–1198.

Arabic philosopher. Born in Córdoba, Spain. His Latin name was a corruption of Ibn Rushd. Like Avicenna (*q.v.*) both physician and philosopher, he held important official posts, served as judge, and was often entrusted with diplomatic missions. At times intimate with the Emirs of Spain, he was at other times in disgrace and under penalty of banishment. Opposed by both Christian and Moslem theologians, the opposition he encountered was a tribute to the influence his writing had begun to have. Famous for his commentaries on Aristotle, he became known through much of the Middle Ages simply as the Commentator, and Aquinas adopted the form of commentary employed by Averroës.

Principal writings: Commentaries on Aristotle's *Categories* (T); *Posterior Analytics*; *The Physics* (T); *On the Heavens*; *On Generation and Corruption* (T); *On the Soul*; *The Short Physical Treatises* (T); *Metaphysics*; *Politics*; *Rhetoric*; also a treatise against Al-Ghazzali's *Destruction of Philosophy*, titled *The Destruction of the Destruction* or *The Incoherence of the Incoherence* (T); *A Commentary on Plato's Republic* (T); *The Middle Commentary on Porphyry's Isagoge* (T); *On the Harmony of Religion and Philosophy* (T); as well as a medical encyclopedia titled *Generalities*.

(1) Both God and the world are eternal. In terms of duration matter is as eternal as God. But the world is, nonetheless, the effect of God's power, created from eternity. The world is eternal but caused, while God is eternal and without cause, knowing in His own essence things in their most exalted state. The world is the *natura naturata* (*q.v.*) of God who is its first cause.

(2) Again like Avicenna, although different in detail, Averroës has a Neoplatonic scheme of emanations from the necessary Being. The first emanation is the first cause, from which emanate the intelligences guiding the celestial spheres, leading down to the world, and individuals. A single, definitive power from the first cause controls all things.

(3) The sciences are eternal by virtue of their generality. The intelligence finds a single conception, the quiddity of the species, when understanding any individual thing. And this conception is not divided, and is therefore not subject to birth or destruction. It is merely an accident of time that knowledge is subject to discovery and to loss.

(4) Universals, quiddities, general ideas have their proper locus in a realm of intelligences. Man's active intellect allows man union with this realm and even though he moves toward the universal from his passive intellect, which has a condition of individuality, it is the non-individual active intellect which is eternal. The individual man is thus not immortal in his individuality, but only in fusion with the universal active intellect. Although this was Averroës' interpretation of Aristotle, and there is much in Aristotle to support the interpretation, this was the most heavily criticized point in the Commentator's system.

(5) Just as the world must always contain prophets and mystics to bring men into relation with the world beyond, so there must be always some great philosophers in order that the active intellect, in which eternal truth exists, may be always actual.

(6) It is not true that the philosophers oppose the doctrine of the Resurrection as Al-Ghazzali had claimed. Philosophers are committed to the doctrine both by religious law and their commitment to guide the people. Averroës suggested that we shall be resurrected in another life not with our present bodies but with representations of them. The presumed inconsistency of this point with (4) above has led many to the presumption of a doctrine of double truth in Averroës—that what is true in religion may be false in philosophy and vice-versa. But the doctrine is nowhere stated as such by the author.

AVERROISM.

The influence of Averroës was felt both by Jewish philosophy and by Scholasticism. Translated into Hebrew, his commentaries produced Averroists until the 15th century. First translated into Latin between 1130 and 1150, translations were still emerging in 1256. No philosophy was more frequently condemned by church leaders and in Christian councils than Averroism. It was condemned in 1209, 1215, 1240, 1270, and 1277. The eternity of matter, the absence of personal immortality, and the presumed doctrine of double truth were in the center of the attack. Albertus Magnus relied heavily on Averroës' commentaries on Aristotle, while noting certain difficulties. Utilizing William of Moerbecke's translations of Aristotle from Greek texts, Aquinas criticized Averroës more intensively still. But nonetheless schools of Averroists continued to appear. Siger of Brabant was the most prominent of the Averroists. In northern Italy Averroism continued to have influence until the 16th century.

AVESTA.

Avestan term meaning "knowledge." The term applies to the sacred scriptures of the Zoroastrian religion. In the West these scriptures were for a time termed "Zend-Avesta," apparently meaning "the tradition of knowledge" or "commentary

on knowledge," but the term seems to have derived from a mistake in translation by Hyde in 1700. For further details *q.v.* Zoroastrianism (4).

AVICEBRON, SOLOMON IBN GABIROL. 1020–1070.

Jewish philosopher. Born in Málaga. Lived in Saragossa. Also a poet and theologian. Neoplatonic in orientation, his view was opposed by Aquinas very early, but found favor with Franciscans and 13th-century Augustinians.

Principal writings: *The Fountain of Life* (*Fons Vitae*) (T); *The Improvement of the Moral Qualities* (T); and a volume of poetry which has become important in Sephardic liturgy, *The Kingly Crown* (T).

(1) Everywhere in the universe one finds a union of form and matter, even in spiritual substances. Matter, then, is to be understood as essentially potentiality, with corporeality its characteristic only on a certain level. Hence, matter cannot be the principle of individuation, and there must be individual spiritual substances. That is to say, form (not matter) must be the principle of individuation.

(2) More than one form is or can be present in the individual thing. There can be a plurality of substantial forms shaping the individuality of the thing.

(3) The world comes from the divine unity in a series of emanations. The mediator between God and the world is to be found in the divine will proceeding from God. This will both creates and sustains the world. From the will comes form, which is essentially united to matter as we have seen. In a different rendering one would say that from the universal intelligence comes the soul, and from the soul comes nature, while from nature come the bodies of the temporal world.

(4) God in his essence remains beyond man's comprehension; but it is our goal in life through knowledge and religion to achieve salvation by triumphing over our sensual natures. This is all the more important since life, on any other grounds, is meaningless—as the pessimistic tone of his poetry suggests.

AVICENNA. 980–1037.

(The Arabic form of his name is Ibn Sina.) Islamic philosopher and physician. Born in Persia. A brilliant student, he had become a practicing physician by the age of 16, and at 17 had mastered most of the available knowledge of his day. Vizier to sultans, he led an active, adventurous, and restless life in both Persia and Iran. Just before his death at 57 he freed his slaves. It was the translation of his writings into Latin that initiated the great Aristotle revival in the 12th and 13th centuries. Known to the Arab world as the "Third Aristotle," Avicenna combined Aristotelian and Neoplatonic themes in his philosophy, having taken an Arabic version of Plotinus' *Enneads* to be the work of Aristotle (*q.v.* Baghdad School). Very early he had been influenced by Al-Farabi's commentary on Aristotle's *Metaphysics*. His treatise on medicine was the most influential work in that field so far as European universities were concerned, remaining dominant from the 12th to the 17th centuries, and yet it was merely an Aristotelian version of Galen. His philosophical influence was especially strong in Europe during the 13th and 14th centuries.

Principal writings: *The Healing* (al-Shifa) (T in part); *The Deliverance* (Najat), a shortened and rearranged version of the *al-Shifa*; *The Canons of Medicine* (T); *The Directives and Remarks*, a concise statement of his philosophy; *The Divisions of the Intellectual Sciences*; *Oriental Philosophy* (Al-hikmat al-mashriqiyah), introduction alone extant; and many other treatises allegedly numbering more than 100.

(1) The public, or rational, side of his philosophy was heavily influenced by Aristotle, distinguishing and describing the roles of sense and reason in knowledge, definition, species, difference, property, accident, and the four causes. His distinction between first and second understanding (*q.v.* Logic 7) seems to have been the origin of the distinction between First and second intentions (*q.v.* Intentionality 1).

(2) He divides the sciences into theoretical (physics, mathematics, theology) and practical (applied physics, mechanics, art, ethics). Opposed to atomism, he believed bodies divisible to infinity. Believing the world finite, he thought that beyond its boundaries lay absolute nothingness.

(3) His psychology, like that of Aristotle, stressed the differences between vegetable, animal, and rational functions.

(4) A realist on the question of universals, he follows Aristotle in believing that our active intellect frees the universal from the particulars of sense. But this operation endows it with no more than potential existence. In order actually to grasp the universal our minds must come in contact with a superior intelligence, superior, that is, to man himself. And at this point epistemology leads into metaphysics.

(5) Between the world and God the scale of being, which begins in this world, continues up to God, the perfect, unitary, and necessary being. The intermediate distance is bridged by ten intelligences, emanating from God and activating the spheres of the heavens. The spheres are also regarded as ensouled, so the analogy between soul and active intellect is exact, as between men and the heavenly spheres. The tenth intelligence, source of the sublunary world, is the active reason. It is this with which our minds come in contact in comprehending the universal.

(6) But the existence of God is not merely assumed. It is the conclusion of an argument consisting of three steps: (a) Anything that can possibly come to be must come to be as a result of a cause. (b) Causes can neither be linked together in an infinite series, nor can they be linked to each other in a great circle. (c) Therefore, the series of causes must lead to a necessary being.

(7) God's nature has been proved to be necessary. He is complete, absolute, and perfect in truth, goodness, love, and life itself. Since God is the necessary being, in Him essence and existence are identical. And since He is absolute goodness He must share His perfection. Hence, the creation is also necessary and, indeed, from eternity. God creates by producing the first intelligence, similar to God yet, as a being that has received existence, one in which essence and existence are not identical but distinct. As other intelligences come in sequence, multiplicity increases. The work of the tenth intelligence is to provide forms, the universal in another relationship, to be received in matter, *i.e.*, potentiality, and capable of multiplication within species. Hence, matter is here the principle of individuation.

(8) Since creation is necessary, so is everything which occurs within creation.

All things are necessary, but God—in whom essence and existence are identical—is necessary in Himself. In other beings essence does not require existence. Such beings are contingent, yet necessary, their existence having been determined by the necessary action of an external cause (*q.v.* Leibniz 13).

(9) Although evil is to be found in individual things, it is an accident of existence, flowing from want, physical suffering, or sin. Evil touches only the individual and not the species; and, of course, it does not touch God. Furthermore, in the case of anything evil, there is always available a superior point of view from which the evil may be seen to be good (*q.v.* Augustine 8).

(10) The creation of the soul takes place at the same time as the creation of the body, and is in harmony with it, although the soul is immortal and the body is not. Since man's true goal is the attainment of a perfect happiness or bliss which can be realized only after death, and since the resurrection of the body is denied, the concept is that of personal immortality.

(11) A bridge to the esoteric, imaginal, aspect of his philosophy occurs in his discussion of prophetic knowledge. Prophetic awareness receives from the active intelligence in a single vision what the ordinary intellect must work out step by step. The prophetic awareness "flares up," and in this context the symbolism of light becomes central. The ten intelligences reflect a divine light which is transmitted to the world of forms which, in turn, give existence to matter (in itself, darkness). The world thus becomes an interplay of light and darkness, the prophetic adding to its light.

(12) Historically, the distinction between the relation of essence to existence in created things and in God (*q.v.* 7 and 8 above), already present in the philosophy of Al-Farabi (*q.v.* 2), becomes a key doctrine in medieval philosophy, having a part to play in the thought of St. Bonaventure (*q.v.* 9), Aquinas (*q.v.* 6), and many others.

AVIDYA.

Sanskrit term meaning "nescience" or "ignorance." A synonym is *maya*. Specifically, *Avidya* is ignorance of the identity of *atman* (*q.v.*) and Brahman (*q.v.*) in Indian philosophy, and therefore of belief in the separate nature of self. Among others, the concept of *avidya* was held by Buddha (*q.v.* 2), Shunyavadins (*q.v.*), Yoga (*q.v.* 3), Gaudapada (*q.v.* 2), and Shankara (*q.v.* 2, 3, 7, 11).

AVYAKTA.

From the Sanskrit meaning "un-manifest." A term used in the *Upanishads* (*q.v.* *Vedas* 4) and in the *Bhagavad-Gita* (*q.v.*), along with the term *Prakriti* (*q.v.*) to refer to the unmanifest power of God, or to Brahman before creation in the state of superabundance, or to the unborn universe. These terms are further specialized as the Indian schools of philosophy develop.

AXIOLOGICAL ETHICS.

One of the types of ethics (*q.v.*) to be contrasted with deontological, teleological, intuitionistic, and formalistic types. The view interprets rightness in terms of value or goodness, so that the judgment of rightness in an action depends upon the value of the action, or the value of its motive or consequences.

AXIOLOGY.

From the Greek *axios* ("value") and *logos* ("knowledge" or "theory"). Although value has been considered in virtually every system of philosophy ever constructed, "Axiology" or "Value Theory" as a separate study is relatively new. (1) The term seems to have been introduced by the French philosopher, Paul Lapie, in his *Logic of the Will*, 1902. (2) Eduard von Hartmann (*q.v.* 4) used the term in the title of Part V of his *System of Philosophy in Outline*, the "Syllabus of Axiology," 1908. (3) The term has been employed by W.M. Urban (*q.v.* 2) and many others, although less than a majority of those interested in the field of value theory. (4) Whatever the term used, the significant point is that the analysis of value in the 20th century brings into a single analysis values of various types: ethical, aesthetic, political, logical, organic, etc. We here follow the most widespread usage and treat the topic under the heading, Value Theory (*q.v.*).

AXIOM.

From the Greek *axioun* ("to think worthy"). Undemonstrable but necessary propositions at the foundation of a given system. One of a family of terms, including assumption (*q.v.*), hypothesis (*q.v.*), postulate (*q.v*), and definition (*q.v.*). The term closest in meaning to "axiom" of this group is "postulate."

(1) Aristotle (*q.v.* 2) thinks of axioms as the primary premises of demonstration, propositions which we must necessarily believe and which are, as suggested above, indemonstrable. Postulates have the same primary position but are demonstrable, even though used without demonstration.

(2) Euclid (*q.v.* 1) called axioms "common notions" which cannot be doubted, once again lying at the base of demonstration. Euclid's "common notions" were not necessarily geometrical. His postulates, on the other hand, were all geometrical while being neither demonstrable nor self-evident.

(3) Wolff (*q.v.* 4) meant by axiom any indemonstrable, theoretical and thus universal proposition, while postulate was for him an indemonstrable, practical, and particular proposition.

(4) Kant (*q.v.* 3) follows Wolff's distinctions in the main. He speaks of the "axioms of intuition." These are *a priori* principles of the pure understanding. One example is that all phenomena have extension.

(5) In the strongest view of the role of axioms four claims interfuse: (a) they are the indemonstrable propositions from which one must begin in building a system of a certain kind; (b) these principles are self-evidently certain to anyone who takes the time to reflect upon them with care; (c) not only are they subjectively certain but also objectively true; (d) they are not merely derived from experience, but are somehow innate and called forth by experience.

(6) Plato, Descartes, and Leibniz would affirm all four of the claims. Aristotle and Locke would drop the claim of innateness. Systems like those of Kant drop the third claim, affirming (a), (b), and (d). The advance of empiricism changed the climate of opinion in recent philosophy to the extent that the dominant position drops claims (c) and (d), affirming only (a) and (b) or (a) alone. Hume may have affirmed (a) and (b) together, but perhaps only (a). Certainly Mill and Russell affirm (a) by itself.

(7) The criterion of truth announced by Descartes (*q.v.* 3) in the second chapter of his *Meditations* that everything he perceives "clearly and distinctly" is true, attempts to substantiate claim (c) on the basis of claim (b). It attempts, that is to say, to gain objective certainty from subjective certainty. The difficulties in making this transition seem reasonable led to its wide rejection.

(8) The challenge directed against claim (d) by John Locke (*q.v.* 1–2) in the first book of his *Essay* was responsible in large part for the change of opinion concerning it in the Western world, although Leibniz' defense of innate ideas against Locke in the former's *New Essays on Human Understanding* (*q.v.* Leibniz 14) had great merit.

(9) Kant's use of human nature as a source for the self-evident in *The Critique of Pure Reason* (*q.v.* Kant 3) failed to find general favor due to its assumption of an invariantly common human nature.

(10) This leaves (a) as alone indubitable, relativizing the axioms to the system, viewing axioms as the primitive propositions with which one must begin in developing particular systems. The phrase "axiomatic method" refers to this usage of the term, designating deductive system construction by specified rules from as small a set of primitive statements as possible. The primitive statements become the axioms or postulates of the system.

AXIOMA.

The term used by Ramus (*q.v.* 4) as the general name for statements. He distinguished *axioma simplex, axioma generale, axioma particulara,* and *axioma proprium.*

AXIOMATIC METHOD.

Q.v. Axiom (10).

AXIOM OF CHOICE.

Q.v. Zermelo (2, 4, 5).

AXIOM OF REDUCIBILITY.

Q.v. Frank Ramsey.

AYAM ATMA BRAHMA.

Sanskrit term meaning "This self is Brahman." *Q.v. Vedas* (4).

AYER, ALFRED J. 1910–1989.

English philosopher. Born in London.

Educated in Oxford. Taught at the University of London before returning to a post at Oxford. His principal contribution has been that of expositor and interpreter of logical positivism or, as he prefers to call his position, logical empiricism, in Britain and the English-speaking world.

Principal writings: *Language, Truth, and Logic*, 1936; 2nd ed., 1946; *The Foundations of Empirical Knowledge*, 1940; *Philosophical Essays*, 1954; *The Problem of Knowledge*, 1956; *Philosophy and Language*, 1960; *The Concept of a Person*, 1963; *The Origins of Pragmatism*, 1968; *Russell and Moore*, 1971; *Probability and Evidence*, 1972; *Philosophy In the Twentieth Century*, 1982; *Wittgenstein*,1985; *The Meaning of Life and Other Essays*, 1990.

(1) In the tradition of David Hume (*q.v.* 5) Ayer holds that all genuine statements are either empirical or analytic (*q.v.* Analytic Judgment). The truths of logic and mathematics are analytic and devoid of factual content. At the same time, Ayer holds, they are not arbitrary. He specifically says that the rules of logic are necessary.

(2) He is less skeptical than Hume concerning the alleged circularity in the principle of induction (*q.v.* Hume 3), holding that "by our own standards" experienced probabilities do provide a guide to the future. Errors occur only in the combinations of facts "imaginatively projected," since we are the ones weighting those projections.

(3) Ayer has considered at great length the criterion which should apply to genuine empirical statements or, as he put it early, genuine factual propositions. Ayer holds that the appropriate criterion has to do with the verifiability of the statement or proposition. But the appropriate expression of the principle has been extremely difficult to obtain. According to Ayer, the criterion of verifiability, as advanced by logical positivists, held that a sentence is significant if one knows how to verify the proposition which the sentence expresses. Ayer holds that it is enough that the proposition be "verifiable in principle." According to Ayer, logical positivists required that the proposition in question be conclusively established in experience; that is, that the strong sense of "verifiable" be used. Ayer holds it is sufficient that the proposition be "rendered probable by experience"; that is, that the weak sense of "verifiable" be used. Finally, Ayer holds, it is not essential that a genuine factual proposition be *equivalent* to an experiential proposition. It is enough that some experiential propositions can be deduced from it in conjunction with certain other premises without being deducible from these premises alone. On the basis of these modifications of the doctrine of logical positivism, Ayer calls himself a logical empiricist.

(4) The verifiability criterion was subject to further qualification in the second edition of *Language, Truth, and Logic*. In this revision the criterion is more complex than in its original form. Any literally meaningful statement, which is not analytic, he held, must be verifiable either directly or indirectly. A statement is directly verifiable if it is an observation statement, or if it is a statement which—joined to at least one observation statement—entails at least one further observation statement without being deducible from the initial observation statement or statements alone. And a statement is indirectly verifiable if, with other premises, it entails at least one directly verifiable statement (not deducible from the other premises alone), and that the other premises consist of statements which are either analytic, directly verifiable, or indirectly verifiable.

(5) Any empirical, or non-analytic, statement which does not meet the demands of the verifiability criterion is to be regarded as meaningless. He believed that statements of metaphysics, theology, ethics, and aesthetics are alike in failing to pass the test. In the latter two fields the statements are regarded by Ayer as emotive with a note of command implicit in them.

(6) Given the criterion of verifiability, what is left of the function of philosophy in this view? Ayer believes that this function consists of analysis. And analysis is the clarification of statements and their interrelations. The procedure involves the translation of the statement needing clarification into other statements which contain neither the key words of the original statement nor synonyms for them. Ayer believes that this is in fact what the British empiricists did, and what

Russell (*q.v.* 4) described so clearly in his theory of descriptions.

(7) In practice, philosophical analysis becomes for Ayer often a translation of sentences about material objects into a sense-datum language. On the basis of this some have regarded him as a phenomenalist. But he grants that statements about material objects can never be fully analyzed into sets of statements about sense-data. The point would seem to be that in becoming aware of the possibilities of partial translation, philosophical insights can occur.

(8) Philosophy in the 20th century, he believes, has advanced to the point where it centers on the study and evaluation of evidence; other styles of philosophizing are ancillary to epistemological analysis, or somehow misguided.

(9) Repelled and attracted, in different ways, by the early and late Wittgenstein—he likes the realism, but not the "irrealism," and rejects the private language argument (*q.v.* Wittgenstein 8)—nonetheless, among 20th century philosophers he finds Wittgenstein to be second only to Russell in "brilliance and originality."

BAAL.

(1) A Semitic term, *i.e.*, one found in most Semitic languages, meaning "possessor." A title of divinity in the history of many Semitic peoples, *baal* signifies the possessor of a place, object, or attribute, but not of a person. Deities of individuals and tribes bear other names, such as "Elohim." The term normally occurs in the plural; reference would be made to the *baalim* of sacred places and objects. The concept is considered to have appeared at a polydaemonistic stage of religious development.

(2) In the Canaanite religion the name of the god of weather and of vegetation. His consort was Ashtoreth, the goddess of fertility. Life resumed in the spring due to the sexual union of Baal and Ashtoreth. The emphasis on fertility was carried over into religious rites and festivals. The 9th century prophets, including Elijah, campaigned to eliminate the shrines of this religion, pressing the Israelites to choose between Baal and Yahweh.

BABEUF, FRANÇOIS.
Q.v. Communism (2).

BABISM.
Q.v. Bahaism.

BABOUVISM.
Q.v. Communism (2).

BACON, FRANCIS. 1561–1626.

English philosopher, legalist, and political figure. Educated at Trinity College in Cambridge, and admitted to the bar in 1575. He took his first seat in Parliament, 1584. He was prominent in an issue against the Queen's subsidy which offended her royal person and delayed his advancement. His defense, Essex, he later prosecuted for treason. In 1603 James ascended the throne granting knighthood to Bacon. In 1603 he was appointed to the king's Learned Council. In 1607 he was made Solicitor General; in 1613 Attorney General; in 1616 Privy Councillor; in 1617 Lord Keeper and Chancellor; in 1618 he was made a Baron and in 1620 Viscount St. Albans. In 1621 he was convicted of taking bribes and removed from office.

Principal writings: *Essays* (first published 1597); *Two Books on the Advancement of Learning*, 1605; *The New Organon*, 1620. A number of works were published posthumously, such as *The New Atlantis*, 1627.

(1) Providing in his philosophy a platform supporting empirical method, or induction (*q.v.* 3), Bacon argued against excessive generalization. He urged that men think in terms of "operations" rather than seek abstract truths, and held that the aim of science is to endow man with new power. But truth and utility are two sides of the same coin, so in gaining one we also find the other. But before it is possible to introduce the new approach to knowledge it is necessary to warn men away from the major sources of error.

(2) Bacon finds four basic *Idola*, erroneous ways of looking at nature: (a) *Idola Tribus*, or idols of the tribe—these are errors natural to man as a member of the human race, *e.g.* the tendency to

generalize from few instances, to give reality to mere abstractions, to fail to recognize the weakness of the senses, to draw conclusions on the assumption that man is the measure of all things. (b) *Idola Specus*, or idols of the cave—errors due to individual bias. These are as numerous as individuals; but a generally corrective rule is to hold in suspicion whatever one's mind dwells on with particular satisfaction. (c) *Idola Fori*, or idols of the market place—errors arising from the influence of words on the mind, *e.g.*, assuming there is an object because there is a word; words confusedly applied to one kind of thing, and to others only vaguely analogous to the original referent, (d) *Idola Theatri*, or idols of the theater—errors in thinking which come from the influence of traditional systems of philosophy, and poorly contrived methods of demonstration, *e.g.*, the sophistical (Aristotle, forcing nature into his science); the empirical insofar as it reaches general conclusions from scattered observations, or by simple enumeration (concluding that since every known A is a B, therefore all A's are B's; or that there is a causal connection between A and B); the superstitious (injecting into philosophy poetical and theological notions).

(3) Believing that to know anything is to understand its causes, and believing that the complex phenomena of experience are produced by a fundamental set of forms or causes, relatively few in number, working in combination and contained in the phenomena themselves, he held that a careful sifting of what appears will serve to bring the causes of things to light. Accordingly, he urged that the conduct of inquiry required the forming of a number of tables: (a) A table of *Essence and Presence* containing instances where the nature under investigation is present. (b) A table of *Absence in Proximity* consisting of instances generally alike, yet lacking the nature under investigation. (c) A table of *Degrees*, or *Comparison*, consisting of instances in which the nature is present in different degrees either in the same or in different subjects. By examining the tables and excluding irrelevant data, Bacon believed one would be led to the discovery of the cause of the nature under investigation.

(4) More generally, it was his conviction that use of the method would not only lead to the discovery of individual causes, but also of the interrelations of the sciences, which in his view would form (in a state of complete information) an organic whole. Accordingly, at the foundation of the sciences he placed "first philosophy," a body of truth containing the axioms common to several of the sciences, the laws of reasoning, and certain very general concepts. Rising from this are the sciences in order: natural history, physics, and metaphysics. The last, concerned with the law binding nature together, may be beyond human capabilities. Natural history is that part of history dealing with the non-human part of the world; and history is defined as the study treating what is circumscribed in place and time, using memory as its essential instrument.

(5) His goal was the Great Instauration, restoring man to mastery over the natural world. His philosophy of science was a blueprint for the accumulation of the knowledge leading to that goal. In the *New Atlantis* he projected an ideal society in keeping with his scientific principles. In that society, science was regarded as the key to happiness, and was fostered under state guidance and control. The society featured a college of experimental science, called Solomon's House, which has been considered by many to be an anticipation of the Royal Society.

BACON, ROGER. 1214–1294.

English philosopher. Born in Somerset. Studied at Oxford and University of Paris concentrating on science through the Arab writers. Lectured both at Oxford and University of Paris. Suspected of unorthodoxy. In 1257, Bonaventure, the head of his order, forbade his Oxford lectures and placed him under non-publishing supervision in Paris. This continued for ten years until Pope Clement IV wrote asking Bacon to compose and send a treatise on the sciences. In the next 18 months he composed the *Opus Majus*, *Opus Minus*, and *Opus Tertium* for the Pope. In 1268 he was allowed to return to Oxford. In 1278, his books were condemned by the head of the Franciscans, and Bacon was imprisoned 14 years.

Principal writings: *Opus Majus* (T), 1267; *Opus Minus*, 1267; *Opus Tertium*, 1267;

Compendium of Studies in Philosophy, 1271; *Compendium of Studies in Theology*, 1292; as well as commentaries on many of Aristotle's works.

(1) Four chief causes of error among men are: (a) authority, (b) custom, (c) the opinion of the unskilled majority, (d) concealment of ignorance under the pretense of wisdom.

(2) The sciences rest on mathematics, and advance only when their facts are subsumed under mathematical principles. Mathematics is termed "the alphabet of philosophy." Speculative argument is never sufficient to establish a conclusion. Direct inspection is necessary. This means that experimental science is superior to speculative science, holding these advantages: (a) It verifies its conclusions by experiment. (b) It establishes truths which could not otherwise be reached. (c) Probing the secrets of nature, it provides us with knowledge, also, of the past and future. He illustrates his method with an analysis of the cause of the rainbow.

(3) But experiment concerns external experience. Also to be considered is internal experience with respect to which divine illumination is possible. Here, philosophy passes beyond experimental science to theology. Leaving behind its imperfect knowledge of created things, it turns toward its true end, which is knowledge of the Creator.

Also *q.v.* Logic (10).

BACONIAN METHOD.

The inductive method of Francis Bacon (*q.v.* 3).

BADARAYANA.

Q.v. Vedanta; Hinduism (6c).

BADEN SCHOOL.

Q.v. Neo-Kantianism (4).

BAER (DOB) OF MESERITZ.

Q.v. Cabala (3g).

BAGHDAD SCHOOL. Est. 832 A.D.

A famous school of translators located in Baghdad. The school, originated in the conscious effort of the Ommaiades dynasties, succeeding the Abbasid in 750, to establish a community of court scholars. The group of Syrian scholars, resulting from this effort, took it as their mission to translate into Arabic the Greek writings thought to be most significant, starting with medical works and continuing with philosophical treatises. Translations were made of Plato, Aristotle, Alexander of Aphrodisias, Themistius, Porphyry, and Ammonius. The Baghdad School translations of Plotinus' *Enneads*, Books 4 to 6—improperly titled *The Theology of Aristotle* and improperly attributed to Aristotle—and Proclus' *Institutio Theologica* (called the *Liber de Causis* or *Book of Causes*), likewise improperly attributed to Aristotle, were responsible for the Neoplatonic misinterpretations of Aristotle which were corrected only in the 13th century.

BAHAISM.

A religious movement initiated in Persia in the second half of the 19th century by Baha u'llah. An offshoot of Islam, its preparatory stage occurred between 1844 (the date when the predecessor of the Baha u'llah, who referred to himself as the "Bab" or "Gate", began to teach the coming of "Him whom God shall make manifest") and 1850 (the date of the Bab's martyrdom). His adherents were said to be members of the Babi faith or Babism. The movement gained definition in 1863 with the realization and announcement by Baha u'llah that he was the manifestation of God prophesied by the Bab. By the time of Baha u'llah's death in 1892 the Bahai faith or Bahaism, as it now came to be known, had become an international religion. The central tenet of the group is that God's essence is beyond our comprehension; and we can know only his "manifestations," *i.e.*, Abraham, Moses, David, Christ, Mohammed, and the Baha u' llah. The manifestations are in essence one, and the teaching one; but expressed in different form for different periods of the world. When one manifestation is outgrown, a new one appears and to this series there shall be no end.

BAHYA BEN JOSEPH IBN PAQUDA. 11th cent. A.D.

Jewish philosopher. Born in Saragossa, Spain, during the Moslem domination. One of the Jewish thinkers who appreciated the possibility of scientific studies and wished to harmonize Jewish religious thought with a scientific outlook. Inclined to Neoplatonic themes he found in Judaism a great spiritual truth defensible through reason, revelation and tradition. The design in nature shows that God exists and is one. He exists since nonexistent things cannot create an existent thing; and He is one since the task of creation demands it. Only God's negative attributes can be known by man. His ethics rests on thankfulness to, and love of, God. *Q.v.* Judaism (7).

Principal writings: *Guide to the Duties of the Heart.*

BAIN, ALEXANDER. 1818–1903.

Scottish philosopher. Educated at Aberdeen. Taught at Glasgow and Aberdeen. Influenced by John Stuart Mill, he is considered a Utilitarian. Discarding faculty psychology and stressing introspection, he utilized the laws of association in the analysis of mental states. Approving laboratory techniques, Bain is regarded as one of the founders of modern psychology.

Principal writings: *The Senses and the Intellect,* 1855; *The Emotions and the Will,* 1859; *Manual of Rhetoric,* 1864; *Logic, Deductive and Inductive,* 1870.

BAKUNIN, MIKHAIL. 1814–1876.

Russian philosopher. Studied in Germany; involved in the Dresden uprising of 1849; imprisoned eight years in Russia; exiled to Siberia, from which he escaped to Europe, making Switzerland his major base. Expelled from the International in 1872.

Principal writings: *The State and Anarchy,* 1873; *God and the State* (T), 1882.

(1) Holding that any privileged person is depraved in intellect and heart, it follows that the destruction of privilege—both political and economic—is a constructive act. The revolutionist should allow neither morality, religion, nor patriotism to turn him from his mission of destruction.

(2) The only laws one need obey are the laws of nature. When one recognizes these laws one will obey them since they are the laws of one's own nature. The need for any political organization will disappear.

BALLOU, HOSEA.

Q.v. Universalism (2).

BALMES, JAMES.

Q.v. Toleration (13).

BAMALIP.

Valid syllogism in AAI mood, fourth figure. *Q.v.* Syllogism (4).

BAPTISM.

From the Greek *baptizein* ("to dip in water"). The rite, religious or tribal, in which a liquid (usually water but sometimes oil, blood, urine, etc.) is applied to the human form by immersion, washing, pouring, or sprinkling, to ward off evil effects or purify from sin. The ritual is world-wide, and is to be found in most religions. Baptism by water gained sacramental status in Roman Catholicism, and retains such status in most varieties of Protestantism (*q.v.* Sacrament).

BAPTISTS.

A major Protestant organization of congregational form, originating within English Congregationalism in the early 17th century, over the issue of the proper form of Baptism. Baptists stress the importance of personal religious experience. The denomination has many sub-groups within it.

BARBARA.

Valid syllogism in AAA mood, first figure. *Q.v.* Syllogism (4).

BARDO.

From Tibetan ("intermediate state" or "state of uncertainty").

(1) In Tibetan Buddhism *Bardo* is the state of a person in the 49 day period between death and rebirth. By extension, it includes all the stages of existence from conception to rebirth in the following manner: conception to the onset of death (the natural *bardo*); death itself (the painful *bardo*); the period of time immediately following death (the luminous *bardo*); the period of time in which karmic projections are active (the karmic *bardo*).

(2) The fourth stage leads to rebirth, as a human being, animal, god, demigod, hungry ghost, or hell-being (*i.e.,* demon). Corollary to each realm, as they are called, is its main negative emotion. In keeping with Buddhist non-attachment, the human negative emotion is desire. The others, in order, are ignorance, pride, jealousy, greed, and anger. One's goal is to escape from rebirth and reach the

Western Paradise of Amitabha.

(3) The *Bardo Tödrol Chenmo* ("the great liberation through hearing in the *bardo*"), named by its Western translator *The Tibetan Book of the Dead*, contains instruction for liberation, and is read by a lama (ideally, one's master) to the dying, the corpse, finally to a picture or effigy of the dead person, the reading at times extending throughout the 49 day period.

(4) The efficacy of the reading requires that the tranquility of mind necessary for liberation be achieved. This is accomplished by sensing the identity between the luminosity of one's mind and the luminosity of Nirvana, or the ultimate void (in the luminous *bardo*), and understanding that the angry demons one confronts in the karmic *bardo* are merely projections of one's own karmic forces. As the text says, referring to the luminous *bardo*: "Now the Ground Luminosity is dawning." In the recognition, and acceptance, of that "clear light" lies the great hope of liberation.

BARE PARTICULAR.
Q.v. Russell (4).

BAR KOKHBA, SIMON. fl. 130.
The Messianic name of Shimon Bar Kosiva, leader of the final Judean revolt against Rome, 132–135. In the opinion of Ben Joseph Akiba, the most prominent rabbi of the time, Bar Kokhba was the prophesied king who would lead Israel to freedom and rebuild the temple. Whether the insurgents captured Jerusalem is problematic; but they did defeat the Roman forces who were in place, organized an independent state, and issued coinage. Within a year, however, Roman troops had been shifted from other provinces; and eventually the insurgents were under Roman siege in a mountain stronghold named Betar "not very far from Jerusalem." According to Roman accounts the casualties of the war included 580,000 Jews and "many Romans." One reason for the revolt had been a Roman plan to erect a temple to Jupiter on the site of the destroyed Jewish temple. That project now went forward as planned and the land renamed Palestine. In Jewish literature Bar Kokhba (or Bar Kosiva) is regarded as a great military hero and, alternately, as a false

messiah, or an incomplete messiah, a step on the way to the true Messiah.

BAR KOSIVA.
Q.v. Bar Kokhba.

BAROCO.
Valid syllogism in AOO mood, second figure. *Q.v.* Syllogism (4).

BARREDA, GABINO.
Q.v. Latin American Philosophy (4).

BARRETO, LUIS PEREIRA.
Q.v. Latin American Philosophy (5).

BARRETO, TOBIAS.
Q.v. Latin American Philosophy (5).

BARTH, KARL. 1886–1968.
Swiss reformed theologian. Born in Basel. Pastor and professor, he taught at Göttingen, Münster, and Bonn, before locating in Basel in 1935. He was the leading exponent of "Crisis Theology."

Principal writings: *Epistle to the Romans* (T), 1919; *Word of God and Word of Man* (T), 1928; *Anselm* (T), 1931; *Church Dogmatics*, 4 vols., (T), 1932–53; *Credo* (T), 1935; *Dogmatics in Outline* (T), 1947; *Evangelical Theology, An Introduction* (T), 1962.

(1) God is the "Wholly Different One" by whom all human things are put under question. At the same time God and the things of God cannot be explained in rational terms.

(2) Interpreting the ontological argument as faith seeking understanding, the argument becomes equivalent to faith confounding from its own resources. Thus one must turn to the revealed word, opposing a scriptural theology to all natural theology. The result is a "Dialectical Theology," which emphasizes the contradiction between God and the world.

(3) Since the truth is thus the result of grace, the rationalistic "analogy of being" is replaced by the "analogy of faith."

BARTHES, ROLAND. 1915–1980.
French philosopher and literary critic. Born in Cherbourg, France. Taught at the École Pratique des Haute Études and Collège de France. Having succeeded in conquering tuberculosis after decades of struggle, his death followed from an accident in which he was struck by a

laundry truck while crossing the street in front of the *Collège de France.*

Principal writings: *Writing Degree Zero* (T), 1953; *Mythologies* (T), 1957; *On Racine* (T), 1963; *Elements of Semiology*, (T), 1964; *Fashion Systems* (T), 1967; *The Empire of Signs*, 1970; *S/Z* (T), 1970; *Sade/Fourier/ Loyola* (T), 1971; *The Pleasures of the Text* (T), 1973; *Roland Barthes* (T), 1975; *Camera Lucida* (T), 1980.

(1) Contemporary poetry is writing at degree zero where the word explodes into all its potentialities, pregnant with all past and future specifications. This is a radical use of language, related to individuality, contrasting with its social function, already patterned into repressive forms. The Eiffel Tower, he comments, is zero degree in terms of monuments; in itself, a framework, a "nothing," it serves as vantage point for multiplying the visual perspectives of Paris.

(2) Interest in language led to his *Elements of Semiology*, influenced by de Saussure and not by Peirce (*q.v.* 16), even though Barthes' semiology has the breadth of Peirce's semiotics. It takes account of all systems of signs, involving images, gestures, musical sounds, objects, as well as their complex associations. The structuralist (*q.v.* 5) implications of this, Barthes called "translinguistics"; signs operate within systems of interrelated significations where "the world of signifieds is none other than" the world of language. The task of criticism, then, is internal to the systems of significations making up any work.

(3) Translinguistics also applies outside of texts. In *Mythologies* Barthes applied it to such diverse phenomena as films, fashions, and food. It also applies to social philosophy, since myth is viewed as a second-order semiological system which makes contingency appear eternal, masking all distortions.

(4) The repressive uses of language, then, begin as myth and end as "ideology." Capitalism is one such ideology so pervasive in (French) society that it makes no obvious appearance. But the myth/ ideology transfer is ubiquitous. Even traditional literature is an "undoubted mythical system" which functions as an ideology.

(5) One interested in individuality must simply "outplay" the servile uses of language, the stereotypes "sleeping" in each sign, the "linguistic masks" on all sides. The problem is that speech, once uttered even in the subject's deepest privacy, enters "the service of power." The move is to become aware of how much we have been used by power and have "the courage to abjure" servility.

(6) It is within speech that speech must be fought for it is there that servility and power intermingle. That outcropping of speech and "fabric of signifiers," the text, must be the locus of the struggle, "the great mass of language upon which men work and which works on them."

(7) *S/Z* provides a case study of the contrast between writing and reading, the results of a two-year seminar devoted to Balzac's *Sarrasine*. Interspersing 561 numbered fragments from the text with 93 passages commenting on, or digressing from, the reading, Barthes traces his preference for the readerly over the writerly, and the presence of open codes in both. The culmination of all his work, *S/Z* is considered by others, and by Barthes himself, as the point when his view stopped being structuralist, and became post-structuralist. The reason is that in this work he did not reveal an underlying structure but explored how the *Sarrasine*, due to its conflicting codes, differed from itself. At least in photography he holds himself to be a realist, since the photograph is "an image without code" (*Camera Lucida*, p. 36). If there are "emanation(s) of past reality" in perception also, then there is a touch of realism in his view, however it is further described.

(8) This marks a transition from a writerly mode of analysis, where the writer is presumed to be in control to a readerly mode where the reader is expected to determine the final code. The birth of the reader must be at the cost of the death of the author.

(9) In the mode of readerly authority, pleasure is derived from application of the reader's own determinative code to the text. This is the text of pleasure (*plaisir*). When no code applies, and one's relations with language are in crisis, one arrives at the text of ecstasy (*jouissance*). Both states are pleasures of the body, and part of Barthes' program to break with the Cartesian emphasis on awareness and return to hedonism.

(10) The opposition to Cartesianism (*q.v.*) allows Barthes to think of the person as a plurality of codes; and to say that since "who speaks is not who writes, and who writes is not who is," the "I" itself is to be unmasked and dismantled.

(11) The view that the social sciences contain a "diachrony" of metalanguages, and that every science contains "the seeds of its own death" in the language code chosen for its expression, was held by Barthes throughout his work. It perhaps explains his having said, although only in an interview, that literary study should be the only subject in the university.

BASIC SENTENCES.
Q.v. Protocol Sentence.

BASILIDES. 2nd cent. A.D.
Gnostic teacher. Taught in Alexandria. Along with Valentinus one of the most famous of the Gnostic teachers.

Principal writings: He seems to have composed a Gospel, and an exposition on this Gospel in 24 books. The writings are not extant.

(1) Holding God to be above existence, Basilides disavowed the emanational view of creation in favor of creation out of nothing. God created a seed, the Divine Word, containing the manifold forms of being of the universe. From the world seed, including a three-fold sonship, the world and all its firmaments arose.

(2) In his view the incarnation involved both divine illumination and integration of all the spheres of being, making possible eternal existence and the restitution of all things.

(3) At the same time he held that suffering presupposes sin, and that this requires the doctrine of transmigration.

(4) Finally, he taught that man must conquer his desires, neither loving nor hating anything.

BASILIDIANS.
The followers of Basilides (*q.v.*), a 2nd-century Gnostic of Alexandria. The Basilidians celebrated the day of Jesus' baptism as the time when Jesus became divine, or when the Divine Savior (in Basilides' terms the divine *Nous*) entered the human figure of Jesus.

BASIL OF CAPPADOCIA.
Q.v. Patristics (10).

BAULS OF BENGAL.
Q.v. Hinduism (5c); Tagore.

BAUMGARTEN, ALEXANDER.
1714–1762.
German philosopher. Born in Berlin. Studied at Halle, where he later taught. He also taught at Frankfurt an der Oder. A follower of Leibniz and Christian Wolff.

Principal writings: *Philosophical Meditations on Poetry* (T), 1735; *Metaphysics*, 1739; *Philosophical Ethics*, 1740; *Aesthetics*, 2 vols., 1750–58; *Practical Philosophy*, 1760; *Natural Law*, 1765; *General Philosophy*, 1770.

(1) Baumgarten contributed a great deal to philosophy by his introduction of terms and classifications. Following Wolff in using the term "ontology" he held that study to concern "the most general or abstract predicates" of things in general. It was Baumgarten who introduced the term "aesthetics" to philosophy and is considered the founder of that study as a formal discipline.

(2) He divided philosophy into three main branches: (a) Theory of Knowledge, subdivided into logic and Aesthetics, (b) Theoretical philosophy, consisting of the fields of Physics and Metaphysics, (c) Practical philosophy, consisting of Ethics, Philosophy of Law, Theory of Conduct, and Theory of Expression.

(3) While Logic dealt with the higher or intellectual reaches of Theory of Knowledge, Aesthetics dealt with sense-knowledge or sensible knowledge, in Baumgarten's view the lower aspect of the discipline. And though he intended the study to apply to perception generally, his own work in the area centered on the beautiful, thus establishing the modern use of the term.

(4) Treating the topics of artistic genius and knowledge, he held the beautiful to be sensitive knowledge of the truth and perfectly lively. Where the intellectual takes intensive clarity as its goal, the aesthetic, resting on "sensitive representations," involving feeling, knowledge and will, has as its goal "extensive clarity." This seems to imply interconnections with many things, and a fusing of their characteristics into some kind of appreciative unity.

BAUTAIN, LOUIS, ABBÉ. 1796–1867.

French Catholic philosopher. Born in Paris. Drifted from Catholicism into philosophical skepticism. Reconverted in 1821 while continuing to accept Kant's objections to the possibility of rational arguments for God. Bautain replaced these arguments with fideism, a doctrine that God can be known through faith, feeling, and mystic insight; and only in these ways. He taught that faith precedes reason, and that reason is in itself metaphysically incompetent. The doctrine of fideism was officially condemned in 1840 by Gregory XVI. Bautain signed a recantation affirming that reason "can prove with certitude the existence of God and the infinity of His perfections."

Principal writings: *The Philosophy of Christianity*, 2 vols., 1833; *Experimental Psychology*, 2 vols., 1839; *Moral Philosophy*, 2 vols., 1842; *Religion and Liberty*, 1848; *The Human Spirit and its Faculties*, 2 vols., 1859.

BAYES' LAW.

Q.v. Probability (4).

BAYLE, PIERRE. 1647–1706.

French philosopher. Author of the celebrated *Historical and Critical Dictionary*. A great educational force. Included a form of Biblical criticism in his entries concerning Scriptural events. Supported freedom of religious interpretation. Remained agnostic on questions beyond the power of reason to decide. Avowedly neutral, he would tend to give more space to arguments favoring skepticism than those favoring traditional beliefs. Denying that the ethical life required a Christian basis, he supported a naturalistic ethics.

Principal writings: *An Historical and Critical Dictionary* (T), 1702.

BAYLE'S DICTIONARY.

Q.v. Pierre Bayle.

BEARDSLEY, MONROE. C. 1915–1985.

American philosopher. Born in Bridgeport, Ct. Educated at Yale. Taught at Yale, Mt. Holyoke, Swarthmore, and Temple University.

Principal writings: *Practical Logic* (shortened version, *Thinking Straight*), 1950; *Aesthetics*, 1958; *Aesthetics from Classical Greece to the Present*, 1966; *Modes of Ar-*

gument, 1967; *The Possibility of Criticism*, 1970; *Essays in Aesthetics* (ed. J. Fisher), 1983.

(1) Aesthetic value has special character, something aesthetic objects have. Art is an intentional arrangement of conditions designed to produce aesthetic value. The objective qualities of art, leading to this goal, are intensity, unity, and complexity. The aesthetic experience is the subjective experiencing of these qualities.

(2) Using the two-subject theory of metaphor (*q.v.* 12–14) Beardsley's specific suggestion is that an indirect contradiction exists in the connotations of the two subjects which the reader resolves by selecting out those connotations having a hidden kinship.

(3) The intentional and affective fallacies, to be avoided in aesthetic criticism (formulated with W. K. Wimsatt) are discussed in New Criticism (*q.v.*).

BEATIFICATION.

From the Latin *beatus* ("blessed") and *facere* ("to make"). That stage in the Roman Catholic process of canonization (*q.v.*) whereby a candidate for sainthood is declared one of the "blessed" and entitled to public religious honor.

BEATIFIC VISION.

In Christianity the immediate vision of God enjoyed by the faithful in heaven.

BEATITUDES.

The declarations of the Sermon on the Mount (*Matt.* 5:3–11; *Luke* 6: 20–22) dealing with blessedness and naming the virtues which lead thereto.

BEAUTY.

Q.v. Aesthetics.

BEAUVOIR, SIMONE DE. 1908–1986.

French philosopher. Educated at University of Paris. Taught in lycee, 1931-43. Colleague of Jean Paul Sartre.

Principal philosophical writings: *The Ethics of Ambiguity* (T), 1947; *Existentialism and the Wisdom of Nations*, 1948; *The Second Sex* (T), 1949; *Letters to Sartre* (T), 1990; in addition, novels and autobiographies.

(1) Finding no physical or biological reason sufficient to account for woman's status as "other" rather than as "subject" (the status of the male), Beauvoir explains this otherness by the intense bond woman

has for the very being who opresses her, man.

(2) Women need to find a unity among themselves in order to assert themselves as subject. Although the way of doing this is not spelled out, the ontological conditions are the same for men and women. Humans live in ambiguity wishing to, while knowing they cannot, be absolute. But if we can learn to work toward an infinite future through finite presence we shall have succeeded in applying the ethics of ambiguity, and be in the way of winning the game of human life.

BECHER, J.J.
Q.v. Phlogiston Theory.

BECOMING.
In philosophy, the passage of events in time including the coming into being and going out of being of any quality. Process, orderly change, in contrast to changeless being. The contrast holds nicely in contrasting Parmenidean being with Heraclitean flux. Both categories are present in Plato (*q.v.* 8), joining the movable and the immovable. The third category in Hegel's lengthy deduction of the categories, synthesizing in a distinctive way the first two categorical ideas of being and nothing (*q.v.* Hegel 7).

BEGGING THE QUESTION.
Q.v. Fallacies (20).

BEHAVIORISM.
A modern psychology stemming from Pavlov in Russia and J.B. Watson (*q.v.*) in America. In this perspective the study of behavior replaces introspective techniques, and the vocabulary of mentalistic terms is dropped altogether. The point of view is related to American naturalism and some of the varieties of American pragmatism. Skinner (*q.v.* 1) continues Watsonian behaviorism under the name "Operationism." Chomsky (*q.v.* 5) has challenged Skinner, arguing that the stimulus-response categories of behaviorism are inadequate. Also *q.v.* Psychology (8); E.B. Holt (4).

BEING.
From the Greek *ousia* and *ontos*; in Latin *esse, essentia,* and *substantia* are the basic referents to "being."

(1) In philosophy the search for what underlies appearance led in Parmenides (*q.v.* 1–4) to the claim that "being is and non-being is not." For Parmenides being is changeless, rational, and one.

(2) Plato (*q.v.* 8–9) associated being with the changeless ideas, and contrasted being with becoming (*q.v.*), relating the latter to the changing world.

(3) Aristotle (*q.v.* 6–7) chose *ousia* or "substance" as his basic category, regarding "being" as an analogical concept, applying to different things in different ways (*q.v.* Analogy 2; Genus 3). For example, "substance" is composed of "matter" and "form," and each of these has its own quality of being.

(4) In the Middle Ages the Aristotelian distinctions, especially, were carried on and developed. For Thomas Aquinas (*q.v.* 4–6), since matter-and-form constituted an essence to which existence had then to be added, the terminology had to be more complex: *Esse* means "existence." *Essentia* means the nature, or "being this," of formed matter. *Essentia* is also *esse quid, i.e.,* an existence of a certain kind. The most general kind of referent to being is *ens,* and *ens* can designate the being of substance, essence, or ideas in the mind (*ens rationis*). *Res* or "thing" is used synonymously with *ens*.

(5) Duns Scotus (*q.v.* 1, 5) substituted the word *realitas* for his predecessors' terms for being and *haecceitas* ("thisness"), or *entitas singularis* ("individual being") for substance, arguing that by virtue of the *haecceitas* the being in question is *this* being.

(6) For Hegel (*q.v.* 6–7) "being" is the most abstract idea, and the starting point of his deduction of the categories.

(7) The interest in being diminished in the modern world until relatively recent years. Max Wundt (*q.v.*) distinguished pure being from ordinary being, claiming that only the latter is within our reach, and that there is a dialectical interplay between the two types of being.

(8) The distinction between types of being appears again in Jaspers (*q.v.* 1, 4, 6) who distinguished between *Dasein* (ordinary being), *Existenz* (authentic being), and Being (the transcending).

(9) Heidegger (*q.v.* 1, 3, 4) distinguishes *Dasein* (or being there), the kind of being ordinarily available to us, from *Eksistenz* (once again, authentic being), and

"transcending Being" which is akin to the holy.

(10) Paul Weiss (*q.v.*) views reality as consisting of four modes of being—actuality, ideality, existence, and God—all interrelating and yet also opposed.

(11) In modern logic being is related to instantiation of logical forms. Quine (*q.v.* 2) therefore holds that to be is to be the value of a variable.

BEING, THE GREAT CHAIN OF.

The phrase, used by A.O. Lovejoy (*q.v.* 2) as the title of his influential book, serves to introduce a concept of importance running from Neoplatonism through the medieval period; that is, the concept of a graded reality embodying all of the possibilities in a continuum running from pure matter to pure spirit, from sheer potentiality to pure actuality. Among others, Isaac of Stella (*q.v.*) used the concept.

BELIEF.

A term roughly synonymous with opinion (*q.v.*), and related to other terms such as "faith" (*q.v.*), "knowledge" (*q.v.*), "probability" (*q.v.*) and "truth" (*q.v.*).

(1) In the "ethics of belief" Clifford (*q.v.* 1) held that one must withhold acceptance of a statement unless all evidence pointed to its truth.

(2) Ortega y Gasset (*q.v.* 2) looked on belief as the power behind ideas. Ideas need to be rooted in prerational belief. In combination, ideas and beliefs constitute "vital reason."

BELLAMY, EDWARD.

Q.v. Utopia (9).

BELL, CLIVE.

Q.v. Aesthetics (28).

BENEDICTINE RULE.

Q.v. Monasticism.

BENEDICT OF NURSIA, ST.

Q.v. Monasticism.

BENEKE, FRIEDRICH. 1798–1854.

German philosopher. Born in Berlin. Educated at Halle and Berlin. Taught at Berlin and Göttingen. Along with Herbart (*q.v.*), one of the anti-Hegelians in the period of Hegel's greatest influence. Beneke responded to the philosophies of Kant and Locke, regarding himself as a disciple of the latter. Believing in an associationalist psychology (*q.v.* 3), he argued that all philosophy derives from psychological analysis.

Selected writings: *The Empirical Doctrine of the Soul as the Basis of all Knowledge*, 1820; *New Basis for Metaphysics*, 1822.

BENEVOLENCE.

From the Latin *bene* ("well") and *volens* ("wishing"). In philosophy a principle taken to support social interest and oppose self-interest. The principle is utilized by Cumberland (*q.v.* 3), Shaftesbury (*q.v.* 3), Hutcheson (*q.v.* 3–4), Jonathan Edwards *q.v.* 5), Hume (*q.v.* 6), Godwin (*q.v.* 3), Herbart (*q.v.* 4c), and Sidgwick (*q.v.* 2).

BENJAMIN, WALTER. 1892–1940.

Q.v. Adorno (5); Frankfurt School, The. A.

BENTHAM, JEREMY. 1748–1832.

English philosopher. Born in London. educated at Oxford. Son of a successful attorney, he studied Latin at three, and received his college degree from Queens College at 15. He studied law at Lincoln's Inn, but never practiced, being led rather into analysis of its philosophical basis. The founder of Utilitarianism (*q.v.*) and leader of the Philosophical Radicals (the reform group based on utilitarian principles) he became the center of a philosophical coterie which included the Mills, both father and son. He was made a French citizen in 1792. In 1824 he founded the *Westminster Review*.

Principal writings: *A Fragment on Government*, 1776; *Principles of Morals and Legislation*, 1789; *Handbook of Political Fallacies*, 1824; *Rationale of Judicial Evidence*, 1827; *Outline of a New System of Logic*, 1827; *Deontology or the Science of Morality*, 1834; *Bentham's Theory of Fictions*, ed. C.K. Ogden, 1932.

(1) The end of individual life is taken to be the pursuit of pleasure and the avoidance of pain. That we seek the one and avoid the other is for Bentham a fact of nature.

(2) The end of life, ethically speaking, is "the greatest good for the greatest number." When this phrase is interpreted we find it means "the greatest sum of pleasure," and when we consider how

to apply this criterion it turns out that we calculate the pleasures in the consequences of our behavior.

(3) This utilitarian, or hedonic, calculus considers the consequences, in seven respects: (a) the intensity of the pleasure or pain; (b) the duration of the pleasure or pain; (c) the certainty or uncertainty of the pleasure or pain; (d) the propinquity or remoteness of the pleasure or pain; (e) the fecundity of the pleasure or pain; (f) the purity of the pleasure or pain; (g) the extent of the pleasure or pain. *i.e.*, the number to whom it extends.

(4) Using these considerations, and the "greatest happiness" principle, we weigh the possible alternatives in a given situation; ethical behavior consists in selecting an alternative likely to yield the largest sum of pleasure or the smallest sum of pain, taking into account all the pleasures and pains which may ensue.

(5) Applied to the state, it turns out that the public interest is nothing but the "mass of the interests of individuals," the result of a hedonic calculus in which the pleasures and pains of individuals are summed up.

(6) According to his "doctrine of fictions," a tremendous number of words in ordinary use refer to fictitious entities. If sentences containing fictions cannot be translated into sentences referring to real entities, they are without meaning. If they can be so translated—he calls the process "definition by paraphrasis"—mental confusion is reduced.

(7) Doctrines of natural rights, natural law, and social contract theory are fictions of the untranslatable sort.

BERDYAEV, NICOLAS. 1874–1948.

Russian philosopher of religion. Born in Kiev. Professor of Philosophy, University of Moscow, 1917. Twice exiled, in 1922 established a school of religious philosophy in Berlin; later moved to Paris, publishing a journal. Russian Orthodox and mystical by temperament, his thought resembles gnosticism to some extent while having affinities with Boehme and Schelling; a prominent critic of Marxist philosophy.

Principal writings: *The Meaning of History* (T), 1923; *The Destiny of Man* (T), 1931; *Freedom and the Spirit* (T), 1935; *Solitude and Society* (T), 1939; *Slavery and Freedom*

(T), 1940; *The Beginning and the End* (T), 1947; *The Russian Idea* (T), 1949; *Dream and Reality* (T), 1951.

(1) Man, like God, is creative, and all creation is out of nothing. In addition to an eternal God there is an eternal *Ungrund*, a nothingness out of which creation comes.

(2) Human freedom, then, is self-creation, creation out of nothing. It is our completion of our Creator's work, our answer to His call, and is thus ultimate.

(3) Creation is, hence, continuous, and development occurs both in man and God. Furthermore, the experiences of suffering, and of satisfaction, are part of the life of each.

(4) Evil results from freedom, and is its degeneration. Good is somehow creativeness and spontaneity, guided by love. This is the case in man, and, in the world, the tragedy of freedom become degenerate is overcome through love by the tragedy of the cross.

(5) In some sense, too, the human time through which we live is a false, disintegrated time, and to be contrasted with an authentic, integrated, divine time. The divine time, or history, is also called eternal.

(6) Finally, man cannot be man apart from community, and this community—including other men—must include as well communion with God.

BERGMANN, GUSTAV. 1906– .

Austrian-American philosopher. Born in Vienna. Bergmann studied at the University of Vienna as one of the second generation Logical Positivists. Coming to the United States in 1938, he taught at the University of Iowa.

Principal writings: *The Metaphysics of Logical Positivism*, 1954; *Philosophy of Science*, 1958; *Meaning and Existence*, 1960; *Logic and Reality*, 1964; *Realism: A Critique of Brentano and Meinong*, 1967.

(1) Arguing that all Logical Positivists are either Materialists or Phenomenalists, Bergmann traces his own course of thought from that of reluctant Phenomenalist to Phenomenological Realist to a Realism with the "phenomenological dross" removed. Ontology is held to be primary, and epistemology is regarded as the ontology of the knowing situation.

(2) Committed to the "linguistic turn" in philosophy on which ordinary

language and ideal language philosophers agree, Bergmann employed the construction of ideal languages as a means of making clear the nature of one's ontological commitments. It is his view that any language will have ontological implications. They will be found in the "undefined descriptive signs" of the ideal language, that is, the signs one uses to define everything else. The point is not only that ideal languages clarify one's ontological commitments, they also serve as a kind of Ockham's razor indicating the commitments which cannot be eliminated easily, those whose elimination comes at too high a price, and possibly those which cannot be eliminated at all.

BERGSON, HENRI. 1859–1941.

French philosopher. Studied mathematics; attracted to the use of evolutionary data in philosophy. A very popular lecturer, teaching at the College of France from 1901 to 1921.

Principal writings: *Essay on the Immediate Given of Awareness* (T), 1889; *Time and Free Will* (T), 1889; *Matter and Memory* (T), 1896; *Laughter* (T), 1900; *Introduction to Metaphysics* (T), 1903; *Creative Evolution* (T), 1907; *The Two Sources of Morality* (T), 1932; *Thought and the Moving* (T), 1934.

(1) Philosophy must form itself according to what is given in experience. We are given reason and intuition, the first tending toward a static view of things, the second tending toward flexibility and change. But the dynamism is the more basic. Stripping away the layers of consciousness, one will find at its center sheer fluidity.

(2) When one grasps the world through ideation instead of intuition one falsifies it. The paradoxes of Zeno result from interpreting the fluidity of time by the static categories of reason. This is "spatializing time."

(3) To a certain extent one must spatialize time, our reason allowing us to approximate, but never reach, the nature of its object by multiplying the number of its aspects in awareness. But the act of reason, creating being, also creates nothingness. At this extreme both are false ideas. The idea of Nothing is in fact dissatisfaction with what is. And

finally we avoid such false problems when we learn to grasp the object by intuitive awareness in which we somehow identify with the object itself. The mode of expression natural to reason is the concept; the mode natural to intuition is the metaphor.

(4) The dynamic and static facets of experience are paralleled by similar facets of the world. The world in its temporal aspect is fluid, dynamic, and continuous. Spatially, however, the world is static and discontinuous. Bergson identifies the temporal aspect of things with the spirit; and the spatial aspect of things, the material aspect, with effete spirit. He illustrates the point using a fountain as his simile. The water shooting forth is spirit; the water falling back is matter.

(5) This means that God works in the processes of evolution; and He is the force, the *Élan Vital*, which makes it go.

(6) It means, also, that evolution is purposive, and adventuring. One of its goals, Bergson states, was freedom. But each new achievement fell back into mechanism until the creation of man when, through heightened complexity, and mechanism cancelling out mechanism, the breakthrough into freedom was gained.

(7) The view of time consistent with these claims is one in which the future is open, and being decided moment by moment. Time is qualitative change. Were the details of the temporal process already settled, time could accelerate toward instantaneity. But these details aren't settled, and time has its own pace.

(8) The future is not in existence, and both man and God create the alternatives and then act upon them; this insures freedom.

(9) The past continues to exist, internal to the present. In man it exists as memory. Bergson compares the situation to a rolling snowball in which its present state contains all its earlier states.

(10) In a way similar to his contrast of spirit and matter, Bergson finds a contrast between a societal ethic, and one which is intuitive; as well as a contrast between an institutional religion, and one which is ecstatic.

BERIGARD, CLAUDE. 1578–1633.

French philosopher. Studied in Paris,

but lived and worked in Italy. Revived the Epicurean philosophy (*q.v.* Epicureanism) although with a cosmology different from the traditional Epicurean affirmation of atoms and the void. Berigard held a view of the void as packed with punctiform atoms, each occupying the dimension of a point. Movement and change involve the transmission of sensible qualities from one atom or set of atoms to another.

Principal writings: *The Circle of Pisa; Doubts Concerning the Dialogues of Galileo.*

BERKELEY, GEORGE. 1685–1753.

Irish philosopher and bishop. Philosophical idealist. Educated at Trinity College, Dublin. Named a fellow in 1707 he served the college in various capacities for five years including lecturer in Divinity. From 1713 to 1720 he traveled in Europe as a chaplain and tutor. He returned to London in 1720. Some years later, he obtained from Parliament a promise of 20,000 pounds to establish a missionary college in the Bermudas; he devoted five years, 1728–33, to this project, including a three-year period of residence in Rhode Island. In 1734 he became Bishop of Cloyne and spent the next twenty years raising his family in a "remote corner of Inokelly." In 1752 he moved to Oxford where his son was studying. He died there in 1753.

Principal writings: *A New Theory of Vision,* 1709; *Treatise Concerning the Principles of Human Knowledge,* 1710; *Three Dialogues Between Hylas and Philonous,* 1713; *Alciphron or the Minute Philosopher,* 1733; *The Theory of Vision or Visual Language, Vindicated and Explained,* 1733; *Siris,* 1744.

(1) "We have first raised a dust, and then complain we cannot see." If this famous statement is taken as the key to Berkeley, his mission in philosophy was reform centering around the artificial problems philosophers have created for themselves; but this concern led him so quickly into the development of an idealist metaphysics, designed as a metaphysical defense of the Christian faith, that we must regard his motivation as double. The transition from his epistemological concern to his metaphysical concern is accomplished by means of an identification of being and perception,

"*Esse est percipi*" ("to be is to be perceived"). He called his view, "Immaterialism," claiming that nothing material exists. Agreeing with Locke that all ideas originate in sense experience, it follows, according to Berkeley, that we have no immediate perception of a three-dimensional world. Instead, we perceive our sensations, and through experience by means of the cooperation of the several senses, including touch, learn to refer these sensations to their appropriate spatial distances, and to interpret their magnitude correctly.

(2) Agreeing with Locke on the origin of our ideas, he vigorously disagrees with Locke's doctrine of abstraction. Through abstraction, Locke (*q.v.* 4) presumes to gain general ideas of man-in-general, triangle-in-general, anything-else-in-general. Berkeley is certain that it is not possible to be aware of a man with color, but no particular color; stature but no particular stature, "and so of the rest"; or to be aware of a triangle "which is neither oblique nor rectangle, equilateral, equicrural nor scalenon, but all and none of these at once." In place of Locke's abstract idea, then, Berkeley substitutes a group of particular ideas joined together by principles of association, and a name. Resemblance, or similarity, is the most important of these principles; and through its use, particular ideas become ranked in kinds, or sorts, and the names attached to them become general names. The claim is that generality is possible without abstract ideas. He also advances causality, and coexistence or contiguity, as related principles of association.

(3) Berkeley next calls into question Locke's distinction of primary and secondary qualities. Where Locke (*q.v.* 6) had referred primary qualities to externally existing things, independent of being experienced, and secondary qualities as dependent on being experienced, Berkeley finds no distinction between the status of color, taste, smell, and the status of primary qualities such as extension, figure, and motion. Just as we can do without abstract ideas so we can do without "substances," the something-one-knows-not-what to which primary qualities are referred. But this step puts all ideas on the same footing; they are equally dependent upon

experience. And at this point Berkeley is able to announce his "*esse est percipi*."

(4) But if "*esse est percipi*," ("to be is to be perceived"), still I am aware that not all of my ideas are my creation; some ideas are unwelcome to me, and yet I experience them all the same. Further, one has done little to avoid artificial problems by committing oneself to belief in a world which fades into existence, and out again, as one's awareness changes. On the other hand, if to be is to be perceived, one cannot allow ideas to exist without the mind. Berkeley's solution to this dilemma is to allow the existence of ideas, which, while not dependent upon my mind are dependent upon a part of a divine mind. Hence, reality is made up of ideas, finite spirits and an infinite spirit.

(5) From all of this it follows that "We eat and drink ideas, and are clothed with ideas." But this is only to say that we eat, drink, and clothe ourselves with the immediate objects of sense. Nature is, itself, "the visible series of effects or sensations imprinted on our minds by the infinite Being." And the laws of nature are nothing more than the regularity of the occurrence of these ideas. Neither time nor space, then, is anything apart from the perceptions of our ideas.

(6) In his final work, *Siris*, Berkeley adds a category of "notions," that is, ideas (such as soul and God) which cannot be handled by his earlier treatment of ideas.

BERLIN, ISAIAH. 1909– .

British political philosopher and historian of ideas. Born in Latvia. Educated at Oxford. Taught at Oxford. Many visiting professorships in the United States.

Principal writings: *The Hedgehog and the Fox* 1953; *Historical Inevitability*, 1954; *The Age of Enlightenment*, 1956; *Two Concepts of Liberty*, 1957; *Four Essays on Liberty*, 1969; *Vico and Herder*, 1976; *Concepts and Categories*, 1979; *Against the Current*, 1980; *The Crooked Timber of Humanity* (ed. H. Hardy), 1990; *Conversations with Isaiah Berlin* (ed. R. Jahanbegloo), 1992.

(1) Taking a fragment from the Greek poet, Archilochus that "the fox knows many things, but the hedgehog . . . one big thing," to refer to the contrast between those who relate everything to a single, organizing principle, and those whose lives and ends reflect plurality, Berlin divides the worlds of intellect and art into hedgehogs and foxes.

(2) In philosophy this is the distinction between those who take a monistic and those who take a pluralistic, view of the world. Although preferring pluralism he found monism to be the central feature of European philosophy, rooted in Plato and extending through Marx. In one or another version the monist-pluralist opposition provides the framework for most of Berlin's thought. It provides, for example, his way of distinguishing negative from positive liberty. Negative liberty is freedom as non-interference, the provision of an area where one can do as one chooses. This is the freedom of the fox to realize a plurality of goals. Positive liberty, on the other hand, is the freedom of the hedgehog, that there is a single principle to be realized, a true self to be followed, and that freedom means acting in terms of that true or higher self. Although Berlin affirms both negative liberty as the removal of obstructions and positive liberty as the realization of ideals, it is clear that he prefers the pluralism of negative liberty.

(3) The term also applies to morality where a loose kind of pluralism of values is to be affirmed, and a monism of values to be denied. Defense of a liberal, or free, or open society rests on a view of the pluralism of values since the more unitary the social structure the greater the range of genuine values which are excluded.

BERNARD OF CHARTRES. c. 1080–1167.

Scholastic philosopher and Platonist. Taught at Chartres in France for five years, beginning in 1114; rose to be Chancellor 1119–24. Holding that ideas are eternally real in the mind of God (although not coeternal with God), he labeled the copies of these forms in things *formae nativae* or "native forms." He combined this robust realism with a "return to nature" theme foreshadowing the early Renaissance.

BERNARD OF CLAIRVAUX. 1090–1153.

Entered Cistercian Order, 1112; became Abbot of Clairvaux, 1115. His support of Innocent II in 1130 secured the Pope's power. In Rome, 1132–35. In 1145 a pupil of Bernard's became Pope Eugenius

III; and Bernard could justly be regarded as the most powerful man in Europe at this time. At the request of Eugenius, Bernard preached and organized the Second Crusade, 1146. His power was sometimes used recklessly due to a hatred of heresy which became in practice a hatred of reason itself. He engaged in controversy with Abelard (*q.v.*) where this trait was exhibited and also with Gilbert de la Porrée. Yet Bernard also possessed the mystic vision of a rhapsodic love in which the Church is described in erotic terms as the bride of Christ.

Principal writings: *On the Love of God*, 1126; *On Grace and Free Will*, 1127; *On Contemplation*, 1150–52; *Sermons on the Song of Songs*, 1135–53.

(1) Fallen man has a formal freedom; otherwise guilt is inexplicable. Man must consent to the grace which comes upon him. Merit lies in the union of grace with freedom.

(2) Truth is received through faith; and the only function of reason is to add a measure of clarity, "unwrapping" the gift of faith.

(3) The highest knowledge, then, results from intuition, not intellect. One must abase himself; and through the stages of meditation he can receive everything that is possible for the human reason, and much more.

(4) There are four stages of love: carnal or self-love; a selfish love of God resulting from suffering; an unselfish or integral love of God; union with God, and the annihilation-deification of the self.

BERNAYS, PAUL.
    Q.v. Set Theory (12).

BERNOULLI'S THEOREM.
    Q.v. Probability (4).

BERNSTEIN, RICHARD.
    Q.v. Praxis (14).

BERTOCCI, P.A.
    Q.v. Brightman.

BESANT, ANNIE.
    Q.v. Theosophy.

BETTI, EMILIO.
    Q.v. Hermeneutics (9).

BEZA, THEODORE.
    Q.v. Gallican Confession.

BHAGAVAD-GITA.
From Sanskrit meaning the "Song of the Blessed." Title of the philosophical poem, in Book Six of the *Mahabharata*, an epic poem thought to date from the 6th century B.C. The poem is a dialogue between Arjuna, advancing into battle at the head of his family in opposition to a hostile family, and the God Krishna who acts as Arjuna's charioteer. The two families are rival claimants to the throne, and a principal part of the discussion is concerned with problems of ethics.

The main theme of the poem is that love of God, whether expressed through knowledge, devotion or unswerving attention to duty, leads to salvation, which is identified with Nirvana (*q.v.*). Although the path of duty is held to be higher, all of these paths can be successful, and have the same goal. The direction one takes depends on choice and thus within this life freedom and individual responsibility are maintained.

The divine appears in two forms in the poem: as Brahman, the impersonal absolute; and as Krishna, an incarnation of the divine in human form. We are told that, liberated from earthly existence, individual awareness continues in the presence of God; and that salvation (when the divine is viewed as impersonal absolute) implies the loss of individual identity.

    Q.v. Vaiṣnavism (2b); Hinduism (2).

BHAGAVATAS.
    Q.v. Vaiṣnavism (2a).

BHAIRAVA.
In Hinduism a name of Shiva (*q.v.*) meaning "fearful." The name of the third member of the Hindu trinity in his "fear" form. A dozen forms of this Bhairava-Shiva relationship are known, the most common being "Bhairava the Black" and "Bhairava the Dog."

BHAKTI.
From Sanskrit root, *bhaj* ("to adore"). The name given to the way of devotion in Hinduism (*q.v.* 5c); also, then, the name of those sects of Hinduism stressing devotional faith as the way to salvation, rather than either the path of works (*karma*), or knowledge (*jnana*). Vishnuite Hinduism, its major vehicle, counts its adherents in the hundred millions. This movement, whose roots are present even

in the early *Vedas*, although making common cause with Brahmanism—as in the successful struggle with Buddhism—has its origin and essential support in the non-Brahmanical sectors of Indian society.

(1) One of the types of Yoga (*q.v.* 5), which moves to liberation through devotion.

(2) Ramanuja (*q.v.*) was one of the philosophers whose analysis remained rooted in the *bhakti* experience and tradition. *Q.v.* Vaiṣnavism (2).

BHARTṚHARI (BHARTRIHARI).
Q.v. Vedanta (1); Time (19).

BHAVA.
Sanskrit, "becoming." *Q.v.* Buddha (2).

BHAVACAKRA.
Sanskrit for "wheel of becoming." A Buddhist depiction of the cycle of rebirth in the form of a 5-spoked or 6-spoked wheel. The rim names (and pictures) the twelve links in the chain of Dependent Origination (*q.v.*). The spokes represent the possible rebirth destinations. In the case of the five-spoked wheel these are rebirth as a god, a man, a beast, a ghost, or a resident in hell. The six-spoked wheel adds rebel gods or titans as a sixth destination. The hub of the wheel names the three evil dispositions, passion, hatred, and stupidity, pictured as dove, serpent, and pig. *Q.v. Karma* (4).

BHAVANI.
Q.v. Śakti; Vaiṣnavism (4a).

BIBLE.
From the Greek *biblia* ("the books"), derived from the name of the Phoenician city, Byblos, an important source of papyrus. The term refers to the scriptures of the Jews (divided into the Law, Prophets and Writings) as well as to those of the Christians (39 books of the Old Testament and 27 of the New Testament). From the 4th century until the rise of Protestantism the Latin Vulgate (*q.v.*) was the basic Christian Bible. Wycliffe (*q.v.* 4) and his assistants translated the Vulgate into English (1382, 1384) producing the first English Bible. A French translation of the Vulgate, its New Testament portion published in Rheims in 1582 and the Old Testament published in Douai in 1609, was known as the Douai Bible. Other translations, largely from Greek and Hebrew sources, include those of Luther (*q.v.* 4), William Tyndale (the New Testament in 1525 and the Pentateuch in 1530). Myles Coverdale (1535 and 1539), Thomas Matthew (1537), as well as the Geneva Bible of 1560 (translated into English by Protestant exiles), and the King James Bible (also known as the Authorized Version) produced by a committee of scholars appointed by James I in 1604. Beginning with the English Revised Version (New Testament in 1881 and Old Testament in 1885) numerous modern translations have appeared.

BIBLICAL CRITICISM.
The application to the Bible of linguistic and historiographic tools in order to purify the text and provide a sound basis for its interpretation. This criticism often pointed out inconsistencies in the Biblical text. Spinoza's (*q.v.*) *Theological-Political Treatise* did this. In *The Age of Reason* Thomas Paine (*q.v.* 5) argued that inconsistencies in the Old Testament and discrepancies in the New point to their human origin. Jefferson (*q.v.* 8–9), believing that Jesus claimed no quality beyond the human, separated Jesus' teachings from their background context which, for him, restored the primitive and genuine doctrines. That, of course, would be a subclass of Biblical criticism called New Testament criticism. Strauss (*q.v.*) treated Jesus in human terms as did Renan (*q.v.*). Schweitzer's (*q.v.* 3) *Quest of the Historical Jesus* summarizes the results of 150 years of New Testament criticism, while presenting his own view of Jesus as a Messianic figure. Bultmann (*q.v.*) was one of the most important New Testament critics of the 20th century. He held that the New Testament must be "demythologized."

BIBLICISM.
Adherence to the Bible as authoritative in a literal sense.

BICONDITIONAL
The binary connective "if and only if" in modern logic (*q.v.* Truth Tables 4). Written in many ways, the sign we shall use is "≡" "p ≡ q," for example, "Louise is the wife of William ≡ William is the husband of Louise." From the bicon-

ditional two implications can be gained, p $\supset$ q, (p implies q) and q $\supset$ p, (q implies p). For example, "Louise is the wife of William $\supset$ William is the husband of Louise," and "William is the husband of Louise $\supset$ Louise is the wife of William." The biconditional is hence a stronger statement than the statement of material implication (q.v.).

BIEL, GABRIEL. 1425–1495.

German Scholastic. Born in Speier. Taught at Tübingen. Twice Rector of Tübingen. A follower of Ockham and an opponent of Pelagianism (q.v.), his expositions of Ockham—expanding the area of faith in relation to that of reason—became influential in German universities, including Wittenberg. This view of God's dominance, the absolute and arbitrary nature of His will, over and in contrast to human wills, influenced the thought of Luther (q.v. 9) and Melanchthon on predestination and free will.

Principal writings: *Commentary on Ockham in Four Books of Sentences*, 1508.

BIOGRAPHISM.

Q.v. New Criticism.

BIOLOGY.

From the Greek *bios* ("life") and *logia* ("knowledge of").

A. The study of biology was central to the Lyceum (q.v.) of Aristotle, and conducted on an experimental basis. Where the study of physics remained speculative and theoretical, knowledge of living forms was gained inductively and by dissection.

B. Only in the modern world did the study of biology become a discipline entirely separate from philosophy. Even in this situation biology remains one of the concerns of Philosophy of Science, and the theoretical interpretations of biology make up the subject matter of the Philosophy of Biology. In the Philosophy of Biology there are three basic interpretations of biological phenomena: Reductionism (q.v.), Vitalism (q.v.), and Organismic Biology (q.v.).

(1) Reductionism, or the view that biological phenomena can be adequately treated solely within the categories of Chemistry and Physics, has as its actual or potential adherents all the followers of either Materialism (q.v.) or Mechanism (q.v.).

(2) Vitalism is the doctrine that there is some controlling vital force within organic forms which is not reducible to physiochemical interpretation. A representative of the view is Hans Driesch (q.v.) who uses Aristotle's term *entelechy* as the name of that force operating within organic life. Vitalists claim Aristotle as their own, yet Aristotle's view seems consonant not only with Vitalism, but also with the Organismic view.

(3) Organismic Biology denies both Reductionism and Vitalism, while holding that the actions of the whole organism cannot be understood simply as the sum of the actions of its parts.

BION OF BORYSTHENES. 3rd cent. B.C. fl. 230.

Greek philosopher. Although a disciple of the Academician Crates (q.v. 1), the Cyrenaic Theodorus (q.v. Theodorus the Atheist), and of the Peripatetic philosopher Theophrastus (q.v.), Bion was an adherent of the Cynic philosophy, popularizing its doctrines, and introducing the form of the diatribe. At the same time he softened the harshness of the Cynic doctrine, moving it toward skepticism and away from asceticism.

BIO THE CYRENAIC.

Q.v. Cyrenaicism (2).

BIVALENCE.

Q.v. Dummet (4).

BLACK, MAX.

Q.v. Metaphor (13).

BLANC, LOUIS.

Q.v. Socialism (5).

BLANSHARD, BRAND. 1892–1987.

American philosopher. Born in Fredericksburg, Ohio. Professor at the University of Michigan, Swarthmore College, and Yale University. An Idealist, Blanshard's thought centers in problems of epistemology and ethics.

Principal writings: *The Nature of Thought*, 2 vols., 1941; *On Philosophical Style*, 1954; *The Impasse in Ethics and a Way Out*, 1955; *Reason and Goodness*, 1961; *Reason and Analysis*, 1964; *The Uses of a Liberal Education*, 1973; *Reason and Belief*, 1975; *Four Reasonable Men*, 1987.

(1) Taking his stand on the autonomy of reason, and its requirements of coherence and consistency, Blanshard moved to conclusions which in every case utilized the framework of necessary and intelligible wholes of experience. In the background, one senses, reality is to be conceived after such a model characterized by internal relations and concrete universals.

(2) The method of reason is his working tool; and in the foreground one finds Blanshard applying this method to problems of epistemology (where ideas are given a universal and metaphysical status and truth is interpreted in terms of coherence), of human freedom (only determinism is really intelligible) and questions of ethical concern (the right is interpreted in terms of teleology, and goodness in terms of satisfaction and fulfillment).

BLAVATSKY, MADAME.
Q.v. Theosophy.

BLOCH, ERNST. 1885–1977.
German social philosopher. Born in Ludwigshaften. Studied at the universities of Munich, Würzburg, Berlin, and Heidelberg. Taught at the universities of Leipzig and Tübingen. A Marxist, although never a member of the Communist party Bloch, the "theologian of the revolution," combined dialectical materialism with that utopian end-point of history, known theologically as eschatology and the coming of the kingdom. His work on the German peasant revolt sided with Thomas Münzer, who supported it, rather than with Luther, who opposed it. His philosophical analysis of the utopian promise is that humanity and nature "co-produce" the future, as humans blend their "subjective possibilities" in with the "real-objective possibilities" of nature. The ontology of the position is founded and "forever refounded," on "the-being-of-that-which-is-not-yet." When declared a revisionist at his East German university, his works condemned, the philosophy journal he edited suppressed, forbidden to publish, he defected to West Germany, teaching at the University of Tübingen.

Principal writings: *On the Spirit of Utopia*, 1918; *Thomas Muenzer as Theologian of Revolution*, 1921; *The Principle of Hope*, 3 vols., 1954–59; *Basic Philosophical Questions: on the Ontology of the Not-yet Being*, 1961; *A Philosophy of the Future* (T), 1963; *Man on His Own* (T), 1978.

BLONDEL, MAURICE. 1861–1949.
French "spiritualistic" philosopher. Born in Dijon. Taught in universities of Lille and Aix-Marseille.

Principle writings: *Action*, 2 vols., 1893; *Thought*, 2 vols., 1933–34; *Being and the Beings*, 1935; *Philosophy and the Christian Spirit*, 2 vols., 1944–46; *Philosophical Requirements of Christianity*, 1950.

(1) Developing a "Philosophy of Action" in which intellect and the contemplative life gain point and meaning in the activities which precede and terminate thought, Blondel's problem is to find the appropriate balance between theory and practice.

(2) Without action thought proceeds interminably. But internal to any activity are its principles; and these are the ideas which can provide the synthesizing criteria for the vast array of ideas, and contradictions, of contemporary thought.

(3) The analysis finally turns on the idea of pure work. Since thought is itself a type of work, the two are combined in a vision of God, at once the height of contemplation, and a transcendent immanence in the world.

BLOOMFIELD, LEONARD.
Q.v. Language (18); Semantics (5); Chomsky (1).

BOAS, FRANZ.
Q.v. Language (15).

BOAS, GEORGE. 1891–1980.
American philosopher. Born in Providence, Rhode Island. Studied at Brown, Columbia, and Harvard; Ph.D. from University of California, 1917. Professor at Johns Hopkins University, 1920–1957. A follower of A.O. Lovejoy, oriented toward the history of ideas.

Selected writings: *Primitivism and Related Ideas in Antiquity*, 1935 (with A.O. Lovejoy); *The Happy Beast in French Thought of the Seventeenth Century*, 1933; *Essays on Primitivism and Related Ideas in the Middle Ages*, 1948; *Dominant Themes in Modern Philosophy*, 1957; *The Inquiring Mind*, 1959; *Rationalism in Greek Philoso-*

phy, 1961; *The Heaven of Invention,* 1962; *The History of Ideas,* 1969; *Vox Populi,* 1969.

(1) It is the object of the historian of ideas to determine the role ideas have played in history.

(2) Man attempts to superimpose his world of logic upon the world of history, and fails due to the existence of time. The world in which we live has no universals; the world about which we reason has no individuals. And it is the world of individuals which provides the basic metaphors out of which we build explanations.

(3) Ideas generally have their origin as figures of speech. They begin as metaphors, and some grow into myths.

(4) The idea of cause, when used in explanation, is the residue of a metaphor which in turn is the residue of a myth. The idea of purpose, when applied to nature, is the residue of a myth. Mechanism and teleology are thus expanded beyond their legitimate spheres.

(5) Certain abstract terms, likewise, become "concentrated emblems" and play a role involving human feelings and "prizings" as well as thought. The term "nature" is one of these, as are such terms as Truth, Beauty, Law, Order, Cosmos.

(6) Periodization, once again, in history moves into something like myth or metaphor in reifying history.

(7) The same can happen to explanatory systems of ideas. Darwinian theory, for example, became a generalized mode of explanation, extended to value theory and many diverse aspects of experience.

(8) The historian of ideas is to work his way through all of the ambiguities he meets, taking the attitude of benevolent skepticism, recognizing that even so he carries a philosophy of history, and so is viewing the world from a certain perspective, somewhat irrationally.

BOCARDO.

Valid syllogism in OAO mood, third figure. *Q.v.* Syllogism (4).

BODHI.

A Sanskrit term meaning "wisdom" or "enlightenment." Widely used in Indian philosophy, the term's opposite is *avidya* (*q.v.*) or ignorance. Also *q.v. Bodhisattva.*

BODHIDHARMA. c. 460–c. 534.

The founder of Zen Buddhism (*q.v.* 1).

BODHISATTVA.

In Sanskrit *bodhi* ("wisdom") and *sattva* ("existence in"). In Buddhism those who defer Buddhahood for the sake of others. The doctrine is to be found in both Hinayana and Mahayana Buddhism; but it is much more central to the latter. *Q.v.* Buddhism, Mahayana (1–2).

BODIN, JEAN. 1530–1596.

French political philosopher. Born at Angers. Educated in Toulouse. A lawyer, he served the Parliament of Paris as advocate, and later the Duke of Alençon as secretary. He was appointed King's attorney in 1576.

Principal writings: *Method for the Easy Comprehension of History* (T), 1566; *The Response* (T), 1568; *The Six Books of the Republic,* (T), 1576; *The Theater of Nature,* 1596.

(1) Dividing knowledge into human history, natural history and divine history (*i.e.,* anthropology, physics, and theology), he devoted his attention largely to the first division.

(2) Defending the French system, Bodin argued for monarchy as the best form of government. In his view the state is made up of households whose heads are citizens, and whose sovereign is its personification and absolute power. The force of civil law lies in his person. He holds the power of life and death even when the law requires death. Sovereignty is indivisible, and the authority of the sovereign is limited only by the requirements of justice.

(3) He found geography influencing the nature of those living in a given area and, by implication. the forms of government.

BODY.

Q.v. Mind-Body Problem. For Descartes (*q.v.* 8) body is extended and has reference to space, time, and motion, standing in contrast to mind, which altogether lacks the first reference, has the second only accidentally, retaining the third in a metaphorical sense.

BOEHME, JACOB. 1575–1624.

German mystic and religious philosopher. Born and lived in Saxony, especially in Görlitz. Raised in the Lutheran faith and lacking formal education, Boehme nonetheless exercised a clearly discernible influence on later religious and philosophical thought. Called the German Philosopher. Often in trouble with the Orthodox elements of the community, he was once banished from Görlitz. Examined for heresy, he was allowed to return to his community under the protection of the elector. Many learned men visited him as his fame spread, one of whom induced him to study Paracelsus whose influence thus entered his work.

Principal writings: *Aurora, or The Dawn* (T), 1612; *De Tribus Principiis, or Description of the Three Principles of Divine Being*, 1619; *De Triplici Vita Hominis, or Concerning the Three Divisions in the Lives of Men* (T), 1620; *The Signature of All Things* (T), 1622; *The Great Mystery, or an Explanation of the First Book of Moses*, 1623.

(1) Behind reality is an *Ungrund* or Abyss, which is God Himself; out of the *Ungrund* came the Trinity and a spiritual universe which in turn generated the physical universe. The primal will of universal light was simple being and essence, containing all that arose later as pure potentiality.

(2) Against this light a second will arose, resulting in a primal darkening.

(3) Out of this darkening the first form of nature arose, "harshness," which on a personal spiritual level is self-centeredness and inertia.

(4) The first will, now seeking to return to its primal state produces instead nature's second form, "attraction."

(5) The two forms, in conflict, produce a third, "bitterness," which on the spiritual level is discontent.

(6) Bitterness increases in intensity, producing a fourth form, "fire." Fire is the dim light of the external man.

(7) It can increase in intensity until it produces the fifth form, "light." In this case the bitterness and raging cease, and one sees things as they are. In this case, too, the first three forms become harmonious and pleasant. In theological terms Christ is God manifest as light. Or from this point the false direction of self-will can be taken, in which case the fierce rage and fury of fire remain dominant; in Lucifer the might of fire became dominant and in the fallen Adam the light was only hidden. Lucifer is God manifest as the principle of darkness.

(8) But if love wins out against self-will, producing the fifth form, then, too, the sixth form, "sound," is attained. Light fixes the direction of things toward the good; consequently, the qualities of things begin to be expressed in speech, cries, colors, scents, tastes, feeling, lightness, heaviness, and so forth.

(9) The seventh form of nature is called figure. "Here the qualities of things having been attained, they have achieved their essences," which leads to embodiment for the six forms, and beings marked with the signature" of God.

(10) Each man, of course, has in him a mixture of light and darkness, the one seeking to lift him up, the other seeking to draw him down. By the inclination of his imagination, each decides the one to which he will belong.

(11) It is notable that in the process a creative principle of negation has been presumed to exist within the divine Being. Thus, a creative process exists in God, and the world is presumed to be merely a reflection of the life of God.

BOETHIUS. 480–525.

Roman philosopher. Philosophically eclectic, he attempted a synthesis of Hellenistic, Roman, and Christian thought, "saving" the best of the old, and using it to engender the new. Termed the last Roman and the first Scholastic. Consul of Rome and minister to Theodoric, king of the Ostrogoths, he was at last accused of treason, imprisoned, and executed. While awaiting execution he composed the first work listed below.

Principal writings: *On the Consolation of Philosophy* (T); *On the Difference of Nature and Person*. In addition, numerous treatises in logic and theology (including *On the Trinity*, T); translated Aristotle's works on logic, as well as commentaries by Porphyry, Cicero, and Victorinus.

(1) His contribution to the development of philosophy concerned the development of philosophical terminology in Latin, pointing toward the appearance of Scholasticism, *e.g.*, "theology" as the application of the canons of Aristotelian logic to the idea of God, "eternity" as "*totum simul*"; "person"; and "essence." Equating "hypostasis" (*q.v.*) with "person," Boethius defined the latter term as "an individual substance of rational nature."

(2) Distinguishing between abstraction and composition, he held that the former (*i.e.* the ideas of genus and species) are true ideas while the latter (*e.g.* a centaur) are false. The former subsist in sensible things but, as thought, are universals. His discussion of the question, including his comments on Porphyry (*q.v.*), initiated the medieval discussion of universals (*q.v.* 7).

(3) The central contrast of his work on the consolation of philosophy is between the transient, shifting values of this world, and the eternal values of philosophy and theology, of the contemplative life and faith in providence.

Also *Q.v.* Logic (5).

BOGDANOV, A. (A.A. MALINOVSKI). 1873–1928.

Russian Marxist philosopher. Considered an extreme revisionist, Bogdanov declared himself an empiricist and materialist, employing the idea of the dialectic as the principle of universal development. Calling his view *Empiriomonism* to distinguish it from *Empiriocriticism*, Bogdanov held the psychic to be individually organized experience, and the physical to be collectively organized experience.

Principal writings: *Empiriomonism*; *Articles on Philosophy*, 3 vols., 1904–6; *A Philosophy of Living Experience*, 1912.

BOGOMILS.

Q.v. Paulicians.

BOLZANO, BERNARD. 1781–1848.

Philosopher of logic and mathematics. Born in Prague. Sometime professor at the University of Prague.

Principal writings: *Scientific Doctrine*, 1837; *The Paradoxes of Infinity*, 1851 (posthumously).

(1) Standing against the tendency of his time to reduce propositions to the judgments in which they occur, Bolzano held to a firm distinction between thinker and thought, the proposition being an independent constituent of the judgment.

(2) The attitude or insight anticipated Brentano (*q.v.*) and modern phenomenology. His views in *The Paradoxes of Infinity* to some extent anticipated Cantor's doctrine of transfinite numbers.

BONALD, LOUIS DE. 1754–1840.

French philosopher. Born in Millau. One of the chief representatives of Traditionalism or Ultramontanism, de Bonald argued that the entire 18th-century Enlightenment was a mistake. Breaking the relationship between man and God the atheism of the movement led to empiricism, popular sovereignty, and revolution. The only way to undo the damage is through a return to the political supremacy of the papacy, absolute monarchy, innate ideas, and Christian dogma.

Principal writings: *Theory of Political and Religious Power in Civil Society*, 3 vols., 1796.

BONAVENTURE, ST. (GIOVANNI FIDANZA). 1217–1274.

Born at Bagnorea in Tuscany. Became a Franciscan, studied under Alexander of Hales in Paris. Augustinian in orientation. Along with Aquinas, accepted in 1257 as Professor of Theology at University of Paris. He did not teach there, however, since he was at the same time elected minister general of his order. Appointed Bishop of Albano and cardinal in 1273.

Principal writings: *Commentary on the Sentences of Peter Lombard* (T in part), 1250–1; *On Charity and the Last Things*, 1253–7; *On Christ's Knowledge* 1253–7; *On the Mystery of the Trinity*, 1253–7; *The Journey of the Mind to God* (T), 1259; *Two Lives of St. Francis*, 1261; *On the Ten Commandments*, 1267; *On the Seven Gifts of the Holy Spirit*, 1268; *On the Six Days of Creation*, 1273.

(1) For St. Bonaventure, philosophy culminates in mysticism, and faith is an essential element. To philosophize without faith is to insure error in one's results. Faith assists one in posing the appropriate questions and avoiding false alternatives.

(2) Every person contains an implicit awareness and knowledge of God. This awareness may become explicit through interior reflection, and such reflection can be aided by reflecting on the things of sense. Hence, he does frame arguments moving from causation to a first cause, composite being to simplicity, changing being to unchanging being, possible to necessary being, and from either truths or errors to the truth itself. But the reason

such arguments can be formed is that we already know dimly what it is we seek.

(3) From this standpoint the most appropriate argument for the existence of God is the ontological argument of St. Anselm which St. Bonaventure supports, while finding the starting point of this argument to be an idea of perfect being innate to our minds, God's imprint as it were. Indeed, not only is there an intellectual contradiction in denying God's existence, there is a practical contradiction as well. Since every person seeks happiness, and this is found in achieving the good—which relates to, and in its supreme form is, God—to deny God verbally is to contradict what one's will affirms.

(4) But not only has man an innate idea of God; he has, too, an innate idea of virtue and the good. Of course, this is only an aspect of the idea of God, but by interior reflection one is able to discern the appropriate judgments concerning values. While the innateness in both cases is a matter of having the capacity and predispositions to arrive at the ideas of God and virtue, the point is that neither idea comes from observation.

(5) Most of our ideas do come from observation, and St. Bonaventure holds that with respect to ordinary experience—*i.e.*, to experience of sensible objects—the mind is initially a blank tablet. And yet ordinary experience is laced with principles of interpretation, first principles, if one will. How do these arise? Man possesses a natural light of reason allowing one to discern the universality of such principles once the relevant ideas have been acquired through observation.

(6) Furthermore, in the experience of sensible things, and in our principles of interpretation, we often have the truth. But the mutability and change in both the world and man effectually preclude our discovery of truth. Hence, its presence calls upon us to interpret the natural light of reason in a rather special manner. We call upon the Augustinian doctrine of illumination at this point. There is in our thought, according to this view, the influence of a divine illumination. Something like the normative and regulative Platonic ideas are at work in relation to our ideas; but these exemplars of our ideas are understood to be the divine eternal ideas of God. And these are further understood as the *Logos*, the Word of God, at work in us, that is to say, the interior Christ. In the ascent from sensible to spiritual things, the influence of the Word increases until God's power is dominant in us and reason has given way to faith.

(7) The doctrine of illumination leads to the view that God stands to the world in the relation of exemplar, and to man in a rather special form of this relationship. Every created thing is a manifestation of God, exemplatum to the divine Exemplar, bearing some analogy of proportionality to Him. But in created things apart from man the proportion is extrinsic. In man it is intrinsic. Other things bear a vestige or trace of God, a *vestigium dei*. Man bears an image of God, the *imago dei*. The trinity of persons in God, for example, is imaged in man's trinity of powers.

(8) The special nature of this relationship is seen in God's immediate creation of the soul out of nothing. The soul's immortality follows from this act, and St. Bonaventure's reflections on immortality turn around the natural tendencies, and purposes, of the soul. Knowing of man's desire for perfect and unending happiness is to know that the soul is immortal. But since Bonaventure also agrees with Aristotle that the soul is the form of the body, he commits himself to a double principle of interpretation. In one sense the souls is the form and actuality of the body, the person being the substance composed of soul and body, form and matter. But in another sense the soul is a spiritual substance composed of spiritual form and spiritual matter. This decision allows him in another application to speak of pluralities of angels within one species. In the analysis of human nature the decision establishes the principle that more than one form can exist in one substance, a point to which we shall return below. But if the soul is a substance and can exist in its own right, why is it joined to the body? Bonaventure's answer is that it has a natural inclination to be so joined; and the body has a similar inclination to be "informed" by the soul. The double principle allows him to argue that the soul becomes more actual as it grows in grace.

(9) The principle of multiple form is employed again, in working out the relationship between God as Creator, and His creation. Agreeing with Aristotle that all things are made up of matter and form, he holds in addition that both matter and form are created by God out of nothing. The creation could be understood, naturally enough, as a reflection of God's ideas. But God might have chosen a different, and indeed a better, creation. But matter is to be understood merely as possibility or potentiality, a seed-bed of virtual forms. These are the seminal reasons, *rationes seminales*, activating the material creation. The activating and perfecting of forms is central to the hierarchy of being, and increasingly so in its higher reaches. All bodies possess the form of light, the principle of activity and first substantial form. To this, other forms are added, depending on the place in the hierarchy occupied by the thing.

(10) The principle of individuation is not the function of matter or form, taken separately. Rather, it is a function of the union of the two, appropriating each other, adding multiplicity to definitude.

(11) The being who is pure form, and pure act, exemplar and author of matter and form, in knowing Himself knows all things in an eternal non-successive cognition. It is this being toward whom we move as we find happiness, truth, reality, actualizing within ourselves the perfections possible to man; while beyond our vision lies a mystical darkness produced by super-abundant illumination, which can become a vision of God beyond this life.

BONHOEFFER, DIETRICH. 1906–1945.

German theologian. Active in the resistance to Hitler, and in the Ecumenical movement, Bonhoeffer died in a concentration camp.

Principal writings: *The Communion of Saints* (T), 1930; *Act and Being* (T), 1931; *The Cost of Discipleship* (T), 1937; *Ethics* (T), 1949; *Resistance and Submission*, (T), 1951.

(1) Emphasizing the historical event of the revelation in Jesus Christ, against either the Act philosophies (which emphasize man), or the Being philosophies (which emphasize God, although in an ahistorical manner), Bonhoeffer reflected an enduring equivocal attitude toward philosophy.

(2) On the one hand, he stated that the languages of ontology and Biblical theology are complementary, and together serve diverse needs of the Church.

(3) On the other hand, holding that philosophy increasingly asserts man's autonomy over himself and the world, Bonhoeffer argued that the Christian is truest to his vocation when he separates himself altogether from the enterprise of philosophy, and especially including ethics and ontology.

BONIFORM FACULTY.

Q.v. Henry More (5).

BOODIN, JOHN ELOF. 1869–1950.

American philosopher. Born in Sweden; he studied at the universities of Colorado and Minnesota, Brown University, and under Royce at Harvard, his mature philosophy combining "empirical realism and cosmic idealism." He taught at Brown University, Harvard, Grinnell College, University of Kansas, Carleton College, and U.C.L.A.

Principal writings: *Time and Reality*, 1904; *Truth and Reality*, 1911; *A Realistic Universe*, 1916; *Cosmic Evolution*, 1925; *God and Creation*, 2 vols., 1934; *Three Interpretations of the Universe*, 1934; *The Social Mind*, 1939; *A Cosmic Philosophy*, 1947.

(1) Creation is an eternal process and evolution a process of spiritualization.

(2) The cosmos is interpreted under the concept of fields, both hierarchically and by way of interpenetration or overlapping.

(3) The hierarchies, a concept of emergent evolution, are the fields of physics, organic life, conscious awareness, and society.

(4) The fields have as their attributes, being, time, space, consciousness (an attribute which, given certain conditions, "lights up" a portion of reality), and form (the ground of organization and structure).

(5) The interpenetration, or overlapping. of fields of conscious awareness makes knowledge and society possible. And, finally, God is that spiritual field in which all of us live and move and have our being, and which extends throughout both space and time.

BOOK OF CHANGES, THE.

(Or *I Ching*). One of the basic Chinese classics. The book arose in relation to the practice of divination, and was formed between the 6th and the 3rd centuries B.C. The book consists of sixty-four hexagrams, based on eight trigrams of three lines each. The trigram for heaven is ≡. That for earth is ≡≡. A divided line stands for the concept of *Yin*; an undivided line stands for *Yang*. The trigrams are combined into all the possible hexagrams, and are supposed to symbolize all possible situations. The hexagram formed by placing the trigram for water ≡ over the trigram for fire ≡≡ symbolizes conquest, triumph, or success. The hexagrams are followed by examination and commentary.

(1) In the beginning is the Great Ultimate. The Great Ultimate gives rise to *Yin* and *Yang*, the elements female and male, or passive and active. *Yin* and *Yang* give rise to the four forms, *i.e.*, major and minor *Yin* and *Yang*. But also to all patterns, symbols, and ideas. Hence, all culture develops from the Great Ultimate through *Yin* and *Yang*.

(2) The process of change is a process of production and reproduction. The movements of *Yin* and *Yang*, constituting the way, renovate all things.

(3) One becomes identified with nature in fulfilling one's own nature, and one's nature is fulfilled through the investigation of principle, and self-development, that is, by following the way.

BOOK OF COMMON PRAYER.

Q.v. Thomas Cranmer.

BOOK OF CONCORD.

Q.v. Schmalkald Articles; Luther (16b).

BOOK OF THE DEAD.

In Egyptian religion a book of formulae, prayers and hymns designed to assist the deceased in meeting the challenges of passage into the after-world. Copies of the book were entombed with the deceased, or portions of the text were carved into the sarcophagus or painted on the walls of the tomb.

BOOLE, GEORGE. 1815–1864.

British logician and mathematician. Born in Lincoln, England. Self-educated.

In 1849, appointed to the chair of mathematics at Queen's College, Cork. Widely regarded as one of the founders of mathematical logic, his achievement consisted of developing an algebra of classes in which the variables x, y, z, etc., stand for classes, and the operations of addition and multiplication are basic.

Principal writings: *The Mathematical Analysis of Logic*, 1847; *An Investigation of the Laws of Thought*, 1854; *Studies in Logic and Probability*, ed. Rush Rhees, 1952.

(1) In this algebra, letters such as x, y, z, etc., stand for classes. X, y, z, etc., are called "elective symbols." X is the result, that is to say, of electing all the x's in the universe. Y and z elect in a comparable manner.

(2) The "=" sign between two letters, say x and y, indicates that the classes have the same members.

(3) If we elect from the universe all of the x's, and then from this select the y's we shall have the overlap of the two classes x and y. The product of the two operations is represented by x × y or xy.

(4) The operation of aggregation is represented by the sign "+", and is expressible by "either . . . or." Boole took disjunction in the strict sense to mean "either . . . or (but not both)"; hence for him "x + y" meant the class of things either x or y, excluding those things which are both x and y. This seems an artificial exclusion; and the aggregation sign in Boolean algebra is now taken to represent the weak sense of disjunction so that "x + y" denotes the class of things x or y or both x and y. Boole also introduced processes of subtraction and division, but they have been dropped as having no value for the algebra.

(5) In addition to classes of the familiar sort Boole introduces a universe class and a null class represented by the numbers "1" and "0." The former is expected to contain everything in the universe, although in practice Boole restricted this to what De Morgan termed "the universe of discourse." The latter has no members. The product of the universe class and any particular class is, as one would wish, simply that particular class, *i.e.*, $1 \times x = x$; the product of the null class and any particular class is also what one would expect, "0"; *i.e.*, $0 \times x = 0$.

(6) Each class has as its complement everything not that class, i.e., "1-x."

(7) Given the foregoing the rules of the ordinary numerical algebra apply to the calculus, i.e.: (a) $xy = yx$, (b) $x + y = y + x$, (c) $(y+z) = xy + xz$, (d) $x (y - z) = xy-xz$, (e) If $x = y$, then $xz = yz$, (f) If $x = y$, then $x + z = y + z$, (g) If $x = y$, then $x-z = y-z$.

(8) Boolean algebra is different from ordinary algebra, however, in a number of ways. For example, the repeating of the operation of election gives the same result; i.e., $xx=x$, or $x^2 = x$. Also in this system $(1-x)=0$.

(9) The calculus extends over the theory of the syllogism. A, E, I, and O propositions are expressed in the following manner:

All x is y: $x (1-y) = 0$
No x is y: $xy = 0$
Some x is y: $xy \neq 0$
Some x is not y: $x(1-y) \neq 0$

The A and E propositions are interpreted as lacking existential import. (Boole expressed I and O propositions in a more circuitous manner, but with the same end result as that given here.)

(10) In the revised Boolean algebra three changes were made in the structure of the calculus: (a) Introduction of the weak sense of disjunction provided the new law "$x + x = x$" strictly analogous to "$xx = x$." This allowed a systematic connection of sums and products. (b) The process of subtraction and division were eliminated. (c) The relation of inclusion of one class in another, "All x is y," symbolized "$x \subset y$" was added to the system by Peirce, replacing the notation "$x(1-y) = 0$." Among contributors to the revised Boolean algebra may be named De Morgan, Jevons, Venn (q.v.), Peirce (q.v.), Huntington (q.v.), and Sheffer (q.v.). The development of the algebra still continues with the work of Tarski (q.v.) and Leśniewski (q.v.).

BOOLEAN ALGEBRA.
Q.v. Immediate Inference (6); George Boole; E.V. Huntington, H.M. Sheffer (2).

BOSANQUET, BERNARD. 1848–1923.
British philosopher. Born in Altwick, England. Taught at Oxford briefly, leaving to concentrate on his writing and social work.

Principal writings: *Logic, or the Morphology of Knowledge*, 2 vols., 1888; *A History of Aesthetic*, 1892; *The Philosophical Theory of the State*, 1899; *The Principle of Individuality and Value*, 1912; *The Value and Destiny of the Individual*, 1913; *Three Lectures on Aesthetics*, 1915.

(1) Influenced mainly by Hegel, and associated with the neo-Hegelian Idealists, Green and Bradley, Bosanquet was intent on developing this tradition in such a way that individuality might be strengthened thereby.

(2) The means to this end is through an understanding of the difference between abstract and concrete universals. The former are exemplified in the language of science where general laws are stressed and differences are ignored. The latter are to be found in communities of persons; indeed, they are persons. Now, a person is a unity or harmony of a variety of experiences, a unity in difference. But the single individual is only partially individual, concrete, and real. The urge for the real directs one beyond oneself to the concrete universal of the community or state (he appears to make no distinction between the two ideas), and finally to the only adequate individual, and reality—the absolute itself.

(3) Imperfection and evil are—in this view—identified with the partial, and the limited, and disappear in relation to the whole.

(4) Beauty, meanwhile, is an expression of the concrete universal, discovered and embodied by the imagination, and calling out human feelings.

BOSCOVICH, RUDJER.
Q.v. Dynamism.

BOSSUET, JACQUES-BENIGNE.
Q.v. Divine Right of Kings.

BOUNDARY MAINTENANCE.
Q.v. Parsons (3).

BOUNDARY SITUATION.
From the German *Grenzsituation*, a term used by Jaspers (q.v. 7) to refer to those situations which set the limits of one's historical being, i.e., death, suffering, struggle, and guilt.

BOUNDLESS, THE.
A translation of the Greek *apeiron*.

Underlying principle of change in the philosophy of Anaximander (*q.v.* 1).

BOUTROUX, EMILE. 1845–1921.

French philosopher. Born in Montrouge. Taught at the Sorbonne. Influenced by the philosophical thought stemming from Maine de Biran (*q.v.*) and Jules Lachelier (*q.v.*), Boutroux was part of the French "spiritualistic" movement in philosophy. Both Bergson and M. Blondel were among his students.

Principal writings: *The Contingency of the Laws of Nature* (T), 1874; *The Idea of Natural Law in Science and Contemporary Philosophy*, 1895; *The Psychology of Mysticism*, 1902; *Science and Religion in Contemporary Philosophy* (T), 1908.

(1) Opposing the mechanistic naturalism dominant in his time, Boutroux called for greater faithfulness to the peculiarities of experience. An appropriate measure of fidelity allows one to affirm the reality both of liberty and contingency.

(2) The means of accomplishing this is an analysis of levels of reality which, beginning with the most fundamental are: absolute necessity, relative necessity, being, genera, matter, life, and conscience.

(3) Each stage involves a leap, and each leap admits contingency and the occurrence of novelty supports the point. Finally, the maximum freedom is to be found in the moral life, a necessary step on the way to the religious life.

(4) The ideals of beauty and good, indeed, the pure ideals of perfection, exercise an attraction over the hierarchies of being, even the lowest, similar to the role which—in more traditional systems—God is said to exercise over His creation.

BOWNE, BORDEN PARKER. 1845–1910.

American Personalistic philosopher. Born in Leonardsville, New Jersey. Professor at Boston University beginning in 1876.

Principal writings: *Metaphysics*, 1882; *Philosophy of Theism*, 1887; *The Theory of Thought and Knowledge*, 1897; *Theism*, 1902; *Personalism*, 1908.

(1) Holding that no form of "impersonal" metaphysics can do justice to the data of experience—and citing especially naturalism or materialism, and absolute idealism—Bowne insists that personality is that unique concept capable of yield-

ing the ultimate explanation of reality.

(2) Personality is neither an abstraction from experience, nor a composite concept but the result, rather, of a careful reading of experience.

(3) Nor is the human person the sole result of the concept of personality. Theism is another, since there can be nothing impersonal behind experience.

(4) The resulting point of view can be called "Personalism." It is a species of Idealism, but a Personal Idealism rather than one which is abstract or absolute.

BOYLE, ROBERT. 1627–1691.

English natural philosopher. The author of Boyle's Law and one of the early workers in the field of chemistry. His approach to experimental science was strongly influenced by Bacon's *Novum Organum*.

Selected writings: *New Experiments Physico-Mechanical*, 1660; *Certain Physiological Essays*, 1661; *The Sceptical Chemist*, 1661; *The Experimental History of Colours*, 1663; *The Origin of Forms and Colours*, 1666.

(1) Adopting the Corpuscular Theory of Matter, he believed that the world operated on mechanical principles, although with some help from the Divine Being.

(2) He worked out the Doctrine of Primary and Secondary Qualities before Locke, and even used the terms. The qualities of size, shape, and motion or rest of its particles, belong to the material object, while its color is a "secondary quality."

"BRACKETING" EXISTENCE.

Q.v. Husserl (6).

BRADLEY, FRANCIS HERBERT. 1846–1924.

English philosopher. British Absolute Idealist. Born in Clapham, Glasbury. Educated at Oxford. Athletic as a youth, from 1871 until his death he was an invalid. His life was limited rather severely to his work. He was the first philosopher to receive the Order of Merit.

Principal writings: *Ethical Studies*, 1876; *The Principles of Logic*, 2 vols., 1883; *Appearance and Reality*, 1893; *Essays on Truth and Reality*, 1914.

(1) Bradley assumes (a) ". . . only what satisfies the intellect can be real or true"

and (b) the most valuable is the most real.

(2) If the individual's total experience violates these assumptions, Bradley believed it would be rational to infer from the inconsistencies of experience to the presence of an absolute behind experience.

(3) We predicate one thing of another. If in saying that x is y, x and y are the same, then we are uttering a bare tautology, "x is x." If x and y are different, we are saying that x is what it is not, and this clearly will not do. Not only the relation of judgment but all relations share the same inner difficulties. If x is related to y—any x, any y, and any relation—either the relation is something additional to x and y, or it is not. If it is not something additional, then the relation must be internal to x or y. But if the relation is internal on one side, so must it be on the other, and x and y become identical. If the relation is external, it has no anchor in x and y; and so the internal relation must relate to x and y by two further relations; and at this point the same alternatives recur. It is the object of this analysis to show that our human ideas of time, causality, change, the human self, and God are inconsistent no matter how we view them.

(4) The attempt of intellect to work through its problems is an attempt on its part to overcome the inconsistent, relational, evershifting, appearances of things, and to reach what Bradley calls the Absolute. Without even knowing its nature, we can know that it will be identical with the real and the true. But we can know part of its nature. It will, for example, be characterized by consistency and permanence. Since thought seeks necessities, not mere contingencies, the Absolute will be characterized by inner necessity. It will be complete and harmonious. It will be a non-tautologous unity, that is, a unity which includes diversity, and the basic clue we have for that is conscious experience. In conscious experience unity and diversity coexist, although imperfectly. In the complete experience this coexistence will be perfectly adequate; by virtue of the "concrete universals" appropriate to this experience, complete individuality and universality will both apply to it, and in full measure.

(5) If there is no total experience beyond individual experience, one ends in Solipsism (*q.v.*). One's own experience is then all there is, and one is experiencing the states of one's own self. But one's own experience can be transcended in terms of the experience of the Absolute, which must contain the total diversity of the world of appearance, and this diversity must be held in unity. This is in principle possible on grounds analogous to the way in which a thing's being red and green will be contradictory from one standpoint but not from another; so in a system of the requisite breadth, all the contradictions we have noted may be overcome.

(6) Thus far, this is the argument of *Appearance and Reality*. In his first book, *Ethical Studies*, a self-realization view of ethics, relating the individual to his community, and leading to religion, was developed. His essay, "My Station and its Duties," argued in Hegelian terms that duties derive from one's place and function in society. And late in life he strengthened his theory of degrees of truth, supporting the positive value of the partial truths in various categories of our partial experience.

BRADWARDINE, THOMAS. c. 1290–1349.

English philosopher and theologian. Born in Sussex. Educated at Oxford. Chancellor of the university, in 1349 he became Archbishop of Canterbury. Called "the Profound Doctor." He countered the "modern Pelagians" by viewing God's will, the first cause, as more immediately responsible for all effects in this world—even human actions—than the proximate or second causes. He likewise criticized the Aristotelian law of motion.

Principal writings: *On the Divine Causality against the Pelagians*, 1344; *On Proportion* (T), 1495; *On Speculative Geometry*, 1516.

BRAHE, TYCHO. 1546–1601.

Danish astronomer. Born at Knudstrup. Studied at Copenhagen, Leipzig, Rostock, and Augsburg. For twenty-one years he made astronomical observations in Denmark, thereafter working at Benatky near Prague. Kepler (*q.v.*) served as his assistant and, after his death, published his astronomical observations. He vastly improved the precision of such observations, providing the material needed by Kepler in perfecting the Copernican revolution.

BRAHMA.
Along with Vishnu (*q.v.*) and Shiva (*q.v.*) the Gods making up the Hindu trinity. Brahma is the Creator god (*q.v.* Doctrine of the Trinity, 17).

BRAHMACARIN.
From Sanskrit, "wandering about in Brahman." The student in the first *ashrama* (stage of life), which is called *Brahmacharya. Q.v. Aśramas* (2); Hinduism (3a).

BRAHMAN.
Sanskrit term, etymology uncertain, the Sanskrit root, "*brh*," meaning "to grow, swell, become great." Initially analogous to *Mana* (*q.v.*), the term came to mean something like "magic," referring to the gaining of magical results from the correct performance of Hindu rituals and sacrifices.

(1) In the *Vedas* (*q.v.*) *brahman* is identified with the power of the Vedic sacrifices, with wind, breath, sun, and with the syllable *Om* (*q.v.*) regarded as the mystic essence of the *Vedas*; also with the power of the Brahmins who presided over the sacrifices.

(2) Finally, *brahman* developed beyond the holy power of the sacrifices into the no less holy power of the universe, essentially pure, unchangeable, and eternal, in which all things have their origin and end. In this extension some *Upanishads* treated *brahman* as an impersonal absolute, others as a personal God. This conception becomes central to the *Upanishads*, (*q.v. Vedas* 4) and in the philosophy of the Vedanta (*q.v.*) system.

(3) The term Brahmanism is sometimes used to refer to the religio-philosophical position of the *Upanishads*, described in Hinduism (5b), and culminating in the identification of *Atman* (*q.v.*), the inner self, with Brahman. This evolution of thought allowed the Vedic priests a religious philosophy capable of competing with the emergent religious perspectives of Buddhism (*q.v.*) and Jainism (*q.v.*).

(4) Shankara (*q.v.* 4–5) retains both the personal and impersonal sense of Brah-

man, distinguishing between Saguna Brahman, or "Brahman with qualities," and Nirguna Brahman, or "Brahman without qualities," regarding the former as delusive, and the latter as veridical.

(5) Ramanuja (*q.v.* 1–6) made the distinction between the two qualities, a difference in epochs of the constantly developing and returning stages of the world.

(6) Aurobindo (*q.v.* 1) associates Brahman with the term Absolute.

BRAHMANAS, THE.
Q.v. Vedas (2).

BRAHMANISM.
Q.v. Brahman (3).

BRAHMA SUTRA.
Q.v. Vedanta.

BRAHMINS (BRAHMANS).
The ruling class in Indian tradition. *Q.v.* Hinduism (4); *Mahabharata* (3); *Laws of Manu* (2).

BRAITHWAITE, R.B. 1900– .
English philosopher. Born in Banbury. Educated at Cambridge where he has taught since 1924. A philosopher of science who has tried to extend the results of his analysis to problems of ethics.

Principal writings: *Scientific Explanation,* 1946; *An Empiricist's View of the Nature of Religious Belief,* 1955; *Theory of Games as a Tool for the Moral Philosopher,* 1955.

(1) Regarding scientific theories as calculi with multiple levels of generalization, whose terms are only partially interpreted by experience, Braithwaite holds explanation to be the implication of a lower-level generalization by one of higher level. At the same time the lower-level generalizations, interpreted by experience, indirectly and partially interpret those of higher level.

(2) He provides his own version of a "frequency view of probability." It contains a rejection rule to be applied when observed relative frequencies vary too greatly from the probabilities initially postulated. It likewise contains a "prudential policy" for choosing between two alternative statistical hypotheses. Since a number can be assigned to the probability of a correct choice for each strategy for deciding among alternative hypotheses, given first the truth of one and then the

truth of the other, one will select the smaller of the two numbers for each strategy, and then the strategy represented by the largest of these numbers. The procedure is called "maximizing the minimum mathematical expectation." The strategy represented by the largest of these smaller numbers he regards as the optimum strategy.

(3) He argues that there is no vicious circle in the problem of induction, since the movement of thought is from a mere belief in the reliability of induction to a reasonable belief, based on evidence, in this reliability.

(4) He has applied the principles of game theory—especially those of the generalized two-person game—to the analysis of judicial decisions and to problems of morality.

(5) Religion combines morality with a mythology consisting of religious stories. The stories, while an essential element in belonging to a religion, need not be believed. The only essential element in practicing the religion is commitment to its moral principles.

BRANDT, RICHARD B. 1910– .

American philosopher. Born in Wilmington, Ohio. Educated at Denison, Cambridge, Tübingen, Yale. Taught at Swarthmore and Michigan.

Principal writings: *The Philosophy of Schleiermacher*, 1941; *Hopi Ethics*, 1954; *Ethical Theory*, 1959; *Value and Obligation*, 1961; "Some Merits of One Form of Rule-Utilitarianism," 1967; *A Theory of the Good and the Right*, 1979; *Morality, Utilitarianism and Rights*, 1992.

(1) Since act Utilitarianism, maximizing utility with respect to individual acts, requires in some cases breaking promises and every other moral rule, Brandt suggested that ideal rule Utilitarianism be considered in its place. In this alternative the rightness of an act is measured, not directly by its utility, but indirectly by its conformity to the set of rules which would maximize utility, given the institutional setting of one's society.

(2) This set of rules makes up the ideal moral code of the society, the utility measure insuring that the currency of these rules would produce at least as much good per person in that society as any other set of rules.

(3) The apparent relativism of ordering the rules to the institutional arrangements of different societies is diminished by Brandt's recognition of two additional rules: the obligation of humanity (if one is in a position to relieve serious distress which no one else is likely to relieve, one should do so), and the obligation of fairness (one must discharge one's institutional obligations fairly).

BRENTANO, FRANZ. 1838–1917.

German-Austrian philosopher-psychologist. Born in Marienburg. Taught at Würzburg and Vienna. Last years in Florence. Had many disciples, among them A. von Meinong and E. Husserl.

Principal writings: *Psychology from an Empirical Standpoint* (T in part), 1874; *On the Origin of Moral Knowledge* (T), 1889; *On the Future of Philosophy*, 1893; *The Four Phases of Philosophy*, 1895; *An Investigation of the Psychology of the Senses*, 1907; *Truth and Evidence* (ed. O. Kraus), 1930; *The Basis and Structure of Ethics*, (ed. Mayer-Hildebrand), 1952.

(1) It was Brentano's object to produce a purely descriptive psychology, proceeding without prior assumptions and leading to a new classification of psychical phenomena.

(2) He finds psychical phenomena to be characterized by "intentional inexistence" which requires reference to a context, and directedness to an object. Involving reference to something beyond themselves, mental acts are relation-like. Whatever is before the mind will be a representation (*i.e.*, a mere being present to awareness), a judgment (*i.e.*, a representation accepted as true, or rejected as false), or a phenomenon of love or hate (*i.e.*, a representation accepted or rejected on an emotive level). In every case there is an object, concrete or abstract, real or imagined, with which the mental activity is concerned. At first he allowed some kind of existence to noexistent objects so long as they are before the mind. Later, he held such references to be descriptions of the mental content of those thinking of them.

(3) All judgments concern things. "Existence" is not a predicate but a *synsemantic* term enabling us to express our acceptance or rejection of things.

(4) Value judgments rest on internal

evidence with respect to the relation "better than" and can be objective.

(5) He defended both the soul and God, and believed that philosophy tends to go through phases of decline between its periods of vitality. The phases include transfer of interest to practical matters, skepticism, and finally, mysticism.

BRETHREN OF THE COMMON LIFE.

A 14th-century monastic order one of whose founders was Gerhard Groote (*q.v.*), probable author of *The Imitation of Christ* (*q.v.*). The order, devoted to the cultivation of personal religion, was open equally to men and women.

BRHASPATI (BRIHASPATI).

Q.v. Jayaraśi (1); Indian Philosophy (2).

BRIDGMAN, P.W. 1882–1963.

American physicist and operational philosopher. Born in Cambridge, Massachusetts. Taught at Harvard University, 1908–1954. Received the Nobel Prize in Physics, 1946. The meaning of any concept, according to Bridgman, is the set of operations one will use in "fixing" that concept. The concept of length, for example, is identical with the operations of measuring. More abstract concepts will have mental operations, or paper and pencil operations, providing their significance.

Principal writings: *The Logic of Modern Physics*, 1927; *The Nature of Physical Theory*, 1936; *Reflections of a Physicist*, 1950; *The Nature of Some of Our Physical Concepts*, 1952.

BRIGHTMAN, EDGAR SHEFFIELD. 1884–1952.

American Personalistic philosopher. Born in Holbrook, Massachusetts. Professor at Boston University as Bowne's successor and follower.

Principal writings: *An Introduction to Philosophy*, 1925; *A Philosophy of Ideals*, 1928; *The Problem of God*, 1930; *A Philosophy of Religion*, 1940; *Nature and Values*, 1945; *Person and Reality*, (ed. P.A. Bertocci), 1958.

(1) Holding, as did Bowne (*q.v.* 1–4), to the inadequacy of impersonal categories to explain experience, Brightman welcomed phenomenological and existentialistic analyses, finding in them support for Personalism (*q.v.*).

(2) Supporting the idea of individuality, the sovereignty of God is not allowed to over-balance human freedom.

(3) The problem of evil is solved by affirming the finitude of God; and viewing evil and tragedy as a "given" on which God must work.

BROAD, CHARLES DUNBAR. 1887–1971.

British philosopher. Born in London. Professor in the Universities of St. Andrews, Dundee, Bristol, and from 1933–53, Professor of Moral Philosophy at Cambridge. Continued the tradition of earlier Cambridge philosophers, such as Russell, Moore, W.E. Johnson and McTaggart.

Principal writings: *Perception, Physics, and Reality*, 1914; *Scientific Thought*, 1923; *The Mind and its Place in Nature*, 1925; *Five Types of Ethical Theory*, 1930; *Examination of McTaggart's Philosophy*, 2 vols., 1933–38; *Ethics and the History of Philosophy*, 1952; *Religion, Philosophy, and Psychical Research*, 1953; *Lectures on Psychical Research*, 1962; *Induction, Probability, and Causation*, 1968.

(1) Assuming, in a qualified sense, the stance of the synoptic and speculative philosopher, Broad believes that one never arrives at certainty but, when successful, one reaches a view with a favorable balance of probabilities; and that a considerable advance in critical philosophy must precede the development of speculative systems.

(2) Broad considers his work as contributing to the development of critical philosophy, and consisting in the exploration of possible alternatives to basic problems, *e.g.*, the seventeen alternate theories of the relation between mind and nature examined in the second of the publications named above.

(3) The most probable alternative in terms of normal facts is "emergent materialism" in which the world has no non-material component, consciousness is generated by the appropriate set of physical conditions; primary and secondary qualities are emergents of different sorts; and *sensa* are short-lived existents, neither physical nor mental. Beyond the normal facts the most promising theory would explain mind as a compound of bodily factors and a "psychic factor" with sufficient persistence after death to ex-

plain the best attested paranormal phenomena and some form of metempsychosis (*q.v.*).

(4) Among these themes some are dealt with at greater length than others. Broad gave considerable attention to a description of the *sensa* of our awareness, which seemed to him among the essential elements in the causal theory of perception. *Sensa* are never identical with their objects; the former change from different perspectives while the latter remain unchanged. The properties of *sensa* are, indeed, different from the properties of objects in various ways.

BROKMEYER, HENRY C.
Q.v. Saint Louis Hegelians.

BROOKS, CLEANTH.
Q.v. New Criticism.

BROTHERHOOD OF THE COMMON LIFE.
Q.v. Gerhard Groote.

BROUWER, L.E.J. 1881–1966.
Dutch mathematician. Born in Overschie. Professor of Mathematics, University of Amsterdam, beginning in 1912. Founder of the Intuitionist School of Modern Mathematics.

Principal writings: "Intuitionism and Formalism," 1912; "The Foundations of Set Theory," 1918–19; "The Foundations of Intuitionist Mathematics," 1926–27; "Mathematics, Science, and Speech," 1929.

(1) An "urintuition," a basic or primitive intuition of temporal counting, lies at the base of mathematics. This is, in fact, the Kantian *a priori* time, and is recognized as the falling apart of moments of life into qualitatively different parts, which are reunited while remaining separated by time, giving an intuition of two-oneness. Out of this intuition the number series can be generated.

(2) Mathematical entities are, thus, constructible from intuition. And since the meaning of the mathematical entity depends on its construction, Brouwer denies the validity of the law of excluded middle. Because of the construction requirement the truth of a proposition is not, in general, equivalent to the falsity of its contradictory.

BRUNNER, EMIL. 1899–1966.
Swiss Protestant theologian. Taught at Zurich.

Principal writings: *The Symbolical in Religious Knowledge*; 1914; *The Mystic and the Word*, 1924; *The Philosophy of Religion of Evangelical Theology* (T), 1927; *The Mediator* (T), 1927; *The Divine Imperative* (T), 1932; *Man in Revolt* (T), 1937; *Christianity and Civilization*, 2 vols., 1948–9.

(1) Occupying a position midway between liberal Protestant theology and the crisis theology of Karl Barth (*q.v.*), Brunner held that while man could not provide his own salvation, he does possess certain natural powers of responding to God.

(2) From the standpoint of reason there are contradictions in man's situation with respect to revelation, but this merely points to the dialectical nature of revelation itself, which takes man beyond reason.

(3) Both technologically and politically, modern societies tend to depersonalize man; the Christian revelation, directed toward persons, provides a key to the true nature of community.

BRUNO, GIORDANO. 1548–1600.
Italian philosopher. Born in Naples. A Dominican monk, he fell into heresy by way of the new astronomy. Excommunicated, he wandered from one university center to another, often holding provisional professorial status. In this manner he visited Geneva, Lyons, Toulouse, Paris, London, Oxford, Wittenberg, Prague, Helmstadt, Frankfurt and Zurich. Unhappily, venturing to Venice in 1592, he was seized by the Inquisition and imprisoned in Rome from 1593 until 1599. Refusing to recant his philosophical opinions, he was condemned to death, and burned alive in the Campo Dei Fiori on February 17, 1600.

Principal writings: *The Ash Wednesday Supper* (I), 1584; *Concerning the Cause, Principle and One* (T), 1584; *On the Infinite Universe and Worlds* (T), 1584; *The Expulsion of the Triumphant Beast* (T), 1584; *On Heroic Enthusiasms* (T), 1585; *Points Against the Mathematicians* (L), 1588; *Concerning the Minimum* (L), 1591; *Concerning the Monad* (L), 1591; *Concerning the Boundless* (L), 1591; *The Summa of Metaphysical*

Terms (L), 1609; in addition, commentaries and summaries such as those on Aristotle's *Physics*.

(1) The universe is infinite in extent and in diversity, so that center is everywhere and nowhere. Nowhere is there permanence, for all is alive, and the condition of life is change.

(2) The souls of things are monads; and of these there are three kinds: God, the monad of monads; souls; and atoms, the simple elements of matter. And all of these are immortal. The simplest monads are animated, and the worlds have lives of their own.

(3) God is both transcendent and immanent, source of the universe and in every part. Indeed, the universe itself can be considered as one, and that one, God. To do so is to consider reality as *Natura Naturans*. To consider reality in its multiplicity is to consider it as *Natura Naturata*.

(4) In another sense the universe is a going forth and return of the divine nature, a going forth into the display of infinite potentialities, a return marked by the human mind whose discovery of unity, simplicity, changelessness, and eternality in the diverse, complex changing scenes of time marks the return toward God.

(5) Through the development of his reason and inspired by love, man has the possibility upon death of return to, and eternal union with, God.

BRUNSCHVICG, LÉON. 1869–1944.

French philosopher. Born in Paris. Educated at the École Normale Supérieure and at the Sorbonne. Taught at the Sorbonne. A Critical Idealist, Brunschvicg held reality to be a function of thought, and mind to have progressed through history. The double emphasis allowed him to view human progress toward self-consciousness as laying down the conditions for science and mathematics. And the double sense of *conscience* in French ("consciousness" and "conscience") allowed him to view this progress as a movement toward spiritual values.

Principal writings: *The Modality of Judgment*, 1897; *Introduction to the Life of the Spirit*, 1900; *The Stages of Mathematical Philosophy*, 1912; *Human Experience and Physical Causality*, 1922; *Spinoza and His Contemporaries*, 1923; *The Progress of Consciousness in Western Philosophy*, 2 vols., 1927; *On Self-Knowledge*, 1931; *The Ages of Intelligence*, 1934; *Philosophical Writings*, 2 vols., 1951, 1954.

BRYSON, SON OF STILPO.

Q.v. Megarian School of Philosophy.

BUBER, MARTIN. 1878–1965.

Jewish philosopher and mystic. Born in Vienna. Studied in Vienna and Berlin. Professor of religion, University of Frankfurt am Main, 1923–33; after 1938, professor of philosophy, Hebrew University in Jerusalem. Influenced by the teachings of the Hasidim, and by the work of Kierkegaard. While appropriating the mysticism of the Hasidim he has also given world-wide currency to that movement of Jewish mysticism (*q.v.* Hasidism).

Principal writings: *I and Thou* (T), 1922; *Religion and Philosophy* (G), 1931; *The Kingdom of God* (G), 1932; *Between Man and Man* (T), 1936; *The Prophetic Faith* (T), 1942; *The Tales of the Hasidim* (T), 2 vols., 1947–8; *Two Types of Faith* (T), 1950; *Good and Evil* (T), 1952; *The Eclipse of God* (T), 1953; *Hasidism and Modern Man* (E), 1958; *The Origin and Meaning of Hasidism* (E), 1960.

(1) Buber's dominant theme concerns how one is to relate oneself properly to the world, other persons, and God. He distinguishes two possible relations: "I-Thou" and "I-It." One relates oneself to another properly in recognizing the other as a "Thou"; improperly, in regarding the other person as an "It."

(2) The life of dialogue is an "I-Thou" relation in which, progressively, self-revelation occurs. In this relationship, as distinct from the other, all of one's being is involved. The relationship involves otherness and the unpredictability of human freedom.

(3) Beyond the context of social relation, in the ultimate context of things, one confronts reality appropriately in finding there an eternal "Thou" in relation to the "I" of one's life. Although we can allow another person to become an "It" for us, God by definition can never be transformed into an "It."

(4) Since the eternal "Thou" can be spoken to but not about, faith has no content in the epistemological sense. In

this relationship ordinary knowledge claims are to be replaced by unconditional trust.

(5) Buber countered the impersonal socialism of Marxism with its historical controls, with the personal socialism of the communities which recognize the "I-Thou" relationship. He found the social form of the *kibbutz* sensitive to this relationship.

BUCHMANISM.

A non-creedal, 20th-century movement of religious awakening also known as the Oxford Group, and Moral Rearmament. Founded by Frank Buchman, a Lutheran minister, the group originally centered in Oxford University seeking true morality in Christian surrender.

BÜCHNER, LUDWIG. 1824–1899.

German philosopher. Born in Darmstadt. *Privatdocent*, University of Tübingen. The outcry against the materialism of his first book forced him into private life. Trained as a physician he practiced medicine in Darmstadt while continuing to publish his philosophical views.

Selected writings: *Force and Matter* (T), 1855; *Nature and Spirit*, 1857; *The Place of Man In Nature* (T), 1869; *Last Words on Materialism and Kindred Subjects* (T), 1901.

(1) Insisting that all reality is material, and that force and matter are the same thing considered from different points of view, Büchner perforce denies the possibility of a God, and reduces mind or soul to cerebral functioning.

(2) Material reality is, however, dynamic and, by adopting Darwinian evolution, Büchner finds it possible to explain the appearance of "higher" forms of life and culture.

(3) His ethical views looked for the largest amount of human happiness on the basis of a respect for human rights, both private and general.

BUDDHA, GAUTAMA SIDDHARTHA. 560–477 B.C.

Founder of the Buddhist faith. Born in South Nepal, India, in the foothills of the eastern Himalayas. Son of a king of the Shakya clan. He is said to have made the great renunciation after the birth of his first child. For six years he sought enlightenment through ascetic practices; convinced it was not to be found in that manner he resumed the life of a beggar living on alms. It was at this time that the quest for enlightenment, sitting under the Bo tree, occurred. Facing east, and resolving not to stir until he had succeeded, he is said to have spent seven weeks in a posture of meditation. At the end of this period he had become Buddha "The Enlightened One." Five companions with whom he had practiced asceticism became the first members of the Buddhist order of monks. The number of his disciples increased rapidly. An order of Buddhist nuns was later permitted at the insistence of some of his female followers. At a ripe age, after a productive ministry, aware of the approach of death, he had a couch placed between two trees, and spent his last hours attended by, and giving counsel to, his disciples, closing with the words, "And now, brethren, I take my leave of you. It is in the nature of all things that take form to dissolve again. Strive with your whole being to attain perfection." Thereupon he passed into a trance, and from one trance state to a higher, finally passing into Nirvana.

These details are fancifully elaborated in the Buddhist tradition; *e.g.*, his mother, Queen Muhamaya, conceived him after a dream in which she beheld the future Buddha descending from heaven and entering her womb in the form of a white elephant. As the time for his birth drew near, healing miracles occurred; heavenly music was heard; delicious scents filled the air; the ocean water lost its saltiness. At the moment of his birth he uttered a shout of victory, took seven steps forward, and found in none of the ten directions a being equal to himself. It is this tradition which has his father attempting to shield him from the four signs the sight of which will lead him to renounce the world—"A decrepit old man, a diseased man, a dead man, and a monk." Buddha sees the signs, realizes the impermanence of earthly things, and makes the renunciation.

Because of Buddha's belief that many questions "tend not to edification" and should not be discussed, more than one interpretation of his position was possible; after his death the early schools of Buddhism, of which only the Theravada school now continues, preached an austere doctrine like that of Buddha himself. Eventually a more elaborate form of Buddhism arose, calling itself Mahayana ("great vehicle"), and the early schools Hinayana ("small vehicle"). The ideas attributable to Buddha himself include the following:

(1) The key to the problem of salvation and enlightenment is the presence of suffering. Misery, pain, or suffering is not merely one among many other equally prominent features of experience. It is its chief and overriding feature. And all other aspects of experience also contain suffering. If one is to experience enlightenment, then one must address oneself to the elimination of suffering.

(2) In the *Discourse to Katyayana* Buddha says that: "Dependent upon ignorance (*avidya*) arise dispositions (*samskara*). In the same way from dispositions consciousness (*vijnana*) arises, from consciousness the psychophysical personality (*nama-rupa*), from personality the six senses (*saddayatana*), from the six senses contact (*sparśa*), from contact feeling (*vedana*), from feeling craving (*tṛsna*), from craving grasping (*upadana*), from grasping becoming (*bhava*), from becoming birth (*jati*), from "birth arise old age and death, grief, lamentation, suffering, dejection and despair."

This is the law of dependent origination. To eliminate these effects one must eliminate their causes. Going the other way: on the cessation of ignorance karmic dispositions cease; on the cessation of karmic dispositions consciousness ceases; on the cessation of consciousness there follows a cessation of "name and form" (*i.e.*, a cessation of sensation, perception, intellection, and their bodily correlates in the way of activity); the cessation of name and form leads to cessation of the six organs of sense (the usual five, plus an inner sense); cessation of the six organs of sense means cessation of sense-object contact; cessation of sense-object contact means a cessation of sensation; cessation of sensation leads to cessation of desire; cessation of desire leads to cessation of any sense of attachment to the world; cessation of attachment leads to a cessation of existence; cessation of existence means a cessation of birth; and cessation of birth means cessation of old age, death,

sorrow, lamentation, misery, grief, and despair. Thus does the cessation of ignorance imply the cessation of suffering.

(3) Now the cessation of ignorance occurs through the avoiding of extremes, and following a middle path. This, the "Noble Eightfold Path," consists of eight steps: (a) right faith, (b) right resolve, (c) right speech, (d) right action, (e) right living, (f) right effort, (g) right thought and (h) right concentration. Despite, however, Buddha's explicit rejection of both asceticism and self-indulgence, and the similarity between the Eightfold path and Aristotle's Golden Mean, Buddhists, both male and female, seriously seeking enlightenment, became monastics.

(4) In achieving enlightenment one becomes a Buddha, and in the blissful state of enlightenment the realization arises that one's *karma* is used up, that one will not be born again and will enter Nirvana. But the nature of Nirvana is never established. Buddha held that whatever is denied of Nirvana is wrong, and whatever is affirmed of it is also wrong. There are, however, what would seem to pass as two metaphysical doctrines, one concerning the soul, the other concerning matter, which seem to belong to the earliest tradition.

(5) The soul or ego is not an entity, and in the substantive sense there is no personal identity; consciousness is an aggregate, whose constituents are called *skandhas* (*q.v.*). But just as the flame of a torch can be passed from one faggot to another, so the characteristics of the self can be transmitted from one aggregate to another. Even in rebirth, so it is claimed, the character of a person can be transmitted into a new existence without a substantive soul, or ego. The impermanent nature of the ego signals that it is relative and false; and hence not an object of attachment.

(6) In the same sense there is no material substance. Impermanence (*anitya*) applies both to the soul and to matter. And anything you may name is in flux, an aggregate of changing parts.

BUDDHADHARMA.
  Q.v. Dharma (6).

BUDDHI.
  Q.v. Sankhya (5b).

BUDDHISM.

The religion founded by Gautama Buddha in the 6th century B.C. Arising in the Eastern provinces, far from the Indus Valley, center of Vedic culture. Founded in the same period as Jainism, and like Jainism by a Kshatriya, Buddhism became the state religion in the 3rd century B.C. Eventually it disappeared from the Indian scene, becoming dominant in China and other Eastern nations. In a deeper sense Buddhism did not disappear from India, but was assimilated by Hinduism, each of its tenets having been accepted by large numbers of Hindus for whom Buddha is one of the avatars spreading Enlightenment to all creatures.

Buddhism is anti-Vedic and anti-caste. Its two main branches are Hinayana (Theravada) Buddhism and Mahayana Buddhism. The doctrines of these schools are set forth below.

BUDDHISM, HINAYANA.

Q.v. Buddhism, Theravada.

BUDDHISM, MAHAYANA. 0–500 A.D. (Formative period).

The later, more popular and more elaborate of the two interpretations of Buddhism which arose after the death of the founder, Gautama Buddha. Members of the movement gave themselves the name "Mahayana" meaning "the great vehicle." To be contrasted with the term "Hinayana" meaning "the small vehicle" which they applied to the earlier and more strict interpretation of the teachings of Buddha. Reference should be made to the following leaders who contributed to the development of this form of Buddhism between the 1st and 5th centuries A.D.: Aśvaghoṣa, Nagarjuna, Asanga, and Vasubandhu.

(1) The basic difference distinguishing all forms of Mahayana Buddhism from Hinayana is belief in the institution of the *bodhisattva*, *i.e.*, the Savior who with universal love for all beings postpones Nirvana in order to work through countless additional rebirths for their salvation. In some versions of Mahayana, Bodhisattvahood is optional; in other versions anyone on the way to Buddhahood must pass through the *bodhisattva* stage. But in every version, while Hinayana Buddhism is indivi-dualistic, Mahayana engenders and expresses an ethic of universal compassion and concern.

(2) Buddhahood is the universal goal and, given sufficient aeons of time, universal salvation will be possible. In those versions where every person will some day assume the role of universal savior, each must pass through the ten stages of Bodhisattvahood, *i.e.*, delight; purity; brightness of intellect; destruction of any sediments of ignorance and evil passion; living in equanimity, seeing eternity in time; seeing the inmost changeless essence of things beneath their evil, ignorance, and particularity; gaining the ability to produce whatever means are necessary for the work of salvation; saintly innocence and immediate knowledge; a still higher stage of perfect knowledge benefiting sentient beings but beyond their power to follow; finally, the *bodhisattva* arriving at the summit, is love and sympathy personified, omniscience, virtue, wisdom, and operative justice.

(3) In corresponding manner the goal of Nirvana is no longer negative but positive. It means first of all the achievement of universal love and profound wisdom in this life for the sake of others. It means, too, the perfect tranquility at the heart of all things. Finally, it means absolute eternal bliss for that one who has completed one's cycle of births and deaths.

(4) Through meditation Four Immeasurable Attitudes are to be cultivated: friendliness (*maitri*), giving pleasure and happiness to others; compassion (*karuna*) uprooting pain and suffering; sympathetic joy (*mudita*) over the happiness of others; equanimity (*upekṣa*) freeing one from attachment to these attitudes in order to foster their impartial implementations.

(5) The transcendental career of Buddha has, furthermore, become determinate in Mahayana Buddhism; and a marked similarity is to be noticed between the Buddhist Trikaya (*q.v.*) and the Christian Trinity. Buddha is to be understood as having three manifestations; as the Body of Transformation, the Body of Bliss, and the Body of Dharma. The first of these is, roughly speaking, the historical Buddha. The second would seem to be an intermediate reality, sharing in the qualities of the physical

world and of ultimate reality, while mysteriously working out schemes of salvation in all times and places. The third is similar to the conception of the God-head, the *Dharmakaya* which is at once the ultimate reality, and the cosmic body of Buddha, yet beyond the physical. It is the immortal in us, in Gautama Buddha, and in all other Buddhas.

(6) In the final analysis the subject-object dualism is resolved by admitting the reality of consciousness only.

(7) In Shin Buddhism the goal is immortal existence in a "Pure Land." The most complete description of this feature of Mahayana centers around Amitabha, a Tathagata whose pure land and its inhabitants are far away to the "West." But in fact there are as many pure lands as there are bodhisattvas and Tathagatas.

(8) The pivotal conception of emptiness came into Mahayana Buddhism very early, reshaping the sense of its doctrines not only in India but also in China and Japan. Both compassion and ultimate knowledge (*prajnaparamita*) have their source in emptiness (*q.v.*, and *Śunya*).

Also, *q.v.* Suzuki (2).

BUDDHISM, THERAVADA (HINAYANA).

Theravada (Pali, "the way of the elders," the Sanskrit equivalent being *Sthaviravada*) is the name of the only remaining school of early Buddhism. Eighteen (or 20) early schools had emerged through the divisiveness of the many centuries of Buddhist history (although countered by Buddhist Councils, *q.v.*). Theravada remains the dominant form of Buddhism in Sri Lanka, Burma, Thailand, Laos, and Cambodia. The devotees of *Mahayana* (Skt., "great vehicle") Buddhism (*q.v.*) appropriated the honorific phrase, "great vehicle," to themselves, pejoratively naming their opponents as followers of *Hinayana* (Skt., "small vehicle") Buddhism. The name does suggest the simpler, less fanciful, doctrines of the early stages of a religion. The ideas which were generally agreed upon by the early schools we have summarized in the entry on Gautama Buddha (*q.v.*) although, as elsewhere, certainty on these matters is not to be expected. The doctrines of the early schools do provide a starker contrast to the central concepts of Hinduism. One

can avoid the pejorative by identifying early Buddhism with the Theravada school; but this is not entirely satisfactory either. Although the Theravadins claimed to have preserved the original teachings of Buddha, the history of the movement does not support the claim. The Theravada school was, in fact, a missionary school established in Sri Lanka by the son of the Indian Buddhist king, Ashoka (3rd cent. B.C.), whose "conquest by *dharma*" both extended the borders of India and stimulated the international spread of Buddhism. One of the issues of the Third Buddhist Council, convened by Ashoka, was heresy in the *Sthaviravada* school. The "heretics" were driven out, and they migrated to the northwest, becoming a further school, the *Sarvas-tivadins*. The *Sthaviravadins* then took the name *Vibhajyavadins* ("distinctionists"), and this was the school implanted in Sri Lanka by Ashoka's son.

Within a century the mission school had taken the name *Theravada*, the Pali equivalent of *Sthaviravada*, thus claiming for itself the mantle of primitive Buddhism. The canon of scriptures, which had been retained in oral form, was written down between 29 and 17 B.C. when Sri Lanka was threatened by invasion. The language of the area was not Sanskrit but Pali; the Pali canon was thus produced in three divisions (or three baskets, *tipitaka* in Pali): the first basket, the sermons and sayings of Buddha; the second, rules of monastic discipline, the third a treatise on doctrine (*q.v. Abhidhamma* 1–2). This is the collection of Buddhist scriptures which has survived virtually intact. By the end of the first millennium A.D. when the revival of Hinduism, combined with Muslim attacks on monasteries, had eliminated Buddhism from India Theravada Buddhism continued to flourish outside India, and does so even today. We shall use the term *Theravada* for the surviving school of early Buddhism, and at times *Hinayana* to refer to common agreement among the early schools.

Four of the schools were mainly important: in addition to the Theravada, the Sarvastivada (*q.v.*), the Sautrantika (*q.v.*), and the Vaibhashika. We confine ourselves here to four Theravada doctrines representative of, if not precisely reflecting, the positions of all the early schools. Note, for example, in (3) below, that the Sarvastivada school held a more extreme form of the doctrine of impermanence. Differences between these doctrines and the position held by Buddha himself on the one hand, and that of Mahayana Buddhism will also be obvious.

(1) The four doctrines of Theravada Buddhism, deserving attention, are *Duhkha* (Skt., "suffering," *Dukkha* in Pali); *Anitya* (Skt., "impermanence," *Anicca* in Pali); *Anatman* (Skt., "no soul," *Anatta* in Pali); *Arhat* (Skt., "worthy or deserving one," *Arahant* in Pali).

(2) From one's first to last moment existence is characterized by *Duhkha*, or bodily and mental suffering. One suffers directly, indirectly, manifestly, and even unmanifestly (when the pain and its cause are not apparent). The source of this suffering lies in chance, and so in the impermanence of things.

(3) Among the conditions of enlightenment is becoming aware of *anitya*, or the pervasive fact of impermanence. The *Sarvastivada* school interpreted *anitya* as "radical momentariness."

(4) The realization of *anitya* brings with it the doctrine of *anatman*. Hinduism had centered on the unborn and undying soul, the *atman*, which is identical with Brahman. Countering the Hindu doctrine is *anatman*, the conception of the self as an aggregate of bodily form, sensation, perception, predisposition (the *Karma* of past lives), and consciousness, one is a succession of contrasting or similar feelings and thoughts. From the features of similarity in this succession one is tempted to make the imperceptive leap to the doctrine of *atman*, or of a persistent self or soul. In fact, recognition of *anatman* is among the necessary conditions for release from the cycle of rebirth.

(5) One who succeeds in doing this will pass into Nirvana. Thus far the ideas are different in no way from the teachings of Buddha. But where Buddha dismissed questions about the nature of Nirvana as "unedifying," here the view is definite that Nirvana means extinction. It is compared to the blowing out of a lamp.

(6) The human goal of life is arhatship, the achievement of freedom of mind and heart, true knowledge including knowledge of past, present, and future, and the thirty-seven factors of enlightenment; the overcoming of desire and passion; reaching the goal of Nirvana (*nibbana* in Pali). As these extraordinary qualities are achieved, one moves through four stages of sanctification: "stream-enterer," "once-returner," "never-returner," and "*arhat*." In Burma eight *arahants* (the Pali term) are venerated, one for each day of the Burmese week. Tradition lists eight *arahants* associated with Buddha during his lifetime. As in the case of saints, candidates for arhatship are put forward from the company of holy monks; protective amulets bearing their images are worn; relics are prized.

BUDDHIST COUNCILS.

Two councils are accepted by all Buddhists, and three by most. The first was a seven-month session held in 483 B.C. following Buddha's death. The place was Rajagha, 500 monks attending. The second, lasting 18 months, was held in 383 B.C. The place was Vesali, 700 monks attending. The third council, lasting nine months, was held in 240 B.C., the place was Pataliputta, 1000 monks attending. The councils had to do with fixing the canon of Buddhist literature and meeting questions of discipline. Northern Buddhists added a fourth council, meeting in Kashmir or Jalandhara in the latter half of the 1st century A.D. The most recent Buddhist Council was held in Burma (now Myanmar) from May, 1954, through May, 1956, the assembly of monks, including representatives from Cambodia, India, Laos, Myanmar, Nepal, Pakistan, Sri Lanka, and Thailand. Buddhists disagree among themselves on the numbering of their councils, those from Sri Lanka and Myanmar counting the 1954 council as the "sixth," those from Thailand as the "tenth."

BULLINGER, HEINRICH.
Q.v. Helvetic Confessions.

BULL, PAPAL.
Q.v. Papal Encyclical.

BULLOUGH, EDWARD.
Q.v. Aesthetics (20).

BULTMANN, RUDOLF. 1884–1976.
German Protestant theologian. Born in Wiefelsted. Studied at Marburg, Tübingen

and Berlin. Taught at Marburg. Heavily influenced by Heidegger, Bultmann is an existentialist theologian.

Principal writings: *Jesus and the Word* (T), 1926; *Belief and Understanding* (T), 2 vols., 1933, 1952; "The New Testament and Mythology" (T) in *Kerygma and Myth* (ed. Bartsch), vol. I, 1948; *Theology of the New Testament* (T), 2 vols., 1948–53; *The Question of Demythologizing* (with K. Jaspers), 1954; *History and Eschatology* (E), 1957; *Jesus Christ and Mythology* (E), 1958.

(1) Bultmann takes the position that the New Testament needs to be "demythologized" in order to be relevant to the contemporary world. The sole item excluded from this sifting process is the claim that God spoke, and speaks, through Christ. At this point we have gotten beyond mythology to truth.

(2) The central Gospel message of salvation, called the *Kerygma*, is reinterpreted in the existentialist language of freedom, *Angst* (*q.v.*), and authenticity. According to Bultmann, authenticity is possible only through the word as revealed in Christ.

BUNGE, MARIO.

Q.v. Philosophy of Science (30).

BUNYAN, JOHN. 1628–1688.

English nonconformist minister. Born in Elstow near Bedford. Served in Cromwell's Army. His conversion to evangelical Christianity occurred gradually between 1650 and 1655. He entered into controversy with the Quakers, and is mentioned by George Fox, their leader. Upon the restoration of Charles II he was imprisoned for his nonconformist ministry. Jailed from 1660–72 and again in 1677, Bunyan wrote religious allegories of great power. The most influential of these is *Pilgrim's Progress*, telling the story of Christian's pilgrimage from the City of Destruction to the Celestial City. Written from prison, the allegory personifies Bunyan's inner struggle, and contains persons and places such as Worldly Wiseman, the foul fiend Apollyon, Vanity Fair, the Slough of Despond, the Delectable Mountains, and the River of Death.

Principal writings: *Grace Abounding to the Chief of Sinners*, 1666; *The Pilgrim's Progress*, 1678; Part II, 1684; *The Life and Death of Mr. Badman*, 1680; *The Holy War for Mansoul*, 1682; as well as numerous theological and devotional tracts.

BURIDAN, JOHN. c. 1295–1356.

French philosopher. Studied at Paris with William of Ockham (*q.v.*). A professor at the University of Paris he served two terms as rector. A moderate nominalist in philosophy, he was a logician who, following Ockham, introduced the distinction between connotation (*q.v.*) and denotation (*q.v.*). He also cultivated a special interest in the modal syllogism. Against Aristotle, he seems to have conceived of a non-local force permeating space and acting on local bodies. He discussed the problem of the relation between the will and reason, and is known for the striking example of "Buridan's ass," starving midway between two identical bales of hay, unable to go to either one since there is no reason to choose one over the other. Unhappily, the illustration is not to be found in any of his surviving writings, although he does offer the comparable illustration of a dog between two equally attractive portions of food.

Principal writings: *Summulae de Dialectica; Consequentiae; Sophismata; Questions on the Four Books of the Heavens and the Earth*; as well as other Commentaries on Aristotle's works.

BURIDAN'S ASS.

Q.v. John Buridan.

BURKE, EDMUND. 1729–1797.

British statesman and philosophical writer. Born in Dublin, Ireland. Educated at Trinity College, Dublin. Beginning his career as a writer and philosopher, politics turned him aside from "active philosophy" and he entered the House of Commons in 1766, remaining a power in the Whig party for a quarter century.

Principal writings: *On the Sublime and the Beautiful*, 1756; *Reflections on the Revolution in France*, 1790.

(1) Burke distinguished the sublime from the beautiful in psychological terms. While the beautiful is finite and produces unmixed delight, the sublime is infinite and produces delight mixed with, or qualified by, terror or pain. His work on the sublime influenced Moses Mendelssohn and was translated into German by

Lessing, influencing the movement of Romanticism (q.v.).

(2) Burke defended the American, while opposing the French, Revolution. Both positions flowed, in his view, from the same principle of conservatism. Traditional rights and liberties are to be preserved, the point of the American rebellion, but the French Revolution was directed toward the destruction of tradition in the name of an imaginary ideal.

BURLEIGH, WALTER. 1275–c. 1343.

English philosopher. A Franciscan, Burleigh taught at Oxford and the University of Paris. An opponent of Ockham in most respects, he employed and vastly elaborated the theory of suppositions (q.v. Suppositio) to which Ockham also contributed. The theory, which would be classed today under that division of logic called Semantics, deals with the types of relations which obtain between terms and what they designate. Such relations are called "suppositions."

Principal writings: Commentaries on Aristotle; On Matter and Form; On Intention and the Remission of Form; On the Purity of the Logical Arts.

(1) Burleigh first divides suppositions into those which are proper and those which are improper. Proper suppositions are those where terms are used in a univocal sense. Improper suppositions include the use of metaphor and figurative speech.

(2) Proper suppositions are divided into material and formal. Material suppositions are those wherein reference is made to the term itself; e.g., "God" is a three-letter word. Formal suppositions are those which refer to extra-linguistic entities or properties; e.g., God is love.

(3) Material suppositions are either reflexive or transitive.

(4) Formal suppositions are either simple (spoken terms), or personal (mental entities).

(5) Simple suppositions subdivide into absolute, comparative, or relative types.

(6) Personal suppositions divide into those which are discrete and those which are common.

(7) Common suppositions are definite or confused. Confused suppositions are pure or distributive; and the distributives are either fixed or changing.

BUSHIDO.

From the Japanese bushi ("warrior") and do ("way" or "principle"). The term refers to the chivalric code (Confucian and Zen Buddhist in origin) of the warrior-knight in feudal Japan.

BUTLER, JOSEPH. 1692–1752.

British bishop and philosopher. Born at Wantage. Oxford educated. Bishop of Bristol, 1738; and Dean of St. Paul's. Bishop of Durham, 1750.

Principal writings: Fifteen Sermons, 1726; The Analogy of Religion and Dissertation upon the Nature of Virtue, 1736.

(1) The criterion of right and wrong is the voice of conscience; and conscience is a reflective and rational principle operating within man. The principle operates only in relation to many other aspects of human nature; the promptings of hunger and thirst, appetitions, are "particular passions" regulated by benevolence and self-love. These last-named principles are not in essential conflict, agreeing for the most part now, and perfectly in the world beyond. Conscience controls all of this in a subtle manner not reducible to a single maxim or criterion, thus intuitive rather than utilitarian or formal.

(2) Defending the Christian position against Deism, he found the latter escaped none of the difficulties of the former, while lacking some of its virtues. Here he is not arguing against atheism; he is accepting the limited affirmations of the Deists, including their view that there is providential design in nature, and attempting to demonstrate that it is reasonable to venture beyond these affirmations in the direction of necessitarianism and revelation. In this venture he found it possible to defend miracles by relating them to an infinite order and knowledge beyond our own.

BUTLER, SAMUEL.

Q.v. Utopia (9).

BYZANTINE CHURCH.

In a strict sense those congregations falling under the jurisdiction of the Church of Constantinople. In a looser sense the entire group of Eastern Orthodox Churches (q.v.).

CABALA.

From the Hebrew meaning the "received" or "traditional." The term originally denoted the Prophets and Hagiographs as opposed to the Pentateuch. By extension it came to include any emphasis on spirit as against law, feeling as against reason. The term is employed somewhat as a collective noun to designate a set of mystical doctrines which developed within Judaism between the last pre-Christian centuries and the 14th century, and the collection of books written in support of these doctrines. The Cabala developed in contrast to orthodox Jewish doctrine, emphasizing exactly the elements rejected by the orthodox.

(1) The doctrines of the Cabala include: (a) A doctrine of emanations relating a transcendent God to the world. (b) A doctrine of the spheres, the *sefiroth*, mediating between the infinite light and creation. These spheres are identified with the Neoplatonic grades of wisdom. (c) Ranks of angels and demiurges facilitating the communion between man and God. (d) A belief in metempsychosis. (e) An understanding of sin as separation from the divine being, and of perfection as overcoming this separation. (f) A belief in Adam Kadmon, or primordial man, from whom the earthly man is derived. This being is a union of sexes not reflecting the earthly division into male and female. (g) A belief in man as a microcosm of the macrocosm. (h) Belief in a dualism of right and left, light and darkness, purity and impurity, male and female; the syzygies, or pairs, characterize everything and imply the harmony of the universe. (i) The use of amulets, numbers and letters with special significance, the casting of lots for divination and changing one's name in illness or out of penitence.

(2) The books in which Cabalistic doctrine centered are: (a) The *Sefer Yesira*, dealing with permutations of numbers, letters, and emanations. Originated during 6th century A.D. Basis of the *Zohar* (*cf.* d, below). (b) *Sefer hab-Bahir*. Commentary on early chapters of Genesis. Holds to the eternity of matter. Attributed to Isaac the Blind, 13th century. (c) *Hekhaloth*, the greater and the less, concerning the *Book of Enoch*. Attributed to Solomon ben Elisha. (d) *Zohar* (*The Book of Splendor*). Allegorical commentary on the Pentateuch. Written in Aramaic, the chief Cabalistic document. Composed by many hands, among them Moses ben Shem Tob de Leon, 1250–1305. (e) *The Book of Raziel*. Directions for preparing amulets. (f) *Shi'ur Koma*. Dimensions and members of the Deity. (g) *Gilgulim*. Lists of transmigrations of souls.

(3) Among the Cabalists of note may be mentioned: (a) Aaron ben Samuel in the 9th century carried the Cabala from Babylon to Europe. (b) Moses ben Nahman, Spanish rabbi, 1194–1270. The influence of the Cabala is marked in his commentary on the Pentateuch. (c) Abraham ben Samuel Abuliafa, 1240–1291, was one of the founders of the Spanish Cabala. (d) Isaac Luria (Arl), 1534–1572. Originated the modern Cabala. He has had many followers. Luria anticipated the thesis-antithesis-synthesis structure of Hegel with his *Tzimtzum* ("contradiction"), *shevirat ha'keilin* ("breaking of the vessels"), *tikkun* ("restoration"). (e) Hayyim Vital, 1543–1620, was a pupil of Luria and his successor. He was a visionary and alchemist. (f) Israel ben Eliezer, Ba'al Shem Tov (Besht) 1700–1760, was founder of the Hasidim, the sect appearing during the final stages of the Cabala's development. (g) Baer (Dob) of Meseritz, 1710–1772, was successor to Besht as the leader of the Hasidim, continuing opposition to the Talmudists.

CABANIS, PIERRE. 1757–1808.

French philosopher and physician. Born in Limousin. Professor of Medicine in Paris. One of the leaders of the French *Idéologues* (*q.v.*).

Principal writings: *The Relations of the Physical and Ethical in Man*, 2 vols., 1802.

(1) Although thought is the product of cerebral activity, and there is no essential difference between the physical and psychical, still the two influence each other, so that the physiological structure of man is influenced by psychical events. Indeed, depending upon one's emphasis the doctrine can become materialistic or spiritualistic. And while no certainty is to be found in metaphysical assumptions,

Cabanis' view tends toward something like pantheism, while emphasizing the fundamental nature of the ethical.

(2) In agreement with most of his colleagues, Cabanis believed in the idea of progress and held that a new era was opening in which the best of man's hopes would be realized.

CABET, ETIENNE.

Q.v. Utopia (7).

CAIRD, EDWARD. 1835–1908.

Scottish philosopher. Born in Greenock. Educated at Glasgow and Oxford. Taught at Oxford and Glasgow. Basing his philosophy on that of Kant, he developed the latter's system in Idealistic terms—removing the distinction between phenomena and noumena. He is thus known as an English Hegelian.

Principal writings: *A Critical Account of the Philosophy of Kant*, 1877; *Hegel*, 1883; *The Social Philosophy and Religion of Comte*, 1885; *The Critical Philosophy of Immanuel Kant*, 1889; *The Evolution of Religion*, 1893.

CAJETAN (THOMAS DE VIO). 1468–1534.

Cardinal. Italian Thomistic philosopher. Born in Gaeta. He became a Dominican in 1480. Professor in Padua and Pavia. Dominican master-general 1508. Cardinal 1517. Papal legate to Hungary, Bohemia, Poland. Served under Pope Clement VII as Cardinal stationed in Rome. One of the most distinguished commentators of Aquinas' *Summa Theologica*.

Principal writings: *On the Analogy of Names and the Concept of Being* (T), 1498; *On the Subject of Natural Philosophy*, 1499; *On the Concept of Being*, 1509; *Whether Power is to be Granted to Natural Beings*, 1510. Plus his famous commentaries on Aristotle and Thomas Aquinas, as well as exegetical works.

(1) When names are used to designate objects, they can be used univocally, equivocally, or analogically. When the name carries the same meaning in its various uses it is being used univocally. When the name carries a different meaning in its different uses the name is being used equivocally. When the name carries a meaning in some ways different, and in other ways the same, the name is being used analogically.

(2) The two main types of analogy are the analogy of attribution and the analogy of proportionality. (a) The analogy of attribution turns on the difference between primary and secondary, or original and derivative meanings. The term "health" for example, applies to medicine, urine, and animal, each in a different but related way. Medicine is the cause of health, urine the sign of health, and the animal the subject of health. The primary analogate is here the animal; the meaning "health" applies intrinsically or fully to this analogate, and extrinsically or derivatively to the secondary analogates. (b) The analogy of proportionality has two forms. One is the metaphorical analogy. In "a smiling meadow" we find one meaning which applies to a true smile, and is metaphorically analogous to a blooming meadow. But the proper sense of this kind of analogy occurs when the common name and its meaning apply to both analogates without metaphors, and proportionally. In the proportion, "2 is to 4 as 4 is to 8" there is a common meaning which applies to each analogate, but proportionally. Similarly, when we say that "God is good" we are employing this form of analogy. We are saying that the goodness which exists in creatures pre-exists in God proportionally. According to Cajetan, the proper analogy of proportionality is an indispensable resource for metaphysical thought.

CALAUCAU.

Q.v. Gnosticism.

CALCULUS.

A system of symbols so organized that inferences can be made by manipulating the symbols of the system according to rule. The elements of any calculus are: symbols, definitions, axioms, and rules of inference. Some of these symbols must be primitive, or undefined; the rest will be defined in terms of those which are undefined. Through the appropriate combination of symbols, well-formed formulae and, through the manipulation of such formulae, the theorems of the calculus, can be gained. Any specific kind of calculus is logically subordinate to one or more of the following types of logical calculus: (1) the sentential or propositional calculus (*q.v.*); (2) the calculus of quantification (*q.v.*); (3) the calculus of identity; (4) the calculus of classes (*q.v.* Set Theory); (5); the calculus of relations (*q.v.*). Questions of completeness (*q.v.*), consistency (*q.v.*), decidability (*q.v.*) and criteria for decisions concerning these matters are of great importance among the theoretical considerations of this subject. *Q.v.* Logic (20–24).

CALEMES.
Valid syllogism in AEE mood, fourth figure. *Q.v.* Syllogism (4).

CALLICLES. 4th cent. B.C.
A Greek philosopher and politician, Callicles enters Plato's dialogue, *Gorgias*, as one of Socrates' contemporaries. One of the Sophists (*q.v.*), he argues that the natural law by which the strong rule is also a natural right and an expression of natural justice. The conventions of society attempt to enslave the strong and thus subvert natural justice. He also argues for pleasure as the goal of life.

CALVIN, JOHN. 1509–1564.
French Protestant theologian. Born in Picardy. Studied philosophy, University of Paris, 1523–27; studied also at Orleans and Bourges. Converted to Protestantism. Moved to Basel where he wrote and published his *Institutes*, 1536. Moved to Geneva and by 1541 had established there a theocracy, ruled by Presbyters, controlling the faith and morals of the people. Responsible for the execution of Michael Servetus, an important scientist and Protestant, who was burned at the stake for heresy (1553), although Calvin opposed the manner of execution. John Knox followed Calvin's teachings in carrying out the Scottish Protestant Reformation. In 1561 the Calvinists and Lutherans separated. Calvin's principles are central to the Presbyterian and the Reformed Protestant churches.

Principal writings: *Institutes of the Christian Religion*, 1536.

(1) God is the absolute and unconditioned cause of all things. Both in the mind of man and in nature God's nature is revealed—as compassion, goodness, mercy, justice, judgment, and truth. Since man is blinded by his state of sin he requires the more explicit revelation of Scripture.

(2) God ordains whatever is to come to pass, but in such manner that it does not do violence to the liberty of creatures, some things being necessary, some contingent, some free.

(3) Man was made a pure being, in his Creator's image, but is fallen and corrupted through his willful turning from the good; even so, part of God's image still remains in man. What remains is not sufficient for salvation.

(4) Christ, the Redeemer, is therefore necessary to the scheme.

(5) Man is dependent on God's twofold predestination, the predestination of some to salvation, and of others to destruction. Men are saved by an unmerited grace on God's part, but condemned on the ground of their own sin. God's grace renews the will, restoring to it its true freedom.

(6) All believers are equal before God, and Scripture alone is recognized as the authority for belief.

CALVINISM.
The movement of thought and practice following from Calvin's work. Initially it developed into theocratic orders as in the church-state of Geneva, the Presbyterians of Scotland, and the Puritans of New England. The Huguenots of France, the Reformed Church, and the Puritans of England are also among its expressions. Karl Barth (*q.v.*) and Emil Brunner (*q.v.*) represent a revival of Calvinist thought.

CAMBRIDGE PLATONISTS.
An English intellectual movement centering in Cambridge University in the third quarter of the 17th century. Centering around problems in the philosophy of religion, the group stood largely in the tradition of Neoplatonism, citing especially Plato, Proclus, and Plotinus. Jacob Boehme, Descartes, and Malebranche also received attention. The group was also anti-Hobbesian and its philosophy can perhaps be regarded as an intellectualized puritanism. The most prominent members of the group were Ralph Cudworth (*q.v.*) and Henry More (*q.v.*); others were Whichcote (*q.v.*), the spiritual founder; Culverwell, Cumberland, Ruts, Smith (*q.v.*), and Stillingfleet. The main emphases of the group included: the re-

lation of faith and reason, the ultimacy of the distinction between right and wrong, the role of mysticism in experience, evidence for the existence of God, and Cudworth's concept of "plastic natures."

CAMESTRES.
Valid syllogism in AEE mood, second figure. *Q.v.* Syllogism (4).

CAMPANELLA, TOMASSO. 1568–1639.
Italian philosopher. Born in Calabria. Entered Dominican order, 1582. Accused of heresy because of his enthusiasm for Telesio (*q.v.*) in 1591. He was accused of conspiring against the Spanish control of Calabria and imprisoned from 1599 to 1626. He composed his principal writings while in prison. Nominally freed he was detained by the Inquisition until 1629. Thereafter he lived in Rome for several years spending his last 5 years in Paris.

Principal writings: *A Philosophy of Perception Demonstrated*, 1596; *City of the Sun* (T), before 1602; *On Sense Objects and More*, 1620; *The Monarchy of the Messiah*, 1633; *General Philosophy*, 1638; *Philosophies of the Rational and the Real*, 1638.

(1) The only trustworthy datum of experience one possesses is the feeling of one's own existence; this datum stands against any doubt which may be brought against it; and the only trustworthy knowledge comes in tracing out the implications of this experience. The most secure part of one's knowledge is innate (*notitia innata*); the knowledge of other things is acquired (*notitia illata*).

(2) My self-certainty, when analyzed, yields knowledge of both God and the world: of the world because I know myself as part of a larger whole, and my sensations as caused by this whole; of God, because I know myself as wisdom, power, and love in a limited sense; and that the whole must contain these qualities without limitation. Hence, a reality exists, including God and world.

(3) But reality does not move in jumps. From matter to God there is a graded reality, embodying perfection in different degrees. All things possess, in their different degrees, the "primalities" of knowledge, power, and love. These are the first principles of all things. And infused through the whole is the love of God, and the desire to be one with Him.

(4) Following Plato, Campanella describes his City of the Sun. It features communal living, state control of eugenics, and provisions for establishing a class of guardians who will be both philosophers and priests.

(5) Believing in the supremacy of the pope both spiritually and temporally, he urged the political supremacy of the pope over mankind. At different times he offered the political administration of this universal spiritual and temporal monarchy to the kings of Spain and France.

CAMPBELL, GEORGE.
Q.v. Rhetoric (16).

CAMPBELL, N.R. 1880–1949.
English physicist and philosopher of science. For Campbell, theory construction interrelates laws and empirical generalizations by means of hypotheses, a dictionary correlating theoretical and empirical concepts, and an analogy relating the phenomena in question to phenomena already understood.

Principal writings: *The Principles of Electricity*, 1912; *Physics: The Elements*, 1920; *What is Science?*, 1921.

CAMPBELL, THOMAS AND ALEXANDER.
Q.v. Disciples of Christ.

CAMUS, ALBERT. 1913–1960.
French writer. Born in Algeria. Educated at the University of Algiers. Moved to Paris in 1940. Active in the French Resistance of the Second World War. The author of a number of philosophical novels and essays, he was for a time associated with Sartre (*q.v.*).

Principal philosophical writings: *The Myth of Sisyphus* (T), 1942; *Letters to a German Friend* (T), 1945; *The Rebel* (T), 1951; *Reflections on Capital Punishment* (T), 1960.

(1) Arguing against suicide on the grounds that it is an inadequate response to the absurdity of life, Camus holds that the adequate response is to continue living while realizing its absurdity, and thus fulfill one's humanity.

(2) Holding human solidarity as a final value, Camus argues that all political change must have this as its goal. He rejects as unjustified what he terms

"metaphysical revolt." Both suicide and nihilism, exemplifying destruction for its own sake, are instances. They lie outside any admissible framework. At last, he regarded capital punishment as likewise inadmissible.

CANON.

A Latin term meaning "measuring line," "rule," or "model," derived from the Greek *kanon* ("rule" or "rod").

(1) Canons of scripture are those writings regarded as authoritative for a given religion. The Jewish or Hebrew canon consists of the Law, Prophets, and Writings. The Christian canon, or Bible (*q.v.*), consists of 39 books of the Old Testament and 27 of the New.

(2) Canon Law. The most authoritative law of the Roman Catholic Church, bearing the authority of Scripture, pope, or council. To be distinguished from decrees of bishops, church-state concordats, and church law resting on custom. The body of Canon Law was published in 1582 by Gregory XIII as the *Corpus Juris Canonici*. A new codification, known as the *Codex Juris Canonici*, was promulgated under Benedict XV in 1917.

CANONIZATION.

In Roman Catholicism the decree placing a person in the catalogue or canon of saints and commending that he be venerated. Necessary to canonization is the prior achievement of beatification (*q.v.*) and the authentication of at least two miracles by intercession of the person, always deceased, under consideration.

CANTOR, GEORG. 1845–1918.

German mathematician. Born in St. Petersburg. Professor at the University of Halle, 1872–1913. Famed for his definition of transfinite numbers, his theory of infinity, and his ground-breaking work in set theory. All of these being part of a single achievement. *Q.v.* Russell (5).

Principal writings: *Groundwork for a Theory of Sets*, 1883; *Contributions to the Founding of the Theory of Transfinite Numbers* (T), 1885–92.

(1) Two finite sets of things have the same number when they can be put into a one-one correspondence.

(2) The characteristic distinguishing any set in one-to-one correspondence from all other sets is the cardinal number of that set.

(3) The cardinal numbers of finite sets are called natural numbers, the cardinal numbers of infinite sets are called "transfinite cardinal numbers."

(4) An example of a transfinite cardinal number is "aleph-null" or $\aleph$, the number of denumerably infinite sets, *i.e.*, the set of all things that can be put into one-one correspondence with the totality of natural numbers.

(5) But not only is the set of all natural numbers denumerably infinite, so is the set of all even numbers, as can be seen by the correspondence:

1	2	3	4	5	6
2	4	6	8	10	12.

Hence, the even numbers also bear the cardinal number, $\aleph$. This is true of some other sub-sets of the set of natural numbers. But merely taking the correspondence with which we had begun it is clear that we have here a meaning for infinity in series or sets; a set, or series, is infinite when it shares a cardinal number with one of its sub-sets, or sub-series.

(6) Cantor discovered, too, that the cardinal number of the set of real numbers is larger than $\aleph$. He called this number "the power of the continuum"; it is not denumerable, not algebraic, hence, transcendental. This is the cardinal number of the points of a straight line, the points of a plane, the points of any three-dimensional space, and the points of any n-dimensional space.

(7) Further, there are infinitely many different transfinite cardinal numbers, since—given any set—a set of higher cardinal number can at once be indicated (the sub-sets of the given set having a higher cardinal number than the given set). The smallest transfinite cadinal number is $\aleph$. It is followed by $\aleph_1, \aleph_2, \ldots \aleph_{10}, \aleph_{100}, \aleph_{1000} \ldots$ etc. Cantor has shown this, and that there is a transfinite cardinal number larger than any of these (*i.e.*, larger than any aleph with a natural number as its index). He called it $\aleph_w$. This is followed by $\aleph_{w+1}$, and the process continues.

CAPITALISM.

That economic system which stresses the role of capital, *i.e.*, wealth of all sorts including economic goods utilized in the production of other goods.

(1) The classical expression of Capitalism is credited to Adam Smith (*q.v.* 2) who argued for the free play of a self-regulating market and who believed that, given competition, the operation of an "invisible hand" would move prices to "natural" levels and induce labor and capital to move from less to more profitable enterprises. In short, man's competitive strivings would be transmuted automatically into the common good.

(2) The French term *laissez-faire* ("let do" or "let make"), derived from the Physiocrats (*q.v.*), came to be attached to "capitalism" as a qualifying phrase. The total phrase "*laissez-faire* capitalism" emphasized the point that in this system economic interests were to be let alone to continue their development without government control and with a minimum of regulation.

(3) Max Weber (*q.v.*) found the rise of capitalism and that of Protestantism to be related, the former standing as a secularized version of the latter's emphasis on individualism, and the necessity that one work out one's own salvation.

(4) The chief critic of capitalism has been Karl Marx (*q.v.*).

CARDAN, GIROLAMO. 1501–1576.

Italian mathematician, physician, and astrologer. Held to an organic view of the world, combined with mysticism and pantheism.

Selected writings: *On the Subtlety of Things*, 1551; *On the Diversity of Things*, 1557.

CAPUCHINS.

Q.v. Francis of Assisi (4).

CARDENAL, ERNESTO.

Q.v. Theology of Liberation (3, 6).

CARDINAL NUMBER.

Q.v. Cantor (3), Frege (2).

CARDINAL VIRTUES.

A term introduced by St. Ambrose, having come across Plato's classification of the natural virtues in the writings of Cicero.

(1) Among the Greeks, and for Plato, the virtues were "wisdom," "courage," "temperance," and "justice."

(2) Among the Scholastics the cardinal virtues were seven in number. They included the foregoing, termed natural virtues, and three additional "theological" virtues: "faith," "hope," and "charity."

(3) Geulincx (*q.v.* 3) held the cardinal virtues to be diligence, obedience, justice, and humility.

Q.v. Virtue.

CARLYLE, THOMAS. 1795–1881.

Scottish essayist. Born in Ecclefechan. Schoolmaster, tutor, rector of the University of Edinburgh, Carlyle was primarily a struggling man of letters.

Principal writings: *Sartor Resartus*, 1834; *French Revolution*, 1837; *On Heroes, Hero-worship, and the Heroic in History*, 1811.

(1) Preaching a doctrine of renunciation and work, of doing what it is in oneself to do, Carlyle moved to a natural appreciation of genius and of the hero who contributes greatly to human history.

(2) The result was a "great man" theory of history. The hope of man lies in the heroic act, which sets conditions within which the rest of us can find our places. One consequence of the doctrine is that for Carlyle biography became the essence of history.

(3) He opposed materialism and utilitarianism as contributing to degeneracy; and generally found the evils of the time outweighing its merits. He defined freedom as the right of the ignorant man to be governed by the wiser.

CARNAP, RUDOLF. 1891–1970.

German-born Logical Positivist. Born in Westphalia. One of the leaders of the Vienna Circle of Logical Positivists. Professor at the University of Vienna, Prague, Chicago, and Los Angeles.

Principal writings: *The Logical Construction of the World* (T), 1928: *Pseudo-Problems in Philosophy* (T), 1928; *Summary of Logistic* (T), 1929; *The Unity of Science* (T), 1932; *The Logical Syntax of Language* (T), 1934; and the following works written in English: *Philosophy and Logical Syntax*, 1935; *Foundations of Logic and Mathematics*, 1939; *Introduction to Semantics*, 1942; *Meaning and Necessity*, 1947; *Logical Foundations of Probability*, 1950; *The Continuum of Inductive Methods*, 1952.

(1) While remaining experimental in approach, Carnap has been motivated by

an unchanging conviction of the meaning-lessness of metaphysics, and the importance of science. His work has turned on certain major problems in the philosophy of science, and consideration of the role of philosophy in relation to the sciences. In method he has always been a formalist, applying symbolic logic to the problems he considers.

(2) His initial attempt was to make a logical construction (*Aufbau*) of the world. He builds the world from "primitive ideas" (cross-sections of the stream of experience) and "primitive relations" (*e.g.*, the "recognition of similarity"). The formal constitution of quality classes, sense-classes, sensory fields, and things is developed. The construction was abandoned by Carnap, apparently because of the difficulty of reaching the public world, required by science, from the starting point of private experience.

(3) The next experiment distinguished "protocol sentences" (describing directly given experience) from all other sentences. Convinced that physics is the language of science, and that all scientific statements can be expressed in the language of physics, Carnap argued that "protocol statements" were also thus expressible. Let one adopt a physicalistic language, and all experiences can be translated into statements about the states of one's body. "Red, now" is equivalent to "the body S is now seeing red." If protocol statements can be so translated the public world has been achieved.

(4) In this case, sentences can be distinguished into three types: syntactical sentences, object sentences, and pseudo-object sentences. The first describe a language; the second describe physical objects; the third appear to be object sentences but are in fact syntactical. The statements of philosophers are of the third type; they are phrased in the "material mode," speaking of things, when they should be speaking of thing-words. Thus many needless confusions are engendered.

(5) In order to avoid such difficulties one must distinguish internal from external questions. Questions internal to an identifiable framework of numbers, propositions, etc., do not lead to difficulty, and here one can choose the linguistic forms one wishes according to a "principle of tolerance." Philosophical

disputes, when not meaningless, are alternate proposals concerning syntax, and philosophy then consists of the form of language of science, its formation and transformation rules being part of science itself, especially of combinatorial analysis and applied mathematics. The uncontrollable questions are those asked outside an identifiable framework. Referring to external, rather than merely internal, objects, such questions have ontological implications, and are to be avoided.

(6) Although initially adhering to a verifiability theory of meaning, this becomes now a recommendation to construct a language which dispenses with non-verifiable assertions, that is, a thing language with reduction pairs to provide for disposition predicates (*i.e.*, "x is soluble" means that "if x is put into water at time t, x dissolves at time t"). Propositions are meaningless unless they have some empirical consequences; and "verifiability" is dropped in favor of "testability" and "confirmability." These positions are expressed in the period of his interest in the syntax of language.

(7) In his later writings Carnap has accepted C.W. Morris' (*q.v.* 2) valuation of the importance of semiotic (*q.v.*) with its branches of "syntactics, semantics, and pragmatics." Philosophy now becomes the semiotical analysis of the structure of cognitive discourse, and more closely identified with semantics than syntax.

(8) In *Meaning and Necessity* Carnap outlines a modal logic which understands the latter as a branch of semantics. Based on C.I. Lewis' (*q.v.* 1) work, Carnap distinguishes between propositions and sentences. The modal properties of propositions are necessity, possibility, contingency, and their opposites. One determines the modal property of a given proposition by examining the sentences which express that proposition in some system of sentences S. The sentences will have semantic properties which can be correlated to the modal properties we have named. Using "L" to stand for "logically" the correlation is as follows: Necessity: the sentence is "L-true." Possibility: the sentence is not "L-false." Contingency: the sentence is factually true. Impossibility: the sentence is "L-false."

(9) He employs the notion of L-truth to explicate the meanings of analyticity

and synonymy. Two sentences are synonymous when their corresponding terms are intensionally isomorphic and when the two sentences have the same intensional structure. Terms have intensional isomorphism when they are logically equivalent (L-equivalent), and sentences have the same intensional structure when they are composed of intensionally isomorphic terms and corresponding designators.

(10) In his discussions of probability Carnap distinguishes two varieties. One of these is frequency-probability; this kind of probability is appropriate to statistical problems. The other variety of probability is confirmation-probability. This is the kind of probability which is appropriate to typical cases of inductive inference, i.e., "It is probable on the evidence that x is true." Despite the difference of kinds one is able to test claims that the degree of confirmation of hypothesis *h* on the evidence *e* is *r* (where *r* is a number). These methods constitute the logic of induction. In this respect Carnap distinguishes five kinds of inference. These are discussed under Induction (10).

(11) In Carnap's extensional semantics a state description is a class of statements containing for every atomic sentence in a semantical system, S, either the given atomic sentence or its negation. A true state description describes the state of the universe, containing all the true atomic sentences and the negations of those which are false. To avoid contradiction certain stipulations must be observed: (a) the primitive individual constants of S must designate separate individuals; (b) the primitive predicates must designate properties and relations which are independent of each other; (c) the values for variables in S must be the individuals designated by the primitive individuals and constants. The range of a sentence is defined as the class of all state descriptions in which the sentence is true. In this context a sentence is L-true or analytic in S if its range is universal, i.e., it belongs to every state description of S. It is L-false, or contradictory, if its range is null, i.e., it belongs to no state description of S. It is L-determinate in S if it is either L-true or L-false; otherwise, it is L-indeterminate. When these concepts are combined with the semantic concept of

truth the L-indeterminate sentences become candidates for being F-true (factually true) or F-false (factually false). Not only the notions of analytic and synthetic, but also those of implication, equivalence, disjunction, etc. may be derived from this approach.

CARNEADES. 214–129 B.C.

Greek philosophical Skeptic. Born in Cyrene. Founder of the Third Academy in 156. Stood in opposition to Stoic philosophy, especially its theory of knowledge. The most powerful of the Skeptics, he opposed Chrysippus, while agreeing with Arcesilaus.

(1) We are not aware of things, but only of our impressions, and it is not possible to distinguish between true and false impressions. This being so, a wise man will suspend judgment, not even being sure that he can be sure of nothing. But Carneades held that there are degrees of probability: (a) an impression may be probable in itself (apparently on account of its strength); (b) probable and uncontradicted (in harmony with one's other impressions); (c) probable, uncontradicted, and confirmed.

(2) In opposition to the idea of divine providence, he pointed to the disharmonies of things. So far as the universe is orderly this can be explained in natural terms.

(3) The idea of god is a tissue of inconsistencies. The attributes of infinity and individuality cannot belong to the same being. Nor can God be either corporeal or incorporeal. If corporeal, God must be simple or composite. If simple, he would be incapable of life and thought; if composite, he could not be indestructible. If incorporeal, God could neither act nor feel. Finally, no assertion of any kind can be made concerning him.

(4) With respect to uncaused action, Caneades held that such events do not have an antecedent cause in the usual sense; they are caused by the person and thus are not literally without a cause.

CARNEGIE, ANDREW.

Q.v. Social Darwinism (1, 3).

CARTESIANISM.

From Renatus Cartesius, the Latinized form of the name of René Descartes. The term refers to all philosophies inspired by the methods and assumptions of Descartes. It includes, then, the thought of Descartes (*q.v.*), Spinoza (*q.v.*), Malebranche (*q.v.*), the Occasionalists (*q.v.*) and, more generally, any system emphasizing the openness of reality to the human mind, mathematical exactness in metaphysics, and the categorical ultimacy of a thought-extension dualism.

CARTHUSIANS.

An order of Christian monks, founded by St. Bruno in 1084 in France, devoted to a simple rule of life.

CARUS, PAUL. 1852–1919.

American philosopher. Born in Germany. Studied at Tübingen and taught at Dresden. Coming to America in 1885, he became editor of *The Open Court*, a periodical, which he developed into a publishing company specializing in philosophy. He founded *The Monist* in 1888.

CARVAKA (CHARVAKA).

Indian philosophical system of Materialism, traceable to the *Rgveda*. Its principal development came in 600 B.C. in the no longer extant *Brhaspati Sutra*. The doctrine of Materialism, also called *lokayata* (*q.v.*), has had many adherents since that time.

(1) The principles of all things are earth, air, fire, and water.

(2) That which cannot be perceived does not exist; to exist is to be perceivable.

(3) Intelligence is only body disposed in a certain manner and the soul is only the body as distinguished by intelligence.

(4) The only end of man is the enjoyment of sensual pleasure, and the avoidance of pain. Heaven and hell are the inventions of stupid men.

(5) The practice of religion has its sufficient explanation in providing a good living for the priests, and the authors of the *Vedas* were "buffoons, knaves, and demons."

(6) Even so-called universal ideas and relations are to be understood through perceptual connections, reinforced by memory. And this feature reduces the power of inference.

(7) The connection of cause and effect must be understood perceptually, also, and when we do so, its basis disappears

for we may perceive the two horns of a cow successively and one horn would not seem to be the cause of the other.

(8) Finally, neither the existence nor non-existence of anything can be firmly established.

CASO, ANTONIO.

Q.v. Latin American Philosophy (12).

CASSIODORUS.

Q.v. Rhetoric (11).

CASSIRER, ERNST. 1874–1945.

German philosopher. Born in Breslau. Taught at the universities of Berlin and Hamburg. On Hitler's rise to power he moved successively to England, Sweden, and then to the United States where he taught at Columbia and Yale. A representative of the Marburg School of neo-Kantian philosophy (*q.v.*).

Principal writings: *The Problem of Knowledge in the Philosophy and Science of Modern Times*, 4 vols. (vol. 4 T), 1906–20; *Substance and Function* (T), 1910; *Philosophy of Symbolic Forms*, 3 vols. (T), 1923–29; *The Individual and the Cosmos in Renaissance Philosophy* (T), 1927; *The Philosophy of the Enlightenment* (T), 1932; *The Platonic Renaissance in England* (T), 1932; *Determinism and Indeterminism in Modern Physics* (T), 1936; and the following works written in English: *An Essay on Man*, 1945; *The Myth of the State*, 1947.

(1) Cassirer's neo-Kantianism situates man's apprehension of reality in phenomena, and especially in experience as mediated by symbolic forms. This is evident in the definition of man as the "symbolizing animal."

(2) Tracing out the development of symbolic forms from mythical thought through art, mathematics, and the sciences in addition to philosophy, Cassirer found therein stages of mimetic, analogical, and symbolic expression.

(3) The initial stage is the stage of myth proper. Here the image is the reality; through the image, language becomes a self-contained world. Names are realities. To have the name is to have power over the thing. As cultural evolution continues, the power of myth diminishes while that of symbolic expression increases.

(4) Another way of making the point is to relate the contrast between religious

and mythical thinking on the one hand and scientific thinking on the other to a contrast between metaphor and concept. Scientific thinking is a tidy universalizing of ideas which lie side by side, or extend over each other in recognizable ways. Religious thinking is essentially metaphorical. The idea of the sacred is the concentration of a multiplicity of meanings at a point, *e.g.*, in the sacred tree. He seems to suggest that the poetic enterprise exercises that function in the modern world.

(5) In one sense the satisfaction of the philosophical quest lies in nothing more than satisfaction in the apprehension of the development of cultural forms. But beyond this there is for Cassirer, despite his strictures against Hegel, a sense in which what has occurred has occurred appropriately so that the norms and goals of various periods are self-justifying.

CASTE.

From the Latin *castus* ("pure" or "pious"). A term adopted by the Portuguese in the 16th century to denote the social system they found in India. The original Sanskrit term is *varna* ("color"); but the terms differentiate the lighter-skinned Aryan invaders from the darker native Dravidians, and since the highest caste, the *Brahmins*, reserved the role of religious teacher, in general, impurity is a consequence of contact with a lower caste, especially in relation to the preparation or consumption of food. The *Brahmin* must be concerned about such contact with respect to three lower castes, as well as the untouchable, the *Kshatriya* ("warrior class") concerning two, the *Vaishya* (merchant) with one, the *Shudra* only with the native untouchable, named by Gandhi the *harijan* ("children of god"). The term *jati* ("birth group" or "family") is sometimes used as a synonym of *varna*, or as a term for the sub-groups making up a *varna*. *Q.v. Aśramas*; Hinduism (4); *Laws of Manu* (2); *The Mahabharata* (3).

CASUALISM.

From the Latin *casus* ("fall," "accident"). Taken literally, although the usage tends to be obsolete, the doctrine that all things result from chance.

CASUISTRY.

From the Latin *casus*, meaning "case."

(1) In an earlier age the science, so-called, of resolving problems of ethical decision by applying to specific cases principles drawn from Scripture, canon law, traditions of the church, the laws of society, and the light of reason. Difficulties in accepting these bases as authoritative have rendered the discipline puerile for many of the contemporary philosophical traditions (*q.v.* Conscience 3–4; Toulmin 2).

(2) The term, fallen into disrepute, now refers to specious or sophistical reasoning with respect to law or ethics. *E.g.*, "No casuistry will persuade me that your cruelty was intended as an act of kindness."

CATECHISM.

From the Greek *katexein* ("teach by word of mouth"). A compendium of essential religious instruction arranged in the form of questions and answers. Although common to many religions, in Western usage the term refers to practices of Jewish, Eastern Orthodox, Roman Catholic, and Protestant religious instruction.

CATEGOREMATIC TERMS.

Q.v. William of Ockham (1).

CATEGORICAL IMPERATIVE.

Q.v. Kant (6).

CATEGORICAL PROPOSITIONS.

Q.v. Proposition (1).

CATEGORY.

From the Greek *kategoria*, composed of *kata* ("against") and *agoreuein* ("to assert"). The term came to mean an assertion, or predication, and then "an ultimate concept or form of thought" or "a major form of predication." Among systematic philosophers, categories have importance as the set of fundamental ideas in terms of which all other ideas can be expressed.

(1) Aristotle (*q.v.* 6) meant by categories that set of expressions capable of classifying all other expressions. His basic category was substance. In addition to substance he elaborated now six, then nine, other expressions of the set.

(2) Gilbert of Poitiers (*q.v.* 1) divided Aristotle's categories into two sets, one primary and the other secondary. This was regarded by many as completing Aristotle's analysis.

(3) Kant (*q.v.* 3) found his categories in a set of expressions exhaustive of the logical classification of judgments. Finding three such categories in each of four divisions—Quantity, Quality, Relation, Modality—Kant elaborated twelve categories in all.

(4) Hegel (*q.v.* 7) meant by categories the ideas which explicate reality. Using a triadic principle of generating these ideas, he derived something in the neighborhood of 272 categories of thought.

(5) Peirce (*q.v.* 2) held categories to be the most general terms into which experience can be divided. Alternatively, he held them to reflect the three types of predicates or relations into which logic can be divided. On both readings he found the same three basic categories, which he termed "firstness," "secondness," and "thirdness." On the first reading above these terms stand for "quality," "reaction," and "generality." On the second reading they stand for "monadic," "dyadic," and "polyadic" predicates or relations.

(6) Russell (*q.v.* 3) essentially substituted a theory of types for a theory of categories, the classificatory scheme for one language existing in a more abstract language. The development of metalanguages (*q.v.*) is a development of Russell's interest in this regard.

(7) Whitehead (*q.v.* 9) moved in a more traditional framework; he elaborated a set of 37 categories in whose terms it should be possible to explicate all experience. In his Categories of Existence the types of entities are set forth, while the Categories of Explanation detail the principles of their operation.

(8) Using the term "category" as a synonym of "word type," Ryle (*q.v.* 1) holds the enterprise of philosophy to consist of the making of category mistakes by some philosophers, and their correction by others, who better understand what they are about.

Also *q.v.* Chang Tung-Sun (3–4).

CATHARI.
  Q.v. Paulicians.

CATHARSIS.
  From the Greek *katharsis* ("purification"). Aristotle (*q.v.* 13) held that the function of tragedy is a purging of the viewer's emotions of pity and fear. Also *q.v.* Tragedy (1).

CATO, MARCUS PORCIUS. 95–46 B.C.
  Roman Stoic philosopher. Became tribune. His defense of the ancient free Roman state made it desirable for Caesar and the other triumvirs to rid themselves of him. In this connection he committed suicide under heroic circumstances, thus becoming the patron saint of Roman Stoicism. Finally Marcus Aurelius, himself a Stoic, gained the imperial throne.

CAUSA.
  Latin term meaning "cause." Among Latin phrases embodying the term the following are to be noted. *Causa cognoscendi* refers to the cause of our knowledge of an event, and is to be distinguished from *causa essendi*, the cause of the event itself. *Causa immanens*, referring to a change produced in an entity by its own activity, is to be distinguished from *causa transiens*, a change produced in an entity by another. *Causa sui* ("cause of itself") and *causa immanens* were used by Spinoza (*q.v.* 2) to refer to God as the one Being who is cause of Himself and needs no other in order to exist. *Vera causa* means "true cause." Newton spoke of *verae causae* as the causes which exist in nature, and are the true and sufficient explanations of things.

CAUSAL EFFICACY.
  Q.v. Whitehead (24).

CAUSE.
  From Latin *causa*. A term correlative to the term "effect." That which occasions, determines, produces, or conditions an effect; or is the necessary antecedent of an effect. The appropriate definition depends upon the point of view of the philosopher in question.

(1) An Eastern claim of the Sankhya (*q.v.* 6) system is that the condition of intelligibility is that every effect must pre-exist in its cause. Otherwise, anything could come from anything.

(2) In the East Buddha (*q.v.* 2) developed a concept of causation which he termed "dependent co-arising," (*q.v.*). Modern interpreters (*e.g.*, J. Macy, *Mutual Causality*, 1991) regard this type of causation

as relational and non-linear, although he intermixed psycho-physiological with physical causal factors.

(3) In the West, shortly after, Aristotle (*q.v.* 9) presented a four-fold analysis of causality in which he distinguished efficient, material, final, and formal causes. Later concepts of causality, at least until Hume, were derived from Aristotle's analysis, by omission.

(4) Buddha's concept of cause led to a dispute concerning momentariness in the early schools of Buddhism. The Sautrantikas (*q.v.*) found the elements of reality, psycho-physiological as well as physical, to self-destruct upon occurrence. Given the self-destruction no momentary event could lead to any other. Causation thus became sequential occurrence and nothing more. The Sarvastivadins (*q.v.*) held a somewhat less extreme version of the doctrine. The regularity interpretation of causation developed by the Sautrantikas was more extreme than that of Hume (*cf.* 11 below), but the Sarvastivadin inter–pretation somewhat less extreme.

(5) Nagarjuna (*q.v.* 2) argues that causation, due to its paradoxical nature, is impossible, and one among many appearances in the world.

(6) William of Ockham (*q.v.* 9) found efficient cause the most useful of Aristotle's four types, and perhaps began the common sense identification of cause with efficient cause.

(7) Hobbes (*q.v.* 1) identified causation with the transmission of motion, thus featuring efficient causality.

(8) For Geulincx (*q.v.* 3) God became the sole cause of the universe and practically the sole reality.

(9) This does not remove the value of, for instance, Locke's (*q.v.* 8) observation that the idea of cause probably originates in our sensed control over our bodies, the movement of our limbs following upon our inner volition.

(10) Leibniz' (*q.v.* 4) principle of sufficient reason represents an emphasis on formal cause, and the teleology of his system an emphasis on final cause.

(11) Hume's (*q.v.* 2–3) contribution to the discussion, finding the source of the necessity we attribute to causes in the constant conjunction of events, is widely admired.

(12) Kant's (*q.v.* 3) suggestion that causality is one of the *a priori* categories of the understanding infused by men into their interpretation of experience is less widely recognized in an age of common sense realism. For a parallel Eastern view *q.v.* Carvaka (7).

(13) Fichte (*q.v.* 2) regarded cause as a posited element of the world.

(14) Trendelenburg (*q.v.*), returning to Aristotle, emphasized final as well as efficient cause, finding this consonant with science.

(15) John Stuart Mill (*q.v.* 6), on this as well as a number of other points, reverted to Hume, defining cause as an invariable and unconditional antecedent.

(16) Petzoldt (*q.v.*) substituted the idea of "functional dependence" for that of cause.

(17) Whitehead's (*q.v.* 24) concepts, of causal efficacy, and of multiple causation, any present occurrence bearing relation—positively or negatively—to the entire antecedent universe, returned to the realist tradition.

(18) Ducasse (*q.v.* 1–2) distinguished four kinds of causal relations since either the physical or mental can be cause or effect.

(19) But the general tendency of our age is to equate the idea of cause with necessary and sufficient conditions. By a "necessary condition" we mean a condition in the absence of which no effect occurs. By a "sufficient condition" we mean a condition in the presence of which the effect always occurs. But a "sufficient condition" and a "necessary condition" are quite different since, *e.g.*, rain may be a sufficient condition for wet streets but not a necessary one, and citizenship may be a necessary condition for becoming president, but it is not a sufficient condition. From this standpoint, by "cause" would be meant either the "sufficient condition" or the "sufficient and necessary conditions."

CAVELL, STANLEY. 1926– .

Born in Atlanta (Ga.). Educated at Berkeley, U.C.L.A., and Harvard. Has taught at Berkeley and Harvard.

Principal philosophical writings: *Must We Mean What We Say?*, 1969; *The Senses of Walden*, 1972; *The Claim of Reason*, 1979; *Disowning Knowledge in Six Plays of Shakespeare*, 1987; *In Quest of the Ordinary*,

1988; *This New Yet Unapproachable America*, 1989; *Conditions Handsome and Unhandsome*, 1990.

(1) Shaped by Austin (*q.v*) and Wittgenstein, Cavell has applied their insights both as riposte to contemporary philosophers and to philosophy of culture.

(2) Taking the later Wittgenstein (*q.v.* 5–11) as providing a nonprofessionalizable method for bringing philosophy to an end over and over, philosophy becomes a personal endeavor to retain or regain one's balance despite the conceptual stumbling which occurs in us every day.

(3) The philosopher become skeptic, for example, sets the standards of knowledge so high that nothing counts as knowledge. The motivation for doing this is not, or not just, intellectual scrupulousness. Personal emotional problems are also a factor, *e.g.*, a prized self-image. For this reason what appears in philosophy as Skepticism occurs in literature as tragedy (his reference is to *Othello*).

(4) Similarly, Wittgenstein's dicussions of "criteria" rest not on evidence but on "claims to community," which are used to strengthen self-identity, reason, and community itself.

(5) For this reason the philosopher as critic joins artists and others as interpreters of human culture to the end of both objectifying and reflecting human subjectivity.

CELARENT.
Valid syllogism in EAE mood, first figure. *Q.v.* Syllogism (4).

CELSUS. 2nd cent. A.D.
A Platonic philosopher of dualistic tendency who held that the contact between man and God could occur only in the highest part of the soul, and whose belief in the divine transcendence was such that a hierarchy of spiritual beings was needed to be a bridge between God and the world. His book against Christianity was answered by Origen of Alexandria (*q.v.*). For Platonists of the same period *q.v.* Atticus and Nicostratus.

Principal writings: Fragments of his *The True Doctrine* survive.

CENSOR.
Q.v. Freud (3).

CERTAINTY.
From the Latin *cernere* and the Greek *krinein* ("to decide").

(1) Logical certainty is a property of valid conclusions in deductive inference (*q.v.* Logic), the property being simply that the conclusion follows necessarily from the premises. Since one is interested in true conclusions, however, it is necessary to have true premises as well as valid reasoning.

(2) Psychological certainty is a state of belief in the truth or falsity of a given proposition; and this state does not insure truth in one's conclusions, even should the latter be gained by valid reasoning.

CERUTTI, HORACIO.
Q.v. Theology of Liberation (9).

CESARE.
Valid syllogism in EAE mood, second figure. *Q.v.* Syllogism (4).

CETERIS PARIBUS.
Latin phrase meaning "other things being equal."

CHABARITES.
An Islamic (*q.v.* 6) school of thought espousing absolute fatalism.

CHAIN OF BEING.
Q.v. Aquinas (5); Lovejoy (2).

CHALCEDON, COUNCIL OF. 451 A.D.
Fourth Ecumenical Council of the Catholic Church. Reaffirmed Nicene and Constantinopolitan creeds, the Ephesine Formula of 431, and the Christological statement of the *Epistola Dogmatica* of Leo I. to Flavianus, patriarch of Constantinople. *Q.v.* Christianity (3); Christology (3).

CHALCHONDYLAS, DEMETRIOS.
Q.v. Florentine Academy.

CHALDEAN ORACLES.
Q.v. Oracles, Chaldean.

CHALLENGE AND RESPONSE.
Q.v. Toynbee (2).

CHAMPEAUX, WILLIAM OF.
Q.v. William of Champeaux.

CH'AN BUDDHISM.
Q.v. Zen Buddhism.

CHANCE.
From the Latin *cadere* ("to fall"), applying especially to dice and fortune. An uncalculated, and possibly incalculable, element of existence; the contingent as opposed to the necessary aspects of existence. Aristotle (*q.v.* 9) regarded chance events to be those occurring at the intersection of independent causal chains, *e.g.*, the unexpected meeting of a friend in the market-place. John Stuart Mill (*q.v.* 6) and Ardigó (*q.v.* 4) held the Aristotelian view. For Epicurus (*q.v.* 5) and Lucretius (*q.v.* 3) chance meant an uncaused happening, *i.e.*, the swerving of an atom by its own inner power. Cournot (*q.v.* 1, 4) and Peirce (*q.v.* 4) followed this interpretation. Also *q.v.* Necessity (5–9); Nagel (1).

CHANDOGYA UPANIṢAD (UPANISHAD).
Source of the famous saying: "*Tat tvam asi*" (*q.v.*), identifying the inner self and Brahman.

CHANGE.
The opposite of permanence, and one of the basic categorial ideas.
(1) Heraclitus (*q.v.* 2) held to the universality of constant change, explaining that it takes place by opposites. His example was the tension of the drawn bow.
(2) Parmenides (*q.v.* 5), Zeno (*q.v.* 4–5), and Nagarjuna (*q.v.* 3) argued for permanence and against the possibility of change.
(3) Aristotle (*q.v.* 8) distinguished three types of change: alteration, growth or diminution, and locomotion.
(4) Bergson (*q.v.* 4) and Whitehead (*q.v.* 9) made the category of becoming (*q.v.*) or process (*q.v.*) central to their philosophies.
(5) For Buddha (*q.v.* 6) all things are in flux.

CHANG TSAI. 1020–1077.
Chinese neo-Confucian philosopher. A native of Chang-An in Shense. Son of a magistrate. Received the "Presented Scholar" degree in 1057. Appointed magistrate in 1057, he became a collator in the imperial library in 1069; and in 1077 director of the Board of Imperial Sacrifices. From the latter two posts he resigned. His personal search described a circle from Confucianism through Buddhism, Taoism, and back to Confucianism.
Principal writings: *The Western Inscription* (T); *Correcting Youthful Ignorance* (T).
(1) Material force is identified with the great ultimate; *Yin* and *Yang* are regarded as aspects of material force, furnishing an opposition which constitutes the dynamism and balance of the universe. Material force is both "The Great Vacuity" and "The Great Harmony." In different modes of existence it is both a positive and a negative spiritual force following laws of growth and destruction.
(2) Making all of these identifications with force, Chang found it desirable to discard spiritualistic ideas of spiritual beings, spirits of the deceased, Buddhistic annihilation, and Taoist non-being.
(3) The principal idea of *The Western Inscription* is to extend the idea of *jen* as love to the entire universe, and to set all human relations in a cosmic framework of filial piety and respect.
(4) Evil results from the fact that one's physical nature, as differentiated, contains the possibility of excess, should one—by choice—depart from the mean.

CHANG TUNG-SUN. 1886–1979.
Chinese philosopher. A native of Chekiang. Self-educated. Editor of newspapers and magazines. University professor in Shanghai, Canton, Peking. Leader of the State Socialist Party. Imprisoned by Japanese during World War II. Post-war, he joined the Leftist Democratic League, 1949 and became a member of the Central Committee of the People's Government in Peking.
Principal writings: *Epistemological Pluralism* (T), 1932; *Knowledge and Culture*, 1946.
(1) Calling himself an Epistemological Pluralist, Chang held both the world we know and the knowing mind to be the result of construction, and yet in both cases there are elements of order and content which are not a result of construction.
(2) Syntheses occur continually both on the level of sensation and on the level of conception. Four levels are marked out: sensory fusion (on the level of sensation),

configuration (on the level of perception), unification (on the level of conception), regulation (on the level of universal categories).

(3) There is a natural progression from sensation to the other levels. The original perception leaves a trace which becomes attenuated into a sign; and the sign, when gaining the mobility of transfer to another person, is known as a symbol. The symbol, or concept, has, among its other characteristics, a property called "normalizing power." The concept with the strongest normalizing power controls, and reduces to its type, other similar concepts. So every concept becomes at once a group of related concepts. The level of sensation, however, retains the power of collapsing concepts by offering conflicting types. The most general level in this progression is the category.

(4) In the category one discovers that sensation is not the sole control over concepts, but that social needs also play a considerable role. "God," "Substance," "the Absolute," help provide the cohesive force needed in society. Thus, our most general ideas reflect not only the world, but the needs and conflicts of the society in which we live.

CHANNING, WILLIAM ELLERY.
1780–1842.

American religious leader. Born in Newport, Rhode Island. Educated at Harvard. A Unitarian minister, Channing found Calvinism immoral and Trinitarianism without Biblical or philosophical support. He is counted among the New England Transcendentalists (*q.v.* Transcendent 4).

CHAOS.

A Greek term, meaning "space," therefore, too, any gulf, chasm, abyss. For Hesiod it is the rude unformed mass of primal existence; for Genesis 1 the earth "without form and void." In Greek mythology, also the scarcely personified parent of night and death. In both East and West, order and chaos are opposed, so that chaos is disorder. In the early *Vedas, rita* (*q.v.*) is the principle of order, protected by the gods and fostered by ritual correctness. In Hinduism Vishnu is the principle of order and Shiva (*q.v.* Vaiṣṇavism 3) that of disorder. In

Śhaktism (*q.v.* śakti, Vaiṣṇavism 4) there are numerous goddesses of destruction as well as goddesses of beneficence. In Western mysticism Jacob Boehme (*q.v.* 1, 11) sensed the order of things contingently poised against the *ungrund* or abyss, a principle of both freedom and destruction. Berdyaev (*q.v.* 1, 2) finds an *ungrund* over against God, allowing divine creation, and human freedom.

CHAOS THEORY.

A mathematical approach to the less predictable aspects of the universe. Although chaos theory is traced back to Newton's method of approximations, and Cantor's method of establishing infinity (by exclusion), the field has burgeoned in the 20th century with the work of the French mathematicians Gaston Julia and Pierre Fatou; meteorologist Edward Lorenz, and physicist-mathematician Mitchell Feigenbaum in the United States. This work was brought together by Benoit Mandelbrot. Contributing to the success of the area in this century has been the power of computers to make the necessary calculations, and of computer graphics to display them.

Selected writings: Edward Lorenz, "Deterministic Nonperiodic Flow," 1963; "The Mechanics of Vacillation," 1963; "The Problem of Deducing the Climate from the Governing Equations," 1964. Mitchell J. Feigenbaum, "Universal Behavior in Nonlinear Systems," 1981. Benoit B. Mandelbrot, *The Fractal Geometry of Nature*, 1983. James Gleick, *Chaos: Making a New Science*, 1987. Also the video, "Fractals, an animated Discussion with Edward Lorenz and Benoit B. Mandelbrot," 1990.

(1) Science concentrated, initially, on those features of the world, such as eclipses, where high predictability was possible. Systems with low predictability, such as cloud formations, weather systems generally, earthquakes, river systems, the formation of snow flakes, the branching of blood vessels, and coastlines were ignored, for the time.

(2) Among the differences between the two types of system is that in high predictability systems a single parameter is under investigation, initial conditions can be specified precisely, the influence of random external events can

be isolated or safely ignored, and the governing laws are known. These are ideal, and exceptional, conditions.

(3) Chaos theorists argue that traditional science abstracted a very thin slice from the more plentiful rough, pocked, pitted, tangled, and strewn aspects of existence. In the more ordinary situation many parameters have to be dealt with simultaneously, initial conditions cannot be precisely specified, external events intrude into the system, making a difference, and covering laws, if they exist, are not well known. Consequently, predictability is low. This means to chaos theorists only that ordinary systems are more complex than those on which scientists had initially concentrated.

(4) Part of nature can be described in terms of the regular, integral figures of Euclidean geometry, where the equations are linear, having definite once and for all solutions, and mappable by way of Cartesian coordinates. The figures of chaos theory are, however, irregular, and belong to what Mandelbrot called fractal (Latin, *frango, frangere*, "to break, fracture, fraction") geometry. Fractal geometry is the geometry of irregular figures, and of fractional equations. The equations of fractal geometry are nonlinear, meaning that they do not have definitive solutions but are recursive, iterating themselves fractionally, producing endless approximations with a difference of scale.

(5) The explicit formulae of linear differential equations are typical of ordinary geometry; the approach by approximations of nonlinear differential equations is typical of fractal geometry, which is called the geometry of chaos. Nonlinear systems are also called dynamical systems and chaos theory is also called dynamical systems theory.

(6) The endless approximations of chaos theory derive from a property of self-similarity shared by fractals (as the objects of fractal geometry are called). The properties of a part of a cauliflower repeat the features of the whole cauliflower; so do the properties of a part of a part. The same is true of clouds, earthquakes, rivers, and coastlines. How far down self-similarity goes is an open question. In the case of coastlines, bays and estuaries repeat as the scale is reduced, and one would never run out of coastline since the length

of the coastline depends on the length of the measuring rod. Halve the rod and the length triples, given an irregular coastline. Make the measuring rod small enough and the coastline becomes infinite in length (presumably continuing to display coastline bay and estuary features).

(7) Mandelbrot discovered that he could produce a set of equations which contained all of the Julia sets, as well as the Feigenbaum bifurcations. The simple, nonlinear equation consisted of producing a number by taking a starting number, multiplying it by itself, and adding the original number, where "c" is the starting number and "z" the target number "$z \rightarrow z^2 + c$." The target number becomes the starting number and the calculation goes on. A further calculation is made to determine whether the target number is going to run away to infinity, or "stick around." If it sticks around it is a member of the Mandelbrot set and plotted on the complex plane (stretching from minus infinity to infinity both east to west and north to south, with zero at the center). When these are plotted, the images of the set—resembling sea horse tails, shells, fireworks in the sky, clouds, coastlines with cliffs—string together, repeating on a diminishing scale. They can be sampled in the video on fractals.

(8) Chaos theory concerns itself with a state of things intermediate between the formless chaos (*q.v.*) of Genesis I where nothing happens, and the determinism of linear equations whose events are predictable. In the "deterministic chaos" of nonlinear equations, randomness emerges from order, and out of randomness a new yet similar underlying order appears.

(9) The repeating images are explained in terms of the "Lorenz attractor," also called the "strange attractor." An attractor is the most stable point in "phase space" (so called because we are now thinking of phases of transition). In the case of a plumb bob, revolving in a tight circle, the attractor is the point in the center of the circle where the bob will come to rest. The equation in this example would be linear. Instances of chaos require at least three strange attractors, and are nonlinear. The images of the Mandelbrot set are produced by the churning equations apparently being drawn toward one

attractor, and then another. The process would end by coming to rest in one of the attractors. If the process is unending, provisional solutions and images continue to be produced.

(10) Chaos theorists believe that much of nature has fractal order, and can be decoded by simple rules. DNA would be capable of specifying the bifurcation and development of blood vessels, which also occurs in river systems. Both vascular and nervous systems appear to be chaos ruled.

(11) The unpredictability of chaotic systems indicates that they are not deterministic in the sense of Laplace's (*q.v.* 3) strong predictability. They appear to be compatible with Peirce's (*q.v.* 4) view of chance (*q.v.*) as an objective feature of the universe. Whether human freedom is a human corollary of objective chance, as Peirce believed, remains an open question.

CHARACTER COMPLEX.

The term for "sense-datum" (*q.v.*), employed in the movement of Critical Realism (*q.v.* 1).

CHARACTERISTICA UNIVERSALIS.

Q.v. Leibniz (11).

CHARISMATA.

From the Greek *charisma* ("gift"). In early Christianity the term applied to the "gifts of the Spirit," especially the gift of "speaking in tongues." Paul (*q.v.* 7) carefully broadened the application of the term, insisting that love is the very highest *charisma*.

CHARVAKA.

Q.v. Carvaka.

CHASIDISM.

Q.v. Hasidism.

CH'ENG HAO. 1032–1085.

Chinese philosopher. Born in Honan. A neo-Confucianist, he was one of the Ch'eng brothers, two outstanding 11th-century Chinese philosophers. His father was a state official. He received the "Presented Scholar" degree in 1057, and served as keeper of records, magistrate, and undersecretary of the heir apparent, and councilor to the emperors Shen-Tsung and Che-Tsung.

Principal writings: *Surviving Works; Additional Works; Collection of Literary Works by Ch'eng Hao; Pure Words.*

(1) Ch'eng took *li* as the primary principle, finding it everywhere and in all things as a law of nature, uniting the multiplicity of the world, and serving as the reason for all creativity and production.

(2) But principle and mind are one. Thus, through sincerity, seriousness and inner mental cultivation, principle is served, and the virtue of humanity (*jen*) which removes the distinctions of self and other is achieved.

(3) Sincerity includes wisdom, humanity, and courage. And *jen* is to be understood as involving righteousness, propriety, wisdom, and faithfulness. All of these qualities one is to make part of oneself.

(4) One arrives at the point where, eliminating all opposition between self and not-self, the whole universe becomes one organic unity, continually productive, creative, and engaged in processes of growth.

CH'ENG I. 1033–1107.

Chinese philosopher. Born in Honan. A neo-Confucianist he was the younger of the Ch'eng brothers. He received the "Presented Scholar" degree in 1059. He declined many high offices. In 1086 he began a series of lectures before the emperor on Confucian principles which continued for 20 months. He was supervisor of the Directorate of Education in 1087, 1092, and 1100. He had many followers, the most famous being Chu Hsi.

Principal writings: *Surviving Works; Additional Works; Collection of Literary Works by Ch'eng I; Commentary on the Book of Changes; Explanations of the Classics; Pure Words.*

(1) Like his brother, Ch'eng Hao, Ch'eng I stressed the importance of principle (*li*), holding to its unitary presence in all things, a unitary principle with a plurality of manifestations.

(2) But the universe is essentially productive, and the productive force in man is called *jen*. *Jen* includes the virtues of righteousness, propriety, wisdom, and faithfulness. In following *jen* man achieves unity with all things, thus overcoming evil.

(3) The achievement of unity means understanding all that is in terms of the principles they exhibit. This includes self-

knowledge, or self-cultivation, and the investigation of things.

CH'I.
Q.v. Li (2).

CHIH-I. 538–597.
Chinese philosopher. A native of Chekiang, and founder of the T'ien-T'ai school of Buddhist philosophy, named after the mountain where Chih-I taught. The outstanding Buddhist priest of his time, Chih-I was frequently invited to lecture by various dynastic rulers, *e.g.*, in the palace at Nanking, 583. Chih-I held that the elements of ordinary existence have their basis in illusion and imagination. What exists in reality is the one Pure Mind, called True Thusness. This exists changelessly and without differentiation. Enlightenment consists of understanding one's unity with the Pure Mind.

CHIH TAO-LIN. 314–366.
Chinese Buddhist philosopher. *Q.v.* Seven Early Chinese Buddhist Schools (3).

CHILIASM.
From the Greek term *chiliad* meaning "thousand." The millenarian doctrine that Christ would soon return to initiate a thousand-year reign on earth prior to the end of time.

CHINESE "LOGICIANS," THE.
A 4th-century B.C. school of philosophers carrying the traditional Chinese concern with rectification of names in the direction of logical analysis. One of the smallest of the schools, the Logicians were without influence after their own time. Hui Shih (*q.v.*) and Kung-Sun Lung (*q.v.*) were the school's most noted thinkers.

CHINESE PHILOSOPHY. 6th cent. B.C. to the present.
Until recent years the factors related in the philosophical history of this culture have been Confucianism, Taoism, Moism, the Logicians, Legalism, the *Yin Yang* School, and Chinese Buddhism.
(1) For Confucianism *q.v.* Confucius, Mencius, Hsün Tzu.
(2) For Taoism *q.v.* Taoism and Lao Tzu, Yang Chu, Chuang Tzu, Huai-nan Tzu.
(3) For schools neither Confucian nor Taoistic, *q.v.* Mo Tzu, Chinese Logicians,

the Legalist School, and the *Yin Yang* School. For the last of these references *q.v. Yin* and *Yang* (2). These names mark developments between the 6th and 2nd centuries B.C.
(4) For neo-Taoism beginning in the 3rd century B.C. *q.v.* Wang Pi, and Ho Yen.
(5) For the mingling of these influences, especially Confucianism and Taoism, beginning in the 2nd century *q.v.* Huai-nan Tzu, Tung Chung-Shu, Wang Ch'ung, Lieh Tzu, and Kuo Hsiang.
(6) For the development of Chinese Buddhism beginning in the 3rd and 4th centuries A.D. *q.v.* Kumarajiva, Seng-Chao, Chi-Tsang, Hsuang-Tsang, and Chih-I. Also *q.v.* the Hua-Yen School, the T'ien-T'ai School, and the school of Ch'an (Zen Buddhism).
(7) For the development of neo-Confucianism from the 8th century A.D. to the present *q.v.* Han Yu, Li Ao, Chou Tun-i, Shao Yung, Ch'eng I, Ch'eng Hao, Lu Hsiang-Shan, Chu Hsi, Wang Yang-Ming, Tai Chen, K'ang Yu-Wei, T'an Ssu-T'ung, Chang Tung-Sun, Fung Yu-Lan, and Hsiung Shih-Li.

CHINESE ROOM, THE.
Q.v. Searle (5).

CHISHOLM, RODERICK M. 1916– .
American philosopher. Born in N. Attleboro, Mass. Educated at Harvard. Has taught at the University of Pennsylvania. Currently, and since 1947, at Brown.
Principal writings: *Perceiving*, 1957; *Realism and the Background of Phenomenology*, 1960; "Contrary-to Duty Imperatives and Deontic Logic," 1963; "The Ethics of Requirement," 1964; *Theory of Knowledge*, 1966; *The Problem of the Criterion*, 1973; *Person and Object*, 1976; *The First Person*, 1981; *The Foundations of Knowing*, 1982; *Brentano and Intrinsic Value*, 1986; *On Metaphysics*, 1989.
(1) Accepting Brentano's (*q.v.* 2) notion of the "intentional inexistence" of the psychical, Chisholm holds that sentences are intentional when they use substantival expressions in such a way that neither the sentence nor its contradictory implies the existence or non-existence of that to which the sentence applies. And he criticizes both positivism and behaviorism for their inability to explicate

and use the notion of intentionality.

(2) Taking propositions and events to be sub-categories of states of affairs, he presents an ontology in which the final stuff of the universe is made up of everlastingly existent states of affairs.

(3) Holding that we need both the thing perceived, and appropriate observation conditions to gain appearance statements, Chisholm argues that the phenomenalist thesis (thing statements can be translated into appearance statements) is not true. Indeed, appearance statements are rewritten in his "adverbial theory of sensing" so that, for example, "he senses a red appearance" is to be read as "he is appeared redly to."

(4) On the problem of the criterion of knowledge, Chisholm holds that it is nondefective justified true belief.

(5) This led to his becoming a "foundationalist" in epistemology, the foundation of knowledge consisting of self-presenting propositions (following Meinong) about one's present state of mind.

(6) Concerning the problems of deontic logic (*q.v.*) Chisholm noted the presence of "contrary-to-duty imperatives" seemingly leading us to cases where we ought not to do what we ought to do. To handle such cases Chisholm placed a concept of "requirement" at the base of this branch of logic which, operating in the manner of Ross' (*q.v.* 2) "*prima facie* duties," points to the requirement in a given situation.

CHIT.
Q.v. Sat (1); Hinduism (5b).

CHI-TSANG. 549–623.
Chinese philosopher. A native of Nanking. He became a Buddhist monk and a Buddhist philosopher. Honored in his lifetime by Chinese emperors, he continued and systematized the work of Seng-Chao, carrying on the development of the Three-Treatise or Madhyamika School of Mahayana Buddhism founded by Nagarjuna, known in China as San-Lun. The doctrine was dominant in China from the 4th to 7th century, and declined in the 9th century.

Principal writings: *Treatise on the Two Levels of Truth* (T in part); *Profound Meaning of the Three Treatises* (T in part).

(1) Following Nagarjuna's middle path of eight-fold negation, Chi-Tsang argues that the *Dharmas,* or elements of existence, are not instances of being, or non-being, nor both being and non-being, nor neither being nor non-being.

(2) The constructive point is to arrive at an "emptiness" free from names and character, incapable of being verbalized or thought.

CHOICE.
Q.v. Freedom.

CHOICE, ZERMELO'S AXIOM OF.
Q.v.. Zermelo.

CHOMSKY, A. NOAM. 1928– .
American linguistic philosopher. Born in Philadelphia. Educated at the University of Pennsylvania. Teaches at M.I.T.

Principal philosophic writings: *Morphophonemics of Modern Hebrew*, 1951; *Syntactic Structures*, 1957; *Current Issues in Linguistic Theory*, 1964; *Aspects of the Theory of Syntax*, 1965; *Cartesian Linguistics*, 1966; *Topics in the Theory of Generative Grammar* (with M. Hale), 1966; *Language and Mind*, 1968; *Studies on Semantics in Generative Grammar*, 1972; *The Logical Structure of Linguistic Theory*, 1975; *Reflections on Language*, 1975; *Essays on Form and Interpretation*, 1977; *Barriers*, 1986; *Knowledge of Language*, 1986; *Language and the Problems of Knowledge: the Managua Lectures*, 1988.

(1) Chomsky believes that linguistic theory has as its basic task the provision of criteria for choosing among alternative grammars. Departing from the rigidities of Bloomfieldian linguistics (*q.v.* Semantics 5) Chomsky moved in the direction of generative grammar. The idea of generative grammar is that the grammar of a language should generate all and only the sentences of that language. Formalizing several systems of the grammar, he rejected the finite state and phrase structure alternatives as inadequate, and proposed transformational grammar in their place. The mark of transformational grammar is the presence in it of transformational rules governing phrase structures and allowing more possibilities in the generation of sentences.

(2) Distinguishing between "competence" and "performance," Chomsky relates the first to the total set of sentences generated by the grammar of a language.

By "performance" he means the utterances produced under normal conditions by the native speakers of a language.

(3) Distinguishing likewise between the surface structure of a language and its deep structure, Chomsky regards, for example, the grammatical subject of a sentence as relating to the surface structure of a language, and the logical subject as relating to its deep structure.

(4) Regarding philosophical semantics as internal to the study of linguistics, he operates on the view that the meanings of sentences are derived mainly from the deep structure of the language by rules of semantic interpretation. It is the base of the grammar, then, that accounts for the semantically relevant options.

(5) Chomsky finds B.F. Skinner's behaviorism inadequate on the ground that the stimulus-response categories of this alternative fail to account for the human ability to form new sentences.

(6) Chomsky speaks of substantive and formal universals. By the former he means the recurrent phonological, syntactic, and semantic elements of language. By the latter he means the principles determining the form of the rules in the grammars of particular languages, and the manner in which the rules are to be applied.

(7) Finally, arguing that the principles of universal grammar are highly restrictive, much more so than can be explained by the influence of common external stimuli or common physiological structures, Chomsky concludes that humans are genetically endowed with a highly specific "language faculty," which is to be understood as a "mental organ" whose growth is post-natal, developing (like other organs) both structure and function. He regards this conclusion to be in harmony with the rationalist tradition in philosophy, and especially on the side of those who use "innateness" in their explanations of mental functioning.

CHOU TUN-I. 1017–1073.

Chinese neo-Confucian philosopher, and pioneer of neo-Confucianism. Native to Tao-Chou in Hunan. The famous Ch'eng brothers were his students.

Principal writings: *An Explanation of the Diagram of the Great Ultimate* (T in part); *Penetrating the Book of Changes* (T in part).

(1) The Great Ultimate by activity gen- erates *yang*; at the limit of activity tranquillity ensues, and *yin* is generated. The two modes alternate, and water, fire, wood, metal and air arise; then Heaven and Earth arise, the male and female elements; the two principles provide for endless production, and transformation. In all of this man arises; there are five moral principles to his nature: *jen* (humanity), righteousness, *li* (propriety), wisdom, and faithfulness. Among men the sage appears, conducting his life by the principles of the mean, correctness, humanity, and righteousness.

(2) The one and the many balance each other in the world. The many are ultimately one, and the one is differentiated into many; each has an important place in the scheme of things.

CHRIST, JESUS. 4 B.C.–29 A.D.

Founder of the Christian religion. Born in Bethlehem; childhood in Nazareth. Began his ministry at the age of thirty, or at thirty-two. His ministry lasted, then, one to three years. On charges of blasphemy and sedition he was tried and executed on the authority of Rome.

(1) Jesus' teachings center on the kingdom of God. In one phase of his thought the kingdom is to come gradually as the people of Israel repent. In the second phase, which must have occurred later, the kingdom is at hand, and it is urgent that one now repent. His language is that the *kairos* (*q.v.* 1), a special term for time, is fulfilled. The following points apply to both phases.

(2) Life is to be lived in the light of an absolute perfection which requires of persons a similar, but proportional, perfection. They are to live with utter integrity—called purity of heart; they are to live with a whole-heartedness which excludes pride of any kind; they are to be sensitive to others—to their sufferings, hopes, and needs—sensing the oneness of oneself and others, and ministering to human needs. They are to love one another.

(3) The point of such behavior is, not only that it is right and pleasing to God but also, that it establishes a new form of human community. Similarly, one is simply to ignore human actions and responses motivated in any other manner; one accepts persecution, turns the other

cheek, and loves one's enemy. The rule
is: Do unto others as you would have
others do unto you. In so acting one
denies the authority, and in a sense the
reality, of the false forms of community.

(4) It is as though the spiritual order
overlies, and is part of, the physical order so that a deepening of purpose, a
reversion to the reality of oneself in childhood, for example, is enough to effect a
change from one to the other.

(5) The spiritual order is to gain full
sway over the world. Jesus sensed a personal role in the bringing of the kingdom in a temporal sense.

(6) The center of this spiritual reality
is God, whose providential care controls
the world in any case. As we are to love
one another so we are to love God; the
approach to God is through the values
of the deepest and most spiritual family
life. The appropriate name for God is
Father.

(7) To depart from these high standards of thought, word, and deed is to
sin. And though we face a kind of judgment now through the winnowing of life,
there is to be a final judgment at the
coming of the kingdom.

(8) Jesus clearly affirms the continued
survival of the individual person beyond
this life; and it is often said that his is a
doctrine of the resurrection of the body.
But if this is the case, there are other
passages such as the "many mansions"
reference, and the resurrection scene itself, whose natural interpretation is the
immortality of the soul.

Also *q.v.* Christology; Strauss; Renan;
Schweitzer (3); Schillebeeckx (4, 6).

CHRIST, THE PHILOSOPHY OF.
Q.v. Erasmus (1).

CHRISTIANITY.
The major religion of the Western
world, its founder being Jesus Christ. This
religion, and Western philosophical traditions, mutually influencing each other,
account for many of the peculiar characteristics of Western culture, including
its ideal of progress, its doctrine of temporal passage, its ethical meliorism, and
the development of science and technology.

Its scriptures are the Old and New
Testaments, the latter representing the
prophetic fulfillment of the former.

A. Its history has led to its division
into three main groups—the Roman
Catholic Church, the Eastern Orthodox
Church, and the many communions
known as Protestant, having repudiated
the authority of the Roman Catholic
Church. This history is divisible into the
following stages:

(1) The Apostolic Age (1st cent. A.D.).
The Christ figure emerges, partly through
the work of Paul (*q.v.*) and the Christian
Church is separated from the Jewish
people.

(2) 100–313 A.D. The Church strengthens its position in the Roman Empire until
Constantine (313 A.D.) gives it official
status. The age witnessed a struggle of
the Church with Gnosticism (*q.v.*). Important theologians of the period were
Irenaeus, Origen, and Tertullian.

(3) 313–590. From Constantine to
Gregory I the Church gains supremacy,
and formulates its creeds. For the determination of doctrine the following councils were held: Council of Nicaea, 325
with the Nicene Creed; Council of Constantinople (I), 381; Council of Ephesus,
431; Council of Chalcedon, 451; Council
of Constantinople (II), 553. Monasticism
developed partly as a rational solution
to the ascetic excesses of the devout in
the first three periods we have mentioned.
The heresies of Arianism, Nestorianism,
Monophysitism, and Pelagianism were
identified and combatted.

(4) 590–800. Gregory I to Charlemagne;
Christianizing of Germanic peoples; loss
of Egypt, Africa, and Spain to the Muslims. Council of Constantinople (III), 680;
Council of Nicaea (II), 787.

(5) 800–1073. Charlemagne to Pope
Gregory VII. Growing power of the papacy. Council of Constantinople (IV), 869;
1054, separation of Eastern and Western
branches of the Church over the "*Filioque*"
of the Nicene Creed.

(6) 1073–1294. Gregory VII to Boniface
VIII, pope at zenith of power in Europe.
Four Lateran Councils, 1123, 1139, 1179,
1214; two Lyon Councils, 1245, 1274. The
seven Crusades designed to win back the
Holy Land, 1096–1270. The rise of Scholasticism with Anselm, Thomas Aquinas,
and Duns Scotus. 1232, Inquisition
founded.

(7) 1294–1517. Boniface VII to the posting of Luther's theses. Council of Vienne,

1311; John Wycliffe (*q.v.*); Council of Constance (John Huss, *q.v.*), 1414–18; Council of Basel, 1431; Fall of Constantinople, 1453; Fifth Lateran Council, 1512–17.

(8) 1517–1648. Luther's theses to Peace of Westphalia. Work of Luther, Calvin, Zwingli. Council of Trent, 1545–63.

(9) 1648 to the present. Development of both Catholic and Protestant Churches, English Act of Toleration, 1689. Vatican Council, 1869. Ecumenical Movement, increasing in strength since the early 1900's. Philosophy continues to have a role in shaping the religious life—through Thomism, recognized since the Vatican Council as the official philosophical standpoint of the Roman Catholic Church; and through the interest of Protestant theologians in philosophy.

B. Among the philosophers who have expressed an opinion on Christianity we include the following:

(10) Tindal (*q.v.* 2), calling himself a Christian deist, held that Christianity is to be interpreted in terms of its moral teachings and, so interpreted, it is as "old as creation."

(11) Holbach (*q.v.* 7) held Christianity to be a superstition fostered by priests.

(12) For Herder (*q.v.* 3) Christianity, like other religions, is an attempt to explain the world. It differs from primitive religions, however, in its level of moral exaltation.

(13) Saint-Simon (*q.v.* 4) argued for a distinction between a "new Christianity" centered in ethics, and a "degenerate Christianity" centered in dogma.

(14) For Hegel (*q.v.* 21–22) Christianity is the absolute truth in picture form, and the proof of Christianity is the entire Hegelian system.

(15) Reinhold Niebuhr (*q.v.* 2) combined the insights of neo-Orthodoxy in a view he termed "Christian realism."

CHRISTIAN SITUATIONISM.

Q.v. Situation Ethics.

CHRISTOLOGY.

Doctrines concerning the person of Christ. The subject held much importance in the early centuries of Christianity's development, and may be said to have dominated the early councils of the Church (*q.v.* Christianity). The subject is most easily organized in relation to the councils.

(1) Prior to the Council of Nicaea (*q.v.*) the following doctrines, many of them influenced by Neoplatonism, were current: *Ebionism* (*q.v.*): Jewish in origin; denial of the incarnation; Jesus as a human being solely. *Docetism* (*q.v.*): Gnostic in origin; Christ divine and his human nature a phantasm. Basilidians (*q.v.*): Christ becomes divine at the moment of baptism. *Alogi* and *Artemonites*; Jesus as human, but a divine power energizing within him. *Patripassianism* (*q.v.*): the same God being Father and Son, God himself was crucified. *Sabellianism* (*q.v.*): the Son is one of three modes in which the divine substance became manifest.

(2) *Arianism* (*q.v.*): the Christology in opposition to which the Nicene Creed (holding Christ to be begotten, not made, and of one substance with the father) was formulated. Arius held that Christ possessed both divine and human natures, was created at a definite time by an act of God's will, that this time was prior to creation, that Christ is subordinate to God, and of a different substance.

(3) Christologies leading to the Council of Chalcedon, 451: *Apollinarianism* (*q.v.*): Christ possesses a human body, but the Logos (*q.v.*) replaces soul in his case. *Nestorianism* (*q.v.*): Christ has both human and divine natures, existing side by side without intercommunication. *Eutychianism* (*q.v.*): Christ possesses the two natures, but his human nature is completely informed and transformed by his divine nature. All of these views were condemned, and in their place the Nicene doctrine was restated and elaborated.

(4) Christologies leading to the Council of Constantinople, III, 689 A.D.: *Monophysitism* (*q.v.*): Christ has one nature, the human being a contingent quality of the divine. *Monothelitism* (*q.v.*): since Christ is one person he has but one will. Constantinople opposed these doctrines, condemning the latter while affirming and developing the stand taken at Chalcedon.

(5) Protestantism (*q.v.*) in its various branches and representatives, contains many Christologies, some of them quite close to the official Catholic position, others similar to some of the heretical positions listed above.

CHRYSIPPUS. c. 280–206 B.C.

Greek philosopher. Born in Cilicia.

Studied in Athens under Cleanthes and Zeno. The third leader of the Stoics, and head of the School from 232 to 208, Chrysippus systematized the doctrine of Zeno and Cleanthes. Not only was it given to him to organize the system of Stoicism, but to defend this new system against the criticism of the Academy; he performed this task with great skill for Diogenes Laertius said of him: "If the gods use dialectic, they can use none other than that of Chrysippus." He also said that without Chrysippus Stoicism would not have existed. In the process of defending the Stoic position he produced an immense literature. The general doctrines of Stoicism are treated under Zeno, Cleanthes, and Stoicism (*q.v.*).

Principal writings: He is credited with some seven hundred and fifty treatises; fragments survive in J. von Arnim, *Stoicorum veterum fragmenta*, 3 vols., 1903–24.

(1) Credited with creating the Stoic logic, Chrysippus went beyond Aristotle in anticipating the propositional calculus (*q.v.*). The five valid inference schemata (called "indemonstrables"), recognized by Chrysippus which now form part of that calculus are:

(a) If the first, then the second; but the first; therefore the second.

(b) If the first, then the second; but not the second; therefore not the first.

(c) Not both the first and the second; but the first; therefore not the second.

(d) Either the first or the second; but the first; therefore not the second.

(e) Either the first or the second; but not the second; therefore the first.

(2) He contributed, also, to definitions of modality (*q.v.*). According to Cicero, Chrysippus followed Philo of Megara's definition of the possible as the self-consistent. According to Diogenes Laertius he defined the possible as that which will be true when external circumstances don't prevent its being so, and the necessary as that which is true, and cannot become false either in itself or through external circumstances.

(3) Chrysippus likewise dealt with the problem of the criterion for truth, relating it both to "presentations" and to "common notions" which all men bear in their awareness.

(4) Chrysippus also contributed some thoughts on good and evil as essential

contraries related to rationality and irrationality. In the larger sense evil is that which opposes the world reason. The path to the good is therefore life according to reason, both one's own and that of the universe.

(5) Regarding God as a material being endowed with reason and extending throughout the universe, Chrysippus also identified God with fire, and in the Heraclitean cycles of the world year (*q.v.* Heraclitus 8) held that all things are consumed into fire, *i.e.*, into God, as the cycle moves to its end and new beginning.

CHUANG TZU. Bet. 399–295 B.C.

Chinese Taoistic philosopher. Little is known of his life. Supposedly a minor state official, he is said to have refused the Post of prime minister in order to retain his freedom. Ignored by Confucian thinkers, Chuang Tzu has had great influence on the development of Taoism and Zen Buddhism.

Principal writings: *The Chuan Tzu* (by Chuang Tzu and his followers.)

(1) From one point of view, there is a relativity of knowledge, such that a thing is so or not so because it is claimed to be so or not so. But this makes opposites true together, and the deeper fact is that opposites produce, imply, and are identical with each other.

(2) From another point of view, the whole of nature expresses continuous flux, and all of life is the result of development from simpler forms. From a deeper point of view although there is a myriad of things, their order is one.

(3) One can relate to both of these aspects of things by relating oneself to the Tao. This is possible through vacuity, tranquillity, mellowness, quietness, and taking no action (*wu wei*). When one takes this attitude the Tao is able to operate in all things, adjusting them to each other. And the Tao is in all things, even the lowest, such as excrement and urine.

(4) At the beginning of things is nonbeing. From non-being the One originates, allowing things their individual character and virtue. The One is the operation of destiny and divides into *Yin* and *Yang*, producing all things through movement and rest. When one cultivates his own nature he returns to virtue. Through virtue he unites with the One, becoming vac-

uous and receptive, and hence great and superior.

(5) Once he dreamed that he was a butterfly. Suddenly awaking, he could not tell if he was a man dreaming he was a butterfly or a butterly dreaming he was a man. "This is called the transformation of things."

CHUBB, THOMAS. 1679–1746.

English deist. Born at East Harnham. Self-educated. Regarding himself as a Christian deist, Chubb believed in natural religion, and free will, while remaining skeptical of prophecy, miracle, special revelation, and the efficacy of prayer. His work was referred to by Voltaire and his view of free will was "refuted" by Jonathan Edwards.

Principal writings: *The Supremacy of the Father Asserted*, 1715; *A Discourse Concerning Reason*, 1731; *The True Gospel of Jesus Christ Asserted*, 1732; *The True Gospel of Jesus Christ Vindicated*, 1739.

CHU HSI. 1130–1200.

Chinese Confucian philosopher. A native of Anhui. Spent most of his life as temple guardian in one locality or another. His writings dominated Chinese, Korean, and Japanese thought for centuries.

Principal writings: *Collection of Literary Works by Chu Hsi; Complete Works of Chu Hsi; Classified Conversations of Chu Hsi*; and anthologies, including *Supplement to the Reflections on Things at Hand*.

(1) Synthesizing the basic doctrines of Confucian philosophers into a coherent unity, Chu Hsi's arrangement of the Confucian classics, stressing the *Analects*, and the *Book of Mencius*, the *Great Learning*, and the *Doctrine of the Mean* were the basis of the Chinese civil service examinations from 1313 to 1905. The elements of this synthesis were: the Great Ultimate, principle, material force, nature, investigation, and humanity.

(2) How was the synthesis achieved? The Great Ultimate is principle in its totality. Principle and actualization require each other; and actualization involves both principle and material force. The former relates to a thing's universality and the latter to its individuality. The nature of mind is its principle, while the nature of a physical thing is its principle plus its material force. Investiga-

tion results from both observation and intuition, its success resting upon the identity in principle between man's mind and the mind of the universe. But the highest understanding depends upon this connection in another way, centering on *jen*. Chu Hsi combines two earlier views, interpreting *jen* both substantially and functionally. As substance, *jen* is the character of man's mind; as function it is the principle of love. It is the specific virtue of "benevolence," and the general virtue which is the basis of all goodness. The synthesis retained, of course, many Confucian and neo-Confucian doctrines, often developed in a novel manner.

(3) He retained, for example, the neo-Confucian balanced system in which the opposites of the One and Many, the principles of *Yin* and *Yang* both continuously apply to reality. The Great Ultimate requires both principle and material force, but is essentially and primarily principle. But while principle remains one, its manifestations are many; principle remains absolute while its manifestations are caught up in the relativities of temporal existence; thus, although one finds principle and material force always together, principle has priority.

(4) This priority gives mind priority over the rest of nature since mind and principle are intimately related. The human problem in making principle effective in an ethical sense requires a kind of clarification of what one is: this requires us to control our selfish desires, to be "serious" within ourselves, to allow mind and principle their own clarity and creativity.

CHUNG YUNG.

Q.v. Doctrine of the Mean.

CHURCH.

Interpretation of the nature of the Christian Church, including its relation to the state, varies with the branch or denomination of Christianity under consideration. Reference should thus be made to Catholicism, Protestantism, Lutheranism, etc. for such considerations. Among specific references to the Church, however, we include the following:

(1) John Huss (*q.v.*) defined the Church as "the body of the predestinate."

(2) Sebastian Franck (*q.v.*) declared al-

legiance to the "church universal" (*q.v.*), rather than to any specific church.

(3) Hooker (*q.v.* 3) viewed church and state as aspects of the same government with the power of the state extending over the church.

(4) Pufendorf (*q.v.* 2) held that the supreme jurisdiction of religious matters rests in the state, while ecclesiastical power resides in the Church.

(5) Jefferson's (*q.v.* 6) Virginia Act for Religious Freedom became a model for other states, leading to the separation of church and state by 1834.

(6) Gioberti (*q.v.* 3) looked upon the Church as the consummation of the ideal of perfection, and hence essential to man's well-being on earth.

CHURCH, ALONZO. 1903– .

American logician. Born in Washington, D.C. Professor of mathematics, Princeton University and U.C.L.A.; editor since 1936 of *The Journal of Symbolic Logic*. An important contributor to the foundations of formal logic, Church developed the role of the logical *lambda* of the calculus and contributed the proof in 1936 that the calculus of elementary quantification theory or, as he terms it, the pure functional first-order calculus, is not decidable (*q.v.* Decidability and Logic 22). Following Gödel he identified mechanical calculability with recursiveness. Such an identification is known as "Church's thesis." Furthermore, he is among those who understand by "proposition" the common content of the given sentence, and its translations into all other languages.

Principal writings: "Alternatives to Zermelo's Assumption," 1927; "A Note on the Entscheidungs Problem," 1936; "An Unsolvable Problem of Elementary Number Theory," 1936; "The Calculi of Lambda Conversion," 1941; *Introduction to Mathematical Logic*, 1944 (rev. ed., 1956).

CHURCH FATHERS.

Q.v. Patristics.

CHURCH OF ENGLAND.

The term refers, first of all, to the historic British Catholic Church established in the 2nd and 3rd centuries A.D., and strengthened by the arrival of the 6th century St. Augustine in 594. The term refers, second and currently, to the independent English Catholic Church which emerged after Henry VIII's break with the pope in the 16th century. This was a break, communicants claim, with the pope but not with the Catholic faith. In 1534 Parliament named the English monarch head of the English Church. The Book of Common Prayer (1549, 1662) and the Thirty-Nine Articles (1571) shape the Church's liturgy and doctrine. Church governance is episcopal in form, divided into the two provinces of Canterbury and York, headed by two archbishops, that of Canterbury having preeminence. Spreading through the world with the expansion of British interests, the Church of England developed into what is now known as the Anglican Communion. The Church of England stands as the mother church of this communion whose presence is world-wide and especially marked wherever the British flag has flown. Canterbury continues to exercise a special influence. Problems of the Anglican Communion are dealt with at the Lambeth Conference, held every ten years at Canterbury.

CHURCH UNIVERSAL.

A term applying to one or more of the following groups: the whole body of Catholic believers; the whole body of Christian believers without regard to denominational boundaries; the ideal church, a community of the faithful, crossing denominational boundaries, and including only real and not nominal believers.

CHWISTEK, LEON. 1884–1944.

Polish philosopher. Born in Cracow. Taught at Cracow and Lvov. A member of the Warsaw Circle (*q.v.*), Chwistek attempted to solve the problem of impredicative definitions (*q.v.* Paradox 8) as a nominalist and a constructivist. Centering his concept of semantics on the foundations of mathematics, he worked at developing a system of "rational metamathematics" which, apparently, resolves the problem at the price of great complexity.

Principal writings: "The Theory of Constructive Types" (T), 1921; *The Limits of Science* (T), 1935; *Philosophical and Logical Writings* (P), 2 vols., ed. Pasenkiewicz, 1961–63.

CICERO, MARCUS TULLIUS. 106–43 B.C.
Roman eclectic philosopher. Through his translations and expositions of Greek philosophy he made the insights of Plato, Aristotle, and the leading schools—the Skeptics, Stoics, and Epicureans—available to the Roman people, while the gracefulness of his style lent added charm to the material.

Principal writings: *On the Nature of the Gods* (T); *On Duties* (T); *On Divination* (T); *On the Greatest Good and Evil* (T); *On Friendship* (T); *On the Republic* (T); *On Laws* (T).

(1) If there is one word which might be taken to characterize the philosophy of Cicero that word is "moderation." He espoused a moderate skepticism, rejecting both dogmatism and extreme skepticism in theory of knowledge. He espoused a Stoic ethic while moderating the rigor of its asceticism. He insisted on the importance of traditions while seeing the equal importance of their progressive transformation; he wished to see peaceful change without violence.

(2) He pictured men living in a harmonious universe controlled by a rational deity. The decisions of this being, built into the universe, constitute a natural law which stands above the positive laws of human societies, and gives them measure.

(3) Holding Rhetoric to be not merely the art of speech but an art of thought related to all of the sciences, and especially to philosophy, Cicero regarded systems of persuasion not so founded as empty verbalism. In his elaboration of the techniques of effective speech he held that the good orator must be a good man, and the perfect orator a perfect man.

CIEZKOWSKI, AUGUST VON.
Q.v. Praxis (3).

CIRCULAR ARGUMENT.
Q.v. Fallacies (20).

CIRCULUS IN DEFINIENDO.
Q.v. Vicious Circle (2).

CIRCULUS IN PROBANDO.
Q.v. Vicious Circle (1).

CIRCULUS VITIOSUS.
Q.v. Vicious Circle.

CITTA.
Sanskrit term meaning "mind stuff." A key term in the interpretation of the ego in the Yoga system (*q.v.* Yoga 3).

CITY OF GOD.
Q.v. St. Augustine (13). The city of God stands in tension to the city of man, two opposed principles in history, the former relating to eternity, the latter to time.

CIVIL DISOBEDIENCE.
Q.v. Thoreau; Gandhi (1); Passive Resistance.

CIVILIZATION.
Often regarded as synonymous with "culture" (*q.v.*), Spengler (*q.v.* 2) distinguished between the two, finding civilization the final stage in a society's development. Alfred Weber (*q.v.*) distinguished between the "civilization process" and the "culture process," regarding the former as continuous and the latter as sporadic.

CLARKE, SAMUEL. 1675–1729.
English philosopher. Born in Norwich. Cambridge educated, he studied Descartes and mastered the system of Newton, whose *Optics* he translated. Taking orders in the Church of England, he was Chaplain to Queen Anne, and held several rectories. He published extensively on theological and religious matters. His correspondence with Leibniz has been published as *The Leibniz-Clarke Correspondence*.

Principal writings: *A Discourse Concerning the Being and Attributes of God*, 1704–5; *Scripture Doctrine of the Trinity*, 1712.

(1) He contended against Leibniz and in agreement with Newton, before Newton had written his famous *Scholium* on the infinity of space and time, that space and time are attributes of an infinite, immaterial, and spiritual Being.

(2) His proof of God rests on the following propositions: (a) something has existed from eternity; (b) it is immutable, and independent; (c) it is self-existent, a necessary being; (d) its essence is incomprehensible to us, but we can demonstrate some of its attributes, such as: its eternality, its infinity and omnipresence, its unity, its intelligence, its possessing the power of liberty and choice, its infinite power, infinite wisdom, infinite goodness, justice, truth and all other moral perfections.

(3) His ethical theory rested on a concept of fitness, which allows us to expect a "mutual consistency" among ethical actions, and a set of self-evident relations between situations and the actions they demand. God has arranged this unity among actions just as he arranged unity among the laws of nature.

CLASS.

From the Latin *classis*. There is no single all-encompassing term in Greek (*q.v.* 1 below). Any multiplicity of entities sharing a common characteristic. The idea of classes arose in the development of logic (*q.v.*), and is present in all major cultures (*q.v.* Nyaya, Chinese Logicians).

(1) For Aristotle (*q.v.* 4–5) classes appear in the form of genus, species, property, difference, and accident. These came to be known as the predicables (*q.v.*), Porphyry (*q.v.* 1) assisting in their canonization. Similarly, while Aristotle originated syllogistic logic (*q.v.* Syllogism) medieval scholars participated in its development.

(2) A class is taken "in extension" when it is defined in terms of the individual entities in the multiplicity (*q.v.* Extension 2). A class is taken "in intension" (*q.v.*) when it is defined in terms of the characteristics distinguishing it from other classes. The interpretation of the syllogism, beginning in Aristotle's logic of predication, tended toward an emphasis on classes taken in extension (*q.v.* Euler Diagrams and Venn Diagrams).

(3) The most recent developments in the idea of classes lie in mathematics, and in symbolic logic in the algebra of classes, including the concepts of class inclusion and exclusion, class complement (*q.v.* Negation 1), class sum, class product, the universal class (*q.v.*), and the null class (*q.v.*). For these concepts *q.v.* Logic (23); Set Theory (1–8).

CLASS STRUGGLE.

Q.v. Marx (5); Marxism (1b).

CLAUBERG, JOHANNES. 1622–1665.

German philosopher. One of the first to introduce the term "Ontology" (*q.v.* 1) into philosophy, he was one of the Occasionalist philosophers (*q.v.* Occasionalism).

Principal writings: *Elements of Philosophy or Ontosophia*, 1647; *Cartesian Defense*, 1652.

CLEANTHES. 331–232 B.C.

Greek Stoic philosopher. Born in Assos. A disciple of Zeno, the founder of Stoicism, in Athens, and after Zeno's death, head of the school. Chrysippus (*q.v.*) was one of his disciples.

Principal writings: Only fragments remain, the most substantial being his *Hymn to Zeus*.

(1) He divided philosophy into six divisions rather than Zeno's three: dialectic, rhetoric, ethics, politics, physics, and theology.

(2) He held the sun to be God's abode, the seat of the vivifying fire and intelligence of the universe. He also said that the world is God.

(3) He held that the vitality of the soul after death depends upon its vitality in this life.

CLEARCO. c. 340 B.C.

Greek philosopher. An Aristotelian or Peripatetic. Wrote interpretations of Plato, as well as treatises on the emotions, and on many aspects of the natural sciences.

CLEMENT OF ALEXANDRIA. c. 150–215.

Christian theologian. Probably born in Athens. Presbyter in the church of Alexandria, he followed Pantaenus as head of the Catechetical school. Teacher of Origen, and the Alexander who became Bishop of Jerusalem.

Principal writings: *Protrepticus, A Hortatory Address to the Greeks; The Teacher Stromata (Patch-Work)*.

(1) The aim of Christianity, like the aim of Greek philosophy, is a nobler, holier life; but what the philosophers glimpsed imperfectly is perfectly revealed in Christ, the *Logos*.

(2) God the Father is the Absolute, the Monad, devoid of all characteristics because superior to sensible distinctions.

(3) Through Christ men are to pass from faith through love, to knowledge. In the process they gain such self-control that they are free from passion, and give no thought to pleasure, becoming the perfect Gnostic.

(4) Not only individual men, but the world, too, goes through stages of development in preparation for Christianity.

(5) Philosophy comes to the Christians directly from God, and to the Greeks indirectly by way of the human reason.

Philosophy is a testament to the Greeks, preparing them for Christianity, just as the Law prepared the Hebrews.

(6) The faults of Greek philosophy lie in its incompleteness. The instrument of Christian belief is needed for the sifting out of truth. The true Gnostic is the Christian whose knowledge is enlightened by the *Logos* and illumined with love. The Christian should use the tools of dialectic in the passage from faith to knowledge mentioned above.

CLIFFORD, W.K. 1845–1879.

English philosopher. Born in Exeter. Educated at Cambridge. Taught at Cambridge and King's College, London.

Principal writings: *Lectures and Essays*, (ed. F. Pollock), 2 vols., 1879; *Mathematical Papers* (ed. H.J. Smith), 1882; *The Common Sense of the Exact Sciences* (ed. K. Pearson), 1885.

(1) The ethics of belief compels one to withhold acceptance of a statement unless all the evidence points to its truth.

(2) Distinguishing between "objects" which may be part of one's consciousness and "ejects" which cannot be part of one's consciousness, Clifford held the world to be composed of "ejects." He held ejects to be "mind-stuff" and to possess the quality of feeling.

CLITOMACHUS. 157–110 B.C.

Greek philosopher. Born in Carthage, he came to Athens at the age of 24, studying principally under Carneades, the Skeptic, whose views he disseminated in some 400 treatises, and whom he succeeded as head of the New or Third Academy in 129 B.C.

Principal writings: Almost nothing of his treatises is left. Cicero expresses a debt to Clitomachus' treatise *On the Suspension of Judgment*.

COELESTIUS.

Q.v. Pelagius.

COESTABLISHED HARMONY.

Q.v. Swedenborg (2).

COGITABILITAS, PRINCIPLE OF.

Q.v. Crusius (1).

COGITATIO.

Latin term for "the faculty of thought or reflection." The term was used by Spinoza (*q.v.* 6) to designate, along with extension, the two attributes of God known to man.

COGITO, ERGO SUM.

A Latin phrase meaning, "I think, therefore I am." The famous first certainty of Descartes (*q.v.* 2), turning around the thrust of skepticism. The argument was anticipated by the *Si fallor, sum* ("If I am deceived, then I exist") of St. Augustine (*q.v.* 4) in *The City of God*. Campanella (*q.v.* 1–2) used a similar approach. One's only certainty is that of one's own existence; but upon analysis this contains knowledge of both the world and God.

COGNITION.

From the Latin *cognitio* ("knowledge" or "recognition"). The term refers both to the act or process of knowing and to knowledge (*q.v.*) itself. Competing theories of knowledge are the subject matter of epistemology (*q.v.*). Cognition involves perception, memory, intuition, and judgment.

COGNITIVE SCIENCE.

An interface discipline directed toward the exploration of intelligent systems. Its subject matter centers on representation both in human cognition, and in computer simulations of human intelligence. Energized by the computer revolution of the 1960's, the fields from which cognitive science draws include cognitive anthropology; computer science (AI, *q.v.*); theoretical linguistics; mathematics of dynamical systems; neurological biology; cognitive and developmental psychology; and philosophy (by virtue of its traditional subject matter in epistemology and philosophy of mind).

Q.v. Folk Psychology.

COGNOSCENDUM.

From the Latin *cognoscere* ("to know"). Any object of a cognition whether veridical, fictive, abstract, or ideal.

COHEN, HERMANN. 1842–1918.

German neo-Kantian philosopher. Born in Coswig. Professor, University of Marburg. Founder of the Marburg School of neo-Kantianism (*q.v.*).

Principal writings: *Kant's Theory of Experience*, 1871; *Kant's Foundation of Aesthetics*, 1884; *System of Philosophy* (3 vols.): *Logic of Pure Knowledge*, 1902; *Ethics of Pure*

Will, 1904; *Aesthetics of Pure Feeling*, 1911.

(1) Opposing the notion of any "givens" in knowledge, Cohen dispensed with the concept of Kant's thing-in-itself. In his view the process of thinking provides content as well as form. Hence, science is simply a production of the scientific community through the ages, and there is nothing behind it.

(2) Philosophy and knowledge as such develop from the categories of the understanding into the forms of culture, and Cohen sets himself the task of providing an analysis of these forms. He does this by applying Kantian analyses to the three areas of logic, ethics, and aesthetics.

(3) Logic is for him an elaboration of the categories of the physical and mathematical understanding.

(4) Ethics is a formal science of the moral categories, resting on the pure will and the idea of obligation.

(5) Aesthetics is a formal science of the categories of pure feeling.

COHEN, MORRIS RAPHAEL. 1880–1947.

American philosopher. Born in Russia. Emigrated to America in his youth. Professor at the College of the City of New York.

Principal writings: *Reason and Nature*, 1931; *Law and the Social Order*, 1933; *An Introduction to Logic and Scientific Method* (with Ernest Nagel), 1934; *A Preface to Logic*, 1944; *The Meaning of Human History*, 1947; *Reason and Law*, 1950.

(1) Believing that progress in philosophy depends on clearly formulating problems of manageable scope, he opposed dogmatism both in its rationalistic and empiricistic forms.

(2) Holding that science in its progress discovers objective relations in the flux of experience, the philosophical task becomes one of setting the framework for this movement.

(3) The rules of logic, for instance, represent invariant relations for all possible objects (thus he supported logical realism), while scientific laws are invariant only in specialized domains.

(4) In this, and in many other connections, he found a principle of polarity philosophically indispensable, reducing apparent contradictions to balancing contrasts.

COHERENCE THEORY OF TRUTH.

Q.v. Epistemology (2–5); Truth (1, 4 and *passim*).

COHN, JONAS. 1869–1947.

German philosopher. Born in Görlitz. Taught at Freiburg. Worked closely with the Heidelberg School of neo-Kantianism (*q.v.* Neo-Kantianism 4), and was strongly influenced by Rickert (*q.v.*).

Principal writings: *General Aesthetics*, 1911; *Theory of Dialectic*, 1923; *Science of Value*, 3 vols., 1932–33.

COINCIDENTIA OPPOSITORUM.

Latin phrase meaning "coincidence of opposites," a principle utilized by Nicholas of Cusa (*q.v.* 2).

COLBY, K.M.

Q. v. Artificial Intelligence (2).

COLERIDGE, SAMUEL TAYLOR. 1772–1834.

English poet. Born in Devonshire. Attended Cambridge.

Principal prose writings: *Biographia Literaria*, 1818; *Aids to Reflection*, 1825; and *Confessions of an Inquiring Spirit* (posthumously), 1840.

(1) In the popular mind he recovered his Christian faith after passing through rationalism, Unitarianism, and German critical and transcendental philosophy. And, indeed, he was—by his own testimony—successively under the influence of Voltaire, Lessing, Socinianism, Schelling, and orthodox Christianity.

(2) Whether the poles be Unitarianism and pantheism, or orthodox doctrine and transcendental Neoplatonism, Coleridge's thought would seem to represent in the main a version of Schelling's philosophy.

(3) He distinguished between "fancy" and "constructive imagination," relating the former to instances of less sustained control, somewhat random associations, and the latter to an "esemplastic" power to shape details into unity according to a controlling plan.

(4) Imagination is both projective and receptive. All things result from combinations of its two phases. Also, *q.v.* I.A. Richards.

COLET, JOHN

Q.v. Platonism (9).

COLLECTIVE.

Q.v. Probability (10).

COLLECTIVE REPRESENTATIONS.

Q.v. Emile Durkheim.

COLLIGATION.

From the Latin *col* ("together") and *ligare* ("to bind").

(1) For Whewell (*q.v.* 1) the placing of isolated information under a general conception. The manner in which an elliptical orbit organized separate observations of planetary position was cited by Whewell as an example of colligation.

(2) J.S. Mill pointed out that every instance of induction is colligation, although some instances of colligation, *e.g.*, those involved in immediate or intuitive knowledge, may not be induction.

(3) Peirce (*q.v.* 8) held the term to its literal meaning and associated the term with deduction rather than induction, holding that in deduction one colligates premises, and then determines what can be derived from them.

COLLINGWOOD, ROBIN GEORGE. 1889–1943.

English philosopher. Born at Cartwell Fell. Student, fellow, professor at Oxford University. Influenced by Cook Wilson and Prichard. Eminent in the archaeology and history of Roman Britain.

Principal writings: *Speculum Mentis*, 1924; *Essay on Philosophical Method*, 1933; *The Principles of Art*, 1938; *An Essay on Metaphysics*, 1940; *The Idea of Nature*, 1945; *The Idea of History*, 1946.

(1) Collingwood's view of the nature of philosophy changed between the writing of his *Essay on Philosophical Method* and his *Essay on Metaphysics*. In the former work, philosophy is a transmutation into systematic form of the contents of human knowledge. Philosophy differs from science in that its concepts overlap each other, requiring special methods of approach and the using of special problems.

(2) In the *Essay on Metaphysics* it is the function of philosophy to bring to light the absolute presuppositions of human thought in one or another period of history.

(3) Each field of human experience—art, religion, science, history philosophy—contains a partial aspect of the truth. Each is by itself one-sided, although for Collingwood the historical perspective has in the end more validity than the others.

COMBINATORY LOGIC.

An approach to logic substituting function symbols for variables. *Q.v.* H.B. Curry.

COMENIUS, JOHN AMOS. 1592–1671.

Moravian philosopher. A pastor and bishop of the Moravian Brethren, Comenius' most important insight concerned educational reform. He emphasized student participation, logical interconnection of subject matter, and close correlation between educational content and the mental maturity of the student. He was the first to teach languages through culture and conversation. Internationally known as an educator, he spent several years in Sweden at the invitation of the government, preparing an educational plan for Swedish schools. He believed in universal education as a means to world reform.

Principal writings: *The Door of Languages Unlocked*, 1631; *The Labyrinth of the World* (T), 1631; *The Great Didactic* (T), 1657; *The Way of Light* (T), 1668.

COMMISSIVES.

Q.v. Searle (2).

COMMON NOTIONS.

From the Latin *notiones communes*. This in turn is Cicero's translation of the Greek phrase *Koinai ennoiai*, used by the Stoic philosophers. The concept held that all men possess a common set of basic ideas serving as the starting point of knowledge (*q.v.* Stoicism 1). The notions, not literally innate, included ideas of good, evil, and of God's existence. Herbert of Cherbury (*q.v.* 2) was an adherent of the view, using the Latin *notitiae communes*. The view has some affinities with Common Sense Realism (*q.v.*).

COMMON SENSE REALISM.

The view that we are able to perceive the external world directly, and that sense-data (*q.v.* Sense-datum) either do not exist or play a subordinate role in perception. *Q.v.* Realism (4, 6, 10). The view was presented by Thomas Reid (*q.v.*), and Dugald Stewart (*q.v.*), although an early anticipation of the position is to be found in Philo of Larissa (*q.v.*). Also *q.v.* Royer-Collard; G.E. Moore (1).

COMMUNISM.

From the Latin *communis* ("common," "universal," "public"). A social structure where all things are held in common.

According to Aristotle, communism was first advanced by Phaleas of Chalcedon and Hippodamus of Miletus.

(1) It was first given systematic form, however, in the *Republic* of Plato (*q.v.* 5e) where communism is to characterize at least the governing class and—when he speaks of starting society over again—one interpretation is that communism is then to characterize all of society.

(2) Advocated during the French Revolution by François Babeuf (1760–1797), the doctrine bore for a time the name, "Babouvism."

(3) The term is today associated primarily with the work of Marx (*q.v.*) and Engels (*q.v.*) who regarded communism as the final stage of social development, a state to be reached after socialism (*q.v.* 6) has been achieved. In the canons of Marxist doctrines (*q.v.* Marxism 1) society began with a "primitive communism" and will end with the "withering away" of the state. To reach this goal the stages of revolution and the "dictatorship of the proletariat" must occur.

COMMUNITY OF INQUIRY.
Q.v. Peirce (13).

COMMUNITY OF INTERPRETATION.
Q.v. Royce (7).

COMMUTATION.
The logical or mathematical operations whose result remains unchanged although the sequence of operations is changed. Many arithmetical and algebraic operations are commutative. Conjunction, disjunction, equivalence, and many other operations are commutative in the Propositional Calculus (*q.v.* 14); and in the algebra of classes (*q.v.* Logic 23) there are comparable operations. An instance from the Propositional Calculus would be that "p and q" is equivalent to "q and p."

COMMUTATIVE LAW.
Q.v. Commutation; Propositional Calculus (14).

COMPENSATION, PRINCIPLE OF.
Q.v. Emerson (4).

COMPETENCE.
Q.v. Chomsky (2).

COMPLEMENT.
For the distinction between a class and its complement *q.v.* Negation (1).

COMPLETENESS.
Along with Decidability (*q.v.*) and Consistency (*q.v.*) one of the basic concepts of contemporary metalogic. A calculus or system is complete when (1) each of its wellformed formulae, or their negates, is a theorem of the calculus; or (2) when any well-formed formula can either be proved in the system or else introduces inconsistency into it. Gödel (*q.v.* 1-2, 4) demonstrated that with respect to mathematical and logistic systems Completeness and Consistency are not compatible.

COMPLEX CONSTRUCTIVE AND DESTRUCTIVE DILEMMAS.
Q.v. Dilemma.

COMPOSITION, FALLACY OF.
Q.v. Fallacies (4).

COMPOSSIBILITY.
A Leibnizian principle of coherence defining a possible world, and the possible coexistence of its contents. *Q.v.* Leibniz (9).

COMPREHENSION.
A term used by John Stuart Mill (*q.v.* 10) to signify what is usually called Intension (*q.v.*). Also *q.v.* Logic (16); C.I. Lewis (4d); Connotation (7).

COMTE, AUGUSTE. 1789–1857.
French philosopher. Born in Montpellier. Briefly attended the École Polytechnique in Paris. Secretary to, and decisively influenced by, Saint-Simon with whom he worked from 1817 to 1824. The founder of the Positivistic Philosophy, he began his first series of public lectures on Positivism in 1826. They were interrupted by mental derangement lasting almost two years. The lectures were renewed in 1828, and the first volume of the course appeared in 1830. In later life Comte advocated, alongside his Positivism, a religion of humanity with the object of worship symbolized by the female form and with busts of humanity's benefactors in the chapels, in whose honor there were to be festival days, according to a Positivist calendar.

He is credited with having coined the term "altruism."

Principal writings: *Course on the Positive Philosophy* (T) 6 vols., 1830–42; *System of Positive Polity* (T) 4 vols., 1851–54; *Catechism of Positivism* (T), 1852; *The Subjective Synthesis*, 1856.

(1) Every science, and every society, must pass through theological and metaphysical states or stages, on the way to the positive, scientific stage which is their proper goal. In the theological stage explanations are given in terms of the gods. In the metaphysical stage explanations are given in terms of the most general abstractions. In the scientific stage explanations consist of correlating the facts of observation with each other.

(2) One field of study after another has reached the scientific stage, the simpler and more abstract before the more complex and concrete. The order of development has been mathematics, astronomy, physics and chemistry, and biology (including psychology). The one area still to be developed is sociology. Each science goes through the three stages, and each depends upon those preceding it in the order. It follows that sociology, and social relations, will have the longest theological and metaphysical stages.

(3) But the key to progress in society is intellectual development. And this development must secure for society the triumph of altruism over egoism. To bring intellect and feeling together a religion of humanity is needed as the crown of the Positivist stage.

(4) One of Comte's most significant contributions lay in his shifting the focus of analysis from the state to society. He was one of the first to hold an organic view of society, arguing that a society can no more be decomposed into individuals than can a surface into lines, or a line into points.

(5) In one sense, however, the organic structure of society is a goal to be achieved. Some periods of society have been characterized by order (*e.g.*, the feudal period); other periods by progress (*e.g.*, Protestantism through the French Revolution). The twin ideals of order and progress will be synthesized in the dawning age of science. In this stage the individual ideals of the period of progress—toleration, liberty, individual

conscience—will be replaced by a shared adherence to scientific law.

CONATUS.

From Latin *conari* meaning "to attempt." The term refers to an inborn desire or endeavor. In Spinoza's philosophy all things are animated by *conatus*, the desire to perpetuate their being. *Q.v.* Spinoza (4-5).

CONCEPT.

From the Latin *con* ("together") and *capere* ("to seize or tame"). An idea (*q.v.*) as distinguished from a percept (*q.v.*) or sensation (*q.v.*). Perhaps "sensation" is the better term to use for contrast, inasmuch as perception (*q.v.*) is normally construed to include both percepts (or sensations) and concepts. Whatever term is used, the line between the two types is in borderline cases quite uncertain. For some (*e.g.* Locke, *q.v.* 4) the distinction between the two depends on generality; for others (*e.g.* Hume, *q.v.* 1) the distinction is drawn in terms of vividness. The alternative positions with respect to concept are identical to the basic positions concerning universals (*q.v.*) and are extensively treated under that heading. In addition to the spectrum of positions from realism (*q.v.*) through conceptualism (*q.v.*) to nominalism (*q.v.*), the Kantian view—interpreting concepts as schema (*q.v.* Kant 3, 11c)—deserves special mention. The functions (*q.v.*) of logic and mathematics are instances of the interpretation of concepts as schema of various sorts.

CONCEPTUALISM.

The position with respect to universals (*q.v.*) that they exist as entities in the mind but have no extra-mental existence. The position stands between the extremes of Nominalism (*q.v.*) and Realism (*q.v.*). The position of Conceptualism is extremely difficult to distinguish from some versions of Nominalism on the one hand, and from moderate Realism on the other. Any philosopher listed as a Conceptualist might be assigned and probably has been assigned elsewhere either to Nominalism or Realism. A case can be made, however, that the following hold the position of Conceptualism with respect to universals: Abelard (*q.v.* 1–3 and Universals 13), Hugh of Saint Victor (*q.v.* and Universals 15), John of Salisbury (*q.v.*), Locke (*q.v.* 4 and Universals 25), possibly Berkeley (*q.v.* 2 and Universals 26), possibly Reid (*q.v.* 2 and Universals 29), Kant (*q.v.* 3, 11 c and f, and Universals 30), John Stuart Mill (*q.v.* 1, 10, and Universals 32), and possibly Quine (*q.v.* 3 and Universals 42).

CONCILIAR MOVEMENT.

A movement within the Roman Catholic Church asserting the authority of councils in church matters. Among philosophers, Marsilius of Padua (*q.v.* 4) and William of Ockham (*q.v.* 16) advanced conciliar principles. The movement came to fruition in the Council of Constance (*q.v.*), which asserted that conciliar authority is derived from Christ and is binding over the pope.

CONCOMITANT VARIATIONS METHOD OF.

Q.v. Mill, John Stuart (4).

CONCRETE UNIVERSALS.

Q.v. Hegel (6); Bradley (4); Bosanquet (2); Royce (7); Croce (3); possibly Blanshard (1); Universals (31, 34).

CONCRETISM.

Q.v. Masaryk (3); Kotarbinski (1).

CONCUPISCENCE.

Q.v. Aquinas (7).

CONDILLAC, ETIENNE. 1715–1780.

French philosopher. Born in Grenoble. Educated at Saint-Sulpice and the Sorbonne. He took holy orders but became a philosopher and, indeed, one of the Encyclopedists. A friend of Rousseau and a disciple of Locke, his views were very popular in France during his time, temporarily supplanting the position of Descartes. He was tutor to the young Duke of Parma, Louis XV's grandson, and elected to the French Academy in 1768.

Principal writings: *Essays on the Origin of the Human Understanding*, 1746; *Treatise on Systems*, 1749; *Treatise on Sensations*, 1754; *Treatise on Animals*, 1755; *Course of Study for the Instruction of the Prince of Parma*, 13 vols., 1769–73.

(1) Knowledge begins with sensations and there are no innate ideas. But even though all ideas originate in experience, judgments imply a judger; and hence one must grant the existence of soul, "the simple and indivisible subject of various perceptions."

(2) In his "fictions of the statue," Condillac proposed the gradual complication of the statue's world until it reached our own in subtlety and complexity. Unstop the nostrils, and confront our statue's original awareness with a rose. For it the world will consist of the aroma of rose. Replace this with a sample of asafoetida. Now the world is a plurality of qualities, containing contrast. Memory has been stimulated, and expectation will follow. Pleasure and pain, the basis of value, have also appeared, the smell of the former being pleasant, and that of the latter unpleasant.

(3) Condillac found in habit the basis of all intellectual functions, including attention, recall, comparison, judgment, imagination, and recognition. Through habit desires become passions, and collections of sensations become things.

(4) Through repeated association signs become attached to things, and to each other, allowing the intellect to develop, and allowing our reason to proceed in the absence of the things signified. He distinguished three classes of signs: accidental signs, natural signs, and conventional signs. It is the last class, instituted by man, which has the most importance, lying at the base of science, and providing the possibility of progressive series making mathematics possible.

(5) Because we know only our own thoughts, strictly speaking, there can be no proof of an external world. But in shrinking from unpleasant sensations, and moving toward pleasant sensations, one becomes aware of one's own body. The next step is to discover the difference between one's own and other bodies. Let one press one's hands together. One will experience a sense of resistance along with two sensations. Let one press one's hand against a foreign body. One will experience a sense of resistance, and one sensation. The missing sensation locates an external object.

CONDITIONAL STATEMENT.

In the Propositional Calculus (*q.v.* 19) the name given to the binary connection "if ... then," often symbolized by the horseshoe, "⊃." "If it rains then the streets will be wet" would be written "it rains ⊃ the streets will be wet." The general form of the connection is "p⊃q." The truth table for the conditional statement shows statements of this sort to be true in all save the case where the antecedent is true and the consequent false. *Q.v.* Truth Tables (3). Also *q.v.* Counterfactual Statement.

CONDORCET, JEAN ANTOINE. 1743–1794.

French philosopher. Born in Ribemont. Educated at the College of Navarre. A prominent member of the group of Encyclopedists. An excellent mathematician, he was made a member of the French Academy in 1769. An early supporter of the Revolution, siding with the Gironde, he was condemned to death by the Jacobins and went into hiding, writing out at this time his philosophy of history as progress. Captured, he died in prison, possibly a victim of poisoning.

Principal writings: *Essay on the Application of Analysis to the Probability of Majority Decisions,* 1785; *Life of Turgot,* 1786; *Life of Voltaire,* 1787; *Sketch for a Historical Picture of the Process of the Human Mind* (T), 1794.

(1) Hailing probability theory as the necessary link between the natural and the social sciences, Condorcet believed that "social mathematics" would allow precise evaluation to replace instinctive and habitual behavior. In an application of probability theory to parliamentary decision, with the dubious assumptions that men's decisions are independent of each other and correct 5/8 of the time, Condorcet concluded that a 2/3 vote of a legislature of 300 would be wrong less than once in a billion times.

(2) He is best known for his philosophy of history as progress. Believing in a general tendency in man toward perfectibility, he traced the path whereby, starting from sheer barbarism, man has moved through nine stages toward enlightenment, virtue and happiness. The stages have been those of (a) the hunter, (b) the pastoralist, (c) the agriculturalist, (d) Greece, (e) Rome, (f) the Roman Empire to the Crusades, (g) Crusades to the invention of printing, (h) the revolution in printing to Descartes, (i) the period from Descartes to the Revolution of 1789, in which the true system of the physical and social universe has been discovered.

(3) In the tenth stage, now dawning in the revolutionary period, three tendencies of the past will be carried to completion, i.e. (a) the destruction of inequality among nations, (b) the destruction of inequality among classes, and (c) the indefinite perfectibility of man—intellectually, morally, and physically.

CONE, JAMES H.

Q.v. Theology of Liberation (7).

CONFESSION.

Q.v. Penance (1).

CONFUCIANISM.

Q.v. Chinese Philosophy (1).

CONFUCIUS. 551–479 B.C.

Chinese philosopher. Born in the state of Lu and the town of Tsou, southwestern Shantung Province, probably of aristocratic, but impoverished ancestry. Confucius became the first professional teacher in Chinese history. His students were also his disciples, and early records name twenty-four who can be described as student-disciples. After years of study with Confucius—principally humanistic, covering the available literature (especially poetry and ritual), history (including "tradition"), and philosophy—his "graduates" received administrative positions of some importance in various Chinese cities and states. Confucius himself, as his "school" became recognized, arranged for the more important of these posts. For some years between 502 and 492, Confucius accepted a post in the state of Lu. Virtually a sinecure, honorable in title but modest in responsibility, it is not surprising that the nature of the post itself helped Confucius reach the decision that he must leave the state of Lu, and find a state where his principles might be tried. Confucius was nearing sixty then. In his travels, which occupied about ten years, Confucius spent time in the states of Wei, Ch'en, Ts'ai, and had returned to Wei a second time when his students, high now in the government of Lu, sent messengers to Confucius asking him to return to Lu. He returned, and took up his teaching once again.

Although gaining some influence even in his own lifetime, the triumph of Confucianism in China finally occurred in the 2nd century B.C.

Principal writings: His sayings are collected in the *Lun Yü*, called the *Analects*, compiled by Confucius' students, and his students' students.

(1) Centering his attention on man in his present life, Confucius had as his goal the achievement of a good society characterized by harmonious social relations.

(2) Harmonious social relations depend upon establishing the conditions of propriety. This is the way of good taste. It is called *Li*. It is the way of the gentleman, yet more than an external show of polished manners. It involves the keeping of rites and ceremonies, but also carrying out the functions of one's position in life, preserving the five cardinal relations: sovereign and subject, father and son, elder and younger brother, husband and wife, friend and friend. Filial piety, one of the cornerstones of the system, emerges from the second of these relations.

(3) Propriety, that is to say, must lead to the development of character. Confucius named the study of poetry and music, along with *Li*, as important in character development. Character was to be stimulated by poetry, established by *Li*, finished by music. The homophone of *Li* on the other hand, meaning "benefit" or "gain," was condemned.

(4) In dealing with others one is to take righteousness as his standard. Put negatively, it can be stated, "What you do not want done to yourself, do not do to others." Put positively this means "Let one establish his own character, and also establish the character of others."

(5) Somewhat more generally, we are enjoined to develop our humanity or *Jen*. This involves propriety, righteousness, love of fellowmen, respect, sincerity, loyalty, liberality, truthfulness, diligence, generosity, and mental cultivation. So to use one's energy is to follow the *Tao*, or Way, which makes one a superior man, relates him to society, and to the will of heaven, lending a somewhat cosmic dimension to his life.

(6) *T'ien*, or heaven, seems to have been regarded by Confucius as an impersonal standard of justice, allowing one man—even when in a minority or alone—to be

right. The way of heaven, then, appears to be a kind of ethical providence to which one can relate his life, although this providence is not necessarily destined to triumph in this world.

(7) The way to reform society is to reform the individual. If order is established in the lives of individuals and families, it will be present in the state. But rulers have to provide in themselves an example of this reform. Announcing openly that state officials up to the king should be selected on merit, Confucius may have believed that rulers, too, should be selected on the basis of merit rather than through heredity or force of arms. Shortly after Confucius' death, at any rate, this view was a tenet of the Confucian school.

CONGREGATIONALISM.

A Protestant movement, originating in England in the late 16th and 17th centuries, with the goal of either purifying (the Puritans) or separating from (the Separatists) the Established Church. In its early stages members of this movement were also known as Independents, non-Conformists, or Dissenters. Stressing the autonomy of the individual congregation, which they believed to be the pattern of the early church, their theology was initially Calvinistic. Persecuted under Elizabeth I, they flourished in the period of the Commonwealth, Oliver Cromwell counting himself among their number. With the Restoration, persecution was renewed with greater intensity. During periods of persecution, groups of early Congregationalists were forced into exile on the Continent, centering in Holland or Geneva. The Puritans who settled in Plymouth Bay in 1620 sailed to the New World after a period of exile in Leiden, Holland. Congregationalism became dominant in New England, for a time making theocratic states of the New England communities; among its leaders were the Mather (*q.v.*) family and Jonathan Edwards (*q.v.*). As the nation developed westward, Congregationalism was unable to retain its preeminence. Possibly the principle of local church autonomy did not permit successful competition with the more centrally organized polity of Methodism (*q.v.*). Possibly, too, the rise of Unitarianism (*q.v.* 3), taking over twelve of the original fourteen Congregational churches of Boston—the original seat of Congregational hegemony—prevented concentrated attention to the problems and possibilities of the frontier. The long-range tendency of Congregationalism has been away from Calvinism and toward a liberal interpretation of Christianity. English, Welsh, and American Congregationalists number somewhat more than two million communicants. The American branch of the movement, having united with the Evangelical and Reformed Church in 1961, is known as the United Church of Christ.

CONGRUISM.

Q.v. Suarez (4). The doctrine that grace leads the elect to yield themselves to God congruently with their own free will.

CONJUNCTION.

In the Propositional Calculus (*q.v.* 10) the name given to the binary connection "... and ..." often symbolized by a dot. "It rains, and the streets are wet" would be written "It rains · the streets are wet." The general form of the connective is (p · q). The truth table for conjunction shows that conjunctive propositions are true only when both constituent propositions are true, not otherwise. *Q.v.* Truth Tables (2).

CONNECTIONISM.

Q.v. Artificial Intelligence (4); Folk Psychology (2).

CONNEXITY.

Q.v. Logic of Relations (17).

CONNOTATION.

From the Latin *con* ("with") and *notare* ("to note or mark"). The word thus refers to the group of characteristics or qualities essential to a term. The usual correlate of connotation is "denotation" (*q.v.*), the set of things to which the term refers. Intension (*q.v.*), signification (*q.v.*), and comprehension (*q.v.*) are often treated as synonymous with "connotation."

(1) The meanings cited above are not in accord, however, with those used in the Middle Ages. William of Ockham (*q.v.* 4), for example, distinguished between absolute terms and "connotative" terms, viewing the former but not the latter as univocal; connotative terms have primary and secondary modes. The term, "just,"

for example, an instance of a connotative term, stands primarily for a quality and secondarily for the subject of that quality.

(2) Jean Buridan (*q.v.*) pushed beyond Ockham's usage in such a way that connoting was identified, or almost identified, at any rate, with naming, and denoting with the qualities of the things named.

(3) James Mill (*q.v.*) continued Ockham's distinction between primary and secondary reference in connotation, regarding the term "white horse" as denoting the color "white" and "connoting" horse.

(4) It was John S. Mill (*q.v.* 11) whose analysis of his father's usage led to the contemporary distinctions listed above. Connotation turns out to be a set of characteristics and denotation a set of things marked out by the connotation.

(5) There are terms with different connotations but identical denotations. Frege (*q.v.* 6) offered "the evening star" and "the morning star" as an instance of this type.

(6) Further, although most terms have both connotation and denotation, proper names have only denotation—lacking connotation. And other terms, such as "unicorn," have connotation but lack denotation.

(7) And what of the characteristics connected with a term but not essential to it? Are such characteristics part of the term's connotation or not? Does the denotation of a term, *e.g.* "tree," refer only to existent things (existent trees), or does it refer to all the things of a given kind which ever existed or ever will exist? C.I. Lewis (*q.v.* 4) felt the situation called for four distinct words: connotation (the conjunction of a term's characteristics); signification (the conjunction of a term's necessary and sufficient characteristics); denotation (the class of existent things); and comprehension (the class of existent, once existent, and possible things).

CONSCIENCE.

From the Latin *con* ("with") and *scire* ("to know"). The Greek quivalent is *syneidesis*. At one time identical with the term, "consciousness" (consider the French *conscience* where this identity continues), the English term "conscience" has gained the restriction of standing for consciousness of right and wrong as known inwardly.

(1) Socrates (*q.v.* 1) identified conscience with an inner warning voice which he regarded as having its origin in God.

(2) Among the Stoics (*q.v.* Epictetus 3; Marcus Aurelius 2) conscience is simply the voice of reason, a divine spark in man, deriving from the universal reason and capable of providing guidance in life.

(3) Throughout the Middle Ages the term for conscience, initiated by St. Jerome, was *synderesis*(*q.v.*), apparently a modification of the Greek term. More precisely, *synderesis* referred to man's consciousness of universally binding rules of conduct. *Conscientia* was reserved for consideration of the relation of the general rules to particular cases (the phrase *scintilla conscientiae*, "spark of conscience," was also used). The "science" of *casuistry* (*q.v.*) arose to order the insights of the application of moral rules in concrete situations.

(4) In the modern world both *synderesis* and *casuistry* disappeared, leaving the field to conscience, which came to include both universal rule and particular case. Bishop Butler (*q.v.* 1) is to be singled out especially as one who viewed conscience as a faculty of the mind—indeed, the faculty of reason—capable of distinguishing between right and wrong. The Moral Sense Theorists (*q.v.*), although tending to regard conscience as a special faculty (not reason), must also be mentioned in this regard. In recent times the idea of conscience has become assimilated under other names to the major ethical doctrines, especially those which are intuitionistic or deontic in character (*q.v.* Ethics 3–4).

(5) For a view of conscience as related to religious assent *q.v.* Newman (8).

(6) For Freud (*q.v.* 2) conscience is man's Super-ego, the admonitions and requirements of one's society, internalized.

CONSCIOUSNESS.

From the Latin *con* ("with") and *scire* ("to know"). At one time identical with "conscience" (*q.v.*). The claims of consciousness are recognized both in Idealism (*q.v.*) and Dualism (*q.v.*), and likewise registered in our discussions of soul (*q.v.*), self (*q.v.*) and psyche (*q.v.*).

(1) The Consciousness-Only School, also known as the Way of Yoga estab-

lished by Asanga (*q.v.*) and systematized by Vasubandhu (*q.v.*), holds that existence belongs neither to external objects nor to the empirical ego but to a Pure Consciousness. We may attain this consciousness through liberation. Hsuan-Tsang (*q.v.* 4) was an adherent of the doctrine.

(2) Galluppi (*q.v.*) argued, against solipsists, that consciousness involves a simultaneous awareness of self or ego and thing.

(3) William James (*q.v.* 3) presented the view that consciousness is not an entity but a function. He held it to be a "stream" whose later states are able to grasp their antecedents.

CONSENSUS GENTIUM.

Latin phrase meaning "the agreement of mankind." *Q.v.* Truth (2).

CONSERVATISM.

Any movement or tendency to conserve the values of the past. In history and theology the movements of Traditionalism (*q.v.*) and Ultramontanism (*q.v.*). Edmund Burke (*q.v.* 2) defended the position in discussing the American and French revolutions. *Q.v.* Liberalism.

CONSILIENCE.

From the Latin *con* plus *salire* ("jumping together"). A term used by Whewell (*q.v.* 2) in the phrase "consilience of inductions" to describe the unifications which occur in experience.

CONSILIENCE OF INDUCTIONS.

Q.v. Whewell (2).

CONSISTENCY.

From the Latin *con* ("with") and *sistere* ("to stand" or "cause to stand"). The characteristic, then, of being capable of standing together, or in harmony.

A. Consistency has been long regarded as one of the criteria for the truth of a system or theory. Those adhering to the Coherence Theory of Truth (*q.v.*) make consistency, along with adequacy, the chief criterion of the truth of a system of philosophy.

B. In recent years the problem of consistency has been explored in relation to the foundations of logic and mathematics where it plays a significant role along with Completeness (*q.v.*) and Decidability (*q.v.*).

(1) The discovery of paradoxes in the

assumptions of Set Theory, Cantor's paradox and Russell's paradox, for example, generates the problem. Russell (*q.v.* 3) restored consistency by means of his famous theory of types; but the theory leads to cumbersome results.

(2) The Intuitionists reached the same result by regarding mathematical entities as constructed by the mind, and by rejecting the law of excluded middle (*q.v.* Brouwer 2).

(3) Zermelo (*q.v.* 3) sought to restore consistency by dropping the principle of unrestricted set existence, and Von Neumann by introducing the principle that only certain entities can be members of sets. Hilbert (*q.v.*) gained the same result by completely formalizing the system, regarding its axioms and theorems merely as strings of marks capable of producing additional strings of marks.

(4) But it was Godel (*q.v.* 3–4) who in 1931 demonstrated that any system rich enough to express the theory of natural numbers, for example, can be consistent only at the price of being incomplete, and will be inconsistent if complete.

CONSPICUOUS CONSUMPTION.
Q.v. Veblen (1).

CONSPICUOUS WASTE.
Q.v. Veblen (1).

CONSTANCE, COUNCIL OF. 1414–1418.
The Council which asserted that the authority of church councils is from Christ and binds the papacy. The Council ended the then current scandal of three popes (representing Rome, Avignon, and a former Council) and which, among other orders of business, anathematized the errors of John Wycliffe (*q.v.*) and executed his disciple, John Huss (*q.v.*).

CONSTANT.
From the Latin *con* ("to") and *stare* ("stand"). Hence, the quality of standing firm.

(1) In science this quality is exhibited by the physical constants, so called, of the speed of light, for example, or of the quantum of energy (Planck's constant: *q.v.* Mechanics 2).

(2) In logic and mathematics constants are to be contrasted with variables. The values of variables are constants—"1, 2, 3" compared with "x, y, z," a determinate compared with an indeterminate number. The same situation occurs in logic where in propositional functions the variables, x, y, z, replaced by constant values, yield propositions. It is not only the values of variables that are regarded as constants, however. So are the valid mathematical operations and relations of addition, multiplication, equality, and their signs; and in logic this is the case with implication, disjunction, conjunction, equivalence, etc., as well as with quantifiers and their signs.

CONSTANTINE THE GREAT. 280's–337.
Roman emperor. Constantine's conversion to Christianity probably aided him in his drive to become emperor; certainly he credits the Christian God with his triumph, and it led to the official recognition of Christianity. Constantine called the Council of Nicaea (*q.v.*) in 325. He moved the capital city of the Empire from Rome to Constantinople.

CONSTANTINOPLE, COUNCIL OF. 381 A.D.
Called by Emperor Theodosius, this was the second general council of the Church, and the first of three to be held in Constantinople. Its historic importance lies in its concluding the Arian controversy by its condemnation of Arianism (*q.v.*); and its endorsement of the *homoousian* formula, holding that the Son is of the same substance as the Father. This formula was the main outcome of the first general council, that of Nicaea (*q.v.*). At the second council the phrase "who proceedeth from the Father" was appended to the term "Holy Spirit" in the Nicene Creed. This addition led to a later controversy splitting the Church into two divisions. This controversy concerned the addition of the phrase "and the Son" to the phrase mentioned above. The addition of the "*Filioque*" (*q.v.*) was made by the Western Church under Charlemagne, but was not accepted by the Eastern Church.

CONSTATIVE UTTERANCE.
Q.v. Austin (3).

CONSTRUCTIVE DILEMMA.
Q.v. Propositional Calculus (7).

CONSUBSTANTIATION.

From the Latin *con* ("with") and *substantia* ("substance"). The Lutheran doctrine of the Eucharist to the effect that the body and blood of Christ are "in real substantial presence" with the bread and wine. To be contrasted with transubstantiation (*q.v.*).

CONTEMPLATION.

From the Latin *con* and *templum* (a space set aside for the observation and interpretation of signs and portents). Although the interpretation of the term has changed, its religious origin has not been entirely lost. The interpretation of *theoria*, or theory, in Greek philosophy, merely enlarged it with a truth-related aspect.

(1) For Plato (*q.v.* 1) contemplation is of the true, the good, and beautiful in an "upward" movement toward theory.

(2) In Aristotle (*q.v.* 1, 10) contemplation relates to theory, and is differentiated from practical and poetic activity. Contemplation in man is, in effect, an imitation of the divine activity which can be described as a "thinking on thinking."

(3) For Plotinus (*q.v.* 6) contemplation is, at once, spiritual and intellectual, and its goal is union with the divine and primal unity.

(4) Hugh of St. Victor (*q.v.* 1) regarded *contemplatio* as the third and final stage of knowledge in the ascent of the soul, which must first pass through *cogitatio* and then through *meditatio* in preparation.

(5) The 17th-century movement of Quietism (*q.v.*) equated one moment's contemplation with a thousand years' good works.

(6) In the broader scheme of things the tradition of mysticism (*q.v.*), both of the East and of the West, has for millennia stressed contemplation or meditation as the means to enlightenment (*q.v.*), *moksha* (*q.v.*), or *satori* (*q.v.*).

CONTEXT OF DISCOVERY.

Q.v. Logic of Discovery (2).

CONTEXT OF JUSTIFICATION.

Q.v. Logic of Discovery (2).

CONTEXTUAL DEFINITION.

For Russell (*q.v.* 5) the kind of definition appropriate to an incomplete symbol (*q.v.* Symbol 4). Since the incomplete symbol disappears into its description, the definition in context construes the incomplete symbol as a substitute for its description.

CONTEXTUALISM.

Q.v. S.C. Pepper (2).

CONTIGUITY.

Togetherness in time or place. A basic principle of the Association of Ideas (*q.v.* 1, 2, 5, 6, 7).

CONTINENTAL PHILOSOPHY.

Q.v. Philosophy (45).

CONTINGENCY.

From the Latin *contingere* meaning "to happen."

The meaning of "contingent" must be made out in contrast to "necessary" (*q.v.* Necessity 2, 12, 14) and in relation to "possible" and "impossible" (*q.v.* Modality 1, 6).

(1) An event is contingent if it might not have occurred; otherwise, it is necessary. A being is contingent (*q.v.* Aristotle 10) if it might not have existed; otherwise, it is a necessary being—indeed, in the language of Aristotle and the Scholastics who used this distinction, the Necessary Being or God. A proposition is contingent if the events which control its truth and falsity are contingent. If the events are necessary, so would be the proposition. Contingency in events, beings, and propositions is not identical with their possibility. A possible event, being, or proposition might be contingent, and might be necessary. And the denial of contingency in event, being, and proposition might mean either necessity or impossibility.

(2) Avicenna (*q.v.* 8) regards all things as necessary: God as necessary in Himself, things in the world as contingent, yet also necessary in that they are determined by the action of external causes.

(3) A somewhat different manner of setting the contingency-necessity contrast is that of Leibniz (*q.v.* 10–11) in his distinction of truths of fact and truths of reason. Truths of fact are contingent, since they might have been otherwise. In Leibniz' view truths of fact are contingent upon God's choice of a certain

world but, given that choice, they could not have been otherwise. Truths of reason on the other hand are necessary, true in any world, and hence not contingent upon any given world.

(4) There is also the position held by Lequier (*q.v.* 3), Cournot (*q.v.* 4), Whitehead (*q.v.* 17), and Hartshorne (*q.v.* 5) that the future is contingent, and hence cannot be known in detail even by God. In this view the necessary refers to generic features of the world, and to that which, becoming definite in the present, continues as part of a changeless past.

(5) Boutroux (*q.v.* 1–3) held that there is contingency at every level of the universe, and that as one moves toward life and intelligence the amount of contingency increases.

(6) Another manner of expressing necessity is that of Wittgenstein (*q.v.* 2), Carnap (*q.v.* 8), and others who identify necessity with logical truths, and regard the latter as tautologies true for all truth values (*q.v.* Tautology). Carnap calls logically true propositions "L-true." Contingent propositions are factually true. In his early work Wittgenstein held that such propositions "picture" facts.

CONTINUANT.
Q.v. W.E. Johnson (3).

CONTINUITY.
From the Latin *continere*, meaning "to hold together." The problem of continuity arises whenever one is concerned with series or fields. It arises, therefore, with respect to numbers, lines, planes, and solids. In a physical sense it arises with respect to magnitudes, and so with respect to space and time.

(1) For a discussion of paradoxes on both of these levels, *q.v.* Zeno of Elea.

(2) Aristotle (*q.v.* 8) attempts to resolve the problem by defining the continuous as that subdivision of the contiguous whose touching limits are one and the same, and contained in each other. This implies, he points out, that nothing continuous can be composed of indivisibles; that is, continuity implies infinite divisibility.

(3) Leibniz (*q.v.* 5) found a law of continuity in both thought and reality, in geometry and in nature. Because of this law rationality applies to reality, and

other laws are possible. As a result of this law we can expect a fullness or plenitude in nature, such that there will be no discontinuous changes.

(4) Problems of continuity and discontinuity arise with respect to the concept of fields in modern physics. In modern mathematics the idea of compact or dense order, asserting that between any two distinct members of a class or arguments of a function there is always a third, has great importance, and is to be attributed in part to Dedekind (*q.v.* 2) and Cantor (*q.v.* 6). In set theory a continuum is a nondenumerable infinite set.

CONTINUUM.
The concept of a reality, or a dimension of reality, without breaks, thus exemplifying continuity (*q.v.*).

(1) Dewey (*q.v.* 4) substituted the concept of a "means-end continuum" for the traditional view that there are fixed ends in nature.

(2) Whitehead (*q.v.* 7, 10–11) regarded space-time events as occurring in an "extensive continuum."

CONTRADICTIO IN ADJECTO.
From the Latin meaning a "contradiction in what is added." A logical fallacy wherein there is a contradiction between the noun and adjective of a descriptive phrase, *e.g.*, a dimensionless area. *Q.v.* Fallacies (22).

CONTRADICTION, PRINCIPLE OF.
Along with the principles of identity and excluded middle, one of the three laws of thought.

(1) It is, according to Aristotle (*q.v.* 5), one of the "most certain of all principles" that "the same attribute cannot at the same time belong and not belong to the same subject in the same respect." This law of thought is sometimes stated as a law of being: the same thing cannot both be and not be at the same time in the same respect. Aristotle accepted both applications.

(2) Since the point is that if a given proposition is true its contradiction is false, it is not the case that the given proposition and its negation can both be held to be true, *i.e.*, "~ (p·~p)." For the truth table of this statement form *q.v.* Tautology (1).

(3) Nicolas of Autrecort (*q.v.*) held this principle to be the only test for certainty.

(4) Nicholas of Cusa (*q.v.* 2) granted that the principle applied to finite entities; but he held that with respect to infinities—and especially with respect to God—opposites apply simultaneously.

(5) According to Leibniz (*q.v.* 10) the denial of truths of reason—or analytic judgments (*q.v.*)—leads to contradiction. They are, then, to be regarded as true in all possible worlds.

(6) Lévy-Bruhl (*q.v.* 3) pointed out that the principle is denied in the world-view of primitive peoples, and that a principle of "participation" exists in its place.

(7) Carnap (*q.v.* 11) in his extensional semantics derives the principle of contradiction from that of state description.

CONTRADICTORY.
    Q.v. Immediate Inference (1).

CONTRAPONEND.
    Q.v. Immediate Inference (4).

CONTRAPOSITIVE.
    Q.v. Immediate Inference (4).

CONTRARY.
    Q.v. Immediate Inference (1).

CONTRARY-TO-FACT CONDITIONAL.
    Q.v. Counterfactual Statements.

CONTRITION.
    Q.v. Penance (1).

CONVENTIONALISM.
    From the Latin *con* ("together") and *venire* ("to come"), hence, in its philosophic sense a convention is a decision resting on common agreement. The conventional often stands in contrast to the natural, or the real, or the true.

(1) Those for whom the conventional is opposed to the natural, include Sophists such as Thrasymachus (*q.v.*) and Callicles (*q.v.*) for whom moral standards are conventional; and Rousseau (*q.v.* 1–2) for whom, in contrast to the natural, conventional standards are debilitating.

(2) Those for whom the conventional is opposed to the real include Democritus (*q.v.* 3) for whom, *e.g.*, taste and color are by convention whereas in reality there are atoms and the void. One thinks also of Locke (*q.v.* 6) for whom secondary

qualities are in a sense conventional, while primary qualities are part of the real world.

(3) Those for whom the conventional is opposed to the true, include the Sophist, Protagoras (*q.v.*), with his "Man is the measure of all things," and the Sophist, Gorgias (*q.v.*). The Kantian reduction of ideas to regulative principles is a move toward conventionalism (*q.v.* Kant 4) allowing the development of Vaihinger's (*q.v.* 1) fictionalism. Mach (*q.v.* 4) held the pictorial aspect of a theory to be conventional and the mathematical aspect to be essential. Poincaré (*q.v.* 2) held that the axioms of geometry and the principles of science are conventional, but the laws of science are not.

(4) In the development of modern schemes of metalogic and metamathematics it is convenient to regard the initial choices of rules and axioms as conventional. Carnap's (*q.v.* 5) principle of tolerance, and Zermelo's (*q.v.* 5) principle of choice look in this direction.

CONVENTION T.
    Q.v. Davidson (6, 7).

CONVENTUALS.
    Q.v. Francis of Assisi (4).

CONVERSION.
    Q.v. Immediate Inference (2).

CONVERTEND.
    Q.v. Immediate Inference (2).

COPERNICUS, NICOLAS. 1473–1543.
    Polish astronomer. Born at Torun. Educated at Cracow, Bologna, Padua, and Ferrara. Architect of the heliocentric theory of the solar system, Copernicus found it necessary to retain seventeen of Ptolemy's epicycles, while supposing that planetary orbits were circular. The later work of Tycho Brahe (*q.v.*) and Kepler (*q.v.*) dropped the epicycles entirely and transformed the orbits into ellipses.

    Principal writings: *Commentarius* (T), 1512; *On the Revolutions of the Celestial Orbs* (T), 1543.

COPULA.
    From the Latin *co* ("together") and *apere* ("to bind"). In traditional logic, a form of the verb "to be" (plus "not" in negative propositions) connecting the subject

and predicate terms of a proposition. In "Socrates is snub-nosed" the subject term, copula, and predicate term are clearly evident. In "Socrates dances" they are not evident; but all such propositions can be rewritten, in this case as "Socrates is a dancer." Non-standard propositions, indeed, must be rewritten in standard form in order for the rules of syllogistic inference to apply.

It is important to notice that the copula can relate a characteristic to an entity ("Socrates is snub-nosed"), a member to a class ("Socrates is a dancer"); can express class inclusion ("All Athenians are Greeks"); and can express identity ("Socrates is the teacher of Plato").

CORNEILLE, PIERRE.
Q.v. Tragedy (2).

CORPUS HERMETICUM.
A body of Neoplatonic, astrological, and alchemical writings falsely supposed to derive from the Egyptian equivalent of the Greek god Hermes. The position of Hermetism which came from this material was of influence in the late Greek and Roman periods.

CORRESPONDENCE, DOCTRINE OF.
Q.v. Swedenborg (3).

CORRESPONDENCE THEORY OF TRUTH.
Q.v. Epistemology (2–5); Truth (1 and *passim*).

CORRUPTION.
Q.v. Generation.

COSMOGONY.
From the Greek *kosmos* ("world") and *gignesthai* ("to be born"). The term refers to accounts of the origins of worlds, and applies equally to the speculative accounts of modern astronomers, and the less sophisticated mythical accounts of ancient peoples. In both cases, hypotheses of creation and evolutionary development are advanced. The creation story of the Bible with God subduing chaos, separating light from darkness, creating sun, moon, and stars, is an ancient cosmogony. The explanation of the origin of worlds from a cloud of dust by the principles of evolution is similarly cosmogonic.

COSMOLOGICAL ARGUMENT.
One of the three standard arguments for God, along with the teleological (*q.v.*) and ontological (*q.v.*) arguments. The cosmological argument argues that the cosmos is not self-explanatory, and requires an unconditioned being, God, as its explanation. Typically, the argument proceeds from the condition of motion, causality, or the contingency of the world to the conclusion that an unmoved mover, first cause, and necessary being must exist.

(1) In the *Laws* Plato (*q.v.* 10) argued from the insufficiency of derivative motion to the primacy of self-motion, identified with God.

(2) Aristotle (*q.v.* 10) formalized the argument, concluding from the impossibility of an infinite regress of motions or causes to God who is unmoved mover and first cause.

(3) Avicenna (*q.v.* 6) used the Aristotelian causal argument, and Bonaventure (*q.v.* 2) used the arguments from motion, cause, and contingency.

(4) Aquinas (*q.v.* 2–3) presented five arguments for God. Three of them are cosmological; *i.e.*, the arguments from motion, cause, and contingency.

(5) William of Ockham (*q.v.* 12) rejected the arguments from motion and cause, and Suarez (*q.v.* 2) rejected the argument from motion.

(6) Descartes (*q.v.* 8) used the cosmological argument in the sense of explaining how a substance continues to exist; or to conserve its being.

(7) Locke (*q.v.* 8), Newton (*q.v.* 6) and Leibniz (*q.v.* 8) all used versions of the argument.

(8) Hume (*q.v.* 7), Kant (*q.v.* 5), and J.S. Mill (*q.v.* 9) found the arguments to be fallacious, the first and third on the grounds that infinite regress is more sensible than is the conclusion to a first cause, while Kant held that the argument moves fallaciously from phenomena to noumena while depending on the ontological argument which is itself invalid.

COSMOLOGY.
From the Greek *kosmos* ("world") and *logos* ("reason concerning"). Traditionally, cosmology is considered to be that branch of metaphysics which concerns questions of the origin and structure of the universe, its creation or everlastingness, vitalism

or mechanism, The nature of law, space, time, and causality. The task of cosmology can perhaps be distinguished from that of ontology (*q.v.*) by a difference of level, the cosmological analysis seeking to discover what is true for this world, and the ontological analysis attempting to discover relations and distinctions which would be valid in any world.

(1) Wolff (*q.v.* 6) initiated the philosophical use of the term, defining it as the science of the world or universe in general, as distinct from ontology (*q.v.*), theology, or psychology.

(2) Scholastic thought from the 18th century on has adopted Wolff's usage, considering the study a part of special metaphysics, along with psychology and natural theology.

(3) Hegel (*q.v.*) included in the study of cosmology the contingency, necessity, eternity, limitations, and formal laws of the world, as well as questions of human freedom and the origin of evil.

(4) A.E. Taylor (*q.v.* 1) included in cosmology the analysis of all of the general concepts, such as motion, change, quality, etc., which would be needed in explicating the structure of the world.

(5) Whitehead's (*q.v.*) subtitle for *Process and Reality*, "an Essay in Cosmology," would seem to have identified cosmology and metaphysics. The aim of the volume is to construct a scheme of general ideas in terms of which every element of our experience can be interpreted.

(6) In recent years, with the relative decline of speculative philosophy, the cosmologists have tended to be scientists—astronomers, theoretical physicists, and mathematicians, such scientists as Bondi, Gold, Hoyle, and Gamow—speculating on the origin and development of the universe as well as its present structure, and thus intersecting the concerns of the ancient cosmogonies.

COSMOPOLIS.
Q.v. Stoicism (4).

COSTA, URIEL DA. 1585–1640.
Jewish freethinker. Born in Portugal. Lived in Amsterdam with periods of time in Hamburg for business reasons. His first book claimed that the idea of immortality was foreign to the law of Moses, and introduced into Judaism by the Pharisees.

In 1623 Semuel da Silva acquired chapters 23–25, the heart of his argument, prior to publication, printing the material and an answer to it. When da Costa's book appeared in 1624 it was burned by the Jewish authorities. Da Costa was excommunicated by the synagogue in both Venice and Hamburg. The excommunication was confirmed in Amsterdam. Da Costa's argument was not accepted in his lifetime. He committed suicide in 1640.

Principal writings: *Examination of the Tradition of the Pharisees Compared with the Written Law*, 1624; *Example of a Human Life* (T), 1687.

COUNCILS, CHURCH.
In Buddhism and Christianity, especially, councils have played an important role in shaping the development of the religious movement.

(1) Buddhist Councils (*q.v.*) were held between the 5th century B.C. and the 1st century A.D. for the purpose of settling on the canon, and solving questions of procedure and discipline.

(2) In the Western Church, councils have been an instrument of church order from the 4th century A.D. to the present formulating creeds, determining orthodoxy, anathematizing heretics, and deciding a variety of other matters (*q.v.* Christianity 3–9; Christology 1–4).

COUNTER-DOMAIN.
Q.v. Logic of Relations (2).

COUNTERFACTUAL CONDITIONALS.
The fuse blows and the light goes out; the fuse does not blow and the light does not go out. These statements provide two obvious lines in the truth table (*q.v.* 4) of the indicative conditional: "If the fuse blows, the light goes out." But how are we to understand the more interesting counterfactual, or subjunctive, conditional: "If the fuse were to blow, the light would go out"? One possibility is to form the analysis in terms of causal laws or a causal system. Another is to involve a possible worlds analysis.

(1) Nelson Goodman, drawing a distinction between lawlike and non-lawlike generalizations, pointed out that counterfactual conditionals rest on the former. If all the coins in my pocket are silver, it does not follow that this penny, were

it in my pocket, would also be silver. But we approach a lawlike generalization with: If this penny were a dime it would be made of silver. He also argued that since we have no independent access to possible worlds, whatever we say about them comes from hypothetical reasoning and so is dependent upon our knowledge of counterfactuals. ("The Problem of Counterfactual Conditionals," 1947). It would seem prudent, then, to build an account of counterfactuals from lawlike generalizations rather than from possible worlds.

(2) Reichenbach follows the path of attempting to assimilate counterfactuals to causal laws. Such laws must be "demonstrably true, fully exhaustive, and universal" (*Elements of Symbolic Logic*, 1947). He believed he had solved the problem of "counterfactuals of non-interference," that is, "when 'a' is false and 'b' is true, we then assert that if 'a' had been true, 'b' would still be true." If an airplane arrives safely, but one of its passengers is dead from heart failure, which occurred during the trip, one would say: "If the plane had crashed into the mountains, the man would also be dead," that is, "'a' does not interfere with 'b.'" Since regular counterfactuals do interfere; the analysis of these, he suggests, must be restricted to "implications which are true without exceptions."

(3) Brian Ellis (*Rational Belief Systems*, 1979) holds that subjunctive conditionals can be assimilated to ordinary, that is, indicative, conditionals since the former are a variation of the latter, appropriate to use when a supposition has not been realized. (a) Simple conditionals: "If x occurs on occasion o, then y will occur on this occasion." (b) Simple past conditional: "If x occurred on occasion o, then y would have occurred." (c) Pluperfect conditional: "If x had occurred on occasion o, then y would have occurred on this occasion." This is the same conditional as (b), but with the prediction made retrospectively, along with "background knowledge that it did not occur." (d) Subjunctive conditional: "If x were to occur on occasion o, then y would have occurred." The subjunctive conditional and pluperfect conditional are, then, two ways of saying the same thing. Both can be handled, Ellis feels, through causal laws so long as the conditionals

are considered to be "variably strict conditionals" (using only the first two lines of the truth table for material implication, *q.v.* Truth Tables 4) so that the paradoxes of material implication will not arise.

(4) If the analysis is made in terms of possibilities, one would first consider views denying objective modality. John L. Mackie allows that "possibilities only exist as the contents" of our considering (*Truth, Probability and Paradox*, 1973). Bas Van Frassen, similarly, holds there is "no objective modality in nature" (*The Scientific Image*, 1980), while Robert Adams assimilates "maximal consistent sets of propositions," to "world stories" stating that so called "nonactual possibles" "must be reducible to statements in which the only things there are said to be are things which are in the actual world. . . ." ("Theories of Actuality," 1974). Against this extreme nominalism it might be argued that whatever, in fact, becomes actual must in fact have been possible prior to its becoming actual; and that implies some form of objective modality. Among those holding to a realistic view of possibilities, David Lewis offers an extreme, and Robert Stalnaker a modest, realism. Both develop their positions in terms of counterfactuals.

(5) Holding counterfactuals to be "variably strict conditionals," as strict, within limits, as they must be to escape vacuity, David Lewis (*q.v.* 3–6) casts his account in terms of the comparative similarity of accessible possible worlds. Using a "limit assumption" that there will be a set of antecedent worlds (worlds in which the antecedent of the conditional is true) closest to our world (with no other antecedent world closer), and a "presupposition on determinate uniqueness" to resolve borderline untruths, it turns out that a counterfactual conditional is true "only if its consequent is true in the most similar world in which the antecedent is true" (*Counterfactuals*, 1973).

(6) Robert Stalnaker's attenuated version of the Lewis program utilizes only the limit assumption ("For any proposition A which is possibly true, there is a non empty set of closest worlds in which A is true"). The incontestable fact is that some counterfactuals are both irreducible and determinately true or false; and that the possible worlds analysis is useful at

a certain level of abstraction although "not a metaphysical conception."

(7) Causality and the similarity criterion can work together, of course, and presumably do so in all realist systems. This is explicitly stated by F.C. Jackson ("A Causal Theory of Counterfactuals," 1977) who tells us that "a $\square \to$ b" (a necessarily implies b) is true in the actual world if there is a possible world with the same causal laws as our world in which both "a" and "b" are true and which is more similar to the actual world than to any such world in which "a" is true and "b" is false.

(8) For J. J. C. Smart (7) counterfactuals are to be found in a metalanguage related to the object language which refers to the world.

COUNTERFACTUAL STATEMENT.

A conditional statement (*q.v.*) whose antecedent is false and whose consequent is conditionally true. An instance would be, "If it had rained, then the streets would be wet." More generally, "If x had occurred, then y would have occurred." Counterfactuals cannot be analyzed in truth-functional terms since the antecedent of every counterfactual statement is false and therefore, according to the truth table for material implication (*q.v.* Truth Tables 4), every such statement is true. Also *q.v.* Counterfactual Conditionals.

COUNTERPART RELATIONS.

Q.v. David Lewis (4).

COUNTER-REFORMATION.

A movement within the Roman Catholic Church in the 16th and 17th centuries designed to purify the Church and to halt the progress of Protestantism. The Society of Jesus or Jesuits (*q.v.*), founded in 1534, was actively involved in both goals. In the first portion of his papal tenure Paul III (1534–49) encouraged Church purification; in the second portion his resolve to halt Protestantism led him to strengthen the Inquisition (*q.v.*). A third agency of the Counter-Reformation was the Council of Trent (1545–63) which directed its attention to the elimination of abuses within the Church, as well as to the continuing definition of its thought.

COURAGE.

From the Latin *cor* ("heart"). One of the four Greek cardinal virtues along with wisdom, temperance, and justice.

(1) In Plato's *Republic* (*q.v.* Plato 5c), courage is viewed as the specific virtue of the guardian class.

(2) For Aristotle (*q.v.* 11) courage is the mean between the deficiency of cowardice and the excess of foolhardiness.

(3) Tillich (*q.v.* 5) regarded the various forms of courage as a means of approaching the ultimate.

COURNOT, ANTOINE A. 1801–1877.

French philosopher and mathematician. Born in Gray. Taught at Paris, Lyon, and Grenoble; rector of the Academy at Grenoble (1835), and of the Academy at Dijon (1854).

Selected writings: *Researches into the Mathematical Principles of the Theory of Wealth* (T), 1838; *Exposition of the Theory of Chance and of Probability*, 1843; *An Essay on the Foundations of our Knowledge* (T), 2 vols., 1851; *Treatise on the Linkage of Fundamental Ideas in the Sciences and in History*, 1881.

(1) Taking the position that chance and discontinuity are as real as order and continuity, Cournot argues that nonetheless we can more and more closely approximate that limit of adequate understanding which would be knowledge of a thing as it is in itself.

(2) The method of approach is that life of the intellect in which through more comprehensive and powerful principles the connections of apparently discrete phenomena and fields become established.

(3) And the task of philosophy is to elaborate the categories, *e.g.*, form, unity, simplicity, symmetry, in terms of which these connections can be expressed.

(4) In this analysis one discovers living beings to be characterized by a finality and vitality not reducible to physics and chemistry; and on a still higher level one finds God whose superiority does not lie in knowing the total future (since that is contingent), but in having, unlike human beings, a sure sense of what is contingent and what is not.

COUSIN, VICTOR. 1792–1867.

French philosopher. Born in Paris where he was also educated. Professor at the Normal School of Paris and at the Sorbonne. In 1840 he became Minister of Public Instruction, Director of the Normal School, and a member of the Institut de France. A spokesman for the *Juste Milieu*, which in fact stood for philosophical eclecticism. He was influenced, in turn by Locke and Condillac, the Scottish Commonsense Philosophy of Thomas Reid and Ferguson, Maine De Biran, Schelling, and Hegel. Out of these elements he was able to create a fusion of ideas turning philosophy in the direction of "Spiritualism."

Principal writings: *Philosophical Fragments*, 1826; *Course in the History of Philosophy*, 3 vols., 1829; *Course in the History of Modern Philosophy*, 5 vols., 1841; *On the True, the Good, and the Beautiful*, 1853. In addition he published, among other ventures, the works of Proclus in six volumes, the works of Descartes in eleven, and a translation of Plato in thirteen volumes.

(1) It is the function of philosophy to classify and interpret the universal experience of humanity as expressed in common sense beliefs; the tools to be used are observation, induction, and analysis.

(2) In the act of creation, and in ordinary life, a spontaneity is to be found which is its own cause, and the source of freedom. In a "spontaneous apperception" we are able to gain by impersonal observation the laws of reason—primarily, substance and causality; and these laws allow us to pass from psychology to ontology.

(3) This passage yields not only a nature, but also God as absolute cause, absolute substance, and absolute spontaneity, the divine activity occurring without deliberation.

(4) The history of philosophy is made up of numerous systems each representing one of the four types—sensualism, idealism, skepticism, or mysticism. No system of philosophy is false, but all systems are incomplete; and part of the function of the philosopher is to unite these incomplete systems, thus providing a philosophy adequate to the totality of consciousness.

COUTURAT, LOUIS. 1868–1915.

French philosopher. Born in Paris. Professor in the University of Toulouse, Caen, and in the Collége de France. Heav-

ily indebted to Leibniz, and a defender of the *Mathesis universalis* (*q.v.*), he argued for the development of symbolic logic as the appropriate tool for an adequate approach to philosophy, opposing Poincaré, and defending Cantor.

Principal writings: *On Mathematical Infinity*, 1896; *The Logic of Leibniz*, 1901; *History of the Universal Language* (with M. Leau), 1903; *Opuscules et fragments inedits de Leibniz*, 1903.

COVENANT.

In religious parlance a formal agreement entered into between man and God.

(1) The Israelites interpreted their history as centering in a covenant made with Yahweh on Mount Sinai (*q.v.* Judaism A.)

(2) Christian theology distinguished between an old covenant resting on law, and a new covenant of grace. The distinction derives from the Apostle Paul's (*q.v.*) belief that in his time the old dispensation of law had been replaced by a new dispensation of the spirit.

(3) In Islamic thought, to the old and new covenants was added a last covenant given by God to Mohammed.

(4) In some strands of Protestant thought, especially in the theology of Calvin and among the Puritans, the idea of covenant became prominent once more.

(5) In New England the Halfway Covenant referred to a special arrangement allowing the baptism of children whose parents supported the church, even though the latter had not met the rigid standards required for full church membership.

COVERDALE, MYLES.

Q.v. Bible.

COVERING-LAW MODEL.

Q.v. Hempel (1); Explanation (2).

CRANMER, THOMAS. 1489–1556.

English Protestant reformer. The first Reformed Archbishop of Canterbury, Cranmer assisted Henry VIII in the latter's first five divorce proceedings–indeed, Canterbury was his award for having defended (in an analysis heavy with quotations from Scripture, the Church Fathers and the decrees of General Councils) Henry's right to divorce Catherine of Aragon. Cranmer is to be credited with having promoted the publication of an English Bible, with having taken the decisive part in the preparation of the 1549 and 1552 editions of the Book of Common Prayer (whose 1662 edition is still in use in the Anglican Communion), and in the preparation of the Forty-Two Articles of 1553 (later reduced to Thirty-Nine) which solidified the doctrinal formula of the Anglican Church. With Mary's accession to power in 1553 Cranmer was imprisoned, taken to Oxford with Latimer (*q.v.*) and Ridley (*q.v.*) in 1554, required to witness their martyrdom in 1555, and convicted of heresy in 1556. Forced six times to recant, at his burning on March 21, 1556 he disavowed the recantations and held his right hand, the offending member that signed the recantations, in the fire until it was consumed.

CRANTOR.

Greek philosopher. Born in Soli. Probably studied under Xenocrates (*q.v.*) and Polemon (*q.v.*). A member of the First Academy (*q.v.* Plato's Academy 1), his basic interest was in ethical questions, although he composed the first known commentary on Plato's *Timaeus*.

Principal writings: *On Pain*; commentary on the *Timaeas*.

CRATES.

The name of three Greek philosophers.

(1) Crates of Athens succeeded Polemon as leader of the original Academy from 270–268 B.C. Interested in ethical theory.

(2) Crates of Mallus, 2nd-century B.C. Stoic philosopher. Head of the Library of Pergamon. Opposed Aristarchus, leader of the Alexandrian school.

(3) Crates of Thebes. Cynic philosopher, latter half 4th century B.C. Diogenes' famous pupil and the last great representative of Cynicism. Helped to develop the satiric essay, a standard means of expression of this school.

CRATYLUS. fl. 410 B.C.

Greek philosopher. According to Aristotle, Cratylus, one of the Sophists (*q.v.* 10), developed an extreme form of the Heraclitean doctrine, holding that you could not step into the same river even once. This influenced Plato to believe that knowledge of the physical world is not available. In Plato's *Cratylus* he defends

the Heraclitean view that a thing's nature is frequently discoverable through its name, that there is a natural correctness in the names of things. In the effort to avoid error Cratylus is supposed eventually to have foregone speech, substituting gestures where required.

CREATIO EX NIHILO.

Latin phrase meaning "creation out of nothing." The Christian doctrine of creation (*q.v.* 1). Q.v. Nothing (7).

CREATION.

From the Latin *creare*, "to produce, bring forth, beget." The term has had its primary philosophic usage in relation to the creation of the world and of man. In most world religions creation is understood as the production of the world from a prior state, whether a cosmic egg, chaos, or the body of deity.

A. Philosophically, there are at least four positions:

(1) *Creatio ex nihilo*. The Christian doctrine of creation out of nothing, becoming dominant in the early centuries of the Christian era, had its reason in the belief that the eternal Logos should not have as counterpart an equally eternal matter. The Gnostic, Basilides (*q.v.* 1), anticipated the doctrine. Hierocles of Alexandria (*q.v.*) held a version of this view. This alternative stresses relatively greater dependence on God than the other alternatives. And even within this alternative, degrees of dependence are to be found. For Thomas Aquinas (*q.v.* 6), God created a world of substances which He sustained in a general way. For Descartes (*q.v.* 8) God's sustaining power is such that the world is virtually created anew in every moment; and each state of the world is radically dependent on God.

(2) The production of the world as an emanation of the Divine Nature. This view, to be found among the Gnostics and Neoplatonists (*q.v.*), is also the view of many Eastern religious philosophies, especially those growing out of Hinduism. In the Eastern view the world has been many times produced through great world cycles only to be reabsorbed at length into Brahman. The motive for creation, as given by Ramanuja (*q.v.* 5), is that it is Brahman's play.

(3) The position that reality is perma-

nent, although undergoing ceaseless modifications. In this case reality has an eternal being even though its individual aspects may be involved in change. This point of view has exercised a powerful suasion over Western philosophers. Aristotle (*q.v.* 10) held this view; Thomas Aquinas agreed that from the standpoint of reason no other view than the eternality of the world was possible, and that belief in creation depended on an act of faith. For Spinoza and many others the rationality of the view of an everlasting reality has proven decisive.

(4) But Kant's (*q.v.* 4) first antinomy bears on the problem of creation; he concludes that human reason simply cannot solve the problem. Any first moment of time requires a moment before the first to explain the first moment, and yet the infinite past constructed in this manner seems inconsistent with our being now in the present. For we should have then gotten through an infinite series, which is by definition impossible.

B. Related points:

(5) Saadia (*q.v.*) argued for the doctrine of creation from the perspective of a finite universe. And Berdyaev (*q.v.* 2–3) stressed the idea of human freedom as self-creation; and our role as co-creators with God in a continuous process. Both are versions of the first position.

(6) Boodin (*q.v.* 1) held creation to be an eternal process, always going on through evolution, a version of the third position.

(7) An approach, dealing with themes common to positions (2) and (4) but more ancient than any of the above, goes back to the *Atharvaveda* (*q.v.*), *xix*, 54. There it is urged that a primordial time, which is pure energy, has brought everything into being, including Brahman and (with the creation of the sun) also measured time. Having brought the universe into being, primordial time sees to its maintenance, as well as to its eventual destruction. *Q.v.* Anaximander (2) for what may be a similar view.

CREATIONISM.

The doctrine that God creates a soul for every human being. Among others, Bonaventure (*q.v.* 8), Avicenna (*q.v.* 10), and Aquinas (*q.v.* 7) held to the doctrine of the creation of the soul out of nothing.

Creationism was the dominant doctrine of the Eastern Church, and of the Western Church during the Middle Ages. The doctrine is to be contrasted with Traducianism (*q.v.*), a doctrine advanced by Tertullian (*q.v.* 5) to the effect that souls are generated from souls when and as bodies are generated from bodies; and with Pre-Existence (*q.v.*), a doctrine held by Origen (*q.v.* 3) that souls pre-exist the body. Although Luther could not decide between Creationism and Traducianism, Lutherans generally have preferred Traducianism.

CREATIVE EVENT.

Q.v. H.N. Wieman.

CREATIVE MINORITY.

Q.v. Toynbee (2).

CREATIVITY.

A process resulting in novelty stressed by some philosophers.

(1) Freud (*q.v.* 4) gave an analysis of personal creativity in terms of sublimation and emergence of the sublimated in a novel form.

(2) Whitehead (*q.v.* 9) held that creativity is the Category of the Ultimate, and that the universe is involved from moment to moment in a creative advance.

(3) Lossky (*q.v.* 2) regarded creativity as the essential characteristic of both God and man.

(4) Berdyaev (*q.v.* 1–4) likewise stressed self-creation as characterizing man and God. In his analysis it is in both cases creation out of nothing.

(5) Wieman (*q.v.*) has centered on the creative event, consisting of four sub-events, and resulting in "creative good." He identifies the creative event with God.

CREDO.

Latin for "I believe." A creed (*q.v.*) or confession of faith. A number of Latin phrases beginning with "credo" have been used as slogans by theologians and by some philosophers.

(1) "*Credo quia absurdum est*" ("I believe because it is absurd"), and "*Credo quia impossibile est*" ("I believe because it is impossible") have been formed from the thought of Tertullian (*q.v.* 1) as apt characterizations of his position.

(2) "*Credo ut intelligam*" ("I believe in order to understand"), the position of St. Augustine (*q.v.* 11) that belief must pre-

cede knowledge, was likewise accepted by St. Anselm (*q.v.* 8), and by a majority of medieval thinkers.

CREED.

From the Latin *credo* ("I believe.") A doctrinal formula accepted by a religious group as binding. Creeds have been elaborated in many religions, invariably arising from situations containing disagreement or danger, for the sake of insuring unity among believers. Among Western creeds the Apostle's Creed (*q.v.*), the Nicene Creed (*q.v.* and Christianity 1, 3), the Athanasian Creed (*q.v.*), the Augsburg Confession (*q.v.* and *q.v.* Luther 12, 16), and the Westminster Confession (*q.v.*) may be mentioned. In the East, creedal statements are less in evidence; perhaps the eightfold path of Buddhism (*q.v.* Buddha 3) functions in some sense as a creed. Maimonides (*q.v.* Judaism 11) framed a creed of the Jewish faith which has had great influence.

CRESCAS, HASDAI BEN ABRAHAM. 1340–1410.

Spanish Jewish philosopher. Born in Barcelona. He opposed the rationalism and Aristotelianism of Maimonides and Gersonides (*q.v.* Judaism 13–15) with a philosophy stressing the centrality of love and the need for revelation. Spinoza accepted Crescas' distinction between attribute and property, and his ideas with respect to creation and free will, (*q.v.* Spinoza 6, 7, 9).

Principal writings: *The Light of the Lord* (T), 1556; *Treatise.*

CRISIS OF CAPITALISM.

Q.v. Marx (13).

CRITERION.

From the Greek *krinein* ("to judge, discern"). The rule or body of rules by which decisions may be reached on the truth or falsity of judgments. Thus, the problem of the criterion usually relates to Epistemology (*q.v.*).

(1) Historically, the term made its appearance after Aristotle in the epistemological debates between the Stoics who claimed knowledge to be certifiable and the Skeptics who doubted its possibility. The term goes back at least to Chrysippus (*q.v.* 3), whose solution invokes "common notions."

(2) Gassendi (*q.v.* 5) argued that Descartes' criterion of clarity and distinctness, required in turn a criterion, and so an infinite regress of criteria.

(3) Later the term was used by Vico (*q.v.* 1) who likewise attacked Descartes' "criterion" of clear and distinct ideas as an inadequate test for truth.

(4) In his logic, Kant held that there could be no "material criterion" for truth and that its "formal criterion" is logical consistency.

(5) Désiré Mercier (*q.v.* 1) made his University of Louvain the center of studies in Criteriology, both "general" and "special." He felt he had discovered an "inner criterion" which refuted both Positivism and Skepticism.

(6) Wittgenstein (*q.v.* 8) discussed the importance of the criterion with respect to "inner" processes, including the possibility (which he disallowed) of a private language. (Also *q.v.* Cavell 4).

(7) The problem of the criterion is central in contemporary philosophy. The interchange on the Gettier problem (*q.v.*), for example, concerns the criterion for "justified true belief."

CRITIAS OF ATHENS. 5th cent. B.C.

Greek philosopher. Born in Athens. One of the Sophists (*q.v.* 9), Critias studied under Gorgias and Socrates. Becoming a political leader he was banished from Athens, returning as one of the overseers of the city. Regarded as the most unscrupulous of the thirty tyrants, he contributed a version of social philosophy in which the laws of the state and the inventions of religion transform men from savages to citizens by means of the fear of punishment. In his view both law and religion are inventions by those in authority to control the people.

CRITICAL IDEALISM.

The name Immanuel Kant gave to his philosophy, an Idealism based upon a critique of the powers of reason.

CRITICAL LOGIC.

Q.v. Peirce (16).

CRITICAL REALISM.

A theory of perception which developed in response to the movement of New Realism (*q.v.*) in the second decade of this century.

(1) In 1920 a group of American philosophers, D. Drake, A.O. Lovejoy, J.B. Pratt, A.K. Rogers, G. Santayana, R.W. Sellars, and C.A. Strong, published a volume titled *Essays in Critical Realism*. Pointing out that the New Realists had lost the "things" of common sense, whatever their intention, this group restored the triadic interpretation of perception which had consisted of "thing," sensedatum, and act of perception. The identification of thing and sense-datum had led the New Realists to a world of things, fuzzy and ambiguous in the extreme. United in what they opposed, the Critical Realists were very diverse in what they affirmed. Their argument ended in holding that the sense-datum (which they called a "character complex"), yielding a complex set of characters to awareness, somehow points to the object perceived, and that hence we are not cut off from affirming that things are, and knowing what they are.

(2) The disagreement within the group had to do with whether the sense-datum should be viewed as a mental existent (Lovejoy, Pratt, Sellars), or as an essence or universal (Drake, Rogers, Santayana, and Strong).

(3) Lovejoy (*q.v.* 1) developed what he thought to be a workable form of dualism, including among its applications a necessary duality of sense-datum and object. The duality is carefully drawn in order not to suggest an impassable gulf between the two.

(4) R.W. Sellars, (*q.v.* 1, 2) seems to have been the author of the term "Critical Realism," having used it in print several years prior to the date of the published volume. *Sensa*, he argued, can be viewed from an external as well as an internal standpoint, and this suggests that they do not stand as a screen between man and the world.

(5) Santayana (*q.v.* 2–6), on the other hand, can serve as our example of the essence-oriented Critical Realists. In perception we are aware of essences rather than sense-data, and one gets from essence to a material world by means of animal faith and the substitution of action for thought.

(6) It should be noted that the position was anticipated by certain neo-Kantians, such as Aloys Riehl (*q.v.* 2), in their struggle against Idealism.

CRITICAL SYMBOLISM.
Q.v. Sabatier (2).

CRITICAL THEORY.
Q.v. Frankfurt School (1, 6, 10); Gramsci (2); Horkheimer (2); Habermas (1, 4, 6).

CRITICISM.
From the Greek *krinein* ("to judge, discern").

(1) In philosophy the term applies most directly to the critical philosophy of Immanuel Kant (*q.v.*) as reflected in his *Critique of Pure Reason, Critique of Practical Reason*, and *Critique of Judgment*. Kant's object was to investigate the nature and limits of human understanding.

(2) In religion one must distinguish textual criticism (aimed at producing an authentic text) from higher criticism (fitting the text into its historical context.) Spinoza (*q.v.*) is regarded as one of the forerunners of higher criticism (in his *Tractatus* or *Theological-Political Treatise*). The method experienced its real development in the latter part of the 19th century. The works on Jesus of both Renan (*q.v.*) and Schweitzer (*q.v.*) reflect, at least in part, this approach.

CROCE, BENEDETTO. 1866–1952.
Italian philosopher. Born in Pescasseroli; mainly resident in Naples. Historian and art critic, Croce held no academic post, founded the journal, *La Critica*, 1903. He served as senator, cabinet member, and twice Italian Minister of Education, although during the period of fascism Croce separated himself from public life.

Principal writings: *Philosophy of the Spirit*, 4 vols., including: *Aesthetic* (T), 1902; *Logic* (T), 1905; *Philosophy of the Practical* (T), 1909; *History—Its Theory and Practice* (T), 1917; *What is Living and What is Dead in the Philosophy of Hegel* (T), 1907; *The Philosophy of Giambattista Vico* (T), 1911; *The Essence of Aesthetic* (T), 1913; *The Conduct of Life* (T), 1918; *Politics and Morals* (T), 1922; *Poetry*, 1936; *History as the Story of Liberty* (T), 1938; *My Philosophy* (T), 1949.

(1) Philosophy and history cannot be separated. Both concern the development of the spirit. Croce called his view the philosophy of the spirit, and distinguished four spheres: aesthetics, logic, economics, and ethics.

(2) For Croce the heart of the aesthetic is individuality; and this individuality is engendered within the imagination of the artist. This intuition, successfully expressed, is the work of art; and the physical work acts to engender in the imagination of the auditor a similar aesthetic response. More generally, all individual embodiment is aesthetic, and all language is the medium of aesthetic expression.

(3) The sphere of logic is the sphere of the universal; this, too, is the sphere of truth, but Croce is interested not in abstract, but in concrete, universals, and in the conceptual comprehension of the singular. Rather than following Hegel's Dialectic of Opposites (q.v. Hegel 3), he called for a "Dialectic of the Distincts."

(4) The sphere of economics is the sphere of practical experience governed by "utility." Law, governed by social utility, fits under the category of the instrumental and economic.

(5) The sphere of ethics, however, is the sphere of practical experience concerned with the universal. It embodies awareness of the spirit as a whole and, deriving from this, a sense of duty overriding private inclinations.

(6) It is the togetherness of these realms which is the spirit, and whose description is philosophy.

CROMWELL, OLIVER.

Q.v. Congregationalism.

CRUSIUS, CHRISTIAN AUGUST. 1712–1775.

German philosopher and theologian. Born in Leuna, near Merseburg. Educated at Leipzig where he later taught, finally becoming rector of the university. The most forceful opponent in Germany of the Leibniz-Wolff tradition, Crusius followed in the Pietistic tradition of Christian Thomasius (q.v.). A leader in the Pietistic movement, Crusius exercised considerable influence over Kant, who referred to Crusius in his early writings.

Principal writings: *Instructions for a Reasonable Life*, 1744; *Sketch of Necessary Rational Truths*, 1745; *The Way to Certainty and Reliability of Human Knowledge*, 1747.

(1) The logical principles of identity and contradiction rest on a principle of *cogitabilitas*, or thinkability. What cannot

be thought false is true; what cannot be thought at all is false.

(2) Between the two poles are most propositions about which we have only "moral certitude," resting on induction, hypothesis, and testimony.

(3) Arguing that all we know of causality derives from our experience of the constant conjunction of events, Crusius defends free will. His defense is based on the ground that determinism cannot handle satisfactorily the question of moral evil.

(4) Rejecting the ontological argument, he finds only moral evidence appropriate to the question of God's existence.

(5) He claimed that one cannot found ontology in logic since one's logic will contain an ontology in any case.

(6) Behind any other distinctions is Scriptural revelation, the ultimate source of truth.

CUDWORTH, RALPH. 1617–1688.

English Platonistic philosopher, born in Aller, Somersetshire. Successively a student, fellow and professor at Cambridge, and finally Master of Christ's College. One of the most influential leaders of the Cambridge Platonists, he was consulted by Cromwell's government, and was not without influence following the Restoration.

Principal writings: *The True Intellectual System of the Universe*, 1678; *A Treatise Concerning Eternal and Immutable Morality*, 1731; *A Treatise of Free Will*, 1838.

(1) The intellectual system of the universe consists of (a) the existence of God, (b) the naturalness of moral distinctions, (c) the reality of human freedom. Atheists, and fatalists, including Hobbes, have opposed these points; and atomic atheism is given particular attention.

(2) Atomic atheism combines atomism and corporealism (the doctrine that only the body exists); but the Stoics were corporealists, so this can be a theistic doctrine. Atomism was held by most ancient philosophers, and was distorted into atheism only by Democritus.

(3) Even so, mechanical principles do not suffice to explain nature, and it is necessary to posit between the material and spiritual orders, "plastic natures" relating the two. The plastic nature is an organic principle and plays a role comparable to

that of the world soul for Plato.

(4) Knowledge is more than a collection of sense impressions; this "more" is an eternal and self-subsistent factor in the mind of God. Hence, moral distinctions have an eternal and immutable aspect, and are not created by the state, as Hobbes believed.

CULTURE.

From the Latin *colere* meaning "to till or cultivate." The term is sometimes used to include all of the creative expressions of man in all fields of human endeavor. At other times it is confined to creative expression in the areas of the liberal arts. In the second of these senses the term is sometimes extended to personal cultivation. Although the term came into use only in the 18th century, there are antecedents going back to the Greeks.

(1) Plato and Aristotle in the Academy (*q.v.*) and Lyceum (*q.v.*) established centers for the production and transmission of the forms of culture in the second of our senses.

(2) The School of Cynicism (*q.v.*), in turning from human society to nature, regarded human culture in both of the above senses as degenerate and corrupting. The Stoics limited the nature of their response to society, but in Stoicism (*q.v.*) a sense of world culture emerged. One was a citizen of the universe, and not merely of his city-state.

(3) The ideals of Greek culture were perpetuated from the days of Alcuin although Boethius and others set the terminology in the seven Liberal Arts, made up of the *Trivium*, and *Quadrivium*. The former consisted of grammar, dialectic, and rhetoric, the latter included arithmetic, geometry, astronomy, and music.

(4) The Romantic notion of culture in terms of genius, and the refinement of aesthetic sensibilities, is said to have been set by Immanuel Kant (*q.v.* 9) in his *Critique of Judgment*.

(5) For the view that speech is important in the development of culture, *q.v.* Herder (1–2).

(6) Saint Simon (*q.v.* 2) distinguished between "critical epochs" and "organic epochs" in the matter of cultural change.

(7) Fichte (*q.v.* 7) believed man's goal to be the development of an ethical world culture.

(8) Hegel (*q.v.* 9–22), developing the idea of the Spirit as a central theme of philosophy, made the idea of culture an object of much more concern than it had ever been.

(9) Schlegel (*q.v.* 2) regarded the vitality of culture as dependent upon the fusion of science and life.

(10) Matthew Arnold (*q.v.* 1) was a 19th-century apostle of culture, identifying it with the goal of "total perfection" and giving it a role in overcoming the barbarism and philistinism of society.

(11) Spengler (*q.v.* 2) distinguished "culture" from "civilization," regarding the former as the vital possibilities of a society, and the latter as the mere external form of their achievement.

(12) Sociologists differ concerning whether or not "culture" and "civilization" are to be understood as identical. E.B. Tylor (*Primitive Culture*, 1871) held the two concepts to be identical, and including knowledge, belief, art, morals, laws, and customs. Alfred Weber (*q.v.*) in his "Culture-sociology" distinguished the terms, relating the former to philosophy, religion, and art; and the latter to science and technology.

(13) Plekhanov (*q.v.* 2), taking a materialist conception of history, came closer than any other dialectical materialist to holding that the cultural product of a nation is dependent upon its economic substructure.

(14) Huizinga (*q.v.*) emphasized the "play" element in culture.

CULTURE PROCESS.
Q.v. Alfred Weber.

CULVERWEL, NATHANAEL. c. 1618–1651.

English philosopher. Born in London. Educated at Cambridge. Taught at Cambridge. Although exposed to Cambridge Platonism, studying under Whichcote (*q.v.*), along with Cudworth (*q.v.*), Culverwel combined an interest in Aristotle, Plato (intermixed with Neoplatonism), Scholasticism, and Calvinism, in a philosophy stressing God's absolute authority with respect to ethics and natural law no less than to divine election.

Principal writings: *Spiritual Opticks*, 1651; *An Elegant and Learned Discourse of the Light of Nature*, 1652.

CUMBERLAND, RICHARD. 1631–1718.

English philosopher. Born in London. Educated at Cambridge. A churchman, he was appointed one of Cambridge's official preachers, and in 1691 Bishop of Peterborough. He thought of his philosophy as a refutation of Thomas Hobbes. His "greatest good" principal anticipated Utilitarianism (*q.v.*).

Principal writings: *De Legibus Naturae* (T), 1672.

(1) Holding that morality rests on natural laws which are "immutably true propositions" carrying obligation with them apart from civil law or governmental compacts, Cumberland found the basis for these propositions in the character of rational beings. To deduce natural law from the character of rational beings is to establish such laws through their causes. They can also be generalized from their effects (*i.e.*, the testimony of people, and laws of nations in all ages); but Cumberland believed that the former approach carried more conviction with it.

(2) In the character of man as a rational agent Cumberland found a natural tendency, shared by brute animals, to seek the welfare of their fellows. The law is that the pursuit of the good of all contributes to the good of each and brings one happiness, while the opposite behavior results in social and personal misery.

(3) From this he derived a principle of universal benevolence ("No action can be morally good which does not in its own nature contribute somewhat to the happiness of men"), and a utilitarian criterion for right action ("the greatest good of the universe of rational beings").

(4) He believed that all the virtues could be deduced from these principles, that ethical and mathematical propositions and systems are analogous, and that the sanctions for ethics are happiness, misery, and future retribution.

CURRY, H.B. 1900–1982.

American mathematician. Born in Millis, Mass. Educated at Harvard, M.I.T., and Göttingen. Taught at Harvard, Princeton, and Penn. State. Developing the alternative of combinatory logic, he experimented with the elimination of variables, replacing them with function symbols. Interested in the formalist program concerning the foundation of mathematics, he called his view "empirical formalism," stressing empirical adequacy and simplicity rather than mere consistency.

Principal writings: *A Theory of Formal Deducibility*, 1950; *L-Semantics as a Formal System*, 1951; *Outlines of a Formalist Philosophy of Mathematics*, 1951; *Combinatory Logic*, 1958; *Foundations of Mathematical Logic*, 1963.

CUSA, NICHOLAS OF.

Q.v. Nicholas.

CUSTOM.

From the Greek *con* and probably *suere* ("to make one's own"). Thus, a course of action which has become habitual. The term has played a number of roles in philosophical thought.

(1) Montesquieu (*q.v.* 1–2), deeply impressed by the role of custom in shaping societies and the tendency of those societies to equate their customs with universal norms and truths, wrote his *Persian Letters* in an effort to bring these facts home to 18th-century French society.

(2) David Hume (*q.v.* 3) vastly extended the philosophical use of "custom," placing this idea at the base of the idea of causation, and thus also of the principle of induction. It is custom which leads us to expect in the future the conjunction of ideas which have been conjoined in the past.

(3) W.G. Sumner (*q.v.* 1–2) found it desirable to distinguish between "folkways" and "mores" in explaining how "spontaneous" patterns of behavior become "principles" of truth and right.

(4) Westermarck (*q.v.* 1), arguing for ethical relativism, traced the role of custom to an "objectivising" tendency in man which gives a false appearance of rationality to ethical beliefs.

CYBELE-ATTIS.

Q.v. Mystery Religions (2).

CYBERNETICS.

From the Greek *kybernetes* ("steersman"). The term was introduced by Norbert Wiener and Arturo Rosenblueth for the study of machines in terms of feedback mechanisms. The appearance of computers, able to alter their "behavior" to take account of negative feedback, raises philosophical problems with respect to the nature of both human and machine intelligence. A.M. Turing has urged that it will be possible to construct machines whose behavior cannot be distinguished from human behavior; and when this happens it will be necessary to grant that machines can think.

CYNICISM. c. 5th cent. B.C.-5th cent. A.D.

From the Greek *kinikos* meaning "doglike" or from "Cynosarges," the name of the building in Athens which first housed this school of Greek philosophy. Teaching that virtue is the only good, the Cynics led a life of independent simplicity and self-control, believing any influence which might compromise the austere independence of the will is positively harmful. The conventions of society, and possessions, were either ignored or despised. As a result the Cynics provoked opposition in both Greek and Roman society.

A. There are two interpretations concerning the origin of the school.

(1) The traditional interpretation, supported by Diogenes Laertius (*q.v.*), holds that the school was founded by Antisthenes (*q.v.*), a pupil of Socrates and the teacher of Diogenes of Sinope (*q.v.*). The latter was regarded as the popularizer of the philosophy.

(2) A more recent interpretation holds that the succession from Socrates was arranged by later Cynics for the sake of prestige, and that Diogenes was in fact the founder of the school. This seems the more reliable interpretation.

B. On either reading, however, the later history of the movement is the same.

(3) Diogenes' immediate followers in the 4th century B.C. included Crates of Thebes (*q.v.*) who originated the Cynic mode of parody in writing, Onesicritus (*q.v.*), and Monimus of Syracuse (*q.v.*).

(4) Zeno of Citium (*q.v.*), the founder of Stoicism (*q.v.*), was a disciple of Crates and adapted Cynic views to his own purpose in the early years of the 3rd century B.C.

(5) Other 3rd century Cynic leaders include Menippus of Gadara (*q.v.*) and Bion of Borysthenes (*q.v.*) who developed more fully the style of sarcasm and burlesque initiated by Crates. Bion is credited with the development of the diatribe as a literary form.

(6) A revitalized Cynicism in the 1st century A.D. could count among its representatives Demetrius (*q.v.*) and Dion Chrysostom (*q.v.*). The latter has left numerous instances of the diatribe form.

(7) In the 2nd century, Oenomaus of Gadara (*q.v.*) and Demonax of Cyprus (*q.v.*) opposed the Stoic emphasis on fatalism. Lucian of Samosata (*q.v.*) became known for his satirical dialogues. And Peregrinus Proteus (*q.v.*) mingled an interest in mysticism in his reversion to the ancient Cynic doctrines.

(8) Maximus of Alexandria (*q.v.*) is an instance of Christian Cynicism. Bishop of Constantinople, he was able to fuse Christian and Cynic doctrines into a single framework.

(9) In the 5th century, Sallustius (*q.v.*) combined Cynicism with religious mysticism, mingling the former view with Neoplatonism.

CYRENAICISM. 4th and 3rd centuries B.C.

One of three philosophical schools resulting, in the traditional interpretation, from the influence of Socrates (*q.v.* also Cynicism, Megarianism). Named from the city of Cyrene in Libya, the birthplace of Aristippus (*q.v.*), founder of the school.

A. In the 4th century the views of Aristippus, a student of Socrates, dominated the school.

(1) Influenced by Socrates' teaching that happiness is one of the ends of moral action, Aristippus interpreted this to mean that pleasure is the sole end of life. He found the sole criterion of pleasure to be intensity, and held that bodily pleasures are to be preferred to intellectual pleasures. Pleasure-pain was accepted as the criterion of right and wrong, although prudence was admitted as desirable in the conduct of life. Knowledge was interpreted positivistically as that which is supported by sensation.

(2) In addition to Aristippus, the leaders of the school in the 4th century include Arete, the wife of Aristippus; Aristippus the younger, a grandson; Bio; and Euhemerus (*q.v.*).

B. In the 3rd century the early interpretations gained modifications, leading to somewhat rival sects within the school.

(3) Hegesias (*q.v.*) stressed the avoidance of pain rather than the cultivation of pleasure.

(4) Annikeris (*q.v.*) modified the view by admitting the pleasures of social relationships as desirable.

(5) Theodorus the Atheist (*q.v.*) denied the existence of anything divine, and held the end of life to be an enduring emotion of joy rather than momentary feelings of pleasure.

C. Against the more solidly based philosophy of Epicureanism (*q.v.*) the school languished and finally disappeared.

CYRIL OF ALEXANDRIA. 376–444.
Patriarch of Alexandria from 414. An advocate of the veneration of the Virgin Mary, he vigorously opposed the Nestorian heresy. It was principally his opposition that led to the condemnation of Nestorianism (*q.v.*) at the Councils of Ephesus and Chalcedon.

DA COSTA, URIEL.
Q.v. Costa, Uriel da.

DADU.
Q.v. Hinduism (5c).

DALAI LAMA.
Q.v. Lamaism.

D'ALEMBERT, JEAN LE ROND.
Q.v. Alembert, Jean le Rond d'.

DALY, MARY. 1928– .
American theologian. Born in Schenectady, (N.Y.). Educated at the College of St. Rose, Catholic University, St. Mary's (Notre Dame), and Freibourg (Switzerland). Teaching posts: Cardinal Cushing College, Boston College. Taking feminism as the key to opposing the oppressive structures of human society, Daly's criticism has included the secondary status of women in the Catholic Church, and the anti-feminism of the movement of Christianity as well as of religions and cultures generally. The source of the oppression is identified as patriarchy which she attempts to counter through a project of serious renaming leading to a new and more powerful feminist vocabulary.

Selected writings: *The Church and the Second Sex*, 1968 (rev. ed., 1985); *Beyond God the Father*, 1973 (2nd rev. ed., 1985); *Gyn/Ecology: The Metaethics of Radical Feminism*, 1978; *Pure Lust: Elemental Feminist Philosophy*, 1984; *Webster's First New Intergalactic Wickedary of the English Language* (with Jane Caputi), 1987; *Outercourse*, 1992.

DAMASCIUS. c. 470–(530?).
Hellenic philosopher. Last head of the Neoplatonic School of Athens (*q.v.*), he went into Persian exile when Justin closed the school in 529. For Damascius, the One can be determined neither positively nor negatively, since the nature of the infinite and perfect cannot be approached from the standpoint of the finite and imperfect. One must thus resort to mysticism in reaching toward the One.

Principal writings: *Life of Isidore, the Philosopher; Difficulties and Solutions Concerning First Principles; Difficulties and Solutions in Plato's "Parmenides."*

DANTE, ALIGHIERI. 1265–1321.
Italian poet. Born in Florence to a Guelph family. He studied poetry, classics, philosophy, and theology. Embroiled in the Guelph-Ghibelline controversy, Dante was exiled as a Guelph in 1302. Forbidden in Florence he wandered through Italy, dying in Ravenna.

Principal writings: *New Life*, 1292; *On Plebeian Eloquence*, about 1305; *The Banquet*, 1308; *Of Monarchy* (T), 1309; *Divine Comedy* (T), completed in the last years of his life.

(1) If the *Vita Nuova*, or *New Life*, a poem celebrating Dante's love for Beatrice, can be said to have a philosophic theme, it would be the capacity for earthly love to spiritualize its object.

(2) The philosophic counterpart of this theme is present in the *Convivio*, or *Banquet*, relating all knowledge to the natural and spiritual realms.

(3) The *De Vulgari Eloquentia*, or on eloquence in ordinary speech, examining French, Provençal, and Italian, seems to be concerned with discovering a linguistic form capable of expressing a national ideal.

(4) The *De Monarchia* or *Of Monarchy*, argues that the world requires a universal monarch, capable of assuring liberty and universal peace. The aim of such a monarchy is fulfillment of human potentialities. Church and state are to be independent, but the church is in a sense superior since the goal of life eternal is superior to the goal of temporal felicity.

(5) In the *Divine Comedy* the temporal and spiritual realms are considered in relation to the individual soul. Through choice in this life the great human drama is begun, but its completion lies beyond this life. The further drama is rehearsed in the person of Dante, guided through the nine circles of hell, up the seven terraces of purgatory, through the nine heavens of preparation, into the true paradise, and toward the moment of complete fulfillment in the beatific vision.

DARAPTI.

Valid syllogism in AAI mood, third figure. *Q.v.* Syllogism (4).

DARII.

Valid syllogism in AII mood, first figure. *Q.v.* Syllogism (4).

DARK NIGHT OF THE SOUL.

Q.v. St. John of the Cross.

DARŚANA (DARSHANA).

Sanskrit term meaning "knowledge," "vision," or "the instrument of vision." In fact, these meanings coalesce since, in Indian philosophy, an immediate or intuitive vision of reality is the goal of every system. Philosophy and religious practice thus tend to become identical. The term is also used to describe each of the six orthodox systems of philosophy which present themselves as interpretations of the Vedic scriptures. *Q.v.* Indian Philosophy (3).

DARWIN, CHARLES. 1809–1882.

English scientist. Born in Shrewsbury. Educated at Cambridge. Graduating in 1831, he began in December of that year his five-year voyage on the "Beagle." His position was that of naturalist on this surveying trip which covered both the Atlantic and Pacific oceans. His theory of evolution emerged from the data collected on his trip, and was stimulated by the reading of Malthus' *Essay on Population* in 1838. In 1858 he received from Wallace an essay which was a virtual abstract of his own theory. He then set to work in earnest, his great work on the origin of species appearing November 24, 1859.

Principal writings: *The Origin of Species*, 1859; *The Variation of Animals and Plants Under Domestication*, 1868; *The Descent of Man*, 1871.

(1) The species of living things are mutable: they come into existence, change, and not infrequently perish altogether.

(2) Organic beings increase at such a rate that the progeny of any single pair would crowd the earth were their multiplication not checked.

(3) But this multiplication is checked by the competitive efforts of other beings to survive and reproduce, both within and beyond the species in question. Such competition constitutes a struggle for existence on the part of every species.

(4) All organic beings tend to vary in all the parts, organs, and functions of life. They also have a tendency to pass on these variations by inheritance.

(5) The above conditions, taken together, provide a principle of natural selection, to the effect that favorable variations, and those possessing them, survive, while unfavorable variations, and those possessing them, are eliminated; they also explain how new species come into existence.

(6) Darwin held that the origin and history of man, like that of all other animals, is explained by this hypothesis.

DARWINISM.

In the narrow sense the doctrines of organic evolution proposed by Charles Darwin (*q.v.*). In the broader sense, those doctrines influenced by Darwin's view. In this sense Darwinism would include the doctrines of A.R. Wallace (*q.v.*) who in part anticipated Darwin, Chauncey Wright (*q.v.*), Spencer (*q.v.*), Stephen (*q.v.*). T.H. Huxley (*q.v.*), Haeckel (*q.v.*), W.G. Sumner (*q.v.* 4) who laid the basis for Social Darwinism (*q.v.*), and even American Pragmatism (*q.v.* Peirce 4–5 and Dewey). Also *q.v.* Evolution (16–21, 26).

DASEIN.

Q.v. Heidegger (1, 3); Jaspers (1, 6).

DATISI.

Valid syllogism in AII mood, third figure. *Q.v.* Syllogism (4).

DATUM.

From the Latin *datus*, past participle of *dare*, "to give," hence, the "given." Decision concerning what is immediately given provides one of the critical distinctions among philosophies.

(1) The view of Naive Realism (*q.v.*) is that the world is immediately given to our awareness.

(2) The more critical the philosophy the less likely that the world will be regarded as immediately given. In New Realism (*q.v.*) and Critical Realism (*q.v.*) our immediate awareness is of sense-data from which the world is inferred or constructed.

(3) The Scholastic tradition and Hobbes (*q.v.* 3) speak of our awareness of phantasms. Locke (*q.v.* 2) speaks of ideas of sensation, Hume (*q.v.* 1) of impressions, Kant (*q.v.* 2) of phenomena.

(4) For Mach (*q.v.* 1) our world is our construction from the components of sense data.

(5) One of the efforts of ordinary language philosophy (*q.v.*) is to do away with the sense-datum, reverting with heightened sophistication to the position that the world is the immediately given.

DAVID OF DINANT. Late 12th to early 13th cent.

Scholastic philosopher. Probably influenced by Erigena (*q.v.*), David developed a pantheistic philosophy. He is referred to in the writings of Albertus Magnus, Thomas Aquinas, and Nicholas of Cusa. Condemned for heresy in 1210, he went into exile. His book was burned, and has disappeared.

Principal writings: *On Separations, that is, On Divisions.*

(1) In a manner anticipating Spinoza (*q.v.* 1–8), David held that bodies are modes of matter, souls are modes of mind, and eternal substances are modes of God. Furthermore, mind, body, and God are identical, as shown in the following argument.

(2) Arguing that neither God nor matter possesses form, since to be so characterized is to be a composite substance, David concludes that God and matter are identical. This being so, our knowledge of God and matter cannot be due to our awareness of their forms. We can know them only because we are identical with them.

DAVIDSON, DONALD. 1917– .

American philosopher. Born in Springfield, Ma. Educated at Harvard. Has taught at Queens College, Stanford, Princeton, Rockefeller University, University of Chicago, and University of Cal. (Berkeley).

Principal writings: *Decision-Making: an Experimental Approach* (with P. Suppers), 1957; *Essays on Actions and Events*, 1980; *Inquiries into Truth and Interpretation*, 1984.

(1) Philosophizing by journal article, Davidson has remained alert to the issues of the day. In action theory he has responded to the debate on identity theory (*q.v.*), and Anscombe's (*q.v.*) analysis of "intention," including her view that events may bear alternate descriptions, arriving at a distinctive view he termed "anomalous monism." In semantic theory he took Tarski's "correspondence" theory of truth, " 'Snow is white' if and only if snow is white," turning it into a verifiability theory of meaning whose problems he moderated with holism. The result is that both correspondence and coherence play a role in his theory of meaning.

(2) To begin with action theory, the topic of his 1980 collection, Davidson presents an event ontology under which an event may be intentional under one description and nonintentional under another. The resultant anomalous monism is a nonreductive psysicalism with the ontological bias that it allows for "the possibility that not all events are mental, while insisting that all events are physical."

(3) The physicalism is nonreductive because while there is a physical (nonintentional) description of every event, and a psychological (intentional) description only of some, psychological descriptions, while supervenient (*q.v.*) upon physical descriptions, can never be replaced by the latter.

(4) They cannot be replaced by the latter because psychological predicates are anomalous, that is, lawless. They do not have the same extensions as physical predicates; nor can their precision be increased indefinitely, as can the preci-

sion of predicates relating to the physical world. Where physical predicates respond to analyses in terms of law-like behavior and causality, mental, or psychological, predicates relate to a background of reasons, beliefs, and intentions. The former homonomic (subject to the same law); the latter heteronomic. Heteronomic, too, are all statements attempting to link the mental with the physical.

(5) In 1984 the essays on semantic theory were published. Since his interest in this topic goes back to 1953, it seems clear that the two interests are to be viewed as part of a single effort.

(6) Approaching meaning through truth-conditions he defends Tarski's "Convention T," expressing it as: "(T) the sentence s of L is true if and only if p" (where s is $e.g.$, the sentence, "Snow is white" (in the metalanguage), L the language and p the statement to be verified in the object language, namely that snow is white). This is considered to be a provable theorem, and there is to be a comparable theorem for every sentence in the language, the whole to be governed by a finite set of axioms ($i.e.$ a "finitely axiomatized theory of truth"). The sentences governed by Convention T he calls T-sentences.

(7) Davidson holds that Convention T can serve as a truth-conditional theory of meaning (or something like meaning) in which: "(M) the sentence s means p." In this context the meaning of the sentence derives from the meaning of its parts. The claim is, for example, that to understand the truth conditions of sentences in English is to understand English. This inverts Tarski's approach. Tarski's object was to find the meaning of the word "true." Davidson assumes truth and takes Tarski's truth-conditioned approach to illuminate the meaning of terms and sentences in the object language.

(8) On the lower levels of generality it would seem that this approach might work along the lines of Quine's ($q.v.$ 5) stimulus-meaning ($q.v.$ 5, Radical Translation 1), although Davidson denies this, remarking that features of the world "alter in conjunction with changes in attitude towards the truth of sentences." Given the establishment of meaning on the lower levels, recursive generation of

truth conditions would allow the extension of meaning to these sentences, also. But the situation is a bit more complicated. There are finally two principles at work here. One is truth-conditional correspondence. The other, as "formal structure" is imposed on the "thin little bits of evidence" (the T-sentences), is a principle of holistic constraint (which surely involves coherence). This is necessary because Davidson believes "we can give the meaning of any sentence only by giving (the) meaning of every sentence in the language."

(9) Davidson's ideas are still fluid, but it seems possibly fair to say, with respect to radical translation, $i.e.$, translation from a foreign language, that with a correct theory of truth (which would involve knowing all the T-sentences in the language), and with the principle of charity, that the beliefs of native speakers are "largely consistent and true by our standards," the resulting indeterminacy of translation ($q.v.$ Radical Translation 1, 2) will be slight enough that possible interpretations will result. The possibility of moving about between less and more complex locutions within one's own language is even more promising.

DEATH OF GOD.

The 19th-century claim, offered first by Mainländer ($q.v.$ 1), then by Nietzsche ($q.v.$ 4) and Sartre ($q.v.$ 3), that God is dead. The claim seems an exuberant manner of saying that there is no God and that the belief in God is losing credibility. In recent years an American group of "death of God" theologians ($q.v.$ Theology 20) revived the claim. Calling their view Radical Theology, they propose to be religious without God while awaiting in a "sacred void" some new word.

DECALOGUE.

The Ten Commandments. The best-known version is to be found in $Exodus$ 20:2–17. A second version is in $Deuteronomy$ 5:6–21. Attributed to Moses, it is more likely that the Decalogue was a product of centuries of deliberation with additions being made even in the 7th century B.C.

DECIDABILITY.

One of the basic concepts of contemporary metalogic, along with "completeness" (q.v.) and "consistency" (q.v.). The decidability or undecidability of a formula or sentence in a given system concerns the presence or absence within that system of a method of proof applicable to the formula or sentence, and completable within a finite number of steps. (For more on decidability q.v. Tarski 4 and Gödel 4). Church (q.v.) proved in 1936 that the calculus of elementary quantification theory is not decidable.

DECISION THEORY.
A relatively new branch of probability theory concerned with methods of making optimal decisions in a state of incomplete information. John von Neuman's analysis of game theory (*Theory of Games and Economic Behavior*, with O. Morgenstern, 1944), and that of Kenneth Arrow concerning voting behavior (*Social Choice and Individual Values*, 1951) are among the important contributions to this area.

DECLARATION OF FAITH OF THE REFORMED CHURCH IN FRANCE.
Q.v. Gallican Confession.

DECLARATION OF THE CLERGY OF FRANCE.
Q.v. Gallican Articles.

DECLARATIONS.
Q.v. Searle (2).

DECONSTRUCTION.
A movement of literary criticism and philosophic thought, French in origin, appearing as a reaction to Structuralism (q.v.). The presiding genius of the movement is Jacques Derrida (q.v.). Its basic theses are that the primary relation of signs are to each other, that the world is structured in languages, and that the act of criticism is essentially negative.

(1) Many Deconstructionists recognize Gaston Bachelard (1884–1962) as the initial member of their group. Although formally a philosopher of science at the University of Paris, Bachelard's interests extended to epistemology, psychoanalysis, literary anthropology, and a type of literary criticism with which deconstructionists could identify.

(2) Derrida, however, is the founder of the movement. He developed de Saussure's (q.v.) idea of "difference" into

the somewhat more radical "*différance*" (q.v. and q.v. Derrida, *passim*). The view is developed in terms of "the metaphysics of presence," the "trace," "erasure," and the "supplement" (Derrida q.v., *passim*).

(3) The themes of Derrida have been played out remarkably in the United States by a deconstruction movement centered in the Yale Department of English. The difference lies in Derrida's usual choice of philosophy, and the Yale critic's (4–7 below) choice of literature, as the kind of text to be deconstructed.

(4) The moving force in the Yale Department was Paul de Man (1919–83), who found in the literary criticism then current in the United States (the New Criticism, q.v.) a patient, meticulous, "close reading" of the text, a "resistance to theory" and "premature absolutes" which related easily to Derrida. "Resistance to theory" became a characteristic of de Man's style of criticism ("The Resistance to Literary Theory," 1982). The impossibility of an authoritative interpretation is reflected in his discovery of an "unreadability" in the text, which "should not be taken too lightly," equally affecting characters, readers, and authors (*Allegories of Reading*, 1979). There are other things: that sign and meaning never coincide, that literature alone is able to avoid the "fallacy of unmediated expression" through the "literary" use of language, that all true literature occurs in the mode of crisis (*Blindness and Insight*, 1971).

(5) Partially adopting deconstruction, J. Hillis Miller (1928–) wrote new prefaces "deconstructing" his already published phenomenological criticism (*The Disappearance of God*, 1963, new preface, 1976; *The Form of Victorian Fiction*, 1968, 2nd ed., new preface, 1980). Against "totalizing and totalitarian tendencies of criticism," his partial conversion continued to recognize the objective structures of individual texts (*Fiction and Repetition*, 1982).

(6) Geoffrey Hartman's (1929–) arguably gifted neologisms—where "deconstruction" becomes "Derridadaism" and its radical practitioner a "boadeconstructor"—are as ironic as should be expected when philosophy is edification (q.v. 8 below). The critic, while resisting

"nomological readings" and revealing the "uncanniness" of the text, is at the same time reexamining and rewriting the traditions which have become attached to and enshrined in it (*Criticism in the Wilderness*, 1980). Equally, however, although here he has antecedents, in deconstruction the undoing is the preserving of the text (*Beyond Formalism*, 1970; *Saving the Text*, 1981).

(7) Harold Bloom (1930–) argues that every strong reading is a misreading, that weak readings yield neither understanding nor self-knowledge (*A Map of Misreading*, 1975). By "strong misprision" poets "wrest" from their precursors newly canonical texts providing their own claims to authority (*The Anxiety of Influence*, 1973), even though the authors are themselves merely "the site of contending meanings" (*Poetry and Repression*, 1976; *The Flight to Lucifer*, 1979; *Agon*, 1982).

(8) Richard Rorty's (*q.v.*) argument against systematic, and his approval of edifying, philosophy (*Philosophy and the Mirror of Nature*, 1979) target so precisely what deconstructionists oppose as logocentrism that Rorty has been widely accepted as the literary critic's handmaiden to Derrida. In fact his scope is wider than that.

DECREATION.
   Q.v. Simone Weil.

DECRETAL.
   From the Latin *decernere* ("to decide"). In ecclesiastical history the term referred, initially, to papal decrees as distinguished from the decrees of the Councils. The Benedictine monk Gratian's collection of decrees (the *Decretum Gratiani*, c. 1140) included both types and that usage has continued. The *Corpus Juris Canonici* and the *Codex Juris Canonici* (*q.v.* Canon 2) are thus regarded as collections of decretals. The decretal, having the force of general law, is to be distinguished from the rescript (*q.v.*) which applies only to a specific case.

DECURTATE SYLLOGISM.
   From the Latin *decurtatus* ("curtailed" or "shortened"). Hence, "decurtate syllogism" is a synonym for "enthymeme" (*q.v.*), a syllogism with a suppressed premise. *Q.v.* Syllogism (7).

DEDEKIND CUT.
   Q.v. Dedekind (1).

DEDEKIND, JULIUS WILLIAM RICHARD. 1831–1916.
   German mathematician. Teacher, Brunswick Technical High School, 1862–94.
   Principal writings: *Continuity and Irrational Numbers*, 1872; *What Are Numbers and What Should They Be* (T), 1888.
   (1) Dedekind's major contribution to the theory of algebraic numbers is the "Dedekind Cut," allowing us to define irrational numbers in terms of rational numbers. An irrational number, *e.g.*, $\sqrt{2}$ or π, cannot be expressed either precisely or periodically in decimal form. The analogy between rational numbers and the points of a straight line is defective unless irrational numbers are included. The line is continuous but the set of rational numbers alone is not. The inclusion of irrational numbers insures the requisite continuity, and adds to the unity of number theory. An irrational number is defined as standing between all the rational numbers greater than and less than itself. The "Dedekind Cut" marks the place of the irrational number in the number series dividing the series into the two sets of rational numbers we have mentioned.
   (2) The "Dedekind Cut" implies that the order of the number series is compact, and hence characterized by continuity (*q.v.*).

DE DICTO NECESSITY.
   Q.v. Plantinga (1).

DEDUCTION.
   From the Latin *de* ("from") and *ducere* ("to lead"). The Latin term *deductio* was patterned after Aristotle's term *apagoge*. It is commonly taken as referring to those instances of reasoning in which the conclusion follows from the premises necessarily. Deduction can proceed from the general to the particular, general to general, or particular to particular.
   (1) Aristotle (*q.v.* 5) is regarded as the inventor of deduction. Kant held that in 2,000 years logic had not had to retrace a single step. There have of course been numerous interpretations of systems of deduction.
   (2) According to John Stuart Mill (*q.v.* 2) deduction is either verbal transformation,

as in the case of immediate inference, or else it is a probable inference, ultimately inductive, in disguised form.

(3) For Peirce (*q.v.* 8) deduction has to do with the colligation of premises to determine what they may produce in formal terms.

(4) The deductive relation stands in contrast to induction (*q.v.*).

Also *q.v.* Logic; Inference; Syllogism; Propositional Calculus; Quantification Theory.

DEDUCTIVE-NOMOLOGICAL MODEL.
Q.v. Hempel (1); Explanation (2).

DEFINIENDUM.
Q.v. Definition (1).

DEFINIENS.
Q.v. Definition (1).

DEFINITE DESCRIPTIONS, THEORY OF.
A theory developed by Russell (*q.v.* 4) giving an analysis of descriptive phrases beginning with "the"; *e.g.*, "the author of Waverley" or "the present king of France." Strawson (*q.v.* 2) presents a criticism of Russell's theory.

DEFINITION.
From the Latin *de* and *finire* ("to limit"). In both informal and formal logic, it is necessary to provide explanations of the manner in which key terms are going to be employed.

(1) In a definition the term to be defined is called the *definiendum* while the defining term is called the *definiens* (that which does the defining). Often definitions are set forth in the form: "Man" (*definiendum*) = df "rational animal" (*definiens*). One of the ways a definition can be tested is by replacing the *definiendum* with the *definiens* in a sentence. The substitution should result in an intelligible sentence without any change in meaning.

(2) Definitions can be divided into *lexical* definitions which follow common usage, and *stipulative* definitions which assign meanings to words, or a combination of the two. One often begins with usage but eliminates areas of vagueness, possibly in terms of a theoretical analysis. Think, for example, of the manner in which the precision of the concept of

temperature, beginning with feelings of hot and cold, has been increased by theoretical analysis leading to exact measurements.

(3) Definitions can be framed by reference to the things covered by the definition. One can refer to what the definition designates in several ways; *e.g.*, in ostensive definition that is accomplished by pointing. W.E. Johnson (*q.v.* 2) has shown that proper names must be defined ostensively. One can define by example or by enumeration of the relevant sub-classes.

(4) Definitions can be framed by reference to the characteristics of the things covered by the definition. Definition by synonym implicitly calls for reference to such characteristics. Aristotle's definition by genus and difference (*q.v.* Aristotle 4) explicitly isolates a general characteristic of the genus to which the term being defined belongs. The difference or *differentia* supplies a general characteristic of the term being defined which distinguishes it from all other terms belonging to the same genus. When Aristotle defined man as a "rational animal," this was a definition by genus and difference. Man belongs to the genus "animal" and is distinguished from other species belonging to that genus by "rationality."

(5) Bentham (*q.v.* 6) suggested a definition by *paraphrasis* to determine the meaning of a word, phrase, or sentence. The procedure consists of replacing the questionable material with material referring to real entities.

(6) J.S. Mill (*q.v.* 3; Logic 20) held definitions to be nominal only, yielding information only about the uses of language.

(7) Poincaré (*q.v.* 4) placed the restriction on definitions that they could not refer to the whole of the class in which the thing being defined was a member. Definitions in violation of the rule were called Impredicative Definitions. It was his intention to resolve logical paradoxes through this restriction. *Q.v.* Paradox (8).

(8) Charles Stevenson (*q.v.* 3) presents the concept of Persuasive Definitions. These, while seeming to be one of the preceding types, are in fact designed merely to elicit approval or disapproval from those addressed.

DE INESSE.

Latin phrase from *inesse* ("being in"). A technical term used by the Schoolmen in two senses: (1) Propositions were said to be *de inesse* in the simple categorical form where a predicate is affirmed (*est in*), or denied (*non est in*) of a subject. Thus, propositions in the assertoric mode were said to be *de inesse* in contrast to propositions in the modalities of possibility and necessity (*q.v.* Modality). (2) Since accidents of substances were held not to exist in their own right (*in se*), but in something else (*in alio*), their mode of being with respect to substance was said to be a mode *de inesse*.

DEISM.

From the Latin *deus* ("god"). The term was introduced by the Socinians (*q.v.*) in the 16th century to characterize their view in contrast to theism (*q.v.* 1) and atheism. But the term is now taken to apply to a movement of thought in the 17th and 18th centuries, predominantly English, which attempted to replace revelation with the light of reason. In sum —although the summary will not reflect exactly the views of every member—the movement held to a belief in: one God who created the world but does not intervene in its present functioning, either by way of revelation or miracle; an objective difference between right and wrong; the duty of life as support of the right; the immortality of the soul; and our condition in the life to come as related to ethical conduct in this life.

(1) Herbert of Cherbury (*q.v.* 1), the founder of deism, expressed essentially the position set out above in his famous "five pillars of deism." He did allow, however, both natural revelation (akin to insight) and personal revelations concerning the conduct of life.

(2) Matthew Tindal (*q.v.* 2), who called himself a Christian deist, and whose *Christianity as Old as the Creation* was called the Deist Bible, identified Christianity with natural religion.

(3) William Wollaston (*q.v.*) identified natural religion and reason, holding that to follow nature is to follow God.

(4) John Toland (*q.v.* 1) stressed the reasonableness of Christianity, and held that truth was his only orthodoxy.

(5) Thomas Woolston (*q.v.*) argued for the allegorical interpretation of religion and against both prophecy and miracle.

(6) Thomas Chubb (*q.v.*) continued the point of view of Christian deism in the sense earlier established by Herbert of Cherbury and Tindal.

(7) Voltaire (*q.v.* 3), known as the French Deist, paid close attention to the English deists, referring to them in his writings.

(8) The opposition to deism was intense. Among its opponents we mention Bishop Butler (*q.v.* 2) who defended the possibility of miracles.

(9) Paine (*q.v.* 5) held deism to be the only religion compatible with democracy.

(10) Jefferson (*q.v.* 7) was among the members of the Constitutional Convention for whom deism was an attractive alternative.

DEITY.

From the Latin *deus* ("god"). *Q.v.* God; S. Alexander (5).

DELPHIC ORACLE.

The oracle of Apollo at Delphi in Greece was famous from the 6th century B.C. for her cryptic advice on political, as well as religious matters. The priestess answered questions from a trance-like state. Important in philosophy because of the Delphic claim that Socrates (*q.v.* 1) was the wisest man in Greece, and for Socrates' having sanctioned the Delphic motto, "Know thyself."

DEMETER-PERSEPHONE.

Q.v. Mystery Religions (1).

DEMETRIUS OF PHALERUM. c. 345–283 B.C.

Greek philosopher. Disciple of Theophrastus (*q.v.*) and member of the Lyceum (*q.v.*), he wrote on ethics, politics, rhetoric, as well as biography. In addition he governed the city of Athens from 317 to 307 on behalf of the Macedonian king. Upon the restoration of democracy he was forced into exile.

Principal writings: Fragments remain of his writings on the constitution of Athens, rhetoric, and on the life of Socrates.

DEMETRIUS THE CYNIC. 1st cent. A.D.

Greek philosopher. Born at Sunium. While insisting upon the development of a cosmic perspective similar to that of

Stoicism, he yet retained the Cynic insistence upon the role of effort in gaining wisdom; without adversity and the overcoming of obstacles no wisdom is possible. He depreciated scientific knowledge. The Emperor Caligula, we are told, wishing to gain his friendship, sent him a large present. Demetrius replied, "If Caligula had intended to bribe me, he should have offered me his crown." Banished by Vespasian, he laughed at the emperor, mocking his anger.

DEMIURGE.

From the Greek *demiourgos* ("craftsman"). In Plato's *Timaeus*, the maker of the world, according to the eternal forms, in the intractable receptacle of space-time. Plato does not claim exactitude for his account insisting, indeed, that what he is telling amounts to a "likely story," or a fable. There is disagreement concerning how seriously Plato intended the conception of the demiurge to be taken (*q.v.* Plato 9). Also, *q.v.* Marcion of Sinope (1–3).

DEMOCRACY.

From the Greek *demos* ("the people") and *kratein* ("to rule"). Rule by the people may be exercised either directly, as in pure democracy, or through representatives of the people, as in representative democracy. Listed along with monarchy and oligarchy as one of the basic types of government, democracy has been evaluated very differently by philosophers.

(1) Democritus (*q.v.* 12) supported democracy.

(2) In the *Republic* Plato (*q.v.* 5f) held democracy to be at one remove from tyranny, and having the tendency to lead to tyranny. Elsewhere he said that it was the "worst of all lawful governments and the best of all lawless ones."

(3) For Aristotle (*q.v.* 12) democracy is the degenerate form of polity, and the "most tolerable" of the three degenerate forms of government, the other two being tyranny and oligarchy.

(4) The post-Renaissance developments of the idea of sovereignty (*q.v.*), social contract theory (*q.v.*), and the doctrine of natural rights (*q.v.*) supported the development of democracy even though many of those contributing, including Locke (*q.v.* 9) himself, had in mind a limited monarchy.

(5) Spinoza (*q.v.* 10) found democracy preferable to monarchy, since liberty must be guaranteed to citizens, and democracy is more compatible with such liberty.

(6) Montesquieu (*q.v.* 6), who introduced the doctrine of the separation of powers, opted for constitutional monarchy. In fact, he believed that the ideal form of government would be classical democracy building on a base of civic virtue. He also believed that the ideal was not attainable.

(7) Rousseau (*q.v.* 5) supported man's freedom and sovereignty, while holding that the form of government must depend upon a variety of historical considerations. At the same time his analysis and his insistence upon freedom contributed to democratic thought.

(8) The American experiment drew ideas from most of those cited above, constructing a "representative democracy" deriving its powers from the people. Representative government was not only suited to the size of the country to be governed; it also provided a cure for the pressures of the over-bearing majority.

(9) John Stuart Mill (*q.v.* 8) argued for representative government and a maximum of liberty for the citizens of the state. He feared the tyranny of the majority, sensing its power in suppressing liberty; for this reason he wanted the more responsible to have a greater voice in government than the rest.

(10) Dewey (*q.v.* 8) believed democracy to be the one method of organizing society which is in keeping with the method of inquiry.

Also *q.v.* Du Bois (3).

DEMOCRITUS. 460–370 B.C.

Greek philosopher. Born in Abdera. A disciple of Leucippus. It is impossible to separate the doctrines of these two men, which appear here as a single piece of work under Democritus' name. Democritus was as famous as Plato or Aristotle in his own time, but none of his works has survived in original form. In contrast to Protagoras' triumphal tour of Athens, Democritus complained, "I went to Athens and no one knew me." His philosophy is known as atomism.

(1) The ultimate constituents of reality are atoms. "Atom" means the uncuttable, or inseparable, from *a* ("not") and *tome*

("cut, separation"). The impossibility of internal change is explained by the character of atoms as internally solid, simple, homogeneous and without void. Any process of cutting occurs through the penetration of a blade into empty places; without void a thing would be infinitely hard.

(2) The two ultimate explanatory principles, then, are atoms and the void. All composite things are combinations of atoms in the void. The idea of the void is the idea of empty space, the existence of that in which nothing exists and through which existent things can move.

(3) The atoms are naturally and inherently in motion; and differ among themselves in size, shape, and velocity; that is to say, their differences are quantitative; and all qualitative differences are derivative from these.

(4) The atoms move about, collide, and when they have shapes capable of interlocking, combine. Democritus thinks of this in mechanical terms, even suggesting the presence of hook-and-eye relations among the atoms.

(5) There is a causal necessity governing the arrangements and changes among the atoms. The present situation is the outcome of antecedent situations, and the motions of the atoms leading to those situations and from those situations to the present one.

(6) Through collisions of atoms, vortices are set up out of which worlds are generated. There are worlds in process of formation, and worlds in process of dissolution. Just as worlds are generated through collisions of atoms, so worlds may be destroyed by collision with larger worlds. When writing about natural processes he remarks correctly that lunar markings are the shadows cast by mountains.

(7) Life develops out of primeval slime, and is related to warmth and fire. Indeed, fire and soul atoms are similar in nature being smaller and more spherical than the others.

(8) This allows Democritus to believe that thought is a kind of motion, and so is able to cause motion in other things.

(9) Consciousness is a function of the soul atoms which are diffused throughout our bodies, and which we inhale and exhale. A slight loss in their number causes us to sleep; a more radical loss occurs in fainting, and a total loss in death.

(10) Perception or sensation is a physical process, and occurs through the impact of images or *eidola* upon our sense-organs, the images being something like detached outlines of the objects we perceive.

(11) Personal immortality is not possible in this philosophy; and the value theory of Democritus is hedonistic. The end we naturally seek is enjoyment, and we naturally avoid pain. The way to determine good and bad, useful and harmful, is in terms of the pleasure and pain involved. But not all pleasures are equally good; the pleasures of the mind are more enduring than pleasures of sense. Moderation is the appropriate means for reaching a general well-being and cheerfulness, a state of untroubled pleasure known as *ataraxia* (*q.v.*).

(12) Democritus supported democracy as the most appropriate social ordering.

DEMONAX OF CYPRUS. c. 80–180.

Greek philosopher. A disciple of Epictetus (*q.v.*), Demonax was somewhat eclectic in his point of view. Because he, along with Oenomaus of Gadara (*q.v.*), opposed the fatalism of the Stoics, and the consultation of oracles, he is regarded as a member of the Cynic school (*q.v.* Cynicism). His central positive emphasis was on moderation and wisdom.

DEMONOLOGY.

Initially, the view that there are demons (Latin *daemon*, Greek *daimon*, meaning "spirit" or "divinity"), superhuman beings inferior to the gods, who help or harm men. In its development in Zoroastrianism, Judaism, Christianity, and Islam, hierarchies of demons were presumed to exist, malevolent in nature, the angels of the devil acting in opposition to the angels of God.

Q.v. Zoroaster (2); Gnosticism.

DE MORGAN, AUGUSTUS. 1806–1871.

English mathematician and logician. Educated at Cambridge. Professor of mathematics in University College, London. Founder and first president of the London Mathematical Society.

Principal writings: *An Essay on Probabilities*, 1838; *Formal Logic*, 1847; *Syllabus* of a *Proposed System of Logic,* 1860; *A Budget of Paradoxes,* 1872.

(1) Credited with introducing the phrase "universe of discourse" to refer to the set of classes relevant to a given argument, and one of the founders of the logic of relations, he elaborated an algebra of logic similar in many respects to that of Boole (*q.v.*).

(2) Two basic equivalences of the Propositional Calculus (*q.v.* 13) are known as De Morgan's Theorems: "~ (p · q) ≡ (~ pv ~ q)" and "~ (pvq) ≡ (~ p · ~ q)."

(3) In his work on probability De Morgan followed Laplace (*q.v.* 3), while approaching the subject from the side of formal logic. As a result the subjective approach to probability, already implicit in Laplace, became explicit. Probability attaches to those propositions which are less than certain, and is a measure of the degree of belief a rational being should have in a given proposition of this type. The method of calculating probability in this sense is the inverse theorem which begins with deduced consequences and attempts to estimate the probable truth of the hypothesis from which the consequences were derived.

DE MORGAN'S THEOREMS.

Q.v. De Morgan (2); Propositional Calculus (13).

DEMYTHOLOGIZING THE NEW TESTAMENT.

Q.v. Bultmann (1).

DENNET, DANIEL C. 1947– .

American philosopher, born in Boston. Educated at Harvard and Oxford. Has taught at Oxford College of Technology, University of California at Irvine, and since 1971, at Tufts University.

Principal writings: *Content and Consciousness,* 1969; *Brainstorms,* 1978; *The Mind's Eye* (with D.R. Hofstadter), 1981; *Elbow Room: the Varieties of Free Will Worth Wanting,* 1984; *The Intentional Stance,* 1987; *Consciousness Explained,* 1991.

(1) Having as his goal the development of "a theory of the mind," Dennett is a serious student of both psychology and cognitive science. In philosophy he is "a sort of realist," accepts Quinian (*q.v.* 5) indeterminacy, eliminative materialism (*q.v.* Materialism 22), and appears to be-

lieve in at least a slight amount of cosmic indeterminism ("undetermined choice points in the causal chain").

(2) The areas he struggles to bring together are "intentional system theory" and "subpersonal cognitive psychology." The first begins on the level of Folk Psychology (*q.v.*) where our language is strongly intentional; here we are "believers, desirers, expecters, and intenders." The language of scientific psychology, however, is mechanistic, predictive, subpersonal, and not yet in place.

(3) In this situation one makes up explanations on the intentional level, taking out "intelligence loans" to be cashed out when replacement mechanisms are discovered. For example, not knowing the design of a computer, we think of it as an intentional system and on this basis are often able to predict its behavior. We may even think of an *homunculus* (*q.v.*) in part of the system ("a little man in the machine") freeing us to work out the mechanism of other parts of the program. Study of "nonlanguage-using" animals likewise requires the use of intelligence loans, and the assumption of rationality helps the analysis.

(4) Computer programs of whose design we are ignorant, and subpersonal animals fit among the levels of explanation lying between the personal and the mechanistic. Dennett's project for bringing the two levels together is to move "down" from the intelligent intentional system of folk psychology through successively more "stupid" intentional systems to one sufficiently low-level that it can be characterized without strain in mechanistic terms.

(5) That most stupid system may or may not be what one means by mechanistic determinism. In either case one wonders if the personhood, morality, responsibility, and freedom which he finds on the level of folk psychology remain defensible in the most stupid final system.

(6) With respect to free will, he conducts the argument from the intentional level, concluding that we can have what we want when we want free will, even should it be the case (something we cannot know) that it does not exist as a metaphysical absolute.

DENOTATION.

From the Latin *de* and *notare* ("to note" or "mark"). Correlative to the term "connotation" (*q.v.*), the denotation of a term is the thing or set of things to which the term refers. The denotation of "table" is all the tables that exist, have existed, or will exist. *Q.v.* J.S. Mill (11); G. Frege (4). C.I. Lewis (*q.v.* 4c) holds a somewhat different view. Also (*q.v.*) Jakobson.

DENYING THE ANTECEDENT.

Q.v. Fallacies (28).

DENYING THE CONSEQUENT.

Q.v. Syllogism (10).

DEONTIC LOGIC.

From the Greek *deon* ("necessity," "obligation"). A sub-branch of Modal Logic (*q.v.* and *q.v.* Logic 25), deontic logic studies the type of necessity present in statements of obligation. The present stage of the discipline is experimental, testing out a great number of alternate ways of expressing obligation. Among those prominent in the discussions of the area are G.H. von Wright (*q.v.* 1), Alan R. Anderson, Jaako Hintikka (*q.v.* 3), and R.M. Chisholm (*q.v.* 6).

DEONTOLOGY.

From the Greek *deon* ("necessity," "obligation"). Thus, the term means literally something like "theory of obligation." Jeremy Bentham (*q.v.*) titled his work on ethics *Deontology or the Science of Morality*. Although Bentham's system of ethics was axiological and teleological, the term "deontological ethics" has come to characterize those systems where rightness is determined without regard to consequences, and thus the systems of such philosophers as Immanuel Kant (*q.v.* 6–7), W.D. Ross (*q.v.*), and Rule Utilitarians (*q.v.* Utilitarianism). The distinctions between axiological, teleological, and formalistic approaches are discussed in Ethics (1–3).

DEPENDENCY THEORY.

Q.v. Theology of Liberation (8c).

DEPENDENT CO-ARISING.

English translation of Sanskrit term, *pratitya-samutpada* (Pali *paticca samuppada*). The concept of causality most reasonably attributed to Buddha (*q.v.* 2) in whose entry the 12-fold formula, also called the twelve causal links of Dependent Origination (better phrased, dependent co-origination), are given. "Dependent co-arising," however, matches the dynamism and reciprocity of the factors which swarm together in this multiply-sourced, nonlinear view of causality, the factors involved in producing an effect, as well as the effects, are characterized by *anitya* (impermanence), *duhkha* (suffering), and *anatman* (no self). His discussion centered on causation as related to the problem of the self, the causal factors of his treatment including feeling, perception, volition, consciousness and ignorance, as well as becoming, birth, and death. Buddha's more general purpose is to describe how, through ignorance, suffering arises. This knowledge points one to the path of its elimination. The problem is, of course, *samsara* (*q.v.*), the cycle of existence, and this came to be depicted as a wheel, *bhavacakra* (*q.v.*) (Skt., "wheel of becoming"); implying repeated cycles of existence until emancipation is achieved.

DEPENDENT ORIGINATION.

Q.v. Dependent Co-arising.

DEPTH PSYCHOLOGY.

Q.v. Psychology (10); Freud (1).

DE RE NECESSITY.

Q.v. Plantinga (1).

DERRIDA, JACQUES. 1930– .

Born in El Biar, Algeria. Educated at École Normale Supérieure, University of Paris, Harvard University. Has taught at École Normale Supérieure, École des Hautes Études Sciences Sociales.

Principal writings: *Of Grammatology* (T), 1967; *Speech and Phenomena and Other Essays on Husserl's Theory of Signs* (T), 1967; *Writing and Difference* (T), 1967; *Dissemination* (T), 1972; *Margins of Philosophy* (T), 1972; *Positions* (T), 1972; *The Archaeology of the Frivolous* (T), 1973; *Glas* (T), 1974; *Limited Inc: abc* (T), 1977; *Truth in Painting* (T), 1978; *The Post Card* (T), 1980; *On the Right to Philosophy*, 1990; *Given Time;* (T), 1991; *Memoirs of the Blind* (T), 1991; *Raising the Tone of Philosophy* (ed. P. Fenves) (T), 1993 (on Kant's late essays).

(1) Citing (in his essay on "Différance," 1968) de Saussure's (*q.v.*) discovery that speech is a system of differences between signs, Derrida invented the term *différance* to stand for the double fact that for signs to function they must "differ" from each other; and, since there is no way of bringing any chain of signification to an end, signs must "defer" to one another endlessly. This is the free play of signifiers, which he addressed, first of all, in relation to three major philosophers.

(2) From Plato, and Greek metaphysics generally, he developed the idea of "presence." Plato preferred speech to writing because of the presence in dialogue of speakers to each other. For Plato inner speech is pure self-immediacy, a dialogue of the soul with itself; the dialogue of two different speakers has shared immediacy. Whether one is present to oneself or to another, both types of dialogue feature speech (*phone*); they are "phonocentric."

(3) When speech is written down, the speaker is normally absent, and the interpretation is controlled by the reader; Socrates/Plato pointed out that what is written down can be maltreated and abused. Derrida found a bias toward the spoken word in Greek metaphysics and in Western culture generally. In fact, however, he also argued that Western thought assumes self-presence in both spoken and written discourse. Consider, in Greek metaphysics, the timeless present, the immortal soul, eternal forms, the primacy of Being, and the eternal God. Such concepts, presuming presence, are viewed by Derrida as "logocentric" (from *logos*, "word, speech, reason," also "the *word* of God"). Logocentrism supposes that truth and reality can be made present to one, and tries to insure this by following a logic of identity, non-contradiction, and excluded middle. But in all these cases, in written, as well as spoken, discourse, absence has clearly intruded. All such logocentrisms deconstruct before the differential play of signifiers, *i.e.*, before *différance*.

(4) Derrida finds logocentrism also in Husserl's (*q.v.* 4, 6) pure intuitions of essence, which are, equally, pure intuitions of presence. Husserl regarded intuited essences as expressions, and contrasted them with signs which indicate things through distance and absence. Derrida argued that absence is equally present in expressions and in indications. When Husserl finally granted that the quest for timeless essence was a failure he would seem to have agreed.

(5) The mixture of presence and absence runs throughout philosophy, appearing in the oppositions of identity/difference, being/nothing, same/other, truth/falsity, even life/death. In every case, however, *différance* maintains our relationship with what is absent through "the play of the trace" in what we necessarily misconstrue. The free play of signifiers allows us this.

(6) Derrida approves of the manner in which Heidegger treats this problem. In his later writings Heidegger tries to overcome the "ontotheological" bias of Greek philosophy by putting Being under erasure (*sous rature*). Whenever he wrote down the word "Being," he at once cancelled it by drawing a large "X" across the surface of the word, allowing the word and its cancellation to stand in contradiction. Behind the cancelled sign Heidegger found a hidden play of metaphors.

(7) The conclusion of these points is Derrida's view that all words are inaccurate and need to be cancelled out. All words are under erasure, yet both word and cancellation need to be retained to mark the trace element of deferred presence, the "forever absent" the word was intended to make present. In this sense *différance* is "the play of the trace" as well as "a trace of the erasure of the trace." Because everything is under erasure a new kind of linguistics is called for, which Derrida named "Grammatology." The point of Grammatology is to encourage the deconstruction of texts. It is accompanied by a logic of non-identity; rather than, the either-or of the principle of excluded middle, the operative principle is neither-nor (or both-and).

(8) In deconstruction decidable concepts are translated into undecidable traces. The author, concerned to create a united text, but aware of its inner oppositions, invokes one member of the opposition as a "supplement" to the one with which he had begun. The supplement presents itself, however, not only as an addition to, but also as a substitute for, the original concept. It stands

for both. Every text, then, has a second message coming from "the logic of the supplement." Every text is other than itself. There is "alterity," a play of otherness diffusing every text.

(9) In this mixture of fiction with truth the careful critic knows that the problems of the text must be made clear. The difference between the author's description and declaration, that is, the duplicity of the text, must be brought out while staying within the text, and avoiding the temptation to resolve the ambiguities and oppositions introduced by *différance*. Deconstruction can make the bias clear but has no grounds for reconstruction.

(10) Since "lived experience" turns at once into text, Derrida holds that there is nothing outside the text. One might imagine that outside the text is a "something I know not what" which feeds textuality, but Derrida doesn't say this. Even the speaking (thinking, conscious) subject is a "function of language." The "self-presence" of consciousness, then, has the same problems as any other text, so that doubt is cast on its primacy and integrity. It is not that the subject is denied but, rather, opened to alterity, the playful desire for what is other than oneself.

(11) *Glas* is representative of the later Derrida. In *Glas* the reader is presented with a double column text, one column featuring Genet's *Our Lady of the Flowers* and other novels, the other Hegel's *Phenomenology of the Spirit*. The two columns "haunt" each other, the preoccupation of the Hegel column centers in Hegel's discussion of the nature of Judaism and Christianity, the preoccupation of the other in carnal, especially homosexual, love. In their run of some 300 pages the columns instantiate many of Derrida's views on deconstruction and *différance*. One example of this instantiation: The Hegel column begins with the question: "what, after all, of the remain(s), today" of Hegel? The Genet column with: "what remained of a Rembrandt torn into small, very regular squares?" and ends with "the debris of" (*"le debris de"*) (Derrida?), suggesting the demise of his name, Rembrandt's, and (symbolically) all proper names. Since, along the way, he has told us: "do not rely on the proper name," this demise of proper names may exemplify his view that the death knell of the proper name is the birth of the literary text.

DERVISH.

From the Persian *darvish* ("beggar"). A member of a Muslim religious order resembling Western monasticism, sometimes mendicant, originating in the 12th century A.D., whose rituals stress hypnotism and ecstatic trance, often involving wandering, howling, or whirling. The accelerated turning of the whirling dervishes (called *Malawiyya* in Arabic) is expected to develop an openess to divine grace. Whirling away earthly ties, they believe, enables them to reach the infinite.

DESCARTES, RENÉ. 1596–1650.

French philosopher, rationalist rather than empiricist in approach. Born at La Haye. Educated in the Jesuit School of La Flèche. Dissatisfied with the traditional nature of his schooling, he turned to the book of the world, following a military career for a number of years. Returning to scholarship he lived first in Paris, then in Holland from 1629–1649. He invented Analytic Geometry, and applied a geometrical method to philosophy. The last year of his life was spent in Sweden tutoring Queen Christina in philosophy, and planning an academy of the sciences. Contracting an inflammation of the lungs, he died there in 1650.

Principal writings: *Discourse On Method* (T), 1637; *Geometry* (T), 1637; *The Meditations* (T), 1641; *Principles of Philosophy* (T), 1644; *The Passions of the Soul* (T), 1649; *Letters* (T in part), 1657–67; *The World, or Treatise on Light*, 1664; *Rules for the Direction of the Mind* (T), 1701.

(1) The possibility of certain knowledge depends upon getting beyond the point of skepticism; and this can be done only, if at all, through pushing skepticism to its final limits. One is sometimes deceived by one's senses. How does one know that this is not a constant occurrence? How does one know that one's present experience is not a dream, or that an evil genius is not deceiving one at every moment, and in every way, with respect both to external and internal appearances? If this is so, only one thing is certain; namely, that nothing is certain.

(2) But if one is doubtful of everything,

one must exist to do the doubting. Hence, we come to the famous formula, "*Cogito, ergo sum.*" To say "I think, therefore I am" is to assert that there is at least one proposition which can stand against the skepticism of doubt.

(3) Examining the nature of his certainty of self, Descartes finds it lies in the clarity and distinctness of the idea he has of himself; and hence lays down the rule that "Whatever is apprehended clearly and distinctly is true." By a clear idea he seems to mean one which we recognize in various contexts; and by a distinct idea one which is clear in every sense, and which we never confuse with another.

(4) Making an inventory of his ideas, seeking another instance as clear as the idea of himself he finds it possible to classify his ideas into those which are innate, adventitious, and factitious. (a) Innate ideas originate from within himself, such as the idea of himself. (b) Adventitious ideas come, or seem to come, through the senses. (c) Factitious ideas are made up from the elements of the ideas of other things. On examination it seems to him that all of the ideas in his mind, other than the idea of himself and one other, may be either factitious or adventitious ideas.

(5) The other exception is the idea of God. He has an idea of "a substance that is infinite, eternal, immutable, independent, all-powerful, and by which I myself and everything else, if anything else does exist, have been created." And on reflection he finds that the perfection present in this idea is such that it could not have come from the ideas of other things, or have been manufactured from ideas of himself. This meant that it was innate; and, on reflection, he discovers that it is, in a sense, the reverse side of the coin, whose obverse is his innate idea of himself as a thinking but limited being. Reflection on the fact of his doubt teaches him of his imperfection; and comparison of his imperfect being with the perfection present in the idea of God in his mind convinces him that (a) the idea of himself as imperfect is derivative from the idea of God as perfect; (b) he can by limitation get the idea of himself from the idea of God, but not the idea of God from the idea of himself, or of other

things; hence, (c) the source of the idea of God must be found in God himself. (d) Just as the idea of a mountain requires the idea of a valley; just as the idea of a triangle requires the idea that its internal angles will be equal to 180 degrees; so the idea of a perfect being requires the idea that this being exists. Hence, God cannot be conceived except as existing; and God can be conceived. This is of course, a statement of the ontological argument. Descartes presented two versions, one is in the *Meditations*, the other in the *Reply to Objections.*

(6) Now, if God exists, and is good, he could not be a deceiver. Hence, it is possible to dismiss the suggestion that one is being deceived at every moment. It follows that while one cannot trust every perception, one can trust all of those where one observes with care.

(7) What then is the condition for error? It lies in the fact that the will is free; and this freedom is something of which one is aware at every moment of decision, the feeling that one could be doing something else. This freedom is what leads to error, when the will has outrun reason. When the reason proceeds with care, however, it can reach truth. Why this confidence in the reason? It derives, perhaps, from one's firm adherence to the view that the objective is that which is present in thought (*idealiter in intellectu*) while the subjective is that which is in the things themselves (*formaliter in se ipsius*). His theory of perception stressed the view that perception is itself an intellectual act.

(8) Avoiding such errors, however, it is now possible to posit the existence of an external world, including both minds and bodies, our own, and those other than ourselves. A clear difference is discernible between minds and bodies. (a) Body is extended, a *res extensa*, and has reference to space and time, and motion. Indeed, Descartes identifies matter with extension, and elaborates a corpuscular theory of the universe on this basis. Descartes' theory holds that all of space is filled, and yet motion is possible on the part of the corpuscles which fill it. (b) Mind is just the opposite, without extension, and with no essential need for reference to space and time. It is a *res cogitans* or "thinking thing." Thus he

holds thought and extension to be the two chief attributes of reality. More precisely, thought is the attribute of mind and extension is the attribute of body, while the modes of mind and body are the "accidental" forms in which they may exist. Imagination, sensation and will are modes of thought, for example. Minds and bodies are created substances. God alone, as the self-subsistent Being, is substance in the fullest sense; and he advances a version of the cosmological argument concerning the dependence of created substance on God for the conservation of its being.

(9) It is obvious that since life involves this conjunction of mind and body, their separation allows both to continue; hence, an idea of immortality is rather close to the surface of this philosophy. The result of Descartes' having so completely separated mind and body was the conviction on the part of many that in that situation mind and body could not influence each other. A doctrine of Occasionalism soon appeared, held by Malebranche and others. The basic idea of Occasionalism was that God came in between mind and body, enabling the two to interact; the mind would make its decision and God would move the body.

(10) In the *Discourse on Method* Descartes recommended an approach to all problems something like that which he utilized in the *Meditations*. One is to break a complex problem down into its simplest parts, arrange the parts in an appropriate order from simple to complex, begin at the beginning, demonstrating each point, and continuing to the end. Ideas are also broken down into their clear and distinct, indecomposable *simple natures*; the solution of problems has to do with the rearranging of these ideas. At the same time Descartes did speak, on occasion, of hypotheses. His normal usage is that hypotheses are simply convenient starting points for deductions, and that their truth or falsity is not established.

(11) In *The Passions of the Soul* he tells us that the passions are modes of the thinking substance. He analyzes man's emotional life in terms of the six key passions of admiration, love, hate, desire or appetite, happiness, and sadness.

DESCRIPTION, KNOWLEDGE BY.
Q.v. Russell (6).

DESCRIPTIONS, DEFINITE.
Q.v. Russell (4); Frege (4, 6).

DESCRIPTIVE PSYCHOLOGY.
Q.v. Psychology (17); Brentano (1).

DESIGN ARGUMENT.
Q.v. Teleological Argument.

DESIGNATUM.
From the Latin *designo* ("to mark out or trace"). The referent of a word, symbol, or expression.

**DESTUTT DE TRACY, ANTOINE.
1758–1836.**
French philosopher. Born in Paris. Educated at Strasbourg. Living through the Revolution, he served in the States-General and was imprisoned under the Terror. Influenced by Condillac and Locke, he was on friendly terms with Condorcet and Cabanis. He named his philosophy, Ideology, and a philosophical group, the Idéologues, gathered around him. Meaning by Ideology an analysis of ideas into their sensory elements—the view that they are so composed he found especially in Locke (*q.v.* 5) but also in Condillac (*q.v.* 2, 4)—Destutt urged that such analysis replace logic and be applied in all fields of knowledge. His view became influential both in the École Normale and in the Institut National. The Institut was a young Organization, and in 1803 Napoleon "suppressed" its sec-ond class, finding Destutt's philosophy dangerous to religion. His final work was translated into English by Thomas Jefferson and published in Philadelphia.

Principal writings: *Elements of Ideology*, 4 vols., 1801–15 (consisting of *Ideology*, 1801; *General Grammar*, 1803; *Logic*, 1805; *Treatise on the Will*, 1815); *Commentary on the Spirit of the Laws of Montesquieu* (T), 1817.

DETERMINABLE.
Q.v. W.E. Johnson (4).

DETERMINANT.
Q.v. W.E. Johnson (4).

DETERMINISM.

From the Latin *determinare* ("to set bounds or limits.") The word entered philosophical terminology through Sir William Hamilton who applied the term to Thomas Hobbes in order to distinguish Hobbes' position from fatalism. The position holds that every event or occurrence is "determined," *i.e.*, could not have happened other than it did. The term is opposed to indeterminism (*q.v.*), and to many definitions of free will.

(1) Democritus (*q.v.* 5) is an early adherent of physical determinism, holding to causal necessity as the explanation of any event.

(2) Epicurus (*q.v.* 5) follows Democritus, while departing from strict determinism in allowing the atoms a power to swerve slightly and spontaneously off course, creating swirling motions and, eventually, worlds. Lucretius (*q.v.* 3) followed Epicurus in all respects (*q.v.* Epicureanism).

(3) Diodorus Cronos (*q.v.* 3), the Megarian, based his determinism on the logical grounds that the idea of unactualized possibility is incoherent.

(4) Stoicism (*q.v.* 1) held that the world, including man, is rationally determined by the universal reason, and that it is man's responsibility to understand and accept his place in the scheme of things. The determinism is both rational and physical, indissolubly linked together.

(5) Carneades (*q.v.* 4), an opponent of Stoicism, added the idea of self-determination to the analysis, holding that so-called uncaused action is caused by the person himself.

(6) Vanini (*q.v.*) believed in an immanent God ruling a determined universe.

(7) Hobbes (*q.v.* 1–2) defends the notion of strict physical determinism based on causal necessity.

(8) Spinoza (*q.v.* 8–9) carried on the Stoic conception where both rational and physical determination apply to every event. For Spinoza the feeling of being free is simply the state of ignorance concerning the cause.

(9) Hume (*q.v.* 2–3) supported a conception of determinism altered by the fact that causality means for him simply regularity in the expected succession of events. This kind of determinism can be consistent with his definition of freedom (*q.v.* 11).

(10) Priestley (*q.v.* 2) held that only determinism is consistent with the greatest happiness principle.

(11) Laplace (*q.v.* 3) expressed his view of determinism with the claim that were there an intelligence with knowledge of the position, direction, and velocity of every particle of the universe, this intelligence would be able to predict by means of a single formula every detail of the total future as well as of the total past. For an updated version of this view, *q.v.* Minkowski (2), Einstein (4).

(12) The analysis of Freud (*q.v.* 3), insisting upon the presence of unconscious determinants in human action, has led to a doctrine of psychological determinism: namely, that any alternative selected by any individual is the effect of multiple determinants, of some of which we are aware, of others of which we are not aware. Together, however, they determine what will be chosen.

(13) Ducasse (*q.v.* 1) held indeterminism to be self-contradictory.

(14) For a view of the sciences as deterministic, including quantum mechanics, biology, psychology, and history, *q.v.* Nagel (1–4).

(15) A distinction is often drawn between hard and soft determinism, the former following the lines of Laplace and Hobbes, the latter including the notion of self-determination introduced by Carneades.

(16) For an Eastern view of determinism *q.v.* Ajivikas (1).

Also *q.v.* Materialism.

DEUS ABSCONDITUS.

A Latin term meaning "the hidden God." In contrast to a rationalistic and humanistic approach to theology Luther (*q.v.* 9) found the divine hiddenness as much a part of religious experience as the divine presence. The contrast may be drawn between the "enlightenment" attitude of Erasmus (*q.v.*) and Luther's struggle to achieve salvation by faith, and that alone, in a dark and fallen world.

DEUS EX MACHINA.

A Latin phrase meaning literally "a god from a machine." Referring originally to the maneuver in some classical tragedies of bringing a god on stage to solve the problems of the plot, it refers to anything artificially introduced, as into a philosophy, to solve its inherent difficulties.

DEUS SIVE NATURA.

Latin phrase meaning "God or nature." A concept used in the philosophy of Spinoza (*q.v.* 3).

DEÚSTUA, ALEJANDRO O.

Q.v. Latin American Philosophy (8).

DEVA.

A Sanskrit term meaning "bright heavenly one." Originally designating the nature gods of the Vedic religion, sons of the sky father, Dyaus. Later, the designation for God in Hinduism and Buddhism and of the evil spirits in Zoroastrianism. In the latter religion the *devas* became the *daevas* or demons (*q.v.* Demonology), allies of Ahriman, the evil deity in the world struggle between good and evil (*q.v.* Zoroaster 1, 3). The Indo-European root of the term becomes *deus* in Latin, *theos* in Greek, and devil in both languages.

DEVI.

Q.v. Mahadevi.

DEWEY, JOHN. 1859–1952.

American philosopher. Born in Burlington, Vermont. Educated at Vermont and Johns Hopkins. Taught at Michigan, Minnesota, Chicago, and Columbia University. Initially Hegelian, he was much influenced by William James' *Principles of Psychology*. Interested in education Dewey, while in Chicago, organized an experimental elementary school under the auspices of the Philosophy Department. At Columbia he related himself both to the Philosophy Department and Teachers' College, developing both interests throughout his life.

Principle writings: *Psychology*, 1887; *Studies in Logical Theory*, 1903; *Ethics* (with Tufts), 1908; *How We Think*, 1910; *Essays in Experimental Logic*, 1916; *Reconstruction in Philosophy*, 1920; *Human Nature and Conduct*, 1922; *Experience and Nature*, 1925; *The Quest for Certainty*, 1929; *Art as Experience*, 1934; *A Common Faith*, 1934; *The Teacher and Society*, 1937; *Experience and Education*, 1938; *Logic: The Theory of Inquiry*, 1939; *Theory of Valuation*, 1939.

(1) "Philosophy recovers itself when it ceases to be a device for dealing with the problems of philosophers and becomes a method, cultivated by philosophers, for dealing with the problems of men." Not satisfied with the philosophy of his age he called for a reconstruction, which would return philosophy to experience, eliminate absolutes, and foster the idea of control by creative intelligence. The publication of Darwin's *The Origin of Species* sets the stage for philosophy's reconstruction, requiring us to view ourselves as creatures who must adapt to each other and to environing conditions in order to survive. The emphasis on adaptation requires a shift in philosophic emphasis from system to method, from fixed result to the process of inquiry.

(2) Inquiry, properly speaking, begins in situations which are indeterminate, disturbed, troubled, ambiguous, obscure, or full of conflict. It is the object of inquiry to transform the indeterminate situation into one which is determinate. Given such a situation, and such an outcome, the intervening steps outlined by Dewey are: (a) locating and defining the problem of the situation; insight is as important in stating the problem as in any subsequent step; (b) setting out the relevant possible solutions to this problem, an "either-or" stage; (c) developing the consequences of the possible solutions, an "if-then" stage; (d) relating these developed alternatives to further observation and experiment; (e) concluding with the alternative which unifies the situation.

(3) With experience one begins and to experience one returns. If the goal of inquiry is not some species of abstract truth, but a transformed situation, the evidence which moves one along toward this goal—called by Dewey "warranted assertibility"—suggests rather more flexibility of attitude than is expected in more traditional modes of justification.

(4) The elimination of fixed ends from nature, one of the lessons to be learned from Darwin, has its corollary in the elimination of fixed ends from human nature. For such fixed ends Dewey substitutes "the means-end continuum." The ends we posit for ourselves are final only until achieved, and become means for further ends which we then project. Ideas are instruments which lead to action, and are to be understood in terms of the actions to which they do or may lead, thus the name, Instrumentalism, which this philosophy often bears.

(5) But Dewey characterizes his philosophy as naturalism, quite as often as he calls his view Instrumentalism. Believing that values, as well as facts, can be discovered in, and sanctioned by, experience, he is a naturalist in ethical theory. Ethical naturalism holds that questions of right and wrong can be settled by the adducing of evidence. He believes that in the process of inquiry the "better" can emerge.

(6) In his discussions of "art as experience," and in his later discussions of logic, experience is divided into instrumental and consummatory phases. The "unified whole" in which successful inquiry terminates, and unity of esthetic appreciation are instances of experience in its consummatory phase; and, indeed, they share many characteristics. Dewey says that the consummatory phase of experience is desired for itself alone.

(7) Combining many of the standard definitions of freedom, Dewey presents freedom as the ability to make intelligent choices, and to act upon them, while acting from the base of one's own individuality.

(8) In social philosophy Dewey argues for democracy as the one means of social organization which is in keeping with the method of inquiry. It is also in keeping with the goal of freedom. Nor are democracy and national planning antithetical; rather, this application of intelligence can provide the conditions for a more genuine type of freedom.

(9) It is not untoward to retain the idea of God if the term is redefined to stand for that active relation between the actual and the ideal. If one is to mean no more than this by the term, its use, Dewey recognizes, will lead to misunderstanding; and Dewey did not himself favor the term in his own writing.

(10) Dewey's philosophy of education is simply his philosophy in application, turning especially on his view of inquiry (*q.v.* 2 above). The result is a view of education centering around the needs of individuals and the prospects for their development. As in the rest of Dewey's philosophy, fixed ends are eliminated, experimentation is encouraged, and the future plays a larger role than does the past.

DHAMMAPADA, THE.

A Pali term meaning "the path of virtue." The *Dhammapada* is an early Buddhist document discussing the chief values of life and the path which leads to enlightenment. Moving within the framework of *karma* (*q.v.*) and rebirth, the four noble truths of Buddha and eightfold path, the *Dhammapada* provides meditations concerning the practice of the way to salvation.

(1) Non-attachment, freedom from desire, serenity, calm, self-control, and self-possession mark the man who is approaching his goal. In this state he will be without fear, and characterized by the highest standards of personal purity.

(2) Such a person is the true Brahmin, ready for Nirvana. Others are bound to the wheel of rebirth. The reward of heaven and hell are also mentioned, but the final goal is Nirvana.

(3) In pursuance of this goal there are chapters on vigilance, thought, the wise man, the *arahant* (saint), the Buddha, happiness, righteousness, the eightfold path, the mendicant, the Brahmin, the elimination of craving and related topics.

DHARANA.

The sixth step in Yogic meditation. *Q.v.* Yoga (4).

DHARMA.

From the Sanskrit *dhr* ("to sustain, support, uphold"). An open-ended term with many related meanings: appropriate ritual, duty, truth, and the elements of ontology; also law, righteousness, property, that which is proper, fate, that one's role in life is metaphysically determined, that the orders of human life and of the universe are intimately related and interactive.

A. The term was introduced within Hinduism, and with shifting meanings in various portions of Hindu scriptures.

(1) In the *Ṛgveda* the term is associated most often with ritual activity and sacrifice as prescribed, which were understood as contributing to the maintenance of the cosmic order.

(2) In the *Brahmanas* the priestly performance of rituals is related to one's well-being in the world to come, and *dharma* gains a normative dimension, referring to the obligations flowing from

one's caste and one's stage of life (*asrama* *q.v.*). One's *dharma* is the sum of these obligations, called *varnashramadharma*.

(3) In addition, there is *sadharanadharma* ("obligations pertaining to everyone"). These are basic ethical rules of human relations (*q.v. Kautilya* 3).

(4) When human obligations were related to karmic order, and the goal of life came to be release from *samsara* (*q.v.*), a conflict appeared between *dharma* and release (*mokṣa*, *q.v.*). The conflict was overcome in various ways, one of which held the world to be illusion (*q.v.* Śankara).

B. The Buddhist use of the term provided other ways out of the conflict.

(5) The normative sense of *dharma* in Buddhism began with Buddha's teachings in which *dharmas* are ethical prescriptions. Elaborated into ethical doctrines the Buddhist approach was able to avoid the conflicts of (2)–(4) above because, for one thing, since Buddhism was anti-caste, the ethical obligations were the same for everyone. The distinction between (2) and (3) above did not exist, so that right action could relate directly to release through the avoidance of bad karma.

(6) *Dharma* is also associated with true doctrine, and so, once again, with the teachings of Buddha. The texts which record the teachings were called *dharmas*. By association Buddha was called a *dharma*, and the *Buddhadharma* led to the Mahayana idea of the *dharmakaya* (*q.v.*) or "body of *dharma*," that is, the Buddha as absolute underlying reality.

(7) There is a second Buddhist identification of *dharma* with reality, the Buddhist doctrine of aggregates supposes that reality is composed of many elements. These elements are called *dharmas*, and existence is viewed as a flux of *dharmas*. (a) In the Sarvastivada (*q.v.*) school there are 72 conditioned *dharmas* subject to the law of dependent origination (causality), and three which are not. The 72 conditioned *dharmas* perpetuate one's conditioned existence. The three unconditioned *dharmas* contribute to release. But also, the flux is perpetuated by an attitude of ignorance (*avidya*), and lessened when related to through intuitive wisdom. Conditioned *dharmas* include the elements of physical reality, the elements of cognition, the properties of things. The unconditioned *dharmas* are space, and two

forms of enlightenment. The *dharma* analysis thus puts together items which the western mind tends to separate; and makes distinctions where the western mind would not. (b) The Theravada school lists 81 conditioned *dharmas* and one unconditioned *dharma*, Nirvana. (c) The analysis differs, of course, from school to school, the numbers of *dharmas* changing with each analysis, rising to 550 in one listing and 1,011 in another.

C. The *dharma* analysis of Jainism (*q.v.*) parallels that of Buddhism but with less complexity.

(8) As in Buddhism *dharma* relates to the true, the moral, and to the basic constituents of the universe.

(9) Differing from the Jains hold both *dharma* sis, however, the Jains hold both *dharma* and *adharma* (non-dharma) to represent real elements of the universe, the first standing for the "condition" of movement, the second for the condition of rest.

(10) Liberation requires the establishment of *adharma*, which is the goal of the liberated self somehow beyond the phenomenal world. For the *Dharma Sutras* *q.v. Vedas* (5). Also *q.v.* T'ien T'ai School (3); Hinduism; the Hua-Yen School (*q.v.* 1–4) of Buddhism; Chi-Tsang (1).

DHARMAKAYA.

Q.v. Trikaya (1); *Dharma* (6); Mahayana Buddhism (5).

DHARMAKIRTI. 600–670.

South Indian Buddhist logician. Taught at Nalanda University. A student of Dignaga's (*q.v.*) logic, he is viewed as having brought it to completion.

Principal writings: Seventeen treatises, mostly on logic. His most noted work is a commentary on Dignaga's logic, the *Pramanavartikki* ("commentary on the means of valid cognition") (T in part, in German).

(1) His commentaries on Dignaga superseded the latter's work in popularity, becoming the standard logic texts for Indian and Tibetan Buddhism. The four chapters of the *Pramanavartikki* deal with inference, valid knowledge, sense perception, and syllogism.

(2) His syllogism had 4 steps: major premise, example, minor premise, and conclusion. He recognized 3 valid types of middle term: those related to the major

term by identity, by causation, and by non-perception. From the third the denial of the major premise can be inferred.

(3) Since nothing else is real, valid cognition can be established only with respect to the Buddha. Perception and inference, then, are valid only in that context. Still, there are degrees of reliability in the relations of false constructs to reality.

DHYANA.

A Sanskrit term meaning "meditation" (*q.v.* 5). Central to the practice of Hinduism, Buddhism, and Jainism, *Dhyana* forms the seventh stage of yogic meditation, leading to the final stage of *Samadhi* or "absorption" (*q.v.* Yoga 4).

DIACHRONY.

Q.v. Structuralism (9); de Saussure (1); Lacan (5).

DIALECTIC.

From the Greek *dialektos* ("discourse," "debate"). The art or science of dialectic begins in the drawing of rigorous distinctions. The procedure brings to light contradictions, and other types of opposition not sensed before. The origin of dialectic may be appropriately attributed to Zeno, Socrates, and Plato, with the Sophists in a supporting role. The role of dialectic, the interpretation of its nature, and the estimate of its importance alter widely in the course of the history of philosophy, depending on the epistemological position of the philosopher in question.

(1) For Plato (*q.v.* 1) dialectic embodied the highest knowledge, and was the coping stone of the sciences.

(2) For Aristotle (*q.v.* 5) dialectic proceeds from the opinions of men, and is less reliable than demonstration which proceeds from first principles. Dialectic is here bracketed with sophistry; but he also finds dialectic capable of providing a method of criticism in which the principles of inquiry may be educed.

(3) In Neoplatonism, dialectic becomes part of the method of ascent toward the One (*q.v.* Plotinus 6).

(4) The Stoics (*q.v.* Stoicism) divided logic into rhetoric and dialectic, so that from the time of Stoic ascendency until the close of the Middle Ages dialectic was assimilated to the discipline of logic, and

formed part of the trivium of the Liberal Arts.

(5) In the hands of Abelard (*q.v.* 4) and others dialectical method became the method of Scholasticism.

(6) But this was not without opposition. Peter Damian (*q.v.* 2) was not the only medieval figure to declare himself against dialectic as exhibiting the sin of pride.

(7) For Kant (*q.v.* 4) dialectic becomes the name of man's misguided effort to apply the principles governing phenomena to "things-in-themselves."

(8) Fichte (*q.v.* 3) first presented the process of dialectic as involving the triad of Thesis, Antithesis, Synthesis. He likewise viewed the process as one of Posit, Counterposit, and Synthesis.

(9) For Hegel (*q.v.* 4, 5), who accepted Fichte's triad, reality at all levels exemplifies an unending dialectical process.

(10) In Marxism, (*q.v.* 1a, 3) Engels especially utilized the idea of dialectic, and provided us with the phrase, "dialectical materialism." The phrase contains the following central ideas: (a) The dialectical process occurs in a material context. (b) Quantitative changes hence lead to qualitative change. (c) Since everything is becoming, the historical sense is a key to understanding reality. (d) The process of thesis-antithesis-synthesis occurs in human societies through class-conflict. (*Q.v.* Engels 1).

(11) Croce (*q.v.* 3) called for a Dialectic of the Distincts to replace the Dialectic of Opposites he found in Hegel.

(12) For a view of a dialectic between value and truth, *q.v.* Jonas Cohn.

(13) Lenin (*q.v.* 3) supported a more severe dialectic dedicated to the destruction of the thesis by whatever means.

(14) Sartre (*q.v.* 8) developed his dialectical opposition through the concepts of scarcity and antagonism.

DIALECTICAL MATERIALISM.

Q.v. Dialectic (10); Engels (1).

DIALECTIC OF HISTORY.

Q.v. Marx (16).

DIALLELON.

From the Greek *diallelos* ("crossing"). The Greek term for "circular definition" (*q.v.* Vicious Circle 2; also *q.v.* Tropes).

DIALLELUS.
From the Greek *diallelos* ("crossing").
The Greek term for "circular argument"
(*q.v.* Vicious Circle 1; also *q.v.* Tropes).

DIALOGUE.
From the same Greek root as "dialectic," meaning "discourse."
(1) The term usually refers to the Socratic method of philosophizing through
discussion (*q.v.* Socrates 1–2) as set forth
in Plato's early dialogues featuring the
Socratic figure (*q.v.* Plato A). Although
Plato's analysis of dialogue form came
to be known as dialectic (*q.v.* 1) and has
had a long history, if one simply refers
to the dialogues themselves it would appear that the form consists of beginning
with a random solution to a problem, and
strengthening that solution through repeated criticism and reformulation.
(2) The instances of use of the dialogue
form in Western philosophy are many,
and too numerous to mention.
(3) Buber (*q.v.* 2) regards dialogue as
the mutual revelation of self through an
I-thou relationship.

DIANOETIC VIRTUES.
From the Greek *dianoia* ("intellect" or
"mind"). Thus, the intellectual virtues. In
Aristotle (*q.v.* 11) a distinction is made
between intellectual and moral virtues.
The former relate to the reasoning function and the apprehension through intellect of rational principles. The latter
concern rational control of man's affective nature.

DIATRIBE.
Q.v. Bion of Borysthenes; and Dion
Chrysostom.

DICAEARCHUS. 4th cent. B.C.
Greek philosopher. Born in Messina.
A follower of Aristotle and friend of
Aristoxenos (*q.v.*), he applied the doctrine
of harmony to the fields of music, psy-
chology, and government. He held that
Sparta represented the appropriate
harmonic blend of aristocracy, monarchy,
and democracy. He tried to prove that
the soul is mortal. He discussed life in
Greece at length, and did excellent work
in the geography of measurement.
Principal writings: *Life in Greece; The
Polity of Sparta or Tripoliticos; Concerning*

Harmony in Music; Description of the World.

DICENT INDEXICAL LEGISIGN.
Q.v. Peirce (16).

DICENT SINSIGN.
Q.v. Peirce (16).

DICENT SYMBOL.
Q.v. Peirce (16).

DICTO, MODALITY DE.
Q.v. Modality (8).

DICTUM.
Latin term meaning "expression" or
"statement." Used by the Scholastics in
relation to modal propositions (*q.v.* Modality 3).

DICTUM DE OMNI ET NULLO.
Latin phrase meaning "principle of everything and nothing." This is the principle of syllogistic inference as formulated
by the Scholastics and grounded in Aristotle. What is predicated universally of
a subject or class is predicated of everything falling under the subject or belonging
to the class. What is denied universally
of a subject or class is denied of everything falling under the subject or
belonging to the class. Accepted as
validating the basic moods of the syllogism in its first figure, the dictum led to
the investigations reducing the other figures to the first figure (*q.v.* Syllogism 3
and 4). The dictum is sometimes mislead-
ingly termed "Aristotle's Dictum."

DIDEROT, DENIS. 1713–1784. French
philosopher. Born in Langres. Educated
in the Jesuit college, Louis-le-Grand, in
Paris. Encyclopedist and editor of the
famous French *Encyclopédie*, he was co-
editor with D'Alembert (*q.v.*) until 1757
when the latter withdrew. Diderot wrote
on philosophy, religion, political theory,
literature, commerce, and the applied
sciences. A follower of Locke, he was a
professed empiricist, opposed to metaphysics and the claims of revealed
religion. A materialist of sorts, he endowed matter with sensitivity in order
to account for life and thought. He held
free will to be a delusion.
Principal writings: *Encyclopédie*, 1750– 65;
Philosophical Thoughts, 1746; *Letter on the
Blind*, 1749; *Thoughts on the Interpretation*

of Nature, 1754; *Letters on Deaf Mutes*, 1759; *Rameau's Nephew* (T) (written 1761, published 1805).

DIETRICH OF FREIBERG.
c. 1250 – c. 1310.

German Scholastic. Born in Freiberg. Educated in Paris. Taught in Paris. In his thought he combined Aristotelian and Augustinian ideas with those of Proclus and Avicenna in such a manner that his doctrines are often opposed to those of Thomas. He wrote on a vast number of scientific as well as philosophic subjects.

Principal writings: *On Light and Its Origin; On Being and Essence; On Accidents; On the Subject of Theology.*

DIFFÉRANCE.

From the French *différer* which means both "differing" and "deferring," the term "*différance*," created by Jacques Derrida (*q.v, passim*), combines both meanings. There must be a "difference" between any two signs for signifying to occur (this point comes from de Saussure, *q.v.*). Equally, however, because the signifier can provide no more than a trace of what is signified, the latter becomes itself a signifier, whose function it is to defer to another signifier, so that the play of signifiers is endless. Along with "difference" and "deferring," the "pure movement" of signifying requires the "trace," a hint within the present of the other (alterity). "The (pure) trace is *différance*." The "a" of the created term is silent; it is not part of the pronunciation; furthermore, the *ance* ending in French "is neither simply active nor simply passive," somewhat resembling the middle voice in Greek which has "a certain nonsensitivity." Derrida suggests that philosophy may have "distributed" this original middle voice "into an active and a passive voice, thereby constituting itself by means of this repression" ("Différance," 1968).

DIFFERENCE, METHOD OF.
Q.v. Mill, John Stuart (4).

DIFFERENTIA.
Q.v. Definition (4); Aristotle (4).

DIGAMBARAS.
Q.v. Jainism (8).

DIGNAGA. c. 480–540.

Buddhist logician. Born near Kanci (southern India). A Brahmin, and Vijnanavadin (also known as Yogacharias, *q.v.*), he probably studied under Vasubandhu in northern India. At least he developed the logic of Vasubandhu (*q.v.* 3) and wrote about him just as Dharmakirti (*q.v.*) wrote about and developed the system of Dignaga.

Principal writings: Of Dignaga's 22 works, most on logic and epistemology, the Sanskrit originals are largely lost, while copies of many exist in Tibetan or Chinese translation. The most important is his last treatise, the *Pramanasamuccaya* ("compendium of the means of valid cognition") (T in part), along with his *Vṛtti* ("commentary") on the compendium.

(1) Writing to refute all non-Vijnanavadin logic, Dignaga examined the *pramanas* ("means" or "instruments") of cognition which he recognized, perception and inference. He defined the former in chapter one as a type of knowledge free from all conceptual construction.

(2) The remaining five chapters treat various aspects of inference, including fallacies or "futile arguments." He arrived at his own positions through criticism of the doctrines of other schools. He followed Vasubandhu in removing two steps from the 5-step Nyaya syllogism, achieving the 3-step Aristotelian syllogism, complete with middle term.

(3) In the Compendium, as well as in two other works, he set down the *hetucakra* ("wheel of reasons"), detailing nine possible relations between reasons and conclusions, two of them valid, two contradictory, and the rest uncertain. In the valid conclusions the middle term covers the minor premise, being present in all "similar instances." Apparently, this is the same relation known in Aristotelian logic as a distributed middle term (*q.v.* Syllogism 6).

DILEMMA.

From the Greek *dis* ("twice") and *lemma* ("assumption" or "premise"). A form of inference of great rhetorical power, the premises consisting of two hypothetical propositions, and one disjunctive proposition; and the conclusion being either a disjunctive proposition or a categorical proposition. To illustrate, one thinks of the dilemma allegedly offered by the Muslim caliph who ordered that the furnaces of the baths of Alexandria be stoked with books from the library of Alexandria: If these books merely repeat what is in the Qur'an they are superfluous; if they report something other than what is contained in the Qur'an, they are meretricious. But they must either repeat, or report something other than, what is contained in the Qur'an. Therefore, the books are either superfluous or meretricious.

The story is a fabrication with a complicated history; but the reasoning illustrates a complex constructive dilemma. It has the form, "If p then q: if r then s: but either p or r: therefore either q or s." That is, $p \supset q, r \supset s, p \vee r, \therefore q \vee s$. (q.v. Propositional Calculus 7).

Three additional forms of the dilemma are:

Simple constructive dilemma: $p \supset q$, $r \supset q, p \vee r, \therefore q$.

Complex destructive dilemma: $p \supset q$, $r \supset s, \sim q \vee \sim s, \therefore \sim p \vee \sim r$. (q.v. Propositional Calculus 8).

Simple destructive dilemma: $p \supset q$, $p \supset r, \sim q \vee \sim r, \therefore \sim p$.

(1) Escaping between the horns: If one discovered an added alternative, either a new hypothetical proposition altogether, or a new consequent for one of the antecedents given, he would have used this form of escape.

(2) Grasping one of the horns: If one can show that the antecedent of one of the hypothetical propositions leads to a consequent not stated, he may be able to use this fact to destroy the power of the dilemma.

(3) Rebutting the dilemma: This device is used when a counter dilemma is framed whose conclusion contradicts the conclusion of the original dilemma.

Although the dilemma is a valid argument form, its interest to logicians is relatively slight, and its role is played largely in the field of rhetoric.

DILTHEY, WILHELM. 1833–1911.

German philosopher. Born in Biebrich. Educated at Heidelberg and Berlin. Taught at Basel, Kiel, and Breslau. His professional career led him by 1882 to a professorship in the History of Philosophy at the University of Berlin. From this post he contributed greatly to the broadening of the scope of philosophy. Directing attention to the *Geisteswissenschaften*, or science in the broadest sense, including history, spirit, and culture, Dilthey exerted a wide influence not only in philosophy, but also in psychology, and the social sciences generally. Related to Windelband (q.v.) and Rickert (q.v.), Dilthey is regarded as a neo-Kantian philosopher, extending the Kantian analysis to history (q.v. neo-Kantianism 6).

Principal writings: *Introduction to the Sciences of the Spirit*, 1883; *Experience and Poetry*, 1905; *Studies on the Foundation of the Sciences of the Spirit*, 1905; *The Essence of Philosophy* (T), 1907; *The Types of World View*, 1911.

(1) Setting himself the task of completing the Kantian set of critiques with a critique of the historical reason, Dilthey separated the natural sciences from the sciences of the spirit whose content is known somehow with one's whole life, and not in the abstract, partial manner in which we gain knowledge of the natural sciences.

(2) But our lives are part of the life of society and of history, a result of evolutionary processes. Substantive human natures are replaced by historical relations. The sciences of the spirit are, therefore, primarily historical. And the information they seek cannot be gained apart from the method of understanding called *Verstehen*. This is the meaning experienced in situations. Such subtle and elusive meaningfulness qualifies the conclusions of the cultural or spiritual sciences.

(3) The three fundamental types of philosophy are naturalism (with materialistic, phenomenalistic, positivistic subtypes), voluntaristic idealism, and objective idealism. The development of these types is a transcendental awareness emerging from (and also in process of being undermined by) history.

(4) The point is that historical judgments and systems of philosophy, once defined, become inert; and history, since it is relative, has no final authority. Dilthey holds, in fact, that historians are bound by the judgments of the ages in which they live—the doctrine is called Historicism—and one can transcend his age only by entering imaginatively and

uncritically into other ages. Thus, neither the historical judgment nor the philosophical system has the final word.

(5) Introducing the term *"Weltanschaung"* (world-view) to philosophy, Dilthey defined it as a comprehensive view of the universe and of man's place in it. World-views are projections of dominant personality traits: intellect dominant/naturalism; will dominant/libertarian idealism; feeling dominant/objective idealism. He believed individuals could combine two of the three types, and that Descartes and Kant, for example, combined intellect and will.

DIMATIS.

Valid syllogism in IAI mood, fourth figure. *Q.v.* Syllogism (4).

DING AN SICH.

A German phrase meaning "thing-in-itself." Introduced by Kant (*q.v.* 2) the *Ding an sich* is the *noumenon* lying behind reality. The question of the *Ding an sich*, and especially whether the concept is expendable, assumed importance in neo-Kantianism (*q.v.* 1).

DINGLER, HUGO. 1881–1954.

German philosopher. Born in Munich. Educated at Erlangen, Munich, and Göttingen. Taught at Munich and in the Technical High School at Darmstadt. A philosopher of science who developed his own type of operationalism, Dingler went to great lengths to show how the exact sciences could be derived, beginning from the zero situation of "freedom from presuppositions."

Principal writings: *Philosophy of Logic and Arithmetic*, 1931; *The Foundations of Geometry*, 1933; *The Method of Physics*, 1938; *From Animal to Human Souls*, 1941; *Outline of Methodical Philosophy*, 1949; *The Grasping of Reality*, 1955.

DIODOROS CRONOS. 4th cent. B.C.

Greek philosopher of the Megarian School.

(1) Diodoros Cronos argued that the possible does not exist either in the present or in the future, since all that is, is real (and therefore actual). Part of his defense, called the *Kurieon*, a term of authority, was as follows: The impossible cannot result from the possible, and a past event cannot become other than

it is; but if an event now actual had, at a given moment, been possible, from the possible something impossible would have resulted. Hence, the event thought possible was really impossible.

(2) He is credited with having added temporal variables to modal propositions (*q.v.* Modality) so that one is to speak of the possibility, impossibility, necessity, and non-necessity of such propositions at a given time t.

(3) The restriction of the possible to the actual world appears to contain a defense of determinism, since there are no unactualized possibilities in his view.

DIOGENES LAERTIUS. 3rd cent. A.D.

Famous biographer, whose extensive compilation of material on ancient Greek philosophy through the schools of Platonism, Epicureanism, Stoicism, and Skepticism provides our major source of information concerning much of this period. Although many such works had been written, most had been lost, while that of Diogenes Laertius survived.

Principal writings: *Lives of Eminent Philosophers*, 2 vols., (T).

DIOGENES OF APOLLONIA. 5th cent. B.C.

Greek Ionian philosopher. A follower of Anaximenes and Anaxagoras, Diogenes held that air is the basic element, becoming all other things by condensation and rarefaction. He also held this primal material to be endowed with consciousness and to perform a directive function. He believed, indeed, that analyses of man and the world provided conclusive evidence of an over-arching teleology.

Principal writings: *On Nature* (only fragments remain).

DIOGENES OF IONOANDA. 2nd and 3rd cent. A.D.

Hellenic philosopher. A follower of Epicurus, Diogenes' interest was in Epicureanism as an answer to the fear of death and of the gods. He argued against the Stoic doctrine of providence.

DIOGENES OF SINOPE. 413–327 B.C.

Greek philosopher. Born in Sinope. A Cynic and possibly founder of the school (*q.v.* Cynicism 2). According to legend he lived in a tub at the temple of Cybele; on seeing a slave boy drink from his hands, he destroyed the single wooden bowl he possessed. Alexander the Great offered him a service, and Diogenes requested that Alexander not stand between him and the sun. He preached the doctrine of virtuous self-control, holding that morality implies a return to natural simplicity; the artificiality of society is not compatible with truth or goodness; virtue requires the avoidance of physical pleasure; both pain and hunger are positive aids in the attainment of virtue.

DIOGENIANUS. 2nd cent. A.D.
Hellenic philosopher. Born in Heraclea. A follower of Epicurus and a polemicist against the Stoic philosopher, Chrysippus (*q.v.*), Eusebius (*q.v.*) adopted some of Diogenianus' arguments against the Stoic concept of a cosmic destiny.

DION CHRYSOSTOM. c. 40–120.
Greek philosopher. Born in Prusa, Bythinia. Exiled from Bythinia to Italy, apparently for political reasons, he was converted to Cynicism (*q.v.*), which he then took back to his native land. He developed the diatribe form, introduced by Bion of Borysthenes (*q.v.*), and left a group of 78 orations giving us much information concerning the opinions of the Cynics and of the political situation of the time. His point of view called for a cosmic perspective, similar to that of Stoicism (*q.v.*) and unlike the individualism of the early Cynics.
Principal writings: *The Orations.*

DIONYSIUS AREOPAGITICUS (DIONYSIUS THE AREOPAGITE).
Q.v. The Pseudo-Dionysius.

DIONYSUS.
From the Greek *dios* ("god") and Thracian *nusos* ("son of" or in some interpretations "tree"). Thus, alternatively "tree god" or "son of god" in literal translation.
(1) The Greek god of wine and nature, introduced from Thrace. Supposedly twice-born from Zeus. In other versions a dying and rising savior whose journeys to the underworld and back correspond to the coming of winter and of spring. Two great festivals were held annually in his honor—the lesser Dionysia in late December, the greater Dionysia at the end of March. There is some evidence that the orgiastic rites culminating in the death

of an animal, torn apart by the hands of communicants and eaten raw as a sacramental meal, may point back to human sacrifice.
(2) The *psyche* in this religion, contrasting with the Homeric conception, was regarded as the superior principle of man's nature, exiled from some world beyond the stars, into a human body. In ecstasy and frenzy it briefly escapes imprisonment in the body, and effects union with the god.
(3) Nietzsche (*q.v.* 1) found in Greek tragedy a combination of a Dionysian element, representing passion, and an orderly rational element, which he termed Apollonian.
Also *q.v.* Mystery Religions (4).

DIPOLARITY.
For dipolarity in God *q.v.* Ramanuja (4); Nanak; Socinus; Whitehead (18); Berdyaev (1); Radhakrishnan (3); Hartshorne (3, 5).

DIRECTIVES.
Q.v. Searle (2).

DISAMIS.
Valid syllogism in IAI mood, third figure. *Q.v.* Syllogism (4).

DISCALCED CARMELITES.
Q.v. Saint Teresa.

DISCIPLES OF CHRIST.
A religious group of American origin founded in 1809 by Thomas and Alexander Campbell. Because of their emphasis on the union of all Christians, the members of this group do not like to think of themselves as a denomination. The largest "denomination" of American origin is congregational in organization, and stresses doctrinal simplicity, essentially directing members to the Bible for their articles of belief.

DISCIPLINARY MATRIX.
Q.v. Kuhn (1).

DISCURSUS.
Q.v. Herbert of Cherbury (2d).

DISINTERESTED BENEVOLENCE.
Q.v. Jonathan Edwards (5).

DISJUNCTION.
From the Latin *disjungere* ("to disjoin"). In logic, disjunctive propositions are

always compound or "molecular," and feature the connective "either-or." There are strong and weak disjunctions, and in traditional logic weak disjunction is termed "alternation." The difference between the two types of propositions is discussed under Proposition (3), and the differences between alternative and disjunctive syllogisms under Syllogism (11, 12). In modern logic only the weak form of disjunction is used; thus the form traditionally called "alternation" is called "disjunction" in modern logic, as in the treatment of that form by means of Truth Tables (*q.v.* 3), as well as the treatment of the Disjunctive Syllogism in the Propositional Calculus (*q.v.* 6).

DISJUNCTS.
Q.v. Syllogism (11–12).

DISPUTATION.
From the Latin *dis* and *putare* ("to reckon" or "to think"). The term originated in the Scholastic *disputatio* of the 13th century, a formal procedure for settling disputed questions (*quaestiones disputatae*). The form consisted of the setting forth of a thesis and its proof in syllogistic form, an attack on the thesis by denying one of its premises or restricting the range of a premise, and a determination of the question by the teacher. In the *Disputatio quodlibetal* the audience participated in selecting the question. In the writings of St. Thomas Aquinas (*q.v.*), as in the case of many of the Scholastics, there are instances of both *Quaestiones disputatae* and *Quaestiones quodlibetales*.

DISSENTER.
The term which, in England after the Restoration, was used to replace Puritan or Separatist, the latter having come into disrepute. It referred to anyone dissenting from the Anglican Church (*q.v.* Puritanism, Congregationalism).

DISTINCTIO FORMALIS A PARTE REI.
Latin phrase meaning "objective formal distinction." *Q.v.* Duns Scotus (6).

DISTINCTION, FORMAL.
Q.v. Scotus (6).

DISTRIBUTION OF TERMS.
Q.v. Syllogism (6).

DISTRIBUTIVE LAW.
Q.v. Propositional Calculus (16).

DIVINE RIGHT OF KINGS.
Derived from the medieval doctrine of the two swords, which latter traced all authority to God, the spiritual sword being granted to the Church and the temporal sword to the state, the divine right of kings held that all authority, spiritual no less than temporal, belongs to the monarch and has been granted him by God. This doctrine of the one sword made its appearance with the rise of the national state. In 17th-century England Sir Robert Filmer (*q.v.*) argued in this vein from Scripture on behalf of Charles I. Locke (*q.v.* 9) answered Filmer directly in the first of his treatises on civil government, and provided an alternative view in the second of these treatises. In France, Jacques-Bénigne Bossuet (1627–1704), tutor to the Dauphin and counsellor to the sun king, Louis XIV, argued in his *Polity Drawn from the Words of Scripture Itself* (1681) that the authority of every legally constituted government is sacred and any rebellion against it is criminal.

DIVISION OF POWERS, POLITICAL DOCTRINE OF.
Q.v. Montesquieu (7).

DOCETISM.
From the Greek *dokeo* ("to seem or appear"). A Christological doctrine appearing in early Christianity and apparently influenced by Gnosticism (*q.v.*), to the effect that the suffering and death of Jesus was only an appearance. These events occurred with respect to a phantom body or shadow. Q.v. Christology (1).

DOCTA IGNORANTIA.
Latin phrase meaning "learned ignorance," a concept employed by Nicholas of Cusa (*q.v.* 1).

DOCTRINE OF THE MEAN.
(*Chung Yung* in Chinese). The most philosophical of the ancient Chinese documents, the *Doctrine of the Mean* existed in the early Han dynasty. Inconsistencies of style and thought suggest it may be the work of more than one person, as with the *Great Learning* (*q.v.*). It was Chu Hsi (*q.v.*) who brought the book into prominence, recognizing it as one of the

four classics. From 1313 until 1905 these classics were the basis of the Chinese Civil Service Examinations.

(1) It is man's goal in life to follow the Way. This means achieving equilibrium and harmony. Equilibrium is the state before feelings of pleasure, anger, sorrow, and joy are aroused. Harmony is the state in which they are aroused in due measure and degree.

(2) One's conduct should strike the appropriate mean between deficiency and excess: to serve one's father as one would expect one's son to serve oneself; to serve one's ruler as one expects one's ministers to serve oneself; to serve elder brothers as one expects one's younger brothers to serve oneself; to be the first to treat friends as one would expect to be treated by them. And in all cases one is to do what is proper to his position, and does not go beyond it.

(3) The three universal virtues are wisdom, humanity, and courage. The five relations they govern are the relations between ruler and minister, father and son, husband and wife, elder and younger brothers, and the relations among friends.

(4) One is to seek sincerity in his personal life; this requires study which should be continuous, thorough, and persistent. Sufficient persistence will render even a stupid man intelligent, and lead to absolute sincerity, which in turn allows a developed nature. A developed nature in oneself allows one to develop the natures of others, assisting in the transforming processes of heaven and earth, and forming a trinity with them. He shall then have become a sage.

DOGEN.
Q.v. Zen Buddhism (4).

DOGMA.
A Greek term meaning "opinion" or "decree."

(1) In substantive form the term has had philosophical use, Dogmatism naming the position of the Fourth Academy (q.v. Plato's Academy 4), developed by Philo of Larissa (q.v.).

(2) Christian dogma is constituted by creeds and doctrines formulated within the body of the Church and accepted in Councils, and Dogmatic Theology is a systematic ordering of such doctrines. Q.v.

Christianity; Christology; Creed.

DOGMATISM.
The philosophical position of the Fourth Academy (q.v. Dogma 1).

DOMAIN.
Q.v. logic of Relations (2); Function (1).

DOMINICAN ORDER.
An order of mendicant friars founded in the early 13th century. Also called the Order of Preachers, the Dominicans were founded with the object of reforming the quality of the individual Christian's life. Dominicans have also worked effectively in many fields of scholarship, as the membership of St. Thomas Aquinas and others attest.

DOMINIC GUNDISALVO.
Q.v. Gundisalvo, Dominic.

DOMINION.
Deriving from God. Q.v. John Wycliffe (2).

DONATION OF CONSTANTINE.
A spurious document representing Constantine as giving to Pope Sylvester I sovereignty over the western part of the Roman Empire. The basis for papal claims of temporal authority, it was shown to be spurious in 1440 by Lorenzo Valla (q.v.).

DONATISM.
A schismatic sect, rising in the early part of the 4th century in Carthage, and taking its name from Bishop Donatus. Declared heretical in 405 A.D., the principal tenet of the sect was that the validity of the sacraments depended upon the merit of the priest administering them. St. Augustine, as their most illustrious opponent, wrote against the Donatists.

DONOSO CORTÉS, JOHN.
Q.v., Toleration (12); Traditionalism (5).

DORDRECHT CONFESSION OF FAITH.
The confession adopted by the Dutch Mennonites in 1632 at a conference in Dordrecht, Holland. The principal articles concern the washing of the saints' feet, forceful defense, the swearing of oaths, and the shunning of those expelled from the faith.

DORT, SYNOD OF.
    Q.v. Predestination (7).

DOUBLE NEGATION.
    Q.v. Negation (3); Propositional Calculus (17).

DOUBLE TRUTH, DOCTRINE OF.
    The doctrine that what is true in religion may not be true in philosophy, and vice versa. A doctrine imputed to Averroës (*q.v.* 6), but never stated openly, at least, in his writings. The belief that Averroës and his followers held to the doctrine, however, is one of the principal reasons for the succession of condemnations which it received (*q.v.* Averroism).

DOUBT.
    The state of withholding assent from a proposition, and from its contradictory. Moderate doubt is usually known as Skepticism (*q.v.*), and its extreme form is known as Pyrrhonism (*q.v.*). Methodical doubt was recommended by Descartes (*q.v.* 1–2), and used by him in discovering the starting point of philosophy.

DOXA.
    A Greek term meaning "opinion" (*q.v.*).

DOXASTIC.
    From the Greek *doxazein*, "to conjecture." The adjective refers to individual belief which is not firmly established, and so of the nature of opinion (*doxa*). The term is used in contrast with epistemic belief (from *episteme*, "knowledge") which is thus, presumably, known.

DREAD.
    Q.v. Angst.

DREAMS.
    Q.v. Freud (4); Lacan (5).

DRIESCH, HANS. 1867–1941.
    German philosopher and biologist. Born in Kreuznach. Studied at Jena. Taught in Aberdeen, Heidelberg, Cologne, and Leipzig.
    Principal writings: *Biology as an Autonomous Basic Science*, 1893; *Vitalism as History and Doctrine*, 1906; *The Science and the Philosophy of the Organism*, 1908; *Theory of Order*, 1912; *The Machine and the Organism*, 1935.
    (1) Arguing that in organic processes

the whole is in the part, Driesch holds that such processes are characterized by directing and sustaining entelechies (*q.v.*).
    (2) With respect to causality, mechanical causality is not denied; but the more adequate interpretation with respect to organisms is that mechanical causality is embedded in an entelechial causality which operates in a non-mechanical way.
    (3) Finally, he introduced God as the superpersonal entelechy of the world. He believed in human freedom and in some form of immortality.

DROYSEN, JOHANN G.
    Q.v. Hermeneutics (4).

DUALISM.
    From the Latin *dualis* ("containing two"). The term seems to have been introduced in 1700 by Thomas Hyde (*The Ancient Persian Religions*) to characterize the good-evil conflict of Ormazd and Ahriman in Zoroastrianism (*q.v.* Zoroaster 1). Christian Wolff (*q.v.* 6) was the first to apply the term to the metaphysical opposition of mind and matter. The term has since been applied to many types of opposition in religion, metaphysics, and epistemology.
    (1) In religion the term has been applied to the good-evil opposition in Manichaeism (*q.v.*) and Gnosticism (*q.v.* 1) generally, the Taoist and neo-Confucian contrast of *Yin* and *Yang* (*q.v.*), among numerous examples.
    (2) The earliest complete metaphysical dualism is that of Plato (*q.v.* 3). Attributing true existence to ideas, he nonetheless recognized an inferior but, opposing principle. His metaphysical dualism was likewise ethical insofar as he identified the good with the former and evil with the latter.
    (3) Aristotle (*q.v.* 7) attempted to avoid Plato's extreme dualism while retaining a complementarity of form and matter.
    (4) Metaphysical dualism was present in the Eastern paired school of Sankhya-Yoga (*q.v.*, and Hinduism 6b) where mind (*puruṣa*) and matter (*prakṛti*) are recognized as fundamental and ultimate. Other systems, *e.g.*, Advaita Vedanta (*q.v.*) and Zen (*q.v.* Intuition 15), claim to have overcome such dualisms.
    (5) Neoplatonism (*q.v.*) continued the Platonic dualism while attempting

through the idea of emanation to bridge the conceptual gulf between matter and the truly existent One.

(6) A thoroughgoing dualism appeared once more in Descartes (*q.v.* 8), distinguishing between the *res cogitans* and the *res extensa*. So extreme was the opposition that a special doctrine of Occasionalism (*q.v.*) arose, calling upon God to mediate at each moment between mind and body.

(7) Spinoza (*q.v.* 2, 6), attempting to rid himself of the Cartesian dualism, forced thought and extension into attributes of a single substance, and mind and body into its modes.

(8) Kant's revolution within philosophy forced this contrast out of metaphysics and into epistemology. It became the contrast between formal and material, transcendental and empirical, analytic and synthetic elements of experience; and Kant (*q.v.* 1) bridged his epistemological dualism by means of *synthetic a priori* judgments.

(9) Laurie (*q.v.*) called for a return to dualism, regarding it as inevitable.

(10) Avenarius (*q.v.* 2) and William James (*q.v.* 10) are among those who have attempted to avoid dualism by accepting a doctrine of "pure experience."

(11) Whitehead (*q.v.* 9–25) attempted to avoid dualism through his philosophy of *organism*.

(12) Lovejoy (*q.v.* 1) on the other hand opposed what he called "the revolt against dualism," insisting that duality must be recognized in the very nature of time and experience.

(13) Merleau-Ponty (*q.v.* 1–2) substituted for the Cartesian mind-body dualism a variety of conceptual levels of which the physical and the mental are but two. Thus, he hoped to substitute for rigid classifications a variety of ways of taking account of phenomena.

(14) Abe (*q.v.* Emptiness) has provided an interpretation of nonduality in Buddhism, turning on the concept of Emptiness, which he finds central to Mahayana Buddhism, and going back even to Gautama Buddha (*q.v.*).

DU BOIS, W.E.B. 1868–1963.

American sociologist and social philosopher. Born in Great Barrington, Mass. Educated at Fisk University (Nashville), Harvard, and the University of Berlin. Taught at Wilberforce University (Ohio), University of Pennsylvania, and Atlanta University. Director of the Atlanta University Conferences on human problems faced by blacks, and editor of the Conference volumes (1898–1913). Participating founder of the NAACP, and editor of the NAACP journal *Crisis* (1910–1934). Called the father of Pan-Africanism, he organized 5 Pan-African Congresses between 1919 and 1945, all but one held in England, on the Continent, or both.

Selected writings: *Suppression of the African Slave Trade*, 1896; *The Philadelphia Negro*, 1899; *Negro Landholders of Georgia*, 1901; *The Souls of Black Folk*, 1903; *John Brown*, 1909; *The Negro*, 1915; *Black Reconstruction in America*, 1935; *Dusk of Dawn*, 1940; *The Autobiography of W.E.B. Du Bois*, 1968; *Negro and Social Reconstruction*, 1985.

(1) Although deeply involved in philosophy at Harvard, studying under Santayana, Royce, and James, the last-named whose protegé he was, convinced him to take his graduate degree in a discipline more practical than philosophy. Du Bois turned to Sociology and by virtue of his first publications became the leading social scientist of black America.

(2) His social philosophy, resting on social equality for blacks as an absolute ("Either extermination root and branch, or absolute equality. There can be no compromise"), included four themes: democracy, social pluralism (later, called "cultural pluralism"), Pan-Africanism, and socialism.

(3) Democracy was a given for Du Bois. Most of his life was energized by the assumption that, given political rights, the economic opportunities necessary for achieving equality could be developed by the Talented Tenth. These were committed, industrious, exceptionally capable blacks who would prepare themselves intellectually, and provide a base of opportunities in terms of which the rest of the Negro community, as he termed it, could rise.

(4) The point of social pluralism is to provide an opening for the race to become fully conscious of its special gifts. This means developing the double consciousness of being both Negro and

American. The immediate goal is not integration, but voluntary segregation in order to foster "one great unity" among Negroes.

(5) Pan-Africanism provides a reference point for blacks. It is for them what Zionism is for Jews. As the Negro fatherland, the history and culture of Africa make a valuable contribution to American civilization. Furthermore, African nations require the help of American Negroes.

(6) Becoming disillusioned in the Talented Tenth, most of whom had failed to provide the necessary leadership, Du Bois began to suspect that a new distribution of wealth would be needed to make "the rise of our group possible." He was encouraged by Roosevelt's initiatives, especially the TVA, and a caring welfare state. He was comfortable with Soviet-American cooperation in World War II, and troubled by the cold war. He began saying that he believed in socialism as well as in democracy; and finally, deciding that full equality for Negroes would never be possible under capitalism: "I believe in Communism." This belief was strengthened by his observations of life in trips to the Soviet Union and China, and the warmth of his reception everywhere in the Socialist world.

(7) Brought to trial in New York City for sponsoring the Stockholm Peace Petition, and denied permission to attend conferences outside the country, he accepted at once when in 1962 Nkrumah invited him to Ghana as director of a proposed multivolume *Encyclopedia Africana*. This time he was allowed to leave the country. Before doing so he joined the American Communist Party. In Ghana, when his passport expired, the American consulate refused to renew it. His response was to become a citizen of Ghana. Numerous African leaders came to him for advice. His Pan-Africanism was developing on many fronts when the cancer against which he had been struggling for several years, claimed his life on August 27, 1963.

DUCASSE, CURT J. 1881–1969.

American philosopher. Born in France. Educated at the University of Washington and Harvard. Taught at Washington and Brown.

Principal writings: *Causation and the Types of Necessity*, 1924; *Philosophy of Art*, 1929; *Philosophy as a Science*, 1941; *Art, the Critics and You*, 1944; *Nature, Mind and Death*, 1951; *A Philosophical Scrutiny of Religion*, 1953; *A Critical Examination of the Belief in a Life after Death*, 1961. *Paranormal Phenomena*, 1969; *Truth, Knowledge and Causation*, 1969.

(1) Regarding causality as a "fundamental category," Ducasse held indeterminism to be self-contradictory, and the only appropriate definition of freedom to be one consistent with determinism, *i.e.*, as one's being able sometimes to do what one wills to do (*q.v.* Freedom B).

(2) Believing mind not reducible to matter, he distinguished four kinds of causal relations—those where cause and effect are both physical, where the cause is physical but the effect mental, where the cause is mental but the effect physical, and where both cause and effect are mental—Ducasse named these alternatives respectively the "physicophysical," the "physicopsychical," the "psychophysical," and the "psychopsychical." His analyses of the mind-body problem, secondary qualities, and *sensa* support his claim that clarity of analysis can be aided by these distinctions.

(3) Although not a theist, he held the survival of the mind after death to be a logical possibility supported but not established by paranormal phenomena.

DUCLOS.

Q.v. Encyclopedists.

DUHEM, PIERRE. 1861–1916.

French philosopher of science. Born in Paris. Professor at the University of Bordeaux.

Principal writings: *The Sources of Physical Theories*, 2 vols, 1905–1906; *Physical Theory, its Object and its Structure* (T), 1906; *Absolute and Relative Movement*, 1909; *The System of the World*, 5 vols., 1913–17.

(1) Holding a physical theory to be a system of mathematical propositions representing a set of experimental laws, Duhem cast his analysis in the language of appearances. The object of science is to discover the relations holding among appearances. In the construction of scientific theory, one relates conventional signs to appearances, interrelates such

signs in convenient and consistent patterns to form hypotheses, and combines the hypotheses mathematically to yield consequences which can be translated back into the language of appearances. If the translation is successful, that is, matches the appropriate appearances, science has obtained its objective.

(2) Furthermore, since every hypothesis is part of a larger theory the concept of a "crucial experiment," decisively eliminating one hypothesis in favor of another, must be given up. The choice is, at last, between theories—and theories are infinitely amendable.

(3) Despite all of this, Duhem is not to be considered either a positivist, or a phenomenalist. Even though science is limited to appearances, he believed that metaphysics can make statements about reality. He found reality to follow the lines of a purified Aristotelianism.

DUHKHA.

From Sanskrit, "suffering;" (*dukkha* in Pali). One of the three principal doctrines of Theravada Buddhism (*q.v.* 1, 2).

DÜHRING, EUGEN. 1833–1901.

German economist-philosopher. Born in Berlin. *Privatdocent* at University of Berlin until 1874. His final position held that matter is the sole reality; thought is adequate to things; yet the end of nature is the production of conscious beings. Sympathy is the basis of morality; and pain exists to provide a contrast with pleasure. The Darwinian "struggle for survival" is a partial reading of the facts; and capitalism is to be purified, not eliminated, since there is an ultimate harmony of interest between capitalist and laborer. Attacked by Marx and Engels.

Principal writings: *Capital and Work*, 1865; *Natural Dialectic*, 1865; *The Worth of Life*, 1865; *Critical History of the National Economy and of Socialism*, 1871; *Critical History of the General principles of Mechanics*, 1872; *Reality Philosophy*, 1878; *The Substitute for Religion*, 1883.

DUMMET, MICHAEL. 1925– .

British philosopher. Born in London. Educated at Oxford. Has taught at Birmingham and Oxford.

Principal writings: *Frege: Philosophy of Language*, 1973; *The Justification of Deduction*, 1973; *William James Lectures*, 1976; *Elements of Intuitionism*, 1977; *Truth and Other Enigmas*, 1978; *The Interpretation of Frege's Philosophy*, 1981; *Frege and Other Philosophers*, 1991; *The Logical Basis of Metaphysics*, 1991.

(1) Evincing a career-long devotion to Frege, Dummet finds theory of meaning the key to progress in philosophy, and addresses the many problems endemic to the working out of that theory. Because of the depth of these problems, and the patient labor necessary in working through them, Dummet's philosophizing is better characterized by the areas of his concern rather than by the statement of formulations to which he may give credence at a particular time.

(2) Frege's (*q.v.* 4, 6) distinction of sense and reference led Dummet to the view that theory of meaning requires both a theory of sense and a theory of reference. The latter leads to problems about realism, the former to a holistic view of language and various types of anti-realism. Where realism requires reference to a world, holism refers bits of language to other bits of language. Dummet's interest in Frege is counterbalanced by a continuing, if less consuming, interest in the later Wittgenstein whose language-games are holistic (one must know all the rules of chess to play chess), whose meaning in use contrasts with meaning as reference, and whose dictum— "to understand a sentence is to understand a language"—is cited by Dummet.

(3) Sometimes regarded as an anti-realist ("meaning" comes via some other route than reference to a world), Dummet's stance is rather that anti-realist arguments merit serious consideration, and that no adequate justification of realism has yet been supplied. Dummet works through many permutations of realism, anti-realism and their combinations. One may be a realist with respect to the physical world, and anti-realist concerning abstract objects (*e.g.*, the entities of mathematics). One may be a global anti-realist (extreme phenomenalism, *q.v.*, would be an example).

(4) Which way one goes depends upon what one does with the principle of bivalence, the question whether all declarative sentences are either true or false including sentences referring to the future and those characterized by vagueness.

To the extent that the principle holds, realism becomes the preferred option; to the extent that it does not, anti-realism gains in relevance. The principle is weakened in the constructivist techniques of intuitionistic mathematics. The greater the departure from bivalence, and the weaker the case for realism, the greater is the tendency to depart from the classical laws of logic. Dummet does not believe, however, that vagueness by itself requires departure from the accepted laws of logic.

(5) So far as one is a realist verificationism is an appropriate approach to meaning, although not all statements are capable of conclusive verification. So far as one is an anti-realist, the holistic theory of meaning, linguistic holism, is appropriate. In the first case the sense of a sentence will be "systematically derivable" from the sense of its constituents. In the second case that sense will come from the place the sentence occupies in a "conceptual network," and the need for a representation of content will be wholly, or largely, rejected.

(6) Since a minimum of holism is indispensable, and since a theory of reference requires a theory of sense, some combination of holism and realism would seem to be indicated.

(7) One also has the option of adopting a modest, or full-blooded, theory of meaning. In the former case a great deal is assumed; in the latter, one is working out "what we must know to know a language and what it is to have that knowledge." In both cases, theory of meaning is part of philosophy of language with the aim of showing what it is for a whole language to function as a language.

DUNS SCOTUS, JOHN. 1266–1308.

Scholastic philosopher. Born in Maxton, Scotland. Entering the Franciscan order in 1278, he was ordained priest in 1291. He studied briefly at Oxford, and then at Paris for three years. Between 1296 and 1307 he probably alternated teaching at Oxford and in Paris. In 1307–8 he taught in Cologne. In 1305 he received his doctorate in theology from the University of Paris. Although historically Duns Scotus stands as an important link between Thomas Aquinas and William of Ockham, in the annals of philosophy his stature is not that of a transitional figure, but a

thinker of the first rank. Not for nothing was he called the "Subtle Doctor."

Principal writings: *Questions on Aristotle's Book "On the Soul"*; *Quaestiones in Metaphysicam subtilissimae*; *On the First Principle* (T); *Quaestiones in quattuor libros sententiarum*; *Quaestiones quodlibetales.*

(1) Since the primary object of intellect is being, which he preferred to call *realitas*, every being falls within the scope of the intellect. This includes both God and self-knowledge, although in this life there are "hindrances" to the adequate knowledge of either of these.

(2) All knowledge arises from sensation, and the intellect begins as a *tabula nuda*. In sensation we know the individual thing by first intention. Our intellect is ordered by second intention to the universals abstracted from individual things. And since the higher power knows more perfectly than the lower, the intellect, in knowing universals, also knows intuitively the singular things from which the universals were derived.

(3) Reliable inductive knowledge is possible due to the operation of natural causes. When an effect is frequently produced by the same cause we can assume a natural cause is at work, and the effect will be always so produced.

(4) Deductive knowledge results from the intellectual act of bringing together terms derived from sense-experience. Even though there are no innate principles, when the simple terms are understood and so combined, first principles which are certain and beyond error (*e.g.*, the notions of "whole" and "part") result. Indeed, the intellect cannot be mistaken concerning the first principles clearly apprehended, and the principles and conclusions which follow clearly from them.

(5) Arguing that Thomas Aquinas' attempt to make prime matter the principle of individuation failed, since prime matter is itself indeterminate, Scotus substitutes the *haecceitas*, that is, "thisness" or *entitas singularis* ("individual being"), standing to the *entitas naturae* ("being of nature") as the specific difference stands to the genus. Although the *haecceitas* adds no qualitative determination, it is by virtue of it that the being in question is *this* being.

(6) Scotus found it necessary to add the notion of a "formal distinction"

(*distinctio formalis a parte rei*) to that of "real distinction" (a distinction between two separable things) and virtual distinction (purely mental with no objective distinction in the thing itself). By "formal distinction" Scotus means an objective distinction relating to two inseparable things. As instances of formal distinctions Scotus advances the distinction between God's attributes, between essence and existence, and between the nature or universal of a thing and its *haecceitas*. To take the last case, for the sake of illustration, it turns out that there is a formal distinction between the universal "human nature" and the "*haecceitas*" of Socrates. We cannot say simply that the universal is in the thing or that it is not. It is grounded in the "*haecceitas*" of the thing.

(7) Scotus also differed from Aquinas in holding that there is a real distinction between form and matter, that matter, therefore, can exist by itself (at least through God's help).

(8) Metaphysical knowledge of God is possible because there exists a univocal concept of being, applicable to God and creatures. There are also univocal concepts of unity, truth, and goodness. Indeed, the attributes of God are formed by the removal of imperfections from attributes found in creatures. If it were not legitimate to do this, no knowledge of God would be possible. Combining these concepts we are able to form a composite quidditative, *i.e.*, unique, idea of God.

(9) That God exists may be demonstrated in many ways, including the argument from contingency to the existence of a necessary being. Finally, any series of causes, infinite in length or not, requires an actual transcendent necessary and unitary cause, the simplest way to describe this cause is as the absolutely infinite being.

(10) In this connection he finds it possible to use Anselm's ontological argument. God, he says, is that than which a greater cannot be thought without contradiction; He is the *summum cogitabile*, and therefore possible. But if God is possible He must exist, since what exists is more thinkable (*majus cogitabile*), standing as a possible object of intuition and intellect, than an object of intellect alone. But this argument is regarded as a "probable persuasion," not a demonstrative proof.

(11) The binding force of morality, its quality of obligation, derives from God's will; but it does not follow that the will of God is arbitrary. The divine intellect, perceiving what conforms with human nature, provides one content of the moral law; but the sanction of God's will forces us to regard its transgression not as an irrationality merely, but as a sin.

(12) The human will is essentially free, and it would not have been possible for God to have created a rational will incapable of sin.

(13) God's will is free with respect to contingent things, so the reason for creation is God's free choice. At the same time there is necessity in God; this, too, is compatible with liberty. If a person hurls himself over a precipice and, while falling, necessarily continues to will that fall, liberty and necessity are compatible. This identity of natural necessity and liberty are to be found in God.

(14) Finally, Scotus suggested that political authority rests on free consent, and has its end in the common good.

DURANDO OF SAINT POURCAIN.
c. 1275–1334.

Scholastic philosopher. Born in France. A Dominican and Bishop of Le Puy and Meaux, he opposed Thomism and tended toward Nominalism (*q.v.*) holding the universal to be a mental abstraction or indeterminate form of the individual thing.

Principal writings: *Commentary on the Sentences; On the Source of Authority; On the Vision of God.*

DURATION.

From the Latin *durare* ("to last or endure"). Thus, a stretch of time.

(1) Whatever the genesis of the concept, its philosophical use appears to be related to the contrast of time with eternity. St. Augustine (*q.v.* 10, 12) analyzed the spread of time in psychological terms, finding this concept less clear than that of God's eternity, while St. Thomas Aquinas (*q.v.* 4) found the term, "duration," applicable both to time and eternity. Duration and succession apply to time, while eternity is characterized by duration without succession.

(2) For Spinoza (*q.v.* 2, 5c) duration characterizes created things, and time is the measure of that duration while eternity is, so to speak, the measure of the divine existence.

(3) Locke (*q.v.* 5c) reverted to something like the psychological approach of St. Augustine in his analysis, regarding duration as the distance between two ideas in the succession making up man's mental life.

(4) For Newton (*q.v.* 3) duration was an indispensable concept used to characterize the flow of absolute time.

(5) In the view of Leibniz (*q.v.* 2) duration is to time as extension is to space, the quality relating to an order of succession rather than the unity of an aggregate.

(6) William James (*q.v.* 2) found a minimal duration in every instance of the "specious present."

(7) Finally, for Bergson (*q.v.* 2, 7) duration is the defining characteristic of time, and there is no eternity standing in contrast to time. In one sense the spatialization of duration gives rise to the false, mathematical sense of time. In another sense, spatialized duration is Bergson's description of the origin of matter.

DURGA.
Q.v. Śakti, Vaiṣṇavism (4a).

DURKHEIM, ÉMILE. 1858–1917.
French positivistic sociologist. Born in Alsace. Professor in Bordeaux and the Sorbonne. Influencing French sociology in an empirical direction, he stressed the importance of the group as the origin of the norms and goals of individuals, and the source and reference of religious symbols. The function of religion in his view is the creation and maintenance of social solidarity. The symbols making possible social cohesion are "collective representations" with which individuals identify. They can be studied by means of social facts, and lead to a "collective conscience" in society.

Principal writings: *On the Division of Social Work*, 1893; *The Rules of Sociological Method* (T), 1895; *Suicide* (T), 1897; *The Elementary Forms of the Religious Life* (T), 1912; *Education and Sociology* (T), 1922; *Sociology and Philosophy* (T), 1924; *Moral Education* (T), 1925; *Lessons of Sociology* (T), 1950.

DUSSEL, ENRIQUE.
Q.v. Theology of Liberation (8).

DUTY.
From the Latin *debere* ("to owe"). The sense of "duty" vies with that of "good" or "value" for the honor of serving as the foundation conception of ethics. Ethical systems taking "duty" as basic are called "formalistic" or "deontological," rather than "teleological" or "axiological" (*q.v.* Deontology, and Ethics 1–3).

(1) Stoicism (*q.v.* 3) stands in contrast to Epicureanism in emphasizing obligation over value satisfaction.

(2) In the Kantian ethic, duty comprises the ultimate end of life and is defined by the categorical and practical imperatives (*q.v.* Kant 6–7).

(3) F.H. Bradley (*q.v.* 6) argued in Hegelian terms that one's duties are set by one's place and functions in a society which is more than a collection of individuals.

(4) Royce (*q.v.* 1) found moral obligation, and an argument for the Absolute, even in human pessimism.

(5) H.A. Prichard (*q.v.*) held, as an intuitionist, that we have an immediate knowledge of our duties and that general theories of duty should not even be attempted.

(6) W.D. Ross (*q.v.* 2) modified the Kantian viewpoint to allow for a hierarchy of duties, one's absolute duty being the highest "*prima facie* duty" in any situation.

DU VAIR, GUILLAUME. 1556–1621.
French philosopher. Born in Paris. A lawyer who became Bishop of Lisieux, Du Vair was—along with Lipsius (*q.v.*)— a neo-Stoic. He emphasized the Stoic maxims, especially those of Epictetus (*q.v.*), relating them to Christianity.

Principal writings: *The Moral Philosophy of the Stoics* (T), 1585; *On Constancy and Consolation*, 1589; *On French Eloquence*, 1595; *The Holy Philosophy*, 1603.

DVEṢA (DVESHA).
Sanskrit term signifying the antipathy man develops toward unpleasant things. One of the five kinds of delusive attachment of the Yoga system (*q.v.* Yoga 3).

DWORKIN, RONALD M. 1931– .

American philosopher of law. Born in Worcester, Mass. Educated at Harvard and Oxford. Has taught at Yale, New York University, Cornell, and Oxford.

Principal writings: *Taking Rights Seriously*, 1977; *A Matter of Principle*, 1985; *Law's Empire*, 1986; *A Bill of Rights for Britain*, 1990; *Life's Dominion*, 1993.

(1) Attacking the positivist approach to law as a set of rules, Dworkin takes H.L.A. Hart (*q.v.*) as target "when a particular target is needed." In Hart's version of legal positivism there are primary rules which grant rights and impose obligations, and secondary rules stipulating how primary rules are to be recognized. Among the ways of recognizing primary rules, *i.e.*, among the "rules of recognition," are: what the king commands, or what the constitution requires. Rules deriving from the sanctioning agency of secondary rules are called "legal rules."

(2) For Dworkin laws are not simply transcripts of established rules, as the positivists would have it, nor simply prescriptive. Principles and policies play a role, and the enterprise resembles a web of many elements hanging together. Each judge must look afresh for "the nature of the enterprise," a kind of essence hidden in the web, and each judge is part of the hermeneutic circle (*q.v.*) with a responsibility to contribute an interpretation capturing the "legal truth" of past decisions while advancing the enterprise.

(3) Through successive reconstructions the coherence, clarity, rationality and legal truth of the interpretation increases. Two different contemporary interpretations, to be sure, may fit all available legal material. In this case the one which provides more support for the human right to equality of concern and respect is to be preferred. Thus a prescriptive element enters into the interpretation.

(4) Taking the right to equal concern and respect as fundamental, the right to treatment as an equal follows, and this supports programs of affirmative action. Decisions about abortion and euthanasia, on the other hand, must be left to individual decision because the inviolability and sacredness of human life are religious ideas, and the separation of church and state prohibits legislation with respect to them.

DYAD.

From the Greek *duas* ("two"). In Pythagoreanism the number two, represented by the line, *i.e.*, two points which do not coincide (*q.v.* Pythagoras 7).

DYAUS.

From the Sanskrit *dyaus* ("sky," "day"). In the Vedic religion, the god of the shining sky and father to other celestial divinities; equivalent in position to the Greek Zeus and the Roman Jupiter. *Q.v. Deva*.

DYNAMICAL SYSTEMS.

Q.v. Chaos Theory (5).

DYNAMIS.

Q.v. Energeia.

DYNAMISM.

From the Greek *dynamis* ("power"). In a general sense any world-view asserting the existence of forces in things not reducible to matter in motion. Thus, any philosophy opposed to mechanism (*q.v.*). In this sense the term applies to the philosophy of Leibniz (*q.v.* 1). More specifically, the term is applied to the *Theory of Natural Philosophy* (T), 1763, of Rudjer Boscovich whose substitution of point-like centers of force for atoms removed the last vestiges of mechanism from the Newtonian world-view.

DYOPHYSITE.

One who holds in contrast to Monophysitism (*q.v.*), the doctrine that two natures, one divine and one human, united in the person of Christ.

DYOTHELITE.

One who holds, in contrast to Monothelitism (*q.v.*), the doctrine that two wills, one divine and one human, united in the person of Christ.

DYSON, FREEMAN.

Q.v. Artificial Intelligence (3).

EASTERN ORTHODOX CHURCHES.

Those Christian churches whose orthodoxy is determined by the first seven Ecumenical Councils and whose final separation from the Roman Church occurred in 1054. There are today fifteen Eastern Orthodox Churches, each with its own bishop. They are the Churches of Constantinople, Alexandria, Antioch, Jerusalem, Russia, Georgia, Serbia, Romania, Bulgaria, Cyprus, Greece, Albania, Poland, Czechoslovakia, and America. The communicants number between 100 and 150 million.

EBIONISM.

The doctrine of the Ebionites, who were the Jewish Christians in Jerusalem and later merely a sect among them. They recognized Jesus as Messiah while denying his divinity; thus, they were also led to reject the Apostle Paul whom they anathematised. *Q.v.* Christology (1).

ECKHART, MEISTER. 1260–1327.

German mystic. Born in Hochheim. Educated at Cologne and Paris. Taught in Paris. A Dominican, he received a doctor's degree from Pope Boniface VIII in 1302, served as Dominican provincial for Saxony, 1304, and Vicar General for Bohemia, 1307. Summoned before the Inquisition in Cologne in 1327, he seems to have recanted whatever in his works could be shown to be erroneous, and by 1329—after his death—certain of his theses were condemned as erroneous. Aristotelian by training, Eckhart is Neoplatonic in the speculative mysticism he elaborated. Although powerfully original, his work shows traces of the influence of Plotinus, Augustine, the Pseudo-Dionysius, and Scotus Erigena.

Principal writings: *Three Part Work* (L), 1314; *Parisian Questions* (L); *German Sermons* (G).

(1) God is pure being, the final ultimate reality. Nothing is so dissimilar as God and his creatures; also, nothing is so similar.

(2) In comparison with the fullness of God's being or *Istigkeit* ("Is-ness") "All things are a mere nothing."

(3) The basis of conscience and of religious awareness is the *Seelenfünklein*, or spark of the soul. It is through this that union with God is able to occur. It is also, once created, indestructible.

(4) The begetting of the Son by the Father, and the procession of the Holy Spirit from both, takes place eternally; and since God is in the soul through grace, this begetting procession takes place in the soul at the highest reaches of the mystical experience.

(5) To allow the process to begin one must annihilate self-interest, and empty oneself out; when one comes to be as a desert, empty of things, he will be full of God.

ECLECTICISM.

From the Greek *ek* ("out") and *lego* ("select"). An attitude which leads to philosophizing by selection, seeking to bring into harmony what is valid from all philosophers while eliminating the mistaken doctrines of the sources. Among eclectic schools of philosophy one would note the Fourth Academy (*q.v.* Plato's Academy 4), the Middle and New Schools of Stoicism (*q.v.* 2, 3), the Alexandrian School of Neoplatonism (*q.v.* 9), and the 19th-century Spiritualistic School of Victor Cousin (*q.v.*).

ECONOMICS, BASED ON FREE TRADE.

Q.v. Adam Smith (2).

ECSTASY.

From the Greek *ex* ("out") and *histanai* ("to stand"). Thus, to stand outside oneself. In mysticism, a psychological state characterized by intense mental absorption, a sense of rapture, a loss of voluntary control and the capacity to respond to sense-perceptions. The state is often identified with religious enlightenment, or union of the soul with a higher reality.

ECUMENISM.

A movement, also called the Ecumenical Movement, toward increasing cooperation among the churches and religious orders of the world. Beginning in the West, and still concentrated there, the movement seeks to reverse the Western fragmentation of religious witness. The Ecumenical Movement is usually regarded as having originated in a meeting of Protestant missionaries in Edinburgh,

Scotland in 1910. Seventeen years later the World Conference on Faith and Order was held in Lausanne, Switzerland, exploring the possibilities of joint social action. In 1948 at Amsterdam, Holland, the World Council of Churches was formed, consisting initially of 148 churches (Protestant and Eastern Orthodox); thus the Ecumenical effort became institutionalized. The next general meeting, called the Second General Assembly, was held in Evanston, Ill. in 1954. The Third World Council General Assembly was held in New Delhi, India in 1960. At this meeting the Roman Catholic Church was represented by five observers. Since that time Catholic participation in Ecumenical matters has continued to increase. Pope John XXIII, indeed, created a Secretariat for the Promotion of Christian Unity and called the Second Vatican Council (1962–5) to prepare for such unity. This council voted a decree on Ecumenism calling for a common effort toward regaining Christian unity, and recognizing common responsibility for past divisions. Ecumenical meetings continue to be held with increasing effect on local, national and world levels.

EDDINGTON, ARTHUR S. 1882–1944.

English scientist. Educated at Cambridge. Taught at Cambridge. His contributions to physics and astronomy apart, Eddington believed that the Heisenberg indeterminacy principle implied free will, that reality is "mind-stuff" whose structure conforms in a Kantian way to rational principles, and that God exists.

Principal writings: *Space, Time, and Gravitation*, 1920; *Nature of the Physical World*, 1928; *Science and the Unseen World*, 1929; *New Pathways in Science*, 1935; *The Philosophy of Physical Science*, 1939.

EDICT OF MILAN.

The proclamation signed in 313 by emperors Constantine the Great and Licinius, extending toleration to Christians and ordering the restoration of their personal and corporate property.

EDUCATION, PHILOSOPHY OF.

Although an attitude toward education is perhaps implicit in most philosophies, only a small minority have made open declaration of its nature.

(1) Plato (*q.v.* 5c), building his Republic around a developing sense of wisdom, or "knowledge of the whole," would be the first. He regarded education as the instrument for achieving an ideal state.

(2) Comenius (*q.v.*) in the 17th century argued that a properly graded system of universal education could lead to international understanding, and lead in solving the problems that beset mankind.

(3) Rousseau (*q.v.* 7) used similar developmental ideas, urging that education must utilize natural desires, teach by means of the natural relations of cause and effect, and prune away artificial and impractical elements.

(4) Jefferson (*q.v.* 4) proposed a scheme of public education, through the university level, designed to help the talented come into their own.

(5) Pestalozzi (*q.v.*) believed the end of education to be the development of each individual's "truth," and that this involved both social and religious experience.

(6) Herbart (*q.v.* 4, 5) related the developmental theme to the achievement of five ethical goals, including "internal freedom" and "benevolence." In terms of method he held that after the reception of new ideas, placed in the appropriate context by association and reinforcement, the student be led to a stage in which the information is applied in new situations.

(7) Froebel (*q.v.*), who studied with Pestalozzi, continued the developmental theme. He held it to be the function of the teacher to stimulate "voluntary activity."

(8) John Dewey (*q.v.* 10) stands as the culmination of the emphasis on individual development, due to his concept of inquiry as problem-solving, and his constant emphasis on experience. Fixed ends are eliminated; experimentation is encouraged; and the emphasis is on the future rather than the past.

Also *q.v.* Gandhi (5).

EDUCTION.

A term now rare, once used to designate immediate inference (*q.v.*); also used to signify the manner in which the substantial form was drawn from matter in the Aristotelian system.

EDWARDS, JONATHAN. 1703–1758.

American philosopher-theologian. Born

in Connecticut. Graduated from Yale, 1720. Pastor in Northhampton, Massachusetts, 1720–50. He completed most of his theological work while serving as missionary to the Stockbridge Indian Mission, 1751–58. In the last month of his life he had accepted a call to the presidency of the College of New Jersey in Princeton.

Principal writings: *Notes on the Mind; Religious Affections*, 1746; *Dissertation Concerning the Nature of True Virtue; Freedom of the Will*, 1754; *Original Sin*, 1758.

(1) Finding a point of convergence for the ideas of Newton, Locke, Cambridge Platonism, and New England Puritanism, Edwards very early adopted an idealistic philosophy in which God and space are, as it were, identified; and all things exist as ideas in the divine mind.

(2) Such existence serves to emphasize the supremacy of God, but not to deprive the things we experience of their existence. Here he made the same point as had Berkeley. It turns out, too, that all things are immediately caused and held in being by God. His analysis of causality in the ordinary sense has much of the conventionality of David Hume.

(3) Freedom, or liberty, must be identified with the absence of constraint, or the power one has "to do as he pleases." But this is clearly a freedom which is consistent with necessity, and with the strictest predestinarian claims. One has the power to do what one will, although that will is determined by God.

(4) He explained original sin by holding that Adam had an added gift of divine grace which he lost through rebellion, as did all mankind through their identity with him.

(5) Virtue is the beauty of moral qualities, and beauty is the agreement of being with being. Virtue is finally, then, a disposition to benevolence toward being in general, disinterested benevolence. Since God is the ultimate being, virtue consists in love of God.

(6) And, since God's virtue would consist in love of Himself, the end of creation is God's own glory.

E=MC²

Q.v. Einstein (2).

EFFECT.

Q.v. Cause.

EFFICIENT CAUSE.

Q.v. Aristotle (9).

EFFLUXES, THEORY OF.

The doctrine that perception occurs through an efflux of images from things, or an influx of such images into the sensory organs. *Q.v.* Empedocles (5); Democritus (10); Epicurus (8).

EGIDIO OF LESSINES. c. 1230–c.1304.

Scholastic philosopher. Born in Belgium. A Dominican, he studied under Albert the Great. He defended the Thomistic doctrine of the unity of form against the arguments of Robert Kilwardby (*q.v.*).

Principal writings: *On the Unity of Form*, 1278.

EGIDIO ROMANO. c. 1247–1316.

Scholastic philosopher. Born in Rome. Educated in Paris. Taught in Paris. A member of the Order of the Hermits of St. Augustine, he became Vicar General in 1295, and bishop of Bourges. He argued for the Thomistic doctrine of the unity of substantial form, and defended the idea of a real distinction between essence and existence. He went beyond Thomism in many ways, however, in the direction of Proclus and St. Augustine.

Principal writings: *Disputed Questions of Essence and Existence; Quaestiones quodlibetales; Theoremata; On the Possible Intellect; On Grades of Forms; On Ecclesiastical Power*; as well as commentaries on Aristotle, the *Book of Causes*, and the *Sentences*.

EGO.

From the Latin *ego* meaning "I." Thus, the individual self. However conceived, generally, the self or ego has been regarded as a harmony of bodily functioning, an entity in its own right, or as the form of the body. It has also been regarded, as in much Eastern thought, as an illusion engendered by false seeing.

(1) The soul as the harmony of bodily functioning appeared among the latter Pythagorean physicians (*q.v.* Pythagoreanism), and among the Sophists. Socrates opposed it in the *Phaedo*. It is the view most compatible with naturalism or materialism. The aggregate theory of Buddhism is similar to, but more subtle than, this conception (*q.v.* Buddha 5). The

Freudian division into *id*, *ego*, and *super-ego* also belongs to the present category (*q.v.* Freud 1–3). Also *q.v.* Jung 3–4.

(2) The soul as an entity in its own right is the conception of all dualistic and idealistic Western views, the conception of most of the high religions including Hinduism, Jainism, and of the philosophies connected with these religions. It was the view defended by Socrates (*q.v.* 5) in the *Phaedo*. For Kant (*q.v.* 11d) and Husserl (*q.v.* 6), our empirical awareness is an entity, but with transcendental implications.

(3) The soul as the form of the body is the Aristotelian (*q.v.* Aristotle 7) and with some qualifications, the Thomistic (*q.v.* Aquinas 6) doctrine. At least in the Aristotelian rendering, the soul as form is not an entity in its own right, and yet, far from being a harmony of the body, it had a directive function.

(4) The illusory nature of the empirical self or ego may be illustrated widely in Eastern thought. In Yoga (*q.v.* 3), for example, the destruction of the sense of the ego reveals the self.

(5) For Fichte (*q.v.* 3) the ego results from a posit, which each of us makes.

EGO, THE SPECULAR.
   Q.v. Lacan (3).

EGOCENTRIC PREDICAMENT.
   In a general sense the problem that we wish to know and interpret the world, and must do so from the perspectives available to us, perspectives centered in ourselves or our egos. In a technical sense the term was introduced by R.B. Perry (*q.v.* 1) who applied the term to the tendencies of Idealists to move from the fact that everything they know is in their minds to the conclusion that everything is mental.

EGOISM.
   The doctrine that all of one's actions either are or ought to be self-directed. Compare with Altruism (*q.v.*).
   (1) Hobbes (*q.v.* 6–7) presented a view of human nature in which each individual could do no other than seek his own ends.
   (2) Giulio Clement Scotti in his satire, *La Monarchie des solipses*, 1652, depicted a society of self-seekers. Directed against the Jesuits, the effect for a time was to

cause the terms "egoist" and "solipsist" to be used interchangeably.
   (3) For the claim that Egoism is the end of life *q.v.* Max Stirner (1).

EHRENFELS, CHRISTIAN. 1859–1932.
   Austrian psychologist and value theorist. Born in Rodaun, Austria. Disciple of Meinong; one of the leaders of the Brentano School; professor in Prague. Opposed to associationalism, Ehrenfels supported the notion of the Gestalt quality of perception; he extended this into value theory, developing the role of desire or pleasure in valuation. Late in life he elaborated a dualistic metaphysics.
   Principal writings: *System of Value Theory*, 2 vols., 1897, 1898; *Basic Ideas of Ethics*, 1907; *Cosmogony* (T), 1916; *The Religion of the Future*, 1929.

EIDETIC.
   From the Greek *eidos* ("form," "shape," "figure"). In philosophy the term is associated largely with Husserl (*q.v.* 4–6). Starting from Plato's (*q.v.* 1) identification of the *eidos* of a thing with its essence or form, Husserl advanced a method of "eidetic reduction," designed to arrive at essence. In the method one "brackets" the question of existence. Given the requisite attention the essence then shines forth. One comes in contact with the essence by "eidetic intuition," and expresses it in "eidetic judgment," *i.e.*, judgment which does not posit individual existence. "Eidetic sciences," similarly, are sciences of essence, not existence (logic and mathematics are examples); and all factual science rests on a foundation of eidetic science.

EIDOLA.
   A Greek term for "images." In the accounts of perception given by Democritus (*q.v.* 10) and Epicurus (*q.v.* 8) "detached outlines" given off by objects and received by our senses.

EIDOLOGY.
   Q.v. Herbart (3).

EINFÜHLUNG.
   A German term meaning "empathy." *Q.v.* Theodor Lipps; Aesthetics (21).

EINSTEIN, ALBERT. 1879–1955.
   Theoretical physicist. Born in Ulm, Ger-

many. Studied in Zurich's Federal Institute of Technology. Official in Bern Patent Office, 1902–1909. Doctorate from University of Zurich, 1905. Professor in Zurich, Prague, and from 1913–33 in the University of Berlin. He was also Director of Physical Theory in the Kaiser Wilhelm Institute. In 1921 he received the Nobel Prize for his scientific work. Deprived of his office and citizenship in 1933, he accepted a position in the Institute of Advanced Studies, Princeton, New Jersey, where he spent the rest of his life. Philosophically, he was influenced by Spinoza, Hume, and Mach.

Principal writings: "A Contemporary Viewpoint on the Production and Transformation of Light," 1905; "Electrodynamic Bodily Movement," 1905; "Toward a Theory of Brownian Motion," 1906; "Theory of Light Production and Absorption," 1906; "The Principle of Relativity and its Deducible Consequences," 1907; "Sketch of a General Theory of Relativity and a Theory of Gravitation," 1913; *Groundwork of the General Theory of Relativity*, 1916; *On the Special and General Theories of Relativity, a Popular Exposition* (T), 1917; "Cosmological Considerations of General Relativity Theory," 1917; *The Meaning of Relativity* (E), 1921; *On the Method of Theoretical Physics* (E), 1933; "Motion of Particles in General Relativity Theory" (E), (with Infeld), 1949; *Out of My Later Years* (E), 1950.

(1) Although having made significant contributions to Photo-Electric theory (essentially "discovering" the photon), the theory of Brownian movement, and statistical mechanics, Einstein's fame rests on his special and general theories of relativity.

(2) In the Special Theory of Relativity, the basic work first appearing in 1905 and 1907, Einstein dropped the assumption of an absolute space and time. The move restored a considerable measure of unity to the field of physics, and led to numerous fruitful consequences. The new view holds that simultanity can be established only within a given inertial system, and will not be valid for observers in systems in motion relative to the given system. Since on this view the energy of any mass is the product of the mass and the square of the velocity of light ($E=MC^2$), every particle of matter contains a vast quantity of energy. Not only has this consequence of the theory been demonstrated, but many others as well. In this theory the velocity of light is constant. Mass increases and time slows down as velocity increases, and time is regarded as a fourth dimension. The Special Theory has the surprising consequences that the same event, viewed from inertial systems in motion with respect to each other will occur at different times, bodies will measure out at different lengths, and clocks will run at different speeds.

(3) The General Theory of 1916 generalized the results of the Special Theory from inertial systems to non-linear transformations of coordinates. This was necessary in order to account for the proportionality between gravitational mass and inert mass. In the theory, gravitation is reduced to or is an effect of space-time curvature, and depends upon the masses distributed through the universe. Thus the concept of action at a distance is discarded. Confirmation of the general theory is much less strong than that of the special theory, but the bending of light rays as they pass through a strong field of gravitation has apparently been observed, and the theory is naturally consonant with the cosmological picture of an expanding universe. One consequence of the General Theory is that the universe is finite but unbounded.

(4) As a further step, Einstein attempted to construct a unified field theory, expressing the properties of matter and energy in a single formula. The effort ran counter to the probabilistic features of Quantum Theory (*q.v.* Mechanics 2), and was not successful. The unsuccessful attempt was motivated in part by a preference for a predictable, determined universe. This preference had many roots. He had accepted his teacher Minkowski's (*q.v.* 2) conception of world lines leading to the view of space-time as a four-dimensional continuum in which future events are already determinately present. Theologically, Einstein believed that God would not play dice with the universe, and he cited with approval the philosophy of Spinoza whose God expresses himself in the orderly harmony of all being.

(5) Throughout his life Einstein sup-

ported the causes of pacifism and passive resistance (except against militant fascism), freedom of conscience, Zionism, the international control of atomic energy, and the need for an international political order.

Also *q.v.* Whitehead (8).

EISAI.
Q.v. Zen Buddhism (4).

EJECTS.
Q.v. W.K. Clifford (2).

EK-SISTENZ.
German neologism coined by Heidegger (*q.v.* 4–6) to emphasize the "standing forth" character of authentic existence.

ÉLAN VITAL.
For Bergson (*q.v.* 5) the prime mover working in the world, and active in evolutionary processes.

ELEATICS.
Among the early Greek philosophers (5th and 6th cent. B.C.) a group of thinkers, centering in Elea, believing in the unity and eternity of being. The Eleatics relegated change and motion to the level of appearance, and offered very subtle arguments for their view. *Q.v.* Parmenides; Zeno of Elea; Xenophanes; Melissus of Samos.

ELECTRA COMPLEX.
Q.v. Freud (5).

ELENCHUS.
From the Greek *elegxos* ("a means of testing"). Thus a refutation by argument. *Q.v. Ignoratio Elenchi.*

ELEUSINIAN MYSTERIES.
Q.v. Mystery Religions (1).

ELIOT, T.S.
Q.v. New Criticism.

ELITES, THEORY OF.
Q.v. Pareto (1).

ELLIS, BRIAN.
Q.v. Induction (15).

ELYSIUM.
Greek term for paradise. Located by Homer on the western edge of the world, by Hesiod and Pindar in the Isles of the Blessed (located in the western ocean), and, by later poets, in the underworld.

EMANATION.
From the Latin *e* ("from") and *mano* ("flow"). Emanation is a doctrine of the production of the world as due to the overflowing superabundance of the divine. An alternative to the doctrine of creation. The concept of emanation connects the eternal and temporal orders, usually through intermediate stages. In the West, Gnosticism (*q.v.* 2) and Neoplatonism are emanationistic philosophies. *Q.v.* Plotinus (2–5), Proclus (1), Erigena (2). Pantheistic philosophies tend in this direction. A similar ordering of ideas is present in Hindu philosophy as well.

EMERGENT EVOLUTION.
The doctrine that novel qualities, not reducible to their antecedents, appear in the course of evolution. The doctrine was held by C. Lloyd Morgan (*q.v.* 2), Boodin (*q.v.* 3), Smuts (*q.v.* 2), S. Alexander (*q.v.* 2–5), G.H. Lewes, and others. A criticism of mechanism is implicit in this view, since mechanism must explain the appearance of life and mind without the doctrine of emergent levels of quality. The most thorough of the emergentists is S. Alexander who begins with space-time, and gains everything else through emergence.

EMERSON, RALPH WALDO. 1803–1882.
American philosopher and essayist. Born in Boston, Massachusetts. Graduated from Harvard, 1821. After three years' teaching, Emerson entered the Harvard Divinity School, becoming pastor of the Second Church, Unitarian, in Boston in 1829. He resigned after some years over the symbolism of the Communion Service. He began his career as lecturer in 1833, becoming the central figure of the New England Transcendentalists (*q.v.* The Transcendent 4). He moved to Concord in 1835. His courses of lectures on "Great Men," "English Literature," "Philosophy of History," and others, including his Phi Beta Kappa address of 1837 on "The American Scholar" and his Harvard Divinity School address, spread his fame. Most of the material for his books came from his

public lectures which took him across America and into England. Harvard conferred an LL.D. on him in 1866.

Principal writings: *Nature*, 1836; *Essays*, 2 vols., 1841, 1844; *Poems*, 1846; *Representative Men*, 1850; *English Traits*, 1856; *The Conduct of Life*, 1860; *May Day and other Pieces*, 1867; *Society and Solitude*, 1870; *Letters and Social Aims*, 1876.

(1) Wanting to "teach the finite to know its master," and seeing the procession of all humanity as lame and blind and deaf through ages past, and the American over-emphasis on commercialism as deteriorating and degrading, Emerson set up a secular pulpit in the lecture halls of America.

(2) The corrective for all these ills, in Emerson's view, is for one to turn to oneself, to conform one's life not to the world but to the pure idea in one's mind. Then one's life will begin to "unfold its great proportions," and the world will correspondingly alter to support and nourish one's development. This is, of course, Emerson's emphasis on self-reliance.

(3) Correspondingly, there is an emphasis, like that in Carlyle, on the great men of history, more particularly of culture, but with the interesting turn that their self-discovery can be of benefit to the rest of us.

(4) Emerson's interest was in individual self-development; and he believed that there were resources in every man allowing him this privilege. He held man to be something like a microcosm of the macrocosm; there is, he taught, a correspondence between the human soul and everything in the universe. He believed, further, that somehow by design a principle of compensation was at work. If a man lacked one gift, nature provided him with another; and a great gift in one area required a deficiency in some other. His interest was in the act of philosophizing rather than in the result; and he seems to have held that systematic results were beside the point. A man need only work over and extract the wisdom from the resources immediately available to him— in himself, in society, letters, and nature— in order to come to himself.

(5) This sense of environing support Emerson symbolized in the conception of an Over-soul from which, especially through nature, the individual might draw insight and strength.

(6) Associating Transcendentalism with an intuitive approach to reality, he related this to Kant's beginning his philosophy with certain intuitions of the mind. Emerson gave a much more literary meaning to intuition than had Kant— a meaning, indeed, which Kant had disavowed. The sense of transcendentalism Emerson supported is closer to Kant's idealistic successors, and to the movement of Romanticism.

(7) Emerson believed that the development of culture was a more worthy end of government than the development of commerce; and that a destiny of world leadership lay in store for any nation— he seems to have had America in mind— whose citizens would stand for the interests of general justice and humanity.

EMMET, DOROTHY. 1904– .

English philosopher. Studied at Oxford and Radcliffe College (Cambridge, Mass.). Taught at King's College, Newcastle upon Tyne, and the University of Manchester.

Principal writings: *Whitehead's Philosophy of Organism*, 1932; *Philosophy and Faith*, 1936; *The Nature of Metaphysical Thinking*, 1945; *Function, Purpose, and Powers*, 1958; *Rules, Roles and Relations*, 1966; *The Moral Prism*, 1979; *The Effectiveness of Causes*, 1985; *The Passage of Nature*, 1992.

(1) Author of an appreciative exposition of Whitehead, Emmet is best known for her defense of the validity of metaphysical thinking. She finds analogical thinking widespread, and of value to all areas of thought, including the sciences; but the manner in which metaphysics relates to all disciplines causes analogical thinking, and its vehicle, the metaphor, to be especially significant in this area.

(2) Metaphysics is the most abstract of the disciplines, having the task of expressing a coherence of all experience, including all scientific theory. One type of metaphysics does only this, utilizing analogies which contain a sense of self-evidence. A second type of metaphysics performs the function already stated, while also making a transcendent reference beyond ordinary experience. Both types contain a value-orientation, which Emmet (following Whitehead) calls a "judgment of importance."

(3) Emmet urges that the disciplines of ethics and sociology have overlapping concerns, and should be capable of joint exploration by representatives of both fields.

EMOTIVIST THEORY.

The theory that value terms are grounded in emotional attitudes. Applying initially to the field of ethics, the view has been extended to other areas where values are central, such as aesthetics and social philosophy.

(1) The view is usually traced to the connection between ethical terms and attitudes of approval and disapproval suggested by David Hume (*q.v.* 6).

(2) The sanction of the Vienna Circle of Logical Positivists (*q.v.*) has made the view central to modern discussions of value.

(3) Ayer (*q.v.* 5) championed emotivism, applying it to aesthetics as well as ethics.

(4) Kelsen (*q.v.*) extended emotivism to legal concepts in the philosophy of law.

(5) The classical statement of the view is to be found in the work of Charles Stevenson (*q.v.* 2).

EMPATHY.

From the Greek *en* ("in") and *patheia* ("feeling," "emotion," "experience"). The English term is a translation into Greek of the German *Einfühlung*. The term has had a role in both psychological and aesthetic analyses. It has been taken as an important key to aesthetic experience by such thinkers as Theodor Lipps (*q.v.*) and W. Worringer (*Abstraction and Empathy*, T, 1917). In this context empathy or *Einfühlung* refers to a state of partial identification with the art object in such fashion that one's relation to the object combines the senses of both identity and distance.

EMPEDOCLES. c. 490–430 B.C.

Greek philosopher. Born and lived in Agrigentum, Sicily. He was considered a god by the people, who honored him whenever he appeared in public. Legends abound concerning his miraculous deeds. After having helped to overthrow an oligarchy, and having refused the kingship offered by grateful citizens, a change in the balance of power forced him into exile where he died.

Principal writings: *On the Nature of Things; Hymns of Purification.* (Both works are poems, and several hundred lines of each survive.)

(1) Coming into being and going out of being are impossible. Genesis and destruction are to be understood as processes of mixture and separation.

(2) The roots of this mixture (*i.e.*, the table of elements) are earth, air, fire, and water. All qualitative distinctions are produced by a mixing of the four elements. The character of the elements causes some combinations to be more likely than others.

(3) The motive power for the mixture and separation is provided by a cosmic principle of attraction and repulsion. The twin forces of love and strife act alternatively through a succession of four phases: (a) the elements are in perfect mixture due to the attractive power of love; (b) strife enters, and the partial separation of the elements takes place; (c) strife is dominant, and the elements are completely separated; (d) love enters and the uniting of the mixture takes place, leading to the first phase once again.

(4) Life is possible in the second and fourth phases, and is explained as a result of chance and evolutionary processes. Indeed, Empedocles utilizes the principle of evolution not only to explain life, but to explain the myths about monsters, centaurs, gorgons, etc. Organs and parts of bodies grow up separately in the strife-filled phase, fusing together on contact, thus providing all varieties of strange mismatching. Those forms whose parts are happily placed are able to survive.

(5) Empedocles' doctrine of perception trades on the idea of similarity, perception occurring by means of a matching of the elements in us with elements in the things perceived.

(6) Thought is a corollary to, and a continuation of, sensation.

(7) The blood circulates, on Empedocles' view, in a pulsation from the center to the surface of the body, and return.

EMPIRICAL PSYCHOLOGY.

Q.v. Psychology (2, 3).

EMPIRICISM.

From the Greek *empeiria* (from *empeiros*:

"experienced in," "acquainted with," "skilled at"). The Latin translation is *experientia* ("experience"). Empiricism is the doctrine that the source of all knowledge is to be found in experience. One of the major theories of the origin of knowledge (*q.v.* Epistemology 2–6), empiricism is usually contrasted with rationalism (*q.v.*), the doctrine that reason is the sole, or at least the primary, source of knowledge. Most philosophers grant the importance of both experience and reason. The empirical philosophers, then, are those whose stress on experience is heavier than most.

(1) In the matter of comparative stress it is sometimes held that Plato is a rationalist (*q.v.* Rationalism 1) and Aristotle (*q.v.* 1–3) an empiricist. Simply as a matter of stress the claim has something to recommend it. Plato was more at home in mathematics and dialectic where Aristotle concentrated on the inductive sciences; yet both of these classical philosophers, and indeed Platonists and Aristotelians in all ages, combine rationalism with empiricism.

(2) To find a pure or full empiricism it is necessary to seek out traditions where observation, rather than idea or essence, is given the key role in inquiry. Among the Greeks Democritus (*q.v.* 10) and Epicurus (*q.v.* 8) belong to such a tradition. They trace all knowledge to an influx of images from things perceived, and all knowledge to a residue of this material. In the medieval period the requisite tradition appears once again. Among the disputants over the problem of universals one position, that of Nominalism (*q.v.*), held the universal to be nothing but a name. The decision displaces the idea or essence from its traditional position. William of Ockham (*q.v.* 11) belonged to this group; he provided an enduring distinction between two kinds of knowledge: that evident by the meaning of terms, and that which is evident from experience. Note that the kind of knowledge one can gain from an essence or idea is now reduced to definitions; the view will later be called tautology (*q.v.*).

(3) Empiricism developed through naturalistic and nominalistic traditions into its greatest flowering in a movement known as British empiricism. Roger Bacon (*q.v.* 2) called for "direct inspection" and "experimental science." Francis Bacon (*q.v.* 1, 3) worked out "tables of induction" and inveighed against rationalism in all its forms. Locke (*q.v.* 2–3) traced all ideas to experience and argued against innate ideas. Berkeley (*q.v.* 1) identified being with the perceived. Hume (*q.v.* 1–5) continued Locke's emphasis along with that of Ockham, distinguishing between matters of fact and relations of ideas. On the Continent, meanwhile, Gassendi (*q.v.* 6) was reviving the Epicurean image-analysis of knowledge.

(4) In the 18th century, British empiricism was exported to the Continent, the French *philosophes* following the British lead. Condillac (*q.v.* 1–3) was a disciple of Locke; and d'Alembert (*q.v.* 1–2) anticipated J.S. Mill by finding even mathematics to be empirical.

(5) Although the 19th century tended toward rationalism in philosophy, the British J.S. Mill (*q.v.* 1–4) stressed inductive logic, developing empirical methods of analyzing causal relations. He believed mathematics to be an empirical discipline, and held matter to be nothing more than the permanent possibility of sensation.

(6) The movement of pragmatism (*q.v.*) in the late 19th and early 20th century made empiricism a test of meaning as well as of truth; and one member of the school, William James (*q.v.* 8), termed his theory of knowledge "radical empiricism."

(7) In the 20th century the logical positivism of the Vienna Circle can be interpreted as an effort to purify philosophy of its nonempirical elements. Two of the members of the circle, A.J. Ayer (*q.v.* 1, 3), and Herbert Feigl (*q.v.*), call their view "logical empiricism"; and Ayer, at least, is quite insistent about tracing his philosophical lineage back to David Hume. The distinction between analytic and synthetic statements, continuing Hume's "relations of ideas" and "matters of fact," is held by and beyond the circle of positivists (*q.v.* Russell 8 and Wittgenstein 1–3, for example).

(8) The movement of Phenomenalism (*q.v.*), containing some of the figures mentioned above, is an attempt to construct the world from empirical data alone. H.H. Price's (*q.v.* 1) interpretation of the "standard solid" as a convergence of families of sense-data is also in this vein.

(9) Among those challenging empiricism are Lévi-Strauss (*q.v.* 2) who holds that empiricism is not applicable to the analysis of myth, and Feyerabend (*q.v.*) who holds that it cannot be made the universal basis of factual knowledge.

EMPIRIOCRITICISM.

(1) A term used by Avenarius (*q.v.* 1) to designate his program of eliminating metaphysical assumptions and doctrines from philosophy in favor of a philosophy of pure experience.

(2) The sensationalism of Mach (*q.v.*) had a similar goal, although he did not employ the term.

(3) Lenin (*q.v.* 2), finding the doctrine penetrating Russian thought, attacked it under the name Empiriocriticism, as reactionary and bourgeois. Against this doctrine he supported epistemological realism as alone consonant with Marxism.

(4) Petzoldt (*q.v.*) supported empiriocriticism, influenced by the views of Mach as well as by the position of Avenarius.

EMPIRIOMONISM.

Q.v. Bogdanov.

EMPSON, WILLIAM. 1906–1984.

English poet and critic. Born in Howden, England. Educated at Winchester College and Cambridge University. Taught at Cambridge. A mathematician turned poet, and student of I.A. Richards (*q.v.*), he has been called one of the leading Cambridge critics.

Principal philosophical writing: *Seven Types of Ambiguity*, 1930.

(1) Meaning by ambiguity "any verbal nuance, however slight, which gives room for alternative reactions to the same piece of language," Empson applied the definition to poetry, writing that all poetry is ambiguous. His application of the seven types to instances of poetry has led to his being classed one of the New Critics (*q.v.* New Criticism).

(2) The seven types of ambiguity, to each of which Empson devotes a chapter, along with strategies for handling them, are:

(a) First-type: when a detail is effective in several ways at once: comparisons with several points of likeness; antithesis with several points of difference.

(b) Second-type: when two or more alternative meanings are resolved into one meaning.

(c) Third-type: two apparently unconnected meanings are given simultaneously.

(d) Fourth-type: the alternative meanings combine to make clear a complicated state of mind in the author.

(e) Fifth-type: a fortunate confusion, *e.g.*, the author discovers his idea in the act of writing; or does not have it all in mind at once.

(f) Sixth-type: what is said is contradictory or irrelevant, and the reader must invent interpretations.

(g) Seventh-type: Full contradiction, showing a fundamental division in the author's mind.

EMPTINESS.

English translation of the Sanskrit *śunya* (*q.v.*). Although the concept predates Nagarjuna, according to Masao Abe (*Zen and Western Thought*, 1985) Nagarjuna (*q.v.*) arrived at the concept of emptiness when he denied both actuality and its negation, thus centering on the distinctive characteristic of Mahayana Buddhism. In this view emptiness as non-dual locates transcendence and eternity in the immediate moment, replaces God, provides the possibility of Egolessness, and an ethic of selfless behavior. It is the concept at the basis of Buddha's (*q.v.* 2–3) doctrine of Dependent Origination and his teaching of the eight-fold path. Should this be so, it would appear, too, that the *koan* (*q.v.*) is designed to lead the individual through the double negation.

ENCYCLICAL, PAPAL.

From the Greek *enguklios* ("in a circle"). A letter of instruction sent by the pope to a circle of dioceses and, in matters of grave importance, to the entire world. Like the Papal Bull, the Encyclical is named from the initial words of its text. The content of the former is, however, not instruction but dogma.

ENCYCLOPÉDIE.

Q.v. Encyclopedists.

ENCYCLOPEDISTS.

In philosophy the term is usually reserved for the group of 18th-century French philosophers, known as *les philosophes* who, motivated by the view that social evils could be eliminated through the spread of knowledge, collaborated in the project of composing the thirty-five volume French *Encyclopédie* (1751–80) designed to bring all knowledge into a single compass. Editor of the encyclopedia was Denis Diderot (*q.v.*) who wrote most of the articles on religion, ancient history, and political theory. His coeditor was Jean d'Alembert (*q.v.*) who wrote many of the mathematical and literary articles, but withdrew as editor before the completion of the project. Both of them wrote on philosophical themes. Among others who contributed articles to the project are Rousseau (*q.v.*), Voltaire (*q.v.*), Duclos, Quesnay, Turgot (*q.v.*), d'Holbach (*q.v.*), and Toussaint. Hampered by conflicts with defenders of church and court as well as by the Sorbonne, the encyclopedia was suppressed in both 1752 and 1759 during the process of its publication. It was likewise attacked in pamphlet and play. The cause of these difficulties was the skepticism its authors felt to be inherent in their commitment to the spirit of reason. Diderot stood firm throughout the attacks and brought the publication of the first seventeen volumes to completion in 1772.

ENDOSEMIOTIC.
Q.v. Semiotic (13).

ENERGEIA.
A Greek term meaning "energy," "action," or "operation." As utilized by Aristotle the term signifies both a state of realized potentiality and the activity leading to that state. In both senses the term stands in marked contrast to *dynamis* ("unrealized potentiality"). The relationship between *energeia* and *entelecheia* is more subtle. When *entelecheia* is defined as "the full realization of essence," the latter is identical to *energeia* in the first sense given above, and the means by which *entelecheia* is reached in the second of the two usages. When *entelecheia* is defined as "the completed or perfect realization of *energeia*" both senses of the latter term are present.

ENGELS, FRIEDRICH. 1820–1895.
Marxist philosopher. Born in Barmen, Germany. Son of an industrialist who had extensive interests in Manchester, England, he was cofounder of the Marxist

movement, and Karl Marx's most intimate friend and life-long collaborator. Meeting Marx in the forties, he thereafter not only devoted himself to the structure of the Marxist movement, but also to the well-being of his collaborator. After Marx's death he edited volumes 2 and 3 of *Capital* and prepared them for publication.

Principal writings: *Herr Eugen Dühring's Revolution in Science*, also known as *Anti-Dühring* (T), 1878; *Socialism: Utopian and Scientific* (T), 1883; *The Origin of the Family, Private Property, and the State* (T), 1884; *Ludwig Feuerbach and the Outcome of Classical German Philosophy* (T), 1888; *Principles of Communism* (T), 1919; *Dialectics of Nature* (T), 1925.

(1) Although most of Engel's work was done in direct collaboration with Marx, and the basic ideas are summarized under the heading Marxism (*q.v.* 3), among Engels' contributions to the subject one must count the notion of dialectical materialism. The thesis-antithesis-synthesis pattern, never mentioned as such by Marx, was presumed by Engels to be working at all levels of reality. In nature this dialectical process generates new qualities; *e.g.*, matter gains the qualities of life and mind. In history the pattern works toward the elimination of classes, and the establishment of the harmonious, classless society.

(2) Even though he held the economic structure to have great importance in the shaping of cultural forms, he did not believe the former completely determines the latter. It seems rather to have been his view that there is a reciprocal influence between these two aspects of society.

ENLIGHTENMENT.
A term used to refer both to the achievement of knowledge, and of religious insight. The nested word, "light," serves as metaphor in both uses. In the East the reference points mainly to religion where, for both Hinduism and Buddhism, enlightenment allows one release from endless cycles of existence (*q.v.* Samsara). Consider, however, the involvement of both cultures in the entry, Divine Illumination (*q.v.*). The most canonical reference of the term in the West is to a distinctive flowering of culture in the 18th-century.
A. In the East the term is to be found

in the Hindu way of *jnana*, or knowledge (*q.v.* Hinduism 5b and Yoga 5c), in Taoism (*q.v. Tao-Te-Ching* 2), in all forms of Buddhism where the term Nirvana (*q.v.*) is a rough equivalent, in Theravada Buddhism (*q.v.* 3) where the recognition of impermanence is one of its conditions, and in Zen Buddhism (*q.v.* 2, 5–7) where its equivalent is *satori*.

B. In the West the enlightenment, taking as its motto (according to Kant) "Dare to know," shaped human life in England, France, and Germany. It was characterized by great optimism with respect to the possibilities of reason in controlling human life. The Enlightenment was carried by the Encyclopedists (*q.v.*) in France, by the Deists (*q.v.* Deism) and empiricistic followers of Locke (*q.v.*) in England, and by their successors at a somewhat later time in the German *Aufklärung* (*q.v.*). Every phase of culture felt the impact of illumination by reason. The same spirit of reason which touched Newton's science, Locke's philosophy, and the Deist's religion, is present in the literature of Corneille, Racine, Molière, the music of Bach, the symmetry of Versailles, and the controlling rationality of Rembrandt. The optimism of the Enlightenment gave way in the 19th century to the forces of Romanticism (*q.v.*). Germany felt the influence of both currents almost simultaneously. Among the 19th-century opponents to the Enlightenment should be mentioned the Romantic poet Novalis (*q.v.* 2) who felt that the Enlightenment's hard and fast distinctions did not allow the proper poetic relationship of finite and infinite.

ENNEADS.
    Q.v. Plotinus.

ENS.
    From the Latin, the present participle of the verb *esse*, meaning "to be" or "being." This Scholastic term refers to being of any kind in any mode, that which exists or can exist, within or without the mind. Hence, it divides into *ens reale*, existing independently of mind; *ens in potentia*, potential being; *ens in acto*, realized being; and *ens rationis*, the being or reason within the mind.

EN-SOF.
    Q.v. Isaac Luria (1).

EN-SOI.
    A French term meaning "in itself." A translation of the Latin *in se*, and the German *an sich* (*q.v. Ding an sich*). The *En-soi* is contrasted with the *Pour-soi* by Sartre (*q.v.* 5).

ENS REALISSIMUM.
    A Latin term meaning "most real being." A definition of God. *Q.v.* Kant (5c).

ENTELECHEIA.
    Q.v. Energeia.

ENTELECHY.
    From the Greek *entelecheia*, a compound of *en* and *telos* ("actuality" or "reality") with *echein* ("to have" or "to hold").
    (1) For Aristotle (*q.v.* 8) the entelechy of a thing is both its complete reality and the power of the developing thing to achieve completeness or perfection. Also, *q.v. Energeia*.
    (2) Leibniz (*q.v.* 2) applied the term to the monads of his system, apparently because they possess both of the qualities mentioned in (1) above.
    (3) In the Vitalism (*q.v.*) of Hans Driesch (*q.v.*) the term is used to refer to the inner controlling force of biological organisms.

ENTHYMEME.
    From the Greek *en* ("in") and *thymos* ("mind"). Its common meaning now is "incomplete syllogism," an inference in which one of the premises, or the conclusion, is implicit. *Q.v.* Syllogism (7).

ENTIA NATURAE.
    Latin phrase meaning "things of nature." *Q.v.* Nature (5).

ENTIA RATIONIS.
    Latin phrase meaning "things of reason." *Q.v.* Nature (5).

ENTITY.
    From the Latin *ens, entis* ("thing"). In Scholastic philosophy, initially, any real being. Later, whatever has sufficient separateness of being, whether in reality or thought, to support predications.

ENUMERATION.
    The term has at least two philosophical connections.
    (1) One of the forms of definition (*q.v.*

3) is "definition by enumeration." This is a definition by listing the individuals or sub-classes making up the denotation of the term.

(2) One of the forms of induction (*q.v.* 1a, 3) is "induction by simple enumeration" (also called perfect or complete induction). The form was criticized by Francis Bacon who argued for the "experimental method."

EPAGOGE.

From the Greek meaning "a bringing in." A Greek and Aristotelian term for induction (*q.v.* 1). Instances of induction are sometimes called "epagogic demonstrations" or "epagogic syllogisms."

EPICHEIREMA.

From the Greek *epicherein* ("to attempt to prove"). For Aristotle a dialectical, as opposed to an apodictic or eristic, syllogism. Later, a syllogism in which statements supporting one or both of the premises are introduced along with the premises themselves.

EPICTETUS. 60–138.

Greek philosopher. Born in Hierapolis. Attended lectures of the Stoic philosopher, Musonius Rufus. One of the best known Stoic philosophers, Epictetus began his teaching career as a slave in Rome. Eventually freed, he was expelled from Rome with all other philosophers by Domitian, 90 A.D. He settled, then, in southern Epirus. Throughout his life he was lame and sickly. His student, Flavius Arrianus, took down his teaching, a substantial part of which has survived.

Principal writings: *Discourses of Epictetus* (8 books extant); *Encheiridion* (a "handbook," summarizing the doctrines of the *Discourses*).

(1) The sole inquiry of importance concerns the conduct of life. The proper conduct of life lies in learning how to distinguish between what does, and what does not, lie within our power.

(2) What lies within our power is our will and inner purpose. Nothing external can force us to act against our will. If we submit, we have willed to submit.

(3) The rationality of man is the God within one. Following reason, one senses one's position as a member of one's own nation, and of the true city of gods and men. He also recognizes the pointlessness of depending upon any external thing.

(4) One will simply try to understand the reality in which one finds oneself, setting up in one's own mind an order of ideas corresponding to the order of nature, for the thought of God directs the universe, and it is our part to accept what happens with intelligence.

(5) Epictetus thus develops the conception that there is a given role for each individual to play in life. He uses the term "person" (*q.v.*) to refer to the individual as playing this role. From Stoic usage the term entered Roman law.

EPICUREANISM.

A school of philosophy founded in Athens in 306 B.C. by Epicurus (*q.v.*). The school, stressing atomic theory, empiricism, and hedonism, remained an influential factor in the cultural life of Greece and Rome from the time of Epicurus in the 4th century B.C. until the 5th century A.D. During this period there is a long record of the polemic between the Epicureans on the one hand and the Stoics (*q.v.*), Skeptics (*q.v.*), and the Aristotelian or Peripatetic philosophers (*q.v.*) on the other.

(1) The initial successors of Epicurus, heading the school, were first Hermarchus and then Polystratus. In its early period the school stressed the value theory in which pleasure is regarded as the highest good, and the ethical philosophy derivable from this.

(2) In the 1st century B.C. a number of remarkable philosophers appeared in the movement more or less simultaneously: Lucretius (*q.v.*), Philodemus (*q.v.*), and Asclepiades (*q.v.*). This was the period in which the school stressed its empirical approach to logic, finding the Stoic logic excessively rational in design. Both the Peripatetics and the Skeptics were likewise criticized on the grounds of using vacuous, rational arguments. This was also the period of Cicero (*q.v.*) whose eclecticism included Epicureanism as one of its major components.

(3) In the 2nd and 3rd centuries A.D. there was a reversion to the ethical philosophy of the initial period. Diogenes of Oinoanda (*q.v.*) and Diogenianus (*q.v.*) are representatives of the period.

(4) In the 15th and 16th centuries a so-called Christian epicureanism appeared in the writings of Lorenzo Valla (*q.v.*) and Erasmus (*q.v.* 3). Here again the ethical side of the movement was stressed. Thomas More (*q.v.*) acquired the epicurean ground of his *Utopia* from these sources.

(5) In the 17th century a strong interest in the atomism of the system developed. Among others this interest was present in Berigard (*q.v.*), Gassendi (*q.v.*), and Maignan (*q.v.*).

EPICURUS. 341–270 B.C.

Greek philosopher. Born in Samos. Influenced by Democritus. He began his school in Athens in 306, after having purchased its garden campus for 80 minae. The student body was coeducational, and the mode of life plain. Many ancient writers testify to the "crowds of Epicureans" attracted by the doctrine.

Principal writings: *On Nature* (in thirty-seven books, fragments of nine extant); the *Canon*; and letters to Herodotus, Pitocles, and Menoeccus. Some three hundred works have been attributed to Epicurus.

(1) Dividing philosophy into the canonical, physics, and ethics, Epicurus meant by the first division something like theory of knowledge. It was treated in the *Canon*. For Epicurus the appropriate philosophical method is to begin with the clear evidence of sense, "plain facts," the burden of perception, and accept, refute, and shape one's opinions in terms of this evidence. When an opinion falls outside the area of possible perception one then adds to the method both analogy and non-contradiction. Theory is expected to elucidate what is perceived.

(2) In application an atomism owing much to Democritus emerged. We are to believe in a permanent subject of change, and this is clearly not any composite body. To account for permanence there must be elements of a solid nature out of which all composite things are formed. As there is a smallest thing to be seen, so there is a minimum level of existence; these simple non-composite entities, the atoms, must be regarded, then, as containing no void, for this would make them composite. The atoms vary indefinitely in size and shape, but not infinitely,

although there is an infinite number of each kind or type.

(3) The atoms, infinite in number, exist in an infinite void, Epicurus' word for space. Motion is possible because of the void; and place is a necessity once one admits the existence of bodies. Space is called "the intangible nature," and is the only intangible nature. The basic entities are atoms and the void; and anything that can act, or be acted upon, hence, for example, soul, must be a body.

(4) The qualities of objects are properties or modifications of bodies. Differences in quality are traceable to the addition or subtraction of atoms, or changes in location. The quantitative aspects of things are, hence, more deeply situated in nature than the qualitative aspects. But the view of Democritus that such qualities are conventional is not the view of Epicurus. The qualities are not things in their own right, nor conventions; but objective products of the atomic constituents of composite things.

(5) The atoms are in ceaseless motion; and these motions explain every sort of change in composite things. The natural motion of unattached atoms is a downward motion. The atoms also, however, have a curious power to swerve, uncaused by anything else; hence, due to chance, apparently. The power of collision among atoms, and the combination of the two motions produces a swirling movement. This in turn accounts for the formation of worlds; and all upward and other motions in the bargain.

(6) Relying chiefly on efficient causation, operating through the change of position, collision and conjunction of atomic particles, the swerve of the atom allows causation of another sort, which allows freedom in man, and keeps Epicurus from determinism. For this power to initiate a causal situation, spread throughout the universe, means that it is not possible even in principle to predict the total future. Hence, the future is in some measure open; partly fixed, partly free.

(7) Soul and mind are understood as concentrations of fine, swiftly moving atoms of special sorts; the soul atoms exist throughout the body; those allowing rationality are concentrated in the chest. But personal immortality is out of the question, since such atoms require the

protection of the body in order to be-have in their characteristic ways.

(8) Perception is possible by means of the outlines of things, *i.e.*, images or *eidola*, which come to us from the composite bodies through our senses, though these outlines are so fine and thin that we can-not see them but only through them. Error is to be explained by the collisions of these outlines before reaching the observer. The realistic basis of epistemol-ogy utilized by Epicurus allows him to believe in the gods, or perhaps more accurately, in the divine. Since men have a deep-seated belief in the gods this ar-gues for there being evidence for the belief; and this must mean that we are receiving "outlines" of the divine at every moment although these outlines are so exceedingly subtle that we cannot well separate them out from the other deliv-eries of sense. We become directly aware of them usually in dreams when the re-ceipt of other outlines has been reduced.

(9) The real question concerns not the existence of the divine, but its nature; and here it is to be said that the divine is composed of atoms, as is all else, and existing in perfect bliss in the spaces between the worlds. His usual reference is in the plural, so that we are to think of more than one such blissful and eter-nally happy nature, no more concerned with us than they have reason to be.

(10) The goal of life is happiness. The material of happiness is understood to be *ataraxia*, a state of pleasure enjoyed in tranquility, free from mental or phys-ical disturbance. Prudence is, then, the guide to happiness, the foundation of the virtues and more precious than philoso-phy. "We cannot live pleasantly without living wisely and nobly and righteously."

EPIPHANY.

From the Greek *epi* ("on," "over," "at," "after") and *phainein* ("to show, bring to light, cause to appear"), hence a mani-festation.

(1) In Greek tragedy the appearance of a divine being, sometimes airborne, relating the play to the ritual at its base.

(2) The name of the Christian feast held on January 6, and widely observed by 325 A.D. Now celebrated in the West as the visit of the Magi, earlier Christian traditions observed this day as the Nativity, or as Jesus' Baptism, or both. In the Eastern Church Jan. 6 is still ob-served as the date of the Baptism. Any one of these occasions can be taken as a manifestation of the divine. If baptism is the original tradition, the day prob-ably relates to pre-Christian beliefs that water was dangerous at the turn of the year, and became available for conse-crated purposes only as the days began to lengthen.

(3) A secularized experience of epiph-any developed in the modern period. Emerson (*q.v.* 5–6) used the term in some-thing like its modern sense when hold-ing that the aroused intellect can experience "an epiphany of God" in the dullest facts. James Joyce, however, fixed the modern usage, having Stephen Hero describe epiphany as a spiritual mani-festation occurring in an evanescent mo-ment, and having Stephen Daedalus define epiphany as "a sudden spiritual manifestation." The latter went on to describe it, using Aquinas' aesthetics (*q.v.* 6), as the moment when the *claritas* (ra-diance) of a thing is discovered to be its *quidditas* (whatness): "This is the moment which I call epiphany." Joyce found epiphany in the "significance of trivial things," as had Emerson.

(4) Although Wordsworth did not use the term, he wrote in "The Prelude" of the "spots of time" scattered everywhere which give us "profoundest knowledge." This celebration of the commonplace has led students of literature to credit him with the origin of the modern concept. More generally, it was attributed to him as a representative of the Romantic move-ment. Artistic inspiration, beginning as religiously epiphanic, was for Schopen-hauer "as if" by inspiration.

(5) If this is a matter of the mutual enfoldment of the temporal and the eter-nal, *q.v.* Novalis (1–2). The experience would have antecedents in Spinoza's (*q.v.* 5) living under the aspect of eternity, Giordano Bruno's (*q.v.* 4) passion for the infinity of the universe, Nicholas of Cusa's (*q.v.* 2, 5) identity of opposites, Boethius' *totum simul* (*q.v.*), and repre-senting Zen Buddhism, Suzuki's (*q.v.* 5) description of *satori*.

EPIPHENOMENALISM.

From the Greek *epi* ("side") and

phainomenon ("appearance"). Thus, a "side appearance" or an "incidental appearance." The doctrine that consciousness is an incidental effect of neural processes, and not a cause. *Q.v.* T.H. Huxley; Shadworth Hodgson; Théodule Ribot; George Santayana (6).

EPISCOPAL CHURCH.
Q.v. Church of England.

EPISTEME.
Q.v. Foucault (3).

EPISTEMIC CORRELATIONS.
Q.v. Northrop (2).

EPISTEMOLOGICAL SOLIPSISM.
Q.v. Solipsism.

EPISTEMOLOGY.
From the Greek *episteme* ("knowledge" or "science") and *logos* ("knowledge" or "information"). The Greek components thus suggest a second order concern with knowledge about knowledge; and this area of philosophy is, indeed, sometimes called "theory of knowledge."

A. We shall consider the topic through a number of ways in which the field may be divided.

(1) The basic contrast between theories of knowledge is the contrast between the methods of Rationalism (*q.v.*), stressed by such thinkers as Parmenides (*q.v.* 1–3), Plato (*q.v.* 1), Descartes (*q.v.* 10), Spinoza (*q.v.* 5b), Leibniz (*q.v.* 1–12) on the one hand, and the theories of Empiricism (*q.v.*), stressed by Francis Bacon (*q.v.* 1, 3), Locke (*q.v.* 1–2), Berkeley (*q.v.* 1), Hume (*q.v.* 1–2), etc. on the other. Since the most promising instances of knowledge are scientific in character, one might argue that the method most consonant with science is to be accepted; but of course some areas of science are more empirical than others. It is quite possible that the contrast between Rationalism and Empiricism is a false contrast, and engenders a false problem.

(2) Empiricism can, generally, be identified with a Correspondence Theory of truth, and Rationalism with a Coherence Theory of truth. The Correspondence Theory (*q.v.* Truth, 1; Aristotle, 1; Aquinas, 4, 6) seems the more reasonable view to ordinary apprehension. It holds that statements are true when they correspond to the world, and ideas are correlated with reality by means of the perceptions we receive from the world.

(3) The Rationalist, typically, is expected to respond that considerable naïveté is present in the supposition that such correspondences can be established. Doubtless, one enters the knowledge-situation with an idea or set of ideas one wishes to check against reality. But since in the nature of the case one can know only ideas, the most one can accomplish is the checking of one idea against another—an idea from memory, for example, with an idea just received from the senses—and that simply was not the intention. Operating with the contention that we know only ideas, the Rationalist who holds the Coherence Theory (*q.v.* Truth 1, 23; Plato, 1; F.H. Bradley, 1, 4) stresses not correspondence, but logical criteria in evaluating a theory or explanation. The adherent of the Coherence Theory would be interested in the question of the internal consistency of each affirmation, or explanation, making up the theory; the external consistency of the affirmations with each other; and the relations of deducibility among the affirmations, permitting us to move from one to the other, and providing evidence that we have not allowed lacunae in our theory.

(4) The counter-criticism of the Correspondence theorist is that there are many instances of systems of ideas, internally coherent and preserving relations of deducibility, yet having no connection with reality. As cases in point one may cite the multiple systems of geometry, each with different axiomatic starting points, each developed with great unity and coherence, yet—since they are inconsistent with each other—not all of them can be true of the world.

(5) The Coherence theorist's answer to this is that the criticism misses the intention of the Coherence theory, for the coherence of ideas includes not only the abstract panoply of systematic ideas, but also the ideas we receive from the whole untidy flux of experience. It is the coherence of all of these ideas which is in question.

(6) The dispute may not be resolvable, but in practical terms it seems obvious that the claims of both rationality and observation must be honored. There is a

related dispute between Realism and Idealism in epistemology. Epistemological doctrines stressing the objectivity of the knowledge relation are sometimes termed "realistic": Representative Realism (q.v.)—ideas represent an objective reality. Naive Realism (q.v.)—our common-sense ideas represent reality as it is. Critical Realism (q.v.)—our ideas indirectly represent an objective reality. New Realism (q.v.)—we come into direct contact with the world through the knowledge relation. All of these are instances of Epistemological Realism, since in each alternative the datum is identified with the object. In Epistemological Idealism, on the other hand, the object would be identified with the datum.

(7) One may likewise distinguish dualists and monists in epistemology: Epistemological Dualism—a duality exists between the sense-datum and the object known. Epistemological Monism—the datum and the object known are identical. In this sense the distinctions of epistemology parallel those of metaphysics or ontology.

(8) There is also the epistemological issue of Foundationalism versus Contextualism, the former holding that knowledge requires an ultimate basis, and the latter not. Chisholm (q.v. 5) believed the foundation to consist of self-presenting propositions.

B. Entries which do not fit the foregoing pattern are set forth here:

(9) Piaget (q.v. 1), interested in the analysis of epistemological ideas in children, developed an approach called Genetic Epistemology.

(10) For a discussion of knowledge as justified true belief, q.v. The Gettier Problem.

Also q.v. Gadamer (3); Foucault (5).

EPISYLLOGISM.

A syllogism one or both of whose premises forms the conclusion of a preceding syllogism.

EPOCHÉ.

A Greek term for "suspense of judgment."

(1) The term was used both by Skeptics (q.v. Pyrrho 2) and members of the Academy (q.v. Plato's Academy 2–3) as the appropriate response to the problem of knowledge. "Suspense of judgment" was regarded as leading to *ataraxia*, or pleasure in tranquility.

(2) Husserl (q.v. 6) has adopted the term, insisting upon *epoché*, or suspense of judgment, as a stage in the phenomenological reduction.

"E" PROPOSITION.

Q.v. Proposition (1); Syllogism (3, 6b).

EQUALITY.

Most analyses of the human condition do not find humans equal, although the claim in the natural rights (q.v.) doctrine is that all have equal rights. Rousseau (q.v. 1) held equality to be "unnatural." Helvetius (q.v. 4) is almost alone in claiming intellectual equality for all human beings, their differences being due to education and motivation. The Jeffersonian claim of "equal creation" can be translated, apparently, into a claim for equal rights. Emerson (q.v. 4) offers a principle of "compensation" which alleges a kind of human equality since what one lacks in one area is compensated for in another. Dworkin (q.v. 4) interprets equality as the fundamental right to equal concern and respect.

EQUILIBRIUM.

Q.v. Harmony (1).

EQUIPOLLENCE.

From the Latin *aequus* ("equal") and *pollens* ("strength"). In logic a synonym for equivalence (q.v.).

EQUIVALENCE.

From the Latin *aequus* ("equal") and *valere* ("to be strong," "to be worth").

(1) In the Propositional Calculus (q.v. 20) "material equivalence" is represented by the sign "≡" between the propositions. The sign is to be read "if and only if." The import of this bi-conditional sign is that the truth values for the propositions "p" and "q" in "p≡q" must be the same if the combined proposition is to be true. And the combined proposition is true when the constituents "p" and "q" are either both true or both false. The details of material equivalence are worked out in Truth Tables (5).

(2) In Modal Logic (q.v. 3) the sign " ≡ " is used to express "strictly equivalent to." "P≡q" is to be read "p strictly

implies q and q strictly implies p." Strict implication contains a sense of necessary implication. For this reason strict equivalence is a stronger relation than material equivalence.

EQUIVOCATION.
From the Latin *aequus* ("equal") and *vocare* ("to call"). The sense is that of regarding a word used in two senses as carrying the same meaning when, in fact, the meanings differ. One of the fallacies of diction and shifting sense (*q.v.* Fallacies 3), the term has been used historically in contrast to univocity (*q.v.*) and analogy (*q.v.*). Cajetan (*q.v.* 1) provided an analysis of the threefold distinction concerning the use of words.

ERASMUS, DESIDERIUS. 1467–1536.
Renaissance man of letters and humanist. Born in Holland. Studied in Paris, Oxford, Louvain, and Turin. Taught in Cambridge briefly. In 1514 he moved to Basel, to work with Froben and publish his works. His influential Greek New Testament was in print by 1516. After living in England again and Louvain he returned to Basel as general editor of the Froben Publishing interests, where he spent the remainder of his life save for a six-year visit to Freiburg. In all of this time he was meeting the demands of an intellectual and literary celebrity. His life was filled with incessant activity. Honors and gifts came to him in considerable abundance. Where Luther had the ear of the common man, Erasmus held the attention of the educated. Both wished the reform of the Church, but Erasmus wished reform through learning, and drew back from the crude, evangelical fervor which surrounded the rise of Protestantism.

Principal writings: *The Contempt of the World*, 1490; *Chiliades Adagidrum*, 1507; *In Praise of Folly* (T), 1509; *Diatribe on Free Will* (T in part), 1524; *The Epicurean*, 1533. In addition, among many other projects, he published the Greek text of the New Testament, 1516; and between 1516 and 1536 the series of the Fathers, including Jerome, Cyprian, Pseudo-Arnobius, Hilarius, Irenaeus, Ambrose, Augustine, Chrysostom, Basil, and Origen.

(1) A moderate by nature, Erasmus' humanism was conciliatory, a middle way of Church reform in contrast to the radical program of Luther. He termed his point of view a "philosophy of Christ," stressing simple piety, eschewing fine theological distinctions, and basing itself on a New Testament morality.

(2) His defense of the freedom of the will drew a vigorous response from Luther (*q.v.* 9) who opposed the concept. Erasmus' defense involved an espousal of the principles of skepticism. The problem exceeds the possibilities of human reason, and the sensible recourse is to follow the doctrines of the Church; and those doctrines require the freedom of the will.

(3) Erasmus also supported a Christian Epicureanism, translating the pleasure-principle of Epicurus into Christian morality by adding the values of faith and immortality to the this-worldly values of the Epicurean. His interest in this project is reflected in his publications of 1490 and 1533.

ERASTIANISM.
The doctrine of the supremacy of the state in religious as well as civil matters. The doctrine is attributed to Thomas Erastus (1524–1583) who argued that the sins of professing Christians are to be punished by civil authority rather than by the "withholding of sacraments." Attracting a considerable number of adherents in 17th-century England, Thomas Hobbes' *Leviathan*—giving the state full power in religious matters—is considered an instance of the doctrine.

ERASTUS, THOMAS.
Q.v. Erastianism.

ERIGENA, JOHN SCOTUS. 810–877.
Irish churchman and philosopher. Born in Ireland. Educated in an Irish monastery. By 850 he was in France at the court of Charles the Bald, and teaching in the Palatine School. By 855 he had begun his translation of the writings of the Pseudo-Dionysius (*q.v.*) from Greek into Latin, and his production of commentaries on this material. A follower of St. Augustine and of the Pseudo-Dionysius, Erigena elaborated a system of ideas which appears on occasion to be pantheistic, in any case both dialectical and with pronounced mystical overtones.

Principal writings: *On Divine Predestination; On the Divisions of Nature.* In addition, translations and commentaries.

(1) Holding nature to consist of the totality of things which are, and which are not, Erigena divides nature into four parts: (a) nature which creates and is not created, (b) nature which is created and creates, (c) nature which is created and does not create, (d) nature which neither creates nor is created. Since God is both (a) and (d), God is to be thought of as a part of nature; yet this must be in a very special sense since Erigena thinks of God also as above nature. The second division includes the eternal ideas, patterns, and acts of divine will by means of which individual things are formed. The third division is the world of created things. The four divisions thus mark the divine theophany moving from God as Creator to God as the final end and goal of all things.

(2) Man is a microcosm of the universe, sharing with plants the power of growth and nutrition, with animals sensation and emotional understanding, with angels the power of reason, so that one might expect to find a correspondence between man's career and that of other created things. Fallen man is redeemed by the incarnate logos, Christ. This means that all men achieve some kind of glorified union with God and immortality, existing in a spiritualized form, no longer sexually differentiated as indeed they were not before the Fall. In cosmic terms the return seems to occur by a process exactly counter to that of creation. Individual created things, including men, return into the eternal ideas and patterns of the second division described above, and these patterns return to God. The fourth stage, then, includes the first two, but occurring in reverse sequence.

(3) The affirmative and negative ways of approaching the idea of God Erigena borrowed from the Pseudo-Dionysius. By the affirmative way we take some significant property of existence or life and because of its significance attribute this property to God, *i.e.,* "God is wise." But he is also not wise. This seems to be a contradiction, but in fact both assertions are correct. God is wise and not-wise because he is super-wisdom, and so too with other properties. God is super-

substance, super-essence, super-goodness. And although human categories do not apply to God the use of the positive and negative ways does point a direction.

(4) The clearest statement which can be made about God is that God is the essence of all things. This allows Erigena to relate God to all that is, while denying that the categories of substance—quality, quantity, time, space, etc.—apply to him. Use of the positive and negative ways would seem to result in the infinite being, existing in essence and eternal, changeless, etc. Erigena does hold that the world is within God, that it is both eternal and created, and that God and creatures are not distinct, but he is here thinking of the super-essentiality of God, of his extended idea of nature, and of the divine theophany and procession of all things from their eternal position in essence in God through existence and back again into eternity.

ERISTIC.

From the Greek *eris* ("strife"). In Aristotle (*q.v.* 5) a mode of argument having as its goal victory in disputation, and thus to be distinguished both from science and from dialectic. The Megarian School of Philosophy (*q.v.*) is associated with Eristic. *Q.v.* Euclid of Megara.

EROS.

Q.v. Freud (8).

ERROR.

Originally, a Latin term meaning "a wandering about." Since to fall into error means that one has missed the truth (*q.v.*) what is said under the latter entry applies here as well. How one falls into error has been the subject of philosophical discussion.

(1) Socrates (*q.v.* 1), arguing for the related point that one never does evil knowingly, would seem to relate error to ignorance. It is a consequence of the absence of knowledge.

(2) In the *Theaetetus*, Plato associated error with mistaken identification. One reaches into the aviary of memory and, whether due to the absence of light, the movement of the birds, or some other factor, simply draws forth an inappropriate content.

(3) Descartes (*q.v.* 7) explained error

as due not merely to a deficiency of knowledge but to an excess of will. One falls into error when the will has outrun, or run ahead of, one's reason.

(4) Granting that we are in error on many things, Royce (*q.v.* 1b) made this fact the premise of an argument for God. Since error implies truth or knowledge, and knowledge implies a knower (able to correct our errors), the fact of error implies the existence of God.

ESCHATOLOGY.

From the Greek *eschatos* ("last things") and *logos* ("knowledge of"). The late Jewish and early Christian doctrine of last or final things such as death, resurrection, immortality, the end of the age, judgment, the future state and, for Christianity, the second coming of Christ. The apparently contradictory beliefs in resurrection and immortality are present both in Jewish and in Christian eschatology.

ESEMPLASTIC.

Q.v. Coleridge (3).

ESOTERISM.

From the Greek *esoteros* ("inner," "interior"). The doctrine that ancient wisdom contains an esoteric part, separate from public writings or lectures available to all (the exoteric part). Applied to Oriental thought, the Pythagoreans and Plato, the Stoics and many other schools, the thesis can be extended to include Aristotle. But where the former may distinguish between a secret and an open teaching, Aristotle distinguishes between the technical and the popular, leading in a somewhat different direction.

L'ESPRIT DE FINESSE.

Q.v. Pascal (3).

L'ESPRIT GÉOMETRIQUE.

Q.v. Pascal (3).

ESSE EST PERCIPI.

Latin phrase meaning "To be is to be perceived." A slogan of Berkeley (*q.v.* 3–4), the statement has had importance for other philosophers as well. For example, *q.v.* G.E. Moore (3).

ESSENCE.

From the Latin *essentia* (from *esse*, "to be"). The corresponding term in Greek is *ousia*. The essence is that by which a thing is what it is, as distinguished from its existence, and accidents. Essence refers to the more permanent and fixed aspects of a thing in contrast to the variable, partial, or phenomenal. In logic the essence has traditionally referred to the properties every member of a species or class must have to belong to that species or class. The contrasting term is existence (*q.v.*).

(1) Plato (*q.v.* 1) finds the essence of a thing in its eternal idea.

(2) Aristotle (*q.v.* 7, 9) identifies it with the form (*eidos*) as cause, thus offering a connection with Plato's ideas.

(3) Avicenna (*q.v.* 8) distinguishes between God in whom essence and existence are identical; and all other beings in whom or in which the two are distinct. This distinction began in Al-Farabi (*q.v.* 1–2), was developed by Avicenna, is present in St. Bonaventure (*q.v.* 9, 11), and attained its classical form in Aquinas.

(4) Aquinas (*q.v.* 6) advanced a double composition theory of essence and existence.

(5) Godfrey of Fontaines (*q.v.*) refused to admit the essence-existence distinction.

(6) If as with Locke (*q.v.* 7) one's awareness is almost entirely of nominal essences, then, one will have only or mostly nominal definitions (*q.v.* Locke 7).

(7) Husserl (*q.v.* 1, 2, 6) developed a philosophy concerned almost entirely with the exploration of essences.

(8) Santayana (*q.v.* 6) employed the term in such a way that experience is saturated with essences. Essences always have subsistence and sometimes existence as well.

ESSENES.

Jewish monastic order dating from at least the 2nd century B.C. exemplifying great purity of spirit; quite possibly the first society in the world to condemn slavery both in principle and practice. The order was communal, esoteric, and severely ascetic; they lived away from settled places, favoring arid regions such as the region of the Dead Sea.

ESSENTIAL PROPERTY.

Q.v. Plantinga (4).

ETCKW.

Q.v. Hartshorne (3).

ETERNAL OBJECT.
Q.v. Whitehead (10).

ETERNAL RECURRENCE.
A doctrine, holding that time is cyclical, to be found in both East and West: in Hinduism (*q.v.*, for example, Śankara 4 and Ramanuja 4); in Greek philosophy (*q.v.* for example, the Great Year as viewed by Heraclitus, 8); in some medieval thinkers (for example, Erigena, *q.v.* 1–2); and in modern philosophy (for example, Nietzsche, *q.v.* 8–9, who deduced exact recurrence from the concept of a finite universe which is everlasting).

ETERNITY.
From the Latin *aeternus* (from *aeviternus*, in turn from *aevum*, "age"). The problem of time (*q.v.*) and eternity turns, at least in part, on the ideas of permanence and change. Time is the order of change and eternity is the order of changelessness. Heraclitus (*q.v.* 1) exemplifies the first of these and Parmenides (*q.v.* 4) the second.

(1) In Plato (*q.v.* 9) the two orders are related, and time becomes the moving image of eternity, while eternity is the realm of the patterns exemplified in time.

(2) In Neoplatonism (*q.v.* Plotinus 2) and St. Augustine (*q.v.* 10) eternity is the "infinite life" characterized by permanence and indivisible unity.

(3) Finally, Boethius (*q.v.* 1) added to the developing concept the "*totum simul*" so that the Infinite Awareness was understood to comprehend in Himself all at once the details spread out in time for our finite awarenesses.

(4) Thomas Aquinas (*q.v.* 4) accepted this complex conception and defended it in his philosophy.

(5) Faustus Socinus (*q.v.* 3) held that the *totum simul*, obliterating time, should be replaced by the concept of everlasting endurance.

(6) John Locke (*q.v.* 5c) attempted to explicate the concept by means of the psychological feeling of endlessness in ordered series, but that would seem to yield at most the concept of everlastingness.

(7) Royce (*q.v.* 5) held that the temporal implies the eternal.

(8) For a concept of eternity as concentrated in the immediate moment *q.v.* Suzuki (5) and Abe, who so interpret Zen Buddhism (*q.v.*). Also *q.v.* Emptiness.

ETHICAL CULTURE.
A movement stressing ethics as the center of religion. Introduced in New York City by Felix Adler (1851–1933), the organization now counts societies in a number of the larger cities in America and abroad. The Sunday services of the societies consist of music, readings, an ethical address, and perhaps a period of meditation.

ETHICAL IDEALISM.
Q.v. Messer (3).

ETHICAL INTUITIONISM.
The view that ethical terms are primary and underived, *i.e.*, different in nature from all non-ethical terms and thereby not wholly definable. For G.E. Moore (*q.v.* 6) "good" is a simple property, like yellow, subject only to ostensive definition. Prichard (*q.v.*) makes the same kind of argument with respect to "duty," and A.C. Ewing (*q.v.* Ethics 31) for the referent of "ought." *Q.v.* Ethics (4).

ETHICAL NATURALISM.
The view that ethics is a part of the natural world, and that ethical issues can be settled by an appeal to facts. Dewey (*q.v.* 5) is the best-known adherent of the doctrine. G.E. Moore in his "Naturalistic fallacy" has registered the most famous objection to the doctrine (*q.v.* Moore, 6, and Naturalistic Fallacy). Moore's objection was raised against the pleasure principle of the Utilitarians; hence, Utilitarians may likewise be classed as ethical naturalists (*q.v.* Ethics 4).

ETHICAL OBJECTIVISM.
Q.v. Ethics (4).

ETHICAL RELATIVISM.
Q.v. Ethics (5, 29); Westermarck; H.R. Niebuhr.

ETHICAL SUBJECTIVISM.
Q.v. Ethics (4–5).

ETHICS.
From the Greek *ethikos* (from *ethos* meaning "custom" or "usage"). As employed by Aristotle, the term included both the idea of "character" and that of "disposition." *Moralis* was introduced into the vocabulary of philosophy by Cicero who regarded it as the Latin equivalent

of Aristotle's *ethikos*. Both terms imply a connection with practical activity.

A. It is widely understood that ethical behavior concerns acting in terms of the good and the right. Ethical analysis has tended to center on these terms.

(1) Philosophers in their analyses of this behavior may be classified as doing Normative Ethics, *i.e.*, building systems designed to provide guidance in making decisions concerning good and evil, right and wrong, or Meta-ethics, analyzing the logic of usage with respect to "good" and "evil," "right" and "wrong." Traditionally, ethical philosophers have combined these two functions in their systems of ethics. More recently, a considerable number of philosophers have regarded their task as that of doing Meta-ethics alone. When we consider the kinds of ethical systems philosophers have constructed, we are in the area of Meta-ethics, although each of these systems, taken as a guide to conduct, is an instance of Normative Ethics.

(2) When the good is taken to be the key to ethical behavior, the ethical theory resulting is characterized by value fulfillment, and the right becomes one aspect of that fulfillment, namely the set of obligations to others which must be respected in reaching the good. Such theories of ethics are termed Axiological (stressing their value aspect) or Teleological (stressing their orientation to final goals). Utilitarianism (*q.v.*, and 21, 22, 37 below) is the basic form taken by teleological approaches. In Utilitarianism (*q.v.*) note the distinction between act and rule versions of this approach.

(3) When the right is taken to be the key to ethical behavior then ethics becomes oriented to ideas of obligation and duty, centering around the statement of principles of behavior, rather than, as in the former case, in the tracing of consequences. Such theories are termed Deontological (stressing obligation), or Formalistic (stressing principle).

(4) But both the good and the right can be viewed as either objective, standing for a real factor in things, or subjective, simply standing for a human proposal: thus, Ethical Objectivism or Ethical Subjectivism. Those ethical theories which regard the good and/or right as objective must be. divided once again; the

natural principle of division turns on the epistemological question of how the good and right are known. Those who claim that the good and right can be known as natural objects are known, and that empirical verification is possible in ethics, are called Ethical Naturalists. Those who claim that the good and/or right can be known only by a special intuition are called Ethical Intuitionists.

(5) Those whose theories hold that ethical terms do not stand for anything objective, may be called Non-Cognitivists, since for this group ethical terms and judgments stand for emotions, attitudes, proposals, recommendations, etc. The Non-Cognitivists can be further subdivided. Those who ground ethical terms in emotions expressing attitudes of approval or disapproval have been called Emotivists. The form of Non-Cognitivism in which the attitudes of the group determine the meaning and the force of value terms may be called Cultural Relativism, or Ethical Relativism.

B. These distinctions are not, of course, to be taken as exhaustive nor as finally authoritative, but they do suggest the complexity of the studies which have been made. We shall briefly mention the major historical figures in ethical theory, relating them to these distinctions where it is appropriate to do so, while adding other distinctions where that is appropriate.

(6) Democritus (*q.v.* 11) held pleasure to be our valuational goal, and an evaluation of pleasure and pain the way to determine good and right. Hedonist, naturalist, teleologist.

(7) Socrates (*q.v.* 3–4) holding it is always better to suffer than to do evil, offers a view looking not to consequences but to inner principle. At the same time pleasure is one of its components. Formalist, naturalist, or intuitionist.

(8) Plato (*q.v.* 1) makes the good an eternal form to be realized in human life. Teleologist, intuitionist.

(9) For Aristotle (*q.v.* 11), the goal of life is happiness or well-being (*eudaimonia*), and virtue is found by finding the Golden Mean. Teleologist, naturalist.

(10) For Epicurus (*q.v.* 10), as for Democritus, pleasure is the key to the good and right. Hedonist, naturalist, teleologist.

(11) For the Stoics (Marcus Aurelius *q.v.* 1–2, Epictetus *q.v.* 1–2) ethical behavior

lies in rationality, relating one's will to the universal reason. Formalist, naturalist, or intuitionist.

(12) St. Augustine (*q.v.* 1, 5, 6, 8, 12) puts the happiness principle in a universal context, joined to God's perfection. Teleologist, intuitionist.

(13) St. Thomas Aquinas (*q.v.* 8) follows St. Augustine and Aristotle while introducing a natural law motif. Teleologist, naturalist.

(14) William of Ockham (*q.v.* 15) rested all of ethics upon the will of God. It is the divine command or prohibition that constitutes the rightness or wrongness of an action. Teleologist, cosmic emotivism.

(15) Shaftesbury (*q.v.* 1) and Hutcheson (*q.v.* 1–2) proposed a Moral Sense theory of ethics. The innate moral sense is a feeling or sentiment resting on man's natural sympathy and leading to the goal of social harmony. Formalist or emotivist, intuitionist.

(16) Samuel Clarke (*q.v.* 3) rested his ethical theory on a concept of fitness, leading to an expectation of "mutual consistency" among ethical actions.

(17) Bishop Butler (*q.v.* 1) held that man's conscience, when not subverted or deranged, naturally makes the appropriate ethical decisions. Formalist, intuitionist.

(18) David Hume (*q.v.* 6) was influenced by the Moral Sense theory of Hutcheson. He combined the element of sympathy in men with the ideas of hedonism, and utility, thus bridging between the Moral Sense theorist and Utilitarians (*q.v.* 21, 22, below). Teleologist, emotivist.

(19) Adam Smith (*q.v.* 1) continued the emphasis on sympathy as the basis of ethics.

(20) Kant (*q.v.* 6) constructs his theory on the ground of principle emerging from the idea of law, and leading to the categorical and practical imperatives. Formalist.

(21) Bentham, founder of Utilitarianism, (*q.v.* 1–4) taking the greatest good for the greatest number as the goal to be achieved, and hedonism as the way of understanding the good, asks us to calculate the balance of pleasure and pain in determining ethical questions. Teleologist, naturalist.

(22) John Stuart Mill (*q.v.* 7) defended Utilitarianism, while modifying the doctrine so that one calculates for the greatest sum of higher pleasures. Teleologist, naturalist.

(23) Herbert Spencer (*q.v.* 3) developed a view of evolutionary Utilitarianism.

(24) T.H. Green (*q.v.*) holds the developed self to be the end which defines the good, and all ethical terms to be formed in relation to that end. Teleologist and, in a sense, formalist.

(25) Sidgwick (*q.v.* 4) combined hedonistic Utilitarianism with certain moral intuitions from which ethical principles, *e.g.*, the principle of benevolence, were derived. Teleologist, intuitionist, formalist.

(26) Nietzsche (*q.v.* 2–6) held life's appropriate goal to be the will to power translated into an excellence beyond the ordinary dimensions of good and evil. Teleologist, intuitionist.

(27) Dewey (*q.v.* 5) was a naturalist in ethical theory, believing that questions of right and wrong could be settled by inquiry.

(28) Sorel (*q.v.* 3) breaks the traditional ethical categories, contrasting the ethics of producers with ethics of consumers.

(29) Westermarck (*q.v.*) presented a view of Ethical Relativism, considering an ethical system as a reflection of social conditions.

(30) Santayana (*q.v.* 8) finds rational ethics deriving from pre-rational morality and yielding to post-rational morality.

(31) G.E. Moore (*q.v.* 6) held the good to be a simple property, not definable in non-ethical terms. The view is called Ethical Intuitionism. Prichard (*q.v.*) related Ethical Intuitionism to the idea of duty. A.C. Ewing, who shares membership in the group, finds "ought" to be the primary unanalyzable term. Intuitionist.

(32) W.D. Ross (*q.v.*), an intuitionist, distinguished the right from the good, and elaborated the concept of *prima facie* duties.

(33) A.J. Ayer (*q.v.* 5) holds the basis of ethical judgments to be emotive rather than factual. Emotivist.

(34) Stevenson (*q.v.* 1–2) holds that ethical judgments are mixtures of descriptive and emotive meaning, but the most basic feature of the judgment is its expression of emotion. Ethical disagreements are, therefore, basically disagreements over attitudes, not disagreements about facts. Emotivist.

(35) Blanshard (*q.v.*) combined in his ethical system satisfaction and self-fulfillment. Teleologist, naturalist, or formalist.

(36) Levinas (*q.v.* 1–2) founded his ethical transcendentalism on a relation to the other which he held to be beyond being.

(37) Brandt (*q.v.*), in order to avoid the paradoxes of act Utilitarianism, suggested the option of ideal rule Utilitarianism.

(38) Sartre (*q.v.* 4) identifies the ethical with authentic choice.

(39) R.M. Hare (*q.v.*), while finding evaluative meanings primary in ethical discourse, felt that study of the logical behavior of value words and value expressions is the key to progress in ethical theory. Emotivist, meta-ethicist.

(40) Nowell-Smith (*q.v.*) likewise encouraged a meta-ethical approach while adopting a modified teleological theory of ethics. Teleologist, meta-ethicist.

(41) Stephen Toulmin (*q.v.* 1) may be taken as representative of the Good Reason approach to ethics, stressing the question of justification. His own position is that we are to follow those rules which produce the least amount of avoidable suffering. Teleologist, meta-ethicist.

(42) For a view critical of Utilitarianism and supportive of Kantian formalism, *q.v.* John Rawls (1–4).

(43) Putnam's (*q.v.* 7) philosophy of science extends to the objectivity of ethical principles.

(44) Habermas (*q.v.*) experiments with a "minimal ethics" resting on the principle of communication.

Q.v. Foucault (7).

ETHICS OF BELIEF.

Q.v. Belief (1); Clifford (1).

ETIOLOGY.

From the Greek *aitia* ("cause") and *logos* ("theory of"). Thus, the study of causality, usually as restricted to a given class of phenomena: *e.g.*, "the etiology of pathology," "the etiology of history."

EUBULIDES.

Megarian philosopher. Initiated the Liar's Paradox. *Q.v.* Paradox (2); Megarian School of Philosophy.

EUCHARIST.

From the Greek *eucharistia* ("thanksgiving"). Another name for the sacrament of the Lord's Supper. Gradually the meaning of the rite developed, or altered, from commemoration of Christ's passion to its reenactment, leading by the 13th century to the doctrine of transubstantiation (*q.v.*). Among Protestants the Eucharist was interpreted in several ways, from consubstantiation (*q.v.*) to a return to regarding it as an act of commemoration.

EUCKEN, RUDOLF. 1846–1926.

German philosopher. Born in Aurich. Educated at Göttingen. Taught at Basel and Jena. He was awarded the Nobel Prize for literature in 1908. All philosophy is "philosophy of life," applying religious inspiration to social problems. He called his doctrine "actionism," and criticized both naturalism and socialism for their failure to recognize man's spiritual autonomy. His position is sometimes viewed as a philosophical expression of Pietism (*q.v.*).

Principal writings: *The Unity of the Spiritual Life*, 1888; *The Meaning and Value of Life* (T), 1909; *Knowledge and Life* (T), 1913; *Man and World* (T), 1918; *Socialism* (T), 1920; *Prolegomena and Epilogue to a Philosophy of the Spiritual Life*, 1922.

EUCLID OF ALEXANDRIA. 3rd cent. B.C.

Greek mathematician. The founder of Euclidean geometry, and probable founder of the Alexandrian School of geometry, he lived and worked in Alexandria. Possibly, too, Alexandria was the place of his birth, although this is not known to be the case.

Principal writings: *The Elements* (T), 13 books; numerous other mathematical and philosophical works, most of them not extant, are attributed to Euclid by ancient writers.

(1) Euclidean method consists of the proving of theorems on the basis of an initial set of definitions, axioms, and postulates. The axioms are "common notions," and are often broader than geometry; they are, apparently, regarded by him as true, and not subject to doubt. Euclid's postulates, on the other hand, are all geometrical in content, are neither demonstrable nor self-evident, but are necessary for the subsequent demonstration.

(2) For over 2,000 years Euclid's work

in geometry retained unlimited validity. Euclid was known as the "Elementator," named from *The Elements*, and portions of that work are still used in the study of geometry. Even with the development of non-Euclidean systems of geometry, Euclid's work retains great mathematical importance.

EUCLID OF MEGARA. 450–374 B.C.

Greek philosopher. A native of Megara, and founder of the Megarian School. A disciple of Socrates, Euclid combined a devotion to his master with the Eleatic philosophy. The result was a view identifying being and goodness. He defended his version of the philosophy of being with Zeno's method of *reductio ad absurdum*, thus providing a line leading to the Eristic (*q.v.*) philosophy.

EUDAEMONISM.

From the Greek *eudaimonia* ("happiness"). The term refers literally to the condition of being blessed by the protection of a benign spirit. Applied to all ethical theories taking happiness as man's chief end, the term is attributed primarily, and most commonly, to the ethics formulated by Aristotle (*q.v.* 11).

(1) *Eudaemonia* refers in Aristotle to a special kind of self-realization involving activity and the exercise of one's reason, accompanied by pleasure.

(2) The ethic of Augustine (*q.v.* 12) is likewise eudaemonistic although qualified by the simultaneous presence in man of original sin.

(3) Aquinas (*q.v.* 8) continued the Aristotelian tradition while identifying the end of life with divine beatitude.

(4) In its Latin and English translations the term has lost the special character given it by Aristotle, dropping the stress on the exercise of reason.

(5) In the modern world Schlick (*q.v.* 4) argued for a eudaemonistic basis for ethics.

EUDEMUS. 4th cent. B.C.

Greek philosopher. Born in Rhodes. A disciple of Aristotle. On the death of Aristotle, Theophrastus (*q.v.*) became head of the Lyceum (*q.v.*); but Aristotle is said to have held these two most significant of his followers in equal esteem. The famous writing listed below, once attributed to Aristotle, is regarded as his work.

Principal writings: *The Eudemian Ethics*; and fragments.

EUDORUS OF ALEXANDRIA. 1st cent. B.C.

Greek philosopher. A member of the Fourth Academy (*q.v.* Plato's Academy 4), Eudorus combined Platonism with Pythagorean and Stoic influences. He divided philosophy into logic, ethics, and physics; and seems to have identified the soul with God, and God with the One in a manner anticipating Neoplatonism (*q.v.*).

Principal writings: *On the End*; *On the Categories*; a *Commentary* on Plato's *Timaeus*.

EUDOXUS OF CNIDOS. 408–355 B.C.

Greek philosopher. A Pythagorean and Platonist, Eudoxus seems to have held, against Plato, that the Ideas are immanent in things, and that the Good is pleasure. He elaborated a theory of astronomy involving the motion of concentric spheres; also, he was known as a mathematician and physician.

EUHEMERISM.

The view that the gods originated from popular heroes. *Q.v.* Euhemerus.

EUHEMERUS. 3rd cent. B.C.

Greek philosopher. Born in Sicily. Close to the Cyrenaic outlook generally, he is best known for his thesis that the popular gods had their origin in popular heroes who gradually became the object of common veneration. The doctrine spread widely. Christians appealed to it to support their view that the Greek and Roman gods were human inventions. Known as "Euhemerism," the view had many adherents even in the 18th century. *Q.v.* Cyrenaicism (2).

Principal writings: *Sacred History*.

EULER DIAGRAMS.

Q.v. Leonhard Euler (2); Syllogism (1–2, 6).

EULER, LEONHARD. 1707–1783.

Swiss mathematician. Born in Basel. Educated at the University of Basel. A student of Bernoulli. He taught at St. Petersburg and Berlin. From 1766 until the end of his life he was active in the Academy of St. Petersburg.

Principal writings: *Introduction to the*

Analysis of Infinity (L), 2 vols., 1748; *Principles of the Differential Calculus* (L), 1755; *Letters to a German Princess on Some Subjects of Physics and Philosophy*, 3 vols. (F), 1768–72.

(1) Although he wrote on many subjects within and beyond mathematics, his interest for us lies in his representation of class relations by spatial relations called Euler Diagrams. The notions of class, class complement, class inclusion and exclusion, sum, product, and equality can be represented by overlapping regions, *e.g.*, circles or ellipses in space.

(2) The spatial representations of class relations appeared in the second of the three volumes of letters dedicated to the German princess. A, E, I, and O propositions were represented in the following manner:

All A is B:
No A is B:
Some A is B:
Some A is not B:
Also *q.v.* Syllogism (1–2, 6).

EULOGON.

The doctrine of Arcesilas (*q.v.*) that probability is the guide to life. The doctrine was held in a somewhat different sense by Arcesilas' successor, Philo of Larissa (*q.v.*).

EUSEBIUS OF CAESERIA. 265–340.

Christian thinker and historian. Born in Caeseria, Palestine. Studied under Pamphilus. Bishop of Caeseria in 314 he was regarded as the most learned man of his age. At the Council of Nicaea in 325 he was seated at the Emperor's right hand and gave the oration in his honor. He submitted the first draft of the Nicene Creed. Initially he tended toward the Arian view due to the influence of Origen's writings on his thought; later he decided the Nicene position best preserved the divinity and subordination of the Son. He regarded Plato as a Greek Moses whose thought contained much Christian truth, although mixed with error. His great contribution, however, was his history of the Christian Church, which gained him recognition as the father of church history. *Q.v.* Apologists (11).

Principal writings: *Ecclesiastical History*; *Against Hierocles*; *Preparation for the Evangel*; *Demonstration of the Evangel*; *Theophany*.

EUTHANASIA.

Q.v. Dworkin (4).

EUTYCHIANISM.

The Christological doctrine that at the incarnation Christ's human nature was absorbed into the divine nature. The doctrine was introduced by Eutychus, head of a monastery outside Constantinople, between 448 and 451 A.D. Since Eutychianism denied that Christ had two distinct natures, and implied that God Himself was tempted, suffered, and died, the doctrine was condemned and Eutychus was excommunicated. *Q.v.* Christology (3).

EUTYCHUS.

Q.v. Eutychianism.

EVANGELICAL AND REFORMED CHURCH.

Q.v. Congregationalism.

EVENT.

From the Latin *evenire* ("to happen"). In traditional ontologies, events are the adventures of substances. In event ontologies, things derive from events (*q.v.* Whitehead 7, 9).

EVENT, CREATIVE.

Q.v. H.N. Wieman.

EVENT-PARTICLE.

For Whitehead (*q.v.* 7) the finite abstractive element gained by "extensive abstraction" in terms of which all geometrical elements are defined.

EVIDENCE.

That which proves or contributes to the proof of a conclusion. The problem of evidence involves the question of the criterion (*q.v.*) for truth.

(1) Some propositions (*e.g.*, that the whole is equal to the sum of its parts) have been regarded as self-evident. The Stoics have called such propositions "common notions" (*q.v.*). The claim of self-evidence must be qualified by the awareness that the certainty claimed may be only psychological (*q.v.* Certainty 2).

(2) William of Ockham (*q.v.* 11) distinguished between two kinds of evidence for general propositions, that *per se nota*, evident by the meaning of the terms; and that *nota per experientiam*, evident by experience. This is identical to the distinc-

tion between analytic and synthetic judgments (*q.v.*). Also *q.v.* Truth (15–18).

EVIL.

From Anglo-Saxon *yfel*. The opposite
and complement of good, the term is
almost always defined negatively. Evil
has been treated from both religious and
philosophical points of view.

(1) According to Zoroastrianism (*q.v.*)
and Manichaeism (*q.v.*) evil is a force in
the universe at war with the good.

(2) On the other hand, from the standpoint of Buddhism (*q.v.*), evil roots in
desire and its control lies in the elimination of desire.

(3) Among philosophers, Socrates (*q.v.*
4) associated evil with ignorance, claiming that it is impossible for a man to
know the good and fail to do it.

(4) Chrysippus (*q.v.* 4), the Stoic, regarded
evil as that which is contrary to the world
reason. It thus turned out to be something like the ultimate irrationality.

(5) In Plotinus (*q.v.* 5) evil is regarded
as a necessary concomitant of the material principle. The good-evil contrast thus
becomes but one aspect of the mind-body
or spirit-matter dualism.

(6) Porphyry (*q.v.* 2), on the other hand,
interpreted evil as a lack of control by
the intelligible principle, a control which
can be gained by purification.

(7) St. Augustine (*q.v.* 8) presented a
double interpretation of evil. It is non-
being, a privation, and nothing positive.
It is also a context viewed from a limited
perspective.

(8) Avicenna (*q.v.* 9) held that evil
touches only the individual and not the
species. He followed St. Augustine in
believing that there is always a larger
perspective from which the evil will be
seen as good.

(9) Chang Tsai (*q.v.* 4) regarded evil as
resulting from the fact that man has the
choice of departing from the mean, *i.e.*, of
going to excess through human freedom.

(10) The problem of God's responsibility for evil has been much discussed.
The problem was especially acute for
Ramanuja (*q.v.* 6) who, in pantheistic
fashion, regarded the world as forming
part of God. Ramanuja solved the problem by limiting evil to God's body.

(11) William of Ockham (*q.v.* 15) defined evil in terms of failed obligation.

It is the doing of one thing while under
obligation to do another.

(12) Among evils Leibniz (*q.v.* 9) distinguished metaphysical, physical, and
moral types. The first type relates to the
incompossibilities of things, the second
to natural misfortunes, and the third to
situations of choice.

(13) Schelling (*q.v.* 7) argued that evil
is a first principle of the universe and
in no sense derivative.

(14) Rashdall (*q.v.* 3) was one of a siz-
able group who solved the problem of
God's responsibility for evil by limiting
God's power.

(15) Berdyaev (*q.v.* 4) regarded evil as
resulting from a degenerate freedom.

(16) Brightman (*q.v.* 3) likewise responded to the issue of the divine responsibility for evil by a concept of the finitude
of God, and of the evil as a "given" which
defines His redemptive task.

EVOLUTION.

From the Latin *e* ("out") and *volvere* ("to
roll"). The idea of evolution is, in a general sense, a subdivision of the problem
of the one and the many, or the problem of permanence and change. If the
concept of evolutionary development is
taken with sufficient generality it can be
shown to have characterized philosophical thought from the beginning, and almost continuously.

(1) Indian philosophy, for example,
from a very early time conceived of a
relation between Brahman and cosmic
development. And in the Sankhya system (*q.v.*) the process is described in
quasi-materialistic terms.

(2) Among the pre-Socratic philosophers the framework of thought is almost
always implicitly evolutionistic, and often explicitly so. One thinks especially
of Anaximander (*q.v.* 1 ,9) positing an
order of progression among living things,
Heraclitus (*q.v.* 2, 5, 8) with his upward
and downward ways evolving through
the great world year, Empedocles (*q.v.*
4) with his stages of development and
his principle of adaptation, Democritus
(*q.v.* 6–7) with a mechanical atomic process underlying the increasing complexity
of development.

(3) The system of Plato would seem
to be antithetical to the idea of evolution, yet Plato sometimes refers to great

cycles of time involving the death and rebirth, at least of cultures; but he apparently viewed the process as devolving, not evolving, in its current stage.

(4) Aristotle (*q.v.* 8–9), although believing in the fixity of species, contributed the idea of potentiality (*q.v.*) to philosophy; and it is by means of potentiality that the idea of development is formulated. Aristotle's belief in the fixity of species limits the application of the idea of development to the individual within the species. Within these limits the analysis is subtle and satisfying.

(5) The Stoic world-view (*q.v.* Stoicism 1) is also cyclical, worlds originating and ending in the element of fire which is also universal reason.

(6) The Epicureans followed Democritus, adding to his scheme only a power to swerve on the part of individual atoms (*q.v.* Epicurus 5; Lucretius 3).

(7) For Neoplatonists evolution is, strictly speaking, devolution since the path of becoming is downward from the divine perfection (*q.v.* Plotinus).

(8) Bruno (*q.v.* 1, 4) on the basis of modern science and Greek learning offered a view of multiverses all in processes of becoming under the provenance of God.

(9) The French *Philosophes* (*q.v.*), generally wishing to derive the world from naturalistic principles, elaborated evolutionary doctrines implicitly or explicitly, employing the scale of increasing complexity as an explanatory device. Holbach's work also included man and his development in the scheme. And again, generally, the *Philosophes* held progress to be the goal of historical development.

(10) Leibniz (*q.v.*) presented a system of thought with great dynamism in the monadic constituents of all things, yet the development of the whole proceeded not by its own dynamism, but by God's choice of a world pattern. He presents a scale of existence which is vertical rather than horizontal, analytical rather than temporal.

(11) Vico (*q.v.*) concentrated on the development of man in society, holding it to be both progressive and cyclical, proceeding from poetical wisdom to the forms it assumes in developed societies.

(12) Herder (*q.v.* 4) applied the genetic method to culture, viewing lower stages as conditions of higher, and earlier as conditions of later stages. He suggested that survival depends upon adaptation.

(13) Hegel (*q.v.* 2–3) also considered existence to be identical with process, although he found the means of self-evolvement in an immanent dialectic.

(14) Schelling (*q.v.* 2, 4) interpreted existence as a process moving through a succession of stages; its principle of development being vitalistic, not mechanical, a process of organic self-evolution.

(15) Comte (*q.v.* 1–3), like Herder, concentrated on cultural evolution; Comte advanced his law of the three stages, holding that cultural evolution has its end in scientific inquiry.

(16) But the decisive work on the problem had to be accomplished on the biological level. It was done by Charles Darwin (*q.v.*) and A.R. Wallace (*q.v.*) who with their theory of natural selection and survival of the fittest, established the view of the mutability of all species of living things. Chauncey Wright (*q.v.*) contributed to the theory from the American side.

(17) Spencer (*q.v.* 1–2) viewed evolution as a law of nature, a movement from "incoherent homogeneity to coherent heterogeneity." Spencer and Stephen (*q.v.*) applied the concept to ethics.

(18) T.H. Huxley (*q.v.*) was an immediate proponent of the view of evolution held by Darwin.

(19) Charles Peirce (*q.v.* 4–5) applied the principles of evolution still more broadly, holding that the laws of the universe, themselves, are in process of development through vast periods of time.

(20) W.G. Sumner (*q.v.* 4) laid the basis for Social Darwinism by applying the doctrine of the survival of the fit to economic matters.

(21) Haeckel (*q.v.*) applied Darwinian evolution to metaphysics, building a monistic and pantheistic naturalism.

(22) Kropotkin (*q.v.* 1) held mutual aid to be as significant a factor as Darwin's competition in the explanation of survival.

(23) John Fiske (*q.v.*) followed Spencer, developing an evolutionary theism.

(24) S. Alexander (*q.v.* 2–5) can be given as an example of an emergentist. For Alexander, beginning with space-time, every other quality and thing can be ex-

plained as due to evolutionary process (*q.v.* Emergent Evolution).

(25) Bergson (*q.v.* 5–6), extrapolating from biology, associates evolutionary change with the nature of time, and finds in nature an *élan vital*, empowering evolution and pushing the world into novelty.

(26) American pragmatists have always oriented themselves very closely to the Darwinian revolution. Dewey (*q.v.*), for example, takes this as the most decisive watershed of intellectual thought.

(27) A.N. Whitehead (*q.v.*) may be suggested as an example of a recent philosopher whose metaphysics has assimilated the Darwinian view, presenting biological change in a context also compatible with the insights of modern physics.

(28) Boodin (*q.v.* 3) held to a concept of emergent evolution in which irreducible qualities emerged at different levels.

(29) Smuts (*q.v.* 2) held that evolution occurred through a series of "creative leaps from the physical to the mental."

(30) Teilhard de Chardin (*q.v.*) proposed a theory of evolution proceeding from the inorganic through the organic into the sphere of mental evolution, which he called the "noosphere."

(31) R.W. Sellars (*q.v.* 3) held a doctrine of evolutionary naturalism.

EWING, A.C.
Q.v. Ethics (31).

EX CATHEDRA.
A Latin term meaning "from the chair." Any statement of the pope defining a doctrine of faith or morals issuing from his office as pastor and teacher of all Christians. Any such statement is regarded as infallible due to the pope's "supreme apostolic authority."

EXCLUDED MIDDLE, PRINCIPLE OF.
One of the three laws of thought. The principle holds that, as Aristotle said, there is nothing between the two parts of a contradiction. Either the proposition p is true, or the contradictory of p is true. *Q.v.* Aristotle (5); Laws of Thought (1–3); Tautology (2).

EXEMPLARISM.
From the Latin *exemplum* ("model" or "example"). The term refers to the Platonic-inspired doctrine that finite things are copies of divine ideas. The phrase,

"exemplary cause," similarly, refers to the causal role of exemplars.

EXISTENCE.
From the Latin *ex* and *sistere* ("to step forth, emerge"). Philosophical analyses of the concept of existence are in some respects similar to analyses of the concept of matter. As "matter" stands in contrast to "form," so "existence" stands in contrast to "essence." And since mental activity is concerned with the characteristics of things the latter terms, "form" and "essence," seem less puzzling than "matter" and "existence." If "existence" cannot be characterized, how is one to discuss it; and if it can be characterized how does it stand in contrast to "essence"? The puzzle is not far removed from the following analyses.

(1) For Plato (*q.v.* 1) form or essence, taken by itself, has more reality than when participated in a material way. Assimilating existence to essence, matter became associated with non-being.

(2) Aristotle (*q.v.* 7) used a dual distinction. He associated existence with formed matter, *i.e.*, substance, while associating essence with form and with the constituents of a true definition.

(3) Thomas Aquinas (*q.v.* 5, 6) held to a double composition of essence and existence. In the first composition formed matter is identified with the essence of a thing; in the second composition existence—as an added gift—translates the essence into actuality.

(4) Duns Scotus (*q.v.* 5), utilizing the notion of *haecceitas* as his principle of individuation, moved in the direction of essentializing existence, since a thing has existence by virtue of its *haecceity*.

(5) Kant (*q.v.* 5) moved in the other direction, holding that existence is not a predicate, since the addition of existence to the idea of a hundred dollars does not add one cent to the concept in one's mind.

(6) Hegel (*q.v.* 5, 6) is regarded as the most completely essentialistic of all philosophers. At least it is widely thought that in equating the rational and the real, he has somehow reduced existence to essence.

(7) Kierkegaard (*q.v.* 1, 7) opposed Hegel's essentialism. Indeed, he is regarded as the first existentialist. As we had suggested initially, if existence is re-

garded as completely separated from essence, it becomes incomprehensible and in some sense irrational. This is the move of Kierkegaard. Even the possibility of an ontology of existence is withdrawn; individual things are recognized but not existence; and existential decision replaces speculation.

(8) Brentano (*q.v.* 3) extended Kant's analysis, holding existence to be not a predicate but a *synsemantic* term.

(9) Husserl (*q.v.* 6) may be regarded as an essentialist who did not identify the rational with the real. Instead, he "bracketed" all questions of existence, to facilitate the discovery of essences in phenomena.

(10) Russell (*q.v.* 4) speaks of existence in relation to arguments which satisfy a function; his analysis of definite descriptions was developed in order that we not make unintentional attributions of existence.

(11) Heidegger (*q.v.* 1, 4, 5 *passim*) concentrated upon human existence whose general name is *Dasein*, and whose authentic form is *Ek-sistenz*, pointing toward truth. In Jaspers (*q.v.* 2) the terms *Dasein* and *Existenz* bear the same meanings as Heidegger's terms.

(12) For Weiss (*q.v.*) existence is one of four modes of being, standing alongside actuality, ideality, and God.

(13) Sartre (*q.v.* 2), an existentialist, held that "existence precedes essence."

(14) Quine (*q.v.* 2) follows Russell's lead, analyzing existence in the framework of modern logic. This is evident in his remark that to be is to be the value of a variable.

EXISTENTIALISM.
A philosophical movement challenging essentialism (*q.v.* Existence 6, 9), and concentrating attention on the human situation. Theistic existentialism is usually regarded as beginning with Kierkegaard and atheistic existentialism with Nietzsche.

(1) Kierkegaard (*q.v.* 1, 5, 6, 7) set many of the themes of existentialism. The act of challenging the Hegelian philosophy signalled the substitution of another approach, replacing essentialism. Specifically, he contributed an emphasis on the individual, the importance of subjectivity, and *Angst* or anguish as the central emotion of human life. With respect to God

he stressed the need for a "leap of faith."

(2) Nietzsche (*q.v.* 4–5) contributed to the movement the theme that "God is dead," and that each individual must seek his own values, providing a bridge to the future.

(3) Unamuno (*q.v.* 1–3) stressed many of the emphases of Kierkegaard: the concrete individual (*i.e.*, the man of "flesh and bone"), the "tragic sense of life," and the substitution of true belief for objective truth.

(4) Ortega (*q.v.* 1–3) might be regarded as a secularized Unamuno. He emphasized the concrete individual, and the "vital reason." Man has no nature but only a history, yet his goal is authenticity.

(5) Heidegger (*q.v.* 1–6) is regarded as one of the most important of the Existentialists. He stressed human freedom, authenticity, *Sorge* or care, and *das Nichts* or Nothingness as a basic, and positive, category.

(6) Jaspers (*q.v.* 2, 7), who denied being an Existentialist or having any connection with Heidegger, nonetheless built his *Existenz-Philosophy* around the idea of authenticity, likewise stressing man's freedom and historicity.

(7) Bultmann (*q.v.* 1–2) recognized the influence of Heidegger, and worked with Jaspers. An existentialist theologian, he stressed freedom, *Angst*, authenticity, and called for the "demythologizing" of the New Testament.

(8) Marcel (*q.v.*), called a theistic existentialist, stressed the concrete over the abstract, and the mystery of being.

(9) Tillich (*q.v.*), an existentialist theologian, drew heavily on Heidegger, developing a systematic theology of considerable interest.

(10) Sartre (*q.v.*) brings together all of the themes of atheistic existentialism: man's radical freedom, and his position as a "noughting nought"; the death of God; the invention of value; authenticity; the presence of *Angst*; and Nothingness as a basic category.

EXISTENTIALIST PSYCHOANALYSIS.
A form of psychoanalysis resting on existentialist rather than Freudian thought.

EXISTENTIAL QUANTIFIER.
The notation used in Existential Gen-

eralization and Instantiation. *Q.v.* Quantification Theory (6).

EXISTENZ PHILOSOPHY.
Q.v. Jaspers (2–3).

EX NIHILO NIHIL FIT.
Latin phrase, meaning "Out of nothing nothing comes." *Q.v.* Nothing (7).

EX OPERE OPERATO.
A Latin phrase meaning "from the work wrought." The Roman Catholic doctrine that the efficacy of sacraments does not depend upon the merits either of the priest or of the recipient.

EXOSEMIOTIC.
Q.v. Semiotic (13).

EXOTERIC.
From the Greek *exoterikos* ("ouside"). *Q.v.* Esoterism.

EXPERIENCE.
From the Latin *experior* ("to prove" or "to put to the test"). The usual use of the term is to refer to information gained from the senses rather than from reason. Although used earlier (*q.v.* Empiricism) the term had its greatest currency in the late 19th and early 20th century.

(1) Locke (*q.v.* 1–2) regarded experience as the origin of all ideas, and the mind as a blank tablet on which experience writes. Even Locke's ideas of reflection are a result of internal experience.

(2) Avenarius (*q.v.* 1) introduced the term "pure experience" as the basis of his philosophy of Empiriocriticism. He meant by the phrase simply the given, devoid of assumptions.

(3) In the later stages of his thought William James (*q.v.* 10) adopted the term, explaining body as well as mind in terms of "pure experience."

(4) Ward (*q.v.* 2) divided mental experience into cognitive, affective, and conative types.

(5) The category of experience has been much used by modern Idealists. Bradley (*q.v.* 4–5), for example, thought of the Absolute as an "absolute experience"; and Royce (*q.v.* 1, 3) argued from the fragmentary character of human experience to an absolute experience.

(6) Dewey (*q.v.* 1–4, 6, 9) has used the term more frequently than any other modern philosopher. It would seem to have been his basic category. Both observation and reasoning occur within experience and, together, constitute it. All possible distinctions are therefore distinctions within experience, which has both instrumental and consummatory phases.

(7) Petzoldt (*q.v.*) followed Avenarius, developing a philosophy of pure experience.

EXPERIMENTAL PSYCHOLOGY.
Q.v. Psychology (4); Wilhelm Wundt (1).

EXPERIMENTALISM.
The name given by John Stuart Mill (*q.v.* 1) to his form of empiricism.

EXPLANANDUM.
That which is to be explained. *Q.v.* Explanation.

EXPLANANS.
That which provides the explanation. *Q.v.* Explanation.

EXPLANATION.
From the Latin *ex* and *planare* ("to make level or plain"). The procedure of making a matter clear consists of dividing a complex idea into its simpler parts, or in demonstrating that the idea in question can be deduced from certain premises, or that a state of affairs would have resulted from certain causes, or in a combination of these procedures. That which is to be explained is called the *explanandum*; that which provides the explanation is called the *explanans*.

(1) For Braithwaite (*q.v.* 1) explanation always involves the implication of a lower-level generalization by a higher level generalization.

(2) Hempel (*q.v.* 1) is associated with the covering-law model of explanation, also known as the deductive-nomological model. In this model, which he regards as adequate for all types of scientific explanation, the explanans consists of the appropriate laws and theoretical principles
$$L_1, L_2, L_3 \ldots, L_m$$
as well as statements of the appropriate empirical circumstances
$$C_1, C_2, C_3 \ldots, C_n$$
These together serve as the premises from which the explanandum
$$E$$
can be deduced.

The inductive-probabilistic model of explanation will have the same form except for the fact that some of the laws of the explanans will be statistical in character.

(3) Nagel (*q.v.* 2–4) holds that explanation is deterministic wherever it occurs, in quantum mechanics as well as in classical mechanics: in biology, psychology, and history, as well as in physics.

(4) Popper (*q.v.* 1) is closely associated with the general modes of explanation mentioned above, while stressing the value of "falsifiability" over "verifiability."

(5) For Lévi-Strauss (*q.v.* 3) language models are primary in explanation and adaptable to all other relations.

EXPLICATIVE JUDGMENT.
Q.v. Analytic Judgment.

EXPORTATION.
Q.v. Propositional Calculus (21).

EXPRESSIONS.
Q.v. Frege (5).

EXPRESSIVES.
Q.v. Searle (2).

EXTENSION.
From the Latin *ex* ("out") and *tendere* ("to stretch").

(1) In 17th-century metaphysics the categorial correlate of thought. For Descartes (*q.v.* 8, 9) thinking and extended things, *res cogitans* and *res extensa*, are basic substances. For Spinoza (*q.v.* 2) thought and extension are the two attributes of God, or infinite Substance, known to us.

(2) In logic, extension is the correlate of intension, the denotation of a term in contrast to its connotation, the set of things to which the term refers in contrast to the set of characteristics belonging to the term (*q.v.* Logic 16). The intension of a term determines its extension, but also the extension of a term determines its intension. Sometimes, different intensions can have the same extension. Frege (*q.v.* 6) mentions "the evening star" and "the morning star" (*i.e.*, Venus) as a case in point. But apparently it is senseless to say that two different extensions have the same intension, for if they had the same intension the two would constitute the single extension of that term as intended.

(3) Nominalistic systems stress extension over intension. For an instance of this approach *q.v.* Nelson Goodman (1, 2).

EXTERNAL RELATION.
A relation independent of its terms. The discussion of external relation was of importance in the late 19th and early 20th centuries.

(1) The argument of the monist (*q.v.* Bradley 3) was that relation, to be intelligible, had to be internal to its terms.

(2) Pluralists (*q.v.* James) held the opposite, supporting the idea of external relations.

EXTERNAL WORLD, ARGUMENTS FOR.
Although skeptics have held the evidence insufficient to conclude with certainty that there is an external world (*q.v.* Skepticism; Vasubandhu), other philosophers have advanced arguments to that end.

(1) Descartes (*q.v.* 6–8) asserted the existence of such a world on the ground that God is not a deceiver, and that thus the total evidence of our senses cannot support illusion.

(2) Locke (*q.v.* 8c) held that we know the external world through sensitive knowledge, through the unwilled sensory evidence which comes to us, and the corroborative evidence of the various senses.

(3) Condillac (*q.v.* 5) argued from the sense of resistance, to the external world, and Destutt De Tracy (*q.v.*) followed him on this as well as many other points.

(4) Common-sense realism (*q.v.*) claims that the truth of such propositions like the one concerning the external world's existence is so clear that no argument is needed. G. E. Moore (*q.v.* 2) was apparently taking such a line with his "argument," "Here is one hand . . . and here is the other."

EXTREME UNCTION.
Roman Catholic sacrament (*q.v.* 1) for those in danger of dying. Holy oil is applied to, and forgiveness asked for, offences committed by the sense organs, hands, and feet.

EXTRINSIC VALUE.
Correlate of intrinsic value (*q.v.*). The phrase applies to things or states of being

valuable not in themselves but in their consequences. "Instrumental value" is a synonym. The contrast between intrinsic and extrinsic value was developed in Greek philosophy (*q.v.* Plato 14). The validity of the distinction between the two types of value has been challenged by Dewey (*q.v.* 4) in his conception of the means-end continuum. *Q.v.* Theory of Value.

F

FA CHIA.

A Chinese term meaning "legalist school." One of the ancient Chinese schools of philosophy. *Q.v.* Legalist School.

FACTIVE.

Q.v. Grice (2).

FACULTY PSYCHOLOGY.

From the Latin *facere* ("to make"). A view of psychology in which mind, psyche, or soul is analyzed into the separate faculties, or powers, of reason, will, and sensibility.

(1) The tripartite analysis of the soul is present in Plato (*q.v.* 3), but he was far from compartmentalizing the soul and, of course, did not use the term.

(2) Aristotle (*q.v.* 7, 11) and Aquinas (*q.v.* 7) thought in terms of potentialities or potencies of the soul, which can bear a functional interpretation as readily as one that presumes faculties. Furthermore, while Aquinas did speak of "powers" as "proper accidents" of the soul, his list of powers was divided into vegetative, sensory, locomotive, and rational—with many subdivisions—hardly the expected arrangement of the "faculty psychology."

(3) The deduction of mental faculties, powers, or functions in Rational Psychology (*q.v.* Psychology 1–2, 14) may be a source for the position referred to as "faculty psychology."

(4) Whatever its origin, the received opinion is that when soul is viewed as a substance, it is natural to divide its operations into faculties, and that this is outmoded.

FA-HSIANG.

Q.v. Śunya (6).

FAITH.

From the Latin *fidere* ("to trust"). An attitude of belief which goes beyond the available evidence. There are both religious and non-religious forms of faith.

A. Religious faith enters philosophy as a significant problem, especially in relation to the claims of inquiry. The problem of faith and reason has had a long and continuing history.

(1) The Apostle Paul (*q.v.* 1), announcing the end of the era of Mosaic Law, held that justification was henceforth to be by faith, not works.

(2) Against the attitude of the Greek philosophers for whom reason was the single means of determining what is to be believed, Tertullian (*q.v.* 1) asserted "*Credo quia absurdum est*" (I believe because it is absurd). Faith thus had the determinative role in contrast to reason.

(3) St. Augustine (*q.v.* 11) stated the necessity of belief as a pre-requisite for understanding in his "*Credo ut intelligam*" (I believe in order to understand). The principle was accepted by St. Anselm (*q.v.* 8) among many others.

(4) The standard and most durable relationship between faith and reason was elaborated by St. Thomas Aquinas (*q.v.* 1). In this relationship faith and reason are held to be complementary, consistent, and to a large extent, alternate means to an identical goal. Although reason can carry some much further than others there are propositions, the articles of faith, beyond the reach of the reason of any human being.

(5) Bonaventure (*q.v.* 1) held that faith helps one to pose the right questions, and so avoid false alternatives.

(6) Herbert of Cherbury (*q.v.* 3) argued that one should begin with reason, proceeding thence only to a faith clear and evident to all humanity.

(7) Pascal (*q.v.* 3) distinguished between two kinds of reason: the geometric reason of logic, and the *esprit de finesse* of intuition. He believed that faith related more closely to the latter, and its reasons of the heart "that reason knows not of."

(8) John Toland (*q.v.* 1) held that faith requires the confirmation of reason.

(9) Ritschl (*q.v.* 1–2) held that faith and

reason are autonomous, each being pre-eminent in its own sphere.

(10) Troeltsch (*q.v.*) believed that a unique deposit of the Christian faith, absolute and invariable, emerged from a dialectic between historical studies and the religious life.

(11) Unamuno (*q.v.* 2), found the conflict of faith and reason leading to the "tragic sense of life."

(12) Buber (*q.v.* 4) claimed that in faith knowledge claims are to be replaced by unconditional trust.

(13) Tillich (*q.v.* 2) grounded reason in faith. This is his theonomous reason, different from autonomous and heteronymous forms, by virtue of its relation to the ground of being.

B. In a more general sense one takes on faith many beliefs which go beyond the evidence, from the existence of one's room when out of it to the principle of induction.

(14) The "will to believe" of William James (*q.v.* 4) allows one to believe beyond the evidence when the option before one is living, forced, and momentous.

(15) Santayana (*q.v.* 3) invoked "animal faith" as the motivating force taking one out of the solipsism of the present moment.

(16) Tennant (*q.v.* 1) interpreted faith as the volitional element in all knowledge.

FALLACIES.

From the Latin *fallacia* ("deceit," "trick," or "fraud"). The problem of validity in logic has its other side in the recognition of types of invalidity. Since fallacies are instances of reasoning which violate the requirements of validity, and since there exists an indefinitely great number of possible ways of reasoning improperly, there can be no comprehensive list of fallacies. A list of those most often cited is set forth below, divided into three sections: (A) Fallacies of diction and shifting sense. These departures from validity are occasioned by difficulties in the use of language. (B) Fallacies of relevance. These are, in one way or another, instances of straying from the point. (C) Fallacies of structure. These are, more properly, distortions of the procedures of valid reasoning—a failure to follow its rules, and appreciate its requirements.

*A List of the Major Fallacies
of Speech and Thought*

A. Fallacies of Diction and Shifting Sense

(1) The Fallacy of Amphiboly—a fallacy committed when the awkward construction of one's sentences allows one's words to be interpreted in more than one sense. "Being in a dilapidated condition, he was able to buy the house at a bargain."

(2) The Fallacy of Accent—a fallacy committed when words are allowed to shift in meaning during an argument as a result of the degree of emphasis or stress used.
"Save soap and waste paper."

(3) The Fallacy of Equivocation—a fallacy committed when a word is used first in one sense and then another during the course of an argument, allowing a conclusion which would not otherwise be possible. "The medicine the doctor gave me made my eyes smart."
"You should have used it on your head."

(4) The Fallacy of Composition—a fallacy committed when one reasons from the properties of the parts of a whole to properties of the whole itself; when this is not warranted; or when one reasons from properties possessed by the members of a collection to the properties of the collection or class as such, when this is not warranted.
"I can't understand why I'm so tired. Reaching up to pick fruit is an easy job."

(5) The Fallacy of Division—a fallacy committed in reasoning from the properties of a whole to the properties of its parts; or from the properties of a class or collection to properties of its members, when these transitions are not warranted.
"Mr. Jones must be quite well off. His state has the highest per capita income in the nation."

(6) The Fallacy of Slanting (*Argumentum ad Populum*)—the fallacy is committed when a conclusion is pointed toward not by evidence, but by the use of persuasively emotive language.
"The war mongering character of this flood of propaganda is very clear. But the shining reputation of our nation is impervious to slander, and we shall persevere."

(7) The Fallacy of Reification or Hypostatization—the fallacy consists in making a thing out of what is not a thing, an entity out of an abstraction, for instance, and drawing a conclusion from it. One of its common forms is personification.

"Flowers complete the gay occasions of today. They speak the language of love and cheer."

B. Fallacies of Relevance are instances of *ignoratio elenchi* or "irrelevant reasoning."

(8) The Appeal to Force (*Argumentum ad Baculum*)—the fallacy committed when one appeals to force or the threat of force to cause acceptance of a conclusion.

"That law is unfair to labor, Senator, and ought to be repealed. The unions have gone on record against it; and there are a quarter of a million union members in your constituency."

(9) Poisoning the Well (*Argumentum ad Hominem*)—the fallacy committed when one directs one's argument to the person instead of directing it to the point at issue. The Genetic Fallacy, dismissing the result of a process because of its origin, is another manner of poisoning the well.

"The case sounds convincing, but remember the evidence has been announced by the police; and all of us know how reactionary they are."

(10) The Appeal to Pity (*Argumentum ad Misericordiam*)—the fallacy committed when an appeal is made to one's pity to accept a given conclusion rather than to any evidence.

"If elected, Brown will give this state an efficient and economical administration. He was wounded twice in the war, and is the sole support of an invalid mother."

(11) *Ipse Dixit*, or the Argument from Authority (*Argumentum ad Verecundiam*)—the fallacy committed in appealing to the feeling of respect people have for the famous in order to win their assent to a conclusion. Not every appeal to authority commits this fallacy, but every appeal to an authority with respect to matters outside one's special province commits the fallacy.

"These pills must be safe and effective for reducing. They have been endorsed by Mr. X, star of stage, screen and television."

(12) The Argument from False Cause (a narrower version of this fallacy is called *Post hoc ergo propter hoc*, "after this, therefore because of this," *e.g.*, "Democrats are the war party, for the major wars have occurred after their election to national office") is the fallacy committed when one incorrectly attempts to establish a causal connection.

"There are more churches in New York City than in any other city in the world; and more crimes are committed in New York than anywhere else. This makes it clear that to eliminate crimes we must abolish the church."

(13) The Fallacy of Complex Question— a fallacy committed when it is not detected that the answer to a given question presupposes a prior answer to a prior question.

"Have you given up your evil ways?"

(14) The Argument from Ignorance (*Argumentum ad Ignorantiam*)—the fallacy committed when one argues that something is true on the basis that it has not been proven false, or false on the basis that it has not been proven true.

"Faith healing must work. No one has ever been able to show that it doesn't."

C. Fallacies of Structure.

(15) The Black-or-White Fallacy—this fallacy is committed when we are told to choose between two alternatives, and the presence of other alternatives is ignored; it is insisted that we must choose between black and white, when in fact there are many shades of gray which might also be chosen.

"To any and all who think they love Communism better than Americanism, let them buy a one-way ticket to China and stay there. Either we are loyal Americans or we are Communists.

(16) The Fallacy of Hasty Generalization—a fallacy committed when one draws an inductive conclusion from too little evidence, or too small a sample.

"He'll never play the recorder he got for Christmas. He hasn't so far."

(17) The Fallacy of False Analogy—it is the business of analogy to illustrate, or suggest, not demonstrate; the fallacy is committed when one argues from the analogy to a conclusion claimed to follow necessarily; the fallacy is more pronounced the more differences there are in the cases compared.

"Ambulances and police cars can go through red lights if they are in a hurry; I should be able to do the same thing when I'm in a hurry."

(18) The Fallacy of Unnecessarily Complex Hypothesis—the fallacy is committed when the more complex of two hypotheses is adopted, even though the less complex hypothesis is adequate to explain all of the facts.

"I did not receive a Christmas card from Mrs. Jones this year. She must have fled the country due to trouble with the Internal Revenue Service."

(19) The Fallacy of the Contrary-to-Fact Hypothesis (also called Speculative Argument)—the fallacy consists in adopting an hypothesis contrary to fact, and then arguing about what would have followed had this been true.
"If Florence Nightingale had not started the Red Cross many disaster victims would not be cared for today."

(20) The Fallacy of Circular Argument (Begging the Question, *Petitio Principii*)—the fallacy is committed when one assumes among one's premises what one is supposed to prove.
Three thieves are arguing over the division of seven very fine pearls. One of them hands two to the man on his right, then two to the man on his left.
"I," he says, "will keep three."
The man on his right says, "How come you keep three?"
"Because I am the leader."
"Oh, but how come you are the leader?"
"Because I have more pearls."
Also *q.v.* Vicious Circle.

(21) The Fallacy of False Dilemma— the fallacy is committed when there is a third alternative which one can adopt, or when the consequences alleged to follow from the alternatives given do not, in fact, follow. Consider the line of reasoning allegedly offered by the Muslim caliph who ordered that the furnaces of the baths of Alexandria be stoked with books from the library of Alexandria: "If these books merely repeat what is in the Koran, they are superfluous. If they say something other than the Koran, they are meretricious. But either they will repeat the Koran, or say something in addition to it. Hence, these books are either superfluous or meretricious." For further analysis of this form of reasoning, *q.v.* Dilemma.

(22) The Fallacy of *Contradictio in Adjecto* is committed when a modifying adjective is inconsistent with the noun it modifies. The phrase "round square" provides a hackneyed instance of the fallacy. More subtle instances depend on context; it is necessary to establish the meaning of terms in context to see if a specific sample of reasoning does or does not commit the fallacy.

(23) The Fallacy of the Undistributed Middle Term—the fallacy is committed when your reasoning has done nothing more than relate two ideas to a third idea, when your conclusion claims you have also related them to each other. This is a fallacy of the syllogism (*q.v.*). The major and minor terms have been related to the middle term but not to each other. Although one can be misled by this fallacy, its invalidity can be intuitively sensed in the following example: "All dogs are mammals. All cats are mammals. Therefore, all cats are dogs."

(24) The Fallacy of Four Terms (*Quaternia Terminorum*). Every syllogism (*q.v.*) is expected to have three terms. When the middle term is ambiguous it is sometimes the case that it is taken in a different sense in the major premise and the minor premise. When this occurs there has been an equivocation (*q.v.* 3 above) in the middle terms. Consequently, even though one has the appearance of three terms, there are really four. This is also called a fallacy of the ambiguous middle term. "The end of a thing is its perfection. Death is the end of life. Therefore, death is the perfection of life."

(25) The Fallacy of Illicit Major. The fallacy is committed when in a syllogism the major term is related to the minor term in a manner which goes beyond the relations of these terms established by the premises: "All Representatives are political figures. No governors are Congressmen. Therefore, no governors are political figures."

(26) The Fallacy of Illicit Minor. The fallacy is committed when in a syllogism the minor term is related to the major term in a manner which goes beyond the relations of these terms established by the premises:
"All fraternity men are lovers of strong drink. All fraternity men are college students. Therefore, all college students are lovers of strong drink."

(27) The Fallacy of Affirming the Consequent. The fallacy is committed when, in an hypothetical syllogism, one affirms the consequent, and on the basis of this affirmation, affirms the antecedent:
(Antecedent)   (Consequent)
"If it rains, then the streets will be wet,
The streets are wet.
Therefore, it has rained."

(28) The Fallacy of Denying the Antecedent. The fallacy is committed when, in an hypothetical syllogism, one denies the antecedent and on the basis of this denial, likewise denies the consequent:

(Antecedent)   (Consequent)
"If it rains, then the streets will be wet.
It has not rained.
Therefore, the streets are not wet."

(29) The Fallacy of the Alternative Syllogism: affirming and denying. The alternative syllogism is built on a weak sense of either-or. The sense is that at least one of the disjuncts must be accepted, and perhaps both, or however many disjuncts there may be. Given this sense, it is clear that one cannot affirm: Either A or B. B. Therefore not A (Q.v. Truth Tables 3, 7; Syllogism 11).

"Either green beans or cauliflower.
I wish green beans.
Therefore, I cannot have cauliflower."

(30) The Fallacy of the Disjunctive Syllogism: denying and affirming. The disjunctive syllogism utilizes a stronger sense of either-or, that of mutual exclusion. When the intention of the premises is to assert: Not both A and B, it is clear that one cannot argue "Not A. Therefore, B." (Q.v. Syllogism 12). For example, on the dinner menu one may have a choice of green beans or cauliflower. It would not do to argue:

"Either green beans or cauliflower.
I do not care for green beans.
Therefore, I must take cauliflower."

FALLIBILISM.

A doctrine of the pragmaticist, Charles Peirce (q.v. 10), that absolute certainty, exactitude, or universality is available in no area of human concern or inquiry, but that movement toward these characteristics is available in every case. Q.v. Logic of Discovery and Logic of Justification.

FALSE ANALOGY, FALLACY OF.

Q.v. Fallacies (17).

FALSIFIABILITY.

Q.v. Popper (1).

FARABI, AL.

Q.v. Al-Farabi.

FARIAS BRITO, RAIMUNDO DE.

Q.v. Latin American Philosophy (7).

FASCISM.

From the Latin *fascis*, the bundle of rods—including an ax with blade projecting—carried as a symbol of authority before the magistrates of Rome. The name of an Italian political organization founded by Mussolini in 1919, bringing him to power in 1922. Gentile (q.v. 4) and Ugo Spirito contributed to the theory of the corporate state which Fascists held to be their goal.

FA-SHEN.

Q.v. Seven Early Chinese Buddhist Schools (2).

FATALISM.

The doctrine that all things happen according to an inexorable fate (q.v.). The doctrine is both pre-philosophical and pre-theological. The equivalent doctrine in theological thought is predestination (q.v.), and in philosophy its equivalent is determinism (q.v.). Also q.v. Necessity.

FATE.

From the Latin *fatum* (the Greek term is *moira*), both terms meaning "a prophetic declaration or oracle." The fated is that which is destined or decreed to come to pass. The term is pre-philosophical, deriving from mythology. In Greek mythology it is the decision of Zeus; in Roman mythology, the spoken word of Jupiter. In both fate is depicted as the three goddesses (the *Fata* in Latin; the *Moirai* in Greek), determining the course of human life. One spins the thread of life; the second twists it; the third snips it. The concept is important in Greek tragedy where all human concerns are subject to the gods, and sometimes even the gods are subject to a controlling necessity. In Arabic the term is *kismet*; it means "fate," "destiny," "the will of Allah.

For an Eastern view of fate q.v. Ajivikas (1).

FATHERS, CHURCH.

Q.v. Patristics.

FATOU, PIERRE.

Q.v. Chaos Theory.

FA-TSANG. 643–712.

Chinese Buddhist philosopher. Founder of the Hua-Yen school. He became a monk at 28, enjoying the favor and support of

Empress Wu. He wrote 60 works, the most important of them explicating and supporting the Hua-Yen School (*q.v.*).

Principal writings: *Treatise on the Golden Lion* (T); *Hundred Gates to the Sea of Ideas of the Flowery Splendor Scripture* (T in part).

FAVORINUS. c. 80–150.

Greek philosopher. Born in Arelatus. A teacher of rhetoric, he probably studied under Epictetus and Dion Chrysostom (*q.v.*). A friend of Plutarch and a member of Hadrian's inner circle, he was an eclectic in philosophy, combining themes from Plato, Aristotle, the skepticism of the New Academy, and Pyrrhonism. Felicitous in turning a phrase, once after Hadrian had bested him in argument and Favorinus' friends were asking why he had not made certain moves, he replied that it was foolish to criticize the logic of the master of thirty legions. And when the Athenians had pulled down his statue to express their displeasure of him, he merely commented that had Socrates had a statue in Athens he might have escaped the hemlock.

Principal writings: *On Epictetus*; *Pyrrhonean Tropes*; only fragments remain.

FA-WEN.

Q.v. Seven Early Chinese Buddhist Schools (4).

FECHNER, GUSTAV THEODOR. 1801–1887.

German philosopher-psychologist. Born in Gross-Särchen, Lower Lusatia. Educated at Leipzig, he became professor of physics at the University of Leipzig in 1834. His interests gradually shifted to physiological psychology. In 1839 a period of suffering began, including temporary blindness, which led him to panpsychism (*q.v.*) and panentheism (*q.v.*).

Principal writings: *The Little Book of Life after Death* (T), 1836; *Nanna or Concerning the Soul-Life of Plants*, 1848; *Zendavesta, or Concerning the Things of Heaven and the World to Come*, 1851; *On Physical and Philosophical Atomic Theory*, 1853; *The Three Motives and Grounds of Faith*, 1863; *Elementary Course in Aesthetics*, 1876; *The Daylight View over Against the Night View*, 1879.

(1) Contributing to experimental psychology the Weber-Fechner Law that the intensity of sensation increases by a certain proportion in relation to increase in stimulus, Fechner developed the conception of psychology as an exact science capable of mathematical treatment. He attempted to discover by experiment the natural proportion of aesthetic preference which he believed to exist.

(2) It was Fechner who introduced the term "psychophysical parallelism," contending that there is a one to one correlation of psychical and physical events. From an external point of view everything is quantitative but internally all is life and soul. Both views are true, but the internal view is more fundamental. As a living cell exists in the body of a living thing, so reality is a continuum of nested souls or cells from the outwardly inorganic to the all-inclusive being of God.

(3) The organismic analogy allowed Fechner to insist upon the compatibility of God's dominance with man's freedom, as a bodily cell might have autonomy within limits while yet serving the general bodily economy. It allowed him to view God as suffering the tragedy of the world, while locating the source of evil in the actions of creatures; and to combine the conceptions of a supreme being and an open future.

(4) This led him to view God as a being whose goodness requires that He Himself be involved in the process of constantly surpassing Himself, though no other being has the possibility of doing so. Thus, there is implicit in Fechner the idea of a growing perfection.

(5) More exactly, Fechner adhered to a principle of polarity in God whereby the divine being can be regarded either in terms of His absolute unchanging essence or in terms of His changing and growing existence.

FEDERALIST PAPERS. 1787–1788.

A series of 85 essays, 51 of them by Alexander Hamilton, 26 by James Madison, 5 by John Jay, arguing for passage of the newly framed American Constitution. The essays were first published in New York City newspapers between late October, 1787, and late May, 1788, under the pseudonym "Publius."

(1) The Federalists might well have called themselves nationalists since their

position, defending a strong central government (not a compact among states) was so-called in the discussions of the Constitutional Convention. The strong central government advocates, instead, chose the name Federalists, leaving for their opponents the puzzling name, anti-Federalists. Governor Clinton of New York was vigorously anti-Federalist; and in the New York convention, held in June of 1788, anti-Federalist delegates outnumbered their Federalist opponents 46–19. By June, however, 10 states had ratified the Constitution, a sufficient number to call the Union into existence. The only question left for New York was whether it would join the Union or stand alone. In this situation the Federalists won handily.

(2) While Federalists and anti-Federalists agreed on many features of the Constitution (*e.g.*, separation of powers, checks and balances, one house based on population the other with equal representation), the Federalists were more inclined to strong, central government and a powerful executive. During the Philadelphia convention the Federalists had argued that representation in the Senate, as well as the House, should be based on population. Many of them, including Hamilton, saw populist dangers in the guarantees implicit in a Bill of Rights. It was argued, especially by Madison in the 10th essay that, although historically republics had been small, the concept of representative democracy made it possible for a republic to govern over a wide area without excessive factionalism.

(3) During Washington's two terms the struggle between Federalist and anti-Federalist was defined by Hamilton's drive for industrialization over against Jefferson's preference for an agrarian economy. A second issue concerned the Bill of Rights, sponsored by James Madison, and ratified by the states in December, 1791.

(4) Although American leaders had wished to govern without political parties, a Federalist party formed around Washington, Hamilton, and Adams, and a Republican party (called Jeffersonian Republicans as distinct from members of the Republican party organized in 1854) formed around Jefferson and Madison. Jefferson's presidential selection in 1800 sent the Federalist party into eclipse.

FEELING.
Any portion of one's awareness characterized by sensation or emotion. Feeling has been subject to a number of interpretations.

(1) For Aristotle (*q.v.* 11) and Aquinas (*q.v.* 7) the sensory level includes both external and internal senses, and the sensory appetites both concupiscible and irascible.

(2) Descartes (*q.v.* 7, 11) approaches this area from the standpoint of intellect. Not only is the valid part of a sensation ideational, but passions are defined as modes of the thinking substance.

(3) Condillac (*q.v.* 2–3), as a good empiricist, attempts to derive everything from sensation, not only ideas but also emotions or passions and the will.

(4) Schopenhauer (*q.v.* 2–3) made the will primary, so that both reason and feeling are manifestations.

(5) Theobald Ziegler (*q.v.*) made feeling the basic psychological process from which both reason and will are derived.
Also *q.v.* Passion.

FEIGENBAUM, MITCHELL.
Q.v. Chaos Theory.

FEIGL, HERBERT. 1902– .
Austrian-American philosopher. Born in Reichenberg, Austria. Educated at the University of Munich. Taught at Vienna, Harvard, Iowa, and Minnesota. Director, Minn. Center for the Philosophy of Science, beginning 1973. He was one of the original circle of Logical Positivists, or, as he preferred to call them, "logical empiricists." Feigl began his association with the University of Minnesota in 1932.
Principal writings: *Readings in Philosophical Analysis* (edited with W. Sellars), 1949; *Readings in Philosophy of Science* (edited with M. Brodbeck), 1953; *Minnesota Studies in Philosophy of Science*, 5 vols. (edited with others), 1956–69; *The "Mental" and the "Physical"—The Essay and a Postscript*, 1967; *New Readings in Philosophical Analysis* (edited with W. Sellars, K. Lehrer), 1972; *Inquiries and Provocations: Selected Writings* (ed. Robert S. Cohen), 1981.

(1) Starting with Behaviorism, Feigl argues that when one moves beyond "observables" to "central states" it is possible to identify such states both with introspective reports of direct experience

and with the referents of neurophysiological terms.

(2) The common referents of these terms are "raw feels" which are expressible in terms of physicalism.

(3) Holding that ultimate principles are not susceptible to cognitive justification, Feigl suggests that principles are "vindicated," not validated, although with their use various kinds of validation are possible. Thus he distinguishes between two types of justification: validation (*justificatio cognitionis*) which takes place in the application of the principles of deduction, induction, morality, etc.; and vindication, a pragmatic justification (*justificatio actionis*) of the principles themselves. The difference is that in vindication it is appropriate that account be taken of practical and valuational considerations.

FELAPTON.
Valid syllogism in EAO mood, third figure. *Q.v.* Syllogism (4).

FEMINISM.
Q.v. Simone De Beauvoir; Mary Daly.

FÉNELON, FRANÇOIS.
Q.v. Quietism.

FERGUSON, ADAM. 1723–1816.
Scottish philosopher. Educated at St. Andrews University and Edinburgh. A member of the Scottish Common Sense school of Thomas Reid (*q.v.*), Ferguson attempted to reconcile all ethical systems by introducing a principle of "perfection" as the goal of individual human life and of societies, and the criterion of right and wrong. Cousin (*q.v.*) regarded Ferguson's principle as superior to either benevolence or sympathy, placing Ferguson "as a moralist above all his predecessors." Principal writings: *Institutes of Moral Philosophy*, 1769; *Principles of Moral and Political Science*, 1792.

FERIO.
Valid syllogism in EIO mood, first figure. *Q.v.* Syllogism (4).

FERISON.
Valid syllogism in EIO mood, third figure. *Q.v.* Syllogism (4).

FERMAT.
Q.v. Probability (3).

FESAPO.
Valid syllogism in EAO mood, fourth figure. *Q.v.* Syllogism (4).

FESTINO.
Valid syllogism in EIO mood, second figure. *Q.v.* Syllogism (4).

FETISHISM OF COMMODITIES.
Q.v. Marx (10).

FEUERBACH, LUDWIG. 1804–1872.
German philosopher. Born in Landshut, Bavaria. Educated at Heidelberg, Berlin and Erlangen. At Berlin he studied under Hegel. Unattached to a university but sometimes giving public lectures, he was supported through most of his adult life by his wife's fractional interest in a porcelain works.
Principal writings: *Thoughts on Death and Immortality*, 1830; *On Philosophy and Christianity*, 1839; *The Essence of Christianity* (T), 1841; *The Essence of Religion*, 1845.

(1) The essence of religion consists in a projection of human qualities into an object of worship. The Trinity, for example, is a projection into infinity of the human faculties of reason, will, and love.

(2) Only when the projection is withdrawn—in a state, then, of atheism—can our human limitations and possibilities be assessed. In this state one discovers that the appropriate object of worship is humanity itself. The individual human being is, of course, limited and imperfect. But humanity in its entire stretch from past to future is not limited, nor is it characterized by the imperfections of individual human beings; the religious projection should be directed toward humanity, and religion should become the Religion of Humanity.

(3) Needless to say, it was Feuerbach's position, emphasized even in the first book listed above, that immortality is an idle dream.

(4) The foregoing ideas are supported by an ontology which is basically materialistic, and an epistemology holding to the harmonious inter-working of sensation and reason although with the emphasis on sensation.

FEYERABEND, PAUL K.
Q.v. Philosophy of Science (30).

FICHTE, IMMANUEL H.
Q.v. Weisse.

FICHTE, JOHANN GOTTLIEB. 1762–1814.

German philosopher. Born in Rammenku, upper Lusatia. Studied theology at Jena, 1780–88; introduced to Kantian philosophy in Leipzig, 1790. Journeyed to Königsberg to meet Kant and wrote a *Critique of Revelation* along Kantian lines. When published in 1792, Fichte's name was omitted from the title page by inadvertence, and the book was widely attributed to Kant. When Kant corrected the mistake while commending the work, Fichte's reputation was assured. He became professor at Jena 1794–99. As a result of certain lectures and pamphlets on the freedom of thought and religion, Fichte became the center of a dispute known as the *Atheismusstreit* which led to his dismissal from the university. He lectured at Erlangen, Berlin, and Königsberg. From 1810 to 1812 he served as rector of the University of Berlin.

Principal writings: *Attempt at a Critique Of all Revelation*, 1792; *Basis of all Theory of Science*, 1794; *On the Idea of a Theory of Science*, 1794; *The Foundation of Natural Rights* (T), 1796; *A System of Ethics*, 1798; *The Vocation of Man* (T), 1800; *Characteristics of the Present Age* (T), 1804; *Way to a Blessed Life* (T), 1806; *Addresses to the German Nation* (T), 1808.

(1) Strongly influenced by Immanuel Kant, and known as the founder of German Idealism, he derived his philosophy from Kant by making the practical reason determinative over the theoretical reason, a step it seems Kant himself never quite took. The result is an Idealism emerging from the moral will. The steps Fichte takes in reaching his conclusion are set forth in *The Vocation of Man*, a book written for non-philosophers. The first point of his argument is that if everything happens by causal necessity, then we are not responsible either for the good or evil that we do; for the source of our actions will be nature, and not ourselves.

(2) Instead of saying that one knows one is perceiving an object it would be more accurate to say that one knows that one thinks one sees an object; and this, so far as we can know anything, is a fact about the one perceiving. If a person who has not reflected on the problem is asked to give a reason for believing in an external world the causal principle will be invoked. What one perceives requires a cause, one may say. And having said this one cannot also say that one observes causality operating in an external world. It was through causality that one was led to posit the world. "Shall the earth rest on the great elephant and the great elephant again rest upon the earth?" The only acceptable answer is that we posit the principle of causality just as we posit the world.

(3) But since our awareness is constituted by our perceptions, we are not more directly aware of the "I" than of the world. We posit the Ego as well as the non-Ego, although Fichte recognizes, as prior to the posit, an "absolute Ego." He points out that the necessity involved in all of these positings is a teleological and dialectical necessity. It was Fichte, indeed, not Hegel, who first presented the process of the dialectic as consisting of Thesis, Antithesis, and Synthesis, and so-named the stages. The activity of reason itself requires that posit, counterposit, and synthesis mark its progress.

(4) Since the necessity which we seemed at first to find in nature exists only in our own thought, we need not take it, or nature, as seriously as we did initially. Indeed, the moral consciousness, telling us that we are free, and alone responsible for our actions, is not in the same class as our positing of causality, and is given primacy over the latter.

(5) The primacy of the moral consciousness requires not a world of "pictures" but a world in which we can act responsibly and fulfill our duties to others—a spiritual world, that is to say, as over against the sensual world of objects determined in space and time.

(6) But why should we posit the sensible world at all? We do so in order to be able to increase our virtue in meeting the obstacles this world places in our way.

(7) The exercise of our duties toward each other leads us to our human vocation, which would seem to be an ethical world culture dedicated to the preservation of the freedom and rights of every man. The states in which we now live

have their true purpose in providing for our rights and freedoms.

(8) And beyond this vocation, and our moral consciousness, is that spiritual and moral order, which can be identified with God himself—God not as a separate Being, Creator, or Cause of the world, but as the Word, or *Logos*, in all that truly is. Since God (Fichte also calls Him "Being" and "Absolute") includes all there is, creation is not compatible with His nature. And since He is eternal, all is completed within Him. And since both myself and other humans are now part of the moral order which is one with God, we are even now one with God, our wills with His will, and with each other, and not God alone, but even I am "unchangeable, firm, and completed for all eternity; for this is no existence assumed from without—it is my own true, essential life and being." And so in the end, Fichte presents us with the paradox of philosophical Idealism, that double focus in which human life and the world generally struggle toward an ideal which, in fact, has already been achieved.

FICINO, MARSILIO. 1433–1499.

Italian philosopher, born at Figline. Educated in Florence. He was received into the household of Cosimo de'Medici who made Marsilio head of the Florentine Academy patterned after Plato's Academy in Athens. Surrounded by Renaissance Platonists and Greek scholars, Ficino began his translations of Plato and Plotinus. At 40 he became a priest, and was given the canonry of S. Lorenzo; he preached in his curé of Novoli, and in the cathedral and church of the Anteli in Florence.

Principal writings: *Commentary on Plato's Symposium* (T), 1469; *On the Christian Religion*, 1474; *Platonic Theology*, 1482; as well as his translation of Plato's works, pub. 1483, and a translation of Plotinus, pub. 1492.

(1) Ficino's goal was one of uniting Christian thought and Hellenistic philosophy along Platonic lines. This is accomplished through stressing the common elements in Platonic and Christian love, while also stressing natural revelation in addition to special revelation, and finding natural revelation especially prominent in Plato and Plotinus. Indeed, true philosophy and true religion are identical for Ficino.

(2) The goal of both is union with God through an internal ascent. He stressed the doctrine of innate ideas, Plato's Doctrine of Reminiscence, and the immortality of the soul.

FICTIONALISM.

For Hans Vaihinger (*q.v.* 1, 3) the doctrine that fictitious entities, useful but imaginary concepts and principles, lie at the basis of mathematics, science, philosophy, law, and religion.

FICTIONS OF THE STATUE.

Q.v. Condillac (2).

FIDEISM.

In Catholic thought the view of Abbé Louis Bautain (*q.v.*) that faith precedes reason with respect to knowledge of God, and that in this respect reason is metaphysically incompetent. The doctrine was condemned in an 1855 decretal.

FIDENS QUAERENS INTELLECTUM.

Latin phrase meaning "faith seeking understanding." The position held by St. Augustine (*q.v.* 11) and St. Anselm (*q.v.* 8) among others.

'FIDO'-FIDO FALLACY.

A fallacy ascribed by Ryle to Carnap, consisting of thinking that every expression is a kind of name. Austin assigns the view to Plato, and Dummet extends this assignment to Frege, who applied the term "name" to every logically unitary expression. This contrasts with the de Saussure and Wittgenstein position that words get their sense by relation of their uses to the uses of other words.

FIELD.

Q.v. Logic of Relations (2).

FIGURE, GALENIAN.

The fourth figure of the syllogism named after Galen who added it to the three figures of Aristotle. *Q.v.* Syllogism (3); Galen.

FIGURE, SYLLOGISTIC.

Q.v. Syllogism (3).

FILIOQUE.

Latin term meaning "and the Son." The

term or phrase, added to the Nicene Creed at the Third Council of Toledo, 589, probably as a result of the continuing Arian controversy, led to the final separation of the Eastern and Western churches. The added term raised theological issues concerning the nature of the Trinity, and the single or double procession of the Holy Spirit. The disputed passage of the creed reads, "I believe in the Holy Ghost, the Lord and Giver of life, who proceedeth from the Father and the Son."

FILMER, SIR ROBERT. c. 1588–1653.

English political writer. Educated at Cambridge. Knighted by Charles I at the beginning of the latter's reign, his house was plundered many times by the Parliamentarians. Filmer nonetheless remained a firm supporter of the king, and of the doctrine of the divine right of kings. It is for the latter that Filmer is principally known, being recognized as its principal advocate in his time. John Locke (*q.v.* 9) for this reason directed his two treatises on government against Filmer. Filmer's argument was largely Biblical, attempting to trace a succession from Noah to the rulers of the states of Europe.

Principal writings: *Freeholder's Grand Inquest*, 1648; *Anarchy of a Limited and Mixed Monarchy*, 1648; *Observations*, 1652; *The Power of Kings*, 1680; *Patriarcha*, 1680.

FINAL CAUSE.

(1) That one of Aristotle's four causes which supports the hylozoistic interpretation of matter (*q.v.* Hylozoism). Final cause has human purposiveness as its paradigm, and generalizes purpose beyond the human realm. One must suppose, with Aristotle, that the unattained state of the oak can exercise causal power over the acorn (*q.v.* Aristotle 9).

(2) Scholastic philosophy continued the Aristotelian philosophy, including emphasis on final cause.

(3) The monadology of Leibniz (*q.v.* 1) emphasized final cause to the exclusion of efficient causation in the unfolding of the inner history of each monad.

(4) Modern science in its development reduced the operative sphere of final causation to living forms. Kant (*q.v.* 11g) analyzed the resultant situation in his *Critique of Judgment*.

(5) Bergson (*q.v.* 4–6) and Whitehead (*q.v.* 16–17, 24) both effect a balance between efficient and final causation, treating the former as operating from the past, and the latter as operating, in some sense, from the future. Also *q.v.* Teleology.

FINITE.

Q.v. Infinite.

FIRST CAUSE.

One of the names of God, derived from the argument—formulated by Aristotle (*q.v.* 10)—that every causal chain requires a first, uncaused cause. *Q.v.* God (B.); Cosmological Argument.

FIRST HEAVEN.

For Aristotle, the outermost sphere, identified with the region of the fixed stars.

FIRST INTENTION, TERMS OF.

Q.v. William of Ockham (2); Intentionality (1–2).

FIRST PHILOSOPHY.

In Aristotle's sense the study of being as being. This, along with Theology, is the name Aristotle gave to the book we now call *Metaphysics*, and to the discipline as well, a study of the concepts existing within and extending beyond specific fields of inquiry.

FISCHER, KUNO.

Q.v. Trendelenburg.

FISKE, JOHN. 1842–1901.

American philosopher. Born in Hartford, Connecticut. Educated at Harvard. Lecturer and Librarian at Harvard. Adopting and, to some extent, developing Spencer's view of evolution, Fiske upheld an evolutionary theism which stands as precursor to the doctrine of emergent evolution.

Principal writings: *Outlines of Cosmic Philosophy*, 2 vols., 1874; *The Unseen World*, 1876; *The Destiny of Man*, 1884; *The Idea of God*, 1885; *Through Nature to God*, 1899.

FIVE PILLARS OF DEISM.

Q.v. Herbert of Cherbury (1).

FLAGELLANTS.

A penitential movement in the Middle Ages characterized by processions of men scourging themselves with leather thongs and iron whips. Outpourings of this sort into the streets of Europe occurred in 1259 and 1349.

FLATUS VOCIS.

Latin phrase meaning "mere word." Anselm (*q.v.* 7) and Abelard (*q.v.* 1) charged that Roscelin (*q.v.*) held the universal to be a mere word, thus opening the issue of nominalism (*q.v.*) with respect to the problem of universals (*q.v.* 11).

FLAVIUS ARRIANUS.

Q.v. Epictetus.

FLETCHER, JOSEPH.

Q.v. Situation Ethics.

FLEWELLING, R.T.

Q.v. Personalism (9).

FLORENTINE ACADEMY. 15th century.

An attempt to duplicate in Florence, the cultural center of the Renaissance, the famous Academy established by Plato in Athens, the cultural center of the ancient world. A meeting in Florence of the Council for the Union of Greek and Latin Churches brought to Florence the Neoplatonist Gemistos Plethon (*q.v.*) who lectured on Plato and the Alexandrian mystics. When Florentine society responded to his lectures with enthusiasm he suggested reviving in Florence the Platonic Academy. Cosimo de' Medici responded positively, naming Marsilio Ficino (*q.v.*) as its head. Among the members of the academy, apart from the Medici family, were Angelo Poliziano, Cristoforo Landino, Demetrios Chalchondylas, and Giovanni Pico della Mirandola (*q.v.*). The academy served to relate Florence to the whole field of scholarship providing an important service of translating Greek and Alexandrian works; the Neoplatonism of the academy, especially Ficino's concept of Platonic love, exercised a strong influence over 16th-century European literature.

FLUDD, ROBERT. 1574–1637.

English mystical philosopher. Born in Milgate, Kent. Educated at Oxford. Influenced by Paracelsus (*q.v.*) and the then-new movement of Rosicrucianism (*q.v.*), Fludd divided the cosmos into an archetypal world, a macrocosm, and the microcosm. Man, the microcosm, relates to the macrocosm and the divine archetypal world by sympathetic correspondences. Fludd's more extreme views were attacked by a list of notable thinkers including Kepler, Mersenne, and Gassendi. His writings are in Latin.

Principal writings: *Defense of the Fraternity of the Roseate Cross*, 1616; *Account of Both Worlds, Greater and Lesser*, 1617–21.

FLUX.

Q.v. Buddha (6); Heraclitus (1).

FOCAL, THE.

Q.v. Polanyi (2).

FODOR, JERRY A. 1935– .

American philosopher, born in New York City. Educated at Columbia and Princeton. Has taught at Illinois and M.I.T.; currently at the City University of New York.

Principal writings: *Psychological Explanation*, 1965; *The Language of Thought*, 1975; *Representations*, 1981; *Modularity of Mind*, 1983; *Psychosemantics*, 1987; *A Theory of Content and Other Essays*, 1990.

(1) Applying a variant of Chomsky's (*q.v.* 7) innatism to psychological explanations, while denying operationalism and behaviorism, Fodor defends a representational theory of mind in which thought is computational, following its own internal code.

(2) This "language of thought," analogous to the machine language of computers, is involved in all concept learning. Since logical intension implies intentionality (*q.v.* 3–4) the language of thought may be said to have "intrinsic intentionality," its mental representations feeding content into our sentences.

(3) These "*bona fide* mental phenomena," even though computational, are not Turing machines (*q.v.*). They are parts of one's private language, *contra* Wittgenstein's (*q.v.* 8) arguments against this possibility.

(4) We effect changes in the world by manipulating the syntax of our internal representational systems. This means that the physical states of our organisms can, and (often) do, obey the constraints of language, although "no adequate account" of how this happens is yet available.

Q.v. Folk Psychology (2); Semantics (7).

FOLK PSYCHOLOGY.

The untutored level of interaction in which we approach each other as intentional systems, *i.e.*, as individuals of desire, belief, hope, and expectation. To be distinguished from cognitive psychology which presumes a nonintentional and perhaps mechanistic level of analysis. The distinction between the two approaches has become important as cognitive science (*q.v.*) has developed.

(1) The folk-psychological (*i.e.*, commonsense) view of propositions is that they are discrete mental entities, possessing causal force, capable of interacting with other propositions to produce conclusions and behavioral consequences. The same was held to be true of the broader category of propositional attitudes—beliefs, desires, hopes, fears, etc.

(2) In cognitive psychology, or cognitive science, the connectionist model of representation replaces discrete propositions with subsymbolic, transient, and shifting nodes in a network of encoded information. While Jerry Fodor (*q.v.* 2–3) and Z. W. Pylyshyn (*Computation and Cognition*, 1984) defend the language of thought, doubting that strict connectionism is viable (Fodor and Pylyshyn, "Connectionism and Cognitive Architecture," 1988), Stephen Stich (*q.v.*) (*From Folk Psychology to Cognitive Science*, 1983) suspects that, strictly speaking, the propositions and propositional attitudes of folk psychology do not even exist. Daniel Dennett (*q.v.* 2–5) uses the device of *homunculi* (*q.v.*) to bridge between the emphases of folk psychology and connectionism.

FOLKWAYS.

Q.v. Sumner (1).

FOLLESDAL, DAGFINN.

Q.v. Quantifying In (4).

FONSECA, PETER. 1528–1599.

Portuguese philosopher. Taught at Coimbra. A neo-Scholastic, he was known as the Portuguese Aristotle. His works are in Latin.

Principal writings: *Commentary on the Books of the Metaphysics*, 4 vols., 1577–89, 1604, 1612; *Introduction to Philosophy*, 1591.

FONS VITAE.

Q.v. Avicebron.

FONTENELLE, BERNARD. 1657–1757.

French philosopher and man of letters. Born at Rouen. Educated in Rouen. Lived in Paris. A nephew of Pierre Corneille (*q.v.*), the founder of French tragedy, Fontanelle combined in himself interests and abilities in literature, science, and philosophy. He was thus able to bridge between the 17th-century French period of science and *belles lettres*, and the 18th-century *philosophes* (*q.v.*) for whom he in a sense prepared the way.

Principal writings: *New Dialogues of the Dead*, 1683; *Conversations on the Plurality of Worlds*, 1686; *Elements of the Infinitesimal Calculus*, 1727; *Defense of the Cartesian Vortices*, 1752.

FORCE.

From the Latin *fortis* ("strong"). In physics the cause of the acceleration in the movement of material bodies. As the etymology of the word suggests, the conception had its origin in human effort, and was transferred to the physical world.

(1) Aristotle (*q.v.* 8), making locomotion the primary motion, was led to interpret force in mechanical terms, requiring contact between bodies. In his view there is a direct proportional relation between force, time, and distance. The view was immensely influential, and only gradually were other alternatives suggested.

(2) In the 14th century Bradwardine found a mathematical difficulty in the Aristotelian view when force and resistance are equal.

(3) At about the same time Buridan (*q.v.*) seems to have anticipated the modern conception of force by regarding it as a space-permeating power able to affect non-contiguous bodies.

(4) Kepler (*q.v.* 2) moved from Pythagorean and Platonic conceptions to the view that force can act at a distance, although its power diminishes with the increase of distance.

(5) Galileo (*q.v.* 2) worked with the mathematical interrelations of motion and force, regarding weight as a continuous force attracted toward the center of the earth.

(6) The three laws of motion expressed by Newton (*q.v.* 2), applied to the idea of gravitation, required a conception of force acting not by contiguity but at a

distance. The conception was for a time qualified by the view that action through an ether restored the notion of contiguity.

FOREKNOWLEDGE.

The doctrine that God has knowledge of the future, divine eternal awareness containing all events in *totum simul* (*q.v.*). It is sometimes argued that in this manner divine omniscience (*q.v.*) is compatible with human freedom.

FORGE, LOUIS DE LA. 17th cent.

French philosopher. One of the Occasionalists (*q.v.*), Forge held that God did not intervene whenever there was a motion from body to mind or mind to body; rather, in a Leibnizian manner, he arranged the harmony of the two happenings in the creation of the universe.

Principal writings: *Treatise on the Human Soul*, 1661.

FORM.

From the Latin *forma* (probably from *ferire* "to strike, hew," thus to create a recognizable thing). *Forma* is a translation of the Greek term *idea* or *eidos*.

(1) For Plato (*q.v.* 1, 9) the individual thing with its class character is explained by the interaction of form and receptacle. The form is received in matter. This constitutes the individual thing and makes it an imitation of the eternal form in which it participates. In this view the eternal forms possess a higher reality than do their temporal imitations.

(2) Aristotle (*q.v.* 7) eliminated separable forms, except for God and other unmoved movers, leaving only the imitations, that is, the instances of formed matter. Individual substances, apart from the exceptions noted, now became the highest reality. Form is more real than matter but since in this view form is not able to exist by itself it is less real than the individual substance.

(3) Avicebron (*q.v.* 1) held that since matter could not be the principle of individuation, form must perform this function. This implies that individual spiritual substances are possible.

(4) Gilbert of Poiters (*q.v.* 2) argued for "native forms," as the ground of species and genus, having their exemplars in the mind of God.

(5) Thomas Aquinas (*q.v.* 5) and other

Scholastics followed Aristotle so closely with respect to the way in which the term "form" is used that one might well speak of the Aristotelian-Thomistic, or Aristotelian-Scholastic, tradition. The term "form" is used in many ways in this tradition: (a) "Substantial form" determines the being to a definite kind or class; for Aristotle "substantial form" and essence (*q.v.*) have the same meaning. For Aquinas it is "substantial form" and prime matter which constitute essence. (b) The properties of a thing are forms or aspects of forms, part of its essence, or determined by its essence. (c) "Accidental form" is a characteristic or quality of a thing not determined by the essence of the thing. (d) "Sensible form" is the form of outward objects separated from matter through sense-perception. (e) "Universals" (*q.v.*) are forms rising in sense-perception, and made intelligible by reason. (f) "Formal cause" is the essence or nature of a thing as a constituent of being. (g) "Natural forms" are distinguished from "artificial" (*i.e.*, manmade) forms. (h) Sometimes "physical form" (*i.e.*, the form of an individual thing) is distinguished from "metaphysical form" (*i.e.*, the form of the genus of a thing). (i) "Non-subsistent" or material form (existing only in matter) is distinguished from "subsistent" form which can exist separately from matter (*q.v.* Subsistence 1).

(6) Duns Scotus (*q.v.* 5, 7) followed the lead of Avicebron, stressing the *quidditas* in substances of all types. Scotus laid stress on the term *haecceitas*, or "this-ness" of individual being.

(7) William of Ockham (*q.v.* 9) held form to be the structure of the material parts of a body.

(8) For Immanuel Kant (*q.v.* 3) form and matter are equivalent to structure and content. (a) Matter is identified with sensation, and form with the conceptions which order sensation. (b) Space and time are presented as the pure forms of sensibility. (c) The categories are presented as the pure forms of the understanding. (d) Reason is viewed as regulative over, and not beyond, phenomena.

(9) For Cassirer (*q.v.* 2) the task of philosophy is that of tracing out the development of symbolic forms in all areas of thought.

FORMAL CAUSE.
Q.v. Aristotle (9); Form (5f).

FORMAL DISTINCTION.
Q.v. Duns Scotus (6).

FORMALISM.
The tendency to emphasize form as over against content.

(1) In ethics (*q.v.* 3) the tendency is most pronounced in Kant (*q.v.* 6) and in Deontological Ethics (*q.v.* Deontology) generally.

(2) In mathematics, formalism refers to a program of deriving all of mathematics from the smallest possible number of axioms by rules of formation and rules of inference. Frege (*q.v.* 1) first showed that it was possible to formalize arithmetic in terms of logic alone. Gödel's (*q.v.* 1) incompleteness theorem showed that a proof of consistency for a logical system cannot be formalized within the system. H.B. Curry (*q.v.*) substituted "empirical formalism" for the alternative approaches stressing consistency alone.

FORMALITER IN SE IPSIUS.
Q.v. Descartes (7).

FORMISM.
Q.v. S.C. Pepper (1).

FORMS OF LIFE.
A term introduced by Wittgenstein (*q.v.* 8) and employed extensively by Peter Winch (1926–) (*The Idea of a Social Science*, 1958; "Understanding a Primitive Society," 1964). In Wittgenstein's use "forms of life" are implicit in language (including the language of mathematics) and relate to the agreement among users of a language to follow certain rules. In speaking a language one participates in a form of life. Winch extends the analysis to say that religion, art, history, the sciences, as well as certain life styles, are forms of life whose principles, percepts, definitions, formulae, criteria of intelligibility, and views of reality are internal and not external.

FORMULA OF CONCORD.
Q.v. Luther (16b).

FOUCAULT, MICHEL. 1926–1984.
French philosopher, and psychologist. Born in Poitiers. Educated at the École Normale Supérieure and the University of Paris. Taught at the universities of Clermont-Ferrand, Paris-Vincennes and at the Collège de France. Initially a structuralist (*q.v.*), he is now regarded by many as post-structuralist (*q.v.*).

Principal writings: *Mental Illness and Psychology*, rev. ed., (T), 1954; *Madness and Civilization*, rev. ed., (T), 1961; *The Birth of the Clinic: an Archaeology of Medical Perception* (T), 1963; *The Order of Things: an Archaeology of the Human Sciences* (T), 1966; *The Archaeology of Knowledge* (T), 1969; *This Is Not a Pipe* (T), 1973; *Discipline and Punish* (T), 1975; *History of Sexuality* (T), 3 vols., 1976–84; *Language, Counter-Memory, Practice: Selected Essays and Interviews* (T), 1977; *Power/Knowledge: Selected Interviews and Other Writings, 1972–77* (T), 1980; "On the Genealogy of Ethics: an Overview of Work in Progress" (T), 1983; *Politics, Philosophy, Culture, 1977–84* (T), 1988.

(1) Reflecting, in his initial writings, the structuralist (*q.v.* 6) thesis which tends to equate reality with language, he had changed, by the 1970's to a post-structuralist (*q.v.*) view where knowledge is seen to be enmeshed in power relations. He has said both that his philosophical position lies at the intersection of "Nietzsche, Freud, Marx"; and that his philosophical heritage comes from Hegel and the Frankfurt School, passing through Nietzsche and Weber. The strongest influence would seem to be that of Nietzsche and especially his "genealogical" method which was also appreciated by Horkheimer and Adorno in the Frankfurt School (*q.v.* A.).

(2) Ideas being context-dependent call for an "archaeology of knowledge." One moves through the archaeological investigation, tracing the "genealogies" of the ideas involved, discovering the manner in which they are linked to and shaped by "systems of power."

(3) Foucault calls the historical shaping of a concept at a given time its *episteme*. Since "knowledge" is context-dependent it can be used in the plural. There are different *epistemes* at work at different times. This means that there are different procedures for "the production, regulation, distribution and operation of statements" at these times. In a succession of books he has reported on his ar-

chaeological investigation of mental illness, medicine, the human sciences, punishment, and sexuality. He has also pointed out that capitalist and Marxist economies have the same genealogy. Marxism simply offers a utopian version, and the capitalist Ricardo, a pessimistic version, of the same economic *episteme*.

(4) Since the will to truth is everywhere determined by the exercise of power, Foucault applies his genealogical method to what he calls "power/knowledge." Sometimes he calls it an "analytics of power."

(5) One might say that Foucault refuses to address the epistemological question. Since the wills to truth and power are always intermixed, Foucault will only speak of regimes of truth. The "regime" of truth within a given society is empowered and deployed by "multiple forms of constraint," including accepted types of discourse, mechanisms for distinguishing true from false statements, and the status granted to those charged with saying what is true.

(6) Although dealing with history almost exclusively, his concern is not antiquarian. The history he writes is a "history of the present." At times he says he is doing an "ontology of the present." But his avowed interest is the definition of the self, that human subject produced historically from the social world.

(7) The constraints of power may be moderated by an approach to ethics and self-definition interpreted as an "aesthetics of existence." In this approach, one shapes one's existence into "a work of art," through attention to one's body and its feelings. The element of self-control in aesthetic self-definition is what Foucault means by ethics.

FOUCHER, SIMON. 1644–1696.

French philosopher. Born at Dijon. Educated at the Sorbonne. An opponent of Malebranche and critic of both Descartes and Leibniz, Foucher revived the skeptical arguments of the Academy (*q.v.* Plato's Academy 4), directing them against contemporary philosophers. The fundamental doctrines of the Church seemed to him intuitively evident, and his philosophical goal was to reconcile his religion with philosophy.

Principal writings: *On the Wisdom of the Ancients*, 1682; *Essays in the Search for the Truth*, 1693.

FOUILLÉE, ALFRED. 1838–1912.

French philosopher. An historian of philosophy concentrating especially on Socrates and Plato, he viewed his own system as "voluntaristic idealism." He argued for the reality of human freedom on the basis of *idée force* (thought-force), crediting the mind with a power of efficient causality through the tendency of ideas to realize themselves.

Selected writings: *The Evolution of Thought-Forces*, 1890; *The Psychology of Thought-Forces*, 1893; *The Ethics of Thought-Forces*, 1908.

FOUNDATIONALISM.

Q.v. Epistemology (8).

FOUR ELEMENTS, THE.

Earth, air, fire, and water were regarded as the basic constituents of the universe in many ancient cosmologies (*q.v.* Empedocles 2; Hinduism 6).

FOURIER, FRANÇOIS CHARLES MARIE. 1772–1837.

French socialist writer. Born at Besançon, and educated in its college. Although his economic resources were always very limited his entire life was spent in working out his theories.

Principal writings: *Theory of the Four Movements*, 1808; *Theory of Universal Unity*, 2 vols., 1822; *The New Industrial World*, 1829; *Snares and Charlatanism in the Two Sects of Saint-Simon and Owen*, 1831; *The False Industry*, 2 vols., 1835.

(1) Holding that the exercise of the passions is normal and good, for our passional nature has come from God, Fourier finds a natural harmony among them. Misery and vice originate in the unnatural restraints imposed by society upon men, destroying the natural harmony of the passions. Society must be reconstructed; and the principle of its reconstruction is co-operative industry, which in his view required a division of society into *phalanges* of 1600 persons, each *phalange* occupying a common building or *Phalanstère*. The central occupation of each *phalange* was to be agricultural; but on his principle of harmony each person should be able to select an occupation

to his taste, and work need never be irksome.

(2) The revenue of the *phalange* was to be first divided so as to give each member subsistence; the revenue remaining after this was to be divided, with 5/12 going to labor, 4/12 to capital, 3/12 to talent.

(3) Private property was not to be abolished, but rich and poor were to be intermingled in the *phalanstères*. While holding to the abolition of the institution of marriage, he suggested that private apartments in the *phalanstères* would allow private family life to continue where desired.

(4) A few *phalanges* were organized in Europe; between 1840 and 1850, 41 were organized in the United States of which the Brook Farm experiment is best known.

FOX, GEORGE. 1624–1691.

Founder of the "Society of Friends" (Quakers). Born at Drayton, Leicestershire, England. After a religious childhood, he in 1643 "at the command of God" broke off all relationship with old and young. There followed four years of wandering, ending in 1647 with the hearing of a voice: "There is one, even Christ Jesus, that can speak to thy condition." Following this he preached for the first time. Imprisoned eight times on such charges as disturbing the peace, blasphemy, attending meetings forbidden by law or, in his words, for "declaring truth," he used the time thus made available in writing. It was at the end of one of these terms of imprisonment that he made his inexplicable barefoot walk through the streets of Litchfield calling out, "Woe to the bloody city of Litchfield." But it is worth pointing out that Lord Cromwell interviewed him in 1655, finding his character and tenets blameless. And William Penn, during Fox's two-year visit to America found him "civil beyond all forms of breeding." Besides preaching throughout England, he led preaching missions to Barbados, Jamaica, North America, Holland and Germany.

Principal writings: *Journal*, 1694.

(1) The truth which "opened" to him led to the doctrine of the inner light, an immediate relationship with God with an authority beyond that of any institution, whether church or state. One's loyalties and obligations to the Supreme Being, defined by direct revelation, have a bearing on one's loyalties and obligations within society. And Fox refused to take an oath, bear arms, or remove his hat in deference to any person. Quaker pacifism likewise reflects the doctrine of the inner light. Fox helped shape the governing system of monthly (local), quarterly (sub-regional), and yearly (regional) meetings. The structure of the service provides ample opportunity to avail oneself of the inner light.

(2) Quakers were to be found throughout the colonies by the time of Fox's visit in 1671, with their center in Rhode Island. With the 1681 grant of Pennsylvania to the distinguished Quaker, William Penn, the center gravitated southward. In the ensuing years, divisions occurred within the society between evangelical and orthodox Quakers; but their testimony has been consistently humanitarian and peaceful.

FRACTALS.

Q.v. Chaos Theory (4–7).

FRANCISCANS.

Q.v. Francis of Assisi.

FRANCIS OF ASSISI, ST. 1182–1226.

Founder of the Franciscans. Born in Assisi, a town in Umbria. Son of a prosperous cloth merchant, he led an active life, social and military, until the onset of a serious illness in 1203. Between 1203 and 1209 solitude, prayer, a pilgrimage to Rome, ministering to lepers and outcasts, disinheriting himself from his father, prepared Francis for the call to begin his mission preaching to the poor. He gained disciples almost at once, and soon Pope Innocent III gave his sanction to Francis' program of preaching and work among the poor. Throughout Umbria a powerful religious revival testified to the validity of the Franciscan testimony.

(1) The order of friars increased in number, extending throughout Italy, and into other countries. In 1212 the "Second Order," that of the nuns, was instituted. In his final years the "Third Order" (Tertiaries), called the "Brothers and Sisters of Penance," was organized. The "Third Order" consisted of committed laity, men and women living out to the best of their

ability the Franciscan principles without withdrawing from the world.

(2) Between 1212 and 1220 Francis made three trips to the Holy Land to preach to the Saracens and Moors. The third trip was the most successful. In 1224 after a vision the stigmata are said to have appeared on his body.

(3) Francis carried through life what has been characterized as "an enthusiastic love of poverty." This was one aspect, apparently, of a spirit of continual rejoicing present in Francis, and enforced as a precept in his order. His rapturous love of nature was another consequence of this spirit.

(4) In drawing up the rule for the Franciscans, Francis insisted on the strictest observance of the vows of chastity, poverty, and obedience. In 1220 Francis resigned as head of the order over disagreement within the order concerning the strictness of the rule. Disagreements continued and, today, in addition to the divisions already discussed, the Franciscans exist as the Friars Minor, the Friars Minor Conventual, and the Friars Minor Capuchin. The Friars Minor preserve the strict rule of St. Francis. The Friars Minor Conventual, or simply Conventuals, favored the holding of property in common, and utilizing the income. Consequently, their churches and other buildings manifest a greater richness of material and decoration. The order of the Capuchins appeared in 1526, founded by Friar Matteo de Bascio in an effort to restore the strict austerity of St. Francis.

FRANCIS OF PAULA, ST.
Q.v. Minimi.

FRANCK, SEBASTIAN. 1499–1542.

A Dominican turned Lutheran, Franck was not accepted by Luther and Melanchthon due to his heretical leanings. Luther called him a "devil's mouth." Franck left Lutheranism eventually, holding that his allegiance was to the "church universal" rather than to any single denomination.

FRANK, PHILIPP. 1884–1966.

Austrian-American philosopher of science. One of the founders of the Vienna Circle (q.v.).

Principal writings: The Law of Causality and its Boundaries, 1932; The Aim of Mechanistic Physics, 1935; Between Physics and Philosophy (E), 1941; Modern Science and its Philosophy (E), 1949; "Comments on Realistic Versus Phenomenalistic Interpretations" (E), 1950.

FRANKFURT SCHOOL, THE. 1923–72.

A movement in German social thought initiated by the establishment of the Institute of Social Relations at the University of Frankfurt in the early days of the Weimar Republic. One reason for its appearance was the felt need to rethink what Marxism should be in the aftermath of the Russian Revolution. The School had three distinct periods, which can be only roughly indicated by its successive relocations.

A. The first period runs from the time of its foundation in 1923, until 1933 when its headquarters and personnel moved to New York City. The first director, Carl Grünberg, was an economist and social historian; under him the school concentrated on empirical analysis. The type of work produced in this period can be illustrated by citing Grossmann's The Laws of Accumulation and Breakdown of Capitalist Systems, and Friedrich Pollock's Soviet Planning and Automation, both 1929. Others of Pollock's essays, including those of the 1930's and '40's were published as The Economic and Social Consequences of Automation (T), 1957, and as The Stages of Capitalism, 1975. Also, Franz Neumann's Behemoth: The Structure and Practice of National Socialism '33–'34, 1944. Otto Kirchheimer's Punishment and Social Structure (with G. Rusche) was published by the Institute in 1939; his Political Justice appeared in 1961. Most of the early members were Frankfurt educated, Pollock, for example, having been a founding member. Leo Lowenthal was a senior research associate of the Institute from 1926–33, and Kirchheimer from 1934–42. The emphasis turned to social philosophy when Max Horkheimer became director in January, 1931. His inaugural address described social philosophy as the source of important questions to be investigated by the specialized social sciences. Erich Fromm was a member, lecturing at the Institute (on social psychology) from 1929–32; and Fromm's interest in relating Freud and Marx would bear later fruit in the Institute's history. Finally Walter Benjamin, significant literary critic and collaborator with members of the Institute, and research associate of the Paris branch, worked with questions of aesthetics and theory of culture, preceding the work of Theodor Adorno who began his association with the Institute in 1928.

B. All of these themes were underway when Hitler became Chancellor of Germany in 1933. Reading the future with unusual prescience, the School responded by relocating in Geneva (Feb., 1933), then going into exile in New York City in 1935, establishing an affiliation with Columbia University which endured until its return to Frankfurt, Germany in 1950. Otto Kirchheimer, an exile from Nazi Germany, was a co-worker in the Institute during these years (1934–42), although his major writings, *e.g.*, *Political Justice* (1861), are of later date. Horkheimer continued as director throughout this period, with Adorno becoming his close associate. During these years the School gained definition.

(1) Horkheimer was the protagonist, attacking positivism, scientism, and modern empiricism. The Vienna Circle of Logical Positivists (*q.v.*) provided a convenient target. Positivism, he argued, places humans in a false position, separating fact from value, and knowledge from all other human interests. This approach is a reflection of bourgeois society and needs to be replaced by a "dialectical theory" capable of reflecting reality in its totality. The replacement would be a "critical theory" of society, superseding the "traditional theory" of positivism and empiricism (see "The Latest Attack on Metaphysics," and "Traditional and Critical Theory," both 1937 essays collected in *Critical Theory* (T), 1972). This general emphasis was continued and developed throughout the movement.

(2) Horkheimer and Adorno collaborated in the development of this thesis in the *Dialectic of Enlightenment* (T), 1944, where the Enlightenment itself was viewed as containing the seeds of its own destruction. The "self-destruction of the Enlightenment" proceeded from the "false clarity" of its theory of knowledge harboring, as they claimed, both positiv-

ism and scientism. This false ideal, indeed, is the cause of the cultural decline and descent into the barbarism of the present age.

(3) The descent is illustrated by their radical claim that the movement of National Socialism is to be thought of as primarily a movement of anti-semitism. This is to be contrasted with the analysis of the German system in A. above: Franz Neumann's view of Germany as a late stage of capitalism which he termed "totalitarian monopoly capitalism," (*Behemoth, Supra*), and Pollock's view of the system as a "state capitalism" in which power replaces profit and with technical rationality as its guiding principle. Horkheimer, too, spoke of the domination of "technological rationality" in the system, controlled by politics rather than economics; that is simply another side of the claim that anti-semitism is the paranoia of the Enlightenment. Otto Kirchheimer (1905–1965) had lamented the consequence of National Socialism with its antagonism toward "individual rights" in the last issue of the Frankfurt School's journal, *Zeitschrift für Sozialforschung* (1932–65, although published in English, 1939–41, under the name *Studies in Philosophy and Social Science*).

(4) The Horkheimer-Adorno position finally had a triple thrust: a critique of positivism and scientism in theory of knowledge, especially in the social sciences; the presence of technical or technological rationality as a new form of domination; the development of a "culture industry" giving impetus to the phenomenon of "mass culture," with power to abort and silence all criticism.

(5) In the first issue of the Frankfurt School journal (1932), Horkheimer had argued for interpreting psychology with Marxist social theory, and Erich Fromm held that psychoanalysis could provide the needed connection. A number of studies were conducted in the 1930's with this in mind, Fromm functioning either as project director or participant. To make the connection, however, Fromm interpreted Marx in terms of his early writings on alienation (the *Economic and Philosophic Manuscripts*), while revising Freud's analysis, dropping the death wish, the Oedipus complex, and the libido theory. When Horkheimer and

Adorno criticized publicly this "revisionist" interpretation of Freud, Fromm withdrew from the Institute (1939). Fromm's interests came to fruition, first of all, in his influential analysis of Hitler's authoritarian personality in *Escape From Freedom* (1941). Related work soon followed (*q.v.* Fromm).

(6) Herbert Marcuse became a member of the Institute in Europe in 1933, emigrating to the United States and continuing with the group at Columbia. Having worked with Heidegger, serving as his assistant from 1928 to 1932, it was natural that his first attempt to revise Marxist social theory would be by way of synthesis with Heidegger's existentialism. When Marx's *Economic and Philosophical Manuscripts* was published in 1932, however, he found in the early Marx the version of Marxism for which he had been looking. Once in the Institute he helped develop the principles of critical theory ("Philosophical and Critical Theory," in *Critical Theory*); he argued that positivism was a more likely cause of Nazism than Hegelian thought, which latter leads, instead, to Marxist social theory (*Reason and Revolution*, 1941). *Eros and Civilization*, 1951, gave his synthesis of Marx and Freud, in which the achievement of abundance is seen to allow the elimination of "surplus-repression." Finally, in *One Dimensional Man*, (1964), Marcuse continued the Horkheimer-Adorno criticism of advanced industrial societies in which modern technology is responsible for one-dimensional mass conformity. During the period of student unrest in the 1960's, Marcuse briefly believed that student activists, ethnic minorities in the United States, and the poor of the underdeveloped world would fill the revolutionary role Marx had predicted for the proletariat, centering the opposition to the "administered" society. By this time, of course the School had returned to Frankfurt, while Marcuse continued his career in America.

C. Back in Frankfurt Horkheimer's role as director continued until 1958. Although Horkheimer and Adorno were equally prominent in the Institute in 1950, Adorno's role gradually increased. He became co-director in 1955. Horkheimer spent a number of years teaching in the United States, and returned in 1959.

Adorno became director, continuing in that role until his death in 1969. The Institute gradually came to reflect Adorno's views which differed from those of Horkheimer in several respects.

(7) The anti-positivism of Horkheimer was continued by Adorno, both in papers presented to social scientists ("Contemporary German Sociology," early 1950's) and in what was presented as a debate with Karl Popper (see the introduction by Adorno to *The Positive Dispute in German Sociology*, 1969; as Popper claimed, his own view was never really considered).

(8) Since Adorno (*q.v.* 1, 5) rejected totality as a vestige of the identity thinking which must be left behind, he could agree with Horkheimer that the weakness of positivism lay in its failure to put facts into a total structure, but the weakness was not unique to philosophy. It reflected the inescapable fragmentation of human life.

(9) The rejection is made explicit in Adorno's *Negative Dialectics*, and derives from his philosophy of aesthetics. Where science merely reflects existing reality, in authentic art one finds intimations of subjectivity and freedom which become lost in its formal organization. These intimations combine superior cognition with subversive potentiality. Similarly in society, insights emerge (and are at once repressed) concerning what life could be under other conditions.

D. Most prominent among the second generation members of the Frankfurt School, Jürgen Habermas (*q.v.*) studied with Adorno in the 1950's and carried the interests of the School into the 1970's. Formally resigning from the Frankfurt School in 1972 (and joining the Max Planck Institute), his total body of work can be seen as a fulfillment of the Frankfurt legacy.

(10) Where Adorno had stepped outside the Marxist framework in his negative dialectics, Habermas returned to the total problem, regarding himself a "Marxist theoretician" working under changed historical circumstances, still directing himself toward discovery of the appropriate "Critical Theory" of society.

(11) He continued the Frankfurt critique of positivism, participating in continued dialogue with Karl Popper in the

1960's. His own corrective to positivism differed from Horkheimer's in totality, and from Adorno's fragmented insight. Like Horkheimer, Habermas found the corrective in "dialectical theory," but he is much clearer in the way he relates the details of scientific theory to social criteria. Empirical science, with positivism and technological reason in its train is used by powerful social interests, while hermeneutical science (cultural science), capable of relieving the fact-value tension, stresses symbolic communication and intersubjectivity. Both approaches to knowledge are based on human interests. There is nothing more foundational than that; but the hermeneutic, cultural approach is more adequate. He never supposed that anything else was superior to science, as did Horkheimer who put "philosophy" in that position, and Adorno "art." In recent years however, Habermas has continued to specify responses to the issues which defined the School. Some of that material is to be found under his name.

FRANKLIN, MRS. CHRISTINE LADD.
Q.v. Antilogism.

FRAVASHI.
Guardian angels of the faithful in Zoroastrianism (*q.v.* 1).

FREEDOM.
From the Middle English *fredom* ("the state of being free"). The quality of not being constrained by fate, necessity, or circumstance in one's decisions and actions. In the history of philosophy it is possible to distinguish at least four different meanings of freedom. Before one can begin to face the question of whether freedom exists, the definition in use must be elicited, nor is there agreement concerning the meaning of freedom most widely used.

A. Certainly one of the most basic meanings of freedom turns on the idea of significant choice. In this sense freedom means the power of selecting any one of two or more alternatives. If one is free in this sense then, even though choosing "a" in the situation containing "a," "b," and "c," were that identical situation back again one could have chosen "b" or "c," that is, one could have

done other than one did do in that situation. If we have the power to do other than we have done in most of the situations which confront us in life, then we are free in this sense. If one holds this view of freedom it is natural to think of the future as open, or indeterminate. Hence, indeterminism is a natural corollary of this view of freedom.

(1) Although it is somewhat difficult to determine Plato's view here, Aristotle's recognition of the sphere of the voluntary fits into this meaning of freedom. The power of atoms to swerve as postulated by the Epicureans, both Epicurus (*q.v.* 5) and Lucretius (*q.v.* 3), is one manner of expressing indeterminism.

(2) The positions of both St. Augustine (*q.v.* 12) and St. Thomas (*q.v.* 4) support the reality of choice in human life; but in their view freedom of choice is combined with divine foreknowledge, and so with a determined future. It is argued that the inconsistency is only apparent and results from blurring the distinctions between the eternal and temporal realms. St. Augustine, indeed, distinguishes between *liberum arbitrium*, the free choice which implies the power to do evil, and *libertas*, which is the good use of that choice. The divine freedom is that of *libertas*, and not the *liberum arbitrium*.

(3) William of Ockham (*q.v.* 14) believed so strongly in the power of man to cause or not cause effects that he held future events to be contingent (although somehow known by God).

(4) Pico della Mirandola (*q.v.* 3) held that man's freedom of choice gave him a privileged position in the universe.

(5) Descartes (*q.v.* 7) supported freedom as choice, pointing to the sense that one could be doing otherwise, a feeling all of us have in most situations of choice, as evidence supporting the reality of freedom.

(6) Cousin (*q.v.* 2) found the source of freedom in a spontaneity which is its own cause.

(7) Martineau (*q.v.* 3) altered this definition slightly, believing freedom to be the capacity to select among competing motives.

(8) Both Charles Peirce (*q.v.* 6) and William James (*q.v.* 8) believed in freedom as choice, the former supporting

indeterminism with a theory of *tychism* (*q.v.*) and the latter by means of a claim that things are related for the most part by external relations; the claim was embodied in the doctrine of pluralism (*q.v.*).

(9) Bergson (*q.v.* 6–8), Berdyaev (*q.v.* 2) and Whitehead (*q.v.* 9, 15–16) adhered to this doctrine in such fashion that choice and becoming through time are closely related. It is through a selection from the possible, the "maybe's" of the future, that the past becomes determinate, and this happens from moment to moment.

(10) The existentialists, generally, hold to a most extensive freedom of choice. Freedom is inescapable, but often uncomfortable. Sartre (*q.v.* 1–2) stresses the human ambivalence of attitude toward freedom, its vast extent in human life, and the escapist character of doctrines of determinism. A more limited version of the same point of view is to be found in Merleau-Ponty (*q.v.* 3).

B. A second meaning of freedom, consistent with doctrines of determinism, identifies freedom with doing as one wishes. Clearly, whether or not determinism is the case one has wishes. When a wish is gratified by one's own action, even if the having of the wish was determined by a set of causes, one is free on this view.

(11) Holding this view, David Hume (*q.v.* 4) believed liberty to be compatible with necessity, and that the opposite of liberty was not necessity but constraint.

(12) Thomas Hobbes (*q.v.* 2) agreed, finding persons sometimes able to do what they will although the will is shaped by causes proceeding ultimately from the hand of God. He compared freedom to water running freely to the sea.

(13) A theological expression of this view is to be found in Luther (*q.v.* 9) and Jonathan Edwards (*q.v.* 3). Human beings do what they will but their will is determined by God.

(14) Voltaire (*q.v.* 4) in his usual position, found the idea of free choice incomprehensible; we can do what we choose, but what we choose we must necessarily choose, and this is freedom enough.

(15) Many contemporary philosophers of the analytic school tend toward this definition of freedom, and toward necessitarianism; but since they likewise tend to be less metaphysical than their predecessors, the results of their analyses are never given universal statement. Among these may be mentioned Ducasse (*q.v.* 1).

(16) Searle (*q.v.* 6) argued that every intentional action supports freedom in the first definition, although in fact we possess freedom only as "psychological libertarianism" compatible with physical determinism.

C. A third meaning of freedom turns on action which proceeds from internal rather than external motives. This alternative requires a doctrine of man such that man has an underlying nature, or self, in terms of which he can act, rather than acting in conformity with the outer world. This meaning is often connected with the interpretation of freedom as choice, and perhaps the two should be so connected.

(17) Although we have placed Aristotle in the group championing freedom as choice, it is clear that the free man for Aristotle chooses in terms of a developed rational nature. Among the Stoics especially (*q.v.* Stoicism 1) this view is emphasized. Man is free when true to his reasonable nature. Freedom, then, consists partly in limitation, and partly in rational fulfillment; together these qualities allow a life of independence.

(18) Action in terms of one's basic nature is fairly clearly manifest in the Neoplatonic tradition, and possibly in Plato as well. In this tradition freedom and autonomy are found in relation; and this supposes the realizing in the self of the quality of the eternal to which the self belongs in any event.

(19) Spinoza (*q.v.* 9) finds man's freedom in living under the aspect of eternity, sensing the universal in the particular experiences of one's life. He finds it possible to combine this sort of rational autonomy with a causal determinism of the most extreme sort.

(20) Kant (*q.v.* 6) also identifies freedom with autonomy, a quality of human life apparently available to all of us, but at considerable psychic depth. It may be that he combines this view with our first meaning for freedom, since he suggests the presence of determinism in the phenomenal world, and freedom in relation to the noumenal world.

(21) Hegel's (*q.v.* 10, 17) view of freedom is rather complicated but it clearly requires development of what one potentially is, so that one's goal is one's basic reality. Nietzsche (*q.v.* 6) viewed humans as having potential selves which, given the opportunity, would become actual.

D. It is perhaps worthwhile to notice a fourth meaning for freedom.

(22) In St. Augustine (*q.v.* 12) and St. Thomas (*q.v.* 4) one also notices an identification between freedom and the Good. The free act acquires a normative connotation, so that freedom means doing what one ought to do. In this sense God who is perfectly good, and could not be otherwise, is also perfectly free. This is the sense of freedom as *libertas* (*q.v.* 2 above).

(23) Milton (*q.v.* 1–2) made an investigation of freedom in this sense virtually a lifelong occupation, especially in his poetic creations. True liberty requires character, and this means choosing the spiritual over nonspiritual alternatives.

(24) When Rousseau (*q.v.* 5e) associated the general will with the common good, and argued that following the general will retains individual freedom, he was endorsing the fourth definition of freedom, possibly combined with some version of the third definition.

(25) Although Boutroux (*q.v.* 1–3) identifies freedom with contingency (*q.v.* A. above), he fits this section in believing that the maximum freedom is to be found in the moral life.

E. Significant entries concerning freedom which do not fit the classifications used above are set down here.

(26) Epicurus (*q.v.* 6) defined freedom as the power to initiate causes.

(27) Victor Cousin (*q.v.* 2) held that freedom rested on "spontaneous apperception."

(28) Carlyle (*q.v.* 3) defined freedom as "the right of the ignorant to be governed by the wise."

(29) For Ardigó (*q.v.* 4) freedom consists in the fact that chance exists at the intersections of individual causal series.

(30) Tracing the issue to neurocerebral processes, Hodgson (*q.v.*) held freedom and determinism to be compatible.

(31) Dewey (*q.v.* 7) defined freedom as the ability to make intelligent choices.

FREE WILL.

The term, "free will," is often the signal for a discussion of freedom in a religious context. The question is whether man can be free and yet God have foreknowledge, or there is a question of free will and divine predestination. A number of these issues have been discussed under freedom.

(1) St. Augustine (*q.v.* 12), although troubled by the problem, believed that free will and divine foreknowledge were compatible; and this view was accepted by a great part of the Middle Ages.

(2) Valla (*q.v.* 2), discussing free will and divine foreknowledge, found it necessary to sacrifice the first in order to preserve the second.

(3) Gabriel Biel's (*q.v.*) exposition of Ockham, asserting the absolute nature of the divine will, diminished the role of human willing. Biel's analysis influenced Luther.

(4) The argument between Luther (*q.v.* 9) and Erasmus (*q.v.* 2) over free will saw the former denying and the latter affirming its presence in man.

(5) Voltaire (*q.v.* 4) found "free will" incomprehensible, although he accepted a guarded definition of human freedom.

FREGE, FRIEDRICH LUDWIG GOTTLOB. 1848–1925.

German mathematician-logician. Born in Weimar. Professor of mathematics, University of Jena, 1879–1918. Founder, along with Boole, of modern mathematical logic, he stimulated contemporary attempts to form an ideal language.

Principal writings: *Begriffschrift* (T), 1879; *The Foundations of Arithmetic* (T), 1884; *Function and Concept* (T), 1891; *Basic Laws of Arithmetic*, 2 vols., (T in part), 1893, 1903.

(1) Providing the basic inspiration for the philosophical contributions of Bertrand Russell (*q.v.* 2), Frege established the general frame in which modern logic has since developed, demonstrating that arithmetic can be derived from the concepts and transformations of logic alone. The significance of the demonstration relates to the fact that in the course of the 19th century mathematicians had succeeded in showing that all of the rest of mathematics can be defined in terms of integers and arithmetical operations. To

reduce arithmetic to logic, then, is equivalent to showing that all of mathematics can be derived from logic.

(2) The key definition from which Frege's derivation largely follows is the definition of cardinal number as the class of all classes whose members can be put into a one-to-one relationship. The cardinal number "0" is the class of all classes which can be put into a one-to-one relationship with an empty class. A class with one member is a unit class; and the cardinal number 1 is the class of all classes which can be put into a one-to-one mapping relation with a unit class, and so on. Other definitions are required, of course, including the ancestral relation, or hereditary property necessary to mathematical induction.

(3) In addition, however, to providing a new orientation to arithmetic, Frege also provided a new orientation to logic, including a way of handling the problems of generality by means of variables and quantifiers. The introduction of quantifiers binding variables has been termed the greatest intellectual achievement of the 19th century. He introduced the sign " ⊢ " as an assertion sign, to be placed to the left of any proposition asserted as true. He introduced functions made up of a small Greek letter "gap" sign and a capital Greek letter property sign, i.e., $\Phi(\varepsilon)$. Development of the new logic was carried out by Whitehead and Russell in the collaboration leading to *Principia Mathematica*, and the development continues along the same line to this day.

(4) Frege's insights have had implications beyond logic and mathematics. For example, he distinguished between the color, sense (*Sinne*) and denotation (*Bedeutung*) or reference of a word. The color of a word is the train of images and associations the word calls up; hence, it is subjective. The sense of a word is objective, and is that feature of its meaning which permits us to determine the truth value of sentences containing the word. The denotation or reference of a word is something "in the world." The reference of a singular term is an "object." The reference of a predicate is a "concept." The reference of a functional expression is a "function." But all of these are features of the world, only the features are of different kinds.

(5) There are, so to speak, saturated and unsaturated features of the world, which are the correlates of saturated and unsaturated expressions. Singular terms and complete sentences are saturated expressions. There is nothing indefinite about them. Concepts, functions, and relations are unsaturated with a great deal still to be defined. Indeed, all unsaturated expressions are types of functions, needing to be filled in to make saturated expressions of them.

(6) Distinguishing sense from reference, it follows that two expressions may differ in sense but have the same reference (the evening star and morning star both have Venus for reference); they may have sense but not reference (although Frege considered this a defect of language); part of the expression can be replaced by another part with the same sense without changing the sense of the whole expression; two expressions having the same sense will have the same reference; and the replacement of part of an expression by another with the same reference will not change the reference.

(7) As it turns out, the sentences we take seriously have reference as well as sense, and this reference is their truth value, the circumstance that they are true or false. Every declarative sentence of the expected sort is to be regarded as a proper name. This is a way of saying that it is complete. And every function—i.e., incomplete or unsaturated expression— is completable by one or more proper names to make a new proper name.

FREIRE, PAULO.
Q.v. Theology of Liberation (2–3).

FREQUENCY THEORY OF PROBABILITY.

An interpretation of probability (*q.v.* 5,8, 10–13) applicable to sequences of events. The probability of an event's occurring is its relative frequency in a total sequence of events, *i.e.*, the frequency of heads in a total sequence of coin tosses. More exactly, as von Mises and others state, it is the limit of the frequency of that event as the number of trials approaches infinity. *Q.v.* Laplace (3); Peirce (9); Reichenbach (1); Carnap (10); Braithwaite (2).

FRESISON.
Valid syllogism in EIO mood, fourth figure. *Q.v.* Syllogism (4).

FREUD, SIGMUND. 1856–1939.
Austrian medical psychologist and founder of psychoanalysis. Born in Freiberg, Moravia. Educated in Vienna where he studied medicine. Studied in Paris, 1885–86, under J.M. Charcot. He was led to psychoanalysis through a study of the effects of hypnosis on hysteria, published with J. Breuer in 1895. He founded the *Yearbook for Psychoanalytical and Psychopathological Research*, 1908, and the International Psychoanalytical Association, 1910.

Principal writings: *Studies in Hysteria* (T), 1895; *The Interpretation of Dreams* (T), 1899; *The Psychopathology of Everyday Life* (T), 1904; *Humor and its Relation to the Unconscious* (T), 1905; *Totem and Tabu* (T), 1913; *Introductory Lectures in Psychoanalysis* (T), 1916–18; *The Ego and the Id* (T), 1923; *The Future of an Illusion* (T), 1927; *Civilization and its Discontents* (T), 1930; *The Problem of Anxiety* (T), 1936; *Moses and Monotheism* (T), 1939.

(1) Primarily interested in psychological therapy, it was necessary for Freud to develop an hypothesis of human nature, now termed depth psychology, in terms of which the therapy might be carried out. In his later writings the implications of this hypothesis were developed. In man's psychological structure he distinguished three factors, the *Id, Ego,* and *Super-ego*. These, added to the concepts of the unconscious—the censor, repression, sublimation, and hypotheses concerning the role of sexuality in human life—make up the framework of his point of view.

(2) The *ego* is the center of rational awareness and effective action. The *superego* is a distillate of the pressures and requirements of society; it is hence the source of moral prescriptions and directives. The *id* is the source of the flow of libido into the psyche. Since this energy is essentially sexual in nature the *ego* is trapped, as it were, between the pressures of the *id* and those of the *superego*. In this situation the *ego* seeks ways of bringing these pressures into harmony, satisfying some, and rejecting some.

(3) When a demand of the *id* is too blatantly at variance with the *super-ego*, the *ego* and the *super-ego* rid themselves of it by repressing this content into the unconscious of the psyche. The repressive act is called the censor. Although broadening the notion of the psyche to include both conscious and unconscious contents, Freud remains on the side of empiricism by insisting that any unconscious content was once a conscious content entering the psyche through conscious experience.

(4) Since repressed contents retain their efficacy, they influence our conscious life in hidden ways. Indeed, the source of creativity in all fields is explained by means of the sublimation of this store of energy into accepted and fruitful channels. Neurosis occurs when the normal repression-sublimation channel does not function for some reason; in this situation the return to normalcy may occur through psychoanalysis, a process of probing the unconscious with an analyst for guide, stimulating recall, utilizing dream fragments to recover and understand the objectionable content which caused the blockage. The assumption is that the troublesome content, once synthesized into consciousness, will lose its power to interfere with the normal functioning of the psyche.

(5) Among the most troublesome and standard of the repressed contents are those centering around incestuous relations, especially the *Oedipus* and *Electra* complexes (desire of son for mother, and daughter for father).

(6) One means of avoiding both individual neurosis and maturity is the practice of religion. Religion is the projection of the father with his prohibitions and commands into cosmic dimensions. Through religion, one is able to insure oneself the security of childhood in adult life, and to prolong one's infancy throughout life. By clinging to an illusion, by participating in a mass neurosis, one may often escape individual neurosis.

(7) Maturity, for Freud, would consist, however, in substituting a *reality principle* for the comfort and discomfort of all illusions, and a *pleasure principle*, taking sexual fulfillment as its paradigm, as the goal of life.

(8) Thinking of *Eros*, or pleasure, as the

life instinct, Freud placed beside it, and in opposition, *Thanatos*, the death instinct. Speaking mythologically, he was willing to regard human history as the result of the struggle between the two principles.

FRIARS MINOR.
Q.v. Francis of Assisi (4).

FRIENDS OF GOD.
The name of a 14th-century society of German mystics largely of lay persons. John Tauler (*q.v.*) and Henry Suso (*q.v.*) were chiefly responsible for the group.

FRIENDS, SOCIETY OF.
The official name of the religious movement, also known as Quakers, and founded by George Fox (*q.v.*). Beginning in England in the middle of the 17th century, the society spread at once to the American colonies which is now the world center of the movement.

FRIES, JAKOB FRIEDRICH. 1773–1843.
German philosopher. Born in Barby, Saxony. Educated at Leipzig and Jena. Taught at Heidelberg and Jena. His interpretation of Kant inspired a Friesian school and eventually the Göttingen school of neo-Kantianism (*q.v.* 3). The latter is sometimes called the neo-Friesian school.

Principal writings: *Reinhold, Fichte and Schelling*, 1803; *Knowledge, Faith and Presentiment*, 1805; *New or Anthropological Critique of Reason*, 3 vols., 1807; *Handbook of Practical Philosophy*, 2 vols., 1818, 1832; *The Mathematical Philosophy of Nature*, 1822; *System of Metaphysics*, 1824; *History of Philosophy*, 2 vols., 1837–40.

(1) Agreeing with Kant that phenomena must be divided into a *posteriori* and *a priori* parts, Fries interpreted the *a priori* not as transcendental features of all experience, but as the constant feature of the thinker's own inner experience; hence, his emphasis on the *anthropological* critique of reason. This has been regarded as an instance of the psychologizing of philosophy.

(2) He further held, this time in agreement with Jacobi (*q.v.*), that immediate certitude, not demonstration, is the ultimate ground of knowledge; and hence, finally, of the principles of reason.

(3) We know the appearance of things, their phenomenal nature; we believe in their true natures; by presentiment we recognize the being in the appearance, the suprasensible in the sensible.

FROEBEL, FRIEDRICH WILHELM AUGUST. 1782–1852.
German philosopher of education. Born at Oberweissbach. Essentially self-educated. 1807–09 worked in Pestalozzi's school at Iverdon. Conducted his own experimental schools in a number of localities in Germany and Switzerland, also holding courses for elementary teachers. Established the first kindergarten in 1837. His educational theory, like that of Comenius (*q.v.*) and Pestalozzi (*q.v.*), held education to be a natural development. Froebel's original emphasis was that learning must proceed from inner impulse; it is the function of the teacher to stimulate "voluntary activity," and this is possible since every subject-matter, from science to language, is a natural development of the human spirit.

Principal writings: *The Education of Man* (T), 1826; *Pedagogy for Kindergarten*, 1862.

FROMM, ERICH. 1900–1980.
Psychoanalyst and social philosopher. Born in Frankfurt, Germany. Educated at Frankfurt, Heidelberg, Berlin. His major philosophical contribution occurred in relation to the Frankfurt School (*q.v.* 5), of which he was a member from 1928–38, resigning in 1939.

Selected writings: *The Dogma of Christ*, 1931; *The Sane Society*, 1935; *Escape From Freedom*, 1941; *Man for Himself*, 1947; *Psychoanalysis and Religion*, 1950; *The Art of Loving*, 1956; *Beyond the Chains of Illusion*, 1962; *Socialist Humanism* (ed.), 1965.

(1) Fromm's early studies on the authoritarian personality bore fruit in his influential study of national socialism, *Escape From Freedom*, in which the two ways of escaping from loneliness are to join with others in a spirit of love and social productivity, or submit to authority conforming to society. The subjects of totalitarian regimes are pictured as having chosen the latter.

(2) His neo-Marxian, neo-Freudian interpretations of culture found expression in most of his other works, where he combined the emphasis on alienation of the early Marx with a revisionist Freud.

Accepting the latter's analysis of the human condition as exactly what one would expect under capitalism, he regarded Freud's pessimism about human emancipation from these conditions as a reflection of the conditions, and believed they could be overcome.

(3) In *Man for Himself* he returned to loneliness, finding its attempted escape in five types of character, the last of which he supports: (a) receptive (taking but not giving), (b) hoarding (keeping, not sharing), (c) exploitative (taking through force and cunning), (d) marketing (self, a commodity to be bought and sold), (e) productive (realizing one's potentialities in a social and supportive manner).

(4) Distinguishing between authoritarian and humanistic religion, he found psychoanalysis as cure of the soul no threat to the latter, while the former is in any case equivalent to idolatry.

(5) In *Socialist Humanism* he found support for his humanistic socialism among the Marxists of Eastern Europe who contributed to this symposium.

FRONDIZI, RISIERI.
Q.v. Latin American Philosophy (9).

FRY, ROGER.
Q.v. Aesthetics (29).

F-TRUTH.
For a discussion of F-true and F-false sentences where "F" stands for "factually," *q.v.* Carnap (11).

FULBERT.
Founder of the School of Chartres. *Q.v.* Gerbert of Aurillac.

FULLER, MARGARET. 1810–1850.
American writer and philosopher. Born at Cambridgeport, Mass. Educated by her father, she read Latin at six, and all of the languages of Europe by the time she was through her teens. Initially a language teacher, she also conducted conversation classes for women containing much philosophical content. In 1840 she founded *The Dial*, principally as an organ of the New England Transcendentalists. Working intimately with Emerson, Channing, Hawthorne, and others in the movement, she was known as "the Priestess of Transcendentalism."

Principal writings: *Collected Works*, 1855; *Life Without and Life Within*, 1860.

FUNCTION.
From the Latin *functio* (from *fungi*, "to perform, execute"). In symbolic logic, an expression involving one or more variable terms whose meaning or truth is determined when the values of the variables are specified.

(1) The term was introduced into mathematics by Leibniz in 1694, used by Bernoulli in 1698, although functions had made their appearance in Descartes' analytic geometry in 1637. The now standard notation, "f(x)" for a function of a variable x, was introduced by Euler in 1734. Modern mathematics is saturated with functions of different types and levels of complexity. Taken very simply the concept of function introduces a number of interrelated factors including: variables, dependent and independent; values or arguments of the variables; the domain of the variable; and a rule for assigning values to the variables. If the expression is simply

$$y=f(x)$$

since y is here a function of x, the values of y will depend on the values given x. This being so, y is dependent on x; y is the dependent variable and x the independent variable. The domain of the variable is fixed by the set of things recognized as values or arguments in any given application of the function; "y=f(x)" provides no rule for determining the values, or discovering the arguments, of x and y. The expression "y=2(x)" provides a rule for determining y, once x is given, and one could find an endless number of theoretical contexts providing rules for determining how x is to be selected.

(2) Propositional functions are functions taking only propositions as values or arguments. The concept of propositional function was introduced by Frege in 1879, developed by Russell in his studies on mathematical logic, and in his collaboration with Whitehead on *Principia Mathematica*. As Russell points out, the expression, "the hardest proposition in A's mathematical treatise," is not a propositional function although its values are propositions. In this context propositions, says Russell, are merely

described. In propositional functions propositions are *enunciated;* "x is human," for example, is a propositional function which becomes a proposition when a value is assigned to x. Given this assignment, the expression becomes either true or false. Mathematical equations are, equally, propositional functions since they become true or false when values are given to the variables of the equation. In logic we are interested not only in these but also in propositional functions which become sentences in ordinary language when determinate. "X is human" becomes a singular proposition when a value is assigned to x. But propositional functions can be made into propositions in another manner. Propositional functions true in all cases can be made into universal propositions and propositional functions true in some cases can be made into particular propositions. To say "all s is p" is to say that the compound propositional function "$\phi x \supset \psi x$" is always true and to say "some s is p" is to say that "ϕx and ψx" is sometimes true. Out of such functions Quantification Theory (*q.v.*) has been developed.

(3) The Logic of Relations (*q.v.* Logic 24) presents functions in a different dress. Given the expression "xRy," and "R" as the function, "x" will be the value of R for the argument "y," and "y" will be the argument of R, hence, "xRy" may be seen to be a different manner of writing $y=(f)x$.

FUNCTIONALISM.
Q.v. Putnam (10).

FUNCTIONAL PSYCHOLOGY.
Q.v. Psychology (5).

FUNG YU-LAN. 1895–1990.
Chinese philosopher. Born in Honan. Educated at Peking and Columbia universities. Has taught at Southwest Associated and Peking universities, in both of which he served as dean.

Principal writings: *History of Chinese Philosophy* (T), 1931; *China's Road to Freedom,* 1939; *The New Rational Philosophy,* 1939; *A New Treatise on the Way of Life,* 1940; *A New Treatise on the Nature of Man,* 1942; *The Spirit of Chinese Philosophy* (T), 1944; *A New Treatise on the Methodology of Metaphysics,* 1946; *A Short History of Chinese Philosophy* (T), 1948.

(1) Standing as a reconstruction of the rationalistic side of neo-Confucianism, Fung Yu-Lan's system rests on four traditional metaphysical ideas: Principle, Material Force, the *Tao,* and the Great Whole.

(2) Because things exist, so also exist the principles they follow. And principles are universals, always real, but not always actual when not embodied. Because things exist, material force must also exist, although not in itself. The universe is in process of incessant change, daily renewed.

(3) The goal of life is to serve heaven. One advances to this fulfillment through the stages of innocence where one does not know what one is doing, to the stage of utilitarian self-benefit, to the stage of moral service to society, and finally to the transcendental sphere of becoming a citizen of heaven, and so of serving heaven.

FUTURE.
Along with past (*q.v.*) and present (*q.v.*), one of the three divisions of time. Determinists (*q.v.*) generally hold that the future is closed, although not yet occurrent; indeterminists hold that it is open. Minkowski (*q.v.* 2) is a clear example of the first position, holding that future events are already present in the space-time continuum. Lequier (*q.v.* 2), Bergson (*q.v.* 8), and Whitehead (*q.v.* 16–17) exemplify the second position, holding that future events do not yet exist and are still to be determined. Mead (*q.v.* 4) held that both past and future change, depending upon the nature of the present.

GABIROL, SOLOMON IBN.
Q.v. Avicebron.

GABRIEL BIEL.
Q.v. Biel.

GADAMER, HANS-GEORG. 1900– .
German philosopher. Born in Marburg an der Lahn. Studied at University of Munich, and University of Marburg.

Taught at Marburg, Leipzig, Frankfurt, Heidelberg.

Principal writings: *Plato's Dialectical Ethics* (T), 1931 (on the *Philebus*); *Truth and Method* (T), 1960; *Philosophical Hermeneutics* (T), 1964; *Hegel's Dialectic: Five Hermeneutical Studies* (T), 1971; *Hermeneutics and the Critique of Ideology*, 1971; *Truth and Historicity*, 1972; *Reason In the Age of Science* (T), 1976; *Dialogue and Dialectic, Eight Hermeneutical Studies On Plato* (T), collected in translation 1980.

(1) Characterizing his philosophy as "studies in hermeneutics," Gadamer begins his principal work, *Truth and Method*, with a history of the subject (part of which we have included in the entry on hermeneutics, *q.v.*), and ends with a discussion of language as the "horizon of a hermeneutic ontology."

(2) Holding the hermeneutic problem to be "universal and basic for all interhuman experience," Gadamer describes the unending nature of the hermeneutic process. We have presented his view on this in Hermeneutics (6). The universality of the view raises a problem concerning the natural sciences whose goal is elimination of the subjective elements of the cognitive process. The hermeneutic analysis applies to all works of art and their criticism. It applies to the cultural sciences because these sciences are based on history, and there is an inner unity between criticism and historical studies. But the objectivizations of the natural sciences represent an attempt to dominate and dehumanize experience; the Greek conception of science did not do this. One gains the impression that Gadamer felt it to be superior.

(3) One advantage of the Greek approach is that it supports the view that the three elements of hermeneutics—understanding, interpretation, and application—go together and require each other. At the end of any hermeneutic cycle is *praxis* (*q.v.* 13), an "applicative moment" doing justice to particular situations in their particularity. *Praxis* requires that we turn *episteme*, or scientific knowledge into *phronesis*, the "practical reason" of Aristotle.

(4) A debate between Gadamer and Habermas (*q.v.* 6) over hermeneutics and critical theory began in 1967 and continued until 1971. Gadamer held that Habermas overplays the power of reason and underplays the role of language. Language is not one social dimension among others, but the condition of the possibility of all thought. Gadamer's position is set forth in *Hermeneutics and the Critique of Ideology*.

(5) Gadamer's position begins to resemble the themes of the Frankfurt School (*q.v.* 1, 4), however, when he worries about modern societies replacing *praxis* with *techne* as the expert replaces the responsible individual and takes over the role of *phronesis*. He also resembles the post-structuralists or deconstructionists when he holds that we belong to tradition, history, and language in a more definitive sense than they belong to us.

(6) In so far as Gadamer has an ethic it centers on the "solidarity" which is embedded in every historical situation and is made up of the ethical norms which the individuals in that situation hold in common.

GAIUS. 2nd cent. A.D.

Head of an eclectic Platonic school associated in time and content with the Fourth Academy (*q.v.* Plato's Academy 4). Synthesizing Platonism with Stoicism he interpreted Plato in a religious and mystical sense. Among his students were Albinus (*q.v.*) and Apuleius. His work influenced the Neoplatonists Proclus (*q.v.*) and Priscianus.

Principal writings: *Outline of Platonic Doctrines*.

GALEN, CLAUDIUS. 130–200.

Greek physician and philosopher. Born at Pergamon, Mysia. Traveled widely and studied in the major philosophical schools. The second half of his life centered in Rome where, as physician, he attended the family of Marcus Aurelius. An Aristotelian in medicine, logic, ethics, and grammar, his writings on medicine remained standard until the 16th century. The Galenian figure, a fourth figure of the syllogism (*q.v.* 4), added to Aristotle's three, was first attributed to Galen by Averroës. There is no evidence, however, that Galen was in fact responsible for the fourth figure. Many of Galen's writings have been lost; others exist only in Arabic copies; critical editions and translations of his work have been recent and the work is still in progress.

Principal writings: *The Writings of Hippocrates and Galen* (T), 1846; *Minor Writings*, 3 vols., 1884–93; *Institutio Logica* (T), 1896; *On the Natural Faculties* (T), 1916; *Galen on Medical Experience* (T), 1946; *Galen's Compendium on the Timaeus*, 1951; *On Anatomical Procedures* (T), 2 vols., 1956, 1962; *On the Passions and Errors of the Soul* (T), 1964; *Galen on the Usefulness of the Parts of the Body* (T), 1968; *On the Doctrines of Hippocrates and Plato* (T), 1978; *Galen on Respiration and the Arteries* (T), 1984; *On the Therapeutic Method* (T), 1991.

GALENIAN FIGURE.

The fourth figure of the syllogism. *Q.v.* Galen; Syllogism (4).

GALILEO GALILEI. 1564–1642.

Italian astronomer and natural philosopher. Born in Pisa. Principally educated in the monastery of Vallombrosa near Florence; studied at the University of Pisa, 1581-85; shortly thereafter lectured for a time, Florentine Academy; lectured in mathematics, University of Pisa 1592–1610; philosopher and mathematician to the Grand Duke of Tuscany from 1610 to the end of his life. Censured by the consulting theologians of the Holy Office in 1616 for his adherence to the new astronomy, he was admonished not to hold, teach, or defend the condemned doctrine. To this he agreed; the censure action was never confirmed by the pope, but in 1632, following publication of his dialogue on the alternative world systems, Galileo was ordered to Rome by the Inquisition. He arrived in February 1633, was examined June 21 on the charge that the publication of 1632 contravened the decree of 1616. On June 22 Galileo read his recantation, and was sentenced to incarceration at the pleasure of the tribunal. Allowed to return to his villa in Florence under conditions of strict seclusion, the remaining eight years of his life were spent in continued scientific study and experiment.

Principal writings: *The Assayer* (T), 1623; *Dialogue Concerning the Two Chief World Systems* (T), 1632; *Dialogues Concerning Two New Sciences* (T), 1636.

(1) Among his scientific discoveries the following may be noted: the isochronism of the pendulum, 1581; the hydrostatic balance, 1586; the principles of dynamics, 1589–91; the proportional compass and thermometer, 1597. Although not the inventer of the telescope he vastly improved it, and was able to describe the mountains of the moon, the Milky Way as a vast constellation of stars, the satellites of Jupiter, the phases of Venus, and the so-called solar spots. These discoveries occurred between 1609 and 1613, the rings of Jupiter proving to be the most powerful in the public mind, and supplying in microcosm dramatic proof of the new astronomy. In 1637, only months before his blindness, he described the diurnal libration of the moon. Even though blind he developed in theory the application of the pendulum to clockwork.

(2) The interdependence of motion and force, and the consequent invariability of relations of cause and effect introduced a new mental perspective on the world in terms of which the new philosophy would develop. That all bodies are heavy, that weight is a continuous force attracting toward the center of the earth, that in a vacuum all bodies would fall with equal velocity, that inertia implies continuance of motion as well as of rest, that stars and planets are no less corruptible than the earth, and that one should tend to notions with the qualities of decidability; here was the path into the future. In method he related empirical and formal considerations in such a way that mathematical analysis was appropriate to the problem at hand; experiment and calculation were combined to produce results capable of confirming or disconfirming the theory.

(3) In general philosophy he found atomism consonant with these procedures. Emphasizing the quantitative aspects of nature, and pointing out that the tickle is not in the feather, Galileo made the distinction between primary and secondary qualities which we now associate with the name of Locke (*q.v.* 6). The objectivity of the measurable and the subjectivity of the non-measurable, powerfully revived by Galileo, have remained standard and virtually unassailable notions.

GALLICAN ARTICLES.

The Four Articles of the Declaration of

the Clergy of France, sanctioned by Louis XIV, in 1682. The articles claimed autonomy from Rome for the French Church, and defended royal and lay rights against the pope and clergy.

GALLICAN CONFESSION.

A forty-article confession of faith and order of discipline written by Calvin; adopted by the First National Synod of the Reformed Churches of France, at Paris in 1559; revised by Theodore Beza (1519-1605), Calvin's successor in Geneva; ratified at the Seventh National Reformed Synod at La Rochelle in 1571; and finally superseded by the Declaration of Faith of the Reformed Church in France, 1872.

GALLICANISM.

The movement leading to the Gallican Articles (q.v.).

GALLUPPI, PASQUALE. 1770–1846.

Italian philosopher. Born in Tropea. Educated at Naples. Taught at Naples. An Italian representative of the French eclecticism and Spiritualism (q.v. 1) of Cousin (q.v.), Royer-Collard (q.v. 1), and Maine de Biran (q.v. 1), Galluppi argued that consciousness involves a simultaneous awareness of self and thing; thus, one is never in the position of solipsism.

Principal writings: *Philosophical Essay on the Critique of Knowledge*, 6 vols., 1819–23; *Elements of Philosophy*, 4 vols., 1820–7.

GALTON, FRANCIS.

Q.v. Image (5).

GANDHI, MOHANDAS K. 1869–1948.

Indian religious and national leader. Born in Porbandar. Educated in London. In the last 8 of his 21 years in South Africa, where he practised law, he developed the techniques of passive resistance in a struggle against the second-class status of Indians in that country. Having achieved his goals through a series of compromise agreements, in 1915 he returned to India to direct the same measures against the British in the cause of Indian independence. The campaign moved through the phases of non-cooperation (in the 1920's) and civil disobedience (the 1930's) to "quit India" (the 1940's). Independence was conceded in 1947; months later, on January 30, 1948, Gandhi was assassinated by a Hindu fanatic over the separation of Pakistan from India.

Selected writings: *Non-Violence in Peace and War*, 2 vols., 1942, 1949; *Gita the Mother* (ed. J.P. Chander), 1944; *Fellowship of Faiths and Unity of Religions* (ed. A.M. Khan), 1947; *The Gandhi Sutras* (Arr. D.S. Sarma), 1949; *Basic Education*, 1951; *In Search of the Supreme*, 3 vols., 1961–62; *Gandhi: Essential Writings* (ed. V.V.R. Murti), 1970; *The Moral and Political Writings of Mahatma Gandhi* (ed. R. Iyer), 1986.

(1) Called *Mahatma* ("great soul"), which he gently denied, Gandhi combined Hindu, Christian, and philosophic principles in a version of pacifism (q.v.) which spelled out the notion of "passive resistance." Thoreau and Tolstoy are specifically credited with having contributed to his thinking. Gandhi's term for the attitude one must cultivate in dealing with social problems was *satyagraha*, which means "truth-force" or "truth-firmness." He was willing to accept "civil disobedience" as a translation for this term because of its connection with Thoreau; but that doesn't carry the sense of inner discipline Gandhi had in mind which required training and involved fearless inner calm, self-restraint, and respect for the spirit of the law.

(2) One should not overestimate the Western contribution to this concept. The attitude Gandhi had in mind can be glossed as an application to human relations of the idea of *ahimsa* ("non-injury"), and although he credits Tolstoy's book on the kingdom of God with having made him a "firm believer" in *ahimsa*, the concept had its early, and most complete development in Hinduism, Jainism, and Buddhism. It required a sense of identification with all being, living and nonliving, chastity, simplicity of life, self-control, and self-purification. It was both a condition for truth, and a means of relating to the divine.

(3) He believed truth, God, and non-violence to be inseparable. Truth is God, and "non-violence—*ahimsa*—love" is the only means to truth. He also held that all of the religions of the world are true; they are "beautiful flowers" from the same garden, and mutually supportive.

(4) Among those he was especially concerned to champion on the way to independence were the untouchables whom

he called the *harijans* ("children of God") and helped to legal status (granted in the Indian constitution of 1949).

(5) Throughout his career Gandhi proposed a goal of organic education in which the physical and spiritual faculties of the person are considered as an indivisible whole. It centered on the teaching of a craft to which all other subjects were related. Tried out in the educational program established in South Africa on the Tolstoy Farm, he presented the program in India as a means of restoring village life following the disruptions of British rule. Gandhi proposed the craft of spinning and weaving, which he viewed as central to village life.

GARRIGOU-LAGRANGE, R.M. 1877–1964.

French philosopher and theologian. A Dominican, he participated in the revival of Thomism in the 20th century, and can thus be termed neo-Thomist or neo-Scholastic,

Selected writings: *God, His Existence and His Nature* (T), 2 vols., 1915; *Providence* (T), 1937; *Predestination* (T), 1939; *The Thomistic Synthesis* (T), 1945; six-volumes of commentary on Aquinas' *Summa Theologica*, 1948, five of them now in translation; *Last Writings of Reginald Garrigou-Lagrange* (T), 1969.

GASSENDI, PIERRE. 1592–1655.

French philosopher, scientist, and mathematician. Born in Champtercier, Provence. Professor of Philosophy at Aix. Provost Cathedral Church, Diegne. In 1645 he accepted the chair of mathematics at the Collège Royale in Paris. He is principally known today as author of the fifth set of objections to Descartes' *Meditations*.

Principal writings: *Discourses on the Paradoxes of the Aristotelians*, 1624–59; *Commentary on the Life, Customs, and Opinions of Epicurus*, 1649; *Anticartesian Inquiries*, 1649; *The Basis of the Epicurean Philosophy*, 1659.

(1) The position which Gassendi attempted to develop was anti-Aristotelian, anti-Cartesian, and committed to the thesis that a revival of Epicureanism with its atomism was the alternative best suited to the new science. Gassendi endeavored to reconcile this view with the teachings of the Church.

(2) Finding the orderliness of atomic combinations evidence for God, who becomes first and final cause, he asserted both mechanical causation and that the atoms are centers of force.

(3) He departed from Epicureanism in holding that the human being is composed of body and an immaterial immortal soul. Harmony between soul and body is provided for by a doctrine of pre-established harmony. He supported Epicurus in the view that the end of life is tranquility of soul, and the Church in holding that such tranquility is perhaps impossible in this life, but possible in the life to come.

(4) Contending for the reality of space and time he supported, against Descartes, the necessity of the void or vacuum in the explanation of change, that is, motion.

(5) He also argued, against Descartes, that the doctrine of clear and distinct ideas required a criterion to separate the ideas which are really clear and distinct from those which merely seem to be so. There must also, however, be a criterion of the criterion etc., *ad infinitum*.

(6) Finally, although stressing empiricism and often repeating the maxim that *nihil in intellectu quod non prius fuerit in sensu*, that there is nothing in the intellect that was not first in experience, he in fact held to the need for sense and reason to remain in balance.

GATHAS.

The hymns ascribed to Zoroaster in the *Avesta*, sacred scriptures of Zoroastrianism (*q.v.* 4).

GAUDAPADA. 6th or 8th cent. A.D.

Indian philosopher. The first known systematic exponent of Advaita Vedanta (*q.v.*), the non-dualistic interpretation of the Vedanta philosophy. Influenced by Nagarjuna and Vasubandhu, Gaudapada's basic attachment was to the *Upanishads*. One thrust of his work lies in showing that both Buddhism and Vedanta are rooted in the Upanishadic literature.

Principal writings: One basic work known as the *Mandukya Verses*.

(1) Arguing against all variations of the doctrine of creation—that the world is the expansion of God, his will, his sport, a function of time, a dream, an illusion—Gaudapada urges the doctrine of No-

origination or *Ajativada*. That anything should originate from the Absolute Is simply impossible. The non-dual Absolute cannot tolerate any distinction.

(2) That we find a world in our experience is like mistaking the rope for a snake. There is an illusion here, but it is our illusion. No shadow of that illusion exists in reality. At the same time, however, even our illusions must somehow be explained. Real water is less unreal than the water of a dream. The difference would seem to be that the latter is simply our imagination while the former is the imagination of the underlying self, and he finally holds, with the Shunyavadins, later developed by Shankara, that the world is *Avidya*, i.e., unreal because essentially indescribable or unthinkable as either existent or non-existent.

(3) Identifying Brahman with the non-dual Absolute, Gaudapada holds that Brahman can be realized by Asparshayoga, i.e., Pure Knowledge, or Uncontaminated Meditation. This is a state in which all categories merge, the subject-object duality is transcended, and the subject becomes one with Pure Consciousness.

GAUNILO. 11th cent.

Benedictine scholar who objected to the Ontological argument of Anselm (*q.v.* 2). Gaunilo's objection is called the "*Pro Insipiente*" from the title of his reply to Anselm, the *Liber pro insipiente* ("Book in behalf of the fool").

GAUTAMA BUDDHA.

Q.v. Buddha.

GAUTAMA THE NYAYA.

Q.v. Nyaya.

GAUTHIER, F.P.

Q.v. Maine de Biran.

GAY, JOHN. 1699–1745.

English philosopher. Educated at Cambridge. One of the forerunners of Utilitarianism (*q.v.*), Gay derived from the will of God the ethical criterion of human happiness.

Principal writings: *Dissertation Concerning the Fundamental Principle of Virtue or Morality*, 1731.

GEHENNA.

From the Hebrew *Ge Hinnom* ("the Valley of Hinnom"). The New Testament term for "hell," apparently from the fact that the city dump of Jerusalem was located in the valley and fires burned there constantly. It was likewise considered a place of abomination since, according to tradition, children had been sacrificed there to the god Moloch. A Canaanite deity, Moloch demanded the first-born.

GEISTESWISSENSCHAFTEN.

German term meaning "sciences of culture or spirit." The term first appeared in von Schiel's 1863 German translation of John Stuart Mill's *Logic*, as an equivalent to Mill's term "moral sciences." In von Schiel's translation the title of Book Six on the applications of inductive logic read "On the Logic of the *Geisteswissenschaften* or Moral Sciences." Dilthey (*q.v.*) broadened the term to include history, spirit, and culture. Also *q.v. Verstehen* (1).

GEMARA.

An Aramaic term meaning "completion." A body of literature amplifying the *Mishnah* (*q.v.*). Also *q.v.* Judaism (2b).

GEMEINSCHAFT.

Q.v. Ferdinand Tönnies (1).

GENERAL WILL, THE.

A translation of the French term, "*la volonté générale*." The term was used by Rousseau (*q.v.* 5d) to apply both to the ideal judgment of a society and to its sovereign power.

GENERATION.

From the Latin *generare* ("to beget, create"). One of the Aristotelian types of change. Its opposite is "corruption." Generation is a change from non-being to being, while corruption is a change from being to non-being. Relative generation and corruption are types of alteration or change of quality, regarded by Aristotle (*q.v.* 8) as one of the three basic types of change. Absolute generation and corruption, although recognized by Aristotle, remain something of a mystery within his system.

GENERIC IMAGE.

Q.v. Image (5).

GENETIC.

From the Greek *genesis* ("origin").

(1) As an adjective the term applies to an investigation into origins: *e.g.*, the genetic method of history (*q.v* Herder 1), Genetic Psychology (*q.v.* Ward 1), Genetic Epistemology (*q.v.* Piaget 1).

(2) The Genetic Fallacy is committed when the latter stages of a process are evaluated only in terms of its earlier stages (*q.v.* Fallacies 9).

GENTILE, GIOVANNI. 1875–1944.

Italian philosopher. Born in Castelvetrano, Sicily. Educated at Pisa. Professor of philosophy at the universities of Palermo, Pisa, and Rome. He reformed Italy's system of instruction as Minister of Public Instruction, 1922–24. A self-styled "Philosopher of Fascism," he was assassinated in 1944.

Principal writings: *The Philosophy of Marx: a Critical Study*, 1899; *The Scientific Concept of Education*, 1901; *The Reform of Hegelian Dialectic*, 1913; *Summary of Education as a Philosophical Science*, 2 vols., 1913; *The General Theory of the Spirit as Pure Act* (T), 1916; *The Origin of Contemporary Philosophy in Italy*, 3 vols., 1917, 1925; *System of Logic as Theory of Knowing*, 2 vols., 1917, 1923; *The Philosophy of Art*, 1931; *The Genesis and Structure of Society*. (T), 1946.

(1) Gentile proposed a philosophy of the pure act, called Actualism, or Actual Idealism. The philosophy is reminiscent of Hegelian Idealism (*q.v.* Hegel 3) in a number of ways. The pure act is the Absolute or Spirit realizing itself in the world. But Gentile moves into this conception by extending the sphere of the subject. The awareness of a subject includes both form and content; it includes not only what is internal to the subject but what is external as well. Gentile believed that Idealism emerges inevitably as one makes clear the logical structure of one's actual experience.

(2) Extension of the sphere of the subject situates the act in a position of ontological primacy; indeed, there is virtually no other category. The object, insofar as one must attend to it at all, exists at the ideal limit of experience. The category of the act thus relates very naturally to human freedom as the self-caused. Self-awareness and self-creation are seen to be identical.

(3) The dialectic of history is a dialectic of thought thinking. Following Hegel (*q.v.* 8–9), philosophy is seen as a synthesis between subjective and objective, art and religion. But in distinction from Hegel, the phases of art, religion, and philosophy are made the basis of a philosophy of education. Art and religion become central to elementary education, and their philosophical synthesis the task of secondary education.

(4) Two movements emerged from his work; one with a religious orientation, finally becoming known as Christian Spiritualism; the other with a political orientation concerned with the theory of the corporate state. The leader of the second group is Ugo Spirito who in addition to advancing, under the name, Problematicism, the view that the function of philosophy is clarification, criticism, and existential confrontation, published a number of studies of "corporativism" and national socialism.

GENUS.

From the Greek *genos* meaning "race, stock, offspring." In logic the term is a synonym for "kind" or "class" (*q.v.*).

(1) In Aristotelian logic the genus is a class of a certain kind; namely, one divisible into other classes, called species (*q.v.* and Aristotle 4). In this tradition, natural classes are recognized, at once generating the concepts of the *summum genus* and the *infima species*. But, of course, the significance of the concepts of most inclusive genus and smallest species alters greatly depending upon whether or not the distinctions drawn are regarded as belonging to the nature of things.

(2) By tradition, definitions are constructed by genus and difference, and since any species will belong to some genus, possessing a characteristic difference from other species within the genus, it is appropriate in this context to speak of real definitions.

(3) The term "being" as most inclusive genus is on this view incapable of definition.

(4) The contemporary tendency is to regard principles of classification as conventional; when so regarded the terms used above, and the classes which result from their use, gain their viability from convenience rather than from reflecting

distinctions which exist in the nature of things.

GEOMETRY, FRACTAL.

Q.v. Chaos Theory (4–6).

GERBERT OF AURILLAC. c. 938–1003.

French philosopher and Churchman. Born in Auvergne. Educated in Rheims; bishop in Rheims and in Ravenna. As Sylvester II he became Pope in 999. He contributed to the logical literature on essential and accidental predicates and held to the unity of faith and reason, and of theory and practice. Among his disciples was Fulbert, founder of the School of Chartres. His influence lent new impetus to the development of speculative philosophy in this period.

Principal writings: *On the Reasonable and the Use of Reason*; *On the Body and Blood of the Lord*; *Letters of Gerbert* (T).

GERGONNE, J. D. 1772–1859.

French mathematician. Born in Nancy. Taught at Montpellier. Rector at Montpellier.

Principal writings: "An Essay on Rational Dialectic," 1816–17.

(1) Beginning with the Euler Diagrams (*q.v.*), Gergonne interpreted them in the following manner:

ⓐ ⓑ   aHb ("H" meaning "Outside of")

ⓐⓑ   aXb ("X" meaning "overlapping")

ⓐⓑ   aIb ("I" meaning "identical with")

ⓐ b   a⊂b ("⊂" meaning "is contained in")

ⓑ a   a⊃b ("⊃" meaning "contains")

(2) On this basis Gergonne was able to show alternate meanings in the traditional A, E, I, and O propositions (*q.v.* Syllogism 1, 2).

"All a is b" can mean either "aIb or a⊂b"

"No a is b" means "aHb"

"Some a is b" can mean either "aXb," "aIb," "a⊂b," or "a⊃b."

"Some a is not b" can mean either "aHb" or "aXb."

On the basis of these more precise distinctions he worked out his theory of the syllogism.

GERMAN PHILOSOPHY, THE.

A phrase sometimes applied to the philosophic movement allied with Pietism, and opposed to the Leibniz-Wolff movement. The contest of the two traditions occurred within the German universities in the 17th and 18th centuries, and was ended by the rise of the Kantian philosophy. Kant was himself a product of the Pietistic tradition, and is regarded as the culmination of the German philosophy. His predecessors include Christian Thomasius (*q.v*), Andreas Rüdiger (*q.v.*), A.F. Hoffman (1703–1741), the last of whom began a new reform of Pietist philosophy after the Leibniz-Wolff forces had gained dominance within the German universities, and Christian August Crusius (*q.v.*) who exerted a direct influence over Immanuel Kant.

GERMAN THEOLOGY, THE.

A late 14th-century mystical treatise of unknown authorship, but probably influenced by the Friends of God (*q.v.*). The work is devoted to the means of growth toward perfection in the Christian life. The work's title was provided by Martin Luther who was also responsible for its initial publication.

GERSON, JEAN DE. 1363–1429.

French churchman and mystic. Born in Gerson. Educated in Paris. Taught at the University of Paris. Chancellor of the University for thirty-four years, he actually defended the rights of the university against king and pope, using the power of the university to end the Great Schism. His main instrument to this end was the calling of Councils, and Gerson was chiefly responsible for the calling of the Councils of Pisa and Constance. The latter, in addition to deposing Pope John XXIII, also tried Huss. Gerson directed both operations, while also seeking at the Council a political judgment against the French House of Burgundy. On the latter issue he failed, and could not return to Paris. He moved eventually to Lyon (where his brother was Prior of a Celestine abbey), teaching children and writing on mystical theology. He believed that the end of contemplation is a union of love with God, and that the love component is the Holy Spirit.

Principal writings: *Mystical Theology*;

The Mountain of Contemplation; On the Consolations of Theology; Against Vain Curiosity in Matters of Faith; essays on university reform and the state of the Church.

GERSON, LEVI BEN.

Q.v. Gersonides.

GERSONIDES (GERSON, LEVI BEN). 1288–1344.

French philosopher. Born in Bagnols, Languedoc, and lived at Orange and Avignon. He was a practicing physician, a mathematician, and astronomer, as well as a philosopher. He followed Aristotle and Averroës philosophically; and was successor to Maimonides in upholding reason and science in the Jewish community. Among other evidences of his influence, Pope Clement VI in 1342 arranged to have some of his astronomical studies translated into Latin; and Spinoza adopted his theory of miracles.

Principal writings: *Book on Astronomy; Wars of the Lord.* In addition, commentaries on the Bible, and on the first five books of Euclid.

(1) The philosophical treatise of Levi ben Gerson is divided into six parts: (a) theory of the soul, (b) prophecy, (c) God's omniscience, (d) providence, (e) astronomy, physics, and metaphysics; (f) creation and miracles.

(2) Beginning from Aristotle's distinction of the active and passive intellect, Levi holds not only that the active intellect is immortal, but the passive intellect (although developed in and relative to each individual) is made up of universals which have a real existence. Hence man in his individuality can be said to be immortal, although intellectual achievement is in some measure a condition for achieving this goal.

(3) Prophecy occurs through the active intellect; hence, the true prophet will evidence moral and intellectual perfections.

(4) God's knowledge includes all cosmic law, and the causal influences of celestial on terrestrial things; since it does not extend to the details of the terrestrial world, man's will remains free.

(5) Some humans are under a general providence; others are under a special providence, the amount of special providence depending on the relation of the person to the active intellect.

(6) Since neither matter nor motion is infinite the world had a beginning, but it will have no end. Rejecting Ptolemaic-style astronomy as impossible, Levi held to a scheme of 48 spheres and 8 planets, each guided by an intelligence. He believed, furthermore, in astrology.

(7) While defending miracles, he severely limited their role. They cannot occur in the celestial spheres, since they are inconsistent with God's absoluteness. Their occurrence thus relates to the terrestrial sphere, and somehow are a result of the working of natural laws. At the same time, he held that miracles cannot contain a self-contradiction, and that their effects cannot endure.

GESELLSCHAFT.

Q.v. Ferdinand Tonnies (1).

GESTALT.

A German term meaning "form, shape, or figure." The term stands for the principle that perceptual content is a series of configurations or totalities, rather than a series of simple perceptual elements. In this sense the school of Gestalt psychology (headed by Max Wertheimer, *q.v.*, Kurt Koffka, *q.v.* and Wolfgang Köhler, *q.v.*) offers an alternative to the associationistic psychology originating with British Empiricists. Once introduced, the Gestalt principle has shown itself capable of application to theories of structure in many fields.

GETTIER, EDMUND L.

Q.v. The Gettier Problem.

GETTIER PROBLEM, THE.

An epistemological problem raised by Edmund L. Gettier in his 1963 *Analysis* article, "Is justified true belief knowledge?" The analysis had emerged that when one says of a certain person S that at a certain time t one knows that a certain statement h is true, three things are involved: One believes that h is true; h is true; and it is evident to S that h is true. Gettier provides a counter-example in which S believes that there is a sheep in the field; one mistakes a dog for a sheep; and there is an unseen sheep in the field. The three conditions appear to have been satisfied yet, since S has mistaken a dog for a sheep, one would not say that one knows there is a sheep in the field. In response to the problem it has been argued that the counter-example fails because the third condition of knowledge as justified true belief (listed above) has not been satisfied. Others strengthen the definition of knowledge, adding requirements of "nondefectiveness" or "indefeasibility," *e.g.*, for Roderick Chisholm (*q.v.* 4) knowledge is nondefective justified true belief; for Keith Lehrer it is indefeasible justified true belief.

GEULINCX, ARNOLD. 1625–1669.

Belgian philosopher. Born in Antwerp. Educated at the University of Louvain. Taught at Louvain 1646–58. Converted to Calvinism he moved to Leiden where he held a post in the university. Precursor to Malebranche and Spinoza, he systematized the doctrine of Occasionalism, and made several notable contributions to logic (*q.v.* 15).

Principal writings: *Quaestiones quodlibeticae*, 1653; *Fundamentals of Logic*, 1662; *Ethics*, 1685; *True Physics*, 1688; *True Metaphysics*, 1691.

(1) Extension and thought, being utterly different, cannot act on each other. Body and mind may be compared to two clocks which act together, because their actions have been synchronized. God is the power synchronizing the actions of mind and body. A mental decision on my part is merely the occasion on which God produces a physical occurrence in my body. Conversely, the physical occurrence is the occasion on which God provides in me the appropriate mental state.

(2) On this view God becomes the sole cause of the universe, and approaches the status of the sole reality. No fact is ground for any other; nothing can exist apart from God; man's thoughts and volitions are the thoughts and volitions of God.

(3) The end of living is "resigned optimism," and right reason the supreme virtue. The cardinal virtues are diligence, obedience, justice, and humility. Humility is chief of these, confessing our helplessness and submission to God.

GHAZZALI.
Q.v. Al-Ghazzali.

GHIBELLINES.
Q.v. Guelfs.

GHOSE, AUROBINDO.
Q.v. Sri Aurobindo.

GIGNOMENE.
Q.v. Theodor Zieher.

GILBERT OF POITIERS (GILBERTUS PORRETANUS). 1076–1154.

French Scholastic philosopher. Born in Poitiers. Educated under Bernard of Chartres. Taught at Chartres, Paris, and Poitiers. In 1142 he became Bishop of Poitiers. In 1148, the Synod of Rheims condemned his works pending their correction, his doctrine of the Trinity having been thought heterodox. Bernard of Clairvaux was one of those opposing him. Gilbert withdrew the offensive material. The first book listed below was long attributed to Gilbert, but is now disputed.

Principal writings: *Book of the Six Principles; Commentary on Boethius' De Trinitate.*

(1) Dividing the ten categories of Aristotle into two classes, one primary, the other derivative, Gilbert places substance, quantity, quality, and relation in the former class, and place, time, situation, condition, action, and passion in the latter. The former categories inhere in objects; the latter do not.

(2) One must distinguish between the individualized essence of a thing and the "native forms" which are the same in individuals of the same species or genus. The native forms have their exemplars in the mind of God. On the other hand it is by collecting and comparing that we form the ideas of species and genus.

(3) God is pure being, the pure form of existence. The three persons of the Trinity are God by participation in pure form. Since the pure form is one and the persons three, a distinction must be drawn between God as pure being and God as triune. It was this distinction which led to Gilbert's condemnation.

GILES OF ROME. c. 1247–1316.

Scholastic philosopher. Born in Rome. Educated at Paris. Taught at Paris 1285–92. An Augustinian, he defended Thomisim against the condemnation of 1277. He was made Archbishop of Bourges in 1295. A critic of Aristotelian physics, his analyses of motion, especially the problem of falling bodies, led toward modern conceptions.

Principal writings: *Quodlibeta*; *On the Soul*; *On the Power of the Church*; commentaries on Aristotle.

GILGAMESH EPIC.

A work of Assyrian-Babylonian literature going back to Sumerian legends 3000 years before Christ. The narrative of the wanderings of Gilgamesh and his friend, Engidu (half-man—half-bull), contains an account of a flood, called the Babylonian Flood Story, of which the Biblical account is a variant.

GILLIGAN, CAROL. 1936– .

Psychologist and ethical philosopher. Born in New York City. Educated at Swarthmore and Harvard. Taught at Chicago, presently at Harvard.

Principal writings in philosophy: *In a Different Voice*, 1982; "Do the Social Sciences Have an Adequate Theory of Moral Development?" 1983; *Meeting at the Crossroads* (with L.M. Brown), 1992.

(1) Noticing that the research sample utilized by Lawrence Kohlberg (*q.v.*) in developing his stages of moral development included only males, Gilligan posed Kohlberg's problems but with "the voices of women." The result was an ethic of "care," contrasting with Kohlberg's ethic of justice. While the latter had an analytic logic, the former turned on a "contextual understanding of relationship."

(2) Gilligan distinguished three levels of moral development in the ethic of care and responsibility: (a) Friendship guiding the decision concerning whom to care for. Friend as source of personal gratification; egocentric and unreflective; liking and not liking. (b) Shift to the criterion of "hurting and not hurting," self-identification with others. Understanding feelings and needs of others; and needs of others fused to needs of self. (c) Interdependence; self reemerges; equal stress on self and others.

(3) "As we have listened for centuries to the voices of men" so more recently it has been possible to hear that "in the different voice of women lies the truth of an ethic of care, the tie between relationship and responsibility, and the origins of aggression in the failure of connection." The ethic of care is pictured as restoring the concept of love to the moral domain. The tension between the contrasting ethics of justice and care is a tension between two modes of ethical thought which are properly in dialogue, requiring each other, tying reflection to relationship and uniting cognition with affect.

GILSON, ETIENNE. 1884–1978.

French philosopher. Born in Paris. Educated at the University of Paris. Taught at the University of Strasbourg, the University of Paris, the Collège de France, and the Toronto Institute for Medieval Studies. Committed to the development and demonstration of the viability of neo-Thomism as a metaphysical alternative, Gilson has directed much of his attention to historical studies. These studies, valuable in themselves, have also brought Platonic, Aristotelian, Augustinian, and other sources to bear on the development of neo-Thomism. In particular Gilson stressed both the essentialism and existentialism of the alternative. The two dimensions of reality can be brought together in existential judgment, linking being and cognition.

Principal writings: *Thomism*, 1920; *The Philosophy of Saint Bonaventure* (T), 1924; *Saint Thomas Aquinas* (T), 1927; *Introduction to the Study of Saint Augustine*, 1929; *The Spirit of Medieval Philosophy* (T), 2 vols., 1932; *Christianity and Philosophy* (T), 1936; *The Unity of Philosophical Experience* (E), 1937; *Heloise and Abelard* (T), 1938; *Dante* (T), 1939; *God and Philosophy* (E), 1941; *The Christian Philosophy of Saint Augustine* (T), 1947; *Being and Essence*, 1948; *Being and Some Philosophers* (E), 1949; *Jean Duns Scotus: Introduction to his Fundamental Positions*, 1952; *History of Christian Philosophy in the Middle Ages* (E), 1955; *Painting and Reality* (E), 1955; *The Spirit of Thomism* (E), 1964.

GIOBERTI, VINCENZO. 1801–1852.

Italian philosopher and statesman. Born in Turin. Educated for the priesthood; he was ordained in 1825. Taught at Turin from 1825 to 1833. In 1834 he was named Chaplain to the king, but was

banished from the country almost immediately because of his liberalism. Until
1845 he taught in Brussels, returning to
Turin under amnesty in 1848. In quick
succession he then became President of
the Chamber of Deputies, Minister of
Public Instruction, and President of the
Council.

Principal writings: *The Theory of Natural Sovereignty*, 1838; *Introduction to the
Study of Philosophy*, 3 vols., 1839-40; *On
the Religious Doctrines of Victor Cousin*,
1840; *The Philosophy of Revelation*, 1856;
On Protologia, 2 vols., 1857.

(1) The proper entry into philosophy
is ontology, not epistemology, since all
that is, is the work of the supremely real
being.

(2) Through mental intuition we can
gain insight into the nature of being,
explicating in language the relation of
ideas so gained. The ideal order can be
partially traced, including its three dimensions of first philosophy, first ontology, and first psychology.

(3) The ideal element in knowledge
carries us into the sphere of religion.
Religion is the direct expression of the
ideal; civilization has perfection as its
goal, and religion is the consummation
of this tendency. The Church is, hence,
essential to man's well-being on this
earth.

GIVEN, THE.
Q.v. Wahle (1); Brightman (3); C.I.
Lewis (5).

GLANVILL, JOSEPH. 1636-1680.
English philosopher. Born in Plymouth.
Educated at Oxford. A divine, he employed skepticism for the defense of faith,
along the way anticipating very closely
Hume's analysis of causality. In separate
publications he supported witchcraft and
the work of the Royal Society.

Principal writings: *The Vanity of Dog-
matizing*, 1661; *Philosophical Considerations
concerning the Existence of Sorcerers and
Sorcery*, 1666; *Plus Ultra, or the Progress
and Advancement of Science since the Time
of Aristotle*, 1668.

GLEICK, JAMES.
Q.v. Chaos Theory.

GLOSSOGONOUS METAPHYSICS.
Q.v. Adolf Stöhr.

GNANA YOGA.
Q.v. Jnana Yoga under Yoga (5c).

GNOSTICISM.
From the Greek *gignoskein* meaning "to
know." Gnosticism is not, as the name
implies, a movement committed to the
increase of genuine knowledge, but a
philosophic-religious movement related
to the mystery religions (*q.v.*) and directed
toward personal salvation. Gnosticism,
like the mystery religions, claimed an
esoteric wisdom, sharply distinguishing
between the uninitiated and the initiated.
Mystic rites and magic words, *e.g.*,
"Calaucau," served to protect the initiated from all the realms of demons.
Gnosticism stood in competition with
Christianity, reaching its highest point in
the latter part of the 2nd century A.D.
Irenaeus (*q.v.*), for example, wrote against
the position. The movement waned in the
3rd century and the Manichaean (*q.v.*)
movement replaced it in point of influence. The variety of Gnostic sects, schools,
and practices was very great.

The following should be included
among Gnostics: the Ophites of Celsus, the
Nicolaitans, the Archontici, the Sethites,
the Carpocratians, the Naasseni, the
Simoniani, the Barbelognostics, the Bar-
desanesians, the Basilidians (*q.v.*), the
Marcionites (*q.v.* Marcion of Sinope), the
Cerinthus, the Valentinians (*q.v.* Valentinus), the Ebionites (*q.v.* Ebionism), and
the Elkesaites.

The above-mentioned groups each
adhered to some selection of the following themes:

(1) Reality displays a marked dualism
between good and evil, light and darkness, a material world of evil, and a spiritual world of goodness. The dualism,
once posited, is in a measure overcome
either by the fall of the Godhead, or a
system of emanations reaching from the
spiritual to the material.

(2) The seven quasi-evil, quasi-hostile
world-creating powers, or angels, are the
last emanations of God; and derived from
them are powers of darkness.

(3) The Great Mother, Goddess of
Heaven, often known as *Sophia*, descends
into the material world, giving birth to
the seven powers.

(4) The Primal Man, existing before the
world, comes into the world to make war

on darkness, and with his appearance the drama of world-history begins. He is partly vanquished by darkness but subsequently is set free, or sets himself free.

(5) The *Soter*, or Savior, is often the Primal Man whose setting free is not only for himself but for the Gnostic initiate. In some systems the task of the Primal Man was to free *Sophia*; and their union signals the salvation of the elect.

(6) Through the appropriate knowledge, and through ascetic separation from the lower world, Gnostics endeavored to lift themselves toward the God of the upper world. In the Gnostic sects where the Great Mother played a prominent role, religious prostitution played a central part, sometimes in relation to the *Soter*.

GOBINEAU, ARTHUR. 1816–1882.

French philosopher. Born near Paris. A diplomat and nobleman, he is best known for his introducing into the philosophy of history the premise of Aryan supremacy. In Gobineau's view only the Aryan has the capacity for culture, thus wherever culture appears Gobineau expects to find Aryan influence. When an Aryan cause cannot be found, he assumes one, giving the argument a circular form. Since the Aryan possesses all the virtues, *i.e.*, beauty, intelligence, and strength, and since racial mixture results in the loss of one or more of these qualities, the purity of the Aryan race is defended.

Principal writings: *Essay on the Inequality of the Human Races* (T in part), 4 vols., 1853–55; *The Religions and the Philosophies in Central Asia*, 1865.

GOCLENIUS, RUDOLF. 1547–1628.

German philosopher. Followed Melanchthon and Peter Ramus. His contributions were largely terminological, including introduction of the term "psychology." He is credited with the Goclenian Sorites (*q.v.* Sorites 2).

Principal writings: *Psychology*, 1590; *Lexicon of Philosophy*, 1613: *Lexicon of Greek Philosophy*, 1615.

GOD.

An Anglo-Saxon term of Teutonic origin referring to the object of religious worship. Its meaning, therefore, is as varied as human culture itself. The concept has developed in different ways in different settings. A great deal of evidence supports the view that the origin of the conception lies in the numinous feeling linking primitive man and the world, issuing in animism, *mana*, and sympathetic magic. It is tempting to say, although arranging cultural stages is hazardous, that the end of this development, given polytheism as an intermediate late stage, is monotheism. Monotheism was reached in the Egyptian concept of the sun god Ra, in the Indian concept of Brahma, the Jewish concept of Yahweh, and the Moslem concept of Allah. The growth of Christian monotheism was aided by a Greek philosophical monotheism beginning with Xenophanes, and exemplified in classical Greek philosophy, especially by Aristotle's concept of the unmoved mover.

A. Philosophically speaking, conceptions of God have stressed absoluteness or relativity, tending to favor absoluteness.

(1) In the *Samhitas* (*q.v. Vedas* 1) Brahman (*q.v.*) is said to be of the nature of intuition, and reached by means of intuition, residing everywhere and in all things, beyond definition, of pure and infinite bliss. In the *Upanishads* (*q.v. Vedas* 4) the inward identification of one's self (*q.v. atman*) with Brahman, the soul of all things, is made. Shankara (*q.v.*) repeats both of these ideas.

(2) Xenophanes (*q.v.* 2–3) regarded God as "unmoving" and the unity of the universe.

(3) Plato (*q.v.* 4, 10) stressed God's absoluteness in his early dialogues, God's relation to the world of change in his middle dialogues, and both emphases occur in balance in his final work.

(4) Aristotle (*q.v.* 10) stressed God's absoluteness, understanding the divine to be the unmoved mover and final cause to which all is related, while remaining in its self-sufficiency and perfection unrelated to anything.

(5) Epicurus (*q.v.* 9) looked upon the gods as existing in perfect bliss and unconcern.

(6) Plotinus (*q.v.* 2–4) stressed the divine absoluteness, holding God to be the One, an absolute unity superior to existence or idea, yet the source from which emanates all that is.

(7) St. Augustine (*q.v.* 6) taught the presence of an inward path, through the

depths of the self, to God. He also (*q.v.* 10) held God's infinite being to be so richly endowed that apparently contradictory statements can be true of Him. The absolutely infinite being of St. Augustine is accepted by his medieval successors.

(8) Erigena (*q.v.* 4) viewed God as the essence of all things.

(9) Avicenna (*q.v.* 7–8) held that God has an identity of essence and existence which, in all other beings, are distinct.

(10) Averroës (*q.v.* 1–2) viewed God as eternal and absolute, yet knowing things in their essence.

(11) Peter Damian (*q.v.* 2) held God to be absolutely infinite and omnipotent, so completely so that human reason simply could not treat of God's nature.

(12) St. Anselm (*q.v.* 4) defined God as the Supreme Being, absolute yet all-knowing.

(13) Thomas Aquinas (*q.v.* 1–4) took a similar position. Although a follower of Aristotle, he held that God has knowledge of particular things through His knowledge of Himself, and of the essences of things included in that knowledge. Aquinas adopted Avicenna's point concerning the identity of essence and existence in God.

(14) William of Ockham (*q.v.* 13) in order to preserve the omnipotence and freedom of God, held that the order of nature as well as that of grace are radically dependent on God's will.

(15) Nicholas of Cusa (*q.v.* 2, 4) held that with respect to infinite being, and especially God, there is a coincidence of opposites so that some kinds of contradictory statements are equally true, *i.e.*, that God is the absolute maximum and the absolute minimum, both transcendent and immanent.

(16) Pico della Mirandola (*q.v.* 5) defined God as Being in itself, as distinct from "participated being."

(17) Calvin (*q.v.* 1) held God to be the absolute and unconditioned cause of all things.

(18) Giordano Bruno (*q.v.* 3) held God to be both transcendent and immanent.

(19) Descartes (*q.v.* 5) provided a definition of God as infinite substance.

(20) Spinoza (*q.v.* 2–3) can be accepted as a representative of that form of pantheism which identifies the conception of an absolute God with the conception of nature. Schleiermacher (*q.v.* 2) continued this definition of God as the infinite whole.

(21) In the East, Shankara (*q.v.* 4–5), stressing the reality of Brahman, the divine being as the sole reality, found it necessary—along with others in the Advaita tradition—to reduce the world to something illusory if not an out and out illusion.

(22) Swedenborg (*q.v.* 4) found three degrees of being in God, and viewed him as the highest being in an organic reality.

(23) Ramanuja (*q.v.* 1–4) retained Brahman's spiritual absoluteness and unrelatedness while recognizing individual souls and bodies as constituting the body of Brahman.

(24) Hegel (*q.v.* 3, 21) would seem to have viewed God as the absolute idea which is the source and culmination of temporal process.

(25) A number of modern thinkers, including Schelling (*q.v.* 8), Fechner (*q.v.* 3–5), Radhakrishnan (*q.v.* 3), Whitehead (*q.v.* 16–17), and Hartshorne (*q.v.* 5) have viewed God as both transcendent and immanent, absolute and relative, each in an appropriate respect.

(26) Among those who have viewed God as a finite being are John Stuart Mill (*q.v.* 9) who suggested that we may regard God as limited but benevolent. In addition there is William James (*q.v.* 12) who pictures God as relative to existence, immured in change, and engaged in struggle. Brightman (*q.v.* 3), regarding evil as a "given" in God's nature, also held to the finitude of God.

(27) S. Alexander (*q.v.* 5) regarded deity as the next stage in evolution. Teilhard de Chardin (*q.v.*) held a similar view with respect to the Omega point. Both held to a more general view of God as well.

(28) Dewey (*q.v.* 9) defined God as the "active relation" between the actual and the ideal.

(29) Boodin (*q.v.* 5) held God to be that spiritual field in which we live, move, and have our being.

(30) Holding truth to be God, and to be inseparable from non-violence, Gandhi (*q.v.* 1–3) taught that "truth-force" both leads to God and is the principal instrument of social change.

(31) Suzuki (*q.v.* 5) believed that the

term "God" (which he preferred not to use), when divested of its mythological trappings, becomes the Absolute Present, the Self within ourselves, and the infinity which pervades the finite.

(32) Schweitzer (*q.v.* 2) viewed God as ethical will and impersonal force.

(33) Buber (*q.v.* 3–4) regarded God as the eternal Thou. Since God can never become an It or object, and since knowing is of objects, our relation to God has no knowledge content in the usual sense.

(34) Karl Barth (*q.v.* 1), approaching the divine through theology, held God to be beyond explanation in rational terms.

(35) Tillich (*q.v.* 3, 4), viewing God as the ground of being, seems to wish to make God available to existence without relativizing Him to existence.

(36) Paul Weiss (*q.v.*) regards God as one of four modes of being.

(37) For Levinas (*q.v.* 4) God, who is beyond being, speaks through the face of the other.

B. The problem of God's existence has been resolved by faith, or reason, or some combination of faith and reason. Emphasis on faith leads into theology; emphasis on reason leads to arguments for God.

(38) In *The Laws* Plato (*q.v.* 10) first offered an argument for God resting on the appearance of design in nature, combined with an argument for the primacy of self-motion.

(39) The arguments offered by Aristotle (*q.v.* 10) turn on the impossibility of infinite regress in series of causes and motions.

(40) Although fully appreciated only 1,000 years later, the view that there are both negative and positive arguments for God was initiated in the West by Philo Judaeus (*q.v.* 2). The position was developed by Maimonides (*q.v.* 2–3), and Aquinas (*q.v.* 2). The positive and negative ways of the West are paralleled in the East by the *neti neti* (*q.v.*) of the *Bṛhadaranyaka Upaniṣad*, also present in Shankara (*q.v.* 4).

(41) Plotinus (*q.v.* 8) offered at least the outline of an aesthetic argument for God, moving from the unity of created objects and the structure of aesthetic experience to an affirmation about the divine.

(42) St. Augustine (*q.v.* 5–7), similarly, provides the outline of an epistemological argument for God, moving from the

idea of truth to the affirmation of God's existence. He also offered arguments from design and motion.

(43) In the 4th century Vaisheshika (*q.v.*) school Prashastapada offers a causal argument for God, combined with the claim that as the immaterial self moves the body, so an immaterial, intelligent being must supply the motive power for inanimate objects.

(44) In the 10th century Saadia (*q.v.*) argued to God from the impossibility of an infinite past. A few decades later Avicenna (*q.v.* 6) offered a refined version of Aristotle's causal argument.

(45) The 10th century Nyaya (*q.v.*) thinker, Udayana Acarya, in the *Kusumanjali* set down both causal and teleological arguments for God's existence, as well as an argument from universal practice.

(46) St. Anselm (*q.v.* 1) introduced a fully developed argument for God called the Ontological Argument. Anselm gives two versions of the argument which moves from the conception of God to the conclusion that God exists. In one version God is that than which no greater can be conceived. In the other version God is the necessary being.

(47) Bonaventure (*q.v.* 2, 3) used the arguments from cause, change, and contingency to God; but held that the reason the arguments work is that we have a dim idea of God from the very beginning. From this standpoint the ontological argument is the strongest, since there is both an intellectual and a practical contradiction in denying God's existence.

(48) Saint Thomas Aquinas (*q.v.* 2–3) brought together five arguments into his *Quinque Viae*: (a) the argument that series of motions cannot continue to infinity, (b) the argument that series of causes cannot go on to infinity, (c) the argument that the conception of a totally contingent world is inconsistent, and that it implies the existence of a necessary being, (d) the argument that the normative aspects of experience imply the existence of a normative being, and (e) the argument that the teleological aspects of existence imply an intelligent director.

(49) William of Ockham (*q.v.* 12), while rejecting the traditional arguments for God, especially those from motion and cause, argued from the conservation of

a thing in being to its conserver. This argument seemed to him valid since its denial implied an actually infinite series, and this is impossible.

(50) Telesio (*q.v.* 3) rejected Aristotle's argument from motion, since matter in his view is intrinsically in motion. He accepted, however, an argument from the order of the universe.

(51) Vásquez (*q.v.*) was the first person to rely upon the moral argument for the existence of God.

(52) Suarez (*q.v.* 2) also rejected the argument from motion and held that even valid proofs for God are beyond finite rationality.

(53) Descartes (*q.v.* 5) revived the ontological argument of Anselm, likewise presenting two versions of the argument. He used the cosmological argument in the sense that the conservation of a substance in being requires a non-contingent being, *i.e.*, God.

(54) John Locke (*q.v.* 8) presented a cosmological argument for God's existence, holding that anyone who exists could not have come from nothing, and must then have his ultimate explanation in eternal being.

(55) Newton (*q.v.* 6) found it necessary not only to posit God to explain creation, but also to explain the continuing functioning of the universe.

(56) Leibniz (*q.v.* 8) supported his own versions of the teleological, cosmological, and ontological arguments, utilizing the Principle of Sufficient Reason and his own analysis of perfection.

(57) Norris (*q.v.* 1) held that ideas are eternal, and this implies that God exists as their locus.

(58) Joseph Butler (*q.v.* 2) argued to Christianity from the presence in nature of "providential design."

(59) Hume (*q.v.* 7) found that ontological, cosmological, and teleological arguments all fail, leading us toward skepticism.

(60) Immanuel Kant (*q.v.* 5) must be mentioned in three connections: (a) His claim that the physico-theological (design, teleology) and cosmological (motion, cause) arguments reduce to the ontological argument has been influential. (b) His criticism of the ontological argument on the grounds that "Existence is not a predicate" has been often accepted as decisive.

(c) He provided a moral argument for God, beginning with the requirement of moral autonomy, and concluding with God as the only manner of satisfying that requirement.

(61) Paley (*q.v.* 2) argued that as a watch requires a watchmaker so the universe required a designer. He carried the argument through numerous instances of design in nature. Voltaire (*q.v.* 3) accepted this analogy as well as the first cause argument.

(62) John Stuart Mill (*q.v.* 9) provided an argument for a limited God on the basis of the design of the universe; but he rejected the cosmological argument on the ground that an infinite regress of causes is more reasonable than is a first cause.

(63) Josiah Royce (*q.v.* 2, 5) improved on the epistemological argument of St. Augustine, attempting to show that the recognition of error implies the existence of God.

(64) Whitehead (*q.v.* 16–19) argued in a manner somewhat similar to that of Newton, holding that God is needed to complete the system of world process.

(65) F.R. Tennant (*q.v.* 2) returned to the teleological argument, raising its level of sophistication and adducing a wider variety of types of evidence.

(66) Lonergan (*q.v.* 7) presented an argument for God based on "complete intelligibility."

C. Once again, a number of philosophers have held God to be nothing more than a projection of human awareness.

(67) The popular conception of God, according to Xenophanes (*q.v.* 1) is such a projection.

(68) The doctrine of *anitya* ("impermanence," "ceaseless change"), which can be traced back to Buddha himself, implies that permanent, unchanging, divine beings cannot exist.

(69) In Hinayana Buddhism (*q.v.*) a dilemma, which cannot be traced back to Buddha argues that, given the injustice, deceit, and falsehood of the world, either God is evil, or does not exist.

(70) Carneades (*q.v.* 3) held that the idea of God is a tissue of contradictions and so stands for nothing.

(71) A member of the Purva Mimamsa (*q.v.*) school (Kumarila Bhatta, 7th century), argued against the existence of God

on the ground that the world is eternal. He also offered the dilemma that if God had a body it would be composite and have to be created by something else; and if God is immaterial it would not be possible for him to control the world.

(72) Feuerbach (*q.v.* 1) considered God to be a projection of human knowledge, will, and love.

(73) For Nietzsche (*q.v.* 4) God was a projection of man's uneasy conscience.

(74) Sartre (*q.v.* 6) held God to be an unthreatened awareness, an impossible ideal which humans would like to have for themselves.

(75) The "Death of God" theologians (*q.v.*) seem also to view the traditional conception of God as a projection which is losing its credibility.

Also, *q.v.* Ontological argument; Teleological argument; Cosmological argument.

GÖDEL, KURT. 1906–1978.

Czechoslovakian mathematician and logician. Educated in Vienna; from 1940 through 1976 he was a member of the Institute of Advanced Study in Princeton, New Jersey.

Principal writings: "The Completeness of the Axioms of the Logical Functional Calculus," 1930; "On the Formal Undecidability Thesis of *Principia Mathematica* and related Systems," 1931; "On Intuitive Arithmetic and Number Theory," 1932; "The Consistency of the Axiom of Choice and of the Generalized Continuous Hypothesis with the Axioms of Set Theory" (E), 1940; "Russell's Mathematical Logic" (E) in *The Philosophy of Bertrand Russell*, 1914.

(1) It was Gödel's great achievement to demonstrate that the axiomatic method of mathematics cannot yield information concerning both the completeness and the consistency of the system axiomatized. This is true of the arithmetic of cardinal numbers, of all other mathematical systems of this or any greater degree of complexity, and except for the first order, of logical systems such as that one developed in the Whitehead-Russell *Principia Mathematica* (*q.v.*). He was able to demonstrate completeness with respect to first-order logic.

(2) With respect to completeness he demonstrated that, given any consistent set of arithmetical axioms whatever, there are true arithmetical statements which cannot be derived from this set of axioms. And however much the set of axioms is augmented, there will always be further true statements not derivable from the set.

(3) With respect to consistency he demonstrated that no proof of the formal consistency of the systems we here envision is possible, except by means of additional principles of inference whose consistency is as fully open to question as the consistency of the system itself.

(4) The proof is elegant but cannot be reproduced here. Gödel's strategy consists of mapping into the formalized arithmetical system, the meta-mathematical statements which explain the system. The elements of the meta-mathematical statements are mapped into the arithmetical system by associating each elementary sign of the system with a unique number. Since each element has a number, it will be possible to associate each formula or expression of the system with a number. In order that the Gödel numbers of the expressions may be unique, and so recoverable, the elements of any expression are also associated—in order of their occurrence—with the first ten prime numbers. For example, since the variables, "p" and "q" have been assigned the numbers "12" and "15," and the connective "⊃" the number "3," the expression "p⊃q" will be uniquely characterized by the number $2^{12} \times 3^3 \times 5^{15}$, taking each assignment as the power of the appropriate prime number. In a similar manner a sequence of formulae will also have a unique Gödel number. With the whole of meta-mathematics thus mapped into the arithmetical system, Gödel proceeds to demonstrate that meta-mathematical statements concerning the completeness and consistency of the system, are not demonstrable within the system; *i.e.*, if the axioms are consistent these statements are "undecidable" and the system is incomplete; but furthermore the consistency of the system cannot be determined by the axiomatic method.

Q.v. Modal Logic (6).

GÖDEL'S PROOF.

Q.v. Kurt Gödel.

GODFREY OF FONTAINES.
c. 1260–c. 1320.

Scholastic philosopher and theologian. Born in Fontaine-les-Hozémont. Educated in Paris, he became Professor of Theology at the Sorbonne, and the Bishop of Tournai. Generally adhering to the lines of Thomistic philosophy, Godfrey separated himself from this philosophy insofar as he stressed the absence of a distinction between essence and existence in the constitution of things, the passivity of the passive intellect which he regarded as moved uniquely by its object, and found the principle of individuation in the substantial form.

Principal writings: *Quaestiones quodlibetales; Ordinary Questions; Disputed Questions Concerning Virtue.*

GODWIN, WILLIAM. 1756–1836.

English political writer and social philosopher. Born at Wisbeach. Educated at Hoxton. After a short time as a Non-conformist minister, he was converted by French Encyclopedism (*q.v.*) and left the ministry. His writings helped engender the movement of Philosophical Radicalism (*q.v.*).

Principal philosophical writings: *The Inquiry Concerning Political Justice*, 1793; *Of Population*, 1820; *Thoughts on Man*, 1831.

(1) Suspicious of government but with confidence in man, Godwin held that all social institutions corrupt those involved in them. The rules and institutions regulating punishment, property, and marriage are all unjust in themselves and lead to further injustices. The solution is to achieve societies able to operate without compulsion.

(2) Such societies will be possible only when its members have so perfected themselves that when they do what is right in their own eyes, it will also be best for society. One of the steps in moving toward the goal is elimination of the categories which create ranks and distinctions in society.

(3) A Utilitarian (*q.v.*) in his ethical orientation, he held that all one does should be for the general happiness, and that this principle is incompatible with self-interest. On the other hand, he held that one's natural emotions were those of benevolence, pity, and affection. Merely providing full information about others

is enough to stimulate these emotions, and lead one to virtuous action.

GOETHE, JOHANN WOLFGANG.
1749–1832.

German Romantic-Classical poet and philosopher. Born at Frankfurt-am-Main. Educated at the universities of Leipzig and Strassburg. He was influenced by Spinoza, Herder, and Schiller. From 1775 on, Goethe's life centered in Weimar as adviser and minister of state to the Duke of Saxe-Weimar. Added to his poetic and dramatic production, and his work as statesman, he studied in the fields of botany, anatomy, optics, and geology, producing hypotheses of varying worth in these areas.

Principal writings: *The Sorrows of Young Werther* (T), 1774; *Iphigenia in Taurus* (T), 1787; *Essay on the Metamorphosis of Plants* (T), 1790; *Faust* (T), 1790–1833; *Contributions to Optics* (T), 1791–2; *Wilhelm Meister's Wander Years* (T), 1795-6; *On Color Theory*, 1810; *Poetry and Truth* (T), 4 vols., 1811–33.

(1) Setting forth in his early writings the *Sturm und Drang* (Storm and Stress) principles of German Romanticism, Goethe became at once the model of German Romantic writers. Implicit in his writings of the period is the idea that the world belongs to the strong, and that convention is to be defied in the interests of spontaneity and inner authenticity. *The Sorrows of Young Werther*, and the first part of *Faust* (composed at this time), reflect these themes.

(2) An extended visit to Italy in 1786 led Goethe to a new point of view in which Romanticism and Classicism, paganism and humanism, were to be held in balance. This point of view is reflected, for example, in the figures of Wilhelm Meister and the mature Faust. He criticized Aristotle's "spectator-theory" of catharsis on the ground that expiation and reconciliation of the tragic figures themselves is more to the point.

(3) His theory of light and color, written in opposition to Newton, has no more than historic interest; his hypothesis of plant morphology in which a teleology of implicit formal types is developed fares somewhat better. And his hypothesis of *Urpflanze*, the primal plant after which all other plants are patterned, is both

reminiscent of Plato and somewhat anticipatory of Darwin.

(4) He attempted no formal contribution to metaphysics, finding the work of Spinoza, as he said, perfectly congenial to his nature. This relates Goethe to pantheism (*q.v.*). His organic view of nature, with its premise that there is a striving upward of all forms, combined with his acceptance of Leibnizian monads, with their own internal principles of animation, suggests the position of panpsychism (*q.v.*).

(5) Goethe valued the intuitive over the rational, and the ability to see the whole in its parts, the idea or form in its concrete reality, as humanity's highest gift, almost as a revelation to consciousness offering a hint of one's likeness to God.

GOLDEN AGE.

The view that the ideal age has already occurred, in the past. The terminology was provided by Hesiod (*q.v.* 2), but the concept was held by Plato and many other ancient philosophers. In a religious sense the same concept is expressed by the ideas of original sin and the fall of man.

GOLDEN MEAN.

Q.v. Aristotle (11); Mean, Doctrine of the (1); Tragedy (6).

GOLDEN RULE.

Stated negatively by Confucius (*q.v.* 4) "What you do not want done to yourself, do not do to others," and positively by Jesus (*q.v.* Christ 3), "Do unto others, as you would have others do unto you," the rule is widely held to be the basis of all morality. Hillel (*q.v.*) anticipated Jesus in his rule, "Do not do unto your neighbor what you would not have him do unto you," although he, like Confucius, expressed the rule negatively. Kant (*q.v.* 6) believed that his Categorical Imperative expresses the basis of the rule, while strengthening it.

GOMPERZ, THEODOR. 1832–1912.

German historian of philosophy and philologist. A positivist, Gomperz utilized the techniques of both philology and modern criticism in his works on the history of philosophy.

Principal writings: *Contributions to the Criticism and Interpretation of Greek Authors*, 7 vols., 1875–1900; *Platonic Essays*, 3 vols., 1887–1905; *Greek Thinkers; A History of Ancient Philosophy* (T), 2 vols., 1893, 1902; *Hellenica*, 2 vols., 1912.

GOOD.

From Anglo-Saxon *god*, Latin *bonum*, and Greek *agathon*. The idea of the good, or of value, plays a role in all philosophical areas but primarily in Ethics, Aesthetics, and Axiology.

(1) The distinction between instrumental and intrinsic goodness, or value, begins with the Greeks (*q.v.* Plato 14). Intrinsic goods are those things good in themselves; instrumental goods have their value in making possible another good.

(2) The idea of intrinsic good hence merges with the conception of a highest good or *summum bonum* (*q.v.*).

Philosophers have offered competing interpretations of the highest good. Compare, for example, Aristotle's suggestion that happiness (*eudaimonia*) is the final good (*q.v.* Aristotle 11) with the Epicurean choice of pleasure (*q.v.* Epicurus 10) and the Stoic insistence (*q.v.* Marcus Aurelius 1) upon serene resignation (*apathia*) as the final good. Other alternatives may be cited: the Christian emphasis on love (*q.v.*), the Confucian emphasis on *li* (*q.v.*). A catalog of such goods is treated under Final Value (*q.v.*).

(3) For Plato (*q.v.* 1) himself, however, the final good was understood to be an efficacious transcendental principle acting upon the world.

(4) Aquinas (*q.v.* 8) defined the good as that which is naturally satisfying to the appetites. He also (*q.v.* Aquinas 4) included the good as one of the transcendentals, applying in some sense to everything.

(5) The idea of the good is also to be considered in Ethics (*q.v.* A.) by way of contrast to the idea of the right. In this connection the good is a conception of greater breadth than that of the right. The right concerns what ought to be done in the way of conduct where the actions of individuals intersect. The good includes those actions but extends beyond them to other realms: for example, to the aesthetic, that which deserves to be appreciated; and the true, that which deserves to be believed.

(6) Helvetius (*q.v.* 2) identified the public good with collective pleasure.

(7) For Hegel (*q.v.* 16) goodness is the coincidence of a human will with the universal, *i.e.*, the rational.

(8) For Westermarck (*q.v.* 2) the good derives from attitudes of approval in society, and the right from attitudes of disapproval, *i.e.*, as prohibitions, initially.

(9) G.E. Moore (*q.v.* 6) held the good to be a simple, unanalyzable quality like yellow, which has to be intuited. Thus, ethical intuitionism.

(10) Berdyaev (*q.v.* 4) identified the good with creativeness and spontaneity.

(11) For Wieman (*q.v.*) the basic distinction is between creative and created good.

(12) Blanshard (*q.v.*) combined in goodness the components of satisfaction and fulfillment.

GOODMAN, NELSON. 1906– .

American philosopher. Born in Somerville, Massachusetts. Studied at Harvard, receiving a B.S. degree in 1928, and after a career in industry returned for his Ph.D. degree which he received in 1941. He has taught at Tufts, the University of Pennsylvania, Brandeis, and Harvard University.

Principal writings: *The Structure of Appearance*, 1951; *Fact, Fiction and Forecast*, 1954; *Languages of Art*, 1968; *Problems and Projects*, 1972; *Ways of Worldmaking*, 1978; *Of Mind and Other Matters*, 1984; *Reconceptions in Philosophy and Other Arts and Sciences* (with C. Elgin), 1988; *How Classification Works* (ed. M. Douglas and David Hull), 1992.

(1) Although Goodman has worked extensively with the problems involved in the construction of phenomenalistic systems, including a detailed examination and criticism of Carnap's early attempt at such construction (*q.v.* Carnap 2), his commitment is in fact to the position of nominalism. Only individuals exist, and classes are the result of construction. Given this position, it is clear that classes will be interpreted in terms of their extensions, and that generally considerable attention will be given to the notion of extensionality.

(2) One of the areas in which extensionality plays a key role concerns the question of synonymy. It is Goodman's view that no two predicates are "exactly synonymous." If one tries to identify sameness of meaning with sameness of extension, the consequence is that all predicates with null extension have the same meaning. It might seem, however, that this case apart, sameness of meaning and extension can be maintained. In addition to the primary extension of any predicate, however, *i.e.*, the individuals to which the predicate applies, there is a secondary extension which includes even the inscription of the term itself; and since each of two apparently synonymous terms will have a different inscription, their secondary extensions will differ. Taking into account both primary and secondary extensions, no two terms will have exactly the same extension, and therefore no two predicates can have exactly the same meaning.

(3) In the construction of a system some decision must be made with respect to the set of predicates which will serve as the primitive, that is, undefined, basis of the system. Goodman has contributed to the discussion of the importance of simplicity as one of the criteria for this decision. One can see that simplicity is a factor by conceiving the case where simplicity has diminished to zero. In this case no predicate will extend over any other. In this case, too, the idea of system has vanished.

(4) Inductive validity in Goodman's view depends not alone on the data with which one is dealing, but also upon how well-entrenched are the predicates that we employ in our hypotheses. It is his claim that in general the hypotheses employing the better-entrenched predicates are preferable to those employing less well-entrenched predicates. His example turns on the color of the next emerald to be seen after time t. Let us form two hypotheses, one employing the predicate "green," and the other a made-up predicate "grue." We shall take green in its normal sense, and we shall take "grue" to apply to any blue thing not examined before time t, and anything examined before time t and found to be green. The hypotheses will be: "The next emerald to be examined after time t will be grue" and "The next emerald to be examined after time t will be green." Although the evidence pertinent to the

two hypotheses is equally extensive and equally strong, hypotheses including the predicate "green" have been much more frequently projected than those employing the predicate "grue" (or another term with the same primary extension). The second hypothesis, then, is seen to be better-entrenched than the first, and hence is preferable.

(5) Approaching aesthetics through the symbols employed in art, he finds that aesthetic symbols have greater density, repleteness, exemplification (standing as samples of what they represent), and more multiple and complex reference, than their non-aesthetic counterparts. Aesthetic structures are also world-making, and worlds differ in entities, emphasis, and ordering. One may be made from another by deletion, supplementation, or deformation, and any approach to universal accord is exceptional.

GOPALA-KRṢNA (KRISHNA).
Q.v. Vaiṣnavism (2a).

GORGIAS. 483–380 B.C.
Greek philosopher. Born in Leontini, Sicily. Sent in 427 to ask Athenian support against Syracuse, he eventually settled in Athens as a teacher of rhetoric, the introduction of rhetoric to Athens standing as his claim to a place in history. Classed as a Sophist, he is the central figure of the Platonic dialogue, *Gorgias*.

Principal writings: *On Nature or the Non-existent*, a lost work.

(1) Nothing exists, for if it did, it would have to come from nothing or from something. It is irrational to say that something can come from nothing and to have it come from something else is not possible either (on the grounds laid out by Eleatic philosophers.)

(2) If anything did exist it could not be known because of the difference between thought and thing.

(3) If anything could be known it could not be communicated because of the difference between intention and understanding.

(4) In the Socratic dialogue which bears his name, rhetoric is defined as the art of persuasion which yields belief about things just and unjust.

GOSALA, MAKKHALI.
Q.v. Ajivikas.

GOSPEL OF WEALTH.
Q.v. Social Darwinism (3).

GOTAMA.
Alternate spelling for Gautama Buddha (*q.v.* Buddha), and Gautama the Nyaya (*q.v.* Nyaya).

GÖTTINGEN SCHOOL.
One of the schools of neo-Kantian philosophy active during the last part of the 19th and the first part of the 20th century. Located at the University of Göttingen it followed Jacob Friedrich Fries (*q.v.*) in making a psychological, rather than a transcendental, approach, to Kant. *Q.v.* Neo-Kantianism (3).

GOVERNMENT, FORMS OF.
Q.v. State; Monarchy; Democracy; Aristocracy.

GOVIND SINGH.
Q.v. Sikhism.

GRACE.
From the Latin *gratus* ("beloved, agreeable"). The term entered theology obliquely by way of the three graces, fate (*q.v.*), fortune, and providence (*q.v.*). In theology, grace is the favor, relating to salvation, shown to humans by God.

(1) The theological concept is derived from the Old Testament conception of God as a being who avenges iniquity and yet is compassionate, gracious, and slow to anger.

(2) For the Apostle Paul (*q.v.* 1–4) the new dispensation was characterized by the working of divine grace, the order of the Mosaic law having been swept away. Man does not merit grace and, since Paul held to predestination (*q.v.*), the role of the individual in receiving divine grace seems rather slight.

(3) The view of St. Augustine (*q.v.* 12), argued against Pelagius (*q.v.*), in no way relaxes the strictness of the Pauline view. Since, to those who are saved, God not only provides grace but the will to receive it (a doctrine known as prevenient grace, *gratia praeveniens*), it is difficult to see how any individual could refuse it. If it cannot be refused then grace is irresistible, and the doctrine is so named (irresistible grace).

(4) As the institution of the sacraments (*q.v.*) developed, grace came to be related to them. Grace, as dispensed through the sacraments, led to a doctrine of sacramental grace. The sacrament is the outward sign of an inner grace.

(5) John Tauler (*q.v.*), although not in the main line of the development of the concept, would seem not to have believed in the strictest interpretation of grace, since he found ascetic practice and divine grace both elements in the "return to God."

(6) Luther (*q.v. passim*) revived the strict interpretation of the Pauline, Augustinian view. His denial of human free will went beyond Augustine.

(7) Melanchthon (*q.v.* 2) attempted to soften the implications of the strict interpretation with his doctrine of Synergism, according to which there are three factors involved and cooperating in the working of grace: the Holy Spirit, the Word, and the human will. The opposing doctrine in the language of the day, that the Holy Spirit is the only factor, called Monergism, is apparently the view held by Luther, although he did not use the term.

(8) Calvin (*q.v.* 5) held to the strict interpretation, and his views were much admired by Luther.

(9) Suarez (*q.v.* 4) was among those seeking some manner of reducing the strictness of the doctrine. His own view, named Congruism, insisted upon a congruence between free human decision, and the infallible yielding of one's will to God through grace.

(10) Jonathan Edwards (*q.v.* 3) returned to the doctrine of prevenient grace. One is free to do as one wills, but one's will is predetermined by God.

(11) More recently A.E. Taylor (*q.v.* 4) has held that there must be an eternal initiative matching the initiative of the individual and leading to immortality.

GRACIÁN, BALTASAR. 1601–1658.

Spanish moralist. Born in Belmonte de Calatayud, Aragón. A Jesuit, and the author of several books analyzing various aspects of society, his most important work was a satire on European society, containing the thesis that humanity is created pure but corrupted by civilization. The work influenced Voltaire, Schopenhauer, and Nietzsche.

Principal writings: *The Critic* (T), 1651–7.

GRAMMAR.

The study of grammar as ancillary to philosophical analysis began at least with the Sophists (*q.v.*), continued in the Middle Ages with Speculative Grammar (*q.v.*; also *q.v.* Peirce (16) who used the term to name one of the branches of semiotic), and is currently represented by Chomsky's (*q.v.* 1) analyses of generative, finite state, phrase structure, and transformational grammars. For Montague Grammar, *q.v.* Richard Montague (2).

GRAMMAR, SPECULATIVE.

Q.v. Speculative Grammar.

GRAMSCI, ANTONIO. 1891–1937.

Italian social philosopher. Born in Sardinia. Studied at the University of Turin. Active in Turin factory strikes (1916–19). Founder and elected secretary of the Italian Communist Party and of its newspaper, *Ordine Nuovo*. A member of parliament in 1924. Jailed from 1926, while a member of parliament and presumably immune from prosecution, until a week before his death in 1937. In prison, Gramsci filled 32 notebooks detailing his point of view, combining Crocean idealism with Marx.

Principal writings: *Works*, 6 vols., 1947–54. Several volumes of selections have been published from *Works*: e.g., *The Modern Prince and Other Writings* (T), 1957; *Prison Notebooks: Selections* (T), 1971.

(1) Adapting Croce to Marx, Gramsci succeeded in adding flexibility to the Marxist dialectic. Through cultural manipulation the economic class achieves "ideological hegemony" (Croce's term) over society. Class interests mask themselves as cultural values, become expressed in images and myths, extend through the media, education, and religion, end in a popular consensus so that everyone in society willingly conforms to the interests of the dominant class. "Culture" is transformed into "nature." Gramsci says "Americanism" is the clearest instance of this phenomenon.

(2) The manipulated consensus will have different profiles in different nations, so different revolutionary strategies will be appropriate. In each case a "counter-

hegemony consciousness" is needed, and a "critical theory" to guide the way. The theory should be directed toward a transformation of human potential issuing in a new awareness. Since the revolution is intellectual, intellectuals must lead it.

(3) No successful Communist revolution has yet occurred because of bourgeois manipulation. "A war of movement" being impossible, only "a war of position" is left. Counter-hegemonic action must be encouraged at all levels, and in all relations of life, including the use of participatory democracy. One must not remain aloof from democratic reforms through misguided "Pontiuspilatism."

(4) Believing ideas to be indispensable to historical change, and drawing on Croce's respect for freedom of the will and responsibility, he urged that philosophy must become a mass movement leading to the self-realization of a people, and a "philosophy of *praxis*."

GRANDY, RICHARD.
Q.v. Radical Translation (4).

GRANTH.
Q.v. Adi Granth.

GRATIAN.
Q.v. Decretal.

GRATIA PRAEVENIENS.
Q.v. Grace (3).

GREAT AWAKENING.
A religious revival that swept the colonies from the 1720's through the 1740's. Working in Calvinist-related denominations, the revival introduced an evangelical Calvinism. Jonathan Edwards (q.v.) and George Whitefield (q.v.) were among its protagonists.

GREATEST HAPPINESS PRINCIPLE.
Q.v. Utilitarianism.

GREAT INSTAURATION.
Q.v. Bacon (5).

GREAT LEARNING, THE.
Chinese philosophical classic of unknown origin, but of great influence in neo-Confucian philosophy. Attention was first called to this treatise in the 11th century A.D. It was Chu Hsi (q.v.), however, in the 12th century who gave this

book a place among the four classics, along with the *Analects*, the *Book of Mencius*, and the *Doctrine of the Mean*. From 1313 until 1915 these classics were the basis of the Chinese civil service examinations.

(1) The cultivation of personal life is the root of good and order in the world. Bringing order to the state means first bringing order to families; and bringing order to families means cultivating the personal lives of the members of the families; and such cultivation requires a rectification of the minds of those involved. But to rectify one's mind means making one's will sincere; and to make one's will sincere, one's knowledge must be extended. To extend knowledge things must be investigated. Their investigation leads to the extension of knowledge, the sincere will, the rectified mind, a cultivated personal life, a regulated family, an orderly state, and peace throughout the world.

(2) If one can renovate oneself for one day, one can do so every day. One will serve one's ruler with filial piety, one's elders with brotherly respect, the multitude with deep love. Thus one will succeed in the three items: manifesting character, loving the people, abiding in the highest good.

GREAT MOTHER, THE.
(*Mater Deum Magna*). Central figure of a religious cult making its way from Phrygia into Greece and Rome. Entering Thrace by the 6th century B.C. and Attica by the 4th, it had gained prominence in Rome by the end of the Republic, and under the Empire the cult of the Great Mother had become one of the three most important in the Roman world. Only the cults of Mithras (q.v. Mithraism) and Isis (q.v.) were as prominent.

The Great Mother, called Cybele, Dindymene, Mater Idaea, Sipylene, Agolistis, Ammas, Rhea, Gaia, Demeter, Maia, Ops, Tellus, and Ceres, was the parent of gods and men. She is the All-begetter and the All-nourisher, the fertile earth itself. She had a special relation to wild nature. Her faithful companions were lions. Centers of her worship were on mountains and in caves. Her rites of worship were orgiastic. Her attendants were the Corybantes, her priests eunuchs in female attire. Self-emasculation on the part of candidates for her priesthood not infrequently occurred at the climax of the frenzy during the services of worship. She was also regarded as a chaste and celibate deity.

Under the Empire her public festivals took place from March 15 to March 27. A sacred meteor stone, set in the head of the image of the goddess, was carried in procession. In developed form the worship of Attis was joined to worship of the Great Mother, the two representing a divine duality. Among the rites was a literal baptism of blood from the sacrifice of a bull and a ram with a promise of spiritual regeneration.

The final appearance of the cult was under Eugenius in 394 A.D.

Also *q.v.* Gnosticism (3, 5–6).

GREAT SCHISM, THE.

The separation of the Eastern and Western Churches in 1054 which lasts to this day. The immediate cause of the schism was the demand of Leo IX that the supreme jurisdiction of the Holy See at Rome be recognized. When the demand was ignored a bull of excommunication was left on the high altar of St. Sophia in Constantinople.

GREAT ULTIMATE, THE.

In Chinese thought a basic underlying principle interpreted in two different ways.

(1) Shao Yung (*q.v.* 1) is an example of those thinkers who regarded the principle as engendering *yang* and *yin* (*q.v.*) number, form, and all things.

(2) Chu Hsi (*q.v.* 1–2) regarded the Great Ultimate as a principle in its totality and thus identical with all things.

(3) In both cases it is also identified with mind, reason, and moral law.

GREEK PHILOSOPHY.

The period of Greek philosophy can be said to run from around 600 B.C. to 600 A.D. In this period of greater than a thousand years not only were all the philosophical alternatives of the Western world sketched out, but many of the scientific theories which have gained acceptance since that time: among these are the atomic theory, the heliocentric view of the solar system, and organic evolution. The philosophical alternatives occur usu-ally in schools of philosophy.

(1) The Milesian or Ionian philosophers are to be placed in the early part of the 6th century B.C. Asking for the nature of reality, they understood their question as one seeking to identify a basic substance. (a) Thales (*q.v.* 1) held this substance to be water. (b) Anaximander (*q.v.* 1) said it was the *Apeiron*, or boundless, and (c) Anaximenes (*q.v.* 1) held it to be air.

(2) The Pythagoreans (*q.v.*) existed as a school from 550–430 B.C., and as a philosophical force for several centuries beyond this time. They made many contributions to philosophical thought, chief among them being the insight that number applies to reality in a very intimate manner, and provides a key for our understanding of it.

(3) At the end of the 6th century B.C. Heraclitus (*q.v.*) of Ephesus found reality's chief feature to be its endless processes of change, and found in fire and *logos* the explanatory keys to this matter.

(4) The school of Eleatic philosophers, existing in the early half of the 5th century B.C., was founded by Parmenides (*q.v.*) and counted among its members Melissus (*q.v.*), Zeno of Elea (*q.v.*), and possibly Xenophanes (*q.v.*). The Eleatic philosophers were convinced, against the doctrine of Heraclitus, and on rational grounds, of the changeless nature of reality, and the erroneous character of sense experience.

(5) In the second half of the 5th century B.C. a solution to the conflict of permanence and change appeared with the philosophies of pluralism and atomism. The central point of the doctrine was to combine a permanence of the part with a change in the manner in which these parts are combined. The point was developed in many ways: (a) Empedocles (*q.v.*) of Agrigentum thought of earth, air, fire, and water as the elemental "roots" which in varying combinations make up all other things. (b) Anaxagoras (*q.v.*) of Clazomenae, settling in Athens, 480 B.C., held that the qualities of things go down to the constituent "seeds" or particles which make them up, that the quality of the whole depends upon the nature of the mixture, and that *Nous* or mind orders the world. (c) The Atomists, Leucippus

and Democritus (*q.v.*), understood reality to be made up of atoms and the void. The atoms are infinite in number, impenetrable, having only primary qualities. Secondary qualities, and processes of change and development, take place through configurations of atoms.

(6) Also in the second half of the 5th century B.C. the Sophists (*q.v.*) made their appearance, teaching the practical arts of life, and often advancing relativistic theses. Among these Sophists may be mentioned Protagoras (*q.v.*).—"Man is the measure of all things," Prodicus (*q.v.*)—the naturalistic origin of religion, Hippias (*q.v.*)—the artificiality of civil law, Gorgias (*q.v.*)—the renunciation of philosophy, and Thrasymachus (*q.v.*)—justice as the interest of the stronger.

(7) The classical period of Greek philosophy includes the works of Socrates (*q.v.*), Plato (*q.v.*), and Aristotle (*q.v.*), extending from about 450 to 321 B.C. In this period the natural philosophy of the pre-Socratics was synthesized with the cultural philosophy of the Sophists so that it became one important objective of philosophy to determine man's place in the universe.

(8) The influence of Socrates was continued not only in Plato's work, but also through the minor Socratic schools: the Megarian School (*q.v.*), stressing dialectic and the *reductio ad absurdum*; the Elean-Eretrian School; the early Cynic School (*q.v.* Cynicism) including Antisthenes (*q.v.*)—only individuals exist, and Diogenes (*q.v.*)—asceticism, as the means to freedom; the Cyrenaic School (*q.v.* Cyrenaicism), with Aristippus (*q.v.*) as founder—present pleasure as the goal of life.

(9) Plato's Academy (*q.v.*) and Aristotle's Lyceum (*q.v.*) continued long after the deaths of their founders, the Academy still existing under Antiochus in 68 B.C. The influence of both men continued far beyond their schools.

(10) Stoicism (*q.v.*) developed from the early Cynic School, perpetuating Socrates' influence. Its cosmology came from Heraclitus. The school was founded by Zeno of Citium (*q.v.*) around 300 B.C., and its existence continued beyond the death of Marcus Aurelius in 180 A.D.

(11) Epicureanism (*q.v.*) was founded by Epicurus (*q.v.*) in Athens in 317 B.C.

and existed beyond the time of Lucretius (*q.v.*) who died in 55 B.C. Its view concerning the end of life came from the Cyrenaics; its cosmology came from the atomists.

(12) Skepticism (*q.v.*) was founded by Pyrrho (*q.v.*), also in the second half of the 4th century B.C., and its influence was great, affecting other schools of thought; and continuing for centuries.

(13) The Roman interest in practice, as opposed to theory, led to a general tendency toward eclecticism, visible from the 3rd century B.C. on, and seen in men such as Cicero (*q.v.*), Varro (*q.v.*), Seneca (*q.v.*), and others.

(14) The final speculative effort of Greek philosophy was Neoplatonism (*q.v.*) and the period from the 3rd to the 6th century A.D. is characterized by this attempt to combine all philosophical and religious doctrines into a single system. Plotinus (*q.v.*) was the founder of the school whose influence continued into the Middle Ages.

GREEK RELIGION.

The religion of the Hellenes begins in polytheism and ends in mysticism.

(1) The religion of the Greeks, as with the people themselves, originates in an inter-mixture of the populations from the north along with Achaean, Minoan, and other influences. As a matter of varying probabilities we can relate the Greek deities to these origins: Rhea and Artemis (Minoan); Athena (Mycenean); Zeus, Hestia (Greek); Hermes, Demeter, Kore (Aegean); Aphrodite (Cyprian); Apollo, Hephaistus (Anatolian); Poseidon (Greek or Helladic); Hera (Ionian); Dionysus and Ares (Thrace). Out of this variety there emerged a pluralistic system in which Zeus is the dominant deity. But the whole pantheon of gods is necessary to the relation of worship and sacrifice, libation, and prayer; the divine beings live on Mt. Olympus, help or hinder human action, and communicate with men through divination and dreams. Zeus rules the world of gods and men with justice, not unmixed with vengeance. Ruling the whole, including Zeus, is also a sense of fate (*q.v.*) and in the background of the essentially cheerful picture there exist the chthonic powers of a nether world; there is the chance that the

Erinys, the Furies, may appear to answer the curse of the wronged. Homer and Hesiod (*q.v.*) helped to make this the common religion of the Greeks, although the system continued to develop after their time, both Dionysus (*q.v.*) and Asclepius gaining high places.

(2) Between the 7th and 4th centuries B.C. religious cults appeared with a markedly different spirit. The celebrant life was insufficient for many, and the quest for salvation replaced it. In an unfamiliar form this is the case with the orgiastic rites of Dionysus. Hellas was dotted with mystic brotherhoods. The Eleusinian mysteries (*q.v.*) of Demeter were the most prominent among them, and the Orphic Brotherhood was a special case. Promising salvation and mystic communion with God, along with many others, Orphism (*q.v.*) broke through all parochial barriers, addressing its gospel to bond and free, Greek and Barbarian alike. *Q.v.* Mystery Religions.

GREEN, THOMAS HILL. 1836–1882.

English philosopher. Born in Birkin, Yorkshire. Educated at Oxford. A neo-Hegelian, Green opposed the views of the British empiricists and Utilitarians from the standpoint of Kant and Hegel.

Principal writings: *Introduction to the Philosophical Works of David Hume*, 2 vols., (ed. Green and Grose), 1874–5; *Prolegomena to Ethics*, (ed. A.C. Bradley), 1883; *Lectures on the Principles of Political Obligation*, (vol. 2 of Nettleship's *Works of T.H. Green*), 1886.

(1) Taking mind, or self-awareness, as a clue to the nature of things, Green viewed the distinction between appearance and reality not as a distinction between the mental and what lies outside the mind, but rather as the distinction between mind as limited and mind as absolute. The universe thus comes to be construed as a divine mind.

(2) Rejecting the isolated sensations of the empiricists, he rejected also isolated desires. In each desire one seeks one's satisfaction as a whole, and this satisfaction is one's complete self-realization. Every motive has this as its goal.

(3) Given self-realization as each person's goal, since one person's claim is as valid as another's, it follows that the end of social organization is "human

perfection." On the other hand, although he viewed society and institutions in organic terms, Green insisted that it was the function of the state to provide conditions for individual development, thus rejecting the view that the citizen is subordinate to the state. A conception of human rights, including the right of revolution, and human duties, flows from this conception.

GREGORY OF NAZIANZUS. c. 329–390.

Christian theologian. Born in Cappadocia. He was made Bishop of Sasima in 370, and of Constantinople in 379. Along with Basil and Gregory of Nyssa, one of the three great Cappadocians. His theological method consisted of illuminating truths of faith by reason when reason is guided by the Scriptures. He believed, however, that certain absolute mysteries, *e.g.*, the Trinity, had simply to be accepted on faith.

Principal writings: *Forty-five Sermons*.

GREGORY OF NYSSA. c. 335–c. 398.

Christian theologian. Born in Cappadocia. He became Bishop of Nyssa. One of the three great Cappadocians, along with his brother Basil and Gregory of Nazianzus, he followed Origen (*q.v.*) in the belief in universal redemption. He believed the universe exhibited a harmonious order reflected from the supreme harmony of God. He denied the Platonic doctrine of pre-existence of souls, believing them to be created by God. He likewise drew a distinction between philosophy and theology, while holding that there should be agreement between the two orders, that of reason and that of faith.

Principal writings: *Dialogue with his Sister Macrina concerning the Resurrection; Logical Catechism*.

GREGORY OF RIMINI. c. 1300–1358.

Scholastic philosopher. Born in Italy. Studied in Paris. Taught first in Italy, and later in Paris. A member of the Eremites of Saint Augustine, he became head of the order in his later years. Both Augustinian and Ockhamite in his formation, he was more strongly influenced by the former than the latter movement. In particular he claimed, against Ockham, both the inner existence of a source for innate principles and the certainty that God, although unconstrained, always acted in terms of His perfections.

Principal writings: *Commentary on the Sentences; On Usury.*

GREGORY THE GREAT. 540–604.

Italian Churchman. Born in Rome. Augustinian in emphasis, he was elected to the papacy in 590 A.D. as Pope Gregory I. Among his achievements are the centralization of papal administration, the establishment of religious missions in England, and reform of the mass. The last-named led to his being credited with the Gregorian chant, the plainsong chants of the Church. He is also regarded as having originated the listing of the Seven Deadly Sins (*q.v.* Sin 1).

Principal writings: *Book of Rules for Pastors* (T); *Morals on the Book of Job* (T).

GRELLING PARADOX.

Q.v. Paradox (4).

GRENZSITUATIONEN.

A German term meaning "ultimate situations" or "limit situations." *Q.v.* Jaspers (7).

GRHASTHA (GRIHASTHA).

From Sanskrit, "householder." *Q.v.* Aśrama (2), Hinduism (3b).

GRICE, H. PAUL. 1913–1988.

British philosopher of language. Studied at Oxford. Taught at Oxford, and University of California (Berkeley). A proponent in the United States of Oxford ordinary language philosophy.

Principal writing: *Studies in the Way of Words*, 1989; *The Conception of Value*, 1991.

(1) Principally known for his doctrine of nonnatural meaning (meaning$_{NN}$), Grice says that the distinction between natural and nonnatural meaning is roughly that between "natural" and "conventional" signs. An instance of natural meaning is "Black clouds mean rain." While an instance of meaning$_{NN}$ is "His gesture meant he was fed up."

(2) In both cases some y is a consequence of some x: but the first is factive and the second is non-factive. Quotes are inappropriate for the first but not for the second. It is "comfortable" to introduce quotation marks in the nonnatural case: "His gesture meant: 'I'm fed up.'" In the

natural case it would be odd to say: "Those black clouds mean: 'It will rain.'" Natural meaning is involuntary; non-natural meaning is voluntary. Natural meaning has nothing to do with intention. Nonnatural meaning supposes the intention to communicate. More than this, the speaker's utterance is intended to produce an effect on the hearer by means of recognizing the speaker's intention. The speaker, then, intends the hearer to recognize the gesture as conveying the speaker's intention of being fed up.

(3) Under the rubric of "Conversational Implicative" Grice extends his analysis to metaphor, meiosis (understatement), hyperbole, deflation, and various forms of ambiguity, distinguishing between what is said and what is implied.

GROOTE, GERHARD. 1340–1384.

Dutch religious leader and philosopher. Born in Deventer near Utrecht. Taught at Cologne. Influenced by Jan van Ruysbroeck (*q.v.*), the Flemish mystic, he founded the Brotherhood of the Common Life.

Principal writings: Some hold that the *Admonitions Concerning Interior Things*, the principal part of the *Imitation of Christ* (*q.v.*), was the work of Groote. Thus, the authorship of Thomas à Kempis (*q.v.*) is in dispute.

GROSSETESTE, ROBERT. c. 1168–1253.

English philosopher, scientist, and divine. Born at Stradbrook in Suffolk. Educated at Oxford, where he eventually taught and became the first chancellor of that university. He became bishop of the see of Lincoln in 1235. Praised by Roger Bacon for his learning in the natural sciences, he was widely regarded as the first mathematician and physicist of his age. There is no question but that his descriptions of scientific method, involving analysis followed by synthesis, had a continuing influence. He held light to be the first principle of the physical universe, capable of transformation into other elements, providing both motion and intelligibility to the universe.

Principal writings: *Light; Corporal Motion and Light; The Sphere; Lines, Angles, and Figures; The Nature of Places;* as well as commentaries on Aristotle's *Physics* and *Posterior Analytics*.

GROTE, JOHN. 1813–1866.

English philosopher. Born at Beckenham. Educated at Cambridge. Taught at Cambridge. Defending the coherence view of truth, and holding that philosophy and science were complementary, he criticized Utilitarianism for omitting the "ideal" element from ethical theory.

Principal writings: *Exploratio Philosophica*, 2 vols., 1866, 1900; *Examination of the Utilitarian Philosophy*, 1870; *Treatise on the Moral Ideals*, 1876.

GROTIUS, HUGO. 1583–1645.

Dutch jurist and legal philosopher. Born in Delft, Holland. Educated at the University of London. He wrote Latin verses at nine, entered the University at 12, and received his Doctor of Laws degree at 16. He was historiographer of the United Provinces of the Netherlands at 20, and Advocate-general for Holland and Zeeland at 24. In 1613, he represented Holland before King James of England. When a theological dispute over predestination between the two hostile parties of the Netherlands, the Remonstrants (*q.v.*) and the anti-Remonstrants, developed political overtones, Grotius attempted to serve as mediator. Finally, unable to preserve neutrality, he sided with the Arminian (*q.v.*) Remonstrants against the Calvinist (*q.v.*) anti-Remonstrants. When the anti-Remonstrants gained the upper hand, Grotius was arrested, and sentenced to life imprisonment. Only thereafter was the charge defined as treason. In prison he continued his research into the basis of the law of nations. Eventually he escaped to Paris, being carried from jail in the chest normally containing the books with which he had finished. Received a pension from King Louis XIII of France in 1621. There he completed his famous work *On the Law of War and Peace*. Accepted service as Swedish ambassador to France. Died following shipwreck off the coast of Sweden.

Principal writings: *On the Law of Booty*, 1604; *On the Law of War and Peace* (T), 1625; *On the Truth of the Christian Religion*, 1627.

(1) The theme of his first book, *On the Law of Booty*, held the ocean to be free to all nations. The analysis concerned the seizure of a Portuguese galleon by a captain of the Dutch East India Company.

Influential in its own right, this analysis led him to the theme of his life work.

(2) The rules which govern the relations among men are not products of convention, but are founded in the nature of man as a social animal endowed with reason. To rational beings these rules are self-evident. The rationally discernible set of principles constitutes a natural law binding on citizens, rulers, and God alike. The power of God could no more cause an intrinsic evil to be an intrinsic good than He could cause the product of two times two to be something other than four.

(3) The power of reason led Grotius to adopt the view that each society had contracted early in its history for a specific form of government. Once chosen, the contract remains in force and cannot be revoked.

(4) The, *Jus Naturale* controls all other types of law—the *Jus Civile, Jus Gentium*, and Jus Divinum. This being the case whether nations recognize it or not, there is a Law of Nations, constituting a system of public law relating the subjects of different nations to each other.

(5) He felt that the same attitude of respect for reason provided a basis for a reconciliation of Protestant and Catholic.

(6) He held a Governmental Theory of the Atonement, viewing the sufferings and death of the Son of God not as an expiation of God's wrath but as a demonstration of His hatred of moral evil, a lesson which contributes to the divine government of the world.

GRUE.

Q.v. Nelson Goodman (4).

GRÜNBAUM, ADOLF. 1923– .

American philosopher of science. Born in Germany. Educated at Wesleyan and Yale. Taught at Lehigh and the University of Pittsburgh, providing indispensable help in establishing the Pittsburgh Center for Philosophy of Science.

Principal writings: *Philosophical Problems of Space and Time*, 1963 (enlarged second ed., 1973); *Modern Science and Zeno's Paradoxes*, 1967; *Geometry and Chronometry in Philosophical Perspective*, 1968; *The Foundations of Psychoanalysis*, 1984; *Validation in the Clinical Theory of Psychoanalysis*, 1993.

(1) Elements of conventionalism, which are to be recognized in philosophy of science, based on relativity theory, include: "the intrinsic metric amorphousness of the spatial continuum," and the postulated value of the speed of light.

(2) In his metrical paradoxes of extension Zeno (*q.v.* 2 and 3) supposed the enumerability of infinite point sets. Concentrating with Cantor (*q.v.* 6), on their non-denumerability requires us to substitute "linear continuum of points" for "point," avoiding the paradoxes.

(3) Extending his interest to psychoanalysis Grünbaum argued that clinical data, while not probatively irrelevant, cannot justify the Freudian theory of repression, including the explanation of dreams as repressed infantile desires, free association discovering "pathogens," and the sexual origin of slips of memory, tongue, ear, and pen. The data are too obviously flawed by patient suggestibility and the hypothesis of the placebo effect.

GRÜNBERG, KARL.
Q.v. Frankfurt School, The, A.

GUELFS.
A term in use in the 13th and 14th century to signify those who favored the spiritual power in contrast with the Ghibellines who favored temporal power. The terms were used throughout Italy and Germany, referring to the struggles between papacy and feudal nobility, and the emerging urban classes against the feudal lords. In 1334 Pope Benedict XII forbade, to no effect, the use of the terms.

GUIZOT, FRANCIS.
Q.v. Toleration (10).

GUNA.
Sanskrit for "strand" or "thread." In the Sankhya (*q.v.* 4) school the *gunas* are the three constituents of *prakriti*, or material substance. Differences in the mixtures of *gunas* account for different individual substances. In the Vaisheshika (*q.v.* 1) school *gunas* are the fleeting qualities of substances, (*e.g.*, color, taste, sound, smell, texture). In Jainism (*q.v.* 1) they are the general features of substances (*e.g.*, earthy, hot, heavy).

GUNDISALVO, DOMINIC. 12th cent.
Scholastic philosopher. A member of the school of translators of Toledo, he provided a classification of the sciences derived from an Arabic interpretation of Aristotle. Science is first divided into human and divine, the former deriving from human faculties and the latter from revelation. The human sciences are comprised by the science of eloquence, the middle science (mathematics), and the science of wisdom. The latter in turn consists of theoretical philosophy and practical philosophy. Theoretical philosophy consists of physics, mathematics, and first philosophy. Practical philosophy consists of politics, family government, and ethics. His metaphysics contained a concept of reality divided into successive grades of being.

Principal writings: *On the Divisions of Philosophy*; *On the Procession of the World*; *On Unity*; *On the Soul*.

GUTIERREZ, GUSTAVO.
Q.v. Theology of Liberation (1, 6).

GUYAU, JEAN-MARIE. 1854–1888.
French philosopher. Born in Laval. Concentrating on ethical theory, he defended an ethic of spontaneity against the traditional ethics of obligation. Most ethical systems, in his view, not only that of Kant but also Utilitarianism, are traditional ethics of obligation. One should look instead toward the natural impulse to creation. Adopting Fouilleé's (*q.v.*) concept of "thought-force," Guyau held that even thinking out one's ideals is a force leading in the direction of their realization. Both art and religion, properly understood, likewise center in spontaneity.

Principal writings: *Epicurean Morality*, 1878; *Contemporary English Morality*, 1879; *The Problems of Contemporary Aesthetics*, 1884; *Outline of a Morality without Obligation or Sanction*, 1885; *The Irreligion of the Future* (T), 1887; *Art from the Sociological Point of View*, 1889; *Education and Heredity* (T), 1889.

GUYON, JEANNE MARIE. 1648–1717.
French mystic. Born at Montargis. Interested in mysticism from convent school days, Guyon was the center of the Quietist movement in France (*q.v.* Quietism.)

Convincing in her discourses and writings about mysticism, Guyon made Quietism her life-purpose, travelling for five years through southern France, eastern Switzerland, and northern Italy, presenting that mystical alternative to the populace with great effect. For a time Archbishop Fénelon (*q.v.*) supported her cause and learned from her; and for a time she had influence with ladies of the French court. At length she was suspected of heresy, imprisoned five years in the Bastille, and then released under surveillance to live on her son's estate near Blois. The estate at once became a center for pilgrimages not only by the French, but by admirers from many parts of Europe.

Principal writings: *Works* (T in part), 40 vols., 1767–91.

H

HABERMAS, JÜRGEN. 1929– .

Born in Düsseldorf, Germany. Studied at Göttingen, Zurich, and Bonn. Taught at Heidelberg and Frankfurt. Now with the Max Planck Institute in Starnberg. A member of the Frankfurt School (*q.v.* D., 10–11) from the late 1950's until 1972.

Principal writings: *The Structural Transformation of the Public Sphere* (T), 1962; *Theory and Practice* (T), 1963; *On the Logic of the Social Sciences* (T), 1967; *Knowledge and Human Interests* (T), 1968; "Technology and Science as 'Ideology,'" in *Towards a Rational Society* (T), 1968; *Legitimation Crisis* (T), 1973; *Philosophical Hermeneutics* (T), 1976 (a collection trans. from *Kleine Schriften*); *The Reconstruction of Historical Materialism*, 1976; *Communication and the Evolution of Society* (T), 1979; *Theory of Communication*, 1981; *Philosophical Discourse on Modernity* (T), 1985; *The Theory of Communicative Action*, 1985; *Postmetaphysical Thinking* (T), 1988; *Moral Consciousness and Communicative Action* (T), 1990; *Justification and Application: Remarks on Discourse Ethics* (T and compiled from German essays published in 1990–91), 1993.

(1) It can be argued that Habermas' lifelong project has been to reposition the criticism of society he gained from Marxism and from the Frankfurt movement, called "critical theory," so that it would be a relevant instrument of analysis. The first step in this repositioning occurred before 1972. Where the usual Frankfurt critique of positivism had urged a return from empirical to hermeneutic science in order to resolve the fact/value tension, Habermas traced both science and norms to social interests. The problem, then, was to understand the contrasting values reflected in scientific and other enterprises.

(2) In *Legitimation Crisis* Habermas points out that capitalism utilizes economic exchange as its basic steering mechanism. Crises occur when economic steering problems are not solved. Legitimation crises occur when the interpretive systems of society are not acceptable to large numbers; at such times it is no longer possible to maintain effective normative structures by administrative means. There are many kinds of legitimation deficits in capitalist society, even though class-compromise has replaced class-conflict.

(3) While the claim of the theoreticians of advanced capitalism is that the ideological clash of the past has been overcome, the fact is that instrumental reason has given us a managed society characterized by systematic distortion and concealed domination. This is, of course, the Frankfurt theme of technological rationality; but Habermas sees the problem operant in both of the alternatives open to us, bureaucratic capitalism and bureaucratic socialism.

(4) Marx was wrong in believing that changes in the mode of production would lead to socialism or that such a transition would be emancipatory. Processes of democratization are needed in both systems. This in turn will be possible only when free and open mutual communication is possible at all levels without the subtle distortions now shaping us in society. This would be an "ideal speech situation." It does not now exist, yet it is Habermas' answer to what the "critical theory" of society must be, that is, "comprehensive theory of communicative action and rationality," also termed a "universal pragmatics." It rests upon the belief that a stubborn transcendent power is to be found in "communicative rea-

son," and supposes a partiality for rationality in human beings.

(5) Because philosophy is "a totalizing knowledge" the search for communicative reason, he has argued, must take place within the framework of sociology, where philosophy of history becomes "genetic structuralism." Another alternative is of course, to view philosophy as not totalizing, and intimately related to the social sciences; and that is Habermas' usual position.

(6) A debate between Habermas and Gadamer (q.v. 4) over hermeneutics and critical theory, which began in 1967, continued until 1971. Habermas held that Gadamer overplays the role of tradition, underplays the power of reason to "shake the dogmatism of life-practice," and fails to see that hermeneutic inquiry requires philosophy of history, taken as a practical enterprise. Habermas' position is given in "On the Scope and Function of Hermeneutical Reflection," in *Philosophical Hermeneutics*.

(7) The ethics of Habermas, which he terms "communicative ethics" or "minimal ethics," concerns fair procedures in adjudicatory normative claims. This is related to a concept of rationality open to "the value standard through which desires and feelings are interpreted," to "decentered unbound subjectivity," to esthetics, and to prerational and unconscious prompting.

HABIT.

From the Latin *habitus* ("state or appearance") from *habere* ("to have, be in a condition"). The Greek term *lexis* is Aristotle's term for this state or condition of body or mind.

(1) Aristotle (q.v. 11) utilized the concept of habit in his ethics to explain how a disposition to act virtuously is developed from the mere capacity to so act. The disposition to act virtuously results from virtuous habits, and the habit is built upon virtuous activity. The circularity seems not to be vicious. Thomas Aquinas (q.v. 8) follows Aristotle here.

(2) In the empirical tradition habit gains additional functions in the forming of conceptions. Condillac (q.v. 3) placed it at the basis of all intellectual functions. In Hume's (q.v. 3) analysis it is the force of habit which explains causality, and thus the building up of any world at all.

(3) Charles Peirce (q.v. 5) generalized the role of habit to its limit, finding one of its applications in the tendency of the universe to become orderly.

(4) The role of habit is, of course, basic to the discipline of psychology (q.v. 3, 5, 8) where, by means of repetition, the patterned response systems of individual life are formed.

HAECCEITAS.

Q.v. Duns Scotus (5–6); Haecceity.

HAECCEITY.

From the Latin *haecceitas* meaning "thisness" or "specificity." The principle of individuation in Duns Scotus (q.v. 5–6). Approximations to the view are to be found also in other Schoolmen, especially those of the Oxford school. "Thisness" is presented as an alternate to matter as the means of understanding the step from *infima species* (the smallest species) to individual thing.

HAECKEL, ERNST. 1834–1919.

German biologist and philosopher. Born in Potsdam. Educated at Würzburg, Berlin, and Vienna. Taught at Jena. A scientist turned philosopher, Haeckel accepted Darwinian evolution as the key to philosophic truth. His philosophy was naturalistic, monistic, and pantheistic. He was a lifelong admirer of Spinoza and Goethe.

Principal writings: *General Morphology of Organisms*, 2 vols., 1866; *The History of Creation* (T), 1868; *On the Origin and Genealogical Tree of the Human Species*, 1868; *Anthropogenie* (T, *The Evolution of Man*), 1874; *Ends and Goals of the Present History of Evolution*, 1875; *Free Science and Free Teaching* (T), 1878; *Monism as the Bond between Science and Religion* (T), 1893; *Systematic Phylogeny.*, 3 vols., 1894–6; *Wonders of Life* (T), 1894; *The Riddle of the Universe* (T), 1899.

(1) In extending the principles of evolution to the lowest inorganic levels, Haeckel filled what seemed to him to be gaps with two *ad hoc* entities: *monera* and *gastrae*. The former primitive, protoplasmic organisms he regarded as coming from inorganic matter by spontaneous generation. The latter fill a gap between

single-celled protozoa and multicellular metazoa. Now rejected, these hypotheses were treated with respect for a period of time.

(2) Haeckel believed that all matter, and even the ether, possessed low-grade will and sensibility. This hylozoistic (*q.v.*) or pan-psychistic (*q.v.*) hypothesis supported his naturalistic interpretation of reality, allowing him to view human consciousness as a function of human organism, facilitated by the presence of a central nervous system.

(3) He argued for a "monistic religion," and for pantheism as the "world-system" of modern science.

HÄGERSTRÖM, AXEL. 1868–1939.

Swedish philosopher. Calling his view "enlightened materialism," Hägerström worked for the elimination of metaphysical statements from philosophy, law, philosophy of history, and the sciences; he held that judgments of value and obligation lack truth value, consisting of an idea linked to an emotion. He is recognized as the founder of the anti-metaphysical Uppsala School of Philosophy.

Selected writings: *The Principle of Science* (G), 1908; *Inquiries into the Nature of Law and Morals* (T, by C.D. Broad), 1953; *Philosophy and Science* (S), 1957.

HAGGADAH.

From the Hebrew *higgyd* ("to relate"). *Q.v.* Judaism (2c).

HAGIOGRAPHA.

A Greek term meaning "holy writings." The term is of Christian origin and refers to the third division of the Old Testament, also known simply as "the Writings."

HAGIOGRAPHY.

Writings first appearing in early Christian times on the lives of the saints and lives of martyrs.

HAHN, HANS.

Q.v. Vienna Circle of Logical Positivists (2).

HALAKHA.

A Hebrew term meaning "practice" or "rule." *Q.v.* Judaism (2c).

HALEVI (HA-LEVI), JUDAH OR YEHUDA. c. 1070–1143.

Jewish philosopher. Born in Tudela, Spain. Traveling widely Halevi lived in Córdoba, Granada, Cairo and, perhaps, Jerusalem. He argued for Judaism as bearer of the "true revelation" in contrast to the beliefs of the Christian and Moslem communities. Much studied in the Middle Ages, he attacked the Aristotelian doctrine of the eternity of matter as well as the doctrine of emanation. He held to a limited free will, and to a doctrine of intermediary causes between God and any final effect. He believed in direct revelation and its preservation through tradition, that the doctrine of the immortality of the soul was essential to religion, and in the insufficiency of philosophy and the primacy of faith. His poetry is venerated as among the most highly inspired in the Hebrew language. His writings were originally in Arabic and Hebrew. *Q.v.* Judaism (9).

Principal writings: *Kuzari: Proofs and Arguments in Defense of the Despised Religion* (T); *Hymn of the Creation.*

HALFWAY COVENANT.

Q.v. Covenant (5).

HAMANN, JOHANN GEORG. 1730–1788.

German philosopher-theologian. Born at Königsberg, Prussia. Studied theology and law. Hamann's thought is oracular and unsystematic, but he influenced Herder, Jacobi, Goethe, and Hegel. Accepting Hume's analysis of experience as a helpful first step in constructive theology, Hamann felt that Kant's separation of sense and understanding, matter and form, resulted in empty abstraction. Concreteness is indispensable, and this is available through the idea of an identity of contraries, which he found in Giordano Bruno. The problems of Kant's first critique may be overcome, he felt, through attention to language.

Principal writings: Numerous brief monographs collected in his *Works*, 9 vols., 1821–43.

HAMILTON, ALEXANDER.

Q.v. Federalist Papers.

HAMILTON, WILLIAM. 1788–1856.

Scottish philosopher. Born in Glasgow.

Educated at Oxford. Taught at Edinburgh. He was influenced by Reid, Stewart, and Immanuel Kant.

Principal writings: *Philosophy of the Unconditioned*, 1829; *New Analytic of Logical Forms*, 1846; *Discussions in Philosophy, Literature, and Education*, 1852–3; *Lectures on Metaphysics and Logic*, (ed. Mansel and Veitch), 4 vols., 1859–60.

(1) Hamilton attempted to improve on Aristotle's system of logic by his decision to provide for the Quantification of the Predicate. This allows eight different forms of statement:

(a) All A is all B
(b) All A is some B
(c) Some A is all B
(d) Some A is some B
(e) Any A is not any B
(f) Any A is not some B
(g) Some A is not any B
(h) Some A is not some B

(2) In epistemology, Hamilton agreed with Reid that objective knowledge is possible because "the root of our nature cannot be a lie." The starting point of objective knowledge, however, is an empirical "phenomenology" of the human spirit, which he identified with descriptive psychology, and which provides a basis for logic.

(3) But since an object is known through its relations to other objects, *i.e.*, as conditioned, there can be no knowledge of the infinite, whether in time, space, or power.

(4) This limitation opens a sphere for faith, or the Unconditioned, providing the object reason demands but cannot conceive.

HAMILTON, WILLIAM.

American theologian. *Q.v.* Death of God Theologians; Theology (20).

HAMMURABI, CODE OF.

Originating between 2100 and 1800 B.C., the Hammurabi Code is based on still more ancient material. Consisting of 282 laws allegedly given to King Hammurabi by the Babylonian god, Shamash, for the governing of the people, the Code was discovered in 1902. Based on similarity of content, the Code would appear to have influenced the Mosaic law.

HAN FEI TZU. 3rd century B.C.

Chinese philosopher. The Prince of Han, and systematizer of the Legalist School (*q.v.*) of philosophy, Han Fei Tzu committed suicide in 233 B.C., apparently because the king of Ch'in refused his offer of service.

Principal writings: *Complete Works* (T).

(1) Virtue and kindness are insufficient to end disorder, while awe-inspiring power is capable of doing so. Occasionally there is a naturally good man, but the ruler must work with all men. Hence, he must practice straightening and bending, using the two handles of punishment and kindness.

(2) Confucianism and Moism, lauding humanity and righteousness, are overly optimistic. Their references to sage kings cannot be verified and, generally, successful rulers rely on power, not humanity.

(3) At the same time the *Tao* does operate in the world, controlling all things, and exercising its dominance by means of material force. The sage understands this and utilizes its operations everywhere.

HANSON, N.R.

Q.v. Philosophy of Science (28).

HAN YU. 768–824.

Chinese neo-Confucian philosopher. Along with Li Ao (*q.v.*) he determined the direction of neo-Confucian philosophy, restoring its historic emphasis on human nature, and possibly saving it from annihilation by Taoism and Buddhism.

Principal writings: *An Inquiry on Human Nature* (T in part); *An Inquiry on the Tao* (T in part).

HAPPINESS.

From middle English *hap*, old Norse *happ* meaning "good luck." Also in Greek *eudaimonia* means "to be prosperous or well-off" as well as "to be happy."

(1) In fulfillment theories of valuation, happiness, as a state of being somehow different from a sum of pleasures, stands as the end of life. Aristotle's view of happiness (*q.v.* 4) sets the pattern in this respect. Epicurus (*q.v.* 10) defined happiness, largely at least, in terms of pleasure with prudence an important ancillary value. Aquinas (*q.v.* 8) followed Aristotle

although adding a theological dimension.

(2) The "greatest happiness" principle for Bentham (*q.v.* 2) and the Utilitarians, on the other hand, means the "greatest sum of pleasures" (*q.v.* Utilitarianism).

(3) Norris (*q.v.* 1) may be cited among the many who have held that the highest happiness lies in the contemplative love of God.

(4) Kant's (*q.v.* 8) conviction that virtue and happiness belong together led him to postulate both immortality and the existence of God.

HARE, R.M. 1919– .

English philosopher. Educated at Oxford. Has taught at Oxford and the University of Florida (Gainesville).

Principal writings: *The Language of Morals*, 1952; *Freedom and Reason*, 1963; *Essays on Philosophical Method*, 1971; *Practical Inferences*, 1971; *Applications of Moral Philosophy*, 1972; *Essays on the Moral Concepts*, 1972; *Moral Thinking*, 1981; *Essays on Ethical Theory*, 1989; *Essays on Political Morality*, 1989; *Essays on Religion and Education*, 1992.

(1) Directing attention to the complex logical behavior of value words as a key to the understanding of ethical behavior, Hare holds that while ethical terms have both descriptive and evaluative meanings, the evaluative meanings are primary.

(2) When the logic imposed by moral concepts is understood and followed, what emerges is a "rational universal prescriptivism" capable of illuminating important practical moral problems.

(3) He distinguishes the *phrastic* element of a sentence, common to both commands and statements, from a *neustic* element which has a different bearing in the two kinds of sentences. The former is the pointing out or indicative element of the sentences. The latter is the assenting aspect of the sentence. Assenting to a command has a very different structure from assenting to a statement.

(4) In philosophy of religion Hare subscribes to a "minimum Braithwaitian position" deriving from Braithwaite's (*q.v.* 5) interpreting religion, specifically Christianity, as moral endeavor.

HARIJANS.

Sanskrit for "children of God," a term used by Gandhi to designate those formerly called outcastes. The class consisted of those excluded from the four Hindu castes. The reason was ritual pollution (for example, people who consume animal flesh, or whose work involves the handling of human or animal waste products) and the outcastes were often segregated, and sometimes forced to lead a nocturnal existence.

Q.v. Caste; Gandhi (4).

HARMONY.

From the Greek *harmos* ("a fitting or joining"). The principle has played a role, modest but continuing, in the philosophy both of the East and of the West.

(1) In the ancient Chinese *Doctrine of the Mean* (*q.v.* 1) the term is defined as a state in which the feelings of pleasure, anger, sorrow and joy are aroused in "due measure and degree," and contrasted with "equilibrium," the state prior to the arousal of such feelings.

(2) For the Pythagoreans the term is given cosmic application. The regularities present in astronomy led them to a concept of the "music of the spheres." Harmony was also held to be the most basic requirement of a healthy body (*q.v.* Pythagoras 4; Pythagoreanism).

(3) For Aquinas (*q.v.* 10) harmony, or *consonantia*, is one of the essential factors in the experience and explanation of beauty.

(4) In Leibniz (*q.v.* 7) the order of the universe is explained by a doctrine of pre-established harmony.

HARNACK, ADOLF VON. 1851–1930.

German Lutheran church historian.

Principal writings: *History of Dogma* (T), 7 vols., 1889–1922; *The Apostle's Creed* (T), 1892; *The Essence of Christianity* (T), 1900; *Marcion*, 1921.

HARRINGTON, JAMES.

Q.v. Utopia (7).

HARRINGTON, MICHAEL. 1928–1989.

Born in St. Louis, Missouri. Studied at Holy Cross, Chicago, and Yale. Taught at Queens College. A major figure in American Socialism.

Principal writings: *Labor in a Free Society*, 1959; *The Other America*, 1962; *The Accidental Century*, 1965; *Toward a Democratic Left*, 1968; *Socialism*, 1972. *The Twi-*

light of Capitalism, 1976; *The Next America*, 1981; *The Politics at God's Funeral*, 1983; *The New American Poverty*, 1984.

(1) Returning to the orthodoxy of Marx, Harrington holds that socialism requires a proletariat as the vehicle of revolutionary change, and that therefore the contemporary surrogates of peasants, party cadres, and military are unsatisfactory, do not realize the intended goal, and betray Marx's vision.

(2) He also views socialism in moral terms. It is to be achieved through the slow development of a free and worthy people. Thus, gradualism becomes central, and the "dictatorship of the proletariat" becomes peripheral, and is perhaps transformed into something like a metaphor.

HARRIS, WILLIAM TORREY. 1835–1909.

American philosopher. Born in North Killingly, Conn. Educated at Yale. Teacher and administrator in the Saint Louis public school system. A leader of the Saint Louis Hegelians (*q.v.*), Harris founded and edited *The Journal of Speculative Philosophy* (1867–93), directed the Concord School of Philosophy from 1879–87, and served as the first U.S. Commissioner of Education, 1889–1906. An enthusiastic Hegelian, he applied the dialectic both to American history and the problems of public school education.

Principal writings: *Hegel's Logic*, 1890; *Introduction to the Study of Philosophy* (ed. Kies), 1890.

HARRIS, ZELIG.

Q.v. Semantics (5).

HART, H.L.A. 1907– .

English philosopher of law. Professor of jurisprudence at Oxford. Coming out of the tradition of Wittgenstein and Austin, Hart centers on the analysis of legal concepts. He separates law from morality, allowing natural law only the point that survival requires that certain minimal conditions be met. He sees law as a union of two sets of rules: the primary rules which impose duties upon us, and secondary rules instructing us on how to recognize, change, and adjudicate the primary rules. Also *q.v.* Dworkin (1).

Principal writings: "The Ascription of Responsibilities and Rights," 1948–49; "Definition and Theory in Jurisprudence,"

1954; *Causation in the Law* (with Honoré), 1959; *The Concept of Law*, 1961; *Law, Liberty and Morality*, 1963.

HARTLEY, DAVID. 1705–1757.

English philosopher and psychologist. Born in Luddenden. Educated at Cambridge. Influenced by Locke and Newton, Hartley developed the "association of ideas" of the former into an associationist psychology. Regarded as the founder of that form of psychology, it was his program to demonstrate that by repeated use of the law of contiguity all states of consciousness—memory, emotion, reasoning, and voluntary and involuntary actions—can be derived from sensation. He believed, further, that disinterested sentiment is possible for one, and grows from self-regarding motives; and that religious belief in the existence of God and immortality is consistent with an associational approach. Hartley's analysis influenced Bentham and the Mills (*q.v.* John Stuart Mill 1).

Principal writings: *Enquiry into the Origin of the Human Appetites and Affections*, 1747; *Observations on Man*, 2 vols., 1749.

HARTMAN, GEOFFREY.

Q.v. Deconstruction (6).

HARTMANN, EDUARD VON. 1842–1906.

German philosopher. Born in Berlin. A military man who turned to philosophical writing in 1865, Hartmann published his *Philosophy of the Unconscious* shortly thereafter. This gave him immediate fame, and shaped his later writings.

Principal writings: *Philosophy of the Unconscious* (T), 3 vols., 1869; *The Unconscious from the Standpoint of Physiology and Heredity Theory*, 1877; *Phenomenology of the Moral Consciousness*, 1879; *Theory of the Categories*, 1898; *System of Philosophy in Outline*, 8 vols., 1907–9.

(1) Hartmann's major point resulted from combining Schopenhauer's blind will with Hegel's rational idea, so that the poles of cosmic, cultural, and individual development are unconscious striving on the one hand and conscious fulfillment on the other, pain and suffering on the one hand and salvation on the other. The presence of levels of un-

conscious striving in the individual was accepted and developed by Freud.

(2) The formal structure of this process of development was worked out in Hartmann's *Theory of the Categories.*

(3) Hartmann believed that a phenomenology of the moral consciousness, by which he meant an inventory of the empirical facts of moral awareness, was an essential preliminary to the discovery of moral principles.

(4) Hartmann was one of the first to use the term "Axiology" to apply to the study of all types of value.

HARTMANN, NICOLAI. 1882–1950.

German philosopher. Born in Riga, Latvia. Educated at St. Petersburg, Dorpat, and Marburg. Taught at Marburg, Cologne, Berlin, and Göttingen. Trained in the neo-Kantian School of Marburg, Hartmann also incorporated in his thought Hegelian and neo-Hegelian influences, combining critical and phenomenological techniques in an original manner.

Principal writings: *Outlines of a Metaphysic of Knowledge,* 1921; *Ethics* (T), 3 vols., 1926; *Foundations of Ontology,* 1935; *Possibility and Reality,* 1938; *The Structure of the Real World,* 1940; *New Ways of Ontology* (T), 1942; *Philosophy of Nature: Outlines of the Special Doctrine of Categories,* 1950; *Teleological Thought,* 1951.

(1) Insisting that it is the role of the philosopher to be faithful to the problem and not the system, Hartmann developed an approach offering insights on ontology, epistemology, ethics, aesthetics, logic, and philosophy of history.

(2) Phenomenological analysis played an important role in the analysis of oppositions which are resolved by means of the philosophical imagination. For example, the subject-object opposition is resolved by viewing each of these as a partial manifestation of being. The contrast between epistemology and ontology leads to the inclusion of the former in the latter, and hence to a realistic ontology in which the basic categories of explanation have ontological status.

(3) The categories are granted different levels of value and are interrelated. The interior categories have the greater strength; the superior categories have the greater autonomy; the categories of superior level contain many of the properties of those below them, but the reverse is not the case.

(4) The combination of points 2 and 3 yields a notion of transcendence in Hartmann leading to his philosophy of the spirit, liberty, and human individuality. In another connection the yield is a conception of transcendent being beyond understanding.

(5) Hartmann's analysis of ethics bases moral value on the disposition of the agent. His analysis of the virtues is reminiscent of the analysis of Aristotle. Virtues and values are viewed both hierarchically and as possessing objective validity.

HARTSHORNE, CHARLES. 1897– .

American philosopher. Born in Kittanning, Penna. Educated at Haverford College and Harvard University, he taught at the University of Chicago, Emory, and the University of Texas.

Principal writings: *The Collected Papers of Charles Sanders Peirce,* 6 vols., 1931–35 (ed. with Paul Weiss); *The Philosophy and Psychology of Sensation,* 1934; *Beyond Humanism,* 1937; *Man's Vision of God and the Logic of Theism,* 1941; *The Divine Relativity,* 1947; *Reality as Social Process,* 1953; *Philosophers Speak of God* (with William L. Reese), 1953; *The Logic of Perfection,* 1962; *Anselm's Discovery,* 1965; *A Natural Theology for our Time,* 1967; *Creative Synthesis and Philosophic Method,* 1970; *Aquinas to Whitehead,* 1976; *Whitehead's View of Reality,* 1981; *Insights and Oversights of Great Thinkers,* 1983; *Creativity in American Philosophy,* 1984; *Omnipotence and other Theological Mistakes,* 1984; *Wisdom as Moderation,* 1987.

(1) The world is interpreted as a society panpsychic in nature, from God to the smallest pulse of experience.

(2) Our sensations are understood to be feelings of feelings; thus the qualitative nature of experience is not illusive but psychic. At the same time the world is viewed as organic and the present as inclusive of the past.

(3) Pointing out that the classical conception of God stressed the category of absoluteness almost exclusively, leading to an asymmetrical relation between God and the world where the world is related to God but not God to the world,

Hartshorne argued for a dipolar conception of God stressing both absoluteness and relativity. In this conception God is eternal, temporal, a conscious being, knowing the world, and world-inclusive; in abbreviated neologism, ETCKW. Other conceptions may be expressed by eliminating one or another of these properties. God is understood to be the surrelatively perfect Being, *i.e.*, the concept is that of a growing perfection. This conception of perfection is required since not all possible values are compossible at one time, but may be so in different times. Hence, if God is to represent the absolute maximum, this implies that God will be the absolute maximum in each time. This means, further, that while no other being can surpass God, God must in fact be self-surpassing. God is also the all-inclusive being who includes the entire world as we include parts thereof. The example is often employed that we are as cells in the divine organism, having a certain amount of autonomy, and yet included in a larger whole. Hartshorne supports panentheism (*q.v.*) in philosophy; all is in God, yet "God" and "world" do not form an identity.

(4) All of the traditional arguments for the existence of God show us something; they need, indeed, to be taken together and not separately. The ontological argument shows that either the idea of God is meaningless or that God exists. Finding in Anselm two versions of the ontological argument Hartshorne views the second version, turning on necessary existence as sound and the first, turning on existence as a perfection, as flawed.

(5) God's nature has been described in (3) above as dipolar. God is characterized by both absolute and relative, necessary and contingent aspects. The world has a similar dipolarity in that the future is contingent while the past is necessary. The contingent future entails that God's knowledge embraces the facts of the past and present, and the possibilities of the future.

HASIDISM.
From the Hebrew *hasid* ("pious"). A movement of Jewish mysticism, originating in Poland in the 18th century. Founded by Israel ben Eliezer (*q.v.* Cabala 3f), Hasidism reached its greatest power in the first half of the 19th century. Through Ravel, Bloch, Singer, and Buber (*q.v.*) Hasidism helped to shape the music, literature and philosophy of the Jewish community. The emphasis of the movement on God's immanence, and of the possibility of man's constant communion with Him, led to a strong sense of joy in worship and a release of human energies. Working within the forms of Judaism, the movement so transformed its spirit that the orthodox feared the dangers of Hasidic enthusiasm. Indeed, the *hasidim* were persecuted throughout the second half of the 18th century. The movement declined in the latter half of the 19th century.

HATHA YOGA.
One of the four types of yoga which stresses discipline of the body as the means to liberation (*q.v.* Yoga 5).

HAYYIM VITAL.
Q.v. Cabala (3e).

HEBREO, LEON.
Q.v. Leon Hebreo.

HEDGEHOG AND THE FOX, THE.
Q.v. Berlin (1).

HEDONIC CALCULUS.
Q.v. Jeremy Bentham (3).

HEDONISM.
From the Greek *hedone* meaning "delight, enjoyment, pleasure." Among those who have held that pleasure is the end of human life and action, or ought to be the end, or both, one would wish to mention the following:

(1) The Cyrenaics with their founder, Aristippus (*q.v.*).

(2) The Epicureans and their founder, Epicurus (*q.v.*).

(3) The Christian Epicureanism of Valla (*q.v.* 1) and Erasmus, (*q.v.*).

(4) The Utopian Epicureanism of Sir Thomas More (*q.v.*).

(5) Hobbes (*q.v.* 6) who taught that pleasure and pain emerge from physical sources.

(6) The Utilitarians, both their founder, Jeremy Bentham (*q.v.* 1–2), and principal exponent, John Stuart Mill (*q.v.*).

(7) The naturalistic French *philosophes* of the 18th century, Helvetius (*q.v.* 1),

Holbach (*q.v.*) and de La Mettrie (*q.v.*), for example.

(8) Any system of philosophy or human nature whose categories are wholly naturalistic or materialistic; behavioristic psychology, for example.

(9) In fact, a number of types of hedonism exist, and they are seldom distinguished from one another. Psychological hedonism holds that one always acts, and must act, from a desire for pleasure.

(10) Egoistic ethical hedonism holds that one always ought to act in whatever manner will bring one the most pleasure in the long run.

(11) Universal ethical hedonism holds, and Utilitarianism is an instance of this view, that one ought always to act in whatever manner will bring the most pleasure to the greatest number in the long run.

(12) Barthes (*q.v.* 9) returns to hedonism in the mode of readerly authority.

HEGEL, GEORG WILHELM FRIEDRICH. 1770–1831.

German philosopher. Born in Stuttgart. From 1788–93 he studied theology at Tübingen University with Schelling and Hölderlin. Associated with Schelling at the University of Jena from 1801 to 1807, together they published a journal of philosophy. He was rector of the Gymnasium at Nuremberg, 1808–16, Professor of Philosophy at Heidelberg, 1816–18, and the University of Berlin, 1818–31. Influenced by the rationalism of Spinoza and Kant, the idealism of Fichte and Schelling, and the theology of his youth, Hegel reached his own original conclusions, vastly strengthening the position of Idealistic philosophy.

Principal writings: *System of Science*, Part I, *The Phenomenology of Mind* (T), 1807; *Science of Logic* (T), Part I, *The Objective Logic*, 2 vols., 1812, 1813; Part II, *The Subjective Logic*, 1816; *Encyclopedia of the Philosophical Sciences in Outline* (T), 1817; *Philosophy of Right* (T), 1821. Hegel's lecture courses on the *Philosophy of Religion* (T), 2 vols., 1832, *History of Philosophy*, 2 vols., 1833, 1836, *Philosophy of Fine Art* (T), 2 vols., 1835, 1838 and *Philosophy of History* (T), 1837, were published posthumously, having been reconstructed from student notes.

(1) The philosophy of Hegel emerged from the unique ordering of a set of distinctive themes. The first of these was his affirmation not only that reason is the guide to reality but, finally, that the rational is the real, and conversely. The rational and the real are identified.

(2) The second theme concerns the constancy of change in the universe. In the manner of Heraclitus (*q.v.*) emphasis is given to the role of opposites, and of opposition, in the analysis of change.

(3) Add to these a belief in progress and a belief in God. One can discern the outline of a system of thought in which these themes can be affirmed jointly. The view would stress process over product; the process would embody progress; but the progress could come only through opposition; it would be a troubled process leading to the unfolding of new qualities through the tension of the opposites involved in the process itself, and the emergent quality might preserve the relevant values of the opposed points of view within a higher synthesis. The pattern of opposition in physical processes and in reason would need to be identical in structure. And every achieved standpoint would be partial and one-sided, neither utterly false nor utterly true; the process would continue indefinitely, empowered by its own partiality, so to speak. And if the world is under the control of God then the entire process might be appropriately interpreted as the divine Reason realizing itself in history. The term "history" should be emphasized in this context, for Hegel is credited with increasing the attention paid to history. In one sense Hegel has historicized the world.

(4) Hegel's dialectic came from Kant's tendency to classify material into triads; the pattern of the dialectic—thesis, antithesis, synthesis—likewise came from Kant as reflected through Fichte. From Fichte, too, came the suggestion for Hegel's unifying theme. The basic Hegelian themes are held together by a posited end, which is the development of the Idea, Truth, or Spirit, into unity. But where Fichte has man's Ego posit another, the world, for the sake of his own development, Hegel substitutes the dia-

lectical process in which Spirit (or Idea, or Truth) posits its more particular other, and rises to a synthesis over and over again. The end is the same as Fichte's—the development of Spirit—but Hegel's choice of instrumentation avoids Fichte's subjective idealism. In his early work, *The Phenomenology of the Spirit*, Hegel develops the successive steps by which spirit rises from individual sensation to universal reason.

(5) Hegel finds the pattern very widely applicable, stressing dialectic as his chief instrument of analysis. Why does he do so? It is not because he was unacquainted with formal deductive systems. Such systems, however, he finds chiefly appropriate in mathematics, the area of "formal" truth, and appropriate there because of the "poverty" of the aim of mathematics as a discipline. He remarks that such deductions are mechanical, and could be done by machines. But all significant problems require the open-textured approach of dialectic, where the terms of the problem and its contest change as one moves toward the solution. Ideas which can be kept apart with a mathematical or quasi-mathematical tidiness he calls the work of the Understanding; the ideas for which dialectical treatment is appropriate call for the employment of the Reason. He is here using Kantian terms, but establishing a different point of view. Kant preferred the tidiness of the Understanding to the vagaries of Reason. Hegel gives preferred status to the Reason: at one level of abstraction our ideals will be the work of the Understanding; and at a more profound level they will be the work of the Reason.

(6) While the abstract universals of the Understanding are inert and "lifeless," the ideas of Reason have something like careers and lives of their own. The ideas of Reason are Notions, which are at once implicitly universal, particular, and singular. They relate to other universal ideas, to further ideational specification, and to particular instances of themselves. No-

tions are self-specifying and self-particularizing; Hegel calls them "concrete universals," and their unusual nature is what makes the Dialectic possible and necessary. Hegel's deductions in his philosophy are not arbitrary, but simply reveal the specifications and development which the Notions themselves dictate. In both the Logic and the Encyclopedia Hegel endeavors in all earnestness to deduce the Categories of thought. Beginning with the most abstract idea, that of Being, Hegel moves through better than 270 categories before he has satisfied himself that he has found the salient ideas of his philosophical system. It is probably not possible to understand what Hegel is about without spending some time considering this material. A classification is to be found in the chart of Hegel's categories prepared by W.T. Stace, and printed in his *The Philosophy of Hegel* (London: Macmillan & Co., 1924).

(7) The top third of the chart fits under the category "The Idea in Itself, or Logical Idea." The first deduction gains the ideas of Nothing and Becoming from the idea of Being. We begin with the idea of Being, since there can be no idea more general than this. Applying to all there is, Being seems to have great fullness of meaning. And yet because it makes no distinctions, the idea of Being reveals its emptiness turning into its opposite, Nothing. But, then, the passage of Nothing into Being, is what we mean by Becoming. Hegel calls the successive phases of the deduction its moments. These are the factors making up each phase. Being and Nothing are the moments of the third phase, Becoming; and Becoming is the concluding moment of the initial deduction. The chain of deductions with its logical moments continues through 272 categories. One can sense something of the arrangement of triads within triads by examining a portion of this top third of the chart. The triads read downward in the manner of the Being-Nothing-Becoming derivation:

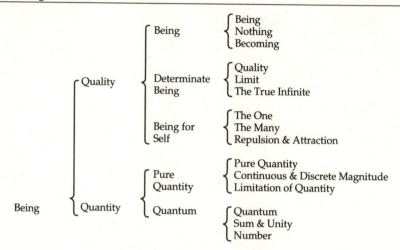

(8) The deduction of the categories in the middle third of the chart, belonging to "The Idea outside itself, or Nature" is extremely awkward and we omit it for that reason. Here Hegel is attempting to deduce scientific ideas, and the scientific context gives evidence of being almost entirely dated.

(9) The material in the bottom third of the chart, labelled "The Idea In and For Itself, or Spirit," lends itself most readily to Hegel's method. The larger divisions of this part of the deduction are:

Because the strength of the Hegelian philosophy lies in this part of the deduction if anywhere, we shall give in a curtailed form many of the conclusions of this part. We shall confine our attention to those parts labeled "Objective Spirit" and "Absolute Spirit"; and first we shall see the whole set of topics under these two headings (q.v. chart on page 214. Sections 10–22 below explicate this chart).

(10) By Objective Spirit Hegel understands a willing of the universal, which is the mark of an autonomous, or free, will; and the source of institutions.

(11) The law of abstract right is: "Be a person and respect others as persons."

(12) Because things are not persons they can be possessed by persons as property. Property is, indeed, the first

embodiment of freedom, and in itself a substantive end.

(13) As a possession, property can be relinquished in favor of another by contract.

(14) Acting in terms of private goals opposed to the universal will of right is what one means by legal wrong (in crime the individual will is pitted against the common or universal will), requiring punishment.

(15) But morality is not an outward matter, as the preceding points clearly are, but an inward matter; it is the identity of one with what one "ought" to be.

(16) Through the kind of purpose and intention in which one's will coincides with the universal, i.e., the rational, the state of goodness has been achieved. Its

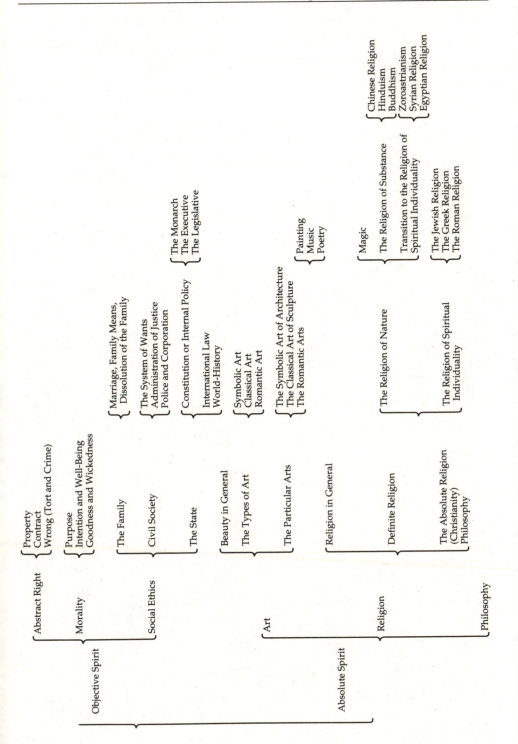

opposite is wickedness and irrationality.

(17) When we put together abstract right and morality we have combined objective and subjective morality into the living unity of social ethics, which is rationality objectified. Hegel then shows how the family entails civil society which entails the state; and in the state universality and particularity find their proper relationship in individuality; so that the state is the supreme embodiment of freedom (even though states may be disfigured in various ways). States are organisms, he says. Life is present in every cell. Thought and consciousness belong essentially to the mature state. States relate to each other as persons, each embodying a developing idea, and together constituting the process of world-history. The state is "the march of God in the world," and while the bad state is finite, the rational state is inherently infinite.

(18) Absolute Spirit is the healing of the division of Spirit into subjective and objective, where Spirit has only Spirit as its object; this is the case in Art, Religion, and Philosophy. The shining of the Absolute through the veils of the sense world as apprehended by Mind or Spirit is Beauty. Put otherwise, Beauty is truth seen in sensuous form. There is Beauty in nature but it is often of a low grade; and the proper subject of aesthetics is Beauty in Art.

(19) A work of art has form and content—spiritual content and material form. Ideally, the two are in perfect accord. But in *Symbolic* art it is the form which dominates. A meaning is suggested which is not expressed, and this drives us on from symbolic art, the art of the Hindus, Egyptians, and Hebrews, to *Classical* art in which the accord of form with content is achieved. Greek art provides an instance of this accord. But Classical art is defective since it presents a finite, finished form, when in fact the spiritual content to be expressed is infinite. And this calls forth *Romantic* art in which spirit predominates over the material form, leaving its sensuous embodiment behind. This is a higher mode of spiritual development than Classical art, but it is in a sense a transitional stage in passage toward the still higher stage of religion. Christian art, Gothic art, 19th-century art, tend to be Romantic. Triadic structures

are present within the general analysis of types of art. Tragedy, for example, is motivated by a conflict of two great, justified, divine-embodying moral forces which the hero must reconcile, transmuting them into "ethical substance." The distinctions Hegel has made concerning the kinds of art not only distinguish the styles of various historic periods; but distinguish the particular arts from each other since architecture tends to be Symbolic, sculpture Classical, while painting, music, and poetry tend toward the Romantic.

(20) Art, we have discovered, provides an inadequate embodiment of spirit. Religion, in general, is a step toward the universality of thought; it proceeds not through pure abstractions but through picture-thinking. And picture-thinking is the highest type of thought of which the masses are capable. Religion, then, would seem to be a substitute for pure philosophy. But each religion has an inner thought-content which remains when its figurative and sensuous form has been removed.

(21) Religion, like art, has passed through a number of stages; and the lowest stages tend to be also the earliest. In the religion of nature, God is not yet conceived as spirit. Magical religion clearly fits this category. But also when God is conceived as pure being, and all else a nonessential modification, God is the only substance. This is pantheism, the religion of substance. He places Chinese religion (not further specified), Hinduism, and Buddhism (he seems to be thinking of its latter stages) in this category. The religions in transition to spiritual individuality—Zoroastrian, Syrian, and Egyptian—are characterized, so Hegel claims, by an increasing spirituality. In the religion of spiritual individuality—Jewish, Greek, and Roman—God is personal. But in the Jewish religion God is everything and man nothing so that man's appropriate response to God is fear. In the Greek religion God appears in the sensuous, and this is, hence, a religion of beauty. The Roman religion is entirely different from the Greek even though many of the gods are identical. The Roman divinity, like the Hebrew, serves a single universal end; but, as in the Greek religion, the end is finite. An end, both finite and universal, can only be the state,

to which the Roman religion was ordered. In Christianity the increasing spirituality we have noticed becomes Absolute, and God truly personal. Christianity presents the Absolute truth in pictorial form. The dogmas of the church—the Trinity, Incarnation, Redemption, Resurrection—provide these pictures.

(22) But we must advance one stage more—to philosophy. And philosophy presents the Absolute truth in its Absolute form—as pure thought. This does not happen at once, but only through the historical development of the discipline, which really means that philosophy reaches Absolute truth in Hegel. And the final proof of Christianity, let it be noticed, is the entire Hegelian system. The Idea now has itself for its object, which had been the goal of the deduction all along.

(23) To this point it would seem that Hegel is simply another rationalistic philosopher. And in terms of his system reason is pushed to the limit. On the other hand, however, he remarked that the history of the world was a "Bacchanalian revel" where not a soul was sober. He remarked on the wisdom that lies in power; and, while regarding passion as the subjective and formal side of the energy of the will, he held that nothing great had ever been accomplished without passion.

HEGESIAS. 3rd cent. B.C.

Greek philosopher. A leader of the Cyrenaic school (*q.v.* Cyrenaicism), Hegesias accepted as central the pleasure principle of this school. But since on his analysis the pains of life outweigh the pleasures, the task of philosophy was to teach how pain is to be avoided. The method is to cultivate indifference toward one's situation, whether it be high or low, fortunate or unfortunate. His lectures were so dramatic that he was called the "lawyer of death," and they were banned by Ptolemy I.

HEIDEGGER, MARTIN. 1884–1976

German philosopher. Born in Messkirch. Studied philosophy under Husserl at the University of Freiburg where he was considered a Phenomenologist. His main work, *Being and Time*, was published in Husserl's *Jahrbuch* in 1927, and dedicated to his master, but he is now considered the central figure in existentialism.

During Hitler's ascendancy Heidegger accepted the Rektorat of the University of Freiburg, praising Hitler in his inaugural address. His motives during this period have been variously interpreted, and while the discussion has not interfered with the tremendous vogue his writing has enjoyed, a question of propriety has been left in the minds of some. In his latter years Heidegger lived in the hills above Freiburg, on rare occasions descending to lecture at the university.

Principal writings: *The Theory of Categories and Meaning in Duns Scotus*, 1916; *Being and Time* (T), 1927; *Kant and the Problem of Metaphysics* (T), 1929; *On the Essence of Reason*, 1929; *What is Metaphysics?* (T), 1929; *The Self-Assertion of the German University*, 1933; *Hölderlin and the Essence of Poetry* (T), 1936; *On the Essence of Truth*, 1943; *Plato's Theory of Truth*, 1947; *Cart Tracks: A Collection of Lectures* (T in part), 1949; *Introduction to Metaphysics* (T), 1953; *What is Thinking?* (T), 1954; *On the Question of Being* (T), 1955; *What is Philosophy?* (T), 1956; *Identity and Difference* (T), 1957; *Composure*, 1959; *On the Way to Speech*, 1959; *The Question Concerning the Thing* (T), 1962; *Phenomenology and Theology*, 1970; *Views*, 1970.

(1) The focus of Heidegger's phenomenological analysis is human existence, although the object of the quest is a rediscovery of Being (*sein*). In the ontological perspective one looks at the world from the standpoint of Being. This is also the existential standpoint. His term for human existence is *Dasein*, meaning simply "being there." The term signals at once both the mystery and arbitrariness in one's being where and as one is. But even if one is hurled (from *werfen*) into the world, still one possesses freedom; Heidegger's philosophy centers in the uses of this freedom.

(2) One decides, for example, to live authentically, or allows oneself to be inauthentic. To live authentically is to discover oneself in direct relation to the things-that-are; it is to be capable of genuine understanding and originative thinking; and it is to be capable of genuine discourse. To be inauthentic is to be characterized by a kind of ambiguity in which one's relation is to the crowd and the requirements of daily life rather than to oneself; one substitutes curiosity and

calculative thinking for genuine understanding; (and one substitutes "prattle" for discourse).

(3) Authenticity is possible only for one who has the attitude of *Sorge*, that is, "care." And the attitude of care is possible only for one who throws one's being into question through *Angst* (anxiety). Through anguish one discovers one's radical finite nothingness. Then one is able to accept oneself as being destined to die, as Being-toward-Death. Such acceptance makes possible for the first time a life of conscience, for conscience is the voice of care, the address of the authentic *Dasein* to oneself.

(4) The fulfillment of *Dasein* is authentic *Ek-sistenz* grasping and reflecting the nature of one's essential finitude. Even time is to be viewed as a projection of *Dasein*, either authentic or inauthentic, hence more or less completely bridging the way to *Eksistenz*. The *extases* of time are its modes of future, present, and past. (a) The future takes its characteristic shape from *Sorge*, the caring nature of the *Dasein*. Its authentic form concerns the development of human potentialities and sensing them as in a sense present now. The inauthentic form of the future, time is a set of discrete moments lacking internal transparency and interconnection. (b) The past, through Being-toward-Death, becomes the possession of the *Dasein* which is able to accept one's own arbitrariness, one's being thrown (*geworfen*) into the world, one's guilt, and obligations. In this sense the past is drawn into the present as a *now*. In its inauthentic form the past is the set of discrete moments beyond recall. (c) The present, as authentic, involves the dynamic interplay and interpenetration of past, present, and future. It is related to a past-made-present, and a future already possessed in projection. The inauthentic present orients itself to the palpable presence or absence of particular things.

(5) To live authentically, grasping the structure of time, being there among the things that are, while appreciating the possible, is living with *Verstehen*. *Verstehen* relates one in devotion to *seiendes*, the things that are. To experience the world from this standpoint is to take the ontic perspective. It is also the *existenziell* standpoint. *Verstehen* (*q.v.*) leads to *Ek-sistenz*.

This stands in contrast to the life in which one relates to the things that are by concern for the *Zuhandenen*, the instruments which provide control of things and take up one's time.

(6) The movement, leading to *Ek-sistenz*, grasping one's finitude, relates oneself also to *das Nichts*. Indeed, the project of *Dasein* was already a projection into the nothingness of past and future out of need and by means of freedom. One becomes aware of Nothingness initially through the dread one feels over one's own prospective non-being. Heidegger further holds that logical negation is possible because there was first of all Nothing. Again, he holds the basic philosophical question to be "Why is there anything at all and not rather Nothing?" In all of this, Nothing is given ontological status and active power so that Heidegger claims that the Nothing nots ("*Das Nichts nichtet*."). In authentic projection, however, Being is disclosed.

(7) The task of ontology, in the middle period, is discovery of the constitution of existence—that is, its finitude, and its dependence on Being, which is itself in the embrace of the Nothing. This task gradually transforms itself into a quest for revelation through the word, and a mythologizing of Being.

(8) It is in this sense that the significance of the word is to be understood, for the word occurs in discourse, and in originative thinking. The "word" is revelatory. It discloses Being, yet it seems to have its origin in the wandering, needful, projective, and finite *Dasein*. It is poetic rather than calculative, although in *Ek-sistenz* poet and thinker support each other: the thinker pronounces Being; the poet names the Holy. The two actions are connected, and the opening toward the revelation, or truth, is a function, in part at least, of human freedom.

HEIDELBERG SCHOOL.

One of the schools of neo-Kantian philosophy active during the last part of the 19th and the first part of the 20th century. Located at the University of Heidelberg, the school took an axiological approach to Kant, holding value to be the key to epistemology. For characterizations of members of the school, *q.v.* Neo-Kantianism (4).

HEILSGESCHICHTE.

A German term meaning "holy history" or the "history of holiness." A Protestant view of history, arising under this name in the 18th century, which held that the purpose of history is the gradual formation of the Chosen People under the guidance of the Holy Spirit.

HEISENBERG, WERNER. 1901–1976.

German physicist. Born in Würzburg. Educated at Munich. Taught at Göttingen, Copenhagen and Berlin. Awarded the Nobel prize in physics, 1932, he has served as director of the Max Planck Institute for Physics, first in Göttingen and then in Munich. Intimately involved in the development of quantum mechanics, Heisenberg is credited with the concept of "uncertainty relations." This is the view that on the microcosmic level the expected quantitative measurement by means of space-time coordinates cannot be supplied. The position and momentum of an electron cannot be determined simultaneously; and an increase in the accuracy of one coordinate is gained at the expense of the other. Also known as the Heisenberg principle of indeterminacy, the discovery limits the scope of classical physics, and perhaps that of the principle of determinism. He believes that modern physics favors Plato over Democritus, supporting the former's view that physical objects are finally forms or ideas, expressible in mathematical language.

Principal writings: *The Physical Principles of Quantum Theory* (T), 1930; *Physics and Philosophy* (E), 1959; *Introduction to the Unified Field Theory of Elementary Particles* (E), 1966; *Natural Law and the Structure of Matter* (E), 1970; *Across the Frontiers* (T), 1974.

HELMHOLTZ, HERMANN VON. 1821–1894.

German scientist and philosopher. Born in Potsdam. Professor of Physiology in Königsberg, Bonn, and Heidelberg (1849–71); and beginning in 1871 Professor of Physics in Berlin. Helmholtz contributed to many areas of science: physics, physiology, biology, chemistry, psychology, and mathematics. Philosophically he was neo-Kantian, supporting the position by means of a physiology of the senses. He agreed with Kant that space was a form of intuition. His knowledge of non-Euclidean geometries led him to deny that its characteristics were Euclidean. The *a priori* elements of the understanding are viewed as rules of method enabling us to manipulate phenomena. The goal of science is the discovery of the ultimate invariable causes of natural processes, and this entails the reduction of phenomena to simple forces. *Q.v.* Neo-Kantianism (1).

Principal writings: Among his many scientific publications we mention only his famous work, *On the Sensations of Tone* (T), 1863. Among philosophical works we name: *Induction and Deduction*, 1873; *Number and Mass*, 1887; *Papers on the Theory of Knowledge* (ed. P. Hertz and M. Schlick), 1921.

HELMONT, J.B. VAN and F.M. VAN, father and son.

Born in Brussels, the Van Helmonts, living between 1577–1644 and 1618–1699, were followers of Paracelsus (*q.v.*). They thought of nature as a dynamic system, the father regarding it as an organism (*q.v.*), and the son developing this view into a monadology (*q.v.*), arranged hierarchically, with God as the directing monad of the whole. It is known that Leibniz (*q.v.*) was in contact with the Van Helmonts.

HELVETIC CONFESSIONS.

The confessions of faith of the Swiss Protestant churches. The first was written in 1536 by disciples of Zwingli (*q.v.*) settling for the conviction that the word of God "alone contains all piety and the whole rule of life." The second was the work of Heinrich Bullinger (1504–1575), successor to Zwingli as chief pastor of Zurich. The second confession appeared between 1562 and 1564, and was widely adopted by Reformed Churches in Switzerland, Poland, Hungary, France, and Scotland.

HELVETIUS, CLAUDE ADRIEN. 1715–1771.

French philosopher. Born in Paris. Due to court preferment he occupied a position of great responsibility and financial reward in the state. Retired to the country when his fortune was assured. His well-known book, *De l'esprit*, appeared in 1758. It was condemned by the Sorbonne, publicly burned by the hangman, and quickly translated into all the languages of Europe.

Principal writings: *On the Mind*, 1758; *On Man, His Intellectual Faculties, and His Education* (T), 1772.

(1) Man's single motivation is the desire for pleasure and for the avoidance of pain. All human actions, even self-sacrifice, are to be explained on these grounds.

(2) Moral ideas are to be traced to custom, yet Helvetius identified the public good with collective pleasure, and held that there was or ought to be an identity between individual and collective interests.

(3) One of the principal tasks of the state is to effect this identity. Since "religious prejudices" often stand in the way of this identity, the sanctions of the state must be utilized against religious traditions.

(4) Helvetius held to the intellectual equality of men, and attributed their apparent differences to differences in education and motivation.

HEMPEL, CARL. 1905– .

German-American philosopher. Born in Oranienburg. Studied at Göttingen, Heidelberg, and Berlin. Initially at Yale, he taught at Princeton 1955–77. Influenced by Reichenbach, Schlick, and Carnap, he has made important contributions to the philosophy of science.

Principal writings: *Fundamentals of Concept Formation in Empirical Science*, 1952; "Deductive-Nomological vs. Statistical Explanation," 1962; "Explanation and Prediction by Covering Laws," 1963; *Aspects of Scientific Explanation*, 1965; *Philosophy of Natural Science*, 1966.

(1) Regarding both deductive-nomological and inductive-probabilistic models of scientific explanation as "covering-law models," Hempel argues that the difference between the two models lies in the character of the laws invoked, and hence in the logical character of the inference linking the statement of the phenomenon to the explanatory information. The first type invokes universal laws; in the second type at least some of the laws are not strictly universal, but statistical in nature. In both cases, however, the phenomenon is deduced from the covering laws—either by necessity or with some degree of probability.

(2) He has also advanced a "translatability" criterion of meaning according to which a sentence has meaning to the extent that it can be translated into an empiricist language.

HENADS, DOCTRINE OF.

Q.v. Proclus (2).

HENOTHEISM.

From the Greek *henos* ("one") and *theos* ("god"). The view that one god is supreme, while not denying the existence of other gods. Often taken to be an intermediate stage between polytheism and monotheism.

HENRY OF GHENT. c. 1217–1293.

French philosopher. Born in Ghent, or in Tournai. Taught at Paris. He participated in the commission leading to the 1277 condemnation of Averroism (*q.v.*). An Augustinian with influences from Aristotle and Avicenna, Henry infused a doctrine of divine illumination into his theory of knowledge, and supported the doctrine of the plurality of forms in material beings. Duns Scotus was among those influenced by his work.

Principal writings: *Quodlibeta*; *Summa Theologica*.

HERACLIDES OF PONTUS. 4th century B.C.

Greek philosopher. Born at Heraclea in Pontus. Member of the Platonic Academy under Speusippus. His doctrines included atomistic and Pythagorean themes. His ontology centered on atoms and the void, but the atoms differed qualitatively as well as quantitatively, the source of their motion residing in God. He held the Pythagorean doctrine that the earth, suspended in the center of the universe, revolves on its axis. Influenced Asclepiades (*q.v.*).

HERACLITUS. c. 540–475 B.C.

Greek philosopher. Born in the city of Ephesus of distinguished family. Resigned an hereditary priestly-political office in favor of metaphysics. Called the "weeping philosopher," "the dark philosopher," "the obscure," Heraclitus opposed the popular religions, the pretensions of democracy, and even Homer and Hesiod.

Principal writings: A considerable number of fragments of his thought remain.

(1) All things are in flux, changing in

such a way that it is not possible to step into the same river twice; for "other and yet other waters are flowing on."

(2) Change takes place by means of opposites, compared to the tension of the bow in shooting an arrow, of the string against the frame in playing the harp, of the river constantly filling and as constantly emptying. Similarly, night and day, good and evil, birth and death, and all the other opposites produce the pattern of change.

(3) This pattern is operative justice. Heraclitus calls it a controlling *logos*, an operative wisdom in things.

(4) Value is generated in conflict and "war is the father of all things," while peace and degeneration are identified.

(5) The tension of opposites in the physical world produces the upward and downward ways between fire and earth. In physical terms fire is the basic element that becomes all things. Earth liquefies into sea, sea into storm cloud, vapor, and fire. This is the upward way, utilized by Heraclitus to explain day and night.

(6) The sun is a bowl in the sky, its concave surface toward us. Fiery vapors from the earth gather there and burn themselves out. Eclipses represent a tipping of the bowl. The moon and its phases are similarly explained. The world on the upward way gives us summer; and winter is the converse movement.

(7) Attacking the superstitions of the popular religions, he held that praying to an image was like conversing with a house while its occupant was away. He found it incredible that men should lament the deaths of their gods: If they are gods, why lament them? If they are lamented why consider them gods?

(8) The changes of things occur finally in a vast cycle of time comprising 360 generations, known as the world year. Figuring each generation at 30 years, the cycle of time bringing things back to their original positions, covers 10,800 ordinary years.

HERBART, JOHANN FRIEDRICH. 1776–1841.

German philosopher. Born in Oldenburg. Studied with Fichte at Jena. From 1809–33 he held Kant's chair at Königsberg before and after which he taught at Göttingen.

Principal writings: *General Theory of Education*, 1806; *General Practical Philosophy*, 1808; *Main Points of Metaphysics*, 1808; *Introduction to Philosophy*, 1813; *Compendium of Psychology*, 1816; *Psychology as a Science*, 1824–25; *General Metaphysics*, 1828–29; *Psychological Investigations*, 1838–40.

(1) Dividing philosophy into Logic, Metaphysics, and Aesthetics, he held that each of the three areas concerns the reworking of concepts.

(2) The criterion of the reworking of concepts in Logic is the gaining of conceptual clarity and distinctness.

(3) Metaphysics, having as its goal the ordering, or reordering of knowledge, has four subdivisions: Methodology, Ontoloy, Synechiology, and Eidology. a) *Methodology* is designed to reduce the contradictions present in the "given." It does this by treating the opposing attributes of inherence and change as different relations among pluralities of real things. (b) *Ontology* is the study of being, and being—according to Herbart—is by definition noncontradictory. To explicate its noncontradictory nature Herbart adopts "pluralistic realism" as his point of view. In this view reality is made up of simple qualitative units, called "reals," which interrelate in various ways. Rather than speaking of things and their properties, Herbart suggests that we substitute statements about syntheses of simple "reals." (c) *Synechiology* is designed to provide the foundation for natural philosophy in that it shows how one reaches the space-time world, beginning with the "reals" of ontology. In ontology the "reals" are divorced from space, time, and motion— all of which are necessary for natural philosophy. By means of the concept of continuity one is able to generate the concepts one needs, such as "intelligible space" and matter. In any ultimate sense, however, these concepts are constructions, and the simple "reals" of ontology alone represent reality. (d) *Eidology* is Herbart's term for epistemology. It is a study of relations, both conceptual and perceptual, of the conjunction and separation of the "reals." As natural philosophy comes out of *synechiology* so psychology comes out of *eidology*. The ego is regarded as itself one of the simple "reals" which, in contact with others, produces presentations, pleasures and pains, ideas, and the first-

person self able to remember the past and form "resolves" for the future.

(4) Aesthetics is for Herbart the study of valuation or judgments of pleasure and pain: thus, it rests on psychology and *eidology*. Ethics is the chief division of aesthetics. The ethics of Herbart depends upon five basic relations of the will: (a) internal freedom requiring harmony within the will, (b) perfection, or a concentrated harmony of the will yielding intensity of feeling and power, (c) benevolence, or a harmony between one's own will and the wills of others, (d) law, or concordance of the wills of persons who desire the same thing, and (e) equity, or a correction of an imbalance between two wills in conflict.

(5) Herbart's philosophy of education, resting on his ethics and his psychology, has as its goal the developed individual characterized by internal freedom and moral virtue. His educational method includes the presentation of ideas, their relation to other ideas by association, the elimination of misleading associations and reemphasis of those most relevant, and the application of the information to new situations.

HERBERT OF CHERBURY, EDWARD. 1583–1648.

English philosopher. Born in Eyton, Shropshire. Educated at Oxford. Knighted by James I, he served as ambassador to France. He was on intimate terms with the royalty of several countries. He became Baron of Cherbury in 1629. In 1644 he was forced to surrender his castle to the parliamentary forces. He is known as the founder of Deism (*q.v.*) His philosophical writings were in Latin.

Principal writings: *On Truth* (T), 1624; *On the Cause of Errors*, 1645; *On the Religion of Laymen*, (T), 1645; *To the Priests on Lay Religion*, 1645; *On the Religion of the Gentiles* (T), 1663.

(1) Especially well-known as author of the five pillars or articles of Deism, in this respect Herbert held: (a) a supreme being exists; (b) He is worthy of our worship; (c) we are to relate ourselves to Him through virtue and piety; (d) sin is to be expiated through repentance; (e) justice demands that we receive punishment or reward after death for our deeds in this life. He found these five articles

universally present in the religions of humankind.

(2) But although most of the interest in Herbert centers upon his role as the founder of Deism, he had much to say in the area of epistemology. He treated the powers of the mind in four parts: (a) The most certain grouping is that of "natural instinct." Here Herbert treats of certain *notitiae communes* which are innate, indisputable and divine in origin. These common notions are distinguished by the marks of priority, independence, universality, certainty, necessity, and immediacy. They make it possible to organize experience (serving the same function as the Kantian categories) and are to be found at the base of all the significant areas of experience: *e.g.*, in religion (*cf.* 1 above), in law, and in ethics. (b) The group standing next in order of certainty relates to the *sensus internus*, or internal sense. Here Herbert treats love, hate, fear, and free will. He also treats the nature of conscience, finding *notitiae communes* there lending structure to ethical distinctions. (c) Third, he treats the *sensus externus*, or external sense. (d) Finally, he treats of *discursis*, reasoning, the least certain of the four, proceeding by division and analysis and requiring at each step the aid of the other three powers. Reason is the source of most human errors, but this is because it can be badly used. Properly treated, no human faculty leads to error; and in any case the corrective power of natural instinct is always available.

(3) With respect to faith and reason he argued that one should begin with reason, passing thence to a faith clear and evident to all humanity.

HERDER, JOHANN GOTTFRIED VON. 1744–1803.

German philosopher. Born in Mohrungen, East Prussia. Studied at Königsberg under Kant and J.G. Hamann. Tutor and pastor in his early years, in 1776 through Goethe's influence he became court preacher at Weimar where he passed the rest of his life. A close friend and disciple of Lessing, he became with Goethe one of the leaders of the *Sturm und Drang* movement, and influential in the developing movement of Romanticism.

Principal writings: *Treatise on the Origin*

of Language (T), 1772; *On Perception and Feeling in Man* (T), 1778; *Ideas on a Philosophy of the History of Man* (T), 1784–91; *Reason and Experience, Reason and Speech, a Meta-Criticism of Pure Reason,* 1799; *Kalligone,* 1800; *Adrastea,* 1809.

(1) Believing the culture of a people to rest on its distinctive intellectual and emotional life which in turn rests upon physical factors including the conditions of the material environment, Herder in effect founded the genetic method of historical analysis. In addition, this belief led him to advocate that poets should turn from classical forms to natural and spontaneous modes of expression.

(2) He finds speech, a principal instrument in the development of culture, to be a natural and necessary outcome of human life, beginning in imitation of the sounds of nature.

(3) Religion, similarly, is a natural outgrowth of the human condition, and more particularly of the first human attempts to explain the world. Early religions are closely related to myth and poetry. The power of Christianity rests on the added element of moral exaltation.

(4) Applying evolutionary principles to human history, Herder somewhat less clearly pictures the lower forms of life as prefiguring humanity, and suggests that survival depends on adaptation.

(5) Herder's philosophy is value-impregnated. The end of society is a rational order based on justice, and the process of evolution is directed by a being in whom goodness and intelligence combine.

HERESY.

From the Greek *hairesis* ("a taking for oneself," "choice," "sect"). In the religious tradition of the West the term has come to mean the denial of a revealed truth. The nature of such truth not always having been evident, a succession of councils (*q.v.* Christianity 3–9; Christology) has been necessary to determine the orthodox position on a variety of questions. The number of positions defined as heretical is not minute. Jeremy Taylor (*q.v.*) held that heresy is not an error of the intellect but of the will.

HERMAGORAS OF TEMNOS.

Q.v. Rhetoric (5).

HERMARCHUS.

Q.v. Epicureanism (1).

HERMENEUTIC CIRCLE.

Q.v. Hermeneutics; Ricoeur (5).

HERMENEUTICS.

From the Greek *hermeneía*, "interpretation," or "explanation." The adjectival form is *hermeneutikós.* The art of interpretation (called by Schleiermacher "the art of understanding" and by Gadamer (*q.v.*) "the art or technique of understanding and interpretation"). Deriving from the need for interpretation in the studies of rhetoric and of scripture, the art came to be applied to any text. Even scientists, to make the scope of hermeneutics universal, may be said to be studying the text of nature. The task of interpretation is said to be never-ending. One reads the text, and makes an interpretation of what one has read; but just as the text was not self-evident, neither is the interpretation; so the text, perhaps indeed in light of the interpretation, requires a new interpretation, which also requires interpretation. This process is sometimes called the hermeneutic circle (*q.v.* Ricoeur 5). One might suppose with Charles Peirce (*q.v.* 12, 17) that the succession of interpretations is moving toward truth; for Peirce, however, the series, although not a circle, is infinite, each interpretant requiring another. This may still be viewed as a circle in the sense that the position of the interpreter is such that no matter what one does another interpretation will be needed, even though the circle of interpretation continues to expand, one is moving to the whole from the part, and no matter what one does the whole recedes.

(1) Hans-Georg Gadamer (*q.v.* 1) has centered his attention on hermeneutics, including calling attention to the historical antecedents of his own analysis. He mentions that Dilthey, for example, held that the initial stages of hermeneutics, both in its Biblical and literary forms, were defensive, focusing on discovery of the original meaning of an indispensable text. In one case the text was from the Scriptures, in the other from classical literature.

(2) Vico (*q.v.* 1) provided an indispensable element in the growth of hermeneutics

by shifting the center of epistemological attention from Cartesian ideas to history, as what conforms more to human capacities since we have made it.

(3) Schleiermacher (*q.v.* 6) expanded hermeneutic techniques by adding psychological to grammatical interpretation, arguing that to understand a text one must finally place oneself in the mind of the author, a projection which is possible because there is a little of everyone in each of us. The success of such projections is confirmed by increased intelligibility in the resultant understanding. Although Schleiermacher was interested primarily in the interpretation of Scripture, his method was applicable, irrespective of content, to any text and even beyond.

(4) Johann G. Droysen (1808–84) is regarded as broadening hermeneutics to historical thought. In *Historik* (1937) he held that an understanding is historical, selective, and fragmentary, in which something is added and something lost. It is written from the standpoint of the present yet has "relative objectivity," broadening and enriching "our ephemeral existence."

(5) Separating the human sciences (*Geisteswissenschaften*) from the natural sciences (*naturwissenschaften*) Dilthey (*q.v.* 1), following both Vico and Schleiermacher, related the former to historical knowledge, finding spirit and life in the configurations of history, so that the historical world itself became a text to be deciphered. Spranger (*q.v.*), a follower of Dilthey, looked upon psychology as a hermeneutic of the spirit.

(6) The final step was taken by Heidegger (*q.v.* 1, 5) who defined hermeneutics as "the analytic of the existentiality of existence," grounding every text in the question of the meaning of being. The consequence was to merge hermeneutics and ontology, historicize natural being, and bring the natural sciences into the hermeneutic circle, along with the social sciences and humanities. The merging of hermeneutics and ontology turns the world into a text, and lends intelligibility to the claim that our being-in-the-world, engaged in interpretive understanding, can listen to being which "speaks" to us, disclosing its nature.

(7) Rudolf Bultmann (*q.v.*) applied Heidegger's view on interpretation to theology, although in truth the influence was mutual. The result in Bultmann's case was the existential interpretation involved in the project of demythologizing.

(8) Gadamer has devoted himself to carrying out the implications of the universality of hermeneutics. History does not belong to us; "we belong to history"; and the "Being which can be understood is language." In Heideggerian fashion we are to open ourselves to whatever is before us—work of art, text, tradition, person, form of life—so that it can "speak" to us. The claim of truth it makes will contrast with our pre-judgments, and thus make possible a change in our own perspective. Each of us enters every hermeneutic situation with prejudices. By allowing our initial perspective to merge with the perspective carried by the presented claim, the horizons of both can be fused, leading to a more generous perspective on our part. The more experienced a person is, indeed, the more "radically undogmatic" that person can be. The process of fusing horizons is, of course, unending except in the sense that fusion effects a kind of closure which is as much a part of the process as understanding and interpretation.

(9) The Italian hermeneuticist, Emilio Betti, argues that Heidegger and his followers including Gadamer, have overstressed the subjective aspects of interpretation to the point that its objective aspect has been lost. In *Validity of Interpretation* (1967) E.D. Hirsch claims in the same vein that the only valid foundation for criticism is that "philological effort to find out what the author meant."

(10) Hermeneutic interpretation is a controlling feature of Ricoeur's (*q.v.* 1, 4) thought.

HERMETISM.
Q.v. Corpus Hermeticum.

HERMOGENES OF TARSUS.
Q.v. Rhetoric (8).

HERRNHUT.
Q.v. Zinzendorf.

HERTZ, HEINRICH. 1857–1894.
German physicist and philosopher of science. Born in Hamburg. Studied in

Berlin. Taught at Kiel, Karlsruhe, and Bonn, having studied under Helmholtz (*q.v.*) the neo-Kantian physicist and physiologist. Hertz contributed to the development of philosophy of science, preparing the ground for Poincaré (*q.v.*). A productive physicist, Hertz took classical mechanics as the locus of his exploration in philosophy of science. He held a scientific theory to be a system from which conclusions are deduced and tested by observation. The primitive concepts of a scientific theory, moreover, should be empirical, or empirical-like, concepts—*e.g.*, not "force" and "energy," but "space," "time," and "mass." The former can enter the system as definitions constructed in terms of the primitive concepts.

Principal writings: *Electric Waves* (T), 1892; *The Principles of Mechanics* (T), 1894.

HERZL, THEODOR.
Q.v. Zionism.

HESIOD. c. 8th cent. B.C.
Greek poet. Born at Ascra in Boeotia. Apparently a shepherd poet who wrote first about his life and work, and later about the gods.

Principal writings: *Works and Days* (T); *The Theogony* (T).

(1) Although the form is poetic, Hesiod introduces numerous philosophical or semi-philosophical ideas. For example, he contrasted Order with Chaos, and held that Order came out of Chaos through the power of Eros; each such concept is introduced as a divine being.

(2) The belief that the past was better than the present has a strong claim on universality; but the universality, allowing us to conceive of a golden age in the past, was provided by Hesiod. He held to a succession of deteriorating ages beginning with the golden, followed by ages of silver, brass, and iron.

(3) In *The Theogony* Hesiod, or a member of his school, attempted to work out in poetic form a system of the gods based on biological relationships as reported in legend.

HETEROLOGICAL.
Q.v. Paradox (4).

HETERONOMIC PREDICATES.
Q.v. Davidson (4).

HETERONOMY.
From the Greek *heteros* and *nomos* meaning "the rule of another." Contrasted with autonomy (*q.v.*) the term is used by Kant (*q.v.* 6–7) to characterize ethical systems whose principles derive from a source outside the person. In the autonomous system of Kant the self determines itself by means of its own law. Tillich (*q.v.* 2) applied the term to a mode of specious reasoning which took its principles from outside itself.

HETEROSYNTHESIS.
Ardigó (*q.v.* 3) defined "things" as a "heterosynthesis" of neutral elements.

HETUCAKRA.
Q.v. Dignaga (3).

HEXAPLA.
Q.v. Origen.

HIEROCLES OF ALEXANDRIA.
fl. around 430 A.D.
Hellenic philosopher. A student of Plutarch who founded the School of Athens (*q.v.*), Hierocles was a member of the Alexandrian School of Neoplatonism. Essentially eclectic, mixing Stoic and Aristotelian themes into his Neoplatonism, Hierocles wrote on the themes of providence and human destiny, attempting to reconcile the Christian idea of providence and the Greek idea of fate. He held with Christianity that the world was created from nothing rather than by emanation, although in his view it was the demiurge that created the world by an act of will.

HIEROCLES THE STOIC. fl. c. 120 A.D.
A Stoic philosopher intermixing the doctrines of the old and the new schools, he wrote on virtue and obligation, defending the presence of an instinct for self-preservation.

Principal writings: *Elements of Ethics;* fragments remain.

HILBERT, DAVID. 1862–1943.
German mathematician and logician. Born in Königsberg, professor in Königsberg and Göttingen. A formalist in the area of philosophy of mathematics, Hilbert worked on the foundations of Euclidean geometry, the axiomatization of arithmetic and consistency proof in

logical systems. Demonstrating the power of formalization, Hilbert took the formulae of the system as signs without signification. The system thus remained uninterpreted.

Principal writings: *Foundations of Geometry*, 1899; *Main Features of Theoretical Logic*, 1928; *Collected Works*, 3 vols., 1932–35; *Foundations of Mathematics* (with Bernays), 2 vols., 1934, 1939.

HILLEL (THE ELDER). 1st cent. B.C.

Jewish rabbi. Born in Babylon. Lived in Jerusalem. A member of the Sanhedrin, Hillel provided seven rules for interpretation of the Scriptures, and helped to shape the traditions of Jewish thought by injunction and example. Revered as a great teacher, many of his sayings have New Testament parallels: *e.g.*, "Judge not thy neighbor until thou art in his place"; and "Do not unto your neighbor what you would not have him do unto you; this is the whole law; the rest is mere commentary."

Principal writings: *Maxims*.

HINAYANA BUDDHISM.

·*Q.v.* Buddhism, Theravada (Hinayana).

HINDUISM. 1500 B.C. to the present.

The native religious system of India. A religion without a founder, Hinduism reflects in itself the cultural history and social conditions of the Indian people from the time civilization flowered in the Indus Valley to our day. The various levels of religious insight from magic to ethical idealism coexist in Hindu scriptures and practices.

It is sometimes said that Hinduism is a *Dharma* (*q.v.*) (right action) instead of a religion. Conduct and belief here intermingle. Different modes of conduct and belief co-exist in Hinduism; the apparent inconsistencies which result may be moderated by the Hindu insight that the One expresses itself and is expressed in many ways. Accept the point and the apparent polytheism of Hindu thought disappears for there are different ways of reaching the Supreme Being, and the gods are merely different names for the one God and different paths leading to the same goal. The *Trimurti*, or trinity, of later Hindu mythology, representing three aspects of the Supreme Being—

Brahma, the creator; Vishnu the preserver; and Shiva the destroyer—is thus also consistent with a strict monotheism; as are the successions of divine incarnations which are said in the *Bhagavad-Gita* to occur whenever "the law fails and lawlessness uprises." In any case, Hinduism is a natural growth characterized by richness but not a doctrine shaped into logical coherence.

(1) The scriptures of Hinduism, called *Vedas* (meaning "knowledge") consist of three parts: (a) the *Samhitas* (meaning "collections") include the *Rgveda*, a collection of hymns in praise of the gods; the *Samaveda*, melodies relating to these hymns; the *Yajurveda*, sacrificial formulae; and the *Atharvaveda*, magical formulae; (b) the *Brahamanas*, texts dealing with ritual and sacrifice, their meaning and value; (c) the *Upanishads*, essentially philosophical discourses, and the primary source for insight into Hindu philosophy.

(2) Comparable to, although more vast in scope than, the position held in Greek culture by the *Iliad* and *Odyssey* are the *Ramayana* (*q.v.*) and the *Mahabharata* (*q.v.*) In process of formation throughout the 1st millennium B.C., their compilation had probably taken place by 200 A.D. The *Mahabharata* tells of the conflicts between the Kurus and Pandavas, two branches of the same family. The *Ramayana* tells the story of the good king Rama whose wife is taken by the King of Ceylon, and later rescued. The framework of the stories is employed to provide a setting for much moral and religious teaching, including the doctrine of the divine incarnation. The *Mahabharata* contains the *Bhagavad-Gita* (*q.v.*) or *Song of the Lord*, a discussion between the incarnate Krishna and a great warrior (one of the Pandavas), Arjuna, on the battlefield of Kurukshetra, and just before the battle is to begin. The war is with the Kurus, and Arjuna is revolted at the thought of what he is about to do. The problems of individual and social ethics are discussed: the values of duty and activity are praised by Krishna, and the immortality of the soul defended.

(3) But the Hindu system of values is much more complex than the preceding comments may suggest, the ideal of life of man requiring a succession of stages, or *ashramas*, each of which is to

be mastered in its turn. These stages are: (a) the life of discipline and education (*brahmacarin*). Here the stress is on knowledge and discipline, one of the three paths to God (*cf* 5 below); (b) the life of the householder (*grhastha*) and active worker; in practical terms this is the most important of the four stages, since it is the stage in which provision is made for the maintenance of the social structure; in this stage it is one's duty to lead an active married life discharging social responsibilities including the duty of serving one's fellow men; (c) a period of retreat from the world (*vanaprastha*) for the loosening of one's social bonds. Study of the *Vedas* is now mandatory. The place of retreat was expected to be in a forest. If the forest-dweller is accompanied by his wife they are to remain chaste. This leads to the fourth stage; (d) the life of the hermit or renouncer (Skt., *sannyasin*). The hermit is to be alone, homeless, nameless, without possessions, separating himself from desire. Renunciation is the energizing ideal of the third and fourth stages. Renunciation is also possible for women, although they are not specifically included in the scheme. For the Hindu "renunciation" is a means whereby the hold of existence is broken. It represents, then, both freedom and fullness.

(4) The caste system of India, like all other aspects of its culture, is reflected in and supported by its scriptures, although not unreservedly. The system, reflecting the realities of military conquest, especially the Aryan incursions, contains four castes: the *Brahmana*, who were priests and religious teachers; the *Kshatriya*, who were kings and warriors; the *Vaishya*, who were the people of commerce and the professions; and the *Shudra*, who were farmers and laboring people. The three higher castes were regarded as "twice born" (once naturally, the second from study of the *Vedas*), and allowed to wear the sacred thread (purple for the *Brahmins*, red for the *Kshatriyas*, yellow for the *Vaishyas*). But the castes were never completely isolated and the followers of the path of devotion (*bhakti cf.* 5c below) have tended to be anti-caste.

(5) Among the ways to God recognized in Hinduism are three main paths sustaining long traditions. They are the way of works (*karma*), the way of meditation and knowledge (*jnana*), and the way of devotion (*bhakti*):

(a) the original *Vedas*, and what is commonly even now understood as the *Vedas*, is that part called the *Samhitas*, mentioned in (1a) above. Originally, and for those who support the way of works (*karma vidhi* or *karma marga*), man's life is closely dependent upon the gods, to be lowered or raised by the correct performance of sacrifices. The ordinary method of sacrifice required the throwing of offerings into the sacrificial fire—foods and animals prized by the owner, for example; the sacrificial act is susceptible of various interpretations, from propitiation of the gods to personal renunciation. Similarly, however, the way of works can be interpreted ritualistically or in an ethical sense, and both senses must now be included even though the second is later in development. And yet as the rituals multiplied beyond comprehension the other paths to God became increasingly important.

(b) The way of knowledge (*jnana marga*) can be correlated fairly closely with the *Upanishads*, originating about 800 B.C., and having as its goal personal enlightenment. Implicitly monotheistic, it is the message of the *Upanishads* that the indwelling all-pervading Supreme Being, or Brahman, is identical with the individual self, or *Atman*. Through the cycle of births one moves toward realization of the identity of *Atman* and Brahman, which we realize in Being (*Sat*), Consciousness (*Chit*), and Delight (*Ananda*). The ethical doctrine of these writings equates suffering and limitation with ignorance. Illumination removes these blocks; and the pervasive *Atman-Brahman* identity engenders an ethical unity of being. From the *Vedas* to the *Upanishads*, from works to knowledge, is also a transition from sacrifice to the ethical life. But the way to God through knowledge could appeal in the nature of the case only to the upper classes. The third alternative emerged, in fact, from the lower castes.

(c) *Bhakti*, the way of devotion, begins as do the other two with the *Vedas*; but *Bhakti* increases gradually in strength, reaching its most flourishing period in the post-Vedic period. Carried essentially by the non-Aryan tradition, it was in its initial stages, an anti-caste movement spurned by the *Brahmins* although, as it developed, losing to some extent its anti-caste cast, *Brahmins* flocked to it. Cutting through the necessity for ritual and sacrifice, substituting the warmth of the human emotions of love and adoration for knowledge, it was natural enough for the substitution of a personal God for the Brahmanic principle to occur along this path; and also for this alternative to lead to mysticism, as it did at last.

The way of devotion incorporated the non-Vedic and possibly non-Aryan idea of the avatar. The divine incarnation takes place differently depending on the *Bhakti* school. The chief schools are the Vaishnavas or Vishnuites and the Shaivas, so named for their respective avatars, Vishnu and Shiva. The exact relations are in flux, however, and ten incarnations of Vishnu are mentioned, including Krishna, Rama, and Buddha. Finally, Vishnu and Shiva became the Supreme Being for their respective schools. The Vaishnava Bhakti movement grew strong in many centers of India, and produced a considerable body of very eloquent devotional literature; this literature often supports the idea of the equality of man and the movement at least engendered tendencies toward liberalization of caste distinctions. Ramanuja and Madhva are the intellectual leaders of this tradition. The Shaiva Bhakti movement was less widespread than the foregoing one but followed a similar pattern.

Another manifestation of *Bhakti* is discoverable in the mysticism of northern India. A product of the mingling of Bhakti followers and Islamic Sufis, as seen in the line, "O God, whether Allah or Rama, I live by thy Name," this tradition dates from the 12th century when the first Sufi teachers came to India. Ramananda (1370–1440) as a Hindu gave the composite movement its initial impetus, preaching direct inspiration. Kabir was the most important of his disciples (he is supposed to have had 12 principal disciples). Nanak (1469–1539) (*q.v.*), founder of the Sikh religion, was strongly influenced by Kabir. The feeling of the movement can perhaps be sensed in the line from Dadu, another influential follower of Kabir: "Who can know You, O Invisible, Unapproachable, Unfathomable? Dadu has

no desire to know; he is satisfied to remain enraptured with all this beauty of yours, and to rejoice in it with you." Most of these mystics came from the lower classes; writing and speaking in the vernacular Hindu instead of Sanskrit, they gave important impetus to local literary traditions.

But the most complete dedication to *Bhakti*, and the most complete divorce from ritual and knowledge, is to be found in the Bauls of Bengal, a cult which grew out of the destruction of Buddhism, Tantra, and Vaishnavism, forming itself from the lowest stratum of Indian society. Believing that one's body is the temple of God, and something like conscience is the scriptures, they allow no external form of worship whatever, keep no records, and sustain no visible forms of organization, other than the informal guru-pupil relationship. Their goal is simplicity, freedom, the avoidance of manmade distinctions, and the inward practice to direct relation to God. Rabindranath Tagore was influenced by the Baul poets.

(6) By about 200 A.D. six systems of philosophy had evolved. They can be treated in three pairs because of their inner similarities: the Nyaya-Vaisheshika, the Sankhya-Yoga, and the Purva-Mimamsa-Vedanta (but also *q.v.* each as a separate entry).

(a) The Nyaya-Vaisheshika together admit four sources of knowledge (perception, inference, analogy, credible testimony), accept causation including multiple causation, four kinds of atomic constituents (earth, air, fire, and water), and nine substances (the four atoms and space, time, ether, mind, and soul). God created the world by fashioning the nine substances into an ordered universe. The Nyaya (*q.v.*) view was expounded by Gautama (not the Buddha) as early as the 3rd century B.C. Kanada produced the *Vaiśeṣika Sutra* at about the same time.

(b) The Sankhya-Yoga pair relate as cosmology to mental discipline. The Sankhya system has two basic categories, *purusha* or eternal spirits, and *prakriti* or the basis of the natural order, including all the potentialities of nature, psychical as well as physical. The world evolves out of *prakriti* with the help of *purusha*. Causation is stressed, and the pre-

existence of the effect in the cause. Evolution proceeds from matter to spirit,
prakriti to *purusha;* and three very special
qualities play a role in this development:
sattva (light, purity, harmonious existence)
empowers the evolution of *prakriti; rajas*
(energy, passion) provides the motive
power for all activity; and *tamas* (inertia, darkness) provides a principle of
resistance. The order of spiritual development is from intellect to self-sense, ego-
feeling, the five cognitive organs, the five
motor organs, the disciplined mind. Rebirth is due to ignorance; knowledge of
the difference between *prakriti* and
purusha leads to disinterested living; and
at death emancipation from the wheel of
rebirth. Beginning with an agnostic position as in Kapila's *Sankhya-pravacana
Sutra,* Sankhya thinkers later accepted
God's existence. Yoga has God as the
guiding principle of evolution, periodically dissolving the cosmos and reiniti-
ating the process. Yoga holds that mental
discipline in terms of habits of concentration needs to be added to discursive
knowledge of the nature of things to effect emancipation. To that end are the
yoga exercises directed.

(c) The Purva-Mimamsa-Vedanta pair
relate closely to Hindu scriptures. The
Purva-Mimamsa system is concerned with
the correct interpretation of the *Vedas,*
which are taken as the absolute authority for conduct. Its main philosophical
support is the *Purva-Mimamsa Sutra* of
Jaimini, written around 400 B.C. The
Vedanta system rests on the Upanishadic
doctrine of the Brahman, having as its
principal texts the *Upanishads,* the
Bhagavad-Gita, and the *Brahma Sutra* (by
its founder Badarayana). One of the
school's early teachers, Gaudapada (*q.v.*),
held the entire world to be an illusion
and Brahman to be the sole reality. In a
less extreme form Shankara (*q.v.*) held the
world to be the appearance whose reality
is Brahman. The Vedanta philosophy has
been the most influential of the systems.

(7) For a division of the sacred books
(*sastras*) into *shruti, smriti, durana,* and
tantra, including the *Vedas* but going
beyond them, *q.v. Sastras.*

HINTIKKA, JAAKKO. 1929– .
   Finnish philosopher. Born in Helsinki.
Educated at Helsinki and Harvard. Has

taught at Helsinki, Stanford, Florida State,
and Boston University. His writings are
in English.

   Principal writings: *Distributive Normal
Forms in the Calculus of Predicates,* 1953;
Two Papers on Symbolic Logic, 1955; *Knowl-
edge and Belief,* 1962; *Aspects of Inductive
Logic,* 1966; *Models for Modalities,* 1969;
Philosophy of Mathematics, 1969; *Logic,
Language Games and Information,* 1973; *Time
and Necessity,* 1973; *Knowledge and the
Known,* 1974; *The Method of Analysis,* 1974;
The Semantics of Questions, 1976; *The Game
of Language* (with J. Kulas), 1983; *Anaphora
and Definite Descriptions* (with J. Kulas),
1985; *Investigating Wittgenstein* (with M.
Hintikka), 1986. In addition, many edited works.

(1) In order to handle propositional
attitudes (statements containing "knows,"
"believes," "remembers," "wishes,"
"strives," "desires") Hintikka developed
epistemic logic. Using the notation Kap
(*a* knows that p), Bap (*a* believes that p),
Pap (it is possible, for all *a* knows, that
p), and Cap (it is compatible with everything *a* believes that p), the semantical
system is worked out in terms of
"epistemically possible worlds," *i.e.,* all
of the possible courses of events compatible with everything *a* knows. Bap, for
example, is interpreted as asserting it is
the case that p in all of the possible
worlds is compatible with everything *a*
believes.

(2) Analysis in terms of modal logic
was then extended to the logic of perception, since perceptual statements can
be treated along the same lines as statements containing epistemic propositional
attitudes. "*A* perceives that p" asserts that
in all possible worlds compatible with
what *a* perceives, it is the case that p.

(3) Ethics also benefits from this approach by way of deontic logic (*q.v.*),
through the addition of a possible world
in which all norms are satisfied. One of
the results is that while "ought" does not
follow from "is" in general, *prima facie*
(*q.v.*) oughts can be derived from factual
premises, and this is often all that our
ethical intuitions suggest. He is also credited with the paradox of deontic logic that
"if it is impossible to do a given thing,
it is wrong to do it."

(4) Finally, he has proposed a game-
theoretical semantics, duplicating the

posture of game-theory (plus an original interpretation of Wittgenstein's language-games), working out logical theory in the context of a struggle for truth with a malicious opponent, which is nature itself. The individual wishes to bring about a true sentence, and nature a false one, logical connectives are interpreted as allowing for some, the individual and for others, nature to make the initial move. For "x and y" nature chooses one of the conjuncts and the game continues. For "x or y" the individual chooses one of the disjuncts and the game continues. The claim is made that numerous semantic problems and paradoxes can be sorted out in this context where the individual and nature seek winning strategies.

Also *q.v.* Quantifying In (5); Modal Logic (8).

HIPPASUS OF METAPONTUM. 6th and 5th cent. B.C.

Greek philosopher. Regarded as one of the earliest of Pythagoras' disciples, even though on many points he seems closer to Heraclitus; *e.g.*, in his beliefs that fire is the basic element, and that the soul is composed of fire.

HIPPIAS OF ELIS.

Greek philosopher. Born middle 5th century B.C. One of the famous Sophists and a contemporary of Protagoras, he is mentioned in a number of Platonic dialogues: *e.g.*, the *Hippias Major*, *Hippias Minor*, and *Protagoras*. Interested in literary style and extemporaneous speech, he is credited with encyclopedic knowledge and contributing to the advance of mathematics. He drew a fundamental distinction between the eternal validity of natural law and the contingent nature of conventional law, siding with nature against convention.

HIPPODAMUS OF MILETUS.

Q.v. Communism.

HIPPOLYTUS. c. 160–c. 236.

Christian writer. A disciple of Irenaeus, Hippolytus followed his teacher in writing against Gnosticism (*q.v.*) which he described as a mixture of Greek philosophy and astral religion.

Principal writings: *Refutation of all the Heresies* (also known by its first part,

Philosophoumena); *Against the Greeks and Plato*.

HIRSCH, E.D.

Q.v. Hermeneutics (9).

HISTORICISM.

From the German *Historismus*, a term signifying an emphasis (or overemphasis) on history. The term was introduced by Mannheim and Troeltsch (*q.v.* neo-Kantianism 6) and was from the start ambiguous. Applied usually to approaches such as that of Vico (*q.v.* 1) who asserted that "everything is history," and Dilthey (*q.v.* 4) who argued that even historians are captive to the assumptions of the age in which they write, the net of its application is sometimes extended to Hegel, Marx, Croce, Collingwood, and Heidegger. When used pejoratively, the term is taken as an instance of the genetic fallacy (*q.v.*), explaining a phenomenon away by reference to its origin.

HISTORICITY.

Q.v. Jaspers (7).

HISTORISMUS.

Q.v. Historicism.

HISTORY.

From the Greek *historia* ("information" or "inquiry"). The phrase "historical inquiry," although redundant, is necessary to distinguish the kind of research dealing with past events in a sequential or temporal manner from that kind of scientific inquiry treating data and their governing laws atemporally. As we shall see in (C.) below there is a position between history as a sequential study of events and theoretical science as a study of governing laws. Those occupying this position claim to find laws, often viewed as stages of development, in the events of history. In a somewhat arbitrary manner we have classed some of these claims under history in (A.) below, and others under philosophy of history in (C.) below, depending upon whether or not the particular claim seemed to be fecund for the study of history.

A. History.

(1) Aristotle (*q.v.* 13) distinguished history from both poetry and philosophy, holding that the former deals with the particular and the latter with the

universal, the former with what has actually happened and the latter with what is or might be.

(2) Francis Bacon (*q.v.* 4) divided history into natural, civil, ecclesiastical, and literary, the first treating the non-human part of the world. History is distinguished from other disciplines by its subject matter; history studies what is circumscribed in time and place, using memory as an essential instrument.

(3) Vico (*q.v.* 1) is the first philosopher to insist that history is humanity's primary discipline. He argued that humans can understand only what humans have themselves made. Since they have made history, this must be central to their understanding.

(4) Herder (*q.v.* 1), assuming for the first time the individuality of each age and culture, founded the genetic method of historical analysis.

(5) Hegel (*q.v.* 3) makes history even more central, regarding history as the locus in which the activity of the divine reason is to be observed.

(6) Schelling (*q.v.* 4) utilized a periodicity, finding three stages in the movement of history.

(7) Carlyle (*q.v.* 2) presented a "great man" theory of history, interpreting the genius of great men as the decisive factor in historical change.

(8) Dilthey (*q.v.* 4) argued for the important point that the historian is limited by the perspectives of the age. The point of view, known as Historicism, rejects the possibility of objective history.

(9) Ritschl (*q.v.*) and Troeltsch (*q.v.*) struggled with the problems of the relations between history and religious faith. They defended the point of view that Christianity emerged from history but is not dependent on it.

(10) Windelband (*q.v.* 2) applied the term "ideographic" to history as one of the cultural sciences. These are the sciences of "individual form."

(11) Max Weber (*q.v.*) and Edward Spranger (*q.v.*) held that "ideal types" can be extrapolated from history, and made the basis of studies in the social sciences. This reference, along with the three preceding, relates to neo-Kantians (*q.v.* Neo-Kantianism 6).

(12) Rudolf Otto (*q.v.*), a neo-Kantian of the Göttingen School, used history to gain the concepts needed in his area of Philosophy of Religion, which he then developed systematically. The members of the Göttingen School (*q.v.* Neo-Kantianism 3) often took this approach to history.

(13) Croce (*q.v.* 1) held philosophy and history to be inseparable elements in the development of the life of the spirit. In practice this meant viewing philosophy in historical terms rather than the converse.

(14) Collingwood (*q.v.* 3) gave the historical perspective a privileged place among the many fields of human experience, while granting that each contains an aspect of the truth.

B. The History of Philosophy. A number of philosophers have considered the history of philosophy as a special problem.

(15) Hegel (*q.v.* 2, 3) found the dialectical pattern of thesis-antithesis-synthesis characterizing the progression of philosophical systems in the history of philosophy.

(16) Cousin (*q.v.* 4) classified all systems of philosophy as representing one of four types: sensualism, idealism, skepticism, or mysticism.

(17) Brentano (*q.v.* 5) believed that philosophy went through stages of practicality, skepticism, and mysticism between its periods of full vitality.

(18) S.C. Pepper (*q.v.* 1) suggested that all systems of metaphysics can be characterized as examples of Formism, Mechanism, Organicism, or Contextualism.

(19) R.P. McKeon (*q.v.* 1) finds a recurrent cycle in the history of philosophy. Philosophy turns to epistemology when metaphysical systems multiply, and then to language study as epistemologies likewise multiply.

C. We distinguish between the study of History and the study of Philosophy of History, on the grounds that the latter finds in history repeated patterns or laws of some kind.

(20) On this ground the early version of time as moving in great cycles, held in both East and West, leading to the decline and rebirth of human societies, qualifies as a philosophy of history. In the East the cycle consists of the birth of the universe from God, and its eventual reabsorption (*q.v.* Ramanuja 4). The Greeks held to a view of the world, including human societies, going through periods of rise and decline (*q.v.* Heraclitus 8; Plato

13). A modern representative of the cyclical view is Nietzsche (*q.v.* 7) with his doctrine of eternal recurrence.

(21) The Judeo-Christian tradition changed the periodization of time from cycle to progression or from circle to the concept of time's arrow. In St. Augustine (*q.v.* 13) the ages of the world represent a fall and return characterized by paradise, expulsion, period of the law, and the Second Coming.

(22) Joachim of Floris (*q.v.* 1) found three periods in history: the Age of Law, the Age of the Gospel, and the Age of the Spirit.

(23) By the 18th century the progression had been secularized, moving from primitive animality to utopia. The French *philosophes* helped to popularize this ideal. Condorcet (*q.v.* 2–3), for example, found ten stages of human progress, society now being in the final stage.

(24) Vico (*q.v.* 3) held to a double perspective. Human societies move through three stages: from the age of gods through the age of heroes into the age of men. Meanwhile, behind the scenes, an ideal history is occurring with divine providence in control.

(25) Auguste Comte (*q.v.* 1) introduced three stages in his view of human progress. Societies pass from a theological stage through a metaphysical into a final scientific stage. In this stage whatever problems humans face will yield to scientific inquiry.

(26) Hegel (*q.v.* 3, 22) traced human progress through a troubled dialectic, featuring oppositions and their resolution, as the Absolute realizes its nature in the history of the world.

(27) Schlegel (*q.v.* 2) likewise regarded history as an expression of the divine.

(28) Marx and Engels (*q.v.* Marxism 1), turning Hegel on his head, developed a Dialectical Materialism moving toward an ideal end through class conflicts, and their resolutions. The ideal goal, a classless society, is inexorable. The human function is merely to hasten its arrival.

(29) Spengler (*q.v.*) reverted to the cyclical concept as applied to individual societies. Denying the possibility of universal history (a cumulative idea), he argued that each society must be considered in its own terms. Societies may, however, be compared structurally, *i.e.*,

each society goes through a cycle marked by birth, growth, old age, and death; and the history of each society divides into the stages, first, of culture, and then of civilization.

(30) Toynbee (*q.v.*) adopted Spengler's view that the unit of analysis is the individual society while modifying the theme of inevitability of decline. At the same time, Toynbee developed the internal categories of the analysis: challenge and response, withdrawal and return, creative minority and transmissive majority.

HISTORY, PHILOSOPHY OF.
   Q.v. History (C).

HOBBES, THOMAS. 1588–1679.
   English philosopher. Born in Westport. Educated at Oxford. Upon graduation he became tutor in the Cavendish family, a lifelong connection. The world of the new science began to open to him during a tour of Europe in 1610. Ben Jonson, Francis Bacon and Herbert of Cherbury were among his friends. In 1636 he met Galileo in Florence; and spent eight months in Paris in discussions with Mersenne and his circle of scientists and philosophers. Returning to England, Hobbes worked out a draft of his monarchist political theory. When the Long Parliament began in 1640, Hobbes began an 11-year, self-imposed exile in Paris, sensing he was a marked man due to his political views. Received back into Mersenne's circle he wrote the third set of objections to Descartes' *Meditations*, and finished *De Cive*, his book on the citizen, in 1641 (but not published until 1647). He was tutor to the exiled Prince Charles of Wales, 1646–48. During these years he was working on the *Leviathan*, which was published in the middle of the year 1651. The book, an immediate success, estranged him from the exiled Royalists and the French authorities because of its thorough-going secularism. He fled to England and was accepted as a private citizen by the revolutionary government. Upon the Restoration, Hobbes became a friend of the court, Charles assigning him a pension. Following the great fire of London in 1666, the House of Commons passed a law against atheism, mentioning Hobbes by name. From that point on, little of his writing could be published in England.

Principal writings: *De Cive*, 1647 (English edition titled *Philosophical Rudiments*, 1651); *De Corpore Politico, or the Elements of Law Moral and Politic*, 1650; *Human Nature, or the Fundamental Elements of Policy*, 1650; *Leviathan, or the Matter, Form and Power of a Commonwealth, Ecclesiastical and Civil*, 1651; *Questions Concerning Liberty, Necessity, and Chance*, 1656; *De Homine*, 1658.

(1) The sequence in which Hobbes intended to present the divisions of his philosophy to the world, and the sequence, to a great extent, in which it did in fact develop, begins with a consideration of the nature of body, followed by a doctrine of man, and concluding with a political philosophy. With respect to body he held that all reality is corporeal, and is controlled by rigid causal laws. Causality is to be explained in terms of the transmission of motion from one body to another by means of contact. The most attenuated body is the ether. The idea of spirit or soul is a contradiction in terms; it is calling for an "immaterial material." All other concepts are to be understood in terms of the least common denominators of matter and motion, and are reducible to them.

(2) When we understand humans as material beings acted upon by the world, it turns out that their activity must be always in accord with the greatest force of experience. We are governed by appetites, passions, imaginations, and emotions. But since reality is causal, every event has its sufficient reason; as part of a causally determined whole we too are causally determined. In the common sense meaning of freedom, then, we are not free; Hobbes compared human freedom to that of water running freely to the sea. In an analogous sense one can be said to be at liberty although one's actions are determined.

(3) The object of perception is at last motion which has gained entrance to our minds. Put otherwise, matter in motion, external to man, becomes light, figure, color, sound, odor, savour, heat, cold, hardness, softness, in man himself. There is no conception in a man's mind which did not first come through the sense organs. After the object is removed, or the eye shut, the brain retains an image of the thing seen, though more obscure.

Memory and imagination (or "simple" and "compounded" imagination, as he calls them) are, therefore, "decaying sense" which Hobbes calls phantasms and all of our thinking is made up of such material.

(4) When language is added, computation with words becomes possible. This computation involves an associating of ideas which is sometimes random and sometimes controlled. When controlled, names become signs.

(5) Hobbes believed that only the present has a being in nature; the past has being only in memory; things to come have no being at all. Furthermore, the things of the world are individual and singular; names are sometimes singular and sometimes universal. Thought follows procedures with words similar to the procedures with numbers, which are appropriate to arithmetic. Truth, then, consists in the right ordering of names in our affirmations. All of our conceptions are finite. When we say a thing is infinite, we signify only that we are not able to conceive its ends and bounds. Further, we cannot have a thought representing anything not subject to sense. Some of our thought is rooted in science; he calls this *sapientia*. Other thought is rooted in experience; he calls this *prudentia*. Prudence (*prudentia*) requires an amplitude of personal experience, and leads to action.

(6) Memories which are harmful, when stimulated by a new sensation, produce the feeling of aversion; memories which are beneficial, when restimulated, produce a feeling of pleasure or desire. In this way valuations and volitions appear, pleasure and pain emerging from the physical forces of attraction and repulsion, and "will" standing for the last link in the appetite-aversion chain leading toward action. Desire and aversion are rooted finally in man's instinct to survive.

(7) Understanding man in this way it is clear that he prefers himself to all others. Indeed, the underlying condition of human existence is a "war of every man, against every man" and self-interest is the universal rule. In this state of things, man's "natural state," life is "solitary, poor, nasty, brutish, and short." In the state of nature man has a right to anything he can gain; having this right, he

also has the right to transfer it to another. And to avoid the unsettled state we have been describing, men contract with each other and with a man or assembly to be their ruler.

(8) In the state of nature there is also a law of nature. In Hobbes the contrast between natural law (*q.v.*) and civil law has become a contrast between the disadvantages of the state of nature and the advantages of civil society. The application of reason to the state of nature leads to the conclusion that this state must be replaced by that of an ordered society. This seems to be the burden of the nineteen precepts of natural law set forth by Hobbes. He does say that the law of nature and civil law contain each other and are of equal extent; but since the latter is written down and enforceable and the former unwritten and unenforceable, he concludes that the former are merely "qualities disposing men to peace and obedience." Indeed, all moral virtues are derived from the desire for peace. The lesson is that in Hobbes the idea of natural law has given way to that of the social contract. Its power lies in "sovereignty," the artificial soul of Leviathan, who is an "artificial man" and a "mortal God." A government whose sovereign power is in the hands of one person is called "monarchy," in the hands of a few "aristocracy," in the hands of all "democracy." "Tyranny" and "oligarchy" are not additional forms of government, but the names for "monarchy" and "aristocracy" if you "mislike" them.

(9) In any case the social contract involves the subordination of individual rights to the sovereign power whatever its form. In Hobbes' view the most advantageous form of contract is that in which society contracts to assign its rights to an absolute sovereign or absolute monarch. Such power, once assigned, reverts to man only in case the power of the state deteriorates so badly that its continued existence is in question. Then man has the right to arrange a new contract. This rests on the only natural right man possesses both in the state of nature and in civil society; this is the right to life. One has no right to disobey the laws of society, but one does have the right to use force in repelling force in defense of one's life. Hobbes argues that

to make the social contract with an absolute monarch is quite appropriate. Since the monarch possesses absolute power, he is above the battle, and thus able to adjudicate the quarrels of other men impartially.

(10) Although the state of nature has been replaced by a variety of social contracts, it is clear that individual man preserves this state within himself in some sense. The state of nature also characterizes the relations of the nations of the world among themselves.

(11) Dividing the sciences into those deriving from fact and those deriving from reason, he puts historical and empirical subject-matter in the first classification, and formal studies in the second.

HOBHOUSE, L.T. 1864–1929.

British philosopher. Born in Cornwall. Professor in Oxford, moving to London University in 1907. Wishing to provide a point of view which could unite naturalism and idealism, empiricism and rationalism, Hobhouse tended toward an organicistic view of the world, which he traced out in detail in its ethical and social implications.

Principal writings: *The Theory of Knowledge*, 1896; *Mind in Evolution*, 1901; *Democracy and Reaction*, 1904; *Morals in Evolution*, 2 vols., 1906; *Social Evolution and Political Theory*, 1911; *Liberalism*, 1911; *Principles of Sociology*, 4 vols.: *The Metaphysical Theory of The State*, 1918; *The Rational Good*, 1921; *The Elements of Social Justice*, 1922; *Social Development, its Nature and Conditions*, 1924.

HOCKING, W.E. 1873–1966.

American philosopher. Born in Cleveland, Ohio. Taught at California, Yale, and Harvard. Shaped by the currents of idealistic, pragmatic, and realistic thought, Hocking united them to a doctrine of personal worth, providing sensitive analyses of humanity, society, and God.

Principal writings: *The Meaning of God in Human Experience*, 1912; *Human Nature and its Remaking*, 1918; *Man and the State*, 1926; *The Self: its Body and Freedom*, 1928; *Types of Philosophy*, 1929; *The Lasting Elements of Individualism*, 1937; *Thoughts on Death and Life*, 1937; *Science and the Idea of God*, 1944.

HODGSON, SHADWORTH. 1832–1912.
British philosopher. Born in Boston, England. Founder of the Aristotelian Society, and its president for fourteen years, he took upon himself the problem of reshaping the Kantian critique of experience in the direction of increased rigor. The approach to experience through categories is retained, however, and explication of the moral sphere leads him in the direction of metaphysical idealism. With respect to free will he believed that while we determine our own actions, the determining factor is a neurocerebral condition accompanied by awareness. On this ground he held freedom and determinism to be compatible. Indeed, since consciousness always accompanies but never determines, his position is that of Epiphenomenalism. In addition to the writings set forth below, volumes one through eight of the *Proceedings of the Aristotelian Society* contain vast quantities of his work.
Principal writings: *Time and Space*, 1865; *The Theory of Practice*, 2 vols., 1870; *The Philosophy of Reflection*, 2 vols., 1878; *The Metaphysic of Experience*, 4 vols., 1898.

HÖFFDING, HARALD. 1843–1931.
Danish philosopher. Born in Copenhagen. Educated at Copenhagen. Taught at Copenhagen. Combining a tendency toward the scientific positivism of the 19th century with an early influence deriving from Kierkegaard, Höffding held that metaphysical systems result from the inevitable value-determinations present in an individual's interpretation of the world. He did not believe metaphysical systems to be invalidated by relativization to the situations in which they are written. He distinguished religions in terms of the values they enshrine, holding this to be their most essential characteristic.
Principal writings: *Outlines of a Psychology Based in Experience* (T), 1882; *Ethics*, 1887; *History of Modern Philosophy* (T), 2 vols., 1894; *Rousseau*, 1896; *Philosophy of Religion* (T), 1901; *Human Thought*, 1910; *Bergson*, 1914; *Totality as Category*, 1917; *Relation as Category*, 1921; *The Idea of Analogy*, 1923.

HÖFLER, ALOIS. 1853–1922.
German philosopher. Born in Kirchdorf. Taught at Vienna. A follower of Meinong (*q.v.*), Höfler based logic on descriptive psychology. From another standpoint he regarded it as a branch of descriptive ontology. Both logic and psychology are held to contribute to theory of knowledge. These disciplines and their interrelations provide the point of departure for metaphysics.
Principal writings: *Fundamental Doctrines of Logic*, 1890; *Philosophical Propaedeutic I, Logic*. 1890; *Psychology*, 1897; *Fundamental Doctrines of Psychology*, 1898; *Fundamental Doctrines of Logic and Psychology*, 1903; *On Contemporary Philosophy of Nature*, 1904; *Science and Philosophy*, 1920.

HOFFMAN, A.F.
Q.v. The German Philosophy; Rüdiger.

HOLBACH, PAUL HENRI D'(BARON). 1723–1789.
French philosopher. Born in Edesheim, Germany. Educated at Leiden. He lived in Paris from an early age. Closely associated with the famous *Encyclopédie*, to which he contributed many translations. Holbach was friend to d'Alembert, Diderot, Condillac, Helvetius, Hume, Rousseau, and many others. His philosophical writings were published anonymously or under assumed names, and outside France. His most notable book, *The System of Nature*, drew answers from both Voltaire and Frederick the Great.
Principal writings: *Christianity Unveiled* (T), 1767; *The System of Nature* (T), 1770; *Common Sense, or Natural Ideas Opposed to Supernatural Ideas* (T), 1772; *Social System*, 1773; *Natural Politics*, 1774; *Universal Morality*, 1776.
(1) Not only is the human being a machine as described by La Mettrie, the world as a whole is a machine; and a machine which does not require a machinist.
(2) The world is a system of material particles operating according to fixed laws of motion in such a way that necessity rules everywhere, free will is a delusion, and the sum of existence remains always the same even though individuals and worlds form and disintegrate in fixed cycles.
(3) The chief qualities of things are the qualities of matter; and these include extension, divisibility, impenetrability, configuration, and mobility.

(4) Each person is motivated by self-interest, and happiness is a state of uninterrupted pleasure; hence, a healthy, well-adjusted organism is the first condition for happiness. A natural ethic stressing pleasure-pain can be derived from these principles.

(5) It is the job of education to make virtue advantageous; and the power of the state must be put behind the program.

(6) Knowledge rests on sensation, and this means one must put science in the place formerly held by religion as the source of explanation, for religion has no certain knowledge.

(7) Indeed, Christianity is only a superstition fostered by priests who wish to retain their power over the people, aided by princes who are thus relieved of the need for governing wisely. It presents an ethical system which proceeds from false assumptions, asking that we love others above ourselves, a thing which is not possible.

Q.v. Meslier (1).

HÖLDERLIN, JOHANN C.F. 1770–1843.
German poet. Born at Lauffen. Educated at Tübingen. A friend of Hegel, Schelling, and Schiller, Hölderlin's romantic poetry mediates between the finite and the infinite, the latter represented by the presence of nature. His work has influenced Heidegger, among others.

Principal writings: *Hymns to the Ideals of Mankind*, 1793; *Hyperion*, 1797–9; *Lyrical Poems*, 1826. There are translated editions of his poetry.

HOLISM.
Q.v. Smuts (1); Davidson (1, 7–8); Dummet (5–6).

HOLOSCOPIC.
Q.v. Mckeon (4).

HOLT, E.B. 1873–1946.
American philosopher. Taught at Harvard and Princeton. Although better known in later life as a psychologist, we cite him here for his participation in the movement of New Realism (*q.v.*).

Principal writings: (symposiast) *The New Realism*, 1912; *The Concept of Consciousness*, 1914; *The Freudian Wish and its Place in Ethics*, 1915.

(1) Holt combined a staunch philosophic realism with the neutral monism (*q.v.*) which he found implicit in James' (*q.v.* 10) doctrine of pure experience. His realism held to the numerical identity of the content of knowledge and the thing known. In fact, the identity was for him partial. The distinction between thought and object is that thought grasps only a portion of its object.

(2) His neutral monism held that reality is neither mental nor physical, but that both mental and physical entities are made up of "elements of being" which have their locus in a timeless realm, and which can function either conceptually or materially.

(3) As instances of elements of being, Holt was fond of citing the concepts of logic and mathematics. In addition, however, the realm had to include also secondary qualities, and even the errors, hallucinations, and illusions of awareness.

(4) At length, Holt renounced the position, and moved toward behaviorism and materialism.

HOLY, IDEA OF THE.
Q.v. Otto, Rudolf (2).

HOLY SPIRIT.
The third member of the Christian Trinity (*q.v.* Doctrine of the Trinity, A). Paul the Apostle (*q.v.* 1) made the Holy Spirit the alter ego of Christ, the guide and help of Christians, first manifesting itself on the day of Pentecost.

HOMER. 8th cent. B.C.
Author, whether single or multiple is open to question, of the *Iliad* and *Odyssey*. The poems provide a comprehensive view of the pantheon of Greek gods, whose principal members were Zeus, Apollo, Poseidon, Ares, Hera, Athena, Aphrodite, Helios, and Hermes. The gods relate to Mount Olympus but intervene at times in human affairs, and can be approached by means of prayer and burnt offering. The concept of *moira*, or fate, in Homer means at times simply the will of the gods and at others a necessity binding even upon them. The poems likewise present a scheme of values, and a view of popular morality. Both Heraclitus (*q.v.*) and Xenophanes (*q.v.*) criticize Homer by name, and he was much cited by other Greek philosophers.

HOMOIOUSIAN.

From the Greek *homoi* ("like") and *ousia* ("substance"). The doctrine defeated in the Council of Nicaea and later that the Son is of similar, but not identical, essence or substance as the Father. *Q.v.* Arianism.

HOMO LUDENS.

Q.v. Huizinga.

HOMO MENSURA.

From Latin meaning "man the measure." The phrase applied to the doctrine of the Greek sophist, Protagoras (*q.v.* 1), that all standards and judgments are relative to man. The doctrine is sometimes interpreted as an individual and sometimes as a collective relativity.

HOMONOMIC PREDICATES.

Q.v. Davidson (4).

HOMOOUSIAN.

From the Greek *homos* ("the same") and *ousia* ("substance"). The doctrine established at the Council of Nicaea (*q.v.*) that the Son is of the same essence or substance as the Father.

HOMO VIATOR.

Latin phrase meaning "man the traveler." *Q.v.* Marcel (4).

HOMUNCULUS.

From the Latin, "little man." Used by Skinner (*q.v.* 4) in defending operational explanations; the attack on explanations as specious when they involve "little demons or goblins" goes back to Leibniz' *New Essays*. Dennett (*q.v.* 3) defends the *homunculus* as an "intentional" placemarker to be cashed out by a replacement mechanical explanation.

HOOK, SIDNEY. 1902–89.

American philosopher. Born in Brooklyn. Studied at the College of the City of New York and Columbia University. Taught at New York University (1927–73). Senior Research Fellow, Hoover Institution (Stanford) (1973–89).

Principal writings: *The Metaphysics of Pragmatism*, 1927; *Toward the Understanding of Karl Marx*, 1933; *From Hegel to Marx*, 1936; *John Dewey: An Intellectual Portrait*, 1938; *Reason, Social Myths and Democracy*, 1940; *The Hero in History*, 1943; *Education for Modern Man*, 1946; *Heresy, Yes—Conspiracy No*, 1953; *Marx and the Marxists: The Ambiguous Legacy*, 1955; *Political Power and Personal Freedom*, 1959; *The Quest for Being*, 1961; *The Paradoxes of Freedom*, 1962; *Religion in a Free Society*, 1967; *Academic Freedom and Academic Anarchy*, 1970; *Education and the Taming of Power*, 1973; *Pragmatism and the Tragic Sense of Life*, 1975; *Philosophy and Public Philosophy*, 1980; *Marxism and Beyond*, 1983; *Out of Step: an Unquiet Life in the XXth Century*, 1987.

(1) Hook's commitment to the Pragmatism of John Dewey, and his desire to contribute to it theoretically, collided with the attractiveness exerted by Marxism in the heart of the Great Depression of the 1930's. He worked at both commitments, but the issues of public philosophy consumed most of his considerable energies, diverting him from his planned technical analysis of Dewey's philosophy. Collaborating with Dewey on a number of practical issues, including an American investigation of the Moscow Treason Trials of 1936–37, Dewey not only joined the investigating commission but travelled to Mexico to interview Trotsky.

(2) The shock of the Moscow trials turned Hook from "fellow-traveler" into "social democrat." In this role he fought the cultural cold war against communists who had not yet awakened from the socialist dream. Through the years he defended the principles of democratic liberalism against attack from whatever quarter. Among his targets, however, were Americans who refused to testify before the Congressional committees, the Adler-Hutchins neo-Thomistic experiments in education, and college administrations who, in a time of student disturbances, failed to preserve the principles of academic freedom in their institutions.

(3) He called his philosophical position "pragmatic naturalism." A virtual mirror of Dewey's pragmatism, the position differed from that of Dewey only in emphasis. Less optimistic than his mentor about human prospects, he was also less permissive about the religious use of the term "God." Hook emphasized the inescapable human tragedy implicit in the incompossibility of goods, and avowed an "open-minded" atheism.

HOOKER, RICHARD. 1553–1600.

English philosopher and theologian. Born at Heavitree. Educated at Oxford. Taking orders in the Church of England, he devoted himself throughout most of his life to a treatise on ecclesiastical and civil law. His purpose was to articulate a view of law supporting the relations of church and state as they had developed in the Church of England, while answering the objections of the Presbyterians. In addition, he provided a basis for the social philosophy of John Locke as articulated in the latter's *Treatise on Civil Government*.

Principal writings: *The Laws of Ecclesiastical Polity*, 8 vols., 1594–1662.

(1) Following Thomas Aquinas' distinctions between eternal, natural, and positive law (*q.v.* Natural Law 4), Hooker assigned to reason—the discoverer of natural law and the interpreter of eternal law—a more significant role than had his predecessors.

(2) All government, whether civil or ecclesiastic, rests on public approbation given directly, or indirectly through inheritance from one's ancestors. Consent is both given, and revoked, through universal agreement.

(3) It follows that church and state are different aspects of the same government. He argued that, at least in England, the royal power—relating directly to the matter of consent—extends over religious as well as civic matters.

HORIZON.

Q.v. Jaspers (4).

HORKHEIMER, MAX. 1895–1973.

German social philosopher. Born in Stuttgart, Germany. Educated at the universities of Munich, Freiburg, Frankfurt am Main. Taught at University of Frankfurt, and associated with Columbia, 1933–48. A long-term member of the Frankfurt School (*q.v.* A.-C.), and director of its Institute For Social Research, 1931–59, Horkheimer presided over its fortunes for almost thirty years, including its move to New York in 1933, and its return to Frankfurt in 1950. For this reason many of the details of his life and thought are to be found in that entry.

Principal writings: Most of his writing was cooperative, appearing, along with essays from other members, in the Institute journal, *Zeitschrift für Sozialforschung* (1932–65) and in cooperative volumes, resulting from Institute studies: for example, *Authority and Family*, 1936; and the Research Project on Social Discrimination (Adorno co-director), leading to the cooperative volume titled *The Authoritarian Personality*, (1959); with Adorno he wrote *Dialectic of Enlightenment* (1944 edition titled *Philosophical Fragments*), elaborating on the same themes in *Eclipse of Reason*, (1947).

(1) Horkheimer is associated with the Frankfurt School attacks on the Vienna Circle of Logical Positivism (*q.v.*) in the 1930's. He regarded positivism as simplistic, unable to distinguish surface from core facts, urging in its place a "dialectical theory" in which facts relate to "totality."

(2) He introduced the phrase "critical theory" as the aim of the School's position with respect to capitalism in his *Zeitschrift* article, "Traditional and Critical Theory," (1937). This was adopted generally by members of the School, and is still used by Habermas (*q.v.* 4).

(3) He supported and developed, if he did not introduce, the idea of technological reason as an instrument of domination in modern society. In *Dialectic of Enlightenment* technological reason is traced to De Sade, for whom reason was an instrument neutral in regard to ends. Culture itself was viewed as the result of "evoked and manipulable demands," embodied in a "culture industry."

HORMIC PSYCHOLOGY.

Q.v. McDougall; Psychology (13).

HOSSO.

Q.v. Śunya (6).

HOWISON, G. H. 1834–1916.

American philosopher. Born in Montgomery County, Maryland. Studied at Marietta College and Lane Theological Seminary. Taught at Washington University (St. Louis), M.I.T., University of Michigan, and the University of California (Berkeley), 1884–1909, where he established the Philosophical Union. Related to the St. Louis Hegelians and their Journal of Speculative Philosophy, the Concord School of Philosophy, and many of the Harvard philosophers. Calling his system Personal Idealism, he viewed the world as a spiritual plurality, developing teleologically in relation to God who is final cause and goal of the process.

Principal writings: *A Treatise on Analytic Geometry*, 1869; *The Conception of God* (with Royce and others, a publication of the Philosophical Union), 1897; *Limits of Evolution, and other Essays in Philosophy*, 1901 (2nd edition, 1904); *Philosophy—Its Fundamental Conceptions and Its Methods*, 1905.

HO YEN. 3rd cent. A.D.

Chinese philosopher. Known as a brilliant young man, and once a minister of state. A neo-Taoist he nonetheless recognized Confucius rather than Lao Tzu as the Sage.

Principal writings: *Treatise on Tao; Treatise on the Nameless*.

(1) The Tao, or ultimate reality, is beyond description, or any name, yet it works in and shapes all things.

(2) The Sage has a name, and yet, in relation to the Tao, is nameless. In possessing nothing he possesses everything. Confucius praised Sage-emperor Yao saying, "The people could find no name for him." Even so is greatness beyond naming.

HSIUNG SHIH-LI. 1885–1968.

Chinese philosopher. Born in Hupei. Educated at the Nanking Institute of Buddhism. Taught at Peking. Turned his attention to the *Book of Changes* and borrowing elements from Western philosophy, he produced a reconstruction of the rationalistic or idealistic side of neo-Confucianism.

Principal writings: *New Doctrine of Consciousness-Only* (T in part), 1944; *An Inquiry on Confucianism* (T in part), 1956.

(1) Reality is a "great functioning," universally operating without cease, passing through transformations of "closing" and "opening," the former transformation representing a tendency to merge, or combine, which may be viewed as material; the latter representing a tendency to maintain an identity or nature, which may be viewed as mental. The latter is to be regarded as more fundamental than the former.

(2) Principle is viewed as primary, and material force is viewed, not as derivative, but as partial. "Principle" includes both substance and function, while "material force" refers only to function. In effect, this allows reality to be viewed in mental terms. Substance and function are viewed as the relation between the ocean and its waves.

(3) The principles of the "great functioning" are present in its manifestations, so that the thousands of individual things and their unchanging principles are present together.

(4) Humanity is not only a virtue, but somehow the foundation of all things, the source of all transformations, and the "original mind" common to all things.

HSUAN-TSANG. 596–664.

Chinese philosopher. Entered monastery of the Pure Land School at 13. From 618 to 629, he traveled from monastery to monastery, finding conflicting doctrines. He spent 16 years, from 629 to 645 in India, seeking the true doctrine. Returning in 645 with 657 Buddhist works, under imperial patronage he set up a school of translation and devoted the next 20 years to the translation of 75 of these works, most of these belonging to the Yogachara tradition.

Principal writings: *Treatise on the Establishment of the Doctrine of Consciousness-Only* (T in part).

(1) The world of our experience is the result of a complex set of discriminations based on Dharma-characters, elements of existence, some real and some unreal. The real elements have no specifiable characteristics, being of the nature of "thusness" or "suchness." The unreal elements are those provided by imagination, and those caused by other elements, having no existence of their own. To explore and understand the nature of reality we must turn to an analysis of the nature of consciousness.

(2) The world is built up by consciousness by means of a very complex process resulting from various reintegrations of the "seen" with the "seeing," and our witnessing and rewitnessing of our seeing the seen. These four modes of consciousness are provided in turn by the parts of consciousness.

(3) The eight parts of consciousness

responsible for its complex functioning include: (a) the five senses, (b) an internal center of sense from which conceptions emerge, (c) a center of thought from which emerge processes of both willing and reasoning on a self-centered basis, and (d) a "storehouse consciousness" responsible for memory but also for good and evil deeds in a karmic sense, extending back indefinitely through earlier existences. The storehouse is being constantly shaped by incoming sensations and ideas. At the same time the storehouse is shaping these sensations and ideas with its own energy. But the storehouse consciousness is not the only transformative agent. The thought-center reflects, uninterruptedly, shaping thoughts on the false basis that the storehouse consciousness is the self. Its products are hence warped by self-delusion, the view that the self exists, self-conceit, and self-love. And the five senses with the internal sense form a center of delusion as well. The five senses contribute to the sixth sense which has the whole external world as its object. It thus becomes a self-center, but is less delusive than the thought-center which does not have the world as its object. All of these transformations are governed by cause and effect, shaping each other, and doing so delusively.

(4) What, then, is the final view? Neither the self nor external objects exist. There is only inner consciousness producing what appears externally. But only in the state of the *arhat* or saint, can this be realized. This is the consciousness-only doctrine. It would seem to be the point that we must work with two levels of truth. On the lower level we are to admit multiple awarenesses, each with a thusness or suchness, the emptiness of true reality. On the higher level true thusness, or perfect reality, is a three-fold nonbeing—a nonbeing of characters, a nonbeing of self-existence, and nonbeing in the highest sense which is beyond description, good, and eternal.

HSÜN TZU. 298–238 B.C.

Chinese philosopher. A native of Chao. A Confucian, he was a contemporary of Mencius. An eminent scholar, he was more influential in the Han dynasty than Mencius. After the Han dynasty his work was subject to neglect until the 19th century. His thought was naturalistic in temper, contrasting with the idealistic temper of Mencius. He was a magistrate of Ch'u in later life.

Principal writings: *The Hsün Tzu* (T in part).

(1) Nature operates with ceaseless regularity. This regularity of nature is the way or Tao, with which one must remain in harmony. If one keeps to the way, nature cannot cause misfortune.

(2) To play his part in the triad with heaven and earth, man must devote his attention to human things. He must play his part through the development of wisdom in order to know how to direct the ten thousand things of the world. Nature is to be regulated rather than to be esteemed.

(3) But man's nature is evil. He seeks personal gain above all else. If his natural tendencies be followed, chaos will result. To prevent this we have the civilizing influence of teachers, laws, and the patterns of propriety and righteousness. Together these result in discipline. Goodness is, therefore, the result of activity. And the sage is a man who has reached that state through accumulated effort. Any inferior man can reach that same state if he is sufficiently persistent.

(4) It is important for the sake of correct thinking and good government that words be used correctly. The sage-kings followed sound principles in the use of names. But now there is a confusion of correct names, and a rectification of names is desirable. Names are conventional. When a convention is established and the custom is formed, the result is a correct name. There are simple names (*e.g.*, horse), compound names (*e.g.*, white horse), general names (*e.g.*, tree in general, thing). By paying attention to the nature and kinds of names, the fallacies of so using names as to confuse names, so using actualities as to confuse names, and so using names as to confuse actualities, can be avoided.

HUAI-NAN TZU. 2nd cent. B.C.

Chinese philosopher. The most important Taoist philosopher between the 4th century B.C. and the neo-Taoism of the 3rd and 4th centuries A.D., he continued the tradition of Lao Tzu (*q.v.*) at a time when Confucianism had an exclusive role in the Imperial government and, generally, in Chinese thought. Plotting a rebellion which failed, he committed suicide.

Principal writings: *The Huai-nan Tzu.* (T).

(1) The Tao is responsible for all things, each according to its nature. The appropriate life is one in harmony with the Tao. This is ultimately the way of non-action (*wu-wei*).

(2) The Tao came from a void which produced the universe of space and time. The universe produced material force. The material forces of heaven and earth combined to form *Yin* and *Yang*. *Yin* and *Yang* became the four seasons; the scattered forces of the four seasons became the myriad things. The hot forces of *Yang* provided fire and the sun. The cold force of *Yin* produced water and the moon. And what remained after producing sun and moon, became the stars and planets.

HUA-YEN SCHOOL. Beginning 5th cent. A.D.

Chinese school of Buddhist philosophy based on the *Hua-Yen Ching* ("flowery splendor scripture"). Contributing to the development of Hua-Yen in China were Tu-Shun (557–640), the nominal founder; and Fa-Tsang (643–712) the real founder.

(1) The *Dharmas* (*q.v.* and 7), or elements of (apparent) existence, arise through the causation of one's own mind. The mind is the primary cause of the *dharma*; and the individual *dharma* is a subsidiary cause of the mind. But the *dharmas* are in fact empty, and have no character.

(2) Nonetheless, the *dharmas* coexist, reflect each other, interrelate and interpenetrate, in such fashion that the world—a world of *dharmas* is a perfect harmony, each *dharma* being a microcosm of the whole.

(3) Since each *dharma* has the characteristics of universality and similarity, in addition to the characteristics of specialty, difference, integration, and disintegration, the collection of *dharmas* is mutually implicative, as well as being mutually interdependent.

(4) An important distinction is drawn between principle and fact. The *dharma* world is characterized equally by the presence therein of static, spaceless, form-less, characterless, empty, and noumenal principles along with dynamic, spatial, temporal, formed, and characterized phenomenal facts. It is the interacting of these two things which provides the harmony of the *dharma* world. (This distinction characterized neo-Confucianism as principle and material force.)

(5) Of course, in the state of enlightenment the *dharma* world is eliminated, giving way to Nirvana (*q.v.*) in which all reality is seen to be mental.

HÜGEL, FRIEDRICH VON. 1852–1925.

English-Austrian philosopher. Born in Florence, Italy. A Roman Catholic, von Hügel combined in his thinking the approach of mysticism and the classical conception of God as transcendent and absolute. His writings are in English.

Principal writings: *Mystical Element of Religion*, 1908; *Eternal Life*, 1912; *Essays and Addresses on the Philosophy of Religion*, 1921; *The Reality of God*, 1931; *Letters to a Niece*, 1950.

HUGH OF SAINT VICTOR. 1096–1141.

Scholastic philosopher and Churchman. Born at Hartingam in Saxony. Member of the Abbey of St. Victor at Marseilles, and then of the Abbey of St. Victor in Paris of which he was canon, and where he died. The mysticism of the School of St. Victor, which he initiated, was the most influential movement of the second half of the 12th century.

Principal writings: *On the Sacraments of Christian Faith*; *Didascalion*; *On the Mystical Ark*; *On the Union of Soul and Body*; *On the Soul*.

(1) The ascent of the soul through *cogitatio, meditatio,* and *contemplatio* is an ascent to faith through reason. The various forms of knowledge form a hierarchy of theory and practice pointing to mystic contemplation.

(2) The hierarchy of knowledge divides into theoretic science (made up of theology, mathematics, physics, arithmetic, music, geometry, and astronomy), practical science (or ethics), mechanical science (the mechanical arts), and science of discourse (dialectic and rhetoric).

(3) With respect to the controversy over universals (*q.v.* 10–15), Hugh followed Abelard (*q.v.*), holding a position of moderate realism. We gain universals by

abstraction, although the forms of sensible things do not exist in universals outside the mind.

(4) His analysis of the seven sacraments was accepted by Peter Lombard, and became definitive for the Catholic church.

HUGUENOTS.

The term was given to French Protestants, apparently from a common meeting place in Tours near the gate of King Hugo. French Protestantism met vigorous persecution. The Huguenots became politically involved, and the issues led the nation to a succession of eight civil wars during the 16th century. These are called the Wars of Religion. In 1562 the Massacre of St. Bartholomew occurred. The period ended with the Edict of Nantes which in 1598 recognized the principle of religious toleration.

HUI-NENG. 638–713.

Early leader of Zen Buddhism (q.v. 3).

HUI SHIH. c. 380–c. 305 B.C.

Chinese philosopher. A native of Sung. Contemporary and friend of Chuang Tzu (q.v.). A "logician," he served as Prime Minister to King Hui of Liang. Our knowledge of his ideas comes from the *Chuang Tzu*.

(1) Collectively, all things form one body called "The Great One." Distributively, each thing is made up of the small units which have nothing within themselves.

(2) The paradoxes of magnitude, height, direction, time, similarity, and difference show that these distinctions are unreal. In the course of elaborating these paradoxes, he held that there are moments when an arrow in flight is neither at rest nor in motion; and that a stick one foot long could be halved daily for ten thousand generations without end. Not only were his paradoxes similar to those of the Western philosopher, Zeno of Elea (q.v.), his intent appears to have been similar, i.e., calling attention to "The Great One."

HUI-SSU.

Q.v. T'ien-T'ai School.

HUI-WEN.

Q.v. T'ien-T'ai School.

HUIZINGA, JOHANN. 1872–1945.

Dutch philosopher and historian of culture. Born in Groningen. Taught at Göttingen and Leiden. Concentrating especially on the forms of life and thought in the late Middle Ages, Huizinga believed that society requires a balance of material and spiritual values infused by an ideal of harmony. His study of the play element in culture has emphasized the definition of man in terms of play, *homo ludens*. Identifying play with the creative element in culture, Huizinga believed that creative epochs (e.g., the medieval and contemporary periods) harbor a heightened spirit of play. The 19th century was, he held, essentially serious.

Principal writings: *The Waning of the Middle Ages* (T), 1919; *Erasmus* (T), 1924–5; *In the Shadow of Tomorrow* (T), 1936; *Homo Ludens* (T), 1938.

HUMANISM.

A term employed in contrast to an opposing term e.g., "absolutism," "theism," in which human values and appreciations are presumably less central.

(1) The doctrine of Protagoras, taking men as the measure, stands in contrast to various types of absolutism, especially of an epistemological nature.

(2) In the Renaissance (q.v. Petrarch 1, Erasmus) the term signified a return to the Greek sources and individual criticism and interpretation in contrast to the tradition of Scholasticism and religious authority.

(3) In more recent centuries the term has been often used in contrast to theism, locating in humanity the source of goodness and creativity. August Comte is an extreme example of this usage, having formalized an ecclesiastical framework for "the worship of humanity."

(4) In the usage of F.C.S. Schiller (q.v. 1) and William James (q.v. 8), humanism is taken as the view which stands in contrast to philosophical absolutism. This does not quite return us to the position of Protagoras, since the humanism of Schiller and James is defined against metaphysical rather than epistemological absolutes, i.e., against the block universe of absolute idealism. The stress is, hence, upon an open universe, pluralism, and human freedom.

(5) Bertrand Russell (*q.v.*) developed the position now called "secular humanism" in which humanity must stand for its ideals in the face of an indifferent, or hostile, universe.

(6) For a contemporary viewpoint opposed to humanism *q.v.* Structuralism (6) and Derrida (3).

HUMANITY.

From the Latin *humanitas* ("human nature, feeling, or kindness"). The term is less used in philosophy than its cognates, although Stoicism (*q.v.* 4) in viewing man as a citizen of the cosmos had clearly arrived at the concept. One of the basic translations of *jen* (*q.v.*) in Confucianism is "humanity."

(1) In the final development of his point of view Comte (*q.v.*) called for a religion of humanity. Churches dedicated to this religion were established in a number of countries.

(2) Feuerbach (*q.v.* 2) regarded humanity as unlimited and capable of achieving any quality, even though individual men are finite. Indeed, according to Feuerbach, men—beginning with this unlimited quality of humanity—have mistakenly projected the idea of God.

HUMBOLDT, WILHELM VON. 1767–1835.

German philologist. Born at Potsdam. Educated at Berlin, Göttingen, and Jena. Humboldt contributed to linguistic study the concept of *Sprachform*, the idea that each language has its own individual inner form, providing a characteristic world outlook for that language.

Principal writings: *On the Heterogeneity of Language and its Influence on the Intellectual Development of Mankind* (T), 1836.

HUME, DAVID. 1711–1776.

British philosopher. Born in Edinburgh. Attended the University of Edinburgh. After trying law and business he spent three years in France, beginning in 1734, working out his *Treatise of Human Nature*. Appearing in 1739, it fell "dead-born from the press," according to Hume. Two volumes of *Essays* in 1741 and 1742 were well received. Failing in 1744 to gain the Chair of Moral Philosophy at the University of Edinburgh, he served as tutor to the Marquis of Annandale, and then

secretary to General St. Clair. In 1748 his *Inquiry Concerning Human Understanding* appeared. This is the *Treatise* rewritten and simplified. At the time it attracted little more notice than the earlier work. In 1751 he moved to Edinburgh; failing once more in his attempt to gain a professorship, he became librarian in the Advocate's Library of Edinburgh. There he worked out his monumental *History of England*. In 1763 he performed the duties of secretary to the British Embassy in Paris; French intellectual society received him with great enthusiasm. He returned to Edinburgh in 1766, only to leave for London in 1767 where he spent two years as undersecretary to General Conway. Returning to Edinburgh in 1769, Hume became the central figure of the intellectual and cultural life of the city until his death on August 25, 1776.

Principal writings: *Treatise of Human Nature*, 1739; *Essays*, 2 vols., 1741, 1742; *An Inquiry Concerning Human Understanding*, 1748; *Political Discourses*, 1751; *Inquiry Concerning the Principles of Morals*, 1751; *History of England*, 4 vols, 1753–61; *Four Dissertations: The Natural History of Religion, of the Passions, of Tragedy, of the Standard of Taste*, 1757; *Dialogues Concerning Natural Religion*, 1779.

(1) Experience is composed of impressions and ideas. The former have the greater force and vivacity; the latter have less force and are derived from the former. Correspondingly, ideas of memory have less force than present experience. Simple ideas are copies of simple impressions. Complex ideas result from complex impressions or from the compounding and manipulating of simple ideas. Although ideas can be traced to impressions, we cannot trace impressions to their source. The vulgar assumption is that our impressions take their rise from an external world; but this we cannot know from experience.

(2) The principles of association, governing our manipulation of ideas, are: resemblance, contiguity, and cause and effect. The first of these principles explains how abstraction can occur. To resembling particular ideas we attach the same term. All ideas are particular. And in the place of general ideas we have a general term attached to a group of particular ideas. The third of these principles

does, in fact, reduce to the second. It is clear that we never observe more, in those relations we term causal, than the constant conjunction of two or more successive impressions.

(3) What leads us to connect two successive events in a causal manner is a habit or custom which has developed in us through experience. This is the origin of the sense of necessity we feel. A similar tendency to go beyond experience leads us to believe in the existence of substances as the source of our impressions, and their continued existence when not related to us through experience. Our belief in the probability that what has held in the past will continue to hold in the future requires the additional premise "that instances of which we have had no experience must resemble those of which we have had experience, and that the course of nature continues always uniformly the same." But the premise cannot be demonstrated, nor even be shown to be probable, since all evidence for it must come from the past, we are engaged in a circular argument, and have no basis for the so-called principle of induction.

(4) The problem of personal identity, or psychical substance, is in exactly the same case. Experience reveals us to be a succession of impressions, ideas, and emotions, memories and anticipations; and one does not experience a unifying framework for this succession. It is memory which leads us to believe in our identity through time; but memory lapses with consciousness. Even the sense of our identity is not continuous. Consistent with these uncertainties, liberty is defined as action in keeping with our desires or wishes, in contrast to constraint, and not essentially opposed to the idea of necessity.

(5) Distinguishing between matters of fact and relations of ideas, Hume held that necessity inhered only in the latter. Relations of ideas, today called analytic statements, yield no information about the world. Hume held, as philosophers do today, that statements of logic and mathematics are analytic.

(6) The valuational side of human life is built up in a fashion somewhat comparable to its ideational side, and indeed fusing with it. By Hume's direct state-ment one must hold the valuational side to be primary. He says that "reason is and ought only to be the slave of the passions, and can never pretend to any other office than to serve and obey them." The primary feelings of pleasure and pain develop into reflective impressions of great complexity (grief, joy, malice, generosity, etc.) by means of the principles of association discussed above (*cf.* 2). In addition to a propensity toward pleasure, humans possess a natural sentiment of sympathy for others. Out of these two propensities benevolence can develop when one's interest relates to the whole of society. Thus value becomes social; and the principle of utility becomes an appropriate criterion of morality. The criterion of utility merges with a sense of social approbation, and disutility with social disapprobation. The general orientation of Hume's ethics came from the Moral Sense theorists, Shaftesbury (*q.v.*) and Hutcheson (*q.v.*).

(7) Although Hume's very rich *Dialogues Concerning Natural Religion* does not lend itself to summary, one of the plot lines of the work leads the reader to see how very close to skepticism are both the man of faith and the natural theologian. Both the skeptic and the man of faith hold to the incomprehensibility of the idea of God. Both the skeptic and the natural theologian hold to the anthropomorphic nature of the idea of God, and agree that discussion of his existence is a matter not of necessity, but of probability. Hume really anticipates Kant in his criticism of the arguments for the existence of God. The *a priori* (ontological) argument is invalid, since "necessary existent" has no consistent meaning. The cosmological argument can never get outside the world. The teleological argument at best proves a finite, imperfect deity. Meanwhile the action of the dialogue moves both the man of faith and the natural theologian toward skepticism. Perhaps the world is the first effort of some infant deity, now doing better elsewhere. Perhaps it is the product of a group of gods just as a ship is built by the joint activity of many persons. Perhaps instead of a world soul, the world is more like an animal, or a vegetable. Throughout his career Hume held that no rational answer to skepticism is avail-

able. Carelessness and inattention, action, and absorption in the occupations of common life, contain the only remedy.

(8) This attitude quite naturally leads to a position which denies the possibility of one's ever being able to affirm a miracle on rational grounds. The reason is that, since the laws of nature are established by a fund of experience which is constantly increasing, and miracles are attested to by solitary individuals widely separated in space and time, no evidence adequate to prove a miracle can ever be forthcoming. Furthermore, the greater the marvel the less evidence we have. Miracles must hence be relegated to the realm of superstition.

HUNG-JEN. 601–674.
Early leader of Zen Buddhism (*q.v.* 2).

HUNTINGTON, EDWARD V. 1874–1955.
American mathematician. Born in Clinton, New York. Educated at Harvard and Strassburg. Taught at Williams and Harvard. He contributed to the axiomatization of the Boolean algebra (*q.v.*).

Principal writings: "Sets of Independent Postulates for the Algebra of Logic," 1904, 1933; *The Continuum and other Types of Serial Order*, 1911.

(1) Huntington's first set of postulates for the algebra was:

Ia. If a and b are elements, so too is a + b.

Ib. If a and b are elements, so too is a x b.

IIa. There is an element 0 such that a + 0 = a for every element a.

IIb. There is an element 1 such that a x 1 = a for every element a.

IIIa. a + b = b + a for all elements a and b whose combinations here mentioned are also elements.

IIIb. a x b = b x a for all elements a and b whose combinations here mentioned are also elements.

IVa. a + (b x c) = (a + b) x (a + c) for all elements a, b, and c whose combinations here mentioned are also elements.

IVb. a x (b + c) = (a x b) + (a x c) for all elements a, b, and c whose combinations here mentioned are also elements.

V. If the elements 0 and 1 exist and are unique, there is an element a such that (i) a + $\bar{a}$ = 1 and (ii) a x $\bar{a}$ = 0.

VI. There are at least two elements x and y such that x $\neq$ y.

(2) The fourth set of postulates will be set down for comparison with the above.

(i) If a and b are elements, so too is a + b.

(ii) If a is an element, so too is $\bar{a}$.

(iii) a + b = b + a for all elements a and b whose combinations here mentioned are also elements.

(iv) (a + b) + c = a + (b + c) for all elements a, b, and c whose combinations here mentioned are also elements.

(v) a + a = a for all elements a and b whose combinations here mentioned are also elements.

(vi) -($\bar{a}$ + $\bar{b}$) + -($\bar{a}$ + b) = a, for all elements a and b whose combinations here mentioned are also elements.

HUSS, JOHN. c. 1369–1415.
Bohemian religious leader. Born in Hussinecz, educated at Prague. There he became acquainted with the works of John Wycliffe (*q.v.*), whose influence was great in the University. When Huss began teaching at Prague, he used a number of Wycliffe's books as texts. Named Dean of Philosophy in 1401 and Rector of the university in 1402, he was at the same time a popular preacher in Prague. In the difficulties which arose, political and religious issues intertwined, and Huss responded both as a religious leader and as a nationalist. By 1403 the doctrines of Wycliffe had been condemned by the university; but this was by the German faction which had a three to one vote over the Bohemian faction in controlling the university. By appeal to the king, Huss succeeded in having the proportion reversed. He was reelected Rector; the Germans withdrew, forming a new university (Leipzig). At the same time the German and Roman axis among the clergy succeeded in having an inquisitor appointed to inquire into the extent of Huss' reliance upon the ideas of Wycliffe. The pressure on Huss gradually increased. Wycliffe's books were burned in Prague by the archbishop. Huss was excommunicated. Prague was placed under an interdict because of Huss' presence there. He withdrew from the city that the interdiction might be lifted. Although he had refused a request from the pope to come to Rome, he agreed to attend the Council of Constance, called in part

to hear his case, under an imperial guarantee of safe conduct. He set out for the council on October 14, 1414 with the sense that he was going to his death. The safe-conduct guarantee was disregarded; Huss was taken. After a series of examinations he was sentenced to death and burned at the stake on July 6, 1415. Among the points at issue was Huss' definition of the Church as "the body of the predestinate." Given that definition the pope's authority concerning the sale of indulgences or excommunication was reduced. When word of Huss' death reached Prague, violence broke out. Emperor Sigismund, who had issued the safe-conduct guarantee, threatened to "drown all Wycliffites and Hussites." Shortly before going to Constance, Huss had adopted the view that the faithful were to receive communion in both kinds (*sub utraque specie*), the cup as well as the bread. This became the rallying point for the important central group of Hussites, called Utraquists. The struggle over this religio-political issue, including open warfare and a crusade against Bohemia, continued into the 16th century when the Hussite cause merged with the general movement of Protestantism.

Principal writings: *Commentary on the Sentences; On the Church; Letters.*

HUSSERL, EDMUND. 1859–1938.

German philosopher. Born in Prossnitz. Educated at the University of Vienna. Taught at the Universities of Halle, Göttingen, and Freiburg. The influence of Brentano, his teacher, combined with that of Bolzano, Lotze, and the Cartesian philosophy to produce the framework of Husserl's thought. Beginning his studies in the foundations of mathematics, the founder of phenomenology finally offered an entirely universal and transcendental approach to experience. It will be necessary to consider his thought in its several stages.

Principal writings: *Philosophy of Arithmetic*, I, 1891; *Logical Investigations*, 2 vols. (T), 1900; *Ideas on a Pure Phenomenology and Phenomenological Philosophy* I, (T), 1913; *Lectures on the Phenomenology of the Inner Time Consciousness*, ed. M. Heidegger, 1928; *Formal and Transcendental Logic*, 1929; *Cartesian Meditations* (T), 1931; *The Crisis of European Science and Tran-*

scendental Phenomenology, I, 1936; *Experience and Judgment*, 1939.

A. (1) The problem of Husserl's *Philosophy of Arithmetic* is to understand number in terms of the essences of the numbering concepts which consciousness has produced. This direct seeing into the essences of things led to his phenomenological method.

(2) The first volume of his *Logical Investigations* extended the method into a consideration of logical forms. The independence of logic is maintained; logic is defended from psychologistic and functionalistic interpretations. Logical forms become independent essences exemplified in various matters of fact, and open to phenomenological inspection. Through phenomenology the universal categorial nature of these forms is to be grasped.

(3) In volume 2 of the *Logical Investigations*, especially in the second edition, the method is generalized in such a way that it becomes applicable to metaphysical problems generally. The meaning of phenomenology itself evolved dramatically between the two editions. In the first edition, phenomenology was viewed as a method of descriptive analysis of subjective processes, hence only in certain respects different from psychology. In the second edition, phenomenology had become an eidetic science, *i.e.*, a science concerned with mental images capable of extracting essences from experience or phantasy, and whose concern is the analysis of subjective processes in terms of their content of ideal possibilities. The whole range of phenomenology, thus, gained the status which had been granted to logic in volume one.

(4) In his later writings Husserl spoke of a number of types of purely eidetic sciences: material ontologies of any material region, a formal ontology of possible being, and a universal eidetic science of worldly being. Material ontologies form the basis of all factual sciences. They are regional in the sense that the essences appropriate to one science will not necessarily be those of another science. But all material ontologies have their basis in formal ontology which deals with universal essences. A number of additional steps were still to be taken in the development of the conception of the

nature of phenomenology. For example the term "transcendental" began to figure more prominently. Philosophy came to be viewed as transcendental phenomenology, an analysis of the subjective structures out of which the concrete individual world may be legitimately and intersubjectively formed. It was in this development that phenomenology became or tended to become, or at least appeared to become, a type of metaphysics. Husserl termed his point of view at this stage, "transcendental-phenomenological idealism."

(5) Somewhat apart from the topic of stages of development is the set of ideas essential to the mature stages of his thought. Central to the set is the concept of intentionality or *Intentionalität*. Throughout awareness are the phenomena of our intentions, the things we intend to do. Husserl made this a basic category. In the stream of subjective processes one is aware of a distinction between processes of intending, and of objects as intended. Since all meaning is intentional, and meaning is constituent to consciousness, both sides of this distinction are intentional. That is to say, we are not referring here to objects as things in an outer world, but things intended. Husserl called the "strictly" mental side of the process *noesis*. Adjectivally, this side of intentionality is termed the *noetic*. *Noesis* points beyond itself to "objects." The objective sense of a *noesis* is called *noema*. This side of the intentional act is termed adjectivally the *noematic* or the *hyletic*. The noetic and noematic sides of the stream of consciousness are both intentional. There is a sense in which "objects" point beyond themselves to other objects. References are made, then, both to noetic and to objective intentionality. Husserl came to believe that the concept of an object not intentionally constituted was contradictory; hence, the philosophical position referred to above.

(6) A constant feature of Husserl's phenomenology is its identification with the seeing and fixing of essences. The quest for the essential in experience required a method of eliminating the non-essential or contingent features of experience whether psychological or physical. The essence sought is a structure thought to be invariant in the modifications of experience permeating both actual and possible instances. The process of discovering essence is called the *Epoché*. It begins with the "bracketing" of existence, *i.e.*, suspending for the time the question of existence, and engaging in a series of reductions including: (a) the psychological reduction freeing the essence of consciousness from its factual concretizations; (b) the eidetic reduction aiming at objectivity; (c) the phenomenological reduction leading to a "pure" subject as the subjective term of the act of consciousness, and hence to pure subjectivity; (d) reduction of the pure subject to the transcendental subject by way of the transcendental ego; (e) reduction of the transcendental ego to a "pure flow of consciousness" involving temporality and history in consciousness and processes of constitution.

(7) In general these reductions merely amplify the notion of intentionality discussed above. The process of working out individual essences led to the noetic-noematic distinction, and to others as well. In the *Cartesian Meditations*, Husserl treated this distinction in another manner, The Cartesian discovery was not that of the existence of the individual ego but the existence of transcendental subjectivity as the first absolute datum, one which founds and includes objectivity. Since the conditions and assumptions of being an individual ego had been "bracketed," the first datum must be referred to the transcendental ego. At this point we are given flow and continuity on both sides of the stream. A constant objective identity, and a constant subjective identity. On the one hand we are given the world, and on the other hand transcendental subjectivity, and the two justify each other. Out of this flow we constitute both a concrete ego and individual objects.

(8) The two sides interact in such a way that the concrete individual subject, once constituted, has an individual world over against his subjectivity called the *Umwelt*. The problem of other minds is resolved by means of the objective elements in the individual worlds of concrete subjects. These elements make communication possible, and suggest the presence of a *Kulturwelt* resulting from the community of individuals.

(9) In his later thought Husserl distinguished between the scientific world and the *Lebenswelt* or "lived world," regarding the latter as primary and the former as derivative from it. In this phase of his thought the central task of phenomenology is analysis of the *Lebenswelt*.

HUSSITES.

Q.v. John Huss.

HUTCHESON, FRANCIS. 1694–1746.

Scotch-Irish philosopher. Born in Drumalig, Ulster. Studied at Glasgow. Headed a Presbyterian Academy in Dublin until 1730 when he was invited to the University of Glasgow as Professor of Moral Philosophy. A disciple of Shaftesbury and a friend of Hume, he can be regarded as the systematizer of the Moral Sense theory of ethics. He stands as a link between Locke, whose theory of ideas he accepted, and the Scottish Common-Sense philosophy which derived in part from his work.

Principal writings: *Inquiry into the Original of Our Ideas of Beauty and Virtue*, 1725; *Essay on the Nature and Conduct of the Passions and Affections and Illustrations upon the Moral Sense*, 1728; *A Short Introduction to Moral Philosophy*, 1747; *A System of Moral Philosophy*, 2 vols., 1755.

(1) Hutcheson's analysis of human nature led him to claim the existence of a great number of special senses. In addition to the Moral Sense, and of course the five senses on which everyone agrees, Hutcheson referred to consciousness as a special sense concerning what goes on in our minds: the sense of beauty; a "public sense" of being pleased by the happiness of others, and being uneasy over human misery; the sense of honor or of praise and blame; and a sense of the ridiculous.

(2) He held the sense of beauty to be an internal reflex sense, responding both to external and internal perceptions. He argued that while custom, education, and example may extend or refine this sense, in order for this to happen there must be a natural power to perceive beauty. Beauty is discerned not only in things, but also in universal truths, moral principles, and moral actions.

(3) The same argument is offered with respect to the Moral Sense. While par-

ticular moral judgments are ideas of reflection in the Lockean manner, such ideas are founded on a natural sense capable of making moral distinctions. He argued that the judgments cannot be based on reason for the power to reason is in general too weak to match moral perceptiveness; and moral distinctions are presupposed in the forces of education, custom, and example. Similarly, the fact that benevolence is pleasing must finally be interpreted as saying that there is a moral sense to which benevolent activity is pleasing.

(4) The Moral Sense pronounces immediately on the character of actions, approving those which are virtuous and disapproving the vicious. One aspect of its work is the pleasure which lies in benevolence; the only virtuous actions are those flowing from benevolence. Those flowing from self-love are "morally indifferent" and, in general, subject neither to praise nor blame. The test of virtuous action, however, is not that it gives pleasure, or at least not that alone; Hutcheson suggests, anticipating Utilitarianism (*q.v.*), that the test of right action is "the greatest happiness for the greatest number."

HUXLEY, ALDOUS.

Q.v. Utopia (9).

HUXLEY, T.H. 1825–1895.

English biologist and philosopher. Born in Ealing. Self-educated. He was an effective proponent of Darwinian evolution, tracing the origin of humanity through remote, pre-human forms. It was also his belief that all living forms constitute mechanical systems in such fashion that consciousness is epiphenomenal. It is the effect of bodily processes and the cause of nothing. Insisting that one ought not to believe beyond the evidence, and that satisfactory evidence concerning the nature of the universe is not available, Huxley coined the term "agnostic" to express his position of suspended belief.

Principal writings: *Man's Place in Nature*, 1864; *Hume*, 1879; *Collected Essays*, 9 vols., 1893–4; *Scientific Memoirs*, 5 vols., 1898–1903; *Life and Letters*, (ed. L. Huxley), 3 vols., 1903.

HUYGENS.

Q.v. Probability (4).

HYLETIC.
Q.v. Husserl (5).

HYLOMORPHISM.
From the Greek *hyle* ("matter") and *morphe* ("form"). The doctrine that all physical things are composed of matter and form. Identified with Aristotle (*q.v.* 7) the doctrine likewise characterizes Thomistic philosophy (*q.v.* Thomism). Form is the principle of actuality and activity, while matter is the principle of potentiality and passivity.

HYLOZOISM.
From the Greek *hyle* ("matter") and *zoe* ("life"). A doctrine predicating life of all matter. Held by many early philosophers, among them Thales (*q.v.*); suggestions of the view are to be found in most philosophies which find the world to be teleologically ordered. If all living forms are sentient to some degree, Hylozoism becomes a subclass of Panpsychism (*q.v.*).

HYPOSTASIS.
From the Greek term *hypostasis*, from *hypo* ("under") and *hitasthai* ("to stand").
(1) For Aristotle the individual substance in the perfection of its actuality.
(2) In Christian doctrine the term is taken as a synonym for Person (*q.v.*), and used to explain both the Trinity (*q.v.* 5), and the nature of Christ.
(3) Aquinas applied the term to second substances which subsist in the species.

HYPOTHESIS.
From the Greek *hypo* ("under") and *tithenai* ("to put"), that is, a foundation or supposition.
(1) The term is often taken to mean a provisional explanation which, dependent upon its degree of confirmation, may come to be regarded as an accepted theory or law.
(2) Plato (*q.v.* 1) made hypothesis the third rung in his ladder of truth, that segment dealing with mathematical entities. In its most central application, then, the method of hypothesis for Plato is the method of geometry where, given a geometric property incapable of direct demonstration, one seeks a second property which can be demonstrated and from which the first follows.
(3) Aristotle (*q.v.* 2) holds an hypothesis to be an assertion capable of proof but accepted and used in a demonstration without proof. He also claims that hypotheses postulate facts on the being of which depend the being of the facts inferred.
(4) Descartes (*q.v.* 10) sometimes spoke as though hypotheses were statements not known to be true or false but convenient starting points for deducing sets of conclusions.
(5) It was in response to this use of the term that Newton (*q.v.* 5) claimed that he did not make up hypotheses, ("*Hypotheses non fingo*").
(6) Lotze (*q.v.* 4) regarded hypotheses as the conjectural filling up or out of the logical space between necessary postulates and experience.
(7) Comte and others have used the term "experimental hypothesis" of any statement or set of statements to be confirmed or disconfirmed by experiment. The term stands in contrast to "*ad hoc* hypothesis" (*cf.* 10 below).
(8) Hypotheses are formed, according to Peirce (*q.v.* 8), by the process of abduction (*q.v.*), the mind moving from a given phenomenon to a condition capable of accounting for the phenomenon.
(9) Poincaré (*q.v.* 1) divided hypotheses into those which are second order, those "indifferent," and "real generalizations subject to test."
(10) Hypotheses are confirmed by their capacity to predict phenomena other than those which led to their formulation. *Ad hoc* hypotheses fail in this respect, predicting only their parent phenomena.
(11) The term "hypothesis" is employed in the term "hypothetico-deductive method." This method, normally associated with the procedures of mathematics and physics, consists of making explicit through deduction all that is implicit in a set of premises. When the method is used in confirming an hypothesis, the hypothesis, joined to a set of confirmed premises, is used to deduce observation sentences, *i.e.*, sentences stating something capable of being observed, which can then be tested. The value of the hypothesis depends upon the significance of its role in helping to deduce observation sentences which turn out to be both true and interesting. It has been often remarked that interesting

hypotheses, finally shown to be untrue, can have value in leading the way to other hypotheses which can be confirmed. *Q.v.* Explanation (2).

(12) The term "hypothesis" has also been used traditionally to refer to the antecedent clause of an "if-then" statement, the thought being that the consequent clause was conditioned by the assumption of the antecedent clause. The validity of this usage is weakened to some extent by the fact that in the propositional calculus the two parts of an "if-then" statement need have no relation to each other. Traditionally, hypothetical propositions were placed in contrast to categorical propositions, but the theory of propositions now holds that "All S is P" is to be rewritten, "For any x, if x is S then x is P." Further, since all composite propositions—conjunctive, disjunctive, and conditional—share a common form, all can be regarded as in some sense hypothetical.

(13) In one sense, by hypothetical syllogism is meant reasoning of the form "If p then q; if q then r; if p then r." In the broader sense, by hypothetical syllogism is meant any form of reasoning whose major premise is composite, and whose minor premise affirms or denies one of the parts. *Q.v*, Logic; Propositional Calculus.

HYPOTHESES NON FINGO.
Q.v. Newton (5).

HYPOTHETICAL PROPOSITIONS.
Q.v. Proposition (2); Hypothesis (12).

HYPOTHETICAL SYLLOGISM.
Q.v. Truth Tables (7c); Propositional Calculus (5); Hypothesis (12).

HYPOTHETICO-DEDUCTIVE METHOD.
Q.v. Hypothesis (11).

I

IAMBLICHUS. c. 270–330.
Syrian Neoplatonist. Born in Chalcis, Coele-Syria. Studied under Anatolius and Porphyry. Immensely influential in his own time he was the chief representative of the Syrian school. His name was often accompanied, both in his own time, and also in the 15th and 16th centuries, with the descriptive phrase "the divine."

Principal writings: *On the Pythagorean; The Exhortation to Philosophy; On the General Science of Mathematics; On the Arithmetic of Nicomachus; The Theological Principles of Arithmetic; On the Egyptian Mysteries* (T).

(1) The very complex and ornate system of Iamblichus differs from that of Plotinus (*q.v.*), the master Neoplatonist, largely by way of embellishment. The embellishment seems to derive from his acceptance of the Pythagorean view that number applies to all things.

(2) Among richly figurative details, Iamblichus added to Plotinus' scheme of the One, *Nous*, Soul, and Nature; at least the following: a second unity mediating between the One and *Nous*; the designation of *Nous*, Soul, and Nature, as gods (intellectual, supermundane, and mundane); the division of *Nous* into one triad of intelligible idea-archetype gods, and a second triad of intellectual idea gods; the division of Soul into a triad of psychic gods; the division of nature into a series of hundreds of gods, including heavenly gods, chiefs, nature gods, gods of nations, and individuals. This swarm of gods influences natural events, possesses knowledge of the future, and will respond to prayer and offerings. Thus, theurgy (*q.v.*) is a feature of the system. The scheme of gods is built largely on threes and sevens.

(3) The soul of man descends into the body by necessity, but has freedom of choice, once embodied. Man's task is to return to the supersensible through virtuous activities; five classes of virtues are mentioned: political, purificatory, theoretical, paradigmatic, and priestly. It may be necessary for the soul to pass through several bodies before effecting its return.

IBN BAJJA.
Q.v. Avempace.

IBN DA'UD, ABRAHAM. 12th cent.
Jewish philosopher. Born in Spain. An Aristotelian and disciple of Avicenna (*q.v.*), he followed Avicenna's doctrine of emanation.

Principal writings: *The Book of Sublime Religion*.

IBN EZRA, ABRAHAM BEN MEIR. 1089–1164.

Spanish Jewish philosopher. Born in Toledo. He left Spain in 1140, living in North Africa, Egypt, Italy, France, and England. He is the author of hundreds of poems, 150 of which found their way into the Jewish prayer book. The author of many commentaries on the Bible, his methods anticipated the higher criticism in many details. Philosophically, Ibn Ezra shows Neo-platonic and Pythagorean influences. The universe comprises three worlds: the highest world of the angels; the middle world of sun, moon, and stars; and the world of nature. God is incorporeal and spiritual, knowing only general ideas, *i.e.*, the species of things but not the individuals of the species. God's creative act related only to the world of nature; the other two are everlasting. He thus opposed the *creatio ex nihilo* doctrine. God acts on the world through angels (and certain human beings of angelic character), and the heavenly bodies (the conjunction of planets). Man is nonetheless endowed with free will. *Q.v.* Judaism (10).

Principal writings: *On the Names of God; On the Divisions and Reasons for the Biblical Commandments*, 1158; also poems, and commentaries on the Pentateuch and other books of the Bible. His works are in Hebrew.

IBN GABIROL.
Q.v. Avicebron.

IBN RUSHD.
Q.v. Averroës.

IBN SINA.
Q.v. Avicenna.

I CHING.
A Chinese term meaning "Book of Changes" (*q.v.*).

ICHTIAS.
Q.v. Megarian School of Philosophy.

ICON.
For Peirce (*q.v.* 16) one of the three major classes of signs.

ICONIC LEGISIGN.
Q.v. Peirce (16).

ICONIC SINSIGN.
Q.v. Peirce (16).

ID.
Q.v. Freud (2).

IDEA.
A Greek term, *idea*, originally meaning "vision" or "contemplation." The Greek term *eidos* has the same root, and generally the same meaning.

(1) The atomism of Leucippus and Democritus (*q.v.* 8, 10) stressed the origin of ideation in sense—images (*eidola*), a usage continued by Epicurus (*q.v.* 8). The emphasis, if not the term, is continuous throughout the empirical tradition of Western philosophy.

(2) For Plato (*q.v.* 1, 9) on the other hand, although he used both *idea* and *eidos*, ideas are not "appearances" but the structural elements of things. Sensation may provide an initial clue to ideation, but ideas are thought, not sensed.

(3) Aristotle (*q.v.* 3) and Thomas Aquinas (*q.v.* 5) utilize both approaches; thought begins with the sense-datum or phantasm (from the Greek *phantasma*, "image") and by abstraction the formal element is separated from it.

(4) In Philo (*q.v.* 4) and St. Augustine (*q.v.* 2) the eternal forms are associated with the mind of God, and are compared to the presence of designs in the mind of the artist.

(5) Hobbes (*q.v.* 3–5) associated ideas very intimately with sense-images. By idea he seems to have meant a *phantasma* or appearance in the brain resulting from the impression of an external body on a sense organ.

(6) The rationalists of the 17th century followed Plato in making ideation the judge of sense data rather than the other way around. In consequence, the Platonic doctrine of innate ideas became a cornerstone of their view, Descartes (*q.v.* 4) separating ideas into three types: innate, adventitious, and factitious. Thus, too, arose Descartes' criterion of truth in terms of clear and distinct ideas.

(7) Locke (*q.v.* 1–6) using the term, "idea," very broadly, "to stand for whatsoever is the object of the understanding

when a man thinks," includes in the term *"phantasm, notion, species,* or whatever it is which the mind can be employed about in thinking." Sense-data are thus included among ideas and Locke, distinguishing between simple and complex ideas, discusses three kinds of the latter: modes, substances, and relations. Since any variety of complex ideas can be produced in his view by operating upon sense-data the doctrine of innate ideas is rejected.

(8) Berkeley (*q.v.* 1–3, 5–6) modified but did not add anything of positive value to the concept although his criticism of Locke's doctrine of abstraction has merit.

(9) Hume (*q.v.* 1, 2) distinguished between impressions and ideas while tracing the latter back to their corresponding impressions.

(10) Many of the above, and especially the British empiricists (*q.v.* 7–9 above), are to be credited with developing the principles of association to explain the manner in which ideas emerge from sensation and develop (*q.v.* Association of Ideas). The 18th-century French philosophers (*q.v.* for example, Condillac 1–4) tended to follow the same path as the British empiricists.

(11) Kant (*q.v.* 1–4, 11 b, f) signalled the presence of formal elements in experience, contributed by the mind. These elements, helping to constitute the "objective" world, he called "categories." Kant used the term "ideas of the pure reason" to refer to ideas which go beyond the boundaries of possible experience. There are three such ideas: (a) the absolute unity of the subject (soul), (b) the complete systematization of phenomena (world), (c) the unity of all existence (God). There are also three ideas of practical reason—God, freedom, and immortality—beyond the boundaries of experience.

(12) Hegel (*q.v.* 4–6), following Kant's distinction between ideas of understanding and ideas of reason, centered his attention on the Absolute Idea, a unity of the rational and the real, in process of dialectical development.

(13) The American pragmatists viewed ideas in terms of their consequences so that with Peirce (*q.v.* 1) the meaning of an idea becomes the sum of its consequences, or with James (*q.v.* 6) not only

these but also what the consequences of holding the idea contribute to its sense. John Dewey's program of viewing ideas (*q.v.* 4) as instruments and plans of action belongs to this family as well.

(14) Husserl (*q.v.* 6) combined empiricism and rationalism in an interesting manner. He called for a direct "seeing" of the essence of an idea.

(15) The verification theory of meaning of logical positivism (*q.v.* Vienna Circle of Logical Positivists) blends the pragmatic point with British empiricism.

(16) Ortega y Gasset (*q.v.* 2) distinguished between ideas and beliefs, regarding the former as abstract and without power, appearing when belief begins to fail; and the latter as empowering ideas.

IDEA-FORCE.
Q.v. Fouillée.

IDEAL.
From the Greek *idea* ("vision" or "contemplation"). Deriving from the term Plato (*q.v.* 1) used to designate the eternal ideas or forms, each of which was perfect of its kind, common usage has retained the valuational aspect of the word while discarding its epistemological or metaphysical aspect. The two senses remain together in the technical philosophical use of the term "idealism" (*q.v.*). In the philosophical systems which bear that name, "idea" is a central category; at the same time a concept of perfection is always, or almost always, present in the system. Kant used the phrase, Ideal of Reason, to refer to God, that one of the Ideas of Reason (*q.v.* Kant 11, b, f) which contains in itself the determination of all finite existence.

IDEALISM.
A term first used philosophically by Leibniz at the start of the 18th century. He applied the term to Plato's thought, contrasting it with the materialism of Epicurus. The term thus designates philosophies which regard the mental or ideational as the key to the nature of reality. From the 17th to the beginning of the 20th century, the term has been much used in the classification of philosophies.

A. Various types of idealistic philosophy have been distinguished.

(1) Schelling (*q.v.* 1 a–c) gave the name "subjective idealism" to the philosophy of Fichte, since in Fichte the world is a posit of the judging subject. Solipsism (*q.v.*), then, should also be so classed. Fichte (*q.v.* 1), who rested idealism on the primacy of the moral will, is regarded as the founder of German idealism.

(2) Schelling called his own philosophy in its middle stages "objective idealism," for nature, he held, is simply "visible intelligence." Taking this alternative to apply to all philosophies identifying reality with idea, reason, or spirit, Berkeley (*q.v.*) would be included along with all philosophers believing in panpsychism (*q.v.*). Notice, however, the view of Dilthey (*q.v.* 5) that in objective idealism, feeling is dominant.

(3) Hegel accepted Schelling's classification, turning it to his own uses. Holding subjective and objective idealism to represent thesis and antithesis, respectively, Hegel was able to present his own position, which he called "absolute idealism" as the higher synthesis of these positions. From the time of Hegel many philosophers began to stress the Absolute. Among absolute idealists are F.H. Bradley (*q.v.*), T.H. Green (*q.v.*), Bernard Bosanquet (*q.v.*), and Josiah Royce (*q.v.*).

(4) Kant (*q.v.*) called his position "transcendental idealism," or "critical idealism." In this alternative the contents of direct experience are not presumed to be things in themselves and space and time are forms of our own intuition. Schelling had used the term "transcendental idealism" as an alternative locution to "objective idealism."

(5) The judgment that one makes contact only with ideas, or in any event with psychical entities, has sometimes been called "epistemological idealism." If we accept this identification, then among epistemological idealists one has to count Descartes (*q.v.*) and most rationalists, Locke (*q.v.*) and most empiricists, the French associationalists, as well as all phenomenologists. The category thus introduces confusion since this epistemological alternative would include philosophers who in their metaphysical positions are realists, dualists, materialists or skeptics. On the other hand Berkeley (*q.v.* 3–4) and in another way

Jonathan Edwards (*q.v.* 1), attain truly metaphysical idealisms starting from epistemological idealism.

(6) Likewise engendering confusion is the occasional use of the term, "idealism," to characterize a philosophy which stresses the ideal. In this sense the positions of Plato (*q.v.*) and Aristotle (*q.v.*) are sometimes regarded as instances of idealism.

B. A number of philosophers have developed their own species of idealism.

(7) Howison (*q.v.*) called his system of philosophy "personal idealism."

(8) Fouillée (*q.v.*) developed a system involving "thought-force" which he named "voluntaristic idealism." The position exemplifies what Dilthey (*q.v.* 5) meant by "libertarian idealism."

(9) Ward (*q.v.* 3) named his position "theistic idealism."

(10) Bowne (*q.v.* 5) regarded his philosophy of Personalism as a species of "personal or personalistic idealism."

(11) Paulsen (*q.v.*) called his philosophy "monistic idealism."

(12) Sorley (*q.v.*) held a position which he named "ethical idealism."

(13) Hastings Rashdall (*q.v.* 2) likewise called his system "personal idealism." He meant by this that minds have independent existence, but matter is mind-dependent.

(14) Husserl (*q.v.* 4) elaborated a transcendental-phenomenological idealism of considerable subtlety.

(15) Messer (*q.v.* 3) advocated an "ethical idealism" which he believed had implications for epistemology.

(16) Gentile (*q.v.* 1), deriving from Hegel, called his system—centering on the primacy of the act—"actual idealism."

(17) Rescher (*q.v.* 2) called his position "conceptual idealism."

IDEALISTIC POSITIVISM.
Q.v. Vaihinger (1).

IDEALITY.
As a "mode of being," *q.v.* Weiss.

IDEAL TYPES.
Q.v. Max Weber; Edward Spranger.

IDEALITER IN INTELLECTU.
Q.v. Descartes (7).

IDEATUM.

The object of, as well as that which is represented in the mind by, an idea.

IDENTIFYING DESCRIPTION.

Q.v. Proper Names (4).

IDENTITY OF INDISCERNIBLES.

Q.v. Leibniz (3).

IDENTITY, PERSONAL.

The problem of personal identity is one aspect of the more general problem of permanence and change.

(1) If, as in Plato (*q.v.* 3), permanence is associated with soul and change with body, personal identity is assured.

(2) If, as in Aristotle (*q.v.* 7) and his followers, permanence and continuity are associated with form as a principle of development, and soul is understood to be the form of the body, the problem is solved.

(3) If, as in Kant (*q.v.* 11d–e), a transcendental ego is posited, one understands that a basic unity of self lies behind experience.

(4) If, as in Bergson (*q.v.* 9), the past as memory is ingredient in the present, identity is still assured.

(5) But if, as in the case of Hume (*q.v.* 4), the self is a cluster of shifting impressions, ideas, and capacities, personal identity is not possible.

(6) In the case of Whitehead (*q.v.* 21–23), the principles of Bergson and Hume are, in a sense, combined. The emphasis is on change and on inheritance from one's past; and, although the emphasis is on "becoming," Whitehead held that there is no continuity of becoming. There is only a "becoming of continuity."

(7) In deconstruction (*q.v.* Derrida 10) the self is opened to otherness and identified with textuality.

(8) In Hinduism personal identity is associated with the individuating features of *karma* (*q.v.* 1); and in Theravada Buddhism (*q.v.* 1, 4) the recognition of *anatman* ("no soul") is one of the conditions for release from the cycle of rebirth.

Q.v. Self; Soul; J.J.C. Smart (4).

IDENTITY, PRINCIPLE OF.

One of the three laws of thought, the principle—applied variously to statements and to things—holds that a proposition or a thing is identical with itself

and implies itself. The principle is useful in logic and can in fact be demonstrated. *Q.v.* Laws of Thought (2, 3); Tautology (3).

IDENTITY THEORY.

The view that mental states and brain states are contingently identical. The claim is that this identity is not a matter of definition but scientific discovery.

(1) Herbert Feigl (*q.v.* 1) has elaborated a "central states" physicalism, going beyond Behaviorism.

(2) The Australian Materialists, so called, J.J.C. Smart (*q.v.*), U.T. Place, and D.M. Armstrong, hold all mental concepts to be states of the central nervous system.

(3) Richard Rorty elaborates a "disappearance form" of the theory, not requiring an exact translation between the mental state and the brain state. To speak of sensations rather than brain processes is like speaking of demons instead of germs as the cause of disease. In both cases the former manner of speaking may well disappear into the second.

IDENTITY THEORY OF UNIVERSALS.

Q.v. William of Champeaux.

IDEOGRAPHIC SCIENCES.

Q.v. Windelband (2).

IDÉOLOGUES.

Q.v. Ideology (1); Destutt De Tracy.

IDEOLOGY.

From the Greek *idea* and *logos*, the term literally means "knowledge of ideas." But it has had from the start pejorative associations.

(1) Destutt de Tracy (*q.v.*) introduced the term *Idéologiste* to characterize the philosopher who, like himself, traced ideas back to the impressions from which, on this view, they arose. Napoleon, who found Destutt de Tracy and his group a danger to the empire, used the term, *Idéologue* in a pejorative sense to characterize any philosopher with republican sympathies, and especially Destutt de Tracy's group. The latter then began to use the term *Idéologie*, or ideology, as the name for that particular brand of philosophy.

(2) In the usage of Marx (*q.v.* 3) and Engels (*q.v.* 2) the term refers to a set of beliefs presented as objective whereas in

fact they merely reflect the material conditions of society.

(3) Karl Mannheim (*q.v.*) used the term to refer to those sets of beliefs where there is a difference between announced and underlying motives. He distinguished between partial and total ideology. The former is psychological in origin, while the origin of the latter is social.

(4) For Quine (*q.v.* 2) "ideology" is a near synonym of "meaning." He thus uses the term in something like its literal sense. *Q.v.* Althusser (4).

IDOLA FORI, SPECUS, THEATRI, TRIBUS.

Latin terms meaning "idols of the market place, cave, theatre, tribe" respectively. *Q.v.* Francis Bacon (2).

IFF.

An abbreviation for "if and only if." The abbreviation expresses material equivalence. "P iff q" means "if p then q, and if q then p." It is thus a stronger form than material implication. "Iff" performs the same function as the signs "≡" and "↔" which are more usual in formal expressions. *Q.v.* Propositional Calculus (20); Truth Tables (5).

IGNORATIO ELENCHI.

A Latin phrase literally meaning "reasoning from ignorance." The *ignoratio elenchi* means "irrelevant reasoning," and applies to those cases where it is taken to establish some conclusion other than the one, if any, which can be deduced from its premises. It thus applies to the entire list of "fallacies of relevance" (*q.v.* Fallacies B).

IKHNATON.

Q.v. Monotheism.

ILLATION.

The process of inferring a conclusion from a premise or premises, as well as the conclusion thus inferred.

ILLATIVE SENSE.

Q.v. Newman (5).

ILLICIT MAJOR.

Q.v. Fallacies (25).

ILLICIT MINOR.

Q.v. Fallacies (26).

ILLOCUTIONARY ACT.

Q.v. John Austin (2); Searle (2).

ILLUMINATION, DIVINE.

In the history of philosophy both truth and God have often been described in terms of light, and not seldom all three are merged in a single conception.

A. In the West this identification stems from Plato.

(1) Plato's (*q.v.* 1) image of the cave is one source of the relation of truth to light. Not only is man in darkness in his natural state, but the world of truth is bathed in light; and it is by an unpredictable flash of illumination that one finds fragments of the truth.

(2) Stoicism (*q.v.*) is another source, finding in man a spark of the universal reason; the latter is described, however, not precisely as light, but—following Heraclitus—as fire, the central element of things.

(3) The identification of light with God and truth is most pronounced in the Gospel of John, the most Greek of the gospels.

(4) In Neoplatonism generally light is regarded both as a physical and a spiritual element. The double interpretation is present in Proclus, the Pseudo-Dionysius (*q.v.* 3), and, through these sources, in William of Moerbeke (*q.v.*), Witelo (*q.v.*), and Robert Grosseteste (*q.v.*) among others.

(5) St. Augustine (*q.v.* 6) inherited the tendency to identify God and light from all of the above sources, but principally from (1), (3), and (4). He found within humans a light and radiance capable of leading one to God. Through the entire Middle Ages, wherever Augustine's massive influence was felt, this type of association appeared. One finds it in Bonaventure (*q.v.* 6–7) where the influence of divine illumination leads us to norms and finally to God, in Henry of Ghent (*q.v.*) and elsewhere.

(6) It appears once again in Protestant sects, among Anabaptists, and especially in the Quaker doctrine of the inner light (*q.v.* George Fox 1).

B. In the Near East, Islamic thought contrasted an Oriental philosophy associated with light to an Occidental philosophy associated with darkness.

(7) The school, called *Ishraqiyah* (*q.v.*, from *ishraq*, "illumination," and its

similarity to *mashriq*, "the east"). Blended, while contrasting, classical Greek philosophy and the Zoroastrian identification of light with the divine. The former (Occidental) was exoteric, the latter (Oriental) was esoteric. The former centered in concepts; the latter, centered in symbolic images, especially that of light, specialized in imaginal thinking, which was held to be more profound, and in which God is the "light of lights."

C. In the East there are numerous references connecting light with the spiritual state of enlightenment.

(8) In *jnana* (*q.v.* Hinduism 5b) suffering and limitation are removed by "illumination."

(9) In Mahayana Buddhism (*q.v.* 2) "brightness of intellect" is one of the ten stages of boddhisattvahood.

(10) In the Consciousness-Only School (*q.v.* Asanga) illumination occurs by way of emptiness.

ILLUSION.

From the Latin *illudere* ("to illude," *i.e.* "to deceive, elude, delude"). In philosophy there are many doctrines holding that the world is not as it appears.

(1) In Greek philosophy Parmenides (*q.v.*) and Zeno of Elea (*q.v.*) held reality to be much different from its appearance to us, as indeed did Gorgias (*q.v.*) with his claim that "Nothing exists." In modern philosophy the absolute idealists, for example F.H. Bradley (*q.v.* 3), found the empirical aspects of the world to be illusory.

(2) In Indian philosophy the terms *maya* (*q.v.*) and *avidya* (*q.v.*) are synonyms, standing for "illusion." Ashvaghosha (*q.v.* 2–3) provided in the 1st century A.D. an influential interpretation of the illusory nature of the phenomenal world from the standpoint of Mahayana Buddhism. In the 2nd century Nagarjuna (*q.v.*) developed numerous arguments, paralleling those of (1) above, in support of illusion. The Chinese Buddhist Seng-Chao (*q.v.* 1) followed Nagarjuna in arguing that time is illusory. From the standpoint of the Yogachara School, Asanga (*q.v.*) and Vasubandhu (*q.v.*) provided such interpretations in the 4th and 5th centuries A.D. For an interpretation from the very influential standpoint of Advaita Vedanta (*q.v.*) both Gaudapada (*q.v.* 2) and

Shankara (*q.v.*) are important.

(3) The movement of Skepticism (*q.v.*) cultivated for many centuries the arguments allegedly showing the unreliability of what "appears" to one. These were organized under tropes (*q.v.*). St. Augustine (*q.v.* 4) and Descartes (*q.v.* 2) admitted the point for the sake of argument, using it as a foil to establish the certainty of one's own existence.

IMAGE.

From the Latin *imago* ("imitation").

(1) The term is sometimes used to translate the Greek *eidolon*, as in the references of Democritus (*q.v.* 10) and Epicurus (*q.v.* 8), to the "outlines" sent by objects to our senses in perception.

(2) The Greek term *phantasma* translates indifferently into phantasm or image. Aristotle (*q.v.* 3) referred to ideas in potency as *phantasmata*. And in the Aristotelian-Thomistic tradition generally (*q.v.* Aquinas 7) the active intellect operates on the phantasm to produce a universal nature.

(3) Both Francis Bacon and Hobbes (*q.v.* 3) employed the term, "phantasm," the latter more extensively than the former. But empiricists generally have relied upon something similar to images, such as Locke's (*q.v.* 3–4) simple ideas, Hume's (*q.v.* 1) impressions, or Condillac's (*q.v.* 3) sensations to provide material for the principles of association to transmute into ideas.

(4) Berkeley (*q.v.* 2), using Locke's term "idea" to cover images, claimed that all ideas must be particular.

(5) Francis Galton (1822–1911), on the other hand, introduced the term "generic image" as a bridge between the concrete data of sensation and general concepts. The generic image was presented as a kind of composite photograph, the product of a variety of individual sensations of a particular kind. And Ward (*q.v.* 1) found three stages in the passage from sensation to idea.

(6) Arguments for and against the presence of, need for, or importance of images intersect with those for and against sense-data (*q.v.* Sense-datum). H.H. Price (*q.v.*) argues particularly well for sense-data, and Ryle (*q.v.* 3) and Austin (*q.v.* 4) against them.

IMAGINATION.

Synonymous with the Greek *phantasia* ("imaging").

(1) The type of analysis offered by empiricists stays close to the literal meaning of our term. The British empiricists, for example (*q.v.* Empiricism 3), mean by imagination a reworking of the materials of sense. On this point, at least, Thomas Hobbes (*q.v.* 3) is typical of his English colleagues. Hobbes divided imagination into "simple" and "compounded" types, an instance of the first being an act of now imagining a man or horse seen before, and of the second the act of conceiving a centaur from compounding the sight of a man and the sight of a horse.

(2) Kant (*q.v.* 11c) distinguished between the reproductive and productive imagination. The former takes the helter-skelter data of the senses and gives us whole objects. It completes the incompleteness of objects sensed. The productive imagination does even more. It is the power through which the categories order the material of intuition. Thus it makes possible a unified world and makes understanding possible. It is apparently also the condition for novelty.

(3) Coleridge (*q.v.* 3) divided the imagination into two parts, the "fancy," and the "constructive imagination." The "fancy" is very similar to Hobbes' "compounded" imagination. But the "constructive imagination" goes beyond random associations and essentially creates its own world, shaping details into its own unity according to its own controlling plan. He called this human capacity an "esemplastic" ("shaping into unity") power.

(4) Croce (*q.v.* 2) looked upon imagination as the creation of an individual intuition, and this process was central to aesthetic creation.

IMAGO DEI.

Latin phrase meaning "the image of God." In Genesis 1:26 it is written that Adam was created "in the image of God." Belief in and speculation about the nature of this "image" runs through much of Western thought. To cite examples almost at random, Bonaventure (*q.v.* 7) held that there is an image of God in man which leads to the concept of the Trinity as the divine exemplar of the human trinity of powers; and Calvin (*q.v.*

3) held that despite man's sin, part of God's image still remains within him.

IMAM.

Q.v. Islam (5, 7, 8); Bahaism.

IMITATION.

A translation of the Greek term *mimesis*. The theory of imitation, treated under Mimesis (*q.v.*), represents the application to aesthetics of the metaphysical theory of participation (*q.v.*).

IMITATIONISM.

Q.v. Kotarbinski (2).

IMITATION OF CHRIST, THE.

A 14th-century devotional book said to have been translated into more than fifty languages, and to have been issued in more than 6000 editions. The book is free from any taint of philosophical abstraction. Appealing to religious feeling, the thesis of the book is that "suffering with Christ" is the path toward spiritual truth. Traditionally attributed to Thomas à Kempis (*q.v.*), there is some evidence that the manual was principally written by Gerard Groote (*q.v.*), founder of the Brethren of the Common Life to which Thomas à Kempis belonged.

IMMACULATE CONCEPTION.

A doctrine of the Roman Catholic Church promulgated by Pope Pius IX in 1854 to the effect that the Blessed Virgin Mary—through a unique privilege and in view of her role as the mother of God—was preserved free from original sin from the moment of her conception.

IMMANENCE.

From the Latin *immanere* ("to inhabit"). The term has been used of actions, principles, and in some doctrines of the relation between humanity and God.

(1) In the language of Scholasticism, an immanent action, such as seeing, remains within the subject and does not modify its object. The correlative action modifying its object, is called transitive.

(2) Spinoza (*q.v.* 2) makes a similar distinction, but between *causa immanens* and *causa transiens*, understanding God's causality to be immanent in nature.

(3) In the language of Kant (*q.v.* 4, 11e) a principle is immanent if its application lies entirely within the limits of possible

experience; otherwise it is transcendent. (4) The immanent-transcendent contrast is utilized in a slightly different manner in religious language. God may be viewed as wholly transcendent, partially transcendent and partially immanent, or wholly immanent. Very different theologies ranging from classical theism to pantheism follow from the choice of relation. God's immanence in the world has been stressed by both pantheists (*q.v.* Pantheism) and panentheists (*q.v.* Panentheism); in the East, Indian philosophy (*q.v.*) especially shows this emphasis; and mysticism (*q.v.*) both East and West, has held to the mutual immanence of humanity and God.

IMMANENCE PHILOSOPHY.
Q.v. Schuppe, Wilhelm.

IMMANENTISM.
Q.v. Laberthonnière.

IMMANENT TRANSCENDENCE.
Q.v. Alfred Weber.

IMMATERIALISM.
A term created by Berkeley (*q.v.* 1) to characterize his position that there is no material substance.

IMMODEST INDUCTION.
Q.v. Induction (13).

IMMORTALITY.
The phrase "of the soul" normally follows this term. By "immortality of the soul" is meant the infinitely prolonged existence of that center of awareness to which the term "I" refers. The concept of immortality is usually viewed as Greek in origin, an invention of Socrates or Plato, although it very quickly became an important part of much Christian faith. In Eastern thought the concept is also present, although it is subordinate to a conception of Nirvana in which self-identity is lost.

Historically, the immortality of the soul has been a feature of systems oriented toward value—Idealism, Dualism, Pluralism; and not of materialistic systems since soul or self is therein interpreted as a product of bodily functioning.

(1) Socrates (*q.v.* 5, 6) presented a number of proofs of immortality, *e.g.*, the indivisible unity of the soul, and the eternality of opposites.

(2) Aristotle's (*q.v.* 7) view of the matter is unclear, and his view of the soul can be interpreted either as upholding or denying this doctrine.

(3) Stoicism (*q.v.*) allowed affirmation of a partial immortality, that of the universal reason within the self.

(4) The Schoolmen defended the doctrine, and understood Aristotle in that sense as well. It was a constant embarrassment to their point of view, however, that Averroës, the chief commentator on Aristotle, interpreted the philosopher as holding that only the nonindividual active intellect is immortal while the passive intellect, containing the conditions of individuality, perishes with the body. (*Q.v.* Averroës 4; Averroism.)

(5) On Descartes' (*q.v.* 9) view both mind and matter survive their separation at death.

(6) On the Leibnizian (*q.v.* 1) view all monads are eternal; immortality is hence a natural property of soul monads.

(7) Mendelssohn (*q.v.* 1) deduced the immortality of the soul from the metaphysical idea of a simple substance.

(8) Kant (*q.v.* 8) refuted Mendelssohn, while advancing a proof of his own which ⁑affirmed immortality on the basis of the demands of the moral reason.

(9) A view of conditional immortality was held by Goethe, Fichte, Lotze, and possibly even Spinoza, in which only those worthy of immortality reached it.

(10) Unamuno (*q.v.* 1) while holding proof to be impossible regarded immortality of body and soul to be the central human concern.

(11) Whitehead (*q.v.* 17) presented a doctrine of objective immortality, which identifies the immortal with the modality of the past.

IMPERATIVE.
From the Latin *imperare* ("to command"). The Language of ethics on the level of practice is fairly crowded with imperatives, expressed positively or negatively, singularly or universally. Many of these imperatives are hypothetical ("If you wish to gain the respect of your peers, be honest").

(1) Kant (*q.v.* 6) held that in addition to hypothetical imperatives, ethics requires and exhibits also a Categorical

Imperative. Whether or not there does exist a Categorical Imperative, which binds us without conditions, must be left to the judgment of the reader. But it is true that most contemporary analyses render ethical imperatives as hypothetical and prudential ("If you wish to be a success, boost, don't knock"), hypothetical and approbatory ("If you tell the truth, it will please me"); or hypothetical and disapprobatory ("If you lie, you will be punished").

(2) Ostwald (*q.v.* 2) speaks of an "Energy Imperative," which seemed to him to lie at the basis both of ethics and all practical activity.

Also *q.v.* Deontic Logic.

IMPERATIVE, CATEGORICAL.
Q.v. Imperative (1); Kant (6).

IMPETUS.
Q.v. John Philoponus; Marsilius of Inghen.

IMPLICATION.
The logical notion of Implication has been treated under several headings. Material Implication is discussed under Truth Tables (3), Modal Logic (2), and Propositional Calculus (18). The so-called Paradoxes of Material Implication are likewise discussed under Truth Tables (3). For Strict Implication *q.v.* Modal Logic (3); C.I. Lewis (1). For a distinction between implication and inference *q.v.* W.E. Johnson (1).

IMPLICATIVE, CONVERSATIONAL.
Q.v. Grice (3).

IMPORTATION.
Q.v. Propositional Calculus (21).

IMPOSITION, FIRST AND SECOND.
In Scholastic logic, terms of first imposition consisted of terms of first and second intention (*q.v.* Intentionality 1, 2). Terms of second imposition were grammatical terms, *e.g.*, "noun," "pronoun," "verb," etc.

IMPOSSIBILITY.
Q.v. Plantinga (3).

IMPREDICATIVE DEFINITION.
Q.v. Paradox (8).

IMPRESSION.
Hume's (*q.v.* 1) term for the material of sensation. He divided impressions into simple and complex, leading to simple and complex ideas.

IMPUTATION.
In theology the attribution of guilt or merit to one person on the basis of the guilt or merit of another. The concept applies not only to the doctrine of original sin (*q.v.* 3) but also to that of justification by faith (*q.v.*).

INCARNATION.
From the Latin *in* and *caro* ("flesh"). The term usually refers to the doctrine that God has, or will, become embodied in human form. The doctrine is held in numerous religions.

(1) In Christianity the doctrine that God became incarnate in Christ is one of the articles of faith (*q.v.*), regarded as beyond the reach of reason (*q.v.* Thomas Aquinas 1).

(2) According to Hindu belief Vishnu (*q.v.*) has become incarnate nine times, one of these incarnations being that of Buddha, and the tenth incarnation is approaching. Incarnations or emanations of the divine are present in all three of the principal Hindu sects (*q.v.* Vaiṣnavism).

(3) In Mahayana Buddhism (*q.v.* 1) the *bodhisattvas* who have worked their way to divinity, postpone Nirvana through endless rebirths to succor the spiritual quest of humankind.

(4) In the religion of Lamaism (*q.v.*) the grand lamas, temporal and spiritual heads of the religion, are regarded as incarnations of celestial beings.

(5) In Islam (*q.v.* 5, 7) the Imams are regarded as appointed of Allah; and some sects of the religion expect the Mahdi, or final Imam, to appear and lead the forces of Islam to final victory.

(6) According to Bahaism (*q.v.*), a sectarian division of Islam, there have been either six or seven manifestations of the divine, including Christ and Mohammed.

INCOMPLETENESS.
Q.v. Completeness; Gödel (2).

INCOMPLETE SYMBOL.
Q.v. Russell (5).

INCONSISTENCY.
The negation of consistency (*q.v.*).
(1) In the traditional square of opposition

(q.v. Immediate Inference 1), a property of those propositions which cannot be affirmed together; i.e., both contradictories and contraries.

(2) The "inconsistent triad," or Antilogism (q.v.), is a method of testing the validity of syllogisms by negating their conclusions, and then testing for inconsistency.

(3) In modern logic a set of propositions or propositional functions is said to be inconsistent if one can derive from the set anything whatever.

(4) For Gödel (q.v. 2–3) either inconsistency or incompleteness must characterize any axiomatized mathematical system.

INCONSISTENT TRIAD.

Q.v. Antilogism.

INDECIDABILITY.

Q.v. Gödel (4).

INDEFINITE RELATION.

Q.v.. W.S. Jevons (1).

INDEMONSTRABLES.

From the Greek apodeiktikos. The term was used by the Stoics—Chrysippus (q.v. 1) being credited with its origin, or at least with the formulation of the argument forms it names—to refer to the basic argument forms of the Propositional Calculus (q.v. 3, 4, 6). He derived Modus Ponens, Modus tollens, and the disjunctive syllogism. The forms were thought to be self-evident, not requiring, and not capable of demonstration.

INDETERMINACY, PRINCIPLE OF.

Q.v. Werner Heisenberg.

INDETERMINISM.

Q.v. Freedom (passim); Determinism; Contingency.

INDEX.

For Peirce (q.v. 16) one of the three major classes of signs.

INDIAN PHILOSOPHY.

Four major periods can be traced in Indian philosophy from the origin of the Vedic period around 2500 B.C., to the decline of the tradition around 1700 A.D. All of the schools and most of the key terms mentioned below are treated in their own right and under their own names. Here we shall merely indicate the general structure of the development, and the topics under which further analysis is to be found.

(1) The Vedic period extended from 2500 to 600 B.C. This was the period of the Aryan incursions, and the writing of the Vedic scriptures. The four Vedas are the Rgveda, the Yajurveda, the Samaveda and the Atharvaveda (q.v. the Vedas).

(2) The Epic period, also called Post-Vedic, extended from around 500 or 600 B.C. to 200 A.D. During this period the great epic literature of India was written, the Ramayana and the Mahabharata. The famous Bhagavad-Gita (q.v.) forms part of the Mahabharata. This was the period when the three heterodox (nastika) systems arose: Buddhism (q.v.), Jainism (q.v.), and Charvaka (q.v.). The first followed Gautama Buddha (q.v.); the second followed Mahavira (q.v.); the third, deriving from the Brhaspati Sutra, was materialistic, its central doctrine being lokayata (this world is all there is). These movements were called heterodox because they did not accept the authority of the Vedas.

(3) The Third period was that of the sutras. It extended from 200 to 700 A.D. During this time the six orthodox systems (or astikas) developed: the Nyaya (q.v.) or logical realism; the Vaisheshika (q.v.) or realistic pluralism; the Sankhya (q.v.) or evolutionary dualism; Yoga (q.v.) or disciplined meditation; the Purva Mimamsa interpretations of the Vedas relative to conduct; and the Uttara Mimamsa or Vedanta (q.v.), investigations of the later Vedas relative to knowledge. Because of their similarities the schools are sometimes presented as three; the Nyaya-Vaisheshika, the Sankhya-Yoga, and the Mimamsa-Vedanta. The systems are known as darshanas, or "instruments of vision."

(4) The fourth period may be called the Scholastic period. It extended from 700 A.D. to 1700 A.D. This is the period of the great commentaries on the sutras, the commentaries on commentaries, and so forth. It is also the period of the great commentators: Shankara (q.v.), Ramanuja (q.v.), and Madhva (q.v.).

(5) As instances of contemporary Indian philosophy we mention Sri Aurobindo (q.v.) who claimed his point of view

to be original Vedanta, teaching humans to rend the veil of illusion, and become one with the Absolute; and Sri Radhakrishnan (*q.v.*), equally at home in Western and Eastern philosophy, who brings the traditions together in a spiritual vision of reality.

INDIFFERENCE.

From the Greek *a* ("not") and *diaphoros* ("different"). The term has been applied to a variety of philosophical problems.

(1) Concerning value, for example, Stoics, Cynics, and Skeptics agreed in holding that one could not be indifferent to virtue and vice. Virtue was to be sought and vice avoided. But one should be indifferent with respect to all other attitudes and values.

(2) In the Middle Ages a "doctrine of indifference" was advanced by Adelard of Bath (*q.v.*) in the dispute over universals. It was his contention that an object of the mind became individual or universal, depending upon the manner in which it is viewed.

(3) In this dispute William of Champeaux (*q.v.*) advanced an "indifference theory" of universals according to which the members of a species are not the same essentially, but are the same indifferently.

(4) One associates John Buridan (*q.v.*) with the concept of a "liberty of indifference." It has been sometimes held that the only liberty is that of indifference, where the alternatives are equally desirable or equally undesirable. "Buridan's ass" is a hypothetical creature starving to death because it is situated exactly halfway between two equally desirable stacks of hay. Although Buridan did discuss this issue the striking figure is not to be found in any of his extant writings.

(5) Although Descartes (*q.v.* 7) is associated with the view that freedom derives from the will, he used the "liberty of indifference" concept in two ways. In Book IV of the *Meditations* he held liberty of indifference, in the sense sketched above, to be the lowest degree of freedom. In the *Principles* the phrase is used for the situation where the reason for choosing one alternative is so clear that there is no hesitation whatever. This is regarded as the highest sense of freedom, and associated with the divine being.

(6) In probability theory (*q.v.* Probability 3–14) the "principle of indifference" refers to the tactical move of assigning a probability of one-half to the occurrence, and the same probability to the non-occurrence of an event concerning which one has no antecedent knowledge.

INDIRECT COMMUNICATION.

Q.v. Kierkegaard (4); Jaspers (5).

INDIRECT PROOF.

Q.v. Reductio ad absurdum.

INDISCERNIBLES, IDENTITY OF.

Q.v. Leibniz (3).

INDISTINCT, PHILOSOPHY AS THE.

Q.v. Ardigó (2).

INDIVIDUAL.

From the Latin *individuus* ("undivided or indivisible") translated from the Greek *atomon* ("indivisible"). The concept of the individual has had currency both within logic and metaphysics.

(1) In traditional logic the individual is the logical subject which admits of predicates, and cannot be predicated of anything else; *e.g.*, one says that man is rational, not that rational is man. From Aristotle through Boethius (who introduced into logic the Latin term *individuum*) into modern times this usage is current.

(2) By individual has also been meant that concrete being to which the principle of excluded middle applies with respect to every possible predicate. This is a more metaphysical notion, and discussion of the means of explicating the idea of determinate being runs throughout the history of philosophy. Alternative principles of individuation have been advanced. Aristotle (*q.v.* 7) held that since a single form is common to all of the members of a class, matter must be the principle of individuation.

(3) Thomas Aquinas (*q.v.* 6) makes it still more clear that matter is the principle of individuation in sensible things; not prime matter, however, but signate matter, ordered to three dimensions. The individuality of angels is accounted for in that each angel constitutes a distinct species; hence, each has a different form. These distinctions clarify but do not solve the problem.

(4) Bonaventure (*q.v.* 10) held that individuation is not the function of matter

and form taken separately, but the function of their union.

(5) Godfrey of Fontaines (*q.v.*) held the substantial form to be the principle of individuation.

(6) For Duns Scotus (*q.v.*) the principle of individuation is called the *haecceitas*, a particularization of the essence of each thing differentiating it from every other.

(7) For Suarez (*q.v.* 3) the individual is a "formal unity" composed of two further unities, one material and the other formal.

(8) Leibniz (*q.v.* 3) treats the problem by means of his principle of the identity of indiscernibles, leading him to conclude that there is an essentially intelligible difference between any two things in the universe.

(9) Hegel defines the individual as "the unity of the universal and the particular." It is his view that the universal, when fully developed or expressed, is an individual being.

(10) Schleiermacher (*q.v.* 3) discussed the human individual as distinguished from any other by one's *proprium*, an inward differentiation giving one a "life-unity."

INDIVIDUALITY.

A term which becomes prominent in 19th-century Idealism, apparently as a corrective to emphases on absoluteness and the organic nature of society.

(1) Max Stirner (*q.v.* 1) argued for the uniqueness of each individual, and that the end of life is the development of one's own individuality.

(2) Bosanquet (*q.v.* 1) directed his philosophy toward an analysis of the individual and the strengthening of individuality.

(3) Royce (*q.v.* 2) held that individuality and existence go together as part of an infinite unity.

INDIVIDUATION, PRINCIPLE OF.

From the Latin *principium individuationis*, a phrase introduced into medieval philosophy by Avicenna in his translations of Aristotle. It signifies the principle by which a philosopher attempts to move in thought from the *infima*, or smallest, species to the individual member of that species. Alternative versions of the principle are discussed under Individual (*q.v.* 2–8).

INDRA.

The beneficent storm and fertility god of the Vedic religion. He wields the thunderbolt, brings rain, overcomes his enemies and shares the booty with his friends.

INDUCTION.

From the Latin *in* and *ducere* ("to lead in"), first translated into the Latin probably by Cicero from Aristotle's term, *epagoge*. The widespread distinction between induction as an inference moving from specific facts to general conclusions, and deduction as moving from general premises to specific conclusions is no longer respectable philosophically. This distinction distinguishes one kind of induction from one kind of deduction. It is much more satisfactory to think of induction as probable inference and deduction as necessary inference.

(1) The technical study of induction began with Aristotle (*q.v.* 3). Although his writings carry suggestions of many of the forms of induction, he clearly describes at least two kinds, which have come to be termed *perfect* and *ampliative* induction. (a) In complete or perfect induction the general conclusion rests on knowledge of each instance covered. The conclusion does not go beyond the evidence. This form is also called induction by simple enumeration. (b) In ampliative induction the conclusion takes the instances as a sample of the class and generalizes from the properties of the sample to the properties of the class.

(2) William of Ockham (*q.v.* 11) found the principle of induction to require an assumption of the uniformity of nature, which in turn required the idea of God.

(3) Francis Bacon (*q.v.* 1, 3), wishing to make induction the method of all science, urged the organization of tables of instances (tables of presence and absence), designed to exclude the nonessential and irrelevant. Gradually the general conclusion emerges. Bacon believed that if the collection of instances is exhaustive, the method cannot fail to end in truth. Bacon criticized induction by enumeration, arguing for his experimental method which combines ampliative and enumerative or perfect induction, and where there is a use of positive and negative instances to isolate the cause of a phenomenon.

(4) Hume (*q.v.* 3), on the other hand, found the attempt to establish the principle of induction involved in circularity.

(5) John Stuart Mill (*q.v.* 3, 4), holding induction to be the sole part of logic productive of knowledge, developed Bacon's tables of instances into the "canons of induction." By correlating positive and negative instances with the presence or absence of the phenomenon, Mill proposed that the causes of phenomena can be isolated. The canons or methods are called the Methods of Agreement, Difference, Agreement and Difference, Concomitant Variations, and Residues. In reflecting upon our willingness to generalize from these experiences to laws, Mill suggested that we employ a principle of the uniformity of nature. Thus inductive reasoning for Mill was understood as a kind of syllogism with the principle of the uniformity of nature as the suppressed major premise. Some find circularity in Mill's reasoning since the principle of the uniformity of nature must itself be supported by induction.

(6) Whewell (*q.v.* 1) contributed the term "colligation" to the literature on induction stressing, against Bacon (and also Mill), the importance of the mental act of viewing the facts as together in a certain way. The colligation appears in the process of working with the data as a means of understanding the manner of their relatedness. In this sense it resembles hypothesis (*q.v.*), or Peirce's process of abduction (*cf.* 8 below).

(7) Jevons (*q.v.* 3) took induction to be simply the inverse process of deduction.

(8) Peirce (*q.v.* 8) distinguished three forms of inference. He found these forms to be intimately related, and complementary. The two forms in contrast with deduction are induction and abduction. Peirce means by induction "ampliative inference," generalizing from a sample to the quality of a class. By abduction Peirce means the construction of a hypothesis capable of explaining the phenomenon: "The surprising fact, C, is observed, but if h were true, C would be commonplace. Therefore h has a certain probability of being true."

(9) W.E. Johnson (*q.v.* 5) held that inductive inferences rest on causality and are characterized by probability.

(10) Analyses of induction have pro-

liferated in the 20th century beyond mention. Induction and probability theory have coalesced. Perhaps Carnap (*q.v.* 10) has accomplished more than any other in this respect. He centered inductive logic around the concept of "degree of confirmation" which is one of the two possible centers for developing probability theory. Carnap found five kinds of inductive inference: (a) *Direct* inference, from the population to a sample (from the frequency of a property in the population to its frequency in a sample); (b) *Predictive inference*, from one sample to another not overlapping the first; (c) *Analogical* inference, from one individual to another on the basis of their known similarity; (d) *Inverse* inference, from a sample to the population; (e) *Universal* inference, from a sample to a hypothesis of universal form.

(11) Braithwaite (*q.v.* 3) argued that there is no vicious circle in the problem of induction since the movement is from belief to reasonable belief.

(12) Reichenbach (*q.v.* 1), supporting the straight rule of induction, holds that the relative frequency of successful to the whole set of tries yields knowledge of probabilities in the long run, but says nothing of the short run.

(13) Salmon deals with the short run ("The Short Run," 1955) by assuming that the relative frequency of the short run will reflect the assumed or known long-run relative frequency.

(14) David Lewis (*q.v.*) argues that the straight rule is the only "immodest" inductive method ("Immodest Inductive Methods," 1971), but that in this area immodesty is a virtue.

(15) The position of Brian Ellis (*Rational Belief Systems*, 1979) is that both rules yield "rational preferability" only when no theoretical considerations are relevant. Otherwise, theory itself (*e.g.*, the probability 1/2 in flipping a fair coin) modifies the straight rule in both short and long run.

(16) For a view of induction involving the criterion of "well-entrenched predicates" *q.v.* Nelson Goodman (4).

(17) Finally, *Mathematical* induction must be mentioned. This type of induction would seem to combine features of ampliative and perfect induction. Its power turns on the controlled nature of

mathematical series. If one can show that the property p of a certain number n is also a property of $n+1$ simply by virtue of the fact that $n+1$ is a successor to n, then one can conclude that p is a property of every number. For an instance of this kind of induction *q.v.* Peano (2).

INDULGENCES.
Q.v. Luther (1); John Huss.

INEQUALITY.
Rousseau (*q.v.* 1) held inequality to be natural among men.

INESSE.
Q.v. De Inesse.

INEXISTENCE, INTENTIONAL.
Q.v. Brentano (2); Chisholm (1).

INFALLIBILITY, PAPAL.
A dogma of the Roman Catholic Church decreed by Vatican Council I (*q.v.*) in 1870. When the pope speaks *ex cathedra* (*q.v.*) in matters of doctrine his statements are guaranteed against error by divine assistance. The doctrine had in fact been used prior to its acceptance by the Council, as in the promulgation of the doctrine of the Immaculate Conception (*q.v.*) by Pius IX in 1854. It was also invoked by Pius XII in 1950 in the promulgation of the doctrine of the Assumption of the Blessed Virgin Mary (*q.v.*).
Also *q.v.* Schillebeeckx (5).

INFERENCE.
From the Latin *in* and *ferre* ("to carry or bring"). In logic, the procedure of deriving conclusions from premises. If the conclusion follows from a single premise, the process is said to be one of immediate inference (*q.v.*). If the conclusion follows from two or more premises jointly, the process is said to be one of mediate inference. For analyses of types of mediate inference *q.v.* Propositional Calculus, Truth Tables, Syllogism, Quantification Theory, Induction, Abduction. For a distinction between inference and implication *q.v.* W.E. Johnson (1).

INFERENCE, IMMEDIATE.
The type of inference in which the conclusion follows from a single premise. The forms of immediate inference are many. In the traditional scheme these forms are derived from the standard relations of categorical propositions and their valid permutations.
(1) The relations of the traditional A, E, I, and O propositions (*q.v.* Proposition 1) can be exhibited by means of the traditional square of opposition.

All students are profound
All S is P Superaltern

No Students are profound
No S is P Superaltern

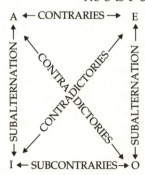

Some students are profound
Some S is P Subaltern

Some students are not profound
Some S is not P Subaltern

Assuming in turn the truth and falsity of the A, E, I, and O propositions, sixteen immediate inferences can be drawn from this set of relations. For all of these inferences to follow, incidentally, it is necessary to assume that the class of things we are talking about—students in this case—has members. (a) If A is true E is false, I is true, O is False. *E.g.*, if "All students are profound," is true, then it is false that "No students are profound," true that "Some students are profound," and false that "Some students are not profound." (b) If E is true, A is false, I is false, O is true. Thus, if "No students are profound" is true, then "All students are profound" is false, etc. (c) If I is true, E is false, while A and O are undetermined. (d) If O is true A is False, E and I being undetermined. (e) If A is false, O is true, E and I being undetermined. (f) If E is false, I is true, A and O being undetermined. (g) If I is false, A is false, E is true, O is true. (h) If O is false, A is true, E is false, I is true. These inferences follow from the four relations set forth in the square of opposition: contradictories cannot be true together or false together; contraries cannot be true together, although they can be false together; subcontraries cannot be false together although they can be true together; the truth of the superaltern determines the truth of its subaltern, and the falsity of the subaltern determines the falsity of its superaltern.

(2) From the valid permutations of categorical propositions additional immediate inferences can be derived. Again it is necessary to assume that the classes in question have members. In the process of conversion (exchanging subject and predicate) three immediate inferences are possible:

Convertend	*Converse*
A. All students are profound	I . Some profound beings are students
E. No students are profound	E. No profound beings are students
I . Some students are profound	I . Some profound beings are students
O. Some students are not profound	— No converse—

(3) The obverse of a proposition is gained by changing the quality of the proposition from affirmative to negative (or from negative to affirmative), and substituting non-P for P in the predicate (or P for non-P).

Obvertend

A. All students are profound
E. No students are profound
I . Some students are profound

O. Some students are not profound

Obverse

E. No students are other than profound
A. All students are other than profound
O. Some students are not other than profound
I . Some students are other than profound

(4) The contrapositive of a proposition is gained by first obverting it, applying conversion to the result, and obverting once again.

Contraponend

A. All students are not profound

E. No students are profound

I . Some students are profound
O. Some students are not profound

Contrapositive

A. All non-profound beings are non-students
O. Some non-profound beings are not non-students
— No contrapositive—
O. Some non-profound beings are not non-students

(5) The inverse of a proposition is valid for only A and E propositions. Each has a full inverse, and a partial inverse. To get the full inverse of an A proposition one converts the contrapositive of the A proposition; and to gain the partial inverse one obverts the full inverse. To get the partial inverse of an E proposition one converts, obverts, and converts again. To get the full inverse one obverts the result.

Invertend

A. All students are profound

E. No students are profound

Inverse

Full: I. Some non-students are other than profound
Partial: O. Some non-students are not profound
Partial: Some non-students are profound
Full: Some non-students are not other than profound

The instances of inversion are obviously the most suspect of the single premise inferences. If we keep in mind the requirement that the classes in question all have members (students, non-students, profound beings, and non-profound beings), the result can be accepted.

(6) If we do not make this assumption, if, indeed, we take the assumption of Boolean algebra that I and O propositions have existential import while A and E propositions do not, the picture changes considerably. A and E propositions can be true together, and are thus not contraries; I and O propositions can be false together, and are thus not subcontraries. A and E propositions can be true while the corresponding I and O propositions are false; thus, subalternation fails. Only the validity of the relation of contradic-

tion remains from the traditional square of opposition. As for the other immediate inferences, conversion remains valid only for E and I propositions; since obversion moves only between A and E, or between I and O, it remains valid altogether; contraposition remains valid for A and O propositions; and the process of inversion is to be rejected altogether.

(7) The valid permutations of non-categorical propositions provide additional immediate inferences. All of the single premise tautological transformations allowed in the propositional, or sentential, calculus are of this nature; for example, the law of contraposition $(p \supset q) \equiv (\sim q \supset \sim p)$. For a list of valid argument forms q.v. Propositional Calculus (3–22).

IN FIERI.

A Latin phrase meaning "to be done, become." A Scholastic term said of anything in process of accomplishment; in contrast with in facto, or accomplished being.

INFIMA SPECIES.

A Latin phrase meaning "the lowest or least species." Thus, the smallest subdivision of a classification. In Aristotelian and Scholastic thought the problem of individuation concerned the principle by which an individual thing is to be distinguished from its infima species. Q.v. Species (3); Genus (1); Individual (2–8).

INFINITE.

From the Latin in ("not") and finis ("boundary," "limit," "end"). Thus that without boundary, limit, or end. Etymologically, the term is gained by negation of the term "finite." There are those, however, (cf. 9 below) who would claim that the conception of the infinite is prior to that of the finite. The conception of the infinite has been associated from the start with series of numbers, magnitudes, times, and spaces. The endlessness of such series provides one conception of infinity, and some (cf. 8 below) hold this to be the basic meaning of the term. If one applies the predicates "finite" and "infinite" to being rather than to series of various sorts, the conception changes; if finite being is limited in extent, properties, etc., infinite being would

be unlimited, or perhaps absolute, in all of these respects. The history of the conception contains speculations both over infinite series and infinite being.

(1) Very early in Greek thought Anaximander (q.v. 1–4) conceived of the source of existence as to apeiron, or "the boundless." Things become determinate out of the indeterminate and endlessly extending apeiron, and are at last resolved once again into its immensity. Anaximander seems to have described an infinite potentiality which he identified with an infinitely extending space and time.

(2) Other pre-Socratic philosophers—among them the Pythagoreans (q.v. Archytas), the Pluralists (q.v. Empedocles, Anaxagoras, Democritus), and Heraclitus (q.v.)—had likewise developed the conception of the endlessness of space and time. Zeno of Elea (q.v. 1–6) explored the paradoxes of infinite series with respect to magnitude and motion, the infinitely small as well as the infinitely large.

(3) Plato (q.v. 1, 9) recognized two kinds of infinity. The "receptacle" of the Timaeus is infinite in the sense of Anaximander's potential infinity which can be structured in an indefinite number of ways (although Plato required a divine agent to do the structuring). The forms on the other hand, together with the absolute God, have the infinity of completeness and perfection.

(4) Among the Greeks it was Aristotle (q.v. 8) who gave the most fruitful analysis of infinity, concentrating especially on the potential aspect of the concept. Potential infinity appears in number series as infinite divisibility, and as the infinite by addition. It applies also to causal series. In all of these cases it is the concept of that beyond which there is another thing. Time, by way of contrast, is a series actually infinite up to the present, and increasing by potential infinity. The infinity of time, joined to his analysis of motion, implies a being who or which must be infinite in at least several actual respects—e.g., independence, eternality, without admixture of potentiality—in order to produce the motion of the world during an infinite time.

(5) In the period between classical Greek philosophy and the Middle Ages

while the in mathematicians—*e.g.*, Archimedes, Eudoxus—were experimenting with methods of analysis which would lead eventually to the calculus, the Neoplatonists (*q.v.* Neoplatonism) were enshrining Plato's two infinities as polar opposites in a metaphysical scheme where positive or actual infinity was represented by the One or God, and potential infinity by matter.

(6) In Thomas Aquinas' (*q.v.* 4) thought, God stands for positive and absolute infinity, while a relative and potential infinity belongs to the order of created things. In the medieval analysis, generally, all perfections, *i.e.*, all positive predicates, belong to the actually infinite Being, sometimes referred to as "the infinite ocean of Being."

(7) Following the Middle Ages, the two orders of infinity, so carefully separated, coalesced. In Giordano Bruno (*q.v.* 1–3) the two orders are to be understood as two ways of viewing the same reality, and this reality is at the same time the actually infinite universe, and the actually infinite divine Being. Nicholas of Cusa's (*q.v.* 2, 4) "coincidence of opposites" has the same effect. In both, the universe becomes an infinite being in full positivity.

(8) In Hobbes (*q.v.* 5) the finite is paramount, and infinity simply means the inability to see an end to some kind of series. At a later time both Locke (*q.v.* 5b) and Berkeley used the same analysis.

(9) Descartes (*q.v.* 5) urged that one's general idea of anything is an idea of infinite being, that we limit this idea to apply to finite things, and that properly speaking the idea of infinity precedes the idea of finitude.

(10) Spinoza (*q.v.* 1–3) followed Bruno's lead, joining the two orders of infinity in a common framework wherein finitude, part, and temporality correspond with infinity, whole, and eternity.

(11) Leibniz (*q.v.* 1–2, 5) represents an attempt to explicate reality in terms of positive infinity alone. God is infinitely great, and the infinitely small is qualitative in nature, the quantitative aspects of the world deriving from the relations of the monads.

(12) It should also be noted that Leibniz and Newton, in developing the calculus, provided a means of handling the potential infinity of finite magnitudes through the concepts of continuity and limit.

(13) Kant (*q.v.* 4) found the idea of infinity involved in the famous antinomies, at least in those of space, time, and God.

(14) For Hegel (*q.v. passim*), as for Bruno and Spinoza, the finite refers to the partial and the infinite to the whole; but in Hegel the emphasis is on process. The true infinite is the synthesis of abstract and concrete, universal and particular, which occurs through development and by means of temporal process.

(15) The idea of positive infinity, a conception different from the potential infinity we have heretofore seen related to series, was introduced into mathematics by Georg Cantor (*q.v.* 5). His positive definition of infinity held that a series is infinite when it shares a cardinal number with one of its subseries. For example, let one notice that the series of even numbers is as great as the series of natural numbers. Should one begin to write down the series of natural numbers, and beneath it the series of even numbers, it would be clear at once that for every natural number, however great, one would find an even number available to set beneath it. Cantor also demonstrated that many orders of transfinite numbers exist.

(16) Royce (*q.v.* 1–6) held that the finite, whether in series or in being, implies the infinite. He found in this numerous arguments for God.

INFRALAPSARIANISM.

Q.v. Predestination (7).

INGARDEN, ROMAN. 1893–1970.

Polish philosopher. Born in Cracow. Educated at Lvov, Göttingen, and Freiburg. Taught at Lvov and Cracow. A member of Husserl's school of phenomenology and of the Warsaw Circle. Ingarden has investigated epistemological, ontological, ethical, and aesthetic problems from this standpoint.

Principal writings: *Remarks on the Idealism-Realism Problem*, 1921; *The Literary Work of Art* (T), 1931; *Essential Problem of Form and its Basic Concepts*, 1946; *Outline of the Philosophy of Literature*, 1947; *The Controversy over the Existence of the World*, 2 vols., (T), 1947–8; *Investigations in the Ontology of Art* (T), 1962; *Time and Modes of Being* (T), 1964; *Man and Value*, (T of a collection of essays from 1970–72, the central essay "Concerning Responsibility"), 1983; *The Work of Music and the Problem of its Identity* (The first section of the *Investigations* plus an appreciation by Max Rieser).

INGENIEROS, JOSÉ.
Q.v. Latin American Philosophy (9).

INGRESSION.
Q.v. Whitehead (5).

INNATENESS.
From the Latin *in* and *natus* ("born"). In philosophy the doctrine that ideas and principles are present in the human mind from birth.

(1) Plato's doctrine of recollection, *anamnesis* (*q.v.*), represents an extreme form of the doctrine.

(2) But both the Stoics (*q.v.* Stoicism 1) and Aristotle (*q.v.* 2) held that basic principles are intuited, and the commonality of such principles suggests an innateness of dispositions, at least in potency or in tendency.

(3) Descartes (*q.v.* 4) held to the presence of innate ideas in the mind along with ideas whose source was adventitious and factitious.

(4) Locke's attack on innate ideas (*q.v.* Locke 1) stimulated the response of Leibniz (*q.v.* 14), a moderate position similar to that in (2) above. But note that in the end Locke's position and that of Leibniz were likewise very similar.

(5) With Kant (*q.v.* 1) the problem of innate ideas was transformed into the problem of *a priori* judgments, and in this form the problem has come down to the present day.

(6) In the contemporary world Chomsky (*q.v.* 7) has revived the Cartesian claim of innateness in relation to the subject matter of linguistics.

INNER LIGHT.
Q.v. George Fox (1).

INQUIRY.
From the Latin *in* and *quaero* ("to seek"). The term appears to have been particularly attractive to American pragmatists.

(1) Charles Peirce (*q.v.* 12–13) regarded inquiry as self-corrective, and more likely than any other method of having opinion lead to the truth. For another version of the self-corrective nature of inquiry *q.v.* Nagel (7).

(2) For John Dewey (*q.v.* 2) inquiry is the heart of philosophic activity and the meaning of intelligence. It is the object of inquiry to transform an indeterminate situation into one which is determinate through a series of stages beginning with the locating of the problem and ending with an appropriate solution.

INQUISITION.
From the Latin *inquirere* ("to inquire"). An institution established within the Roman Catholic Church for the purpose of eliminating heresy, the Inquisition gained its distinctive form over a considerable period of time. In 1163 at the Council of Tours, Pope Alexander III commanded that the clergy seek out heretics on the basis of "inquests," involving the testimony of sworn witnesses. In a series of Councils between 1163 and 1215 inquisitorial procedures were developed and recommended; and in the 13th century the Inquisition came into being in all of Europe, Scandinavia and England excepted. Unlike cases in open court, the accused were never told the sources of the charges against them. Penalties ran from light penances to death by burning; and in 1252 Pope Innocent IV authorized the use of torture in the process of interrogation. The highly organized Spanish Inquisition, under the direct authority of the king exercised authority in Latin America as well as Spain. The Spanish Inquisition was established in 1480 and abolished in 1834. The Holy Office of the Inquisition was established in Rome in 1542, its most notable cases involving Bruno (*q.v.*) and Galileo (*q.v.*). The Office continued in existence, in fact, until 1965 when it was replaced by the Congregation of the Doctrine of the Faith.

INSCRIPTIONS.
A term used by R.M. Martin ("On Inscriptions," 1951; and with Woodger "Toward An Inscriptional Semantics," 1951), interpreting sign-tokens as the typographical characters themselves as they stand on the printed page.

IN SE.

Latin phrase meaning "in itself," standing in contrast to *in alio* ("in another"). Primarily a Scholastic term. A substance, for example, exists *in se*, while accidents exist *in alio*.

INSOLUBILIA.

A Latin term meaning "unsolvables," *i.e.*, "unsolvable problems." The *insolubilia* are semantical and logical paradoxes which began to appear in Greek philosophy, were important in the Middle Ages, and are still current. Sample *insolubilia* are treated under Paradox (2–6).

INSTITUTIONS, AS CORRUPTING.

(1) Rousseau (*q.v.* 2, 4) viewed the development of society as leading to depravity and corruption. The correction for this was to be a different kind of society, as set forth in the *Social Contract*.

(2) Godwin (*q.v.* 1) likewise found social institutions to be corrupting. His solution was a society operating without coercion.

INSTRUMENTALISM.

The self-styled philosophy of John Dewey (*q.v.* 4). Stressing instruments and means over ends, and viewing ideas as instruments of action, Dewey's philosophy is directed toward the clarification and control of experience. For a Dewey-influenced instrumentalism, which is also a naturalism *q.v.* Nagel (5, 6).

INSTRUMENTAL VALUE.

Q.v. Value (1–2).

INTEGRALISM.

Q.v. Sciacca.

INTEGRAL YOGA.

Q.v. Sri Aurobindo (3).

INTELLECT.

From the Latin *intelligere* ("to understand"). The power or faculty of knowing as compared to will or feeling.

(1) The traditional interpretation of the intellect derives from Aristotle (*q.v.* 11) who divided the intellect into two parts, one passive and the other active, the former receiving materials of sense, the latter acting upon them to create and interrelate ideas.

(2) Avempace (*q.v.* 2) made the same distinction, while treating the active intellect as a goal for human striving, a more completely actualized existence.

(3) Averroës (*q.v.* 4) viewed the active intellect as that portion of man which is immortal, although the passive intellect contains the conditions of individuality. The point, apparently depriving man of individual immortality, was heavily criticized. Averroës held this to be, not without reason, Aristotle's view.

(4) Aquinas (*q.v.* 7) likewise followed the Aristotelian distinction. The passive intellect, or *intellectus possibilis*, receives the *phantasmata* of sense, and the active intellect, or *intellectus agens*, grasps the form or essence abstracted from the sense material. On Aquinas' view the intellect is immaterial, and thus capable of existence apart from the body.

(5) William of Ockham (*q.v.* 9) said that he found no reason to believe in the existence of the active intellect, although he accepted it on the authority of the saints and philosophers. Nor did he find (*q.v.* 14) intellect and will to be distinct faculties.

INTELLECTUAL VIRTUES.

Q.v. Dianoetic Virtues.

INTELLIGENCE, ARTIFICIAL.

Q.v. Artificial Intelligence.

INTELLIGIBLE LIGHT.

As a metaphor for God *q.v.* St. Augustine (6).

INTENSION.

From the Latin *in* and *tendere* ("to stretch out"). Intension and extension are the words favored by modern logicians to express respectively the characteristics present in the definition of a term, and the set of objects to which the term refers. Synonyms for "intension" are "comprehension" and "connotation"; a synonym for "extension" is "denotation." *Q.v.* Extension (2).

INTENSIONAL ISOMORPHISM.

Q.v. Carnap (9).

INTENTION.

For a discussion of First and Second Intentions *q.v.* Intentionality (1–2). Searle (*q.v.* 1) likewise relates intention to linguistic communication.

INTENTIONAL FALLACY.
  Q.v. New Criticism.

INTENTIONAL INEXISTENCE.
  Q.v. Brentano (2); Chisholm (1).

INTENTIONALITÄT.
  Q.v. Intentionality (4); Husserl (5).

INTENTIONALITY.
  From the same root as the term, in-tension. Two applications of the idea of intentionality are of special interest to philosophy.
  (1) Thomas Aquinas' distinction between terms of first intention and those of second intention, prepared for by the Arabian philosophers and especially by Avicenna's distinction between first and second understanding (*q.v.* Logic 7), is warmly embraced by modern logicians who find in it anticipations of the theory of types. (Terms of first intention refer to real objects while terms of second intention refer to terms of first intention. These terms are carried by intentional acts.)
  (2) William of Ockham (*q.v.* 2) made the distinction between terms of first and second intention very basic in his understanding of logic and of philosophy generally.
  (3) Brentano (*q.v.* 2), returning to the Scholastic notion of intentionality, characterized all mental phenomena as intentional, containing "an object intentionally within themselves." The mode of existence of those objects, since some will be like unicorns, for example, is "intentional inexistence."
  (4) Following Brentano, Husserl (*q.v.* 5) made *Intentionalität* a basic category of his thought, with processes of intending pointing to objects intended.
  (5) For Romero (*q.v.* 2) intentionality is the essential characteristic of the psychic level.
  (6) Chisholm (*q.v.* 1) carried the problem of intentionality into 20th century philosophy, reviving Brentano's "intentional inexistence."
  (7) Anscombe's discussion of "intention," involving action, events allowing alternate descriptions, some intentional and some not, along with other characteristics (*q.v.* Anscombe), provided the starting point utilized by Davidson in his

analysis of the same concept.
  (8) Davidson's (*q.v.* 1–4) analysis, with events intentional under one description and non-intentional under another, led to his view of anomalous monism.
  (9) For Searle (*q.v.* 3–4) intentionality is a property of mind caused by the microprocesses of the brain. Also *q.v.* Artificial Intelligence (3, 6).

INTERACTIONISM.
  Q.v. Mind-Body Problem (1).

INTERNAL REALISM.
  Q.v. Putnam (8).

INTERNAL RELATIONS.
  Q.v. Relations (8).

INTERPRETANT.
  Q.v. Peirce (17) for a discussion of emotional, dynamic, and symbolic interpretants.

INTRANSITIVE RELATIONS.
  Q.v. The Logic of Relations (14).

INTRINSIC VALUE.
  Correlate of extrinsic value (*q.v.*). The phrase applies to states of being or experience valuable in themselves without regard to their consequences. "Final value" is a synonymous expression. The contrast between intrinsic and extrinsic value was developed in Greek philosophy (*q.v.* Plato 14). The validity of the distinction between the two types of value has been challenged by Dewey (*q.v.* 4) in his conception of the means-end continuum. *Q.v.* Theory of Value.

INTROJECTION.
  Q.v. Avenarius (5).

INTROVERT AND EXTRAVERT.
  Q.v. Jung (1).

INTUITION.
  From the Latin *in* and *tueri* ("to look at"). Direct insight into, or apprehension of, truth. To be contrasted with Empiricism (*q.v.*) and Rationalism (*q.v.*) as sources of knowledge.
  A. In the West intuition relates to the concept of innate ideas, at least when innateness is understood dispositionally, as a tendency (*q.v.* Innateness, 2, 4, 5).
  (1) Sometimes intuition is set in contrast

to discursive reasoning. This is the case with a wide variety of thinkers who are thus able to speak of sensible as well as intelligible intuition, or to speak, as did Leibniz, of intuitive truths of reason and intuitive truths of fact. In this reading we intuit both what we perceive, and the general principles which order our reasoning. Aristotle (*q.v.* 2), Descartes (*q.v.* 4, 10), Locke (*q.v.* 1–2, 8a), and Leibniz (*q.v.* 10, 14) would agree to using the term in this manner. William of Ockham (*q.v.* 10) held that our judgments of contingent fact are gained intuitively, or in his phrase, by *notitia intuitiva*.

(2) Spinoza (*q.v.* 5c) employed the term "*scientia intuitiva*" (intuitive knowledge) to describe the mode of thinking of one who has risen to the third stage of existence, and lives under the aspect of eternity. The point is that this combines in one the principles of the two previous stages, *i.e.*, of empirical and rational intuition.

(3) Kant's (*q.v.* 3–4, 11a) usage differs somewhat, since he distinguished between empirical and pure intuition, the empirical intuition of objects and the pure intuition of space and time as the form of sensibility.

(4) Bergson (*q.v.* 1–2) contrasted intuition with discursive reasoning, insisting that intuition is capable of grasping the world in its essential fluidity, while the discursive reason falsifies it, stops its flow, and spatializes time.

(5) Husserl (*q.v.* 6) contrasted empirical intuition with essential intuition. One begins with empirical intuition, but its contents are appropriately essentialized to reveal its pure essence. To reduce to idea, then, far from distorting reality, reveals it.

(6) In the area of aesthetics (*q.v.* 13), Croce (*q.v.* 2) gave intuition the central role.

(7) In contemporary ethics (*q.v.* 31–32) there exists an intuitionist school headed by G.E. Moore (*q.v.* 6) who held the good to be an intuited property. Prichard (*q.v.*), Ewing, and Ross (*q.v.*) are also intuitionists.

(8) The Intuitionist School of Mathematics (*q.v.* Brouwer 2), placing its reliance on intuition rather than discursive reasoning, restricts the applicability of the principle of excluded middle and the principle of mathematical induction, and rejects the method of indirect proof. This alters, rather substantially, the discipline of mathematics.

B. Intuition in the East, in company with other philosophical ideas, is set in the context of spiritual enlightenment (*q.v.* A.) or release (*q.v. Mokṣa*).

(9) The six orthodox philosophical systems of India, called orthodox because of their acceptance of the Hindu (*q.v.* 6) scriptures, the *Vedas* (*q.v.*), had appeared by 200 A.D. All six accepted intuition, inference and the scriptures as sources of knowledge. In all six intuition was regarded as more reliable than reason, supporting a direct relation between self-consciousness and super-consciousness which is beyond logic and science.

(10) In the *Ahirabudhnya Samhita* (*q.v. Vedas* 1) Brahman is said to be of the nature of intuition, and this is identified with pure and infinite bliss.

(11) In the Nyaya (*q.v.* 2) system, for example, there are two types of intuition (*pratyakṣa*), a perceptual intuition aided by the senses, and yogic intuition unaided by the senses. Both are immediate apprehensions, and the most important of the means of knowledge (*pramanas*).

(12) The Vedanta (*q.v.*) system interpreted the *Upanishads* (*q.v.*) which make up the end of the *Vedas*. For Shankara (*q.v.*), the leader of the school, intuition (*anubhava*) of the conscious self moves in a direction opposite to that of perception. He quotes *Bṛhadaranyaka Upaniṣad* which refers to "the Brahman which is present to intuition, not hidden." Linking the two, intuition reveals the *Atman-Brahman* identification, a single-centered Brahmanic reality which does not exclude other centers reflecting that reality. The reality cannot be called one or many but simply non-dual (*a-dvaita*).

(13) Aurobindo (*q.v.*), a 20th century Advaita Vedantist, puts it that the highest state of knowledge is self-luminous intuitional knowledge.

(14) Radhakrishnan (*q.v.* 2) began with Shankara's position, finding analogues to it in Western Idealism. He supports spiritual intuition as involving direct apprehension of God, an experience as immediate for some as perception of the external world is for others. Conceivably infallible in itself, intuition becomes fallible through the interpretation with

which it is invariably mixed.

(15) Suzuki (*q.v.* 4) held that enlightenment involved a state of knowledge available through *prajna*-intuition (from *prajna*, "transcendental wisdom," and "existential intuition"). This wisdom illumines each of us from within. In *prajna*-intuition the numerous dualisms of ordinary knowledge (subject-object, knower-known, questioner-question, affirmation-negation, set out in linear progressions with one thing known and then another) are overcome. *Prajna* intuition finds in knowledge a oneness which knows things in their totality and unity, breaking the fetters of intellection. It does this by penetrating to the foundations of relative knowledge, the base from which it rises, and which makes it possible. On achieving this goal, one's state is that of *prajnaparamita* ("*prajna* awakended or attained"). This is the perfect enlightenment of Buddha, and the goal of *satori* in Zen (*q.v.*).

INVERSE.
Q.v. Immediate Inference (5).

INVERTEND.
Q.v. Immediate Inference (5).

INVISIBLE HAND.
The metaphor of Adam Smith (*q.v.* 2), justifying his economics of self-interest.

IONIC PHILOSOPHY.
The school of philosophy arising in Ionia during the 6th century B.C., originating the development of Greek philosophy. *Q.v.* Thales; Anaximander; Anaximenes.

"I" PROPOSITION.
Q.v. Syllogism (3, 6c).

IQBAL, MOHAMMAD. 1877–1938.
Pakistani philosopher. Born in Sialkot. Educated at Cambridge and Munich. Influenced by Bergson, as well as by Moslem sources, Iqbal viewed ultimate reality as pure duration. God and man interrelate in an organic universe. Human freedom is interpreted as spontaneity. Iqbal's system can be viewed as an instance of panentheism (*q.v.*).

Principal writings: *Secret of the Self* (T), 1915; *Reconstruction of Religious Thought in Islam* (T), 1934.

IRASCIBLE, THE.
In Aquinas (*q.v.* 7) that appetite in man concerned with the protection of one's satisfactions.

IRENAEUS. c. 125–202.
Christian theologian. Probably born in Smyrna, Asia Minor. Bishop of Lyon. His most influential work was directed against Gnosticism (*q.v.*).

Principal writings: *Revolution and Overthrow of False Knowledge* (or *Against Heresies*), c. 180.

(1) In the process of refutation he developed the first system of Catholic belief, including among other emphases, the following: (a) the authority of the apostolic succession; (b) the presence of God's plan in the Old and New Testament as expounded by the Church, including Christ as redeemer, Christ as the God-Man drawing man unto himself; (c) the presence of God's heavenly body in the elements of the Eucharist.

(2) Relying heavily upon the writings of the apostle Paul, and the fourth gospel, he vastly increased the influence of the Johannine gospel in Christian thought, taking the meaning of *logos* from that context, so that the common designation of the term came to be not the divine "reason," but the "voice" of God as given in His revelations to men.

IRONY.
From the Greek *eironeia* ("dissembler"). The use of irony in philosophy has had both heuristic and revelatory goals. *Q.v.* Metaphor.

(1) "Socratic irony," developed in the famed mission of Socrates (*q.v.* 1) to the state of Athens, is heuristic. It feigns ignorance in order that the ideas of others may be more easily educed and examined.

(2) Novalis (*q.v.* 1) spoke of the romantic irony of the poet as an instrument allowing the true discovery of one's self.

(3) If the above uses are heuristic, that of Kierkegaard seeks a revelation. The irony of Kierkegaard (*q.v.* 1–5) moves by "indirect communication" to the point where a leap of faith is needed.

(4) For the uses of irony in literary criticism *q.v.* New Criticism, Deconstruction (6).

Also, *q.v.* Rorty (5).

IRREFLEXIVE RELATIONS.
   Q.v. The Logic of Relations (8).

ISAAC ISRAELI. Late 9th and early 10th cents.
   Jewish philosopher. Lived in Egypt. Author of a book of definitions, his Aristotelian and Neoplatonic influences helped extend those traditions into the Middle Ages.
   Principal writings: *Book of Definitions.*

ISAAC LURIA (ARL).
   Originator of the modern Cabala (*q.v.* 3d).

ISAAC OF STELLA. c. 1100–c. 1169.
   English philosopher. Educated in England and France. From 1147–69 head of the Cistercian abbey at l'Etoile. Shaped by Aristotelian as well as Neoplatonic influences, he viewed the soul as occupying a position between the body and God, and capable of rising toward God empowered by the reason. Similarly, he spoke of the great chain, or golden chain, of being which includes all beings, including God Himself.
   Principal writings: *Sermons; Letters on the Soul.*

ISAAC THE BLIND.
   Q.v. Cabala (2b).

ISHRAQ.
   Q.v. Suhrawardi (2–3).

ISHRAQIYAH.
   From the Arabic *ishraq* ("illumination"). An Islamic school of esoteric philosophy defending imaginal thinking, especially the symbolic image of light. Figures in the history of the school's development are Ibn Sina (Avicenna, *q.v.* 11), Suhrawardi (*q.v.*) and Mulla Sadra (*q.v.*). Various historical strands merged into the "school of Isfahan" during the Safavid dynasty (1499–1720), becoming a factor in Twelver Shiism (*q.v.* Shia) and Sufism (*q.v.*).

ISHTAR.
   Babylonian and Assyrian goddess. Also known as Astarte and Ashtoreth. Goddess of springs, vegetation, the universe of flocks and herds, sexual love, wedlock and maternity, she also bore a negative aspect as the destroyer of life, goddess of storm and war. Her yearly descent to the underworld in behalf of Tammuz was associated with the death of vegetation. In astrology, Ishtar was identified with the planet Venus.

ISIDORE OF SEVILLE. c. 560–635.
   Spanish philosopher. Born in Cartagena. Bishop of Seville. His interest in the systematization of knowledge led him to produce an important encyclopedia (the first work listed below) which helped to preserve learning, and was very influential in the Middle Ages.
   Principal writings: *Etymologies; Sentences; On the Catholic Faith; On the Nature of Things.*

ISIDORUS.
   Q.v. Rhetoric (11).

ISIS.
   Nature goddess whose cult was prominent in Egypt as early as 1700 B.C. Along with Mithra and the Great Mother, one of the three most formidable antagonists of Christianity in Rome from the 2nd century A.D. until its forcible extirpation. The cult had its mysteries and rewards—purification, forgiveness, communion, regeneration, and immortality. However the connection originated, the Isis-Osiris myth possessed a solar significance; Osiris is slain by his brother Set, enclosed in a chest which is put adrift in the Nile. After much search and sorrow the chest is found by Isis his wife, and mourned by Isis and her sister, Nephthys (the wife of Set). Set gains possession of the body, divides it into fourteen parts, and disperses it about Egypt. Isis gives birth to Horus, and hides him in the marshes of the delta. After much search she recovers and inters the parts of the body of Osiris, who is restored by a magic formula, and becomes god of the dead. Horus takes vengeance on Set for slaying his father, although his life is spared through the entreaty of Isis. Horus and Set appear before the court of the great gods of Egypt, where Horus is assigned the crown and throne of his father, uniting Egypt. In the myth, Osiris is the sun, Set the night, Isis the eastern horizon or dawn, Horus (again) the sun, Nephthys the western horizon or evening. The myth also symbolized the struggle of good with evil, the regeneration of man, and the immortality of the soul.
   Q.v. Mystery Religions (2).

ISIS-OSIRIS.

   Q.v. Mystery Religions (2); Isis.

ISLAM.

   Name of the religion founded by Mohammed (q.v.). The term means "submission to God." According to the tradition, Gabriel asked Mohammed, "Messenger of God, what is Islam?" The prophet replied, "Islam is to believe in God and His Prophet, to say the prescribed prayers, to give alms, to observe the feast of Ramadan, and to make the pilgrimage to Mecca." The faith is characterized by an exclusive monotheism, the worship of Allah as the one true God, and Mohammed as the greatest of his prophets.

   (1) As sources for the religion, in addition to the genius of Mohammed himself, one may cite Zoroastrianism (q.v.) as well as Judaism and Christianity. The influence of the former is to be found in such elements as the portrayal of the judgment where one is tested by having to walk a bridge over hell which, for the faithless, diminishes to the thinness and sharpness of a razor. Depending upon the degree of one's faithfulness and purity, one falls into the tortures of hell or passes over into a life of pleasure and feasting in the company of lovely maidens (q.v. Zoroaster 3). The claim that we are to be resurrected with "living bodies of flesh," stated in the Qur'an, derives from Judaic and Christian influences. The influence of the latter two religions may likewise be seen in the acceptance of Adam, Noah, Abraham, Moses, and Jesus as prophets preparing the way for Mohammed.

   (2) The duties of the communicant, largely worked out by Mohammed during the Medina period of his life, include daily repetition of the confession of faith, a program of prayers—five daily—while facing in the direction of Mecca, dawn to dusk fasting during the month of Ramadan, at least one pilgrimage to the holy city of Mecca, and payment of a 2 $^1/_2$ percent poor tax.

   (3) The ethical impulse of the movement would seem to have been powered more by justice than mercy, something like the *lex talionis* (q.v), although Mohammed is to be credited with the abolition of infanticide, a custom rather widely practiced among 7th-century Arabians in the case of female infants.

   (4) After Mohammed's death the role of leadership was taken up in turn by four of the prophet's closest companions, the last of whom was named Ali. At this point a division arose within Islam over the succession. One group, the Sunnites—now constituting the great majority of Moslems—held that the succession of true leaders ended with Ali. The Shiites recognize the descendants of Ali as belonging to the true succession.

   (5) The Shiites, who look forward to the future appearance of a great leader—the final Imam, called the Mahdi—have given rise to the mystical movement of Sufism (q.v.), the rationalistic sect of the Mutazilites (q.v.), and the ecumenical movement of Bahaism (q.v.).

   (6) In terms of theological doctrine, the most significant contrasts are to be found between the Mutazilites and Qadarites on the one hand, espousing free will, and the Chabarites on the other holding to absolute fatalism. In terms of influence the two most powerful schools are the Mutazilites or Separatists, and the Mutakillim or Orthodox.

   (7) The term "Imam" is used to refer to those in the true succession of Mohammed, and there are differences of interpretation. The Islamic equivalent to the Messiah is the Mahdi, the expected final Imam who will lead Islam to world conquest. According to the tradition of the Shiites, the "hidden Imam," who disappeared in 873 A.D., will appear again as the Mahdi. Numerous claimants to the role have arisen in Islamic history.

   (8) The chief doctrinal difference between Sunni and Shia is that the former find their authority in the Qur'an, supplemented by tradition, and the latter in the pronouncements of the inspired Imams. Both sides provide ecclesiastical interpretation, one of the Qur'an and tradition, and the other of the Imamate, including the pronouncements of the hidden Imam, who remains in touch with agents of his own choosing.

ISLAMIC PHILOSOPHY.

   The philosophy of Islam or of the Arabic world. For many centuries the culture of Greece was known only to the Arab world. During this period, beginning with the decline of Greece and ending with the rise of Scholasticism, the advances in science and medicine, mathematics, literature, and philosophy are to be credited to the Arab world, although the inspiration was clearly Greek.

(1) Most of the intellectual vigor of this culture was concentrated in Alexandria, where by the 3rd century B.C. the famous school, and the beginnings of its library, were in existence (*q.v.* Alexandrian School). To indicate the importance of this center it need only be mentioned that both Euclid and Ptolemy were Alexandrian (*q.v.* Aristotelianism 2).

(2) As the Arabic influence grew, Greek manuscripts were translated into Arabic. And this became a chief function of Alexandrian scholars. Arabic interest in science fostered interest in, and translations of, Aristotle. Arabic mysticism fostered interest in Platonism and Neoplatonism. The great Islamic philosophers appear between the 9th and 12th centuries: Al-Kindi (*q.v.*), Al-Farabi (*q.v.*), Avicenna (*q.v.*), and Avempace (*q.v.*) attempted to synthesize this material into an Aristotelian Neoplatonism. Averroës (*q.v.*) spread Aristotle's influence by means of detailed commentaries. Al-Ghazzali, maintaining an orthodox and non-philosophical mysticism, criticized his predecessors heavily.

(3) This was the material which, translated into Latin, educated Europe in the Aristotelian philosophy in the 12th and 13th centuries, making possible, and requiring, the work of Albertus Magnus and Thomas Aquinas.

Q.v. Philosophy (33).

ISOCRATES. 436–338 B.C.

Greek philosopher and rhetorician. A contemporary of Plato, Isocrates was educated by the Sophists. He established his school near the Lyceum around 392. Among his many students were Speusippus, Plato's successor as head of the Academy.

Principal writings: *Against the Sophists; Antidosis;* plus numerous addresses and letters.

(1) Isocrates is credited with defining rhetoric as the "science of persuasion." Viewing the discipline as technical in nature, he argued against the Sophists whose methods were less technical, and whose outlook was more parochial. He also differed from the Sophists in holding that rhetoric must be oriented to the nobler side of the human spirit. In his school the student was first introduced to the abstract rules and techniques governing the discipline, and then required to apply the rules in practice compositions criticized by the master.

(2) In ethics, he celebrated the profitableness of virtue, holding honesty—and the reciprocity of the golden rule—to be the best policy. He held that virtue can be taught and consists of moderation, and that the moral law is more apt to show its excellence in the life of the state than in the shorter life of the individual. The utilitarian approach of Isocrates anticipates later developments, although Isocrates did not develop his position.

ISOMORPHISM.

From the Greek *iso* ("equal") and *morphe* ("form"). Although the conception of isomorphism has applicability to many areas of science, its relevance to philosophy derives from the discipline of mathematics, and relates to the close association between mathematics and logic. Any two groups of entities may be said to be isomorphic when they have the same structure, that is, when by a one-to-one correspondence the elements of one group can be correlated with the elements of the other. The concept has important applications throughout modern mathematics. It has obvious relevance to the philosophy of science both in the theory of measurement and in the analysis of the problem concerning how different branches of science relate to each other.

ISRAEL BEN ELIEZER, BA'AL SHEM TOB (BESHT).

Founder of the Hasidim. *Q.v.* Cabala (3f).

ISRAELI, ISAAC BEN SOLOMON. Late 9th and early 10th cents.

Jewish philosopher. Born in Egypt. Educated at Kairawan. His philosophy was Neoplatonic utilizing the principle of emanations.

Principal writings: *Book of Elements; Book of Definitions; Book of Substances; Book on Spirit and Soul.*

ISTIGKEIT.
   Q.v. Meister Eckhart (2).

IŚVARA (ISHVARA).
   From the Sanskrit *iś* ("to command, rule") and *vara* ("master, lord"). For Shankara (*q.v.* 4) the phenomenal aspect of Brahman. Also *q.v.* Nyaya (4) and Vaiśeṣika (6) for whom Ishvara is a creator and personal god. For Patanjali (*q.v.*, and *q.v.* Yoga 1) Ishvara serves as an object of meditation and a spiritual ideal.

IŚVARA KṚṢNA (ISHVARA KRISHNA).
   Q.v. Sankhya.

I-THOU AND I-IT RELATIONS.
   Q.v. Buber (1–3).

ITO JINSAI. 1627–1705.
   Japanese philosopher. Born in Kyoto. A Confucian, Ito turned from the neo-Confucianism of Chu Hsi (*q.v.*) to the doctrines of Confucius and Mencius.
   Principal writings: *The Meaning of Terms in the Analects and Mencius; Boys' Questions; Changes in Confucian Teaching, Past and Present* (ed. Ito Togai).

J

JACOBI, FRIEDRICH HEINRICH. 1743–1819.
   German philosopher. Born in Dusseldorf. Educated for a commercial career he devoted himself to business and politics until 1785 when his philosophical productivity began. Holding that the Kantian philosophy leads to solipsism, and that "dogmatic rationalism" leads to Spinozism with its corollaries of pantheism and determinism, Jacobi adopted a philosophy based on intuition, feeling, and faith. Faith (in the sense of an intuition or feeling of immediate certainty) not only provides the basis for God and freedom, ideas of the practical reason, but also the basis for the theoretical reason, and hence for all knowledge. His first publication unleashed a furious controversy over Spinoza, involving Lessing (*q.v.*), Moses Mendelssohn (*q.v.*) and many others (*q.v. Pantheismusstreit*).

Principal writings: *On the Teaching of Spinoza in Letters to Moses Mendelssohn,* 1785; *David Hume on Beliefs, or Idealism and Realism,* 1786; *Open Letters to Fichte,* 1799; *On the Undertaking of Criticism in Reducing the Reason to the Understanding,* 1801; *On Divine Things,* 1811.

JACOBITES.
   Name by which the members of the Syrian National Church are known. Descendants of the Monophysites of Antioch who refused to accept the decisions of the Council of Chalcedon, 451 A.D. The name comes from their leader, Jacob Baradeus, who organized the group during the reign of Justinian and Theodora.

JAEGER, WERNER. 1881–1961.
   German philosopher. Born in Lobberich (the Rhineland). Taught at Basel, Kiel, Berlin and Harvard. Interested in Greek philosophy and culture, especially in the *Paideia,* or educational training of the youth.
   Principal writings: *History of the Evolution of the Metaphysics of Aristotle,* 1912; *Aristotle: Fundamentals of the History of his Development* (T), 1923; *Antiquity and Humanism,* 1925; *Plato's Place in the Formation of Greek Culture,* 1928; *The Spiritual Presence of the Ancients,* 1929; *Paideia, The Forming of the Greek Nature* (T), 3 vols., 1934–44; *The Theology of the Early Greek Philosophers* (T), 1949.

JAIMINI. 5th cent. B.C.
   Author of the *Mimamsa Sutra. Q.v.* Purva Mimamsa; Hinduism (6c).

JAINISM. After 800 B.C.
   Along with Charvakan materialism, one of the heterodox systems of Indian philosophy. Grounded in the doctrine of the *Yajurveda,* as systematized by Vardhamana (Mahavira), but substituting logic and experience for the authority of the *Veda.* Vardhamana, like Buddha, was a *Kshatriya.* Jainism arose in the eastern provinces, distant from the Indus Valley center of Vedic culture. There still exist in India a number of centers of this faith.
   (1) Believing in both atomism and the distinction of soul and body, the analysis of the universe is resolved into the contrasting categories of *jiva* (the conscious), and *ajiva* (the unconscious). *Ajiva* includes matter, motion, rest, space, and

time. All but time are regarded as *astikaya dravyas*, or physical substances, whose physical characteristics are called *gunas*. *Astikaya dravyas* have parts and spacial extension. Time is the only *anastikaya dravya* or nonphysical substance not having constituent parts and extension in space. These, the components of the human being, are themselves everlasting, and independent.

(2) But due to karmic matter, formed by our passions, soul is enmeshed in the body; and its release takes more than a single lifetime. One must stop the inflow of karmic matter, shed its influence, and so achieve release. *Moksha*, or release, is available in only two of the six epochs which repeat themselves in time's vast but endless cycles.

(3) The means of release is provided by the three jewels: right belief (belief in Jainist doctrines); right knowledge (knowledge of nature as it is); and right conduct (practicing the five virtues of nonviolence, truth-speaking, non-stealing, chastity, nonattachment to worldly things).

(4) The Jainist doctrine of knowledge called *Syadvada* (meaning "maybe" or "perhaps") holds that all knowledge is merely probable and partial, and all predictions are relative because reality is multiple. The analysis of knowledge distinguishes the following types: (a) ordinary cognition—memory, recognition, induction; (b) cognition through signs and symbols—involving association, understanding, and aspects of the meaning of things; (c) clairvoyance—direct knowledge across considerable stretches of space and time; (d) telepathy—direct knowledge of the thought of others; (e) perfect knowledge—complete, all-comprehensive.

(5) Important, too, is the Jaina doctrine of *Naya*, of aspects or standpoints. Seven standpoints from which we can view reality in a relative manner are isolated: (a) figurative, or non-literal; (b) general, or as a class concept; (c) distributive, or in terms of a discrimination of subclasses, orders, or kinds; (d) the active condition; (e) descriptive, including grammatical and expressive propriety; (f) specific, rendering the meaning of a work definite; (g) active, understanding a name in terms of the activity connoted by it. The first four of these *Nayas* represent the "object

standpoint." The last three represent a "word standpoint." Each preceding *Naya* has a greater denotative spread than the *Naya* which succeeds it.

(6) Furthermore, one must say of everything it somehow is both perishable and eternal, of similar and dissimilar form, describable and indescribable, existent and nonexistent. But this need not be contradictory, since the two parts of the apparent contradiction can refer to different aspects of the thing. There are seven modes of predication, all of which can be true without contradiction: that a thing exists; that it does not exist; that it both exists and fails to exist; that it is indescribable; that it exists and is indescribable; that it fails to exist and is indescribable; and that it both exists and fails to exist and is indescribable.

(7) In this system there is no God; but the liberated souls achieve something of this status, having immortality and omniscience; and the religious community treats the liberated ones as though they were divine, building temples to them, and venerating their images.

(8) There are two sects of Jainism, agreeing on doctrine, disagreeing on dress, or its lack, the *Shvetambaras* dress in white, the *Digambaras* ("sky clad ones") wear nothing at all. Their reason is the belief that possession of property excludes one from Nirvana, and clothes are property. It is their further belief that women are excluded from Nirvana in any case.

JAKOBSON, ROMAN. 1896–1982.

Born in Moscow. Educated at the Universities of Moscow and Prague. Taught at the University of Masaryk, Columbia, Harvard, and M.I.T. Founder of Prague School of Structural Linguistics.

Principal writing: *Essays on General Linguistics*, 1963.

(1) Jacobson developed his view around six factors which he found to be present in communication: a sender, a message, a receiver, a context or referent, a code (at least partially common to sender and receiver), a contact (a channel connecting sender and receiver). The factors give rise to six functions of communication. When a sender sends a message to a receiver there is a denotative, cognitive function (a referent), an expressive or emotive function (interjections), a conative

function (directed toward making an impression on the receiver), a *phatic* function (designed merely to keep the contact, *e.g.*, talk about the weather), a metalinguistic function (designed to determine if sender and receiver are using the same code), a poetic function (stress on the message itself).

(2) Levi-Strauss (*q.v.*) was influenced by his having said: "There are no things, only relations between things."

JAMBLICHUS.
  Q.v. Iamblichus.

JAMES-LANGE THEORY.
  Q.v. William James (3).

JAMES, WILLIAM. 1842–1910.
American philosopher and psychologist. Born in New York. Educated at Harvard. The brother of Henry James, the novelist. Their father, Henry James Sr., was a Swedenborgian theologian. The brothers had much of their schooling in Europe. William joined the Agassiz expedition to Brazil in 1865–66; received an M.D. from Harvard in 1869; became instructor in anatomy, Harvard, 1873; and began teaching psychology there in 1875. He became Assistant Professor of Physiology in 1876, and Professor of Philosophy in 1885. He was plagued by ill health through much of his life. The term "pragmatism," associated with his name, came from Charles Peirce. The writings of James popularized the term, linking it permanently with American philosophy. *Q.v.* also Russell (9).

Principal writings: *The Principles of Psychology*, 2 vols., 1890; *A Textbook of Psychology; Briefer Course*, 1892; *The Will to Believe*, 1897; *The Varieties of Religious Experience*, 1902; *Pragmatism, A New Name for Some Old Ways of Thinking*. 1907; *A Pluralistic Universe*, 1909; *The Meaning of Truth*, 1909; *Memories and Studies*, 1911; *Some Problems of Philosophy*, 1911; *Essays in Radical Empiricism*, 1912.

The philosophy of William James emerged from the tension between his commitment to science and the attractiveness of religious faith. In a way this is signaled by the fact that his first two books concerned the science of psychology he helped to found, while his next two books had to do with religious be-

lief. It might even be said that in his remaining publications he was seeking the philosophical perspective in which these two focii of experience can be affirmed jointly and respectably. In life, of course, the scheme could not have been so patent. Many of the essays published in his later books had been in the journals much earlier. Even so, the pattern is sufficiently close to being true that we shall use it as the basis of our comments.

A. *The Principles of Psychology* has long been recognized as a classic.

(1) In method the work is empirical, combining intense introspection with a functional, biological approach to psychology. Metaphysical issues were postponed until his later works.

(2) He thought of consciousness as a stream or flow whose later moments are able to grasp and own their predecessors. Indeed, he adopted the term "specious present" to refer to that real duration we are able to grasp at once and which contains in it part of the past and part of the future. But this suggests an organic relatedness although the scientific view recognizes only separate molecules.

(3) He developed at this time, too, what has come to be known as the James-Lange theory of the emotions. On the theory an emotion is the feeling of a bodily state; it must, therefore, follow rather than produce this state. We do not run because we are afraid, then; on the contrary, we are afraid because we run. The view clearly supports a functional theory of consciousness. James took his final step in that direction in his essay of 1914, "Does 'Consciousness' Exist?" He answered that the term does not stand for an entity but that it does most emphatically stand for a function.

B. The other aspect of James' thought pulled in a different direction.

(4) In *The Will to Believe* he argued that when the options of life are forced, living, and momentous, neutrality is impossible, and that in such cases we have a right to believe beyond the evidence. Since not to decide is to decide in the negative, and since our choice is itself part of the evidence, it is necessary to go beyond the evidence. We are asked to have recourse to indirect evidence; *e.g.*, how strongly does life support you now that the choice has been made? In a sense

such options are thus decided by the whole history of the human race. At one point James suggests that our decisions may have some effect upon the universe in the way of shaping it in the direction of our ultimate beliefs.

(5) *The Varieties of Religious Experience* is a careful, sensitive, and concerned study of the religious life based upon the experience both of mystics and ordinary believers. His analyses of the twice-born, of the function of belief in "sick souls," led him to view the religious perspective as relying on something beyond, or other than, reason. At the same time the unity of the religious testimony is sufficient to provide some evidence that the religious hypothesis may be true.

C. The attempt to find the unity of these interests occupied James increasingly.

(6) His adoption of pragmatism as a method is in line with the functionalism of his psychology, while his extension of pragmatism to indirect consequences agrees with his interest in religion and ideality. Taking from Peirce (*q.v.* 1) the pragmatic maxim, and expressing it thus—"The meaning of any proposition can always be brought down to some particular consequence in our future practical experience, whether passive or active"—it is clear that James no less than Peirce wished ideas to be interpreted in terms of their consequences. This meant some ideas would not pass muster; the element of reform was in his mind when he urged that ideas be taken in terms of their "cash value."

(7) At the same time, however, he related the doctrine of meaning to the doctrine of truth: "the true is only the expedient in the way of our thinking, just as the right is only the expedient in the way of our behaving. Truth is a matter of degree. Truth "happens" to an idea. Truth changes and develops through time. In his most defensible development of this doctrine James holds that for a doctrine to be regarded as true it must pass three tests: the test of theoretical consistency, the test of factual support, and the test of giving our practical energies "something to press against." Thus, a doctrine which presents us with a world in which we cannot live meaningfully cannot be true. For James that was the case with atheism.

(8) As for the world in which we live, James combatted monism with his doctrine of pluralism. The world is not absolutely unified. There is looseness in it, sufficient looseness to keep the future open and to allow human freedom. The relations of the world are not all internal—*i.e.*, relations of entailment. Ours is not a block universe. The basic fact is that of external relatedness; and the approach to knowledge is "radical empiricism," an approach which requires no trans-empirical connective support.

(9) Value appears in the claims we make; and ethics consists in discovering the alternatives capable of satisfying most harmoniously the claims present in a situation. Thus, the right is no more absolute than is the true.

(10) Mind and matter are merely two of the different ways in which reality gets organized. James held that the stuff which gets organized is "pure experience." This decision gave him a number of advantages. He could avoid the mind-body dualism; he could see how an object in one person's world could become an object in another's, and how "our minds can meet in a world of objects which they share in common."

(11) He was troubled, also, by the dualism of the sense-datum theory, where objects are duplicated in perception. He suggested that it might be possible to avoid this dualism if we follow out the paradigm case where one item can be part of two realities; *i.e.*, the point situated at the intersection of two lines is on both lines. Let us apply this to the problem of perception. Think of your life as a line extended through space and time; and think of any object of perception, *e.g.*, a tree, as constituting a similar line. At the moment of perception the two lines cross, and there is no need of a sense-datum to duplicate the fact of one's perceiving of the tree. At most, the sense-datum is needed to explain erroneous perception, the seeing of something that isn't there.

(12) The possibility of a meeting of minds also suggested to James the manner in which our awareness might relate to a divine awareness. There could be a "compounding of consciousness." "Pluralistic panpsychism" attracted him ever more strongly. Beyond our awareness there could be a wider awareness of

which we were part. God must be the "deepest power" in the universe; "a power not ourselves" which makes for righteousness and "means" it, and which recognizes us. He must include us, but not in such fashion as to rob us of freedom; He must be somewhat less than all-inclusive, in order that He not be responsible for evil; and He must participate in a real history in order that our temporal concerns not be drained of their significance.

JANSEN, CORNELIUS. 1585–1638.

Dutch theologian. Born at Accoy, Utrecht. Studied at Louvain and Paris. Taught at Louvain. He joined the Augustinians in a struggle going on at Louvain between Jesuits and Augustinians. Out of this struggle came the Jansenist movement. He twice journeyed to Spain, 1624 and 1626, in the interests of his party exposing himself to the dangers of the Inquisition. In 1636 he was appointed Bishop of Ypres. Until his death Jansen worked on his theology of St. Augustine. His volume appeared posthumously.

Principal writings: *St. Augustine's Doctrine of Human Nature*, 1640.

(1) Interested in a reformed church, Jansen found a sterile dialectic in charge of religious belief while worshippers trivialized their religion into pietism, or natural philosophy. But in religion experience, not reason, is the appropriate guide.

(2) Humans are helplessly dependent upon God, requiring a conversion they cannot give themselves. Their fate depends upon God's will. Hence, the doctrine is at last strongly predestinarian.

(3) We are not justified merely by faith, however. The justification must develop also through works.

(4) Finally, the relation of the soul to God is possible only through the authority and sacraments of the Catholic Church.

JANSENISM.

Named for Cornelius Jansen (*q.v.*) whose Augustinian doctrines sparked this 17th-century movement. Jansenism was a dispute within the Catholic Church which deeply involved the Port Royal (*q.v.*) school, and thus both Arnauld (*q.v.*)

and Pascal (*q.v.*). The Jansenist controversy was with the Jesuits over the basis of the religious life. The chief episodes in the dispute were: (1) Du Vergier, Abbot of St. Cyran, expounded Jansen's ideas in France. His student, Antoine Arnauld, published them in book form. The book was *Frequent Communion*, 1643. (2) 1649, the University of Paris condemned five propositions from Jansen's book on Augustine; all of the condemned propositions concerned predestination. (3) 1653, Pope Innocent X declared the five propositions to be heretical. (4) The Jansenists, led by Arnauld, claimed that Jansen had not intended the propositions in the sense in which they were condemned. (5) 1656, Pope Alexander VII held that the propositions had been condemned as intended. (6) Arnauld held that while the Church was competent to make judgments on theological questions, it could not know infallibly what was passing through an author's mind. (7) Pascal wrote the *Provincial Letters* in support of Arnauld, 1656–7. (8) The defense notwithstanding, Arnauld was deprived of his degree by the French government; and in 1661 all suspected Jansenists were forced to sign a renunciation or be sent to the Bastille. This period ended with a kind of peace under Clement IX, 1669. (9) Madame de Longueville, cousin to Louis XIV, was sympathetic to the Jansenists and protected them. After her death in 1679 Arnauld was forced into exile. (10) 1685, Pasquier Quesnel, the new leader of the Jansenists, had to take the same step. (11) 1685, Louis Antoine de Noailles—who had expressed official approval of a well-known devotional manual written by Quesnel—became Archbishop of Paris. (12) 1701, the Jansenists of the Paris divinity school posed the question: Must one accept the condemnation of Jansen with interior assent, or is "respectful silence" sufficient? (13) 1705, Clement XI issued a papal bull condemning the "respectful silence" alternative. (14) 1713, there appeared the papal bull called *Unigenitus* in which 101 propositions from Quesnal's devotional manual were held to be anathema. (15) France became divided into "appellants" and "acceptants," and the battle raged until 1730 when *Unigenitus* became part of French law. But many of the judges found the matter unpalatable, and the struggle continued through much of the 18th century. (16) Meanwhile, many Jansenists followed Quesnel to Holland where they found the Dutch Catholics in sympathy with them. Some Jansenist congregations survive in France, others in Holland.

JAPANESE RELIGION AND PHILOSOPHY.

As in India and China, religion and philosophy in Japan have not been sharply differentiated until recent years. The native religion of Japan, Shinto (q.v.) goes back at least 2000 years although it was not named until Buddhism was introduced from China in the 6th century A.D. Confucianism had been introduced in the 5th century A.D. along with Chinese script.

(1) Confucian influence reached its height in the Tokugawa era (1603–1867). The neo-Confucian philosophers Chu Hsi (q.v.) and Wang Yang-Ming (q.v.) have received special attention and esteem.

(2) All the schools of Buddhism, developed in China, have been imported into Japan. The T'ien-T'ai School (q.v.) gave rise to the most powerful Japanese sect, the Nichiren; and the meditation school of Ch'an or Zen Buddhism (q.v.) has achieved a development in Japan far beyond anything it had achieved in China.

(3) Following the Meiji restoration of 1868, Japan was opened to Western philosophy with the result that Hegel, Eduard Von Hartmann, Windelband, Rickert, T.H. Green, William James, and John Dewey, exercised influence. From the mid-1920's the power of Marxism had steadily grown; and from the mid-1940's the influence of existentialism has been increasing.

JASPERS, KARL. 1883–1973.

German philosopher. Born in Oldenburg. He took his doctorate in medicine in 1909; from 1908–15 he engaged in psychiatric work in Heidelberg. He became *privatdozent* in psychology at Heidelberg in 1913. From psychiatry and psychology Jaspers' interest turned toward metaphysics. He was named professor of philosophy at Heidelberg in 1921, was forbidden to lecture during Hitler's regime and deprived of his professorship in 1937; he was reinstated in 1945, and was named professor of philosophy at Basel in 1948. Although often considered as an existentialist, and indeed its chief German exponent after Heidegger, Jaspers has refused both the label and any connection with the philosophy of Heidegger. He has held the three-volumed *Philosophy*, 1932, to be his magnum opus.

Principal writings: *General Psychopathology* (T), 1913; *Psychology of World Views*, 1919; *Man in the Modern Age* (T), 1931; *Philosophy* (T), 3 vols., 1932; *Reason and Existenz* (T), 1933; *Nietzsche* (T), 1936; *Descartes and Philosophy*, 1937: *Existence Philosophy*, 1938; *The Idea of the University* (T), 1946; *Nietzsche and Christianity*, 1946; *The Question of Guilt* (T), 1946; *Philosophical Logic, On Truth*, vol. 1 (T in part), 1947; *The Perennial Scope of Philosophy* (T), 1948; *The Origin and Goal of History* (T), 1949; *Reason and Anti-Reason in Our Time* (T), 1950; *The Way to Wisdom* (T), 1950; *On Tragedy* (T), 1952; *Myth and Christianity* (T), (with Bultmann), 1954; *On the Conditions and Possibilities of a New Humanism*, 1956; *The Great Philosophers* (T), 1957; *Truth and Science*, 1960; *Nicholas of Cusa*, 1964; *Introduction to Philosophy*, 1966; *Ciphers of Transcendence*, 1970.

(1) It is the whole purpose of Jasper's philosophizing to awaken men to authenticity. All of his terms are to be understood in this way, that they are not intended to convey a doctrine, but to explicate the human situation. In the explication we are told some things about man: (a) Man is *Dasein*, a "being there," that is, an empirical object in space and time. (b) Man is Consciousness (*Bewusstsein Uberhaupt*). (c) Man is *Geist*, that is Spirit, working the material of life into ideal totalities.

(2) But more important than any of these distinctions is the fact that man is *Existenz*. The importance of this concept may be seen in the tendency to refer to Jasper's point of view as *Existenz*-Philosophy. The concept is really a normative one; since man can avoid *Existenz*, it is only a possibility for him. In those times when man achieves authentic self-awareness, standing in history with an attitude of freedom and openness before the Encompassing, an instance of and yet knowing he is less than his possible

transcendence, then man is *Existenz*. Put in another manner, when man becomes himself, he is *Existenz*. The assumption then would seem to be that for each man there is an authentic self for him to be at a given time, taking into account his capacities and history. Man's tendency is to lose the openness, for the awareness to become corrupted and the *Existenz* to be lost; one then sinks back into *Dasein*.

(3) Even in the man who is *Existenz* there is a polarity between Reason and *Existenz*. Reason, lacking *Existenz*, is empty; *Existenz* without Reason is a private dream. Reason has the power to unite diverse *Existenzen* into various kinds of communication; these kinds of union and communication are kinds of truth. But *Existenz* pushes beyond these forms toward transcendence and Being.

(4) The object of the struggle, the transcending, is Being; and the deepest kind of truth is truth of Being. But although this is the direction and the goal one can never expect really to achieve it. Each of us operates within an horizon. Beyond the horizon, our present state of *Existenz*, our conceptual scheme, is the Encompassing. We may succeed in forcing the horizon to recede, but this does not rid us of the horizon or the Encompassing beyond it. The idea of the Encompassing requires that we recognize the partiality and incompleteness of every determinate scheme. All philosophies contain partial truth. But the circularity implicit in systems of thought, their necessary incompleteness, shows their place within the Encompassing, and the need for their transcendence. On the other hand the incompleteness in human life, the fact that there is no *Existenz*, no state of Being, finally satisfactory, calls again for transcendence. This, plus the fact that man is always more than he can ever be said to be, points to the presence of the Encompassing within man as well as beyond him.

(5) Jaspers believes there is a way in which we can read the truth of Being and of transcendence, although it cannot be expressed conceptually; the reading of the face, for example, of one with whom I am in existential communion. And metaphysics is, finally, a reading of the ciphers of transcendence. The cipher is symbol, not sign. Through signs the empirical world speaks to consciousness (1b above); through ciphers or symbols transcendence speaks to *Existenz*. This communication is indirect and apparently similar to intuition although this endless ambiguity is of the very essence of the language of the cipher. Still, in myths and philosophies the primal cipher lies hidden, waiting as it were to be read.

(6) The world of science emerges from the level of *Dasein*. To be an empirical object among other empirical objects is to exist in the space-time world. World orientation, *i.e.*, philosophy on the level of existence, constitutes the world of the sciences. Although reason seeks wholeness in *Dasein*, only separate spheres are possible. Jaspers distinguishes these: the inorganic, the organic, the soul as experience, and spirit (*Geist*), the rational soul of philosophy.

(7) The idea of history has been mentioned several times (*cf.* 2 above). Jaspers thinks of historicity in relation to all that touches empirical existence, and even man's attempts at transcendence. Truth is an historical being, conditioned by existence within the empirical world. As we have indicated, however, freedom is always possible for man, even though man's freedom and the limits of his historical being are set by the ultimate situations (*Grenzsituationen*) of death, suffering, struggle, and guilt.

JATI.
Sanskrit, "birth," "birth group". *Q.v.* Buddha (2); Caste.

JAYARAŚI (JAYARASHI). 7th or 8th cent. A.D.
Indian philosopher. A Brahmin, Jayarashi was born and lived in southern India, as a member of the Lokayata (*q.v.*) school of materialists. What we know of Jayarashi is either established or suggested by internal references in the only work of his now extant, discovered in 1926 in the Patan manuscript library.

Principal writing: *Tattvopaplavasimha*.

(1) Expressing solidarity with Brihaspati, a Lokayatan materialist, in his opening lines Jayarashi insists that Brihaspati's materialism merely reflects the beliefs of the people, and that upon examination, the principles we use in thinking do not stand up.

(2) He demonstrates the point by arguing against the theories of *pramana*, or means of acquiring knowledge, used in all the schools until his time: the Nyaya (*q.v.*), Mimamsa (*q.v.*), Buddhist (*q.v.*), and Sankhya (*q.v.*). Although the lists of *pramanas* differ, chief among them are perception, inference, and testimony.

(3) With respect to inference he argued that, since universals are indemonstrable, major premises cannot be established. Causal arguments fail on the ground that inferences from effect to cause are either unnecessary or impossible. To know something (*e.g.*, smoke) to be an effect, one must know the cause (*e.g.*, fire). If one knows that, the inference is unnecessary. If one does not, it is impossible.

(4) Extending his argument about the elusive nature of evidence to the idea of soul, Jayarashi considers, and believes he has demolished, the theories of soul advanced by Nyaya, Jainism (*q.v.* 1), Sankhya, and Vedanta (*q.v.*).

(5) His book was well-named since *Tattvopaplava* means "the upsetting of all principles." Some refuse to count him a Lokayatan, since Lokayatans accepted the *pramanas*. On Jayarashi's own terms this means only that the materialism of the people harbored a skepticism which emerged upon careful examination, *i.e.*, when Jayarashi joined the school. Upsetting all principles of perception and inference, led him to an extreme form of skepticism, a position which, in the West, is called Pyrrhonism (*q.v.*).

JEANS, JAMES H. 1877–1946.

English physicist and astronomer. Educated at Cambridge. Taught at Cambridge and Princeton. Apart from his scientific work Jeans is known for his popular expositions of science. Taking the idealistic position, he reduces the world to thought, regards it as the contents of the divine mind and then—perhaps taking his cue from Plato—regards this Mind as the Pure Mathematician.

Principal writings: *The Universe Around Us*, 1929; *The Mysterious Universe*, 1930; *Through Space and Time*, 1934; *Physics and Philosophy*, 1942.

JEFFERSON, THOMAS. 1743–1826.

Third President of the United States. Born at Shadwell, Virginia. Educated at the College of William and Mary. Studied law privately for five years. Admitted to the bar in 1767. Member of Virginia legislature, 1769–76. Virginia delegate to the Continental Congress in Philadelphia, 1775–76. In June of 1776 appointed to the committee to draft the Declaration of Independence, becoming its principal author. Virginia legislature, 1776–79. Governor of Virginia, 1779–81. Returned to the Continental Congress in 1782. U.S. Minister to France, 1785–89. Secretary of State under Washington, 1789–94. Vice-president under Adams, 1797–98. President, 1801–09. In his post-presidential years, worked at establishing the University of Virginia which received its charter in 1819 and opened to students in 1825.

In the writings listed below, since most of Jefferson's work was published posthumously, the years given are those of composition. In some few cases, *e.g.*, the Declaration, that is also the year of publication.

Principal writings: "The Declaration of Independence," 1776; *Notes on the State of Virginia*, 1781–85; *The Commonplace Book*, 1764(?)–1824; *Farm Book*, 1774–1826; *The Anas* (1789–94) (written opinions sent to the president by the Secretary of State); *The Life and Morals of Jesus of Nazareth* (*The Jefferson Bible*), 1804–19; *Memoir* (early years to 1790), 1821.

(1) Jefferson believed that civil rights are derived from natural rights, chief of which are life, liberty, and the pursuit of happiness. One of his models was the Virginia Bill of Rights, containing the phrase, "life and liberty, with the means of acquiring and possessing property, and pursuing and obtaining happiness and safety." Jefferson's point is that property is a natural want and although it may follow from natural rights, its dependence upon the civil compact makes it a civil, rather than natural, right.

(2) "I have sworn upon the altar of god, eternal hostility against every form of tyranny over the mind of man," although aimed at the Alien and Sedition Law, is the key to his social philosophy. He endorses the maximal possible liberty without interference in the liberty of another. Beyond that, since the will of the majority must always prevail, since the earth belongs to the living, and since one generation cannot bind another, the

social contract can be abrogated and reshaped in each generation. The instrument is legislation when possible; rebellion when necessary ("A little rebellion, now and then, is a good thing... as necessary in the political world as storms in the physical"); and full scale, generation-spanning revolution when conditions are unbearable ("The tree of liberty must be refreshed from time to time with the blood of patriots and tyrants").

(3) In 1770 he argued, in a court case, that "under the law of nature all men are born free." In the Declaration of Independence he added that they are created equal. Slavery, then, is contrary to the law of nature and should not exist. He made five dramatic moves against slavery; one of them was successful, and another came within one vote of passing. His denunciation of the slave trade in the Declaration was eliminated by Congress. His bill preventing the further importation of slaves into Virginia was passed by the Virginia legislature in 1778. On the other hand, his emancipation bill, prepared for the same legislature in 1779 was withdrawn because "the public mind would not bear the proposition." The emancipation provision embodied in the constitution he drafted for Virginia in 1783 was never even discussed. On the national level, also in 1783, the passage on slavery which he introduced into the Northwest Ordinance would have abolished slavery after 1800 in the states created from the Virginia territories. The passage was discussed, and lost by one vote. He predicted rather exactly the consequences for the nation of not resolving the problem. Throughout all of this, and to the end of his life he was a slaveholder, a model slaveholder, it would appear, who did not allow his slaves to be whipped, and freed them at his death. Still, he believed blacks to be, unlike Indians, intellectually inferior to whites (failing to note at the time that blacks had been deprived of their culture, while Indians had not); for this reason the slave, once freed, was "to be removed beyond the reach of mixture." In 1809 he moderated these views, observing that they had been formed in a state where the opportunities for the development of the race were severely limited.

(4) Jefferson believed in a natural aristocracy of virtue and talent. His plan for "the general diffusion of knowledge" looked to a system of public education to discover and develop these natural aristocrats. The best students from local elementary schools would be sent to district schools for a higher degree of education. The best graduates of district schools would be sent to the four-year university "where all the useful sciences should be taught." These select students would be supported at public expense. In his time only the capstone of the system came into being, the University of Virginia, on whose architectural design, buildings, faculty, and courses he lavished such care in the years following his presidency.

(5) In a letter to Jefferson, John Adams had argued that of the characteristics of beauty, wealth, birth, genius, and virtue, any one of the first three is more powerful than either or both of the last two. Jefferson demurred, finding his natural aristocracy in the last two, and a false aristocracy in the first three. His opposition to the Federalist party generally, and to Alexander Hamilton in particular, was rooted in his fear that their encouragement of the financial sector was creating a false aristocracy of wealth to the detriment of the natural rights of the majority, and since 90 percent of the nation was engaged in agriculture it was natural that he should find them to be his most virtuous citizens, and those most wedded to liberty; second are those who earn their living from the sea; he sensed a certain mendacity in those engaged in commerce and industry. These tend to be the instruments whereby a nation's liberties are overturned. The corruption he sensed might be accounted for, he thought, by their being "piled upon one another" in large cities.

(6) His Act for Religious Freedom, developed between 1776 and 1779, and fought through the Virginia legislature between 1779 and 1786, held that the freedom to profess one's own opinions in matters of religion is a natural right, whose exercise must not be allowed to affect one's "civil capacities" in any way. The statute became a model for the country, so widely enacted that the separation between church and state can be said

to have been complete by 1834.

(7) Since we cannot know in this life whose religion is right, the goodness of a religion must be judged by the goodness of life of the believer. He understood Jesus to hold that the sum of all religion consists in belief in one all perfect god, in a future state of reward and punishment, and in loving God with all one's heart and one's neighbor as one's self. "I am of his theology," said Jefferson, "A sect by myself, as far as I know." Yet the three beliefs he mentioned are among the pillars of Deism (*q.v.*), which he believed to be supported by science, the design revealed by science providing evidence for god.

(8) As for ethics he liked Epictetus and Jesus, the former telling what we owe ourselves, and the latter what we owe to others. Jesus, claiming no quality beyond the human, taught the purest of all moral systems. The teaching is, however, cloaked in a conspiracy of priestcraft and kingcraft against the civil and religious liberties of mankind. The pure principles and artificial vestments coexist in the Gospels. To restore the "primitive and genuine doctrines" of Jesus a separation must be made, and this is no more difficult than distinguishing "diamonds in a dunghill."

(9) To demonstrate the point he separated the teachings of Jesus from its surrounding narrative, discarding the latter. In four parallel columns, the teachings were presented in Greek, Latin, French and English. This is the work now known as *The Jefferson Bible*. Since he had background in all four languages, the manual was obviously his own personal source for meditation and reflection.

JEHOVAH.

Q.v. Yahweh.

JEN.

A Chinese term whose literal meaning is "man in society," the Chinese character combining the signs for "man" and "group." *Jen* is the chief virtue of the Confucian philosophy (*q.v.* Confucius 5); and since for this view man achieves his true value in society, the term may be translated appropriately as "humanity," "true manhood," "human-heartedness." In addition to the above the term has been

translated as "altruism," "benevolence," "love," "goodness," "perfect virtue." Some of these choices are, however, inappropriate; "love" is, for example, the translation of the Chinese *ai* (*q.v.*).

(1) Among Confucianists the term has been used by Mencius (*q.v.*), Chuang Tzu (*q.v.*), Tung Chung-Shu (*q.v.* 3), Han Yu (*q.v.*), and Ch'eng Ming-Tao.

(2) Neo-Confucianists gave the term a more metaphysical meaning. Chang Tsai (*q.v.* 3), for example, extended the idea of *jen* to the entire universe, putting human relations into a cosmic perspective. Among other neo-Confucianists using the term are Chou Tun-I (*q.v.* 1), Chu Hsi (*q.v.* 2), Ch'eng I (*q.v.* 2) and Ch'eng Hao (*q.v.* 2–3), Kaibara Ekken (*q.v.*), K'ang Yu-Wei (5).

(3) The term has also been used by Mo Tzu (*q.v.* 3) for centuries the chief rival to Confucius.

Q.v. Chinese philosophy (1, 7).

JEROME, SAINT. c. 347–420.

Church Father. Born in Dalmatia. Educated in Rome where he was baptized. Traveled extensively, finally settling in Bethlehem where he built a monastery and spent the last thirty-four years of his life. Regarded as the most scholarly of the Latin Church Fathers, his most outstanding achievement was the translation of the Bible into Latin from Hebrew and Greek manuscripts. His translation is known as the Vulgate (*q.v.*), and remained the dominant translation for a thousand years. Also *q.v.* Synderesis.

JESUITS.

Founded by Ignatius Loyola (*q.v.*) in 1534, and approved by Pope Paul III in 1540, the Society of Jesus was designed by its founder to provide a company of men unusually well qualified to provide extraordinary service to the Church. A military conception of obedience runs through the training manual, *Spiritual Exercises*, and is reflected in the organizational structure, of the Jesuits. Headed by a "general" with supreme authority, members of the society pledge "perfect obedience" to the Superior. The term translated "society" is in Spanish *compañia*, suggesting a military unit.

(1) Prepared for any task *ad majorem Dei gloriam* ("to the greater glory of God"),

the Jesuits have been most closely identified in Europe with the Counter-Reformation. The three goals the Jesuits set for themselves were to teach the young, to preach to the ignorant and heathen, and to guide Christians to perfection. How well they succeeded can be seen from the following facts: By the end of the 17th century they had established 769 colleges and universities with enrollments of at least 200,000 students. Further, Jesuit missionaries had established churches or missions in India, Japan, China, Tibet, Africa, Abyssinia and both North and South America. The extent of their success in achieving the third of their goals is perhaps open to question.

(2) The Jesuits served as the target of Pascal's *Provincial Letters* (*q.v.* Pascal); and, as one of the protagonists in the bitter Jansenist controversy (*q.v.* Jansenism), sanctioned the doctrine of free will.

(3) Defending the Christian faith against the doctrines of the Enlightenment, the second half of the 18th century witnessed an astonishing suppression of the Society throughout the world, beginning in Portugal (1759), France (1765), Spain and all of its dependencies (1767). In 1773 the Society was suppressed in its entirety by Pope Clement XIV. The changed climate of opinion engendered by the course of the French Revolution led to the Society's restoration in 1814 by Pope Pius VII.

(4) The most prominent philosophers of the order have been Vásquez (*q.v.*) and Suarez (*q.v.*).

JESUS.
  Q.v. Christ, Jesus.

JEVONS, W.S. 1835–1882.
  British philosopher and economist. Born in Liverpool. Taught at Owens College, Manchester, 1866–76; University College, London, 1876–80; resigned to devote full time to writing.
  Principal writings: *Pure Logic or the Science of Quality Apart From Quantity*, 1864; *The Substitution of Similars*, 1869; *Elementary Lessons in Logic*, 1870; *The Theory of Political Economy*, 1871; *The Principles of Science*, 1874; *Primer of Logic*, 1878; *Studies in Deductive Logic*, 1880.
  (1) Agreeing with Boole that logical operations and mathematical equations

are sufficiently analogous that they can share a common symbolism, Jevons held the basic principle of logic to be "the substitution of similars." Given that A=B, and using the sign "$\emptyset$" to mean "indefinite relation," then the general formula of all inference is:
  From A=B $\emptyset$ C
  A $\emptyset$ C.
  "In whatever relation a thing stands to a second thing, in the same relation it stands to the like or equivalent of that thing."

(2) Realizing that the method of the developing logic allowed mechanization, Jevons constructed a logic machine in 1869 which was demonstrated before the Royal Society where, by pressing keys representing classes or propositions, allowable combinations were made to appear on the face of the machine.

(3) Taking deductive inference as basic, Jevons held induction to be simply the inverse process of deduction as division is the inverse process of multiplication. This meant that induction is to be viewed really as the deduction of some known particular from a general hypothesis. One is to rank the hypotheses from which the given particular can be deduced by their probability, choosing the most probable hypothesis for the inverse deduction.

(4) Following De Morgan (*q.v.* 3) in his interpretation of probability, Jevons looked upon probability as the measure of appropriate belief, determined by the inverse theorem of Bayes. The procedure required deducing the consequences of all the alternative hypotheses, checking these against the evidence, and by the inverse theorem reasoning back to the probability of the truth of the hypotheses.

JEWISH PHILOSOPHY.
  Q.v. Judaism B.

JIVA.
  Q.v. The *Vedas* (1); Jainism (1).

JNANA.
  From the Sanskrit root *jna* ("knowing") (the "j" pronounced as a hard "g"), *jnana* is an episodic knowledge-event which may contribute to *prama* (knowledge in fuller, more usual sense). *Jnana* as specific knowledge events is basic to Nyaya

(*q.v.* 2) and Vaisheshika (*q.v.* 3). This sense is also present in the Buddhist concept in which awareness is one of the constituents of the self (*q.v.* Buddhism, Therayada 4). In relation to salvation (*mokṣa*) the way of *jnana* (*jnana marga*), or knowledge, is one of the three paths to release (*q.v.* Hinduism 5b). One of the four types of Yoga (*q.v.* 5c) is Jnana Yoga.

JOACHIM, H.H.
Q.v. Truth (24).

JOACHIMITES.
Q.v. Joachim of Floris (3).

JOACHIM OF FLORIS. 1145–1202.
Italian mystic theologian. Born in Celico, Calabria. Abbot of the Monastery of Corazzo; founded the Monastery of San Giovanni in Fiore where he also served as abbot. The Order of Floris was approved by Innocent III in 1204.

Principal writings: *Concord of the New and the Old*; *Discourse on the Apocalypse*; *The Ten Stringed Psaltery*; *The Book of Figures*; *On the Articles of Faith*.

(1) Finding three periods in human history—the Age of Law (or the Father), the Age of the Gospel (or the Son), and the Age of the Spirit (or the Holy Ghost)—Joachim held that mankind was then at the initiatory period of the third age which was to begin in 1260.

(2) The third age was to see the purification of the Church, the world triumph of monasticism, and the sabbath day of humanity.

(3) Joachimite ideas spread into the Franciscan order in both Italy and France. Numerous pseudo-Joachimite treatises appeared. Many of them identified the Franciscan order as the harbinger of the third age. Finally, a council held at Arles in 1260 condemned the writings and followers of Joachim.

(4) The promised era provided a suasion over many for centuries. Dante thought enough of Joachim to name him as one of those in Paradise.

JODL, FRIEDRICH. 1849–1914.
German philosopher. Born in Munich. Educated at Munich. Taught at Prague and Vienna. Anti-metaphysical in orientation, he looked upon the task of philosophy as providing a synoptic vision

of the world, based upon the data of the sciences. He argued against phenomenalism and for critical realism (*q.v.*) on the ground that there must be a reality as an object for science. He argued for monism, and a religion of national culture, identifying "God" with human ideals.

Selected writings: *Monism and the Contemporary Problem of Culture*, 1911; *On the True and False Idealism*, 1914; *Critique of Idealism*, 1920.

JOHN DUNS SCOTUS.
Q.v. Duns Scotus, John.

JOHN OF DAMASCUS. c. 675–749.
Christian theologian. Born in Syria. Educated in Damascus. Entered monastic life around 726. A defender of the Orthodox position against a number of heresies, John contributed both method and definition to the Middle Ages. His definitions of Being, Substance, Accident, Essence, Existence, Person, Individual, Nature, and many more, were used by the Scholastics in the 12th and 13th centuries. The final chapter of his systematization of philosophy and theology furnished the model for the *Sentences* of Peter Lombard. This opuscule, titled *On the Orthodox Faith*, was cited frequently by Thomas Aquinas.

Principal writings: *The Fountain of Knowledge*.

JOHN OF JANDUN. c. 1286–c. 1328.
French philosopher. Born in Jandun. Educated at Paris. Taught at Paris. John's chief claim to fame is his collaboration with his colleague at the University of Paris, Marsilius of Padua (*q.v.*), in writing the famed *defensor Pacis*. With Marsilius he sought refuge with Louis of Bavaria when the book was condemned by the papal court; also like Marsilius, he gained preferment when Louis became emperor. His prize was the bishopric of Ferrara. In his own right, however, John was an important follower and interpreter of Averroës. His interpretations of Averroës' commentaries on Aristotle were used for centuries.

Selected writings: Commentaries on Aristotle's *Metaphysics*, *Physics*, *On the Soul*, *De Caelo et mundo*, *Parva naturalia*.

JOHN OF LA ROCHELLE. c. 1190–1245.

Franciscan philosopher. Taught at the University of Paris. A "Summist" of importance, he is credited with authorship of the first and third books of the *Summa of Alexander of Hales* (*q.v.* Alexander of Hales 1).

Principal writings: *Treatise on the Soul and the Virtues; Summa on Vices and Sins; Summa on Gifts; Summa on the Soul.*

JOHN OF MIRECOURT. 14th cent.

A Cistercian whose unpublished commentaries on the Sentences of Peter Lombard (*q.v.*) brought condemnation from the theological faculty of the University of Paris. John was taking the Ockhamist line that there can be no reasoned proof of God's existence, that right and wrong are not objective but depend upon God's arbitrary will, and that evil too is present in the world through the will of God. He held that there are two types of self-evident propositions: those depending upon the principle of contradiction, and those depending upon internal evidence. The proposition that one exists is as strong as any proposition of the absolutely self-evident, or first, category.

JOHN OF SAINT THOMAS. 1589–1647.

Spanish philosopher-theologian. Born in Lisbon. Educated at Coimbra and Louvain. Taught at Alcalá de Henares and Alcalá. Not only is he credited as one of the great Thomistic commentators, but his work in material and formal logic is regarded as important in the development of that subject.

Principal writings: *Philosophy Course; Theology Course.*

JOHN OF SALISBURY. c. 1115–1180.

English philosopher. Born in Salisbury. Educated in France under Abelard, William of Conches, Richard l'Evêque, and Gilbert de la Porrée. He is recognized as one of the principal representatives of the humanistic school of Chartres (*q.v.*). Appointed as secretary to Theobold, Archbishop of Canterbury, he continued as secretary to Thomas Becket when the latter became archbishop in 1161. Under both appointments he was frequently sent on missions of importance; taking an active part in the disputes between Becket and Henry II, he withdrew to France with the former, returned with him in 1170, and was present at his assassination. In 1176 he became Bishop of Chartres. His writings were humanistic in tone, modelled on Cicero; his prose was exceptionally pure. Meliorist and utilitarian in attitude, he combined a mild skepticism concerning the possibilities of human knowledge with acceptance of the truths of faith, just as he combined theory and practice, faith and works. In the controversy over universals (*q.v.* 10–15) he attacked absolute realism, and held a position much like that of Abelard and would seem to have been a conceptualist. He held that genera and species are *figurae rationis* or mental constructions and do not exist as universals in things, although we gain them through abstraction from things, and in the comparison of things.

Principal writings: *Policraticus; Or Concerning the Vain Purposes of Courtiers and the Traditions of Philosophers* (T in part); *Metalogicon* (T); *Historia Pontificalis* (T).

JOHN OF THE CROSS, SAINT. 1542–1592.

Spanish mystic. Member of the Carmelite order and founder (with Saint Teresa, *q.v.*) of the Discalced Carmelites (Barefoot Carmelites) against great opposition. His descriptions of mysticism are regarded as classics. His concept of the dark night of the soul is a description of the despair experienced by the mystic, which he interprets as a means of purgation and purification sent by God.

Principal writings: *The Dark Night of the Soul; Ascent of Mount Carmel.*

JOHN PAUL II, POPE (WOJTYLA, KAROL JOZEF). 1920– .

Born in Wadowice (Poland). Educated at Jagiellonian Univ. (Cracow), and Angelicum (Rome). Taught at universities of Cracow and Lublin. Ordained priest (1946), Cardinal (1967), elected Pope (1978).

Philosophic writings: *The Jeweler's Shop* (T), 1960; *Love and Responsibility* (T), 1960; *Person and Act* (T), 1969 (English title: *The Acting Person*); *The Foundations of Renewal* (T), 1972 (English title: *The Sources of Renewal*).

(1) The writings listed above appeared

prior to Wojtyla's elevation to the papacy. Two of the four are clearly philosophical. The first, described by the author as "a meditation passing on occasion into drama," suggests that existential and transcendental love are related. The latter exercises a providential and salvific function over the former.

(2) The philosophy behind the drama is developed in *Love and Responsibility* on which the argument is made that complete love must possess an ethical character, and matrimony a spiritual dimension. Beyond matrimony, however, is "spiritual virginity," pointing toward eternal union with God. He criticizes the category of "use" in utilitarianism as egoistic, confusing persons with objects.

(3) The third publication, *Person and Act*, is presented as a phenomenal analysis, through Scheler (*q.v.*), of the nature of person, which becomes manifest through action, thereby gaining fulfillment. One also acts "together with others," and the communal action does not negate but supports one's individual action. The commandment of love is regarded as a protection against alienation.

(4) The final treatise was prepared as a study guide to the achievement of the Second Vatican Council; and was published on the tenth anniversary of its inauguration for use in the archdiocese of Cracow.

JOHN SCOTUS ERIGENA.
Q.v. Erigena, John Scotus.

JOHNSON, SAMUEL. 1696–1772.
American philosopher. Born in Guilford, Conn. Educated at New Haven College. Participated in the founding of the University of Pennsylvania, and King's College (Columbia). He served as the first president of the latter institution. An enthusiastic follower of Berkeley, whom he met in Rhode Island.
Principal writings: *Synopsis Philosophiae Naturalis; Logic; Encyclopedia of Philosophy,* 1731; *Elementa Philosophica,* 1752.

JOHNSON, SAMUEL. 1709–1784.
English man of letters.
Q.v. Tragedy (4); Utopia (9).

JOHNSON, W.E. 1858–1931.
English philosopher. Born, was educated, and taught at Cambridge. Among his students were C.D. Broad (*q.v.*) and J.M. Keynes (*q.v.*).
Principal writings: *Logic,* 3 vols., 1921–4; "On Probability," 1932.

(1) Defining logic as the "analysis and criticism of thought," Johnson did not exclude metaphysical considerations from its scope. Distinguishing between implication and inference, he held that the former was hypothetical and the latter categorical, the former resting upon implicative principles of validity and the latter upon applicative principles requiring that the premises be true.

(2) Following the usual distinction between connotation (*q.v.* 4) and denotation (*q.v.*), Johnson pointed out that proper names must be defined ostensively, that they require a connection between an act of pointing and the statement of the name.

(3) In place of the terms "substance" and "accident," he offered the terms "continuant" and "occurrent." Every continuant is, in his analysis, a set of occurrents; but a group of occurrents is a continuant only when characterized by causal unity.

(4) In place of the terms "universal" and particular," he offered "determinable" and "determinant." Abstract nouns, *e.g.,* "color," are determinable while specific attributes, *e.g.,* adjectives such as "red," "blue," "yellow," "green" are determinants.

(5) He regarded inductive inferences as resting on causality and as characterized by probability rather than necessity.

JOIN.
Q.v. Logic of Relations (4).

JOSEPH, H.W.
Q.v. Cook Wilson.

JOUFFROY, THÉODORE. 1796–1842.
French philosopher. Born at Pontets, Doubs. Educated at the École Normale. Taught at the École Normale and the Collège de France. Best known as the French popularizer of the Reid-Stewart "common sense" philosophy whose works he both translated and interpreted.
Principal writings: *The Feelings of the Beautiful and of the Sublime,* 1816; *Philosophical Mélange,* 1833; *Lectures on Natural Right,* 2 vols., 1834–5.

JOURDAIN, P.E.B.
  Q.v. Paradox (3).

**JOURNAL OF SPECULATIVE PHILOS-
OPHY, THE.**
  Q.v. Saint Louis Hegelians; W.T. Harris.

JOYCE, JAMES.
  Q.v. Epiphany (3).

JUDAH IBN GABIROL.
  Q.v. Avicebron.

JUDAISM.
  The religion of the Jewish people, parent religion of both Christianity and Islam. We shall consider Judaism in itself, and in terms of the philosophies developed within its framework.
  A. Religiously, the origin of Judaism is usually traced to a compact between God and Abraham to foster the development of a special people in exchange for their devotion. In fact, this perspective must be associated with the time of the Babylonian exile; at least it was during that period that it was possible to conceive the history of this people as a series of triumphs and defeats, related to their faith and faithlessness in God. And since this view of history is present in the Bible, these are the people of the Book in an unique sense. Be this as it may, the intimate relation of God to the community accounts for the early history of Judaism as presenting an example of theocracy (*q.v.*)
  (1) If we ask for the general philosophical and ethical beliefs characterizing this movement the most outstanding is monotheism, a belief in the absolute and exclusive unity of God. Related to this is the belief that God has revealed Himself to man, that men are responsible for their unrighteousness, that righteousness is the way to salvation, that right will triumph in the world, that it is Israel's divinely appointed task to teach the universal Fatherhood of God, and that justice is measured out in a world to come. The beliefs existed, of course, in a rich matrix of ceremonial and juristic observances, related to the Mosaic law.
  (2) The canon of the Bible was set, it would seem, in response to the emergence of Christianity. The distinction between canonical and apocryphal books is a distinction between the books on whose authority there was agreement, and books whose authority was in dispute. Among the canonical books themselves (the Old Testament from a Christian viewpoint), authority centered in the Books of the Law. (a) The center of Jewish worship and life, then, was the *Torah*, the Mosaic law, comprised in the Pentateuch. The text of the law became fixed in the 5th century, and required interpretation. This was supplied in two further bodies of writing, the *Talmud* and the *Midrash*. (b) The *Talmud* includes the civil and religious laws not present in the *Torah* and explanations and amplifications of the laws of both. The *Talmud* is made up of the *Mishnah*, summing up the oral law from the 5th century B.C. to the 2nd century A.D., and the *Gemara*, which amplifies and explains the *Mishnah*. In another sense the *Talmud* is divisible into the Palestinian *Talmud*, which was completed by the 5th century A.D., (the persecution by Constantine having caused the decay of the Palestinian schools), and the Babylonian *Talmud*, which was completed by the 7th century A.D. (c) The *Midrash* is the body of exegetical material on the Bible which developed between the 4th and 12th centuries A.D. The *Midrash* is made up of the *Halakha*, containing Jewish traditional law and minute precepts not present in the written law; and the *Haggadah* which is made up of free interpretations and especially parables, based on Scripture.
  (3) The importance of the Law for Judaism, and the necessity for new interpretations, called into being a distinctive ecclesiastical structure. (a) The rabbi was both a religious teacher and a civil judge. (b) The priests of the Sanhedrin had both religious and civil power, and at one time the high priest was also head of state. (c) The scribe fixed the text of the Law, and then began the work of its interpretation, determining how tradition required that the Law be carried out. (d) The influential party, the Pharisees, were those willing to apply to their lives the entire tradition of written and oral law.
  (4) If the periods of exile and restoration were marked by the emergence of the written law, and the period of Roman rule and the Diaspora marked Judaism's internal development, then the

fall of the Temple and the beginning of the school of R. Johanan ben Zakkai mark the period of the oral law, the *Talmud*, as well as the final universalizing of Judaism. Through these stages there had come into prominence the doctrines of the survival of the loyal remnant, the coming of the Messiah, the age of universal peace, and the return to Zion. The further development of Judaism involves philosophies as well as priests.

B. The Jewish traditions and institutions have sometimes determined, but usually have only helped to shape, the systems of Jewish philosophers. In addition, some other major philosophical tradition has usually been at work.

(5) In the case of Philo of Alexandria (*q.v.*), 30 B.C.–50 A.D., the goal was to interpret Jewish theology in the terms of Greek philosophy, allegorizing some portions of the Old Testament. Neoplatonic motifs figure prominently in his work.

(6) The writing of Saadia ben Joseph al-Fayyumi (*q.v.*), 892–942, had as its goal the harmony of philosophy and religion; but Saadia's work occurred in the context of the Karaite schism. The Karaites wished a return to the tradition of the *Torah* as sole authority, while Saadia defended the Talmudic and Rabbinic position; this involved a defense of reason.

(7) By the 11th century the philosophical problem concerned the harmony between religious faith and knowledge resting on reason. The center of interest was Spain. Among the Spanish philosophers Bahya ben Joseph ibn Paquda developed a rational theology culminating in an ethic of gratitude to God.

(8) Avicebron (*q.v.*), 1020–1070, born in Málaga, Spain, developed his philosophy without respect to the claims of religion. His work, Neoplatonic in flavor, was often cited by the 13th-century philosophers.

(9) Judah Halevi (*q.v.*), around 1085 to around 1143, born in Toledo, continued the Spanish philosophical tradition. He opposed both the Aristotelian doctrine of the eternity of matter and the Neoplatonic doctrine of emanation. He opposed the Mu'tazilite doctrine of unlimited free will in favor of a limited freedom (the power to do good or evil in matters under one's control). He op-

posed the Karaite group (*cf.* 6 above) in favor of the Rabbinic tradition.

(10) The Ibn Ezra family contributed to philosophy, poetry, grammar, and science. Moses ben Jacob ibn Ezra, born in Granada, *c.* 1070–1138, is more famous for his prayers and poetry than for philosophy. Abraham ben Meir ibn Ezra (*q.v.*), 1092–1167, born in Toledo, became one of the most widely known Jewish scholars of the Middle Ages.

(11) Moses ben Maimon (or Maimonides, *q.v.*), 1135–1204, born in Córdoba, Spain, contributed importantly to the development of Judaism. He supported the claims of both reason and revelation against an encroaching mysticism. He produced a famous philosophical treatise, *Guide For the Perplexed*, and an equally famous compilation, the *Mishnah Torah*, or "second Torah," a systematization of the whole of Judaism, including a thirteen-article creed of the Jewish faith. This famous *halakhic* work (*cf.* 2c, above) retains its value and use to the present day.

(12) Due to his espousal of philosophy and reason, Maimonides was regarded as the protagonist in a dispute with the Cabalists which developed after Maimonides' death. Gnostic mysticism, already present in the *Haggadah*, developed into a revolt against logic, spreading throughout Spain and into Europe. The emphasis was on perfection and self-purification; its instrument was a set of books and practices called the Cabala (*q.v.*).

(13) The dispute between mysticism in the form of the Cabala, and reason as personified by Maimonides, continued until 1305 when a synod at Barcelona banished both secular study and the works of Maimonides. A counter-ban was issued from a synod at Montpellier excommunicating those who prevented anyone from studying science or who abused Maimonides. Since the synods had only local authority, the dispute continued.

(14) One of the great successors to Maimonides was Levi ben Gershon or Gersonides (*q.v.*), 1288–1344. More Aristotelian even than Maimonides, the principle of reason was reflected even more strongly in his work.

(15) Carrying on the opposition to the spirit of rationalism was Hasdai ben Abraham Crescas (*q.v.*), 1340–1410. He

opposed the idea of basing a religious system on Aristotle, and tried to demonstrate the insufficiency of reason, and therefore the necessity for revelation.

(16) The opposition between *Talmud* and Cabala continued in the 17th century, spreading throughout the Jewish communities of Europe and Asia. In reaction to the excesses (especially of the Cabalists), skepticism toward the Judaic tradition appeared here and there. One instance of this was the deism of Uriel da Costa (*q.v.*), 1585–1647. Another was the independence of Spinoza (*q.v.*), 1632–1677, who believed Judaism should have ended with the destruction of the Temple (*cf.* 4 above). Spinoza's philosophy, nonetheless, had deep roots in Jewish thought, and continues to exert an influence over individual Jewish thinkers.

(17) Another reaction to this dispute was actualized in the life of Moses Mendelssohn (*q.v.*), 1729–1786. Convinced that Judaism requires conformity to ceremonial law while tolerating complete liberty of opinion, Mendelssohn worked very productively as a rabbi within the Jewish community, and as a philosopher and writer within the German nation.

(18) The Reform movement in Judaism was the product of the European Enlightenment. Its stress was on reason. The liturgy was revised, the service conducted in the vernacular, and emphasis was given to the scientific interpretation of Scripture and the Oral Law.

(19) The 18th-and 19th-century mystical movement of Hasidism (*q.v.*) influenced many aspects of Jewish culture, especially in the humanities. The 20th-century mystical philosopher, Martin Buber (*q.v.*), is a product of this movement.

(20) In the second half of the 19th century, Hermann Cohen (*q.v.*) established the Marburg School of neo-Kantianism. His student, Franz Rosenzweig, 1886–1929, who collaborated with Buber on a new German translation of the Hebrew Bible, developed a position of religious existentialism.

JUDGMENT.

From the Latin *jus* ("right") and *dicere* ("to determine or say"). The current usage of the term is roughly synonymous to "proposition" (*q.v.*).

(1) As Aristotle used his terms in *De Interpretatione*, a proposition is a significant assertion, either true or false, resulting from a judgment. And when he spoke of the relations of opposition among significant assertions it was of contradiction and contrariety among "propositions," for example.

(2) Thomas Aquinas, holding that "truth resides in the intellect composing and dividing," holding further that judgment is the act of composing and dividing, made judgment the basic unit of knowledge.

(3) The Port Royal logic holds: "We call judging that activity by which our mind, joining various ideas together, affirms that the one is the other, as for example when I have the idea of earth and of round, I affirm that the earth is round or deny that it is round."

(4) Kant. (*q.v.* 1, 9), more than any other Western thinker, made judgment central to his philosophy. Kant asked if synthetic *a priori* judgments were possible, and now to pose the question another way (putting "propositions" for "judgments") sounds inappropriate. For Kant the employment of the mind in judging is indispensable to the construction of the phenomenal world. Further, it is the faculty of judgment from which one derives the aesthetic judgment of beauty and the teleological judgment of purposiveness in nature.

JUDGMENTS, TERMINATING.

Q.v. C.I. Lewis (3).

JUHOS, BÉLA. 1901–71.

Austrian philosopher. Born in Vienna. Educated at the University of Vienna. A member of the Vienna Circle (*q.v.*), publishing eight books on epistemology, logic, and philosophy of physics between 1928 and 1970. A selection of his articles, published between 1931 and 1971, is now in English translation. Juhos distinguished between the logical function of language, which relates to natural events, and its metaphysical function, relating to valuative events. The latter function is rhetorical, rather than logical, and features "sham propositions" which trigger the value experiences which the metaphysician seeks to induce, and to present as "true knowledge."

Selected writings: *Selected Papers on*

Epistemology and Physics (T), ed., G. Frey, 1976.

JULIA, GASTON.
Q.v. Chaos Theory.

JUNG, CARL GUSTAV. 1875–1961.
Swiss psychoanalyst. Born in Kesswil. The son of a Protestant clergyman he first contemplated archaeology; then shifted to medicine. He received his medical degree from Basel in 1912. He joined a psychiatric clinic at the University of Zurich. Along with Freud and Adler, he is regarded as one of the founders of psychoanalytic theory. Breaking with Freud in 1913, Jung pursued a theory more oriented toward the symbolic aspects of human culture. He called the discipline Analytic Psychology. The insights of his private practice in Zurich have found expression in many influential works. Beginning in 1932, he was Professor of Psychiatry at the Federal Polytechnical University in Zurich.

Principal writings: Jung's first publication was in 1912. Beginning in the 1950's the Bollingen Foundation published his work in translation in the following 18 volumes. We have indicated the dates of original publication only where the conditions of American publication have not substantially altered title or contents (*i.e.*, combining in one volume two or more pieces published separately in German): *Psychiatric Studies; Experimental Researches; Psychogenesis in Mental Disease; Freud and Psychoanalysis; Symbols of Transformation* (T), 1912; *Psychological Types* (T), 1921; *Two Essays on Analytical Psychology* (T); *The Structure and Dynamics of the Psyche; Psychology and Religion* (E), 1940; *Psychology and Alchemy* (T), 1944; *Archetypes and the Collective Unconscious* (T), 1950; *Aion; Contributions to the Symbolism of the Self* (T), 1951; *Civilization in Transition; Alchemical Studies; Mysterium Coniunctionis* (T), 1955–6; *The Spirit in Man, Art, and Literature; The Practice of Psychotherapy; The Development of Personality.* In addition, his autobiography) *Memories, Dreams, Reflections* (T), 1973; and vol. 18 of the Bollingen series, *The Symbolic Life, Miscellaneous Writings,* 1976.

(1) Although best known for his distinction between introvert and extravert personality types, Jung's most impressive contribution to human thought consists in discovering a relationship between the patterns of the collective unconscious (present, he believed, in all human beings) its patterns (called archetypes), and the archetypal representations infused in myth, religion, and art.

(2) The archetypal patterns—*mandalas* and their constituents—provide the material for an interesting analysis of human nature. In this analysis the individual is viewed as a plurality of psychic forces, both conscious and unconscious, which sometimes block each other, but which may be mutually reinforcing. The concept of projection is used to help explain the relation of the individual to his or her world.

(3) On the conscious level, the individual consists of an Ego determining the conditions of life, and a *Persona*, appearing before the world in a certain manner.

(4) The male ego will have an archetypal *anima* to project upon the world; the female ego will have an *animus* archetype. Love consists of a double projection, each possessing the other's *animus/anima*. Love is, hence, both blind and idealistic.

(5) Another archetypal projection Jung calls the Shadow. This is a negative principle, corresponding in some respects to the Freudian death wish. In projection it exemplifies a hidden wish toward self-injury, and explains the misfortunes we bring upon ourselves.

(6) Finally, there is the projection of the Self, an archetypal ideal of our developed nature. This in some sense includes the other archetypes, and supposes their having been successfully integrated. The increase of energy which sometimes occurs through religious conversion is a sign that integration of these forces is possible.

(7) In addition to the archetypes mentioned are pictorial elements of the unconscious, such as the snake, the sun, the star, and above all the *mandala*, a symbol of the sought-for unity of self in which the parts are held together in a unity of the whole, *e.g.*, the rose window of the medieval cathedral, and the pictographs of Eastern religions.

(8) Since *mandalas* typically have four parts, Jung believes that quaternity—

rather than trinity—is the symbol of wholeness. But whichever is the case, the symbol results from archetypal projection; and however the rest may be spelled out, God the Father is the projection of the ideal self.

(9) Much of Jung's published work is designed to demonstrate the extent to which human culture, East and West, is infused with archetypal patterns. Since he believes that the basic archetypes have a semi-autonomous life within us, we must respond in some manner to their claims. Coming to know the extent of one's cultural preoccupation with the archetypes is one aspect of Jung's therapy. His final object is, then, not metaphysics or the philosophy of human nature, but the cure of souls.

JUNGIUS, JOACHIM. 1587–1656.

German philosopher. Born in Lübeck. Educated at Rostock, Giessen, Padua. Taught at Rostock and Helmstedt. The first important representative in Germany of the new Galilean science, philosophically he was a mechanist. Jungius' most significant contribution was his treatise on logic.

Principal writings: *The Hamburg Logic*, 1638.

JUS CIVILE.
Latin phrase meaning "Civil Law."

JUS DIVINUM.
Latin phrase meaning "Divine or Eternal Law."

JUS GENTIUM.
Latin phrase meaning "Law of Nations" (*q.v.* Stoicism 4; Vitoria 3).

JUS NATURALE.
Latin phrase meaning "Natural Law" (*q.v.* Stoicism 4).

For references on the use of the four phrases *q.v.* Natural Law (2–5); Aquinas (9); Grotius (4).

JUSTICE.
From the Latin *jus* ("right" or "law"). In philosophy, the most influential analyses of the term were given by Plato and Aristotle.

(1) The context for Plato's analysis was set by the Sophists (*q.v.* 3, 6–8) who contrasted natural and conventional justice,

usually preferring the former. Thrasymachus (*q.v.*) defined Justice as the "interest of the stronger."

(2) Plato (*q.v.* 5b–c) moved beyond the natural-conventional dichotomy, viewing justice in functional terms as the supreme virtue of the state, referring to the condition in which everyone is having and doing what is one's own, and not interfering in that which is another's.

(3) Aristotle (*q.v.* 11) held justice to be a mean between the injustice of interfering with what belongs to another, and suffering interference one's self. He distinguished between two forms of justice: distributive—one's just share of the resources of the state; and retributive—the redress of injury.

(4) Aquinas (*q.v.* 8) and Locke (*q.v.* 9c) agree that there is a natural and rational order, identifiable with equity or justice, discernible through the exercise of reason.

JUSTIFICATIO ACTIONIS.
Q.v. Feigl (3).

JUSTIFICATIO COGNITIONIS.
Q.v. Feigl (3).

JUSTIFICATION, LOGIC OF.
Q.v. Logic of Discovery.

JUSTIFICATION BY FAITH.
In Christianity, the problem of how one is absolved, or acquitted, of one's past actions, or how one acquires one's new being as a Christian.

(1) Paul (*q.v.* 1) in *Galations* and *Romans* contrasts justification by law with justification by faith. The former is justification through obedience and is, strictly speaking, impossible; the latter is justification through Christ, and leads to a new being.

(2) In St. Augustine (*q.v.* 11) the doctrine of justification occurs by means of grace, originating in God but infused through sacramental channels. St. Thomas Aquinas (*q.v.* 8) takes the same view, holding that justifying grace is the foundation of the qualities of faith, hope, and love.

(3) Luther (*q.v.*) proclaimed the Pauline doctrine of "justification by faith" the cardinal doctrine of Christianity.

(4) The doctrine is also to be found in

the movement of the Moravian Brethren, presided over by Zinzendorf (*q.v.*), and in Methodism. John Wesley (*q.v.*) came upon the doctrine both in Luther and in contacts with the Moravian group.

JUSTIN MARTYR. c. 105–c. 165.
Christian Apologist. Born at Flavius Neapolis, Samaria. Through study of the Pythagorean, Platonist, Peripatetic, and Stoic philosophies he became convinced the complete truth lay elsewhere. Converted to Christianity in Ephesus he continued lecturing as a philosopher, particularly in Rome, to bring educated pagans to Christ through philosophy. Suffered martyrdom between 163 and 167.
Principal writings: *Apology; Dialogue with Trypho.*
(1) Greek philosophy was a preparation for the truth which is exemplified by Christianity. The Greek doctrines are not untrue but partial, and therefore insufficient. Indeed, the Divine *Logos* had illumined the Greeks, enabling them to sense the partial truth which exists wholly in the incarnate wisdom, Christ.
(2) The truth of Christianity is attested to by the manner in which prophecies more ancient than Greek philosophy have been fulfilled in the new dispensation, by the moral excellence of its doctrines, and by its good effects upon believers.
Q.v. Apologists (3).

KABBALA.
Q.v. Cabala.

KABIR.
Q.v. Hinduism (5c).

KADDISH.
An Aramaic term meaning "holy." A Jewish prayer with the same opening phrases as the Lord's Prayer. Since the Middle Ages the mourner's declaration of faith.

KAFIR.
An Arabic term meaning "infidel." A term applied by Moslems to all unbelievers.

KAIBARA EKKEN. 1630–1714.
Japanese philosopher. Born in Fukuoka. Educated at Kyoto. A neo-Confucianist, he disagreed with Chu Hsi (*q.v.*), stressing cosmic love as ultimate, and thus increasing the cosmic interpretation of *jen*. Principal writings: *The Great Doubt; The Great Learning for Women.*

KAIROS.
A Greek term meaning "due measure," "right proportion." With respect to place "the right spot." Concerning time "the right time for action," "the critical moment."
(1) The temporal meaning was employed by Jesus (*q.v.* 1) in announcing the kingdom of God: "the *kairos* is fulfilled, and the kingdom of God is at hand; repent and believe in the gospel" (Mk 1:15). The sense is that time has moved through a series of steps and has arrived at a critical juncture. At this juncture it is everyone's urgent responsibility to repent and participate in establishing the kingdom.
(2) When used as critical juncture elsewhere in the New Testament, *kairos* takes on a somewhat different meaning. The *kairos* is in act, but the kingdom will fully arrive only after the second coming of Christ and the final judgment. In the interim one must live with kingdom qualities. This is the plan for "the fullness of time," set forth by God to which Paul refers in Ephesians 1:10 and elsewhere.
(3) For Paul Tillich (*q.v.* 7), who made the term central to his own Christology (*q.v.*) in the 1920's, *kairos* signifies a qualitative shift in time where the more usual Greek term for time, *chronos*, is quantitative. Centering the "great *kairos*" in Jesus' proclamation of the kingdom, as in (1), he eternalizes the moment in which the critical juncture occurs, somewhat as in (2). The great *kairos* of Jesus' proclamation "established the center of history once and for all." Derivative *kairoi* appear whenever religious groups and individuals experience "existential encounters" with the great *kairos*. Such encounters may take place at any chronological time, resulting in "new being" for the individuals and groups concerned.

KALAMUKHAS.
Q.v. Vaiṣnavism (3).

KALI.

Hindu divinity. Pre-Aryan goddess, probably of vegetation and agriculture; therefore, judging from the animal and human sacrifice following in her train, a fertility goddess. The human sacrifice has been banned, yet occasional reports of its occurrence still surface. The animal sacrifice continues. Consort of the god Shiva (*q.v.*), she is known under many names: Kala, Durga, Shakti, Sati, Uma, Parvati. Wearing a necklace of skulls, she greets her devotees with open mouth and protruding fang-like teeth; as Kundalini she is the serpent-power rising from the sexual organs to the crown of the head where the piercing of the thousand-petaled lotus can bring the practitioner of Kundalini Yoga (*q.v.* Yoga 10) to Nirvana. *Q.v.* Śakti, Vaiṣṇavism (4a).

KALLEN, HORACE.

Q.v. Naturalism (5).

KAMA.

From Sanskrit, "desire," "pleasure," "longing." Linked to Agni ("fire" and the god of fire) and also Vishnu, the solar god and literal source of heat, *kama* as the heat of sexual desire is to be contrasted with the heat generated by ascetic practices (*tapas*). One of the four Hindu Aims of Life (*q.v. Puruṣarthas*) *Kama* is also appropriate to the householder stage of the *ashramas* (*q.v.* 2, 3). Pleasure as a value was personified in Kama as a Hindu god, who played a role like that of Cupid in the affairs of both gods and humans. *Q.v. Kama Sutra.*

KAMA SUTRA.

The earliest and best known of numerous Hindu manuals on sexual love, the *Kama Sutra* probably dates from the 3rd or 4th century A.D. Its author (compiler) was Vatsyayana who utilized numerous earlier texts. Treating *kama* as one of the three Aims of Life (before *moksha* appeared), the author takes it upon himself to provide instruction on achieving sexual pleasure. *Kama* at that time stood on an equal footing with *dharma* and *artha* (*q.v. Puruṣarthas*). *Kama* is to be practiced for progeny in the third *ashrama* (*q.v.*), as a householder, as well as for sheer pleasure, and the *sutra* is to be studied by women as well as by men. The penchant

for detailed classification anticipates contemporary manuals on the subject, and the Hindu *sutra* is perhaps somewhat more graphic.

KANADA.

Q.v. Vaiśeṣika.

KANGER, STIG.

Q.v. Modal Logic (8).

K'ANG YU-WEI. 1858–1927.

Chinese philosopher. A native of Kwangtung. A neo-Confucian he obtained the "Presented Scholar" degree in Peking in 1891. From 1888 until near the end of his life, K'ang was active in programs of reform. In 1898 with the aid of the emperor he engineered the Hundred Days Reform. Many edicts were passed urging wholesale reform but the movement collapsed and K'ang went into exile for 16 years, traveling throughout the world. He returned to China in 1912 when the Republic was established. In 1914 he advocated Confucianism as the state religion of China. In 1917 and 1924 he attempted to restore the deposed emperor Hsüan-T'ung.

Principal writings: *Book of Great Unity* (T), 1935.

(1) History evolves through three ages with three rotating phases in each. The ages, attributed to Confucius, are: (a) the age of disorder; (b) the age of rising peace; (c) the age of great unity. Not only are there cycles of order and disorder within this evolutionary movement; there are series of subcycles within subcycles within subcycles. Confucius was born in the age of disorder; we are now in the age of rising peace; the age of great unity lies ahead.

(2) Man's life is largely a life of suffering. Suffering has its source in states, class distinction, racial distinction, distinction of inequality between the sexes, distinction between families, occupational distinctions, unreasonable and unjust systems, distinction between species, distinctions of suffering giving rise to other suffering.

(3) In the period of great unity these sources of suffering will be overcome so that the whole world will become a unity—one race, one family, love among all sentient beings, equality.

(4) Because there must be harmony

between one's acts and the age in which one lives, one cannot now act as one would in the period of great unity, nor could one in the days of disorder. Similarly, it causes great harm in the age of rising peace to act in terms of the age of disorder.

(5) And yet the appropriate underlying value in these matters is humanity (*jen*), and humanity means not being able to bear the sufferings of others. This is the power which brings the great unity.

(6) The principle of humanity is also the power of attraction in the universe, and is somehow involved with the forces of electricity and with the ether.

KANT, IMMANUEL. 1724–1804.

German philosopher. Born in Königsberg, a center of German pietism. In his early years, especially through his mother, Kant felt the influence of this movement. Educated at the University of Königsberg where he later taught, becoming professor of logic and metaphysics. For nine years a private tutor, he received his doctorate and became *privatdozent* in 1755. In that year he published his *Natural History and Theory of the Heavens*, advancing the nebular hypothesis forty-one years before Laplace. He remained in this position fifteen years, refusing offers of positions elsewhere. In 1770 he received his professorship and eleven years later the *Critique of Pure Reason* appeared. Within a few years the Kantian system was being taught and discussed in all of the leading German universities, and Königsberg became a shrine for young philosophers.

Probably because of a frail constitution he spent his entire life in Königsberg, arranging his existence in an extremely orderly way. He arose at five each morning, studied for two hours, then gave his two hours of lectures, and returned to his studies until one; at one he would dine, changing his restaurant frequently to avoid the crowds of strangers who came to catch a glimpse of him. In the afternoon he would walk for an hour. He would spend the evening in light reading after devoting an hour or two to the preparation of his lectures for the next day, and retire by nine or ten in the evening. His servant said that in 30 years Kant never failed to rise at five; it was claimed that townspeople would set their clocks according to the time Kant passed their houses in his daily walk.

Only a few men in the history of philosophy have written as significantly as Immanuel Kant.

Principal writings: *Dissertation concerning the Form and Principles of the Sensible and Intelligible Worlds* (T), 1770; *Critique of Pure Reason* (T), 1781; *Prolegomena to any Future Metaphysics* (T), 1783; *Idea of a Universal History* (T), 1784; *Foundations of the Metaphysics of Morals* (T), 1785; *Metaphysical Principles of Natural Science* (T), 1786; "On the Employment of Teleological Principles in Philosophy," 1788; *Critique of Practical Reason* (T), 1788; *Critique of Judgment* (T), 1790; *Religion within the Limits of Reason Alone* (T), 1793; *Perpetual Peace* (T), 1795: *Metaphysics of Morals* (T), 1797; *Contest of the Faculties*, 1798; *A Pragmatic View of Anthropology*, 1798.

(1) Trained in Leibnizian philosophy, as diffracted through the mind of Christian Wolff, it was not until Hume had roused him from his "dogmatic slumber" that Kant posed the question which led to his original work in philosophy: "How are synthetic *a priori* judgments possible?" Philosophical literature, at least since Leibniz, had contained the distinction between analytic and synthetic, *a priori* and *a posteriori*, judgments. An analytic judgment is one whose predicate merely asserts a characteristic already implicit in the subject, *e.g.*, "All bachelors are unmarried." The assertion follows necessarily from the meaning assigned the term "bachelor." One has this information without looking about the world. The predicate of a synthetic judgment, on the other hand, conveys an idea not implicit in the subject, adding something to the subject. "All books in my case are paperbacks," would be an instance of this kind of judgment. We must look about the world to be able truly to assert such predicates. Analytic judgments are *a priori* in the sense that we know their truth or falsity prior to experience—apart from, or without experience. Synthetic judgments are *a posteriori* in the sense that we know their truth or falsity only after experience—by means of, and through, experience. If we put the expected relations side by side the meaning of Kant's question becomes clear:

| Analytic | *A Priori* |
| Synthetic | *A Posteriori* |

The strength of analytic judgments lies in their necessity, and the weakness of such judgments in that they tell us nothing new. The strength of synthetic judgments lies in their ability to tell us something new; and the weakness of such judgments in their having no necessity.

If we could have judgments providing us with both information and necessity, we should have the best of both worlds. These would be synthetic *a priori* judgments, combining the strengths of synthetic and analytic judgments. Kant did not ask *if* synthetic *a priori* judgments are possible, but *how* they are possible, because he thought he had discovered, in science, judgments which were both informative and necessary: *e.g.*, "7 + 5 = 12," "a straight line is the shortest distance between two points," "in all changes of the physical world the quantity of matter remains unchanged," "in all communication of motion, action and reaction must always be equal."

(2) He comes at the answer to this question by means of a point of view which he regarded as the philosophical equivalent of the Copernican revolution. Copernicus discovered that part of the apparent motion of the planets is due to the motion of the observer. In the same way part of the apparent nature of reality may be due to the nature of the observer.

tion of it is asking, "How does it appear when it doesn't appear?" The question may not even be intelligible. In short, then, we are to give up the attempt to move in thought from the way things appear to the way they are, substituting the more modest goal of moving from the way they do appear to the way they will appear; since we do contribute to experience certain of its features, we can expect our experience to be predictable.

(3) To the raw data of sensation we contribute the forms of space and time. Indeed, Kant holds that space is the form of the external sense, and time the form of the internal sense. We never experience anything except it be in space or time; and yet we never experience space or time. Hence the space and time in which we order phenomena must come not from sensation but from ourselves. From this situation we get certain Axioms of Intuition, such as that all our intuitions are of extensive magnitudes. To the manifold of sense we contribute not only space and time, but structural elements of a conceptual nature. The categories in which we think the world come from the structure of our understanding. Everything sensed and understood has quality, quantity, relation, and modality; and the 12 basic categories are set forth under these terms (*cf.* box).

Quantity	Quality	Relation	Modality
Unity	Positive	Substance-Accident	Possibility-Impossibility
Plurality	Negative	Cause-Effect	Actuality-Non-actuality
Totality	Limited	Reciprocity or Community	Necessity-Contingency

What we know will then be a mixture of physical nature and human nature. Kant accepted this conclusion, and named what we know "phenomena," a blend of two realities (*i.e.*, *noumena*), the noumenal world, and my noumenal self. But though the *noumena* are there, it is hopeless to try to know them directly. We know only a phenomenal blend of noumenal realities. He defined nature as: The sum total of phenomena insofar as they are connected with each other throughout. Notice that nature belongs to the phenomenal order, and that the noumenal order lies behind it. A Kantian synonym for *noumenon* is *Ding an Sich*. Asking what the world is like apart from our observa-

He finds four sets of principles corresponding to the sets of terms. They are: Quantity—Axioms of intuition; Quality—Anticipations of perception; Relation—Analogies of experience; and Modality—Postulates of empirical thought. It is not possible in a brief account to go into all of these sets of principles; but the sort of thing Kant has in mind may become clear through discussion of the third set, termed "Analogies of experience." It may be worth noticing that Kant has gotten these categories out of ordinary logic, and the three sets of terms under "Relation" are derived respectively from categorical propositions with a subject-predicate structure, hypothetical propositions with an if-then structure, and disjunctive propositions with an either-or structure. The principle relating to causality is that it is necessary for humans to view the world in causal terms. The principle relating to reciprocity extends the idea of causal interaction to a community of interacting substances. Similarly, categories of modality derive from the modes of our judgments. When our judgments concern what may be, they are *problematic*. When they concern what is, they are *assertoric*. When they concern what must be, they are *apodeictic*. There are, of course, corresponding negative modes as well, the two sides yielding the categories of possibility-impossibility, actuality-non-actuality, necessity-non-necessity. In formal terms, the possible satisfies the formal conditions of experience; the actual satisfies the material condition of experience (*i.e.*, sensation); the necessary satisfies the universal conditions of experience. His point is that we have no alternative to casting our experiences into these forms and according to these principles. Indeed he calls his philosophy "architectonic" because it follows the general plan of developing a set of categories derived from logic.

(4) Knowledge, then, must be understood as a product of both sense and understanding. Kant points out that "thoughts without content are empty; and intuitions without concepts are blind." But the ideas we contribute to experience are regulative concepts only, having no applicability beyond the reach of possible experience. The attempt to extend our ideas beyond experience, called by Kant "dialectic," leads to contradiction. Kant lists four Antinomies of Reason which fit this description, where the mind, in taking one position is forced by compelling reasons to shift to its opposite: (a) The world has a beginning in time, and is limited with regard to space. (b) Everything compound consists of simple parts, and nothing exists anywhere but the simple, or what is composed of it. (c) There is freedom in the world, and not everything takes place according to the laws of nature. (d) There exists an absolutely necessary Being belonging to the world either as a part of it, or as the cause of it. And when one shifts to the opposite

position there are equally compelling reasons for shifting back again. Hence neither of the positions will do. The corrective to this situation lies, of course, in refraining from posing questions whose answers would require our going beyond possible experience. This corrective consists in regarding ideas as regulative principles.

(5) The fourth antinomy suggests Kant's treatment of the traditional arguments for God. Dividing these arguments into Cosmological, Physico-Theological, and Ontological, Kant argues that the former two arguments depend on the latter, and that the latter argument is not valid: (a) The Cosmological Argument, also called the argument from the contingency of the world, has the structure, "If there exists anything, there must exist an absolutely necessary Being. I, at least, exist: therefore there exists an absolutely necessary Being." Transition to the idea of such a being on the ground of the necessity of everything having a cause and the impossibility of there being an infinite series of causes, uses ideas not as regulative principles but as constitutive principles (*cf.* 4 above). (b) The Physico-Theological argument concludes from order, beauty, and fitness of the world to a sublime and wise intelligence as its cause. But Kant objects that this argument can reach the idea of a supreme being as other than simply a very great being only by using the cosmological argument which in turn uses the ontological argument. (c) The Ontological Argument holds that to deny the existence of the most real Being (*ens realissimum*) is to utter a contradiction. Kant argues that this follows only if existence is taken to be a predicate, property, or characteristic similar to all others, as *e.g.*, whiteness; but "Being is evidently not a real predicate, or a concept of something, that can be added to the concept of a thing." A hundred real dollars contains not one penny more than a hundred possible dollars; the dollars are not at all increased by the existence which is outside the concept. Since existence is not a real predicate, one can deny the existence even of the most real Being without contradiction. The only argument for God he approved was a moral argument, and it rested on the Practical Reason

since morality finally requires that God exist.

(6) Under Transcendental Dialectic, Kant had discussed what he called the Transcendental Paralogisms (or "fallacies"). He also called them the Paralogisms of Pure Reasoning, or simply the Psychological Paralogism. Under whatever name, he was concerned to show that the "I think" which accompanies all of our judgments does not imply the existence of a substantial self or soul, which is simple rather than composite, possessed of continuing personal identity, and capable of existing apart from the body. Each of these conclusions of rational psychology is fallacious. Yet, when he comes to his ethics it seems that human identity is more than a mere place-marker. For example, he distinguishes between the autonomous and heteronymous will, the first acting from an inner principle, the second from an external principle. The will as autonomous reflects the noumenal itself, and is capable of operating without taking account of desires or inclinations. Our sense of obligation derives from this source and indeed Kant constructs his ethics out of the related ideas of "duty," "respect," "the idea of law," the idea of a categorical imperative as opposed to hypothetical imperatives, and the belief that the only thing in the world altogether good is the good (because autonomous) will. The view would today be called a deontological ethics. By "hypothetical imperative" Kant meant an action which would allow one to reach a certain end. One reaches some ends by acting prudently, and others through exercising certain skills; among the hypotheticals there exist technical and prudential imperatives. They have the same form: "If you want to achieve y, do x." Prudence is itself "skill in the choice of means to one's own greatest well being." In addition to hypothetical imperatives there exists an imperative without condition. (a) Kant called it the Categorical Imperative, and this is where ethics appears. Although he expressed this imperative in many ways, most of the expressions are very similar: *Act as if the maxim of thy act were to become by thy will a universal law of nature.* Whatever else might be excluded by this rule, Kant clearly meant to ex-

clude all actions devoid of integrity, forcing one into duplicity, or inner inconsistency. The paradigm case of unethical behavior from this standpoint is the lie. The lie is an instance of duplicity; it throws one into an essential inconsistency. The nature of a lie requires one to except oneself from the principle one's act requires of others. The only way to universalize behavior in this situation is to eliminate the lie. For this reason the imperative might be stated: "Do not except yourself from the principle your act requires of others" (although Kant did not do so). (b) A second manner of expressing the same rule Kant called the Practical Imperative: *Treat every man as an end in himself and never as a means only.* In other words, never use another as an instrument. (c) Out of these two conceptions comes the view of society as a realm of ends, where all are participating in the construction of universal lawfulness. Such participation means that one is sovereign, as well as subject, in the realm of ends, which is the good society. (If this is stated as an imperative, "Recognize that everyone is sovereign as well as subject..." etc., it can be seen as a Cultural Imperative, requiring equal rights, and leading from ethics into social philosophy. The third imperative is implicit in Kant's view but not clearly stated.)

(7) All of this relates to the claim that the only unqualifiedly good thing in the world is the good will. And a will is good if it follows the principles of autonomy, that is, if it takes its law from itself alone; that means following the above-named principles. Such a will is autonomous. If the will takes its principle from outside itself it is heteronomous; it sacrifices both authentic ethics, and its own freedom. Kant argues that human reason is able to sense the unconditional authority of the ethical law; and human will to reject all alternatives incompatible with this. Virtue, indeed, is defined as duties "firmly settled in the character."

(8) In philosophy of religion, beginning with the natural realm of fact, and the intelligible realm of the good, he posits a divine order capable of harmonizing these results of the theoretical and practical reason. In fact, for Kant the ideas of God, freedom, and immortality are Postulates of Practical Reason. It is never

altogether clear, however, that God is to be distinguished from the moral law itself except in this sense: the virtuous man deserves to be happy; and only God can remove the incommensurability which exists in this world between virtue and happiness. At the same time his effort is directed toward confining religion within the bounds of reason alone.

(9) Kant's position on aesthetics is less definitive, internally and externally, than his published positions on the status of human knowledge and of ethics; and yet his work in this area has turned aesthetic theory in a new direction. Kant approaches aesthetics through the aesthetic judgment; and this is a judgment which gives no information, is not connected with desires, and is possessed of no more than subjective universality. Kant theorizes that the aesthetic judgment derives from a harmonizing of the aesthetic object with our faculties of will and understanding; that in this cognition our faculties harmonize with each other; and that this interadaptation is pleasing; when the form of the object is adapted to our faculties, we experience the beautiful. When, instead, our faculties must adapt to the object, due to its force or greatness, what we then experience is the sublime. Comparably, aesthetic creation is the product not of rule but of genius.

(10) His social philosophy supports the social contract as a regulative idea leading to the rule of law. In *Perpetual Peace*, Kant argued that if each person is participant in a process developing a universal legislation, human political organization must reflect this fact; and a form beyond the nation is required. His conception heralded the formation of a "universal union of states" in a "permanent congress of nations."

(11) Thus far we have discussed Kant in terms of the problems he faced, and have paid relatively little attention to the systematic unity of his thought. (a) Kant divides intellect into the faculties of sensibility (*Sinnlichkeit*) and thought (*Denken*). The former involves perception, *i.e.*, awareness accompanied by sensation (the content of sensuous intuition) and leads to the space-time schemata ordering the manifold of sense. This is treated in the Transcendental Aesthetic. (b) Thought divides into understanding (*Verstand*),

judgment (*Urtheilskraft*) and reason (*Vernunft*). From understanding or *Verstand* come the Categories. This is treated in the Transcendental Analytic. (c) The minister of the *Verstand* is the *Einbildungskraft*, or imagination. It is both productive and reproductive, but ultimately creative since it requires the materials of sensibility to function. Mediating between sensibility and understanding, the imagination provides the schema of, *e.g.*, quantity, reality, substance, causality, and reciprocity. (d) But the connectedness of experience is due to the transcendental unity of apperception. This is the presence of the *Ich denke* or "I think" in every datum of experience, connecting the parts and guaranteeing connection in the future. But the *Ich denke* represents nothing more than "A transcendental subject of thought = X, which is known only through the thoughts that are its predicates." Empirical apperception denotes this unity in relation to the empirical ego. Transcendental apperception denotes the same thing in relation to the transcendental ego. (e) In this connection, transcendental means not derived from experience but presupposed by experience. The term has a similar meaning in "Transcendental Aesthetic" and "Transcendental Logic." (f) When we come to the antinomies of *The Critique of Pure Reason* (*cf.* 4 above), thought is pressing beyond Understanding and toward Reason (*Vernunft*): that is to say, thought is calling for a completeness which goes beyond the space-time schemata, beyond the phenomenal world. The *Vernunft* is a power to systematize into unity on the basis of the most inclusive principles. That most inclusive standpoint involves the Ideas of Reason—God, freedom, and immortality (in contrast to the categories of the understanding, *cf.* 3 above). The *Critique of Practical Reason* works out this standpoint; it turns out that the ideas of reason are practically warranted although not theoretically demonstrable. (g) Finally, since *Verstand* gives us the conception of nature, and *Vernunft* gives us the conception of ultimate ends, the two together require the idea of end in nature. This is Judgment (*Urtheilskraft*). When the adaptation of nature to reason is subjective, one has the field of aesthetics. When the adaptation is objective or logical, one has a teleological view of nature, that is, nature as including organic life. These views are developed in *The Critique of Judgment*.

KAPALIKAS.
   Q.v. Vaiṣṇavism (3c).

KAPILA.
   Q.v. Sankhya; Hinduism (6b).

KAPLAN, DAVID.
   Q.v. Quantifying In (3).

KARAITES.
   Hebrew term meaning "Reader of Scriptures." The term applies to a Jewish sect, centering in Babylon, rising in the 8th century A.D. The group repudiated the *Talmud* and accepted the Old Testament as sole authority. The movement, flourishing between the 9th and 12th centuries, stimulated defenses of the Talmudic tradition by the Rabbinic group. The sect still continues but with little influence. *Q.v.* Judaism (6).

KARMA.
   From the Sanskrit *kri* meaning "deed" or "action." The structure of one's life as resulting from one's prior actions in earlier existences. The view, then, requires reincarnation or metempsychosis as its complement.
   (1) In Hinduism (*q.v.* 5a; Yoga 8) *karma* (*karma vidhi* or *karma marga*) is "the way of works." The object of works is to deal with the fact that the soul or self transmigrates, carrying its burden of *karma*, or effects.
   (2) In Jainism (*q.v.* 2, 3), *karma* characterizes reality even down to the atomic level, and the concept of "karmic matter" is central.
   (3) The schools of Theravada (Hinayana) Buddhism (*q.v.*), believing in *karma* but not a transmigrating soul, have exercised considerable ingenuity in explaining the transfer of one without the other.
   (4) In any case the figure widely used for the cycle of rebirth in Buddhism is *bhavacakra* (Skt., "the wheel of becoming"), sometimes depicted with five spokes, representing rebirth destinations in hell, animals, ghosts and men, the hub representing the three evil dispositions, and the rim the twelve causal links of De-

pendent Origination (*q.v.* Buddha 2).
   (5) Although a number of Western philosophers and thinkers have expressed belief in reincarnation—*e.g.*, the Pythagoreans, Plato, the Cabalists (*q.v.* Cabala 1)—the notion of *karma* has not often been explicitly analyzed. In Eastern terms the problem of salvation is to use up in this existence the *karma* one has accumulated without creating further effects.

KARUNA.
   From Sanskrit, "compassion." One of the Four Immeasurable Attitudes to be cultivated through meditation in Mahayana Buddhism (*q.v.* 4). Great compassion (*mahakaruna*) is a mark of buddhahood.

KATHARSIS.
   Q.v. Catharsis.

KATZ, JERROLD.
   Q.v. Semantics (7).

KAUTILYA. 4th–3rd cent. B.C.
   Indian philosopher, minister to the first Mauryan emperor. Contributed to the development of orthodox Brahmanism through his *Arthaśastra*, a study of society from the standpoint of policy and utility, written between 321 and 296 B.C.
   Principal writings: *The Arthaśastra* (T).
   (1) The chief end of life is *artha*, or wealth. All other values depend on an economic foundation. (2) The power of the king depends on many factors, not least of which is the happiness and well-being of his subjects, which should be a king's chief good. (3) Rising above the prudential basis are the common human obligations, or *sadharana*, stated in Book I of the *Arthaśastra*: to refrain from injuring others, to tell the truth, to live purely, to practice goodwill, to be forgiving, to exercise patience.

KAUTSKY, KARL. 1854–1939.
   Czechoslovakian-German Marxist. Born in Prague. Educated at Vienna. Influenced by Haeckel, Marx, and Engels. One of the classic expositors of dialectical materialism, Kautsky resisted all efforts to revise the Marx-Engels position.
   Principal writings: *The Economic Doctrines of Karl Marx* (T), 1887; *Thomas More and his Utopia* (T), 1888; *Forerunners of Modern Socialism*, 1894–1921; *The Agricul-*

tural Question, 1899; The Social Revolution (T), 1903; Ethics and the Materialist Conception of History (T), 1906; The Origin of Christianity (T), 1908; The Materialist Conception of History, 2 vols., 1927; The History of Socialism, 1947.

KELSEN, HANS. 1881–1973.

German-American philosopher of law. Born in Prague. Taught at Vienna, Cologne, Geneva, and Berkeley. Following the traditions of Positivism, Kelsen proposes a "pure theory of law," based on the analysis of legal concepts separated from value judgments and sociological entanglements. Centering on established codes of positive law, Kelsen is able to defend international law since such law rests upon the similarities of national codes of law. These in turn rest on political or moral preferences which are finally emotive in nature. Natural Law doctrines, not resting on any positive legal order, are still more clearly emotively based.

Principal writings: The Doctrine of Pure Law (G), 1934; General Theory of Law and the State (T), 1943; What Is Justice? (E), 1957.

KEMPIS, THOMAS À.

Q.v. Thomas à Kempis.

KENOSIS.

From the Greek kenos meaning "empty." The term begins in a Christological dispute centering around Philippians 2:7 where Christ is said to have "emptied himself, taking the form of a servant." According to some this means that Christ divested himself of his divine attributes during his earthly career. According to others the attributes were retained, although hidden from view. The interpretation of the concept has varied with each Christological (q.v.) option.

KEPLER, JOHANNES. 1571–1630.

German astronomer. Born at Weil. Educated at Tübingen. Taught at Graz. In 1600 he became assistant to Tycho Brahe (q.v.), and after Brahe's death was named to his post. The first astronomer to defend Copernicus' view openly, Kepler's laws of motion are an indispensable part of Newton's (q.v.) system.

Principal writings: Mysterium Cosmographicum, 1597; A New Astronomy 1609; The Harmony of the World, 1618.

(1) Encouraged to believe in the heliocentric theory of the solar system by the Pythagorean example and by Platonic analogies, Kepler swept away the epicycles retained by Copernicus (q.v.), arriving at three laws of planetary motion: (a) that the planets move in ellipses with the sun at one focus; (b) that the planets sweep out equal distances in equal times, and thus move more rapidly nearer the sun; (c) that the squares of the periods of any two planets are proportional to the cubes of their mean distance from the sun, a period being the time required for a complete trip around the sun. The laws fitted the data, and the question concerning why this was so remained.

(2) All of Kepler's explanations supposed that forces could act at a distance, an anti-Aristotelian idea. At the start he spoke of the sun as a "moving soul" of the planetary system whose force was stronger nearby than at more remote distances. Later he dropped the notion of soul, and simply spoke of a force emanating from the sun, diffusing through the space of the universe, diminishing with distance, and subject to mathematical expression.

KERYGMA.

A Greek term meaning the "good news," or "gospel." The New Testament message of salvation. Q.v. Bultmann (2).

KEYNES, JOHN MAYNARD. 1883–1946.

English economist and logician. Born in Cambridge. Educated in King's College, Cambridge, where he was subsequently a Fellow. His work on economics has had immense influence since the 1930's. His work on probability is likewise widely known. Viewing probability as a relation between series of propositions, given the first series one can speak of the degree of probability of the second series. Certainty is the maximum probability; impossibility is the minimum probability. Probability thus is understood as the degree of rationality present in believing the second series on the basis of the first.

Principal writings: The Economic Consequences of Peace, 1919; A Treatise on Probability, 1921; General Theory of Employment, Interest, and Money, 1930.

KEYSERLING, COUNT HERMANN. 1880–1946.

German philosopher. Born in Könno, Estonia. Educated at Dorpat, Geneva, Heidelberg, and Vienna. An intuition-oriented philosopher, interested in Eastern modes of thought, he opposed the category of "life" to mechanism, and "wisdom" to scientific knowledge, founding a "School of Wisdom" in Darmstadt in 1920. He published works, some in German, others in French.

Principal writings: *Immortality* (T), 1907; *The Travel Diary of a Philosopher* (T), 2 vols., 1919; *Philosophy as Art*, 1920; *Creative Understanding* (T), 1922: *Rebirth* (T), 1927; *On the Art of Life*, 1936; *Journey through Time*, 1948.

KHORDA AVESTA.

One of the five parts of the *Avesta*, sacred scriptures of Zoroastrianism (*q.v.* 4).

KIERKEGAARD, SÖREN. 1813–1855.

Danish philosopher-theologian. Born in Copenhagen. Educated at the University of Copenhagen. In addition, he studied philosophy in Berlin with Schelling, 1841–2. Author of 21 books in 12 years, he is considered the father of existentialist philosophy and theology. Physically frail, with a pronounced tendency toward melancholy, turned inward by partial deformity he nonetheless won the love of Regina Olson. His inner conflicts were so powerful that, without ceasing to love Regina, he broke off the engagement. This event marks the beginning of his fantastic intellectual productivity, directed to the end, as he said, of helping men realize what it is to be a Christian. His first writings are "indirect communications," published under pseudonyms. They take up other points of view than the one to which Kierkegaard adhered; through the elaboration of the point of view it is expected that the reader can be brought to realize the author's disaffection with it. His later writings, describing the Christian life, are direct communications, published under his own name. Championing an intensely personal religion, as opposed to institutional religion, brought Kierkegaard into conflict with the Danish Church; his final writings reflect the conflict. His utterances became more extreme.

He argued that by failing to attend church one escapes at least one great sin; one is "not attempting to fool God by calling that the Christianity of the New Testament which is not the Christianity of the New Testament." Shortly after, Kierkegaard fell unconscious in the street, both strength and money entirely spent. He died with the words, "The bomb explodes, and the conflagration will follow."

Principal writings: *The Concept of Irony* (T), 1841; *Either-Or* (T), 1843; *Fear and Trembling* (T), 1843; *Repetition* (T), 1843; *The Concept of Dread* (T), 1844; *Philosophical Fragments* (T), 1844; *Stages on Life's Way* (T), 1845; *Concluding Unscientific Postscript* (T), 1846; *The Present Age* (T), 1847; *Christian Discourses* (T), 1848; *Works of Love* (T), 1848; *Sickness Unto Death* (T), 1849; *Two Short Ethico-Religious Treatises* (T), 1849; *Training in Christianity* (T), 1850; *Armed Neutrality* (T), 1851; *For Self-Examination* (T), 1851; *The Instant* (10 articles) (T), 1854–5.

(1) Setting himself against the Hegelian system of his day, Kierkegaard announced himself as opposed to those who believed that truth could be caught in a system of ideas. Indeed, he championed "truth as subjectivity" over against "truth as objectivity." The latter is characterized by "endless approximation"; the former is characterized by "appropriation." In the latter, one seeks to lose his subjectivity, becoming objective. In the former, one seeks to learn how to become more richly subjective. This is the direction of promise.

(2) The problem of choice can be faced on several levels. Kierkegaard found three levels—the *aesthetic*, the *ethical*, and the *religious*. The aesthetic individual seeks the greatest sum of pleasure, composing his life out of the most exquisite pleasures. The point is that he expects to compose his life, having no inkling that there may be a deeper manner of living in which one's life is composed for him (at the religious level, *cf.* 4 below). Life on the aesthetic level appears to possess maximum freedom; but in fact this is a life lacking in purpose, which falls apart into disconnected desires and satisfactions; the aesthetic individual, far from free, merely responds to the situation in which he finds himself.

(3) But the ordinary man who enters into the relations of life, sensing the obligations they impose, seeking for

example a wife instead of a mistress, has found the ethical stage of life. Containing universal purposes, it is a life also of self-determination, and superior to the aesthetic stage.

(4) Were it the case that every man had the conditions of knowledge within him, he could arrive at the religious stage by continued self-examination. He would need at most a Socratic teacher to serve as midwife. And, indeed, at one point Kierkegaard did discuss a universal religion on the way to Christianity, which would seem to be a development of the ethical stage as the ethical is a development of the aesthetic stage. But in fact there is a leap between the ethical stage and the true religious stage which is Christianity. One of the ways in which Kierkegaard expressed this was by contrasting Socrates and Christ. Socrates is sufficient if we already have within us the conditions of knowledge and of truth; then what is in us needs only to be educed. But if we do not possess these conditions we shall need someone able to provide them. We shall need a far greater teacher than Socrates; not a teacher, but a Savior; not Socrates, but Christ. Similarly, Socratic irony must be replaced by the irony of "indirect communication," cutting away alternatives, leaving a void requiring revelation. The religious level must be approached with fear and trembling; for it can happen that here the requirements of the ethical life can be suspended, at the command of God. Kierkegaard called this the "teleological suspension of the ethical." The example he used is that of Abraham, willing to suspend the ethical and sacrifice his son at the command of God. The religious level cannot be understood in a straightforward logical manner. It is infused with paradoxes, the most ultimate of these being that God should have become man. But the achievement of this level is the achievement of truth as subjectivity.

(5) We have thus far considered human life as a progression toward a goal. But the possibility of this progression occurs in a context fraught with uncertainty. The most central feeling of human life is an anguish or *Angst* which accompanies us at every moment. We wish to avoid the anguish, and so attempt to cast down our identity in the group. We wish to avoid ourselves, when we should choose ourselves. The problem of life can be put more simply than in the preceding points. We live in time, losing ourselves in its contents; but if we face ourselves there is a chance that we shall break through time into eternity, finding God in the eternal moment.

(6) This signals a religious category of Repetition, which is the work of freedom and looks toward the future. If one is able to make the leap of faith and reach the eternal moment, the achievement is not a single act. One must regain this ground over and over in passionate living.

(7) Drawing an interesting contrast between the tragic hero and the man of faith, Kierkegaard regarded the latter as renouncing the universal in order to gain himself, while the former renounces himself in order to express the universal. In Kierkegaard's view, of course, the tragic hero is inferior to the man of faith.

KILWARDBY, ROBERT.

Second half of the 13th-century Scholastic philosopher. Taught theology at Oxford from 1248 until 1261. Thereafter he served as Archbishop of Canterbury and was made a Cardinal. An Augustinian, he opposed the Thomistic philosophy beginning to influence Oxford in his time, arguing for a plurality of forms in things and against the Thomistic doctrine of a unity of form. In 1277 he condemned thirty Thomistic propositions as dangerous and not suitable for teaching. He divided the sciences into those which treat of divine, and those which treat of human, things. The former include natural, metaphysical, and mathematical sciences. The latter include ethics, the mechanical arts, and logic.

Principal writings: *On the Origin of Science* (T); *On the Imaginative Spirit*; *On Conscience*; *On Time*; also, a book on the Trinity as well as commentaries on Porphyry, Aristotle, and the book of *Sentences*.

KINDI, AL.

Q.v. Al-Kindi.

KING.

In the medieval doctrine of the two swords the temporal, in contrast to the spiritual, power. For John Wycliffe (*q.v.* 3) the king was God's vicar on earth. The doctrine of the Divine Right of Kings (*q.v.*) in the 17th century regarded the monarch as possessing spiritual, as well as temporal, authority.

KINGDOM OF GOD.

A Hebrew concept which looked to the future for the fulfillment of God's rule over mankind. Jesus began his ministry with the announcement that the kingdom was at hand, picturing it both as already present and as imminent (*q.v.* Christ, Jesus 1, 4–5).

KIRCHHEIMER, OTTO. 1905–1965.

Q.v. Frankfurt School.

KISMET.

An Arabic term meaning "fate" (*q.v.*).

KLAGES, LUDWIG. 1872–1956.

German philosopher-characterologist. Born in Hanover. Educated at Munich. He established at Munich a center for the study of Characterology, a hopefully projected science of the Spirit based on a classification of psychological types. The center later moved to Kilchberg, near Zurich. A student of Theodor Lipps, and influenced by Nietzsche, Klages conceived life as a struggle of spirit against both body and soul. He identified rationality with the first, and creative vital forces with soul. He attempted to type men psychologically in terms of the balance of soul and spirit in their characters. But the object of his effort was the resurgence of soul and its vital symbols against the deadening effect of science.

Principal writings: *Principles of Characterology* (T, *The Science of Character*), 1910; *On the Cosmogonic Eros*, 1922; *The Psychological Discoveries of Nietzsche*, 1926; *The Spirit as Adversary of the Soul*, 3 vols., 1929–33; *Goethe as Researcher of the Soul*, 1932; *Language as the Source of Soul Knowledge*, 1948.

KNOWLEDGE.

From the Greek *gignoskein* ("to decide upon, determine, or decree"). The theory of knowledge is treated under Epistemology (*q.v.*). Also *q.v.* Rationalism, and Empiricism.

A. We here give some of the uses made of the term in the history of Western philosophy.

(1) For classical Greek philosophy, knowledge (*episteme*) stands in contrast to opinion (*doxa*), (*q.v.* Plato 1). The highest form of knowledge is wisdom (*sophia*) which is knowledge of the whole for Plato, and knowledge of the first principles or first causes of things for Aristotle (*q.v.* 2). Aristotle gave intuition a significant role in this activity.

(2) Weigel (*q.v.*) distinguished between authentic and inauthentic knowledge, relating the former to inward spiritual knowledge, and the latter to external things.

(3) Swedenborg (*q.v.* 2), in a religious adaptation of Plato's doctrine of recollection (*q.v.* 1), claimed that men have total knowledge in their souls, but it has been rendered inoperative through the fall of man. Swedenborg held that the fall separated man's soul from his reason.

(4) The empirical tradition roots knowledge in sensation. Locke (*q.v.* 2, 8) took this approach, while distinguishing knowledge into three types: intuitive, demonstrative, and sensitive. Condillac (*q.v.* 1) is a French representative of this approach. For Eastern empiricism (*q.v.*) Carvaka (2, 6–7).

(5) For Kant (*q.v.* 11b) theoretical knowledge relates to the *Verstand*, requires a categorical structure, and is regulative in nature.

(6) Comte (*q.v.* 2) called attention to the order of development in knowledge, claiming that the order is from the abstract to the concrete, beginning with mathematics and ending with sociology.

(7) Opposing a spectator theory of knowledge, Dewey (*q.v.* 2–3) held that the aim of knowing is to make certain differences in the environment, and that "knowing is seen to be a participant in what is finally known."

(8) Lonergan (*q.v.* 5) related objectivity in knowledge to authentic subjectivity.

(9) Russell (*q.v.* 6) distinguished between "knowledge by acquaintance" and "knowledge by description."

(10) Ortega y Gasset (*q.v.* 2) advanced the thought that knowledge must be rooted in prerational belief.

(11) Plato's (*q.v.* 1) alternate definition of knowledge as "justified true belief" has been much discussed since the 1960's, turning on what is called the Gettier problem (*q.v.*). Many philosophers have written on the anomalies Gettier pointed out, including Chisholm (*q.v.* 4) and Lehrer (*q.v.*).

B. In Eastern thought a multiplicity of terms specify different types of knowledge, and assessments of them.

(12) The word *Veda* itself means knowledge; and in the Vedic period (*q.v. Vedas*) the term *vidya* meant knowledge with no distinction between higher and lower forms. *Jnana Marga* ("the way of Knowledge") is one of the three paths to liberation, and relates to the *Upanishads* (*q.v.* Hinduism 5b). *Darshana* (*q.v.*) ("knowledge," or "instrument of vision"), relates to the six orthodox systems.

(13) For Vedanta (*q.v.*) higher knowledge (*paravidya*) was associated with truth and reality, while lower knowledge (*aparavidya*) designated the phenomenal world.

(14) In the Advaita Vedanta (*q.v.*) Shankara (*q.v.*) equated *paravidya* with Brahman. All else was equivalent to *avidya* or *maya* (*q.v.*).

(15) For Hinayana (*q.v.*) Buddhism *aryaprajna* ("noble knowledge") is identified with Nirvana, in comparison with which all other standpoints, including Brahman as well as *atman*, are extinguished.

(16) The term for ultimate knowledge in Mahayana (*q.v.*) Buddhism, *prajnaparamita*, means emptiness, or even emptiness of emptiness, beyond any form of discursive knowledge.

KNOX, JOHN. c. 1514–1572.

Scotch reformer. Born in Giffordgate. A student at St. Andrews, Knox entered the priesthood prior to 1540, and accepted a call to the Reformed Ministry in 1546. Captured by the French in 1546, he served in the galleys 18 months. He was released by English intervention. In England until 1554, his work there led Carlyle to call him "the Chief Priest and Founder" of English Puritanism. He removed to the Continent in 1554 when Mary became Queen of England. Between 1554 and 1559, he guided congregations in Frankfurt, Geneva, and Dieppe. He visited Scotland from September 1555 to the summer of 1556, preaching and strengthening the reform movement. His final return to Scotland was in 1559. Through civil war and against the opposition of Queen Mary, Knox guided the Scottish Reformation to its end in the establishment of Protestantism as the national religion.

Principal writings: *Epistles and Admo-*

nition, 1554; *On Prayer*, 1554; *On Predestination*, 1554; *On Affliction*, 1556; *The First Blast of the Trumpet against the Monstrous Regiment of Women*, 1558; *The History of the Reformation in Scotland*, 1566; *An Answer to a Scottish Jesuit*, 1572.

KNUDSON, A.C.

Q.v. Personalism (9).

KNUTH, D.E.

Q.v. Algorithm.

KNUTZEN, MARTIN. 1713–1751.

German philosopher. Educated at Königsberg. Taught at Königsberg. A follower of Wolff and a Pietist, Knutzen is principally known for having been the teacher of Immanuel Kant. The extent of his influence on his famous pupil is in dispute. His writings were in Latin.

Principal writings: *Metaphysical Dissertation on the Impossibility of an Eternal World*, 1733; *Philosophical Commentary on the Relation between Mind and Body*, 1744.

KOAN.

From the Chinese *kung-an* ("public notice"). A paradoxical question or statement developed in the Rinzai school of Zen, and used as a stimulus along the path to enlightenment. Resolution of the paradox passes beyond intellectual opposition to *satori* (*q.v.*).

Q.v. Emptiness; Zen Buddhism (7).

KOFFKA, KURT. 1896–1941.

German Psychologist. Born in Berlin. Taught at Giessen, Cornell, University of Wisconsin, and Smith College, emphasized role of insight in Gestalt Psychology. Also *q.v.* Wertheimer, Köhler.

Principal writings: *On the Analysis of Representations and their Laws*, 1912; *The Bases of Mental Development* (T), 1921; *Principles of Gestalt Psychology* (E), 1935.

KOHLBERG, LAWRENCE. 1927–1987.

Psychologist and ethical philosopher. Born in Bronxville, N.Y. Educated at the University of Chicago. Taught at Yale, Chicago, Harvard.

Principal writings: "From Is to Ought," 1971; *Recent Research in Moral Development* (with E. Jurnel), 1973; *Essays in Moral Development*, 1978; *The Meaning and Measurement of Moral Development*, 1981; *The*

Philosophy of Moral Development, vol. 1, 1981; *The Psychology of Moral Development* (with others), 1984; *The Stages of Ethical Development* (with T. Lickona), 1986; *Child Psychology and Childhood Education* (with others), 1987.

(1) Extending Piaget's (*q.v.*) study of the moral judgment of children into adolescence, Kohlberg elaborated a somewhat Kantian view of justice as fairness.

(2) The development of what determines goodness and badness moves through three levels and six moral stages.

I. Preconventional Level.

(a) Punishment and obedience: the physical consequences of action determining goodness/badness.

(b) Instrumental relativist: what satisfies one's own needs and occasionally the needs of others.

II. Conventional Level.

(c) Interpersonal concordance: what pleases or helps others and is approved by them.

(d) "Law and order" orientation: what conforms to authority, maintaining a given social order.

III. Post-conventional Autonomous or Principled Level.

(e) Social-contract legalistic orientation: social utility (generally Utilitarian, *q.v.*) with the agreement of society.

(f) Universal ethical principle: logical comprehensiveness; universality; consistency (*q.v.* Golden Rule, Categorical Imperative, as interpreted through the Practical Imperative).

(3) The stages form a natural sequence and turn up in research findings in all cultures, although (e) and (f) are not to be found in semiliterate and literate village culture. This means to Kohlberg that such cultures require further evolution. On their psychological side the stages represent a "cognitive-developmental" theory which on its philosophical side is a non-relativistic moral theory. The thrust of cultural relativism is parried by the fact that it appears within the scheme and is outgrown by the final stage. Each stage has a more complicated logic than its predecessor, corresponding to a more sophisticated ethical outlook. The two are reciprocal and the individual masters both at the same time. His stage psychology thus supports a moral philosophy with "universally substantive principles."

KÖHLER, WOLFGANG. 1887– .

German psychologist. Born in Tallin, Estonia. Educated at Tübingen, Bonn, and Berlin. Taught at Berlin, Swarthmore College, the University of Pennsylvania, and Dartmouth. A Gestalt psychologist noted for his contributions to animal psychology. Also *q.v.* Wertheimer; Koffka.

Principal writings: *The Mentality of Apes* (T), 1917; *Gestalt Psychology* (E), 1929; *The Place of Value in a World of Facts* (E), 1938; *Dynamics in Psychology* (E), 1940.

KORAN.

Q.v. Qur'an.

KORN, ALEJANDRO. 1860–1936.

Argentine philosopher. Born in Buenos Aires. Initially a practicing psychiatrist-director of a hospital for the insane and professor of anatomy, National College of La Plata. He became professor of philosophy in the University of Buenos Aires in 1906 and for a time served as dean of its faculty of philosophy and letters. He was director of the journal, *Valoraciones*.

Principal writings: *Philosophical Influences in the National Evolution*, 1919; *Creative Liberty*, 1922; *Epistemological Schema*, 1924; *The Concept of Science*, 1926; *Axiology*, 1930; *Philosophical Notes*, 1935.

(1) Opposed to the uncritical forms of the philosophies in his milieu—whether positivism, romantic idealism, or realism—Korn subscribed to a native Argentinian form of positivism compatible with both human freedom and human value.

(2) Indeed, the problem of philosophy is to come to terms with the contrast between objectivity and subjectivity, the scientific point of view and the standpoint of human awareness, necessity and liberty. This cannot in fact be done conceptually, but only in practice.

(3) Human freedom, for example, is not something given but something achieved in struggle with necessity. He understands liberty, incidentally, as having both ethical and economic aspects, neither of which can be eliminated.

(4) The human response to a fact or an event involves valuation. Value is, in fact, part of the struggle for freedom. Even though values are not absolute, they have relevance to the biological, social, and cultural fields of experience in which they have arisen. Each pair of values has

its own historicity and ideality.

(5) He distinguished nine types of valuation: economic, instinctive, erotic, vital, social, religious, ethical, logical, and aesthetic. The fundamental value-polarities belonging to each of these are respectively: useful-useless, agreeable-disagreeable, lovable-hateful, select-vulgar, licit-illicit, holy-profane, good-evil, true-false, and beautiful-ugly. The final value involved in each is respectively: well-being, happiness, love, power, justice, holiness, good, truth, and beauty. Finally, the systems in which these distinctions are enshrined are respectively: Utilitarianism, Hedonism, Mysticism, Pragmatism, sociological systems, Scholasticism, Stoicism, Rationalism, and Intuitionism.

(6) While not taking metaphysical systems at face value, Korn believed, as is evident from the above, that in some form metaphysical speculation remained part of the task of an adequate philosophy.

KOSÍK, KAREL.
Q.v. Praxis (11).

KOTARBINSKI, TADEUSZ. 1886–1981.
Polish philosopher. Born in Warsaw. Educated at Lvov. Taught at Warsaw. Along with Leśniewski (q.v.), a member of the Warsaw Circle, analogous and related to the Vienna Circle of Logical Positivism.

Principal writings: *Elements of the Theory of Knowledge, Formal Logic and Methodology of Science*, 1929; "The Fundamental Ideas of Pansomatism," (E), 1955; *Praxiology: an Introduction to the Sciences of Efficient Action* (T), 1958; "Psychological Propositions," (E), 1965; *Meditations on the Virtuous Life*, 1976.

(1) Holding that only concrete individual objects exist, a view he termed Concretism or Reism, Kotarbinski advocated both Semantic Reism (only the names of concrete objects are genuine; all other names are apparent) and Ontological Reism (every object is a thing, either physical or sentient). The doctrine of Ontological Reism he calls Somatism, an apparent synonym of Physicalism, and he rejects the term, Materialism, as an apparent name. He uses the term, "Pansomatism," to name the doctrine that every sentient entity is a body.

(2) He believes that psychological propositions are known not by introspection but by Imitationism, *i.e.*, imitating the behavior of others or oneself.

(3) The application of these principles to value and action leads to Praxiology, a theory of efficient action.

KOZLOV, ALEXEY A. 1831–1901.
Russian philosopher. Born in Moscow. Taught at Kiev and St. Petersburg. His deepest philosophical influence came from Leibniz by way of Teichmüller. Under this influence he developed a system of Panpsychism, calling it by that name. His view was that of an interacting monadology, a cell-theory of reality, grounded in God.

Principal writings: *Philosophical Studies*, 2 vols., 1876–80; *Philosophy as a Science*, 1877.

KRAMA ŚAIVISM (SHAIVISM).
Q.v. Vaiṣnavism (3d).

KRAUSE, KARL CHRISTIAN FRIEDRICH. 1781–1832.
German philosopher. Born at Eisenberg. Studied at Jena under Hegal and Fichte. Holding the universe to be a divine organism, a view he termed Panentheism (q.v.), Krause taught that reality is progressing toward higher internal unities. God includes in his being, while transcending them, both nature and humanity. Humanity is the highest component; and the progress of society consists in extending organic relations within society, finally to all humanity.

Principal writings: *Sketch of the Philosophic System*, 1804; *System of Morality*, 1810; *The Prototype of Humanity*, 1811; *Lectures on the System of Philosophy*, 1828.

KRIKORIAN, YERVANT.
Q.v. Naturalism.

KRIPKE, SAUL A. 1940– .
American philosopher. Born in Omaha, Nebraska. Studied at Harvard, Oxford, Princeton, and Rockefeller University. Has taught at Rockefeller University, Princeton, and Cornell.

Principal writings: "A Completeness Theorem in Modal Logic," 1959; "Naming and Necessity," 1972 (slightly revised, *Naming and Necessity*, 1980); "Outline of a Theory of Truth," 1975; *Wittgenstein on*

Rules and Private Language, 1982.

(1) A modal logician who has contributed to the field of possible world semantics (*q.v.* 8), Kripke advanced a causal theory of naming in which proper names (*q.v.* 5) designate what their originators intended, and in principle can be traced causally to their "initial baptism."

(2) That initial baptism turns the name into a "rigid designator" with "transworld identity." In every possible world (also called a "Kripke structure") the baptized name will refer to the same individual as in this world.

(3) His theory of truth is directed toward the resolution of semantic paradox in the manner of Tarski (*q.v.*) while utilizing a single truth predicate "ever increasing with increasing levels" until a fixed point is reached where the language contains its own truth predicate without paradox.

(4) Kripke argued that what Wittgenstein (*q.v.* 8) objected to in the private language argument was a "private model" of rule following without reference to the community in which one functions.

KROPOTKIN, PETER. 1842–1921.

Russian author and social philosopher. Born in Moscow. Studied the French Encyclopedists (*q.v.*) at an early age. After working as a geographer for many years he joined the Russian revolutionary party in 1872 and soon thereafter became an avowed anarchist. After imprisonment and escape his efforts became international. He contributed to the development of the socialist movement in Paris, founded and edited a revolutionary newspaper in Switzerland. After a French imprisonment he moved to England where he received recognition for the first time. Returning to Russia in 1917, he denounced the Bolshevik dictatorship which had gained control of the country.

Principal writings: *Words of a Revolutionary,* 1885; *The Conquest of Bread* (T), 1892; *The State, Its Part in History,* 1898; *Mutual Aid* (T), 1902; *The Great Revolution* (T), 1909; *Ethics* (T), 1925.

(1) Believing that the followers of Darwin had stressed the factor of competition in evolution too exclusively, Kropotkin wished to redress the balance, holding that mutual aid is a factor of equal importance, the survival of many species depending upon cooperative endeavor. Humans, of course, belong to such a species.

(2) Morality derives from the factor of mutual aid, generating a disinterested good will which goes beyond the requirements of equity and justice.

(3) Society in its natural state was able to rely upon this natural tendency toward cooperation. But society has been corrupted by authoritarian institutions leading to inequality, crime, and violence.

(4) Anarchism is simply a movement back toward the natural state of society. Kropotkin's vision of anarchist-communism stressed the value of the commune as the natural form of cooperative society with a free-distribution warehouse at its center.

KṚṢNA (KRISHNA).

Along with Rama (*q.v.*) one of the last two incarnations of Vishnu. Their followers constitute a considerable portion of the Hindu people and a majority of the Vishnuites (*q.v.* Vaiṣnavism 2a). Krishna is acknowledged as the supreme God in the *Mahabharata,* the *Harivamśa* and the *Puranas,* yet his actions reveal a Rajput chieftain willing to employ questionable means for the sake of personal ends. Supposing that Krishna, the incarnate God, grew from the figure of the chieftain, how did this happen? The path is somewhat complex. In the Vedic period, Krishna, having begun as a tribal head, is regarded as a wise man seeking religious truth. Vasudeva is mentioned quite early as a God mystically identical with Vishnu. It happened that Krishna became identified with Vasudeva, thus taking over his identification with Vishnu, and thus did a Rajput chieftain become an incarnate God.

KṢATRIYA (KSHATRIYA).

From Sanskrit, ("warrior"). Second in rank of the four castes of Hindu society (*q.v.* Hinduism 4). Numerous religious reformers emerged from this group, among them Gautama Buddha, Mahavira (*q.v.* Jainism), and the protagonist of the *Bhagavad-Gita* (*q.v.*), Arjuna. *Q.v. Mahabharata* (3); *Laws of Manu* (2).

KUHN, THOMAS S. 1922– .

American philosopher and historian of science. Born in Cincinnati. Educated at

Harvard. Has taught at Harvard, Berkeley, Princeton, and M.I.T. Member Institute for Advanced Study, Princeton, 1972–79.

Principal writings: The *Copernican Revolution*, 1957; *The Structure of Scientific Revolution*, 1962; *The Essential Tension*, 1977; *Black-Body Theory and the Quantum Discontinuity, 1894–1912*, 1978; *The Trouble with the Historical Philosophy of Science*, 1992.

(1) Kuhn holds that scientific theories develop around basic paradigms—*i.e.*, models or examples of central importance in interpreting scientific theories. One of these, for example, would be the model of atomic theory in terms of a solar system; but also anything else which can function in the absence of a theory, including shared symbolic generalizations, shared values, and standard solved problems. All such elements are part of a shared disciplinary matrix.

(2) The scientific community determines the line between scientific orthodoxy (normal science) and heresy (revolutionary science) at a given time. Change in orientation of science depends upon convulsions in that community. A paradigm begins to lose explanatory power; various kinds of emendation are made. An attempt occurs to explain away in order to prevent a shift. The champions of heterodox interpretations, bearing a different paradigm, are regarded as heretical, but one or more of them may be the bearers of a new scientific orthodoxy.

(3) Somewhat wary about applying the label "truth," Kuhn is willing to say that of two theories successively abandoned, the later was the better of the two "as a tool for the practice of normal science," but he is not willing to use the language of Peirce (*q.v.* 12) and Popper (*q.v.* 1) that the second also more closely approximates truth.

KÜLPE, OSWALD. 1862–1915.

German psychologist and philosopher. Born in Candau, Latvia. Educated at Leipzig, Berlin, Göttingen, and Dorpat. An associate of Wundt in Leipzig. Taught at Würzburg, Leipzig, Bonn, and Munich. Founder of the Würzburg school of experimental psychology. Continued Fechner's experimental studies in aesthetics. Philosophically, Kulpe was a realist who defined his position in terms of Kant. Against Kant, he believed metaphysics

to be possible. Against the Marburg neo-Kantians he defended realism. His psychological orientation affords many points of contact with phenomenology.

Principal writings: *Outlines of Psychology* (T), 1893; *Immanuel Kant*, 1907; *Theory of Knowledge and Natural Science*, 1910; *The Realization*, 3 vols., 1912–20; *Lectures on Psychology*, 1920; *Foundations of Aesthetics*, 1921; *Lectures on Logic*, 1923.

KULTURWELT.
Q.v. Husserl (8).

KUMARAJIVA. 344–413.

Chinese Buddhist philosopher. Half-Indian and half-Chinese, Kumarajiva became a monk at the age of seven. He became so influential that kings sent armies to bring him to their courts. The title of "National Teacher" was conferred on him. More than 1000 monks attended his daily lectures. In ten years he translated 72 Buddhist books into Chinese. He introduced the Middle Doctrine of Nagarjuna (*q.v.*) into China, where it is the San-Lun school. Among these were the really philosophical Buddhist texts. Hence, he made systematic philosophizing about Buddhism possible.

KUMARILA BHATTA.
Q.v. God (71).

KUNDALINI YOGA.
Q.v. Yoga (10).

KÜNG, HANS. 1928– .

German theologian. Born in Lucerne, Switzerland. Educated at the Pontifical Gregorian University (Rome), and Institut Catholique and the Sorbonne (Paris). Ordained priest, 1954. Taught at universities of Münster and Tübingen. Deprived of the title of "Catholic theologian" by the Vatican (1979), he continues in Tübingen as professor of Ecumenical Theology, and director of the Institute for Ecumenical Research.

Principal philosophical and theological writings: *Justification: the Doctrine of Karl Barth and a Catholic Reflection* (T), 1957; *Freedom Today* (T) (collected), 1966; *The Incarnation of God* (T), 1970; *Infallible? An Inquiry* (T), 1970; *Why Priests?* (T), 1971; *On Being Christian* (T), 1974 (shorter version, *The Christian Challenge*, 1977); *Does God Exist?* (T), 1978; *Freud and the*

Problem of God (T), 1979; *The Church, Maintained in Truth* (T), 1979; *Eternal Life* (T), 1982; *Christianity and the Chinese Religion* (with J. Ching) (E), 1989; *Global Responsibility: In Search of a New World Ethic* (T), 1990; *Judaism: Between Yesterday and Tomorrow* (T), 1991.

(1) Arguing that democratization of the Catholic Church would encourage ecumenical progress, Küng urged an ending of the Index of Forbidden Books, of precensorship of books, and of papal infallibility—substituting for the last-named the "indefectibility" of the community of the faithful, despite the fallibility of its members.

(2) He likewise held that the Gospels contain no support for the idea of apostolic succession, individual centers of worship existing in New Testament times as non-hierarchical spiritual communities.

(3) The articles of faith are to be understood symbolically, which implies their being subject to reevaluation and reinterpretation. The virgin birth, the assumption of Mary into heaven, the incarnation and resurrection are candidates for such treatment (but note the limitation in 4 below).

(4) One knows by critical argument that God exists, although critical argument requires one to include in His nature the feminine-maternal alongside the masculine paternal. We know by enlightened trust that we do not die into nothingness but into God. This trust comes to us from Jesus who lives "through and with God," as signalled by his life, death, and resurrection. (It would seem, then, that Jesus' resurrection can be no more symbolic than his life and death.)

(5) Through Christian experience who God is has become apparent. Because Christianity has a more complete understanding of these matters than other religions, its world mission remains valid— not by holding there is no salvation outside the Church, but by asking the whole world to enter the service of God.

KUNG-SUN LUNG. 4th cent. B.C.

Chinese "Logician" philosopher. A native of Chad. *Q.v.* The Chinese "Logicians."

Principal writings: *The Kung-Sun Lung Tzu* (T).

(1) "A white horse is not a horse." This paradox plays on the differences in the functioning of names and naming phrases on different levels of generality. (2) "All things are marks and no things are marks." This paradox plays on the difference in functioning of things and the names of things. (3) "A hard, white stone is and is not three things." The paradox plays on the differences between different properties, and between property words and entity words. (4) The point of these discussions would seem to be that names are to be distinguished from the actualities they designate, and that care must be taken in determining what names designate.

KUO HSIANG. 3rd–4th cents. A.D.

Chinese neo-Taoist philosopher. A high government official, and an enthusiastic Taoist.

Principal writings: *Commentary on the Chuang Tzu* (T in part). (1) Each thing has its own nature, and its own ultimate to which to adapt. Each thing has its principle and every affair its proper condition. Either there is no Creator or He is incapable of materializing all the forms, for the forms materialize by themselves. Everything creates itself without the direction of any Creator. Things happen by necessity, and principle prevails at all times. If we leave things alone they will accomplish their purpose. Heaven is not something behind the process of nature, but merely its general name. (2) Those who are at ease with their spirits can reach their highest degree while remaining in silent harmony with their ultimate capacities. This is the way to realize one's destiny. (3) Combining the preceding points, one finds the way to govern most effectively—through being at ease and allowing things and persons to act according to their principles.

KURWILLE.

Q.v. Ferdinand Tönnies (1).

KYRIE ELEISON.

A Greek phrase meaning "Lord have mercy." One of the few Greek phrases used in the Roman Mass and the Anglican Communion service, it is of course used in the litanies of the Eastern Church. Its presence in the Western rites may point to a common, vanished litany.

L

LAAS, ERNST. 1837–1885.

German philosopher. Born at Fürstenwalde. Studied under Trendelenburg. Taught at Strassburg. A critic of Kantian transcendentalism, and of Platonism from which he found all transcendentalism to derive, Laas defended positivism as being inductive rather than deductive, natural rather than artificial, its ethic determined by the social interest rather than ascetic self-denial or an inflexible moral law.

Principal writings: *Kant's Analogies of Experience*, 1876; *Idealism and Positivism*, 3 vols., 1879–84; *Literary Remains* (ed. Kerry), 1887.

LABERTHONNIÉRE, LUCIEN. 1860–1932.

French philosopher-theologian. Born in Chazelet. Entered the Order of the Oratory. Wishing an interior and total faith, made and not simply given, Laberthonniére opposed Christian realism to Greek idealism. This led him to stress the divine immanence, however, and to oppose the conception of God as *actus purus*. His "immanentism" was condemned by Pope Pius in the 1907 Encyclical *Pascendi* opposing modernism.

Principal writings: *The Moral Dogmatism*, 1898; *Essays in Religious Philosophy*, 1903; *Christian Realism and Greek Idealism*, 1904; *Positivism and Catholicism*, 1911; *On the Way of Catholicism*, 1912.

LABRIOLA, ANTONIO. 1843–1904.

Italian philosopher. Born in Cassino. Educated at Naples. Taught at Rome. A Marxist, he argued for a philosophy of "things," to replace traditional philosophies of "ideas." Sustaining a personal relationship with Engels, he argued against revisionist tendencies in other Marxists, including his disciples Croce and Sorel. Some of his writings were in French. *Q.v. Praxis* (6).

Principal writings: *On Socialism*, 1889; *Essays on the Materialist Conception of History* (T), 1896–7; *Socialism and Philosophy* (T), 1899; *On the History of Materialism*, 1902; *Writings on Philosophy and Politics* (ed. Croce), 1906; *Letters to Engels*, 1949.

LACAN, JACQUES. 1901–1981.

Born in Paris. Studied at Stanislas College and Paris Medical School. Founder and director of the Freudian School of Paris (1964–1980). His interpretation of Freud has been influential in the movement of Structuralism (*q.v.* 3).

Principal writings: *Paranoiac Psychosis and its Relations to the Personality* (T), 1933 (revised and expanded, 1975); *The Seminar of Jacques Lacan*, numerous volumes, 1953–1980, of which at least the following have been translated into English: *Freud's Papers on Technique* (T), (Sem. I); *Ego in Freudian Theory* (T), (Sem. II); *Psychoses* (T), (Sem. III); *The Four Fundamental Concepts of Psychoanalysis* (T), (Sem. XI); *Encore* (T), (Sem. XX); *Ecrits* (T and compiled), 1966; *Writings*, 1966; *The Language of the Self* (T), 1968; *Feminine Sexuality* (T and compiled), 1982.

(1) Lacan draws a correlation between de Saussure's *parole* and *langue* on the one hand, and Freud's conscious Ego and "unconscious" Id on the other. Holding that "the unconscious is structured like a language," Lacan believes that the "will" of the unconscious (the Id) can express itself in language, and that the conscious Ego should recognize the priority of the Id with its unconscious linguistic depths and plurality of meanings.

(2) This outcome is not easy to achieve however. The conscious Ego is the identity of the person, shaped through immense struggle, its contents passed on by one's official censor. Standard therapy is designed to strengthen the Ego. In that context, however, analyst and analysand come together, both possessed by their unconsciouses, turning their self-aggression, a property each of us has (arising from the inability of the child to be, or have, its other), against each other. They come together repeatedly, each demanding an encore, yet satisfied by "bla bla bla," an arrangement of purposeful incompleteness.

(3) The point of Lacanian therapy is to subvert, rather than reinforce, the Ego. The reason is that the conscious Ego is a patched-up affair, compensating for the sense of loss, going back to infancy, by censorship and repression. To compensate for the loss the failed ego takes two major steps. Having begun as a center of diffuse, undirected need, the infant ego moves

into the imaginary or mirror stage, projecting the mirror image of its failed ego. This image (called both *imago* and "specular ego") lacks the negative features of its source. It is therefore an ideal, often what the mother wishes for the child (the description is stated, in fact, in terms of the son). The symbolic stage follows, a third stage, with apprehension of the father as law-maker and speech-giver, blocking the path to the mother. Unconscious desire is replaced by symbolism; the split in the ego is now complete; and the sense of aggression, engendered by the child's loss, turns into self-aggression. This is the complex to be subverted by therapy.

(4) The subversion, disorienting, or decentering, of the Ego occurs through laying bare the self-aggression of the subject, or, to put it in other terms, uncovering the "split-I." The "split-I" is naturally related to "split" and diverse meanings. Since the language of the unconscious is multiply structured, there is an affinity between the two, so that awareness of the split-I makes the language available to the subject.

(5) The analyst is able to sense this language, not through what the subject says (that is the misleading voice of the ego), but through what is not said: silences, equivocations, omissions, misrememberings. The motive of the language of the unconscious can be understood more clearly from dreams, where the language of the conscious Ego is diachronic, logical, defensive, and censored. The language of the unconscious is synchronic, trans-individual, and incapable of passing the censor. Dreams are an exception, they do at times, pass the censor. They are to be esteemed as signifiers without a signified, to be related to each other in a synchronic system. In the free associations of this system the unconscious speaks.

(6) Lacan found the unconscious also appeared in the synchrony of puns and word play, metaphor and metonymy. These, like the not-said of (5) are signifiers making up a chain of unconscious discourse, silently doubling conscious discourse under the "misrecognition" occasioned by repression. One of the reasons he held that psychoanalysis must open itself to "literature, philosophy, an-

thropology and political theory" is the presence of figured speech in many of these disciplines. In any use the point is to remember the "interminable" play of one's conscious desires, entering "with gaiety" the open-ended order of the symbolic.

LACHELIER, JULES. 1834–1918.

French philosopher. Born in Fontainebleau. Professor in the École Normale Supérieure of Paris. Influenced by Maine de Biran and Ravaisson, he was the teacher of both Boutroux and Bergson. All three are sometimes placed in a neo-Spiritualism movement with Lachelier as founder. Advancing a philosophy of spiritual realism, Lachelier found in the spirit of man and its spontaneity the conception allowing him to avoid the difficulties of materialism and idealism. When these latter are not viewed as the ultimate ends of analysis but as the manner in which the principles of thought and reality manifest themselves, then one is able to make central the creative activity which produced them. Lachelier "solved" the problem of induction by stressing the interrelatedness of efficient and final causes.

Principal writings: *On the Grounds of Induction* (T), 1871; "*Psychology and Metaphysics*" (T), 1885; *Studies on the Syllogism*, 1907.

LACTANTIUS. 4th cent. A.D.

Christian Apologist. Probably born in Italy. Educated in North Africa under Arnobius. Converted in Nicomedia around 300 A.D. Tutor to Constantine's son, Crispus, and adviser to Constantine, he was called "the Christian Cicero." His thought contained Chiliast (*q.v.*) and Manichaean (*q.v.*) emphases. He argued against the value of philosophy. Fragments of truth lie scattered through the philosophers which could yield a coherent body of doctrine in accord with Christian faith, but it is impossible to sift them out without the aid of revelation. *Q.v.* Apologists (11).

Principal writings: *Institutiones divinae*, 7 vols.; *On Death from Persecution; On the Anger of God; On God's Workmanship.*

LAFINUR, JUAN CRISÓSTOMO.

Q.v. Latin American Philosophy (3).

LAKATOS, IMRE. 1922–74.

Hungarian philosopher of science. Born in Debrecen. Educated at Debrecen, Budapest University, Moscow University, and Cambridge. Taught at London School of Economics. In 1947, appointed Secretary in the Ministry of Education charged with the democratic reform of Hungarian higher education. A political prisoner from 1950–53 under the Stalinist puppet government, and freed following Stalin's death. Fled Hungary in 1956, following the Soviet suppression of the Hungarian revolt. Making his way to England, after a period of study in Cambridge he joined Karl Popper at the London School of Economics.

Principal writings: *Proceedings* (Int. colloquium in the Philosophy of Science), ed., 1967–70; *Proofs and Refutations: The Logic of Mathematical Discovery* (ed. J. Worrall, E. Zahar), 1976; *Mathematics, Science and Epistemology: Philosophical Papers*, Vol. II (ed. J. Worrall, G. Currie), 1977; *The Methodology of Scientific Research Programmes: Philosophical Papers*, Vol. I (ed. J. Worrall, G. Currie), 1977.

(1) Advocating a problematic, rather than an axiomatic, approach to mathematics, Lakatos held the axioms of mathematics to be hypotheses whose truth and consistency develop under the challenge of counter-examples, and whose theorems improve as attempts are made to prove them.

(2) While accepting the thrust of Popper's (*q.v.* 1) views on falsifiability, and on conjecture and refutation, he decided that Popper, along with many others (including Kuhn, *q.v.* 1), had overemphasized the importance of individual theories. Lakatos shifted the emphasis to the appraisal of "research programmes" which encompassed a succession of related theories. Research programs progress so long as scientific content is increasing, and degenerate when it is not. The typically defensive response to a refuted theory is to protect its "hard core," while altering any number of its auxiliary assumptions. Since these also change under the influence of a progressive program, defensive modifications can lead to the recovery of a degenerating program.

LALANDE, ANDRÉ. 1867–1964.

French philosopher. Born in Dijon. Educated at the École Normale Supérieure. Taught at the Sorbonne. Interested in the application of evolutionary theory to philosophy. His greatest contributions related to his efforts in behalf of a unified terminology in philosophy: *Vocabulaire technique et critique de la philosophie* (one of the basic sources for the present work); and contact among philosophers both nationally (*Société Française de Philosophie*) and internationally (*The International Congresses of Philosophy*).

Principal writings: *Dissolution Opposed to Evolution in the Physical and Moral Sciences*, 1898; *Technical and Critical Vocabulary of Philosophy*, 1902–23; *Reasoned Précis of Moral Practice*, 1907; *Theories of Induction and Experiment*, 1929; *The Psychology of Judgment of Value*, 1929; *Reason and Norms*, 1948.

LAMAISM.

The system of religious and political doctrine which from the 15th to the 20th centuries ruled Tibet with spiritual influence; also in Mongolia, China, and Siberia.

(1) In the middle of the 15th century, to begin the narrative halfway through, the emperor of China (who also controlled Tibet) named two Buddhist monks to be, one the spiritual ruler, and the other the temporal ruler of Tibet. The spiritual ruler was called the Dalai Lama; the temporal ruler the Panchen Lama. The reason for the move was that this particular sect of Buddhism, a reform movement, had become astonishingly powerful in numbers and influence. The two Grand Lamas are regarded as incarnations of celestial beings; the Dalai Lama of Avalokiteshvara, the Panchen Lama of Amitabha. When either Lama died it was the duty of the other to discover the child in whom the *bodhisattva* had become reincarnate. The names of all male children born shortly after the death of his counterpart would be laid before him. He would choose three names; a council of holy men after a week of prayer would select by lot one of the three to be the future Grand Lama.

(2) The Buddhism of Tibet is Mahayana Buddhism (*q.v.*). The other form of Buddhism, Theravada, has remained free

of belief in *bodhisattvas*, innumerable Buddhas and the like. In fact, five trinities appeared in Mahayana Buddhism. The trinities grew from the fact that the power of a Buddha was explained by the belief that he was the emanation of an ethereal Buddha existing in the skies, a Dhyani Buddha; and, being Buddhas, they had their *bodhisattvas*. In the case of the historical Gautama Buddha, Amitabha was said to be his Dhyani Buddha, and Avalokiteshvara his *bodhisattva*.

(3) Mahayana Buddhism was introduced into Tibet in 622 A.D., the ruler sending to India for the sacred books. After many difficulties, including civil wars, "the second introduction of religion" occurred in the 10th century. It grew in power for 300 years, scoring its greatest triumph when Kubla Khan, Mongol emperor, and grandson of Genghis Khan, became a convert to Tibetan Buddhism. He named a Buddhist abbot as head of the church, and tributary ruler of the country. The head of the church in return crowned Kubla Khan ruler of the Mongol empire. Thus began the temporal sovereignty of the Lamas, under the authority of the emperors of China.

(4) In 1390, Tsongkapa (1357–1419) began a reform movement within Buddhism, raising the spiritual level of the monks, opposing animism and extreme Tantric practices, while restoring the rules of celibacy and simple living. He returned to the yellow or orange robe of Gautama Buddha in preference to the red robes worn by Tibetan monks. The orange-hoods completely overshadowed the red-hoods. It was from this group that the Chinese emperor selected the Grand Lamas in the 15th century. The work of Tsongkapa shaped Tibetan Buddhism for more than 500 years, until the Chinese invasion of 1959 with its destructiveness and the flight of the Dalai Lama to northern India.

(5) A Tantric form of Mahayana Buddhism, known as Vajrayana ("diamond vehicle") or Mantrayana ("mantra vehicle"), promises the possibility of Buddhahood within a single lifetime. This Tibetan alternative is considered by some a final stage of Buddhism, beyond both Hinayana and Mahayana.

LAMAS, THE GRAND.
Q.v. Lamaism.

LAMBERT, JOHANN HEINRICH. 1728–1777.
German mathematician, physicist, and philosopher. Born in Muhlhausen, Alsace. Self-educated. Proved the irrationality of π; proved a number of theorems in conics which bear his name; introduced hyperbolic functions into geometry. Philosophically, he is in some measure a forerunner of Kant. His "new organon" included a study of the laws of thought, of the conditions for arriving at truth, of semiotic or a doctrine of language, and phenomenology (*q.v.* 1) or a doctrine of the phantasms offered to perception. This is included within an architectonic supported by a doctrine of categories.

Principal writings: *Cosmological Letters on the Structure of the Universe*, 1761; *New Organon*, 2 vols., 1764; *Sketch of the Architectonic*, 2 vols., 1771; *Logical and Philosophical Papers*, 1782.

LAMBERT OF AUXERRE. Mid-13th cent.
Scholastic philosopher. One of the representatives of Terminist logic (*q.v.*). He distinguished between logic and dialectic, holding the former to be a method for determining truth and falsity, and the latter a method which arrived at no more than probability.

Principal writings: *Dialectic; Summa of Logic.*

LAMENNAIS, HUGUES FÉLICITÉ ROBERT DE. 1782–1854.
French philosopher and Churchman. Born in Saint Malo. Shocked by the excesses of the French Revolution, Lamennais began his turbulent reformist career, holding that the right of private judgment championed by Descartes, Luther, Rousseau, and the Encyclopedists had ended in atheism, and the solution was a return to revelation and ecclesiastical authority. He held that tradition was the sole test of certitude, and the pope the only sovereign being on the face of the earth. More Ultramontanist than the French Church, which had come partly under the control of the French nation through the Concordat signed by Napoleon and Pius VII, Lamennais ran into difficulties both

with the state and the Church. His periodical, *L'Avenir*, ceased publication when Pope Gregory XVI condemned his policy in the encyclical, *Mirari vos*. From this time he devoted his energies to democracy and socialism, supporting the Revolution of 1848, and sitting on the left in the constituent assembly.

Principal writings: *Essay on Indifference in Matters of Religion*, 4 vols., 1817–23; *On Religion*, 2 vols., 1825–6; *The Progress of the Revolution and of the War Against the Church*, 1828; *Words of a Believer*, 1834; *Sketch of a Philosopher*, 4 vols., 1841–6.

LA METTRIE, JULIAN OFFRAY DE. 1709–1751.

French philosopher and physician. Born in Saint Malo. Studied medicine at Rheims, and the University of Paris. In 1742 he became Surgeon of the Guards in Paris. The outcry against the materialism of his first book was so great that he took refuge in Leiden to compose his second. The reaction to his second forced him to leave Holland. Frederick the Great gave him sanctuary in Berlin, allowed him to practice as a physician, and appointed him court reader.

Principal writings: *Natural History of the Soul*, 1745; *Man a Machine* (T), 1747; *The Man Plant* 1748; *Discourse on Happiness*, 1750; *Reflections on the Origin of Animals*, 1750; *The System of Epicurus*, 1750; *Venus Metaphysic*, 1751.

(1) Starting from one aspect of the Cartesian position, namely that animals are soulless mechanisms, La Mettrie extended this principle to include humans on the clear evidence of the gradual transition from animal to human form leading through the apes.

(2) If, then, man is a mechanism, his psychical awareness and its modifications will be the result of physiological causes. Further, then, the intelligence of a person will be a function of the character of his brain; and the character of a people will be determined by their environment, including the climate in which they live.

(3) Since rational activity depends upon language, and speech is just physical sound, thought can be explained without a rational faculty. For La Mettrie it involved, besides physical sounds, physical images in the brain correlated to sounds. In a certain sense, then, the human soul

became for him a collection of images.

(4) He traced ethics to natural laws playing on and shaping human desires. The goal of life is pleasure; and virtue is a species of self-love which should be directed toward the service of humanity.

(5) He thought it possible that God existed, but the fact seemed to him irrelevant to human life. Indeed, since human life is richer when free of fear, it is better that humans should live without faith in a divine being or an afterlife.

LA MOTHE LE VAYER, FRANÇOIS DE. 1588–1672.

French philosopher. Born in Paris. A skeptic, La Mothe Le Vayer turned skepticism against science, which he held to be both problematical and blasphemous, in order to return nonbelievers to the Christian faith.

Principal writings: *Christian Discourse on the Immortality of the Soul*, 1637; *The Virtue of the Countrymen*, 1642; *Small Skeptical Treatise*, 1647; *Discourse Showing that Skeptical Doubts are of Great Use in the Sciences*, 1669.

LANDINO, CRISTOFORO.

Q.v. Florentine Academy.

LANGE, FRIEDRICH ALBERT. 1828–1875.

German philosopher. Born at Wald, near Solingen. Taught at Bonn, Zürich, and Marburg. Applying the Kantian philosophy to metaphysical systems, Lange regarded them not as true but as embodying human purposes. Materialism, which he studied at length in his *History of Materialism*, has been of service in providing a framework for science, and Idealism has directed human life in the same manner as have poetry and religion. Regarded as an early member of the Marburg School of neo-Kantianism (*q.v.* 2).

Principal writings: *The Labor Question*, 1865; *History of Materialism and Critique of its Present Significance* (T), 1866; *Logical Studies*, 1877.

LANGER, SUSANNE K. 1895–1985.

American philosopher. Born in New York. Studied at Radcliffe College and University of Vienna. Taught at University of Delaware, Columbia, and Connecticut College. Strongly influenced by Cassirer, and interested in symbolic logic.

Principal writings: *An Introduction to Symbolic Logic*, 1937; *Philosophy in a New Key; A Study in the Symbolism of Reason Rite and Art*, 1942; *Feeling and Form: A Theory of Art Developed from Philosophy in a New Key*, 1953; *Problems of Art*, 1957; *Reflections on Art*, 1959; *Philosophical Sketches*, 1962; *Mind: An Essay on Human Feeling*, 3 vols., 1967, 1972, 1982.

(1) Langer defines man as the "symbolific animal" and finds in symbolism a new key to philosophy.

(2) She distinguishes between signs (widespread in the organic realm) and symbols (present to human awareness), noting the tendencies of empiricists to forget the extent to which sense data are infused by symbols. She notes and analyzes the transformation of symbols in psychoanalysis, symbolic logic, and in the structuring of works of art, distinguishing between the open presentational symbols of art and the representational symbols of science tied to dictionary meanings.

(3) Her aesthetics not only stress the importance of "unconsummated" symbols, allowing us the freedom to read into them, but the presence of "virtual" space and time in works of art.

LANGFELD, H.S.

Q.v. Aesthetics (22).

LANGUAGE.

Philosophers, prior to and along with linguists, have concerned themselves with the nature of language.

(1) In the period of Vedic philosophy the confidence in language was so great that the *Vedas* (*q.v.*) were considered to be eternal with Sanskrit its equally eternal instrument. Also *q.v.* Purva Mimamsa (3).

(2) In the *Cratylus*, Plato explored the problem of the relation of names to things. Cratylus held that there is a natural relationship between the two, while his Sophistic opponent argued that names are mere conventions. One of the most widespread convictions of the school of Sophists (*q.v.*) concerned the conventional nature of linguistic signs.

(3) The Confucian emphasis on the "rectification of names" suggests an approach like that of Cratylus, but Hsün Tzu (*q.v.* 4) held both to the doctrine of the rectification of names, and to the view

that names are conventional.

(4) Concern with language, mingled with considerations of logic and epistemology, characterizes the thought of Aristotle, the Stoics, Pyrrhonists, and Scholasticism.

(5) Skepticism over the truth capabilities of language developed, especially, in Buddhist thought. For Nagarjuna (*q.v.* 10), who founded the school of Madhyamika (*q.v.*) Buddhism, we must rise above the subject-object duality of language to the non-dual Absolute which language cannot represent. Among the Madhyamikas the absolute is identified with *shunya* (*q.v.* Śunya), or vacuity.

(6) Vasubandhu (*q.v.*) who, with his brother, Asanga (*q.v.*) founded the Consciousness (*q.v.* 1) Only school, held that we can know only the imagined mental forms of our own construction (*vikalpa*) with their subject-object duality and remoteness from reality.

(7) In Zen Buddhism (*q.v.* 6–7) the paradoxes of language are used against each other in the *koan* (*q.v.*) to reach a direct apprehension of reality. For Suzuki (*q.v.* 4) this is an intuitive understanding.

(8) Hobbes (*q.v.* 4) understood language to be a computation with words, always following the force of experience.

(9) Leibniz (*q.v.* 11) called for a *characteristica universalis*, a universal language applicable to all fields, allowing disputation to be replaced by calculation.

(10) In the movement of Empiricism (*q.v.* 3–4), the analysis of language was equated with passage from impressions to ideas, and the affixing of signs.

(11) Herder (*q.v.* 2) provided a naturalistic interpretation of the origin of language, finding it to lie in imitation of the sounds of nature.

(12) Von Humboldt (*q.v.*) held that each language had a *Sprachform*, an inner form containing implicitly a characteristic world outlook.

(13) Mauthner (*q.v.* 2) held language to be essentially adjectival; the translation of adjectives into nouns rests on "word superstition."

(14) Ferdinand de Saussure (*q.v.*) looked upon language as a storehouse of words and phrases, sentences being a result of free and creative activity.

(15) Franz Boas (1858–1942) followed von Humboldt's lead, finding a unique

grammatical structure in each language. The linguist's task is to discover the appropriate descriptive categories for a given language.

(16) Paul Tillich (*q.v.* 4), a theologian, distinguished between signs and symbols, holding that the language of religion rests on the latter. Symbols, in Tillich's view, have lives of their own and relate to reality in a unique manner.

(17) Edward Sapir (1884–1939) emphasized the cognitive character of language (*Language*, 1921). Among other claims, he argued that all ideas originate in metaphor, clear cognitive expressions standing for dead metaphors.

(18) Leonard Bloomfield (1887–1949), adopting behaviorism as a framework, laid it down that linguistic study is to be descriptive, not prescriptive, and that only usage by native speakers prescribes correctness.

(19) Ludwig Wittgenstein (*q.v.* 1–2) and Russell (*q.v.* 8) at one stage advanced a doctrine of logical atomism which supposed that there ought to be a mirroring relationship between symbols and the facts they symbolize. In his later work Wittgenstein (*q.v.* 5–6) worked in terms of language games, resolving conceptual difficulties into differences among the language games being played.

(20) Finding ordinary language an inadequate vehicle for precise conceptual work Carnap (*q.v.* 3–6) set language rules, thus constructing ideal languages in terms of which conceptual problems might reach definitive solutions.

(21) Benjamin Lee Whorf (1897–1941) developed, along with Sapir, a thesis of linguistic relativity, known as the Sapir-Whorf hypothesis, according to which one's manner of perceiving reality derives from the structure of one's language. Different languages provide different maps of possible ideas, or different "segmentations of experience" (*q.v. Language, Thought, and Reality*, ed. J.B. Carroll, 1956).

(22) Lacan (*q.v.* 4–6) speaks of the language of the unconscious, and for him this is more than a metaphor. The discourse of the unconscious can add profundity to the chain of conscious discourse.

(23) Gustav Bergmann (*q.v.* 2), following a revised positivist line, employs ideal languages as a method of testing philosophical ideas.

(24) Dietrich Bonhoeffer (*q.v.* 2), a theologian, related to the problem of language from a somewhat different angle, claiming differences and yet complementarity between the languages of ontology and biblical theology.

(25) John Austin (*q.v.* 1, 4) centered his attention on language acts, distinguishing locutionary, illocutionary, and perlocutionary types. He believed that close attention to the natural language and its use would provide means for the solution, or dissolution, of philosophic problems.

(26) In his generative grammar. Chomsky (*q.v.* 7) distinguished between the deep structure of a language and its surface structure, holding that humans have a highly specific "language faculty" in some sense innate.

(27) Derrida (*q.v.* 1–3, 7), utilized de Saussure to launch the project of deconstruction (*q.v.*), emphasizing the inability of signs to provide the sense of totality for which we intend them.

Also *q.v.* Structuralism.

LANGUE.

Q.v. de Saussure (1); Lacan (1).

LAO TZU. 6th cent. B.C.

Chinese philosopher. The reputed founder of Taoism, and author of the *Lao Tzu* or *Tao-Te Ching* (*Classic of the Way and its Virtue*), a book of poems explaining Taoism. Details of his life are not known. Ssu-ma Ch'ien in the *Records of the Historian* provides a fairly complete picture of a religious leader impatient with the Confucian principles and seeking something better. Ssu-ma Ch'ien places him in Ch'u, makes him a custodian of the imperial archives, records a visit by Confucius where Confucius is seeking the advice of Lao Tzu, claims that in old age he retired and on his way to his place of retirement paused at the request of a gatekeeper to write out 5,000 words on his philosophy. This document was the famous *Tao-Te Ching*. Some scholars substantially accept this account. Others place Lao Tzu in the 4th or 3rd century B.C., and hold the *Tao-Te Ching* to be a composite work. Since the term Lao Tzu means "the Old One," "the Old Philosopher," or "the Old Philosophers," the composite origin of the work is not unlikely, and the title may refer to a group of Chinese mystics. The *Tao-Te Ching*, and its ideas, led to the major religion of Taoism, no matter who its author, or authors may have been. The ideas of this document are discussed under the heading, *Tao-Te Ching*.

LAPLACE, PIERRE SIMON, MARQUIS DE. 1749–1827.

French mathematician and astronomer. Born at Beaumont-in-Auge, Normandy. Studied theology and mathematics. Through d'Alembert he obtained an appointment as professor of mathematics at the École Militaire of Paris. He was called "the Newton of France" due to his brilliant demonstrations concerning planetary perturbations. It is said that the mathematical genius of his *Celestial Mechanics* ranks second only to *the Principia* of Newton. He became a member of the French Academy of Science in 1785, and thereafter of most of the scientific associations of Europe. Chancellor of the Senate in 1803, and grand officer of the Legion of Honor. He was created a count by Napoleon, and became a Marquis in 1817.

Principal writings: *Exposition of the System of the World* (T), 1796; *Celestial Mechanics* (T), 5 vols., 1799–1825; *A Philosophical Essay on Probabilities* (T), 1812.

(1) In his first papers Laplace demonstrated the invariability of planetary mean motions, and on this basis—in friendly competition with Lagrange—cleared up the anomalies of apparent planetary perturbations; special attention was given to the inequalities of Jupiter and Saturn, and even to the dependence of lunar acceleration upon eccentricities in the earth's orbit.

(2) In the *Exposition of the System of the World and Celestial Mechanics* he systematized the results obtained in the development and application of the laws of gravitation, and the progress achieved in each branch of the subject. He made important experiments in many areas, and laid the foundations of the sciences of heat, electricity, and magnetism.

(3) Starting from the work of Pascal and Fermat he developed the theory of probability, applying it to chance situations, future events, and inquiries into causality. Laplacian probability obviously relates to human knowledge only, since for him the happenings of the world occur by necessity. In his discussion of probabilities Laplace argues that were there an intelligence sufficiently vast to know the forces acting in the universe and the disposition of the beings acted upon by these forces, this intelligence could express in a single formula the movements of every star and every atom; every detail of the future and of the past would be open to its view. Not having this information we must proceed by probability, *i.e.*, by the ratio of the number of favorable cases to all possible cases. Where various cases are not equally possible, the possibility of each must be determined; then the probability will be the sum of the possibilities of each favorable case. If the events are independent, the probability of their conjoint existence is the product of their respective probabilities. If the events depend upon each other, the probability of the existence of the compound event is the product of the probability of the first event, and the probability that, this event having occurred, the second will occur.

LAROMIGUIÈRE, PIERRE. 1756–1837.

French philosopher. Born at Livignac. Professor of logic in the École Normale. A student of Condillac, indebted also to Destutt de Tracy and Cabanis, Laromiguière concentrated on the importance of the act of attention in building up the conception of a world, or of the organon for handling it. Since Condillac wished to build up the nature of the self from sensation, Laromiguière's thesis is radical. He felt it also allowed him to believe in free will and the immortality of the soul.

Principal writings: *Draft of the Elements of Metaphysics*, 1793; *The Paradoxes of Condillac*, 1805; *Lessons of Philosophy*, 1815–17.

LARROYO, FRANCISCO.

Q.v. Latin American Philosophy, (12).

LASK, EMIL. 1875–1915.

German philosopher. Born in Wadowice, Austria. Taught at the University of Heidelberg. Continuing, as he believed, the Kantian analysis, Lask arrived at a category of the categories, an *Urform*, primitive and primary, from which the transcendental logic is deduced which serves as a criterion of truth, and as an Absolute.

Principal writings: *Fichte's Idealism and History*, 1902; *The Logic of Philosophy and the Teaching of the Categories*, 1912; *The Theory of Judgment*, 1913.

LASSALLE, FERDINAND. 1825–1864.

German socialist and philosopher. Born at Breslau. Educated at Breslau and Berlin. An Hegelian, his analysis of human social history was triadic: solidarity without freedom (ancient and feudal periods); freedom without solidarity (since 1789); freedom with solidarity through the principle of association (the goal for the future). In short, he believed that the power of capital could be broken by the establishment of productive workers' associations financed by the state. He thought, further, that the key to such a move was universal suffrage, since workers outnumber capitalists. To this end he established the *Allgemeiner Deutscher Arbeiterverein* ("General German Workers' Association"), centering in Berlin, Leipzig, Frankfurt, and the industrial cities of the Rhine. The association, to which he devoted the last two and one-half years of his life, is regarded as the parent of German socialism. By 1903 the association returned eighty-one representatives to the Reichstag.

Principal writings: *The Philosophy of Heraclitus the Dark of Ephesus*, 1858; *The System of Acquired Rights*, 1861; *The Worker Program*, 1862, and other pamphlets.

LATERAN COUNCILS.

The name given to five Church councils (*q.v.* Christianity 6–7) held at the Lateran palace in Rome. At the fourth Lateran Council the doctrine of transubstantiation was accepted as applying to the Eucharist.

LATIMER, HUGH. c. 1485–1555.

English Protestant reformer. Bishop of Worcester. Martyred at Oxford on October 16, 1555 along with Bishop Ridley (*q.v.*). At the stake Latimer cried out to Ridley "... we shall this day light such a candle, by God's grace, in England as I trust shall never be put out."

LATIN AMERICAN PHILOSOPHY.

The philosophy of Latin America has followed to a great extent the political fortunes of the area. From the beginning of Spanish rule in the 16th century until the expulsion of the Jesuits and the struggles for independence, Scholastic philosophy was in the ascendancy. Alonso de La Veracruz (*q.v.*), working in Mexico, is an outstanding illustration of this fact.

A. The revolt from Scholasticism led in the first half of the 19th century to an interest in the doctrines of the French Enlightenment, to Condillac especially, and to the *Idéologues*.

(1) The development in Cuba, beginning with P. José Augustín Caballero whose *Philosophia electiva*, 1796, marked a shift away from Thomism in philosophy, was continued by Felix Varela (1788–1853) who introduced the philosophies of Locke, Condillac, and Descartes, treating reason and experience as valid sources of truth, while not denying the authority of the Church in matters of dogma. (*Institutiones philosophiae*, 4 vols., 1812–14; *Lessons in Philosophy*, 3 vols., 1818.) Luz y Caballero (1780–1862) continued this development, opposing not only Scholasticism but also the spiritual eclecticism of Cousin which had gained a foothold in Cuba. Philosophy was for him a science of values including, of course, religious values. Religious and philosophical truth are not at last inimical. (*Course in Philosophy*, 1839–43; *Attack on Cousin's Examination of Locke's Essay on the Human Understanding*, 1840 (in part); in full, 1948).

(2) Born in Venezuela, Andrés Bello (*q.v.*) lived in Chile from 1829. Influenced primarily by the British empiricists, his *Philosophy of the Understanding* was an outstanding exposition of an empirical logico-psychological approach to philosophy.

(3) In Argentina a similar development was occurring. Juan Crisóstomo Lafinur (1797–1824) supported Condillac, Cabanis, and Destutt de Tracy against Scholasticism. Against opposition, the teaching spread. Carrying on the work of their teacher were Diego Alcorto and Juan Manuel Fernandez de Agüero.

B. The movement into Positivism occurred in the second half of the 19th century.

(4) Gabino Barreda (1820–1881) of Mexico studied under Auguste Comte, bringing Comtian positivism to Mexico. Not only did his teaching create followers, such as Porfirio Parra and Agustin Aragón; but Barreda's work in drafting the public instruction legislation of 1867 brought his emphasis into the schools. (*On Moral Education*, 1863; *Opúsculus*, 1871.)

(5) Comtian positivism was introduced into Brazil by Luis Pereira Barreto (1840–1923), (*The Teleological Philosophy*, 1874). The doctrine was supported at least in his middle period, by Tobias Barreto (1839–1889), although the latter began as a follower of Cousin, and ended in an attempt to engineer a synthesis of the metaphysical systems of German transcendentalism and idealism. The attempt ran counter to a similar interest he sustained in the philosophy of Haeckel. (*Studies in Law; Contemporary Questions; German Studies*.)

(6) Enrique José Varona (1849–1933) supported positivism in Cuba, combining the emphases of Comte, Spencer, John Stuart Mill and Bain. The theme of skepticism emerged from his work as well as an affirmation of the possibility of human freedom. (*Philosophical Lectures*, 3 vols., 1880; *Lessons in Psychology*, 1901; *Logical Notions*, 1912.)

C. The 20th century has witnessed the attempt to go beyond positivism, finding authentic national or regional philosophies emphasizing value and creative freedom while often reflecting aspects of Leibniz, Kant, Hegel, neo-Kantianism, Bergson, and Croce.

(7) Transitional in the extreme is the figure of Raimundo de Farias Brito (1862–1917). This Brazilian thinker found positivism and Materialism unable to come to terms with the spirit of man revealed in suffering. He found philosophy going beyond science, and approaching religion. (*The Goals of the World*, 3 vols., 1895–1905.)

(8) Alejandro O. Deústua (1849–1945) in Peru developed a philosophy of creative liberty influenced by Krause, Wundt, and Bergson. He understood freedom to be the foundation of all values and the key to the problem of moral values. The development of philosophy in Peru owes much to his teaching. More recently his successors and colleagues in Peru have shown interest in the Baden school of neo-Kantianism, the realism of Nicolai Hartmann, phenomenology (especially problems of intentionality), problems in the philosophy of law and philosophy of science. (*General Aesthetics*, 1923; *Applied Aesthetics*, 1932.)

(9) In Argentina, Alejandro Korn (*q.v.*) (1860–1936) was among those who broadened the framework of positivism, seeking an indigenous philosophy; his point of view emphasized human liberty and its relation to human values. José Ingenieros (1877–1925) supported a form of positivism oriented toward the ongoing processes of science. He found his view consistent with a reordered metaphysics, which might still in some sense go beyond experience. (*Simulation in the Struggle for Life*, 1903; *Genetic Psychology*, 1911; *Mediocre Man*, 1913; *Toward a Morality without Dogma*, 1917; *Propositions Relative to the Future of Philosophy*, 1918; *The Evolution of Argentine Ideas*, 2 vols., 1918–20). Francisco Romero (*q.v.*) (1891–1962) continued the emphasis of Korn and Ingenieros, although also influenced by European philosophers. He added especially an emphasis on intentionality. Coriolano Alberini (1886–1960), while retaining the emphasis on freedom and value, introduced into Argentine philosophy the views of Bergson, Meyerson, Croce, Gentile, James, and Royce. (His publications include, for example, *The Pedagogy of W. James*, 1910; *The Kantian Theory of the Synthetic a Priori Judgment*, 1911; *The Ethical Problem in the Philosophy of Bergson*, 1925.) Risieri Frondizi (1915–1983), with a doctrine of integral experience, likewise broadened the base of Empiricism beyond its positivistic confines in an effort to take account of the legitimate claims of traditional philosophy. Finally, Ángel Vassallo (1902–), influenced especially by Blondel, reintroduced the contrast between finite and infinite being, and the relation of man's spiritual life to the transcendent. (*New Introductions to Metaphysics*, 1938; *Alejandro Korn* (with Romero and Azner). 1940); *Essay on the Ethics of Kant and the Metaphysics of Hegel*, 1945;

The Moral Problem, 1957.) Among other Argentine philosophers one may mention Alberto Rougès (1900–45). (*The Hierarchies of Being and Eternity*, 1943.)

(10) Among the philosophers of Chile, Enrique Molina (1871–1962) (*Tragedy and Realization of the Spirit*, 1952) may be mentioned. Rejecting both Idealism and materialism, Molina held that spirit exists in being potentially, and that humans are called to spiritualize and valorize reality. Influenced by Nietzsche, Guyau, and Bergson, the ideas of Ortega y Gasset. Yves Simon, and the existentialists also contribute to the shaping of Chilean philosophical thought.

(11) The influence of Carlos Vaz Ferreira (1871–1958) (*Living Logic*, 1920; *Fermentario*, 1938) is very much alive among the philosophers of Uruguay. Vaz Ferreira came to terms with positivism by assimilating it to a concrete logic able to deal with normative as well as descriptive, substantive as well as verbal, problems. Problems of human value are important to the philosophers of Uruguay; personalism has some effect in the area.

(12) The new wave of philosophy in Mexico, following the Barreda-led positivism (*cf.* 4 above), was inaugurated principally by Antonio Caso (1883–1946) who found his way beyond positivism in the typical manner— that is, by amplifying its doctrine of experience. He directed attention to the work of Boutroux, Bergson, Husserl, and Meyerson, among others. José Vasconcelos (*q.v.*) (1882–1959), with an intense interest in aesthetics, value, and cultural problems generally, as Rector of the National University and Secretary of Education (1921–3), was able to exert considerable influence on the educational curriculum. Samuel Ramos (born 1897), influenced by Ortega y Gasset and Scheler, has worked especially in philosophical anthropology out of a concern for the individual in modern mechanized societies. Oswaldo Robles (1904–1969) continued the neo-Thomistic tradition while finding some value in existentialism and phenomenology. Francisco Larroyo (1908–1981) served as the principal bearer of neo-Kantian thought in Mexico. Combining the influences of Marburg and Baden, he worked with the problems of ethics and human value. His

influence was extended by means of the journal *La Gaceta filosófica* which he established. Leopoldo Zea (1912–) (*Two Stages of Thought in Hispanic America*, 1949, trans. 1963 as *The Latin American Mind*) has spent many years in the analysis of the history of positivism in Latin America.

(13) The most influential philosopher of law in Latin America is the Brazilian, Miguel Reale (1910–). He calls his view "critical ontognoseological historicism" and holds that there is a dialectical interplay and unity between history and nature, fact and value.

LATITUDINARIANISM.

The position of the Anglicans agreeing to Cromwell's church settlement. They sought a position between Calvinism and Catholicism, allowing more "latitude" of belief and practice. Its influence was greatest in the 17th century. *Q.v.* Toleration (1).

LATTER DAY SAINTS.

Generic name for the six religious sects, also known as Mormons, tracing their foundation to Joseph Smith. The movement dates its origin from 1830 in Fayette, New York, when Smith received a series of revelations, commanding him to establish a new church. Not only did he receive information concerning the Second Coming but also, eventually, a set of golden plates from which the Book of Mormon was translated. The book traces America's initial settlement to the dispersion of mankind following the Tower of Babel, and a group of Israelites six centuries before Christ. After the establishment of a number of colonies Smith was killed in 1844 in Carthage, Ill. Brigham Young assumed leadership, guiding the main group to Utah where Salt Lake City was founded in 1848.

LAUD, WILLIAM. 1573–1645.

English Churchman. Archbishop of Canterbury under Charles I, Laud's persecution of Puritans was one of the causes leading to the English Civil War. In 1640, as the war went on, he was imprisoned; his trial began in 1644; on January 10, 1645 he was beheaded.

LAUDAN, LARRY.

Q.v. Logic of Discovery and Logic of Justification (1).

LAURIE, SIMON. 1829–1909.

Born in Edinburgh. Taught at Edinburgh. Hailing his view as a return to dualism, Laurie tried to show how, from pure feeling (in a dialectical ascent) there arise sensation (with a sense of the external), intuition (where the object and the differences among objects are apprehended as such), perception (where the subject becomes active and the subject-object opposition becomes definitive). The reason, which appears in the third stage, merely validates the distinctions emerging at earlier stages. Man is thus guided not by reason, but by a will-reason. The ascent finally leads to God in whom these dialectical oppositions are resolved.

Principal writings: *On the Philosophy of Ethics*, 1866; *Metaphysica Nova et Vetusta, a Return to Dualism*, 1884; *Ethica, or the Ethics of Reason*, 1885; *Synthetica: Being Meditations Epistemological and Ontological*, 2 vols., 1906.

LAVELLE, LOUIS. 1883–1951.

French philosopher. Born in Saint-Martin-de-Villéreal. Professor in the Collège de France.

Principal writings: *On Being*, 1928; *Self-Awareness*, 1933; *The Total Presence*, 1934; *The Ego and its Destiny*, 1936; *On the Act*, 1937; *The Error of Narcissus*, 1939; *Evil and Suffering*, 1940; *French Philosophy Between the Two Wars*, 1942; *Of Time and Eternity*, 1945; *Introduction to Ontology*, 1947; *The Powers of the Ego*, 1948; *On the Human Soul*, 1951; *Treatise on Values*, 2 vols., 1951, 1955; *Spiritual Inwardness*, 1955.

(1) Developing a metaphysics of "Act," Lavelle built his philosophy around the notion of our participation in the act of being. As we discipline by rational means the natural spontaneity of our instincts, we begin to reach our potentialities and this is the achievement of freedom,

(2) By thus turning inward we relate ourselves to the Absolute act of Being, or God, who is also Absolute freedom. Each of us in an appropriate manner is able to actualize an appropriate but limited act of being, freedom, and value in participation with the Absolute Being.

LAVROV, PETER L. 1823–1900.

Russian socialist and philosopher. Born in Melekhov. Educated in St. Petersburg. Taught in St. Petersburg. A socialist, he was sent to the provinces, and went into exile in Europe in 1870. Holding to self-development as the end of history, and mutual aid as the path to such development, he only partially accepted the Marxist view of economics and class conflict.

Principal writings: *Historical Letters* (T in part), 1868–9; *The State Element in Future Society*, 1876.

LAW.

The term relates to philosophy in many ways. The basic distinction is between descriptive and prescriptive senses of the term's use.

A. In a descriptive sense "law" means "law of nature," an invariant relationship found in phenomena by scientific investigation, and thus presumed to hold in the natural world.

(1) The implications of law in this sense are examined within the discipline of Philosophy of Science (*q.v.*).

(2) For Peirce (*q.v.* 5) natural laws are to be explained by a habit-taking feature of the universe. They evolve, and do not eliminate chance.

(3) Descriptive laws, applying to society and history, are often proposed. August Comte (*q.v.* 1) advanced a law of cultural evolution, called the Law of the Three Stages. It held that culture had to pass through theological and metaphysical stages on the way to a scientific stage of thought. Some proposals of this type seem to lie between descriptive and prescriptive usages (*q.v.* Philosophy of History).

B. There are a number of senses in which one speaks of prescriptive laws.

(4) The Laws of Thought (*q.v.*)— identity, contradiction, and excluded middle—are in some sense prescriptive.

(5) Ethics (*q.v.*) is a prescriptive discipline, and sometimes the phrase "moral law" is used. William of Ockham (*q.v.* 15), for example, regards the moral law as dependent upon the will of God.

(6) While laws of nature are descriptive, civil law is prescriptive. Plato (*q.v.* 5b) viewed law as a disposition of reason, ordering things according to their natures. Thomas Aquinas (*q.v.* 9) distinguished four forms of prescriptive law: positive law, the law of nations, natural law, and

eternal law. These distinctions began with Aristotle (*q.v.* 14) and were developed by the Stoics (*q.v.* Stoicism 4) Grotius (*q.v.* 2–4), Hobbes (*q.v.* 8), Locke (*q.v.* 9), and Montesquieu (*q.v.* 5).

(7) Natural law doctrine is quite extensive, and concerns the alternative that there may be a natural code to which positive law must conform (*q.v.* Natural Law).

C. The Philosophy of Law is a modern discipline subjecting to analysis the prescriptive concepts relating to jurisprudence.

(8) For a view in which law is held to apply to society as mathematics applies to the space-time world *q.v.* Stammler.

(9) Kelsen (*q.v.*) approaches the subject-matter as a positivist, presenting a "pure theory of law."

(10) Miguel Reale (*q.v.* Latin American Philosophy 13) presents a philosophy of law which he calls "critical ontognoseological historicism."

(11) Hart (*q.v.*), working out of the tradition of Wittgenstein and Austin, interprets law as a fusion of two sets of rules: the primary duty-imposing rules, and secondary rules which concern the recognition and adjudication of primary rules.

(12) Dworkin (*q.v.* 1–2) opposes Hart as a legal positivist, arguing that legal interpretation is hermeneutic (*q.v.*) in its nature.

D. An item which does not fit the above framework:

(13) Theodor Ziehen (*q.v.*) believed he could show that causal, mental, and logical laws are rooted in the given of experience.

LAW, INTERNATIONAL.
Q.v. Vitoria (3).

LAW OF THE THREE STAGES.
Q.v. Comte (1).

LAWS OF MANU.
An Indian metrical work of 2,685 verses concerned with the development of the orthodox Brahmanical view in relation to religion, law, custom, and politics.

(1) In a time of social change the Laws of Manu lent support to the traditional four *ashramas* (*q.v.*) or orders of life—student, householder, hermit, and ascetic. The life of the householder, supporting the other three, is declared to be the best. Man should pass through all four stages.

The third, designed to loosen the bonds of life, requires retirement to the forest for meditation in preparation for the final stage in the attempt to gain enlightenment.

(2) The duties of the four castes (*q.v.*) are outlined: *Brahmins*—teaching, studying, performing sacrifices, accepting gifts from pure men. *Kshatriyas*—protection of the order of society, including the caste system. *Vaishyas*—attention to the details of agriculture and trade. *Shudras*—servile labor for one of the higher castes; and if this service is given a Brahmin the Shudra is promised birth into a higher caste in his next existence.

(3) Women are to be honored, but kept in dependence by the males of their families—by father, then husband, and finally, by sons. A faithful wife will share the fate of her husband beyond this life.

(4) The most virtuous and efficacious act is to recognize the self in all created beings. *Q.v. Vedas* (5).

LAWS OF THOUGHT.
In traditional logic one finds stated three principles upon which all logical thinking is held to depend. These are the laws or principles of identity, excluded middle, and contradiction. In modern logic the principles turn out to be tautologies (*q.v.*).

(1) Aristotle (*q.v.* 5) gave clear expression to two of the three principles but not the third. He held to the impossibility of a thing belonging and not belonging to the same thing at the same time in the same respect (the principle of contradiction); and he held to the impossibility of there being anything between the two parts of a contradiction (the principle of excluded middle).

(2) In the traditional logic of the Middle Ages the principles were often expressed in something like the following manner: (a) The Principle of Identity: A is A ("Whatever is, is"). (b) The Principle of Contradiction: A is not not-A ("Contradictories cannot both be true"). (c) The Principle of Excluded Middle (or *tertium non datur*): Everything is either A or not A ("Contradictories cannot both be false"). So stated it is clear that the principles of contradiction and excluded middle derive from the definition of contradictories. It would follow that the

contradictories of the traditional Square of Opposition (*q.v.* Immediate Inference 1) exemplify these two principles.

(3) In the Propositional Calculus the three principles are expressed in the following manner: (a) Principle of Identity: p ⊃ p and p ≡ p. (b) Principle of Contradiction: ~(p·~p). (c) Principle of Excluded Middle: pv~p. *Q.v.* Tautology (for the truth tables demonstrating the truth of the three principles).

(4) Pauler (*q.v.* 2) added the Law of Connection ("Everything is connected with other things") to the original three laws of logic.

(5) Brouwer (*q.v.* 2), and other Intuitionists, deny the validity of the law or principle of excluded middle.

(6) For Quine (*q.v.* 6) the laws of logic are immune to change due to their remoteness from experience.

(7) Rescher (*q.v.* 4) held the laws of logic to be regulative principles.

LAW, WILLIAM. 1686–1761.

English divine and mystic. Born in Northhamptonshire. Educated at Cambridge where he was elected Fellow. Losing his fellowship after three years, on political grounds, he lived with the utmost simplicity, supporting himself by tutoring and private chaplaincies. His early writings had a marked influence on John Wesley (*q.v.*). He became acquainted with the writings of Jacob Boehme (*q.v.*) around 1733; and thereafter his own writings became markedly mystical in tone, and he came to be known as "The English Mystic."

Principal writings: *A Treatise of Christian Perfection*, 1726; *A Serious Call to a Devout and Holy Life*, 1728; *The Case of Reason*, 1732.

LAX, GASPAR. 1487–1560.

Spanish philosopher. Born in Sariñena. Educated at Zaragoza. Taught at Zaragoza and Paris. Interested in logical formalism. His writings are in Latin.

Selected writings: *On Solvables and Unsolvables*, 1511; *Treatise on Syllogisms*, 1519; *Treatise on the Short Logic*, 1521; *Summa on Opposition*, 1528; *Predicables*, 1529; *Summa on Propositions*, 1529.

LAYA YOGA.

Q.v. Yoga (11).

LEARNED IGNORANCE.

Q.v. Nicholas of Cusa (1).

LEARNING.

Q.v. Education, Philosophy of, for alternative theories of learning.

(1) The "method of trial and error" in learning was formulated by C. Lloyd Morgan (*q.v.* 1).

(2) The equation of learning with positive and negative reinforcements, understood in an operationalistic or behavioristic sense, has been pushed most forcefully by Skinner (*q.v.* 1).

LEBENSWELT.

Q.v. Husserl (9).

LECOMTE DU NOÜY, PIERRE A. 1883–1947.

French biophysicist and philosopher. Born in Paris. Educated at the Sorbonne. Conducted research at the Rockefeller Institute (N.Y.) and the Pasteur Institute (Paris). Taking evolution as the framework of his philosophy, Lecomte argued that the earth is too recent for life to have appeared by chance, and that the upward course of evolution contradicts the law of entropy. The conclusion is that only the hypothesis of telefinalism is adequate to explain what has occurred and is occurring; and that hypothesis, with the implication that the universe is achieving ultimate ends, requires one to accept the existence of God.

Principal writings: *Time and Life* (T, *Biological Time*), 1936; *Man Before Science* (T, *The Road to Reason*), 1939; *Human Destiny* (E), 1948.

THE LEGALIST SCHOOL.

A Chinese school of philosophy (the *Fa Chia*) instrumental in bringing to power the authoritarian Ch'in dynasty (221–206 B.C.). In contrast to Confucian principles the Legalists were interested in augmenting the power of the ruler, subordinating the individual to the state, uniformity of thought, and reduction of moral right to positive law. Because of its brutality the Ch'in government fell in 206 B.C. There has been no Legalist tradition in China for the past 2,000 years. For representatives of this school *q.v.* Shang Yang, Han Fei Tzu.

LEHRER, KEITH.
Q.v. The Gettier Problem.

LEIBNIZ, GOTTFRIED WILHELM. 1646–1716.
German philosopher. Born in Leipzig. Son of a professor of moral philosophy, who died in 1652. Essentially, Leibniz was his own teacher, learning Latin at eight and Greek shortly thereafter. Received a doctorate in law from Altdorf in 1666, where he was offered a professorship. In 1667, entered the service of the Elector of Mainz whom he represented throughout Europe (including an unsuccessful effort to persuade Louis XIV that French military aggressiveness could be more properly directed against Egypt than Holland). If his mission to Paris was politically unsuccessful, it was a success personally for he met Arnauld, Malebranche and Christian Huygens. On a mission to London he met Oldenburg, Boyle, and Dell. He exhibited his calculating machine (which in addition to arithmetical operations could extract square roots) before the Paris Academy and the Royal Society of London. He was elected a Fellow of the Royal Society in 1673. In the same year he entered the service of the Brunswick family, and moved to Hanover in 1676 to take charge of the Ducal library. On the way he visited Spinoza, copying extracts from the latter's unpublished *Ethics* manuscript. In Hanover, he helped the Duke of Hanover become an elector; and he produced a history of the family which required a three-year trip through Germany and Italy, 1687–90. While in Rome he was offered, but refused, the headship of the Vatican Library. He attempted to bring about a reconciliation of Catholicism and Protestantism. In 1690, he was appointed librarian by Duke Anton of Brunswick-Wolfenbüttel. In 1700, the Berlin Academy of Science, which he planned, came into being and Leibniz was elected president for life. He drew up the plan for an academy at St. Petersburg, was made privy councillor of justice by the Elector of Hanover, the Elector of Brandenburg, and Peter the Great. In 1712 he became an imperial privy councillor and a baron of the empire. When the Elector George Louis of Hanover became King of England in 1714, Leibniz was disappointed in the expectation that he might serve in England as the king's adviser.

His work on the infinitesimal calculus began after 1673. He published his first paper on the differential calculus in 1684, and on the integral calculus in 1686. Newton and Leibniz had apparently invented the calculus independently, although Newton's method was first published in 1693. Most of Leibniz' writing was done between 1690 and 1716, part of it in correspondence, *i.e.*, the correspondence with Arnauld and with Clark. He wrote the *Theodicy* at the request of the Queen of Prussia, and the *Monadology* for Prince Eugene of Savoy. Despite his many publications, much of his work remained in manuscript form at the time of his death.

Principal writings: *The Principle of Individuation* (T), 1663; *Meditations on Knowledge, Truth and Ideas* (T), 1664; *Sample Philosophical Questions* (T), 1664; *Dissertation on the Combinatory Art* (T), 1666; *New Physical Hypothesis* (T), 1671; *Theory of Motion* (T), 1671; *Discourse on Metaphysics* (T), 1686; *On First Philosophy and the Idea of Substance* (T), 1694; *Considerations on the Doctrine of a Universal Spirit* (T), 1697; *On the Origin of Things* (T), 1697; *On Nature* (T), 1698; *Essays on Theodicy* (T), 1710; *The Monadology* (T), 1714; the Leibniz-Clarke correspondence was published in England in 1717; *Principles of Nature and of Grace Founded on Reason* (T), 1719; *New Essays on Human Understanding* (T), 1765.

(1) The philosophy of Leibniz derives from a number of original decisions. One of the most important was his decision that the ontological unit is primarily a center of force. In this he departed radically from Descartes for whom extension is primary. He came to this conclusion on the grounds that the concept of an "atom" as the "smallest particle of matter" is meaningless. As long as matter is characterized by extension it is divisible. Thus he takes the Zeno paradox seriously and the atom is deprived of its extension. Endowing this extensionless unit with force (on the grounds that the laws of motion so demand) he terms it "monad." The monads are the simple substances out of which everything else is made. Since they lack extension they are not in space. Since they lack parts

they cannot degenerate into something simpler. Leibniz seems to have concluded that, since their existence cannot be extensional it must be intensional. At any rate these centers of force are also centers of feeling, perception, and appetition. The term "monad" had been used earlier both by the Pythagoreans and by Giordano Bruno, but Leibniz' treatment was distinctive. Everything has an inner state. That inner state's awareness of itself he calls "apperception." Its awareness of other things he calls "perception." It is perhaps also important to note that in the 17th century the term "perception" signified the more general relation of "taking account of" as well as our sense of perception as "mirroring" an object. Leibniz identified the two meanings, producing the astonishing doctrine that each monad "mirrors" the entire universe and is hence a microcosm.

(2) Out of this highly reflective doctrine emerge Leibniz' conclusions with respect to space and time. Space is the "order of possible co-existences" while time is the order of possibilities which cannot coexist, and which must hence exist successively. There are different times because each monad is in process of development; it burgeons with the future in coordination with all other monads; and this power to extract its being out of itself is perhaps why Leibniz calls the monads also "entelechies" (*q.v.*). In any case the order of these actualizations establishes temporal order. Thus space and time depend upon the possibilities and incompatibilities of the monads. Space and time are relative. Leibniz sometimes speaks as though space and time have only a phenomenal existence resting upon our perception of the monads. On the other hand since this is a *phenomenon bene fundatum*, or "well-founded phenomenon," and perception is a fairly basic feature of Leibniz' metaphysics, the "phenomenal" cuts rather deeply.

(3) The Principle of Identity of Indiscernibles follows strictly from the derivative reality of space and time. If space and time are derivative there will be a distinction between two things only if they have different properties, and if they have exactly the same properties they will be the same thing.

(4) The Principle of Sufficient Reason also follows from this source. The principle holds that nothing takes place without a reason; for any occurrence, a being with sufficient knowledge would be able to give a reason sufficient to explain why it is as it is and not otherwise. The principle follows from the idea of the consistency of development in time.

(5) Both principles relate to the law of continuity which Leibniz fashioned on the model of the mathematical infinite, according to which there are no breaks in the series "but everything takes place by degrees." If this law is accepted as having relevance for ontology, along with the Identity of Indiscernibles, it follows that there will be a graded hierarchy of monads, from those which are infinitely close to insentience to one monad exemplifying perfect being, that is, God. In Leibniz' language of perception the hierarchy runs from monads whose perceptions are almost totally confused to the monad all of whose perceptions are distinct; in the language of appetency, the hierarchy runs from the almost totally passive to *actus purus*.

(6) This distinction of grade is then utilized in distinguishing soul from body. Rather than the unworkable dualism of Descartes, Leibniz views the soul as a monad of higher grade controlling a colony of monads of lower grade; the ruling monad is the entelechy of the body. The analogy this provides for a possible relation between God and the world should not be overlooked. Furthermore, he suggests that any "physical configuration" is a momentary mind, although lacking memory.

(7) "The monads have no windows by which anything may go in or out." This declaration rests on the initial conception of the monad as a simple substance. Apparently, Leibniz felt, each monad must have a career independent of all the rest. This decision, given the preceding points, yields Leibniz' doctrine of Pre-established Harmony. Just as two clocks can be synchronized to run in harmony, and two choirs can sing from the same score, so the universe can present the appearance of interaction without the reality. Each monad acts out the law of its own being, and God's original choice of a universe accounts for the consistency

of action of the parts.

(8) God is, hence, not only suggested by the law of continuity, but demanded by a teleological argument beginning from the assumption of windowless monads. Leibniz offers a cosmological proof, which begins from the Principle of Sufficient Reason, and concludes that the sufficient reason of the total universe must be a being containing its own reason for existence. Advancing beyond Anselm, Leibniz noted that the ontological argument is valid only if it is shown that the concept "perfect being" is a possible concept. Leibniz accomplishes this in a very interesting manner. He differentiates properties which are perfections from properties that are not. Properties which are perfections must admit of a superlative degree (hence "largest number" fails to be a perfection), and must not rule out any other positive quality (hence "red in color" fails to be a perfection). Properties such as "goodness," "wisdom," "knowledge" are perfections, admitting the idea of a superlative, and of compossible existence. Hence the idea of a perfect being is a possible idea. Since God is not a contingent being, the case in which the idea of God is possible, although God does not exist, is ruled out; and since the concept is possible, it is to be concluded that God exists.

(9) The idea of God as a perfect being, who is creator of the world, entails the decision to create the best of all possible worlds and we must assume that this has been done. But the best of all possible worlds is not a perfect world. It will have a balance of good over evil, but will not be without evil, for the problem of consistency also confronts God in choosing worlds. The principle of the incompossibility of possibilities entails the conclusion that the world will have evil—metaphysical, moral, and physical—but God will choose that possible world with the most fortunate combination or compossibility of "possibles." And this is interpreted to mean the combination allowing the largest number of "possibles" to be actualized together; thus a principle of plenitude makes its appearance. Implicit in this is, of course, his solution to the problem of theodicy (*q.v.*) or the goodness of God in light of the evil of the world.

(10) Leibniz distinguishes between truths of reason and truths of fact. This is the contemporary distinction between analytic and synthetic truths. The former rest on the Principle of Identity, since the negation of a truth of reason is a contradiction. The latter rest on the Principle of Sufficient Reason. The former have their source in the mind as active, the latter in the mind as passive (*i.e.*, as mirroring the world). The former would be true in any possible world. The latter are true in this world. The former are necessary, the latter are contingent. He likewise distinguishes between absolutely necessary truths, the truths of reason, and hypothetical necessity. The latter, like truths of fact, are true only in this world. Certain necessities of this kind, *e.g.*, causality, are given in God's decision to create this world rather than some other.

(11) Truths of reason are more basic than truths of fact. The *characteristica universalis* (universal characteristic) is a development of Leibniz' belief in the primacy of truths of reason. In its most satisfactory form any proposition should be expressible in the form, ABC is A (or AB or B or AC or C or ABC); and any false proposition in the form: ABC is not A (or etc.). Any true proposition would then be analytic; and any false proposition a contradiction. Could an appropriate language, applicable to all fields (including ethics and aesthetics) be devised, the disagreements among philosophers would disappear, and calculation would replace disputation.

(12) The *characteristica universalis* and the *mathesis universalis* (universal mathematics) are two divisions of Leibniz' *ars combinatoria* (the combinatory art or art of discovery). The art of discovery is relevant both to truths of reason and to truths of fact. In the former case it renders explicit what is implicit, and orders the truths so that they follow from each other, the derivative following from the primitive, according to the Principle of Contradiction. In the latter case it orders the primitive truths of fact (from internal experience), inferring derivative truths from them in relation to experience, and by means of the Principle of Sufficient Reason; thus additional truths of fact are brought to light.

(13) For God, indeed, all truths are

truths of reason. This raises the interesting possibility that God alone could use the *characteristica universalis*, since God alone has perceptions sufficiently distinct to read off any state of any monad from its mirroring in the divine nature. From this standpoint the distinction between contingency and necessity would seem to have disappeared; but Leibniz saves the distinction at least partially by pointing out that truths of reason rest on absolute necessity, and truths of fact on a hypothetical necessity, the necessity namely of being among the set of possibilities God has chosen for this world.

(14) In this world God also chose all of the free acts that would ever be performed by human beings; hence the claim that human freedom is also preserved. The monad, which is the human soul, has—along with any other monad—perception, appetite, and spontaneity. In human terms these have become thought, will, and freedom. Freedom, even freedom of choice, consists in following reason, in always exemplifying the Principle of Sufficient Reason. At birth the soul, far from being a *tabula rasa*, is like the unworked block of marble, its hidden veins already containing what it will become through the labor of the sculptor; hence, in response to Locke's "*Nihil est in intellectu quod non prius fuerit in sensu*" (Nothing is in the intellect which was not first in sense), Leibniz added "*nisi intellectus ipse*" (except for the intellect itself). Our perceptions are too confused for us to be aware of the total content of our internal nature. But the life of the soul is its percipient being. The flood of perceptions continues through sleep and in states of shock, the *petites perceptions* beneath the level of awareness maturing into thought.

Also *q.v.* Russell (1).

LEIBNIZ' LAW.

Q.v. Logic (22); Leibniz (3).

LENIN, VLADIMIR ILYICH. 1870–1924.

Russian Marxist. Born in Simbirsk (now Ulianov). Studied at Kazan and St. Petersburg. Imprisoned for revolutionary activity in 1895. Exiled to Siberia in 1897. In exile most of the time between 1900 and 1917. Headed the Soviet Union from 1917–24.

Principal writings: *Materialism and Empirio-criticism* (T), 1909; *Imperialism* (T), 1916; *State and Revolution* (T), 1917.

(1) Lenin dedicated himself to the Marxist philosophy. In this regard his quest was to discover the strongest version of that philosophy. He began with a Marxism closely oriented to that of Marx himself, abjuring the dialectic, while adhering to materialism. He ended, however, in agreeing with all of the propositions of Engels, while contributing a proposition, or at least a clarification, of his own (*q.v.* Marxism 4).

(2) The original emphasis came in his struggles with those Marxists who seemed to him to be departing from materialism. One of these was Bogdanov (*q.v.*) who had combined Marxism with the positivism of Ernst Mach and Richard Avenarius. Another was Plekhanov, who had held to a symbolic theory of perception. Lenin concluded that materialism requires an epistemological realism of the most literal sort and that *Empirio-criticism* was a reactionary epistemology of the bourgeoisie. The concepts and sensations in our minds must be replicas of realities outside the mind. His defense of the thesis has made it a standard claim of orthodox Marxism.

(3) Furthermore, his reflections on the opposition between thesis and antithesis were designed to carry the import of revolutionary struggle and destruction of the thesis, whatever its form. This would seem not quite to be the Hegelian sense of dialectic movement. But Lenin had concluded that the success of the revolutionary movement required the more severe dialectical opposition he supported.

LEON HEBREO (or ABARBANEL).
c. 1460–1520.

Jewish philosopher. Born in Lisbon. His family forced from Lisbon into a transient existence in Spain and Italy, Leon finally centered in Naples. The strongest influence on his thought came from the Florentine Academy (*q.v.*) and especially from Ficino (*q.v.*). Leon composed three famous dialogues on love. In his view love has its origin in God and radiates throughout the universe, unifying it and affecting all beings. Love moves both from inferior to superior, and conversely.

Principal writings: *Dialogues on Love*, 1536.

LEOPOLD, FRIEDRICH.
Q.v. Novalis.

LEQUIER, JULES. 1814–1862.
French philosopher. Born at Quintin. Educated in Paris. Renouvier was his disciple and, through Renouvier, William James.
Principle writings: *The Search for a Primary Truth*, 1865; *Liberty*, 1936.
(1) Knowledge is possible, and since freedom, or liberty, is a condition of knowledge, freedom is possible.
(2) If freedom is possible, then what I choose is not known in advance by God. God can know certainly what has been realized; but can know only conjecturally what is still to be chosen.
(3) It follows that humans have independence, even against God, that God, seeing things change, must change in beholding them; that the future is contingent; and that God and the world have a reciprocal interrelatedness, each affecting the other.

LE ROY, EDOUARD. 1870–1954.
French philosopher. Born in Paris. Educated at the École Normale Supérieure. Taught at the Collège de France. Combining Bergsonian vitalism with Blondel's emphasis on action as opposed to intellect, Le Roy arrived at "pragmatic" interpretations of science and religion. Although Catholic, his pragmatic interpretations of religion were placed on the index of forbidden books.
Principal writings: *Dogma and Criticism*, 1907; *The Idealist Requirement and the Fact of Evolution*, 1927; *Intuitive Thought*, 2 vols., 1929–30; *The Problem of God*, 1929; *Introduction to the Study of the Religious Problem*, 1943; *Attempt at a First Philosophy*, 2 vols., 1956–8.

LE SENNE, RENÉ. 1883–1954.
French philosopher. Born in Elbeuf-sur-Seine. Educated at the École Normale Supérieure. Taught at the Sorbonne. Collaborating with Lavelle (*q.v.*) in an extension of the French tradition of spiritualism, his "philosophy of the spirit" insisted upon the fact of human freedom, and the creation of the willing self, value,

and obligation through obstacles.
Principal writings: *Obstacle and Value*, 1934; *Treatise on General Morality*, 1942; *Treatise on Characterology*, 1945; *Personal Destiny*, 1955.

LEŚNIEWSKI, STANISLAW. 1884–1939.
Polish philosopher and logician. Born in Serpukhov, Russia. Educated at Lvov. Taught at Warsaw. An important member of the Warsaw Circle (*q.v.*), his interest lay in solving the problems raised by Russell and others with respect to the foundations of mathematics. The basis of Leśniewski's logic is the "protothetic," *i.e.*, theory of first principles with equivalence as the only undefined term, leading to a propositional calculus enriched by functorial variables and quantifiers. On this he built "ontology," a doctrine of name variables compatible with Aristotelian syllogistic, and "mereology," a theory of the part-whole relationship. He was the teacher of Tarski. He wrote in Polish and German.
Principal writings: "The Foundations of a General Theory of Manifolds," 1916; "On the Foundations of Mathematics," 1927–30; "On the Foundations of Ontology," 1930; "On the Definitions of the so-called Theory of Deduction," 1931; "Basic Features of a New System of the Foundations of Mathematics," 1938.

LESSING, GOTTHOLD EPHRAIM. 1729–1781.
German litterateur and philosopher. Born at Kamenz, Saxony. Attended University of Leipzig. Beginning in 1748, Lessing maintained himself by literary work. His translations, plays, poems, and essays in literary criticism helped establish the milieu making possible the German *Aufklärung* or Enlightenment in which Goethe participated.
Principal writings: *Laocoön* (T), 1766; *Nathan the Wise* (T), 1779; *The Education of the Human Race*, 1780.
(1) In the *Laocoön* Lessing argued that each art has its own function and its own governing principles; to these it must limit itself if high accomplishment is desired. Poetry, for example, is temporal, while the plastic arts are spatial; and the difference must be respected. The function of art may be discerned from his views on tragedy. Reinterpreting

Aristotle, Lessing held that the poet reveals in "silhouette" the divine plan of creation, that his work is thus a revelation of theodicy connecting the events of the world in a different order, achieving the "general effect of good."

(2) The play, *Nathan the Wise*, argues that since goodness is no respecter of creeds, complete toleration in religious matters is eminently reasonable.

(3) Prior to this he had urged that since the power of Christianity, or any religion, depends upon its ministration to human nature, the religious spirit has nothing to fear from even the boldest speculation.

(4) In the final writing we have listed, *The Education of the Human Race*, Lessing argues that every religion has contributed something to human development; that there is a law of progress in history even though occasional retrogression may be necessary in the human movement toward its goal, and that goal is the stage of a new eternal Gospel according to which humanity will seek the right because it is right and not for an arbitrary reward.

(5) In the year before his death, Lessing apparently told Jacobi (*q.v.*) that he was a follower of Spinoza and a determinist. Jacobi's publication of this statement after Lessing's death initiated an involved controversy known as the *Pantheismusstreit* (*q.v.*).

LEUCIPPUS.

Q.v. Democritus.

LEVELLERS.

A term appearing in England in 1647 referring to a movement principally in Cromwell's army for parliamentary supremacy and the extension of political rights. Some were likewise interested in property reform. "They have given themselves a new name, *viz.*, Levellers, for they intend to set all things straight...."

LEVI BEN GERSON (OR GERSHON).

Q.v. Gersonides.

LEVINAS, EMMANUEL. 1905– .

French philosopher. Born in Kovno, Lithuania. Educated at Strassbourg, Freiburg, and the University of Paris. Became a French citizen in 1930. Has taught at Poiters, Nanterre, and the Sorbonne. Director of the École Normale Israelite Orientale from 1946–1963.

Principal writings: *The Theory of Intuition in Husserl's Phenomenology* (T), 1930; *Existence and Existents* (T), 1947; *On Disclosing Being with Husserl and Heidegger*, 1949; *Totality and Infinity* (T), 1961; *Otherwise Than Being* (T), 1974; *Ethics and Infinity* (T) (conversations with P. Nemo), 1982; *Collected Philosophical Papers* (T), 1987.

(1) Accepting the term "ethical transcendentalism" as descriptive of his approach, Levinas is indebted especially to the phenomenology of Husserl (influenced also by Heidegger). Derrida recognizes him as a force in the development of deconstruction (*q.v.*). Both find a rupture in the analysis of being; but where Derrida invokes *différance* (*q.v.*), Levinas cites the face of the other. In both irruptions philosophy has an opportunity to open itself to "the dimension of otherness" (alterity) and to "transcendence beyond being."

(2) If ontology is the domain of being, relation to the other, being exorbitant, does not fit within being. Levinas holds it comes from beyond being. The face, mutely testifying "you shall not commit murder" and our response "here I am" (*me voici*), found an ethic of justice and of love, establishing self-identity, meaningfulness (meaning appears by virtue of our being in the world with the other), and responsibility.

(3) My infinite responsibility for the other becomes generalized by virtue of the realization that the other also has an other to whom my responsibility likewise extends. That initial responsibility translates into the rights and duties I sustain as a member of community. Among one's duties is building an economy capable of clothing the naked and feeding the hungry.

(4) God, who is beyond being and speaks through the face of the other, calls for a reversal of our nature, giving the other primacy over ourselves. As being is the domain of truth, beyond being (nonbeing) is the domain of justice which is prior to truth. It is also the domain of God whose infinity speaks through the other.

(5) The problem of expressing the infinite from within the domain of being (the finite) is that saying (*le dire*), whose

spontaneity is beyond being, becomes the said (*le dit*) and is at once part of the coherent whole of being. One must then surprise saying, using its upsurge of communication by indiscretion, before it becomes said.

LÉVI-STRAUSS, CLAUDE. 1908– .

French philosopher and anthropologist. Born in Brussels. Educated at the University of Paris. Has taught at the University of São Paulo, New School for Social Research, École Pratique des Hautes Études, Collège de France. Initially a professor of philosophy, he turned his attention to anthropology, engaging in extensive anthropological studies in Brazil. He is now recognized as the founder of a philosophical movement centering in France, known as Structuralism (*q.v.*). His linguistic antecedents have been Ferdinand de Saussure (*q.v.*) and especially Roman Jakobson (*q.v.* 2).

Selected writings: *The Elementary Structures of Kinship* (T), 1949; *Tristes Tropiques* (T), 1955; *Structural Anthropology* (T), 2 vols. 1958; *The Savage Mind* (T), 1962; *Totemism* (T), 1962; *The Raw and the Cooked* (T), 1964; *From Honey to Ashes* (T), 1966; *The Origin of Table Manners* (T), 1968; *Conversations with Claude Lévi-Strauss* (T), 1969 (with G. Charbonnier); *Structure and Misfortune* (selected texts), 1970; *The Naked Man* (T), 1971; *The Symbolic Function* (ed. M. Izard, P. Smith), 1979; *The Way of the Masks* (T), 1979; *The View from Afar* (T), 1983; *The Jealous Potter* (T), 1985; *Anthropology and Myth* (T), 1987; *Conversations with Claude Lévi-Strauss* (T), 1988 (with D. Eribon).

(1) Regarding social structures as objective entities, existing independently of human consciousness, it is his view that different societies reproduce in a partial and incomplete manner the same structure. A social structure is not in fact an empirical reality, but "beyond" that. It is discerned by exploration of the myth, ritual, and religious representation by which individuals try to hide or justify the discrepancies between their actual society and its ideal image. The analysis allows a blend of anthropology, linguistics, philosophy, and psychology. The structure we wish to educe lies, in fact, in our unconscious.

(2) The study of myth poses a non-Cartesian problem, since its difficulties can neither be divided into minute parts nor totalized. In the analysis of myth, empiricism loses its force. A single myth is sufficient to elaborate the grammatical laws appropriate to its analysis. Analysis of myth relates to food supply, kinship systems, and linguistic structures simultaneously. It is myth that holds together the actual and the ideal, reflecting the history of a social system and the elements of society which would otherwise stand in opposition or incoherence.

(3) Using a language model to understand other relations, he regards them all as susceptible to study by linguistic methods. One develops the grammar of a myth and produces thereby a "myth of mythology." Just as language had to be born at a fell swoop, marking a transition between one stage where nothing had meaning and a second stage where everything possessed it, so myth functions as a whole. There is the difference, however, that language has tense while myth is timeless. Marriage relations and kinship systems function as languages, permitting certain kinds of communication, women circulating between groups in place of words.

LÉVY-BRUHL, LUCIEN. 1857–1939.

French philosopher. Born in Paris, where he was also educated. Professor of philosophy at the Sorbonne, beginning in 1899.

Principal writings: *The Philosophy of Jacobi*, 1844; *The Philosophy of August Comte* (T), 1900; *Ethics and Moral Science* (T), 1903; *The Mental Functions in Inferior Societies* (T), 1910; *Primitive Mentality* (T), 1922; *The Primitive Soul* (T), 1927; *Nature and the Supernatural in Primitive Mentality* (T), 1931; *The Primitive Mythology*, 1935; *Mystical Experience and Symbols among the Primitives*, 1938; *The Notebooks of Lucien Lévy-Bruhl*, 1949,

(1) Dedicating much of his life to the study of primitive societies, Lévy-Bruhl found the primitive mentality to be prelogical. Indeed, in contrast to the civilized who guide themselves by the principle of contradiction, primitives employ what Lévy-Bruhl named a principle of participation.

(2) According to the principle of participation any thing or person, in a way

impossible for us to understand, can be both itself and something other than itself; and forces and qualities can be received and transmitted by mystical processes.

(3) The principle of contradiction, which requires clear distinctions, is simply not accepted. The primitive is thus able at times to believe both sides of what we should judge to be a contradiction.

LEWIN, KURT. 1890–1947.

German-American psychologist. Born in Poznan. Educated at Berlin. Taught at Berlin, Cornell, Iowa, and M.I.T. Founder of topological and field theory psychology, he introduced the concept of "life space" as the totality of facts and relationships which define the situation of a person at a given time. Given this setting he likewise urged analysis of the "single case" as more productive of insight than collections of statistics. The writings listed were published in English.

Principal writings: *A Dynamic Theory of Personality*, 1935; *Principles of Topological Psychology*, 1936; *Resolving Social Conflicts*, 1948; *Field Theory in Social Science*, 1951.

LEWIS, CLARENCE IRVING. 1883–1964.

American philosopher. Born in Stoneham, Mass. Studied under Royce. Taught at Harvard University. By his own description a "conceptualistic pragmatist," Lewis recognized especially the contribution of C.S. Peirce to his thinking.

Principal writings: *A Survey of Symbolic Logic*, 1918; *The Pragmatic Elements in Knowledge*, 1926; *Mind and the World Order*, 1929; *Symbolic Logic* (with C.H. Langford), 1932; *An Analysis of Knowledge and Valuation*, 1946; *The Ground and Nature of the Right*, 1955.

(1) Among the contributions of C.I. Lewis to philosophy, the most notable is his exploration of systems of modal logic, going beyond the assertoric modes of the truth and falsity of propositions to add the modes of possibility, impossibility, and necessity. Aristotle and the medieval tradition had such modes of thought, but they had not been included in the propositional calculus (*q.v.*), or in modern quantification theory (*q.v.*) Part of Lewis' motivation for this development was his desire to introduce into modern logic the notion of "strict implication,"

i.e., the notion that p implies q if and only if it is logically impossible for p to be true and q to be false. In the material implication (*q.v.*) of the propositional calculus, where p implies q is true in all cases save when p is true and q is false (*q.v.* Truth Tables 3), certain troublesome paradoxes arise. In Lewis' system there are also paradoxes, but apparently less troublesome. Lewis in fact constructed eight alternate systems of modal logic, numbering them S1 to S8, strengthening them consecutively by the addition of axioms and rules. The notions of possibility and necessity were symbolized in a distinctive manner. "$\Diamond$ p" means "it is possible that p." "$\Box$ p" means "it is necessary that p." This can also be expressed by "$\sim \Diamond \sim$ p." "P strictly implies q" is expressed by "p $\dashv$ q." It is also expressed by "$\sim \Diamond \sim$ (p$\supset$q)." On the basis of these symbols and the more usual connectives, axioms and rules of inference are developed as in any calculus (*q.v.* Propositional Calculus, Modality 5, and Modal Logic.)

(2) In *Mind and the World Order*, philosophy is held to be a reflective examination of experience in which ethics seeks to determine the good, logic the valid, and metaphysics the real. The problem of metaphysics is held to be the problem of the categories, which are implicit in human experience and attitude. Since we use the categories to interpret experience they cannot fail to be exemplified therein. They can alter as basic human interests change, but they can never be refuted. Hence, what is "given" in experience remains in a certain sense ineffable. If it is too much to say that the *a priori* elements of experience are immutable, still they go very deep.

(3) In *An Analysis of Knowledge and Valuation* the depth of analytic truth is related to linguistic convention, the classification imposed by our criteria; and the relations between our criteria of classification and the meanings of our expressions. Lewis finds these relationships beyond "convention or decision." It seems to have been Lewis' intent to reduce the elements of convention in the analytic, *a priori*, and categorial, by this means. Similarly, his concept of "terminating judgments," giving way to action, experiment, and hence to confirmation or

disconfirmation, is related to "objective belief" and would seem to reduce the "ineffability" of the given.

(4) With respect to meaning, Lewis distinguished four aspects to be considered rather than the usual two: (a) the connotation of a term is the conjunction of all the characteristics connected with it; (b) the signification of a term is the conjunction of those characteristics necessary and sufficient for correctly relating the term to its denoted (and comprehended) things; (c) the denotation of a term is the class of existent things connoted and signified by the term; (d) the comprehension of a term is the class of existent and possible things connoted and signified by the term.

(5) He likewise held that the value-disvalue polarity is a mode of experience, and disclosed in experience as an ultimate kind of value-truth, divisible into utility, instrumental, inherent, intrinsic, and contributory types of value. Thus he took his stand as a naturalist in value theory. Three responses may be made to the "given": moral or active, cognitive, or aesthetic. All three are value responses. The disclosed value in experience is indubitable when found, and the final basis and ultimate referent of all judgments of value. That the good life is the "*summum bonum*" is one of the elements thus disclosed. And while the aesthetic relates to the inherent value of immediate experience, ethics refers us to the rational imperative that concerns the whole of life and sets the end to which all particular aims must be subordinated.

LEWIS, DAVID K. 1941– .

American philosopher. Born in Oberlin, Ohio, educated at Swarthmore and Harvard. Has taught at U.C.L.A. and Princeton.

Principal writings: *Convention*, 1969; *Counterfactuals*, 1973; *On the Plurality of Worlds*, 1986; *Parts of Classes*, 1991.

(1) Lewis discovered that his work in modal logic, especially with respect to Counterfactual Conditionals (*q.v.* 4–5), implied a metaphysics of possible worlds.

(2) One might claim that possible worlds are merely "sets of sentences of a language." Against this view he argues that the number of such sets would have to equal "the infinite cardinal of the set

of all subsets of real numbers." Since sentences are "finite strings over a finite alphabet," there are not enough sets of sentences to go around. Possible worlds, then, must be granted their own reality.

(3) To deal with counterfactuals, possible worlds are compared with respect to their "similarity." Although it is inevitable that there will be vagueness in the comparison, "the limited vagueness" involved in comparing possible worlds "accounts nicely for the limited vagueness of counterfactuals," leaving us with one mystery instead of two.

(4) Calling his own view "genuine modal realism with counterparts instead of overlap," the approach of "transworld individuality," because it involves overlap, is an "ersatz modal realism." What transworld individuality supposes is simply that the same individuals which exist in our actual world also exist in other possible worlds. Lewis opposes transworld individuality because it harbors an inconsistency, at the same time claiming and denying literal identity across worlds. In its place he puts the idea of counterparting, which rests on comparative similarity among possible worlds. In this view nothing inhabits more than one world; but some other worlds have conterparts of some of the individuals in this world, which represent them. The representation is sufficiently close "in important respects of intrinsic quality and extrinsic relations" that what something might have done or been, its counterparts do or are, and what is "essential to something is what it has in common with all its counterparts."

(5) Similarity gives rise to comparative possibility and concerns worlds more like our own than other worlds: "It is more possible for a dog to talk than for a stone to talk, since some worlds with talking dogs are more like our own than is any world with talking stones."

(6) It is "closeness" which makes counterfactuals true. When some A-and-C world (*i.e.*, a world in which both antecedent and consequent of a counterfactual conditional are true) is closer to our world than is any not-A-and-not-C world, the counterfactual in question is true at our world.

LEXICAL DEFINITION.
Q.v. Definition (2).

LEX TALIONIS.
Latin phrase meaning "law of retaliation, or recompense." The name given to the Old Testament law of "life for life, eye for eye, tooth for tooth."

LI.
A homophonic term in Chinese philosophy, possessing three distinct meanings, identical only in pronunciation, while being semantically and etymologically unrelated.

(1) For Confucius (*q.v.* 2–3) *Li* stood for "propriety," the outward expression of an inner harmony. The homophone, meaning benefit or gain (*q.v.* 3 below), Confucius condemned.

(2) Among Neo-Confucians *Li* stood for "principle" or "reason," the rational principle of the universe, contrasting with *chi*, the material principle. *Q.v.* Chou Tun-I (1); Chu Hsi (2–3); Ch'eng I (1); Ch'eng Hao (1); Lu Hsiang-shan (1–3); Wang Yang-ming (1).

(3) Among the Moists (*q.v.*) *Li* is the principle of benefit, resulting from universal love; this is especially clear in Mo Tzu (*q.v.* 3). For Mencius (*q.v.*) *Li* as benefit or gain is condemned.

LI AO. 8th and 9th cent. A.D.
Chinese philosopher. Along with Han Yü (*q.v.*), Li Ao determined the direction of neo-Confucian philosophy, restoring its historic emphasis on human nature, possibly saving it from annihilation by Taoism and Buddhism. Held the "Presented Scholar" degree, professor at the Directorate of Education, divisional chief, censor, vice-minister in the Ministry of Justice, and in the Ministry of Revenues and Population. Influential in his time, he added little of philosophic note to the tradition he helped shape.

Principal writings: *Recovery of the Nature* (T in part).

LIBERALISM.
From the Latin *liber* ("free"). Any position or movement directed toward maximizing human freedom. One might expect Liberalism to stand in contrast to Conservatism (*q.v.*), but the multiple definitions of freedom (*q.v.* A.–D.) are reflected in a variety of types of liberalism, forming a cross-classification. Political liberalism, associated with the mechanisms of decision-making within the state, follow definition A., concerned with choice. Economic liberalism follows definition B., enshrining freedom as nonintervention, or laissez-faire. The position, sometimes called libertarian, is reflected in the night watchman state of Nozick (*q.v.*). Ethical or cultural liberalism turns on definitions C. and D. The option of freedom as the development of potentiality is taken as basic in a variety of alternatives, in Rawls (*q.v.* 4), socialism (*q.v.*) and Marxism (*q.v.* Marx 8c).

LIBERATION, PHILOSOPHY OF.
Q.v. Theology of Liberation (8, 9).

LIBERATION, THEOLOGY OF.
Latin American movement, centered in practical theology, or theological *praxis* (*q.v.*), devoted to improving the status of the oppressed. Its period of greatest influence was between 1960 and 1985. Although centered in theology, it was fed by, and responded to, an astonishing range of influences, including that of Marxism.

(1) The centerpiece of the theological movement was Gustavo Gutierrez' *Theology of Liberation* (T), 1971. In that work the Peruvian theologian fused the goal of Christ as a transcendent redeemer with the social action ethics of Jesus. Christ the Redeemer thus became the liberator of the oppressed both in this world and in the world to come.

(2) The social action message of Vatican Council II (*q.v.*), 1962–65, was interpreted as supporting such liberation. Paulo Freire, in the Northeast of Brazil began teaching literacy to adults through consciousness-raising (*conscientizacão*), first described in his *Education as the Practice of Liberty*, 1964. After the military takeover of Brazil in 1964 he was invited to leave the country, continuing his work in Chile. During that period *The Pedagogy of the Oppressed* (T), 1970, was published. Freire is now an international figure and his 1970 work an international classic.

(3) Church base communities began to appear not only in Brazil, but in many areas of Latin America. Adapting the consciousness-raising of Freire, the communities compensated for a critical shortage of parish priests. Worshippers would

meet for scripture reading and discussion, the leaders having had some training by Church officials in conducting the meetings. Jesus' teachings would be discussed, and self-help projects in the community would be implemented. Over a million parishioners in Brazil alone belonged to base communities. Ernesto Cardenal, Sandinista Minister of Culture, was priest in the base community at Solentiname (*The Gospel in Solentiname*, 4 vols., T, 1976). In El Salvador Archbishop Oscar Romero gave strong support to the Salvadoran base communities.

(4) CELAM, the Latin American Conference of Bishops, was organized in 1955. In its 2nd meeting (1968), the Medellin meeting, the bishops urged the Church to participate in the transformation of society, and called for "consciousness-raising" evangelism after the manner of the base communities. In its 3rd meeting (1979), the Puebla meeting, they declared (not without opposition) "the need for a conversion of the whole Church to a preferential option for the poor" directed toward their liberation.

(5) These lines of influence fused with Marxist revolutionary movements from time to time, as suggested in (3) above. Parishioners in base communities would sometimes associate Christ the Redeemer with guerrilla fighters in the hills. Theologians of liberation, in addition to Gutierrez, include the Brazilians, Clodovis and Leonardo Boff, the former producing *Theology and Praxis*, 1978, the latter *Jesus Christ Liberator* (T), 1978, and *Salvation and Liberation* (T), 1979; Franz Hinkelammert in Costa Rica, *The Ideological Weapons of Death* (T), 1977, in which liberation theology, a "theology of life," is contrasted with the antiutopian theology of the rich, the theology of capitalism and of ecclesiastical Christianity which is a "theology of death"; and Juan Luis Segundo of Uruguay, *A Theology for Artisans of a New Humanity* (T), 5 vols., 1975.

(6) In his 1980–85 visits to Latin America Pope John Paul II denounced social injustice, while cautioning against the excesses of liberation theology. Ernesto Cardenal was suspended from the priesthood, Gustavo Gutierrez was summoned to the Vatican for discussions of his position, and Leonardo Boff's right

to teach was suspended. Subsequently, the movement began to lose power.

(7) In *A Black Theology of Liberation* (1970), James H. Cone likewise argues for Christianity as the religion of the oppressed. In his version, however, oppression is black oppression, and both God and Christ are by necessity black: "Any statement about Jesus" in which blackness is not "the *decisive* factor about his person is a denial of the New Testament message."

(8) Enrique Dussel, an Argentine philosopher (now in Mexico), after having published extensively within the context of liberation theology, expanded the framework of the discussion with his book on *Philosophy of Liberation* (T), 1977. Three important points are: (a) Although the philosophers of the developed world play word games while people die, the appropriate role for philosophy is to take the lead in liberating the oppressed. (b) Following Levinas' (*q.v.*) analysis of the face of the other, he held that we are judged by the look of the oppressed. (c) Tracing out dependency theory, in which developed nations are in the center and third world nations on the periphery, Dussel argued for a system in which every nation can turn on its own center.

(9) Other Latin American philosophers have written about philosophy of liberation, among them Horacio Cerutti, likewise from Argentina and teaching in Mexico. His *Latin American Philosophy of Liberation* discusses the concept and reviews the Latin American contributors to the movement.

LIBER DE CAUSIS. c. 9th cent. A.D.

A treatise on God and the world, Neoplatonic in its structure, translated from Greek into Arabic, and thence into Latin (*q.v.* Baghdad School; Neoplatonism 12). Often attributed to Aristotle, the work had considerable influence until the 13th century, and influenced Eckhart in the 14th century. Typically Neoplatonic in its cascading levels of being—intelligence, forms, soul, and matter—its doctrine stands apart in regarding the First Cause as creator of the other levels of being, hence marking a difference of kind between God and the world, and temporalizing the Neoplatonic levels of being. The work in fact was taken in large part from a manuscript by Proclus (*q.v.*) on theology.

LIBERTY.

From the Latin *libertas*, from *libero* ("to set free, liberate"). The term, like freedom (*q.v.*), has two senses: one is the metaphysical capacity to make decisions freely; the other is the social fact of having a certain amount of elbow-room within society. In early modern usage in both French and English the term "liberty" was used to express both of these senses (*q.v.* Freedom 11–14; David Hume 4); and this is the case with the term *liberté* in French to the present day. In English, although both terms are used in both of these senses, the tendency is to use the term "freedom" to refer to the metaphysical situation of choice, and the term "liberty" to refer to the area of non-constraint granted members of society (or which should be granted to them). In his striking essay, *On liberty*, Mill (*q.v.* 8) discussed the benefits accruing to society through maximizing the area of individual non-constraint. In most definitions, as *e.g.*, that of Jefferson (*q.v.* 2), the natural boundary of liberty is the point where one begins to interfere with the liberty of another. (Notice that the "Four Freedoms" likewise refer to the social dimension of the concept.) For the metaphysical analysis of choice, *q.v.* Freedom; Free Will.

LIBERUM ARBITRIUM.

A Latin phrase meaning "free will" (*q.v.*). Also *q.v.* Freedom (2); Liberty.

LIEBMANN, OTTO. 1840–1912.

German philosopher. Born in Löwenburg. Taught at Strassburg and Jena. In 1865 Liebmann sounded the famous call "Back to Kant," which helped announce the neo-Kantian movement (*q.v.* Neo-Kantianism 1). He was calling for a return to sanity from the fantastic speculations of Hegelian idealism. In his view, neither romantic philosophy nor materialism paid sufficient attention to the data of experience, the difference between what is posited and what is given. The return to Kant was thus in his eyes a philosophical reform. He believed that the Kantian "thing-in-itself" stood either for something nonexistent or something unknowable, and in either case

should be removed from the sphere of philosophy.

Principal writings: *Kant and the Epigonen*, 1865; *On the Objective View*, 1869; *The Climax of Theory*, 1884.

LIEH TZU. 5th cent. B.C.

Chinese philosopher. A follower of Taoism (*q.v.*). He taught the complete abandonment of effort, and is thus associated with negative Taoism. In epistemology, he taught skepticism with respect to the possibility of any knowledge.

LIFE, HUMAN.

The concept of human life is implicit in all philosophical and religious discussion. Its explicit treatment is, however, somewhat rare.

(1) In Hinduism (*q.v.* 3) life is divided into a succession of four stages (*aśramas*), each with its duties and expectations.

(2) In Kierkegaard (*q.v.* 2–4) a division is made between the levels of human life. In ascending importance they are: aesthetic, ethical, and religious.

(3) Heidegger (*q.v.* 4b) claims that "Being-toward-Death," *i.e.*, living in such a way that one does not avoid but accepts the fact of one's own death, adds authenticity to life.

(4) Marias (*q.v.* 1) holds that the ultimate category and final reality is not being, but life.

LIGHT.

Light has played a role in philosophy and religion in both East and West, often standing for physical and Divine Illumination (*q.v.*) at the same time.

A. In Western thought the Neoplatonic doctrine treated light in dual terms. It was an emanation of the divine, containing both physical and spiritual aspects. Out of the Neoplatonic tradition, however, other analyses emerged.

(1) Robert Grosseteste (*q.v.*) held light to be the first principle of material things, which transformed itself into other elements.

(2) Witelo (*q.v.*) accepted the Neoplatonic analysis but also studied the phenomenon of light directly through optics.

(3) Descartes and Newton held to a corpuscular theory of light, treating it as a physical phenomenon.

(4) Einstein (*q.v.* 2, 3) demonstrated that the velocity of light is constant, and that its rays would bend when passing through a strong gravitational field.

B. In Near Eastern thought the religious emphasis on light began with the Zoroastrian religion.

(5) From that point it combined with Greek philosophy to produce an Oriental philosophy in which "light" and "existence" are interchangeable terms. *Q.v.* Ishraqiyah; Divine Illumination (7).

C. In the Far East there are numerous references.

(6) In the Chinese contrast between *Yin* and *Yang* (*q.v.*) the darkness of *yin* stands in contrast to the light of *yang*.

(7) In Mahayana Buddhism (*q.v.*) the properties of light and brightness are typically related to the Buddhas as well as to their celestial lands.

(8) In the Sankhya school (*q.v.*, and Hinduism 6b) light (*sattva*) produces the evolution leading from matter to spirit.

LILA.
Q.v. Play (1); Ramanuja (5).

LIMIT.
From the Latin *limen* ("threshold").

(1) For Kant the idea of the *noumenon* (*q.v.* Kant 2) is a "limiting concept" or *Grenzbegriff*. Phenomena point to but do not encompass the noumenal reality.

(2) In his logic Kant used the phrase "Limitative Judgment" to apply to every judgment of the type "Every 'A' is a not 'B.'"

(3) In mathematics and logic generally, by the "limit of a function" is meant the upper and lower values (the "upper limits" and "lower limits") of the set of values of the function.

LINGAYATS.
Q.v. Vaiṣnavism (3a).

LINGUISTICS.
Q.v. Semantics (5–7).

LINGUISTIC TURN.
Q.v. Bergmann (2).

LIN YUTANG. 1895–1976.
Born in Amoy, Fukien Province, China. Educated at St. Johns (Shanghai), Harvard, Jena, and Leipzig. Taught at Peking National University. Lived in the United States from 1936–66. His importance lay in interpreting Chinese culture to the West.

Selected writings: *The Importance of Living*, 1937; *Wisdom of Confucius*, 1938; *Wisdom of China and India*, 1942; *Between Tears and Laughter*, 1943; *Wisdom of Laotse*, 1948; *The Importance of Understanding*, 1961; *The Chinese Theory of Art*, 1967.

LIPPS, THEODOR. 1851–1914.
German philosopher and psychologist. Born in Wallhalban. Educated at Erlangen, Tübingen, Utrecht, and Bonn. Taught at Bonn, Breslau, and Munich. Considering psychology to be the basis of philosophy, and indeed of all questions relating to internal experience, he derived from this basis logic, ethics, aesthetics, and epistemology. His logic was hence psychologistic. On the other hand his ethical standpoint was formalistic, and reminiscent of Kant. His aesthetics benefited most fully from its psychological base. His theory of empathy (*Einfühlung*) emerged from this study. Aesthetic objects possess a kind of life; projecting ourselves into this other life we experience *Einfühlung*. This principle is exemplified in all of the arts.

Principal writings: *Psychological Studies* (T), 1885; *Characteristics of Logic*, 1893; *The Aesthetics of Space and Optical Illusions*, 1897; *Basic Questions of Ethics*, 1899; *Aesthetics*, 2 vols., 1903–6; *Psychological Investigations*, 2 vols., 1907–12; *Philosophy and Reality*, 1908; On *Einfülhlung*, 1913.

LIPSIUS, JUSTUS. 1547–1606.
Belgian humanist and philosopher. Born at Overyssche. Educated at Cologne and Louvain. Taught at Jena, Leiden, and Louvain. He published editions of Seneca, Tacitus, and other Latin authors. He left the Catholic Church, but became reconciled in 1590. Philosophically a neo-Stoic, he defended "constancy" as the highest value, describing it as an inner force which is unaffected by outward circumstance, and which may be developed by reflection and effort. Combining Christian and Stoic doctrines, he defended free will and God's control over human destiny.

Principal writings: *On Constancy*, 1584; *Of Politics*, 1588–9; *Guide to the Stoic Philosophy*, 1604; *Stoic Physiology*, 1604.

LITERARY CRITICISM.
  Q.v. New Criticism; Structuralism (5); Deconstruction.

LITTRÉ, ÉMILE. 1801–1881.
  French philosopher and linguist. Born in Paris. Largely self-educated. A follower of Comte, and at one time heir apparent to the movement, he called for a return to the early Comte, *i.e.*, the thesis of scientific positivism untrammeled by considerations of the ethics and religion of humanity.
  Principal writings: *Reasoned Analysis of the Course in Positive Philosophy of M.A. Comte*, 1845; *Application of the Positive Philosophy to Government*, 1849; *Conservation, Revolution, and Positivism*, 1852; *Remarks on the Positive Philosophy*, 1859; *Auguste Comte and the Positive Philosophy*, 1863; *Fragments of Philosophy and Contemporary Sociology*, 1876.

LITT, THEODOR. 1880–1962.
  German philosopher. Born in Düsseldorf. Taught at Leipzig and Bonn. Influenced by Dilthey and Spranger, Litt was an adherent of the "Philosophy of the Spirit." Opposed to Idealism no less than materialism, Litt emphasized the spirit-nature or ego-world unities from which spring both the "I" and the objective world.
  Principal writing: *History and Life*, 1918; *Individual and Society*, 1919; *Knowledge and Life*, 1923; *Kant and Herder as Interpreters of the Spiritual World*, 1930; *Philosophy and the Spirit of the Times*, 1935; *The Self-Knowledge of Man*, 1938; *Man and World*, 1948; *Modern Problems of Being*, 1948; *Thought and Being*, 1948; *Hegel, Attempt at a Critical Revival*, 1953.

LOCKE, JOHN. 1632–1704.
  English philosopher. Born in Wrington. Studied in Christ Church, Oxford, receiving a bachelor's degree in 1656 and a Master's degree in 1658. In 1660 he became a tutor at Oxford in Greek, rhetoric, and philosophy. Before 1666, not having graduated in medicine, he was nonetheless practicing as a physician in Oxford. He became Secretary to the Earl of Shaftesbury in 1667, moving to London where he was made a member of the Royal Society, serving on its council. He began working on his famous essay in 1670 to clear up some uncertainties about the limits of human understanding after a particularly frustrating evening of philosophical discussion; the process required twenty years. In 1675 Shaftesbury's political difficulties dictated a move to the Continent. For four years Locke lived and studied in and near Paris, meeting many well-known scientists and philosophers. In England from 1679 to 1683, he saw his patron restored to power, committed to the Tower of London, tried, acquitted, suspected, and escaping to Holland where he died in 1683. Locke, also suspect, lived in Holland under the assumed name of Dr. Van der Linden from 1683 to 1688. Beyond the reach of the government, he was deprived of his position at Oxford by order of the King. He published his first article while in Holland at the age of 54. He also became known to William, Prince of Orange, who landed in England, November 1688. Princess Mary followed in February, 1689, Locke returning on the same ship. Turning down an ambassadorship, he became Commissioner of Appeals, while bringing his books to completion. The famous *Essay* appeared in 1690. In 1691 he made his home in the manor house of Otes, the country seat of Sir Francis Masham, to the delight of the Masham family. In 1696 he accepted a commissionership of the Board of Trade. During these years he answered numerous charges against the *Essay*. His interchange with Stillingfleet took place between 1696 and 1699. In 1704 the *Essay*, having gone through four editions, having been translated into French and Latin, was formally condemned by the authorities at Oxford. "I take what has been done," Locke answered, "rather as a recommendation of the book."
  Principal writings: *The Letter on Toleration*, 1689; *Two Treatises on Government*, 1689; *Essay Concerning Human Understanding*, 1690; *Thoughts on Education*, 1693; *Reasonableness of Christianity*, 1695; *The Conduct of the Understanding*, 1706; *Miracles*, 1716; in addition, many replies to attacks on the major works.
  A. In his *Essay* Locke developed the following themes:
  (1) There are no innate ideas stored in the mind at birth. The individual begins in the world as a blank slate, a *tabula*

rasa, on which experience writes. Locke describes this initial condition as a dark closet, requiring to be furnished from without. Even though there are no innate ideas, however, there are "innate practical principles."

(2) The origin of all ideas is traced to experience; and experience is made up of sensation and reflection. Out of these two sources comes all the complexity of mental life.

(3) Although we are at liberty to produce an unlimited number of new complex ideas, no one has the power to invent a new simple idea; we are passive before experience in this respect. Furthermore, all ideas, as they come into the mind, are simple ideas.

(4) Humans have a power to discern and distinguish; they combine simple into complex ideas; they discover relations among ideas by holding them together in the mind; they engage in abstraction, drawing what is common from a set of ideas and in this way producing abstract or general ideas, *i.e.,* universals. He interprets universals in several ways. At times he says that we are aware of them directly, at other times he allows a particular idea or a name to perform the function of directing our attention to a set of similar ideas. In these procedures he is engaging in the association of ideas. It is the process of association which explains the complexity possible to thought.

(5) There are three types of complex ideas: (a) *Modes,* ideas whose objects cannot exist by themselves but must be part of a thing which can self-exist, part of a substance, that is to say. There are simple modes and mixed modes. The idea of a "dozen" is an instance of a simple mode. It is the idea of a unit repeated a number of times; it is held within the boundaries, so to speak, of a simple idea. The idea of "beauty" is an instance of mixed modes, simple ideas of several kinds being necessary to the making up of this idea. (b) *Substances,* ideas whose objects exist by themselves. The idea of a man is an idea of a single substance; the idea of an army, a collective idea of substance. The idea, of substance, in turn, is a "something I know not what" that underlies the ideas presented by experience. (c) *Relations,* the ideas which result

from comparison. By changing the terms of the comparison a substance can have contrary determinations. A person is both, and truly, older and younger, stronger and weaker, etc. It is Locke's claim that all of these complex ideas can be traced back to the simple ideas of which they are composed; he provides numerous examples of such analyses—substance, God, infinity (the sense that another unit can always be added to a given series), duration, time, eternity—leading to the conclusion that our conceptual world is the result of inference, and of construction.

(6) But we are not, as this might suggest, merely living in a world of our own invention. Some of the ideas in our minds stand for the original or primary qualities of the things we have been observing; others stand for secondary, or derived, qualities. The primary qualities, those ideas inseparable from the things observed, are "solidity, extension, figure, motion or rest, and number." The secondary qualities are "nothing" in the objects themselves; but qualities produced in our minds by the primary qualities of things, *i.e.,* colors, sounds, tastes, and the like. Locke remarks that had we microscopes for eyes many of the secondary qualities of color would disappear; and he finds it a sign of divine wisdom that we are so constructed that we can find our way among things in terms of secondary qualities which are not really in the things.

(7) Apparently, then, we can be said to have a purchase of some sort on the world. Indeed, Locke makes a place in his philosophy for the traditional idea of essence. He distinguishes nominal from real essence. The *nominal essence* of any genus or kind is the abstract idea for which the name stands; the *real essence* is the real constitution of the thing on which its properties depend. Clearly, then, our understanding traffics in nominal essences; how often or in what way one knows the real essences of things is not made clear.

(8) Even though inquiry is directed toward the originals of things (called archetypes) which our ideas more or less resemble, the object of our awareness is our ideas themselves, not the world itself. Holding that truth and falsity belong only to propositions, *i.e.,* to

affirmations or denials involving at least two ideas, he distinguishes between "truth of words" and "truths of thought," the former having to do with the joining and separating of words as the ideas they stand for agree or disagree, the latter concerning the joining or separating of ideas according to the realities they represent. At the same time he defines knowledge as "the perception of the connection and agreement, or disagreement and repugnancy of any of our ideas." The content of our knowledge can be subdivided into intuitive, sensitive, and rational kinds. (a) *Intuitive knowledge*, the foundation of all knowledge, is present in the immediate comparison of ideas, perceiving their likeness or difference. (b) *Demonstrative knowledge* rests on the foregoing, and yet is different in that the agreement or disagreement of two ideas may be shown only by moving through intervening steps. (c) *Sensitive knowledge* is an attempt on the part of Locke to gain a connection between our ideas and the outer world, since this kind of knowledge is perception of the existence of particular external things. We have an intuitive knowledge of our own existence; a demonstrative knowledge of God's existence; and sensitive knowledge of the existence of anything else. We have an internal, infallible perception that we are. It should be noted, however, that what we are aware of is our "person," and while this is dependent on the individual substance, "man," supporting our "person," the two concepts have different significations. A person is an intelligent thinking being able to consider itself as the same thinking being in different times and places. One's person, then, extends as far as do one's self-awareness and memory. The possibility remains open that two successive persons might inhabit the same body. Although we have no innate idea of God, beginning with the intuitive knowledge of our own existence, it is possible to demonstrate with certainty that God exists. How would the demonstration proceed? I am an actual thinking being. The "being" of my nature could not have come from nothing, for certainly those ideas are repugnant to each other; to prevent saying that it has come from nothing, I must finally say that it came from eternal being; and

the power of my being from eternal power. Further, it is in a similar sense repugnant to hold that the perception and thought of my being have come from senseless matter. In this instance the agreement and disagreement of ideas can be put to use to show the certain existence of an eternal thinking, feeling, all-powerful being. And while our sensitive knowledge is not as certain as intuitive and demonstrative knowledge, yet that some of our ideas require an exterior cause is for Locke an acceptable conviction on the grounds that we receive such ideas whether we will to receive them or not; and they have about them the same compulsion we sense in our arm when moved by a command of one's mind. Locke finds this experience to be the source of our idea of causality. The ideas of the external world may indeed be received in pain, but remembered without such a reaction; and several senses may attest to each other's report. On these grounds it follows that there is an external world.

B. Many of Locke's ideas are related to the presence of a gracious author of nature who has disposed us and the world in a certain manner. And even though Locke is able to argue for God's existence, the nature of that Being, appearing from time to time both in the *Essay* and the *Treatise,* is clearly shaped by Locke's Protestant heritage.

(9) Even more clearly than the *Essays,* the *Second Treatise on Civil Government* is theistically grounded. The ideas, in brief, are the following: (a) Men possess by nature certain rights which society should recognize, and of which men cannot be arbitrarily deprived. Locke says that these rights are the gift of God; what God has given, men cannot arbitrarily take away. (b) These are the rights to life, liberty, and property. While the two former are clear, the third is not. But the right of property has its origin in God's gift of the world to all mankind. Beginning with the initial common gift, property is carved out by man's adding his labor to some portion thereof. (c) Since these rights apply to all men, an idea of equality of treatment appears; and this requires that society operate according to written law rather than arbitrary command. (d) Placing a social contract at the base of society,

Locke, although not using the term "social contract" must be judged to be one of those philosophers effective in transferring the locus of sovereignty to the people. Officials of state, henceforth, must be viewed as having only a conditional grant of power, remaining responsible to the people and to their well-being. (e) When the state becomes misdirected it is the people's right and duty to redirect the state; and in doing so they may call upon the right of revolution. (f) Underlying both natural rights and the social contract is the idea of natural law. Locke defines natural law as that rule of common reason and equity which God has set to the actions of men for their mutual security. This rule is available to man through the use of his reason. It is not only the law of reason but of nature's God. It is available to man in the state of nature and in society. It ceases not to obligate men in society, says Locke. Positive law must conform to the principles of the law of nature. Similarly, virtue and vice should be coincident with natural and divine law even though they seem everywhere to stand respectively for what is approved and disapproved by a particular society.

C. The writings on religion and education complete Locke's philosophy, both turning within the framework of the *Essay*.

(10) Religion should turn from arid theological speculation to the simplicity of the Gospels whose central point was the practical acknowledgment of Jesus as Messiah. Reasonableness must be our guide in religion as in all else. Persecution must not be permitted. Toleration of religious differences is essential and to be extended to all save atheists (since "the taking away of God dissolves all," including the taking of a valid oath); and indeed the allegiance of the Church of Rome to a foreign sovereign makes that a special case requiring some limitation.

(11) The purpose of education is the development of character and intelligence. The qualities interfering with this development are hasty judgment, bias, lack of respect for evidence, undue regard for authority, excessive love of custom and antiquity, indolence, and skeptical despair.

LOCUTIONARY ACT.
Q.v. John Austin (2).

LOGIC.

The theory of the conditions of valid inference. The term was first used by Alexander of Aphrodisius (2nd century A.D.). Aristotle's logical writings were called the *Organon*, or instrument of science. Inference involves the passage from one or more statements which are called premises to a further statement called the conclusion. When the conclusion follows from the premises necessarily, the process is called deduction—hence, deductive inference, deductive logic. When the conclusion follows from the premises with a degree of probability less than certainty, the process is called induction—hence, inductive inference, inductive logic.

(1) The development of logic spans some 2500 years in the West, and at least as many years in the East. The development has not been continuous by any means, but in that course of time the vigorous and immensely sophisticated contemporary structure came into being. Because the historical order is, perforce, a progression from simple to complex, it is in one sense the most natural means of explanation. Finally, however, we must consider the field in something like its formidable contemporary complexity, and this requires an analytical ordering. To satisfy both requirements we shall consider first the history of logic, and then its contemporary structure.

A. The history of Western logic begins in Greece. Logic could be said to have had its origin in the geometrical demonstrations of the Pythagoreans, the dialectic of Zeno of Elea (*q.v.*) or that of Plato (*q.v.* 1). The *Categories, Topics, On Interpretation, Prior Analytics,* and *Posterior Analytics* of Aristotle (*q.v.* 1–5) developed an analysis of propositions, their interrelations, their quantification, and their use in inference. Although some inferences of other kinds are examined, Aristotle's analysis culminates in the doctrine of the syllogism, and the extension of knowledge is related fairly closely to the search for middle terms.

(2) By way of contrast, and in the same general period when Greek logic was developing the Nyaya (*q.v.*) school of logic, founded by Gautama (variously

reported 250 B.C.–450 A.D.), was beginning in India. The Nyaya syllogism required five propositions instead of three. The school concerned itself with analyses of language and classification of fallacies. The development of Nyaya logic stimulated a corresponding movement within Buddhism. While Nagarjuna (*q.v.*) and Asanga (*q.v.*) wrote short treatises on logic, Vasubandhu (*q.v.* 3) is regarded as the founder of Buddhist logic, both reducing the Nyaya (*q.v.*) 5-step inference to a 3-step syllogism, and arriving at something like the Western notion of term distribution (*q.v.* Syllogism 6). Dignaga (*q.v.*) followed Vasubandhu in these respects while further developing and popularizing the system. Buddhapalita and Bhavaviveka were also active in the field. Dharmakirti (*q.v.*) is viewed as bringing Dignaga's work to completion. These were followed by many other logicians, including Devendrabuddhi (630–690), Jnanagarbha (700–760), Shantirakshita (725–784), Dharmottara (c. 730–800), Kamalashila (740–790), Prajnakaragupta and Jnanshrimitra (11th century). There were also logical traditions in Mimamsa and Jainism.

(3) In the West the Peripatetic School continued to develop Aristotelian logic (but also *q.v.* Theophrastus). It had a rival in the Megarian-Stoic school of logic. The latter tradition, perhaps because of its connection with the dialectic of Zeno the Eleatic, exhibited an interest in developing something similar to the propositional calculus. Concentrating on "if . . . then" and "either . . . or" type connectives, the members of the Megarian-Stoic school worked out the valid inference forms for these connectives (*q.v.* Chrysippus 1–2). Their analyses were at least partially truth-functional in character. The dispute between Philo of Megara (*q.v.*) and Diodorus Cronos (*q.v.*) over the interpretation of the conditional proposition is also an index of the nature of their concern.

(4) A second, although less weighty, rival to the Peripatetic School is to be found in Epicurean logic (*q.v.* Philodemus of Gadara and Asclepiades), where the claim is made that all logical connections are derived empirically, and thus rest on induction or analogy.

(5) The vitality of the major schools of logic continued well into the Middle Ages. The writings of Cicero (*q.v.*), Galen (*q.v.*), Sextus Empiricus (*q.v.*), Alexander of Aphrodisius, and Porphyry (*q.v.*) testify in one manner or another to this fact. Boethius (*q.v.*) occasionally mentioned the logical controversies between Stoics and Aristotelians, invariably siding with Aristotle. It was Boethius' speculation on the manner of existence of species and genus that sparked the medieval discussion of universals.

(6) Alcuin (*q.v.*), John Scotus Erigena (*q.v.*), and Abelard (*q.v.*) all had something to do with logic between the 8th and 12th centuries A.D., Abelard being the most notable of this group. Abelard composed four treatises on logic. He regarded the verb "to be" as the copula of every categorical proposition (although he was not the first to do so), and held that the copula does not predicate existence. His claim that an affirmative categorical proposition is true only when the subject and predicate terms stand for the same things led to the theory of *Suppositio terminorum* ("substitution of terms"). He dealt with some problems of negation and modality. He entered the argument concerning the paradoxes of implication by holding that the antecedent of a true conditional statement must require the consequent intrinsically in order to rule out the truth of such conditionals as "If Socrates is a stone, then he is an ass." Among valid rules for argument he included early versions of *modus ponendo ponens* (*q.v.*) and *modus tollendo tollens* (*q.v.*), transitivity, negation, and the interrelations of modal statements. He abandoned the position of Stoic logicians that disjunction is to be interpreted strongly.

(7) Avicenna (*q.v.* 1) distinguished natural signs of first understanding from abstract notions of second understanding, holding the concern of logic to be with signs of second understanding. This appears to be the origin of the discussion of first and second intentions.

(8) In the 13th century William of Sherwood (*q.v.*) produced a manual of logic in which the valid moods and figures of the syllogism appear in mnemonic verses with the names Barbara, Celarent, Cesare, Felapton, etc. (*q.v.* Syllogism 4). He considered conjunctive, disjunctive, and

conditional propositions in essentially modern terms; and a work on *Syncategoremata*, analyzing "and," "or," "not," "if," "every," "save," "only," is attributed to him.

(9) In the same century Peter of Spain (*q.v.*), later Pope John XXI, composed his *Summulae Logicales*—a logic textbook widely used in the later Middle Ages, and up until the 17th century. Its 166 editions are perhaps better explained by its development of the technique of mnemonic verses than by its analyses of propositions, predicables, categories, syllogisms, topics, fallacies, supposition, relations, ampliation, appellation, restriction, and distribution. The point of view is very similar to that of William of Sherwood.

(10) Roger Bacon (*q.v.*) was not alone in stressing the importance of empirical procedures and experimental research. He had been preceded by Robert Grosseteste (*q.v.*); but the interest was not central to the age.

(11) Raymond Lull (*q.v.*) in the same period advanced an idea for combining concepts mechanically to provide exhaustive listings of alternatives. The method, called the *Ars Magna*, has influenced the development of logic; and certainly it anticipates Leibniz' *Characteristica Universalis* (*cf.* 17 below).

(12) William of Ockham (*q.v.* 1–11) produced a systematic study of terms, propositions, and arguments. William's so-called nominalism derives from his doctrine that all signs represent individual things; although some signs represent many individual things. What he finds incredible is the belief that there are universals existing in many individuals at once. And although the maxim known as Ockham's razor, *Entia non sunt multiplicanda praeter necessitatem*," ("Entities are not to be multiplied beyond necessity") is compatible with what Ockham says, it is apparently not in his published work.

(13) Peter Ramus (*q.v.* 1–5) opposed the influence of Aristotle, and attempted to put together a logic of a different kind. His popularity was such that some 17th-century writers divided logicians into Aristotelians, Ramists, and Semi-Ramists.

(14) The *Novum Organum* of Francis Bacon (*q.v.* 1–4) published in 1620, was also written in opposition to Aristotle, but Bacon—unlike Ramus—had a genuine alternative. He could see that the traditional logic was not an instrument of scientific discovery; and he directed himself toward the task of constructing such an instrument. His influence was immense, while his success was partial.

(15) Arnold Geulincx (*q.v.*) worked at restoring the traditional logic in the middle of the 17th century; in addition, however, he introduced the notion of the antisyllogism, (the denial of the conclusion of a syllogism entails the denial of the conjunct of its premises), held to the weak sense of disjunction, and divined both of what are now called De Morgan's Theorems (*q.v.*).

(16) Antoine Arnauld (*q.v.*, and also Jansenism) and Pierre Nicole (*q.v.*) produced their *La Logique ou l'Art de penser* in 1662. The book, also known as the Port Royal Logic, considers logic the art of managing one's reason. Rejecting both medieval logic and that of Ramus, they accepted Aristotle only in part. In the choice between Aristotle and the new science their enthusiasm is for the latter. The position curiously combines an attitude of earnest piety and concern with modern science; and yet as followers of Descartes their sense of method derives from geometry. Induction, for example, is held to be unreliable. Their distinction between comprehension and extension of general terms is well-known; comprehension—the set of attributes which could not be removed without destruction of the idea; extension—the set of things to which it is applicable. In the spirit of Descartes and Pascal they state eight rules of method: (a) to leave no term obscure for lack of a definition, (b) to employ in definitions only terms perfectly known or already explained, (c) to use as axioms only things perfectly evident, (d) to accept as evident only that easily recognized as true, (e) to prove all obscure propositions by means of preceding definitions, agreed upon axioms, and already demonstrated propositions, (f) to remove equivocation of terms by restrictive definitions, (g) to proceed so far as possible from the most general and simple, passing from genus to species, (h) to divide each genus into all its species, each whole into its parts, each difficulty into its cases.

(17) Leibniz (*q.v.* 10–13) deserves recognition as a great logician. (a) While

respecting Aristotle he found that not all arguments could be brought into syllogistic form. His respect for subject-predicate logic, however, led him to underestimate the role of relational statements, and to construct a curious kind of substance-attribute ontology. (b) He held to the idea of an *Ars Combinatoria* ("art of discovery") as more fundamental than ordinary logic. (c) And the ideal *Characteristica Universalis*, with its philosophically construed grammar and rules of procedure, was to enable one to move easily through all fields of knowledge. (d) Leibniz' attempts to construct a universal calculus were designed to further the interests we have mentioned; the calculus remained fragmentary, but at last an attempt had been made to produce an abstract mathematics.

(18) In the 18th century Leonhard Euler (*q.v.* 2) helped direct the attention of logicians to the extensional interpretation of general statements. This alternative was developed by Gergonne (*q.v.* 1) in the 19th century.

(19) Sir William Hamilton (*q.v.* 1) in the 19th century introduced an approach to logic in which predicates as well as subjects are quantified; but the modification had no important consequences.

(20) John Stuart Mill (*q.v.* 2–4) attracted great attention because of the clear purpose of his *System of Logic* to develop a logic compatible with the empiricist tradition of British philosophy. He held definitions to be identical propositions giving information only about the use of language. Thus he supported the view of nominal definitions. On the other hand he thought of all propositions as conforming to the subject-predicate pattern, yet he also held that every syllogism exhibits a *petitio principii*. All inference is from particular to particular; hence syllogistic reasoning is not properly termed "inference." This clearly puts the emphasis on induction; and Mill's methods of agreement, difference, joint method, etc. attempt to provide an instrument of discovery.

B. The list of those who in the 19th and 20th centuries have contributed to modern logic is long and notable. Among them may be mentioned: *in the algebra of logic*: George Boole (*q.v.* 1–10), J. Venn (*q.v.* Venn Diagrams), W.S. Jevons (*q.v.*

1), C.S. Peirce (*q.v.*, and *cf.* 24 especially, below), E.V. Huntington (*q.v.* 1–2), and H.M. Sheffer (*q.v.* 1–2); *in the theory of relations*: C.S. Peirce, E. Schröder (*q.v.*), Augustus De Morgan (*q.v.* 1–2); *in the logical foundations of arithmetic*: Gottlob Frege (*q.v.* 1–3), Georg Cantor (*q.v.* 1–8), J.W.R. Dedekind (*q.v.* 1), G. Peano (*q.v.* 1–2), A.N. Whitehead (*q.v.* 1–2), Bertrand Russell (*q.v.* 2–3), J. Łukasiewicz (*q.v.*), and S. Leśniewski (*q.v.*); *on set theory*: Boole, Cantor, E. Zermelo (*q.v.* 1–5), Lowenheim, Skolem, John von Neumann, and Paul Bernays (*q.v.* Set Theory 9–12); *on the problems of logical paradoxes*: K. Gödel (*q.v.* 1–4), B. Russell, Zermelo, Alonzo Church (*q.v.*), and W.V. Quine (*q.v.* 1); *on modal logic and strict implication*: C. I. Lewis (*q.v.* 1); on intuitionism in mathematics: L.E.J. Brouwer (*q.v.* 1–2); *on combinatory logic*: H.B. Curry (*q.v.*); and on the distinction between semantics, syntactics, and pragmatics: Charles Morris (*q.v.* 2), Rudolf Carnap (*q.v.* 7), and Alfred Tarski (*q.v.* 1).

These names relate to the analytical treatment of logic given below, but only the most monumental are repeated in context. The basic types of calculus are given below, but each type is treated more fully under its own heading. The discussion of the contributions of philosophers and mathematicians to these calculi is sometimes given below and at other times under the individual entries, as indicated by the cross-references.

(21) Modern logic begins with the Propositional Calculus (*q.v.*). This part of logic is also called the sentential calculus. Its foundations established by Frege and Peirce, this calculus turns on the formalization of the connectives "and," "or," "not," and "if-then." As the name implies it is a calculus of "propositions." The letters "p," "q," "r," etc. are allowed to stand for propositions. The truth functional connectives are symbolized in various ways; and by means of definitions and Truth Tables (*q.v.*) formulae or theorems are derived exhibiting the valid steps which may be taken in manipulating propositions by means of the connectives. A heavily redundant list of these (the less redundant the more difficult their derivation) has been set down under Propositional Calculus (3–22).

(22) The second type of calculus we

may call the Propositional Calculus with Quantification. It is also called the Predicate Calculus, and the Functional Calculus of First Order. We have treated this calculus under the heading, Quantification Theory (q.v.). The letters "x, y, z . . . etc." in this calculus stand for individuals. In addition to individual variables, the calculus contains predicate variables symbolized by capital letters "F, G, H, . . . etc." Individual and predicate variables are used together so that "Fx" will mean an individual with the characteristic "F." Universal and existential quantification are introduced with the symbolism "(x)" and "(∃x)." "(x)" is the universal quantifier and is read, "For all x. . . ." "(∃x)" is the existential quantifier and is read, "There is an x such that . . . ."

By means of the foregoing, in addition to the signs and formulae of the Propositional Calculus (all of which are assimilated), and rules for introducing and removing quantifiers, every syllogistic inference can be treated in this calculus. This treatment is elaborated elsewhere (q.v. Quantification Theory). Let us here only mention how the propositions treated in the theory of the syllogism are to be written:

A. (All humans are mortal):

(x) [Hx ⊃ Mx]

("For all x, if x is human, then x is mortal.")

E. (No humans are angels):

(x) [Mx ⊃ ~ Ax]

("For all x, if x is human, then x is not an angel.")

I. (Some politicians are statesmen):

(∃x) [Px · Sx]

("There exists an x such that x is a politician and x is a statesman.")

O. (Some politicians are not statesmen):

(∃x) [Px · ~ Sx]

("There exists an x such that x is a politician and x is not a statesman.")

For mathematical use, it may be remarked, among the functional constants must be included the sign "=" standing for identity or equality. Church then calls the system "the functional calculus of first order with equality." The law of identity, or Leibniz's law as it is known, may be stated: "x=y if, and only if, x and y have every property in common." Although the formulae of the Propositional Calculus allowed substitutions to be made, they were sentential substitutions, but with the law of identity or equality, given that x=y it is permissible anywhere in the context where the equality holds to replace x with y or y with x; further, it is permissible to replace some of the x's with y's (or the converse) while leaving others unchanged. The introduction of equality thus increases the flexibility and power of the calculus. The laws of reflexivity (x=x), symmetry if x=y, then y=x), and transitivity (if x=y and y=z, then x=z) follow from the law of identity. To the existential and universal quantifiers there may now be added numerical quantifiers. Accepting the existential quantifier as expressing the meaning "there exists at least one thing . . ." satisfying a given condition, we can express "there is at most one thing . . ." as "for any x and y, if x satisfies the given condition and if y satisfied it, then x=y." And "there are at least two things satisfying the condition," as: "There are x and y, such that both satisfy the condition and x ≠ y" (i.e., x is not the same as y).

In discussing the Propositional Calculus (q.v.) it was stated that the method of Truth Tables provided a decision procedure for testing the validity or invalidity of any argument. For the predicate calculus no decision procedure is available. This was demonstrated by Alonzo Church in 1936. Tarski has developed a decision procedure for the elementary algebra of real numbers; but Church has shown there can be no decision procedure in general for this calculus.

(23) The calculus of classes, also known as Set Theory (q.v.), had its origin in the work of George Boole and Georg Cantor. Boole provided the earliest workable class calculus, while Cantor provided analyses of cardinal number, infinity, and order. The dimensions of the calculus have become standard, as developed especially by Zermelo in Axiomatic Set Theory. A summary of its basic structure is given under the heading, Set Theory (q.v. 1–8).

(24) The logic of relatives, or logic of relations, was suggested by Peirce in papers written between 1870 and 1903

(*cf*. his "The Logic of Relations," 1883) and systematically developed by Schröder in his *Lectures on the Algebra of Logic*, vol. 3, 1895. Peirce found his beginning point in Boole and De Morgan. The latter had treated the syllogism as no more than a special case in the theory of the composition of relations. Peirce found De Morgan's treatment lacking the beauty of Boolean algebra, and endeavored to extend the elegance of Boolean algebra to the algebra of relatives. In particular, Peirce contributed the idea of relative product, relative sum, and conversion. He worked out a notation for relations, (*e.g.*, the compound sign "lij" tells us that the person named by the letter "i" loves the person named by the letter "j"), by which relations with several terms could be represented. And he used " Σ " and " π" standing for "some" and "every" to quantify relational expressions. A summary of the basic structure of the calculus of relations is given under the heading "Relations, The Logic of."

(25) Modal logic (*q.v.*) adds to the foregoing calculi symbols and definitions for necessity (" □ "), possibility (" ◇ "), strict implication (" ⊣ "), and strict coimplication (" ≡ "), thus extending the scope of logic to statements of possibility and necessity. Although logical recognition of the modalities of possibility and necessity goes back to Aristotle, C.I. Lewis deserves credit for establishing modal logic as a discipline. Deontic logic (*q.v.*), investigating statements of obligation, has developed as a branch of modal logic.

(26) Tense logic adds operators for "always" and "at some time." "What is always the case is the case now," or "If always p, then p." And "what is the case now is the case at some time," or "if p, then p at some time." In some treatments it leads to a "theory of instants." There are interesting connections between quantification theory, modal logic, and tense logic, such that "everything," "something," "necessarily," "possibly," "always," and "at some time," are all operators which may be used in conjunction with each other. Among others, A.N. Prior (Prior and Fine, *Worlds, Times and Selves*, 1977) has worked with this possibility.

(27) The lurking problems of logical paradoxes have been handled in a number of ways, most notably by Russell

in his theory of types and by Zermelo in his unique treatment of set theory. Further treatment of the matter is to be found under Paradox (2–9).

C. The following entries, while of interest with respect to logic, do not readily fit into the above historical and schematic survey.

(28) W.E. Johnson (*q.v.* 1) defined logic as the "analysis and criticism of thought."

(29) F.C.S. Schiller (*q.v.* 2) regarded the forms of logic as linked indissolubly to use and to be retained only so long as useful.

(30) Reichenbach (*q.v.* 1) argued that the two-valued logic of truth and falsity should be replaced by an infinite-valued logic of probability.

(31) Combinatory logic on the other hand, developed chiefly by H.B. Curry (*q.v.*), seeks to eliminate variables entirely, replacing them with function symbols.

(32) Nagel (*q.v.* 6) defends a view of "logic without ontology," regarding the entities and operations of logic as having context-determination.

(33) Toulmin (*q.v.* 3) regards logic as "generalized jurisprudence."

LOGICAL ATOMISM.
Q.v. Russell (8).

LOGICAL EMPIRICISM.
Q.v. Vienna Circle of Logical Positivists; Ayer (3); Feigl.

LOGICAL FORMS AS ESSENCES.
Q.v. Husserl (2–3).

LOGICAL POSITIVISM.
The point of view of the Vienna Circle of Logical Positivists (*q.v.*). The goal of the school, also known as "logical empiricism," was to purify philosophy—sifting out its metaphysical elements, and reconstituting the discipline with logic as its organon. The goal of philosophy in this sense is working out the implications of the logic of science. Also *q.v.* Ayer (3).

LOGICAL REALISM.
Q.v. Morris Cohen (3); Northrop (2).

LOGIC OF DISCOVERY AND LOGIC OF JUSTIFICATION.
(1) Through much of the 17th and 18th centuries, as Larry Laudan has pointed out (in his "Why Was the Logic of

Discovery Abandoned?" 1980) an effort was made to discover rules to accelerate the pace of scientific advance. These rules would constitute a logic of discovery. The widely accepted view was that this logic would also be a logic of justification. The issue is bound up with fallibilism and infallibilism. For those who believe we can have infallible knowledge, it is reasonable to believe that the two logics are identical. If, however, all knowledge is fallible, it will no longer be so reasonable to identify the logic of discovery with that of justification. There will be no mechanical way of moving from observation to theory. And although there is no royal road to theory it will still be possible to justify theories in terms of their likelihood, that is, in terms of fallible knowledge.

(2) Reichenbach (*q.v.* 6), using the phrases, "context of discovery" and "context of justification," thought of the former as a psychological, and the latter as a logical, process.

LOGIC OF RELATIONS.
Q.v. Relations, Logic of.

LOGIC OF THE SUPPLEMENT.
Q.v. Derrida (8).

LOGOCENTRISM.
From *logos* (speech, reason, logic), thus any discourse ingenuously centered in speech, reason, or logic. The alleged bias in Western thought, favoring the written over the spoken word, presence over absence, and completeness over the incompleteness of actual experience. The bias is insisted upon by Derrida (*q.v.* 3, 4), and supported by deconstructionists, generally (*q.v.* Deconstruction).

LOGOS.
A Greek term meaning "reason, word, speech, discourse, definition, principle, or ratio." The function of the term in philosophy has turned largely on the *logos* as "reason."

(1) Heraclitus (*q.v.* 3) found in the universe a formative and shaping power analogous to the power of reason in man. Man's soul is part of the objective reason or *logos* of things.

(2) From Anaxagoras (*q.v.* 3) through Aristotle, *nous* replaced *logos* as the mo-

tivating principle of the universe, and *nous* is an immaterial power while *logos* is material.

(3) *Logos* reappeared in the system of the Stoics, when their principle of teleology was termed both *logos* and God (*q.v.* Stoicism 1). A subordinate principle was the doctrine of *logos spermatikos*, a principle of active reason working in dead matter. The *logos* in man is the *ratio* within his psyche which becomes *oratio* upon his lips, a distinction utilized by Philo and the Church Fathers.

(4) Even in Judaism there are tendencies to personify the word of God as a creative and partially independent being, *i.e.*, as the creative power of God.

(5) Philo (*q.v.* 4) identified the creative word of the Old Testament with the *logos* of the Stoics. The *logos* thus became a transcendent principle, as the means by which God expresses Himself in the world. But *logos* also had a redemptive function; it was the means to a higher spiritual nature.

(6) In the Gospel of John, the *logos* is both creative and redemptive; the latter aspect is given greater emphasis than the former. In John and in the early Church the principle was assimilated to the idea of an historic person, whose transcendent aspect is as a member of the Trinity.

(7) The *logos* is found among the emanations of many of the Gnostic systems (*q.v.*, for example, Valentinus).

(8) Among the Apologists, Minucius (*q.v.*) found the Christian Trinity prefigured in Greek philosophy, and identified the *logos* of the Greek philosophers with the Son of Christianity.

(9) In modern philosophy, Fichte (*q.v.* 8) stated that God is present as *logos* in all there is; and Hegel's (*q.v.* 4) dialectic—derived from Fichte—is an expression of a working *logos*.

(10) Unamuno (*q.v.* 3) rejected the *logos* as an abstraction, substituting for it the Word as the intimate expression of the man of flesh and bone.

(11) For Heidegger (*q.v.* 8) the *logos* or Word is present in all discourse, capable of revelatory disclosures of Being when properly addressed.

LOISY, ALFRED. 1857–1940.
French Biblical scholar. Born in Ambrières. Taught in the Catholic

Institute of Paris and later in the Collège de France. As one of the leaders of Modernism (q.v. 2) his emphasis was on divine immanence and the importance of individual religious experience. He believed that the sacred books of all religions contained successive revelations of God to man. His books were put on the Index in 1903. His *Author of a Small Book* responded to this action in the same year. In 1907 Pius X issued his encyclical against Modernism, criticizing it as the "synthesis of all heresies." Loisy responded with his *Simple Reflections* in 1908. Finally, Loisy was excommunicated.

Selected writings: *Babylonian Myths and the First Chapters of Genesis*, 1901; *Author of a Small Book*, 1903; *Simple Reflections on the Decree*, 1908; *Religion*, 1917; *Pagan Mysteries and the Christian Mystery*, 1919; *The Acts of the Apostles*, 1920; *Are There Two Sources of Religion and Morals?*, 1933.

LOKAYATA.

Sanskrit term from *loka* ("world"). Name of the doctrine of Indian materialism. A school of thought, developing in India around 800 B.C. in contradiction to Vedic culture, it was precursor to Jainism and Buddhism. Its tenets include the following:

(1) Perception is the only means of knowledge.

(2) Even inference from sense data is to be rejected as unreliable.

(3) Only matter exists, and in the basic forms of the four elements—air, earth, fire, and water.

(4) When the body is constituted by the appropriate intermixture of elements, consciousness appears. When the mixture becomes inappropriate, consciousness becomes utterly nonexistent once again.

(5) Hence, concentration on the present life becomes important.

(6) The value of the *Vedas* is denied; they are said to be characterized by untruthfulness, internal contradiction, and useless repetition.

Q.v. Carvaka.

LOLLARDS.

A name applied to the "poor preachers" of Wycliffe (q.v. 4) who, in the decade after the latter's death, spread across England, challenging the abuses of the Church. They were severely persecuted

by Henry IV, beginning in 1401. Those who survived went underground, the movement becoming open once again at the Reformation.

LOMBARD, PETER.

Q.v. Peter Lombard.

LONERGAN, BERNARD J.F. 1904–1984.

Canadian theologian and philosopher. Born in Buckingham, Quebec. Educated at Loyola College (Montreal), Heythrop College (England), University of London, and Gregorian University. Taught at Loyola College (Montreal), *L'Immaculee Conception* (Montreal), Regis College and Jesuit Seminary (Toronto), Gregorian University, Boston College. Entered the Jesuit order in 1922, ordained in 1936.

Principal writings: *De Constitutione Christi*, 1956; *Insight; a Study of Human Understanding*, 1957; *De Deo Trino*, 1964; *De Verbo Incarnato*, 1964; *Verbum: Word and Idea in Aquinas*, 1967 (ed. D.B. Burrell); *The Subject*, 1968; *Doctrinal Pluralism*, 1971; *Grace and Freedom in Aquinas*, 1971; *Method in Theology*, 1972; *Philosophy of God, and Theology*, 1973; *The Way to Nicea* (T), 1976.

(1) Attracted by the Augustinian strand of interiority in Aquinas' thought (a strand which led Augustine, q.v. 1–6, through immaterial ideas to the divine), Lonergan centered on understanding, or insight as the key concept in human knowing, providing a link between the sensible and intelligible worlds.

(2) Developed first in classical terms, in a set of theological studies on Aquinas, Lonergan's Augustinian interest enabled him to include the modern appreciation of historical consciousness in his analysis.

(3) This breadth of interest, along with his belief that cognition moves not from premise to conclusion but "from data through understanding (or insight) to judgments and decisions," allowed him to call for the reintegration of philosophy, science, and theology after their "long separation." With respect to science, the data of all its subdivisions stand as raw material to be worked over in cognition.

(4) The levels of conscious awareness—experiencing, understanding, judging, and decision-making—naturally repeat the stages of cognition. The normative human level is the "fourth level of waking

consciousness" and includes an appreciation of the good.

(5) The manner in which objectivity and subjectivity interrelate for Lonergan can be sensed in his claim that objectivity in knowledge is a matter of authentic subjectivity, achieved through remaining authentically faithful to the requirements of intelligence. It is likewise present in his view that "the integral structure of proportionate being" which one seeks in metaphysics is to be found in the structural features of one's own cognition.

(6) Self-transcendence is increasingly present in the four levels of awareness, as well as in the three forms of conversion—intellectual, moral, and religious. The third form is totally transcendent, requires grace, and the supernatural.

(7) Lonergan presents a formal argument for God: "If the real is completely intelligible, God exists. But the real is completely intelligible. Therefore, God exists." God thus becomes the "formally unconditioned unrestricted act of understanding," extending far beyond conditioned and limited human understanding. On the intellectual level our knowledge of being points toward transcendent being so, to understand what being is, and what God is, come to the same thing.

(8) Although the argument for God is valid on the intellectual level, and is not necessary on the religious level, moral conversion (with its appreciation of the transcendent good) is, practically speaking, a necessary condition for grasping the validity of the argument.

LONGINUS. c. 213–273.

Greek rhetorician. Born in Syria. Studied in Alexandria under Ammonius Saccas (*q.v.*) and taught in Athens. Although a fellow-student of Plotinus (*q.v.*) in Alexandria, he held—in opposition to Plotinus—that ideas have an independent existence outside the divine mind or *Nous*. Thus, he may be regarded as rather more a Platonist than a Neoplatonist. Long credited with the book *On the Sublime*, it seems that this treatise on impressiveness in style is more properly attributed to an unknown 1st-century author.

Principal writings: *On First Principles; On the Chief End;* a *Commentary* on Plato's *Timaeus; The Art of Rhetoric.*

LOPATIN, LEO M. 1855–1920.

Russian philosopher. Taught at Moscow. Influenced by Schopenhauer, Solovyev, and Leibniz, Lopatin is one of the most noted neo-Leibnizians in Russian philosophy. Believing in human freedom, he regarded the person as creative, and capable of "creative causality," from which all other conceptions of causality are derivative.

Principal writings: *The Positive Tasks of Philosophy*, 2 vols., 1886, 1891; "The Problem of Liberty of the Will," 1889; *Philosophical Characterizations and Addresses* (T in part), 1911.

LORD'S PRAYER OF THE MUSLIMS.
Q.v. Qur'an (5).

LORD'S SUPPER.
Q.v. Eucharist.

LORENZ ATTRACTOR.
Q.v. Chaos Theory (9).

LORENZ, EDWARD.
Q.v. Chaos Theory, and (9).

LOSSKY, NIKOLAI O. 1870–1965.

Russian philosopher. Born in Vitebsk. Studied in St. Petersburg. Professor of philosophy at St. Petersburg, until 1921. Exiled, he lived in Prague and Bratislava, Czechoslovakia, and in New York. His work reflected the influence of Leibniz and Bergson.

Principal writings: *The Intuitive Basis of Knowledge* (T), 1906; *The World as an Organic Whole* (T), 1917; *Freedom of Will* (T), 1927; *Value and Existence* (T), 1935; *History of Russian Philosophy* (E), 1951.

(1) Taking an intuitionistic approach to reality, Lossky held that subject and object must interpenetrate for knowledge to be possible. This requirement led him to interpret the world itself as an organic whole. Intuition extends not only to objects, but also to the cosmic principle or person on which the cosmic order depends.

(2) Holding to the reality of human freedom, Lossky supported the ideas of creativity both on the divine and human levels, finding all things aspiring toward God, each in its own way.

(3) As a kind of necessary complement to real being, Lossky posited ideal being as a source for norms and principles.

(4) He believed in the Absolute as a living God, supporting ideal being.

LOTZE, RUDOLF HERMANN. 1817–1881.

German philosopher. Born in Bautzen. Educated at Leipzig. Taught at Göttingen and Berlin. A student of Fechner, he was at first interested in medicine and the natural sciences, but he turned increasingly to philosophy. His writings helped to shape the field of Axiology.

Principal writings: *Metaphysics* (T), 1841; *Logic* (T), 1843; *On the Idea of Beauty*, 1845; *On the Conditions of Beauty in Art*, 1847; *General Physiology of Corporeal Existence*, 1851; *Medical Psychology or Physiology of the Soul*, 1853; *Microcosmus* (T), 3 vols, 1856–8; *Polemical Writings*, 1857; *The History of Aesthetics in Germany*, 1868; *System of Philosophy* (T), 2 vols., 1874, 1879.

(1) Insisting, against Schelling, that the operation of mechanical laws is not cancelled out in the organic and spiritual realms, he nonetheless held that the reality of such laws is not antithetical to value.

(2) Indeed, the regions of fact, law, and value are separate only in our thoughts; in reality they are together. This togetherness requires at last the idea of God who has chosen the laws through which His ends are to be realized. That is to say, the only intelligible notion of a universe one is able to form—the conception of a plurality of interconnected things governed by a system of laws—bears a strong analogy to one's own mental life with its unity of self and multiplicity of states, and suggests a psychic continuum of souls or monads so ordered that man is a microcosm of the macrocosm, and so is everything else.

(3) The analogy does not prove the existence of God, who at this stage is perhaps better called the Absolute; but the path from the Absolute to God lies in the sensitive appreciation of values by means of which the metaphysical ground of things is sensed as the realization of the holy, beautiful, and good. Such realization is beyond the scope of science, though not for that reason invalid. The appreciation of individual values involves the use and interpretation of signs, which stand as instances of universal and objective value. His analysis of aesthetic value utilizes the concept of empathy.

(4) His use of the terms "postulate" and "hypothesis" has some distinctiveness, since he regarded postulates as the absolutely necessary assumptions without which the content of a given set of observations would contradict the laws of our thought, and hypotheses as the conjectures filling up the postulates by stating the concrete causes, forces, and processes out of which the given phenomena arose in the case being considered.

LOVE.

The Latin terms are *amor* and *caritas*, and the principal Greek terms are *philia*, *eros*, and *agápe*. *Philia* developed the connotation of the kind of love involved in friendship (*jen* standing as the Chinese synonym), *amor* and *eros* the type of love based on desire, and *caritas* and *agápe* the sense of a higher or selfless type of love.

(1) For Hesiod (*q.v.* 1), Eros is a primal deity, bringing order out of chaos.

(2) Empedocles (*q.v.* 3) introduced the complementary principles of love (*philia*) and Strife (*neixos*) as forces governing motion and development in the universe. *Philia* was at this point merely a principle of attraction, lacking the connotation suggested above.

(3) Plato (*q.v.* 1) in the *Symposium* used the term *eros*, claiming, on the authority of the wise Diotima, that all love is love of beauty, its perfect form being the love of the abstract form of beauty itself.

(4) Aristotle (*q.v.* 10, 11) fills a double role in the development of the idea. First, he continues the sense of Platonic love as the desire of the imperfect for the perfect. The primary instance of this is the manner in which the unmoved mover, Aristotle's absolute and perfect deity, moves the entire universe through the love of perfection present in all things. Secondly, in the *Nicomachean Ethics*, Aristotle developed the sense of love as friendship based on the "good, pleasant, or useful."

(5) The Confucian idea of *jen* (*q.v.* Confucius 5), having among its meanings "love of fellow men," appears to be an Eastern equivalent to *philia*.

(6) *Agápe* or "selfless love," seems to have originated in the common meals or "love feasts" of the early Christians. It provides an interesting contrast to the sense of love developed by Plato and

Aristotle. Where the Greek conception is based on the desire of the imperfect for perfection, that of the Christians is a gift freely given. Its paradigm case is God becoming man, giving of Himself with no possibility of return. Its principle is thus in some sense the opposite of the Greek principle; where God is defined as perfect Being, the movement is from perfection to imperfection, as it were.

(7) In Neoplatonism and mystical theology there is a double movement, an emanating of love into the world, and a desire on the part of the order of creation to be united with the divine. In the *Pseudo-Dionysius* (*q.v.* 3), the metaphors of love and light intermingle, illuminating and linking us to each other and to our eternal source.

(8) In St. Augustine (*q.v.* 6, 12, 13), the metaphors of love and light likewise mingle, the light and love of God being identical. His problem in the *Confessions* was his inability to distinguish the "clear brightness of love from the fog of lustfulness"; he defined virtue as the *ordo amoris*, or "order of love"; and saw the opposition between the City of God and the City of Man as a struggle between love of God and love of self.

(9) For Aquinas (*q.v.* 7) there are two forms of natural love, one relating to the passions and the other to the will. He interprets *caritas* as a supernatural love; for one to exhibit such love some "habitual form" must be superadded to his "natural power."

(10) The rise of the Florentine Academy (*q.v.*) led to a resurgence of interest in Platonic love. Among those having written famous essays on the subject are Marsilio Ficino (*q.v.*) and Leon Hebreo (*q.v.*).

(11) For Spinoza (*q.v.* 4, 5c) the "intellectual love of God" is the highest end of life, the paradigm case of love whose definition for Spinoza is "happiness joined to the idea of an external cause."

(12) Malebranche (*q.v.* 5) and Norris (*q.v.* 2) distinguished between self-centered and altruistic love, holding that our relation to God depended upon cultivation of the latter type.

(13) Rousselot (*q.v.*), reviving an ancient theme, held love to be the key to knowledge of the divine.

(14) Caso (*q.v.*) found love the appropriate governing principle for human life,

building on other principles, those of economy and disinterest.

(15) Freud (*q.v.* 7–8) insisted that *Eros*, interpreted as sexual fulfillment, is the nucleus of what is meant by love; and that human history is the struggle between *Eros* and *Thanatos* (the death instinct).

(16) Jung (*q.v.* 4) interpreted romantic love as a double projection which occurs between those afflicted by it.

(17) Nygren (*q.v.*) regarded *agápe* as the distinguishing mark of Christianity, interpreting all of Christian doctrine in its light.

LOVEJOY, ARTHUR O. 1873–1962.

American philosopher. Born in Germany. Educated at Berkeley and Harvard. Taught at Johns Hopkins, 1910–38. Lovejoy combined two interests: epistemology and the history of ideas. Founder of the *Journal of the History of Ideas*.

Principal writings: "Reflections of a Temporalist on the New Realism," 1911; "On Some Novelties of the New Realism," 1913; *Essays in Critical Realism* (symposiast), 1920; *The Revolt Against Dualism*, 1930; *Primitivism and Related Ideas in Antiquity* (with G. Boas), 1935; *The Great Chain of Being*, 1936; *Essays in the History of Ideas*, 1948; *The Reason, the Understanding, and Time*, 1961.

(1) Although interested in New Realism (*q.v.*), Lovejoy found his epistemological home in the movement of Critical Realism (*q.v.* 3), contributing to the 1920 volume. His *Revolt Against Dualism* argued for a dualistic epistemology, holding that in the very nature of time and physiology there must be a duality between the world and what we sense in objects. This also requires, then, the sense-datum theory. He likewise held, somewhat in the manner of Locke, that primary qualities are in things, while secondary qualities are a result of the action of things on us.

(2) As an historian of ideas, Lovejoy concentrated on themes of great historical resonance underlying philosophical decisions. The two themes which he explored most fully were the idea of the chain of being, and primitivism. The first of these ideas rests on "the principle of plenitude" which had its origin in Plato. The principle is that all possibilities are to be realized. In the West the principle

has led to the medieval hierarchical universe with its degrees of being, the infinite universes of Giordano Bruno, and the Leibnizian Principle of Sufficient Reason. The work on primitivism made clear the multiple meanings of the term lying behind its philosophical employment, and the tendency to idealize the past, looking back to golden ages of politics, literature, knowledge, etc.

LOWENHEIM, LEOPOLD.

Q.v. Lowenheim-Skolem Proofs.

LOWENHEIM-SKOLEM PROOFS.

Leopold Lowenheim proved in 1915 that if "F" is a well-formed formula of the first-order predicate calculus with certain predicate variables, then either not-F is provable or F can be satisfied in the natural number series by suitable determinations of the predicate variables. In 1919 Thoralf Skolem proved that for an enumerated set of formulae "F_1," "F_2," "F_3," etc., the whole set of formulae can be satisfied; and since set theory is such a set of formulae, the Lowenheim theorem applies to set theory. It follows that if the axioms are consistent, the relation of membership between the natural numbers can be determined in such a manner that all of the axioms become valid. One consequence of the procedure, however, is that sets cannot be construed as absolute in Cantor's sense. (*Q.v.* Set Theory).

LOWENTHAL, LEO.

Q.v. Frankfurt School, The. A.

LOYALTY.

For Royce (*q.v.* 1a) the ideal of loyalty is a universal, capable of bringing harmony among competing loyalties. The principle of ethics is, from this perspective, "Be loyal to loyalty."

LOYOLA, ST. IGNATIUS OF. 1491–1556.

Founder of the Society of Jesus. Born in the Basque province of Guipuzcoa. At thirteen, a page in the court of Ferdinand and Isabella, he followed a career of arms for almost two decades. Badly wounded in 1521, he was given the last sacraments; then in a long convalescence he saw a likeness of the Virgin Mary, the first of many visions. Dedicating himself as a Knight of Christ he lived in the Domini-

can Convent at Manresa for a year, where he practiced extreme austerity. Gradually, the Society of Jesus formed. In 1534 a group of seven had taken vows of poverty and chastity, pledging themselves to go to the Holy Land as missionaries. In 1537 the vows were renewed. The decision to go to the Holy Land not working out, the group put itself at the disposal of the Pope. In 1540 Pope Paul III officially recognized the Society, and Loyola was elected its first general in 1541. The history of the Society is discussed under the heading, Jesuits.

Principal writings: *The Book of the Spiritual Exercises*, 1548.

(1) Loyola's book is a manual of training to be put into practice. Its first step is the cultivation of a sense of shame and sorrow for one's life. This exercise is to continue for seven to ten days. During this time one is to deprive oneself of light, warmth, contact with one's fellows and unnecessary material goods.

(2) In the second week of the exercises Christ is presented as the Leader one is to aid in reconquering the world from the dominion of sin and the devil. This week closes with the election to leave all things and follow Christ.

(3) In the third week the subject is encouraged to penance and meditation on the passion of Christ.

(4) In the final week one is to allow oneself rest and refreshment while meditating on the Resurrection and the joys of heaven.

L-TRUTH.

For a discussion of L-true and L-false sentences where "L" stands for "logically," and discussion of L-determinate and L-indeterminate concepts, *q.v.* Carnap (8–9, 11).

LUCIAN OF SAMOSATA. c. 125–180.

Greek philosopher. Influenced by the Epicureans, Skeptics, and Cynics, he is closest to the last-named school. His principal influence was that of Demonax of Cyprus (*q.v.*). Emphasizing the satirical style of the Cynics, Lucian is known for his satirical dialogues directed both against philosophical doctrines and religious beliefs. An opponent of enthusiasm, even his praise of certain philosophers is mixed with irony.

Principal writings: Fragments of the dialogues remain.

LUCRETIUS (TITUS LUCRETIUS CARUS). c. 99–55. B.C.

Roman poet and philosopher. Born in Rome. A member of the aristocracy. A student of Greek philosophy and especially of the writings of Epicurus. The account of Suetonius that Lucretius suffered mental illness as the result of taking a powerful love-philtre, that his book was composed during his lucid intervals and corrected by Cicero; and that he died by his own hand at the age of 49, has little to recommend it. Certainly the philosophical poem itself reveals a powerful mind at work.

Principal writings: *On the Nature of Things* (T).

(1) Following Epicurus in most points, Lucretius developed a metaphysics built from the concepts of atoms, motion, and the void. Atoms are indestructible, having size, shape, and weight but no secondary qualities. The different qualities of composite things are due to the difference of the constituent atoms and their arrangements.

(2) Matter and space are infinite; hence, one must posit an infinite number of worlds coming into being, developing to maturity, and perishing.

(3) Atoms are naturally in motion; and this motion, incredibly rapid, is initially downward and in parallel lines. The atoms possess a power, however, to swerve slightly from the downward direction dictated by their weight. This swerving allows the birth of worlds and the appearance of composite things. The same power is called upon by man in mental decisions, allowing free will.

(4) The human psyche has, like everything else, an atomic structure. Hence, there can be no immortality, and the fear of death is unreasonable.

(5) Streams of images leave the surface of things, entering our eyes when these are appropriately turned. The senses receive the images but sometimes the mind misinterprets the content received.

(6) Our world began from an atomic chaos which produced its own order. Living forms have developed from vegetation into animal forms, and at last to the form of man. The criterion of survival has determined what species continue to exist, and many species have perished.

(7) The advance of man from a brutish state into civilization is accompanied by the growth of a natural justice.

(8) Gods exist in the interspaces between worlds, but they are self-sufficient beings, and have nothing to do with us. And since worlds come to be by natural causes no creator is required.

(9) Pleasure is the end of life, but only the pleasures of peace and a pure heart are at last satisfying. These are found, at least in part, in devotion to truth, and the realization that while the world is temporary and man more temporary still, death is nothing to us; and the fear of the unknown can be dissipated along with superstition.

LU HSIANG-SHAN. 1139–1193.

Chinese philosopher. Born in Kiangsi. He achieved the "Presented Scholar" degree in 1172. He was District Keeper of Records and professor at the national university. He returned to his home in Hsiang-Shan to teach and lecture, and was given the honorary name "Master Hsiang-Shan." He also served as magistrate from 1190 until his death. It is said that thousands of scholars gathered to hear his lectures. He carried on the major emphases of Cheng Hao (*q.v.*). Developing the idealistic wing of neo-Confucianism, he stood in opposition to Ch'eng I (*q.v.*) and Chu Hsi (*q.v.*) who represent the rationalistic wing. He opposed Chu Hsi in a famous debate.

Principal writings: *Complete Works of Lu Hsiang-Shan* (T in part).

(1) One's principal task in life is to concentrate on the investigation of one's mind, following principle, and "honoring the moral nature." One can know the fundamentals of things through the principles inherent in one's own mind. And knowing the fundamentals, the six classics become our footnotes.

(2) The traditional twin neo-Confucian goals of following principle and investigating things become one for Lu. He views the mind not only as endowed with innate knowledge of the good, but also with an innate ability to do the good. What permeates the mind emanates from it and extends throughout the universe.

(3) Concrete principle thus fills the entire continuum of time and space constituting the universe. Sages appearing tens of thousands of generations ago, today, and tens of thousands of generations in the future share these principles. The principles are equivalent to *jen* (*q.v.*) or "humanity." The consequence is that the universe is one's mind, and one's mind the universe.

(4) In learning, one should begin in "genuine and personal concern, self-examination, correcting one's mistakes, reforming to do good. That is all."

LUKÁCS, GEORG. 1885–1971.

Hungarian Marxist philosopher. Born in Budapest. Studied at the University of Budapest, Berlin, Heidelberg, and the Soviet Academy of Sciences. Taught at the University of Budapest. Combining intellectual and political activity, Lukács spent 25 years in exile—in Austria, Russia, and finally in Romania—before his final return to Hungary. He was Commissioner of Public Instruction in the government of Béla Kun, and Minister in Imre Nagy's government. Once sentenced to death and once imprisoned by Stalin, for several months in 1941. Despite political engagement he identified himself finally with intellectual work. At times he disavowed earlier works in acts of public self-criticism. Since there were also times when he disavowed his disavowals, it is exceedingly difficult to treat his work as a whole. His intellectual life was largely oriented by a continuing interest in aesthetics. For this reason the points which follow will center on aesthetic theory, although not without attention to his social philosophy.

Principal writings: *Soul and Form* (T), 1910; *Sociology of Modern Drama* (T), 2 vols. abridged, 1911; *Aesthetic Culture* (H), 1913; *The Theory of the Novel* (T), 1916; *History and Class-Consciousness* (T), 1923; *Lenin: a Study on the Unity of his Thought* (T), 1924; *Lenin and the Problem of Culture* (H), 1946; *Goethe and His Time* (T), 1946; *Nietzsche and Fascism* (H), 1946; *Existentialism or Marxism* (T), 1947; *Essays on Realism* (G), 1948; *The Literary Theories of Marx and Engels* (H), 1948; *The Young Hegel* (T), 1948; *Contributions to the History of Aesthetics* (G), 1954; *The Destruction of Reason* (G), 1954; *The Mean-*

ing of Contemporary Realism (T), 1958; *The Specific Nature of the Aesthetic* (G), 2 vols., 1963; *The Young Marx* (G), 1965; *Ideology and Politics* (G), 1967; *Problems of Realism* (G), 3 vols., 1967–71; *Problems of Aesthetics* (G), 1969; *Marxism and Stalinism* (G), 1970; *The Ontological Basis of Human Thought and Action* (G), 1970; *On the Ontology of Social Reality* (T), 2 vols., 1971, 1972; *Writer and Critic and other Essays* (collected and T), 1971; *Marxism and Human Liberation* (collected and T), 1973.

(1) Lukács charted the first 3 stages of his philosophical odyssey as: beginning with "subjective idealism" (neo-Kantianism); moving to "objective idealism" (Hegel); thence to a synthesis of "realist Hegelianism" and Marxist humanism. He also recorded a fourth stage, closer to, if not identical with, doctrinaire Marxism; but since it is in this stage that one must be less certain of Lukács inner opinions, it is worth the effort to attempt to explicate his aesthetic views, utilizing only the first 3 stages.

(2) In the first stage *Soul and Form* is central. The literary analysis relates to the current of "romantic anticapitalism," including Kierkegaard, Novalis, Thomas Mann, and others, and is viewed as an anticipation of 20th century existentialism where individuals, caught in a corrupting world, yearn for lives of authenticity. The romantics, not understanding the dichotomy of poetry and life, turned life into poetry. The two cannot be fused. Despite its positive acceptance, Lukács had moved beyond this stage within the year.

(3) In the *Theory of the Moral*, the Hegelian ideas of "totality" and historicity first appear. The novel represents "extensive totality," yet expresses "the transcendental homelessness of man." Drama allows us to shape the "intensive totality of essentiality" in a nonhistorical manner. (Rejected by Lukács within two years.)

(4) In *History and Class-Consciousness* Lukács entered the third stage: (a) The basic stance is that of Hegelian Marxism. Marx is understood as emphasizing the Hegelian idea of "concrete totality," extending, rather than negating, Hegel. (b) Dialectical method occurs through fusing subjective awareness with the relevant objective features achieving totalities of the available human/reality features.

Dialectical method is historical-social, not primarily a "dialectic of nature." From this standpoint Lukács could criticize empiricism and positivism as naive, taking facts as simply given, while overlooking the point that every set of facts implies an interpretation (*q.v.* Hermeneutics). (c) The dialectic of history moves towards global socialism by way of successive totalities including instances of revolutionary change, and enriched *praxis*. The proletariat is the "identical subject-object," because it is the universal class, universal through its universal suffering, and the object of human liberation. (d) The "objective possibility" of the role of the proletariat is represented by the Communist Party, which acts as an "objectification of the proletariat's will." (e) Meanwhile Lukács argues that "reification" (from *res*, making into a thing) afflicts capitalist society. Reification is Lukács' complement to Marx's (*q.v.* 10) "fetishism of commodities." In the latter commodities are elevated to an undeserved status. In the former, human beings are "dehumanized," reduced to the status of a thing ("thingified," to use a convenient neologism).

Lukács repudiated the work in 1933 as theoretically false and practically dangerous. In 1957 in separate statements he held the work "deservedly forgotten," and also that his repudiation of 1933 was part of the struggle against fascism.

(5) In *The Destruction of Reason*, Lukács traced the self-destruction of German high culture into Nazi barbarism and irrationalism, a German mystical irrationalism evolving through Nietzsche. The work concludes with adulation for Stalin in standing against this destruction.

(6) The five points of the third stage (4 above) remained as the background of his numerous publications on aesthetics for half a century, allowing him both to support and oppose the aesthetic theory of socialist realism. Its support is to be found in the view that art concretizes the historical process (King Lear, for example, demonstrating the collapse of feudalism in the family). All art is realistic in the sense that its appropriate analysis introduces us to the dialectic of history; and great art through intensified subjectivity shows us the way out, reflecting the "species character" of human-

ity, allowing us to defetishize our lives. Great art is not, then, just a reflection of bourgeois ills, or socialist achievements; it points beyond these to a liberated future.

(7) The turn toward ontology in Lukács' final years, surprising since the term, "ontology," had been used dismissively through the 1950's, seems to have been intended to bring the stages of his thought together. He sensed new beginnings and a chance to "start anew." One might have expected a system, affirming individual totality in relation to the species. The attempt to do so led to a massive document, reportedly containing contradictions, satisfying neither Lukács nor the students he had invited to review his work.

ŁUKASIEWICZ, JAN. 1878–1956.
Polish logician. Born in Lvov. Educated in Berlin and Louvain. Taught at Lvov and Warsaw. Leaving Poland during the occupation, he lived in Switzerland and Belgium, finally teaching in the Royal Irish Academy in Dublin from 1946 until his death. He wrote in Polish, German, French, and English.

Principal writings: *On the Principle of Contradiction in Aristotle*, 1910; "On Three-valued Logic," 1920; "Two-valued Logic," 1921; *Elements of Mathematical Logic* (T), 1929; "Philosophical Observations on Polyvalent Systems of the Propositional Calculus," 1930; *Aristotle's Syllogistic from the Standpoint of Modern Formal Logic* (E), 1951; "A System of Modal Logic" (E), 1953; *Problems of Logic and Philosophy* (ed. Slupecki), 1961.

(1) The first to develop a three-valued logic, he introduce—along with "true" and "false"—the valence of the "possible."

(2) Given the three-valued logic, he demonstrated that polyvalence in logic could be extended indefinitely, even to an infinite number of values.

(3) It was Łukasiewicz who developed the symbolic notation of the Polish logicians, accepted as one of the standard notations.

(4) In the history of logic he called attention to the achievements of the Stoic logicians in the Propositional Calculus, and presented an analysis of Aristotelian logic, including modal logic, from the standpoint of modern logical form.

LULL, RAYMOND. 1236–1315.

Philosopher and missionary. Born in Palma, Majorca. Taught several years at Paris. His goal was to state the truths of Christianity so succinctly that the infidels could not possibly deny them. To this end he wrote the Ars Magna, a mechanical method of exhaustively stating the possible relations of a topic. The method requires three concentric circles divided into compartments. One circle is divided into nine relevant subjects; a second circle is divided into nine relevant predicates; the third circle is divided into nine questions; whether? what? whence? why? how large? of what kind? when? where? how? One circle is fixed; the others rotate, providing a complete series of questions, and of statements in relation to them. Lull lectured on his method throughout France, Italy, and Spain. For a time Lullist schools formed in competition with schools of Thomism and Scotism. The hold of Lullism continued over the University of Palma into the 18th century. Lull learned Arabic and engaged in missionary activity in North Africa. The tradition, subject to dispute, holds that he achieved martyrdom there in 1315.

Principal writings: *Book of Contemplation; The Tree of Knowledge; The True Art of Invention; The Great Art; The Art of Contemplation.*

LULLISM.

Q.v. Raymond Lull.

LUMEN GRATIAE, AND LUMEN NATURALE.

Latin phrases meaning the "light of grace" and the "natural light" respectively. The *lumen naturale* is the power of the unaided reason, while the *lumen gratiae* is the divine revelation.

LUNDENSIAN THEOLOGIANS.

Q.v. Anders Nygren.

LURIA, ISAAC. 1534–1572.

Founder of the Lurianic Cabala. Lived in Safed (Afghanistan). In an era when the nations of Europe were forcing Jews into exile, Luria's visions produced a cosmic drama in which God's purpose is to overcome the fractured world where evil forces defy his will. Luria's disci-

ples, especially R. Hayyam Vital (*q.v.* Cabala 3e), placed his visions in writing and they spread rapidly throughout Judaism. The scheme is Neoplatonic.

(1) God (the *En-sof*), wishing creation, contracted away from the "middle," providing an empty space (the *tsimtsum*) for its locus. This was the first exile. But the divine essence was impure, containing potentially evil powers as well as good. In the contraction the evil powers separated out. This purified the divine essence, while leaving the evil powers stuck on the walls of empty space.

(2) In the second stage emanations of the divine light shot into empty space. Expected to give body to the divine vessels, due to the influence of the evil powers the light scattered. He called this failure the *shevirah* ("breaking of the divine vessels"). The emanations returned to God, but sparks of divine light from the *shevirah* were captured by the evil powers, strengthening them.

(3) Ever since, the *En-sof* has endeavored to mend or correct (*tikkun*) the catastrophe by actions which would free the captive sparks. This would eliminate the evil powers since they exist by virtue of the captured divine sparks of the *shevirah*. First, he created Adam, representing the cosmic duality, a divine spirit in a body controlled by evil desires. Instead of *tikkun* Adam committed the original sin. More sparks flew, strengthening the evil forces. Next *En-sof* chose the people of Israel to achieve *tikkun*, but they sinned with the golden calf. Further sparks fell, and *shevirah* continued.

(4) The chosen people retain total responsibility for achieving the *tikkun* through their religious and ethical conduct, even their good and evil thoughts. When they reach their goal, the Messiah will come, and God's exile from his universe will end.

LUTHER, MARTIN. 1483–1546.

German Churchman and reformer. Born at Eisleben in Saxony. Studied classical literature and philosophy at Erfurt, receiving his A.B. degree in 1502, and his M.A. in 1505. In that year he entered the cloister of Augustinian hermits at Erfurt. Ordained to the priesthood in 1507. Between 1508 and 1512 he lectured at the University of Wittenberg on philosophy, the Holy Scriptures, and the *Sentences* of Peter Lombard; and represented Staupitz, the Vicar General of his order, in Rome. In 1512 he received the degree, Doctor of Theology. He interpreted the Old Testament by the New and lectured on the books of *Romans, Galatians,* and *Hebrews.* In this period the Pauline doctrine of justification by faith, the Augustinian doctrine of grace, reinforced by his own experience as a monk, became central to his thinking. In 1515 he was named vicar with responsibilities over eleven monasteries. At this time he became involved in a controversy over indulgences. Since this involvement marks the beginning of a series of interrelated events leading to the establishment of the Lutheran Church, it is appropriate to number these events.

(1) Opposing the sale of indulgences—letters drawing on the superabundant merit of the saints to compensate for inadequate merit on the part of an individual—Luther issued informal protests against the Dominican salesman, John Tetzel, for more than a year. As Tetzel approached Wittenberg, Luther posted his ninety-five theses on the church door (November 1, 1517). The Theses expressed four main points: (a) Indulgences cannot remit guilt of punishment for sin; this power lies in God alone. (b) Indulgences can have no efficacy for souls in purgatory; what the pope can do for souls in purgatory must be done through prayer, not through the power of his office. (c) Since the true treasurehouse of merits is the Holy Ghost, the power of the pope with respect to indulgences can extend only to the remission of ecclesiastical penalties imposed by the Church. (d) Christ demands true repentance; and a truly repentant Christian has already received God's pardon quite apart from an indulgence. The Theses were known throughout Germany within a fortnight, and throughout Europe within a month. The sale of indulgences declined.

(2) Between 1518 and 1520 there were printed interchanges, conferences, and a public disputation in Leipzig. John Eck was his principal opponent in these matters. Luther gradually formulated his position as standing for the spiritual priesthood of *all* believers, while his opposition held to the medieval point that

God can be approached only through a priestly mediator,

(3) Convinced of the final nature of his break with Rome, Luther published in 1520 the three primary treatises: *On the Liberty of a Christian Man; An Address to the Nobility of the German Nation; On the Babylonian Captivity of the Church of God.*

(4) The bull of excommunication was issued June 15, 1520, but did not reach Wittenberg for many months. Luther's response was to post a notice, inviting his students to witness the burning of the papal bull. This occurred on December 10, 1520.

(5) Charles V of Spain had succeeded Alexander as Emperor of Germany, and opened his first diet at Worms, January 22, 1521. Charles wished Luther to be condemned unheard, but the members of the diet proposed that Luther be given a safe-conduct and be heard. Luther appeared before the diet April 17–19. The emperor attempted to have Luther placed under the ban of the empire, but the diet objected. No action was forthcoming, and Luther returned toward Wittenberg with his safe-conduct running out. On the way Luther disappeared, and it was widely believed that he had been slain by papal emissaries. In fact the Elector of Saxony had arranged that Luther be seized and conveyed to a place of safety. When the edict against Luther appeared on May 25 it was already a dead letter.

(6) For the next 10 months Luther was held in the Elector's Wartburg castle. He spent the time translating the New Testament into German. When he returned to Wittenberg March 6, 1522, he was able to bring the manuscript with him. It appeared in September (the entire Bible, Melanchthon and others helping with the translation, appeared in 1532).

(7) It is held by many that between 1521 and 1525 Luther was the real leader of Germany. He bent his efforts toward gradual reformation rather than revolution, succeeding until the outbreak of the Peasants' War in 1525. Although risking his life, he failed to quiet the insurgents. And when their leader urged the peasants "not to let the blood cool on their swords," Luther responded with his call to the princes to suppress the revolt with violence.

(8) On June 13, 1525, Luther married

Catherine Von Bora, daughter of a noble family, and one of a group of Cistercian nuns convinced by Luther's writings of the unlawfulness of monastic vows. Three sons and two daughters were born to them.

(9) It was also in 1525 that Luther opposed free will, responding to Erasmus in his treatise on the bondage of the will. It was his view that superficially one possesses some freedom in matters that do not pertain to salvation, but one has no freedom to save oneself. In fact, although in all matters one acts as one wills, one's will is in fact controlled by God. The dominance of God in all matters requires, as a corollary, predestination. Where Erasmus stood for enlightenment, for Luther the world was dark and irrational, and the God on whom he counted was often hidden.

(10) The Diet of Speyer, 1526, anticipated the peace of Augsburg of 1555. Its principle of allowing each state to make its own religious decisions led to Luther's activity in simplifying the church service, and offering advice on church organization. The Diet of Speyer, 1529, followed the emperor in attempting to restore the earlier ecclesiastical uniformity. The minority declared they would abide by the decision of 1526, and protested the decision of 1529, hence the name "Protestant."

(11) In 1528 and 1529 Luther published his small and large catechisms, centering in an evangelical interpretation of the catechetical material, stemming from the doctrine of justification by faith.

(12) In 1530 Emperor Charles attempted to mediate the problem of which confession was to be used. Three were presented to him: one from Zwingli and another from this time called the Augsburg Confession, written by Melanchthon and agreed to by Luther. The Augsburg Confession summarizes Lutheran thought in 28 articles. Finding reconciliation impossible, Charles again sought to annul Protestantism, attempting to restore Church property by legal means. The answer of the Protestant princes was the Schmalkald League for their mutual protection.

(13) From 1529 to 1536 disputes continued, especially between Luther and Zwingli, over the nature of the sacrament of Communion. Disagreement was finally narrowed to a single point, *i.e.*, whether the body of Christ is extended in space in the sacrament. In the Wittenberg Concord, concluding the discussion, this is left an open question. The Lutheran doctrine, known as consubstantiation, holds the body and blood of Christ to be in real substantial presence with the bread and wine.

(14) In 1537, responding to a request by elector John Frederick of Saxony, Luther composed the Schmalkald Articles summarizing his teaching. Besides emphasizing the sovereignty of God, Christ as Mediator, and justification by faith, he denounced the mass, penance, saints, and relics of the Roman Church and identified the Pope with the antiChrist.

(15) Luther's death occurred on February 18, 1546 while settling a minor dispute in Eisleben.

(16) The Lutheran movement offers considerable variety. Doctrinally, it is held that nine separate creeds form the basis of Lutheranism: (a) from the early Christian Church, The Apostle's Creed, The Nicene Creed (with *Filioque*), and The Athanasian Creed: (b) from the 16th century the Augsburg Confession, an apology for the Augsburg Confession written by Melanchthon in 1531, the Schmalkald Articles, Luther's two catechisms, and the Formula of Concord issued in 1577 by the Lutheran Church of Germany. This material made up the *Book of Concord*, published in 1580. Only the three early creeds and the Augsburg Confession are accepted by all Lutherans. Most Lutherans accept Luther's catechisms. The Formula of Concord is expressly rejected by many.

LUTHERAN AND REFORMED CHURCHES.

The two major Protestant denominations resulting from Luther's work. The basic doctrinal difference between the two concerns the Lord's Supper, Lutherans interpreting the rite consubstantially (*q.v.* Consubstantiation) and the Reformed members symbolically. Lutheranism, initiating in Germany, looks upon Luther (*q.v.* 16) as founder; and the Reformed churches, centering in Geneva, look back to Zwingli and Calvin. Although both denominations have churches in many countries, Lutheranism is the state religion in the Scandinavian countries, and in Germany sustains a consistorial relation to the state.

ŁUTOSLAWSKI, WINCENTY. 1863–1954.

Polish philosopher. Born in Warsaw. Taught in many countries, accepting a professorship at the University of Wilna in 1919. Best known for his study of Plato's logic, he was a Leibnizian in metaphysics, and sustained an interest in the philosophy of culture, especially in the vitality of regional cultural traditions. He wrote in several languages, including English.

Principal writings: *The Origin and Growth of Plato's Logic* (E), 1897; *Between East and West* (E), 1907; *The National Task*, 1922; *The Immortality of the Soul and the Freedom of the Will*, 1925; *The Knowledge of Reality* (E), 1930.

LUZ Y CABALLERO, JOSÉ DE LA.

Q.v. Latin American Philosophy (1).

LYCEUM.

From the Greek *lykeion* meaning "after the neighboring temple of Apollo." This is the name of the school founded by Aristotle in Athens around 339 B.C. The name seems to be derived from the first location of the school in Athens, a description enabling one to find the school. The school was established by Aristotle, after Speusippus rather than Aristotle was named to follow Plato as head of Plato's Academy (*q.v.*). The school was organized as a center of scientific investigation, primarily in the areas of biology as well as other natural sciences. But the interests of the school extended to geography and political science. In the last named field a study was made of 158 constitutions of Greek city states. Philosophical analysis occurred most often in relation to the subject matter of the sciences.

(1) Aristotle was, of course, the first head of the school, and remained so until his death. He named Theophrastus (*q.v.*) as his successor. Other important philosophers from the initial group are Eudemus (*q.v.*) of the *Eudemian Ethics*, Aristoxenos (*q.v.*), and Dicearchus (*q.v.*). Among the disciples of Theophrastus mention should be made of Strato of Lampsacus (*q.v.*) who became the third head of the school, following Theophrastus, and Demetrius of Phaleron (*q.v.*). The fourth head was a disciple of Strato's named Lycon of Laodicea (*q.v.*). Near the end of the 3rd century B.C. Ariston of Chios (*q.v.*) followed Lycon as head. By this time the school was in decline, and indeed dropped out of sight.

(2) It revived as a school in Alexandria, Egypt, in the 1st century B.C. under Andronicus of Rhodes (*q.v.*), but hardly as the Lyceum. And its revival in Athens under the Empire as one of the four official schools is a revival of Aristotelianism (*q.v.*), but not of the Lyceum. Needless to say, the Lyceum has survived as an educational ideal.

LYCON. 3rd cent. B.C.

Greek philosopher. Born in Laodicea. A disciple of Strato (*q.v.*), he studied in the Lyceum (*q.v.*) following Strato as its head around 268 B.C. He guided the school for a period of forty years. Unhappily, this was a period of decline for the Lyceum.

LYCOPHRON.

Q.v. Sophists (5).

LYTTON, BULWER.

Q.v. Utopia (9).

MACH, ERNST. 1836–1916.

Austrian physicist and philosopher. Studied in Vienna. Professor of Mathematics, University of Graz, 1864–67. Professor of Physics, Prague, 1867–95. Professor of History and Theory of Inductive Science, University of Vienna, 1895–1902. Served in the Austrian parliament. Made contributions to many fields of science. Influenced particularly by Berkeley, Hume, and Helmholtz, he provided in his turn one of the chief influences on the Vienna Circle of Logical Positivists (*q.v.*) and on Percy W. Bridgman (*q.v.*). According to Bridgman, Mach exercised an influence over Einstein through his operational approach to the world. A work of Lenin, *Materialism and Empirio-criticism*, was directed against Mach.

Principal writings: "On the Definition of Mass" (T), 1868; *The Science of Mechanics* (T), 1883; *The Analysis of Sensation* (T), 1886; *Popular Scientific Lectures* (T), 1894; *Space and Geometry* (T), 1906; *The Principles of Physical Optics* (T), 1921.

(1) It is Mach's program to get rid of unobservables. All scientific concepts—and by extension, all concepts whatever—must be understood as summaries of sense-experience and a means to put us in touch with further sense-experience.

(2) It follows that explanation consists in calling attention to the sensations or "neutral impressions" from which the concept was derived and for which it stands. Any concept which does not relate to sensations in this manner is metaphysical, and hence unacceptable.

(3) Scientific laws are abridged descriptions of past experience designed to assist us in predicting future experience. Such abridged descriptions are of the pattern of the past phenomena, and hence will be (or will be likely to be?) characteristic of future instances of the same kind.

(4) Scientific theories have quantitative and qualitative aspects. The quantitative aspect enables us to predict future experience, phenomena, or sensations. The qualitative aspect conveys a kind of picture of an unobservable world. The theoretical entities of these qualitative pictures should not be thought of as representing a world behind experience, but rather as instruments or tools helping us formulate the mathematical relations leading to predictions. Even the entities of atomic theory must be construed in this manner.

(5) Finally, for Mach the unity of all of the branches of science consists in the fact that each is a study of sensations of some sort, and of the patterns to be found in their interrelations. The differences among the sciences concern the direction of the investigation.

(6) Although it seems not to be in character with the operational character of his other pronouncements, Mach went so far as to say that the world consists only of our sensations.

MACHIAVELLI, NICCOLO. 1469–1527.

Italian statesman and philosopher. Born in Florence. Well-educated in Latin and Italian classics. In 1494, he became clerk in the second chancery of the commune under Adriani. In 1498, Adriani became chancellor of the republic, and Machiavelli became (1498–1512) second chancellor and secretary. In this post he had much to do with the embassies of the other Italian states; his duties also took him to France and Germany. He worked at developing a national militia for Florence; partly through his efforts the long war with Pisa ended with the latter's surrender in 1509. But in 1512 the Cardinal Giovanni de'Medici with a Spanish army appeared at the gates of Florence. The Florentines opened the gates to the prince of the House of Medici, and Machiavelli's government fell. Machiavelli was imprisoned, to be released only when Giovanni de'Medici was elected pope in March, 1513. Retiring to a farm, Machiavelli utilized his enforced idleness in writing. *The Prince* was completed in 1513. His *Discourses* on the history of Livy, a more general analysis of the nature of states, was begun before the former but completed somewhat later. In these works Machiavelli set the modern usage of the term "state" as an independent political community. His *Art of War* and *Life of Castruccio* were written in 1520. By this time the Medicis were beginning to send Machiavelli on state missions; in 1520 he was commissioned at their insistence to write a history of Florence, and provided with an annual allowance of 100 florins while engaged on the project. The history was not completed by the time of his death. He composed a number of plays; one of them, the *Mandragola*, has been called the most powerful play in the Italian language. In 1526 he inspected the fortifications of Florence for Clement VII, presenting a report on the subject. He performed other missions in the papal service, requiring several visits to Lombardy before his death in 1527.

Principal writings : *The Prince* (T), 1513; *Art of War* (T), 1520; *Life of Castruccio* (T), 1520; *Mandragola* (T), 1524; *History of Florence* (T), 1532; *Discourses on the First Ten Books of Livy* (T), 1532.

(1) In *The Prince*, Machiavelli discussed

the best means of gaining and keeping power, and uniting a state. In the *Discourses* he discussed among other things the best means of government. It is perhaps not possible to find complete consistency in the two accounts.

(2) In the *Discourses* he expressed a preference for popular government, finding it less inconsistent than tyranny. He set forth a doctrine of checks and balances, holding that the three powers— the princes, nobility, and people—should be so arranged in proportion to their real power as to keep each other in check, so that stability is preserved in the state. Liberty is important to a state, and the people generally are wiser than their princes.

(3) But on the other hand, as he also says in the *Discourses*, countries are so corrupt nowadays that only a monarchy with full and absolute powers can curb the ambitious and corrupt elements of the state. And in both the *Discourses* and *The Prince* he provides a view of man as dominated by self-interest and insatiable desires. Man's nature being thus, from this standpoint, too, a powerful ruler is required.

(4) The prince will seek to acquire and maintain power. The virtuous prince will maintain power while satisfying his subjects and keeping them from becoming rebellious. He will keep faith when it pays to do so, but not otherwise (since his people would do the same). He will try to be both feared and loved; but will prefer to be feared than loved since the efficacy of fear is unfailing. He will employ force ruthlessly, committing his cruelties all at once in order to be done with them, while stretching out the granting of benefits in order that they may be more enjoyed. The prince will utilize propaganda, and especially the institutions of religion, in keeping the people satisfied. Thus may the order of the state and the regularity of her laws be insured.

MACHIAVELLI, THE CHINESE.
Q.v. Shang Yang.

MACROBIUS.
Flourished during the reigns of Honorius and Arcadius (395–423). Roman philosopher. Expressed both Stoic and Neoplatonic ideas in his writings, and according to some accounts he was con-

verted to Christianity. His commentary on Cicero's *Dream of Scipio* had currency during the Middle Ages.

Principal writings: *Saturnalia*; *On the Dream of Scipio*; *On the Difference and Associations of Greek and Latin Verbs*.

(1) Macrobius presented the Neoplatonic scheme of emanation (*q.v.* Plotinus) in the form of the Good, the Intelligence, and the Soul. As in other forms of Neoplatonism the earlier principle gives rise to the later. The intelligence contains both names and ideas; the Soul contains, and is the source of, individual souls.

(2) But in another sense individual souls are fallen spirits; and on the way down to incorporation in matter they acquired the characteristics of the three principles, from the Good through the reason to the nutritive elements. They thus remain linked to higher realms to which they return after liberation from the body.

MACROCOSM.
From the Greek *makros* ("great") and *kosmos* ("universe"). The term is contrasted with microcosm, from *mikros* ("small") and *kosmos* ("universe"). Macrocosm, taken to refer to the universe, is set in contrast to man, the microcosm, a little universe.

(1) An Eastern expression of the point of view is to be found in the identification of Brahman, the all-controlling deity, with *Atman*, the individual soul or self, in Indian thought (*q.v.* Vedanta 1–4). Tung Chung-Shu (*q.v.* 4) likewise presented the microcosm-macrocosm contrast.

(2) In the Western world the view is already present at the origins of Greek philosophy. It seems to be implicit in Empedocles' (*q.v.* 5) doctrine of perception that like is known by like. To know the world, then, man must be like the world.

(3) A similar point, but more completely developed, is present in the Platonic doctrine of *Anamnesis*, that all learning is recollection. Knowledge of the whole is, then, somehow originally present in each individual soul (*q.v.* Plato 1).

(4) The Aristotelian doctrine that the soul is in some way everything that it knows suggests the microcosm-macrocosm identification, likewise on epistemological grounds.

(5) The clearest ontological statement of the view emerges among the Stoic philosophers. For them the world-soul is to the world as the individual soul is to the body; furthermore, the rational part of the soul is comparable to the universal reason (*q.v.* Marcus Aurelius 2; Posidonius).

(6) Erigena (*q.v.* 2) found a correspondence between man's career and everything else in the universe, man standing as a microcosm of the whole.

(7) All of those influenced by the mysticism of Meister Eckhart (*q.v.*) express this relationship. Among them one must mention the early Renaissance philosophers, such as Nicholas of Cusa (*q.v.* 5), Paracelsus (*q.v.* 1), Bruno (*q.v.* 4), for example, where every item in the universe is a focal point of the divine and a microcosm of Being. Among their followers were Robert Fludd (*q.v.*).

(8) The Leibnizian monad, mirroring the universe through a predetermined divine harmony, is still another expression of this relationship (Leibniz *q.v.* 1).

(9) Emerson (*q.v.* 4) found a correspondence between the human soul and everything in the universe, and a principle of compensation at work as well.

(10) Lotze (*q.v.* 2) utilized the analogy in his work entitled *Microcosmos*, 3 vols., 1856. All things are here regarded as ensouled, relating to each other and to God, somewhat as Leibniz held.

(11) A contemporary expression of the macrocosm-microcosm idea is to be found in Whitehead's insistence that each actual entity sustains relations to the entire world, and that these relations are perforce present within the constitution of the actual entity (*q.v.* Whitehead 13).

MADHVA. 1197–1276.

Indian Vedantan philosopher. Along with Shankara (*q.v.*) and Ramanuja (*q.v.*), one of the chief commentators on Vedanta philosophy. A dualist (or pluralist), he opposed Shankara's non-dualism. His radical pluralism separated him from Ramanuja. His position is much indebted to the Sankhya school of Indian philosophy. *Q.v.* Vedanta.

Principal writings: *Commentary on the Vedanta Sutras* (T).

(1) The system contains five fundamental differences: (a) A difference between God and the individual self. (b) A difference between God and matter. (c) Differences between individual selves. (d) A difference between individual selves and matter. (e) Differences between individual material substances. The point of view emerges from these distinctions in the following manner.

(2) Permanence characterizes not only God, who in this system is identified with Vishnu, but also selves and the world. All are eternal but the others are dependent on Vishnu, the inner ruler of all selves, and director of the world.

(3) Each self is unique; and the problem of life is to free oneself from impurity, coming to terms with one's burden of *karma*. Even in the state of release, the unique selves or souls are distinguishable.

(4) Salvation is a blissful state of perpetual adoration of the divine. The way to God is through *Vayu*, a principle related to the Vedic element of air.

(5) Each material entity in the universe is different from every other. Hence, so-called universals are merely statements about the similarity of comparable aspects of different things. There are no real universals.

(6) In keeping with the other commentators, Madhva believed that the universe moved through great cycles of generation and destruction under the governance of Vishnu.

MADHYAMIKA.

One of the four chief philosophical schools of Buddhism, the system of the Mean or "middle way." Members of the school are called Madhyamikas. Nagarjuna (*q.v.*) is regarded as its founder. The school of Shunyavada (*q.v.* Śunyavada) was highly influential in shaping Mahayana Buddhism. Chi-Tsang continued the development of the school in China.

(1) According to the Madhyamika school the essential nature of things consists in "vacuity" (*śunya, q.v.*), or "emptiness." Existence produced by causes is void or vacuous existence. The cessation of the production of vacuous existence is Nirvana. Wisdom and truth involve knowledge of the vacuous nature of things.

(2) Some members of the school hold, further, that the *dharmas* or elements do

not simply exist vacuously. They do not exist at all. They are like the hairs that a monk with diseased eyes might see in his empty almsbowl. In this situation absolute truth is perfect silence.

(3) The Svatantrikas ("independents") were a sub-school within Madhyamika. They held that while logic cannot express the deepest truths of emptiness, some statements about emptiness are capable of verification.

MADISON, JAMES.
Q.v. Federalist Papers (3, 4).

MADRID SCHOOL, THE.
The name advanced by Julián Marías (*q.v.*) to characterize the thought of a group of recent and contemporary Spanish philosophers including Miguel de Unamuno, Ortega y Gasset, Xavier Zubiri, Manuel García Morente, and Marías himself.

MAGNA MATER.
A religious cult of the Roman Empire often linked with Mithraism (*q.v.*). Its devotees were largely women, and the sanctuary of the cult often adjoined that of the cult of Mithra. The common practice was to dedicate them jointly to the two divinities, Mithra and the Great Mother (*q.v.*).

MAHABHARATA, THE.
The great Brahman epic poem of the 6th century B.C., which contains the *Bhagavad-Gita* as one of its parts, the *Mahabharata* tells the story of two families, both having claims upon the throne, involved in struggle. In addition to the themes of the *Bhagavad-Gita* (*q.v.*) the poem contains an elaboration of (1) the four aims of life: righteousness, wealth, worldly enjoyment and spiritual freedom. (2) The four *Ashramas* (*q.v.*), or the four stations of life and their duties: the student, householder, forest-dweller, and ascetic. (3) The four castes: *Brahmin* (priest and teacher), *Kshatriya* (warrior), *Vaishya* (merchant), *Shudra* (laborer). *Q.v.* Vaiṣnavism (2b); Hinduism (2).

MAHADEVI.
Sanskrit from *maha* ("great") and *devi* ("goddess"). The tendency to associate the goddesses of the Hindu tradition with a single great goddess responsible for the stability of the world. As *Shakti* ("power") she is the divine energy of Shiva (*q.v.*) her destructive side is Kali (*q.v.*).

MAHAKARUNA.
Q.v. Karuna.

MAHAT.
Q.v. Sankhya (5a).

MAHAVIRA.
Q.v. Vardhamana.

MAHAYANA BUDDHISM.
Q.v. Buddhism, Mahayana.

MAHDI.
From the Arabic meaning "the guided, or well-directed, one." The one who will appear on earth as Allah's representative to lead the hosts of Islam to worldwide victory. He will be the final Imam (*q.v.* Islam 5, 7, 8).

MAIEUTIC.
From the Greek *maia* ("midwife"). Normally used as an adjective, describing Socrates' method of delivering an individual of his ideas. Related by implication to the Socratic or Platonic doctrine of recollection or reminiscence, according to which we have knowledge within us from an eternal existence; and that this knowledge has been obscured by the trauma of birth (*q.v.* Socrates 1). Also, however, *q.v.* Kierkegaard (4).

MAIGNAN, EMMANUEL. 1601–1676.
Spanish philosopher. Born in Toulouse. Joined the order of the Minims. Taught in Rome; then returned to Toulouse for the last twenty-five years of his life. He supported the atomism of Epicurus, positing extended atoms with shape and force at the base of reality. He held that psychical phenomena should be explained in physical terms, and this requires no reference to consciousness.
Principal writings: *Course in Philosophy*, 4 vols., 1652; *Sacred Philosophy*, 1661–72.

MAIMON, SALOMON. 1754–1800.
German philosopher. Born in Polish Lithuania. Studied medicine in Berlin. In 1770 he discovered the Kantian philosophy. Maimon is now best remembered for his criticism of the Kantian point of view, his principal objection being that

the "thing-in-itself" is so completely separated from awareness as to be unthinkable; hence, there is a paradox in asserting it as an element of the transcendental philosophy.

Principal writings: *An Essay on the Transcendental Philosophy*, 1790; *The Categories of Aristotle*, 1794; *Essay on a New Logic or Theory of Thinking*, 1794.

MAIMONIDES. 1135–1204.

Jewish philosopher. Born in Córdoba, Spain during the Muslim hegemony. His Hebrew name, from which the above Latinized version was derived, is Moses ben Maimon. Living in north Africa as a young man Maimonides spent his final years in Cairo as court physician and leader of the Jewish community. Maimonides exercised an immense influence over Jewish, as well as Scholastic, thought during the Middle Ages.

Principal writings: *The Guide for the Perplexed* (written in Arabic; translated into Hebrew in the 12th century; and into Latin in the 13th); a Commentary on the *Mishnah*, including a treatise on ethics ("The Eight Chapters"); *The Mishnah Torah*, a codification of law, including a philosophical system of religious beliefs ("The Book of Knowledge"); medical treatises, including a critique of Galen; and the *Epistle to Yemen*.

(1) Maimonides wrote his guide for those perplexed by the apparent contradictions between philosophic (and hence scientific) truth, and religious faith. He wanted to show that the two are not incompatible, that philosophy properly understood left room for religion. This compatibility seems to be achieved variously in different parts of the *Guide*.

(2) His central approach to this end lies in his development of negative theology. God is radically other than the world; and hence, any ascription we may make to God, coming as it must from something in the world, really describes what God is not. We can know that God is not finite, not composite, not any of the properties we know. And in the sense of existence known to us, we must even say that God is not existent. But to know what God is not, at least separates him from false conceptions; and it opens the way to religious faith.

(3) On the other hand, if one uses a positive theology one arrives at the conception of God as a necessary being who could not have created the world in time, and whose purposes could not change in the process of time, once creation is admitted. But if creation is admitted, one is moving within the religious sphere; and if God can intervene at this point he can do so at others.

(4) He accepts the Aristotelian arguments for God as the prime mover of the universe. Following his Neoplatonic heritage, he moves beyond Aristotle in holding God to be the efficient, formal, and final cause of the universe. Given this identification it seems that Maimonides believes that a certain knowledge of God is possible through the study of nature; and, through an understanding of nature, which entails our living a contemplative, theoretical life, it is possible for one's life to rise to an imitation of God. This does not quite contradict the negative theology, since Maimonides makes a distinction between knowledge of God, and knowledge of God's operations in nature.

(5) He interprets Aristotle's doctrine of the active intellect to mean that only this general and unparticularized aspect of our natures survives death. And, indeed, his view of ethics requires that one act in universal terms, and in disregard of particular, individual situations.

(6) At the same time, while reason leads us to the universal, imagination relates us to the particular. Both prophets and political leaders need to combine reason and imagination.

(7) To act in terms of one's active intellect is to establish union with God, since for Maimonides there exists a hierarchy of beings from God through nine spheres of celestial forms to the active intellect which is the tenth sphere, and relates specifically to the human reason.

MAINE DE BIRAN. (F.P. GAUTHIER). 1766–1824.

French philosopher. Born at Bergerac. Lived in retirement during the horrors of the revolution, immersed in the study of psychology. These studies led him to philosophy. After the Restoration he held the office of treasurer to the Chamber of Deputies, retiring periodically to his estate in Bergerac for philosophic study.

Principal writings: *Influence of Habit on*

the Faculty of Thought, 1802; *Examination of the Philosophical Teachings of M. Laromiguière*, 1817; *New Considerations on the Rapport Between the Physical and the Moral in Maine de Biran*, 4 vols., 1841; *Unedited Works of Maine de Biran*, 3 vols., 1859.

(1) Having begun as a follower of Condillac's sensationalism. Maine de Biran's developed point of view came to be known as *Spiritualism*. To explain experience he found it necessary to posit the self, thinking of it as an active power developed through experience.

(2) The distinction between sensation and perception is the distinction between the forcefulness of the external world, and that of the percipient self. The togetherness of the two is also a fact of experience: active and passive, internal and external, physical and psychological.

(3) From the one, causality is derived, and from the other, the fact of human liberty.

(4) Finally, in mystical experience Maine de Biran finds evidence of the overcoming of physical and corporeal existence in a higher spiritual life.

MAINLÄNDER, PHILIPP. (Born Philipp Batz). 1841–1876.

German philosopher. Born in Offenbach, Main. Follower of Schopenhauer.

Principal writings: *The Philosophy of Redemption*, 1876.

(1) The world begins with the death of God, since God is a principle of unity shattered in the plurality of the world. (2) It is implied that God is also joy, denied in the law of suffering which dominates the world. (3) The original unity and joy persist in the human awareness that nonexistence is better than existence. (4) When humans act on this awareness, refusing to perpetuate themselves, or ending their existence by suicide, they are completing the cycle of redemption.

MAISTRE, JOSEPH DE. 1753–1821.

French philosopher. Born in Chambery (Savoy). Represented Savoy in Turin, Sardinia, and St. Petersburg. Philosophically conservative and an Ultramontanist, he found the 18th-century French *philosophes* particularly objectionable. The anarchism of the French Revolution was likewise anathema to him. He argued that God cannot be measured by human reason, that the foundation of authority lies in God, who alone is sovereign, and whose earthly representatives are Pope and King. The altar and the throne are to be held together; whatever force may be necessary in preserving this union is justified. Whether by force or faith it is one's portion to obey; nor is obedience—even blind obedience—foreign to human nature.

Principal writings: *Study on Sovereignty*, 1791–7; *Considerations on the History of France*, 1797; *The Soirées of Saint Petersburg or Conferences on the Temporal Government of Providence*, 1806; *Essay on the Philosophy of Bacon*, 1815; *On the Gallican Church*, 1821; *On the Pope*, 1821.

MAITREYA.

The expected or future Buddha, prophesied by Gautama Buddha (*q.v.*), whose incarnation will spread the doctrine, restore the good society, and save all beings. According to the prophecy Maitreya is to come in 5,670,000,000 years.

MAITRI.

From Sanskrit, "friendliness." One of the Four Immeasurable Attitudes of Mahayana Buddhism (*q.v.* 4).

MAJOR, JOHN. 1469–1550.

Scotch philosopher and theologian. Attended Cambridge University. Taught at Glasgow, St. Andrews, and the University of Paris. Sympathetic to Ockham and Buridan, he sparked a brief revival of 14th-century nominalism.

Principal writings: Commentaries on Peter of Spain, the *Sentences* of Peter Lombard, and Aristotle's *Ethics* and *Physics*.

MAJOR PREMISE.

Q.v. Syllogism (3).

MAJOR TERM.

Q.v. Syllogism (3).

MALCOLM, NORMAN. 1911– .

North American philosopher. Born in Selden, Kansas. Studied at Harvard, and at Cambridge University. Now teaching at Cornell University. A follower of Wittgenstein (*q.v.*), he has applied Wittgenstein's "method" to problems of epistemology, perception, philosophy of mind, and philosophy of religion.

Principal writings: *Ludwig Wittgenstein: A Memoir*, 1958; *Dreaming*, 1959; *Knowledge and Certainty*, 1963; *Problems of Mind*, 1971.

MALEBRANCHE, NICOLAS. 1638–1715.

French philosopher. Born in Paris. Studied philosophy at the Collège de la Marche, and theology at the Sorbonne. 1660, joined the congregation of the Oratory, becoming a priest in 1664. In the same year he discovered Descartes, and from that moment devoted himself entirely to philosophy. In 1699, he was made an honorary member of the French Academy of Sciences.

Principal writings: *On the Search for Truth*, 3 vols., 1674–5; *Clarifications*, 1678; *Treatise on Nature and on Grace*, 1680; *Treatise on Morality*, 1684; *Conversations on Metaphysics and on Religion* (T), 1688; *Treatise on the Love of God*, 1697; *Conversations on a Chinese Philosophy on the Nature of God*, 1708; *Reflections on Physical Premotion*, 1714.

(1) Knowledge is possible by virtue of the fact that, knowingly or not, men see all things in God. Knowledge begins—though somewhat vaguely—with ideas of the infinite and is adjusted to finite things through specification. Knowledge begins with general ideas, and these are ideas of the infinite being.

(2) Our knowledge of particular things is our knowledge of these things as contained in God. Just as particular ideas are participations of infinite ideas, *i.e.*, ideas of the infinite being, so particular things are merely imperfect participations in the Divine Being. Our knowledge is, hence, always participation in God's knowledge. If we only judge of that which we see clearly we cannot be mistaken. As with Descartes, then, clarity remains a test for truth.

(3) The finite-infinite contrast also characterizes the difference between the power of God compared to the power of the physical world. Extended body is dependent upon God for its force and mobility; hence, Malebranche's doctrine of Occasionalism in which God is the single efficient cause of the movement of things, both among bodies, and between souls and bodies.

(4) The human soul differs from its body in possessing force and freedom, although each decision of the will merely provides the occasion for God's efficacious activity in the realm of extended things.

(5) Malebranche's position on values utilized the same contrast we have noted in his epistemology. Man's love of happiness, of himself, of his fellows is in fact a somewhat vague and perhaps confused sense of his love for God. He utilizes the idea of the Fall to point to the situation which ought to obtain, *i.e.*, where men prefer the universal to the particular, love of God to love of self. The Fall represents a sinking into particularity and finitude, as it were. Our task is to weaken our union with the bodily, and strengthen our union with the universal, that is, with God. Malebranche believes that love of order is the universal ground, making virtuous our habits and dispositions.

(6) In a similar manner Malebranche felt God could be separated from any responsibility for evil by identifying his universal operations with goodness. Evil appears in particular individual existence; and even this, viewed universally, must be seen as good.

MALINOVSKI, A.A.

Q.v. Bogdanov.

MAMMON.

From the Aramaic *mamona* ("riches"). Personified in the New Testament as the evil of wealth, the personification was taken literally by medieval writers. For Milton, Mammon was one of the fallen angels.

MAN.

Since philosophy is a human artifact, all of its basic divisions, Epistemology, Ethics, Aesthetics, etc., include comments upon human nature. We group here a number of references, many of them standing as alternative definitions of that nature. Although it is not our intention to use gendered locutions, in some contexts they are virtually unavoidable. In such contexts we usually find that the gendered masculine term has been accepted as paradigmatic of the human being. In such cases we have retained the term "man" as more faithful to authors' intentions.

(1) Plato (*q.v.* 3) regarded man as essentially a tripartite unity of mind, will, and passions.

(2) Although Aristotle (*q.v.* 4, 7, 11) continued this division, which went on to characterize much of the thinking about man through the medieval period, his view of soul as the form of the body suggested an organic unity which could be defined as "rational animal."

(3) Hsün Tzu (*q.v.* 3) regarded man as naturally evil, and thus requiring the pressures of outward discipline.

(4) Augustine (*q.v.* 12) drew upon 328 Scriptural as well as philosophical sources in viewing man as a union of soul and body, tainted by original sin, and motivated by the happiness principle.

(5) William of Ockham (*q.v.* 14) held man to be a *suppositum intellectuale*, a complete rational being which is self-existent. He believed further that intellect and will in man are not distinct faculties.

(6) For La Mettrie (*q.v.* 1–2) man is a machine or "soulless mechanism."

(7) Holbach (*q.v.* 4) is not alone in having looked upon man as a creature inevitably motivated by self-interest.

(8) Unamuno (*q.v.* 1) rejected the interpretation of man as a reasonable being, believing it to be too abstract. He substituted the view of man as a creature of "flesh and bone."

(9) Cassirer (*q.v.* 1) viewed the human being as the "symbolizing animal," whose nature can be known only indirectly through the study of symbolic forms. Langer (*q.v.* 1) followed him in this definition.

(10) Ortega y Gasset (*q.v.* 5) is among those insisting that man has no nature, but rather a history.

(11) Sartre (*q.v.* 2, 5) defined the human individual as a "noughting nought," a *pour soi* who is not an object but a project, and who is condemned to freedom.

MANA.

Melanesian term referring to a potency immanent in and emanating from all natural objects, and especially from the spirits of the dead.

MANAS.

Sanskrit, "mind." *Q.v.* The *Vedas* (1).

MANDALA.

From Sanskrit, "circle," "round." In Hindu and Buddhist ritual and meditation *mandalas* are diagrams, usually with four parts and inscribed in a circle, representing the gods or their symbols. (1) As the *mandala* is inscribed in sand, paper, or some other medium, incantations are given and spiritual forces are believed to enter the pattern. The patterns are believed to provide access to divine power on the same kind of correspondence theory which underlies the use of *mantras* (*q.v.* 6). The images relate to incantations, which combine appropriate language and sound. Both relate one to reality, and ultimately to the divine. (2) Jung (*q.v.* 2, 7, 8) held the *mandala* form to suggest that with respect to the godhead quaternity is preferable to trinity.

MANDELBROT, BENOIT B.

Q.v. Chaos Theory and (7).

MANDELBROT SET.

Q.v. Chaos Theory (7).

MANDEVILLE, BERNARD DE. 1670–1733.

English philosopher. Born in Dordrecht, Holland. Studied in the Erasmus school at Rotterdam and at Leiden University. Received a medical degree in 1691. Moving to England he produced his *Fable of the Bees* and other satires.

Principal writings: *Free Thoughts on the Religion, Church, and Government*, 1720; *The Fable of the Bees*, or *Private Vices, Public Benefits*, 1723; *Inquiry into the Origin of Man and Usefulness of Christianity*, 1732.

(1) In the fable we learn that "virtue" is detrimental to society; and that "vice" contributes to human progress. By "virtue" Mandeville understands "every performance by which man, contrary to the impulse of nature, should endeavour the benefit of others, or the conquest of his own passions, out of a rational ambition of being good." By "vice" he means self-regarding actions. It follows that "private vices are public benefits."

(2) All social virtues may be traced to the drive for self-preservation. Hence, laws are the result of selfish aggrandizement and of protective alliances among the weak.

(3) Were one to organize a society on the basis of other-regarding or altruistic, motives, it would be characterized by utter apathy.

(4) Since Mandeville stated that he was writing for "the entertainment of people of knowledge and education" it is possible that the foregoing sentiments should be enjoyed but not taken seriously.

MANI. 215–276.

Religious leader. Born in Babylonia. Founder of Manichaeism (*q.v.*).

MANICHAEISM.

The religion of Mani, originating in Babylonia in the 3rd century A.D., and lasting until the Mongol invasions of the 13th century. Mani was born in the early years of the 3rd century, probably around 215, in Babylonia. Convinced that he had been chosen to proclaim a new faith, Mani began his public mission in 242, traveling widely and apparently visiting India and China in addition to the countries of Central Asia. He wrote many books and epistles, only scattered fragments of which survive. The opposition of the Magi, the Zoroastrian priesthood, led to his execution around 276 A.D.

(1) Holding that God has revealed Himself to man through various representatives—Buddha in India, Zoroaster in Persia, Jesus in Israel—Mani held himself to be God's messenger to Babylonia.

(2) The framework of world conflict and world redemption turns on the opposition of good and evil; these are identified with light and darkness. God is Lord of the Kingdom of Light; Satan rules the Kingdom of Darkness. While God is eternal, Satan was produced by the elements of darkness. A terrible struggle has gone on between these two forces. God produced the Primal Man to help him in the struggle, and the Primal Man was vanquished by Satan. Our present world was formed by heavenly powers from the chaos of intermingled light and darkness resulting from this struggle. Even at the inanimate level there is light to be released from darkness. The mechanism of release at any level is the "pillar of glory" by which light ascends to the moon, the sun, and the higher regions. The system of the Zodiac was viewed by the Manichaeans as one of the

mechanisms by which light is freed to begin its ascent to God.

(3) Mankind had its origin in Satan and the powers of darkness in an effort on their part to imprison and keep in their possession as much as possible of the elements of light. Jesus, in this interpretation a heavenly being above suffering, was sent to Adam and Eve to teach them the way of release and to warn them especially about sensuality. The teaching was not entirely successful, and God has sent a succession of prophets to man to teach the true *gnosis* concerning light and darkness.

(4) Man is expected to live in such a way that the light that is in him will make its way to God, and that the darkness can be consigned to hell. The liberation of light is expedited by a life of ascetic purity, and is retarded by idolatry, impurity of action, speech, or thought, the destruction of life, and sexual intercourse.

(5) To provide the maximum release of light a social organization was developed comprising an outer circle of members called "Hearers" or "Combatants," and an inner circle of the "Elect." The Elect abstained from flesh, wine, and the plucking of fruits and vegetables. The Hearers thus supplied the fruit and vegetables on which the Elect subsisted. The Hearers were allowed to eat flesh, though they could not take the life of the animals. Also the Hearers were permitted marriage, and vocations, while marriage and property were denied the Elect.

(6) Upon death the Elect ascend by the "pillar of glory" along the way stations to the realm of light. The Hearers must experience extensive purification before joining the Elect. The souls of the wicked wander in the world until the final separation of dark and light occurs in a world conflagration of 1458 years' duration. At this time the souls of the wicked will find their home in the realm of darkness.

MANIFOLD OF SENSE.

Q.v. Kant (3).

MANNHEIM, KARL. 1893–1947.

European sociologist. Born in Budapest. Taught in Heidelberg, Frankfurt, and

London. His work in the Sociology of Knowledge contains many philosophical implications: for example, his distinction between substantial and functional rationality, the former leading toward reality, the latter fulfilling predetermined institutional ends. Similarly, one may cite his distinction between partial and total ideology, the former stemming from psychological, the latter from social roots. The former rest on delusions where recognition would not further the interests of some individual. The latter reflect the *Weltanschung* (*q.v.*) of an age or social group. Regarded in a general sense as a member of the neo-Kantian movement (*q.v.* Neo-Kantianism 6).

Principal writings: *Man and Society in an Age of Reconstruction* (T), 1935; *Ideology and Utopia* (T), 1936; *Diagnosis of Our Time* (E), 1943; *Freedom, Power, and Democratic Planning* (ed. Gerth and Bramstedt), 1951; *Essays on Sociology and Social Psychology* (ed. Kecskemeti), 1953; *Essays on the Sociology of Culture* (ed. E. Mannheim and Kecskemeti), 1956.

MANSEL, HENRY. 1820–1871.

British philosopher. Born at Cosgrove. An Oxford graduate, he was successively tutor, reader, and professor there, becoming Dean of St. Paul's in 1868.

Principal writings: *Prolegomena logica*, 1851 (2nd ed., 1862); *The Limits of Religious Thought*, 1858; *Metaphysics*, 1860; *The Philosophy of the Conditioned*, 1866; *Letters, Lectures, and Reviews*, (ed. Chandler), 1873; *The Gnostic Heresies*, (ed. Lightfoot), 1875.

(1) Influenced by Aristotle, Kant, and Reid, at least in part as interpreted by William Hamilton and Victor Cousin, Mansel produced an eclectic but interesting, realistic point of view.

(2) While agreeing in general with Kant's critical philosophy, he held that we do have direct experience of our own egos, and that consciousness implies knowledge, also, of the external world.

(3) Logic is regarded as the "science of formal thinking," and logical judgments are held to rest ultimately on psychological judgments. The will enters into cognition by its power to direct our attention; it does not as such falsify cognition, however.

(4) It does follow from this that human knowledge is not absolute, but is limited to the finite and conditioned. Hence, we must remain agnostic in respect to metaphysical and theological questions.

(5) We can and should believe in God's perfect goodness and omnipotence on faith. Since this cannot be understood from the standpoint of our finite goodness and power. Mansel adds a dimension of mystery to the universe. It was on this point that Mansel drew the criticism of Mill, who preferred to solve the paradox rather than invoke a mystery.

MANTRA.

From Sanskrit, *man* ("think"), understood as "vehicle of thought" and eventually "sacred utterance." In Hinduism the term referred initially to the *Rgveda*, then to all four of the *Vedas* (*q.v.* 1). Since the *Vedas* were considered to be related to specific deities, the gods were invoked through the sacred utterances, and then through "seed" syllables of those utterances.

(1) "*Om*," initially the first syllable of the Gayatri *mantra*, a three line verse of the *Rgveda* addressed to the sun, came to represent being itself, and was used to begin and end every Vedic recitation or *mantra*. The second birth of the "twice-born" castes (*q.v.* Hinduism 4) consisted of a ceremony in which the Gayatri *mantra* was "received," after which those receiving it were allowed to perform the obligatory daily rituals.

(2) While the Vedic *mantras* were limited to the twice-born, post-Vedic *mantras* were open to all, invoking various divinities but especially Vishnu, Shiva, and the goddess Devi, the locus of attention shifting from Vedic sacrifice to devotional worship related to the images of the gods in temples and shrines.

(3) The use of *mantras* was especially prominent in the Hindu movement of Tantrism (*q.v.* 2) where the "seed" syllables were often formed around the first letter of the deity's name (*e.g.*, *krim* for Krishna). *Mantras* are inscribed in *mandalas* (*q.v.*) which the devotee's imagination places in various bodily parts, thus increasing the extent of one's identity with the god.

(4) *Mantras* are also used in Mahayana Buddhism appearing in the school of *Mantrayana* (*q.v.*) (Skt., "the vehicle of the *mantra*") in the 7th century and still

continuing. Here the *mantras* and *mandalas* represent Buddhas and *bodhisattvas*, and the goal is to actualize in oneself the "three mysteries of the Buddhas"—their body through ritual gestures (*mudras*), their speech through *mantras*, their mind through meditation (*q.v.* Tantrism 7).

(5) The Pure Land sects of Buddhism used the name of Buddha as a *mantra*.

(6) *Mantras* are powered by a correspondence theory of sound, thought, and language with being. The phonological prejudice which Derrida (*q.v.* 2) found in Plato, is also present here. Sound is primary, held to be the first physical element, arising in space, and the source of everything else. Thus, the appropriate sound of a given spiritual entity relates one at once to the power and reality of that entity.

(7) In *mantra* Yoga (*q.v.* Yoga 9) *om* is the sacred sound.

MANTRAYANA.
Q.v. Lamaism (5); Tantrism (7).

MANU.
A Sanskrit term meaning "man." In Hindu mythology the term refers to a series of progenitors of the human race, each of whom ruled the world for a time. The seventh Manu, from whom derive all men now living, survived (like Noah) the deluge in an ark. *The Laws of Manu* (*q.v.*, and *Vedas* 5), chief ancient Hindu legal code, is attributed to this progenitor.

MARBURG SCHOOL.
One of the schools of neo-Kantian philosophy active during the last part of the 19th and the first part of the 20th century. Located at the University of Marburg, the school specialized in problems of epistemology and analyses of the sciences. For characterizations of members of the school *q.v.* Neo-Kantianism (2).

MARCEL, GABRIEL. 1889–1973.
French philosopher. Born in Paris. Attended the Sorbonne. After several years of teaching, Marcel turned toward the fields of publishing, and of dramatic and literary criticism. His philosophical development continued unbroken. *The Mystery of Being* was produced from his Gifford Lectures of 1949–50.

Principal writings: *Metaphysical Journal* (T), 1927; *Being and Having* (T), 1935; *Creative Fidelity* (T), 1940; *Homo viator* (T), 1944; *The Metaphysics of Royce*, 1945; *The Philosophy of Existence* (T), 1949; *The Mystery of Being* (T), 1950; *Men Against Humanity* (T), 1951; *The Decline of Wisdom*, 1954; *The Problematic Man*, 1955; *The Existential Background of Human Dignity* (E), 1963.

(1) Marcel sets in contrast two main ways in which life can be taken, *i.e.*, as a problem or as a mystery, and two kinds of meaning which flow therefrom. Similarly, "having" can be taken in two ways, as mere possessing or as participating. And existence can be taken in a clear but impoverished sense, or in a somewhat less clear but richer sense. Marcel consistently chooses mystery, participation and richness.

(2) If being is rooted in mystery, then one can speak of the revelation of being; religious terms are no longer alien to ontology, and the subject-object dichotomy is replaced by a sense of encounter.

(3) Terms which have been taken in an impoverished psychological sense (*cf.* 1 above) thus acquire ontological significance. Fidelity provides a basis for the conception of existence, love, admiration, prayer, and communion all help to root the world ontologically.

(4) The new set of relations is designed to help man come to terms with his broken world, and to help man the wanderer—*homo viator*—find in reality his home.

MARCION OF SINOPE. c. 85–c. 165.
Founder of the principal rival in its time to the Catholic Church. The Marcionite Church was Pauline in emphasis, stressing salvation by faith. Marcion was himself a wealthy shipowner who settled in Rome, found his views rejected by the Roman Church, and began his own religious community around 144 A.D. Within a short time numerous congregations had been established throughout the empire, and Marcion devoted much of his time visiting the sister churches. Although influenced by Cerdo, a Gnostic, and often related to Gnosticism, Marcion felt his mission was one of reforming Christianity to the "pure gospel," a goal which he apparently held to the end of his life. In the West the movement

began to die out in the 4th century. In the East it survived until the 7th century.

Principal writings: *The Antitheses.*

(1) Man was created by the Demiurge, a just and wrathful God who placed him under a rule of law. Since man could not keep the law, the whole human race fell under a divine curse.

(2) A higher God, noting man's wretchedness, sent his Son to redeem the human race. The Demiurge, in anger and in ignorance, had Christ crucified.

(3) Since Christ had in fact fulfilled the law, however, the Demiurge had acted inconsistently. The risen Christ appeared before the Demiurge with this charge, and the Demiurge had to release to Christ the souls of those to be redeemed, purchased by his death.

(4) Christ commissioned Paul to be his apostle and to redeem the living. Paul did so through preaching the true gospel, and founding congregations of the faithful.

(5) Since the Church did not remain faithful to this vision it was necessary for Marcion to be next commissioned to preach the true gospel, found new churches, and lead a movement of reform. In this movement Marcion preached that salvation came through renouncing the Demiurge, accepting the good God and his Son, and doing good works in a spirit of love. Beyond this, however, he also preached that one must practice asceticism, shun marriage, and avoid sensuality. In salvation, man's soul alone survives, while the material body perishes.

MARCIONITE CHURCHES.
Q.v. Marcion of Sinope.

MARCUS, RUTH BARCAN.
Q.v. Modal Logic (7); Quantifying In (2).

MARCUS AURELIUS ANTONINUS. 121–180.
Roman emperor and philosopher. The adopted son of Antoninus Pius, Marcus Aurelius was groomed for rule from early youth. His lessons began with rhetoric and poetry. By the time he was 11 he had discovered Stoicism through the philosopher Diognetus. As his studies advanced he specialized in philosophy and law. At 18, the title "Caesar" was conferred upon him, and at 19 he became a consul. The same year he married

Faustina, daughter of Antoninus Pius. At the age of 40, in 161, he became emperor, sharing the title with Commodus, another adopted son of Antoninus Pius. Marcus Aurelius became sole emperor upon the death of Commodus in 169. Although the empire was confronted in these years by a series of disasters—including fire, flood, plague, insurrection, and repeated incursions of barbarians—Aurelius acted with intelligence, patience, and an attitude very like serenity. Near the end of his life he was initiated into the Eleusinian mysteries, and endowed chairs of philosophy in the major philosophical schools of Athens: the Academy, the Lyceum, the Epicurean Garden, and the Stoa. Paradoxically, the Christians were subject to systematic persecution during his reign. A devout adherent of the Roman religion, he found the Christians guilty of sacrilege. At the age of 59, on March 17th, he died in camp during one of the engagements of the German war. He was succeeded by his son, Commodus.

Principal writing: *The Meditations* (T).

(1) Written as a kind of intellectual diary during moments snatched from public life, the *Meditations* interprets Stoicism as a guide to responsible living. The main goal of life is tranquility of mind. This is achieved by living in conformity with nature.

(2) Living in conformity with nature means opposing bodily drives when they oppose reason. It likewise involves accepting as reasonable whatever happens. For reason is the divinity within man, expressing itself as conscience. Reason in the universe is the deity to which human reason relates, and which is expressed in the order of nature.

(3) Aurelius stressed the social nature of man, leading to obligations as a member of society, and as a citizen of the world. He held justice to be the foundation of all the virtues and its own reward. The themes are not new to Stoicism, but Aurelius injects a tone of mutual fellow-feeling, and a sympathy approaching love, into his analysis.

MARCUSE, HERBERT. 1898–1979.
Born in Berlin. Educated at the Universities of Berlin and Freiburg. Assistant to Heidegger, 1928–32. Among his teaching posts were Yale, Brandeis, and the

U. of Cal. at San Diego. A member of the Frankfurt School (*q.v.* 6) from 1932 on, he continued with the group at Columbia, remaining in the United States when the group returned to Frankfurt in 1950. In the 1960's his work stirred interest among student activists.

Principal writings: *Hegel's Ontology* (T), 1932; *Reason and Revolution*, 1941; *Eros and Civilization*, 1951; *Soviet Marxism*, 1958; *One Dimensional Man*, 1964; *An Essay on Liberation*, 1969; *Counter-Revolution and Revolt*, 1972.

MARDUK.

Babylonian deity. As the city of Babylon increased in importance, Marduk was transformed from the patron deity of a city to head of a pantheon of gods, and finally he was regarded as the sole deity, having absorbed the characteristics of the other gods such as Ea and Bel, and manifesting himself in various forms. He created the world through slaying Tiamat, a monster representing primeval chaos, and bringing a reign of law and order. He determined the fate of each individual, and is represented as doing so at the start of each year. The New Year's festival, occurring at the time of the vernal equinox, and representing the stirring of life, was sacred to Marduk. Originally a solar deity, his consort was Sarpanitu, the shining one.

MARÉCHAL, JOSEPH. 1878–1944.

Belgian philosopher. Born in Charleroi. Educated at Louvain. Taught in Louvain, at the Jesuit Scholasticate, 1919–35.

Principal writings: *The Point of Departure of Metaphysics*, 5 vols., 1922–47; *Studies of the Psychology of the Mystics* (T in part), 2 vols., 1924, 1937; *Précis of the History of Modern Philosophy*, 1933; *Mélange Maréchal*, 2 vols., 1950.

(1) A neo-Scholastic, Maréchal began with the critical philosophy of Kant, and attempted to show that it led back to Thomism. His point is that we grasp reality, the noumenal, in our necessary judgments.

(2) The *a priori* is both metaphysical and psychological. The intellect has a natural tendency toward Absolute Being, or Pure Act. The dynamism of human cognition, as a species of act, cannot avoid relation to transcendental truth.

MARIANA, JUAN DE. 1535–1624.

Spanish historian and political philosopher. Anticipated later social theorists in advancing a social contract theory wherein the will of the people retains the authority to depose a bad monarch, and property is seen as the root of social strife.

Principal writings: *History of Spain*, 20 vols., 1592; 10 further vols., 1605; *On the King and the Education of the King* (T), 1599.

MARÍAS, JULIÁN. 1914– .

Spanish philosopher. Born in Valladolid. Studied under Ortega y Gasset in Madrid. Teaches in the Institute of Humanities founded in Madrid in 1948 by Ortega. The intellectual heir of Ortega, even though the latter had broken with organized religion and Marias remains Catholic, he has developed many of the themes announced but not developed by his master.

Selected writings: *History of Philosophy*, 1941; *M. de Unamuno*, 1943; *Introduction to Philosophy* (T, *Reason and Life*), 1947; *Ortega and Three Antipodes*, 1950; *The Idea of Metaphysics*, 1954; *Present-Day Philosophy and Existentialism in Spain*, 1955; *The Social Structure: Theory and Method*, 1955; *The Office of Thought*, 1958; *The School of Madrid*, 1959; *Ortega*, 1960; *The Historic and Social Reality of Linguistic Use*, 1954; *Metaphysical Anthropology*, 1970.

(1) The ultimate category and final reality is not being, but, rather, life. Within this field of life we find both our own life and that of others. Furthermore, other aspects of reality, including elements of transcendence, are involved in this final reality as its conditions.

(2) Metaphysics is the effort to gain certitude through the vital reason. The quest seems inevitably to lead in a religious direction, toward transcendence, a transcendent being, and possibly personal survival.

MARINUS OF NEAPOLIS. 5th cent. A.D.

Neoplatonic philosopher. Disciple of Proclus (*q.v.*) and on the latter's death succeeded to the headship of the school. He wrote a *Life of Proclus* in which he reviewed his master's speculations. His other works include Platonic-style dialogues, and works on mathematics.

MARITAIN, JACQUES. 1882–1973.

French philosopher. Born in Paris. Attended the Sorbonne, and Bergson's lectures at the Collège de France. Converted to Catholicism in 1906. Taught at the Institut Catholique de Paris beginning in 1914. French ambassador to the Holy See, 1945–48. Professor of Philosophy at Princeton, 1948–56. His wife, Raïssa, had shared the adventure of his development from secularism to religious belief, and had collaborated with him not infrequently.

Principal writings: *The Bergsonian Philosophy* (T), 1914; *Art and Scholasticism* (T), 1920; *Elements of Philosophy*, 2 vols., 1920, 1923; *Reflections on Intelligence*, 1924; *Three Reformers* (T), 1925; *The Angelic Doctor St. Thomas Aquinas* (T), 1929; *Religion and Culture*, 1930; *The Degrees of Knowledge* (T), 1932; *The Dream of Descartes* (T), 1932; *On the Christian Philosophy*, 1933; *Seven Lessons on Being and the First Principles of the Speculative Reason* (T, *A Preface to Metaphysics: Seven Lectures on Being*), 1934; *The Frontiers of Poetry* (T), 1935; *The Philosophy of Nature* (T), 1936; *Integral Humanism* (T), 1936; *The Situation of Poetry* (with R. Maritain) (T), 1938; *Confessions of Faith*, 1941; *The Rights of Man and the Natural Law*, 1942; *Christianity and Democracy*, 1943; *Education at the Crossroads* (T), 1943; *From Bergson to Thomas Aquinas*, 1944; *The Person and the Common Good* (T), 1947; *Short Treatise on Existence and the Existent* (T), 1947; *Reason and Reasons*, 1948; *Man and the State* (E), 1951; *Nine Lessons on the First Notions of Moral Philosophy*, 1951; *Creative Intuition in Art and Poetry* (E), 1953; *Approaches to God* (T), 1954; *On the Philosophy of History* (E), 1957; *Moral Philosophy* (T), 1960; *The Responsibility of the Artist* (E), 1960.

(1) As a neo-Thomist, Maritain devotes himself to showing that Thomism is a living system relevant to the contemporary situation. In one sense, then, he is merely delineating the thought of Thomas Aquinas. But in the application of this thought to the contemporary world, new insights make their appearance.

(2) His discussion of epistemology is designed to allow the legitimacy of many kinds of knowing. One can know by logical reason and by intuitive reason. The former kind of knowing includes the science of nature, the philosophy of nature, mathematics, and metaphysics. The object of each of these studies, in turn, is the observable and measurable, the intelligible structure of observable and measurable things, the universe of quantity, and the universe of being as being. The second kind of knowing includes poetic insight, mystical experience, and ordinary knowledge of moral values.

(3) Poetic insight occurs on the level of concrete reality. A flash of reality takes place through an emotion of the poet. The poetic insight is a faint immortalizing of the reality grasped. It relates finally to the eternal source of beauty.

(4) With respect to man, Maritain pointed out that as an individual, man is subordinate to society while as a person (with an immortal soul) he transcends it. As an individual one must assume certain obligations to society. As a person, one has a higher end than society; society must recognize this and establish the relations appropriate to a being with such a goal. In this aspect of his thought Maritain regards his position as one of Christian personalism, since man cannot be explained by any impersonal principle.

(5) Maritain distinguishes between the state and society, defends the concept of an ordered democracy against both the atomistic excesses of liberal thought, and against totalitarian denials of individuality.

(6) He found a "metaphysical intuition of being" at the root of metaphysics. And while accepting Aquinas' five arguments for God, he suggests a sixth. One has the intuition that the "I" of one's active intellect is not temporal. And from this one moves to the existence of that "I" eternally in the act of thinking of the infinite being.

MARIUS VICTORINUS. 4th cent. A.D.

Neoplatonic philosopher. A Latin Christian; by virtue of his translations of and commentaries on Greek texts, and his writings in logic, he made himself a connecting link of some importance between the Greek world and the Middle Ages. Through his work on logic contributed to medieval logic; his doctrine of providence influenced St. Augustine. His view of rhetoric, and his analysis of the Aristotelian categories likewise carried weight for centuries beyond his time.

Principal writings: Translations of Aristotle's *Categories* and *On Interpretation*, Porphyry's *Isagoge*, Cicero's *On Invention*; and the logical writings: *On Definition* and *On the Hypothetical Syllogism*.

MARKOVIĆ, MIHAILO.
Q.v. Praxis (7, 8).

MARKOVIĆ, SVETOZAR. 1846–1875.
Serbian philosopher. Leader of the Socialist movement in Serbia, Marković held that the path to socialism in undeveloped countries was not through capitalism and the proletariat, but from feudalism directly to socialism, with the intelligentsia playing a major role.

Principal writings: *The Principles of the National Economy*, 1874.

MARRANOS.
Term applied to those Jews and Moors who, at the time of the Spanish reconquest, accepted Christianity under duress or to escape persecution.

MARSILIUS OF INGHEN. c. 1330–1396.
Medieval philosopher. Born in Inghen, near Nimega. Taught at Paris, 1362–78, serving two terms as rector. Taught at the University of Heidelberg beginning in 1383, becoming rector in 1386. A disciple of Jean Buridan, he was likewise influenced by William of Ockham, Nicholas of Oresme, and Albert of Saxony. Following his teacher, Buridan, he rejected Aristotle's theory of movement in favor of the theory of impetus. He also held that quantity is not identical with extension. As an Ockhamist he distinguished knowledge from faith, and held that God's nature, the creation of the world, and the resurrection of the body are matters of faith and not of knowledge.

Principal writings: *Quaestiones on the Four Books of the Sentences*, 1501; *Logical Discourses on Supposition, Ampliation, etc.*, 1512, 1516; *Exposition on the First Books*, 1516; *On Generation*, 1518; *Summaries of the Physics*, 1521.

MARSILIUS OF PADUA. c. 1275–1342.
Italian philosopher. Born in Italy. Studied medicine there, perhaps in Padua. Went to Paris, probably in 1311, becoming rector of the University of Paris in 1313. There he met John of Jandun (*q.v.*) with

whom he wrote his famous *Defender of Peace* (*Defensor Pacis*) in 1324. The book was condemned by the papal court in Avignon in 1326, not unnaturally, since its thesis was that as between Empire and Church the former is rightfully supreme. Since Louis of Bavaria, king of the Romans, was engaged in a protracted struggle with Pope John XXII over just this thesis, the two authors sought refuge at the court of Louis in Nuremberg. Marsilius became one of Louis' closest advisers, and lived to see an application of the principles of his book: Louis crowned emperor at Rome not by the pope but by "delegates of the people"; John XXII deposed; and a mendicant friar (Nicholas V) raised to the papacy after a "popular election." For his services Marsilius was made Archbishop of Milan; his collaborator gained the bishopric of Ferrara.

Principal writings: *Defender of Peace* (T), 1324; *Minor Defender*.

(1) The Church has a higher end than the state but its goal must be primarily achieved in another world. (2) The state is to serve the good life. Put positively, its function is to provide a context in which fulfillment—understood in an Aristotelian sense—can be achieved in accordance with justice. Put negatively, the coercive authority of the state is to prevent the conflicts among individuals from destroying society. (3) So far as this world is concerned the power of the state must be supreme over the Church. The papacy and priesthood must hence be subject to the state, confining their attention to administering sacraments and teaching divine law. In any case, religion must be voluntary. (4) The power of the state rests in the people. They, or their most important part, must elect or appoint the head of government whom they may remove for cause. Furthermore, the people of each community must elect their priesthood. The pope must be elected by all of Christendom. And the Church must be guided in all questions of interpretation by elected general councils.

MARSTON, ROGER. c. 1250–1303.
British Scholastic. Born in Marston. Studied at the University of Paris. Taught at Oxford and Cambridge. A provincial

of the English Franciscans, he defended St. Augustine and tradition against Aquinas and Aristotle, often synthesizing apparently opposing views: the Augustinian eternal light with the Aristotelian active intellect; the Aquinian doctrine of a singular form in things with the traditional doctrine holding to a plurality of forms in things (Marston's synthesis: one form with subordinate modifications).

Principal writings: *Disputed Questions.*

MARTIANUS CAPELLA. 5th cent. A.D.

Anticipated and, indeed, influenced, the development of the medieval university curriculum by means of an allegory presenting the union of eloquence and knowledge, witnessed by the seven liberal arts. Eloquence and knowledge were represented by Mercury and Philology; the seven liberal arts were grammar, dialectic, rhetoric, geometry, arithmetic, astronomy, and music.

Principal writings: *On the Marriage of Philology and Mercury* or *Nine Books on the Seven Liberal Arts.* Also titled simply *Satyricon.*

MARTINEAU, JAMES. 1805–1900.

British philosopher and Unitarian leader. Born in Norwich. Attended Manchester College. Held Unitarian churches in Dublin, and then in Liverpool. In 1840 he returned to his college, now named Manchester New College, as professor of mental and moral philosophy, retaining this post until 1885. He served as principal of the college from 1869–85. When the college moved to London, he moved with it. His philosophical studies were carried on along with theological and biblical studies; and his philosophical positions were largely adopted for religious reasons. For example, by 1839 he had broken with necessitarianism, finding it incompatible with Christianity. A year's study in Germany under Trendelenburg in 1848–49 provided him what he termed "a new intellectual birth." Although he published a great deal, his most important work came in later life.

Representative writings: *Studies of Christianity,* 1858; *The Relation Between Ethics and Religion,* 1881; *A Study of Spinoza,* 1882; *Types of Ethical Theory,* 2 vols., 1882; *A Study of Religion,* 2 vols., 1888; *Essays, Reviews and Addresses,* 4 vols., 1890–91;

The Seat of Authority in Religion, 1890.

(1) Breaking with his early associationalism and Utilitarianism, Martineau developed a position with overtones of Common Sense philosophy, Kantianism, and Idealism. In his view one simply accepts the testimony of experience that one has from the start: a self related to a world. One interprets this datum in terms of will, the free will of the individual and the divine will as cause of the world. (2) One interprets the nature of the divine on the basis of the ethical demand—which one finds within human experience—to act in terms of the higher motive. This inner demand is treated as a continuing divine revelation available to every person. Ethics, then, is treated in terms of motives rather than consequences. But consequences play a role in helping us determine the higher motive to which we are committed. (3) Our capacity to select from among opposed and competing motives is what one means by free will. And, indeed, the free will in humans is in microcosm what the divine will is in relation to the universe. (4) He thought of the church as a voluntary association, removed both from religious hierarchy and enforced state uniformity. His scheme to allow the coordination of a diversity of churches under the state, however, was not viable.

MARTIN, R.M.

Q.v. Inscriptions.

MARTY, ANTON. 1847–1914.

Born in Switzerland. Professor at Prague. A member of the Brentano school of philosophy, his principal interest was in the philosophy of language. He distinguished between categorematic and syncategorematic functions of language, held to a linguistic and nonmetaphysical doctrine of the *a priori,* and based logic on linguistic structure. His writings are in German.

Selected writings: *On the Origin of Language,* 1875; *Investigations on the Basis of a Universal Grammar and Philosophy of Language,* 1908; *Toward a Philosophy of Language,* 1910.

MARULIĆ, MARKO. 1450–1524.

Croatian philosopher. Born in Dalmatia. A Christian philosopher, Marulić combined the impress of Renaissance humanism with knowledge of Greek philosophy. His view of Christian ethics, for example, owed much to Stoic and Platonic sources.

Selected writings: *On the Principles of Living Well and Happily by Divine Example*, 1506; *Fifty Parables*, 1510; *Evangelistarium*, 1516; *On the Humility and Glory of Christ*, 1519.

MARVIN, W.T.

Q.v. New Realism (1).

MARX, KARL. 1818–1883.

German philosopher and economist. Born in Trèves (Rhenish Prussia). His father became a Lutheran in 1824, and the entire family followed him, leaving the Jewish faith. Studied at Bonn, Berlin, and Jena, receiving his doctorate from the last-named for his thesis on Epicurus. Editor of the *Rheinische Zeitung* of Cologne, 1842–43. The paper was suppressed, and he moved to Paris in the fall of 1843, becoming co-editor of the *Deutsch-französische Jahrbucher*. Only one issue appeared. It contained two articles by Marx, and two by Friedrich Engels (*q.v.*) who began his long association with Marx in 1844. As one of the contributors to the magazine *Vorwärts*, Marx was asked to leave France in 1845 at the request of the Prussian government. Moving to Brussels, Marx and Engels edited a weekly paper, the *Brüsseller deutsche Zeitung*, and worked with the League of the Just, an organization of German workers dedicated to communism. It was for this group that Marx and Engels wrote the *Communist Manifesto* in 1847. Marx went to France when the revolution of 1848 broke out there, but after some months moved to Cologne where with Engels and others he started the *Neue rheinische Zeitung* as a daily paper with a revolutionary editorial policy. The paper was suspended in the fall of 1848, and Marx was arrested for treason. He was acquitted but expelled from Prussia in May 1849. After similar difficulties in Paris, he settled in London, England for the remainder of his life. There he spent much of his time in the British Museum, working on his book, *Capital* (*Das Kapital*) the first volume of which appeared in 1867. Meanwhile, he reestab-

lished the *Neue rheinische Zeitung*, which lasted this time for six issues. He served as foreign correspondent for Horace Greeley's *New York Tribune*. In 1864 he founded the First International, and dissolved it in 1876, because of its internal conflicts. The second and third volumes of *Capital* were completed by Engels after Marx's death.

Principal writings: *Economic and Philosophic Manuscripts of 1844* (T), (first pub. 1932); *The Holy Family* (with Engels) (T), 1845; *The German Ideology* (T, written 1845–46); *The Poverty of Philosophy* (T), 1847; *The Communist Manifesto* (with Engels) (T), 1848; *The 18th Brumaire of Louis Bonaparte* (T), 1852; *Capital* (T) 3 vols., 1867, 1885, 1895.

A. The themes of his principal books:

(1) The *Economic and Philosophic Manuscripts* provides an overview of the ideas Marx would be developing, unencumbered by statistics. It is implicit in human nature that one externalize oneself. What first occurs as an inner purpose becomes through work an external product, which individuals claim as their own. Thus property arises, separating them from each other. The pricing mechanism gives everything a price, and price begins to replace value. Now alienation appears and the sense of a void in human life. The place to attack the problem is the property relationship, so that property will not divide humans from each other.

(2) *The Holy Family* was directed against a circle of Young Hegelians, led by Bruno and Edgar Bauer. The theme of the book is that, philosophically, Hegel is superior to the Freien (as they were called); and, practically, the radicalism of this group of philosophers is inferior to the genuine radicalism of the socialist and working class movements of Great Britain, France, and Germany.

(3) *The German Ideology*, no less than the foregoing, has a title which is misleading from a contemporary standpoint. The book is a criticism of post-Hegelian German philosophy, utilizing Feuerbach's materialism as an instrument of analysis as well as Marx's growing sensitivity to the importance of class distinctions.

(4) *The Poverty of Philosophy*, likewise polemical, is directed against Proudhon

(*q.v.*) whose socialism was too philosophical, a point common to the three polemical works, and that English socialists and economists had already anticipated what he announced as his discoveries, *e.g.*, a theory of labor value.

(5) *The Communist Manifesto*, calling on the workers of the world to unite, and throw off their chains, was directed to the revolution of 1848. It provides a popular analysis of mid-19th century social conditions, and urges that these conditions imply and require the revolution. It also announces Marx's view that the central element in the history of every society has been class struggle. He argues here, as well as elsewhere, that philosophical, religious, and ethical ideas are a reflection of the material conditions of production and thus form a kind of defense of the status quo.

(6) *The 18th Brumaire of Louis Bonaparte* reviews the failure of the 1848 revolution in France, interpreting the event from the materialist standpoint. Marx began this materialist analysis of history with Hegel's comment that all "world-historical facts" occur twice. Marx added "the first time as tragedy, the second as farce." Napoleon's *coup d'état* was the first occurrence; that of his nephew the second.

(7) *Das Kapital* proposed to show by a scientific analysis that the capital accumulated by owners of industries came through exploitation of the proletariat. The key concept is surplus-value, that portion of the value of a product which does not go to the worker, but is claimed as profit (*q.v.* 11 below). The amount of surplus-value is limited not only by wages (the amount needed to provide normal conditions of existence for the worker), but also by competition. The capitalist responds by absorbing smaller companies. Hence, enterprise is concentrated in fewer and fewer hands, and the class of dependent workers grows ever larger. In the later stages of this development it becomes necessary to expropriate the expropriators, and a cooperative system arises to replace the competitive system of capitalism.

B. These ideas cohere in the following way:

(8) Alienation. Marx finds the worker, under capitalism, subject to three forms of alienation: (a) They are alienated from the products of their work which, though their creations, oppose them as things which are not theirs. (b) They are alienated from their own basic activity in life since, having sold their labor to another, it is no longer theirs. They experience, then, self-alienation. (c) They are alienated from their species. Since the life to which human beings naturally aspire, and in which they are free beings is a life in which the universal powers of the species are developed, this alienation leaves man an isolated, egoistic individual. Life-activity, then, the human "essence," is transformed into a mere means for the continuation of one's existence.

(9) Nature. In his discussion a fourth form of alienation appears whose importance is more evident today than it was when Marx wrote. In treating everything as a means to our continued survival, we treat nature as an instrument to that end. This alienates us from the nature of which we are, in fact, part and which functions as part of our bodies.

10) Fetishism of commodities. The first form of alienation, *i.e.*, the alienation from the products of our labor, gains its revenge on us in a pathological manner. Reduced to isolated egoistic individuals, the world of commodities opposes us. We suppose that we can solve this isolation by gaining control of commodities. The "fetishism of commodities" thus takes control of our lives. We fall under the control of the commodities which oppose us, supposing that by acquisition the first form of alienation can be overcome. Our enthusiasm for things becomes pathological, turning the means of living into its end.

(11) Surplus value. That the economic process takes advantage of the worker is argued by Marx in terms of his concept of "surplus value." The argument contains the following ideas: The economic value of the worker resides in his or her "labouring power." This power is sold to the employer for a price whose lower level allows the worker the bare necessities of life; also, enough to allow the worker to reproduce so that one laborer can be replaced by a successor. The employer, or capitalist, hires the worker on condition that the worker produce a surplus value, over and above what is needed to continue in existence

and maintain strength. That surplus value will be the profit going to the employer, or capitalist.

(12) Surplus value and the elements of capitalism. It is part of Marx's vision to hold that the cost of raw materials, machinery, rent, and interest will also be claiming parts of the surplus value, but that while taking from the surplus value, these elements don't add to it. His reason for confining the creation of surplus value to labor was, it seems clear, to show that capital lived on labor value. It can be argued, on the other hand, that lower rather than higher prices for raw materials, machinery, rent, and interest help in the creation of surplus value. The point seems especially obvious when robotic machines replace human labor, performing the same functions.

(13) The crisis of capitalism. Capitalism contains the seeds of its own demise in that its continued functioning under conditions of competition leads to lower and lower profit levels for employers and increasing levels of suffering for workers, a result which did not always occur. The end point was to be an economic crisis in which revolution would occur by historical necessity.

(14) Productivity after the revolution. The other side of the same point was Marx's conviction that after the revolution, the many forms of alienation to which humans are now subject would disappear. Living and working without the drag of alienation, economic productivity will increase and economic crisis will be a thing of the past.

(15) Marx and feudalism. One might argue that the absence of such economic increase in the cases of the Soviet Union and China is evidence against Marxist theory. On the other hand, since Marx expected the revolution to come out of the development of capitalism, and since both the Soviet and Chinese revolutions occurred in countries where capitalism had not developed, these revolutions do not stand as counter-examples to Marx, whatever they do to the theories of his followers.

(16) Dialectic of history. Although Marx did not use the term "dialectical materialism" (this came from Engels, q.v. 1), he did believe that the material features of societies, i.e., their underlying economic organizations, controlled to a very large extent their superstructures, i.e., their cultural expressions, including their philosophies. In the march of history, the changes in these features could be seen as a dialectic of class conflict from the Greek and Roman opposition between slave and patrician, the Medieval opposition of serf and noble, the modern opposition of capitalist and proletariat. Standing Hegel on his head consisted of concentrating on the more concrete features of society rather than on abstract cultural or "spiritual" features. He did believe that the capitalist/proletarian conflict was the critical one because the industrial revolution was world-wide and capitalism required a world-scene. Consequently when the revolution rising out of capitalism occurred, it too would be world-wide. He also believed that the capitalist/proletarian opposition was the final class conflict and would be followed eventually by a society in which classes had disappeared, the classless society.

MARXISM.

Any of several philosophies deriving from the writings of Karl Marx. Since he regarded his work as scientific in nature, and not philosophic, Marx would not have considered himself a Marxist. There have been many versions of Marxism.

(1) There is a generalized version of Marxism fixed in the popular mind, but whose full set of themes was held neither by Marx nor Engels, nor by any of their followers. The theses include: (a) Dialectical materialism.— In all its parts, and at all levels, reality moves through dialectical processes of opposition, using a thesis-antithesis-synthesis pattern, which introduces new qualities as oppositions are overcome. (b) Primitive communism and class struggle.—Although society was initially characterized by primitive communal unity, it has moved through a number of earlier oppositions to the present climactic opposition between the class capitalists on the one hand, and the working class on the other. (c) The end of this process must necessarily be the elimination of capitalism and the triumph of the working class. With this victory the dialectic must end, since society will have rid itself of its internal contradictions.

(d) It is a law of history that the revolution is to occur at a certain stage of the capitalist-proletarian conflict. Hence, the revolution is international, and is to occur at a certain stage of industrial society. (e) Dictatorship of the proletariat.—On the way to the promised age of harmony a stage must intervene in which the proletariat must rule. This is a stage allowing the remnants of capitalist ideology to be eliminated from society through reeducation. (f) The withering away of the state.—Given the corrective described above, the coercive functions of the state will be increasingly less important. The state, as an organized entity, will be able to disappear into a new communal relationship resembling that in which society had its origin. (g) Dominance of the mode of production.—In all societies characterized by alienation the mode of production controls the cultural achievements of the society. A change in the former leads to a change in the latter. Hence, cultural artifacts are epiphenomenal, and to be interpreted in economic terms.

(2) Even though Marx was mostly concerned with other issues, he does comment, in abbreviated form, on (b) through (f). These may be taken in some sense, as belonging to his point of view. He never mentions dialectical materialism, nor does he say that the mode of production is completely dominant over the forms of cultural expression.

(3) Engels subscribed to (a) through (f), developing each of these theses much more thoroughly than Marx. It was he who contributed the idea of dialectical materialism (q.v. Engels 1). He is often credited with (g) as well; but he seems never to have held to the dominance of the mode of production in an extreme form. The cultural expression can have, in his view, causal power in its own right. It is not, then, merely an expression of the means of production.

(4) Initially, Lenin followed Marx closely, stressing (b) through (f) above. He dismissed (a), terming Engels' preoccupation with the dialectic a vestige of Hegelianism. In stressing the importance of the individual in the revolutionary struggle, he minimized (g). In later years he came to regard the dialectic as integral to the materialism. He likewise

added, or at least clarified, a further proposition important to Marxism, which might be added to the above list: (h) Epistemological realism.—The perceptions and conceptions in human awareness are exact copies of real things. Lenin saw this proposition as important to the defense of materialism, and blocking a possible opening to Idealism (q.v. Lenin 2). In holding this view he also had to hold that awareness is a reflection of the world; and this in turn virtually requires (g) above, rather than a doctrine stressing the importance of individual effort. It can, then, be argued that Lenin must finally be viewed as the quintessential Marxist, holding Propositions (a) through (h).

(5) The immediate non-revisionist followers of Marx and Engels include Kautsky (q.v.) who edited the Die Neue Zeit, official organ of the German Social Democratic party, and who inherited the task of publishing the literary remains of Marx after Engels' death, and who also wrote the theoretical portions of the Erfurt Program; and in Italy Labriola (q.v.).

(6) Among the unorthodox, partial Marxists of importance are Peter Lavrov (q.v.) and Ferdinand Lassalle (q.v.).

(7) Among contemporary existentialists Marxism has had considerable influence. although existentialism is scarcely appropriate material for the generalized version of Marxism sketched in (1) above. Sartre (q.v. 8), for example, holds that his existentialism is an "enclave" within Marxism; but the extent of the indebtedness seems to be the recognition of a "dialectic" of human relationships. And Merleau-Ponty (q.v. 6) even doubts the dialectic, finding instead tendencies in society capable of development in more than a single direction.

Also q.v. Marx; Althusser (3, 5).

MASADA.

From the Hebrew meaning "stronghold" or "fortress." After the fall of Jerusalem in 70 A.D. the Masada garrison refused to surrender. A Roman force numbering almost 15,000 besieged the fortress, defended by fewer than 1,000. The siege lasted until April 15, 73, at which time the fortress fell. As a final act of defiance, the Jewish defenders took their own lives, rather than surrender to the Romans.

MASARYK, THOMAS G. 1850–1937.

Czechoslovakian philosopher and statesman. Born in Hodonin. Studied at Vienna and Leipzig. Became *privatdozent* at Vienna, and professor of philosophy at Prague, beginning in 1882. He combined philosophy and politics for many years, entering the Austro-Hungarian parliament in 1891. When Czechoslovakia was created in 1918, Masaryk became president of the republic, serving in this office for 17 years.

Principal writings: *Suicide as a Mass Social Phenomenon of Modern Civilization*, 1881; *The Calculus of Probabilities and Humean Skepticism*, 1884; *Foundations of a Concrete Logic*, 1885; *The Social Question*, 1898; *Politics as Science and Art*, 1906; *The World Revolution* (T, *The Making of a State*), 1925; *Conversations with T. G. Masaryk* (T, *Masaryk on Thought and Life*), 1931–5.

(1) Beginning his studies with the problem of suicide in modern society, he used the occasion to speculate upon the possibility of a balanced society which would allow development without tension. (2) In general he abjured abstraction, and found the more concrete forms of experience more meaningful. This led him away from German idealism and toward Hume and Comte. (3) It also led him to a philosophy of Concretism, in which the senses, emotions, and will are equal to the reason. His concrete logic contains a classification of the sciences. Philosophy is to work with their relations, and use them as the basis for a new world-view. (4) While agreeing with the goals of Marxism, he found the collectivism implicit in the movement stifling. His tendency toward the concrete led him to assert the claims of the individual against the collective whole. For him this implied democracy, and affinities with Western nations.

MASS.

From the Latin *missa* ("dismissal"). The term seems to have derived from the words of dismissal at the close of the service of the Eucharist (*q.v.*). Primarily used by Roman Catholics, the term also has currency in the Anglican Communion, and in several other Protestant churches.

MATERIAL CAUSE.

Q.v. Aristotle (9).

MATERIAL EQUIVALENCE.

Q.v. Propositional Calculus (20); Truth Tables (5).

MATERIAL IMPLICATION.

Q.v. Truth Tables (4); Propositional Calculus (19); Modal Logic (2); Philo of Megara (1).

MATERIALISM.

Any set of doctrines stressing the primacy of material over spiritual factors in metaphysics, value theory, physiology, epistemology, or historical explanation. The term is probably construed most appropriately in adjectival form, since in each of these areas there exists a range of doctrines from the most spiritualistic or idealistic to the most materialistic. Among the historical representatives of materialism one would include the following:

(1) While the earliest systematic account of Materialism appeared in India between the 9th and 7th centuries B.C., the movement is known only through "refutations" by its opponents. The doctrine is called *Charvaka* (*q.v.*) or *Lokayata* (*q.v.*). These are also the names of the schools in which the doctrine was developed. Some have suggested that its bad repute may derive from a relation to Tantrism (*q.v.*). Also *q.v.* Indian Philosophy (2), and Jayarashi (1). In Jayarashi (*q.v.* 5) (7th or 8th cent. A.D.) materialism turns into skepticism.

(2) Among the 5th-century Greeks, Leucippus and, Democritus (*q.v.*) developed a thorough-going materialism, originating an atomic theory which allowed all change to be expressed in quantitative terms. The spatial and temporal relations of atoms and their motions provided a sufficient explanation of any phenomenon.

(3) Epicurus (*q.v.*) continued the tradition. His interest centered rather more strongly in value-theory than in metaphysics or ontology. Pleasure-pain becomes the common denominator of human values; thus, hedonism and materialism join forces.

(4) Lucretius (*q.v.*) followed Epicurus. He posited more firmly than had his

teacher those voluntary deviant motions in the original fall of atoms through space, which explained the possibility of the development of vortices of atoms, and the development of world systems.

(5) In 11th century China, Chang Tsai (*q.v.* 1) held material force to be the basic explanatory category.

(6) In the 17th century Thomas Hobbes (*q.v.* 1–4) revived materialism, extending it to questions of language and epistemology. In perceptions and mental operations we work with phantasms of sense.

(7) In the same century Pierre Gassendi (*q.v.*) was materialistic in his account of the operations of the physical world, including sensation. But he accepts both an active intellect in human beings, and a God in the universe. His account is thus perhaps more dualistic (*q.v.* Descartes 8) than materialistic.

(8) Meslier (*q.v.* 2) began the 18th century with a system of mechanistic materialism.

(9) In the 18th century La Mettrie (*q.v.* 1) gave a new impulse to materialism, approaching the problem through physiology, and attempting to show that human functioning can be explained in terms of mechanical principles. Diderot (*q.v.*), provided a "softened" materialism by endowing matter with sensitivity. Priestley (*q.v.* 1) is one of the British materialists of the century.

(10) Continuing the kind of analysis given by La Mettrie, but broadening it once again into a metaphysical system, Holbach (*q.v.* 1–3) argued for a strong materialism. Since, however, he allowed the qualities of sympathy and antipathy to characterize the ultimate material particles of the universe, the system is more nearly Lucretian than Democritean.

(11) In the 19th century, materialism is carried forward by numerous figures. One thinks of Jacob Moleschott (*q.v.*), Ludwig Büchner (*q.v.*), Friedrich Lange (*q.v.*), and Ernst Haeckel (*q.v.*). The most interesting contribution to the movement was made by Friedrich Engels (*q.v.* 1) in his theory of dialectical materialism, and his view of the dominance of the material mode of production over human culture (also *q.v.* Marxism 1, 3). In the former we are given an attempt to show that novel qualities of existence can be derived from changing material conditions. In the

second we are reminded of the importance of considering the basic economic structure of society in understanding the cultural product of that society. Plekhanov (*q.v.* 2) followed Engels, and although more of a determinist than the latter, did not claim that economic conditions are wholly determinative of the cultural product.

(12) Büchner (*q.v.* 1–2) held that reality is material, and force and matter are two perspectives of the same thing.

(13) Dühring (*q.v.*) advanced a non-dialectical view of materialism, which supported a purified capitalism, and was attacked by both Marx and Engels.

(14) Hägerstrom (*q.v.* 4) developed an anti-metaphysical philosophy which he named "enlightened materialism."

(15) E.B. Holt (*q.v.* 4), a New Realist (*q.v.*), moved to the position of behaviorism and materialism in later life.

(16) Montague (*q.v.* 2) characterized his point of view as *animistic materialism*.

(17) Broad (*q.v.* 3) held his view to be that of an "emergent materialism." Given the conditions, new properties will arise.

(18) There has also been in the United States a non-dialectical movement of materialism, sometimes called Naturalism (*q.v.*). This movement has had many members including Santayana (*q.v.* 1, 6) and John Dewey (*q.v.* 5).

(19) The 20th century movement of Logical Positivism (*q.v.*), stressing the role of protocol statements in assessing the meaning of any statement, is implicitly materialistic, since protocol statements must be testable and thus must refer to a physical property of something.

(20) More recently, Identity theory (*q.v.*) is attempting to bring together references to mind and brain in such fashion that something reminiscent of materialism is the result.

(21) The Australian materialists, including J.J.C. Smart (*q.v.*). D.M. Armstrong and, for a time, U. T. Place, argue that pain, thoughts, after-images, indeed all mental phenomena, are merely states of the central nervous system.

(22) The two preceding numbers fit into what is often called Eliminative Materialism in which the intentional aspects of explanations are eventually to be replaced by non-intentional mechanisms (*q.v.* Dennett 1 and *passim*).

MATERIAL MODE.
Q.v. Carnap (4).

MATERIAL ONTOLOGIES.
Q.v. Husserl (4).

MATHEMATICS.
Beginning with Aristotle, and continuing for many centuries, mathematics was defined as the science of quantity. But the development in mathematics of increasingly more abstract levels of generality has led to definitions such as that of Benjamin Peirce who suggested that mathematics is the science which draws "necessary conclusions," or of Whitehead who held mathematics to be the science "concerned with the logical deduction of consequences from the general premises of all reasoning." These more general definitions raise the question of the relation between mathematics and logic. Indeed, Whitehead played a significant role in the effort to demonstrate that mathematics can be derived from logic (q.v. below 9).

A. Epistemology. If we consider the subject matter of mathematics from an epistemological standpoint, we find the same range of opinions concerning the status of mathematical entities in the universe that we find in the history of philosophy concerning the status of ideas.

(1) Mathematical entities can be regarded realistically as part of a Platonic realm of ideas. It is necessary to notice, however, that Plato regarded them as intermediate between the intelligible and the sensible realms (q.v. Plato 1). In his Seventh Letter, however, he seems to regard geometrical entities as part of the realm of ideas.

(2) Mathematical entities can be regarded conceptually as having a foundation in reality, but an existence in themselves only when abstracted by an intelligence. Aristotle (q.v. 1, 3) seems to have so regarded the entities of mathematics, and so, too, many of his followers in the Middle Ages.

(3) A different kind of conceptualism is Kant's view (q.v. 1) that mathematical and geometrical entities are the result of construction, but that they are not a result of convention. They are synthetic and a priori at the same time, since they reflect human sensibility, or the nature of the sensible intuition.

(4) John Stuart Mill (q.v. 3) can stand as our example of a nominalist, regarding mathematical entities as having no a priori force, but standing as generalizations of human experience, which in some other world might have come out differently. Also q.v. D'Alembert (2).

B. In the latter part of the 19th century mathematics was moving into a period of increasing axiomatization, and a desire for formalization. This movement required Platonism in mathematics. Platonism led to paradoxes. Attempts were made to resolve the paradoxes by Constructivism and Intuitionism. Dropping Platonism but keeping formalization, Hilbert tried to put mathematics into a single formal system. Gödel's theorems showed that this was impossible, and led to the present nonideological stand-off in contemporary mathematics. This is the scenario we wish to trace. Among the participants in the development are the following:

(5) Peano (q.v.) axiomatized the series of natural numbers.

(6) Cantor contributed to the development of set theory, including work on transfinite cardinal and ordinal numbers (q.v.). This work contained assumptions that mathematical entities in the sets had existence apart from our thought about them.

(7) Dedekind (q.v.) added a method of defining real numbers in terms of rational numbers.

(8) Frege (q.v. 1-3) contributed to the axiomatization of logic, the effort to logicize mathematics, and to formalize arithmetic and analysis in a system of set theory.

(9) Russell (q.v. 2-4) and Whitehead (q.v. 1-2) carried much further the attempt to logicize mathematics, or to include mathematics in a system of set theory.

(10) Russell discovered the paradoxes of set theory (q.v.). The set of all sets not members of themselves leads to a contradiction. It both is and is not a member of itself. Thus it is clear that some limitation must be imposed on the formation and utilization of sets or classes.

(11) One way out of the impasse is through the Intuitionism of Brouwer (q.v. 2). In this alternative, mathematical entities are not recognized as existing until they are generated or constructed. The law of excluded middle, hence, applies

only to mathematical entities, series, and sets which have been constructed.

(12) A second way out was the path chosen by Hilbert (*q.v.*). One could avoid the Platonizing tendency while seeking to do classical mathematics still, building formal systems on a constructivist base, trying to complete them and show them to be consistent.

(13) In 1931 Gödel (*q.v.* 1–4) demonstrated that all formalizations in mathematics must be incomplete. The proof is rigorous and elegant, and strikes a death blow to the attempts to formalize mathematics.

MATHER.

Surname of a highly influential family of Congregational ministers in the 17th and 18th centuries. Their work centered in Boston, and they were supporters of the Halfway Covenant. The three successive generations contributing most significantly to the development of New England Congregationalism consisted of Richard Mather (1596–1669) who migrated to Boston from England in 1635, and who preached in Dorchester from 1636 until his death; his son, Increase Mather (1639–1723), minister of the Second (or North) Church, Boston, from 1662 until his death, serving also as acting president of Harvard College (1681–2, 1685); and Cotton Mather (1663–1728), son of Increase Mather, who became assistant pastor in his father's church in 1681, remaining in the ministry of the Second Church all his life, finally succeeding his father as minister. Disappointed in the growing liberalism of Harvard College, Cotton Mather was instrumental in establishing Yale College in Connecticut, and even in eliciting the substantial gift from the Englishman, Elihu Yale, after whom the new college was named. He defended the verdict in the Salem witchcraft trials of 1692, changing his mind on the issue some years later. He was elected to the Royal Society of London in 1713. Among his numerous works were *Magnalia Christi Americana*, 1702; *Bonifacius* or *Essays to do Good*; 1710, and *Christian Philosopher*, 1721.

MATHESIS UNIVERSALIS.

Latin phrase meaning "universal mathematics." A project of Leibniz (*q.v.* 12), he regarded it as one of his two combinatory arts.

MATHEW OF AQUASPARTA. c. 1240–1302.

Medieval philosopher-theologian. Born in Italy. A disciple of Bonaventure he taught at the University of Paris, then in Bologna and Rome. Minister general of the Franciscans in 1287, he was named a cardinal in 1288.

Principal writings: *Questions of Cognition; Questions of Faith and of Christ; Commentaries on the Sentences.*

(1) He combined Augustinian and Aristotelian emphases in his thought, holding that the soul could not know the intelligible species without a divine illumination, and that at the same time it is the work of the active intellect which gains this intelligible product from the sensible species, roughly speaking, sense-data. (2) He spoke of a singular species by which we have direct knowledge of individual things. (3) He gained from Bonaventure a doctrine of hylomorphism (*q.v.*) which characterized the world of created things.

MATTEO DE BASCIO.

Q.v. Francis of Assisi (4).

MATTER.

From the Greek *hyle* ("construction material" or "woods"). From its original practical sense a number of contrasting interpretations have developed.

(1) Protagoras (*q.v.* 2) is alleged to have held that matter is the sum of its appearances to any and all observers.

(2) In Plato (*q.v.* 9) matter is equated with the space-time receptacle which receives eternal forms, and the combination of the two is a space-time thing.

(3) Aristotle (*q.v.* 7–8) gave us the analysis in which formed matter yields sensible substances. Prime matter is here a principle of indeterminacy awaiting determination, a passive potentiality able to become all things. It is also the principle of individuation (*q.v.*).

(4) The Buddhist, Nagarjuna (*q.v.* 4), who appeared next in time, argued—as did many of his colleagues—for the unreality of matter.

(5) Plotinus (*q.v.* 5) held matter to be the final emanation in the series from

the One, and approaching non-being.

(6) For the Consciousness Only school of Buddhism (*q.v.* Consciousness 1) reality pertains to pure consciousness and external objects do not exist.

(7) Avicebron (*q.v.* 1) anticipated both Aquinas and Duns Scotus in arguing that matter as a principle of potentiality, cannot serve as the principle of individuation.

(8) Averroës (*q.v.* 1) argued for the eternity of matter, although he regarded it as nonetheless the creation of God.

(9) While the Scholastics followed Aristotle in the main (*q.v.* Aquinas 5–6), the double composition theory marks a difference as does the notion of signate matter, ordered to three dimensions.

(10) Duns Scotus (*q.v.* 5), arguing that prime matter cannot explain individuation, called upon a principle of *haecceitas*, or "thisness," to serve this function.

(11) William of Ockham (*q.v.* 9) anticipated the modern conception of matter, defining it as body with spatially distinguishable parts.

(12) Paracelsus (*q.v.*) spoke of *ultimate matter* which seems to have been something like the *apeiron*, or "boundless," of Anaximander (*q.v.*). In addition there is the prime matter of which Aristotle spoke, which has the potentiality to become all things.

(13) The modern doctrine of matter as extended and observable was finally introduced in the writings of Telesio (*q.v.* 1).

(14) Descartes (*q.v.* 8) accepted the new interpretation, identifying matter with the *res extensa*, or extended thing.

(15) Leibniz (*q.v.* 1–2) identified the individual thing with force rather than extension, which in fact requires spacetime matter to be derivative rather than primal in its reality.

(16) Boyle (*q.v.* 1) adopted the Corpuscular Theory of Matter, developing the operations of the system in terms of mechanical principles.

(17) For John Locke (*q.v.* 5b) substance is an "I know not what" that serves as a substratum for the qualities we experience.

(18) Berkeley (*q.v.* 1, 3, 5) finds the notion of substance, or matter, simply unnecessary. At this point the Greek complex of ideas had been reduced to a species of phenomenalism in which the world is composed of a play of ideas.

(19) Holbach (*q.v.* 3) held the chief qualities of things to be the qualities of matter.

(20) John Stuart Mill (*q.v.* 6) defined matter in terms of the phenomena of experience. Separating matter, however, from the evanescent and unreliable types of sensation, he defined matter as "the permanent possibility of sensation."

(21) James (*q.v.* 10), along with Russell (*q.v.* 9), held for a time to a doctrine of neutral monism, wherein the world in itself is some neutral stuff which, organized in one way, results in a material object, while organized in another way is mental.

(22) Whitehead (*q.v.* 8), like Leibniz, held matter to be a derivative idea. Whitehead regarded matter as derivative from events, which are the basic entities of the universe.

(23) For Santayana (*q.v.* 6) matter was the basic category, supporting essence, spirit, and truth.

(24) Aurobindo (*q.v.* 1) argues against Shankara (*q.v.* 7) that reality exists in a graded series, beginning in matter and rising to the Absolute.

MATTHEW, THOMAS.

Q.v. Bible.

MAUPERTUIS, PIERRE-LOUIS MOREAU DE. 1698–1759.

French philosopher and scientist. Born in Saint-Malo, Brittany. Elected to the French Academy of Science in 1723, and to the Royal Society in 1728. In 1736 he directed expeditions to Lapland and Ecuador whose measurements of the meridian helped prove the flattening of the earth at the poles. In this, as in many of his endeavors, he was supporting the scientific theories of Newton. In 1744 at the request of Frederick the Great he began a reorganization of the Berlin Academy, serving as its president from 1746 until his death.

Principal writings: *The Shape of the Earth* (with others), 1738; *The Physics of Venus*, 1745; *Philosophical Reflections on the Origin of Languages and the Signification of Words*, 1748; *Essay on Moral Philosophy*, 1749; *Essay on Cosmology*, 1750; *The System of Nature*, 1751; *Essay on the Formation of the Organized Body*, 1754; *Philosophical Examination of the Proof of the Existence of God*, 1756.

(1) The contributions of Maupertuis to science ranged from confirmation of Newton's laws of gravitation by showing the earth to be a sphere flattened at the poles, the principle of least action which helped to systematize Newtonian mechanics and has since had many additional applications, to anticipations of the biological principle of homeostasis. (2) The philosophical complement to this work remained somewhat eclectic. In keeping with his 18th-century colleagues, he was empirical in tone, stressing the role of sensation, even building mathematics from an empirical base. He also found the structure of language remaining as a deposit in scientific theorizing. In his ethics, hedonistic in tone, he anticipated the utilitarian calculus. (3) His reflections on biology and physics led Maupertuis to the doctrine of panpsychism, that the elementary particles are endowed with "desire, aversion, and memory."

MAUTHNER, FRITZ. 1849–1923.

Bohemian philosopher. Born in Horice, Bohemia. Studied law in the University of Prague. After an initial period as journalist and novelist, Mauthner settled down to study the philosophy of language. He was never a professor, and was in large measure self-taught.

Principal writings: *Contributions to a Critique of Language*, 3 vols., 1901–03; *Aristotle* (T), 1907; *Wordbook of Philosophy*, 2 vols, 1910; *The Three Pictures of the World, an Attempt at Language Criticism*, 1915; *Atheism and its History in the West*, 4 vols., 1920–23; *Godless Mysticism*, 1925.

(1) Because language originates from sense-experience, and since what the senses register is an accident of evolution, and without consistency from one person to another, what we call true is simply what is in agreement with the prevailing speech patterns of the group. (2) Language is essentially adjectival, yet humans tend to transform adjectives into substantives. This is "word superstition." In philosophy and every other field the most constructive approach is a continuing critique to remove this superstition, and to sophisticate the level of understanding within the given area. (3) The conclusion of this process is the realization that nothing finally true can be said,

and that the manner of contacting reality is through a "godless mysticism."

MAXIM.

In ordinary language a rule of action, summing up wisdom in an established context. In Kant, a rule providing ethical guidance (*q.v.* Kant 6).

MAXIMIN RULE.

Q.v. Rawls (2).

MAXIM, PRAGMATIC.

Q.v. Pragmatic Maxim.

MAXIMUS OF ALEXANDRIA. 4th cent. A.D. fl. 380–90.

Bishop of Constantinople. One of the Christian Cynics, Maximus substituted Christ for Hercules as the ideal of life. Despite this substitution in the Cynic pattern, Maximus used the diatribe form of expression typical of Cynicism (*q.v.*), as well as the depreciation of social forms.

MAXIMUS OF SMYRNA. fl. end of 4th cent. A.D.

Greek Neoplatonic philosopher. More interested in influencing the emperor Julian than in philosophy, he practiced theurgy (*q.v.*) and magic. On Julian's demise he was imprisoned and later put to death by Valens.

MAXIMUS OF TYRE. 2nd cent. A.D.

A Platonic philosopher similar to Celsus (*q.v.*), stressing dualism, a hierarchy of intermediate spiritual beings connecting God and the world, the identification of matter with evil, and believing that life is the sleep of the soul from which it awakes at death. Eclectic in tendency, he assimilated Aristotelian, Stoic, and Cynic elements to his basic Platonism.

Principal writings: Fragments remain of the forty-one *Diatribes* he wrote in defense of Platonism.

MAYA.

From the Sanskrit *maya* ("magic"). The term is used in Indian philosophy to refer to the world as an appearance, somehow different from the reality. Indian philosophy contains a range of possible interpretations of the status of the world. On the one extreme of this range, Ramanuja (*q.v.*) holds the world to be perfectly real, although finite; at the other extreme

Shankara (*q.v.* 2, 3, 7, 11) as a representative of the Advaita Vedanta (*q.v.*), holds the world to be an outright illusion. Also *q.v.* the synonymous term, *Avidya*; and Radhakrishnan (1).

MAZDA.

Originally, the term referred to Ahura Mazda, the benevolent but limited deity of Zoroastrianism (*q.v.* Zoroaster 1–3, 5–6). By the 5th century B.C. Mazda had become all-powerful and the center of an Iranian religion known as Mazdaism.

MAZDAISM.

Q.v. Mazda.

McCARTHY, JOHN.

Q.v. Artificial Intelligence (3, 4).

McCOSH, JAMES. 1811–1894.

Scottish philosopher. Born in Ayrshire. Studied in Glasgow and Edinburgh. A minister of the Established Church of Scotland, he was appointed professor of logic and metaphysics, in Queen's College, Belfast, in 1852. From 1868 to 1888 he served as president of the College of New Jersey in Princeton, as well as professor of philosophy. In 1888 he resigned as president, but continued as lecturer in philosophy until his death.

Principal writings: *The Method of the Divine Government*, 1850; *The Intuitions of the Mind Inductively Investigated*, 1860; *The Supernatural in Relation to the Natural*, 1862; *An Examination of Mr. J.S. Mill's Philosophy*, 1866; *Christianity and Positivism*, 1871; *The Scottish Philosophy, Biographical, Expository, Critical, from Hutcheson to Hamilton*, 1874; *First and Fundamental Truths, Being a Treatise on Metaphysics*, 1889.

(1) Holding that God relates to the world not only through the laws he has established but also through special acts of providence, McCosh accepted Darwinian evolution, finding providence in the chance variations of which Darwin spoke, and understanding the struggle for survival as God's instrument of creation.

(2) In epistemology he stood with the Scottish Common-sense philosophy. The natural beliefs we have about the world are not subject to question. Indeed, these beliefs are either necessary principles, such as causation and the idea of good, or they are derived from such principles.

The principles have their origin in experience, but on examination their ineluctable necessity is driven home to us.

McDOUGALL, WILLIAM. 1871–1938.

English psychologist. Born in Chadderton. Educated at Cambridge. Taught at London, Oxford, Harvard, and Duke University. The founder of Hormic Psychology (from the Greek *horme*, or "impulse"), McDougall held that striving for goals is a basic category of psychology, and cannot be explained mechanistically. He believed that human behavior derived from the following out of instincts, among them flight, repulsion, curiosity, self-abasement, self-assertion, and parental love.

Principal writings: *Introduction to Social Psychology*, 1908; *Body and Mind*, 1911; *Psychology, the Study of Behavior*, 1912; *An Outline of Psychology*, 1926; *Character and the Conduct of Life*, 1927.

McGILVARY, E. B. 1864–1953.

American philosopher. Born in Bangkok, Siam. Studied at Davidson College, Princeton, and the University of California from which he received his Ph. D. degree in 1897. Taught at Cornell, 1899–1905, and the University of Wisconsin, 1905–24.

Principal writings: *Toward a Perspective Realism*, 1956.

(1) Seeking to come to terms with the opposition in American philosophy between the New Realists (*q.v.*) and the Critical Realists (*q.v.*), McGilvary stressed the fact of relatedness. (2) He held that anything whatever is simply the totality of its relational characters. (3) Consciousness, too, is relational. It involves the having of a perspective. The relevant perspectives are temporal, spatial, intellectual, moral, and aesthetic. (4) Perspectives do not exist, but inter-sist. The inter-sistence of perspectives can explain sense-qualities, the perception of starlight, reference to the past or retrospectivity, and other epistemological problems, according to McGilvary. The view was termed "objective relativism" by A. E. Murphy.

McKEON, R.P. 1900–1985.

American philosopher. Born in Union Hill, N.J. Educated at Columbia University, and University of Paris. Taught at Columbia and University of Chicago.

Principal writings: *Selections from Medieval Philosophers* (ed.), 2 vols., 1929; *The Basic Works of Aristotle* (ed.), 1941; *Introduction to Aristotle* (ed.) 1947; *Democracy in a World of Tensions* (ed.), 1951; *Freedom and History*, 1952; *Thought, Action and Passion*, 1954; *The Freedom to Read* (with others), 1957; *Rhetoric: Essays in Invention and Discovery* (ed. Mark Backman), 1957.

(1) Finding a recurrent pattern in the history of philosophy, McKeon suggests that metaphysical speculation is the first stage of the cycle. As metaphysical systems multiply, the necessity for deciding among them drives philosophy into an epistemological period. As epistemologies likewise multiply, philosophy moves into a linguistic period, seeking the means of discriminating among epistemologies. Thereafter the circle turns back to metaphysics once again.

(2) McKeon finds four basic parameters of analysis in all philosophical thought. They are: Logistic, Problematic, Dialectic, and Operationalism.

(3) Mckeon believed that a pertinent analysis could be made of any subject matter from the standpoint of the natural sciences, social sciences, and the humanities.

(4) Finally, he distinguished between meroscopic analysis (from Greek *meros*, "part") which takes philosophy as a set of separate problems and holoscopic analysis (from *holos*, "whole") which considers philosophic problems in terms of the whole of reality.

McTAGGART, JOHN ELLIS. 1866–1925.

British philosopher. Born in London. Educated at Trinity College, Cambridge, where he was named a Fellow in 1891, and where he taught continuously from 1897 until 1923. An idealist and Hegelian from the start, he argued vigorously for the position long after philosophical styles had changed.

Principal writings: *Studies in the Hegelian Dialectic*, 1896; *Studies in Hegelian Cosmology*, 1901; *Some Dogmas of Religion*, 1906; *A Commentary on Hegel's Logic*, 1910; *Human Immortality and Pre-existence*, 1915; *The Nature of Existence*, 2 vols., 1921, 1927; *Philosophical Studies*, 1934.

(1) Although his work on Hegel is marked with originality, the best sample of McTaggart's thought would be an attempt to characterize the chain of reasoning in *The Nature of Existence*. We begin, then, with the claim that "Something exists." The claim is defended on Cartesian grounds. If one doubts the claim, the doubt exists. We must then have something that exists, even if it is only doubt (*q.v.* Descartes 2).

(2) What exists must have qualities, since not to have them is to be indistinguishable from nothing.

(3) Since not all qualities are consistent, there are also qualities which this thing does not have. The having of some qualities excludes the having of others. To be green is not to be red.

(4) Having qualities implies the existence of something which is qualified. Hence, we are led to admit the existence of something substantiated, *i.e.*, substance.

(5) There must, indeed, be more than one substance, however, since, if you doubt this claim, you will find at least two—*i.e.*, the doubter and the doubt.

(6) One is led to conclude that there are many substances, similar in that they coexist, different in that they form a plurality. Since similarity and difference are relations, relations must be likewise real.

(7) The community of substances which we now find it necessary to affirm is bound in a variety of relations such that a change anywhere entails a change everywhere. If A affects B in some specific way there exist at once the relations between A and B of affecting, and being affected by, the other; and the class of relations of other substances affecting B as is A, and being affected by A as is B; and the class of things dissimilar from A and B in neither affecting B nor being affected by A. Let the action of A cease and everything in the universe loses the relation of being similar or dissimilar to A or B in the given respect. Hence, there is a universal mutuality of dependence.

(8) Not only is everything a part of the universe with intimate relations to the whole of things, every part is a whole, and consists in turn of parts. Furthermore, there are "determining correspondences" between whole and part such that a "sufficient description" of the whole will apply to any part, or the converse. This kind of relation in our experience is

confined to conscious awareness. And so it turns out that this requirement, added to that of the mutuality of relations, leads to the conclusion that reality is a community of spiritual substances.

(9) But the project has not yet reached its goal, for it is McTaggart's contention that this community of substances is the Absolute, and this requires demonstration of the unreality of matter, space, and time. Matter and space are eliminated because they do not meet the "determining correspondence" criterion. His argument against time involves the distinction of an A-series (past, present, and future) from the B-series (earlier and later). The A-series is more basic, and an inconsistency is to be found in speaking of events as past, present, or future, for these are incompatible characteristics. If we say of event C that it is now future, and will be present, and then past, successively, this won't do, for we are saying that there is a moment in which C is future, a moment in which C is present, a moment in which C is past. And these moments cannot coexist as they must. Hence, time is unreal and reality becomes the Absolute, spiritual in content and timeless, its parts connected by love and understanding.

MEAD, GEORGE HERBERT. 1863–1931.

American philosopher. Born in South Hadley, Mass. Studied at Oberlin, Harvard and in various European universities. Taught briefly at the University of Michigan before coming to the University of Chicago in 1892. Influenced by Royce and James, he formed an important part of the Chicago school of pragmatists.

Principal writings: *The Philosophy the Present* (ed. A.E. Murphy), 1932; *Mind, Self and Society* (ed. C.W. Morris), 1934; *Movements of Thought in the Nineteenth Century* (ed. M.H. Moore), 1936; *The Philosophy of the Act* (ed. C.W. Morris and others), 1938.

(1) Mead traces the emergence of mental activity from the level of gesture, where a movement of a certain sort calls forth a compensatory movement on the part of a second individual. This gesture and response, internalized, leads to language and to rationality.

(2) On this basis Mead distinguishes between the "I" and the "me" in his analysis of the person. The former refers to the individual's capacity for spontaneity, and the latter to the internalized response of the "other." Thinking is the internal dialogue which occurs when the "me" responds to the action or projected action of the "I" and the "I" alters its response in terms of the standpoint of the "me."

(3) His view of perception marks out a path somewhat similar to that whereby gesture led to symbolic meaning. In the case of perception, his point is that the consummatory phase of perception is contact, so that perception can be said to be implicit manipulability. Thus, the idea of substance is generalized from the sense of resistance. Space, time, and mass are derived from contact experiences.

(4) Stressing the importance of the present, Mead stressed also the ubiquitousness of novelty both in the emerging present and the past and future, which likewise become novel in terms of the unique character of that present.

(5) His view of sociality led to a perspectival theory of the universe, centering in the act, in which the present moment is pluralistic due to the multitude of perspectives taken with respect to that moment by different individuals. On the other hand, however, the individuality of these perspectives is reduced by the fact that each of us has the ability also to take the viewpoint of the other.

MEAN, DOCTRINE OF THE.

(1) In the ethics of Aristotle the doctrine that virtue lies between extremes (although closer to excess than to deficiency) (*q.v.* Aristotle 11).

(2) In Chinese philosophy the Middle Way or *Chung Yung* in which every feeling is exercised in its proper degree and in harmony with every other (*q.v.* Doctrine of the Mean 1–2).

(3) In Buddhist philosophy the strategy whereby desire is eliminated and Nirvana gained (*q.v.* Buddha, Gautama).

MEANING.

Theories of meaning are formulated through determining a position on the significance and interrelations of sense-data, words and sentences, the use of words and sentences in ordinary language, ideas, and the problem of reference in regard to words, sentences, and ideas.

(1) The most common view of meaning is that one gets at the meaning of a word or idea by finding its reference in the non-linguistic world. But this view has difficulty with the claim that two meanings can have the same referent (*q.v.* Frege 6), and that there are many words which perform indispensable functions within sentences, but which are not referential (*q.v.* Syncategorematic Terms). The famous Verifiability Criterion (*q.v.*) held the verifiability of a sentence to be a condition of its meaning. But the criterion itself is not verifiable, thus exemplifying the objection mentioned above. Hempel (*q.v.* 2) suggested that a "translatability" criterion would avoid some of the objections of the verifiability criterion. Popper (*q.v.* 1) offered a variation on the same theme, suggesting falsifiability rather than verifiability as the approach to meaning. Reichenbach (*q.v.* 3) held that some propositions have "surplus meaning," in excess of observable consequences.

(2) Another form of the reference theory would be that one gets at the meaning of a word or idea by finding the sense-data which have given rise to the idea. Locke (*q.v.* 5–6), Berkeley (*q.v.* 1–2), and Hume (*q.v.* 1–2), although using different language, and making somewhat different decisions, agree on having words and ideas stand for sense-data. The view would seem to be open to the same objections as our first view.

(3) A third version of the reference theory holds that one gets at the meaning of a word or idea through the theoretical and practical consequences of the word or idea (*q.v.* Peirce 1; Dewey 4).

(4) H. Paul Grice (*q.v.* 1–2) offered a concept of "nonnatural" meaning in which saying that a speaker means something by an utterance is to say that he intends the utterance to produce some effect in a hearer by means of the recognition of this intention.

Also *q.v.* Dummet (1).

MEANING, THEORY OF.
Q.v. Dummet (1, 7).

MEANING-CARRIER.
Q.v. Semiotic (9).

MEANING-UTILIZER.
Q.v. Semiotic (9).

MEANING$_{NN}$.
Q.v. Grice (1).

MEANS-END CONTINUUM.
Q.v. Dewey (4); Hook (3).

MECHANICAL EXPLANATION.
Put negatively, any explanation which avoids teleology and final causation. Put positively, mechanical explanations stress efficient causation and are reducible to laws covering instances of matter in motion. Although this category of explanation arose among Greek philosophers, its period of dominance began with the rise of modern science. According to Spinoza, this is the true and complete explanation; the invocation of teleology is superstition. Mechanical explanation is the principle of explanation utilized by most materialistic systems, and not easily separated from such systems (*q.v.* Materialism). In biology a type of explanation opposed to Vitalism (*q.v.*).

MECHANICS.
That portion of physical science dealing with the action of forces on bodies. Although the science has numerous subdivisions, our interest is in the distinction between classical and quantum mechanics.

(1) Classical mechanics reached maturity in the work of Newton (*q.v.* 1–2) with his three laws of motion. Within the framework of classical mechanics there seemed no barrier to the exact determination of the position and momentum of any particle in the universe. Indeed the principle of determinism, as stated by Laplace (*q.v.* 3), held the entire future of the universe to follow from the present positions and momenta of its particles.

(2) For quantum mechanics this possibility no longer exists, even in principle. As the determination of the position of an electron is rendered more precise, the determination of its momentum must be less precise, and conversely. This principle of indeterminacy, attributed to Heisenberg (*q.v.*), is governed by the consequence that the product of the uncertainty of the two measurements can never be less than a constant h, known as

Planck's Constant. Finally, electrons (and photons) are to be interpreted in some contexts as waves, and in other contexts as particles.

(3) The difference between classical and quantum mechanics is interpreted in various ways. Some hold that the development of quantum mechanics invalidates the principle of determinism. Others disagree; Nagel (*q.v.* 2) holds that the latter is no less deterministic than the former although with a different state description.

MECHANICS OF MOTION.
Q.v. Newton (1).

MECHANISM.
Q.v. Democritus (4); Mersenne (2); Holbach (1); S.C. Pepper (1).

MEDELLIN MEETING.
Q.v. Theology of Liberation (4).

MEDIATION.
The process of connecting two end terms by an intermediary. In logic, mediate inference connects the major and minor terms by means of the middle term (*q.v.* Inference). In Neoplatonism, God and the world are related by mediation. In theology, Christ is the mediator between God and the world.

MEDIEVAL PHILOSOPHY.
Although periodization in history has only the value of convenience, if we are to speak of a medieval period of philosophy, it is reasonable to define it in terms of its highest point, and that is certainly the 13th-century synthesis of thought achieved by Saint Thomas Aquinas. Taking this as our anchor we would then reach back through the centuries to find the preparatory work for this achievement, and look forward until we sense another kind of work holding the center of philosophical attention. Between those two periods we shall find our material for medieval philosophy. It would be reasonable to begin the period with John Scotus Erigena in the 9th century, or with Saint Augustine in the 4th and 5th centuries. In any case the period will extend until new forms of thought become dominant in the Renaissance. Again the date is not definite. We must include William of Ockham in the 14th century. Certainly by the 17th century we have reached

high tide in another mode of philosophic thought.

(1) If the specific problem of the Middle Ages can be said to be the discovery of adequate syntheses between philosophy and the Christian faith, then St. Augustine (354–430) must be regarded as the first figure in this period. He provided a valuable synthesis of Platonic and Neoplatonic thought with Christian doctrine (*q.v.* Augustine 2, 3, 9, 11, 13).

(2) Boethius (480–524/25) remained essentially Platonic in point of view, set the stage for the problem of universals, and provided translations of Aristotle's logic. (*Q.v.* Boethius 2.)

(3) John Scotus Erigena (*c.* 810–*c.* 877), (*q.v.*), was like St. Augustine in viewing the Christian faith through the perspective of Neoplatonism. Among his translations was the *Pseudo-Dionysius* which was very influential during the Middle Ages.

(4) Saint Anselm (1033–1109), (*q.v.* 1), was a follower of St. Augustine. This protagonist of the Ontological Argument (*q.v.*) believed the truths of faith to be capable, to a large degree, of rational proof.

(5) Peter Abelard (1079–1142), (*q.v.*), helped to perfect the Scholastic method of disputation. He was an Augustinian whose interest in the orderly movement of reason led into the age of the Schoolmen.

(6) The 12th-century School of Chartres emphasized the sciences, as present in Platonic sources (of Aristotle they had only the logic), and the Latin classics. Among the members of the school were Fulbert, Bernard, Gilbert of Poitiers (*q.v.*), and John of Salisbury (*q.v.*).

(7) Between 1150 and 1250 Greek, Arabic, and Jewish writings, including the works of Aristotle, were being translated into Latin. Among the Arabian philosophers who contributed to the shaping of the medieval world are Avicenna (980–1037), (*q.v.*), and Averroës (1126–1198), (*q.v.*), whose commentaries on Aristotle were so highly regarded that he was given the title of "The Commentator." Among the Jewish philosophers who contributed similarly we mention Ibn Gabirol (Avicebron) (*c.* 1020–*c.*1070), (*q.v.*), and Moses Maimonides (1135–1204), (*q.v.*).

(8) In the early part of the 13th century

the two focal points of Scholastic philosophy emerged into the status of universities: Oxford and the University of Paris. The former remained Platonic in its outlook; the latter became the center for Aristotelianism. Robert Grosseteste (*q.v.*) was the first chancellor of Oxford, and William of Auvergne (*q.v.*) was the dominant figure at this time at the University of Paris.

(9) Roger Bacon (1214–1292), (*q.v.*), studied and taught first at Paris, and was later attracted to Oxford by the experimental emphases of Robert Grosseteste. To these methods he himself made a great contribution.

(10) St. Bonaventure (1221–1274), (*q.v.*), developed the new Augustinianism which now arose in opposition to the growing Aristotelian school. He developed this point of view among the Franciscans whom he served as Minister General after leaving his post at the University of Paris.

(11) St. Albert the Great (1200–1280), (*q.v.*), who taught both at Cologne and at the University of Paris had a scientific spirit. He attempted to harmonize the philosophies of Aristotle and Plato.

(12) St. Thomas Aquinas (1225–1274), (*q.v.*), who prepared the great synthesis of Aristotelian and Christian thought, was a Dominican, who taught both at the University of Paris and in Italy.

(13) Siger of Brabant (1240–1284) (*q.v.*) and Boetius of Dacia, a contemporary, were Aristotelians teaching at the University of Paris who had no desire to harmonize Aristotle and the Christian faith. Using Averroës as a clue to Aristotle they are called the Latin Averroists.

(14) John Duns Scotus (1266–1308), (*q.v.*), is interested in the unity of philosophy and the Christian faith, but is less confident than was Thomas Aquinas of the power of the unaided reason. His conclusions about these matters are subtle and important.

(15) Peter of Spain (1210–1277), (*q.v.*), developed Aristotelian logic, adding the idea of *supposition*; and William of Sherwood wrote an important treatise on syncategorematic terms.

(16) William of Ockham (1290–1349), (*q.v.*), was a nominalist with respect to the problem of universals, an empiricist in epistemology. He believed in the truth of the Christian faith, but did not believe that this truth was a part of science or of human knowledge. He studied at Oxford.

(17) Meister Eckhart (1260–1327), (*q.v.*), taught at the University of Paris and at Cologne. A disciple of St. Albert the Great, and a German Dominican, he developed Neoplatonism into a Christian mysticism centering in a mystical union with God.

(18) Nicholas of Cusa (1401–1464), (*q.v.*), may be picked, somewhat arbitrarily, to end our catalogue of names whose work can yield an understanding of medieval philosophy. Nicholas studied not at Oxford or the University of Paris but at Heidelberg, Padua, and Cologne. He specifically opposed Aristotelian logic whose principle of non-contradiction does not allow the higher wisdom of the identity of opposites. The mysticism of Nicholas is a call to return to Neoplatonism.

MEDITATION.

From the Latin *meditor* ("to think over, consider, reflect"). Where "contemplation" (*q.v.*) began as a religious term, meditation was a synonym for "thoughtfulness"; something of a reversal has occurred, however. It is more natural to speak of philosophical contemplation and religious meditation than the other way around. That would seem to leave contemplation to the West where philosophy has distanced itself from religion, and meditation to the East, where the two are intermixed. There is something to that, although the case is not so simple, and finally there is no clear manner of demarcating the two terms.

(1) The Western uses of meditation occur in a religious context: Clement (*q.v.* 3, 6) teaching a meditation on the Scriptures, leading to *gnosis*, a special form of knowledge; Bonaventure (*q.v.* 2, 4, 6) calling for an interior reflection, ending in illumination; Loyola (*q.v.*) preparing a manual of meditative spiritual exercises for the Society of Jesus; Teresa (*q.v.*) of Avila and John of the Cross (*q.v.*) teaching their stages of mysticism—a purgative state being the dark night of the soul—to their Barefoot Carmelites. Meditation was also central in the 17th-century movement of Quietism (*q.v.*).

(2) Eastern references are more frequent. The early stages of Taoism (*q.v.* 2 and Tao-Te-Ching), however, may be viewed as contemplative since putting oneself in harmony with nature is, at least in part, conceptual. Through the centuries meditation techniques were developed, including visualization exercises, breath control, and elixirs of immortality.

(3) Numerous meditative techniques flourished in Yoga (*q.v.*), a set of disciplines emerging within Hinduism, and also in Buddhism. Patanjali (*q.v.*) was the founder.

(4) Tantrism (*q.v.*), appearing within Hinduism, Buddhism, and Jainism, operated on the assumption that the universe is diffused with divine energy. The object of Tantric practices is to trap this energy and utilize it for spiritual purposes. *Mantras* (*q.v.*) and *mandalas* (*q.v.*) were employed to facilitate meditation. In the left-handed *Tantra* (*q.v.* Tantrism 4) physical partnering was combined with ritual meditation to achieve spiritual liberation.

(5) Buddha (*q.v.*) became enlightened under the Bo tree, and meditation became a central feature of Buddhism, directed toward the elimination of desire. In Theravada Buddhism (*q.v.*) meditation manuals became standard, based on the remembered sayings of Buddha. Where in *Veda*-based meditations, however, the object was to realize the self (*atman*), in early Buddhism the object is to realize *anatman*, the doctrine that there is no self. In Mahayana Buddhism (*q.v.* 2, 4) the objective shifts again. Wishing to become a *bodhisattva*, serving others through numerous rebirths, the four attitudes to be cultivated through meditation are friendliness, compassion, sympathetic joy, and equanimity. In Madhyamika (*q.v.*) Buddhism meditation turns on realizing "emptiness," and in T'ien T'ai (*q.v.* 1, 3) since all things interpenetrate, the truth of emptiness leads to "true thusness."

(6) Suzuki (*q.v.*) finds Mahayana Buddhism centering its attention on *dhyana* ("meditation absorption") rather than of *sila* ("morality") or *prajna* ("intuitive understanding"). Criticizing the emphasis on *dhyana* as sweeping all mental activity from the field of consciousness, he prefers the meditative technique of Zen Buddhism (*q.v.*) where *dhyana* combines with *prajna*, the combination of contemplating *koans* and meditation leading to an intuitive understanding in which the self is transformed. Thus is the *prajna* eye opened.

(7) In Islam (*q.v.*) as an alternative to the rationalism of the Mutazilites (*q.v.*) Sufism (*q.v.*) arose, seeking mystical union with Allah not only by breath control, repetition of sacred phrases, and visualization of sacred words, but by repetitive motions. The whirling dervishes (*q.v.*) gained trancelike states, losing the sense of self in this manner.

MEGARIAN SCHOOL OF PHILOSOPHY. c. 400–c. 300 B.C.

Centered in Megara the school was shaped partly by the influences of Socrates, and partly by the influence of the Eleatic philosophers. The school seems to have gained more from the latter than the former, presenting many arguments like those of Zeno (*q.v.*) of Elea, disproving commonsense pronouncements. In doing this, a number of semantic paradoxes were discovered and contributions made to logical form.

Among the Megarians were Euclid (*q.v.*), an associate of Socrates and the founder of the school; his disciple, Ichtias; Eubulides of Miletus, the second director of the school, who developed the Paradox of the Liar; his disciple, Philo of Megara (*q.v.*); Stilpo of Megara (*q.v.*), and Diodorus Cronus (*q.v.*), both of whom seem to have been teachers of Zeno the Stoic; and Bryson—son of Stilpo—who is said to have been the teacher of Pyrrho the Skeptic.

MEIER, GEORG FRIEDRICH. 1718–1777.

German philosopher. A follower of Baumgarten (*q.v.*), Meier extended Christian Wolff's (*q.v.*) approach to philosophy, writing treatises on aesthetics, ethics, epistemology, and metaphysics, as well as philosophy of religion.

Selected writings: *Principles of All Beautiful Arts and Sciences*, 3 vols., 1748–50; *Considerations of the Limits of the Human Understanding*, 1775.

MEINONG, ALEXIUS. 1853–1920.

Austrian philosopher. Born in Lemburg, Galicia. Studied under Brentano at the University of Vienna. Taught in Prague and Graz, establishing in the latter city an influential Institute of Psychology, organized for laboratory research.

Principal writings: *Hume Studies*, 2 vols., 1877, 1882; *Psychological-ethical Investigations on Value Theory*, 1894; *On Assumptions*, 1902; *On Object Theory*, 1904; *On Possibility and Probability*, 1915; *On Emotional Presentation*, 1917; *Foundation-work on the General Theory of Value*, 1923.

(1) Meinong in his theory of objects separated the being (*Sein*) of an object from its character (*Sosein*). Thus, golden mountains and round squares are objects even though they have no being. The not-being-the-case of a golden mountain is very different from the not-being-the-case of a round square; their character has to be regarded as independent of our thoughts or expressions about them. The round square is an instance of an impossible object, since it violates the law of contradiction. The golden mountain is an instance of an incomplete object. As an imaginary object it does not either have or fail to have each predicate one can name; thus it violates the law of excluded middle. An incomplete object with almost no character is called a defective object. The basic doctrine, involving the separation of *Sein* from *Sosein* he called the doctrine of *Aussersein*.

(2) The objects of which we have spoken serve as material for use in *objectives*, which are the objects of judgment. Objectives are higher order objects. Thus, "that there are no round squares" has as its objective the nonbeing of round squares. The objective, in turn, has round squares as its constituent. All judgments involve objectives; so do assumptions, or supposings, although the latter are instances of affirmation or denial which do not entail commitment.

(3) In his theory of evidence Meinong distinguishes between direct, certain, *a priori* evidence (any tautology), direct, certain, *a posteriori* evidence (any veridical report of inner perception), direct, but not certain, *a posteriori* evidence. He calls this last type of evidence *Vermutungsevidenz*, or surmise-evidence. The fact that reports of memory and perception can be directly evident, supported indirectly by other items of evidence, yet not be certain, entails that judgments can be directly evident and at the same time

false. Meinong holds that this is important in the analysis of memory, perception, and induction.

(4) In his theory of value Meinong distinguishes four types of feeling: (a) Presentation-act-feelings—sensually liking without concern for the *Sein* or *Sosein* of the object. (b) Presentation-content-feelings—aesthetic feelings concerned with the *Sosein* but not the *Sein* of the object. (c) Judgment-act-feelings—scientific feelings concerned with the *Sein* of the object but not the *Sosein*. (d) Judgment-content-feelings— valuations concerned with both the *Sein* and the *Sosein* of the object. Value-feelings, in turn, are divided into aesthetic, ethical, and other classifications, leading to analyses of various problems.

MELANCHTHON, PHILLIPP. 1497–1560. German theologian. Born in Bretten. Professor of Greek at Wittenberg. Under the influence of Luther, Melanchthon's interests shifted from humanistic studies to theology. Known as the "preceptor of Germany," his thought tended toward moderate positions blending Protestant theology with Aristotelianism and other elements from his broad humanistic culture. He was the author of the Augsburg Confession, the principal creed of Lutheranism.

Principal writings: *On Rhetoric*, 1519; *Commonplaces of Theology*, 1521; *Moral Philosophy*, 1538; *Commentary on the Soul*, 1540.

(1) In the Adiaphoristic controversy, Melanchthon took the position reached in the Augsburg Interim agreement of 1547 that numerous religious practices and beliefs were matters of indifference (*adiaphora*). His interpretation became less permissive in later years; and in any case the controversy was at least officially ended by the Augsburg Peace of 1555.

(2) A second instance of moderation is to be found in the doctrine of *synergism*, held by Melanchthon and defended by his followers. The doctrine holds that the act of regeneration involves the cooperation of three agencies: the Holy Spirit, the preaching of the Word, and the human will. The doctrine, containing a claim about human freedom, was regarded as at least semi-Pelagian, and was the subject of much controversy.

(3) He held logic, physics, and psychology

to be the main branches of philosophy; and his development of each of the subjects followed Aristotle closely.

MELIORISM.

From the Latin *melior* meaning "better." The doctrine that humanity, while incapable of perfection, is capable of an indefinitely extending series of improvements. This applies both to the individual and to the race. It is difficult to locate the doctrine in the history of philosophy. It relates to the doctrine of human perfectibility, and is sometimes used to characterize pragmatic philosophers, *e.g.*, William James.

MELISSUS OF SAMOS. 5th cent. B.C.

Greek philosopher. Born in Samos. As admiral he engaged the Athenian fleet in battle around 440 B.C., and. according to Plutarch, was victorious. One of the Eleatic philosophers, his strategy and arguments are very similar to those of Parmenides and of Zeno. He argued from the spatial and temporal infinity of the world to its changelessness, and from thence to the illusive character of perception.

Principal writing: *On Nature or on Being* (fragments extant).

MEMORY.

One of the topics of Epistemology (*q.v.*) or Theory of Knowledge; the analysis of memory cannot be sharply separated from the analysis of perception. How we know the past is related to the questions of how we know the present and predict the future. The explanation of memory has sometimes centered on the difference between an event remembered and an event perceived, imagined, or thought.

(1) Hobbes (*q.v.* 3) regarded memory as "decaying sense."

(2) Hume (*q.v.* 1) adopted a somewhat similar alternative. Utilizing the notion of differences of force and vivacity, he found ideas of memory to be less intense than the impressions of immediate experience, but more intense than those of imagination.

(3) John Stuart Mill (*q.v.* 6) related memory to the mind's awareness of its past.

(4) William James (*q.v.* 2) explained memory as involving an image or idea in the mind along with feelings of

warmth, intimacy, and past direction in time.

(5) Bergson (*q.v.* 9) supported a realistic view of memory as the past continuing to exist internal to the present state of awareness.

(6) Bertrand Russell interpreted memory as feelings of familiarity and pastness combined with present images and ideas, while holding it to be a form of direct knowledge (*q.v.* Russell 6).

(7) C.I. Lewis held that there is in any ostensible memory event a *prima facie* credibility, which may be increased to a higher degree of probability by the agreement of other ostensible memory events.

(8) Linguistic philosophers, such as Norman Malcolm, are concerned to challenge all representative theories of memory (1, 2, 4, 6, and 7 above), casting their analyses in terms of memory dispositions and memory acts.

MENCIUS. c. 371–c. 289 B.C.

Chinese philosopher. Born in Shantung province. Studied under a disciple of the grandson of Confucius. Basically a teacher and civil servant, his career was markedly similar to that of Confucius, from whom in fact most of Mencius' teachings are derived. Where, however, Confucius failed to raise the question concerning the original goodness of human nature, Mencius made this doctrine the cornerstone of his system. Men are originally good; hence, they must have innate knowledge of the good, and an ability to do it. Every individual has the capacity within him to become a Sage; thus a premise of human equality is also admitted. It was this view, too, which led him to advocate the right of the people to revolt against a state which denies these principles. In contradistinction to the Moist doctrine of universal love, Mencius stressed the dual values of humanity (*jen*), and righteousness (*li*). The homophone of *li*, meaning "benefit" or "gain," is explicitly condemned.

Principal writing: *The Book of Mencius*.

MENDELSSOHN, MOSES. 1729–1786.

German Jewish philosopher. Born at Dessau. Learned his first philosophy from Maimonides' *Guide for the Perplexed*. Philosophically self-taught. Friend of Lessing with whom he once collaborated. The lucidity of his prose style led to his being called "the German Plato." In addition to his philosophical writings he translated the Pentateuch into German with commentaries, as well as many other books of the Jewish Bible. Founded the Jewish Free School in Berlin where the sciences were taught as well as the Bible and the Talmud. He had to defend himself against both Spinozism and his fidelity to the Jewish community.

Principal writings: *Philosophical Conversations*, 1755; *On Evidence in the Science of Metaphysics*, 1763; *"Phaedo" or Concerning the Immortality of the Soul*, 1767; *Jerusalem*, 2 vols., 1783; *Morning Hours or Lectures on the Existence of God*, 1785.

(1) Mendelssohn produced no system of thought. Believing in the existence of God and the immortality of the soul, he offered arguments for both propositions. He deduced the soul's immortality from its nature as a simple substance. (2) He argued for freedom of conscience and that the state had no right to interfere with the religion of its subjects. His reason was that individuals may need different religions, and the test of a religion is nothing other than its effect on conduct. (3) He argued that while Judaism may properly require conformity to ceremonial law, this must be made compatible with complete liberty of opinion. (4) His aesthetic view centered the idea of tragedy in admiration—although it is a "mixed feeling"—rather than in pity and terror. He centered the sense of beauty in a faculty of "approval" which is separate both from intellect and desire. (5) Aesthetic perfection, however, is subjective, man's substitute for the objective metaphysical perfection—the unity in variety of reality—known only to God although the goal of man's striving. (6) He suggested an epistemological combination of reason and common sense as the path to truth.

MENIPPUS OF GADARA. 3rd cent. B.C. fl. 270.

Greek philosopher. Born in Phoenicia. A Cynic philosopher, he developed the tradition of writing in satire and burlesque. Indeed, the Roman world knew a type of satire called Menippean satire; it influenced among others, Varro (*q.v.*) and Seneca himself.

MENNONITES.

An evangelical Protestant religious movement derived from the Anabaptists (*q.v.*) in the 16th century, and named for the Anabaptist elder Menno Simons (1492–1559). The Old Order Amish and the Hutterites are among the many branches of the denomination.

MENNO SIMONS.

Q.v. Mennonites.

MENTALISM.

Any doctrine insisting upon the exclusive reality of minds and their inner states (*q.v.* Idealism *passim*); the term is also applied to those views of mind which distinguish mental states from brain states.

MENTALITY.

The quality of mind is treated under such topics as "idealism" and "soul." But Morgan (*q.v.* 4) held mentality to be the emergent of the psychical correlate. And Whitehead (*q.v.* 15) regarded the "mental pole" as originative of novelty in the universe.

MENTION.

Q.v. Use-Mention Distinction.

ME ON.

Greek term, one of two, for nonbeing. *Q.v.* Nothing.

MERCIER, DÉSIRÉ. 1851–1926.

Belgian philosopher. Born in Brabant. Named professor of Thomistic philosophy at the University of Louvain in 1882. Founded the Institute of Philosophy at Louvain in 1889; this institute became the center of studies in "Criteriology." In 1906 he was made an archbishop, and in 1907 he became Cardinal Mercier. He took as his special mission the relating of Thomism to modern thought, and especially to the sciences.

Principal writings: *Course of Philosophy*, 4 vols. (*Psychology; Logic; General Metaphysics or Ontology; General Criteriology or General Theory of Certitude*), 1892–9; *The Origins of Contemporary Psychology* (T), 1897; "Experimental Psychology and the Spiritualist Philosophy" (T), 1900; *Elementary Treatise of Philosophy* (with Wulf and Nys) (T), *A Manual of Modern Scholastic Philosophy*), 2 vols., 1905; *The Philosophic*

Definition of Life, 1908; *Christianity in Modern Life*, 1918.

(1) Distinguishing between General and Special Criteriology, Mercier investigated criteria for certainty both in an ontological sense and in relation to modern science, especially psychology. He claimed to have found an internal criterion, refuting both skepticism and positivism.

(2) Taking the lead in reassessing Thomism, he defended its claims against all philosophical alternatives, reaffirming its compatibility with revealed truth.

MEREOLOGY.

Q.v. Leśniewski.

MERLEAU-PONTY, MAURICE. 1908–1961.

French philosopher. Born in Rochefort-sur-Mer. Taught at Lyon. Sorbonne and the Collège de France. Along with Jean-Paul Sartre and Simone de Beauvoir, he founded *Les Temps modernes*.

Principal writings: *The Structure of Behavior* (T), 1942; *Phenomenology of Perception* (T), 1945; *Humanism and Terror*, 1947; *Sense and Nonsense* (T), 1948; *In Praise of Philosophy* (T), 1953; *The Adventures of Dialectic*, 1955; *Signs* (T), 1960; *The Primacy of Perception* (T), 1964; *The Visible and the Invisible* (ed. Lefort), 1964.

(1) Influenced both by Gestalt psychology and Husserl's phenomenology, Merleau-Ponty merged and broadened these approaches. The result was a phenomenology of perceptions capable, at least in his view, of coming to terms with the real world. One consequence of his method was his ability to provide an alternative to dualism. Opposing the Cartesian mind-body dualism, Merleau-Ponty presented the elements of the identical problem as a matter of a variety of conceptual levels in the study of human behavior; *e.g.*, the physical level, the biological level, and the mental level. The latter presuppose the former, but are not separable from them.

(2) Given this beginning point, rather than distinguishing pure consciousness from the body one thinks of the body as intending. And since this is the locus of all intentions it follows that all awareness is from some particular perspective, and not universalizable.

(3) Part of this perspective is a fund of accepted and pre-evaluated meanings which is both a condition of and a limitation on the exercise of human freedom.

(4) The limitations of a given perspective are to some extent overcome by the power of language, since language is inter-subjective; and perceptions are sharpened and deepened by an aesthetic mode of viewing the world.

(5) Among the elements of perception are the relations, or relational forms, permitting one to relate sensation and idea to each other in terms of a particular situation. And this is possible not simply for a single individual, but for all who participate in that situation.

(6) Although initially drawn to orthodox Marxism, he finally decided that there was no single logic to history, but that any agency looking toward change in society must pay attention to the multiple tendencies or intentions of society, and seek to direct them in progressive ways.

MEROSCOPIC.

Q.v. Mckeon (4).

MERSENNE, MARIN. 1588–1648.

French philosopher. Born near Bourg d'Oizé. Studied at La Flèche, and later in Paris. Joined the order of Minimi. The so-called "Circle of Mersenne" contained the most illustrious philosophers, scientists, and theologians of Europe. His appreciation for Descartes stemmed not from the latter's metaphysics, but from Descartes' role in diffusing the ideas of the new science.

Principal writings: *The Impiety of the Deists, Atheists, and Libertines*, 2 vols., 1624; *The Truth of the Sciences Against the Skeptics and Pyrrhonians*, 1630; *Universal Harmony*, 1636.

(1) Embracing science as the middle way between skepticism and dogmatism, Mersenne held that the knowledge of phenomena which we have in science refutes the skeptic while making dogmatism unnecessary.

(2) And although he found in science information concerning the work of God, he understood that work to be constructed according to mechanical principles, and associated such principles with scientific understanding.

(3) Consequently, too, he viewed the world of sensible qualities as subjective;

hence, the distinction of primary and secondary qualities is implicit in his point of view.

MESLIER, JEAN. 1664–1729.

French freethinker. Village priest of Etrépigny.

Principal writing: *Testament* (written in the 1720's).

(1) The main thesis of the book is that religion is an instrument of the ruling classes to control and subjugate the rest of society. The material was so tailored to the times that the manuscript circulated widely as an unpublished underground protest; editions were published by Voltaire and by Holbach. These were reprinted many times prior to the publication of the entire manuscript in 1864.

(2) He held atheism to be the only logical position, and found ethical nobility to flow from that point of view. The philosophical corollary of atheism is mechanistic materialism.

(3) A call to revolution is implicit in Meslier's thesis, and for a society lacking nobles, rulers, or priests.

MESSER, AUGUST. 1867–1937.

German philosopher. Taught at the University of Giessen.

Principal writings: *Kant's Ethic* (T), 1904; *Sensation and Thought* (T), 1908; *The Problem of Free Will* (T), 1911; *Faith and Knowledge* (T), 1919; *Critical Realism* (T), 1923.

(1) Interpreting Kant as a critical realist, Messer held that critical realism solved the basic problems of epistemology. (2) He advocated a phenomenological method open to psychological data, and consistent with his realistic approach. (3) He likewise advocated an "ethical idealism" which in his view threw light not only upon problems of ethics, but upon problems of epistemology as well.

MESSIAH.

Q.v. Messianism (1).

MESSIANISM.

(1) Belief in the coming of a personal Messiah ("the anointed one") who would usher in the Kingdom of God. In the 1st century B.C., especially in its second half, the idea gained considerable strength among the Jews.

(2) In the 19th century a Polish national movement bore this name. A not inconsiderable number of the nation's philosophers, poets, and religious thinkers saw Poland's function to be that of building a spiritual community which would establish a pattern of what an "authentic nation" may be, and thus lead the world to universal peace.

META-ETHICS.

A second order discipline taking the field of ethics, or Normative Ethics (*q.v.*), as its subject matter. Its procedure, appropriate to a meta-discipline, is analysis of the ethical statements of moral philosophers as well as those of ordinary persons. Following the Use-Mention Distinction (*q.v.*, and Russell 3), such statements are viewed from the outside. They are mentioned but not used. Among the Meta-Ethicists are R.M. Hare (*q.v.*), Nowell-Smith (*q.v.*), and Stephen Toulmin (*q.v.*). Also *q.v.* Ethics.

METALANGUAGE.

Every language has in it signs which refer to the world, and signs which refer to other signs of the language. This is the Use-Mention Distinction (*q.v.*). To avoid semantic paradox it is possible to distinguish between the language in use, and its meta-language, regarding the latter as that part of the language which refers to the signs of the language itself. A number of philosophers have urged the adoption of the language-metalanguage distinction, and a considerable amount of philosophical work has been done in developing the idea.

(1) Bertrand Russell (*q.v.* 3) first posed this distinction as a corollary of his theory of types. The structure of any language, he claimed, must be discussed from the standpoint of another language; this, in turn, has a structure requiring still another language, etc. without end.

(2) Tarski (*q.v.* 3) related the problem of metalanguages to that of formalized deductive sciences. The structure of a given science must be discussed in a metalanguage which defines the scope of a metascience. Here a hierarchy of metasciences accompanies the language hierarchy.

(3) Carnap (*q.v.* 4–5) discussed the concept in terms of an object language L_1 whose analysis requires a metalanguage

L$_2$. As in the preceding cases the meta-languages can be multiplied to whatever extent may be necessary.

(4) Analysis of a metalanguage must be concerned with the syntactics, semantics, and pragmatics of the language. Syntactics is the structure of the language, and the problems involved in that structure. Semantics is a study of the relation of the language to what it designates. Pragmatics is concerned with the problems of significance.

(5) For the view that there is a single metalanguage including both descriptive and evaluative discourse *q.v.* Northrop (1–2).

(6) For a view of metalanguage as applied to literary criticism *q.v.* Jakobson; Structuralism (5).

METALOGIC.

The term refers simply to the metalanguage (*q.v.*) of logic. It is a study of the structure, signs, connectives, formulae, theorems, and rules of inference of logic from a syntactic, semantic, and pragmatic point of view. The basic concepts, upon which discussion of metalogic has turned in recent years, are decidability (*q.v.*), completeness (*q.v.*), and consistency (*q.v.*).

METAPHILOSOPHY.

The term is derived from the language-metalanguage distinction (*q.v.* Metalanguage) which in contemporary philosophy has replaced to a great extent the physics-metaphysics distinction. But fashion does not settle the question.

(1) In terms of subject-matter, Metaphilosophy is the discussion of the nature of philosophy, including of course the nature of its constituent disciplines of logic, Ethics, Aesthetics, Epistemology, etc.

(2) For those who still adhere to the claim that the discipline of Metaphysics (*q.v.*) is possible, Metaphilosophy becomes a subject within Metaphysics. The metaphysician might argue that this must be the case since, to the extent that one separates Metaphilosophy as a study of what philosophy is from philosophy itself, to that extent the question of an infinite regress of disciplines of this sort must be raised. One might argue that the scientist, reflecting upon the nature of science, does so as a philosopher of science; but the philosopher, reflecting upon the nature of philosophy, continues to stand within the field of philosophy. For this discipline, the claim would be, self-referentiality is not vitiating.

(3) From the metalinguistic standpoint, the scientist, reflecting upon the nature of science, does so as a metascientist, and by means of a metalanguage designed for this purpose (*q.v.* Tarski 3). Similarly, metaphilosophy would be a study of the nature of philosophy by means of a metalanguage appropriate to the study. In Carnap's terms this would be a logically correct language (*q.v.* Carnap 6–8); in Bergmann's terms this would be an ideal language (*q.v.* Bergmann 2).

METAPHOR.

From the Greek *meta* ("beyond" or "over") plus *pherein* ("to bring, bear, or carry"). The initial meaning was that merely of carrying a burden from one place to another. In Plato the meaning was that of translating a term from one language to another. But, of course, Platonic philosophy was highly metaphorical in the modern sense. In that sense "metaphor" is one of the four tropes or figurative uses of speech. The four are metaphor, metonymy, synecdoche, and irony. In three of the four, some type of nonliteral substitution takes place: *e.g.*, effect for cause (metonymy), part for whole or whole for part (synecdoche), the meaning contrary to that intended (irony). In the case of metaphor rather than a substitution we are presented with an unusual identification: "The man is a rock," "The skies are angry." The important question concerns the use of metaphor in philosophical thinking. Everyone will agree that metaphors may be useful in suggesting relationships; but given this as a starting point, what follows?

(1) A great many philosophers, including Aristotle, Hobbes, Locke, and the modern logical positivists, have urged the elimination of metaphorical expressions in philosophy on the grounds of ambiguity and their relating to feeling rather than thought.

(2) But it is often said that Plato (*q.v.*), for example, used metaphor and myth to explain figuratively what he could not explain literally, letting these elements stand as placemarkers, as it were, for the missing analyses.

(3) And Thomas Aquinas (*q.v.* 4) provides a role for something like metaphor in his analogy of being. Between univocal expression and equivocal expression he finds various kinds of analogical expressions which have intellectual uses.

(4) Burleigh (*q.v.* 1) places metaphor in the category of "improper supposition."

(5) Bergson (*q.v.* 3) provides a still more positive role for metaphor. Dividing types of expression into intellectual and intuitive, he suggests that the intellect requires literalness in its expressions, but that the natural language of intuition is metaphorical.

(6) The claim of Collingwood (*q.v.* 1) that philosophy is the discipline whose concepts overlap each other contains the suggestion that metaphorical relations should be natural to philosophy, an essential part of its subject matter.

(7) Ernst Cassirer (*q.v.* 4) distinguished between scientific thinking on the one hand, which strives for clarity, order, and literal meaning in its concepts; and religion and poetry on the other, which concentrate a multiplicity of meanings at a point, hence relying necessarily on metaphor.

(8) W.M. Urban (*q.v.* 4) insisted that metaphysical concepts are essentially metaphorical, and cannot be translated into literal speech. It is a corollary that some insights cannot be translated into literal language; therefore, metaphor can convey truth.

(9) S.C. Pepper (*q.v.* 1) argued that every metaphysical system has a root metaphor from which the system is generated, and in terms of which the system is to be understood.

(10) Dorothy Emmet (*q.v.* 1) found analogical thinking at the basis of metaphysics, and metaphor a natural manner of expressing the analogies.

(11) Polanyi (*q.v.* 3) is among those who find metaphor to be an essential element in art and religion.

(12) I.A. Richards (*q.v.*) in *Philosophy of Rhetoric* proposed a theory of metaphor based on interacting contexts in which every metaphor has two parts, the "tenor" or underlying idea, and the "vehicle" ("the idea under whose sign the first idea is apprehended"). The vehicle is understood through the tenor, although there are dissimilarity, tension, and interaction between the two.

(13) Max Black (*Models and Metaphors*, 1962) continued the interactive analysis, using "focus" and "frame" in place of vehicle and tenor for the principal and subsidiary subjects of the metaphor. The "associated implications" of the subordinate subject are transferred to the principal subject, and there is a backwash of associations the other way.

(14) Monroe Beardsley (*Aesthetics*, 1958; "The Metaphorical Twist," 1962) adds the point that the metaphor presents an implicit (*i.e.*, indirect) contradiction between the two subjects which the reader must resolve by selecting from the opposed sets of connotations those which exhibit hidden kinship. The implicit, is thus resolved into an apparent, contradiction.

(15) For Ricoeur (*q.v.* 2) metaphor combines a semantic impertinence with a code-saving novel pertinence.

METAPHYSICAL FORM.
Q.v. Form (5h).

METAPHYSICAL SOLIPSISM.
Q.v. Solipsism.

METAPHYSICS.

The term, meaning "beyond physics," came from the position of an untitled book by Aristotle in the classification of his works made by Andronicus of Rhodes (*q.v.*). The term thus meant "the book beyond the *Physics*." In a conceptual sense the description of metaphysics as "going beyond" physics is often retained. Metaphysics is, then, thought of as a study of ultimates, of first and last things, its content going beyond physics, or any other discipline. That is not, however, Aristotle's sense of the term (*cf.* 3 below), and in general a variety of approaches has been taken to the subject, as we shall see. Metaphysics does tend toward the building of systems of ideas; and these ideas either give us some judgment about the nature of reality, or a reason why we must be content with knowing something less than the nature of reality, along with a method for taking hold of whatever can be known. We shall name some of the representatives of different approaches to the subject.

(1) The Eleatics were the earliest philosophers to satisfy both of the above

conditions, and Parmenides (*q.v.* 1) was the central figure in the group. Here the method is rational consistency, and the claim is that the real is the rational, even if this does not square with sense experience. Indeed, the Eleatics forced a contrast between appearance and reality. Reality was unitary, eternal, changeless; and the world of ordinary experience was held to be a mere appearance.

(2) Plato (*q.v.* 1) likewise found it appropriate to draw a contrast between appearance and reality. It was his method, however, not simply to deny sense-experience, but to take account of this experience, while correcting it by the principles of reason. One is to use the approach of self-correction until one reaches the point where it is possible for reason to make its way alone. This is the method of dialectic, which would apparently contain not only the truth of all the sciences in deductive form but also a total vision of reality. One supposes that dialectic remains an ideal which we may approach, but never fully realize.

(3) Aristotle (*q.v.* 1, 2, 7–10) relaxes the appearance-reality contrast, thinking of metaphysics (he called it "first philosophy") as the discipline dealing with concepts too general to be treated within one of the special fields of knowledge. The problems of causality and substance, and the analysis of general terms such as potentiality and actuality, are examples of topics or concepts utilized in numerous fields of inquiry, and which can receive their definitive treatment only in the general discipline of metaphysics. For him this is also, however, the study of being as such, whereas the sciences study parts of being.

(4) Plotinus (*q.v.* 1) presents a position much like that of Plato. The most striking difference is that the movement toward reality is at the same time one's movement toward personal salvation. The theme of metaphysics here becomes union with God.

(5) Thomas Aquinas (*q.v.* 5, 6) reflected the position of Aristotle, especially the point that metaphysics is the study of being as such. But it is much more the case that here the study is one of transcendent being, and that means in its primary instance, the being of God Himself.

(6) Descartes (*q.v.* 1–3) found the criterion of metaphysics not in transcendence or in generality, but in certainty. One must find, as he thought he had, a starting point which is indubitable. Beginning from that point one must move carefully by steps equally certain to establish a basis for all knowledge, including then the knowledge of the special sciences.

(7) Spinoza (*q.v.* 5) developed an approach different from any of the above. On the basis of an initial set of definitions and assumptions, he worked out a deductive system whose truth is supported by the consistency of the whole and the rigor of the deductions.

(8) Leibniz (*q.v.* 10) understood metaphysical propositions to be necessary truths whose denial involves a contradiction. They differ from contingent truths in that they would be true in all possible worlds, not merely in the one which happens to exist.

(9) Although Locke (*q.v.* 1–5, 8) allows some arguments which go beyond experience, *e.g.*, an argument for God, he is strongly empirical in approach. His connection with metaphysics is merely the stance he takes toward our knowledge of the world; and his general approach is to try to determine how our complex ideas can be shown to be derived from experience.

(10) Berkeley (*q.v.* 1–4) continued this approach. He retains the validity of the argument for God, is more convinced about the reality of souls than Locke; and is quite certain that Locke is wrong in allowing the idea of substance as a "something" existing in the world.

(11) Hume (*q.v.* 1–3) reduced the scope of what is known to the phenomena one has. Skepticism must invest any claims which go beyond the flood of immediate impressions. Necessity is to be found only in the formalities of reason, *i.e.*, in symbolic structures shaped by us.

(12) Kant (*q.v.* 1–3, 8) found both a way to agree with Hume and to find necessity in scientific knowledge; this involved a further exploration of our relation to phenomena. He also provided a practical reason whose province included the metaphysical propositions concerning God, freedom, and immortality.

(13) Hegel (*q.v.* 6–9) understood the

task of metaphysics to be that of making a set of rational deductions which will encompass and exemplify reality. Unlike the rational systems of Descartes and Spinoza, however, the Hegelian system is dialectical, emerging by opposition and synthesis rather than the more familiar types of inference. Also unusual is the claim that it is finally the Absolute Spirit which is being deduced, and whose life is, indeed, the life of the world.

(14) C.S. Peirce (*q.v.* 2) found metaphysics to be an observational science, involving a careful phenomenology of the general features of existence. The appropriate metaphysical structure will be architectonic, rising from the focal points of our total experience.

(15) Stöhr (*q.v.*) distinguished between pathogonous, glossogonous, and theorogonous types of metaphysics.

(16) R.G. Collingwood (*q.v.* 1–2) understood metaphysics to be a study of the ultimate presuppositions of the systems and schemes advanced in the course of civilization.

(17) Rudolf Carnap (*q.v.* 4–6) and other logical empiricists have regarded metaphysical systems as having no truth value, but having an emotional value.

(18) Henri Bergson (*q.v.* 1–3) found metaphysics to involve an intuitive approach to the world, capable of overcoming the spatializing tendency of reason and grasping the fluidity of temporal process.

(19) A.N. Whitehead (*q.v.* 9–24) believed metaphysics to require imaginative generalization from the total data of human experience in all fields, from the sciences to that of religion. He held the results of such activity to be never more than probable.

(20) Gilbert Ryle (*q.v.* 1) held metaphysical statements to involve category mistakes. The conclusion is possible, or the problem arises, because language has been misused. Many other ordinary-language philosophers have made similar claims.

(21) P.F. Strawson (*q.v.* 3) supports a descriptive metaphysics arising from deeply bounded linguistic distinctions.

(22) Dorothy Emmet (*q.v.* 2) distinguishes two kinds of metaphysics, one stressing coherence, and the second including, in addition, an allegedly transcendent reference.

METASCIENCE.
Q.v. Tarski (3).

METEMPSYCHOSIS.
The passing of soul, spirit, or personality upon death into another body, whether of the same or a different species. A cardinal feature of many forms of Indian philosophy; *q.v.* Hinduism, Jainism, Mahayana Buddhism. Also a part of the Pythagorean (*q.v.* Pythagoras 3) philosophy, and present in the writings of Plato (*q.v.* 1). Finally, the doctrine is to be found in the Jewish Cabala (*q.v.* 1d).

METHODEUTIC.
Q.v. Peirce (16).

METHODISM.
Originally a reform movement within the Church of England, led by John and Charles Wesley (*q.v.*), George Whitefield (*q.v.*), and other representatives of Oxford Methodism. The origin of the movement is to be credited to Charles Wesley who, beginning in 1727, persuaded a group of his fellow students at Oxford to take religion more seriously, whereupon an onlooker exclaimed, "Here is a new set of Methodists sprung up." John shortly joined his brother at Oxford. By 1729 the "Holy Club," John being considered its "father," was formed. The club met at first on Sunday evenings, then every evening. Its members observed the Lord's Supper together every Sunday, fasted every Wednesday, and constantly kept their personal lives under review. Whitefield was one of the approximately twenty-five members of the Holy Club. In retrospect, John Wesley found three "rises" of Methodism. The first was the organization of the club. The second was the society of thirty to forty members formed in Georgia in 1736, when the brothers were briefly part of Governor Oglethorpe's expedition. The "third rise" occurred in 1738 by means of a series of meetings held by Whitefield in the "open air" of Bristol, when the doors of all the churches were closed against him. After six weeks of intense interest and immense crowds, John Wesley joined the meetings. A new society was formed, converts multiplied, and a system of lay assistants, local and travelling preachers, emerged. Whitefield separated from the

Wesleys in 1741 over a theological dispute and, although the rift was healed, Whitefield thereafter worked independently. Beginning in 1747, John devoted six years to establishing the movement in Ireland. In 1751 he began a similar work in Scotland. Methodism spread to North America, first through the emigration of lay assistants and finally, upon appeal, the dispatch of ministers such as Francis Asbury, Thomas Rankin, and Thomas Coke. Methodism was first organized as a separate denomination, the Methodist Episcopal Church, in Baltimore, Maryland, in 1784. From the start the emphasis on direct religious experience was dominant in Methodism; as a corollary, the interest in theology was slight, although it was anti-Calvinist and in support of free will and the possibility of human efficacy in religious matters. The largest Protestant denomination in the United States, the church has world-wide affiliations.

METHODOLOGY.

The problem of method is treated under many entries. The selection of a procedure for reaching an end in view has many aspects.

A. In the most general sense the problem of method is a problem of logic.

(1) Deductive method concerns the gaining of conclusions from premises with a sense of necessity attached to the procedure (*q.v.* Deduction; Syllogism; Aristotle 1, 5).

(2) Inductive method concerns the gaining of conclusions from premises with a sense of probability attached to the procedure (*q.v.* Induction; Mill's Methods; Probability).

(3) Peirce suggested a method of Abduction in which hypotheses were generated from data (*q.v.* Abduction, C.S. Peirce 8).

B. Some combination of the methods of logic is used in coming to philosophical conclusions.

(4) Contrasting approaches to philosophy are discussed under the topic, Epistemology (*q.v.*).

(5) Contrasting systems of philosophy, embodying different approaches, are discussed under the heading Metaphysics (*q.v.*). Also see Dialectical Materialism.

C. Method in the sciences has been the subject of considerable discussion.

(6) For the natural sciences generally, the Hypothetico-Deductive Method is of importance. For this method *q.v.* Hypothesis (11) and Philosophy of Science (2).

(7) For various approaches to mathematics *q.v.* Mathematics as well as Formal Logic.

(8) For approaches to the Social Sciences *q.v.* Induction, Retroduction, and Mill's Methods.

METONYMY.

Q.v. Metaphor.

METTRIE, JULIAN OFFRAY DE LA.

Q.v. La Mettrie.

MEYERSON, ÉMILE. 1858–1933.

French philosopher. Born in Lublin, Poland. Educated in Germany as a scientist. From 1882 he lived in Paris. Although never a professor he became the center of an academic group.

Principal writings: *Identity and Reality* (T), 1908; *Explanation in the Sciences*, 2 vols., 1921; *The Ways of Thought*, 3 vols., 1931; *Essays*, 1936.

(1) It is the tendency of reason to unify. In the process it must simplify, eliminate from consideration, identify. Carried to its natural extreme the goal of explanation would be the homogeneous rounded sphere of Parmenides. Science tends to try to eliminate the factor of time, and assimilate the world to space.

(2) But the world retains irreducible elements. Even time is incapable of elimination. And some of the eliminations we make in theory, such as the elimination of secondary qualities from the world, remain within experience. Nor can one free oneself from the uneasy conflict of experience with reason.

MEZUZAH.

A Hebrew term meaning "door post." In Hebrew custom a tube containing a scroll on which are inscribed *Deuteronomy* 6:4–9 and 11:13–21. These passages not only enjoin love of and faith in the one God, but ask that these words be written on the doorposts of the house. The orthodox response was to attach the tubed scroll to the door post at the entrance of the house.

MICROCOSM.

Q.v. Macrocosm.

MIDDLE TERM.

Q.v. Syllogism (3); Quantification Theory (1).

MIDRASH.

A Hebrew term meaning "explanation." A body of exegetical material on the Jewish scriptures. Q.v. Judaism (2c).

MILESIANS, THE.

Q.v. Thales; Anaximander; and Anaximenes. The earliest Greek philosophers on record, they are known as the Milesians from the name of their city-state, Miletus, on the coast of Asia Minor. They directed their investigations toward the discovery of a primary element at the base of all things.

MILHAUD, GASTON. 1858–1918.

French philosopher. Taught at the University of Paris beginning in 1909. Influenced by Comte and Renouvier, Milhaud stressed the creative or constituent role of human awareness in the development of scientific ideas. His emphasis opposes both positivism and phenomenalism. In this respect he may be compared with Poincaré and Duhem.

Principal writings: Essay on the Conditions and Limits of Logical Certitude, 1894; The Rational, 1898; Positivism and the Progress of the Spirit, 1902; The Philosophy of Charles Renouvier, 1927; Studies on Cournot, 1927.

MILL, JAMES. 1773–1836.

Scotch philosopher. Studied at Edinburgh. Worked for the East India Company. A disciple of Jeremy Bentham, he became one of the leaders in the Utilitarian movement, exercising some influence over the group of Philosophical Radicals (q.v.) and their program of reform. He followed and, in some respects, developed the Associationist Psychology of Hartley (q.v.) and Hume (q.v.). It is interesting that James Mill continued Ockham's view of connotation (q.v. William of Ockham 4), holding that, e.g., the expression "white horse" denotes the color "white" and connotes "horse." This is not, of course, the modern usage which later, in fact, however, was developed by his son, John Stuart Mill (q.v. 11), beginning from his father's position.

Principal writings: History of India, 3 vols., 1817; Elements of Political Economy, 1821; Analysis of the Phenomena of the Human Mind, 1829.

MILL, JOHN STUART. 1806–1873.

English philosopher. Born in London. Educated by his father, his studies of Greek began at the age of three, and Latin at the age of eight. By the age of fourteen he had completed a rigorous classical education. At about this time he discovered Jeremy Bentham (q.v.) whose writings gave him "a creed, a doctrine, a philosophy . . . a religion." In 1823 he began to work for the East India Company and was in charge of relations with Indian states from 1836 until 1856 when the British government took charge of the company. He served in Parliament from 1865–68. Through most of his adult life, beginning in 1831, he cherished the intellectual companionship of Mrs. Harriet Taylor whom he finally married in 1852, three years after the death of her husband. He gave to Mrs. Taylor major credit for his own intellectual achievements. Harriet Taylor died in 1858.

Principal writings: A System of Logic, 2 vols., 1843; Essays On Some Unsettled Questions of Political Economy, 1844; Principles of Political Economy, 1848; On Liberty, 1859; Representative Government, 1861; Utilitarianism, 1863; Examination of Sir William Hamilton's Philosophy, 1865; Auguste Comte and Positivism, 1865; The Subjection of Women, 1869; Autobiography, 1873; Three Essays on Religion, 1874.

(1) Accepting the view of his father, and that of Jeremy Bentham, that the principles of association elaborated in the work of the British empiricists and developed by David Hartley (q.v.) provide the most promising approach to explanation in every area of life and thought, Mill became the chief representative of Empiricism in the 19th century. (Since he associated the term "empiricism" with miscellaneous information, however, he termed his view "experimentalism.")

(2) One consequence of his approach was that Mill regarded inductive inference as the sole part of logic productive of knowledge. He understands deduction to be either merely verbal transformation, as in the case of immediate inference, or as in the case of the syllogism, a summing up of past inductive results encouraging

one to infer beyond these results to new cases. The sentence "All humans are mortal" sums up our past experience; as a result we have confidence in its application to a new case. He likewise regarded every syllogism as a *petitio principii*, or circular argument, its conclusion already stated in the premises (*q.v.* Logic 20).

(3) He held empirical judgments to be merely probable, and necessary judgments to be merely verbal—concerning the manner in which we use our terms and the meanings we assign them. Definitions are nominal, giving us information only about the use of language. Not believing mathematics to consist of verbal operations, Mill takes the other alternative and mathematics, too, becomes inductive. If mathematical equations represent generalizations from experience, it would be possible to have a world in which 2 plus 2 equal 5. If whenever two pairs of things were put together, one had a pair and a triplet, mathematics would be revised to take account of this result. One might claim that there is some logical certainty in the operations of mathematics; but we have already seen that deduction itself rests on inductive probabilities. Furthermore, logical certainty, when not merely verbal, translates into psychological certainty. And, indeed, he regarded logic as a subdivision of the field of psychology. One might charge that one does not really encounter mathematical entities—units, points, lines—in experience. Mill answers that one does encounter such entities, by restricting one's attention to the unitary, positional, linear aspects of things.

(4) Inductive inference advances knowledge through the discovery of causal connections among phenomena. Mill elaborated a set of methods, based on the principles of association, which individuals had long used to separate causal relations from other phenomena. These devices are known as Mill's Methods. (Also *q.v.* Francis Bacon 3).

(a) Method of Agreement: Where two or more instances of a phenomenon have only one circumstance in common, that circumstance is the cause (or effect) of the phenomenon.

Circumstance	Phenomenon
abcde	x
afghi	x
ajklm	x
anopq	x

(b) Method of Difference: If an instance in which the phenomenon occurs, and an instance in which it does not occur, have all circumstances in common save one, that one occurring only in the former, the circumstance in question is the effect, or cause, or part of the effect or cause, of the phenomenon.

Circumstance	Phenomenon
abcde	x
-bcde	—

(c) Joint Method of Agreement and Difference: (Combine the explanations of the separate methods of Agreement and of Difference.)

Circumstance	Phenomenon
abcde	x
afghi	x
ajklm	x
anopq	x

Circumstance	Phenomenon
-bcde	—
-fghi	—
-jklm	—
-nopq	—

(d) Method of Concomitant Variations: If some part of the set of circumstances varies as the phenomenon varies, this part of the set of circumstances is causally related to the phenomenon.

Circumstance	Phenomenon
abcd	Y
⊳bcd	⊰Y
∇bcd	⅄
⊲bcd	⋎

(e) Method of Residues: Take away from the phenomenon what is known by previous inductions to be the effect of certain antecedents; the residue of the phenomenon is the effect of the remaining antecedents.

Circumstances	Phenomenon
abcd	wxyz
abc	wxy
ab	wx
a	w

(5) But the validity of these methods can be accepted only if nature is orderly in such a fashion that given similar causes, similar effects will occur, and dissimilar effects given dissimilar causes. What is the ground for our confidence in the order of nature? In Mill's language, we are adhering to the principles of the uniformity of nature. But if we must believe in the uniformity of nature in order to understand how causal inductions can be made successfully, and if all knowledge is inductive, so that we know of the uniformity of nature by induction, is that not a circle? Mill answers that there is only the appearance of a circle, and this for the reason that the uniformity of nature is attested to by every induction we make, and by all experience. A causal induction tells us both of the cause of the phenomenon we are investigating, and that nature is uniform. Hence, the general principle by virtue of its massive verification can be properly used to support causal induction.

(6) In a manner similar to his antecedents among the British empiricists, Mill comes close at times to sheer phenomenalism, interpreting the world in terms of its phenomena. He defines cause as an "invariable and unconditional antecedent," even though his agreement with Aristotle that chance exists only at the intersection of causal chains seems to require a more substantial notion of causality; in the same phenomenalistic vein he defines matter as "the permanent possibility of sensation." Similarly, he might have interpreted mind as a series of feelings; but since the mind is aware of itself as a past and a future, it cannot be simply regarded as a series. Memory and anticipation show mind to be something more.

(7) Not only did Mill accept the principles of associationalism, but also the hedonic corollary to this point of view. Following Bentham, he explained human activity in terms of the "greatest happiness" principle. But he, at the same time, introduced an important qualification into Bentham's application of the principle. Where Bentham (q.v. 1–2) made the criterion of ethics the production of the greatest amount of pleasure or the least amount of pain, Mill made a distinction between lower and higher, or less and

more valuable, pleasures. "It is better to be a Socrates dissatisfied than a pig satisfied." The consequence is that one no longer seeks to determine which act would yield the greatest sum of pleasure; it is the greatest sum of higher pleasure that one seeks.

(8) The qualitative change introduced by Mill into the Utilitarian ethic is paralleled in his social philosophy. For example, in the striking essay "On Liberty" he argued for a maximum of liberty in society in order that new truths, and novel contributions to society, not be prematurely crushed. In his work on government he argued for a type of representative government in which the better educated and more responsible would have a greater voice than other members of society. His concern in both cases was the tyranny of the majority, a force favoring the conventional.

(9) Mill's writings on religion tend toward a religion of humanity, influenced by the view of Auguste Comte (q.v. 3). But where Comte is atheistic, Mill suggests that we entertain the idea of a deity who is benevolent but limited in power. The argument from design, indeed, provides some evidence for this view. The cosmological argument fails, however, since an infinite regress is more reasonable than a first cause. So far as personal immortality is concerned, there is no evidence either way.

(10) Mill's emphasis on principles of association would lead one to suppose that he would incline toward nominalism (q.v.). In fact, in the Examination he states that properties are universals invariable in nature, and that there are also invariable connections between universals. Both concepts and general terms, he holds, must be construed in comprehension, that is to say intensionally rather than extensionally. These decisions, added to the phenomenalism of his system, require us to class Mill with the defenders of conceptualism (q.v.) in his interpretation of universals.

(11) It was Mill who set contemporary usage for the terms "connotation" and "denotation," relating the former to the characteristics determining the object named, and the latter to the object or objects so named.

MILLENARIANISM.

The doctrine of *Revelation* 20 that Christ will return and rule the earth for 1000 years, prior to the resurrection of the dead and the creation of a new heaven and a new earth.

MILL'S METHODS.

Q.v. John Stuart Mill (4); Induction (5).

MILTON, JOHN. 1608–1674.

English poet. Born in London. Studied at Cambridge. Although trained as an Anglican, he became a Puritan and, indeed, beginning in 1649 served until the Restoration as Latin secretary to the Council of State, overseeing all diplomatic correspondence which at this time was still conducted in Latin. The blindness which descended upon him in 1652 required a gradual curtailment of his activities. His greatest poetic achievements came after this time. Our interest here is in his philosophical and theological ideas.

Principal philosophical writings: *The Reason of Church Government*, 1641; *Areopagitica*, 1644; *Doctrine and Discipline of Divorce*, 1644; *Of Education*, 1644; *Eikonoklastes*, 1649; *Treatise on Christian Doctrine*, 1825 (a manuscript initially proscribed and then forgotten).

(1) Rejecting Calvinism and its corollary of predestination, Milton held that every human has free will, and thus the power to choose good over evil. This power is a gift, of God, part of the grace which puts salvation within human reach.

(2) One of the major Miltonic themes, no less of his poetry than of his prose work, is the attainment of true liberty. This is also the achievement of character, and involves the experience of and rejection of evil. The choice of good over evil is the choice of the spiritual and divine over their opposites.

(3) One's guide in this undertaking is in fact the external and internal scriptures. The Bible contains God's revelation presented in such fashion that fallible men can understand it. In addition there is an internal scripture in the individual conscience, although imperfectly sensed. Under the leading of the Holy Spirit this internal scripture can be sensed more clearly since it is the remnant of the law of nature given to man by God before the fall.

(4) On the ground that it is lacking in Scriptural authority, Milton denies the validity of the Trinity. He believes in the Son and Holy Spirit, but as creations of the one God and thus not sharing in His august status.

MIMAMSA.

Q.v. Purva Mimamsa.

MIMESIS.

A Greek term meaning "imitation." (1) When Plato (*q.v.* 9) held that "time is the moving image of eternity," he was saying that the world is an image or an imitation of the eternal forms or ideas. (2) When the same philosopher held in his *Republic* that art is "an imitation of an imitation," he was elaborating the mimetic theory of art (*q.v.* Plato 5g). (3) When Aristotle (*q.v.* 13) held that art imitated not necessarily an actual thing, but a possible or probable thing, he broadened the mimetic theory almost beyond recognition. (4) It is sometimes said that the mimetic theory of art was dominant in the 18th century. The work on art by Abbé Du Bos, *Critical Reflections on Poetry, Painting and Music* (T), first published in 1719, and often reprinted, held to this conception. *Q.v.* Aesthetics (2, 3).

MIND-BODY PROBLEM.

One of the most persistent problems in the history of philosophy, the mind-body problem concerns how the relationship between mind and body is to be understood. Since the description of mental content is quite different from the description of physical processes, can the two be considered an identity, or can they not? The problem is so deeply rooted that discussion of its possible solutions is tantamount to a discussion of the basic philosophical systems.

(1) Plato (*q.v.* 3), of course, held to a dualism of the mind and body, the former relating to changelessness and the latter to change. The dualism was continued by the Neoplatonists (*q.v.*). The question here is how there can be any interaction of the two in any sense. The views supporting such interaction are called Interactionist Theories, or simply Interactionism. Descartes (*q.v.* 8) likewise held to a dualism and described mind and body as

direct and complete opposites. He assumed the pineal gland to be the point of the interaction of mind and body. The Occasionalists (*q.v.*), not seeing how such extreme opposites could relate to each other in any sense, gave up the hope of any interaction. They invoked God to relate mind to body, intervening between every mental decision and the corresponding movement of the body.

(2) Aristotle (*q.v.* 7) has a different kind of alternative, deriving from his understanding of form and matter. What is form in one sense can be matter in another. Hence the physical body, although formed, is matter in relation to soul which is the form of the body. This view was held in the Middle Ages by Thomas Aquinas (*q.v.* 7) and many Scholastics.

(3) Among other alternatives is Materialism (*q.v.*) which holds that mind is simply brain, so that all processes are physical processes, and the point seems to be that there is then no mind-body problem. The alternative has been developed in the East (*q.v.* Carvaka) as well as in the West (*q.v.* Hobbes, Holbach).

(4) Berkeley and other Idealists solve the mind-body problem by doing away with matter. If only minds and mental contents exist, there can hardly be a problem of the relation of mind to body (*q.v.* Idealism).

(5) A number of points of view can be classed under that of Psychophysical Parallelism (*q.v.*). The term was introduced by Fechner (*q.v.* 2) to characterize the position that every psychical event has its physical counterpart, and the two exist in a one-to-one correspondence. In addition to Fechner, who however favored the psychical side of things, the position has been held by Spinoza (*q.v.* 8) and Leibniz (*q.v.* 6–7).

(6) The alternative of Epiphenomenalism (*q.v.*) recognizes a qualitative distinction between a mental quality, *e.g.*, the sense of justice, and the neural connection that carries this quality. But this view holds that the mental quality is without power. All force lies in the physical system.

(7) There is also the alternative of Neutral Monism (*q.v.*) which holds that mind and body are the same, but organized in different ways or looked at from different standpoints. There are many holding the

view. Paulsen (*q.v.*), for example, calls his view Monistic Idealism, and understands mind and body to be the outer and inner aspects of the same reality.

(8) Merleau-Ponty (*q.v.* 1) regards the mental and the physical as two of many conceptual levels relating to the study of human behavior.

(9) Strawson (*q.v.* 3) argues that "person" is the primitive concept and both mental states and physical properties are ascribable to it.

(10) Identity Theory (*q.v.*) maintains that a relation of identity obtains between mental phenomena and brain events.

(11) Searle (*q.v.* 3) dismisses the problem, distinguishing between a macro (mind) and micro (brain) level with the former as the effect of the latter.

MIND, MOMENTARY.
Q.v. Leibniz (6).

MIND-STUFF.
Q.v. Citta; Clifford; Eddington; Romanes.

MING-CHIA.
Q.v. The Chinese "Logicians."

MINIMI.
From the Latin *minimus* ("least"). A mendicant order founded by St. Francis of Paula in 1453 and patterned after the Friars Minor of St. Francis of Assissi (*q.v.* 4).

MINISTRY.
Q.v. Schillebeeckx (8).

MINKOWSKI, HERMANN. 1864–1909.
German mathematician and physicist. Born in Russia. Educated at Königsberg and Berlin. Taught at Bonn, Königsberg, Zurich, and Göttingen. Known as Einstein's teacher of mathematics, he provided the latter an important bridge between mathematics and physics.

Selected writings: *Geometry of Numbers*, 1896; *Fundamental Equations for Electromagnetic Occurrences*, 1907–8; *Time and Space*, 1909.

(1) Joining the three dimensions of space to a fourth dimension, time, Minkowski regarded the four dimensions as coordinates whose specification provided a precise location for anything whatever. Such location required a set of world-points which became world-lines by virtue of the temporal dimension.

(2) All events and objects are four-dimensional, with a position on some set of world-lines. Since the dimension of time includes both past and future, all events are determinately present in the space-time continuum.

MINOR PREMISE.
Q.v. Syllogism (3).

MINOR TERM.
Q.v. Syllogism (3).

MINSKY, MARVIN.
Q.v. Artificial Intelligence (3).

MINUCIUS FELIX, MARCUS.
Late 2nd- and early 3rd-century, A.D. Christian Apologist. The first of the Apologists to write in Latin, Minucius Felix, who wrote in dialogue form, shows the influence of Cicero. He opposed the polytheism of popular faith with a description of divine omnipresence. His point of view stressed the unity between Christianity and Greek philosophy. He found the Trinity (Father, Son, and Holy Ghost) prefigured in the concepts of *Nous*, *Logos*, and *Pneuma*, respectively, of Greek philosophy. Indeed, he held that the Christians are philosophers and the philosophers, insofar as they adhere to beliefs in immortality and monotheism, are Christians. The only incapacity of the philosophers in this respect is their failure to notice that the Christian purity of life is the practical correlate to the Greek insistence on purity of thought. *Q.v.* Apologists (7).

Principal writings: *Octavius*.

MIRACLE.
The term refers to that which causes wonder. It is ordinarily taken to apply to an event which cannot be understood as part of the natural order. Miracles have gathered around all of the great religious leaders, and yet most of them—including Confucius, Lao-Tzu, Buddha, Mohammed, and Christ in some of his sayings—protested against miracles and refused, at least at times, to give their followers a sign. Within the philosophical tradition there is disagreement concerning whether or not miracles are possible.

(1) The early Christian Apologists (q.v.) sometimes argued for miracles in support of the claims of Christianity.

(2) St. Augustine (q.v. 11) held that miracles are not contrary to nature but only to our knowledge of nature. There is a harmony between nature and the miraculous, since a miracle or portent, should it occur, would occur by the will of God, and nature is itself nothing but the will of God.

(3) St. Thomas Aquinas (q.v. 1) and the Schoolmen continued in the same vein. They distinguished two orders in nature, that order known to us and the order known to God. Those events are properly called miracles which contradict the lower order, while expressing the higher, *i.e.*, that order known to God.

(4) Spinoza (q.v. 8), following Gersonides (q.v. 7), argued that miracles cannot happen. Since the laws of nature are the decrees of God, any violation of the order of nature would mean that God is contradicting himself.

(5) Deism (q.v.) opposed the possibility of miracles on similar grounds. According to deists God created the world to run by fixed laws, and after its creation never intervened Q.v. Thomas Woolston.

(6) Joseph Butler (q.v. 2) answered the Deists essentially in terms of Aquinas and the Schoolmen.

(7) David Hume (q.v. 8) argued that the greater the marvel, the more substantial must be the confirming evidence. But since the great bulk of our evidence attests to the laws of nature, the exceptional testimonies to miracle can never outweigh this experience. Hence, miracles can never be proved, nor even rendered probable.

(8) Schleiermacher (q.v. 4) attempted to combine the two warring ideas, holding that while nature may contain the cause of the miracle, the event occurs only when God calls it forth.

(9) 19th-century historical and Biblical criticism led to numerous interpretations of the life of Christ. Among those writing on the subject we may notice the view of David Strauss (q.v.) that miracles are legendary accretions symbolic of metaphysical ideas, and the view of Renan (q.v.) that miracles were a violence done to Jesus by his age.

MISES, RICHARD VON.
Q.v. Probability (10).

MISHNAH.

A Hebrew term meaning "instruction." A summary of Jewish oral law. Q.v. Judaism (2b).

MITHRAISM.

A religion of great popularity in the Roman Empire in the centuries immediately prior to the Christian era and becoming by 307 A.D. the official religion of the empire. But the victory of Constantine occurred in 312 A.D., and thereafter Mithraism languished. The God, Mithra, of the religion seems to have been derived from the Mitra of the Vedic religion, and to have journeyed to the Mediterranean through Asia Minor. It became the religion of the military forces and was carried by them throughout the empire.

In the mythos of the religion, Mithra slays the great bull and due to its generative power vegetable life springs forth on earth. The sacrifice is dedicated to the sun god who also plays a role in the religion. In its later stages the Roman emperor was the representative of the sun god on earth.

The central act of worship of the religion seems to have been the sacrifice of the bull, whose life-giving blood gave the worshippers a pledge of immortality. There were seven grades of membership with initiations and ceremonies at each stage. Q.v. Mystery Religions (5).

ML.

Q.v. Quine (1).

MNEMIC CAUSATION.

Q.v. Russell (9).

MODALISM.

The theological doctrine that the Son and the Holy Ghost are but "modes" of the Father. Q.v. Sabellius; Monarchianism.

MODALITY.

In logic, the alternatives for classifying propositions with respect to their relations to existence. The three widely recognized modes are those of possibility, actuality, and necessity. Letting "p" stand for any proposition, the mode of possibility is expressed by "It is possible that p," the mode of actuality simply by "p," the mode of necessity by "It is necessary that p." These propositions and their negations are the modal propositions.

(1) Aristotle (q.v. 10) speaks of four modal propositions: those which are possible, impossible, contingent, and necessary. The contingent modality is that which may or may not be actual. Hence, the mode of contingency presupposes the modality of possibility. The necessary, in turn, has the modalities of both the possible and the actual within it. For Aristotle, reasoning with modal propositions belongs to the theory of the syllogism (q.v.).

(2) The Stoic and Megarian contributions to the theory of modality essentially anticipated the contemporary locus of modality as a function of the Propositional Calculus (q.v. Modal Logic). Diodorus Cronos (q.v. 2) is credited with having introduced a time variable into modal propositions. Philo of Megara (q.v. 2), who anticipated in part the Propositional Calculus, offered a definition of possibility resting on consistency. Chrysippus (q.v. 2), who anticipated the entire calculus, defined the possible as that which will be true given the appropriate circumstances, and the necessary as that which is and will be true no matter what the circumstances.

(3) The Scholastics continued the Aristotelian development of modality. They used the terms *modus* and *dictum* to identify the two parts of a modal proposition. The *modus* or mode of the proposition is indicated by the initial words "It is possible that," "It is necessary that," etc. The *dictum* (or expression or statement) of the modal proposition is the proposition following the modal phrase. It is the proposition "p" in "It is possible that 'p.'"

(4) Kant (q.v. 3) defined the possible, actual, and necessary as that which satisfies the formal, material, and universal conditions of experience, respectively.

(5) It was C.I. Lewis (q.v. 1) who put all of this together into a system of modal logic (q.v.). The logic was built on the basis of the Propositional Calculus, and that approach has been standard since his time.

(6) Carnap (q.v. 8) distinguished between the modal property of a proposition and the semantic property of the sentence which expresses it. The proposition is said to be possible, contingent, necessary (and the negations of these) when the expressing sentence is "not-L-

false," "factually true," "L-true" (and their negations), respectively, where "L" stands for "logically."

(7) Reichenbach (*q.v.* 5) identified necessity with nomological statements; impossibility thus became their denial, and possibility the inapplicability of such statements.

(8) Contemporary discussion turns on the distinction between modality *de re* and modality *de dicto*, *i.e.*, modality as a characteristic of a thing and modality as a characteristic of a statement or proposition. The Aristotelian-Thomistic doctrine of essence holds that essential properties are necessary (given the existence of the substance in question); therefore, one can speak of necessity *de re*. Necessity *de dicto*, is to be found in any true statement beginning "It is necessary that...." The truth values of many statements change depending upon the alternative they are held to represent, *e.g.*, "Necessarily, the father of Cain is Adam" is true *de dicto* but false *de re*. In a comparable sense the modes of possibility and actuality can be discussed *de re* or *de dicto*.

MODAL LOGIC.

Although modal logic has received its greatest development in the 20th century with the work especially of C.I. Lewis (*q.v.* 1), its history goes back at least to Aristotle. This material is treated under the heading, Modality (*q.v.*).

A. As it is understood today, Modal logic uses as its base the Propositional Calculus (*q.v.*), adding operators for necessity, possibility, strict implication, strict co-implication, as well as rules for their introduction and elimination.

(1) We introduce the symbol "□" to express necessity and the symbol "◇" to express possibility. "□p" will mean "p is necessarily true," and "◇p" will mean "p is possibly true." Introducing the tilde "~" for "not," "◇p" can be expressed as "~□~p," and "□p" as "~◇~p."

(2) We introduce the symbol "⊰" to express strict implication. "p⊰q" will mean "p strictly implies q." This is a stronger form of implication than material implication (*q.v.*). Rather than merely asserting "p ⊃ q" ("p implies q") it asserts "□ (p ⊃ q)."

(3) We introduce the symbol "≡" to express strict coimplication. "p ≡ q" will

mean "p is strictly equivalent to q." This is a stronger form of equivalence than "p≡q," the equivalence of the Propositional Calculus. One has "p≡q" when "p ⊰ q" and "q ⊰ p."

(4) In addition to the above, we introduce "·" for "and" and "v" for "or," as well as the transformations of the Propositional Calculus. With these schemata it is possible to express and evaluate arguments containing in their premises and conclusions the modalities "it is possible that," "it is necessary that," and their negations.

B. The recent developments of modal logic are highly complex. The following items relate part of that development.

(5) It is said that one of C.I. Lewis' motives for experimenting with strict implication (p strictly implies q if it cannot be the case that p is true and q is false) was to solve the paradoxes of material implication (*q.v.* Truth Tables 4). It was clear to him at once that new paradoxes arose (namely, that "A proposition which is self contradictory or impossible implies any proposition," and "A proposition which is necessarily true is implied by any proposition"). Paradoxes of strict implication apart, however, Lewis (*q.v.* 1) experimented with numerous systems of modal logic, numbered S1 to S8, preferring one of the weaker systems (S2).

(6) Other systems have appeared since Lewis's time: system T, emerging from Kurt Gödel's work; system M from that of G.H. Von Wright, system Q from A.N. Prior.

(7) Beginning with S2 Ruth Barcan Marcus introduced the "all" and "some" quantifiers of first order predicate logic, establishing quantified modal logic ("Functional Calculus of First Order Based on Strict Implication," 1946).

(8) S4 and S5 have received much attention. Saul A. Kripke developed an "extension" of S5, also involving S4 and M ("Semantical Considerations on Modal Logic," 1963). He finds the positions of Stig Kanger (*Probability in Logic*, 1957) and Jaakko Hintikka ("Modality and Quantification," 1961) closest to his "present theory," although others are also cited (in "Semantical Analysis of Modal Logic," 1963).

(9) In his two logic books C.I. Lewis devotes 33 pages to Leibniz, without any

use of "possible world" locutions. Kripke introduces the ordered triple (G, K, R) where K is a set, R a reflexive relation, and G is a member of K. His interest is in set-theoretic considerations, and his explanation is that K is the set of "all possible worlds," G is the "real world," and R is the relation between any two possible worlds.

(10) While possible world semantics are now commonplace among modal logicians, there is a debate over how "possible world" is to be interpreted. Some, like Robert Adams ("Theories of Actuality," 1974), hold possible worlds to be no more than "maximal consistent sets of propositions," or "world stories," others grant them ontological status.

(11) David Lewis (*q.v.* 1–4) dubs his position "genuine modal realism," and views actuality as indexical, what the inhabitants of each possible world call their world, the objects of each world having counterparts in others.

(12) Robert Stalnaker (*q.v.*) who claims to hold a modest realism with respect to possible worlds states that the possible worlds semantics is a "projection strategy" from the requirements of epistemology in explicating "causal and counterfactual locutions."

Q.v. Counterfactual Conditionals.

MODE.

From the Latin *modus* meaning "manner." In philosophy the term refers to the manner of existence of a thing or substance.

(1) Descartes (*q.v.* 8) regarded minds and bodies as the two basic created substances. Each substance has an essence or attribute; that of mind is thought and that of body is extension. The modes of the existence of minds and bodies extend over the accidental properties which may further characterize them. For Descartes, God is, of course, the primal substance; but Descartes did not make it clear how modes and attributes might relate to God.

(2) Spinoza (*q.v.* 1–2, 7) tightened up the framework so that thought and extension are attributes of that which is substance, strictly speaking, *i.e.*, God. Minds and bodies, then, are no longer regarded as substances, but as modes of the divine attributes.

(3) Locke (*q.v.* 5) understood by modes those ideas whose objects cannot exist by themselves. He divided modes into the categories of "simple modes" and "mixed modes," depending upon their complexity.

MODERATE REALISM.

Q.v. Realism (1); Universals (3, 7, 13, 16).

MODERATUS OF GADES. 1st cent. A.D.

Greek philosopher. A neo-Pythagorean along with his contemporary, Apollonius of Tyana (*q.v.*). Moderatus held numbers to stand for principles, thus providing a key to the interpretation of the intelligible realities,

Principal writings: *Pythagorean Scholiae*.

MODERNISM.

Although the term suggests that anyone who takes the norms of modern thought and life as decisive in the interpretation of any matter would be a modernist and believe in modernism, the term in fact has an almost exclusive reference to religious thought.

(1) Among Protestants it stands for a movement rising from the application of modern critical methods to the study of Biblical texts and to the history of dogma. Following the lead of the German church historian Adolf Harnack (*q.v.*) and the no less outstanding German theologian Albrecht Ritschl (*q.v.*), the movement tended to stress the ethical and experiential aspects of Christianity over its creedal and dogmatic aspects.

(2) For the Catholic Church it is the name of a movement of naturalism, some of its roots identical with those in the similar movement in Protestantism, which had begun to take hold among the clergy in the last years of the 19th century and the first years of the 20th century. One of the French modernists was Alfred Loisy (*q.v.*). In 1903 his books were placed on the Index. In 1907 Pope Pius X condemned 65 propositions held by modernists, and in addition issued an encyclical criticizing modernism and directing bishops to examine the tenets of professors under their jurisdiction and books used by students. Vigilance committees were to be appointed to prevent

further inroads of false doctrine. In 1910 he ordered every priest of the church to take an "Oath against Modernism." The requirement is still in force and, indeed, has been extended.

MODES OF BEING.
Q.v. Weiss.

MODUS.
Latin term meaning "mode." Used by the Scholastics in relation to modal propositions (*q.v.* Modality 3).

MODUS PONENS.
A Latin phrase meaning the "mode of affirming." This is a mode of the hypothetical syllogism with the form "If p then q; p; therefore q."
Q.v. Propositional Calculus (3); Syllogism (9); Truth Tables (6b).

MODUS PONENDO TOLLENS.
A Latin phrase meaning the "mode of denying by affirming." This is a mode of the Disjunctive Syllogism with the form "Either A or B; A; therefore, not B" or the form "Either A or B; B; therefore, not A." The mode is valid only in the cases of a strong disjunction where "either-or" has the sense of "not both" *i.e.*, "Not both A and B" or "A and B cannot be true together." This form of disjunction is not basic to the Propositional Calculus where the weaker form of disjunction, called Alternation, is central (*q.v. Modus Tollendo Ponens*); but the form is treated in traditional logic (*q.v.* Syllogism 12).

MODUS TOLLENDO PONENS.
A Latin phrase meaning the "mode of affirming by denying." It is a mode of the alternative syllogism with the form "Either A or B; not A; therefore B" or the form "Either A or B; not B; therefore A." In the Propositional Calculus (*q.v.* 6) it is called the Disjunctive Syllogism. *Q.v.* Syllogism (11); Truth Tables (7a).

MODUS TOLLENDO TOLLENS.
A Latin phrase meaning the "mode of denying by denying." This is a mode of the hypothetical syllogism with the form "If p then q; not q; therefore, not-p." *Q.v.* Propositional Calculus (4); Syllogism (10); Truth Tables (7b).

MOHAMMED (MUHAMMAD). 570–632.
Founder of Islam. Born in Mecca. Believing that there is but one God, and that his name is Allah, Mohammed at the age of 40 began receiving revelations. These convinced him that he had been called to serve as the prophet of Allah. The revelations continued over a period of 23 years. Written down by Mohammed, they form the Qur'an, sacred book of Islam. In the first year of his active ministry, his converts numbered only eight, including his wife and adopted son, and after three years no more than twenty. The turning point came when he decided to overthrow the idols of Mecca. The action aroused so much opposition that he was forced to flee Mecca, where he had preached for a decade with little result. The flight, called the great Hejira, but perhaps better translated as the breaking of relations, marked his transition from Mecca to Medina, which he reached on Sept. 24, 622. In recognition of the Hejira the Islamic calendar begins from June 16, the start of the Arabian year in which the move to Medina occurred. In Medina his role in bringing many of the clans into confederation, diminishing the chronic instability of the area, allowed him to direct the energies of his group outwardly, thus combining religious and military elements in a single organization. In Medina he was able to build both a mosque and an army. This became a characteristic of the movement. From his base at Medina he finally brought Mecca under his control, effecting the reform he had promised and instituting the sole worship of Allah. By the end of his life he had unified Arabia by this method, and Islam had already begun its sweep of the Near East.

MOHISM.
Q.v. Moism.

MOIRAI.
The Greek goddesses of fate, presiding over initiation, marriage, death.

MOISM.
Chinese philosophical movement, resting on the doctrine of universal love, and providing the chief alternative to

Confucianism between the 5th and 3rd centuries B.C. The movement disappeared soon after the 3rd century. The writings of the 5th century philosopher Mo Tzu (*q.v.*), provided the stimulus for this movement.

MOKṢA (MOKSHA).

Sanskrit term meaning "release or deliverance." The term refers to the state of enlightenment which is the goal of all Indian religions. The term first appears in the *Upanishads* where it undergoes a long development. Its basic sense is that of discernment of the identity between the God Brahman and one's own inner self. It also develops into the sense of self-liberation and complete autonomy. In the *Bhagavad-Gita* (*q.v.*) it becomes a means of liberation for those of every class, including women. The idea of *moksha* is likewise central to Buddhist and Jainist thought. *Q.v.* Śankara (1, 5, 11).

MOLESCHOTT, JACOB. 1822–1893.

German philosopher. Born in Holland. A professor of physiology who taught in Heidelberg, Zurich, and later in Rome, Moleschott argued for materialism at a time when the issue was alive and involved in the further question of the freedom of scientific inquiry. His principal doctrines included the assertion of an inseparable bond between force and matter, the physical nature of consciousness, the principle of the conservation of matter, the belief in hard determinism, and a utilitarian ethic based on pleasure. *Q.v.* Materialism (11).

Principal writings: *The Circuit of Life*, 1852.

MOLINA, ENRIQUE.

Q.v. Latin American Philosophy (10).

MOLINA, LUIS DE. 1535–1600.

Spanish Scholastic. Born in Cuenca. Entered the Jesuit Order in 1553. Educated at Coimbra. Taught in Coimbra and Evora.

Principle writings: *The Concord of Free Will with the Gift of Grace*, 1588; *On Justice and Law*, 6 vols., 1593–1609.

(1) In the controversy concerning how predestination and free will are compatible, Molina developed a view which invoked the *Scientia Media*, or middle knowledge. It had long been granted that God possesses knowledge both of existent things and pure possibilities. Molina's middle knowledge refers to God's knowledge of how individuals would respond under various sets of circumstances, including the offer of divine grace. Possessing such knowledge, God merely decrees the desired circumstances and the effect follows without limiting human freedom.

(2) Molinism had considerable influence in the 17th century. Suarez (*q.v.*) was influenced by it, and developed his doctrine of Congruism from it.

MOLINISM.

Q.v. Molina, Luis de (2).

MOLINOS, MIGUEL DE.

Q.v. Quietism.

MOLOCH.

Q.v. Gehenna.

MOMENT.

Q.v. Hegel (7).

MOMENTARINESS, DOCTRINE OF.

Q.v. Sarvastivada; Sautrantika.

MONAD.

From the Greek term *monas* meaning "unit."

(1) The term's first use was in Pythagorean number theory where it was the name of the first number of the series, and thus the number from which all other numbers were derived (*q.v.* Pythagoras 6–8).

(2) Giordano Bruno (*q.v.* 2) used the term as the name of the irreducible ontolo gical unit of which all else is made up.

(3) F.M. Van Helmont (*q.v.*) likewise developed a monadology, apparently on the basis of the thought of Paracelsus.

(4) Leibniz (*q.v.* 1) accepted this usage and gave the term its greatest currency in his *Monadology*.

(5) Kant (*q.v.*) elaborated a monadology in the pre-critical stages of his thought.

(6) Goethe (*q.v.* 4) accepted the Leibnizian monadology as the basis for an organic view of a dynamic nature.

(7) Lotze (*q.v.* 2) likewise interpreted reality from the standpoint of a monadology.

MONADOLOGY.

Q.v. Leibniz; Monad (2–7).

MONARCHIANISM. 2nd and 3rd cents. A. D.

A theological movement within the early Church stressing the unity of God. Two variants are distinguished within the movement, depending upon the interpretation given to the relation of Father and Son. Dynamistic Monarchians held Christ to be a man who became the Son of God due to the divine quality of His wisdom and power. The Alogi (q.v. Christology 1) and Paul of Samosata (q.v.) exemplify this variant. Modalistic Monarchians held that Father and Son were simply designations, names, or modes of the two relations in which the one God stands to the world, the one as Creator and the other as Savior. The Patripassianists (q.v.) and Sabellius (q.v.) are instances of this variant.

MONARCHY.

From the Greek *monos* ("alone") and *archein* ("to be first"). A form of government characterized by the rule of one person.

(1) For Aristotle (q.v. 12) monarchy is that one of the three approved forms where rule is in the hands of one man.

(2) Dante (q.v. 4) proposed a universal monarch to bring liberty to man and peace to the world.

(3) Hobbes (q.v. 9) defined monarchy as the form of government where the sovereign power is in the hands of one person. He argued that absolute monarchy is preferable to any more limited form. Also q.v. Filmer

(4) For Montesquieu (q.v. 6) the most viable form of state is that of the limited or constitutional monarchy.

MONASTICISM.

From the Greek *monazein* ("to be alone"). A discipline of life characterized by withdrawal from the world, meditation, self-abnegation and some degree of asceticism. Present in East and West, and in all religious traditions of long standing, monasticism begins in individual withdrawal—from the fourth stage of Hinduism (q.v. 3) to the Christian anchorites (from the Greek *anachorein*, "to retire") or hermits of the 3rd century A.D.

withdrawing into the Egyptian desert. St. Anthony the Hermit (c. 250–c. 355) is the most notable Christian instance of this type. But monasticism has always developed into ordered communities governed by an established rule of life. Such orders are to be found in Hinduism, all forms of Buddhism, in Judaism (the Hasidim), in Islam (the Dervishes), as well as in Christianity. St. Pachomius (c. 290–346) is credited with having established the first set of rules for Christian monasticism, and nine monasteries in the Egyptian desert. St. Benedict of Nursia (c. 480–c. 547), however, in developing the Benedictine Rule for the monastery at Monte Cassino, in Italy, is regarded as the real founder of Western monastic order. In addition to the Benedictines, a sampling of the names of Western monastic orders would include the Franciscans, Dominicans, Carmelites, Augustinian Hermits, and the Jesuits.

MONERA.

Q.v. Haeckel (1).

MONERGISM.

Q.v. Synergism.

MONIMUS OF SYRACUSE. 4th cent. B.C.

Greek philosopher. A disciple of Diogenes of Sinope (q.v.) as well as of Crates of Thebes (q.v.), Monimus defended the Cynic philosophy by parody and satire.

Principal writings: *On the Impulses*, 2 vols.; and an *Exhortation* to philosophy.

MONISM.

A term introduced by Christian Wolff (q.v. 6) in discussing the mind-body problem. He used the term to designate those philosophers who acknowledge only mind or only body. A number of qualifications are sometimes used.

(1) Parmenides (q.v.) and Spinoza (q.v. 1) can be said to represent substantival monism, *i.e.*, the view that whatever exists is a part of a single substance.

(2) Democritus (q.v. 1, 2), Leibniz (q.v. 1), and contemporary atomic theory may be taken to represent attributive monism, *i.e.*, the view that however many substances may exist they are all of a single kind.

(3) The denial of monism may commit one to Dualism (q.v. 2, 13) or Pluralism (q.v.; also James 8).

(4) On the other hand, one can apparently be a pluralist and a neutral monist. At least Russell (*q.v.* 9), building on a suggestion of William James, adhered for a time to a position he called Neutral Monism (*q.v*). It held that reality is neither mental nor physical but some neutral stuff capable of either type of organization. Ardigó (*q.v.* 3) anticipated both James and Russell in the point of view (but not the name), as indeed did Aloys Riehl (*q.v.* 2) who called his position "philosophical monism."

(5) For Anomalous Monism *q.v.* Davidson (1–4).

Also, *q.v.* Berlin (1–3).

MONOPHYSITISM.

The Christological doctrine, developing between the 5th and 7th centuries A.D. (*i.e.*, between the Councils of Chalcedon and Constantinople), that in Christ the divine and the human form a single nature. In the period indicated there were many formulations of the doctrine, leading in quite different directions; *e.g.*, two natures united in a single energy; or the attributes of Christ's natural body becoming so heightened by the presence of the *Logos* that it became sinless and incorruptible; or that in Christ's death God Himself suffered and died. The doctrine was rejected at the Council of Constantinople in 680.

MONOTHEISM.

From the Greek *mono* ("one") and *theos* ("god"). The doctrine or belief that there is but one god. The first monotheist may have been the Egyptian pharaoh, Ikhnaton (*c.* 1375–1358 B.C.), who worshipped the sun god, Aton, and sought unsuccessfully to bring all of Egypt into the sole worship of Aton. The names of other gods were replaced by the name "Aton" in all inscriptions. Within 25 years, however, Ikhnaton's successors had restored the old cults. In *Moses and Monotheism*, (1939) Freud (*q.v.*) credited Ikhnaton as the source of monotheism in Judaism. If, as some believe, Ikhnaton's position was one of Henotheism (*q.v.*) rather than monotheism, then it was in Judaism that monotheism was achieved. Christianity and Islam are likewise monotheistic.

For Indian monotheism *q.v.* Nanak.

MONOTHELITISM.

A Christological doctrine, developing in the 7th century A.D., to the effect that although Christ had two natures, He had but a single will. In 680 the Council of Constantinople condemned the doctrine, holding that as there are two natures there must be two wills, but the human will conforms itself in every way to the divine will.

MONTAGUE, RICHARD. 1930–1971.

American mathematician and philosopher. Born in Stockton, Calif. Educated at Berkeley. Taught at U.C.L.A.

Principal writings: *Formal Philosophy* (ed. R.H. Thomason), 1974.

(1) Holding that natural and artificial languages can be brought within a single mathematically precise theory, Montague utilized metamathematical materials in his analyses both of the structure of natural languages, and of philosophical problems.

(2) In his metamathematical (also called model-theoretic) approach to language, Montague focused on the problem of ambiguity. He understood grammar to be a list of basic expressions and a list of syntactic rules for making complex expressions from simpler ones. By selecting problematic fragments of English (Montague's natural language), and providing them with syntax, and a semantic and pragmatic interpretation, Montague worked to "disambiguate" the language fragment, so that each complex phrase would have one and only one syntactic structure. Syntax is the prelude to semantics or theory of reference, the latter involving theories of truth and entailment. Montague held that the appropriate semantics must be intensional (sense-related) rather than merely extensional (denotation-related). Intensionality led, in turn, to a possible-worlds semantics supporting the use of modal logic (a necessary statement being true in all possible worlds, a possible statement in at least some). Semantics requires pragmatics (involving contexts of use) to treat "indexical expressions" (*e.g.*, those including the pronoun "I") whose references become clear only in context.

(3) With respect to philosophical analysis, Montague argued that natural languages are inadequate, and that

augmented set theory is contemporary philosophy's proper theoretical framework. One justifies the language necessary for a given analysis, transcending set theory by, *e.g.*, the addition of individuals and empirical predicates. Within the augmented language (and enlarged philosophy) one is able to carry out new philosophical transactions.

MONTAGUE, W.P. 1873–1953.

American philosopher. Born in Chelsea, Mass. Harvard educated, he taught at Barnard and Columbia. Very active in the American epistemological movement known as New Realism (*q.v.*).

Principal writings: "A Realistic Theory of Truth and Error" in *The New Realism*, 1912; *The Ways of Knowing*, 1925; *Belief Unbound*, 1930; *The Ways of Things*, 1940.

(1) Believing that the object of knowledge must be independent of the knower, Montague imparted this point of view to the New Realists. He termed his own view Subsistential Realism, and argued that in addition to the reality of things one must find a way to admit into reality the entire set of things and non-things which function as the object of discourse. He distinguished the merely subsistent from that which has existential subsistence. False statements have the merely subsistent as their reference, while true statements refer to that which has existential subsistence.

(2) His solution to the mind-body problem invoked the doctrine of Animistic Materialism which allowed the conception of a physical soul, and the attribution of a limited psychic aspect to matter.

(3) God has the world as his body and is limited thereby. But this is a limitation in power, and not in goodness.

MONTAIGNE, MICHEL DE. 1533–1592.

French philosopher and essayist. Born in Périgord. Latin was his first language. He studied at Bordeaux and Toulouse. He served as a member of the local parliament and as mayor of Bordeaux for a number of years. Although he never formally held a position in the French court, he was active in attempting to settle Protestant-Catholic differences, and perhaps had some influence in the conversion of Henry IV to the Catholic faith.

Principal writings: *Travel Journal* (T), written in 1580–81, lost almost 200 years and then published from copies, the original having disappeared once more; *Essays* (T), 3 vols., 1588, including the *Apology for Raimond Sebond*.

(1) Humans in their present civilized state, neither value the good nor know the truth. They are vain, ignorant, and immoral. The life of the primitive, or the innocence of the animal, has much more to recommend it.

(2) Taking as his motto "*Que scais-je?*" or "What do I know?" Montaigne decided that with respect to knowledge the only reasonable position is that of skepticism, not the moderate skepticism of the Academy (*q.v.* Plato's Academy 2–3), but the radical skepticism called Pyrrhonism (*q.v.*). The former holds that while we cannot have certainty we can have probability, that some judgments are more probable than others. The Pyrrhonist view that all human reasoning is open to question, and sense experience shot through with variability, is more plausible. Hence, the Pyrrhonists quite correctly suspended judgment on all questions.

(3) Montaigne suggests two responses to this situation. The first recommends a return to nature. Reducing life to simplicity, one may control one's vaulting ambition and egoism, dropping the pretense that lofty truths are possible.

(4) The second response is to say that Pyrrhonism is the one philosophy compatible with the Christian faith. Giving up the pretense that human reason can reach truth, prepares one for the reception of divine grace. Thus it is that out of skepticism one reaches the position of faith, or fideism.

MONTANISM.

The name of a 2nd-century A.D. movement which, along with Gnosticism (*q.v.*), provided the early Church with its greatest challenge. The movement of Montanism, initially led by one Montanus (*q.v.*), was otherworldly, stressed the importance of martyrdom, and awaited the coming of the Lord. In response to this challenge the Church became Catholic, coming to terms with the world and learning to live within it. Although Montanus had begun his work in 156 it was not until the start of an extended period of persecution two decades later that Montanism became for a time an empire-wide movement.

(1) During this period the churches of Asia Minor, surrounding the area of Phrygia where the movement began, had gone over to Montanism except for the larger churches controlled by bishops.

(2) The churches of Gaul sent a letter to Rome asking that communion with the Montanist churches be maintained. According to Tertullian (q.v.) the Pope was considering the move until persuaded against it by Praxeas, a vigorous opponent of the movement in Asia Minor.

(3) In the churches outside Asia Minor, cell groups of Montanists appeared, dedicated to quickening the faith. Tertullian belonged to one such group in Carthage. By 207 he had decided that the Church had entered on a path of secularism from which it could not be turned, and he left the Church to become a Montanist.

(4) In Phrygia, Montanist communities continued to exist in the 4th century. And in Carthage a sect called Tertullianists was in existence in the year 400. By then the influence of the movement had subsided.

MONTANUS. 2nd cent. A.D.

Religious leader. In 156, Montanus announced at Ardabau in Mysia near the Phrygian border that the dispensation of the Holy Spirit had begun, and he was to be its vessel. His movement had as its goal higher standards of morality than those generally required in the Church, especially with respect to obligations concerning marriage, fasting, and martyrdom. He likewise selected two small towns in Phrygia, named Pepuza and Tymion, and there established a religious community waiting for the coming of the Lord. Along with Montanus, two women, Prisca and Maximilla, were regularly moved by the spirit, revealing to the others commands for holiness. For twenty years the movement spread slowly through Phrygia and nearby areas. In 177 a general persecution of Christians began throughout the Roman Empire. This was interpreted as a sign that the end of the world was at hand. And the religious movement of Montanus suddenly became Montanism (q.v.), a movement that spread like fire throughout the Roman Empire.

MONTESQUIEU, CHARLES DE SECONDAT. 1689–1775.

French philosopher and social essayist. Born in La Brède near Bordeaux. A member of the nobility, Baron of La Brède and of Montesquieu, he served as president of the parliament of Bordeaux for twelve years before going to Paris to enter society. He travelled in Italy, the Low Countries, and England whose constitution he called "the mirror of liberty." His political thought was influenced by that of John Locke.

Principal writings: *The Persian Letters* (T), 1721; *Spirit of the Laws* (T), 1748.

(1) In both of his principal writings Montesquieu turned the attention of his readers to the diversity of structures and conditions characterizing society. His first book was a satire on French society carried out by means of a series of letters, ostensibly by two Persian visitors to France. The device allowed Montesquieu to demonstrate that French customs and manners were not universal, but in their own way quite provincial.

(2) His second book gave positive expression to the same theme. Societies, he held, are individual and shaped by a variety of factors including climate, religion, laws, constitutional precedents, commerce, customs, and manners.

(3) Given these factors, he suggested that there is an appropriate form for a society, depending upon the conditions which obtain. If a society is harmonious, it can be regarded as fitting its environment.

(4) In fact, however, such harmony is not possible to maintain. He held a notion similar to that of Rousseau (q.v. 1–4), in which simpler societies, closer to the state of nature, give way to an artificial state of enforced inequality once developed societies have been established. The simpler societies likewise have inequalities, although they are less extreme.

(5) He holds to the natural law doctrine. Before societies were established, before laws were made, there are relations of possible justice. To say that justice begins with laws is to say that before describing the circle, the radii are not equal.

(6) If it were possible to restore the classical type of democracy resting on civic virtue, this would be ideal. But it

is not possible. At the same time despotism is to be avoided. The appropriate and viable form of government, then, is constitutional monarchy. The form of government can be so ordered as to avoid the tyranny of the despot as well as the tyranny of the people.

(7) The safeguard against despotism is provided by the division of powers within the government and by parliament. Parliament provides a balance wheel, and the division of powers into legislative, executive, and judicial insures an equilibrium of opposed forces, and a consequent durability of government.

(8) In any system, however, "political virtue" is to be defined in terms of the love of law and country, and requires a continual preference of the public over private interests. All other virtues can be derived from this one.

(9) Montesquieu believed in God's existence and benevolence, and that human will is free by God's intention.

MOODS, SYLLOGISTIC.
Q.v. Syllogism (3–4).

MOORE, G.E. 1873–1958.
English philosopher. Born in London. Educated at Cambridge, where he taught from 1898–1904, and 1911 until retirement in 1939. Editor of *Mind* 1921–47; he was elected to the British Academy in 1918, and appointed to the Order of Merit in 1951.

Principal writings: *Principia Ethica*, 1903; *Ethics*, 1912; *Philosophical Studies*, 1922; *Some Main Problems of Philosophy*, 1953; *Philosophical Papers*, 1959; *The Common Place Books*, 1962.

(1) Sometimes characterized as a Common Sense Realist, Moore was one of the principal forces in England at the turn of the century engaged in attacking Idealism and reestablishing the credentials of realism in philosophy (*q.v.* New Realism 3). The analysis of the act of knowing requires both a mental act and an object of knowledge which is independent of that act. The remainder of his philosophical career was taken up with the elaboration, refinement, and modification of this position.

(2) His most dramatic argument for the existence of external objects was a reflection of his Common-sensist approach. He held up one hand and then the other, announcing: "Here is one hand . . . and here is the other." The argument would seem to be that we can advance no good reasons for denying that there is one hand, and here the other. Should one try to deny that this is a hand or that a pencil, then the argument shifts to one of probabilities. Which is more probable, that this hand or pencil exists, or that the principles of skepticism are true?

(3) A second line of argument lay in attempting to distinguish sensations from their content. One would then be distinguishing the sense-datum I have of the pencil from the pencil. It would also mean distinguishing the act of sensing yellow from the quality of yellow of the pencil. The Idealists, holding that to be is to be perceived ("*Esse est percipi*"), fail in one or another level to adhere to this distinction. Moore regarded this operation as separating the *esse* from the *percipi*.

(4) The exercise forced Moore into an epistemology which was dualistic, separating sense-datum from object. That separation normally forces one into the position of Representative Realism (*q.v.*); at times he did hold this view. But he tried to go beyond the situation where we are confined to sense-data. For example, he tried valiantly to develop the view that our sense-data are, at least at times, parts of the surfaces of the objects they represent. But he found great difficulty in this alternative, and one must say that at last he failed to find a way of relating sense-data to objects.

(5) He believed also in universals and understood them to be either relations, relational properties, or non-natural properties such as numbers and colors. Initially he held truth to be a simple unanalyzable property which some propositions have and others fail to have, but later he defended a correspondence theory of truth.

(6) He held the good to be a simple unanalyzable quality like "yellow," one which must be simply intuited to be known. Thus, he was the founder of ethical intuitionism. Moore claimed that to equate the good with any other quality than the non-natural quality of good itself is to commit the Naturalistic Fallacy. If it is urged that the good is pleasure, and someone asks, "Yes, but is pleasure

good?" one is clearly not asking if pleasure is pleasure. The upshot is that for Moore good cannot be identified with any natural quality. He found personal affection and aesthetic enjoyment to be among the greatest of goods. His analysis showed the rights and duties usually upheld by ordinary persons to be the appropriate rights and duties.

(7) Moore claimed to be aware of many truths for which he could not supply the "correct analysis." Nor did he claim to be able to supply the correct analysis of how one carries on a "correct analysis."

MORALITY.

In many usages, a synonym of the term, "ethics" (q.v., where most of the issues common to both terms are treated). The items below are those where authors specifically used the term "moral" or "morality."

(1) Shaftesbury (q.v. 4) held morality to be natural, and independent of supernatural sanctions.

(2) Fichte (q.v. 4–5) gave the moral consciousness such primacy that he decided his metaphysics in terms of it.

(3) For the claim that morality derives from an evolved factor of mutual aid, q.v. Kropotkin (2).

(4) For a division of moral systems into two types, that of master or slave morality, q.v. Nietzsche (2).

(5) Santayana (q.v. 8a, 8c) regarded morality as separate from ethics. The latter he regarded as a rational discipline; morality was for him more closely related to custom or habit. He distinguished pre-rational and post-rational forms of morality.

MORAL REARMAMENT.

Q.v. Buchmanism.

MORAL SENSE THEORY.

The ethical theory that we are able to distinguish between right and wrong by a distinctive moral sense. (1) This view is most prominently associated with the name of Shaftesbury (q.v. 1), who held that the moral sense was similar to feeling in nature. (2) Francis Hutcheson (q.v. 1, 3–4) and David Hume (q.v. 6) are regarded as followers of Shaftesbury in this respect.

MORAVIAN BRETHREN.

Q.v. Zinzendorf.

MORE, HENRY. 1614–1687.

English philosopher. Born in Lincolnshire. Educated at Cambridge, where he also taught. Along with Cudworth (q.v.) and Whichcote, one of the most prominent of the Cambridge Platonists (q.v.).

Principal writings: *Philosophical Poems*, 1647; *Several Philosophical Writings*, 1662; *Divine Dialogues*, 1668; *Enchiridion Metaphysicum*, 1671.

(1) Initially enthusiastic about Descartes, he increasingly began to see him as the unknowing leader of the forces tending toward atheism in the 17th century. One of More's ways of opposing this tendency was to deny the Cartesian dichotomy between mind and matter (q.v. Descartes 8, 9). His manner of denial is to hold that spirit is characterized by extension as well as by thought. And he terms all those, including Descartes, who deny extension to spirit, "Nullibilists."

(2) Spirit, or soul, is thus regarded as the sole agent of motion or action. And he holds that it has this property by virtue of something he calls its "Spissitude." Matter is regarded as inert. It is never the case that one object moves another; rather, some power of "Spissitude" is present making the motion occur. For motions which occur on the inorganic level, he calls upon "Seminal Germs," which carry the requisite "Spissitude."

(3) Spirit likewise has the property of being able to penetrate both material objects and other spirits. Thus, both an individual soul and God can be simultaneously present in any physical object.

(4) Space is regarded as an obscure representation of the essence of God. And this is why, although we can modify things in space both physically and conceptually, we cannot alter space itself.

(5) Man possesses a special "Boniform" faculty leading him to "right reason," the central concept in his Aristotelian analysis of virtue.

MORE, THOMAS. 1478–1535.

English statesman and essayist. Born in London. Educated at Oxford. Became a member of Parliament in 1504, and Lord Chancellor of England in 1529. Martyred due to his refusal to recognize Henry VIII as head of the English church.

Principal writings: *Utopia*, 1516; *A Dialogue of Comfort Against Tribulatian*, 1534.

(1) The *Utopia* sketches what More would take to be an ideal society. The ideal owes much to the Christian epicureanism of Lorenzo Valla (*q.v.* 1) and Erasmus (*q.v.*), but even more to Plato's *Republic* and the *Laws*.

(2) The *summum bonum* or greatest good and end in life in the *Utopia* is pleasure. The matter of pleasure consists of the individual goods of life, and the form of pleasure is Platonic communism, but with the family unit remaining, and a premise of the equality of men and women. Only with such an arrangement, it is suggested, can the greatest amount of pleasure be brought into society.

(3) On the individual level one should seek the "natural" pleasures which come from a life of simplicity, eschewing the false pleasures of wealth and status. One should also seek the eternal pleasures which come from divine providence, and relate to life in another world.

MORES.

Q.v. Sumner (2).

MORGAN, AUGUSTUS DE.

Q.v. De Morgan, Augustus.

MORGAN, C. LLOYD. 1852–1936.

English scientist and philosopher. Born in London. Studied under T.H. Huxley. Taught first in South Africa and then at the University of Bristol.

Principal writings: *Emergent Evolution*, 1923; *Life, Mind, and Spirit*, 1926; *Mind at the Crossways*, 1929; *The Emergence of Novelty*, 1933.

(1) Originator of the phrase "method of trial and error" to apply to the capacity to learn from experience across a broad spectrum of organic life, his studies of living forms led him to a concept of emergent evolution.

(2) He believed that evolution occurs at all levels of natural history, not continuously but by discontinuity, in which "emergents" abruptly appear, leading from lower to higher forms of life. Everything emerges from an original space-time matrix, including matter itself. In addition to emergents there are also "resultants," repetitive elements providing

the continuity necessary to the process.

(3) As his system developed, he held that physical and psychical interpretations are correlative and equally applicable at all levels of explanation. He regarded this as an indication of the Spinozism of his system (*q.v.* Spinoza 8).

(4) He held that mentality was the emergent of the psychical correlate. Not emergent, but directing the course of evolution, is God whose purpose is expressed in the entire course of events.

MORGAN, THOMAS. c. 1690–1743.

Welsh deist. An independent minister deprived of his living because of unorthodoxy, Morgan followed the five principles or "Common Notions" of Herbert of Cherbury (*q.v.* 1–2), attacked the priestcraft for instituting superstition and persecution, pioneered in biblical criticism, and defended religious toleration.

Principal writings: *A Letter to Mr. Thomas Chubb*, 1727; *A Defense of Natural and Revealed Religion*, 1728; *The Moral Philosopher*, 1737; *A Vindication of the Moral Philosopher*, 1741.

MORMONS.

Q.v. Latter Day Saints.

MORRIS, CHARLES W. 1901–1979.

American philosopher. Born in Denver. Educated in Chicago. Taught at Chicago and Florida.

Principal writings: *Six Theories of Mind*, 1932; *Logical Positivism, Pragmatism, and Scientific Empiricism*, 1937; *Foundations of the Theory of Signs*, 1938; *Paths of Life*, 1942; *Signs, Language, and Behavior*, 1946; *The Open Self*, 1948.

(1) His specific lifelong goal has been that of relating the achievements of American pragmatism, especially the insights of Charles Peirce and George Herbert Mead, to those of logical positivism.

(2) His most distinctive contribution in this regard has been in the field of Semiotic (*q.v.* 10). Semiotic, or general theory of signs, was subdivided by Morris into three parts: Syntactics, Semantics, and Pragmatics. *Syntactics* is the study of the relations which signs have to each other by virtue of their formal properties. *Semantics* is the study of the relations between signs and what they designate. *Pragmatics* is the study of the

relations between signs and their users, *i.e.*, the modes of response to signs by those who use them. This division has been widely accepted in contemporary philosophy.

(3) Morris made a distinction between pure and descriptive semiotic, the former elaborating a language for discourse about signs, for example the complex matrix of the types of signs in use in the manner of C.S. Peirce (*q.v.* 16); the latter studying existent signs, *i.e.*, signs in the natural languages. This distinction is not widely accepted.

(4) He has conducted extensive investigations attempting to relate types of philosophical belief to types of human physical structure, as well as to differing forms of human culture.

MORRIS, WILLIAM.
Q.v. Utopia (7).

MOSCA, GAETANO. 1858–1941.
Italian social philosopher and theorist. Born in Palermo. Educated at Palermo. Taught at Palermo, Rome, Turin. Member Chamber of Deputies from 1908. Named Senator for life, 1919.

Principal writings: *Elements of Political Science*, 1895 (3rd ed. trans. into English, titled *The Ruling Class*, 1939).

(1) Every organized society consists of a ruling minority and a ruled majority. Societies are organized according to a variety of principles, but in every modern society the professional bureaucracy constitutes an important segment of the ruling class, providing the continuing administration of that society.

(2) The order of society is maintained not really through force of arms but by means of a "political formula" widely accepted by the members of that society. It is the formula which legitimizes the structure of the society.

(3) He notes advantages in the open society characterized by parliamentary government, and the provision of individual rights and liberties. The stability of such societies is increased by the fact that the ruled have an opportunity to become part of the ruling class.

MOSES BEN NAHMAN.
Spanish rabbi. *Q.v.* Cabala (3b).

MOSES BEN SHEM TOB DE LEON.
Q.v. Cabala (2d); Zohar.

MOSLEM.
Q.v. Muslim.

MO TI.
Q.v. Mo Tzu.

MOTION.
Change in the relative positions of bodies.

(1) Parmenides (*q.v.* 6), Zeno (*q.v.* 4–5), Nagarjuna (*q.v.* 2), and Seng-Chao (*q.v.* 1) argued against the possibility of motion.

(2) For Democritus (*q.v.* 3) motion was held to be an inherent property of atoms.

(3) For Aristotle (*q.v.* 8) locomotion, or movement through space, is one of three types of motion.

(4) Newton (*q.v.* 2) elaborated three laws of motion.

MO TZU. 479–381 B.C.
Chinese philosopher. The next major philosopher after Confucius, he was probably at one time a follower of Confucius, turned opponent. His school, known as Moism or the Moist school, flourished until the Han dynasty, during which time it went into decline. The followers of Mo Tzu came from the *hsieh* or knight-errant class rather than the *ju* or literary class, and were thus in opposition to the Confucianists.

Principal writings: *The Mo Tzu* (T in part).

(1) Mo Tzu operates with two kinds of ideas, held together by the usefulness of each set.

(2) On the one hand he held to a leader principle, which emerged from the class to which he and his adherents belonged: (a) Every member of every group must identify himself with the leader of his group. The leader is to identify himself with a higher leader until "the son of Heaven" is reached. It is said that Mo Tzu's group was organized in such a way that the leader held the right of life and death over its members. (b) If the "son of Heaven," or king, has the right principles, so will the rest of society. And if he does not, the displeasure of nature will be manifest through disastrous happenings, including flood and drought. (c) He

believed with some of the Confucians that all officials, even kings, should be selected on the basis of merit.

(3) On the other hand he held to a principle of universal love, "*Ai.*" He does not disavow the Confucian ideal of *jen* (human heartedness) or *li* ("benefit" or "gain"). Indeed, men of *jen* and *li* were those who practice all-embracing love: (a) The chief need of men, ruled and rulers alike, is to practice universal love and mutual benefit. This requires regarding other persons, families, and countries as one's own. When this happens universally, the strong will not oppress the weak, the rich will not insult the poor, the honored will not despise the humble, the cunning will not deceive the ignorant, and all men will live in peace. (b) Loving others we shall be loved in return; benefiting others we shall be benefited in return. This was the way of the sage kings, Mo Tzu argued, and should be practiced today if we want the state to be wealthy and orderly. (c) Not only is such a way of living beneficial, it is also the will of heaven. To practice this way is to use righteousness as a method of control. This is to the emperor what the compass is to the wheelwright, and the square to the carpenter. It is one of the functions of the emperor to bring about a unified conception of right among the people. This view is opposed to the way of fatalism which says that nothing can be done to improve the lot of the people.

(4) The two approaches were held together by the view that whatever is beneficial should be done; and whatever is harmful should be avoided. To engage in music-making is wrong because it takes time from ploughing, planting, weaving, and spinning. It uses up the resources of the people and takes up their time. Elaborate funerals, because of the waste, are also wrong.

MOUNIER, EMMANUEL. 1905–1950.

French philosopher. Born in Grenoble. Studied in Paris. Taught in Brussels, 1933–9. Editor of a journal named *Esprit*.

Principal writings: *The Thought of Charles Péguy*, 1931; *What Is Personalism?* 1947; *Personalism* (T), 1949; *Notebooks along the Way*, 1950-3.

(1) Descartes began his philosophy with the isolated individual thinking, and thus set a tragic pattern for his successors. Starting from this point it is not possible to get either from the individual to community, or from thought to being.

(2) The economic correlate of the isolated individual is capitalism. The correlate is likewise characterized by an absence of community.

(3) In fact, however, the person is a spiritual being who is aware of the Thou along with the I, and who has the unique vocation of bringing about communication with other persons.

(4) Personalism is the philosophy stressing this as the primary goal of persons rather than the conquest of nature, humans interacting with other humans in a process of mutual enrichment.

M-PREDICATES.

Q.v. Strawson (3).

MUDITA.

From Sanskrit, "sympathetic joy." One of the Four Immeasurable Attitudes of Mahayana Buddhism (*q.v.* 4).

MUHAMMAD.

Q.v. Mohammed.

MULLA SADRA. 1571/2–1640.

Muslim philosopher. Born in Shiraz. Studied in Ispahan. Taught in Shiraz. Founded a school of philosophy which remains widely influential in Persia to this day. Babism (*q.v.*) and the Shaikhi Movement represent rival schools of thought. He wrote in Arabic.

Principal writings: *The Exalted Wisdom Concerning the Four Journeys of the Spirit*; *The Book of Metaphysical Penetrations*; *The Divine Witnesses*; *The Book of Theophany Inspired by the Throne*.

(1) In the moment of knowing something truly, one's intellect is identified with the intelligible form of the object known. The state of knowing truly is hence an ontological state, where knowing and being interpenetrate.

(2) As knowing has an ontological correlate in being, so has the human imaginative faculty (faculty of imaging) in an imaginal world. In terms of imaging, the human imagination is a microcosm of a cosmic imagining. This means ultimately that Mulla Sadra finds it important to add a *mundus imaginalis* to the

more common concepts of the *mundus intelligibilis* (*q.v.*) and the *mundus sensibilis* (*q.v.*).

(3) He also held to the primacy of existence, and believed that existence can only be intuited and not conceived. This applies to the idea of God in the sense that the idea of a necessary being does not prove the existence of such a being. God, he says on the other hand, is perfectly his own proof.

(4) Contingent existence was created by a simple divine creation; it is nothing in itself, but is wholly dependent upon God.

MÜLLER, MAX.
Q.v. Myth (8).

MUNDUS IMAGINALIS.
Latin phrase meaning the "world of images." Used by Mulla Sadra (*q.v.*), following the pattern of the *mundus intelligibilis* (*q.v.*) and the *mundus sensibilis* (*q.v.*).

MUNDUS INTELLIGIBILIS.
Latin phrase meaning the "intelligible world." (1) The phrase refers to the Platonic realm of ideas which contains an exemplar idea or form for every kind, sort, or species of thing in the terrestrial world (*q.v.* Plato 1). (2) Equally, however, the phrase applies to the Neoplatonic *Nous* (*q.v.* Plotinus 3) which serves as intermediary between God and the world. (3) In the medieval application of the term the forms become *rationes aeternas*, eternal ideas in the mind of God (*q.v.* St. Augustine 2).

MUNDUS SENSIBILIS.
Latin phrase meaning the "world of sense." The sense world is the terrestrial correlate of the *mundus intelligibilis* (*q.v.*).

MUNRO, THOMAS. 1897–1974.
American philosopher. Born in Omaha, Nebraska. Educated at Columbia University. Director of the Cleveland Museum of Art beginning in 1931, and editor of the *Journal of Aesthetics and Art Criticism* from 1963. Instrumental in the founding of the American Society for Aesthetics. Munro holds that aesthetics is a science, comparable to biology, whose structures have evolved, and must now

be carefully and systematically studied.

Principal writings: *Scientific Method in Aesthetics*, 1928; *The Arts and their Interrelations*, 1949; *Art Education*, 1956; *Toward Science in Aesthetics*, 1956; *Evolution in the Arts*, 1963.

MÜNSTERBERG, HUGO. 1863–1916.
German philosopher and psychologist. Born in Danzig. Taught first in Freiburg and then at Harvard. A member of the Heidelberg School of neo-Kantianism (*q.v.* 4).

Principal writings: *The Origin of Morality*, 1889; *Psychology and Life* (E), 1899; *The Eternal Values* (E), 1908.

(1) According to Münsterberg, values arise spontaneously in life processes, and also through the development of culture and science. The system of values is, nonetheless, absolute.

(2) The absoluteness of the system is defended in Idealistic terms in the manner of Fichte (*q.v.* 2–3). One regards the world as an act of absolute will, and on this act rests the hierarchical unity of the system of logical, aesthetic, and ethical values.

MÜNZER, THOMAS.
Q.v. Anabaptists; Bloch.

MURPHY, A.E. 1901–1962.
American philosopher. Born in Ithaca, New York. Educated at Berkeley. Taught in a succession of universities and finally in the University of Texas.

Principal writings: *The Uses of Reason*, 1943.

(1) Murphy contributed the phrase *Objective Relativism* to philosophy, meaning thereby a point of view in which events have primacy over objects in the interpretation of the world. In the traditional approach, events happen to objects; in objective relativism, objects happen to events, and relations are looked upon as more important than their terms.

(2) Among objective relativists Murphy counted not only himself, Dewey, and Whitehead, but also McGilvary (*q.v.* 4) who advanced the doctrine of perspective realism (*q.v.* Realism 7). The classification suggests that Dewey and Whitehead might be fairly assimilated into the realistic tradition.

MUSIC.

For Schopenhauer (*q.v.* 5) the highest of the arts.

MUSLIM.

Arabic term meaning "one who submits." One who professes the faith of Islam (*q.v.*), *i.e.*, a follower of Mohammed (*q.v.*).

MUSLIM PHILOSOPHY.

Q.v. Islamic Philosophy.

MUSONIUS RUFUS.

Q.v. Epictetus.

MUTAKILLIM.

An Arabic term meaning "debaters." The name of the Orthodox school of Islamic thought. *Q.v.* Islam (6).

MUTAZILITES.

From the Arabic *mutazilah* meaning "seceders." A Shiite sect of Islam (*q.v.* 5, 6) dating from the 8th century. Known as the "party of equity and unity," they held that the Qur'an must be interpreted according to the canons of reason, and that man's free will negates the possibility of divine predestination.

MYSTERIUM FASCINOSUM.

Q.v. Otto (2).

MYSTERIUM TREMENDUM.

Q.v. Otto (2).

MYSTERY RELIGIONS.

The name given to a group of religious cults popular in the Hellenic and Roman periods. The mystery religions were characterized by a body of esoteric knowledge and ceremony which allegedly had the power to purify the initiate and guarantee union with God and personal immortality. Virtually all of the mysteries centered around dying and rising saviors.

(1) The Eleusinian mysteries, taking their name from Eleusis—location of the shrine near Athens—turned on the myth of Demeter and Persephone. The myth concerns the succession of the seasons, and rebirth of life in the spring; but the cult developed until its central theme was personal rebirth.

(2) The mysteries of Isis-Osiris, Cybele-Attis, and Aphrodite-Adonis followed a pattern almost identical to that of the Eleusinian mysteries. In each case the rites had their origin in inducing fertile crops and developed into cults of personal salvation through rites of purification. *Q.v.* Isis.

(3) The Orphic mysteries likewise followed the pattern. Orpheus and Eurydice were the divine pair; and because Orpheus failed to follow exact instructions Eurydice had to return to the underworld. A substantial body of Orphic poetry developed in relation to these mysteries.

(4) The mysteries of Dionysus (*q.v.*) present a contrast to the rest. Here deity is celebrated through song and dance, the virtues of wine, and the ecstasy of full participation in slaughtering and savoring the sacrificial animal. Through ecstasy one seeks union with the God. The soul is regarded as superior to the body and imprisoned therein.

(5) Mithraism (*q.v.*), centering around the slaying of the bull in the name of the hero-god Mithra, was celebrated particularly by Roman soldiers. More elaborate than most of the mysteries, the initiate must rise through seven grades of purification, analogous to the seven heavens through which one bound for paradise must pass.

MYSTICAL THEOLOGY.

Q.v. The Pseudo-Dionysius (2).

MYSTICISM.

From the Greek *mystes* meaning "one initiated into the mysteries." The term is derived from the Greek mystery religions whose initiates bore the name "mystes." And the term "mysticism" seems to have been first used in the Dionysius Areopagitica (*q.v.* Pseudo-Dionysius). It there refers to the technique of the *Via Negativa* (*q.v.*) or negative way, as the method whereby the wholly transcendent God may be approached. Although this usage set the pattern for much of the mysticism of the Western world, there are a number of alternatives to be distinguished.

In general, mysticism can be understood as a spiritual and non-discursive approach to the union of the soul with God, or with whatever is taken to be the central reality of the universe. When this is thought to be a transcendent God, one typical path is inward, away from the world, toward union with the transcendent

One. But introversive mysticism is not the only type. There is also an extraversive mysticism in which the subject senses unity with the universe, with all there is. This is often accompanied, either as cause or as effect, with a pantheistic identification of God with all there is. Finally, meditative techniques, mystical in tone, are used to achieve an enlightened state of being, apart from any concept of the divine. Each of these approaches has been developed in both East and West.

(1) The Indian identification of *Atman* (*q.v.*) with Brahman (*q.v.*), developed in the *Upanishads* (*q.v. Vedas* 4), supposes that the end of life is achieved when individuals become aware of their identity with the divine. This would seem to fit introversive mysticism. Much of the meditative technique of Yoga (*q.v.*) is designed for this end. And in the school of Advaita Vedanta (*q.v.*), the interpretation of Shankara (*q.v.*) reaches this awareness through recognition of the illusory character of the space-time world. In the philosophy of Ramanuja (*q.v.*), where the deity is conceived both as the divine unity and as the world soul, the emphasis is on both introversive and extraversive mysticism.

(2) Buddhism represents the third type of mysticism. In Hinayana (*q.v.*) Buddhism, mystic contemplation is utilized to achieve a state of being which seems not to be describable as union with God. In Mahayana (*q.v.*) Buddhism, although here the divine beings reappear, the goal is identity with the Buddha nature; this is not unlike the goal in Hinayana Buddhism. Once again, in Zen (*q.v.*) Buddhism, which stresses a breakthrough into *satori*, a life of enlightenment, the goal is a state of being rather than identification with a divine being.

(3) Mysticism in the West was prepared by the Mystery religions (*q.v.*) of the Greeks, the movement of Gnosticism (*q.v.*) which reached its highest point in the 2nd century A.D., the early stage of the movement of Neoplatonism (*q.v.*) which combined the emphases of the foregoing movements with Platonism (*q.v. Plotinus*), and the early Christian movement of monasticism which stressed meditative and ascetic practices with personal purification as the goal.

(4) In Islam, Sufism (*q.v.*) is the name of the mystical movement, beginning with Arabic ascetics in the first centuries A.D., and developing into a fellowship within Islam seeking union with Allah through prayer and ascetic practices.

(5) Jewish mysticism centers in the Cabala (*q.v.*), a movement which began in the late pre-Christian world and had reached its distinctive form by the 14th century, and Hasidism (*q.v.*) which began in the 18th century. The former shares many elements with Gnosticism and Neoplatonism (*cf.* 3 above). The latter is a movement of spiritual renewal, ethical in tone, working within Judaism. Buber (*q.v.*) in the present century was influenced by the Hasidim, and has spread widely his appreciation of the movement.

(6) Roman Catholic mysticism began with monasticism (*cf.* 3 above), and developed in the Middle Ages through the meditative experiences of a remarkable group of individuals, including Bernard of Clairvaux (*q.v.*) whose fourth stage of love involves the annihilation-deification of the self; St. Bonaventure (*q.v.* 1) who clarified the mystical implications of the Franciscan-Augustinian tradition and whose mysticism centered on the image of God in man; Meister Eckhart (*q.v.*), a German mystic summoned before the Inquisition during his own day and some of whose doctrines were later condemned; his followers John Tauler (*q.v.*), Henry Suso (*q.v.*), and John Ruysbroeck (*q.v.*) continued this strain of mystic illumination. A number of religious communities emerged from these influences. Tauler and Suso were central to a group called the Friends of God (*q.v.*); out of the influence of this group the *German Theology*, a famous mystical treatise, may well have come. Ruysbroeck established a religious society. Groote (*q.v.*) established the *Brethren of the Common Life* (*q.v.*). from which came the impressive devotional work on *The Imitation of Christ* (*q.v.*). In the 16th century Saint Teresa (*q.v.*) of Avila and Saint John of the Cross (*q.v.*) added to the understanding of mystical literature with their writings.

(7) Among the Protestant mystics it is necessary to mention above all the German mystic of Lutheran faith, Jacob Boehme (*q.v.*). Living in the last quarter

of the 16th century and the first quarter of the 17th, he influenced the German movement of Pietism (*q.v.*), and even the 17th-century movement of Quakerism. George Fox (*q.v.*), the founder of the Quaker doctrine of the inner light, is mystical in nature. William Law (*q.v.*), called "the English mystic," was influenced directly by Boehme and in turn exercised a strong influence upon John Wesley, the founder of Methodism.

(8) In recent decades the claims of mysticism have been defended by thinkers of such diverse orientation as William James (*q.v.* 5), Buber (*q.v.*), and von Hügel (*q.v.*).

MYTH.

From the Greek term *mythos* meaning "legend." Hence, a narrative account taken to be true, but not known to be true. The elaboration of dramatic narratives involving superhuman powers provided the first explanations of the origin and operation of the universe. Myth has some relation to metaphor (*q.v.*), and can be treated as allegory (*cf.* 1 below). A number of different relations between myth and philosophy have had currency in the history of philosophy.

(1) The rise of philosophy signaled a shift from mythical accounts of the universe to rational modes of explanation. Among the early philosophers some specifically attacked the accepted mythical explanations; among these are Heraclitus (*q.v.* 7), and Xenophanes (*q.v.* 1). Among the Sophists (*q.v.*) the practice of allegory began, viewing mythical explanations as cloaking conceptual truth. This manner of dealing with myth was very attractive to Christian thinkers in later centuries.

(2) Plato (*q.v.*), on the other hand, is one of those who found myth an ally in the working out of a philosophy. Not only does myth allow an approximate expression of philosophical insights whose precise expression is not available, it is particularly appropriate for expressing changing features of the indeterminate world of becoming.

(3) The Hellenistic Jews found it helpful to treat the Old Testament as an allegory, purveying in hidden form the philosophical ideas of the Greeks. Philo Judaeus (*q.v.*) is an outstanding representative of this approach.

(4) Christian thinkers, from the early centuries through the Middle Ages, found allegorical interpretation an essential instrument of analysis. St. Augustine (*q.v.* 11) found allegories throughout the Bible, even in the parable of the Good Samaritan. It was standard procedure in the Middle Ages to sort out the allegorical sense, the analogical sense, and the mystical sense of a given passage.

(5) Vico (*q.v.* 2) holds mythology to be the instrument by means of which the history of the race, as present in the customs of its social groups, is retained. Myth is the standard means of expression in the early ages of humankind, and the social reality shapes the myth.

(6) Schelling (*q.v.* 5) reverses Vico's dictum concerning the relation between myth and history in his insistence that the history of a people is determined by its mythology. Myth takes hold of the pure creative potencies of the members of the social group, giving them shape.

(7) Strauss (*q.v.*) regarded the Christian gospels as mythology, representing unconscious human invention which he analyzed in Hegelian terms.

(8) Max Müller, in his linguistic and cultural studies, finds myth to be the "dark shadow" cast by language on thought. The shadow occurs because of verbal ambivalence, *i.e.*, paronymy, the fact that a single word is able to carry several images. For Müller the fact that words are able to carry not only a specific meaning, but figurative suggestions from which myths may be elaborated, is a disease of language, regrettable but also inevitable.

(9) E.B. Tylor explains myth as a product of the confusion of early humans, mixing together without distinction their dream and waking experience.

(10) Sorel (*q.v.* 2) is interested in a particular type of myth, that expressing a social will concerning a preferred future state.

(11) The Freudian interpretation (*q.v.* Freud 5–8) finds the explanation of myth, in intimate family love-hate relationships which are repressed and expressed in cosmic terms.

(12) Jung (*q.v.* 1–2, 7–9) finds the recurrent elements of myth in the human collective unconscious which are superimposed upon the details of experience.

(13) Cassirer (*q.v.* 2–4) revives Schelling's view of the authenticity of myth while concentrating on the critical import of language. In the stage of mythical thinking, word and reality are identified, so that narrative power and power over nature are identical.

(14) For a program of demythologizing the New Testament *q.v.* Bultmann (1).

(15) Lévi-Strauss (*q.v.* 2) revives Vico's claim that myth presents the customs of social groups. The approach of Lévi-Strauss is through anthropology, a more sophisticated instrument than the historical approach available to Vico. Lévi-Strauss, further, found a role for myth in holding the social reality together against social oppositions which could be reconciled in the mythical account. He holds that myth cannot be treated rationally since it poses a non-Cartesian problem; and he regards his analysis as a "myth of mythology."

MYTH OF THE GIVEN.
Q.v. W. Sellars (3).

N

NAGARJUNA. 100–200.
Indian philosopher. A Mahayana Buddhist and the first systematic expounder of an important school, called Shunyavada, holding to the relativity of thought, and the non-duality of the Absolute. The school is also known as the Madhyamika or Middle Doctrine school. There are two aspects to his thought, one negative and the other positive.

Principal writings: *Twenty Verses on the Great Vehicle* (T); *Treatise on the Middle Doctrine* (T); *Treatise on Relativity* (T).

(1) The negative aspect, reminiscent to Westerners of Zeno of Elea, marshals weapons of dialectic with great skill in reducing to absurdity the positions of his opponents. Along the way Nagarjuna demonstrates that nothing can be produced. If it is produced out of itself it is already in existence. And it cannot be produced out of what it is not, since it is not that thing.

(2) Causation is impossible, for either the effect pre-exists in the cause, or it does not. If the effect pre-exists in the cause, then threads should be called cloth. And if the effect does not pre-exist in the cause, cloth could be produced from reeds. The conclusion is that causality is only an appearance. A similar argument is used to show (a) that motion is impossible; and that motion, mover and goal, are equally unreal; and that (b) seer, seen, and sight are illusory.

(3) Change is impossible. If the changeless does not exist, there is nothing to change. And if it does exist, there is no change.

(4) Matter is unreal. Suppose that it exists. If it exists, it has no cause because it is already existent; but uncaused matter is not possible. If it does not exist, it has no cause, being a nonentity. Similar arguments are employed to show that feeling, conception, force, individual consciousness, and the elements of earth, air, fire, water, and space are unreal.

(5) According to Buddha the universe is beginningless and endless. But what does not exist in the beginning or the end, cannot exist in the middle. Hence, the universe is unreal.

(6) On the other hand, if reality does not exist, how are we to account for the fact that something appears; but if it is an appearance, how can it be reality?

(7) Further, Nirvana is an illusion. If Nirvana is existent, it will be subject to birth and death. If Nirvana is nonexistent, it will depend upon existence for its status, since nonexistence depends upon existence. Nor can it be both of these (for reasons of inconsistency) nor neither. Hence Nirvana is an illusion.

(8) What is the upshot? Nagarjuna summarizes his view in eight negations and fourteen antinomies. (a) The eight negations are: no origination, no dissipation, no permanence, no ending, no differentiation, no identity, no coming into existence, no going out of existence. (b) The fourteen antinomies are: we cannot say whether the world is finite or not or both or neither; or permanent or not or both or neither; we cannot say if the Buddha, after Nirvana, is existent or not or both or neither; or whether matter and mind are identical or not.

What, then, can be affirmed?

(9) Reality is beyond intellect and to be realized directly as the non-dual Absolute in which all distinctions merge.

(10) The truth has two aspects. One of these is empirical, and the other Absolute. The empirical truth is a workable makeshift covering for reality. But from the standpoint of the empirical it is more than this; and it is by means of these appearances that one ventures into the Absolute truth. It is knowledge of the Absolute which destroys the wheel of causation. Another way of saying this is to say that identity is itself relative and related to the Absolute on which it depends for its meaning. From this standpoint no doctrine was taught by the Buddha; he descended to the phenomenal level to help all beings rise above the categories of intellect, and to realize directly the non-dual Absolute.

NAGEL, ERNEST. 1901–1985.

American philosopher. Born in Novemesto, Czechoslovakia. Educated at City College and Columbia University. Beginning his teaching career at City College, he taught at Columbia University from 1931 until retirement. He was named John Dewey Professor of Philosophy in 1955. Collaborating with Morris Cohen (q.v.) on his first book, a well-known introduction to logic, he has subscribed to naturalism and instrumentalism throughout his career. He has concerned himself especially with the fields of logic and philosophy of science.

Principal writings: *An Introduction to Logic and Scientific Method* (with M. Cohen), 1934; *Principles of the Theory of Probability*, 1939; *Sovereign Reason*, 1954; *Logic without Metaphysics*, 1956; *Gödel's Proof* (with J. R. Newman), 1958; *The Structure of Science*, 1961; *Observation and Theory in Science* (with others), 1969; *Teleology Revisited*, 1979.

(1) He is a naturalist in the sense that he believes that events or objects with space-time location can be cited for anything that occurs. In addition he holds that, whatever might be said of a chance event, since any series of events corresponds to some mathematical function, any such series can be related to some set of laws or other. Thus, it seems impossible even to express what would be meant by a chance series of events.

(2) For him, in physics, quantum mechanics, no less than classical mechanics, is deterministic; subatomic processes are not acausal. He points out that the state description of classical mechanics, expressed in terms of "position" and "momenta" of particles, is not an appropriate state description for quantum mechanics. Given an appropriate wave-mechanical formulation of the state description, no suggestion of indeterminism arises.

(3) Furthermore, where some have found biological and psychological explanations to be naturally teleological, and in this way different from explanations in physics, Nagel takes the view that teleological explanations are equivalent to nonteleological ones in biology and psychology. One can replace teleological explanations by their non-teleological equivalents with no loss of content. With respect to the specific argument of the Reductionists (q.v. Reductionism) that biology can be reduced to the categories of physics and chemistry, and the argument of the Organismic Biologists (q.v.) that mechanistic explanations fail in biology, Nagel shows that neither claim has been substantiated. The Reductionists have not shown either that all biological terms are definable in the language of physics and chemistry, or that the content of biology is derivable from the propositions of physics and chemistry. The Organismic Biologists, on the other hand, have not shown that in biology the whole is not equal to the sum of the parts, as they claim, nor have they even made clear the nature of the claim.

(4) He holds that despite the paucity of statistical evidence relating to social determinants, there is no reason to suppose that historical explanations differ in kind from those in the natural sciences. We lack an explicitly formulated logic applicable to history, but the selectivity exercised by historians does not imply subjectivity.

(5) Statements of this sort suggest a strong naturalism. On the other hand he is not a materialist in a reductive sense. Poetry, aesthetic appreciation, and value-discriminations of all types are held to be valid and real.

(6) The instrumentalism is suggested by the close attention he has given the

thought of John Dewey, and in his use of the principle of context-determination. It is by virtue of the principle of context-determination that Nagel is able to offer us logic without ontology. Interpreting the principles and concepts of logic contextually, or operationally, one is burdened with no ontological commitments with respect to the status of logical entities and principles.

(7) Agreeing with Peirce (*q.v.* 12–13) that inquiry is self-corrective, Nagel holds not only that the conclusion of every inquiry may be challenged by new theoretical constructions and fresh experimental data, it is also the case that any schema used in such evaluations is subject to revision should it lead to frequently undependable conclusions.

(8) And finally, with respect to the cognitive status of theories he holds that there is only a verbal difference between asking whether a theory is satisfactory, and asking whether it is true. By extension it might be supposed that there is a similar verbal difference between asking whether Nagel is an instrumentalist or a naturalist.

NAIVE REALISM.

The perfectly gratuitous view that all of the qualities we sense in objects—including sounds, colors, tastes, smells, and tactile sensations, as well as shapes and motions—are in fact characteristics of these objects. No one, whether philosopher or non-philosopher, has ever admitted to being a naive realist. Philosophers employ the term largely to illustrate a type of realism to be avoided. Presumably no one has ever believed that the tickle was in the feather; at least Galileo (*q.v.* 3) used the example as a *reductio ad absurdum* argument against this alternative. *Q.v.* Realism for a full listing of the types of realism. Also *q.v.*. Perception (1).

NAMA-RUPA.

Sanskrit, ("psychophysical personality"). *Q.v.* Buddha (2).

NAMING.

Q.v. Kripke (1–2); Proper Names.

NANAK. 1469–1539.

Founder of the Sikh religion. In a synthesis of Hindu and Islamic sources Nanak taught that God was one, unborn,

immortal, omniscient, just, loving, and creator of all things. Dipolar in nature, God is transcendent as well as immanent. As transcendent he is pure potentiality; as immanent, he embodies the world. *Q.v.* Hinduism (5c); Sikhism.

NANTES, EDICT OF. 1598 A.D.

Measure by Henry IV (Henry of Navarre) ending the French religious wars and granting freedom of religion to both the Protestants (Huguenots) and Catholics. When it was revoked by Louis XIV in 1685, hundreds of thousands of Huguenots were forced into exile.

NARAYANA.

Q.v. Vaiṣṇavism (2a).

NASTIKA.

Sanskrit term meaning "denier." It applies to any Indian system of thought not accepting the authority of the *Vedas*. Examples are Charvaka (*q.v.*), and Buddhism (*q.v.*). To be contrasted with the *Astika* (*q.v.*) systems which accept the *Vedas* as authoritative.

NATIVE FORMS.

Q.v. Gilbert of Poitiers (2).

NATORP, PAUL. 1854–1924.

German philosopher. Born in Düsseldorf. Taught at Marburg, beginning as *Privatdozent* in 1881, and becoming professor in 1892. A neo-Kantian disciple of Hermann Cohen (*q.v.*), he became his colleague and one of the principal figures in the Marburg School (*q.v.*).

Principal writings: *Introduction to Psychology According to the Critical Method*, 1884; *Plato's Theory of Ideas: An Introduction to Idealism*, 1903; *The Logical Foundations of the Exact Sciences*, 1910; *Kant and the Marburg School*, 1912.

(1) Accepting as his goal the application of Kant's critical method to the forms of culture, he applied the method to the natural sciences, the social sciences, history and art, but not in the manner of Cohen (*q.v.* 1–4) who followed Kant's guidelines rather closely. His approach rested its analysis on the unity of consciousness in the manner of Fichte (*q.v.* 3), deriving subjectivity and objectivity from a consciousness which is its own posit.

(2) Natorp interpreted Plato as a "Marburg neo-Kantian" whose ideas are

not otherworldly but lie at the base of science, providing its laws and principles. The Platonic ideas are a pure positioning of thought at the basis of the existent world, allowing an identification of thought and being.

NATURAL FORMS.
Q.v. Form (5g).

NATURALISM.
A philosophical perspective, developed in the United States, which came into focus briefly in the 1940's with the publication of Yervant Krikorian's *Naturalism and the Human Spirit*, 1944, although the antecedents of the position date from the early 1900's. Naturalism holds that all explanations must finally make reference to objects and events in space-time. There is no non-natural order to which appeal can be made. The position differs from Materialism (*q.v.*) in denying that all phenomena can be reduced to matter in motion. The qualitative aspects of experience—*e.g.*, the distinctions proper to logic, ethics, and aesthetics—are regarded as valid and in some important sense irreducible.

(1) The group regards Santayana (*q.v.* 1, 6) as an antecedent, even though the latter called himself a materialist and held spirit to be epiphenomenal.

(2) The connection lies in the fact that Woodbridge (*q.v.* 1, 2) found in Santayana an organic antireductionistic metaphysics which, combined with Aristotelianism, became naturalism, the position Woodbridge represented forcefully through the years.

(3) When John Dewey (*q.v.* 5) came to Columbia he began to feel the influence of Woodbridge. In addition to calling his view Instrumentalism, he likewise used the term "empirical naturalism." Whatever the name, his categories of explanation remained this-worldly, and his philosophy was antireductionistic.

(4) Morris Cohen (*q.v.* 5) likewise subscribed to this tradition, as did his student and collaborator Ernest Nagel (*q.v.* 1, 6, 8). The thought of Nagel contains the influence of Dewey as well.

(5) Horace Kallen and Sidney Hook (*q.v.*), among others, may be listed as belonging to this group. The alternative of naturalism, no less than materialism,

is implicitly atheistic. Hook (*q.v.* 3) called himself a "pragmatic naturalist," and subscribed to an "open-minded atheism." Also, however, *q.v.* Dilthey (5).

NATURALISTIC FALLACY.
A phrase coined by G.E. Moore (*q.v.* 6) to describe an error in reasoning which he believed the Utilitarians had committed: they identified the "good" with "pleasure." But even if one should admit that the good is pleasurable, one might ask: Is pleasure good? And since it makes sense to ask the question, apparently "pleasure" and "good" do not have the same meaning; for otherwise one would be asking: Is good good? And no one would ever need to ask that question. Moore believed, in fact, that the fallacy was committed whenever ethical terms were defined in terms of something nonethical; and it was his position that one simply had to intuit—without reductive definitions—the nature of the good.

NATURAL LAW.
In Latin the *lex naturae*, or *jus naturale*. The concept of there being a natural law in some prescriptive sense, in addition to the positive law or written law of a society, runs throughout Western thought.

(1) When Plato (*q.v.* 5b) conceives of law as a disposition of reason ordering things according to their nature, we are already in the sphere of natural law.

(2) Aristotle (*q.v.* 14) referred, in passing, to the permanent and changeless universal law as more important than written laws. He also used the term "law of nature"; but it is not clear that his conception distinguished the *jus gentium* or law of nations, from the *jus naturale*, or law which should order all nations.

(3) The Stoic conception of a universal reason ordering and providing law for the physical universe, communities, and individuals, provides the most explicit support for the idea of natural law (*q.v.* Cicero 2). And it was among Roman lawyers that the distinction between the *jus gentium* and *jus naturale* was finally and explicitly made (*q.v.* Stoicism 4).

(4) Thomas Aquinas (*q.v.* 9) provided the most comprehensive statement of the various forms of law, and it was widely accepted among Scholastics. The *eternal*

law of God is conveyed to man in part through revelations and in part through human reason. What man can discern of the eternal law through reason is *natural law*. Both *positive* (or written) *law* and the *jus gentium* are derived from natural law, the former by way of particularizing its precepts to fit a given society, the latter by the drawing of inferences to fit particular cases.

(5) Vitoria (*q.v.*3) followed the natural law doctrine, relating it to international law and the problems of subject nations.

(6) Hooker (*q.v.* 1) followed the distinctions made by Aquinas, while strengthening the role of reason in interpreting both natural and eternal law.

(7) Grotius (*q.v.* 2–4), interpreting the natural law as the rationally discernible set of principles available to all men, held this sense of law to be determinative not only over the positive or civil law, and the law of nations, but also over the divine or eternal law. This had the effect of secularizing the concept.

(8) With Thomas Hobbes (*q.v.* 8), a contemporary of Grotius, only two types of law enter the discussion, natural law and civil law, and the thrust of his conception elevates civil law above natural law. The eternal law is not discussed since that is the subject matter of theology; the law of nations does not exist since nations are in a state of nature, *i.e.*, in the war of each against all. And natural law, although it is held to be identical to civil law (for this reason it is impossible to think of disobeying a civil law), is really the set of reasons why it is better to form a civil society rather than remain in a state of nature. In this sense, with Hobbes natural law gives way to the social contract doctrine.

(9) Cumberland (*q.v.* 1–2) found natural law in the character of rational beings, and believed that morality rested on these immutable truths.

(10) John Locke (*q.v.* 9) likewise used a social contract theory but he was able to retain much of the traditional meaning of natural law. Since Locke, unlike Hobbes, believed man to be essentially rational, and since, like Aquinas, he believed the law of nature to be not only the law of reason but the law of nature's God, Locke could hold that the rules of positive law must conform to the law of

nature, *i.e.*, to the will of God. He was thus able to place within his view the eternal law, natural law, and positive law.

(11) Montesquieu (*q.v.* 5) held natural law to be the relations of possible justice which positive law implements.

(12) Rousseau (*q.v.* 3–5) placed so much emphasis on the social contract that the state of nature became a state of animal existence, and natural law became an equivocal concept.

NATURAL RIGHTS.

The rights which belong to man, by nature, resting not on custom or convention, but on self-evident principles or fundamental laws of reason. The support for natural rights rests on the doctrine of natural law (*q.v.*). But the assertion of natural rights came at the time when the social contract theory of the origin of government had joined itself to the doctrine of natural law (*q.v.* Social Contract).

(1) For Thomas Hobbes (*q.v.* 9) man has a natural right to life, which no society can abridge arbitrarily. In any situation one can use force to repel force in defense of his life.

(2) For John Locke (*q.v.* 9) the natural rights are life, liberty, and property. The same triad is mentioned in the U.S. Constitution, although in the Declaration of Independence Jefferson (*q.v.* 1) suggested a different triad: life, liberty, and pursuit of happiness. He regarded property as a civil right.

(3) For Rousseau (*q.v.* 5c) we give over our natural rights to act on impulse and instinct as we enter the state, and receive civil rights in return.

(4) The French Declaration of the Rights of Man and the Citizen, and Thomas Paine (*q.v.* 4) who helped frame the Declaration, hold that the natural rights are liberty, equality, security, property, social protection, and resistance to oppression.

(5) Trendelenburg (*q.v.*) explained natural right in terms of Aristotelian final cause.

(6) The United Nations Declaration of Rights has widely expanded every previous listing.

NATURAL SELECTION.

Q.v. A.R. Wallace; Darwin (5); Chauncey Wright.

NATURAL THEOLOGY.

Any theology which purports to rest its case on reason instead of revelation. The program reached the status of a movement in the 17th and 18th centuries. The most vigorous proponent of the doctrine was William Paley (*q.v.* 2) whose book, *Natural Theology*, 1794, had considerable influence.

NATURA NATURANS and NATURA NATURATA.

Latin phrases meaning "nature naturing" and "nature natured," respectively. "Nature naturing" applies to God as the creative principle of created things, or infinite and eternal Being over against finite, temporal beings. "Nature natured" applies to the created things which find their principle in God.

(1) The phrase "*natura naturata*" seems first to have been employed by Averroës (*q.v.* 1) in the above sense. Although he did not use "*natura naturans*," his conception of God as first cause is a near equivalent.

(2) The two phrases were first used together, and in the above senses, by Vicente de Beauvais (*q.v.* 2).

(3) The phrases are employed once again in Giordano Bruno (*q.v.* 3) where they relate to transcendence and immanence in God.

(4) Their most widely noted usage, however, is in Spinoza (*q.v.* 3) where the distinction is between eternal and infinite essence and temporal existents, or between the eternal principle and what follows by necessity from this principle.

NATURE.

From the Latin *natura*, a translation of the Greek word *physis*. Both terms derive from roots suggesting production, growth, and bringing to birth. Thus the early signification of the term concerned that part of reality subject to change; and physics was the name of the study charged with the understanding of this aspect of reality.

(1) The pre-Socratic philosophers directed their attention initially (*q.v.* Milesian Philosophy) to the discovery of some ultimate factor which could explain the changes and transformations of things.

(2) Plato (*q.v.* 2, 9) understood nature as the realm of change, created according to a timeless pattern. But in a second sense the nature of a thing refers to its generating idea, that is, the form it represents.

(3) Aristotle (*q.v.* 7–10) suggests that nature has the following five characteristics: it is that which has not been made, *i.e.*, it is not an artifice; it is not eternal or immutable; it involves matter or potency; it has an immanent principle of movement; and it has form or essence. It is interesting that the list allows us to speak of nature in Plato's terms as a realm of chance, and of the nature of a thing in terms of its essence or definition.

(4) The Stoic philosophy, however, extended the concept of nature to the point where man, finite things, and God formed part of a single system. Nature was the all-inclusive system, and there was nothing beyond nature (*q.v.* Stoicism; Marcus Aurelius 2).

(5) Erigena (*q.v.* 1) divided nature into creative and created parts, regarding it as coming from God as creator and returning to God as final end.

(6) The concept of nature most widely held in the Middle Ages derived from Aristotle. Implicit in Aristotle is the widely held distinction of the Middle Ages between "things of nature" (*entia naturae*) and "things of reason" (*entia rationis*), *i.e.*, entities having their existence in the mind. There was an emphasis, as in Aquinas (*q.v.* 5), on the distinction between the natural and the supernatural. In this conception nature is the order of secondary causes, created by the first cause, but preserved by the operation of secondary causes. Miracles (*q.v.* 3) are possible because surpassing the power of nature simply means action in terms of the primary cause rather than the secondary.

(7) William of Ockham (*q.v.* 13) held the order of nature to be radically dependent upon the will of God.

(8) Descartes (*q.v.* 8–10) uses the term nature in several senses. Clear and distinct ideas, which are not further divisible, he calls "simple natures." Such ideas have a key role in inquiry. Implicit in Descartes, too, is the position that nature is to be understood as the set of bodies with spatial extension which can be ordered mathematically. Both finite souls

and God are, therefore, strictly speaking outside of nature.

(9) Spinoza (*q.v.* 3), on the other hand, followed the Stoics in viewing nature as a system including both man and God. This inclusive system is infinite and may be referred to as "God or Nature" (*Deus sive Natura*). The two aspects are captured in his distinction between *Natura naturans* and *Natura naturata* (*q.v.*).

(10) In all of the views given thus far, except in that of Ockham, nature has some measure of independence. For the Idealist Berkeley (*q.v.* 5) nature is nothing more than a series of ideas imprinted on our minds by God.

(11) Hume (*q.v.* 1, 8) found nature to be what lies outside of our minds, supporting the matters of fact known to us. Our constant experience supports the idea that nature is orderly and thus has laws. Miracles, then, as violations of the laws of nature, are impossible.

(12) Kant (*q.v.* 2) restricts nature to the phenomenal world. It is the order of causal necessity, he agrees, but causality in his view is phenomenal. Human life, on the other hand, is rooted in a supersensible or noumenal order.

(13) Finally, nature is used in the phrase "state of nature" to refer to the relations which obtain among persons apart from the conditions of formal social organization. For the social usage *q.v.* Social Contract.

(14) For Marx (*q.v.* 9) capitalism, in making nature exclusively a means to human survival, provides a fourth form of alienation.

NAYA.

A Sanskrit term meaning "aspect or standpoint." In Jainism (*q.v.* 5) there are seven *nayas* from which one can view reality.

NECESSARY AND SUFFICIENT CONDITION.

These terms apply to both causal and logical explanations. Let "p" and "q" represent events, ideas, or propositions.

(1) Given any p and q, p is a sufficient condition of q if, given p, then q.

(2) Given any p and q, p is a necessary condition of q if, given ~ p, then ~ q.

In causal terms the presence of oxygen is a necessary but not a sufficient condition for fire. Oxygen plus combustibles plus the striking of a match would illustrate a sufficient condition for fire. In logical terms, since a syllogism requires both major and minor premises in order to gain the conclusion, the major and minor premises together constitute a sufficient condition for the conclusion. Each premise taken separately is a necessary condition for the conclusion. Also *q.v.* Fichte (2).

NECESSITARIANISM.

The doctrine that all events happen by necessity, having either logical or causal determination, and that the will is not free. A synonym for "determinism" (*q.v.*).

NECESSITY.

From the Latin *ne* ("not") plus *cedere* ("to go away"). The Greek term is *anagke*, and the original concept probably concerned fate or destiny. Necessity may be affirmed of propositions, of things, or of God.

A. When affirmed of propositions, to say that a proposition is necessary is to say that it is not possible to deny that proposition.

(1) In modal logic (*q.v.* Modality), letting "□" stand for necessary, "◇" for possible, and the tilde "~" for "not," to say that some proposition "p" is necessary ("□ p") is to say "~ ◇ ~ p."

(2) Or, in Aristotle's (*q.v.* 10) language, the contingent is that which can be otherwise, while that which cannot be otherwise is necessarily as it is. The opposite of the contingent is another contingency (in the class of colors the "not-green" will be another color) while the opposite of the necessary is the impossible.

(3) Leibniz (*q.v.* 10) distinguished between absolute necessity, whose denial leads to contradiction, and hypothetical necessity (his example is causal necessity) whose denial does not lead to contradiction. The former are truths of reason, and are analytic.

(4) Kant (*q.v.* 1) found necessity not only in analytic judgments, as he called them, but also in synthetic *a priori* judgments. The latter he regarded as both necessary and non-trivial.

B. When necessity is affirmed of things one is saying that no other state of affairs is possible.

(5) The atomists thus held that the

whirling, world-creating motion of atoms came by necessity from their initially random movements, and that this necessity remained in the world once it was structured (*q.v.* Democritus 5–6).

(6) The view was further developed in Stoicism (*q.v.* 1) where physical causality and an ordering universal reason coalesced to produce a system in which everything is controlled by necessity, and nothing could have been otherwise.

(7) Spinoza (*q.v.* 1–3) represents the perfection of this point of view. Collapsing logical and causal necessity into each other, for Spinoza the existent world follows from the nature of God exactly as demonstrations in geometry follow from the initial definitions and axioms of the system. Wherever there is a cause, there is a reason and conversely.

(8) A variant version of necessity in things is to be found in Hume (*q.v.* 3) who, while holding there is no such thing as chance in the world, explains the idea of necessity as arising from the fact that experience of the constant conjunction of two things establishes a custom of expectation within us.

(9) Holbach (*q.v.* 2) held the world to be a system of material particles operating according to the rule of necessity.

(10) The idea of necessity is dramatized by Laplace's (*q.v.* 3) conception of a superhuman genius able to express the total future of the world in a single formula.

(11) Fichte (*q.v.* 2–3) held that causal necessity has to be "posited" along with the Ego and non-Ego.

C. Affirmed of God, the concept leads to that of a necessary Being.

(12) Aristotle's (*q.v.* 10) analysis led him to the conception of a necessary being, consisting of form alone, purely actual and standing in contrast to all ordinary beings, since such beings are contingent, contain matter and potency, and can thus cease to exist.

(13) Avicenna (*q.v.* 8) distinguished between God as necessary in Himself, and things in the world as necessary since they are determined by external causes.

(14) Aquinas (*q.v.* 4–5) accepted Aristotle's analysis while extending it in certain ways. God's necessity consists in the identity of his essence and existence, and all contingent beings are preserved in being by God's power.

(15) Leibniz's distinction between types of necessity (*cf.* 3 above) leads to a distinction between God as necessary and necessity in the world. The former concerns God's choice of the best possible world, and the latter the necessity in a world once chosen.

(16) The question whether existence can be inferred from the conception of God as a necessary Being is treated under the heading, Ontological Argument (*q.v.*). Anselm (*q.v.* 1–3) and others think so. Aquinas, Kant (*q.v.* 5), and others think not.

NEGATION.

From the Latin term *nego*, meaning "I deny." In philosophy the term applies to the denial of a class or property, statement or proposition.

(1) When denial occurs with respect to a class or property, the effect is to divide the universe of discourse between that class and its complement. If one denies the term "red," attaching to it the prefix "not," one gains a second term "not-red." Every other term may now be fitted either within the original class "red" or its complement "not-red."

(2) With respect to statements or propositions, the denial of affirmative propositions yields negative propositions, and the denial of negative propositions yields affirmative propositions. We shall divide propositions into those of the Propositional Calculus (*q.v.*) and those of syllogistic logic (*q.v.* Syllogism) and Quantification Theory (*q.v.*).

(3) In the Propositional Calculus (also *q.v.* Truth Tables 6), although denial may be indicated in more than one way, the most common is by the placing of a tilde, "~" before any proposition "p." This yields the negative proposition "~ p" (not-p), which may be read "It is not the case that 'p'." Double negation restores the original situation, since "~ ~ p" is equivalent to "p." The consequences of negating compound propositions are more complex. De Morgan (*q.v.*) has shown that the denial of "~ (p and q)," *i.e.*, "It is not the case that p and q," is "~ p or ~ q," *i.e.*, "Either not-p or not-q"; and the denial of "~ (p or q)," *i.e.*, "It is not the case that p or q," is "~ p and ~ q," *i.e.*, "Not-p and not-q." (*Q.v.* Propositional Calculus 13, 17.)

(4) In syllogistic logic, the negative propositions are named "E" and "O" propositions after the two vowels of the Latin term *nego*. The "E" proposition is universal and negative, *i.e.*, "No S is P." The "O" proposition is particular and negative, *i.e.*, "Some S is not P." The relations of affirmation and negation form a Square of Opposition (*q.v.* Inference 1) which was worked out in the Middle Ages. The same expressions are handled in Quantification Theory (*q.v.* 5, 6) by using the tilde as negation sign and certain other conventions.

(5) The discussion of negation sometimes raises the issue of Negative Facts. True empirical statements are factually supported. When the statements are affirmative they are supported by positive facts. When they are negative, are they supported by negative facts? If the ball is not-red, is there a negative fact of its not-redness? Or is the positive fact of its blueness the evidence which verifies the indefinitely extending set of true statements concerning what it is not? The oddity of the former assertion leads most philosophers, if not all, to accept the latter.

Q.v. the entry, Nothing, for the relationship of negation to Ontology.

NEGATIVE FACTS.
Q.v. Negation (5).

NEGATIVE THEOLOGY.
Q.v. The Pseudo-Dionysius (1).

NELSON, LEONARD. 1882–1927.
German philosopher. Born in Berlin. Taught at the University of Göttingen. Influenced by Jacob Friedrich Fries (*q.v.*), he established a neo-Friesian School of thought, also known as the Göttingen School of neo-Kantianism (*q.v.* Neo-Kantianism 3); and in 1904 a journal, the *Abhandlungen der Friesschen Schule, Neue Folge*, where much of his writing appeared.

Principal writings: *The Critical Method and the Relation of Psychology to Philosophy*, 1904; *Kant and Non-Euclidean Geometry*, 1906; *Lessons on Ethics*, 3 vols., 1917–32; *Ethical Realism*, 1921; *Socratic Method and Critical Philosophy: Selected Essays* (T), 1949.

(1) The central problem, as Nelson saw it, is to discover an appropriate manner of using psychology in relation to philosophical analysis without falling into psychologism. He found the solution to be that of reestablishing the subjective deduction of the principles of experience employed by Kant in the first edition of his *Critique*, but omitted in the second edition.

(2) The point, put quite simply, is that we discover in experience—that is, through a psychological process—the principles required in various fields; but we justify these principles metaphysically by making them part of a transcendental deduction. Thus, they assume the status of synthetic *a priori* judgments (*q.v.* Kant 1).

(3) Nelson applied the method to problems of epistemology, political philosophy, philosophy of law, ethics, and practical philosophy. He felt that his colleague, Rudolf Otto (*q.v.*), had made such an analysis in the field of religion.

NEMESIUS. 4th cent. A.D.
Christian Churchman and philosopher. Born in Greece. Bishop of Emesa. A member of the Alexandrian School (*q.v.*) of Neoplatonism, Nemesius combined influences from the Neoplatonists Porphyry and Ammonius with Stoic and Aristotelian themes and the analyses, both physiological and psychological, of Galen, to produce a work in philosophical anthropology. Q.v. Neoplatonism.

Principal writings: *On the Nature of Man.*

NEO-CONFUCIANISM.
Q.v. Chinese Philosophy (7).

NEO-CONNECTIONISM.
Q.v. Artificial Intelligence (4).

NEO-CRITICISM.
Q.v. Renouvier.

NEO-FRIESIAN SCHOOL.
Q.v. Neo-Kantianism (3); Leonard Nelson; Rudolf Otto.

NEO-KANTIANISM.
A remarkable movement of return to Kant, appearing spontaneously in the 1860's and enduring until the 1920's. The mood of the movement was epitomized by the "Back to Kant" slogan of Otto Liebmann (*q.v.* and also *cf.* 1 below), issued in 1865. For most of those who

responded the call meant "back to epistemology" after the metaphysical excesses of 19th-century Idealism and Romanticism. There were neo-Kantian philosophers and movements in all parts of Germany. But the characteristics of an identifiable approach to Kant, a school of Kantian philosophy with its own journal, developed in only a handful of cases.

(1) Prior to the schools, there were eminent philosophers, some later identified with one or another of the schools, who, like Liebmann, called for the return to Kant. Eduard Zeller (*q.v.*) called specifically for a return to epistemology which, he pointed out, meant a return to Kant. Helmholtz (*q.v.*) argued that the Kantian philosophy, unlike the Romantic philosophies, would be a stimulation to the sciences. Liebmann insisted that the Kantian attention to the details of experience was essential, although he believed that Kant's concept of the "thing-in-itself" should be dropped. Aloys Riehl (*q.v.*) believed that it was consistent with the Kantian philosophy to reject metaphysics, although he believed that the "thing-in-itself" is an ineradicable feature of any adequate philosophy. And Wilhelm Wundt (*q.v.*), himself initially a physiologist, exemplified the manner in which Kantianism was consistent with the special sciences by developing a fairly complete neo-Kantian philosophy.

(2) The Marburg School of neo-Kantianism was characterized by an epistemological approach to philosophy in relation to extensive analyses of the sciences. Epistemology and philosophy of science may be said to be the chief interests of the school. Their journal was the *Philosophische Arbeiten*. Among the Marburg neo-Kantians were Friedrich Lange (*q.v.*), who held materialism to be the most scientific doctrine of reality; Hermann Cohen (*q.v.*), who dropped the concept of the "thing-in-itself" and made the thinking of the scientific community constitutive of the scientific reality; Paul Natorp (*q.v.*), who extended Cohen's analysis into Psychology while using the unity of consciousness as a premise; Cassirer (*q.v.*), who continued to extend the analysis—applying it to all symbolic forms including myth and religion; and Stammler (*q.v.*), who applied the Marburg approach to the Philosophy of Law.

(3) The Göttingen School began with a revival of appreciation for the work of Jacob Friedrich Fries (*q.v.*), a Kantian who had interpreted the Master psychologically rather than transcendentally. Indeed, the Göttingen School is also known as the neo-Friesian School. Among the members of the school are Leonard Nelson (*q.v.*), who set himself the task of showing that the psychological approach to Kant can avoid psychologism by means of a rational justification of the principles found through the psychological analysis, and Rudolf Otto (*q.v.*), who applied this approach to religious phenomena.

(4) The Heidelberg School of neo-Kantianism, also called the Baden School, or the Southwest German School, of neo-Kantianism, named its journal *Logos*. The school is characterized by an axiological approach to philosophy, taking value, usually absolute value, to be the key to epistemology. The interpretation was initiated by Wilhelm Windelband (*q.v.*), expanded by Heinrich Rickert (*q.v.*), given a turn in the direction of increasing the importance of logic in the analysis by Jonas Cohn (*q.v.*). Although teaching at Leipzig, Johannes Volkelt (*q.v.*) reflected the Heidelberg thesis in his work. Münsterberg (*q.v.*), teaching first at Freiburg and then at Harvard, argued the thesis of absolute value while defending it in terms of a Fichtean absolute will.

(5) At the University of Halle, Hans Vaihinger (*q.v.*) initiated two journals devoted to Kantian philosophy: *Kantstudien*, which was open to all of the varieties of neo-Kantianism, and the *Annalen der Philosophie und Philosophischer Kritik*, which was devoted to his own version of the critical philosophy, called Idealistic Positivism or Fictionalism.

(6) Not a school in the strict sense, a number of neo-Kantians carried the analysis into the areas of history and society. Sharing the premises of Windelband and Rickert, Dilthey (*q.v.*) in Berlin devoted himself to extending the Kantian analysis to the historical sciences. Max Weber (*q.v.*), related to Heidelberg as well as to Berlin, extended this analysis to sociological studies, initiating the concept of "Ideal Types." Edward Spranger (*q.v.*), related to Berlin and Tübingen, set himself to complete and systematize the work

of Dilthey; in the process of doing so, he developed a typological approach similar to that of Weber. Karl Mannheim (*q.v.*), related for a time to Heidelberg, working with the problem of ideology, used some of the same elements in his own sociology. Troeltsch (*q.v.*) followed Dilthey, finding through history a type of autonomy for the Christian faith, and Ritschl (*q.v.*), combining Kant with Schleiermacher, found the autonomy of faith by separating it sharply from the sciences.

(7) Another loosely structured group was somewhat more inclined to a metaphysical orientation than most Kantians, and a spiritualistic metaphysics at that. Max Wundt (*q.v.*) was the spiritual father of this group. Paulsen (*q.v.*) was influenced by Max Wundt, and Erich Adickes (*q.v.*) by both Paulsen and Wundt. Georg Simmel (*q.v.*), stressing the importance of the creative life, bears some similarity to this group.

(8) In addition to the above, there were neo-Kantian movements in most of the countries of Europe, although without the organization of the German schools. In France, Lachelier (*q.v.*) advanced a doctrine of spiritual realism, having started from Kantian premises; and Renouvier (*q.v.*) elaborated a voluntaristic personalism on these grounds. In England, Edward Caird wrote in the spirit of Kant, but touched with Hegelian idealism.

NEO-ORTHODOXY.

Q.v. Karl Barth; Emil Brunner; Reinhold Niebuhr (1); H.R. Niebuhr.

NEOPLATONISM.

One of the most persistent strands of Western philosophy, Neoplatonism is, as the name suggests, a philosophy which begins from the work of Plato, and interprets him in a special manner. The manner of that interpretation tends to associate God with the principle of unity. As a result God becomes completely transcendent, and related to the world by means of a series of intermediaries, who (or which) derive from the One by a principle of emanation. In this view reality is a graded series from the divine to the material, and man, who has in him some part of the divine, longs for union with the eternal source of things. The

system thus has spiritual as well as intellectual implications.

(1) Although the term is most intimately associated with the philosophy of Plotinus (*cf.* 6 below), the germ of the movement is discernible in Plato's Academy, having made its appearance shortly after the Master's death. Speusippus (*q.v.*), who succeeded Plato as head of the Academy, adhered to the doctrine of a divine process which produced the Good; and Xenocrates (*q.v.* 2), head of the Academy after Speusippus, had already identified God with the primal unity.

(2) Furthermore, the Pythagorean influence, playing upon the Academy and having some effect on the thought of both Speusippus and Xenocrates, increased in the Pythagorean renaissance which lasted from the 1st century B.C. until the 2nd century A.D. Thus, there was a continuing pressure to construe Plato in Pythagorean terms.

(3) Prior to the flowering of Neoplatonism, other figures may be regarded as preparing the way for it. Among them one might mention Philo Judaeus (*q.v.* 5) whose thought, in the 1st century A.D., anticipated Neoplatonism in a number of ways: in his conception of a totally transcendent God, for example, and his interposing a hierarchy of intermediate levels between God and the world.

(4) Numenius of Apamea (*q.v.*), who is regarded as a neo-Pythagorean in the 2nd century A.D., combined so many of the themes characteristic of Neoplatonism that he is regarded by some as its founder before Plotinus.

(5) Ammonius Saccas (*q.v.*), the 3rd-century A.D. teacher of Plotinus, as well as Origen the Neoplatonist (*q.v.*), and many others, are likewise sometimes regarded as the founders of this school of thought.

(6) But Neoplatonism is usually defined primarily in terms of the philosophy of Plotinus (*q.v.*) with its three great levels of the One, the *Nous*, and the World Soul, leading down from pure being through the world of life, and finally down to matter at the lowest end of the scale.

(7) Among the immediate disciples of Plotinus were Amelius (*q.v.*) and Porphyry (*q.v.*), and Iamblichus (*q.v.*) was a disciple of Porphyry. The former tended

largely to memorialize their master, while the latter added embellishments to his thought. Edesius, a disciple of Iamblichus, founded the School of Pergamum.

(8) The most classical school of Neo-platonism was the School of Athens. Existing from about 380 to 529 A.D., this school searched for a single viewpoint in the thinking of Plato, Aristotle, Plotinus, and other strands of thought such as Stoicism. Among its leaders Plutarch of Athens (*q.v.*), Syrianus (*q.v.*), Proclus (*q.v.*), Damascius (*q.v.*), and Simplicius (*q.v.*) deserve to be mentioned. The school, hostile to Christianity, was closed by Justin in 529.

(9) Related to the School of Athens was the Alexandrian School of Neoplatonism (*q.v.*). The dates for this school extend from around 430 A.D. to the Moslem conquest of Alexandria in 642. A number of the members of this school were themselves Christians; the others were amicable to the movement. Among the more significant members of the Alexandrian School were Hierocles (*q.v.*), Hermias (*q.v.*), Ammonius, Asclepius (*q.v.*), and Olimpiodorus (*q.v.*).

(10) The Latin Neoplatonists, so called because of their relations to Rome, include Macrobius (*q.v.*), Marius Victorinus (*q.v.*), and Boethius (*q.v.*). Many of these were Christians; and a recurrent theme was the development of the concept of the Trinity in Neoplatonic terms.

(11) In a variety of ways these schools continued to exert influence on succeeding generations, sometimes indirectly. For example, St. Augustine (*q.v.*) passed through a Neoplatonic stage on the way to Christianity, and a residue of this experience remained as a permanent deposit in his thought, not without influence on the Middle Ages. Again, the writings of the Pseudo-Dionysius (*q.v.*), based on the work of Proclus, were accepted as the writings of Dionysius the Areopagite mentioned in the Book of Acts. It is now known that the writings were composed at the end of the 4th or the beginning of the 5th century. As the work of Dionysius they had immense prestige into the 13th century.

(12) Two other instances may be cited, this time in connection with the Baghdad School (*q.v.*) of Syrian thought. In 832 this school initiated a program to translate various Greek texts into Arabic. Among the translations were a portion of Proclus' work on theology, and Books four to six of Plotinus' *Enneads.* The first of these translations came to be known as the *Book of Causes* (*q.v. Liber de Causis*) and the second as the *Theology of Aristotle* (*q.v.*). Both works circulated widely until the 13th century as works of Aristotle. Since the doctrine of both works was straight Neoplatonism, a vast number of Aristotle's interpreters were led into Neoplatonic thought, elaborating vast hierarchical systems leading from the divine to the temporal world. Among those so influenced were: Al-Kindi (*q.v.*), Al-Farabi (*q.v.* 1), Avicenna (*q.v.* 5, 7), Avicebron (*q.v.* 3), and Averroës (*q.v.* 2).

(13) The system of Erigena (*q.v.*), with its theophany of emanation and return, is a direct expression of the influence of the Pseudo-Dionysius, whose writings he translated into Latin. And the same influence is clearly present in the work of Meister Eckhart (*q.v.*).

(14) In the 15th century the Florentine Academy (*q.v.*), established by the Medicis partly under the influence of the Neoplatonist Plethon, was avowedly Platonic and implicitly Neoplatonic, as indeed was its first head, Marsilius Ficino (*q.v.*).

(15) In the 16th-century Paracelsus (*q.v.*) was shaped by Neoplatonic as well as Gnostic influences.

(16) In the 17th century the Cambridge Platonists (*q.v.*) centered their attention on Plato, Proclus, and Plotinus. Cudworth (*q.v.*) and Henry More (*q.v.*) were among the most prominent members of this group.

(17) In the 19th century Schelling (*q.v.*) and even Hegel (*q.v.*) can be fairly regarded as recipients of this influence.

NEO-PYTHAGOREANISM.
Q.v. Pythagoreanism (2).

NEO-SCHOLASTICISM.
Q.v. Thomism (3).

NEO-SPIRITUALISM.
A late 19th-century movement in French philosophy headed by Lachelier (*q.v.*).

NEO-STOICISM.
Q.v. Lipsius; Du Vair.

NEO-TAOISM.
Q.v. Chinese Philosophy (4, 5).

NEO-THOMISM.
Q.v. Thomism (3).

NESCIENCE.
Q.v. Sankara (6–11).

NESTORIANISM.
A Christological doctrine of the 5th century A.D. advanced by Nestorius, Patriarch of Constantinople. Terming it a *"prosopic* union" of the divine and human (from the Greek term *prosopon* meaning "face"), Nestorius held "the manhood is the face of the Godhead, and the Godhead is the face of the manhood." This was misinterpreted as the doctrine that the God-man is two complete persons. It is this misinterpretation that bears the name, Nestorian heresy. Condemned at the Councils of Ephesus and Chalcedon, and subject to persecution, the Nestorians developed into a separate church, revering Nestorius as a saint, and exercising long-lasting influence throughout Asia. *Q.v.* Christology (3).

NETI NETI.
Sanskrit phrase meaning "not this, not this" (or "not this, not that"). A *Vedanta* (*q.v.*) utterance designed to separate everything transitory from Brahman, thus serving as in the *Bṛhadaranyaka Upaniṣad* (*q.v. Vedas* 4), and by Shankara (*q.v.* 4) as the only appropriate definition of Brahman. For a Western example, *q.v.* Philo of Judaeus (2).

NETTESHEIM.
Q.v. Agrippa von Nettesheim.

NEUMANN, FRANZ.
Q.v. Frankfurt School, The. A.

NEURATH, OTTO. 1882–1945.
Austrian philosopher. One of the original members of the Vienna Circle of Logical Positivists (*q.v.*), Neurath, with Carnap, invented the doctrine of physicalism, stressing the role of protocol sentences— *i.e.*, sentences based on observation and referring to space-time states. He expected this doctrine to lead to a unified science, and worked to establish the *International Encyclopedia of Unified Science* (*q.v.* Vienna Circle 6). He

developed an "empirical sociology" on the foundation of physicalism.
Principal writings: *Scientific World View: The Vienna Circle* (with Carnap and Hahn), 1929; *Empirical Sociology*, 1931; *Foundations of the Social Sciences*, 1944.

NEUROSIS.
Q.v. Freud (4).

NEUSTIC.
Greek term meaning "to nod assent." *Q.v.* Hare (2).

NEUTRAL IMPRESSIONS.
Q.v. Mach (2).

NEUTRAL MONISM.
The doctrine that the basic entities of the world are neither physical nor mental, but of some neutral "stuff" which, organized in one manner, yields physical entities, or bodies, and, when organized in another manner, yields mind. The doctrine was held, at least for a time, by Russell (*q.v.* 9) who found the suggestion for his doctrine in William James' view of "pure" experience. Although they did not use the term, the doctrine was anticipated by Ardigó (*q.v.* 3) and Riehl (*q.v.* 2). Also *q.v.* New Realism (4, 5, 7).

NEVELL, ALAN.
Q.v. Artificial Intelligence (3).

NEW CRITICISM.
A 20th century Anglo-American theory of literary criticism which held that the activity of criticism should concentrate on the text, viewing historical, biographical, and psychological considerations to be irrelevant. The name was supplied by the poet and critic, John Crowe Ransom, in his *The New Criticism*, (1941). Among the New Critics are I.A. Richards (*q.v.*), T.S. Eliot, Cleanth Brooks, René Wellek, Austin Warren, William Empson (*q.v.*), W.K. Wimsatt, and Monroe Beardsley (*q.v.* Metaphor 14). Since most of its members were in the United States the movement is sometimes called the "American New Criticism" and its adherents "American New Critics." With awareness centered on the text critical judgment turns on internal organization, theme, and verbal nuance involving irony, paradox, and tension. Wimsatt and Beardsley formulated two fallacies to be

avoided in criticism; "the intentional fallacy" when the poem is confused with its origins, and "the affective fallacy" when the poem is confused with its effect on an audience ("The Intentional Fallacy" and "The Affective Fallacy," in W.K. Wimsatt, *The Verbal Icon*, pp. 3–18, 21–39, 1954; Monroe C. Beardsley, "Intention and Interpretations: A Fallacy Revisited," *The Aesthetic Point of View*, 1982). The intentional fallacy is committed in "Biographism" where the critic finds the key to the quality of the poem in the poet's life. The supposition on which New Criticism rests, that every text supports an authoritative reading, has been challenged by a rival literary theory called Deconstruction (*q.v.*).

NEW ENGLAND TRANSCENDENTALISM.

Q.v. Transcendent (4).

NEW HAVEN THEOLOGY.

Q.v. Nathaniel Taylor.

NEWMAN, JOHN HENRY. 1801–1890.

English Churchman. Born in London. Studied at Oxford. Entered the Anglican clergy in 1824. Participated in the Oxford Movement, directed toward increasing the vitality of the Christian faith. His activity in this connection led him to doubt the viability of the Anglican alternative, and in 1845 he was converted to Catholicism. In the 1850's he served as Rector of the new Catholic University of Ireland. He was named Cardinal in 1879.

Principal writings: *An Essay on the Development of Christian Doctrine*, 1845; *The Idea of a University*, 1852; *Apologia pro Vita Sua*, 1864; *Essay in Aid of a Grammar of Assent*, 1870.

(1) In his view Christian doctrine passes all of the tests for genuine development: *i.e.*, its principles are influential, have continuity, the capacity to assimilate new data, organize complex social processes, anticipate the future, conserve the past, and retain chronic vigor.

(2) The most strategically placed center for cultural development in the contemporary world, however, is the university. The task of the university is to prepare individuals to determine the direction of history by inculcating in them the basic perspectives of humanistic, scientific, and theological studies.

(3) The *Apologia pro Vita Sua* of 1864 is an autobiographical defense of his conversion to Catholicism. This defense of the course his life had taken, initially published in bimonthly instalments, was the subject of intense interest. The publication removed a considerable amount of distrust which had been accumulating in England since the time of his conversion. Implicit in the *Apology* and explicit in the *Grammar* is the question concerning how one can have a reasonable basis for religious faith. The answer to this question called forth Newman's most original thinking.

(4) First, Newman distinguishes between formal and informal reasoning. Formal reasoning is general and abstract as in mathematics. Informal reasoning is individual and concrete. Formal or abstract reasoning has certitude as its goal. Informal or concrete reasoning has not certitude, but rather certainty, as its goal, the former having a logical and the latter a psychological sense. The problem is to determine how concrete reasoning can lead to certainty.

(5) Since in any case of reasoning it is an individual mind that is doing the reasoning, there is a sense in which concrete reasoning is more basic than abstract reasoning. All good reasoning is produced by the human "illative sense" (the faculty of drawing logical conclusions). Newman argues that the "illative sense" is the "sole and final judgment" of the validity of any instance of concrete reasoning. Religious decision would be an instance of concrete reasoning.

(6) Newman held a somewhat unusual view of probability. Holding that only abstract reasoning can have certitude, it followed that all informal or concrete reasoning is probable. He meant by probable reasoning not an inference falling short of certainty, but the relationship of a person to a concrete situation. A sequence of such reasoning can be probable and yet hold certainty.

(7) With respect to the giving of assent, again there are two types. One can give a notional assent to a proposition or a real assent to a situation. While notional assent is to a proposition, real assent is to the reality to which the

proposition refers. In any important matter notional assent must be perfected by real assent.

(8) Religious decision is the key area where notional assent must be completed by real assent. And Newman believed that the life of conscience relates to such real assent, since conscience comprehends the whole person and for Newman provides a link allowing one to gain a luminous vision of God and also to sustain a relationship with Him.

NEW PHILOSOPHERS, THE.

A group of French social philosophers, coming into prominence in the 1970's. Anti-establishment, anti-Marxist, and anti-ideological, they are the fruit of the May, 1968, student and worker uprising. Among their number are: André Glucksmann (*Strategy and Revolution in France,* 1968); Jean-Marie Benoist (*Marx is Dead,* 1970); Phillipe Nemo (*The Structural Man,* 1975); and Bernard-Henry Lévy (*Barbarism with a Human Face,* 1977).

NEW REALISM.

A movement featuring the resurgence of realism in the early years of this century. The New Realists argued for the independence and external relatedness of objects of knowledge. Their arguments were directed against the powerful currents of Idealism in England and America whose epistemology reduced things to thoughts on the ground that all awareness is mental, and who urged the need for internal relations between objects of knowledge and acts of awareness. The New Realists, wishing to avoid the extremes of Idealism and Materialism, developed the alternative of Neutral Monism (*q.v.*) which posited a neutral kind of entity underlying both material and mental "objects."

(1) Beginning in 1909 the group had a brief period of organized activity in the United States, when six American philosophers—E.B. Holt, W.T. Marvin, W.P. Montague, R.B. Perry, W.B. Pitkin, and E.G. Spaulding—developed a program and platform for the movement. Published in the *Journal of Philosophy* in 1910, the platform was followed in 1912 by a cooperative volume titled *The New Realism.*

(2) Since a number of the philosophers named above moved on to other positions, and since the same was true of Russell and Moore—intellectual associates of the movement—perhaps the clearest point to be made is that at the turn of the century Idealism had reached its crest, and an opportunity existed both in England and in the United States, to provide a new statement of the realist position. The statement, once given, led on to other points of view.

(3) The beginning of the movement's development consisted of the 1902 publication of W.P. Montague's article, "Professor Royce's Refutation of Realism," and the 1903 publication of the article by G.E. Moore (*q.v.* 1) on "The Refutation of Idealism." Both articles made the point that the object of knowledge is not radically dependent upon the knowing relation. At the same time, and with similar intent, Russell (*q.v.* 1) was seeking a non-Idealistic basis for mathematics.

(4) In the United States, William James (*q.v.* 10) was developing a doctrine of pure experience. A neutral category underlying both thoughts and things, pure experience functioned in some relationships as thoughts and in other relationships as things. It was this analysis which allowed the development of the doctrine of neutral monism which the movement needed.

(5) It was E.B. Holt (*q.v.* 1–3) who most fully developed the doctrine of neutral monism. He referred to the neutral entities as elements of being and located them in a timeless realm. His position that even secondary qualities have being was shared by the English philosopher, T.P. Nunn.

(6) E.G. Spaulding and W.P. Montague (*q.v.* 1) contributed the notion of subsistence to the movement. Indeed, Montague called his doctrine Subsistential Realism. Error is explained, in this account, by our taking as existential an object of consciousness which is only subsistential. But the subsistential, that which has subsistence, is no less real than that which has existence. The error consists in having confused two modes of being.

(7) Russell (*q.v.* 9) adopted the doctrine of neutral monism for a time, crediting James with the source of his insight. R.B. Perry (*q.v.* 1), a close student of James, was likewise a neutral monist for a time,

finding his source in James' writings.

(8) Perry's original contribution to the movement, however, consisted in his suggestion that the Idealists had committed the fallacy of inferring from the straightforward idea that for us to know something we must think it, to the very different idea that anything we know is thought, *i.e.*, mental. The situation we are in which does not allow this inference Perry called the Egocentric Predicament (*q.v.*, and Perry 1).

NEWTON, ISAAC. 1642–1727.

English physicist and natural philosopher. Born at Woolsthorpe. Studied at Cambridge, where he became a member of the faculty as professor of mathematics from 1675 to 1701. He was admitted to the Royal Society in 1672; he served in Parliament for a year as representative of Cambridge. He was named Warden of the Mint in 1694, and Master of the Mint in 1697, holding this latter post for the remainder of his life. He was admitted to the French Academy of Science in 1699. He became president of the Royal Society in 1703, and was reelected yearly until his death. He was knighted in 1705. John Locke was a close friend, and Leibniz a European rival. Leibniz and Newton had invented the differential calculus independently; there was an unfortunate quarrel among their followers concerning who should receive the credit. In France, Voltaire defended and popularized the work of Newton. It was Voltaire who first told the story of the falling apple as suggesting to the mind of Newton, meditating on the planets, the principle of universal gravitation. Voltaire got the story from Newton's niece. The event is supposed to have occurred at Newton's birthplace and family home during the summer of 1666.

Principal writings: *Mathematical Principles of Natural Philosophy*, 1687; *Optics*, 1704.

(1) It was Newton's great achievement to have worked out in the *Principia* (the first work mentioned above) the mechanics of motion, both celestial and terrestrial. The achievement gave modern science a solid basis for the continual development which has since occurred. By elaboration of the law of gravitation, showing that the force of attraction between the sun and the planets varies with the inverse square of their distances, he brought order into the new astronomy.

(2) His three laws of motion have been subject to some refinement since his time. (a) The first law, that every body continues in a state of rest or uniform motion in a straight line unless compelled to change that state by forces impressed upon it, is the Principle of Inertia. But Newton identified this property with *vis insita*, or the innate force of matter; this is not quite a modern doctrine. (b) The second law, that the change of motion is proportional to the motive force impressed and in the direction in which the force is impressed, regards force as a real entity which is the cause of acceleration. Here, too, we have a somewhat specialized reading of the matter. (c) The third law, that to every action there is always an equal and opposite reaction, completes the triad.

(3) Newton believed that it was necessary to suppose an absolute space and time as the framework for the motion of bodies. He suggested a number of simple experiments which in his view require one to speak of the absolute motions of bodies, in addition to their relative motions with respect to one another.

(4) In terms of method he was something of a positivist. He gave four rules of reasoning in philosophy: (a) Admit no more causes of natural things than are "true and sufficient" to explain their appearances. (b) To the same natural effects, assign as much as possible the same causes. (c) The qualities of bodies within the reach of our experiments are to be esteemed the universal qualities of all bodies. (d) Propositions established by general induction are to be regarded as true or very nearly so, until these propositions are corrected by additional inductive evidence.

(5) When criticized for having merely worked out the law of gravitation without providing an adequate causal explanation, he responded with "*Hypotheses non fingo*." The verb "*fingo*" has many meanings. Among them are "to fashion," "to invent," and "to feign." And thus Newton was saying "I do not fashion, or invent, or feign hypotheses." The sense of the expression would seem to be that the business of science is not speculative

explanation but the discovery and statement of laws.

(6) He gave his system of mechanics a theistic framework, accepting from Henry More (*q.v.*) the idea that space is the sensorium of God. He found at least three functions for God in relation to his system. God is necessary to explain (a) creation, (b) why the law of gravitation does not draw the stars together into a single mass, (c) the stability of the solar system despite certain observed perturbations of planetary motion.

NEXUS.
Q.v. Whitehead (14).

NF.
Q.v. Quine (1).

NICAEA, COUNCIL OF. 325 A.D.
Called by Constantine to enable the Church to speak with a single voice on matters of faith, the main business of the council was that of determining a position on the relationship of Christ to God. The Trinitarian formula was introduced, and the position of the Alexandrians, argued by Athanasius (*q.v.*)—that Christ was *homoousious*, or of one substance, with God—carried the day. The alternative held by Arius (*q.v.*) that there was a time when the Son was not, was rejected. Arius was sentenced to exile, and his books were condemned to be burned. The Nicene Creed, using the Alexandrian phrase, had its origin in this council. The controversy over this issue continued until the Council of Constantinople (*q.v.*) in 381.

NICENE CREED.
A statement of belief developed in the councils of Nicea (*q.v.*) and Constantinople, gaining further definition until the 11th century. Like the Apostles' Creed (*q.v.*) derived from a baptismal formula. It begins: "I believe in one God the Father Almighty; maker of heaven and earth, and of all things visible and invisible." Its distinctive features include the *homoousian* (*q.v.*) claim that Christ is "of one substance with the Father," and the *Filioque* ("and from the Son") claim, that the Holy Ghost proceeded "from the Father and the Son." The first feature was directed against Arianism (*q.v.*). The second led to a permanent rupture between the Roman and Greek churches. It remains, however, the most widely accepted Christian creed. *Q.v.* Christianity (3).

NICHOLAS OF CUSA (NICHOLAS CUSANUS). 1401–1464.
German philosopher. Born in Cusa. Studied at Heidelberg, Padua, and Cologne. Holding to a conciliar view of Church government, he was often a papal emissary, charged most often with missions pointing toward ecclesiastical reform. Named a cardinal in 1448 and bishop in 1450.

Principal writings: *On Catholic Harmony*, 1433–4; *On Learned Ignorance*, 1440; *On Conjecture*, 1440; *On the Hidden God*, 1444; *Apology for Learned Ignorance*, 1449; *The Idiot*, 1450; *On the Peace of Faith*, 1453; *The Vision of God*, 1453; as well as mathematical treatises.

(1) Since all presumed knowledge is in fact conjecture, the height of wisdom is *docta ignorantia* or "learned ignorance" which recognizes its own impotence.

(2) Holding to a principle of *coincidentia oppositorum*, or the "coincidence of opposites," Nicholas strenuously opposed the Aristotelian principle of noncontradiction. Although the latter principle applies fairly well to finite beings, as one approaches infinity, either in the analysis of the world as a whole, or with respect to God, the opposite principle—that of the "coincidence of opposites"—becomes operative.

(3) The world for Nicholas is, of course, not absolutely infinite but only relatively so—he calls it the "relative maximum." It is boundless in extent and thus without a center. The planet earth, therefore, has no central location, nor is it at rest. It moves with a relative motion in the vastness of space.

(4) God is absolutely infinite, and thus the "absolute maximum." But at this point the "coincidence of opposites" applies. God as the absolute maximum is at the same time the absolute minimum, just as at infinity the arc of a chord is identical to the chord itself, and as at infinity a curve is identical to a straight line. In the case of God the principle leads to the consequence that God both transcends the universe and is immanent in every part, even in the smallest of things.

(5) The general conclusion, however, is that every part of the universe is present in every other part; and man, particularly, is both an image of God and a microcosm in which is reflected the total macrocosm.

NICHOLAS OF DAMASCUS. 1st cent. B.C.

Hellenic philosopher. A member of the Aristotelian school in Alexandria along with Andronicus of Rhodes (*q.v.*) and Ariston of Alexander (*q.v.*), Nicholas wrote commentaries on virtually all fields of knowledge from the sciences to theology as well as a work on Aristotle. He likewise served as counsellor to Herod the Great.

Principal writings: *On Plants*; *On Aristotle*; and fragments.

NICHTS, DAS.

Q.v. Heidegger (6).

NICHTS NICHTET, DAS.

German phrase meaning "the Nothing nots." *Q.v.* Heidegger (6); Nothing (12).

NICOLAS OF AUTRECORT. 14th cent. A.D.

Scholastic philosopher. A severe critic of Aristotle and Averroës, his work was condemned to be burned in 1347, and he was barred from teaching. His opposition to Aristotle rested on his firm acceptance of Aristotle's principle of noncontradiction. Nicolas held the principle to be the only test for certainty. It followed that certainty is not possible with respect to questions of existence. Neither the inference from effect to cause nor from appearance to substance is admissible in his view. Furthermore, he held that atomism is a more plausible view than the substance-attribute view of Aristotle.

Principal writings: *Exigit ordo executionis* (the first words of his treatise).

NICOLE, PIERRE. 1625-1695.

French philosopher. Born in Chartres. A Jansenist (*q.v.* Jansenism) who worked both with Arnauld (*q.v.*) and Pascal (*q.v.*), Nicole taught at the school for boys at Port Royal, Racine being one of his pupils. His initial contact with the school came through his aunt who was for a time abbess of one of the convents of the abbey. Nicole collaborated with Pascal on the *Provincial Letters*, and with Arnauld on the Port Royal Logic. In 1679 he went into exile in Belgium with Arnauld. In 1693 he, although not Arnauld, came to terms with the authorities and returned to Paris. Apart from his collaborators, his writings on morality gave him a reputation in his own right. *Q.v.* Logic (16).

Principal writings: *The Art of Thinking* (with Arnauld), 1662; *The Perpetuity of the Catholic Faith with Respect to the Eucharist* (with Arnauld), 1669; *Moral Essays*, 14 vols., 1671-87.

NICOMACHUS OF GERASA. 2nd cent. A.D.

An Hellenic philosopher born in Arabia. A neo-Pythagorean with an admixture of Platonic and Philonic ideas, Nicomachus held ideas to be numbers, providing the model for creation. The numbers pre-exist in the mind of God in his view. The one, or unity, is itself the principle of reason and the divine, while the two or dyad is the principle of matter. His treatise on arithmetic was translated by Boethius (*q.v.*) and Apuleius, was the subject of numerous commentaries, and was used as a text well into the Renaissance.

Principal writings: *Introduction to Arithmetic*; *Manual of Harmony*; *Life of Pythagoras*.

NICOSTRATUS. 2nd cent. A.D.

Although living in the period of the Fourth Academy (*q.v.* Plato's Academy 4), Nicostratus was able to avoid the tendency then current of forcing the ideas of Plato and Aristotle into a single mold. Instead he remained an orthodox Platonist. Furthermore, he produced a commentary on the *Categories* of Aristotle which was used both by Plotinus and Porphyry. For likeminded philosophers *q.v.* Atticus and Celsus.

Principal writings: Fragments of the *Commentary* on the *Categories* survive.

NIEBUHR, HELMUT RICHARD. 1894-1962.

American theologian. Born in Wright City, Missouri. Educated at Elmhurst College, Eden Theological Seminary, Washington University (St. Louis), the University of Chicago, Yale Divinity School. Taught at Eden Theological

Seminary, and Yale Divinity School. Combining pragmatism and the social gospel with Neo-Orthodoxy, Niebuhr held that humans can encounter an absolute God, although existing within the relativities of history. Ethical relativity, for example, is cancelled out by our "fitting response" to the absolute God, moving us closer to the kingdom.

Principal theological writings: *The Social Sources of Denominationalism*, 1929; *Moral Relativism and the Christian Ethic*, 1929; *The Kingdom of God in America*, 1937; *Christ and Culture*, 1951; *Radical Monotheism and Western Culture*, 1960; *The Responsible Self: An Essay in Christian Moral Philosophy*, 1963.

NIEBUHR, REINHOLD. 1892–1971.

Born in Wright City, Missouri. Studied at Yale University. Held a pastorate in Detroit; notable for his support of the labor movement and of pacifism. A committed Socialist for a time, he later broke with the party. He spent most of his career teaching Christian ethics and theology at Union Theological Seminary. He gave the Gifford Lectures in 1939.

Principal writings: *Moral Man and Immoral Society*, 1932; *An Interpretation of Christian Ethics*, 1935; *Beyond Tragedy*, 1938; *Christianity and Power Politics*, 1940; *The Nature and Destiny of Man*, 2 vols., 1941–3; *The Children of Light and the Children of Darkness*, 1944; *Faith and History*, 1949; *Christian Realism and Political Problems*, 1953; *Pious and Secular America*, 1958.

(1) Developing a Protestant theology called neo-Orthodoxy, in which God is regarded as the "wholly other," Niebuhr stressed the presence of original sin due to the fall of man. Human pride and egotism are the signs of this fall. It is man's tragedy that he can conceive of self-perfection, although he cannot achieve it. And even though man is a free spirit and thus responsible to God for his use of this freedom, there is a demonic element infusing all of his actions. For this reason moral progress simply does not occur in history.

(2) Politically, Niebuhr believed in a liberal realism capable of recognizing man's irrationalities in order to direct them rationally. In this kind of assessment it seemed clear to him that institutional changes were more important than changes of heart in attempting to reach the good society. Although opposed to utopian visions, he believed in the creation of systems of justice, and that social adjustment was needed within the framework of American capitalism. Beyond politics, Niebuhr believed in Christian realism, a point of view that applies to social perspectives the insights of neo-Orthodoxy mentioned in (1) above.

NIETZSCHE, FRIEDRICH. 1844–1900.

Born in Röcken, Prussia. A brilliant student at Leipzig, he was appointed associate professor of classical philology at the University of Basel even before his doctor's degree had been granted, and became a full professor in 1870. He resigned the professorship in 1879 because of ill health, and spent the next ten years largely in solitude as an author, living in Italy and Switzerland. He collapsed on a street in Turin in 1889 and died in 1900 after eleven years of insanity. A friendship with Richard Wagner came to an end prior to 1879 when Wagner's loyalty to the spirit of the new German empire and Nietzsche's cosmopolitanism collided.

Principal writings: *The Birth of Tragedy* (T), 1872; *Human, All Too Human* (T), 1878; *The Gay Science* (T), 1882; *Beyond Good and Evil* (T), 1886; *Toward a Genealogy of Morals* (T), 1887; *The Case of Wagner* (T), 1888; *Götterdämmerung: How One Philosophizes with a Hammer* (T), 1889; *The Twilight of the Idols* (T), 1889; *Thus Spake Zarathustra* (T), 1883–91; *The Antichrist: Attempt at a Critique of Christianity* (T), 1895; *The Will to Power* (T), *posthum.* 1901, 1904 (from notes arranged by his sister); *Ecce Homo* (T), *posthum.* 1908.

(1) In *The Birth of Tragedy*, Nietzsche expounded his discovery that Apollonian calm was not the single source of the greatness that was Greece. He found these people to be characterized not only by the calm rationality of Apollo; but also by the passion of Dionysus. He found a blend of these two elements to be the chief characteristic of Greek tragedy. All of art represents mixtures of these two modes. When the Apollonian mode is dominant, art is rational, classic in its proportions, featuring order and balance. In the Dionysiac mode, art stresses passion and ecstasy, rapture and repulsive-

ness. Apollonian art is a dream of rationality in an irrational world. Dionysiac art tears the veil from appearance, and allows one to see the underlying destructiveness and nihilism of the life-world, and perhaps of all temporal process. But the highest art is to be found in tragedy, which unites the two modes, for tragedy is conceived in Dionysiac debauch and is consummated in Sophoclean calm. He also found, it would seem, that an appropriate blend of reason and passion defined the ideal human life; in his later writings the personality of the Superman contained both Apollonian and Dionysian elements.

(2) In *Beyond Good and Evil*, Nietzsche finds it possible to reduce all moral systems to either a master morality, a slave morality, or a compound of the two, mixing the components in a certain ratio. Master morality, deriving from the rules of society, is a morality of self-affirmation. Slave morality derives from the ruled, is rooted in resentment and the compensatory desire for revenge. Although master morality is closer than slave morality to the ideal, both are partial, and require each other.

(3) If the ideal is to be formulated, it must be done in terms of the "will to power" which Nietzsche claimed to be man's most basic drive. The pure form of this will to power is man's will to bring to perfect fruition all of his capacities. It is the will to be creative rather than merely creaturely. From this standpoint it is possible to see both the master and slave moralities as a falling away from this ideal. If man fails to actuate his will creatively it is possible that by a crude sublimation (a term first used in its modern sense by Nietzsche) he may substitute power over others for his original goal. Master morality fits the description to some extent. A further perversion of man's creative purpose is present in the slave morality which is the will to power of the weak, despising all excellence and elevating the mediocre and low.

(4) It is the slave morality which constitutes the sickness of Europe, elevating a herd morality and a false equality into the foremost place. The result is a loss of standards of excellence, a leveling of humanity to mediocrity and widespread moral nihilism. The sickness is present both in democracy and Christianity. The Christian values of humility and self-abnegation express this leveling tendency; furthermore, Christianity has made sex unclean, and has wrongly deprecated the values of the body, and of this world, in favor of the values of a fictitious soul and fictitious other world. Even the idea of God, when properly understood, is nothing more than a projection of man's uneasy conscience, and as a consequence he has developed a desire for self-torture. Indeed, since "God is dead" we must get on with other alternatives.

(5) In this situation, Nietzsche felt it his special mission to "philosophize with a hammer," breaking up the inferior encrustations of the past, providing an opportunity for development of the authentic kind of will to power. This explains the powerfully aphoristic style which he developed, and his famous phrase calling for a "transvaluation of values." In his conception the present stage of life is transitional. The best that can now be done is to prepare for a more fortunate age. He expressed this by saying that man was the bridge to the Superman.

(6) The Superman for whom we are to prepare is the man who has developed his will to power in an authentic manner; that is, he has become a creator. He will be a person of high integrity, without prejudice, appropriately proud, intellectual, great-souled, considerate toward those who are inferior, and a lover of solitude as one of the conditions of creation. The conditions of life upon the advent of the Superman are not specified. Indeed, since he expected in the 20th century exactly the kind of political devolution which has occurred, it seems evident that Nietzsche was not expecting a utopian transformation of men into Supermen. Possibly, the Superman was posited only as a norm or measure to define our striving. In *Ecce Homo*, however, in discussing "how one becomes what one is" Nietzsche spoke of one's potential self which, given the opportunity, would gradually develop into the position of command.

(7) In *Toward a Genealogy of Morals* Nietzsche explains the multiple meanings of good, bad, evil, and punishment, relating them to the will to power of specific personality types (*e.g.*, the ascetic

priest). The genealogical analysis is an initial stage in the transvaluations prescribed in the previous four points.

(8) But in addition to these points, Nietzsche also believed in the idea of an eternal recurrence of time and its contents through vast cycles. He believed that its series of cycles is everlasting but that the number of its possible configurations is finite. From these two things it followed that the present configuration of the world must be repeated time after time in the future. The great-souled man, affirming reality without resentment, will find satisfaction in such a prospect.

(9) He believed that his view of eternal recurrence was implied by the science of his day, that his philosophy was compatible with science. He likewise held that there is at least partial truth in all of the various perspectives which have been entertained concerning the universe.

NIGIDIUS FIGULUS. 1st cent. B.C.

Graeco-Roman philosopher. According to Cicero, Nigidius was the most prominent neo-Pythagorean of his time. His point of view fused mystical and astrological interests with philosophical concepts from Pythagorean and Platonic traditions.

Principal writings: *On the Gods.*

NIHILISM.

From the Latin *nihil* ("nothing"). A doctrine denying validity to any positive alternative, the term has been applied to metaphysics, epistemology, ethics, politics, and theology. The term was coined by Turgeniev in his novel *Fathers and Children* (1862) to apply to a Russian movement in the second half of the 19th century which pressed for change without a plan and which, at its height, assassinated numbers of Russian officials including the Tsar Alexander II himself.

(1) Metaphysical and epistemological nihilism can be associated with the doctrine of Gorgias (*q.v.* 1–3) that nothing exists; if it did exist it could not be known; and if it were known it could not be communicated.

(2) Epistemological nihilism is best exemplified by that extreme form of skepticism called Pyrrhonism (*q.v.*). Pyrrho adhered to the doctrine that no knowledge is possible.

(3) Ethical nihilism is the doctrine that all value judgments have lost their validity. Schopenhauer's (*q.v.* 6) ethics of pessimism is close to this doctrine although the value of "renunciation" remains positive for Schopenhauer and supplies at least a partial answer to the problem of life.

(4) Nietzsche (*q.v.* 4) found moral nihilism with its negation of life a consequence of the sickness of Europe and its loss of superior values. Nietzsche's own yea-saying alternative with its transvaluation of values was designed, at least in part, to combat such nihilism.

(5) Political nihilism is the doctrine that destruction of the inherited social and political order has positive value and is its own goal. Bakunin (*q.v.* 1) gave philosophical support to this alternative, holding that the act of destruction is itself creative. Camus (*q.v.* 2), on the other hand, held political nihilism to lie outside the admissible framework of behavior.

(6) Theological nihilism is best represented by the Death of God movement in American theology (*q.v.* Death of God Theologians; Theology 20). For this group of theologians the concept of God has lost validity, and they seek reorientation, continuing their worship although with a void where formerly they recognized God.

NIMBARKA.

Q.v. Vedanta (4).

NIRGUNA BRAHMAN.

From the Sanskrit *nir* ("without") plus *guna* ("attributes"). Hence, that form of Brahman (*q.v.*) without attributes or qualities. Also, *q.v. Śankara* (4).

NIRMANAKAYA.

Q.v. Trikaya (3).

NIRVANA.

Sanskrit term meaning "blown out," referring to the extinction of all worldly desires. Referring to the state of release, or salvation, the term is most often associated with Buddhism. (1) Buddha (*q.v.* 4) said that whatever one says about the term, either positively or negatively, will be in error. (2) In Theravada Buddhism (*q.v.* 5) the term seems to be definitely equated with extinction. (3) In Mahayana Buddhism (*q.v.* 3) Nirvana is usually equated with a state of absolute bliss, although Nagarjuna (*q.v.* 7) of the Middle Doctrine School of Mahayana Buddhism holds that Nirvana is itself an illusion. (4) The term seems to have originated in the Vedantic writings. It is mentioned in the *Bhagavad-Gita* (*q.v.*), and elsewhere in the *Vedas*. (5) Schopenhauer (*q.v.* 7) is one of the few Western philosophers to find a place for the concept in his philosophy.

NISHIDA KITHRO. 1870–1945.

Japanese philosopher. A follower of Zen (*q.v.*) whose work bears analogies to Western philosophy and was in fact influenced by neo-Kantianism (*q.v*).

Principal writings: *Intelligibility and the Philosophy of Nothingness*, 1958; *A Study of Good*, 1960.

NISUS.

A Latin term meaning "striving." The term was used by S. Alexander (*q.v.* 4) to express his view that evolution has a tendency to move toward higher levels.

NIYAMA.

The second step of Yogic meditation, that of positive ethical preparation (*q.v.* Yoga 4).

NIYAT.

Q.v. Ajivikas.

NOEMA.

A Greek term meaning "that which is thought." The adjectival form, "noematic," is also used. The term is usually associated with Husserl (*q.v.* 5) who employed the term to refer to the material element, as contrasted with the "thought" element of the act of perception. The latter he termed *noesis* (*q.v.*).

NOESIS.

A Greek term meaning "thought" or "intelligence." The adjectival form. "noetic," is also used. The term is usually associated with Husserl (*q.v.* 5) who employs the term to designate the element of thought within the act of perception. He wishes to distinguish this from the material element within that act, which he terms the *noema* (*q.v.*).

NOETIC SYNTHESIS.

Q.v. G.F. Stout (1).

NOMINALISM.

From the Latin term *nomen* meaning "name." Nominalism represents the minimal position with respect to the problem of Universals (*q.v.*). The position is that universals are not real entities either in the world or in the mind, but names which refer to groups or classes of individual things. The position of Nominalism is difficult to distinguish from some forms of Conceptualism (*q.v.*) and in what follows, although we shall list those philosophers most often regarded as Nominalists, it should be borne in mind that most of those on the list have been regarded by some as belonging to the group of Conceptualists. Among those philosophers whose position with respect to universals can be reasonably interpreted as Nominalism we may include: Roscelin (*q.v.* and Universals 11) with his doctrine of *flatus vocis*, Peter of Aureol (*q.v.* and Universals 18), William of Ockham (*q.v.* 6 and Universals 19), Durando of Saint Pourcain (*q.v.* and Universals 20), Jean Buridan (*q.v.*), Gregory of Rimini (*q.v.*), Jean Gerson (*q.v.*), John Major (*q.v.* and Universals 23), Thomas Hobbes (*q.v.* 3–5 and Universals 24), possibly Hume (*q.v.* 2 and Universals 27), Condillac (*q.v.* 2–4 and Universals 28), possibly Reid (*q.v.* 2 and Universals 29), Nelson Goodman (*q.v.* 1 and Universals 41), and possibly Quine (*q.v.* 3 and Universals 42).

NOMINALISTIC RADICAL EMPIRICISM.

Q.v. Northrop (2).

NOMOTHETIC SCIENCES.

Q.v. Windelband (2).

NONBEING.

Q.v. Nothing. Also *q.v.* Wang Pi; Chuang Tzu (4).

NON CAUSA PRO CAUSA.

Latin phrase designating the fallacy of taking what is "not a cause for a cause." Also known as False Cause (*q.v.* Fallacies 12).

NON-COGNITIVISM.

The view that ethical terms lack cognitive meaning (*q.v.* Ethics 5). The term is often applied to Emotivist theories (*q.v.*) in the field of ethics (*q.v.* Ayer 5,

Stevenson 1–2, and Hare 1); such theories hold that moral utterances are to be understood in terms of attitudes of feeling rather than cognition.

NONCONFORMISTS.
In 17th-century England the term was applied to Protestants who did not conform to the doctrines of the Church of England. Also *q.v.* Dissenters.

NONCONTRADICTION, PRINCIPLE OF.
Probably the better name for that one of the three laws of thought usually called the Principle of Contradiction (*q.v.*). If we accept as its standard statement, "It is not the case that p is true and not-p is true," the principle urges upon us the avoidance of contradiction, and hence the appropriateness of the above name. *Q.v.* Laws of Thought (1–3); Tautology (1).

NONDUALITY.
Q.v. Advaita; Emptiness.

NON-NATURAL PROPERTIES.
For the Intuitionist school of ethics (*q.v.* 4, 31–32), properties apprehended not by sensation but by intuition. G.E. Moore (*q.v.* 6) held "Good" to be a non-natural property or quality.

NONREDUCTIVE PHYSICALISM.
Q.v. Davidson (3).

NON SEQUITUR.
Latin phrase meaning "it does not follow." In logic, a conclusion that does not follow from its premises. In this general sense all of the fallacies (*q.v.*) of reasoning are non sequiturs. The phrase is sometimes restricted, however, to two fallacies (*q.v.* 27, 28), that of affirming the consequent, and that of denying the antecedent.

NON-SUBSISTENT FORM.
Q.v. Form (5i).

NON-VIOLENCE.
Q.v. Leo Tolstoy (2); Thoreau; Gandhi (1–3); Einstein (5).

NOÖSPHERE.
Q.v. Teilhard de Chardin.

NORMATIVE ETHICS.
The traditional view of Ethics (*q.v.*) that it is part of the task of the moral philos-

opher to provide guidance with respect to issues of right and wrong, good and evil. Normative Ethics is to be distinguished from Meta-Ethics (*q.v.*), the analysis of the logic of ethics and the systems of those who treat of Normative Ethics.

NORRIS, JOHN. 1657–1711.
English philosopher. Born at Collingbourne-Kingston in Wiltshire. Oxford-educated and a fellow at All Souls' College from 1680 to 1689, he was ordained in 1684. In 1689 he became minister of Newton St. Loe in Somersetshire. In 1691 he was transferred to Bemerton near Salisbury. Beginning as a Platonist in contact with the Cambridge Platonists (*q.v.*), Norris eventually became known as the English Malebranche (*q.v.*). In addition he responded vigorously to the intellectual currents of his day, producing criticism of Locke, Toland, and others.

Principal writings: *An Idea of Happiness,* 1683; *Poems and Discourses,* 1684; *The Theory and Regulation of Love,* 1688; *Reason and Religion,* 1689; *Practical Discourses,* 3 vols., 1690–8; *Reflections on the Conduct of Human Life,* 1690; *An Account of Reason and Faith,* 1697; *An Essay Towards the Theory of the Ideal or Intelligible World,* 2 vols., 1701, 1704; *A Philosophical Discourse concerning the Natural Immortality of the Soul,* 1708.

(1) Defending in his first two publications a version of Platonism, Norris held that the highest happiness lies in the contemplative love of God, that the eternality of truth implies the reality of eternal ideas, and that these in turn imply the existence of God, inasmuch as the only appropriate locus for such ideas is within the divine mind.

(2) By 1688 Malebranche's distinction between two kinds of love appeared in Norris' work; desire seeking union with its object, and benevolence seeking the good of others.

(3) The first criticism of Locke's theory of ideas was made by Norris. In an appendix to the *Practical Discourses* he questioned Locke's arguments against innateness, attacked the concept of nominal essence, and suggested the possibility of sub-conscious ideation.

(4) By 1695 he had adopted Malebranche's view that we should love only

God, while accepting human relations as occasions for personal happiness.

(5) In his 1697 answer to Toland (*q.v.*) he argued that the human mind is not the measure of truth. Its measure is reason, the divine reason, which differs from human reason in degree but not in kind.

(6) In the 2-volume *Essay* Norris gave a complete exposition of Malebranche's philosophy. At this point Norris broke with the Cambridge Platonists, accepting the Cartesian view of the physical world as a soulless mechanism as well as accepting Descartes' mind-body dualism.

(7) His final publication was a platonically-based defense of immortality against the argument of one Henry Dodwell that the soul is mortal.

NORTHROP, F.S.C. 1893– .

American philosopher. Born in Janesville, Wisconsin. Educated at Beloit College, Yale, and Harvard. Taught at Yale.

Principal writings: *Science and First Principles*, 1931; *The Meeting of East and West*, 1946; *The Logic of the Sciences and the Humanities*, 1947; *The Taming of the Nations*, 1952; *The Complexity of Legal and Ethical Experience*, 1959; *Philosophical Anthropology and Practical Politics*, 1960; *Man, Nature and God*, 1962; *Prolegomena to a Philosophia Naturales*, 1985.

(1) Seeking a common framework or a common metalanguage for all the fields of learning, recognizing both identities and differences in their procedures, Northrop has noted differences in the uses of logic in various fields. Where in the natural and social sciences, descriptive judgments predominate, in law, politics, and the humanities generally, evaluative judgments are central.

(2) Northrop claims that there is a framework or metalanguage appropriate both to evaluative and descriptive language. It is nominalistic radical empiricism in epistemic correlation with logical realism. By "nominalistic radical empiricism" he means the component of observation with its particularity and flux. By "logical realism" he means the conceptual level of mathematics or other abstract theory with a relative freedom from empirical observation. The two levels are kept in contact by "epistemic correlations"—that is connective procedures established by our own epistemological decisions—relating mathematically described physical theory, or otherwise abstractly described theory, to empirical data.

(3) In his work on international culture he held that the East is more closely oriented to the appreciative world of direct experience, the West to abstract theoretical explanation, and the need of both is to achieve a balance of the two orientations.

NOTA NOTAE EST NOTA REI IPSIUS.

Latin phrase whose literal meaning is "the note of a note is a note of the thing itself." The thought is that whatever falls within the comprehension of a component of a thing falls within the comprehension of the thing itself. Kant substituted the "Nota notae" for the traditional *Dictum de omni et nullo* (*q.v.*) as the principle governing valid inference.

NOTA PER EXPERIENTIAM.

Q.v. William of Ockham (11).

NOTHING.

From "no" and "thing"; the Latin is *nihil*. In Greek there are two terms *me on* (that which has no actual being but has potential being) and *ouk on* (the nothing at all). The term is a synonym for the philosophical term, "non-being," and is thus the formal complement to the term, "being" (*q.v.*). The fact of this complementarity has led even those who wish to grant reality only to various kinds of being, to make reference to non-being, or nothing.

(1) When Parmenides (*q.v.* 3) claims that being is and non-being is not, the denial seems to endow the not-being with a kind of reality, despite all intentions. Both Zeno of Elea (*q.v.*) and the Buddhist Nagarjuna (*q.v.*) utilize a dialectic that plays upon the concepts of negation and non-being.

(2) A straightforward reference to the category of the Nothing occurs in Democritus (*q.v.* 2) whose two basic principles are the reality of atoms and the void.

(3) Gorgias (*q.v.* 1) apparently wished to deny both being and non-being with his claim "Nothing exists," but once more the denial has the sound of a kind of affirmation.

(4) Plato (*q.v.* 8) avoided the problems of the term by a doctrine of negation in which denial is interpreted as the affirmation of a different kind or instance of thing. To claim that a thing is not red is thus to claim that it is some other color, or has some property other than a color property. The doctrine of "othering" thus reinterpreted references to not-being in terms of being.

(5) Aristotle (*q.v.* 7–8) essentially followed Plato's lead although he does have a category of privation which indicates the absence of a potentiality in a given thing. And the kind of relative non-existence of potential being is associated with prime matter.

(6) Neoplatonism (*q.v.*) interpreted the principle of matter as virtual non-being, in this sense following Aristotle. Evil was given the same type of interpretation, not only by Neoplatonists, but also by Christian thinkers (*q.v.* Origen 3; and St. Augustine 8).

(7) Against the established Greek motto, "Out of nothing, nothing comes" (known to us in Latin as the principle of *ex nihilo nihil fit*), the Christian tradition held to the creation of the world out of nothing (*creatio ex nihilo*). The doctrine emerged in clarity, however, only after a long struggle with the emanationistic doctrines of Neoplatonism (*q.v.* and also Creation).

(8) The tradition of Mysticism (*q.v.*) in both East and West has provided numerous approaches to non-being. To speak only of the mysticism of the Middle Ages (*q.v.* Mysticism 6), for example, in such mystics as Bernard of Clairvaux (*q.v.* 4) and Meister Eckhart (*q.v.* 5), the soul had to become as nothing, annihilated, in order for the being of God to enter; and in Jacob Boehme (*q.v.* 11), among others, opposition, negation, non-being acquire a positive role in dialectic and in the process of creation, not excepting the divine self-creation.

(9) The Idealists Fichte, Schelling, and Hegel all employ negation in such a way that it vaults beyond logic and enters the world. Fichte (*q.v.* 3) was the first to formalize the dialectic of thesis, antithesis, synthesis. Schelling (*q.v.* 8) finds polarity to characterize God Himself; and Hegel (*q.v.* 7) speaks of the power of the negative, and deduces the idea of Becoming from the thesis of Being, and its antithesis, Nothing.

(10) Bergson (*q.v.* 3), however, explained the Nothing as a pseudo-idea, a dissatisfaction with the being present to us.

(11) Berdyaev (*q.v.* 1–2), on the other hand, reverted to Boehme and Schelling, arguing for the reality of an eternal Nothing out of which creation comes, and holding that the meaning of freedom is creation out of Nothing.

(12) Heidegger (*q.v.* 6), starting from the concept of anxiety or dread—finding this a dread of Nothing—grants ontological status to Nothing, as the basis of negation, coining the phrase "the Nothing nots" ("*Das Nichts nichtet*"), which would seem to grant active power to the Nothing.

(13) Sartre (*q.v.* 2, 7) holds man to be a "noughting nought." In the process he defines himself. Sartre appears to follow Heidegger in recognizing Nothingness as a basic category. His analysis begins in the disappointed expectations mentioned by Bergson above, but moves beyond that level into one which is ontological.

NOTHINGNESS.
For a discussion of this term as a basic philosophical concept, *q.v.* Sartre (7).

NOTION.
Q.v. Berkeley (6); Hegel (6).

NOTIONS, COMMON.
Q.v. Common Notions.

NOTITIAE COMMUNES.
Q.v. Common Notions; Herbert of Cherbury (2a).

NOTITIA ILLATA.
Q.v. Campanella (1).

NOTITIA INNATA.
Q.v. Campanella (1).

NOTITIA INTUITIVA.
Latin phrase employed by William of Ockham (*q.v.* 10) to refer to what we know by immediate awareness, *i.e.*, the world around us and our own acts. Ockham regarded such knowledge as intuitive and carrying its own guarantee.

NOUGHTING NOUGHT.

Sartre's definition of man (*q.v.* Sartre 2, 7). Also *q.v.* Nothing (13).

NOUMENON.

From the Greek *noumenon* which means equally "thing perceived" and "what is known." Plato used the term occasionally, and always in the latter sense, to refer to the intelligibles or "things of thought." The term is most firmly identified with Kant (*q.v.* 2), and although the Kantian philosophy is sometimes interpreted in such a way that the *noumena* are like Platonic forms, the more accepted interpretation is that they are simply things in themselves, whatever their nature may turn out to be. In this interpretation Kant would appear to be using the term in the first sense given above; they are the things perceived as existing but only through a rational apprehension and as a limiting concept. Kant uses the term in contrast to the term "phenomenon" which does appear to sense.

NOUS.

A Greek term signifying "mind" or "reason." The term had extensive use in Greek philosophy.

(1) Anaxagoras (*q.v.* 3–4) invokes the idea of *Nous* as a principle both of order and of animation, accounting for the presence of a universe rather than a chaos.

(2) Although Plato used the term to refer to the highest knowledge or the faculty of highest knowledge, it was Aristotle (*q.v.* 11) who formalized the point, distinguishing between the *nous poietikos* (or "active reason") in man and the *nous pathetikos* (or "passive reason"). The two complement each other as do matter and form. It was also Aristotle who applied the term to God whose activity he describes as *noesis noeseos*, a "thinking on thought" or "thought thinking itself" (*q.v.* Aristotle 10).

(3) The Neoplatonists (*q.v.*) used the term extensively to refer to the intelligible world. Plotinus (*q.v.* 3) regarded the *Nous* as the first emanation from the divine Being, and one of the three hypostases of God, the other two being the One and the World Soul.

NOVALIS. (Pseudonym of Friedrich Leopold). 1772–1801.

German Romantic poet. Born at Oberwiederstedt in Saxony. Studied at Jena, Leipzig, and Wittenberg. Influenced by Goethe, Schiller, Fichte, and Schelling. One of the leaders of the early Romantic movement.

Principal writings: *Blütenstaub (Pollen)*, 1798; *The Novices of Sais*, 1798; *Hymns to the Night*, 1800; *Henry of Ofterdingen*, 1876.

(1) Finding contemporary life in a state of fragmentation, Novalis held that it is the function of the poet through romantic irony to negate the fragmented mechanistic sensible world and make it possible for one to discover, through the liberation of one's imagination, one's true self. The poetic means of liberation is by way of aphorism, pointing to unstated meanings in the depths of things.

(2) Opposing the rationalism of the Enlightenment, the philosophic complement to Novalis' views would be some version of Idealism, that of Fichte (*q.v.*) or Schelling (*q.v*). In the final assessment, Novalis believed that all polarities were reconciled so that the achievement of salvation and the flight into nothingness became identical; and both of these are identical to the discovery of an infinite reality.

NOWELL-SMITH, P.H. 1914– .

English philosopher. Born in Polmeath, Cornwall. Educated at Harvard and Oxford. Has taught at Leicester, Kent, and Toronto.

Principal writings: *Ethics*, 1954.

(1) Arguing for a modified teleological theory of ethics, Nowell-Smith's major thrust has to do with encouraging analyses of moral discourse at the appropriate level of complexity, recognizing the untidiness of ordinary language.

(2) A suggestion of his approach may be seen in his distinction between "A-words" (aptness words), "D-words" (descriptive words), and "G-words" (gerundive words). Examples of the first category are "terrifying," "amusing," "sublime," interpreted as meaning "apt to terrify," "apt to amuse," and "apt to produce feelings of the sublime"; of the second category any descriptive term, *e.g.*, "tall," "short," etc.; and of the third category "praiseworthy," "laudable,"

"damnable," interpreted as meaning "ought to be praised" and "ought to be damned." He holds that each type of word has its own logic; and appreciation of their differences helps sharpen metaethical distinctions and unravel ethical problems.

NOZICK, ROBERT. 1938– .

American social philosopher. Educated at Harvard and Princeton. Has taught at Princeton, Rockefeller University, and Harvard.

Principal writings: *Anarchy, State, and Utopia*, 1974; *Philosophical Explanations*, 1981; *The Examined Life*, 1989; *The Nature of Rationality*, 1993.

(1) Taking the unimpeded exercise of the will to be the goal of human behavior (and implicitly the definition of human freedom, *q.v* B.), Nozick builds the state around the concepts of classical economics including the latter's concern for property rights (both of acquisition and transfer), and the working of an invisible hand in the shaping of the state.

(2) Beginning with the state of nature, Nozick traces the rise of the minimal state from mutual protective associations, one of which becomes the dominant protective association in a given area. As it gains a *de facto* monopoly in the area it becomes an ultraminimal and then a minimal state. The result is a "night watchman" state whose mission is to protect individual and property. He claims that only such a minimal state could come into existence without violating the rights of some individuals.

(3) The clash of individual wills defines the boundary limits between individuals. Boundary crossings are viewed as violations of individual rights, to be rectified by a principle of compensation. The principle appears to presume that every transgression has its price, a point Marx (*q.v.* 1) associated with the late stages of capitalism.

NULL CLASS.

In the algebra of classes the concept of that class in the universe of discourse which has no members. Boole (*q.v.* 5) symbolized this class by "0." In Boolean algebra the null class has many uses. For example, to express "No x is y" in this algebra one says "xy = 0," *i.e.*, the product

of x and y is the null class. Also *q.v.* Null Relation.

NULLIBILIST.

Q.v. Henry More (1).

NULL RELATION.

In the algebra of relations, the relation without instances. The symbol is often "$\wedge$" or "$\overline{\wedge}$" *Q.v.* Null Class; Universal Relation; Logic of Relations (5).

NUMBER.

Beginning with the Pythagorean insight that reality is to be understood in terms of numerical expressions (*q.v.* Pythagoras 4), the status of number and the nature of numerical entities have occupied philosophers no less than have the status and nature of ideas. Indeed, the basic positions of Realism, Conceptualism, and Nominalism, which appear in the discussions of Universals (*q.v.*) reappear in the corresponding discussions of number. In these discussions, however, the terms favored for the respective positions are Platonism, Intuitionism, and Nominalism. For a discussion of these alternatives *q.v.* Mathematics. For a modern definition of number *q.v.* Frege (2); Russell (2). For definitions of finite and transfinite cardinal numbers, *q.v.* Cantor (2–3). It was through his investigation of the "essence" of number that Husserl (*q.v.* 1) was led to his phenomenological method.

NUMENIUS OF APAMEA. 2nd cent. A.D.

Hellenic philosopher. Born in Syria. A neo-Pythagorean sometimes regarded as the founder of Neoplatonism, Numenius combined Pythagorean and Platonic ideas with those of Philo and the Egyptian mystery religions.

(1) His system contained a succession of three Gods. The first God is an absolute transcendent unity and the principle of being.

(2) Related to the first God is the system of Pythagorean numbers. These are identified with Platonic Ideas.

(3) The second God, representing the principle of becoming, creates the world in accordance with the number-forms.

(4) Next is the third God who rules the created world.

(5) Inferior to this divinity is a series of divine and demonic beings of various kinds.

(6) Beneath all of these is the human being composed of soul and body.

(7) The hierarchy of creation finally leads down to prime matter which is closely associated with nonbeing.

(8) The individual, although imprisoned in the body, can through ascetic practices achieve an ecstatic union with the first God who is the principle of being.

NUMINOUS.

From the Latin *numen* ("nod"). Thus, a nod as a sign of command; and from this, the divine will or divine command. The term, "numinous," gained the sense of the felt presence of a divine spirit. Rudolf Otto (*q.v.* 2) used the term to signify the state of feeling of the worshipper in the presence of God.

NUNN, T.P.

Q.v. New Realism (5).

NYAYA.

One of the six systems of Indian thought to arise in the period following the Vedic Age, and the formation of the *Bhagavad-Gita* and many of the sutras. This system was founded by a man named Gautama (variously reported 250 B.C.–450 A.D.), author of the *Nyaya-sutra* and developed by Vatsyayana (3rd–4th cent. A.D.), author of the *Nyaya-baṣya* Nyaya shares with the Vaisheshika system a metaphysics which endorses atomistic pluralism and logical realism. But while Vaisheshika stresses the metaphysical and ontological side of things, Nyaya is directed toward consideration of logical and epistemological problems. Nyaya provided the logic, as it were, for the other systems.

(1) Five elements are recognized in the Nyaya syllogism: (a) the proposition to be established; (b) the affirmative or negative reason, establishing the proposition; (c) an affirmative or negative example, implying that the character in the conclusion is invariably contained in or invariably absent from, such instances; (d) the application of the example to the case or cases present in the proposition to be established; (e) the conclusion, restating the proposition as now supported. It may be noticed that the presence of particular instances in this logic prevents universal propositions from being vacuous.

(2) A number of kinds of perception are recognized by Nyaya logicians. Gautama distinguished determinate perception (in which we recognize the object's genus, and also its specific qualities) from indeterminate perception (simple apprehension of an object). Later, the school recognized four kinds of perception: sense perception, mental perception, self-consciousness, and yogic intuition.

(3) Nyaya logic includes classifications of fallacies in reasoning, and how to oppose them; analyses of language and the parts of speech; and logical analysis of metaphysical arguments, such as the arguments for God, which are held to be valid.

(4) The pluralistic Nyaya universe is ordered by Ishvara, a creator god who dispenses grace to humans.

NYGREN, ANDERS. 1890– .

Swedish theologian. Educated at Lund. Taught at Lund. Distinguishing between *Eros,* and *Agápe,* and identifying the latter with the essential content of Christianity, Nygren became the leader of a group called the Lundensian theologians who interpreted all Christian doctrine from this standpoint.

Principal writings: *Eros and Agápe* (T), 1930; *Commentary on Romans* (T), 1944; *Meaning and Method* (E), 1971.

OBJECT.

From the Latin *ob* ("over against") and *jacere* ("to throw"). One cannot derive the meaning of the term from its etymology alone, however, in part because the meaning has been involved in a remarkable shift. The ordinary current meaning of object is that which exists in its own right, as a thing outside the mind. But, initially, that was the meaning of the word "subject."

(1) When the term came into philosophic use in the Middle Ages the widely

held meaning of object (or *objectum*) was whatever is designated by any intentional reference. Let the reference be cognitive, volitional, or emotive, whatever the term of this thought, that is what one meant by "object."

(2) For Duns Scotus (*q.v.* 2) "objective" means an "object of thought." Thus an object was understood to be within the mind, while the existence of a thing in the world was considered to be subjective.

(3) Descartes (*q.v.* 7) continues this usage, as does Berkeley (*q.v.* 3), who regards the objective existence of a thing to be that thing as perceived.

(4) The reversal of these meanings came with Kant (*q.v.* 2, 11d) who understood objective to be that which is outside any subject, and subjective to mean "that which is within a subject."

(5) Meinong (*q.v.* 2) and Husserl (*q.v.* 5) attempt a return to the original meaning, regarding "object" as whatever can be the subject of a judgment.

(6) Whitehead (*q.v.* 5) distinguishes between sense objects, perceptual objects, physical objects, and scientific objects.

OBJECTIVE INTERIORITY.
Q.v. Sciacca.

OBJECTIVE RELATIVISM.
Q.v. A.E. Murphy (1); E.B. McGilvary (4).

OBJECTIVE SPIRIT.
Q.v. Hegel (9–10).

OBJECTIVES.
Q.v. Meinong (2).

OBJECT LANGUAGE.
In keeping with the Use-Mention distinction (*q.v.*), statements about a given language must be made in a Metalanguage (*q.v.*). The given language calling for the metalanguage is usually called the Object language.

OBLIGATION.
From the Latin *obligare* (from *ob*, "to", and *ligare*, "to bind"). One important tradition in ethics (*q.v.* 3) centers on the ideas of obligation and duty. The theory of obligation is called deontology (*q.v.*) from the Greek *deon* ("obligation"). Deontic logic (*q.v.*) studies the types of necessity present in statements of obligation.

OBVERSE.
Q.v. Immediate Inference (3).

OBVERSION.
Q.v. Immediate Inference (3).

OBVERTEND.
Q.v. Immediate Inference (3).

OCCASIONALISM.
A 17th-century theory that God is the intermediary between soul and body. The problem was posed by the exclusiveness of the mind-body dualism in Cartesian philosophy (*q.v.* Descartes 8–9). If soul and body are utterly unlike, it is impossible to explain how their interaction occurs. According to Malebranche (*q.v.* 3–4), Geulincx (*q.v.* 1) and others, on each occasion of the soul's consent to a given action, God moves the body. It is God, too, who delivers to the soul the awareness of any physical modification of the body. Other occasionalists include Johannes Clauberg (*q.v.*) and Louis de la Forge (*q.v.*). It should be noted that Islamic philosophers had already presented a generalized version of the theory in which God is the intermediary between any two events, effectively replacing the category of causality.

OCCURRENCES, PHILOSOPHY OF.
Q.v. Wahle (1).

OCCURRENT.
Q.v. W.E. Johnson (3).

OCKHAMISM.
The movement of thought initiated by William of Ockham (*q.v.*). It consisted in criticism of Scholasticism, an emphasis on empirical method, and a heightened appreciation of the role of religious faith. Followers of Ockham were active during the 14th century both at Oxford and Paris. The most eminent of those associated with the movement are Nicolas of Autrecourt (*q.v.*), Jean Buridan (*q.v.*), Gregory of Rimini (*q.v.*), and Jean Gerson (*q.v.*).

OCKHAM'S RAZOR.
Synonym for the Principle of Parsimony. Its usual formulation, "Entities are not to be multiplied beyond necessity," is approached but never quite stated in Ockham's writings. The sense of the razor

is to cut away useless or gratuitous ideas in explanation, and to accept the simplest hypothesis which can explain the data. *Q.v.* William of Ockham (8–9).

OEDIPUS COMPLEX.
Q.v. Freud (5).

OENOMAUS OF GADARA. 2nd. cent. A.D.
Greek philosopher. Reverting to the point of view of the ancient Cynics (*q.v.*), he opposed both the Stoic emphasis on fatalism and the religious practice of consulting oracles to read the future. He claimed the latter to be deceptions consciously practiced on the populace.

OLIGARCHY.
From the Greek *oligoi* ("few") and *arche* ("rule"). The term literally signifies a form of government characterized by minority rule. For Plato and Aristotle, however, it stood for that form of government where the wealthy few rule for their own interests.

(1) In the *Republic* Plato (*q.v.* 5f) views oligarchy as a degeneration from timocracy, a form of government in which honorableness is the criterion for rule.

(2) For Aristotle (*q.v.* 12) it represents the degenerate form of aristocracy, the latter being one of his three approved forms of government.

(3) For Hobbes (*q.v.* 8) it is not a separate form of government, but the name one gives to aristocracy when displeased with it.

OLIMPIODORUS. 6th cent. A.D.
Alexandrian philosopher. A Neoplatonist and member of the Alexandrian School (*q.v.*) he studied with Ammonius of that school, and wrote commentaries on the works of Plato and Aristotle.

Principal writings: *Life of Plato; Commentaries* on Plato's *Phaedo, Philebus, Gorgias, Alcibiades I;* and on Aristotle's *Categories* and *Meteorology.*

OLIVI, PETER JOHN. 1248–1298.
French philosopher. Born at Sérignan. Studied at Paris. A Franciscan, Olivi was often cited by Duns Scotus and William of Ockham. He advocated a doctrine of the *ratio realis*, or reason grounded in reality, which provided Peter Aureol (*q.v.*) and Ockham (*q.v.*) an intermediary stage

between general and specific concepts. He rejected the distinction between active and passive intellect.

Principal writings: *Commentarius in IV libros sententiarum, c.* 1287–1290; *Summa quaestionum super sententiarum,* 1295.

OM.
A Sanskrit term connoting assent (thus analogous to "amen"). Originally *aum*, the three letters bearing multiple interpretations: standing respectively for the absolute, the relative, and the relation between them; for the awakened state, the dream state, and dreamless sleep (the syllable as a whole standing for Brahman, "seated in the hearts of all"); for the three gods of the Hindu trinity, Brahma the creator, Vishnu the sustainer, Shiva the dissolver; standing also for the three worlds. *Om* is identified in the *Iśa, Mundaka, Mandukya, Taittiriya,* and *Chandogya Upaniṣads* (*q.v. Vedas* 4) as standing for the whole world and its parts, including past, present, and future, as well as for *atman,* the self of all things. The *Chandogya* also identifies *om* with the "imperishable," the *Maitrayana* with the "primary sound," and the *Katha* asserts that by meditating on *om* one can attain Brahman. *Om* thus becomes the mystic and sacred syllable of all Hinduism, to be repeated at the beginning and the end of every sacred recitation. It also became a *mantra* (*q.v.*) and, in written form a *mandala* (*q.v.*) for use in religious devotion and meditation.

OMEGA POINT.
Q.v. Teilhard de Chardin.

OM MANI PADME HUM.
Sanskrit, ("O, the jewel in the lotus") from *mani* ("jewel") and *padme* ("lotus"). The famous *mantra* (*q.v.*) of the Tibetan prayer wheels, sending forth its multiple invocations through innumerable revolutions. The Sanskrit phrase entered Tibet unchanged in the seventh or eighth centuries from Indian Tantric (*q.v.* 6) Buddhism. The interrelating of jewel and lotus probably referred initially to union of the male and female principles.

(1) In Tibet it is the *mantra* of Avalokiteshvara (*q.v.*), the *Bodhisattva* (*q.v.*) central to Tibetan Buddhism. The turning of the prayer wheel invokes his presence. In meditation, Tibetans envision the

turning prayer wheel in six sections, radiating a light which banishes evil, bringing bliss and peace not only to themselves but to all beings.

(2) The six syllables of the *mantra* are identified with six buddhas, six colors, and six "realms of sentient beings," in the fasting cult of Avalokiteshvara, where the *mantra* is recited six times in each 12 hour period of the day and night.

OMNIPOTENCE.

From the Latin *omnis* ("all") and *potens* ("powerful"). One of the chief attributes of the absolutistic conception of God (*q.v.* 7, 11, 12, 19). That view should be compared with others in which God (*q.v.* 25) is regarded as finite in some respects and infinite in other respects. Nor is the conception of God (*q.v.* 26) as a finite being negligible in Western thought.

OMNIPRESENCE.

One of the traditional attributes of God. If a thing or being is where it works, then the problem of the divine omnipresence becomes part of the problem of omnipotence (*q.v.*), and the distinctions important to that concept likewise apply here.

OMNISCIENCE.

From the Latin *omnis* ("all") and *scire* ("to know"). Traditionally, one of the chief attributes of God (*q.v.* 7–9).

(1) In traditional theology (*q.v.* Aquinas 1–4) the attribute of omniscience includes completely detailed knowledge of the future as well as knowledge of the past and present.

(2) For Faustus Socinus (*q.v.* 4), Lequier (*q.v.* 2) and Charles Hartshorne (*q.v.* 5) omniscience includes detailed knowledge of the past and present, but not of the future, since the future does not yet exist, is not yet made up, and hence is not there to be known.

ONE.

From the Latin *unus* and the Greek *oine*.

(1) In Pythagorean number theory (*q.v.* Pythagoras 7) the "One" and the "Dyad" generate all other numbers.

(2) For Plato (*q.v.* 1) the One interpenetrates with Beauty, Truth, and the Good to make something close to a single eternal principle.

(3) For Chuang Tzu (*q.v.* 4) the One is the principle of being and of virtue.

(4) Hui Shih (*q.v.* 1) regarded all things collectively as the Great One, and their individual reality as illusive.

(5) Aristotle in the Metaphysics held that the term One refers either to the naturally continuous, the whole, the individual, or the universal.

(6) In Neoplatonism (*q.v.* 6) "the One" is the name of God who generates the entire universe by emanation from Its superessential reality. *Q.v.* Plotinus (2).

(7) In the T'ien-T'ai school (*q.v.* 3) and in its founder Chih-I (*q.v.*) reality is identified with the one pure mind, and termed True Thusness.

(8) Chou Tun-I (*q.v.* 2) finds a balance between the one and the many.

(9) Ch'eng Hao (*q.v.* 4) views the universe as a single, organic unity.

(10) Chu Hsi (*q.v.* 3) represents neo-Confucianism in its developed form as a system balanced between the One and the Many, with an interaction between principle and material force.

Q.v. Unity.

ONESICRITUS. 4th cent. B.C. fl. 330.

Greek philosopher. A Cynic and follower of Diogenes of Sinope (*q.v.*). Accompanying Alexander the Great on his expedition to India, Onesicritus was much impressed by the Indian Gymnosophists whose indifference to pain, disregard of custom, and simplicity of life seemed to him to confirm the chief tenets of the Cynic philosophy (*q.v.* Cynicism).

Principal writings: *Life of Alexander; Description of the Coasts of India.*

ONTIC.

Adjective formed from the Greek *on, ontis* ("being").

(1) Heidegger (*q.v.* 5) uses the term to describe the perspective of looking at the world from the standpoint of the entities (*seindes*) which make it up. The attitude of the ontic perspective is *existenziell* (compare with "ontological" and "existential," Heidegger 1).

(2) Quine (*q.v.* 8) uses the phrase "ontic theories" to refer to metaphysical systems.

ONTOLOGICAL ARGUMENT.

An argument for God which moves from the definition of His nature as a perfect being to the conclusion that He exists. The argument has several versions.

(1) It was first formulated by Anselm (*q.v.* 1–3) who gave two different versions of the argument: one from "the being than which none greater can be conceived," the other from the conception of a necessary being, to the existence of that being. Bonaventure (*q.v.* 3) supported Anselm, starting from an innate idea of perfect being.

(2) Descartes (*q.v.* 5) presented the same two versions of the argument.

(3) Spinoza (*q.v.* 1, 2) argued to existence from the concept of that "whose conception does not require the conception of another thing."

(4) Leibniz (*q.v.* 8) moved to validate the argument by first establishing that the idea of God is a "possible concept."

(5) Kant (*q.v.* 5c), holding that "existence is not a predicate," is given credit very widely for having destroyed the credibility of the argument. But he had not distinguished the two versions of the argument to which we have referred; and there is some question whether his refutation is equally fatal to both versions.

(6) Barth (*q.v.* 2) interpreted the argument as a matter of faith seeking understanding.

(7) In the 1960's Charles Hartshorne (*q.v.* 4) revived the argument, noting the differences of the two versions, and including the Leibnizian move.

(8) Norman Malcolm (*q.v.*) and others have also paid attention to the argument, reviving it at least as a subject for discussion.

ONTOLOGICAL PRINCIPLE.
Q.v. Whitehead, (19).

ONTOLOGY.
From the Greek *ontos* ("being") and *logos* ("knowledge"). The term thus means "knowledge of being" and refers to a division of philosophy having such knowledge as its subject matter. The term did not make its appearance until the 17th century when it was introduced by Goclenius in 1636, used by Clauberg in 1647, Micraelius in 1653, and DuHamel in 1663. Accepted by Leibniz, Wolff, and Baumgarten the term had become standard by the century's end. Despite its pedigree, wide agreement on its use has

never existed. The relation between Metaphysics (*q.v.*) and Ontology has remained especially unclear.

(1) Clauberg called ontology "first science," a study of being as being. The study was understood to apply to all entities, no less to God than to created beings, and to underly both theology and physics. The study was to cover the principles and attributes of being, as well as analyses of cause, order, relation, truth, and perfection. He also called this study *ontosophia*, having the same meaning as ontology, and came to prefer this name. For a time ontology and *ontosophia* were used interchangeably.

(2) Wolff (*q.v.* 2) defined ontology as the science of being in general, and used "first philosophy" as its synonym. Its method is deductive, and its goal a system of necessary truth. The principles of noncontradiction (*q.v.*) and sufficient reason (*q.v.*) are to be its organon.

(3) Baumgarten (*q.v.* 1) defined ontology as a study of "the most general or abstract predicates" of things in general. He used the terms "ontosophia," "universal metaphysics," and "first philosophy" as synonyms for ontology.

(4) The term passed easily into Scholastic thought where it became identified with "general metaphysics," the study of the properties of being as such (including the Transcendentals, *q.v.*), and standing in contrast to "special metaphysics" which dealt with those aspects of being within the reach of ordinary experience.

(5) Herbart (*q.v.* 3) contrasted methodology with ontology, regarding the former as charged with reducing the contradictions within the given, and the latter as a method for understanding true (*i.e.*, non-contradictory) reality.

(6) Rosmini-Serbati (*q.v.*) contrasts ontology with theology and cosmology. Ontology is the universal doctrine of being. Theology is the doctrine of absolute being. Cosmology is the doctrine of finite and relative being.

(7) For Gioberti (*q.v.* 1) ontology is the basic philosophic discipline.

(8) Husserl (*q.v.* 4) distinguished formal from material ontology. Both deal with the analysis of essences. Formal ontology, dealing with formal or universal essence, is the ultimate basis of all science. Material ontology, dealing with

material or regional essences, is the basis of all factual sciences. Material ontologies are regional, and regional ontologies have their basis in formal ontology.

(9) Heidegger (*q.v.* 1, 7), on the contrary, understands ontology to be an analysis of existence. Directed toward analysis of the constitution of "the being of existence," it discovers the finitude of existence, and is concerned to discover what makes existence possible.

(10) Leśniewski (*q.v.*) uses the term "ontology" in the area of logic, calling the calculus of classes and relations by this name. For this reason the axiomatic of the calculus is termed an ontological axiomatic. Ontology in this usage stands as a term along with "propositional calculus" and "algebra of classes."

(11) Carnap (*q.v.* 5) regarded all ontological implications as falsely drawn. His view turns on the distinction between internal and external questions, and their corresponding internal and external objects. Questions internal to an identifiable framework of, *e.g.*, numbers, propositions, things, etc., are legitimate and the linguistic forms one uses may be freely chosen according to a principle of tolerance; the objects to which one refers by means of these linguistic forms are internal objects. But when questions are asked concerning the reality of entities in general, outside a specific framework, one is making reference to external objects, and the questions are false questions.

(12) Levinas (*q.v.* 2) distinguishes between ontology and metaphysics, finding the latter to be beyond being.

(13) Bergmann (*q.v.* 2), presuming that any language will have ontological implications, uses ideal languages to test and gain control over the ontology to which one is committing oneself.

(14) Quine (*q.v.* 2) contrasts ontology with ideology, relating the first to theory of reference and the second to theory of signification. For Quine both terms always relate to particular theories. The question of ontology, then, concerns what one is committed to admit in terms of entities in the universe, if one commits oneself to a given theory.

(15) Chisholm (*q.v.* 2) presents an ontology of states of affairs.

ONTOSOPHIA.
Q.v. Ontology (1, 3).

OPAQUE CONTEXTS.
Q.v. Quantifying In; Quine (9–10).

OPEN SOCIETY.
A society structured to allow its members to advance to whatever level their capacities allow.

(1) Mosca (*q.v.* 3) found the open society to be more stable than other societies.

(2) Popper (*q.v.* 3) lauded the open society against the closed society of Plato. He argued the advantages of pluralism over monism as a pattern characterizing the structure of societies.

OPERATIONAL DEFINITIONS.
Q.v. Operationalism.

OPERATIONALISM.
A philosophical position first announced by the physicist, P. W. Bridgman (*q.v.*), to the effect that scientific concepts are to be defined in terms of operations; and the meanings of such concepts are identical to the operations entering into their definitions. His standard example was the manner in which a given length is identical to a set of measuring operations with a ruler. Under pressure, he added pencil and paper operations to allow more abstract definitions. Hugo Dingler (*q.v.*) independently developed a similar approach. Anatol Rapoport supported the view in his *Operational Philosophy*, (1953). Operationalism has been introduced into psychology by B.F. Skinner (*q.v.* 1) and others.

OPHITES OF CELSUS.
From the Greek *ophis* ("serpent"). A Gnostic sect revering the serpent as the font of divine wisdom. The Ophites interpreted the serpent's act in persuading Adam and Eve to eat of the tree of knowledge as friendly and beneficial. *Q.v.* Gnosticism.

OPINION.
From the Greek term *doxa* ("opinion," from *dokeo*, "to suppose, seem, appear").

(1) Parmenides (*q.v.* 2) contrasted opinion with truth, the former relating to sense-experience and dealing with appearance, the latter relating to thought

and dealing with reality and being.

(2) For Plato (*q.v.* 1) opinion represents a position which stands between *agnoia* or ignorance and *episteme* or knowledge. In Plato's twice-divided line the bottom half represents opinion, while the top half represents knowledge or understanding. Opinion can be only probable since its subject is the world of change.

(3) Aristotle (*q.v.* 5) follows Plato in that for him, too, opinion relates to the contingent, and can be no more than probable. That which is held to be true, or popular opinion, is regarded as the starting point of inquiry.

OPPOSITES.

Some systems of philosophy have placed a stress on the role of opposites.

(1) The Pythagoreans (*q.v.* Pythagoras 6) developed a table of opposites reflecting a basic duality in the universe.

(2) Heraclitus (*q.v.* 2) found a "tension of opposites" providing the order and dynamism of the universe.

(3) In Taoism (*q.v.* 1) *Yang* and *Yin* represent opposites in terms of which the universe operates.

(4) Nicholas of Cusa (*q.v.* 2) presented a doctrine called the "coincidence of opposites" which applied to God, the Infinite Being.

(5) Hegel (*q.v.* 3) believed the basic processes of reality and thought moved through contraries into novel unities.

OPPOSITION, SQUARE OF.

Q.v. Immediate Inference (1).

"O" PROPOSITION.

Q.v. Syllogism (3, 6d).

ORACLES, CHALDEAN.

A philosophical poem of the 2nd century A.D. describing the descent of the soul into the realm of matter and its possible rise, after purification, through the concentric circles of the universe toward its eternal home. Containing Platonic, Neoplatonic, and neo-Pythagorean influences, the poem is probably an expression of a neo-Pythagorean mystery religion (*q.v.*).

ORATORIANS.

Members of the Congregation of the Oratory, founded in 1575, and consisting of independent communities of Catholic priests living in obedience to a rule but without vows.

ORDER.

An arrangement in accordance with intention, principle, or rule.

(1) According to Hesiod (*q.v.* 1), order came out of chaos (*q.v.*) through the power of Eros. In addition to *eros* Greek philosophy (*q.v.*) has explored many other possible ordering principles, including mind and chance variation.

(2) Both linear and hierarchical order are implicit in Plato's (*q.v.* 9) notion that the world of change has as its pattern a world of Ideas. The possibility of graded order is likewise present in medieval thought where the idea of order depends upon a relation of adequacy or commensurability between a thing and its idea in the mind of God (*q.v.* Chain of Being). In Leibniz (*q.v.* 5, 9) the principles of plenitude and continuity continue the Platonic and medieval senses of graded order. In altered form the principle is to be found in the philosophy of Whitehead (*q.v.* 16).

(3) Aristotle is not unrelated to the preceding sense of order; but it should be noted that it was he who related the order of a whole to the reciprocal relations of its parts, and this idea continued to be held in the Middle Ages. The Aristotelian idea contains the germ of the modern approach to the idea of order, *i.e.*, an aggregate of some sort controlled by a relation. In the modern world, Peano (*q.v.*) isolated the relation of "successor of." Such series are characterized by relations (*q.v.*) of transitivity, irreflexivity, connexity, and asymmetry, according to Whitehead and Russell.

(4) Where traditional accounts view order and chaos as excluding each other, in chaos theory (*q.v.*) the distinction is placed on a continuum from single-parametered investigations which are amenable to linear equations, and hold the promise of high predictability; to multiply parametered investigations of increasing complexity whose predictability drops as parameters increase, and where nonlinear equations are the rule. Scientists were attracted to single-parametered cases initially, according to chaos theorists, by their high predictability even though the

dynamical systems of nature are typically more complex.

ORDINARY LANGUAGE PHILOSOPHY.
Q.v. Oxford Movement (3).

ORESME, NICHOLAS. c. 1325–1382.
French ecclesiastic and scientist. Born in Normandy. Educated at the University of Paris. Adviser to the king and bishop of Lisieux. He anticipated Galileo's mean-speed and distance theorems. In mathematics he arrived at the concept of an irrational exponent.

Principal writings: *De proportionibus proportionum* (T); *Ad pauca respicientes* (T); *De commensurabilitate vei incommensurabilitate motuum celi* (T); *De cofigurationibus qualitatum* (T); *Quaestiones de sphera* (T).

ORGANICISM.
Q.v. S.C. Pepper (1); and Organism; Philosophy of.

ORGANISM, PHILOSOPHY OF.
Just as some philosophers have taken matter and mind as the key to metaphysics (*q.v.* Materialism and Idealism), others have found the key in the concept of "organism." The philosophy of organism, sometimes called "organicism," is the result.

(1) Greek philosophy exhibited some tendencies toward the philosophy of organism. For example, Plato (*q.v.* 9) in the *Timaeus* found the world to be a living organism; and Aristotle (*q.v.* 9) at least utilized certain organic properties, such as their goal directedness, to construct a teleological system where final cause played an important role.

(2) The 16th century contained a number of such philosophies. Paracelsus (*q.v.* 1–2) held the world to be a vast organism, and man a microcosm of the macrocosm (*q.v.*). The Van Helmonts (*q.v.*), father and son, developed Paracelsus' views into a monadology (*q.v.*).

(3) This in turn influenced the system of Leibniz (*q.v.* 1–2, 6) in the 17th century where, although the world is not an organism, organic motifs are widely present.

(4) In the 19th century Fechner (*q.v.*) presented a view wherein God is the soul of the universe, having as his constituents lesser souls, which in turn contain

hierarchies of souls still more inferior, the whole functioning together in organic terms.

(5) The Russian philosopher, Soloviev (*q.v.* 3), gave an organismic interpretation of reality.

(6) In recent years Lossky (*q.v.* 1), following Leibniz in part, has held the world to be an organic totality. The system of Whitehead (*q.v.* 25) was a self-styled philosophy of organism. Not only did Whitehead use the term; it was used of his view by Dorothy Emmet (*q.v.* 1-2) in evident approval.

ORGANISMIC ANALOGY.
Q.v. Spencer (1).

ORGANISMIC BIOLOGY.
The name of that interpretation of biology which stresses the non-reductionistic nature of the organic level, taking the position that the whole cannot be equated simply with the sum of the activities of the parts. J.H. Woodger (*q.v.*) is a representative of the position. Alternative positions are Vitalism (*q.v.*) and Reductionism (*q.v.*). Also *q.v.* Biology (3). The view has a resemblance to the philosophical doctrine of holism (*q.v.* Smuts 1).

ORGANISMIC METAPHOR.
Q.v. Society (9–13, 16, 18); Spengler (1); Toynbee (1); Popper (4).

ORGANON.
A Greek term meaning "instrument", derived from *ergon* ("work").

(1) The term by which the logical treatises of Aristotle are known. First applied to Aristotle's treatises on logic by Alexander of Aphrodisius (*q.v.*) and John Philoponus (*q.v.*).

(2) Francis Bacon (*q.v.*), setting his inductive logic against the traditional logic, named his work the *New Organon* (*Novum Organum*).

(3) Others have continued the competition; for example, Whewell (*q.v.*) with his *Novum Organum Renovatum*.

ORIGEN. c. 185–254.
Christian theologian. Probably born in Alexandria. Taught in the Catechetical School there. Studied under Clement of Alexandria (*q.v.*) whose work he continued, and probably under Ammonius

Saccas (*q.v.*), the teacher of Plotinus. Some, indeed, hold that Origen, the theologian, and Origen the Neoplatonist (*q.v.*) are the same person. After 232 he moved to Caesarea where he opened his own school.

Principal writings: *On Principles* (T); *Against Celsus* (T); *On Prayer* (T); the *Hexapla* and *Tetrapala*, his famous editions of the Scriptures with Hebrew and Greek versions side by side; and many commentaries on books of the Bible including *The Song of Songs* (T).

(1) Presenting a philosophical-theological system directed toward human redemption, Origen presupposes a premundane fall from grace of each individual soul, activating the world drama.

(2) Of the figures of the Trinity, the Son and the Holy Spirit are subordinate to the Father and derivative from Him, while being at the same time eternal. The Son is both the Logos and the Redeemer of this fallen world; and is, along with the Holy Spirit, a mediator between God and the world.

(3) Believing the soul of man to have pre-existed, and identifying evil with privation and nonbeing, Origen holds that man's presence in a material body is a sign of his sin and his fall, of his having used the liberty God had granted him not for the intended good but for evil purposes. One retains one's initial freedom, although hampered by the body, to turn toward God and goodness.

(4) One's help in this, and the guarantee of one's final success, is the Redeemer, the *Logos* united with a pure human soul, who sacrificed Himself for man's sins. This has made possible a gradual but continuous process of purification which is to culminate at last in the *Apocatastasis* the universal restoration of all to God, and the final destruction of evil.

ORIGEN THE NEOPLATONIST. 3rd cent. A.D.

Hellenic philosopher. A companion of Plotinus he studied with Plotinus under Ammonius Saccas (*q.v.*). Associated with Neoplatonism, he speculated on the relation between the transcendent God and the creator of the world. It is also known that he worked at length on the *Timaeus* of Plato.

Principal writings: *Concerning Demons; That Only the King is Poet.*

ORIGINAL SIN.
Q.v. Sin (3).

ORIGINATION, DEPENDENT.
Q.v. Dependent Origination.

ORMAZD.
Q.v. Ahura Mazda; Zoroaster (1).

ORPHEUS-EURYDICE.
Q.v. Mystery Religions (3).

ORPHIC MYSTERIES.
Q.v. Mystery Religions (3).

ORPHISM.
The doctrine of the Orphic Mysteries (*q.v.* Mystery Religions 3) in which Dionysus is a dying and rising savior. (1) The ascetic and ceremonial requirements of Orphism and Pythagoreanism (*q.v.*) are strikingly similar. (2) The Orphic hymns and poems exercised considerable influence over the development of Neoplatonism (*q.v.*), and were frequently cited in 3rd- and 4th-century controversies between pagan and Christian writers.

ORTEGA Y GASSET, JOSÉ. 1883–1955.
Spanish philosopher. Born in Madrid. Studied under Hermann Cohen in the Marburg neo-Kantian school, without becoming an adherent. Although his thought passed through several stages, his mature point of view might be termed a vital humanism. His close association with *El Espectador* and *Revista de Occidente* spanned two decades beginning in 1916. Much of his work was published in these journals. Associated with Central University in Madrid as Professor of Metaphysics from 1911 until his retirement in 1952. His activities as a teacher ended, however, in 1936.

Principal writings: *Meditations on Quijote* (T), 1914; *Persons, Works, Things,* 1916; *The Theme of our Time* (T), 1921; *Invertebrate Spain* (T), 1922; *The Dehumanization of Art* (T), 1925; *The Spirit of the Letter,* 1927; *The Revolt of the Masses* (T), 1929; *Goethe From Within,* 1934; *Self-absorption and Alteration,* 1939; *Studies on Love* (T), 1939; *Ideas and Beliefs,* 1940; *Youthful Excesses,* 1941; *Theory of Andalusia and Other Essays,* 1942; *Two Prologues,*

1945; *Papers on Velazquez and Goya*, 1950; *Velazquez* (T), 1955; *Man and People* (T), 1957; *What is Philosophy?* (T), 1957; *The Idea of Principle in Leibniz* (T), 1967.

(1) Starting from the point of view that knowledge is rooted in life, Ortega preached the doctrine of a "vital reason." Abstract reason can create abstract systems of thought. But vital reason is the means by which man has been able to survive in the universe. Thus, it is concrete and full, various and multiform.

(2) The difference between ideas and beliefs is a difference between abstract and concrete. Beliefs provide the foundation for life, the context within which it is lived. Ideas are forged when beliefs begin to fail. At the same time ideas, leading to knowledge, need to be founded in belief and all perspectives have some—although partial—validity. Knowledge is one of the forms of thought, which must somewhere be rooted in pre-rational belief. One does not investigate without the belief that there is something there to be investigated. Vital reason requires the combination of belief and idea, thought and knowledge.

(3) But the point is that it is life that requires knowledge on which one can depend. And life is therefore the fundamental reality. The fundamental reality is a continual self-making which seeks authenticity. Insofar as one evades this task one's life is less real and one has failed to discover one's true vocation. There are grades of reality, indeed, depending upon how closely one approaches one's authentic destiny. One may dispense with the idea of transcendence; one's proper transcendence is one's authentic human existence.

(4) One seeks to avoid shipwreck in this life by developing and appropriating the forms of culture. Science, philosophy, religion, and art are analogous to poetic creations, human constructions in the face of a problematic reality. In comparison with the reality, science is itself phantasmagoria. The constructions of art, for example, in this age are highly experimental, seeking a new basis after having used up traditional artistic modes.

(5) Man, then really has no nature. He has a history. Hence he must be approached through the vital reason. The same is true of society. But Ortega's comments on society move in two directions. On the one hand, society is viewed as a form of inauthenticity, from which one must turn. On the other hand, society is viewed sometimes as an instrument requiring our adaptation and at other times as a support for our own liberty, like the flexible skin which contains the organism while permitting freedom of movement. The two directions are perhaps reconciled by the concept of forms of interdependence not completely personal and not completely social.

ORTHODOXY.

From the Greek *orthos* ("right") and *doxa* ("opinion"). Correctness of belief as determined by an authoritative standard. To be contrasted with heterodoxy or heresy (*q.v.*). The concern with orthodoxy is much more pronounced in Western than in Eastern religions. The same may be true in philosophy.

ORWELL, GEORGE.

Q.v. Utopia.

OSIRIS.

Q.v. Mystery Religions (2).

OSTENSIVE DEFINITION.

Q.v. Definition (3).

OSTWALD, WILHELM. 1853–1932.

German chemist and philosopher. Born in Riga. Taught at Leipzig.

Principal writings: *Energy and Its Transformations*, 1888; *Individuality and Immortality* (E), 1906; *The Energetic Basis of the Science of Culture*, 1908; *Energy*, 1908; *Natural Philosophy* (T), 1910; *The Energy Imperative*, 1912; *Philosophy of Value*, 1913; *Science and Belief in God* (ed. Herneck), 1960.

(1) Contending that reality is energy rather than matter, Ostwald argued that his position superseded the older materialisms. Energy is the basic stuff that transforms itself into all other forms and properties.

(2) Since the usable energy of the universe decreases through time, a high value must be placed upon the availability of energy. Ostwald felt that the basic imperative is the accumulation of energy for human use, including that of future generations.

OTHERING.
Plato's concept of negation. *Q.v.* Plato (8) and Nothing (4).

OTHERNESS.
Q.v. Levinas (1–4); Derrida (8).

OTTO, RUDOLF. 1869–1937.
German philosopher. Born in Peine. Taught at Göttingen. A follower of Kant, he was a member of the neo-Friesian School—also known as the Göttingen School—of neo-Kantianism (*q.v.* 3). His interest lay in the philosophy of religion.

Principal writings: *The Philosophy of Religion of Kant-Fries and its Application to Theology* (T), 1909; *Darwinism and Religion* (T), 1910; *The Idea of the Holy* (T), 1917; *Studies Relative to the Numinous,* 1923; *Mysticism East and West* (T), 1926; *Freedom and Necessity,* 1940.

(1) Applying the Kantian analysis of Jacob Fries (*q.v.*)—also sanctioned by Leonard Nelson (*q.v.*)—to religious phenomena, Otto employed history to gain a distillation of concepts which he then developed analytically in his chosen area of philosophy of religion.

(2) The concepts he discovered in this manner became the keys to his interpretation of the phenomena. They included the *numinous,* the *mysterium tremendum,* and the *mysterium fascinosum.* All three terms relate to the religious attitude. The *numinous* is the feeling of awe which takes hold of the worshipper before the sacred object or in the holy place. The *mysterium tremendum* is the fathomless mystery beyond rational analysis which attaches to the sacred being. The *mysterium fascinosum* is the equally deep fascination or enchantment experienced by the worshipper in contemplation of the sacred being. Together, the concepts make up the idea of the holy.

OUK ON.
Greek term, one of two, for nonbeing. *Q.v.* Nothing.

OUSIA.
A Greek term meaning "being," "substance," or "essence."

(1) Aristotle (*q.v.* 7) used the term to refer primarily to the individual, existing thing. This he called *ousia prote* or "first substance." And these are the primary

subjects of propositions. Any other term which can stand in the subject place he calls *ousia deutera* or "second substance." He has in mind, especially, the terms naming species and genera, and regards the former as "more substantial" than the latter. Other general terms are called "second substances" by analogy.

(2) The Arian (*q.v.*) controversy of the 4th century centered on the use of this term. The Arians held that the Son is *homoiousios* ("of similar substance") to the Father, while the orthodox insisted that Father and Son are *homoousios* ("of the same substance").

(3) In Neoplatonism (*q.v.*) God was said to be *hyperousios* ("beyond substance").

OVER-SOUL.
Q.v. Emerson (5).

OWEN, ROBERT. 1771–1858.
English social reformer. Born at Newton, North Wales. At an early age he worked his way into the position of manager and then owner of cotton mills, first in Manchester and then New Lanark. In 1813 he formed a company, Jeremy Bentham participating, which asked only a 5 percent return on the investment. In relation to the mills, he operated stores selling at cost, and introduced schools for children as well; his work at New Lanark gained national and European attention. In 1826 he founded a community in New Harmony, Indiana, according to the social principles he had developed. It failed within two years, taking most of the fortune Owen had accumulated. Returning to England, he terminated his connections with New Lanark, and settled in London where he worked for the improvement of the laboring class. Credited as the founder of English socialism, he organized the Association of all Classes of all Nations in 1835.

Principal writings: *A New View of Society,* 1813; *Debates on the Evidences of Christianity,* 1839; *Revolution in the Mind and Practice of the Human Race,* 1849; *Life of Robert Owen,* 1857; *Threading My Way,* 1874.

(1) Believing that human character is formed by circumstances over which one has no control, Owen stressed the importance of establishing an educational and social system exerting the proper

influences on those in their formative years.

(2) At the same time, the competition between human labor and machinery, leading to the permanent pauperization of great numbers of the working class, called for human action to subordinate machinery to human ends.

(3) He believed that both ends would be achieved through the establishment of voluntary communities of 500 to 3,000 persons, working 1,000 to 1,500 acres with the best machinery and offering every variety of employment. Each family would have its own apartment but the dining areas would be common. At the age of three the education of the child by the community would begin. The communities were to be self-sustaining as much as possible.

(4) Owen called on individuals, parishes, counties, and states to set up such communities. It was his thought that they would multiply freely, federate with each other, and finally unite the world in bonds of common interest.

(5) His opposition to Christianity, expressed in England and in the United States in 1839 through a six-day debate with Alexander Campbell (*q.v.*), worked against acceptance of his social theories.

OXFORD GROUP.
Q.v. Buchmanism.

OXFORD MOVEMENT.
(1) A 19th-century Catholic movement of spiritual renewal at Oxford, one of whose leaders was Cardinal Newman (*q.v.*).

(2) It is worth noting that Oxford has not been without philosophic movements as well, the arrival of the Franciscans in the 13th century signalling the first of them. Roger Bacon (*q.v.*), Duns Scotus (*q.v.*), and Robert Grosseteste (*q.v.*) were among the important philosophers of the group.

(3) One can speak of an Oxford group of philosophers, if not a movement, in mid-20th century. Among the philosophers of the group, characterized by a linguistic approach to the problems of philosophy, one would cite Ryle (*q.v.*), Waismann (*q.v.*), Strawson (*q.v.*), Austin (*q.v.*), and Hare (*q.v.*).

PACHOMIUS, ST.
Q.v. Monasticism.

PACIFISM.
Q.v. George Fox (1); Tolstoy (2); Gandhi (1); Einstein (5).

PAIDEIA.
A Greek term meaning "education," *Q.v.* Werner Jaeger.

PAINE, THOMAS. 1737–1809.
Social reformer. Born in Thetford, England. An autodidact, Paine received an honorary Master of Arts degree from the University of Pennsylvania on July 4, 1780. He came to Philadelphia in 1774, carrying letters of introduction from Benjamin Franklin whom he chanced to have met in England. He supported himself by journalism until his significant writings began to appear. The success of his initial publications led to an honorary Master of Arts degree conferred by the University of Pennsylvania on July 4, 1780. At about the same time he was voted membership in the American Philosophical Society, also located in Philadelphia. All of his writings were stimulated by the political crisis facing the colonies, and the republic which grew out of it. Even his book defending deism is rooted in the view that only a rational religion is compatible with democracy, a view with currency among others involved in framing the Constitution. Paine lived in his writing. The events of the day had reality for him only as they related to the process of his inner thought. He had an unusual capacity for clear statement and powerful argument, involving the emotions of his readers. The capacity was, at times, polarizing, creating enemies as well as friends.

Selected writings: *Common Sense*, Jan. 10, 1776; *The Crisis*, 13 numbers, 1776-83; *Rights of Man*, Parts I and II, 1791, 1792; *The Age of Reason*, Parts I and II, 1794, 1795; *Agrarian Justice*, 1797; *The Writings of Thomas Paine*, 4 vols., 1894-96.

(1) In *Common Sense* Paine argued for an immediate declaration of independence on the ground that a continent

cannot remain tied to an island, that to remain so tied is to court moral corruption, while to declare independence is to begin to fulfill one's moral obligation to the world. In the republic to come law would be king. Concerning freedom, which he said had been hunted around the globe, he urged his fellows to receive the fugitive, and "prepare in time an asylum for mankind." Paine said the pamphlet sold 120,000 copies in three months. The estimate of its total sale is 500,000. Dr. Benjamin Rush said the book, "burst from the press with an effect which has rarely been produced by types and paper in any age or country."

(2) After the July 4 Declaration of Independence Paine joined Washington's army, and during the retreat through New Jersey wrote the initial number of *The Crisis*, "These are the times that try men's souls," allegedly on a drum head around a campfire at night. By Washington's orders it was read to each regiment and each detachment of the army. Some said it was the combined genius of Washington and Paine that brought independence, and that neither could have done it without the other. Congress resolved in 1785 that the timely publications of Thomas Paine "merit the approbation of this Congress."

(3) His *Rights of Man*, Part I dedicated to Washington and Part II dedicated to Lafayette, answered Burke's *Reflections on the Revolution in France* (1790). Paine had returned to Europe in 1787, living alternately in France and England while working on his "pontifical invention," an iron bridge with a single span. At the same time he was fostering the idea of an American-style revolution in both countries. The bridge was built in Yorkshire, England, and was a moderate success. It had the longest span of its time, 110 feet, but far short of the 400 foot span Paine had envisaged. He turned back to social philosophy to answer Burke. Burke defended the American revolution, while attacking the French. Paine defended both. Where Burke believed that one's contract with the state could not be altered, Paine held that individuals enter a compact with each other to form a government, and one generation cannot legitimately bind another. He believed that civil rights rest on natural rights. He

argued for a written constitution and a bill of rights, and believed that the American Constitution was to liberty what "grammar is to language." Finally, he called on the British people to overthrow their monarchy and establish a republic. The book sold 200,000 copies in Britain before it was banned in 1792. Paine was tried for treason, convicted *in absentia*, and outlawed.

(4) By this time he was in France whose National Assembly had made him a citizen, elected him to its National Convention, and appointed him to a select committee to draft a new constitution. The Declaration of Rights, preceding the constitution, seems to have been Paine's work; it held the natural rights to be liberty, equality, security, property, social protection, and resistance to oppression (*q.v.* Natural Rights, 4). As for property, he held (although this is from *Agrarian Justice*) that the earth in its natural state was "the common property of the human race," so in that state everyone was born to property. In any case the draft was never discussed. Soon war broke out and the Reign of Terror descended. In the year he sat with the Convention he organized a Republican Club with the object of converting Convention members to the American system. He argued before the Convention that the royal family not be executed but sentenced to banishment (he thought exile in America would be appropriate). His proposal lost by a narrow margin, more than 300 voting with him. He was also working on *The Age of Reason*, so that when the authorities came to arrest him on Dec. 28, 1793, Part I of the manuscript was complete, and he was able to talk his captors into allowing him to take that part of the manuscript to an American friend who had the book printed in Paris. He was placed in the Luxembourg prison. The underlying reason for his arrest was that his sympathies were with the Girondins, the party of small businessmen, which had fallen, and many of whose members were being executed.

(5) During the imprisonment he worked on Part II of *The Age of Reason*. His urgency in working on this book was his belief that the only religion compatible with democracy was Deism (*q.v.*). It was part of the social pattern for which

he stood, and he saw French anticlericalism slipping into atheism. In Part I he gave his "profession of faith": belief in one god, hope for happiness beyond this life, human equality, religion defined as "doing justice, having mercy, and endeavoring to make our fellow creatures happy." He accepted the arguments from design and first cause, finding in the creation a manifestation of God's power, wisdom, and goodness. All of this is the religion of reason. Revealed religion, on the other hand, with its superstition, is the cause of most of the ills of mankind. In Part II he goes through the books of the Bible successively, "showing" that they lack authenticity. His objective is to point out inconsistencies in the Old Testament, and discrepancies in the New, especially in the Gospels. Even Jesus' ethical teachings fail. They go beyond the dictates of conscience. The injunctions to turn the other cheek, and to love one's enemies, engender hypocrisy and are part of a "feigned and fabulous morality."

(6) He had been in prison for almost a year, and in Britain was thought to have been guillotined. Shortly after James Monroe became Ambassador to France, however, he interceded on Paine's behalf, and secured his release within two days. This was on Nov. 4, 1794. The Monroes took him into their home and nursed him back to health. While recuperating he finished the second part of *The Age of Reason*. The French edition remained largely unsold, even though his reason for writing the book had been to help shape the French Revolution. In England and America it was widely discussed, however, and within four years fifty books were written, countering his arguments. In England, as with the *Rights of Man*, court cases were brought against the book. At least one book seller was jailed. Paine protested from France but without effect. On Decenber 8, his membership in the Convention was restored, and he was offered a pension for "consecrating liberty" in two worlds. He rejected the pension, but returned to his seat in the Convention. On July 7, 1795 he defended his position on the rights of man once more, while criticizing a property qualification in the 1795 constitution.

(7) The Monroes returned to America

in the spring of 1797. Paine intended to sail with them but at Le Havre "British frigates were cruising about," apparently with the design of capturing him. He altered his plans, remaining in France. It was five years until, during the brief Peace of Amiens, he was able to leave. In America he continued to contrast the Religion of Deism with Christianity, but the resonance of his effort was much reduced. Books devolved into articles, and articles into letters to newspapers. *The Age of Reason* had aroused hostility; in addition, he had criticized Washington for allowing him to languish so long in the Luxembourg. He was buried on his farm in New Rochelle, his request for burial in a Quaker cemetery having been turned down by the Society of Friends. Neither France nor America sent an official representative to his funeral.

PALEY, WILLIAM. 1743–1805.

English philosopher-theologian. Born at Peterborough. Educated at Cambridge, where he became fellow and then tutor. After nine years of teaching he went into the ministry, finally becoming Archdeacon of Carlisle. His book on moral and political philosophy was based on his Cambridge lectures; it became the ethics text at Cambridge, and went through fifteen editions during Paley's lifetime. His book on the evidences of Christianity brought him the position of subdean in the cathedral at Lincoln, as well as the rectory of Bishop-wearmouth.

Principal writings: *The Principles of Moral and Political Philosophy*, 1785; *Horae Paulinae*, 1790; *Evidences of Christianity*, 1794; *Natural Theology*, 1802.

(1) Taking the common good to be the will of God, and both the Scriptures and man's natural light the means of interpreting this will, Paley championed a doctrine of "theological Utilitarianism," using the criterion of the general happiness. He believed that prudence and virtue, or egoism and altruism would in the long run coincide.

(2) In his work on natural theology he argued, by analogy, from the evidences of design in nature to an intelligent and beneficent Creator. His basic analogy was that of the watchmaker; just as a watch requires a watchmaker, so the world requires an intelligent designer. The

argument is then supported by adducing instances of design from nature. His favorite instance is the subtle and careful adaptation of the parts of the eye to make sight possible.

PALI CANON.
Q.v. Abhidhamma; Buddhism, Theravada.

PALMER, G.H. 1842–1933.
American philosopher. Born in Boston. Taught at Harvard in the period of James, Royce, and Santayana. An Idealist, he took self-realization to be the end of life, and the criterion for ethics. He located the possibility of human freedom at the intersection of causal chains.

Principal writings: *The Nature of Goodness*, 1903; *The Problem of Freedom*, 1911.

PANAETIUS. c. 180–110 B.C.
Greek philosopher. Born in Rhodes. Educated in Pergamum and Athens (where he studied under Carneades and others). A Stoic of the Middle Period (*q.v.* Stoicism 2), he taught in Rome, becoming an influential member of the circle of Scipio the Younger. After the death of Scipio he returned to Athens (129 B.C.) to become head of the Stoic school. His books were drawn on heavily by Cicero (*q.v.*).

Principal writings: *On Duty; On Providence; On Cheerfulness; On Philosophical Schools;* but only fragments remain.

(1) Modifying the ancient Stoic cosmology, Panaetius abandoned the doctrine of the periodic destruction of the world by fire. In this he seems to have followed the lead of his teacher, Carneades (*q.v.*).

(2) He also modified the ancient ethics, substituting the more positive value of peace of mind for the Stoic *apathia* (*q.v.*), while stressing the positive role of possessions in obtaining happiness.

(3) With respect to human reason he held both that the development of reason implies a universal humanism, transcending our animal nature; and that the theoretical reason is less serviceable to man than his practical reason which, in most matters, deserves priority.

PAN-AFRICANISM.
Q.v. Du Bois (5).

PANCARATRINS.
Q.v. Vaiṣnavism (2a).

PANCHEN LAMA.
Q.v. Lamaism.

PANENTHEISM.
From the Greek *pan* and *theos* meaning "all in God." The view that all reality is part of the being of God. To be distinguished from Pantheism which identifies God with the total reality.

(1) The term was first used by Krause (*q.v.*) for his view that the world is a finite creation within the infinite being of God; and that the whole is a divine organism so constituted that higher organisms have lower organisms as their constituents. Indeed, organic relationships characterize the cosmologies of panentheists.

(2) Fechner (*q.v.* 2–3), who was a panpsychist (*q.v.*) as well as a panentheist, held every entity to be sentient to some extent, and to exist as a component in the life of a more inclusive being. The series ends with the Divine Being whose constituents include all of reality. Just as a cell has a certain freedom within the body, so we have a certain freedom within the Divine Being.

(3) The metaphysics of Whitehead (*q.v.* 13–18), with feeling spread throughout a reality interpreted in organismic terms, is likewise a candidate for panentheism. Deity is dipolar, both absolute and relative, and human immortality is one's continued reality within the consequent nature of God.

(4) Among Eastern philosophers, Iqbal (*q.v.*) has developed a philosophy which fits the themes of panentheism. He did not, however, use the term.

(5) Hartshorne (*q.v.* 3) holds that panentheism is characterized by an organic and panpsychic reality where God includes the world as an organism includes its cells, and where the divine is not simply absolute but dipolar, having absolute and relative aspects.

PANLOGISM.
From the Latin meaning that "all is reason." The term is sometimes applied to the system of Hegel (*q.v.* 1) where the rational and the real are identified.

PANPSYCHISM.
From the Greek *pan* and *psyche* meaning that everything is possessed of soul.

The doctrine that everything is possessed of life is termed Hylozoism (*q.v.*). Although Panpsychism makes a stronger claim, the distinction between possessing soul (or sentience) and possessing life is difficult to maintain in practice.

(1) The early Greek philosophers, viewing matter as intrinsically active, are said to be hylozoistic, yet Thales (*q.v.* 2) in one of the extant fragments of his thought held that all things are full of gods. The fragment at least has a panpsychistic sound.

(2) Even in Aristotle (*q.v.* 9), since the material world responds to God as final cause, it is difficult to choose between the categories of hylozoism and panpsychism. It is usually held, however, that the material world is for him hylozoistic. The same decision, then, is appropriate with respect to the medieval Aristotelians, including Aquinas.

(3) Giordano Bruno (*q.v.* 2) advanced the first clear theory of panpsychism. The basic unit of reality is the monad, animated with its own energy. Souls and gods are likewise monads, and the innumerable worlds of the universe are interpreted in organic terms, as having lives of their own.

(4) Campanella (*q.v.* 3) presented the notion of a graded reality from matter to God, yet each level has to some extent the qualities of knowledge, power, and love.

(5) F.M. Van Helmont (*q.v.*) developed a monadology on the basis of his father's thought and that of Paracelsus (*q.v.*).

(6) Leibniz (*q.v.* 1) accepted the idea of a monadology, describing the basic units as centers of awareness, appetite, and feeling.

(7) Maupertuis (*q.v.* 3) adopted panpsychism, endowing the ultimate particles with "desire, aversion and memory."

(8) Goethe (*q.v.* 4) accepted Leibniz' monadology to help express his view of the dynamic natural world where all forms are striving upward.

(9) Schelling (*q.v.* 2) suggested that dualism can be avoided by regarding all of nature as alive, even if "slumbering" on its lower levels; but all levels of nature are directed toward consciousness.

(10) Schopenhauer (*q.v.* 2–3) presented a similar position. The world is characterized throughout as throbbing will, more or less informed by awareness, depending on the level of reference.

(11) Fechner (*q.v.* 2) suggested that all things are material from an external point of view, but from within all is life and soul.

(12) Lotze (*q.v.* 2) likewise developed a monadology building reality from a psychic continuum of souls.

(13) Kozlov (*q.v.*) provided a particularly clear system of panpsychism, calling it by that name.

(14) W. Wundt (*q.v.* 5) began his thought from the special sciences. In the extension of that thought into metaphysics he believed that the mental and psychical had primacy over the physical in interpreting the nature of reality.

(15) W.K. Clifford (*q.v.* 2) in his later years constructed a speculative system in which reality is composed of "ejects," which he interpreted as "mind-stuff."

(16) In his period of Objective Idealism Charles Peirce (*q.v.* 5) is sometimes classed with the panpsychists on the ground that he interpreted law as a habit-taking character of the universe, and he found it more convincing to explicate matter in terms of mind than conversely.

(17) William James (*q.v.* 12) was attracted to pluralistic panpsychism as a means of relating human to divine awareness through the compounding of consciousness. Ward (*q.v.* 3) and Read (*q.v.*) held a similar point of view; Soloviev (*q.v.* 3), a Russian philosopher, was also a panpsychist.

(18) A.N. Whitehead (*q.v.* 13, 20) made feeling a universal category, and understood the basic relation of prehension as a feeling-relation. At the lowest levels prehensions are blind—at least they lack consciousness—since the latter category is not universal.

(19) Hartshorne (*q.v.* 1) elaborates a system of "societism" in which every entity of the universe is presumed to have awareness to some degree.

PANSOMATISM.

The doctrine of Kotarbinski (*q.v.* 1) that every sentient entity is a body.

PANTAENUS.

Q.v. Alexandrian School (1).

PANTHEISM.

From the Greek *pan* and *theos* meaning "everything is God." The adjective "pantheist" was introduced by John Toland (*q.v.* 3) in 1705 in reference to Socinianism (*q.v.*). In an attack on Toland in 1709, Fay characterized Toland's position as "pantheism." Once introduced, the term was applied to a variety of positions where God and the world are held to be identical. The term is to be distinguished from Panentheism (*q.v.*) where the world is regarded as a constituent of God but not identical with Him. A number of types of Pantheism will be distinguished, first in the West and then in the East.

A. Pantheism in the West arose in the context of philosophical speculation, rather than in the context of religious practice.

(1) The early Greek philosophers were hylozoistic (*q.v.* Hylozoism), finding matter and life inseparable. Although the identity between ruling principle and ontological unit is not fully developed, the position may be termed Hylozoistic Pantheism.

(2) Parmenides (*q.v.* 1) regarded the world to be a changeless Absolute. If this means that the change and variety of the world are apparent only, the position can be termed Acosmic Pantheism. The world of change has disappeared into the changeless Absolute.

(3) Heraclitus (*q.v.* 5) held fire to be the divine and controlling element, working from within a single but basic aspect of the universe. The view may be called Immanentistic Pantheism. Anaxagoras (*q.v.*), substituting *Nous* for fire, shares this classification.

(4) Stoicism (*q.v.*) combined the motifs of Heraclitean fire and a world-soul much like the *Nous* of Anaxagoras. At the same time, however, the theme of determinism by the universal reason introduces a sense of the absoluteness of the divine in relation to the world. The world reason is immanent in men. The view has its own identity and can perhaps be termed Stoic Pantheism (*q.v.* Cleanthes 2; Chrysippus 4).

(5) Neoplatonism (*q.v.*) developed a system which may be termed Emanationistic Pantheism, since all that is comes from the Divine Being, and is that Being in attenuated form.

(6) Throughout the medieval period in the West both Emanationistic and Stoic Pantheism have many representatives. The former is to be found in Avicebron (*q.v.* 3). Erigena (*q.v.* 1–2), Averroës (*q.v.* 2), and the mysticism of the Jewish Cabala (*q.v.* 2). Meister Eckhart (*q.v.* 3–4) shows evidences of both Stoic and Emanationistic Pantheism, but his followers Tauler (*q.v.*), Suso (*q.v.*), and Ruysbroeck (*q.v.*) are more clearly Stoic Pantheists. David of Dinant (*q.v.* 1) anticipated Spinoza's pantheism in the late 12th or early 13th century.

(7) Nicholas of Cusa (*q.v.* 2, 5) in the 15th century carried on many of the emphases already discussed. In addition, he held that in God there is an identity of opposites. This means that contradictory ascriptions apply equally to God. Giordano Bruno (*q.v.* 2–3) who in the 16th century held the same view, applied this to statements concerning God's immanence and transcendence. We shall consider the point of view an Identity of Opposites Pantheism.

(8) In the Renaissance, Paracelsus (*q.v.* 2–3) presented a mixture of Stoic and Emanationistic Pantheism; and Stoic Pantheism is to be found in Ficino (*q.v.*), Weigel (*q.v.*), Pomponazzi (*q.v.*), Cardan (*q.v.*) and many more. Pico Della Mirandolo (*q.v.*) is a representative of Emanationistic Pantheism. Boehme (*q.v.* 11) absorbed a number of the influences we have mentioned; but his belief that the world is merely a reflection of the divine allows one to view his position as that of Acosmic Pantheism.

(9) In the 17th century, Spinoza (*q.v.* 1–3) constructed a highly Monistic Pantheism where time is engulfed by eternity. It was in reference to Spinoza that Hegel coined the term Acosmic Pantheism. But Hegel had overstated the case. The world is not lost in God, but the two concepts exist in an indissoluble unity.

(10) Goethe (*q.v.* 4) represents a mixture of Hylozoistic and Stoic Pantheism. And the French philosopher Cabanis (*q.v.* 1) presented a pantheism that, too, mixed a number of types.

(11) If the deduction of the Hegelian system is taken as a logical sequence, then Hegel (*q.v.* 1–4) represents a Neoplatonic scheme stood on its head. Absolute Spirit emerges at the end. Taken as a temporal process, the system would seem to qualify as Stoic Pantheism. Insofar as the absoluteness of the divine is emphasized,

a hint of Monistic or Acosmic Pantheism may be present.

(12) Certainly it seems to be the case that in Hegel's followers the emphasis on absoluteness is heightened. In our terms, Schleiermacher (*q.v.* 2) represents a Relativistic Monistic Pantheism. The world is real, changing, and in God, although God remains absolute and is not affected by the world. Haeckel (*q.v.*), who claimed to be a Monistic Pantheist, probably fits the present category. F.H. Bradley (*q.v.* 2, 4–5) and Josiah Royce (*q.v.* 2–5) present Absolutistic Monistic Pantheisms. God is both absolute and identical with the world; thus the world—though real—is changeless.

(13) The Russian philosopher, Soloviev (*q.v.* 3), held to a number of pantheistic positions, mingling them with panentheism.

B. In the Near and Far East pantheism first appears in the context of religious devotion.

(14) In the Hindu scriptures, both in the *Vedas* and the *Upanishads*, man's inner self and the divine are held to be identical. The problem is to interpret what this means.

(15) Shankara (*q.v.* 2–5), for whom the world is the phantom of a dream and only the unmanifest Brahman is real, takes the position of Acosmic Pantheism.

(16) Ramanuja (*q.v.* 1–5,), on the other hand, presents a system in which the qualified world emanates from the unmanifest Brahman; but thereafter—until the end of the cycle—is the body of Brahman. The system in the first stage mentioned is Emanationistic Pantheism. In the second, it is Relativistic Monistic Pantheism.

(17) In Buddhism the same distinctions appear. When Ashvaghosha (*q.v.*) holds the world to be waters stirred by the wind when in reality only the Absolute exists, he is taking the position of Acosmic Pantheism.

(18) When the Buddhist Nagarjuna (*q.v.* 9–10) holds that the Absolute and the Void are identical, he is giving us an instance of Identity of Opposites Pantheism.

(19) When Chih-I (*q.v.*), founder of a school of Chinese Buddhism, holds that ordinary existence is based on illusion, and only the Pure Mind exists, once again

we are presented an instance of Acosmic Pantheism.

(20) In the Near East the mystical movement of Sufism (*q.v.*; also Islam 5) developed into a pantheism of the monistic type.

PANTHEISMUSSTREIT.
German for "Pantheism Dispute" or "Pantheism Controversy." A classic 18th-century argument over Spinoza (*q.v.*), whose German reputation had been that of an outright atheist. The involvement was initiated by Jacobi (*q.v.*) who published his correspondence with Moses Mendelssohn concerning the alleged Spinozism of the deceased and revered Lessing (*q.v.* 5). Jacobi claimed this to be Lessing's final philosophical position. Mendelssohn suggested that Jacobi had not caught the irony in Lessing's comments on Spinoza. Others entered the controversy, Kant disagreeing with the philosophical positions of Jacobi, Mendelssohn, and Spinoza; Herder and Goethe (*q.v.* 4) defending Spinoza's theism.

PAPAL BULL.
Q.v. Encyclical, Papal.

PAPINI, GIOVANNI. 1881–1956.
Italian philosopher. Born in Florence. Self-educated. Participated in the founding of a number of Italian cultural journals. An opponent of Positivism (*q.v.*), he found his first response to that approach in a Corridor Theory of Pragmatism (cited by William James) according to which Pragmatism can allow the simultaneous exploration of a hundred alternatives. In later life he found the approach of St. Augustine to his liking.
Principal philosophical writings: *The Twilight of the Philosophers*, 1906; *Pragmatism*, 1913; *St. Augustine*, 1929.

PARACELSUS. 1490–1541.
Swiss physician. Born in Einsiedeln. Largely self-educated, he read the book of the world in extensive travels through Europe. He did, indeed, make some discoveries; but the medical profession of Europe soon rose against his unorthodox ways. His interest for us is his relation to alchemy, the Cabala (*q.v.*), Neoplatonism (*q.v.*), and Gnosticism (*q.v.*).
Principal writings: *Archidoxis*, (c. 1524);

Four Treatises of Theophrastus of Hohenheim (T), 1529; *Philosophia Sagax*, (c. 1536).

(1) Taking the view that man is a microcosm of the macrocosm, Paracelsus held that every part of the world of man has its counterpart in the world of nature. This was his doctrine of signatures.

(2) Both the world and man are characterized by a dynamic, restless creativity and are interpreted in keeping with organic principles. Growth emerges from decay, combination through separation; life comes from death and death from life. Masculine and feminine are two basic opposites in the nature of things. Indeed, the world generally works through opposition.

(3) The universe comes from God through the stages of ultimate matter which by separation becomes prime matter, and by further separation and mixture becomes all other things. The restless tendency of the universe manifests itself in the merging back into ultimate matter and separation out again.

(4) From the above general premises Paracelsus moved into an alchemical analysis of nature which yielded, surprisingly, a chemical analysis of bodily functioning quite modern in tone.

PARACLETE.

From the Greek *parakaleo* ("to call to one"). Hence, a witness, advocate, helper, or comforter. The term is usually applied to the role of the Holy Spirit.

PARADIGM.

From the Greek *paradeigma* ("a pattern, model, or plan").

(1) Plato (*q.v.* 1) used the term with respect to his Ideas or Forms, thus indicating their role in the world.

(2) In contemporary philosophy the center of analysis and criticism is often a paradigm case, presented as exemplifying the issues which are at stake. Disposition of the paradigm case is thus presumed to be tantamount to a resolution of the argument. When Moore (*q.v.* 2) raised his hand, saying "Here is a hand, and here another," he was presenting a paradigm case. The question is whether the principles of skepticism, holding we have no certainty, can deflate that presentation.

(3) Kuhn (*q.v.* 1) holds that scientific theories are constructed around basic paradigms—*e.g.*, the solar system model of an atom—and that shifts in scientific theory require new paradigms.

PARADOX.

From the Greek *para* ("contrary to") and *doxa* ("opinion"). Hence, contrary to received opinion. From this, the term has come to refer to that which is or seems to be contrary to common sense, or contradictory.

A. Sometimes paradoxes have been elaborated in philosophy to prove the opposite of the position leading to the paradoxical result.

(1) Zeno's paradoxes (*q.v.* Zeno of Elea) were of this type. The Chinese philosopher Hui Shi (*q.v.*) independently elaborated the same paradoxes at about the same time. A similar approach was taken somewhat later by the Indian philosopher, Nagarjuna (*q.v.* 1–7).

B. Beginning with the Megarian and Stoic philosophers, a number of semantical and logical paradoxes were discovered. Called *Insolubilia* (*q.v.*) or unsolvable problems in the Middle Ages, such paradoxes survive today as testing procedures at the foundations of semantics, logic, and mathematics. Among such paradoxes are:

(2) Epimenides, the Cretan, claiming that all Cretans are liars. An earlier version of the Liar's Paradox was presented by the Megarian philosopher, Eubulides: "If I am lying, am I telling the truth?"

(3) The card of P. E. B. Jourdain bearing on one side only the words, "The sentence on the other side of this card is true," and on the second side only the words, "The sentence on the other side of this card is false."

(4) The Grelling Paradox distinguishing between predicates which have the properties they denote, *e.g.*, "polysyllabic," and those which do not, *e.g.*, "monosyllabic." We shall call the first type of predicate "autological," and the second type "heterological." The set of autological predicates will then possess the properties they denote, while the set of heterological predicates will lack the properties they denote. The question is whether the predicate "heterological" is autological or heterological.

(5) The Russell (*q.v.* 3) Paradox of class

membership, also termed the Zermelo Paradox (*q.v.* Zermelo 3), distinguishes between classes which are members of themselves and those which are not. The class of pencils is not a member of itself, since the class is not a pencil; but the class of comprehensible things would seem to be a member of itself, since such a class is comprehensible. The question arises concerning the class of all things not members of themselves: Is this class a member of itself or is it not?

(6) In the field of mathematics there are the Burali-Forti Paradox concerning the greatest ordinal number, a Russell Paradox concerning the greatest cardinal number, the Richard Paradox concerning definable and undefinable real numbers, the König Paradox concerning the least undefinable ordinal number.

C. While no general solution to such paradoxes has been found, a number of approaches are possible.

(7) Zeno's paradoxes, and many of the paradoxes of number, turn on the peculiarities of infinity.

(8) Many of the semantical and logical paradoxes turn on statements which are self-referential in a vicious sense. In response to such statements Poincaré (*q.v.* 4) devised his Impredicative Definitions. Proper, or predicative definitions, were not allowed to refer to the whole of the class of which the term being defined was a member. Russell in fact incorporated Poincaré's principle in his theory of types (*q.v.* Type 4, Russell 3). Hermann Weyl (*q.v.*) regarded impredicative definitions as instances of the Vicious Circle (*q.v.*) fallacy. Restricting the scope of sentences so that they refer to other sentences but not to themselves was one of the motives lying behind the development of metalanguages (*q.v.*) as well.

(9) Strawson (*q.v.* 1) offered a solution to the Liar's Paradox by applying to it his performative view of truth. Since saying of a sentence that it is true is the performative act of agreeing with the sentence, it is like saying "ditto." But in this case there is no original sentence to which to say "ditto." Hence, the paradox disappears.

D. The term "paradox" has also been used in the phrase "the paradoxes of material implication," to refer to the unusual consequences which result from the weak sense of implication used in the propositional calculus. These are not true paradoxes. For a discussion of what is involved in the so-called "paradoxes of material implication," *q.v.* Truth Tables (4).

E. For literary use of paradox, *q.v.* New Criticism.

PARALLELISM, PSYCHOPHYSICAL.

(1) The doctrine that there is a one-to-one correspondence of physical and psychical events throughout the universe. The phrase was introduced to philosophy in this extended sense by Fechner (*q.v.* 2), and in this sense seems to characterize the point of view of Spinoza (*q.v.* 8), and Leibniz (*q.v.* 6–7).

(2) Fechner's observations for the doctrine came from his investigations in the area of experimental psychology. In the narrower sense, the doctrine can mean simply that every mental event has a physical correlate. *Q.v.* Mind-Body Problem (4).

PARALOGISM.

From the Greek *para* ("beside") and *logos* ("reason"). Thus, the idea of a conclusion which does not follow reason, *i.e.*, a fallacious syllogism (*q.v.* Fallacies 23–30). Today the term is associated almost entirely with Immanuel Kant (*q.v.* 6) who, in a section of his first Critique on Transcendental Dialectic, distinguished between Formal and Transcendental Paralogisms. By the latter he understood the Fallacies of Rational Psychology which began with the "I think" of experience as premise, and concluded that *man* possesses a substantial, continuous, and separable soul. Kant also termed this the Psychological Paralogism, and the Paralogisms of Pure Reasoning.

PARAMATMAN.

Sanskrit, "universal soul." *Q.v.* The *Vedas* (1).

PARETO, VILFREDO. 1848–1923.

Italian philosopher and social analyst. Born in Paris. Educated in Italy. Lived and taught the last half of his life at the University of Lausanne.

Principal writings: *Course in Political Economy*, 2 vols., 1896–7; *Manual of Political Economy*, 1909; *Treatise on General*

Sociology (T, *The Mind and Society*), 2 vols., 1916; *Facts and Theories*, 1920; *Compendium of General Sociology*, 1920; *The Transformation of Democracy*, 1921.

(1) Holding that every society is ruled by "elites." Pareto distinguishes between two types of elite—the risk-takers, who deal in "combinations," and the defenders of the status quo whose interest is "the persistence of aggregates."

(2) Both types are among the invariable elements of society. He calls all of the recurring elements, whatever their nature, the "residues" of society. The basic structure of human belief and commitment relates to these recurring elements. The variable elements of society he calls "derivations." He holds that humans use "derivations" to justify their "residues," a way of saying that the more things change the more we wish them to remain the same.

PARKER, DEWITT.
Q.v. Aesthetics (4).

PARKER, THEODORE. 1810–1860.
American theologian and minister. Born in Lexington, Mass. Harvard educated, he became a Unitarian minister. A liberal leader, he built religion around the ideas of God, the moral law, and immortality. Active in the emancipation movement. Emerson called him the Savonarola of New England Transcendentalism (*q.v.*).

Principal writings: *A Discourse of Matters Pertaining to Religion*, 1842.

PARMENIDES. c. 515 B.C.–c. 450 B.C.
Greek philosopher. Born in Elea. Influenced by the Pythagoreans. He is said to have prepared the laws for his native city of Elea. Prophet of changelessness, he founded the Eleatic philosophy. It is sometimes said that he wrote in opposition to Heraclitus; this is apparently not known to be the case; but certainly the two philosophies present a marked contrast. His stress on the unity of things makes him one of the earliest defenders of Monism (*q.v.* 1).

Principal writings: *On Nature*; substantial fragments are extant.

(1) Since thought and being are identical, one need only follow out the principle of consistency to gain the truth about reality.

(2) Sense experience, on the other hand, is full of contradiction and hence is mere appearance.

(3) Thought seeks the common, universal and invariant. What is common to all things is the being they have; and what is not-being is not existent. Hence, being is and not-being is not.

(4) If being is and not-being is not, being cannot come from not-being. Hence being is eternal.

(5) If anything changes, something which was not comes to be; since not-being is nonexistent, change is impossible.

(6) If anything moves it must occupy a space where it was not; and since empty space is not-being and nonexistent, motion is impossible.

(7) If things are separate from each other, they are separated by empty space; hence, things cannot be separate from each other.

(8) Hence, finally, being is homogenous throughout like the mass of a rounded sphere "perfected on every side," equally distant from the center at every point. This picture of reality, so different from the world we see, was defended by the paradoxes of Parmenides' ablest student, Zeno of Elea (*q.v.*).

Also, *q.v.* Nagarjuna.

PAROLE.
Q.v. de Saussure (1); Lacan (1).

PARONYMY.
Q.v. Myth (8).

PAROUSIA.
From the Greek meaning "a being present" or an "arrival." Although the term was used by Plato to refer to the presence of the form in a thing, the *Parousia* is usually taken to refer to the return of Christ, his "arrival" and his "presence" on earth.

PARSEISM.
The religion of the 100,000 or more Parsis of western India (a group of Zoroastrians who migrated to India when the Moslems conquered Persia in the 8th century A.D.), concentrated in Bombay. They venerate the Persian religious leader, Zoroaster, as head of their religion. *Q.v.* Zoroaster; Zoroastrianism (5).

PARSIMONY, PRINCIPLE OF.

From the Latin *parsimonia* ("thriftiness").

(1) The principle that, of two explanations, each capable of explaining a given phenomenon, one should choose the simpler of the two. *Q.v.* Ockham's Razor; William of Ockham (8–9).

(2) Quine (*q.v.* 7) holds that conceptual economy is one of the factors in establishing and reshaping the basic conceptual scheme which includes all of science.

PARSONS, TALCOTT. 1902–1979.

American sociologist. Born in Colorado Springs. Educated at London School of Economics and Heidelberg. Taught at Harvard.

Selected writings: *The Structure of Social Action*, 1949; *The Social System*, 1951; *Theories of Society* (with Naegele and Pitts), 1961; *Social Structure and Personality*, 1964; *Politics and Social Structure*, 1969; *The Early Essays* (ed. C. Camic), 1991.

(1) Holding that the central concern of sociology is analysis of the phenomena of "the institutionalization of patterns of value-orientation in the social system," Parsons believed that sociology and economics provide the two major theories of the social system, differentiated by their goals.

(2) Finding the defining characteristic of "society" in a "distinctive institutionalized culture," containing subsystems of various sorts (*e.g.*, political, economic, familial, and educational groupings), the continuing identity of society depends on the maintenance of order and the availability of criteria for member identification.

(3) These requirements, in turn, underline the importance of "boundary maintenance," and hence call forth a tendency for society and state to coincide.

PARTICIPATION.

A translation of the Greek term *methexis*.

(1) The Pythagoreans used the term to describe the manner in which number played a role in the constitution of the world (*q.v.* Pythagoras 4).

(2) Plato (*q.v.* 1, 8) developed a doctrine of participation of the Ideas or Forms as shaping elements of the material world. The intelligible world participated in the sensible world by means of the Forms.

(3) Aristotle expressed his dissatisfaction with Pythagoras and Plato in this regard; and insisted that both held the same doctrine under different names (*Metaphysics* 987a10–987b12).

(4) Lévy-Bruhl (*q.v.* 1–2) found a principle of participation among primitive tribes which stands at variance to the Principle of Contradiction accepted by the civilized. Instead of self-identity and consistency, the primitive believes in multiple identity, multiple location, the transmission and reception of mystic powers.

(5) Lavelle (*q.v.* 1) interpreted human activity as participation in the act of being, and thus related to the Divine.

PARTICULAR PROPOSITIONS.

The "I" and "O" Propositions of syllogistic logic, *e.g.*, "Some politicians are liars," and "Some students are not honest." *Q.v.* Proposition (1d–e).

PARVATI.

Q.v. Vaiṣṇavism (3).

PASCAL, BLAISE. 1623–1662.

French philosopher. Born at Clermont-Ferrand. His family moved to Paris in 1631. A mathematical genius, he reconstituted the proofs of Euclid's *Geometry* up to Proposition 32 at the age of eleven without having read Euclid. In his teens he wrote an original mathematical essay on conic sections which was published in 1610, and also constructed a mechanical calculator. He made intellectual contributions not only to number theory and probability theory, but in physics as well, his studies of barometric pressure and the vacuum breaking new ground. He was intimate with the mathematician Fermat, and known at an early age to the intellectuals of his time. Strongly influenced by the skepticism of Montaigne (*q.v.*), the Stoicism of Epictetus (*q.v.*), and Jansenism (*q.v.*), his life involved a struggle to reconcile the constituent elements of these positions.

His well-known second conversion occurred one night in 1654. From 10:30 to 12:30 he was held by a religious experience which contained the elements of fire, certitude, joy, peace, and a sense of union with Christ. He emerged from the experience with the conviction that the path to God had to be through Christianity rather than through philosophy. As a result of this experience he wrote a message to himself, known as Pascal's amulet ("the God of Abraham, the God of Isaac, the God of Jacob, not of philosophers and scholars"), and wore it sewn into his coat for the remainder of his life. His sister, Jacqueline, had entered one of the Port Royal convents in 1652. The Port Royal abbey, the most important French center of the Jansenist movement, was located in Paris; Pascal joined the group in a lay capacity in 1655. It was at the end of this year that Arnauld (*q.v.*), the most important figure at Port Royal, was condemned by the Sorbonne for heresy. Pascal answered the charges in a series of eighteen letters, published in quick succession, and known as the *Provincial Letters*. Through numerous vicissitudes he continued his scientific work, and began to collect material on what was to be a defense of the Christian faith. The material was published posthumously as the *Pensées*.

Principal writings: *Essay on the Conics* (T), 1640; *New Experiments Concerning the Vacuum* (T), 1647; *Conversations with M. de Saci* (T), 1655; *Provincial Letters* (T), 1656–7; *The Geometric Spirit* (T), 1658; *Pensées* or *Thoughts on Religion* (T), 1669.

(1) For Pascal man occupies an unbearable position in the world. He can neither validate his convictions nor surrender to skepticism. Caught between the infinitely large and the infinitely small, neither of which he understands, he is certain only of his uncertainty. Man is a thinking reed, greater than the universe which crushes him, since he is aware of what is happening and the universe is not. Likewise caught between his possible grandeur and his bestiality, man is an infinite nothing, a contradiction and paradox to himself.

(2) There is no rational way out of man's dilemma. The two major divisions of philosophy, Pascal learned from Montaigne, are dogmatism and skepticism. Reason confounds the former position, and nature the latter. Accepting from Jansenism the corruption of human nature after the fall, he would not expect the operation of the natural reason, apart from grace, to be able to solve the problem.

(3) There are, however, some steps which can be taken along the way. Man has available to him not only the spirit of geometry (*l'esprit géométrique*), but also the spirit of finesse (*l'esprit de finesse*). The former is the method of systematic procedure which begins with definitions and assumptions, using these to demonstrate other propositions. The spirit of finesse, on the other hand, does not utilize a step by step approach. Here comprehension is immediate, sudden, and total. It is, in short, the spirit of intuition. Intuition is the source of the discernment of the principles which may then be employed geometrically. The spirit of finesse is essential to the successful working of the spirit of geometry. It would seem to be the case that when Pascal urges that the heart has reasons that the reason knows not of, he is speaking of this intuitive power in man. If this is the case, then when he holds that God is to be felt by the heart, rather than known by the reason, here too is an application of the spirit of finesse. Not even this spirit, however, is sufficient.

(4) Noting that proofs of God are convincing at most only in the moment of demonstration, Pascal suggests that a rational approach to God leads one either to atheism or to deism. No wonder, since one is attempting to reach by reason the infinitely incomprehensible. But there is a way to use reason to prepare the way for God. Is it worth one's while, in terms of the mathematics of probability, to gamble on religious faith? Addressed to his skeptical and freethinking friends, some of whom were enthusiastic gamblers, Pascal's Wager, as it has come to be known, answers this question. The conditions are that one is already involved in the wager. To believe or not to believe in God's existence is actually to wager that He exists or does not exist. If we believe He exists and He does, the reward is eternal happiness. If we believe God exists and He doesn't, nothing is really lost, and the same is the case if we disbelieve and He doesn't exist. However, if we disbelieve He exists and He does, we are damned for eternity. Thus we have everything to gain

and nothing to lose by wagering God exists. On the mathematics of probability alone every gambler should find the wager irresistible. This does not imply that Pascal approves the calculating attitude involved in the wager. After the way is cleared, the gambler must learn to abase himself, to "stupefy" himself, establishing a way of life making appropriate the gift of divine grace, should God will it. The God who is hidden to fallen man is present in the power of grace. This is the God of Abraham, Isaac, and Jacob central to "the amulet."

PASCAL'S AMULET.
Q.v. Pascal.

PASCAL'S WAGER.
Q.v. Pascal (4).

PASCENDI.
Q.v. Laberthonnière.

PASSION.
From the Latin *passio*, a translation of the Greek *pathos* ("a passive condition").

(1) One of the categories of Aristotle (*q.v.* 6), passion contrasts with action and refers to the condition of a thing as acted upon by other things. The passion of a thing thus refers not to the essence but to the accidents of things, and has a passive sense.

(2) Scholasticism continued the meaning given above, although discussing whether or not the passions of a being are part of the being itself.

(3) By the time of Descartes (*q.v.* 11) the passions had become emotional dispositions. Among the Greeks such dispositions had been described as the consequence of the appetitive element in man (*q.v.* Plato 3). Descartes made appetite or desire one of the six passions of man's emotional life. Something of the original meaning of "passion" was maintained, since it was supposed that these emotions happened to the soul against one's will or reason, even though a result of one's appetitive nature, or animal spirits.

(4) Spinoza (*q.v.* 4), using the term "affect" to mean "a passion of the soul" by which the mind is determined in one direction or another, joined the basic element of desire to happiness and sadness, explaining all other "affects" in terms of these.

(5) For Hegel (*q.v.* 23) passion is the subjective and formal side of the will, providing energy for human accomplishments.

(6) Fourier (*q.v.* 1) goes even further, holding that the passions are natural and good, and naturally harmonious. Human felicity lies in their free exercise. Taking Fourier as a representative of the Romantic period, it seems clear that by this period the initial meaning of passion as "passivity" had been replaced by something like its opposite, the source of activity in man.

PASSIVE RESISTANCE.
Q.v. Tolstoy (2); Thoreau; Gandhi (1); Einstein (5).

PASSOVER.
A Jewish observance beginning on the evening of the fourteenth day of the month Nisan (the first month of the Jewish religious calendar) to commemorate the "passing over" the houses of the Israelites, although the first-born of every Egyptian family was taken (*Exodus* 12).

PAST, THE.
One of the modes of time, the concept of the past has not received a great deal of attention in terms of philosophical analysis.

(1) Bergson (*q.v.* 9) presented a doctrine of the past as internal to the present. His analogy is that of a rolling snowball containing its earlier states.

(2) When pragmatists have analyzed the concept of the past (*q.v.* Mead 4), they have tended to urge that the past is variable, changing with every change in the present.

(3) Whitehead (*q.v.* 17), suggesting there is a sense in which the past is a perpetual perishing, and another sense in which it is a perpetual conservation, relates this second sense to the *consequent nature of god*.

PAŚUPATAS (PASHUPATAS).
Q.v. Vaiṣnavism (3).

PATANJALI. 2nd cent. B.C.
Indian philosopher. Founder or developer of the Yoga system (*q.v.* Yoga 1). He held Yoga to be a method of attaining salvation through the control of the physical and psychical features of human

nature. Author, or one of the authors of the following work which, however, is multiply sourced.

Principal writings: *Yoga Sutras* (T), 4 vols.

PATER, WALTER. 1839–1894.

English literary and social critic. Born in Shadwell. Studied at Oxford where he later taught. The Pre-Raphelite literary group gathered around him, appropriating his "Aestheticism."

Principal writings: *Studies in the History of the Renaissance*, 1878; *Marius the Epicurean*, 1885; *Imaginary Portraits*, 1887; *Appreciations, with an Essay on Style*, 1889; *Plato and Platonism*, 1893; *Greek Studies*, 1895; *Miscellaneous Studies*, 1895.

(1) Channeling all the subject matter he touched into support for his aesthetic view of the world, Pater championed the theme of art for art's sake, found the origin of the Renaissance in the human ability at a given time to stand in nature and find it beautiful, interpreted religion as an aesthetic experience, and philosophy as "philosophy of life," culminating in an epicurean "Aestheticism." The final goal, however, is not an accommodation to circumstances, but maintaining a "candid discontent" in the face of one's achievements; or, as he said in his studies on the Renaissance, living always "with this hard, gemlike flame."

(2) He emphasized the importance of form in aesthetics. Poetry is any literary production giving pleasure "by form as distinct from its matter," and all art tends toward the condition of music where the fusion of form and matter has reached completion.

PATHETIC FALLACY.

Q.v. Anthropopathism.

PATHOGONOUS METAPHYSICS.

Q.v. Adolf Stöhr.

PATRIPASSIANISM.

From the Latin *pater* ("father") and *patior, passus* ("to suffer"). A heresy of the 2nd and 3rd centuries A.D., holding that since the Father and the Son are two modes of the same God, birth, suffering, and death befell the Father as well as the Son. Sabellius (*q.v.*) was among those who held the doctrine. *Q.v.* Christology (1).

PATRISTICS.

From the Latin *pater* ("father"). The term refers to the Church Fathers and their works in the period between the end of the New Testament period, and the beginnings of Scholasticism with Erigena (*q.v.*) in the 9th century. We shall follow the traditional ordering, at least in part, dividing the period of the Church Fathers into the Apostolic Fathers, the Apologists, and the systematizers.

A. The Age of the Apostolic Fathers extended from the end of the New Testament period to the early part of the 2nd century.

(1) The basic material defining the age is a body of non-canonical material including *First and Second Clement*, the *Epistles of Ignatius*, the *Epistle of Barnabus*, the *Epistle of Polycarp*, the *Epistles of Diognetus*, the *Shepherd of Hermes* (an allegory in the form of visions), and the *Teaching of the Twelve Apostles*, a manual of early Church order.

B. The Age of the Apologists (*q.v.*) is essentially the 2nd century, although Apologies were still being written in the 3rd and 4th centuries. The Apologies agreed in being defenses of the Christian faith, but beyond this agreement there are many differences.

(2) A considerable number of the Apologies were directed to emperors, calling for an end to Christian persecution. The Apologies of Aristides (*q.v.*), Justin Martyr (*q.v.*), and Athenagoras (*q.v.*) were of this nature.

(3) Some of the Apologies were directed against the Gnostics (*q.v.*) who were providing a strong challenge to Christianity at this time. Irenaeus (*q.v.*) and his disciple Hippolytus (*q.v.*) took up this challenge, accusing the Gnostics of false knowledge, compared to the true knowledge of the Gospels.

(4) Many of the Apologies were directed against philosophy, the target being the Greek tradition. The objective was to insulate the Christian tradition from philosophical infection. Holding this separatist position, in addition to Tertullian (*q.v.*), were Tatian (*q.v.*). Theophilus of Antioch (*q.v.*), Hermias, Irenaeus (*q.v.*), Hippolytus (*q.v.*), Arnobius (*q.v.*), and Lactantius (*q.v.*). Tertullian occupied the most extreme position of the group, urging that Christianity is to

be believed *because* it is absurd.

(5) Not all of the Apologists took the separatist position, however. Some argued for a considerable measure of truth in Greek philosophy, although the final truth is to be found in Christianity. Justin, Athenagoras and, to a degree, Minucius Felix argue for this position.

C. After the Age of Apologetics came the Age of the Development of Christian Doctrine. Prior to the Council of Nicaea in 325 the development was casual and sporadic. Later it became more self-conscious and systematic.

(6) In 180 A.D. Pantaenus founded the Catechetical School of Alexandria (*q.v.* Alexandrian School 1). As the wave of separatism began to subside, the center of the Patristic movement shifted from the Carthage of Tertullian to Alexandria. Pantaenus had set the pattern of the school with an openness to Greek thought. As he was succeeded as head of the school by his disciple, Clement of Alexandria (*q.v.*), and Clement by his disciple, Origen (*q.v.*), the spirit of openness and conciliation increased. Clement and Origen thought of Christianity as the fulfillment of world culture with the commitment to universal redemption.

(7) The culmination of this development came through the Council of Nicaea. Eusebius of Caeseria (*q.v.*) was one of the chief figures of the Council, sat at the emperor's right hand, and prepared the first draft of the Nicene Creed.

(8) Athanasius (*q.v.*) of Alexandria carried the fight against the Arian heresy (*q.v.* Arius) not only at the Council of Nicaea but throughout his life, thus helping to settle the cardinal doctrine of the relation of the Father to the Son.

(9) Gregory of Nazianzus (*q.v.*) developed a theological method illuminating truths of faith by reason aided by Scripture.

(10) Gregory of Nyssa (*q.v.*), the second great Cappadocian, began to articulate the two orders of philosophy and theology. Advances in articulating the doctrine of the Trinity are credited to the three Cappadocians: the two Gregories and Basil.

(11) Cyril of Alexandria (*q.v.*) helped to settle the orthodox doctrine of Christ, due to his vigorous opposition to the Nestorian (*q.v.*) heresy.

(12) St. Augustine (*q.v.*) received the tradition in this form and brought unity to it, developing widely acceptable positions on faith and reason, grace and predestination, free-will and God's omnipotence, original sin, and the nature of the Trinity.

(13) Nemesius (*q.v.*) and the Pseudo-Dionysius (*q.v.*) deserve mention for their infusion of Neoplatonism into the developing system of thought.

(14) The period closed in the West with Gregory the Great whose talent was administrative; and in the East with John of Damascus (*q.v.*) whose work provided a bridge to Scholasticism. The former lived in the 7th century, the latter in the 8th.

PATRIZZI, FRANCESCO. 1529–1597.
Italian philosopher. Born in Dalmatia. Taught at the Universities of Ferrara and Rome. A Platonist, he was virulently anti-Aristotelian, and argued that Aristotle's views were in direct opposition to Christianity, while Plato, on the other hand, foreshadowed and prepared the way for the true religion. Patrizzi's cosmology held that light, an emanation from God, extends throughout space, and is the reason for all development.

Principal writings: *Discussion of the Peripatetics; A New Philosophy of the Universe.*

PAULER, AKOS VON. 1876–1933.
Hungarian philosopher. Born in Budapest. Educated at the University of Budapest where, from 1915 on, he served as professor of philosophy.

Principal writings: *The Problem of the Thing-in-Itself in Modern Philosophy*, 1902; *The Problem of Epistemological Categories*, 1904; *Toward a Theory of Logical Principles*, 1911; *The Problem of the Concept in Pure Logic*, 1915; *Introduction to Philosophy*, 1920; *Foundations of Philosophy*, 1925; *Logic*, 1925; *Aristotle*, 1933.

(1) Dividing philosophy into Logic, Ethics, Aesthetics, Metaphysics, and Ideology, Pauler regards Logic as an objective discipline forming the basis for the other four.

(2) Elaborating four laws of Logic, he adds a Law of Connection to the traditional principles of identity, contradiction, and excluded middle. The Law of Connection holds that everything is connected with other things, and implies the principles of sufficient reason, classification,

correlativity, and the *dictum de omni et nullo* (*q.v.*). Pauler's Principle of Classification is that everything can be classified, and his Principle of Correlativity holds that everything relative implies an absolute.

(3) The method to be used in metaphysics is called Reduction. It consists in finding the presuppositions necessary to reach valid conclusions about the world.

(4) The field of ideology is the term Pauler used for ontology. He uses the laws of logic to develop a series of regional ontologies, somewhat in the sense of Bolzano and Husserl (*q.v.* 4), within a general, formal ontology.

PAULICIANS.

An evangelical Christian Church widespread in Asia Minor and Armenia from the 5th century on. The name probably derives from Paul of Samosata (*q.v.*), and was initially a term of derision given them by their detractors. Equally probably, the name was accepted as meaning they were followers of St. Paul. And certainly they did reflect his antithesis between law and the spirit. At the same time they held a view much like that of the first-mentioned Paul that Jesus became Christ by merit. For the Paulicians it was at his baptism that Christ gained the "primal raiment of light" which Adam had lost, and they did venerate Christ in their own holy men while opposing veneration of the Virgin and the saints. The Paulicians gave rise to a similar sect in Bulgaria called Bogomils. The Cathari and Albigenses of southern France, movements of the 12th and 13th centuries, bear similarities to the Paulicians.

PAUL OF SAMOSATA. 3rd cent. A.D.

Bishop of Antioch. Born at Samosata. Deposed by a Synod meeting at Antioch in 269. Paul's heresy lay in his view that Jesus was born a man who through the merit of his sufferings became the savior and redeemer of mankind, coalescing inseparably with God.

Principal writings: *Discourses to Sabinus.*

PAULSEN, FRIEDRICH. 1846–1908.

German philosopher. Born in Langenhorn. Taught in Berlin. Succeeded Zeller (*q.v.*) as professor of Moral Philosophy

in 1896. Influenced by Max Wundt (*q.v.*) and Fechner (*q.v.*), he exerted influence in turn over Adickes (*q.v.*). All of those named, apart from Fechner, are regarded as neo-Kantians of the same type (*q.v.* Neo-Kantianism 7). Paulsen regarded philosophy as an inductive generalization from scientific data, and yet his philosophy was a monistic Idealism, designed to solve the mind-body problem by viewing the physical and the psychical as outer and inner aspects of the same reality. The view is reminiscent of Fechner. He likewise held to a voluntarism such that what appears on the conscious level as will is, on the unconscious level, force.

Principal writings: *History of the Development of Kantian Epistemology,* 1875; *System of Ethics* (T), 1889; *Introduction to Philosophy* (T), 1892; *Immanuel Kant* (T), 1898; *Ethics,* 1904; and many works on history and philosophy of education.

PAUL, THE APOSTLE.

1st century A.D. According to the tradition he was born in Tarsus, in Cilicia; reared as a Pharisee; educated in Jerusalem under Gamaliel; and engaged in the persecution of the Christians until the time of his conversion on the road to Damascus. After years of missionary and organizational work among the young churches, tradition has it that he was martyred in Rome.

Principal writings: *The Epistles.*

(1) Announcing that the era of the Mosaic Law has been replaced by a dispensation of the Spirit, Paul held that henceforth justification is by faith rather than by works. The dispensation of law had failed, merely revealing the weakness of the flesh.

(2) Paul traced this weakness to the sin of Adam, which he treated as an event determinative over human life, explaining the inevitability of human suffering and death. Men carry the consequences of this event within themselves as original sin.

(3) The divine response to the hopelessness of the human situation was the sending of Jesus Christ, the Messiah and eternal Son of God, by whom all things were created, who by his life, death, and bodily resurrection overcame sin and death, broke the hold of the law, and

made possible the salvation of mankind. As in Adam all men sinned, so in Christ are they saved. Paul seems to have held that Christ's coming provided a substitute for the punishment men deserved, satisfying the divine standard of righteousness, and providing a vicarious atonement for mankind.

(4) It is by means of baptism that man enters the new order, shares in Christ's death and resurrection, and in the Church becomes one with the mystical body of Christ, henceforth living no longer for oneself but for Christ. To help him in this new life, the power of the Holy Spirit, sent by God, enters his heart.

(5) Paul referred in several passages to divine predestination, resting on God's pleasure. This predestination is part of the drama involving Christ and man's final salvation or damnation.

(6) Paul denied both the essentially Greek doctrine of immortality (*q.v.*), and the view that in the Last Judgment our earthly body would be restored. Standing between the two extremes, he argued that we would on that day be provided with a heavenly body.

(7) In terms of values or virtues, Paul's division into faith, hope, and charity or love came to be known as the theological virtues, the last of which he regarded as the highest gift of the spirit.

PEACE OF GOD.
Q.v. Truce of God.

PEANO, GIUSEPPE. 1858–1932.
Italian mathematician and Logician. Born in Cuneo. Professor of Mathematics at Turin from 1890 until his death.

Principal writings: *The Principles of Arithmetic: A New Method of Exposition*, 1889; *Notations of Mathematical Logic*, 1894; *The Rules of Mathematics*, five versions appearing between 1893 and 1905.

(1) Among Peano's contributions to the field of mathematics was a postulate system, known as Peano's Postulates, from which the entire arithmetic of natural numbers can be derived. In the earliest version of his five postulates for the arithmetic of natural numbers, the first postulate referred to 1 as the first number. In later versions, as here, he began with 0 as the first number.

(2) We present the final version of his

postulate system. Postulate number five expresses the principle of mathematical induction.

P1. 0 is a number.

P2. The successor of any number is a number.

P3. No two numbers have the same successor.

P4. 0 is not the successor of any number.

P5. If P is a property such that: (a) 0 has the property P; (b) whenever a number *n* has the property P, then the successor of *n* also has the property P, then every number has the property P.

Q.v. also Russell (2).

PEANO'S POSTULATES.
Q.v. Peano (1–2).

PEARSON, KARL. 1857–1936.
British scientist and philosopher of science. Born in London. Studied at Cambridge. Taught at University College, London, from 1884 until 1933. He held that science is not explanatory but descriptive, and that its models are for the purpose of facilitating the correlation of data.

Principal philosophical writings: *The Ethic of Free Thought*, 1888; *The Grammar of Science*, (three somewhat different editions between 1892 and 1911).

PEASANTS' WAR.
Q.v. Anabaptists.

PECKHAM, JOHN. c. 1225–1292.
English philosopher. Born in Patcham. Educated at Oxford where he joined the Franciscan order. He taught first at the University of Paris, and later at Oxford. He was named Archbishop of Canterbury in 1279. As an Augustinian he opposed—vainly as it turned out—the growing influence of Aristotle.

Principal writings: *Questions Concerning the Soul; Summa of Being and Essence; Quodlibet Romanum; Treatise on the Soul*.

PEIRCE, CHARLES SANDERS. 1839–1914.
American philosopher. Born in Cambridge, Massachusetts. The son of Harvard mathematician, Benjamin Peirce. Graduated from Harvard in 1859. He worked with the U.S. Coast and Geodetic Survey from 1860 to 1891. He taught logic

at Johns Hopkins University, 1879–84; and for three years was special lecturer in Philosophy of Science at Harvard. He also lectured at the Lowell Institute in Boston. Retired to Milford, Pennsylvania in 1887. For Peirce's contributions to logic, *q.v.* Logic (21, 24).

Principal writings: *The Collected Papers of C.S. Peirce*, vols. 1–6 (ed. C. Hartshorne and P. Weiss), 1931–35; vols. 7–8 (ed. A. Burks), 1958; *Letters to Lady Welby* (ed. I. Lieb), 1953.

(1) Peirce introduced the term, "pragmatism," in 1878 as the name of a theory of meaning whose criterion was the Pragmatic Maxim. Among his statements of the maxim we cite the following: "In order to ascertain the meaning of an intellectual conception one should consider what practical consequences might conceivably result by necessity from the truth of that conception; and the sum of these consequences will constitute the entire meaning of the conception." Years later, in his final treatment of the maxim, he held that it allows for "would-be's," *e.g.*, that a diamond buried in the sea, or forever swathed in cotton, and never put to the test of hardness, is nonetheless to be regarded as hard. In 1905, troubled that the popularizers of pragmatism—including William James—had turned it from a theory of meaning to a theory of action, he renamed his own doctrine Pragmaticism, a name "ugly enough" to be safe from kidnappers.

(2) Although initially inveighing against armchair philosophy, he developed into a metaphysician of considerable power. Among his lifelong interests was the elaboration of three categories which he believed to be relevant to any philosophical analysis. He called them Firstness, Secondness, and Thirdness, identifying these terms with quality, reaction, and generality (and many synonyms of these terms). He found the categories in a phenomenology of his own experience, in an examination of the *phaneron*, in that which is open to sight, evident, and manifest to any awareness. He believed that any philosophy must develop the implications of each of these categories. He decided that past philosophies were often inadequate, developing a point of view stressing only one or two of the categories; but the great systems

tended to stress all three. The conflict of past philosophies has hence been the conflict of one-sided systems. The true approach to philosophy is through an architectonic, letting the system rise from an adequate analysis of experience, and indeed from as many points of experience as one can manage. Hence, the data of all of the sciences must be taken into account.

(3) The three categories have certain implications for understanding the modes of time: future the "can-be," present—the "is"; past—the necessary. The future is, hence, open.

(4) Peirce held to a doctrine of real chance, which he called Tychism. In this doctrine, events without causal antecedent are a real feature of the universe. Novelty is therefore to be admitted as an ultimate aspect of things.

(5) Natural laws are to be explained by a habit-taking feature of the universe which Peirce named Synechism; regularities grow; and the ordered universe might well have emerged from a succession of novel occurrences: Firstnesses, "sporting" freely. Laws thus evolve. This is the basis of the claim that Peirce supports an organic view of the universe, and has some relation to Panpsychism. The general position he called Objective Idealism, "the one intelligible theory of the universe."

(6) Human societies exhibit most fully this development in which both novelties and regularities appear and increase. It follows that man cannot be said to be the product of necessity. Man's ability to produce novel creations indicates his freedom.

(7) Man has no compartmentalized faculties, as reason, will, feeling. Rather, his inner life and his nature are a compound reason-will-feeling. The three interpenetrate. In addition to conscious inferences, there is a semi-conscious process in which inferences continue, feelings develop, attitudes form. No reason is possible without emotion and will; no feeling or willing, which is not also inferring. We are this compound, complex process.

(8) Thinking has three forms which supplement each other in the developing life of the mind—induction, abduction, and deduction. *Induction* has to do

with establishing general premises. *Abduction* provides explanatory hypotheses; it has to do with the discovery of connections among terms. *Deduction* has to do with the colligation of premises to determine what they may yield in formal terms. Taken by itself, deduction is trivial. The same might be said, however, for the other processes as well.

The three processes interweave in the following manner:
Induction:
These beans (an appropriately determined sample) are from this bag.
These beans are white.
∴ All the beans in this bag are white.
Abduction:
All the beans in this bag are white.
These beans are white.
∴ These beans are from this bag.
Deduction:
All the beans in this bag are white.
These beans are from this bag.
∴ These beans are white.

(9) Inductive conclusions, resting on sampling, are no more than probable. And Peirce, rather than following the relative-frequency view of probability, substituted a truth-frequency view where the probability of a given outcome rested on the proportion of true propositions to the total number of propositions in a given class. In finite classes the proportion is established by sampling; when the class is infinite one appeals to the long run. The constant reference to the future in such cases suggests that the three processes of thought will never be able to complete their task.

(10) For this reason no system of philosophy, or science, can be completed. Here, all theory is tentative. One begins where one is with the prejudices one has, and it is the task of reason to refine, crystallize, and criticize the beliefs with which one had begun. And while it could not be the case that one is wrong in all of one's beliefs, there is no belief that might not be false. What is true of man's personal situation applies also to scientific inquiry. The general doctrine of man's fallible and corrigible nature Peirce terms Fallibilism.

(11) But our incomplete sciences are interdependent and dependent upon principles not themselves scientific. These principles come from logic, ethics, and aesthetics. Aesthetics must present the ideal of life; logic the principles of inquiry. The two together provide the rational ideal, or ethics. All three provide a control for science, and a direction which defines for human life the *Summum Bonum*.

(12) Even though man is fallible one need not give up absolutes with respect to truth, beauty, goodness; for inquiry is self-corrective, and however foolish our thought may be at one time, ways can be found to discover any particular absurdity. The truth is what we are fated to believe at the end of inquiry. And the "real" is what will be thus believed.

(13) It is, therefore, the unlimited community of inquirers which will possess the truth. Through unlimited reaches of experience, the truly aesthetic will be more surely sensed. And it is the unlimited community in which the good is to appear, and where it does appear here and there. Indeed, one can speak of Agapism, an objective tendency toward achievement of appropriate human relations in society.

(14) Individuals who put their final confidence in any limited perspective—whether in a person, institution, or nation—will be illogical in all of their inferences collectively. One's final devotion is, properly, to the unlimited community.

(15) The idea of God emerges in Peirce's thought somewhat less clearly than that of the community. The idea of God is an hypothesis, derived by abduction by way of "musement," the latter being a process of free association of the categories as exemplified in the universe. In this conception God is not changeless but grows in the details of his being along with the changing universe.

(16) The categories are utilized once again in providing the structure of Peirce's expanded logic, or Semiotic. Dividing the subject matter into Speculative Grammar, Critical Logic, and Speculative Rhetoric (or Methodeutic), he provides his analysis of signs, also called representamens, in the first division. In the initial application of the categories here, three basic types of signs emerge—icon, index, and symbol. An icon is a sign containing some of the qualities of the

thing signified. An *index* is a sign which calls attention, which is in dynamic relation to the thing signified, and which tells one nothing as such. A *symbol* is a sign with an agreed upon connotation. Every sign has to some degree iconic, indexical, and symbolic aspects. In a further application of the categories to semiotic, ten classes of signs are set forth: the *Qualisign* (any sensory quality); the Iconic Sinsign (an individual diagram); the Rhematic Indexical Sinsign (*e.g.*, a spontaneous cry); the Dicent Sinsign (*e.g.*, a weathercock); the Iconic Legisign (a diagram apart from its factual individuality); the Rhematic Symbol (a common noun); the Rhematic Indexical Legisign (a demonstrative pronoun); the Dicent Indexical Legisign (*e.g.*, a street cry); the Dicent Symbol (an ordinary proposition); the Argument (an ordinary syllogism). In a still later development of his thought the classes of signs were expanded to sixty-six.

(17) There is a relationship between the three categories, the three basic kinds of signs treated above, and thought, will, and feeling in man. The relationship is through the emotional, dynamic, and symbolic interpretants. So far as meaning is concerned, signs are to be considered from the symbolic standpoint. Many so-called concepts from the past have only emotive or dynamic meaning. The pragmatic maxim, having to do with "the conceivable bearing on the conduct of life" of any sign, is designed to separate objective from subjective consequences, and so to exclude all save the symbolic interpretants from the meaning of the sign.

PELAGIANISM.

The doctrine of Pelagius (*q.v.*) and his followers that man has free will, and that divine grace merely helps a Christian to accomplish what is in his power without it. The doctrine was condemned at the Councils of Carthage, 416 and 418. In the 14th century, Bradwardine (*q.v.*) wrote against the "modern Pelagians," as did Biel in the 15th.

PELAGIUS. c. 360–c. 420.

British theologian. Probably of Irish birth. Although a layman, he maintained monastic discipline throughout his life. Coming to Rome near the start of the 5th century he was shocked by the moral laxness he observed, and felt that the doctrine of man's total depravity had permitted an evasion of moral responsibility. On the ground that ability limits obligation, he held there can be no sin where the will is not free. This implied, in his view, that man has free will, and therefore that there is no original sin, except in the sense that Adam has provided us a bad example and influence. As for grace, his view seems to have been that its influence simply makes it easier for the Christian to accomplish what is in his power in any case. And with or without grace it is the human will that must take the initiative in moving toward salvation. St. Augustine found the views of Pelagius heretical, and had them condemned at the Councils of Carthage in 416 and 418. By an imperial edict of 418, it was decreed that Pelagius and Coelestius (his most noted follower) be banned along with all who subscribed to their doctrines, and that their property be confiscated. Pelagius, who had moved from Rome to North Africa when Rome was sacked in 410, and then to Palestine, is not heard of after 420.

PENANCE.

One of the sacraments (*q.v.* 1) in both the Roman Catholic and Eastern Orthodox Churches, relating to the expiation of sins after baptism.

(1) The act of penance is understood to consist of three steps: *contrition, i.e.,* sorrow that one has sinned coupled with intention to abstain therefrom in the future; *confession, i.e.,* acknowledgment of one's sin to a priest; *satisfaction, i.e.,* carrying out works of penance assigned by one's confessor; almsgiving, fasting, prayer, reparation.

(2) Upon completion of the three steps, absolution, or reconciliation with the Church, is granted by the priest as a temporal sign of the sinner's reconciliation with God.

(3) The Roman Church held that, apart from the sacrament of penance, even perfect contrition is insufficient to reconcile the sinner with God; and that with the sacrament even imperfect contrition, termed attrition (sorrow for sin motivated by fear of penalty and not by love of God), is sufficient. This interpretation,

along with that of the power of the priest to determine satisfaction and give absolution, was challenged by the Lutheran doctrine of justification by faith (*q.v.* 3).

PENTATEUCH.

From the Greek *pente* ("five") and *teuchos* ("book"). The first five books of the Hebrew and Christian Bible (*q.v.*), also known as the Books of Law.

PENTECOST.

From the Greek *pentekonta* ("fifty"). For the Jews an observance coming fifty days after the Passover and commemorating Moses' reception of the Law on Mt. Sinai (*Exodus* 19–23). For Christians the Day of Pentecost, coming on the seventh Sunday after Easter, commemorates the outpouring of the Holy Spirit (*Acts* 2).

PENTECOSTAL SECTS.

A group of fundamentalist sects, centered in the United States, whose distinguishing mark is the act of "speaking in tongues" associated with the Day of Pentecost.

PEPPER, STEPHEN C. 1891–1972.

American philosopher. Born in Newark, New Jersey. Educated at Harvard. Taught at Berkeley.

Principal writings: *Aesthetic Quality*, 1938; *World Hypotheses*, 1942; *The Basis of Criticism in the Arts*, 1945; *The Work of Art*, 1955; *The Source of Value*, 1958; *Ethics*, 1960.

(1) According to Pepper every philosophical system has been developed from a root metaphor, controlling the manner in which the basic categories of the system are to be understood. There are four basic root metaphors in the history of philosophy, and thus four basic metaphysical systems. They are Formism (*e.g.*, Aristotle, where form is taken as the key concept), Mechanism (*e.g.*, Hobbes, where the machine is the basic metaphor), Organicism (*e.g.*, Whitehead, where organism is the organizing metaphor), and Contextualism (*e.g.*, Pragmatism, where reference to context is the key).

(2) Initially favoring Contextualism as his principle of interpretation, stressing the role of contextual relations in educing the qualities of a work of art, he later held that in both ethics and aesthetics

there are hedonistic, organic, pragmatic, cultural relativistic, and evolutionary theories, each right in its own way. He thus added a perspectival notion (*q.v.* Perspectivism) to his contextualism.

PERCEPT.

A neologism derived from perception (*q.v.*). A "percept" is the given in perception, as "concept" is the given in conception. The line between percept and concept is exceedingly vague, depending to some extent upon the amount of attention directed to the instance in question.

PERCEPTION.

From the Latin *percipio*, which covers both the obtaining of knowledge through the senses, and apprehension with the mind. Attention has been given to the problem of perception from the early stages of Greek philosophy, continuing to the present day.

(1) Empedocles (*q.v.* 5) held that perception occurred on the basis of the similarity of elements within us to those outside, making up the objects we perceive.

(2) Anaxagoras (*q.v.* 9) claimed, on the contrary, that we perceive by contrast, the qualities of the world being sensed or grasped by contrasting qualities within the perceiver.

(3) Leucippus and Democritus (*q.v.* 10) argued for an image theory of perception which, in the 5th century B.C. anticipated Locke's representative theory of perception (*cf.* 7 below). In this view the images of things are constantly bombarding our senses, and we perceive on the basis of the images which enter into our awareness through our sense-organs.

(4) Aristotle (*q.v.* 3), wishing to explore the connection between sensation and thought, developed the view that in perception our sense organs deliver images, and our mind thinks the form in the image. In abstraction, when properly done, the connection is more direct. By leaving out contingent data, the mind abstracts the form which is present in the images, the idea being that the form which is the substance of things becomes the material of thought. The same view, holding that we abstract form from phantasms carried weight throughout the Middle Ages (*q.v.* Aquinas 7).

(5) Hobbes (*q.v.* 3) regarded perception as matter in motion, returning to the framework of Greek materialism.

(6) Descartes (*q.v.* 7) stressed the intellectual aspect of perception. Perception is an intellectual act, and sensation without intellect is quite formless.

(7) John Locke (*q.v.* 1), regarded as the chief exponent of the Representative Theory of Perception (also called the Causal Theory), speaks of the mind as the blank tablet on which experience writes. He also refers to the "dark closet" of the mind. The point is that from the inscriptions on the tablet, or the ideas entering the dark closet, we are able to make reliable inferences concerning the nature of the world. Such inferences are possible because the ideas entering the mind have been caused by things in the world. Arnauld (*q.v.* 3) presents a somewhat different version of the representative theory.

(8) Leibniz (*q.v.* 1, 7, 14) claimed that perception is a continuing process in man occurring even in deep sleep, and providing man's continuity. He spoke of the *petites perceptions* (little perceptions) constantly occurring in man; but since he also held that *Monads* are windowless, and regulated to each other by a pre-established harmony, it is not clear that perception in its ordinary sense can occur at all.

(9) Kant (*q.v.* 11) defined perception as awareness accompanied by sensation, relating it to the schema of his Transcendental Aesthetic.

(10) Mill (*q.v* 6), defining matter as "the permanent possibility of sensation," provides an instance of phenomenalism (*q.v.*), where the dualism between sensation and object is dropped. Mach (*q.v.* 1, 6) develops the thesis much more self-consciously.

(11) In the early years of this century, the discussions about Realism involved the nature of perception. Naive Realism (*q.v.*) held the qualities we experience in sensation to be present in the world. New Realism (*q.v.*) argued against the 19th-century Idealists for the external relatedness of objects of knowledge. Critical Realism (*q.v.*) argued for a triadic interpretation of perception, consisting of thing, sense-datum, and act of perception.

(12) The term "sense-datum" (*q.v.*) was introduced by Moore (*q.v.* 3–4), employed by Russell (*q.v.* 6–9) and Broad (*q.v.* 4), all three of whom may be regarded as adherents of the Sense-Datum Theory, *i.e.,* that we perceive not things but sense-data.

(13) Still more recently the opponents of Sense-Datum Theory have argued that sense-data are a needless complication, and that we do indeed perceive things. Among the supporters of this view are Ryle (*q.v.* 3) and Austin (*q.v.* 4).

(14) In a different vein, Mead (*q.v.* 3) held perception to be "implicit manipulability."

(15) Merleau-Ponty (*q.v.* 5) offered a phenomenological analysis of perception which concludes that among the elements of perception are relations, or relational forms, and that these explain the possibility of intersubjectivity as well as providing a bridge between sensations and ideas.

PERCIPIENT EVENTS.
Q.v. Whitehead (3).

PEREGRINUS PROTEUS. 2nd cent. A.D.
Greek philosopher. A Cynic in philosophy who, despite an early inclination toward Christianity, reverted to the ancient ideals of Cynicism (*q.v.*). According to Lucian of Samosata (*q.v.*), he opposed all social norms and conventions. He maintained an interest in mysticism. In 165 A.D. he hurled himself into the flames at the Olympic games, ending his life.

PERELMAN, CHAIM.
Q.v. Rhetoric (17).

PERFECTION.
From the Latin *perfectio* meaning "completeness" or "completion." The concept has been applied pimarily to God, and then in a derivative sense to human beings.

(1) The concept is to be found, at least implicitly, in Xenophanes (*q.v.* 2, 3), who made of God a changeless being with the properties of omnipresence and omniscience, since it was inappropriate to think of the divine as changing.

(2) Still more forthrightly, Plato (*q.v.* 4) considered God to be a perfect Being immune to change, since any change

would be for the worse. This description related God to the changeless realm of Ideas, and separated Him from the world of change.

(3) Aristotle (*q.v* 8) provided the longstanding analysis of perfection, differentiating the perfect Being from every other as the Being which is Pure Form, and Pure Act. Having actualized every potentiality, it is without deficiency, while all other beings are mixtures of actuality and potentiality. In this view, too, God's perfection implies changelessness.

(4) Jesus Christ (*q.v.* 2), regarding God the Father as perfect, laid down the eschatological requirement of men that they be likewise perfect. Although the injunction is usually regarded as impossible of fulfillment in this life, it gave rise to a goal of Perfectionism which appears here and there throughout the history of Christian thought and institutions: in Origen (*q.v.* 4), in Roman Catholic monasticism and mysticism, and in numerous Protestant perfectionist sects.

(5) Anselm (*q.v.* 1) made the concept of perfection the basis of his ontological argument for God's existence, defining God as "that than which nothing greater can be conceived."

(6) Aquinas (*q.v.* 3d, 4) argued from the grades of perfection in the world to God as a perfect Being; and in his use of the analogy of proportionality God, as compared to other things, is viewed as pure actuality and perfection.

(7) Leibniz (*q.v.* 8) determines in his own mind that the idea of God is a possible idea by first of all separating out the properties which are perfections and admit of superlative degree, and then defining God as the sum of all perfections.

(8) Ferguson (*q.v.*) introduced the idea of perfection as the criterion of right and wrong as well as the goal of individual and social life.

(9) For Herbart (*q.v.* 4b) perfection is one of the five basic relations of the will.

(10) Fechner (*q.v.* 4) was one of relatively few thinkers who have considered God to be a Being who is self-surpassing, although not surpassed by any other being. Thus, he set the framework for an idea of a growing perfection.

(11) T.H. Green (*q.v.* 3) looks upon human perfection as the objective of social organization.

(12) The conception of the God in process has been developed especially by Hartshorne (*q.v.* 3) who regards God's perfection as surrelative, *i.e.*, He is the absolute Maximum at any given time, but in the process of time He is and must be self-surpassing.

PERFORMANCE.
Q.v. Chomsky (2).

PERFORMATIVE UTTERANCE.
Q.v. John Austin (3).

PERGAMUM, SCHOOL OF.
A 4th-century school of Neoplatonism (*q.v.* 7) founded by Edesius of Cappadocia who had studied under Iamblichus (*q.v.*). The Emperor Julian the Apostate, and Sallustius the Neoplatonist (*q.v.*), belonged to the school.

PERIPATETIC.
From the Greek *peripatos* meaning either "sheltered walkway" or the conversation which occurs during a stroll. The term was applied to the members of Aristotle's school, the Lyceum (*q.v.*), and now signifies any follower of Aristotle. Taking the second meaning of the term, it has been supposed that Aristotle's style of teaching was conversational, and that the teaching took place during leisurely strolls. But this does not accord with what is known of Aristotle's temperament, or the nature of his school. It is perhaps more likely that the school was identified by its location near a sheltered walkway.

PERLOCUTIONARY ACT.
Q.v. John Austin (2).

PERRY, RALPH BARTON. 1876–1957.
American philosopher. Born in Poultney, Vermont. Studied at Harvard. Taught briefly at Williams and Smith colleges prior to a forty-four year (1902–46) career at Harvard.
Principal writings: *The Approach to Philosophy*, 1905; *The Moral Economy*, 1909; (Symposiast), *The New Realism*, 1912; *Present Philosophical Tendencies*, 1912; *General Theory of Value*, 1926; *Philosophy of the Recent Past*, 1926; *The Thought and Character of William James*, 2 vols., 1935, (Pulitzer Prize, 1936), briefer version, 1938; *In the Spirit of William James*, 1938;

Puritanism and Democracy, 1944; *Characteristically American*, 1949; *Realms of Value*, 1954.

(1) Perry contributed to the movement of New Realism (*q.v.* 8) and to philosophy in general his analysis of the Egocentric Predicament. The predicament consists in the fact that it is not possible for us to eliminate from our awareness of an object whatever effect the act of awareness may have had on the object. It is lack of sensitivity to this predicament which has allowed Idealists to move with such facility from the epistemological statement that all that is known is thought, to the ontological statement that thought is all there is.

(2) Perry defined value very broadly as any object of any interest. The definition is designed to allow just as much value-conflict as one finds in experience. But the question of morality requires a diminution of such conflict, requiring us to harmonize our interests internally, and with respect to the interests of other people, through reflective agreement. The act of harmonizing interests naturally leads one to greater value-inclusiveness, and this is for Perry the *summum bonum*.

(3) In his analysis, Perry divided value into eight realms: morality, the arts, science, religion, economics, politics, law, and custom.

PER SE NOTA.

Q.v. William of Ockham (11).

PERSON.

From the Latin *persona*, a translation of the Greek *prosopon*, both words signifying the mask worn by actors onstage. By extension the reference is to the role an individual plays in the drama of life.

(1) The term *prosopon* was used by Epictetus (*q.v.* 5) and other Stoics to refer to the individual human being in his capacity of undertaking a specific role in life as determined by the Universal Reason.

(2) From Stoic usage the term *persona* or "person" entered Roman law to signify the legal subject of rights and duties.

(3) In the Christian doctrine of the Trinity (*q.v.* 6), God is interpreted as three Persons in one Substance. In this formulation "person" and "hypostasis" are used synonymously.

(4) In the standard formulation of Christ's nature the same identification of "person" and "hypostasis" appears, and the contrasting term is "nature" or *phusis*. Christ is understood as being of two natures—one divine and the other human—in one Person.

(5) Boethius (*q.v.* 1) supplied the definition of person which served the Middle Ages both in Christological analyses and beyond. Retaining the identification of hypostasis and person, the latter term is defined as "an individual substance of rational nature."

(6) Locke (*q.v.* 8c) gained a very different basis for the idea of person, identifying it with self-awareness and memory. One is the same person so long as these powers continue our awareness of an identity. The individual substance, man, on which one's person depends, may have, and apparently does have, a longer span of existence than does one's person.

(7) Fichte (*q.v.* 3), holding that we posit the "I" as well as the "non-I," stresses the idea of the person as a construction from the processes of awareness.

(8) Scheler (*q.v.* 3) defined person as the unity of one's concrete being, and held the concept of person to be the basis of metaphysical knowledge.

(9) F.C.S. Schiller (*q.v.* 3) identifies "person" with the spiritual and intensional side of our natures rather than with an entity either natural or spiritual. The term thus refers to functions rather than to a substance.

(10) Caso (*q.v.*) argues that the principles of disinterest and love are appropriately characteristic of the level of "person."

(11) Whitehead (*q.v.* 23) regards the individual human being as a particular kind of "personal order society," having other societies—both organic and inorganic—as constituents.

(12) Sartre (*q.v.* 3) regards the person as an invention with which each of us is charged.

(13) Strawson (*q.v.* 3) regards "person" as a primitive and logically irreducible term to which both mental and physical ascriptions may be made.

(14) Jacques Lacan (*q.v.* Structuralism 3) refers to "person" as the "fading subject."

PERSONA.
Q.v. Jung (3).

PERSONALISM.
A philosophical position taking the concept of "person" as ultimate. Appearing in the latter half of the 19th century and with adherents until around the middle of the present century, the position arose in opposition both to Pantheism (q.v.) and Materialism (q.v.). The term was first used by Schleiermacher (q.v.) in 1799, and then by Feuerbach (q.v.) in 1841, to characterize the position that God is personal, a person rather than an abstract principle. The poet, Walt Whitman, published an essay on "Personalism" in 1868, and Bronson Alcott may have gained the term from Whitman. Among the philosophers who have regarded themselves as Personalists we mention the following:

(1) Alcott used the term of his position, stating that the ultimate reality is a Divine Person who sustains the universe by a continuous act of creative will.

(2) Renouvier (q.v. 3) divided philosophers into two camps, the Personalists and the Impersonalists. The former, with whom he agreed, find their ultimate explanatory principle in human nature; the latter take their ultimate principle from some part of the outer world.

(3) Bowne (q.v. 1, 4) also contrasted personal and impersonal explanatory principles, holding the former to be ultimate. He regarded Personalism as a form of Idealism which he called Personal Idealism.

(4) F.C.S. Schiller (q.v. 3), who initially called himself a Humanist and Pragmatist, regarded himself as a Personalist in his later years.

(5) Wilhelm Stern (q.v.) named his doctrine Critical Personalism, since he restricted the scope of the doctrine to psychology and epistemology, disallowing its metaphysical possibilities.

(6) Brightman (q.v. 1, 3) applied the doctrine especially to the philosophy of religion, presenting a concept of God in some ways finite, and struggling against the "given" evil of the world.

(7) Maritain (q.v. 4), the neo-Scholastic, called his philosophy at times a Christian Personalism, since man is not reducible to natural factors.

(8) Mounier (q.v. 4) was, like Maritain, a Catholic Personalist. Applying the philosophy to the question of life goals, Mounier held that man's goal was increased communication and mutual enrichment, rather than the conquest of nature.

(9) In addition, A.C. Knudson published The Philosophy of Personalism in 1927; and R.T. Flewelling founded and served as editor of The Personalist, a California-based journal of philosophy.

PERSONAL ORDER SOCIETY.
Q.v. Whitehead (23).

PERSONIFICATION.
Q.v. Fallacies (7).

PERSPECTIVISM.
A term introduced by Teichmüller (q.v.) to the effect that every point of view is in some sense true and offers a valuable and unique perspective of the universe. The term has been used by Nietzsche (q.v. 9), Simmel (q.v.), Ortega y Gasset (q.v. 2) and Russell (q.v. 7). Mead (q.v. 5) derived from his philosophy of the act a perspectival theory of the universe.

PERSUASIVE DEFINITION.
Q.v. Definition (8); Charles Stevenson (3).

PESSIMISM, ETHICS OF.
Q.v. Schopenhauer (6).

PESTALOZZI, J.H. 1746–1827.
Swiss philosopher of education. Born in Zurich. Educated at the University of Zurich. Interested in developmental education, allowing students to achieve their own "truth," Pestalozzi believed that the complete development of a person requires the experience of altruism in one's early years, and finally a personal relation to God. He believed the years of primary education to be crucial, and established a number of experimental schools. The most important of the schools was at Neuchatel and attracted international attention.

Principal writings: The Evening Hours of a Hermit, 1780; Leonard and Gertrude (T), 1781; How Gertrude Teaches Her Children (T), 1801; Swan's Song, 1827.

PETER DAMIAN. 1007–1072.
Italian Churchman. Born in Ravenna.

Named Archbishop of Ostia in 1057, he represented the Pope on a number of important missions.

Principal writings: *On Holy Simplicity; On the Order of Things; On Divine Omnipotence* (T in part).

(1) A vigorous opponent of dialectic, by which he meant the application of reason to theology, philosophy, or even science, Peter traced human pretensions in these areas to the sin of pride, regarding them as the work of the devil. Knowledge of the Scriptures alone was exempt from his criticism.

(2) His attack on reason was designed to support the absolute infinity and omnipotence of God. In his view any suggested limitations in this respect merely reflect on the weakness of human reason, man's hope lying not in reason but in religious contemplation, approached in humility and through self-mortification.

PETER LOMBARD. 1100–1160.

Scholastic theologian. Born in Lombardy. Studied in Bologna and Rheims. Locating in Paris, he was associated with Hugh of Saint Victor and Abelard. Named Bishop of Paris shortly before his death.

Principal writings: *Gloss on the Psalms*, 1135–7; *Gloss on the Epistles of St. Paul*, 1139–41; *The Four Books of Sentences*, 1157–8.

(1) It was the great achievement of Peter Lombard to bring the Scholastic method of analysis to maturity, profiting from the sense of method to which many had contributed, especially Abelard (*q.v.*) and Hugh of St. Victor (*q.v.*), but also Gratian, John of Damascus (*q.v.*), and others. The achievement is to be found in the books of the *Sentences*, consisting of texts and opinions of the Fathers and other authorities analyzed, compared, criticized, and conclusions drawn. The four books treat in turn of God, creatures, the virtues and salvation, and the seven sacraments (accepted from Hugh of St. Victor).

(2) The work gained immediate acceptance and great popularity, serving as the basis of theological study not only in Paris, but in most of the European universities during the medieval period. His concept of the sacraments became central both in theology and dogma.

PETER OF AUREOL. 14th cent. A.D.

Scholastic philosopher. A Franciscan, he taught theology, becoming Archbishop of Aix-en-Provence. Opposing Thomas Aquinas and Duns Scotus, he was a precursor to William of Ockham, tending— as did the latter—to avoid unnecessary complexity (*q.v.* Ockham's Razor).

Principal writings: *Commentary in Four Books of Sentences*.

(1) On the ground that it is the essence of form to inform matter, Peter denied the existence of separate forms. Since the existence of such forms was a basic feature of the system of faith and reason worked out by Aquinas and Scotus, philosophers asserting the existence of such forms and theologians helping explicate their nature, Peter's denial of separate forms destroyed the bridge between the two realms. The move, denying a postulate of reason, increased the importance of faith as well as its autonomy, shifting the balance of thought toward St. Augustine. It likewise encouraged an empirical point of view since experience was presupposed in any acquisition of knowledge.

(2) The consequence of Peter's view for the theory of universals is that they became indefinite designations of individuals fabricated by the mind. Hence, Peter may be regarded as a representative of nominalism (*q.v.*).

PETER OF SPAIN (PETRUS HISPANUS). 1226–1277.

Scholastic philosopher. Born in Lisbon. Educated at the University of Paris, probably studying with William of Sherwood (*q.v.*) among others. Taught at Siena. Becoming Bishop Cardinal of Tusculum in 1273, he was elevated to the papacy in 1276 as John XXI. While Pope he countenanced, and perhaps encouraged, the 1277 condemnation of Latin Averroism at the University of Paris. He is best known as a logician, his book on logic serving widely as a text for three centuries and passing through 166 editions.

Principal writings: *Summulae Logicales* (T); *Syncategoremata* (T); *Treatise on the Major Fallacies; On the Soul*.

(1) Holding the Augustinian position of realism (*q.v.*) with respect to the status of universals, his doctrine of the soul combined Avicenna with the Augustinian

emphasis on an inner illumination. The consequence was a substantial soul with the power of existing apart from the body.

(2) His doctrine of the distinction between *significatio* and *suppositio* has historical importance, influencing William of Ockham (*q.v.* 5) among others. By the *significatio* of a term one means the relation of the sign to the thing or class of things signified. By the *suppositio* one means the use of the term in discourse to signify definite individuals. "All men are mortal" has *significatio* but not *suppositio.* "The man died today," referring to a definite individual, has both *significatio* and *suppositio.* The distinction is roughly that between the sense and reference of a term, or its connotation and denotation.

Also *q.v.* Logic (9).

PETER, THE APOSTLE. 1st cent. A.D.

(1) Simon, one of the twelve disciples of Jesus, was given the name Peter, signifying "the rock," by Jesus in honor of his steadfastness.

(2) In the Gospel of Matthew, Jesus acclaims Peter as the rock on which He will build His church. Many Protestant scholars hold the passage to be of doubtful authenticity.

(3) All recognize Peter as the leader of the Church in Jerusalem. Catholic doctrine, in addition, regards Peter as visible head of the Roman Church, and first in an unbroken succession of popes who held the same authority Christ conferred on Peter.

(4) According to tradition, Peter suffered martyrdom in Rome in 64 A.D.

PETITES PERCEPTIONS.

French for "little perceptions." A concept of Leibniz (*q.v.* 14) that perception is occurring constantly, even below the threshold of consciousness.

PETITIO PRINCIPII.

A Latin phrase usually translated as "begging the question." Considered to be one of the Fallacies (*q.v.* 20) of logic.

(1) The sense usually given to the *petitio principii* is that of assuming in the premises the very conclusion one sets out to prove.

(2) Aristotle's meaning was somewhat different. Regarding the *petitio* as a fallacy of disputation, he found it occurring when, instead of presenting a rational argument, one attempts to lead one's opponent to admit the very matter in question.

PETRARCH (FRANCESCO PETRARCA). 1304–1374.

Italian humanist. Born at Arezzo. From 1313 to 1341 his life centered in Avignon. From 1323–6 he studied law in Bologna. By 1340 he had gained international notice as a poet; and thereafter he resided mainly in Italy—in Parma, Vaucluse, Milan, Venice, Padua, and Arqua. He was sent on numerous diplomatic missions by the Milanese, including one to Emperor Charles IV. Petrarch and Boccaccio were close friends.

Principal philosophical writings: *On the Solitary Life* (T), 1356; *On the Secret Conflict of My Worries* (T), 1358; *On the Remedies of Good and Bad Fortune,* 1366; *On His Own Ignorance and That of Many Others* (T), 1367; *Letters* (T in part).

(1) Petrarch is regarded as the earliest representative of Renaissance Humanism, an attitude of mind that turned attention to the recovery of Latin and Greek sources, and fostered appreciation for them. The attitude of mind is not a philosophy; but Petrarch's lifelong devotion to self-culture through literary study and achievement does reflect a value-orientation of some importance. His appreciation of Cicero and Seneca, as well as earlier Stoics, likewise reveals a philosophical bent.

(2) In fact, Petrarch contains a mixture of traditional and modern responses. His "Letter on the Ascent of Mont Ventoux"—in which a robust appreciation of natural beauty alternates with feelings of contrition over his enjoyment (the latter confirmed by his copy of St. Augustine's *Confessions*)—is often cited as evidence of his role as a transitional figure standing between the spirit of the Middle Ages and that of the Renaissance.

PETROVIC, GAJO.

Q.v. Praxis (7, 9).

PETRUS TARTARETUS.

Q.v. Pons Asinorum.

PETZOLDT, JOSEPH. 1862–1929.
German philosopher. Born in Altenburg. Part of the movement of Empiriocriticism (*q.v.*), Petzoldt was influenced by Avenarius (*q.v.*), Mach (*q.v.*) and Schuppe (*q.v.*). Calling his position Relativistic Positivism, he substituted for causality the concept of "functional dependence," and for substance, relatively stable complexes of sense qualities. He defended Psychophysical Parallelism (*q.v.*), regarding mind and body as distinct modes of interpretation of the same phenomena.
Principal writings: *Introduction to the Philosophy of Pure Experience*, 2 vols., 1899, 1904; *The World-Problem from the Standpoint of Relativistic Positivism*, 1906; *The Natural Goal of Human Development*, 1927.

PFÄNDER, ALEXANDER. 1870–1941.
German philosopher. Born in Iserlohn. Taught at the University of Munich. Influenced by Lipps (*q.v.*) and Husserl (*q.v.*), Pfänder developed an independent approach to phenomenology. He developed a phenomenological logic based on ideal, subsistent entities; and an approach to philosophical anthropology resting on dispositions which include both thought and feeling.
Principal writings: *Phenomenology of the Will*, 1900; *Introduction to Psychology*, 1904; *Logic*, 1921; *The Soul of Man*, 1933; *Philosophy of Life Goals*, (ed. Trillhaas), 1948.

PHALANGE.
Q.v. Fourier (1).

PHALANSTÈRE.
Q.v. Fourier (1).

PHALEAS OF CHALCEDON.
Q.v. Communism.

PHANERON.
Q.v. Peirce (2).

PHANTASM.
From the Greek *phantasma* ("an appearance, image, or phantom").
(1) In Aristotle (*q.v.* 3) the image as reflected on by intellect, making possible universal meanings.
(2) In Scholasticism (*q.v.* Aquinas 7) the species of the object as educed by the active intellect from the images of things.
(3) For Hobbes (*q.v.* 3) the image directly given in perception.

PHASE SPACE.
Q.v. Chaos Theory (9).

PHATIC ACT.
Q.v. Austin (2).

PHATIC FUNCTION.
Q.v. Jakobson.

PHEME.
Q.v. Austin (2).

PHENOMENALISM.
From the Greek *phainomenon* ("appearance"). The view that we know only phenomena, and that there are no things behind phenomena causing their appearance. When one separates the phenomena of which one is aware from the objects causing one to have this awareness, the problem arises of determining what these causative objects may be. The difficulties present in the dualism of phenomenon and object have led a number of philosophers to the position of Phenomenalism.
(1) Berkeley (*q.v.* 1) solved the difficulties of Locke's separation of appearance and object by identifying being and being perceived, thus creating the first phenomenalistic system.
(2) Hume (*q.v.* 1) is close to a phenomenalism in the sense that we can trace our ideas only to impressions and must remain skeptical with respect to the source of the impressions.
(3) John Stuart Mill (*q.v.* 6), regarding matter as a permanent possibility of sensation, is usually considered to be a phenomenalist.
(4) Numerous philosophers in the movement of neo-Kantianism (*q.v.* 1, 2) denied the possibility of a Kantian "thing-in-itself," and were thus left with a phenomenalistic view.
(5) Renouvier (*q.v.* 1) is one of the key representatives of phenomenalism. A neo-Kantian, he rejected the idea of the thing-in-itself, building the world from phenomena.
(6) Avenarius (*q.v.* 1–3), author of *Empiriocriticism* (*q.v.*), held that the world must be built from pure experience. Petzoldt (*q.v.*) agreed with Avenarius, and Lenin (*q.v.*) was the principal critic of the view.
(7) Mach (*q.v.* 1, 6) is often cited as the

prime exemplar of phenomenalism. He tells us that reality consists of sensations, and that scientific concepts are summaries of sense-experience, putting us in touch with further sense-experience.

(8) A number of philosophers have passed through a phenomenalist stage. Russell (*q.v.* 7) experimented with the possibility of building the world from *Sensibilia, i.e.,* all possible perspectives that can be taken. Some of these are actual sense-data, and other *Sensibilia* are possible perspectives and so possible sense-data.

(9) Carnap (*q.v.* 2) in his *Aufbau* stage attempted a logical construction of the world out of the stream of experience, but the approach was soon abandoned.

(10) Goodman (*q.v.* 1) has made a detailed examination of Carnap's early phenomenalism, which turned into a close examination of the structure of phenomenalistic systems.

(11) Ayer (*q.v.* 7) is sometimes regarded, although mistakenly, as a phenomenalist, due to his tendency to identify philosophical analysis with the translation of material-object sentences into sense-datum language.

(12) Chisholm (*q.v.* 3) has provided a refutation of the phenomenalist's thesis that physical object statements can be reduced to appearance statements.

PHENOMENOLOGY.

From the Greek *phainomenon* ("appearance") and *logos* ("knowledge of"). In general, phenomenology is an approach to philosophy centering on analysis of the phenomena which flood human awareness.

(1) The term was introduced by J. H. Lambert (*q.v.*) in 1764 to refer to the Theory of Appearance which, along with Theory of Truth, Logic, and Semiotic, made up his four basic philosophical disciplines. Since Lambert the term has been used in many different connections.

(2) Kant (*q.v.*) named part four of his *Metaphysical Principles of Natural Science* "Phenomenology." The section treats motion and rest as general characters of phenomena. In his correspondence, Kant called for a phenomenological study of the distinction between the sensible and intelligible worlds to prevent metaphysical confusion between the two.

(3) Hegel (*q.v.* 4) in his *Phenomenology of the Spirit* details the separate steps by which Western man has risen to the level of universal Reason.

(4) William Hamilton (*q.v.* 2) called for an empirical phenomenology of the human spirit as the starting point of objective knowledge.

(5) Eduard von Hartmann (*q.v.* 2, 5) used the term "phenomenology" as a synonym for "survey," claiming that a phenomenology of moral practice should precede any philosophical conclusions with respect to moral principles.

(6) In 1900 Pfänder (*q.v.*) published his *Phenomenology of the Will,* developing an approach to phenomenological analysis sometimes termed the Munich School of Phenomenology.

(7) Peirce (*q.v.* 2) urged in 1902 that philosophical analysis required an initial phenomenological step consisting of analysis of the *phaneron, i.e.,* the contents of awareness available to any person.

(8) But the central figure is that of Husserl (*q.v.*) whose 1913 work *Ideas Toward a Pure Phenomenology and Phenomenological Philosophy* set the standard usage of the term. One approaches the study "bracketing" questions of existence while exploring the "essences" of the phenomena. The derivation of the method can be traced in vol. 2 of the *Logical Investigations* (*q.v.* Husserl 3).

(9) Messer (*q.v.* 2) is likewise to be counted among those recommending a phenomenological approach.

(10) Max Scheler (*q.v.* 2) applied phenomenological method to the exploration of the nature of value.

(11) Heidegger (*q.v.* 1) studied under Husserl but directed his own phenomenological analyses to the rediscovery of the meaning of Being via an understanding of human nature.

(12) Sartre (*q.v.* 1) used the phrase "An Essay in Phenomenological Ontology," as the subtitle of his central work, *Being and Nothingness,* thus signalling both his relation to phenomenology, and the influence of Heidegger. His discussion, like that of Heidegger, moves from an analysis of the human situation to ontology.

(13) Merleau-Ponty (*q.v.* 1) developed a phenomenological approach blending the emphases of Husserl's phenomenology with those of Gestalt Psychology, the

result being a phenomenology of perception able, in Merleau-Ponty's view, to deal with the real world.

PHENOMENON.

From the Greek *phainomenon* meaning "that which appears."

(1) Kant (*q.v.* 2) uses the term in contrast to "*noumenon*" (*q.v.*) which does not appear to sense.

(2) Brentano (*q.v.* 2) holds that psychical phenomena are characterized by "intentional inexistence."

PHILODEMUS OF GADARA. 1st cent. B.C.

Hellenic philosopher. Born in Syria. Studied in Athens under Zeno of Sidon and Demetrius of Laconia. With Siron he headed a school of Epicurean philosophy in Naples. He engaged in polemic against the Stoics, holding that the relation between sign and thing signified is established in every case empirically, either by induction or analogy. The Stoic position on the matter (*q.v.* Stoicism 1) rests such connections on a relationship of logical necessity. Philodemus, regarding the rules of rhetoric as probable and based on experience, exercised influence on Cicero (*q.v.*).

Principal writings: *On Methods of Inference*.

PHILO JUDAEUS. 30 B.C.–50 A.D.

Hellenic Jewish apologist. Born in Alexandria. A member of the Alexandrian School (*q.v.*), Philo was an outstanding representative of the Jewish Diaspora in Egypt during the Hellenic period. His style of writing was mostly in the nature of commentary on the Jewish Scriptures. *Q.v.* Judaism (5).

Principal writings: *Concerning the Artisan of the World* (T); *That God is an Immutable Being* (T); *On the Contemplative Life* (T); *On the Eternity of the World* (T).

(1) Convinced that the teaching of Moses anticipated the wisdom of the Greeks, especially Platonism and Stoicism, Philo interpreted the Scriptures allegorically in an effort to demonstrate the point.

(2) Founder of the Negative Theology; although he holds God to be Being itself, His transcendence is so complete, beyond virtue and goodness or any other predication, that the only conceptual approach to God is by means of saying what God is not, that is, by the denial of predicates to Him.

(3) Through a nonconceptual rapture or ecstasy, however, the individual may make contact with God, at the same time dealing with man's central problem— learning how to free oneself from sin. He says that the true prophet speaks his revelation with no admixture of his own reason.

(4) God relates to the world through an intermediary, the *Logos*, which proceeded from God, along with the ideas, and intelligible beings. The ideas existed from eternity in the mind of God; and then by emanation, as it were, in their own intelligible realm. The *Logos* created the world, taking as its model the intelligible ideas.

(5) In addition to the foregoing, Philo mentions a hierarchy of other beings including the divine wisdom, the divine Man, the Spirit, and the angels. The hierarchy and style of thought has obvious resemblance to Gnostic and Neoplatonic systems.

PHILOLAUS. 5th cent. B.C.

Greek philosopher. Associated with Croton in Italy. Survived the burning of the Pythagorean school in Croton and brought the philosophy to mainland Greece. Regarded as the systematizer of Pythagoreanism, he held fire to be the central element of reality, nature to be regulated by the opposition of limit and the unlimited, man's soul—a harmony— to be imprisoned in his body due to human sin, and number to be constitutive of reality. The hypothesis concerning number contained the following identifications: 1 = the point; 2 = the line; 3 = the surface; 4 = the solid. With these premises established, he correlated the elements with combinations of the regular solids: fire with the foursided tetrahedron, earth with the cube, air with the octahedron, and water with the 20-sided icosahedron. The 12-sided dodecahedron he assigned either to a fifth element, the aether, or to the universe as a whole. He also held the doctrine that the earth is in motion, and that the solar system contains—in addition to the sun and the planets—a central fire and counter-earth essentially as discussed under Pythagoras (*q.v.* 8); indeed, it is likely that he was the originator of these doctrines.

PHILO OF LARISSA. 2nd–1st cent. B.C.
Greek philosopher. A disciple of Clitomachus (*q.v.*) he was head of the Fourth Academy (*q.v.* Plato's Academy 4) from around 110 to around 88 B.C. He lectured in Rome and was known to Cicero (*q.v.*). Beginning with the position of moderate skepticism supported by his predecessors, especially Arcesilas (*q.v.*) and Carneades (*q.v.*), he evolved a position called Dogmatism, but which appears to have been an anticipation of Common Sense Realism (*q.v.*). It was this position that characterized the Fourth Academy. His point seems to have been that skepticism can never be more than a methodological gambit, and behind it stands the *eulogon*, that is the probable or the reasonable. The conclusion is that the mind has every possibility of being related to some truths. What is true with respect to knowledge holds also with respect to moral skepticism. Positive moral principles may be discovered behind the facade of moral skepticism.

PHILO OF MEGARA. 4th cent. B.C.
Megarian philosopher. Disciple of Diodorus Cronos (*q.v.*) and Zeno of Citium (*q.v.*).
(1) He anticipated the Propositional Calculus (*q.v.*) in his definition of what is now known as material implication: a conditional statement is true in all cases except those where the antecedent is true and the consequent is false.
(2) In modal logic he offered a definition of possibility as that which can be true by virtue of its internal nature.

PHILOPONUS, JOHN. Late 5th and early 6th cent. A.D.
Hellenic philosopher. Born in Caesarea. A member of the Alexandrian School of Neoplatonism, he is held by some to have been a Christian Monophysite, and to have held a doctrine of tritheism (*q.v.*) wherein the triune God is interpreted as virtually three Gods. It is certain that he launched a vigorous attack on Aristotelian thought. He believed the universe to be a creation of God who at the moment of creation imposed the laws by which it operates. He believed the heavenly bodies to be perishable and not divine, and offered arguments based on astronomical evidence for this contention. He advanced a doctrine of impetus, and applied the doctrine to the flow of light. All of these doctrines had a touch of modernity to them, were inconsistent with Aristotelian philosophy, and had influence among Islamic and Scholastic philosophers.
Principal writings: *On the Eternity of the Cosmos Against Proclus; On the Creation of the World; Commentaries on Aristotle's Physics; On Generation and Corruption; Meteorology;* and *On the Soul.*

PHILOSOPHEME.
From the Greek *philosophema* referring to a philosophical proposition or demonstration. Aristotle used the term to distinguish demonstrative reasoning from rhetoric, eristic, and dialectic.

PHILOSOPHERS, THE NEW.
Q.v. New Philosophers, The.

PHILOSOPHES, LES.
French phrase meaning "the philosophers."
Name given the group of 18th-century French philosophers who cooperated in publishing the great French *Encyclopédie. Q.v.* The Encyclopedists; *q.v.* Meslier (*q.v.*) for an instance of an earlier figure championed by Voltaire and Holbach.

PHILOSOPHIA PERENNIS.
A Latin phrase meaning "perennial philosophy." The term was introduced by Steuchen in 1540 to refer to the features common to medieval Scholasticism and the School of Padua. The term has since been used in a variety of senses, sometimes designating Thomism, and at other times what is common to Greek and medieval philosophy. Leibniz (*q.v.* 1) used the phrase to refer to the valid elements of the entire history of philosophy, of which he believed his system to be a continuation. Rosmini-Serbati (*q.v.*) followed in the same vein. Urban (*q.v.* 1) used the term still more broadly to refer to any adequately based philosophy—*e.g.*, Plato, Aristotle, Thomism—where both fact and value are dealt with in the system.

PHILOSOPHICAL ANALYSIS.
Q.v. Analysis, Philosophical.

PHILOSOPHICAL RADICALISM.

Name of the movement initiated by Jeremy Bentham (*q.v.*), James Mill (*q.v.*), William Godwin (*q.v.*), and others. The position is perhaps better known as English Utilitarianism. The initial contributions of the group appeared in the Westminster Review, founded by Jeremy Bentham in 1824. *Q.v.* Utilitarianism (5, 6).

PHILOSOPHY.

From the Greek *philos* ("love of") and *sophia* ("wisdom"). We shall deal in turn with the meanings which have been given to philosophy, the history of philosophy, and its constituent fields.

A. The Senses of Philosophy.

(1) The term was first used by Pythagoras (*q.v.* 2) who noted that men could be divided into three types: those who loved pleasure, those who loved activity, and those who loved wisdom. The end of wisdom in his view, however, concerned progress toward salvation in religious terms.

(2) Socrates (*q.v.* 1) seems to have held self-knowledge, through the gaining of conceptual clarity, to be the function of philosophy.

(3) For Plato (*q.v.* 1) the object of philosophy was the discovery of reality or absolute truth, the two are the same in his view, through dialectic.

(4) Aristotle (*q.v.*), suggesting that philosophy begins in wonder, tells us that this discipline is concerned with the investigation of the causes and principles of things. In this sense of the term, philosophy would seem to be identical with the totality of human knowledge. But, within the general discipline of philosophy there is another discipline, "first philosophy," which he also called "theology," concerned with ultimate principles and causes, which includes the idea of God, the principle of principles and cause of causes.

(5) Following the period of classical Greek thought, philosophy turned practical for a time. The Cyrenaic philosopher, Hegesias (*q.v.*), for example, believed it to be the task of philosophy to teach how pain is to be avoided. Many Epicureans (*q.v.* Epicureanism) would have said the same, and the Stoics would have held the achievement of serenity or *apathia* (*q.v.*) to be philosophy's goal.

(6) Neoplatonism (*q.v.*) believed the goal of philosophy to be union with the Divine.

(7) During the Middle Ages, philosophy was either held to be an interference in the life of faith (*q.v.* Peter Damian), or a handmaiden to theology, conducting us by reason to the point where reason could no longer function, and we must thereafter proceed by faith (*q.v.* Aquinas 1).

(8) For Descartes (*q.v.* 1–3, 10) philosophy is the elucidation of ultimate truth whose starting point is found by pushing skepticism to its limit. At that limit the certainty of one's own existence is revealed.

(9) Locke (*q.v.* 5) believed that philosophy required an analysis of the ideas with which our mind is stocked, and this involved unpacking ideas to reveal their simple constituents.

(10) Saint Simon (*q.v.* 1) believed philosophy to be the instrument for bringing the world into harmony.

(11) Hegel (*q.v.* 6, 22) held that it is the function of philosophy to deduce the categories, *i.e.*, the basic ideas necessary for interpretation of the nature of things, and philosophy, through its history, presents the absolute truth in absolute form.

(12) Cousin (*q.v.* 1) believed the function of philosophy to be that of classifying and interpreting the experience of humanity.

(13) Cournot (*q.v.* 3) described the task of philosophy to be that of elaborating the categories in terms of which the connections of discrete phenomena and fields of knowledge can be expressed.

(14) Spencer (*q.v.* 1) believed philosophy to be a synthetic discipline, resting on the data of separate fields and held together by universal principles. He found Evolution to be the basic, unifying idea.

(15) Nietzsche (*q.v.* 5) believed it was his personal mission to "philosophize with a hammer," feeling that the breaking up of outworn conceptions is itself a positive good.

(16) Husserl (*q.v.* 3) understood philosophy to be a phenomenological analysis directed toward the discovery of the essences within experience.

(17) Bergson (*q.v.* 1) argued that philosophy is basically an intuitive discipline,

since reason falsifies reality. Apparently, however, if the dynamism of intuition is allowed the central role, the static nature of reason can be of help in approximating what has been gained intuitively.

(18) Whitehead (*q.v.* 9) believed it to be the function of philosophy to develop through imaginative generalization a categoreal scheme applicable to all experience.

(19) Croce (*q.v.* 1) found philosophy to relate to the concrete rather than to the abstract. In his view philosophy and history were inseparable.

(20) Cassirer (*q.v.* 2) regarded the philosophical task to be that of tracing out the development of symbolic form in all fields of thought as expressions of humanity.

(21) Schlick (*q.v.* 1) found two tasks for philosophy: exploration of the logic of science and the purification of philosophical language.

(22) Morris Cohen (*q.v.* 2) held that it was the task of philosophy to set the framework for the onward movement of science.

(23) Ortega y Gasset (*q.v.* 1, 4), holding to the importance of the "vital reason," found the deliverances of philosophy—along with other forms of culture—to be poetic creations set up in the face of a problematic reality.

(24) C.D. Broad (*q.v.* 2) distinguished between speculative and critical philosophy. He found his own function to be that of elaborating many alternatives to basic problems, thus contributing to the field of critical philosophy.

(25) Collingwood (*q.v.* 1–2) initially held to the view that philosophy deals with a special set of "overlapping concepts" which require special treatment. Although not forced from this position, he later held it to be the function of philosophy to bring to light the "absolute presuppositions" of human thought.

(26) Heidegger (*q.v.* 1) believes the object of philosophy to be a "rediscovery" of the meaning of Being, a heritage once held in his view by early Greek philosophy.

(27) Wittgenstein (*q.v.* 3, 5) initially held philosophy to be a dispensable analysis, similar to the claim of John Wisdom (*q.v.*) that "philosophy is the disease of which philosophy is the cure." Later, it was his view that philosophy

has its role in the analysis of families of concepts.

(28) Ryle (*q.v.* 1) holds the function of philosophy (in the sophisticated sense) to be the analysis of the category mistakes into which less sophisticated philosophers have fallen.

(29) Bonhoeffer (*q.v.* 1), whose goal it is to exchange philosophy for the Christian faith, distinguishes between the "Act" philosophies which emphasize man and the "Being" philosophies which emphasize an ahistorical deity.

(30) Bergmann (*q.v.* 2) uses a philosophical method that involves the construction—in actuality or at least in principle—of ideal languages to determine the nature of one's commitments. The richness of these alternatives suggests that no one of them is determinative but that they stand as a fund of source materials to stimulate our own efforts to determine where we stand.

B. The History of Western Philosophy. In a general sense every item in this dictionary is a part of the history of philosophy. It would not be possible to mention here all the figures of each period of the history of philosophy. But there may be some point in identifying some of the principal figures of each period.

(31) For Greek philosophy (*q.v.*) Thales (*q.v.*), Anaximander (*q.v.*), Anaximenes (*q.v.*), Xenophanes (*q.v.*), Pythagoras (*q.v.*), Parmenides (*q.v.*), Heraclitus (*q.v.*), Anaxagoras (*q.v.*), Empedocles (*q.v.*), Democritus (*q.v.*) and Protagoras (*q.v.*), may be mentioned in that period of philosophy termed the Pre-Socratic period. The period of time runs from the 7th to the 5th century B.C. Within this period the emphasis of the first philosophers concerned discovery of the basic elements of the Universe. Water, air, fire, the boundless, numbers, atoms, being itself: all of these alternatives were tried out. As for the ordering principle, mind and mechanical causation were both suggested. In the later period of the Pre-Socratics, the Sophists (*q.v.*) appeared, turning their attention away from nature and toward man. The classical period of Greek philosophy, consisting of Socrates (*q.v.*), Plato (*q.v.*) and Aristotle (*q.v.*), runs from 470 to 322 B.C. In this period two classical approaches to philosophy of

enduring value were struck out: the philosophy of Plato with its emphasis on eternal forms, and the philosophy of Aristotle with its emphasis on substance.

Among the schools of philosophy in this period, some emerged from the influence of philosophers already mentioned: *i.e.*, Pythagoreanism (*q.v.*) with its emphasis on the power of number; and the Eleatics (*q.v.*) with their emphasis on being. Three schools are credited to the influence of Socrates: the Megarians, Cyrenaics, and Cynics. The Megarian School (*q.v.*), dealing with semantics and logical form, was founded by Euclides (*q.v.*). Cyrenaicism (*q.v.*), stressing the role of pleasure, was founded by Aristippus (*q.v.*). Cynicism (*q.v.*), opposing the conventions of society and stressing a life of austerity, was traditionally traced to Antisthenes (*q.v.*), a pupil of Socrates, but Diogenes of Sinope (*q.v.*) is now regarded as the more likely founder of the school. Plato's Academy (*q.v.*) and Aristotle's Lyceum (*q.v.*) existed for long periods of time not only as schools of thought but also as functioning educational institutions. In the 4th century B.C. three further schools of great importance came into being: Stoicism (*q.v.*), Epicureanism (*q.v.*) and Skepticism (*q.v.*). The first of these alternatives, stressing man's life as a part of the universal reason, was initiated by Zeno of Citium (*q.v.*). The second, stressing materialism and a life of pleasure, had Epicurus (*q.v.*) as its founder. The third, more a movement than a school, and the principal force in the second and third academies of Plato, was begun by Pyrrho (*q.v.*).

Pythagoreanism, the Academy, the Lyceum, Stoicism, Epicureanism, and Skepticism continued into the Hellenistic era.

(32) The Hellenistic-Roman Period of Philosophy. Cicero (*q.v.*), one of the initiators of the Hellenistic-Roman period of philosophy, reflected influences from all five of the continuing schools of Greek philosophy. His eclecticism (*q.v.*) was typical of the Roman approach to philosophy. Among the Roman representatives of Stoicism, Seneca (*q.v.*), Epictetus (*q.v.*) and Marcus Aurelius (*q.v.*) deserve special mention. One of the new philosophical movements was Neoplatonism. Like the Pythagorean philosophy which influ-

enced it, Neoplatonism had personal salvation as its goal. Plotinus (*q.v.*) was the principal Neoplatonist, although his disciple, Porphyry (*q.v.*), likewise deserves mention. The attempt to assimilate Christianity to the philosophical tradition also began in this period. Alexandria in Egypt became an important cultural center as Greece waned in influence. The Alexandrian School (*q.v.*), in one of its several meanings, provided a locus for Neoplatonists, Jewish philosophers such as Philo (*q.v.*), and Christian thinkers such as Origen (*q.v.*). The speculations of the Church Fathers (*q.v.* Patristics) occurred in the early centuries of the Christian era. Boethius (*q.v.*) and St. Augustine (*q.v.*) are important both for this period and for their contributions to medieval philosophy.

(33) The period of Islamic philosophy. The religion of Islam (*q.v.*) began in the 7th century A.D. and rapidly gained control of the culture of the Near East. Beginning in the 9th century and continuing through the 12th, a remarkable series of philosophers appeared, interpreting the texts of Aristotle and the Neoplatonists. The principal figures were Al-Kindi (*q.v.*), Al-Farabi (*q.v.*), Avicenna (*q.v.*), Al-Ghazzali (*q.v.*), and Averroës (*q.v.*). A theme of esoteric illumination was introduced by Avicenna (*q.v.* 11), and developed by Suhrawardi (*q.v.* 2–3) and Mulla Sadra (*q.v.* 2).

(34) The period of Pre-Scholastic Jewish philosophy. Although the phrase would include Philo Judaeus (*cf.* 32 above), the intention of this section is to call attention to that group of Jewish philosophers, including Avicebron (*q.v.*), Halevi (*q.v.*), Ibn Ezra (*q.v.*) and especially Maimonides (*q.v.*), whose writings, along with those of the Islamic philosophers named above, provided the stimulus leading to the rise of Scholasticism (*q.v.* Jewish Philosophy 2).

(35) Medieval philosophy. The high point of medieval philosophy (*q.v.*) was Scholasticism. Among the figures preparing for this culmination, in addition to those named above, are Erigena (*q.v.*), Anselm (*q.v.*), Abelard (*q.v.*), Grosseteste (*q.v.*), Roger Bacon (*q.v.*), Bonaventure (*q.v.*), and Albert the Great (*q.v.*). The *Summae* of Thomas Aquinas (*q.v.*) bring these influences into a coherent whole.

One must also mention Duns Scotus (*q.v.*), Peter of Spain (*q.v.*), and William of Ockham (*q.v.*).

(36) The philosophy of the Renaissance (*q.v.*) turned from Aristotle to Plato, was attracted by mysticism, and open to the new sciences which were beginning to form. Petrarch (*q.v.* 1), Bruno (*q.v.*) and Nicholas of Cusa (*q.v.*) are typical Renaissance figures.

(37) The key figures of 17th-century rationalism were Descartes (*q.v.*), Spinoza (*q.v.*), and Leibniz (*q.v.*).

(38) The British tradition, although including the materialist Thomas Hobbes (*q.v.*), is basically empirical in character. Among the empiricists are Roger and Francis Bacon (*q.v.*), John Locke (*q.v.*), Berkeley (*q.v.*), an empiricist-idealist, and David Hume (*q.v.*). John Stuart Mill (*q.v.*) in the 19th century likewise fits the empirical tradition.

(39) Turning back to the Continent, Immanuel Kant (*q.v.*) built a distinctive philosophy, responding to the influence of Leibniz through Christian Wolff (*q.v.*), and the skepticism of David Hume. The influence of Kant was reflected in the work of Fichte (*q.v.*), Schelling (*q.v.*) and Hegel (*q.v.*), who developed a very influential Idealistic philosophy.

(40) Responding to Hegel in the 19th century were Kierkegaard (*q.v.*) who wished to substitute an Existentialism for Hegel's essentialism and Marx (*q.v.*) whose wish concerned substituting a Dialectical Materialism for Hegel's Dialectical Idealism. Other Continental 19th-century philosophers of note include Schopenhauer (*q.v.*), Comte (*q.v.*), and Nietzsche (*q.v.*). The movement of neo-Kantianism (*q.v.*) began near the middle of the century and continued into the 20th century.

(41) English followers of Hegel include F.H. Bradley and T.H. Green (*q.v.*). A new kind of analytic philosophy began with G.E. Moore (*q.v.*). Bertrand Russell (*q.v.*) who in the 20th century continued the traditions of British empiricism, made significant contributions to logic. His collaborator was A.N. Whitehead (*q.v.*). Russell's student, Wittgenstein (*q.v.*), helped to turn British philosophy in a linguistic direction.

(42) The contribution of North American philosophy has been Pragmatism. The principal figures have been C.S. Peirce (*q.v.*), William James (*q.v.*), John Dewey (*q.v.*), and C.I. Lewis (*q.v.*). A contemporary logician, Quine (*q.v.*), likewise claims to be a Pragmatist. Other names, not Pragmatists, requiring mention, are Royce (*q.v.*), Santayana (*q.v.*), and A.N. Whitehead (*q.v.*) whose last years were spent at Harvard. The movements of New Realism (*q.v.*) and Critical Realism (*q.v.*) emphasized the Realist tradition in philosophy.

(43) On the Continent, Husserl (*q.v.*) initiated the phenomenological movement (*q.v.* Phenomenology). The movement continues in its own right, while having given rise to other philosophies: the Existentialism (*q.v.*) of Heidegger (*q.v.*) and Sartre (*q.v.*), and the revised Phenomenology of Merleau-Ponty (*q.v.*).

(44) The Vienna Circle of Logical Positivism (*q.v.*) initiated a philosophical reform, seeking to dispense with metaphysics. As a result of the second World War many of its leaders came to the United States. Among those who did so were Carnap (*q.v.*), Feigl (*q.v.*), and Bergmann (*q.v.*).

(45) During somewhat more than half of the 20th century, the West has been divided between Anglo-American and Continental philosophy, the former analytic, the latter in some sense transcendental. Analytic philosophy has turned on the clarification of specific, limited problems, often derived from, or analyzed in terms of, epistemology or symbolic logic; hence, meroscopic (*q.v.* McKeon 4). Continental philosophy has been holoscopic and thematic: *q.v.* Structuralism, Hermeneutics, the Frankfurt School, and Deconstruction. Anglo-American philosophy has been less thematic, although consider Ordinary Language (*q.v.*) philosophy and Identity Theory (*q.v.*). A range of analytic thought may be sampled in Chisholm (*q.v.*), Wilfrid Sellars (*q.v.*), Davidson (*q.v.*), Dennett (*q.v.*), Kripke (*q.v.*), Putnam (*q.v.*), David Lewis (*q.v.*), Searle (*q.v.*), Rescher (*q.v.*), and Van Fraassen (*q.v.*). Near the end of the century attempts to cross the Western divide were being made: from the Continental side Habermas (*q.v.*) and Ricoeur (*q.v.*); from the Anglo-American side, Richard Bernstein and Rorty (*q.v.*).

(46) Latin American philosophy (*q.v.*), treated in its own right, has been

characterized in the past four centuries first by Scholasticism, then by Positivism. The reaction to positivism opened the way to more intuitive and voluntaristic philosophies. At present, existentialist and phenomenological approaches to the world have strength, as does Marxism, with the analytical tradition also represented but less strongly.

C. The History of Non-Western Philosophies.

(47) Only recently recognizing the separation between religion and philosophy so long characteristic of the West, Indian philosophy (*q.v.*) through most of its history has proceeded principally in terms of commentaries on the *Vedas* (*q.v.*). The schools of philosophy, reflecting many of the same distinctions developed in the West—from Materialism (*q.v.* 1) to Idealism—divide according to whether they recognize the authority of the Scriptures. In recent years, of course, Indian philosophies have combined their own traditions with those of Western philosophy.

(48) Chinese philosophy (*q.v.*) presents a variety of options beginning with Confucianism (*q.v.*), Taoism (*q.v.*), Moism (*q.v.*), the Chinese Logicians (*q.v.*), Legalism (*q.v.*), the Yin Yang School (*q.v.* Yin and Yang 2), and Chinese Buddhism (*q.v.* Chinese Philosophy 6). Through time these alternatives interacted with interesting results. Of particular interest has been neo-Confucianism (*q.v.* Chinese Philosophy 7) with a history extending from the 8th century A.D. to the present.

(49) Japanese philosophy has received its long-term influence from China, accepting both Confucian and Buddhist developments. Beginning in 1868, the influence of Western modes of thought has steadily grown (*q.v.* Japanese Religion and Philosophy).

D. The Fields of Philosophy. The areas of philosophy depend both on processes of historical evolution and on the principles of division adopted by philosophers; these factors also have led to agreement on the dividing lines between philosophy and other disciplines.

(50) Aristotle (*q.v.* 1) included among the areas of philosophy: logic, ethics, aesthetics, psychology, political philosophy, physics, and metaphysics. His division of the fields of learning, for him largely a division of the parts of philoso-

phy, was triune: the theoretical sciences, the practical sciences, and the productive sciences.

(51) The Stoics (*q.v.* Stoicism) divided philosophy into logic, physics, and ethics.

(52) Wolff (*q.v.* 1) considered the areas of philosophy to be logic, first philosophy, ontology, theology, cosmology, rational psychology, ethics, and theory of knowledge. He divided these disciplines into theoretical, practical, and criteriological parts.

(53) The fields of philosophy now commonly recognized include most of the above, except that physics and psychology have gained their own charters, political philosophy is often regarded as an area of political science whose philosophical counterpart now tends to be called social philosophy, and theology has been replaced by philosophy of religion. In addition, the responsibility of philosophy to other disciplines has been increasingly recognized through the development of interdisciplinary "philosophy of" studies and courses. The most fully developed of these is Philosophy of Science (*q.v.*), increasingly involving a distinction between Philosophy of the Natural Sciences and Philosophy of the Social Sciences; Philosophy of History (*q.v.* History C.); Philosophy of Religion (*q.v.* Religion C.); Philosophy of Law (*q.v.* Law C.); and Philosophy of Education (*q.v.*).

PHILOSOPHY, AS WEAPON OF REVOLUTION.
Q.v. Althusser (5).

PHILOSOPHY OF BIOLOGY.
Q.v. Biology (B.).

PHILOSOPHY OF EDUCATION.
Q.v. Education, Philosophy of.

PHILOSOPHY OF HISTORY.
Q.v. History (C.).

PHILOSOPHY OF LAW.
Q.v. Law (C.).

PHILOSOPHY OF RELIGION.
Q.v. Religion (C.).

PHILOSOPHY OF SCIENCE.
A discipline which attempts to relate philosophy to the fields of scientific inquiry. Depending upon the orientation

of the philosopher and the area of science, the goal of philosophy of science is to discover the nature of science, or the nature of scientific method, or the logic of science, or to explore the interfaces of the fields of science, or to axiomatize the sciences—*e.g.*, mathematics, physics—which are axiomatizable. In one sense the philosophy of science extends back to the origins of Western philosophy. From the origin of philosophy until the period of the Sophists the emphasis of philosophy was on scientific knowledge. Plato and Aristotle devoted attention to science and its methods. But the development of Philosophy of Science as a discipline required a prior development of the sciences. Hence, it is more appropriate to regard philosophy of science as beginning with the remarkable development of the sciences in the modern period.

A. The first contrast, pitting against each other two approaches to philosophy of science, is between rationalistic and inductivistic attitudes toward science. Already present in the differing approaches of Plato and Aristotle, the contrast becomes extreme in the late 16th and 17th centuries.

(1) The Lord Chancellor of induction was Francis Bacon (*q.v.* 3–4) who, responding to a mistaken interpretation of Aristotle as an *a priori* rationalist, held that a careful, inductive sifting of what is observable is sufficient to lay bare the causes of things.

(2) The rationalistic philosophy of science is implicit in the approach to knowledge of the Continental rationalists. Indeed, the hypothetico-deductive method, where hypotheses are regarded as premises for the deduction of the phenomenon under investigation may be traced to the Cartesian Method (*q.v.* Descartes 10), and to Leibniz (*q.v.* 11–13). Both expressed great reservations concerning observation, and the latter with his "universal characteristic" and "universal mathematics" held that finally (at least from God's standpoint) all truths are truths of reason. For both, deduction is much more important than induction in the attainment of truth.

(3) Locke (*q.v.* 6–8) and Hume (*q.v.* 3), while not concentrating specifically on science, carried the analysis of percep-

tion to the point where the phenomena of awareness separate off from the world, leading to the next step in philosophy of science.

(4) This step was taken by Kant (*q.v.* 1–4) who found a way of maintaining the rationalistic heritage which came to him from Leibniz, while recognizing the achievements of the British empiricists. The result restricted science to exploring the order of phenomena.

(5) The contrast of rationalistic and inductivistic philosophies of science is to be seen in two 19th-century English philosophers who specialized in the study of induction, John Stuart Mill (*q.v.* 2–5) and William Whewell (*q.v.* 1). Mill follows the inductivist tradition from Bacon through Hume, even using a version of Bacon's Table of Comparative Instances for the discovery of causal connections. Whewell, on the other hand, influenced by Kant, interpreted induction as "colligation," *i.e.*, relating a phenomenon to an hypothesis in such a way that the former can be deduced from the latter. He thus defends the hypothetico-deductive method.

(6) The English philosopher, W.S. Jevons (*q.v.* 3), likewise held to the hypothetico-deductive method, regarding induction as nothing more than the inverse process of deduction.

B. A third element in the Philosophy of Science, adding to the alternatives of rationalism and empiricism, is the growth of the movement of Conventionalism (*q.v.*). It is perhaps accurate enough to trace this development from its occurrence in the movement of neo-Kantianism.

(7) Helmholtz (*q.v.*), neo-Kantian physicist and physiologist, worked in terms of the ordering of phenomena, while adding flexibility to the Kantian framework.

(8) His student Hertz (*q.v.*) eliminated non-empirical concepts from the primitives of scientific theory.

(9) Mach (*q.v.*), influenced by Helmholtz, Kant, and the British Empiricists, regarded all scientific concepts as summaries of sense-experience, designed to help us predict future experience.

(10) Poincaré (*q.v.* 2) is best known for the Conventionalist thesis that there are numerous conventionalist elements true by definition not only in mathematics but also in the sciences. The principles of

science are conventional, if the laws are not.

(11) Duhem (*q.v.* 1) continues in the same vein, holding the object of science to be a discovery of the structure of relations holding between appearances.

(12) Pearson (*q.v.*) continued Mach's emphasis on sense-experience, holding that science is descriptive rather than explanatory.

(13) Influenced by Mach and Poincaré, N. R. Campbell (*q.v.*) worked out a highly interesting analysis of scientific theory involving empirical generalizations, along with the elements of a dictionary, an hypothesis, and a basic analogy.

C. A fourth element which has had a minor but continuing influence in Philosophy of Science has been Pragmatism.

(14) Initiated by C.S. Peirce (*q.v.* 1–2, 8), the pragmatic maxim had as its goal the elimination of meaningless statements from philosophy. This reform was pushed much more intensively by the logical positivists (*q.v.* F. below) in their verificationist theory of meaning (*q.v.* Verifiability Criterion). Peirce's emphasis on Abduction (*q.v.*), regarding hypothesis-formation as a process neither inductive nor deductive, was to have influence in a later period of time.

(15) James (*q.v.* 6) and Dewey (*q.v.* 1, 2) continued this emphasis although its relevance for philosophy of science was for a long time quite indirect.

D. (16) An approach to Philosophy of Science which created no school is that of Whitehead (*q.v.* 3) who looked upon the task of this discipline as deducing scientific concepts from the simplest elements of our perceptual knowledge.

E. A fifth element in the developing alternatives making up contemporary Philosophy of Science is the philosophy of logical atomism.

(17) Wittgenstein (*q.v.* 1–4) in his *Tractatus* held that logical truths are tautologies, complex propositions are truth functions of elementary propositions, and that the latter are pictures of reality. These emphases influenced the development of the Vienna Circle (*q.v.*).

(18) Russell (*q.v.* 8) made this the basis of his doctrine of Logical Atomism. The world, he held, consists of atomic facts which can be represented by elementary propositions.

F. Logical Positivism appeared out of the confluence of the Wittgenstein-Russell doctrine and the emphasis on sense-experience of Ernst Mach.

(19) Carnap (*q.v.* 2) made the attempt in his *Aufbau* to construct the world from the concepts of logic on the basis of private experience. The attempt was given up, and Carnap moved in a direction which involved the application of symbolic logic to the problems and methods of the sciences.

(20) Schlick (*q.v.* 1), although considered the founder of logical positivism, was influenced by Mach, Helmholtz, and Poincaré, but the decisive influence of his mature philosophy came from Wittgenstein and Carnap. Nonetheless, Schlick may be credited with shaping the positivistic understanding of the task of philosophy as exploration of the structure of science, and elimination of the obscurity of traditional philosophical language.

(21) Neurath (*q.v.*) helped develop Carnap's second stage of Physicalism (*q.v.* Carnap 3), applying the doctrine especially to sociology. He also worked directly on the project of establishing a unified science.

(22) Also in the original group were Philipp Frank (*q.v.*) and Feigl (*q.v.*). The latter applied the tenets of positivism to psychology. Bergmann (*q.v.*), a second-generation positivist, made the initial application of positivism to psychology, although his interests have now shifted to some extent. Grünbaum (*q.v.* 3) has assumed that mantle with respect to Freudian psychoanalysis.

(23) Reichenbach (*q.v.* 1), a member of the Berlin group of logical positivists, held a much more open view of the verification theory than did his colleagues in Vienna. He related this issue—as he did many others—to probability theory.

(24) Tarski (*q.v.*), a member of the Warsaw group of positivists, developed the analysis of meta-languages and meta-mathematics.

G. The standpoint of Operationalism (*q.v.*), bearing resemblance both to Pragmatism and Positivism, has been welcomed by a number of scientists.

(25) Introduced by the American physicist, P.W. Bridgman (*q.v.*). the position construes meanings or definitions in

terms of operations. Anatol Rapoport titled his 1953 work *Operational Philosophy*. Dingler (*q.v.*) and Skinner (*q.v.* 1) also produced versions of operationalism.

H. (26) Opposing the verificationist theory or the verifiability criterion of meaning, Popper (*q.v.* 1) has offered "falsifiability" as a more apt criterion of meaning than "verifiability."

I. Out of these influences the present situation in philosophy of science may be educed.

(27) Ayer (*q.v.* 3–5) has served as expositor of logical positivism, and defender of the verifiability criterion of meaning. Hempel (*q.v.* 1) continues the rationalistic hypothetico-deductive approach to philosophy of science. Influenced by Reichenbach, Schlick, and Carnap, his "covering law model" of scientific explanation regards induction as assimilable to the same framework as deduction.

(28) A considerable number of contemporary philosophers of science have blended pragmatism with some other tradition in philosophy of science. Charles Morris (*q.v.* 1–2) combined the pragmatism of Peirce and G.H. Mead with logical positivism, gaining a development of semiotic (*q.v.*) in the bargain. Nagel (*q.v.* 1) combined the instrumentalism of Dewey with an independent interest in philosophy of science to produce an analysis of the structure of science pragmatic in tone. Quine (*q.v.* 7) combined an interest in Russell and the *Principia* of Whitehead and Russell with a more general interest in the conceptual scheme of science leading to a pragmatic philosophy of science. N.R. Hanson combined the approach of Russell with the pragmatism of Peirce, supporting, in his *Patterns of Discovery* and elsewhere, a position opposing the hypothetico-deductive method as having the final word. In the manner of Peirce he held retroduction to be an integral method. Michael Scriven, with a background that includes the influence of logical positivism via Feigl, and a period of collaboration with Hanson, opposes the covering law model, arguing for an asymmetry of prediction and retroduction.

(29) The scientific realism of Wilfrid Sellars (*q.v.*) has its origin in Feigl and Bergmann.

(30) Finally, a number of contemporary philosophers of science combine an evaluation of positivism with an appreciation of Popper. Mario Bunge (*Myth of Simplicity*, 1963), who cautions us against the myth of simplicity, argues for metascience—a discipline interested in axiomatizing the foundations of the mature scientific disciplines. Paul K. Feyerabend (*Against Method*, 1975; *Killing Time*, 1995) who sustains a number of relations to logical positivism, argues for a maximization of novelty in theory production and a minimum of uniformity.

Also *q.v.* Science.

PHLOGISTON THEORY.
An 18th-century explanation of combustion which held that every combustible substance contained phlogiston, an inflammable material substance. Phlogiston was thought to be consumed in the process of combustion, leaving the original substance behind. Propounded by J.J. Becher and G.E. Stahl, the theory remained viable for a century until Lavoisier produced his counter theory involving oxygen. Stahl, who defended the theory with great vigor, was influenced in the direction of animism and vitalism by J.B. Van Helmont (*q.v.*).

PHONOCENTRISM.
Q.v. Derrida (2).

PHRASTIC.
Greek term meaning to point out or indicate. *Q.v.* Hare (2).

PHRONESIS.
Greek term meaning "practical wisdom." *Q.v.* Aristotle (11).

PHYLACTERIES.
From the Greek *phylakteria* ("amulet"). "Frontlets" for the forehead and left arm, complementing the mezuzah (*q.v.*), commanded by Scripture (*Deut.* 6:4–9; 11:13–21; and *Ex.* 13:1–10; 11–16); worn by the Orthodox adult male Jews in weekday morning worship.

PHYSICALISM.
A doctrine of the Vienna Circle of Logical Positivists (*q.v.*) requiring the protocol sentences of any hypothesis to be expressed in a physicalistic language. *Q.v.* Otto Neurath; Carnap (3).

PHYSICOPHYSICAL, THE.
  Q.v. Ducasse (2).

PHYSICO-THEOLOGICAL ARGUMENT.
  Kant's (*q.v.* 5b) teleological argument
for the existence of God.

PHYSIOCRATS.
  An 18th-century French school of economics, headed by François Quesnay
(1694–1774). They regarded land as the
central factor in economics and the principal source of wealth; they also held to
the doctrine of *laissez-faire*, or the non-
interference of government in economic
matters.

PIAGET, JEAN. 1896–1980.
  Swiss psychologist. Born in Neuchatel.
Educated at Neuchatel, Zurich, and the
Sorbonne.
  Selected writings: *Language and Thought
of the Child* (T), 1923; *Judgment and Rea-
soning in the Child* (T), 1924; *The Child's
Conception of the World* (T), 1926; *The
Child's Conception of Physical Causality* (T),
1927; *The Child's Conception of Time*
(T), 1927; *The Moral Judgment of the Child*
(T), 1932; *The Child's Conception of Number*
(T), 1941; *The Child's Conception of Move-
ment and Speed* (T), 1946; *The Child's Con-
ception of Space* (T), 1948; *Treatise on Logic*,
1949; *Introduction to Genetic Epistemology*,
3 vols., 1950; *The Genesis of Elementary
Logical Structures*, 1959; *Epistemology,
Mathematics and Psychology* (with E. W.
Beth), 1961; *The Mechanisms of Perception*
(T), 1961; *Six Psychological Studies*, 1964;
Insights and Illusions of Philosophy (T), 1965;
Biology and Knowledge (T), 1967; *On the
Development of Memory and Identity* (E),
1967; *Treatise on Experimental Psychology*
(with P. Frasse) (T), 1967; *Genetic Epistemology* (T), 1968; *Structuralism* (T), 1968;
*The Development of Thought: Equilibration
of Cognitive Structures* (T), 1975.
  (1) Developing an approach to the
analysis of concepts termed "genetic epistemology," Piaget has traced the growth
of concepts from random activity on the
part of the child. He has treated the genesis of the concepts of shape, size, space,
time, causality, chance, velocity, the origin of mathematical concepts in logic, and
the origin of the concepts of logic in classification and relational skills.
  (2) Structures and functions interrelate

in his view, although development requires adaptation and organization (structural change), achieving various kinds of
equilibrium (equilibration) along the way,
both within the organism and in relation
to the world.

PICO DELLA MIRANDOLA. 1463–1494.
  Italian philosopher. Born in Mirandola.
Studied at Bologna, Ferrara, and Padua.
Lived principally in Florence, Paris, and
Rome. After 1488, he settled in the vicinity of Florence, and taught in the
Florentine Academy (*q.v.* Platonism 8).
He came into public view in 1486 with
his invitation to the intellectual world to
attend his defence of 900 theses supporting the position of the unity of knowledge, and the validity of a wide range
of sources from Greek philosophy, mystery religions, the Cabala (*q.v.*), and Zoroastrianism, to Christian scripture and
tradition. When the disputation was prohibited by the Church, Pico wrote a defence of his theses, whereupon all 900
were condemned. Between this occurrence and his being allowed to settle in
Florence, a number of dramatic events
intervened including an ineffective submission to the Church, flight to France,
imprisonment, and release by the French
king. Along with Ficino (*q.v.*), Pico was
a leading Italian Renaissance humanist.
  Principal writings: *The 900 Theses*, 1486;
Apology, 1487; *Heptaplus*, 1489; *On Being
and Unity*, 1491; *Disputations Against Astrology*, 1496; *Oration on the Dignity of Man*
(T), 1496.
  (1) Pico's principal contribution to
Western thought was the attitude of
openness to all aspects of human culture
exemplified in his 900 theses. Although
formally syncretistic, he was pushing
toward a unified perspective recognizing the legitimate insights from the wide
range of sources mentioned above. This
was the Platonic notion that there is a
universal truth implicit in the diversity
of traditions.
  (2) At the same time he seems to have
regarded religion as superior to philosophy although compatible with it. In terms
of relating one to the universal truth,
religion provides the fulfillment for which
philosophy provides the preparation.
  (3) Understanding man's essential attribute to be the power of self-determination,

Pico argued that man possesses a radical freedom of choice. His power is so unique that it gives him a privileged role in the universe, linking the intelligible and physical worlds and standing as a microcosm of the macrocosm.

(4) It is on the basis of the elevated position of man that Pico decided astrology cannot be true. The stars cannot control human destiny because a lower being cannot control a being of higher order.

(5) In formal terms Pico, holding to the coextensivity of "being" and "unity," distinguished between "being in itself" which he identified with God, and "participated being" which he identified with the world. As part of his universal truth he claimed that Plato and Aristotle shared this view.

PIECEMEAL SOCIAL ENGINEERING.
Q.v. Popper (3).

PIETISM.
A 17th-and 18th-century devotional movement which arose within the Lutheran Church. Initiated by Philipp J. Spener (*q.v.*), this movement sought a participative relationship among communicants based on deep religious feeling. Spener's book, *Earnest Desires for a Reform of the Evangelical Church*, 1675, was widely accepted. The movement spread rapidly, leading to the founding of the University of Halle, whose theological chairs were filled with Pietists. The 1727 organization of the Moravian Church was a direct outgrowth of Pietism. Kant (*q.v.*) came from a Pietistic family and the influence of the movement can be seen in Schleiermacher's definition of religion (*q.v.* Schleiermacher 1). Eucken (*q.v.*) gave philosophic expression to a number of the themes of Pietism.

PITKIN, W.B.
Q.v. New Realism (1).

PLACE, U.T.
Q.v. Materialism (21); Identity Theory (2).

PLANCK'S CONSTANT.
Q.v. Mechanics (2).

PLANTINGA, ALVIN. 1932– .
American philosopher. Born in Ann Arbor, Michigan. Studied at Calvin College, University of Michigan, and Yale. Has taught at Yale, Wayne State, Calvin College, and Notre Dame.

Principal writings: *The Ontological Argument* (ed.), 1965; *God and Other Minds*, 1967; *God, Freedom, and Evil*, 1974; *The Nature of Necessity*, 1974; *Does God Have a Nature?*, 1980; *Warrant and Proper Function*, 1993.

(1) Although all of his major works are concerned with the idea of God, *The Nature of Necessity* approaches both modal logic and important theological issues (the problem of evil, the ontological argument) through possible worlds semantics. Writing about necessity (*q.v.*) from the vantage point of modal logic, Plantinga distinguishes between *de dicto* necessity which is a property of propositions, and *de re* necessity which is a property of things. While everyone recognizes the presence of possibilities, impossibilities, and necessities in language Plantinga believes that the *de re* necessity of traditional philosophy can be explicated by way of modal logic, utilizing a possible worlds semantics.

(2) While some have held that possible worlds are actual alternative worlds (*q.v.* David Lewis 2), Plantinga holds possible worlds to be at least compossible sets of possibles, as Leibniz (*q.v.* 9) viewed them. They are states of affairs which are maximally possible or complete. Only one complete state of affairs is actual; that is the possible world which "obtains," in which we exist. The others are the ways the world "could have been." Only logical impossibilities are ruled out; and impossibility "in the broadly logical sense" is used to establish what belongs to a compossible set; yet he also says that while only one possible world has actuality, the others have existence.

(3) An impossible individual or predicate is one which exists in no possible world; an actual individual or predicate is one which exists in this world; a possible individual or predicate exists in at least one possible world (and so is "possible" in every possible world); a necessary individual or predicate exists in every possible world.

(4) In these terms he develops something like an Aristotelian essentialism, accounting for propositions, individuals, properties, essences, and accidents. A

proposition is true in the actual world, if true, and true in a given possible world *W*, if it would have been true had *W* been actual. An individual or property *x* exists in a given possible world *W* if it is impossible that *W* obtain and that *x* fail to exist. Accidents are properties individuals have in some possible worlds, while in others they have the complements to those properties. Essential properties are the properties an object *O* has in all the possible worlds in which it exists; and a given property is an essence of an object if *O* has that property essentially, and in no possible world does an object distinct from *O* have that property.

(5) Applying the system to certain religious questions he treats the problem of theodicy (*q.v.*): how is the presence of evil to be reconciled with divine omnipotence and the necessity that God choose the best of all possible worlds? His solution is to grant significant freedom to human beings, while supposing "transworld depravity" in some of them.

(6) As for Anselm's ontological argument (*q.v.*) he accepts the Hartshorne (*q.v.* 4) and Malcom version of the argument while suggesting this version shows God to be "maximally great" in some possible world, but not in the actual world. His corrective is to urge that "maximal greatness" entails "maximal excellence" (omniscience, omnipotence, moral perfection). These are essential properties, world-indexed, and necessarily true of God. Therefore, God has maximal excellence in every world.

PLASTIC NATURES.
Q.v. Cudworth (3).

PLATO. 428–348 B.C.
Greek philosopher. Born in Athens. Studied under Socrates. Born of a distinguished Athenian family, he early intended to follow a political career, but the trial and death of Socrates turned him toward philosophy. After Socrates' death Plato left Athens, spending some time in travel, including a visit to his friend, Dion of Syracuse, brother-in-law of the tyrant, Dionysius. According to the sources, he intended to use Syracuse as a pilot project for an experiment leading toward his perfect state. There is a legend that this visit ended in his being sold into slav-

ery, and rescued by a friend. In any case, on his return to Athens in 388 he founded his famous Academy, the first true university offering a wide range of studies including all of the then extant sciences. In 367, upon the death of Dionysius I, Dion invited Plato back to supervise the education of Dionysius II. Plato made a brief visit which succeeded at least in establishing a course of royal instruction in mathematics and philosophy. In 361 he visited Syracuse a third time, apparently hoping to gain approval for a federation of Greek city states against Carthage; but this trip, too, ended in failure. He returned to Athens, disappointed by his ventures in practical politics, continuing to spread the influence of the Academy until his death.

Principal writings: *Apology; Crito; Euthyphro; Ion; Protagoras; Gorgias; Meno; Cratylus; Phaedo; Republic; Symposium; Parmenides; Sophist; Theaetetus; Phaedrus; Politicus; Philebus; Timaeus; Critias;* and *Laws.*

Plato wrote dialogues for the public and lectures for his classes at the Academy. The works mentioned above are his dialogues; none of his lectures has survived (the exact opposite is true with respect to Aristotle). The dialogues are works of art, rich in figurative expression. Indeed, the mixture of metaphor and analysis has led some to find metaphor a working part of his method, both illustrating the analysis and serving as a place-marker for an analysis which for the present eludes the thinker. In both cases he regards metaphor and myth as particularly appropriate to the changing nature of the world of becoming, in contrast to the conceptual nature of the eternal world. There is a good deal of disagreement concerning (a) how we are to separate the work of Plato from that of Socrates, since Socrates appears as protagonist in most of Plato's dialogues; (b) whether Plato had a system of philosophy; and if so what is its nature.

It is our conviction that Plato philosophized first of all under the influence of Socrates, setting down as accurately as possible Socrates' encounters with his colleagues, while in later dialogues he developed the implications of Socratic thought. This takes us through the dialogue called the *Republic*, Then there are dialogues which call in question the positions worked out in this first period. In one such dialogue, the *Parmenides,* Socrates loses the contest of ideas and is led about by the older philosopher. Finally there are dialogues where Socrates is no longer the protagonist. In two of these dialogues, the *Timaeus* and the *Laws,* it seems evident that Plato is attempting to achieve a synthesis of the ideas of his Socratic period, and the new insights which came to him in his period of Socratic criticism. It is here that we should look for the clues to his most mature thought.

We shall attempt to look at his philosophy from this perspective. When we adopt this scheme the major dialogues group themselves in the following pattern: (A) The Socratic Period—(1) Socratic dialogues—*Apology, Crito, Euthyphro, Ion, Protagoras,* and possibly Book I of the *Republic.* (2) Socratically based dialogues: *Gorgias, Meno, Cratylus, Phaedo, Republic,* and *Symposium.* (B) Period of transition and criticism—*Parmenides, Sophist, Theaetetus, Phaedrus, Politicus, Philebus.* (C) Final synthesis—*Timaeus, Critias,* and *Laws.*

The basic ideas making up Plato's thought can be fitted to these three periods.

A. At some point in this period the transition between the thought of Socrates and Plato is to be made; and scholars disagree over the location of this point. The problem, however, does not concern us directly since it is Plato's thought we wish to describe. Beginning with the Socratic emphasis on getting one's ideas straight, the Platonic treatment of ideas emerged.

(1) Plato's Doctrine of Ideas found pictorial expression in his myth of the cave (*Rep.,* Bk. VII), where it is clear that man's mental life begins with a flood of images. Plato has it that all mankind initially imprisoned in the cave, manacled by ignorance, able to see only the shadows of objects cast on the wall of the cave. The shadows are cast by individual objects being moved before a fire. The real world is outside the cave, containing the patterns from which the objects were copied, and the principle of the good, whose analogue is the light of the sun. It is man's task to free himself from his shackles and move toward and into this upper world. The means of freedom lies in the power of man's under-

standing. How man is to move toward the upper world by developing his understanding can be made clear, perhaps, by means of the line of truth, Plato's famous twice-divided line. A diagrammatic representation would present this appearance: The vertical line is the line of truth. Its basic division is between opinion and knowledge. Its second division is the division of its two segments. Since we begin at the bottom of the line and work up, our start is in opinion (*doxa*); although our goal is knowledge (*episteme*). Because of a lack of clarity in Plato's discussion many aspects of the twice-divided line remain controversial. But a number of points are clear. The items on the two sides of the line are correlates of each other, left and right-hand sides standing for mental states and their ontological "objects" respectively. The shift in inner process as we approach truth is from unsupported imagination through partially warranted opinion, and supported individual ideas to Plato's process of dialectic moving surely among the relations of ideas with the help of first principles. The shift in "object" is from image to individual things to mathematical and other semi-abstract entities to universal forms. The line presents Plato's belief that the universal and abstract has more reality than the individual concrete thing. One point lacking in clarity concerns the emphasis on mathematical entities in the third segment of the line. Plato was heavily influenced by the Pythagoreans, was sensitive to the value of mathematics, and made the study of mathematics a central feature of his educational system. It might be argued that for Plato the path to truth in every area is through mathematics. On the other hand, although he stresses the importance of number elsewhere, in none of his other discussions of the movement up from the perceptual world to ultimate reality is number given such an important role. This convinces me that we should think of the third level more as a logical than a mathematical process, taking hypothesis—in his sense of a supported position—as our key meaning.

The movement upward is a movement toward theory. The corresponding downward movement is the application of theory to activity, and this is art in the

	Reasoning About First Principles	Universal Forms
Knowledge	Logical & Mathematical Processes; or Hypotheses	Mathematical (& other (?) Semi-Abstract Entities)
	Perceptual Belief (also Partially warranted Belief)	Individual Objects (Images of Universal Forms)
Opinion	Imagination	Images of Appearance

very general sense of controlled and purposive making and doing. The fine arts represent but a small portion of this category. And the sense of beauty is in the *Symposium* given a treatment parallel to that of the twice-divided line. The direction of movement, empowered by *eros*, is from beautiful appearances and individual objects to the beauty in more abstract unities such as constitutions, and laws, (and equations?); this increasing abstractness leads us at last to an intuition of beauty itself, eternal, never diminishing, Absolute. And if we combine what Plato says of the good in the *Republic* with what he says elsewhere—in such dialogues as the *Philebus*—we can make out a similar progression with respect to the good. In the place of images we shall have pleasures, and on the higher levels, leading to the final one, we shall have the categories of moderate satisfaction of appetites, intellectual pleasures, measure, proportion, completeness, and seasonableness, while over these may be discerned that Absolute Good which Plato terms "the author of all things beautiful and right" and the "source of reason and truth in the intellectual world." The discussion of the artist, *Republic*, Book X, provides an additional instance of the same general type of ascent. There is on the lowest level the image of the bed contributed by the artist. But this is really an image of an image, since the bed constructed by the carpenter is itself as individual object, the image of a universal form.

Now if we add to this the emphasis on the One in the *Parmenides*, it is probably correct to hold that the Absolutes of Truth, Beauty, Good, and the One interpenetrate, are at last identical, and stand in a special relation, perhaps in some sense in a generating relation, to the archetypes of individual aspects of the sensible world.

Certain it is that the universal forms "participate" in their imaginal counterparts in the world. Certain it is that the human mind is able to "participate" in the forms. So intimate did Plato find this connection that he propounded, mythically, a doctrine of recollection—the Greek word is *anamnesis*—holding that we had known these universal forms and truths in eternity, but the shock of birth had driven them from conscious awareness. Still, in a vague sort of manner we know everything, and experience enables us to recall this knowledge with some precision. It is in this aspect of his thought that Plato defends the innateness of our ideas and, indeed, transmigration or metempsychosis. Elsewhere, as in the *Theaetetus*, where he defines knowledge as justified, true belief, his view is more thoroughly empirical; but everywhere the stress is on the universal as an entity in its own right, and not on the elusive, partly illusive, and flux-burdened particular.

(2) The emphasis on ideas in the Socratic period gains as its counterpart a world of change formed after the patterns of universal forms and yet sufficiently intractable to the forms that none of the absolutes can be fully exemplified in the world. One knows, for example, the definition of a perfect circle, and yet perfect circularity can never be exactly exemplified in things.

(3) The partial irrationality of things in turn causes Plato to think of change as a quality foreign to rationality so that, as he says, "the soul is dizzy when it touches change." This emphasis on changelessness is also reflected in Plato's claim that the soul is non-composite, hence simple. And as a simple entity it cannot be destroyed, and is therefore immortal. This contrast is the source of Plato's famous dualism of mind and body; the problem of reconciling opposites is here considerable. This picture, to be sure, must be squared with the tripartite nature of the soul, which Plato also presented. The famous figure is in the *Phaedrus*, although the doctrine is already present in the *Republic*: the career of the soul is akin to the passage of a chariot with driver, one well-mannered white steed, and one intractable and plunging black steed. The driver is reason, the white steed the spirited part (related to will), and the black steed represents the appetitive element in man—the element of desire with its lawlessness. The task of reason is to control the will and appetites and provide a unity of function among these elements of the soul. The difficulty, of course, is that only the rational element of the soul appears to fit Plato's description of the soul as changeless, yet survival of the soul in any significantly personal sense requires survival of the total personality.

(4) The emphasis on fixity in the soul is a reflection of the changelessness Plato ascribes to God. God is perfect being, and hence incapable of change, since change in what is already perfect could only introduce imperfection. As perfect being God is cause of the good, and of the good only. This would seem to give God an intimate relation to the interpenetrating absolutes of Good, Truth, and Beauty.

(5) The gradation toward universal forms and absolutes shapes the character of Plato's approved social order.

(a) Plato's *Republic* begins with the cheerful social principle that the object of rule is the good of the people; but of course this is a real and objective good, and not to be confused with what the people may wish.

(b) This good is in fact a just social order, and Plato finds justice in that condition of life where every person is doing the work for which he or she is fitted, and so making a maximum contribution to society. And, indeed, Plato conceives of law as a disposition of reason, ordering things according to their natures.

(c) The educational system provides the means of finding the role one should play in society. Each person will fit in one of three main classes: artisans, soldiers, or rulers. Each of the groups goes further in the educational system than the one preceding. The rulers are expected to have mastered all the sciences, and philosophy, and to have demonstrated their administrative ability through fifteen years of practical experience in service of the state. At the age of 50 these wise persons become philosopher kings and rule the society. The specific virtue of the philosopher king is wisdom, of the soldier, courage, of the artisan, temperance; and of the whole state, when each one is doing that for which one is suited, justice. In this way Plato is able to relate to society the four Greek cardinal virtues: wisdom, courage, temperance, and justice.

(d) Women were to be given equal footing with men in the *Republic*; women would, like men, find their appropriate places in the three classes.

(e) Plato makes a provision for communism in his *Republic*. It is not clear if this provision applies to the whole state, or merely to the two upper classes.

(f) The structure of the state developed in the *Republic* is an aristocracy, *i.e.*, rule by the best in the interest of what is best for society. The degenerate forms of society in order are: *timocracy*, where the criterion of selection is honorableness; *oligarchy*, where the criterion is wealth; *democracy*, where the criterion is popularity; and *tyranny*, where the criterion is simply power. Plato discusses how each of these forms is transmuted into the next.

(g) We have already spoken of Plato's view of beauty (*cf.* 1 above), but his view of art in the *Republic*, while consistent with the view of beauty in the *Symposium*, is nonetheless surprising; for while beauty is an eternal form, art is an imitation of an imitation, hence, removed from reality. It turns out, then, that it is not the artist but the intellectual who is capable of appreciating true beauty; and since the product of the artist is inferior, art is subject to control by the intellectual, *i.e.*, censorship by the philosopher-kings.

(h) By the time he wrote the *Republic*, possibly due to his experiences in Syracuse, Plato was doubtful that the system could be implemented; and later, in the *Laws*, Plato provided a more moderate and realistic—if less ideal—social plan.

B. The dialogues of the Socratic period provide that view of the world usually associated with Plato. The period of transition and criticism, and the final synthesis, are little noted; nor does the transition occur by an abrupt break, but rather by a pointing up of difficulties, and an introduction of new emphases.

(6) The *Parmenides* can be taken as signaling the change. In this dialogue, Socrates is unable to defend his Doctrine of Ideas. The problem of the utter difference between time and eternity sets the problem. As creatures of time it seems that we would have no capacity to know the universal forms, nor can we have, then, any connection with the eternal God, or He with us. Furthermore, if it is on the basis of similarity that we posit a universal form—the idea of man because of the similarities among men—then, are we not required to posit a third man to account for the similarities between individual men and the ideal man? And are we not caught in an endless regress of posited forms? But even with these difficulties the *Parmenides* also emphasizes the idea of abstract unity, the importance of the One.

(7) Where the *Republic* and *Phaedo* stressed the unchanging nature of the soul, the emphasis in the *Phaedrus* is exactly reversed. In this dialogue, soul is the principle of self-motion; and we are told that soul is always in motion, and what is always in motion is immortal. The difference now between spirit and matter is not changelessness in contrast with change, but self-motion, the essence of the soul, in contrast with derived motion. The emphasis on self-motion is continued even in the *Laws*, Plato's final dialogue.

(8) The point, then, is that Plato emphasized, at different stages of his development, different categories as ultimate—the fixity of Being, and the mobility of Becoming. In the *Sophist* one finds evidence of a decision that both of these categories must be given equal play: "As children say entreatingly 'Give us both,' so (the philosopher) will include both the movable and immovable in his definition of being and all." While admitting to the categories of Being and Becoming, it is in the *Sophist* where Plato denies the category of nonbeing. He interprets negations not as referring to nonbeing, but as referring to some other being. Thus, negation is interpreted as "othering." It is also in the *Sophist* that Plato gives his definitive answer to the problem of participation: How is it that the forms participate in the formed objects of the world? They do so without losing their unity simply because the ideas are so completely divorced from anything material or spatial.

C. In the final dialogues, a synthesis of all his preceding themes is achieved, and no major emphasis is sacrificed. The absolute ideas remain, and what we have said about the role of Truth, Beauty, Good, and the One (*cf.* 1 above) can still be affirmed; but the context has altered.

(9) In the *Timaeus*, for example, the category of Being is represented by an eternal God in communion with the universal forms. The category of Becoming is represented by the World Soul, a self-moving initiator of change having the world as its internal environment, and interpreted according to organic principles. It is as though the problem of time and eternity in the *Parmenides* were here being met by a dual interpretation of the divine nature, extending to the divine the Platonic tendency to have counterparts in time of what exists in eternity. The famous Platonic definition of time as the moving image of eternity, offered in the *Timaeus* itself, is perhaps the operative principle. And should the addition of a World Soul be insufficient to effect the bridge between time and eternity, Plato also mentions a demiurge with this function; but the demiurge may be reasonably regarded as a mythical elaboration of the cosmology we are describing, referring especially to the power of the basic absolutes in the system. It is in the

Timaeus that the Pythagorean tendencies of Plato come to the fore. He seeks to understand the elements of nature in terms of number and geometric form. In addition to the eteral and temporal forms of the divine, the elements, the basic absolutes and the universal forms, another element in the scheme is the Receptacle, the material principle of creation, essentially the space-time matrix which receives, and is molded by, the forms.

(10) In the *Laws*, additional suggestions are made, concerning both cosmology and social philosophy. Suggesting the likelihood of a supreme being to account for good, and an evil counterpart to account for evil, Plato nonetheless finds a means of bringing together changelessness and motion in God by utilizing the figure of a globe turned on a lathe, its center fixed, its surface in motion. Along the way he provides arguments for God based both on design and on the primacy of self-motion to derived motion.

(11) The social philosophy of the *Laws* is, Plato tells us, a second best alternative.

(a) It will be a polity, directed to the good of all the citizens, and a government in which law is supreme.

(b) Those in positions of rule must be selected by their personal qualifications, and remain subject to the laws of the state.

(c) The wealth of the citizens is to be moderate, and private property is to be respected.

(d) Provision is made for judicial and legislative functions, including legislative assemblies, and a system of ministers, of which the minister of education has chief importance.

(e) The educational program retains many of the features characterizing it in the *Republic*. Music, gymnastics, mathematics, and the sciences retain importance. Women and men are to be educated in much the same way.

(f) Censorship continues in the state, covering art and religion. Atheism and heresy are criminal offenses.

(g) Slavery is accepted, nationalism encouraged, and travel outside the state restricted.

Many of the details seem an ill-fitting conclusion to the greatness of Plato's thought.

D. Inevitably there are points of importance which have not fitted the division of early, middle, and late dialogues. We shall set them forth here at the end.

(12) There is an anticipation in Plato of the association of ideas. In the *Phaedo* (Par. 73–76) Plato gives instances of the principles of contiguity and similarity.

(13) There is a tacit acceptance of the cyclical nature of time. Just as individual life cycles repeat, although not exactly, so are there cycles of time in the rise and fall of human societies. He looks to the past for the Golden Age; the world is now on a downward way. But the assumption is present that such ages have occurred more than once, and that they will occur again.

(14) He distinguishes in the *Republic* between values which are extrinsic and instrumental, those intrinsic and final, and a class in between of values both extrinsic and intrinsic, instrumental and final, a mixed class.

(15) His analyses of truth and falsity in the *Theaetetus* and *Sophist*, stating that a false proposition is one which asserts "the non-existence of things which are and the existence of things which are not," initiated the Correspondence Theory of truth (*q.v.*).

PLATONISM.

If one means by Platonism that set of philosophies shaped by Plato's thought, then a wide variety of philosophies must be included.

(1) For one thing, of course, Plato's Academy (*q.v.*) existed from 385 B.C. to 529 A.D. and however far it may have strayed from Plato's thought, in the direction of other schools, Plato's name was venerated and some measure of his thought retained.

(2) Aristotle (*q.v.* 7), although critical of Plato's theory of ideas, yet incorporated them as the element of form in sensible substance. Thus, in some sense, Plato's philosophy continued in Aristotle's Lyceum (*q.v.*).

(3) The movement of Neoplatonism (*q.v.*) beginning in the 1st century B.C. and continuing into the 1st century A.D., carried on and accentuated the mystical aspects of Plato's thought.

(4) Philo Judaeus (*q.v.*) combined Platonic thought with the Jewish religious

tradition, placing Plato's realm of forms in the divine mind as the pattern of creation. The forms thus began as ideas in the divine mind. By the principle of emanation they became the realm of forms. Philo thus preserved God's autonomy and Plato's system.

(5) St. Augustine (*q.v.* 2) continued the Philonic tradition; on the basis of his own experience he believed Platonism to be a preliminary and necessary step in the acceptance of Christianity.

(6) Islamic philosophy (*q.v.*) continued the traditions of both Platonic and Aristotelian thought, for a long period interpreting both within the framework of Neoplatonism.

(7) In the Middle Ages the Franciscans tended to perpetuate Augustinian and Platonic modes of thought. This emphasis is noticeable in Erigena, Anselm, and Bonaventure among others.

(8) In the Renaissance one must mention not only Nicholas of Cusa (*q.v.*) and Petrarch (*q.v.*) but the Florentine Academy (*q.v.*), seeking to bring Plato's Academy to life in Italy. Pletho (*q.v.*), Ficino (*q.v.*), and Pico Della Mirandola (*q.v.*) played roles in this revival.

(9) In England John Colet, Thomas More (*q.v.*), and the Cambridge Platonists (*q.v.*), including Ralph Cudworth (*q.v.*), Henry More (*q.v.*), Benjamin Whichcote (*q.v.*), and others, were Platonists.

(10) In recent years A.N. Whitehead (*q.v.* 10), who regarded Western philosophy as a series of footnotes to Plato, introduced into his philosophy "eternal objects," which are markedly similar to Platonic ideas.

PLATO'S ACADEMY. c. 385 B.C.–529 A.D.

The school founded by Plato in Athens. Named from the gardens in which the school was located, a public place dedicated to the Greek hero, Academus. The school specialized in the study of mathematics, music, astronomy, and dialectic. The history of the school may be divided into four parts, although some scholars prefer a tripartite division: the Ancient or First Academy; the Middle or Second Academy; the New or Third Academy; and the Very New or Fourth Academy. In the last stage, that of the Fourth Academy, the Academy is some-

times called the School of Athens (*q.v.*) and is part of the Neoplatonic movement (*q.v.*).

(1) The First Academy reflected a pronounced Pythagorean influence, often identifying the ideas with numbers. The principal figures are Speusippus (*q.v.*), Xenocrates (*q.v.*), Heraclides of Pontus (*q.v.*), Polemon (*q.v.*), Crates (*q.v.* 1), and Crantor (*q.v.*).

(2) The Second Academy continued the stress on epistemology which underlay the work of the school generally, turning the position of the school toward a moderate skepticism. Arcesilas (*q.v.*) is the principal figure.

(3) The Third Academy was somewhat more skeptical than the Second, developing an interest in probability theory. The principal figures are Carneades (*q.v.*) and Clitomachus (*q.v.*).

(4) The Fourth Academy was characterized by eclecticism and Neoplatonism. Among its members are Philo of Larissa (*q.v.*), Antiochus of Ascalon (*q.v.*), Gaius (*q.v.*), Eudorus of Alexandria (*q.v.*), Plutarch of Alexandria, Theon of Smyrna (*q.v.*), Gaius (*q.v.*), Albinus (*q.v.*), Nicostratus (*q.v.*), Atticus (*q.v.*), Celsus (*q.v.*), Maximus of Tyre (*q.v.*), and Severus (*q.v.*).

PLAY.

An activity standing in contrast with work and serious endeavor.

(1) In Hindu philosophy the motive of Brahman in creating a succession of worlds is said to be *lila* ("play" or "sport") (*q.v.* Ramanuja 5). Ramanuja also compares Brahman's motive in creation with the enthusiasm of a monarch, competing in sport with no other objective than amusement.

(2) In the West the poet and philosopher, Friedrich Schiller (*q.v.* 1), held play to be the impulse behind both aesthetic activity, and the idea of freedom.

(3) Huizinga (*q.v.*) found play to be the creative element not only in art but in all of culture.

(4) In Derrida (*q.v.* 1 and 5, 7, 8, 10) the free play of signifiers, and the play of the trace, lead to the play of otherness (*q.v.* Derrida 8), and to playful desire.

(5) Rorty (*q.v.* 6) believes that culture should now celebrate not truth, but play and metaphor.

PLEASURE.

From the Greek *hedone* ("delight, enjoyment"). The doctrine that pleasure is the end of life, or that the pursuit of pleasure is built into human nature, is called Hedonism (*q.v.*). Pleasure has often been advanced as the final human value (*q.v.* 2), and pain the final disvalue, that we seek the one and shun the other. Aristotle (*q.v.* 11) regarded pleasure not as the end of activity, but as a concomitant of successful functioning. Spinoza looked upon pleasure as the feeling we have on passing from a lesser to a greater perfection. Freud (*q.v.* 7) held that humans do and should operate on a "pleasure principle."

PLEKHANOV, GEORGE V. 1856–1918.

Russian Marxist philosopher. Born in Lijseck. An early collaborator of Lenin whom he influenced philosophically. An ideological separation divided the two men in 1903, when Plekhanov joined the Mensheviks; the final break occurred in World War I when Plekhanov urged his followers to support the Western allies. Although his standing in the Soviet Union has fluctuated widely through the years, his influence on Soviet philosophy has been significant.

Principal writings: *Anarchism and Socialism* (T), 1894; *In Defense of Materialism* (T), 1895; *The Materialist Conception of History* (T), 1897; *Fundamental Problems of Marxism* (T), 1908.

(1) While stressing the importance of dialectical materialism, Plekhanov found it necessary to approach the problem of matter in phenomenological terms, *i.e.*, as the cause of our sensations. This "Humean" approach brought down upon his head the criticism of Lenin and countless other Soviet philosophers.

(2) Through his studies in social history, he found an almost total dependence of the cultural product of a nation on its economic substructure. He taught, however, that with the application of reason this need not be the case.

(3) Departing from the simple realism of Marxist thought (*q.v.* Lenin 2), Plekhanov adopted a hieroglyphic theory of sensations. In this view our sensations do not reproduce reality, but rather symbolize it. This view, too, was attacked by Lenin and others, and Plekhanov was dubbed an idealist rather than a materialist.

(4) In the area of aesthetics, he held the value of a work of art to depend upon both the value of its ideas, and of the form in which they are expressed.

PLEROMA.

A Greek term meaning "fullness." Used by both Christians and Gnostics to refer to the fullness of being of the divine life.

PLETHO (GIORGIUS GEMISTUS). c. 1355–1440.

Byzantine pilosopher. Born in Constantinople. Educated in Adrianople. Lived most of his life in Mistra. A Platonist, Pletho is credited with inspiring Cosimo de Medici to support the founding of the Florentine Academy, modeled after Plato's Academy. He apparently lectured on Plato during the 1438 Council of Ferrara-Florence for which he served as philosophical adviser to the Greek delegation. He regarded Plato as superior to Aristotle, but interpreted Plato Neoplatonically as an emanationist. He held that matter might be a result of creation, but that souls emanated from the Ideas which had their origin in the One.

Principal writings: *On the Difference Between the Doctrines of Plato and Aristotle; The Laws.*

PLOTINUS. 205–270.

Egypto-Roman philosopher. Born in Lycopolis, Egypt. Apparently attracted to philosophy by Ammonius Saccas who taught in Alexandria. Traveled in Syria and Persia. Moved to Rome in 245, founding his own school of philosophy. The school attracted students widely from the professions, including senators among them, and even members of the imperial household. He is the principal figure in the movement of Neoplatonism. His writings were collected by his disciple, Porphyry, into six volumes, called the *Enneads.*

Principal writings: *Enneads* (T), 6 vols.

(1) The system of Plotinus can be viewed either from the standpoint of the individual person caught within a space-time world and seeking salvation from it, or from the standpoint of the logical progression in which reality emerged from a primal unity. In the former case, the system becomes a guidebook to the

divine, and hence a religious philosophy. In the second case, the system is an effort to explain how, out of the One, an eternal principle of unity, the temporal order could have arisen.

(2) The One is the undifferentiated divine out of whose being the other elements of reality are derived by emanation. The emanation, logical rather than temporal, occurs due to the refulgence of the original principle.

(3) The initial emanation is that of the *Nous* or Intelligence. This is the realm of forms of Plato. The *Nous* is a reflection into multiplicity of the eternal unity, and it continues to exist—as does everything else—through the power of the One.

(4) The second emanation is that of the World Soul. This is a principle of life and active intelligence. It exists in contemplation of the *Nous*. And like the demiurge of Plato the forms become the patterns of its creation in the space-time world. That world is, in point of fact, its inner existence, since the world soul contains the world as its body. Time is the record of the world soul's attempts to embody in matter the fullness of eternal and infinite being.

(5) The final emanation in the series is that of matter itself which, devoid of form, is the closest approach to nonbeing. The evil in the world, and the evil in man, are viewed as a necessary concomitant of the material principle.

(6) Man, then, combining in himself the material and spiritual orders, is in an uncomfortable position. He has a longing for the eternal forms and for the One, and yet he is caught within a body. The means of his liberation is contemplation, intellectual and spiritual at once. Furthermore, the liberation may require more than a single lifetime.

(7) Plotinus finds evidence of the One diffused in the world of our experience. The existence of anything whatever requires a unity of parts; and this unity can come from no other source than the One.

(8) Similarly, the Plotinian analysis of beauty is traced to a unity of the whole. In this sense an aesthetic argument for God is implicit in the *Enneads*.

(9) Finally, Plotinus held that the object known must be identical with the knowing act. Thus, he offered an identity theory of truth. If the identity does not exist, neither does truth. What truth affirms, it must also be.

Q.v. Evolution (7).

PLOUCQUET, GOTTFRIED. 1716–1790.
German philosopher. Studied at Tübingen where he also taught. A disciple of Wolff and member of the Leibniz-Wolff school, he held to a spiritualistic phenomenology in which things are made real by their divine representations. Ploucquet is also regarded as one of the forerunners of mathematical logic. His writings were in Latin.

Principal writings: *Primary Monadology,* 1748; *Principles of Substances and Phenomena,* 1752; *Fundamentals of Philosophic Speculation,* 1759; *Principles of Theoretical Philosophy,* 1772; *Elements of Contemplative Philosophy,* 1778; *Meditations on Select Philosophies,* 1781; as well as treatises on logic.

PLURALISM.
Any metaphysical view holding that the world must be composed of more than one or two basic kinds of entities. The latter views would be termed Monism (*q.v.*) or Dualism (*q.v.*).

(1) Anaxagoras (*q.v.* 1) held the number of qualitatively different substances to be indefinitely great.

(2) Empedocles (*q.v.* 2) limited their number to four: earth, air, fire, and water.

(3) Herbart (*q.v.* 3) described his ontology as a Pluralistic Realism, meaning thereby that reality is composed of simple qualitative units which he called "reals." These form syntheses, leading to the world we experience.

(4) Among modern self-avowed pluralists one must mention William James (*q.v.* 8) who explained the Pluralism of the world in terms of the dominance of external relations.

(5) Chang Tung-Sun (*q.v.* 1), who combined elements of constructionalism with pluralism, styled his doctrine Epistemological Pluralism.

(6) Ward (*q.v.* 3) regarded his worldview as pluralistic.

(7) Rescher (*q.v.* 6) used the term Orientational Pluralism to signal the position that equally eligible alternatives are to be found on both sides of many philosophical issues.

Also, *q.v.* Berlin (1–3).

PLUTARCH OF ATHENS. c. 350–433.
Hellenic philosopher. First head of the School of Athens (*q.v.*), the Platonic Academy turned Neoplatonic. He studied Plato and Aristotle together, holding Aristotle to be the most appropriate introduction to Plato's thought. He held that communion with God was possible by means of theurgic rites.
Principal writings: *Commentary* on Aristotle's *Of the Soul*.

PLUTARCH OF CHAERONEA. c. 45–125.
Greek philosopher and man of letters. Born in Chaeronea, Boetia. A Platonist, Plutarch studied in Plato's Academy (*q.v.*) in Athens, later establishing his own school in his native town. He lived for some time in Rome lecturing on philosophy. Tradition has him tutor of Hadrian who in return appointed him Procurator of Greece. An archon in the mystery religion of the Pythian Apollo, he believed that the purified soul rose to an eternal world. Best known for his biography of parallel lives, Roman paired with Greek, coming to forty-six in all. He also wrote on questions of popular morality. *Q.v.* Utopia (7).
Principal writings: *Parallel Lives* (T); *Moralia* (T).

PNEUMA.
A Greek term meaning "air." The term was used by Stoic philosophers (*q.v.* Stoicism 1) as a principle of animation for the universe, and the term they preferred to psyche or soul, as the principle of animation in man as well.

POETRY.
As revelatory. *Q.v.* Novalis (1); Heidegger (8). For Wordsworth *q.v.* Epiphany (4).

POIESIS.
A Greek term signifying the activity of creating, making, or producing. In Aristotle (*q.v.* 1) *poiesis* defines one of the three types of science, the productive science; and poietic knowledge correspondingly is set in contrast to theoretical and practical knowledge.

POINCARÉ, HENRI. 1854–1912.
French mathematician and philosopher of science. Born in Nancy. Taught first at Caen, and then at the University of Paris. Principal writings: *Science and Hypoth-*

esis (T), 1902; *The Value of Science* (T), 1905; *Science and Method* (T), 1909; *Last Thoughts* (T), 1912.
(1) Dividing hypotheses into those which are "natural and necessary," those which are "indifferent," and "real generalizations," Poincaré meant by the first those very general judgments which facilitate the making of more specific hypotheses. By the second he meant hypotheses which may be pictorial but cannot be verified by experience. In his view, atomic theory is an instance of an indifferent hypothesis. "Real generalizations" are open to test by experience.
(2) Poincaré is perhaps best known for his Conventionalist thesis. This thesis called attention to the substantial role of definition not only in mathematics, but also in the agreed upon principles of science. He pointed out that the axioms of geometry are a result of definition, and are thus both conventional and unfalsifiable. In most scientific theories there are similar conventional elements.
(3) But if the principles of science are conventional, its laws have to do with the relations of things, and are thus verifiable or disverifiable.
(4) Also known for his solution to the logical paradoxes known as Burali-Forti and Richard, Poincaré introduced the prescription that in defining the member of any class no reference should be made to the totality of members of that class. Definitions in violation of this prescription were known as Impredicative Definitions.

POINT-EVENT.
In Whitehead (*q.v.* 7) the ideal limit of an event with its dimensions uniformly restricted.

POLANYI, MICHAEL. 1891–1976.
Hungarian scientist and philosopher. Born in Budapest. Educated at Budapest and Berlin. Taught in Berlin, Victoria University (Manchester), and Oxford. A scientist whose analyses took an ever-broadening scope, Polanyi's point of view has been of especial interest to scientists, educators, and historians. The writings listed below were all published originally in English.
Principal writings: *Science, Faith, and Society,* 1946; *The Logic of Liberty,* 1951;

Personal Knowledge, 1958; *The Study of Man*, 1959; *The Tacit Dimension*, 1966; *Knowing and Being*, 1969; *Scientific Thought and Social Reality* (ed. F. Schwartz), 1974; *Meaning* (with H. Prosch), 1975.

(1) Stressing the importance of the role of tacit knowledge on all levels of judgment, Polanyi held that an important part of what we know is grasped inchoately, related to our "dwelling in" various contexts including theories, skills, and tools.

(2) The terms "subsidiary" and "focal" are central terms in his analysis of meaning The word being used is called a "subsidiary" and it bears on a "focal" matter; *i.e.*, the word refers to something. Signs and symbols are distinguished from each other. With respect to symbols, *e.g.*, the flag, the focal becomes so by virtue of our embodying various qualities and concerns in the object. When using symbols we project certain qualities into the object, and we do not do so when using signs.

(3) Metaphor is an essential element in both art and religion. The power of religious rites and myths is to be understood by means of the central role of metaphor.

POLARITY, PRINCIPLE OF.
(1) Nicholas of Cusa (*q.v.* 1, 4) held that polar opposites apply at the same time to infinite beings. God is the chief example of the principle's applicability.

(2) Fichte (*q.v.* 3), Hegel (*q.v.* 4), and Marx and his followers (*q.v.* Marxism 1), believed that such opposites were replaced by a synthesis in the process of dialectic.

(3) Schelling (*q.v.* 8) advanced the idea of a basic polarity in God which was itself a permanent and eternal contrast within God. This point of view was followed by Fechner (*q.v.* 5), Whitehead (*q.v.* 18), Przywara (*q.v.*), and Hartshorne (*q.v.* 5).

(4) According to Morris Cohen (*q.v.* 4), the principle of polarity refers to the situation that many analyses require a balancing of two opposing ideas, and that to eliminate either is to run the risk of an inadequate analysis. W.H. Sheldon found the principle important to metaphysical analysis.

POLEMON. 4th–3rd cent. B.C.
Greek philosopher. Born in Athens. Head of the First Academy (*q.v.* Plato's

Academy 1) from 314 to around 276. Interested in problems of ethics, he combined an emphasis upon living a virtuous life in conformity with nature, and using wisdom to select the pleasures for one's enjoyment.

POLITICAL PHILOSOPHY.
Q.v. Social Philosophy.

POLITY.
In Aristotle (*q.v.* 12) one of the three desirable forms of government. Polity seemed to have been Aristotle's preference. It has many of the features of constitutional democracy.

POLIZIANO, ANGELO.
Q.v. Florentine Academy.

POLLOCK, FRIEDRICH.
Q.v. Frankfurt School, The. A.

POLYSTRATUS.
Q.v. Epicureanism (1).

POLYSYLLOGISM.
A systematic series of syllogisms leading to a single conclusion.

POLYTHEISM.
From the Greek *polys* ("many") and *theos* ("god"). The view that there are many gods. Polytheism stands in contrast to Henotheism (*q.v.*) and Monotheism (*q.v.*).

POMPONAZZI, PIETRO. 1462–1525.
Italian philosopher. Born in Mantua. Educated at Mantua and Padua. Taught at the universities of Padua, Ferrara, and Bologna. Becoming acquainted with Averroism at Padua, Pomponazzi developed a position on the immortality of the soul regarded as sufficiently heterodox to have his book on the subject burned in Venice.

Principal writings: *On the Immortality of the Soul* (T), 1516; *Apology*, 1517; *Defense*, 1519; *On Fate, Free Will, and Predestination*, 1520; *On Incantations*, 1520.

(1) Holding the Thomistic interpretation of Aristotle on the soul to be erroneous and the doctrine false, Pomponazzi found similar difficulties with the universal soul of Averroës. He supported the doctrine he attributed to Alexander of Aphrodisius that the soul is absolutely mortal and relatively immortal. Self-

knowledge and knowledge of universals imply some relative sense of immortality. In all of this he was simply reducing the level of the knowledge claim we are justified in making about immortality. He also suggested that this question, like that of the eternality of the world, cannot be settled by reason. It must finally be accepted as an article of faith.

(2) He argued that virtue is its own reward, requiring neither sanction nor punishment beyond this life. Accepting the Stoic doctrine of fate, he attempted to combine it with the Christian doctrine that divine predestination and free will are compatible.

PONS ASINORUM.

A Latin term meaning "bridge of asses." The term has been applied to the fifth proposition of Euclid, and to a logical diagram of Petrus Tartaretus (c. 1480), the idea being that these are conceptions, of intermediate difficulty which the incompetent are unable to grasp. By extension any task of the mentioned sort is a *pons asinorum*.

POPE.

From the Greek *papas* ("father"). Head of the Roman Catholic Church. Bearing the title Pontifex Maximus (meaning "supreme intermediary between man and God"), the pope is regarded by Roman Catholics as successor to Peter as Bishop of Rome, and bearing in himself all of the powers Christ granted Peter. As of 1870 it was decided that infallibility (*q.v.*) characterized the pope's utterances when defining doctrines of faith and morals.

POPE JOHN XXIII.

Q.v. Vatican Council II.

POPE JOHN PAUL II.

Q.v. John Paul II, Pope; Theology of Liberation (6).

POPE PIUS IX.

Q.v. Vatican Council I.

POPKIN, RICHARD.

Q.v. Skepticism (30).

POPPER, KARL. 1902–1994.

Austrian philosopher of science. Born in Vienna. Educated at the universities of Vienna, New Zealand, and London. Taught first in New Zealand and then at the London School of Economics.

Principal writings: *The Logic of Scientific Discovery* (T), 1935; *The Open Society and its Enemies* (E), 2 vols., 1945; *The Poverty of Historcism* (E), 1957; *Conjectures and Refutations* (E), 1963; *Objective Knowledge*, 1972; *The Self and its Brain* (with J.C. Eccles), 1977; *The Open Universe* (with W.W. Bartley), 1982; *Quantum Theory and the Schism in Physics* (with W.W. Bartley), 1982; *Realism and the Aim of Science* (with W.W. Bartley), 1983; *In Search of a Better World* (T), 1992.

(1) Holding that scientific theories emerge by imaginative leaps from many bases—pseudo-science, philosophy, the prejudices of ordinary life—Popper suggests that "falsifiability" is a more reliable criterion of both meaning and truth than is verifiability. We must seek hypotheses which are "falsifiable," which can be disproved by negative instances. Indeed, the more falsifiable the hypothesis, the more valuable it is likely to be. If negative instances are not found we begin to gain confidence in its truth toward which we move by conjecture and refutation.

(2) On this view science is necessarily incomplete and provisional; and probability is interpreted as an assignment of propensity to some part of the natural world rather than as the limit of a frequency.

(3) Defending the concept of an open or pluralistic society against the structured society of Plato, he argues for "piecemeal social engineering" as the only means of change in conformity with what can be known.

(4) Against the holistic or organicist interpretation of society, Popper argues that since social wholes are not physical entities but theoretical entities, they cannot be analyzed as such. Social phenomena are to be analyzed only in terms of individuals, and their actions and relations.

PORPHYRY. 232 or 233–304.

Neoplatonic philosopher. Born in Tyre. Studied in Athens under Longinus, and then in Rome under Plotinus whose disciple he became. It was Porphyry who compiled the *Enneads* of Plotinus, bringing the latter's work into manuscript

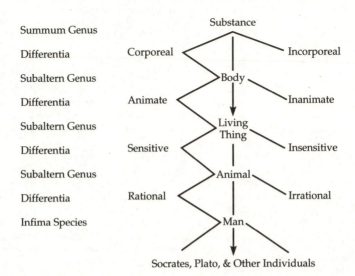

Summum Genus		Substance	
Differentia	Corporeal		Incorporeal
Subaltern Genus		Body	
Differentia	Animate		Inanimate
Subaltern Genus		Living Thing	
Differentia	Sensitive		Insensitive
Subaltern Genus		Animal	
Differentia	Rational		Irrational
Infima Species		Man	

Socrates, Plato, & Other Individuals

form. The author of numerous works, his object was the preparation of the soul for union with the One. His book against the Christians was burned by order of Theodosius II in 435.

Principal writings: *Philosophy of the Oracles*; ed. *Enneads* (T); *Isagoge* (an introduction to Aristotle's *Categories*); *Sentences on the Intelligibles*; *Life of Plotinus*; *Against the Christians*.

(1) Porphyry brought the list of predicables (*q.v.* 1) to five by including "species" among them. He is, however, most widely known for his illustrative manner of relating genus, species, and individuals in the Tree of Porphyry (*Arbor Porphyrii*). The subject is dealt with in the chapter on "Species" in the *Isagoge*. Taking the category of substance as his illustration, Porphyry diagrammed the relationship between this basic category, which is a genus and not a species, terms of lesser generality which are both genus and species terms, the *differentiae* which control these terms, down to the most narrow species which contains individuals as its members. To the right of the diagram one sees the complements of the differential terms. Porphyry seems to have combined Plato's method of division with Aristotle's theory of predicables. The tree came into Latin literature through the translation of Boethius, and exercised great influence during the Middle Ages. Porphyry suggests that it is beyond the power of man

to know whether genus and species are subsistent entities or exist only as concepts.

(2) Although generally in close agreement with his master, Porphyry gave a different explanation of evil. For Plotinus (*q.v.* 5) evil is a property of matter. For Porphyry evil is a lack of control by the intelligible principle. This control can be gained through meditation and ascetic purification. In so doing the soul begins its ascent toward divine union.

(3) There are sets of virtues of ascending rank through which one will pass. One begins one's ascent with civil and political virtues, exchanges these for the virtues of apathy in the Stoic sense. On the third level are the virtues leading the soul toward the *nous* or the intelligible world. On the final level are the virtues of the *nous* itself.

(4) Before meeting Plotinus, Porphyry briefly advocated theurgy (*q.v.*), the use of rites and incantations to control the gods, a practice Plotinus opposed, and Porphyry eventually rejected.

PORT ROYAL.

An abbey founded near Paris in 1204. It moved to the capital in 1626. The philosophical importance of the abbey derives from the simultaneous presence there of Arnauld (*q.v.*), Nicole (*q.v.*), and Pascal (*q.v.*). The three were brought together by the attraction of Jansenism (*q.v.*), an Augustinian type of religious-philosophical movement. Pascal wrote the *Provincial Letters* in support of Arnauld who had been condemned by the Sorbonne for heresy. The *Provincial Letters* were placed on the Index in 1657. Soon thereafter the Jansenist movement was condemned by the Pope. In 1662 Port Royal was closed, and its members were required to sign a renunciation. The other connection in which Port Royal is known relates to the Port Royal logic. This logic was developed in a book composed by Arnauld and Nicole, called *The Art of Thinking*, published in 1662. Unlike traditional logics, it took Descartes' Rules of Method as central to logical analysis (*q.v.* Arnauld 1).

PORT ROYAL LOGIC.
Q.v. Port Royal; Arnauld (1).

POSIDONIUS. c. 135–50 B.C.
Greek philosopher. Born in Apamea in Syria. A Stoic philosopher of the Middle Period, he studied under Panaetius (*q.v.*), founded his own school in Rhodes where Cicero (*q.v.*) is said to have studied, and stressed the philosophies of Plato and Aristotle with respect to most problems. The ascending and descending paths of Heraclitus, with the central element of fire, are also present. He is credited with viewing man as a microcosm of the macrocosm, and as a citizen of the world.

POSIT.
From the Latin *ponere, positum* ("to place"). To posit a proposition is to advance it, or put it in place, as a postulate (*q.v.*). In a somewhat different sense J.G. Fichte (*q.v.* 3) developed a metaphysics in which the Ego posits both itself and the non-Ego.

POSITIVE PHILOSOPHY.
A phrase introduced by Saint-Simon (*q.v.* 1) as a synonym for Positivism, a scientific approach to the world. Schelling (*q.v.* 1e) meant by the term a positive approach to the universe, an approach which was mythological and spiritualistic in tone. With Comte (*q.v.* 1) the term, Positivism, became standard for the scientific approach.

POSITIVE THEOLOGY.
Q.v. The Pseudo-Dionysius (1).

POSITIVISM.
A family of philosophies characterized by an extremely positive evaluation of science and scientific method. In its earlier versions, the methods of science were held to have the potential not only of reforming philosophy but society as well. Later versions have concentrated on the reform of philosophy.

(1) The term was introduced by Saint-Simon (*q.v.* 1–2) for whom the implications of the positive philosophy extended beyond philosophy to political, educational, and religious reforms. He found society alternating between critical and organic epochs.

(2) Comte (*q.v.* 1), who popularized and systematized the use of the terms "positivism" and "positive philosophy," was for seven years Saint-Simon's student and collaborator. Comte argued that societies proceed from a theological stage through a metaphysical stage into a scientific stage where the positive philosophy is dominant.

(3) The term "positive philosophy" was also used by Schelling (*q.v.* 1) who employed it to distinguish the final stage of his philosophy from early stages, which seemed to him largely negative and critical. Since this final stage recognized a philosophical validity in religious experience and mythology, Schelling's use of the term is very different from that of Saint-Simon and Comte, almost the polar opposite in fact. And even though Schelling's usage may have come first both in lecture and manuscript, the material of this stage of his thought was published posthumously. Saint-Simon's usage has primacy in terms both of publication and acceptance.

(4) Taine (*q.v.*), along with Littré (*q.v.*), was the spokesman for Comtian positivism in the second half of the 19th century.

(5) A number of other variant usages may be noted. Vaihinger (*q.v.* 1), working from the basis of Kant's doctrine of regulative ideas, named his own view Idealistic Positivism. The position is usually, however, referred to as Fictionalism.

(6) Korn (*q.v.* 1) applied the idea of positivism to Argentina, finding in the Argentine experience after independence a native form of positivism.

(7) Petzoldt (*q.v.*), influenced by Avenarius' doctrine of experience, while

stressing functional dependence, called his position Relativistic Positivism.

(8) The most powerful development of the positivistic analysis, however, came from the Vienna Circle of Logical Positivists (*q.v.*). The influence of this group, among whose many representatives we cite Schlick (*q.v.* 1) and Carnap (*q.v.*), has been so great that today positivism usually means logical positivism.

(9) Ayer (*q.v.* 3), who worried the verifiability criterion (*q.v.*) of meaning—favored by positivists—through a number of revisions, has been the most persistent English expositor of Logical Positivism.

(10) Kelsen (*q.v.*) is among those applying the doctrines of positivism to the field of law.

(11) Bergmann (*q.v.* 1), a lapsed positivist of the Vienna Circle, argues that all positivists are either materialists or phenomenalists.

(12) For an example of legal positivism *q.v.* Dworkin (1).

POSSIBILITY.

From the Latin *potis* ("able") and *esse* ("to be"). One of three modal terms with a long philosophic history, "possibility" must be treated along with "actuality" and "necessity." The contrasting definitions of these terms, as treated in the history of philosophy, are given under the heading Modality (*q.v.*). In Modal Logic (*q.v.* 1) "possibility" and "necessity" are defined in terms of each other, "possible p" being defined as "not necessarily not p." We shall not repeat those distinctions here, but rather deal with what has been said of possibility in its own right.

(1) One of the most basic distinctions is that between *logical possibility* (any concept, hypothesis, or theory which is self-consistent), and *real possibility* (those possibilities having some rooting in the universe which might well bring them into existence).

(2) A somewhat similar distinction, common in the medieval period, is that between *absolute* (or intrinsic) and *relative* (or extrinsic) *possibilities*. The former are logical possibilities, and the latter are possibilities requiring a cause to bring them into existence.

(3) Aristotle (*q.v.* 10) expresses, at least

implicitly, all of these senses of possibility. Real possibility derives from his conception of existence in potency, one of his chief contributions to philosophy. And extrinsic possibility is very similar to his view of the contingent as that which may or may not be, depending upon the conditions.

(4) The Megarian philosophers are reputed to have restricted the notion of possibility to that of actuality. Diodorus Cronos (*q.v.* 1) argued in the *Kurieon* that the possible and the actual are identical for a past event cannot become other than it is; but if an event now actual had once been merely possible, then from the possible something impossible would have resulted. On the other hand Philo of Megara (*q.v.* 2) seems to have had in mind the broader notion of logical possibility when he defined possibility as that which is true by virtue of its internal nature.

(5) If the Megarians, by and large, restricted the possible to the actual, Platonism subscribed to the view that possibility extends beyond actuality. Plato (*q.v.* 1) seems not to have discussed possibility directly, but his treatment of the ideas or forms as providing patterns for the temporal world entails that there are general possibilities. And in the same sense the treatment philosophers give to universals (*q.v.*) can tell us something of their view of possibility. And when a philosopher adopts the position of Realism (*q.v.*) with respect to universals, as Plato did, one may fairly infer that for this person possibility encompasses more than actuality, *i.e.*, there are unactualized possibilities.

(6) The medieval period distinguished between the eminent, virtual, and formal existence of possibilities. According to Aquinas (*q.v.* 4–5), possibilities are eminently in the divine essence, virtually in the divine potency, and formally in the divine and human understanding. In the divine understanding their existence is primary and in the human understanding their existence is secondary.

(7) Leibniz (*q.v.* 9) embraced the Platonic notion that possibility extends beyond actuality in his doctrine of the "incompossibility of possibilities." Since not all possibilities can be actualized together, it follows that the realm of

possibility is wider than that of actuality.
(8) Whitehead (*q.v.* 10) with his doctrine of eternal objects likewise held the possible to extend beyond the actual. Furthermore, in the process of time, the notions of the relevant and of "real possibilities" become identical.

(9) Rescher (*q.v.* 5) offers a type of Conceptualism in which possibility is mental, adding no "iffiness" to the world.

POSSIBLES, COMPOSSIBILITY OF.
Q.v. Leibniz (9).

POSSIBLE WORLDS.
A phrase used by Leibniz (*q.v.* 9) to refer to the compossible sets of possibilities among which God chose in creating the world. Leibniz held that God would choose the best possible combination. Voltaire (*q.v.* 5) lampooned the concept in *Candide*. The term also appears in current discussions of Modal Logic (*q.v.*). In this context a necessary proposition is true in all possible worlds, a contingent proposition has truth value in some possible world and a necessarily false, or impossible, proposition, is true in no possible world. Also *q.v.* Hintikka (1–3); Proper Names (5); Plantinga (4); David Lewis (1–5).

POST HOC ERGO PROPTER HOC.
A Latin phrase meaning "after this, therefore because of this." The name of one of the Fallacies of Relevance, also known as False Cause (*q.v.* Fallacies 12).

POST-MODERNISM.
Q.v. Toulmin (5).

POSTPREDICAMENTS.
From the Latin *postpraedicamenta* meaning "after the categories." The name given to the terms analyzed by Aristotle following his analysis of the predicaments or categories. The analysis of the postpredicaments begins in Book X of the *Categories* and deals with the basic senses of opposition, contrariety, priority, simultaneity, movement, and possession.

POST-STRUCTURALISM.
A movement of literary criticism and philosophic thought originating, like Structuralism (*q.v.*), in France, agreeing with its predecessor in stressing semiology while placing greater stress on the relations of signs to each other than to some objective reality. In the one case the signifiers of signs are other signs; in the other the signifiers are objective entities.

There are at least two varieties of post-structuralism: anti-constructionist and deconstructionist.

(1) Barthes (*q.v.* 7) represents the anti-constructionist alternative. In *S/Z* he renounced structuralism, thereby constituting himself a post-structuralist. His renunciation rested on the ground that there is no underlying system to reveal. The point is to disentangle the intermingled codes of the text without attempting to decipher them.

(2) The other variety of post-structuralism is deconstruction (*q.v.*). In this alternative the critic demonstrates how discourse undermines the philosophical presuppositions on which they presume to rely. Derrida (*q.v*) is the initiator of deconstruction.

POSTULATE.
From the Latin term *postulatum* meaning "demand," "request," or "claim." The term is usually used to indicate those propositions which form the starting point of inquiry which are neither definitions, nor provisional assumptions, nor so certain that they can be taken as axiomatic. They are laid down as true, and used without demonstration. Thus "postulate" is one of a family of related terms including "definition" (*q.v.*), "assumption" (*q.v.*), "hypothesis" (*q.v.*), and "axiom" (*q.v.*).

(1) Aristotle (*q.v.* 2) held postulates to be among the primary premises of demonstration. He viewed them as demonstrable but used without demonstration.

(2) Euclid (*q.v.* 1) agreed that postulates were among the primary premises of demonstration. For Euclid, postulates are neither demonstrable nor self-evident. While the axioms of Euclid's system are general and non-geometrical, only geometrical statements appear among the postulates in Euclid's system, *e.g.*, "Between any two points a straight line can be drawn."

(3) Wolff (*q.v.* 4) used the term more broadly to signify propositions which were indemonstrable, practical, and particular in nature.

(4) Kant (*q.v.* 3, 8) followed, at least

in part, the lead of Wolff. He referred to his principles of modality as "postulates of empirical thought," and he held the ideas of God, freedom, and immortality to be "postulates of practical reason."

(5) Lotze (*q.v.* 4) regarded postulates as absolutely necessary assumptions. in contrast with hypotheses which are conjectural in nature.

POTENTIALITY.

From the Latin *potentia*, derived from *potens*, meaning "to be powerful" in a certain respect or "to have a capacity" of a certain kind. The Latin term is a translation of the Greek *dynamis*, used by Aristotle (*q.v.* 8–9) as the name of the factor correlative to actuality in the analysis of change.

(1) The distinction between logical and real potentiality is identical to that between logical and real possibility (*q.v.* Possibility 1). But real potentiality is further divisible into active and passive potentiality, the former referring to the process leading to the actualization of a potency, the latter referring to the disposition to receive a determination. An instance of the former would be the acorn in the process of becoming an oak. An instance of the latter would be the wax receiving the impress of the signet ring.

(2) In Leibniz (*q.v.* 1–2) we are given a notion of potentiality in which the present burgeons with the future, and where active potentiality is identified with force.

(3) In Schelling (*q.v.* 2) one encounters the doctrine of *potenzen*, determinate potencies occurring at each level of existence with different qualities.

(4) Whitehead (*q.v.* 11) regards potentiality as the source of continuity, and actuality as atomic in nature.

POTENZEN.

Q.v. Schelling (2).

POUR-SOI.

Q.v. Sartre (5).

P-PREDICATES.

Q.v. Strawson (3)

PRACTICAL IMPERATIVE.

Q.v. Kant (6).

PRACTICAL REASON.

Q.v. Kant (11f).

PRAEDICAMENTA.

From the Latin *praedicamentum* ("category"). In Scholastic logic, the ten categories of Aristotle (*q.v.* 6).

PRAGMATICISM.

The replacement term for Pragmatism, introduced by Peirce (*q.v.* 1) in 1905 after his original term—introduced in 1878—had gained a popular and loose signification.

PRAGMATIC MAXIM.

Q.v. Peirce (1); James (6); Pragmatism (1–2).

PRAGMATICS.

That branch of Semiotic (*q.v.*) concerned with the relations between signs and their users, *i.e.*, with problems of signification. Along with Syntactics (*q.v.*) and Semantics (*q.v.*), the three branches of semiotic laid out by Charles Morris (*q.v.* 2), and adopted by Carnap (*q.v.* 7). Also *q.v.* Metalanguage (4); Richard Montague (2).

PRAGMATIC THEORY OF TRUTH.

Q.v. Truth (1, 21, 22).

PRAGMATISM.

From the Greek *pragma* ("thing, fact, matter, affair"). A philosophical movement of the late 19th and 20th centuries whose emphasis lay in interpreting ideas through their consequences.

(1) The term was adapted from Kant by C.S. Peirce (*q.v.* 1). Kant had distinguished the practical—relating to the will and action—from the pragmatic—relating to consequences. Peirce derived a theory of meaning from this idea. The criterion of meaning was the pragmatic maxim: "Consider what effects, that might conceivably have practical bearings, we conceive the object of our conception to have. Then, our conception of these effects is the whole of our conception of the object." He made this theory of meaning central to his philosophy.

(2) William James (*q.v.* 6–7) stated the maxim more broadly: "The meaning of any proposition can always be brought down to some particular consequence in our future practical experience, whether passive or active." In his application it was clear that the criterion applied to truth as well as meaning, having the power at least to eliminate some hypotheses.

(3) Royce (*q.v.* 8) termed his system, in its later stages, Absolute Pragmatism.

(4) In Italy, Giovanni Papini (*q.v.*) adopted a Corridor Theory of Pragmatism, enshrining a principle of tolerance according to which philosophers can hold competing theories all of which, nonetheless, meet the test of the pragmatic criterion.

(5) Le Roy (*q.v.*) in France gave a pragmatic interpretation both of scientific and religious doctrines.

(6) F.C.S. Schiller (*q.v.*) expounded an English version of pragmatism, more akin to the views of James than Peirce, and possibly more relativistic than the pragmatism of William James. In Schiller's view reality and truth are, at least in part, human constructions.

(7) G.H. Mead (*q.v.* 4) emphasized the primacy of the present and the biological and social context of thought.

(8) John Dewey (*q.v.* 1, 3–4), calling for a "reconstruction in philosophy," turned Pragmatism into Instrumentalism, and truth into "warranted assertibility," while developing an overall theory of inquiry based on criteria of practical and theoretical adjustment.

(9) C.I. Lewis (*q.v.* 2–3) described his own position as Conceptualistic Pragmatism on the ground that mind supplies the categories, concepts, and principles for the organization of experience.

(10) Ernest Nagel (*q.v.* 6–7) has been influenced both by Peirce and Dewey. Peirce's view of inquiry as self-corrective, and Dewey's instrumentalism, have had a great deal to do with the pragmatic naturalism to which he subscribes.

(11) W.V. Quine (*q.v.* 7), rejecting the analytic-synthetic distinction, holds that the conceptual scheme of science is adjustable to contrary experience in many ways; and the only requirement is that the scheme be adjusted in some pragmatically viable manner.

(12) Rescher (*q.v.* 2), using the term Methodological Pragmatism, held that methodology requires pragmatic justification.

PRAJNA.
Q.v. Intuition (15); Meditation (6); Suzuki (4).

PRAJNA-INTUITION.
Q.v. Intuition (15).

PRAJNAPARAMITA.
Q.v. Intuition (15).

PRAKRTI (PRAKRITI).
Sanskrit *pra* ("urge") and *krti* ("producing" and "produced"), thus the "urge to produce." The female energetic principle in tension with the male principle of *purusha* (*q.v.* 1). It is the principle of materiality which stands in contrast to the principle of soul or spirituality. In the Sankhya (*q.v.* 1–5) philosophy these two principles explain the entire phenomenal world. Also *q.v.* Hinduism (6b).

PRALL, D.W.
Q.v. Aesthetics (25).

PRAMA.
Sanskrit for "knowledge." *Q.v. Jnana.*

PRAMANA.
Q.v. Intuition (11); Dignaga (1); Jayarasi (2, 5).

PRANAYAMA.
Sanskrit term meaning "breath control." The fourth step in Yogic meditation (*q.v.* Yoga 4).

PRANTL, KARL. 1820–1888.
German philosopher, born in Ladsberg am Lech. Taught at the University of Munich. He is known for his pioneering studies in the history of logic.
Principal writings: *History of Logic in the West*, 4 vols., 1855–85.

PRAPTI.
Q.v. Sarvastivada.

PRASASTAPADA (PRASHASTAPADA).
Q.v. God (43).

PRATITYA-SAMUTPADA.
Q.v. Dependent Origination; Buddha (2).

PRATYA-BHIJNA.
Q.v. Vaisnavism (3d).

PRATYAHARA.
Sanskrit term meaning "sense-control." The fifth step in Yogic meditation (*q.v.* Yoga 4).

PRATYAKṢA (PRATYAKSHA).
Q.v. Intuition (11).

PRAXIOLOGY.
Q.v. Kotarbinski (3).

PRAXIS.
A Greek term meaning "a doing; transaction, business," from *pratto* or *prasso*: "to do, practise, act, run a business." (*Q.v.* pragmatism, from *pragma*, likewise from *pratto*.) Also, a German term meaning "practice, exercise, usage" with *Praktik* as a synonym, and *praktisch* as its adjective. The problem of the term is to identify the usage intended by an individual writer, whether in Greek or German.

(1) Aristotle (*q.v.* 1) divided activity into *theoria*, devoted to abstract reasoning, and practical activity, subdivided the latter *poiesis* (all forms of making which result in an artifact), and *praxis* (the doing centered in the activity itself, *e.g.*, music, poetry, sport, moral and political activity).

(2) As elsewhere (*q.v.* subject and object) meaning reversal has occurred with some of these terms. "Practice" and "practical" have come to mean activity productive of artifacts, while *poiesis* tends to be associated with the fine arts and the absence of artifacts (unless art objects are called artifacts).

(3) In the 19th century August Von Ciezkowski, a Young Hegelian, used the German term, *Praxis*, to support the view that philosophy must become a concrete activity, related to social and cultural life. "The future role of philosophy," he said, is to become "a philosophy of practical activity, of *Praxis*," so that history will become acts, not facts. This may keep to Aristotle's meaning, but neo-Marxists (*cf.* 6–14 below) have invested this usage with a society-transforming sense of *Praxis*, which they also presume to find in Marx and Engels, going beyond Aristotle.

(4) The intentions of Marx and Engels are not so clear. Since the term *Praxis* in German is the noun standing in contrast to *Theorie*, they use it as a matter of course. And in the *Theses on Feuerbach* Marx says that self-transformation can only be understood as *revolutionäre Praxis* (the italics are in the German text). Further, he identifies "revolutionary" with *praktisch-kritischein* activity (thesis 1), and the

adjectival form of *praktisch* (practical) is used throughout the *Theses*. In the *Communist Manifesto*, where the phrase "revolutionizing practice" is used, the German is *Praktik* and *praktische*. Elsewhere, Marx speaks of the "political *Praxis*" of the aristocracy, and the *Praxis* of scientific method. Engels remarks that Americans are better at *Praxis* than they are at *Theorie*. It is not clear, then, that Marx and Engels have always in mind the transformative conception of *Praxis* which has come to characterize the new reading of Marx.

(5) Kotarbinski (*q.v.* 3) coined the term Praxiology to mean a theory of efficient action.

(6) Antonio Gramsci (*q.v.* 4) used the phrase "philosophy of *praxis*," crediting Antonio Labriola (*q.v.*) with the insight that Marxism is a theory of *Praxis* with the potentiality of becoming a theory of reality.

(7) A group of Yugoslavian philosophers, who called themselves The Praxis Group, expressed their ideas in a journal titled *Praxis*, published in both national and international editions, beginning in 1964. The national edition lasted until the spring of 1975 when the government dismissed all the philosophers from the university at Belgrade. The international edition continued for another decade. Interested in reestablishing the unity of theory and practice, they viewed Marx as having created an "all-embracing critical social theory." They read Marx in terms of the humanism of his early writings and found "free human creativity" to be the central category of his thought. In this context *Praxis* is a normative conception, requiring the transformation of both individual and society. Two of the most prominent leaders of The Praxis Group are Marković and Petrovic. A third member and long-time Yugoslav reinterpreter of Marx is Vranicki. We sample their positions in the following points.

(8) Mihailo Marković defined *praxis* as a form of life in which the following distinctive universal human capacities are realized: sensing, reasoning, imagining, communicating, creating novelty, choosing freely, establishing harmonious relations with others (*From Affluence to Praxis*, 1974).

(9) Gajo Petrovic ("Why *Praxis?*" 1972) identified human creativity with revolutionary activity, since the former implies a challenge to the established order.

(10) Predrag Vranicki, who participated in the Eric Fromm (*q.v.*) volume, *Socialist Humanism*, 1965, sees the Yugoslav-type *Praxis* as continuing an historic development initiated by Marx, and interrupted by Stalin, leading to a new human community transcending class-distinctions. He agreed with Gramsci that workers' councils mark "a new era in the history of the human race" ("The Idea of Self-Management," 1979).

(11) Karel Kosík (*Dialectic of the Concrete*, 1963) is a Czechoslovakian member of the Praxis Group interpreting Marx as having stood for a "philosophy of *Praxis*" whose "concrete totality" fused subjectivity and objectivity, replacing the inauthentic reification of everyday life with truth and authenticity.

(12) The members of the Frankfurt School (*q.v.*), at least beginning with Fromm (*q.v.*) and Marcuse (*q.v.*), had already provided an anticipation of the neo-Marxist conception of *praxis*. The "critical social theory" which was central to Habermas (*q.v.*) had as its corollary an interpretation of Marx as combining a "social *praxis*" providing social insight with a "political *Praxis*" aimed at "overthrowing existing systems of institutions."

(13) Gadamer (*q.v.* 3, 6), on the other hand, uses the term *praxis* in Aristotle's sense, moving into it through the practical syllogism which ends in decision, and whose final goal is human "solidarity," appearing through the resolution of common human problems. He also finds this sense in the *Lebenswelt* writings of the late Husserl, quoting the latter's use of the phrase "universal *praxis*" which he identifies with the "new kind of *Praxis*" of the Yugoslav Philosophers. Although it does not seem likely that Husserl had in mind such a strong sense of the word Gadamer calls it a "phenomenologizing" of humanity.

(14) Richard Bernstein (*Praxis and Action*, 1971) takes the neo-Marxist usage as Marx' own (as does Sanchez Vazquez in *The Philosophy of Praxis* (T), 1966), finding the neo-Marxist *Praxis* everywhere.

PREACHERS, ORDER OF.

Alternate name for the Dominican Order (*q.v.*).

PREDESTINATION.

The doctrine that man's salvation or damnation was predetermined from eternity by God. When the doctrine holds that not only man's eventual disposition, but every event of his life is predestined, the position is identical to a special kind of determinism (*q.v.* 11).

(1) The position can perhaps be traced back indefinitely, but in the Christian world the Apostle Paul (*q.v.* 5) clearly included predestination among the basic themes of his interpretation of Christianity.

(2) Denied by Pelagius (*q.v.*) and his followers, who found predestination inconsistent with free will, it was taken up by St. Augustine (*q.v.* 12) who held the two doctrines to be both true and consistent.

(3) Although St. Augustine advanced no theory explaining how the two doctrines could be consistent, Aquinas (*q.v.* 4), viewing God as the primary cause of all things, distinguished between two kinds of secondary causes: those natural and necessary on the one hand, and those which are voluntary and contingent.

(4) Luther (*q.v.* 9) opposed Erasmus (*q.v.* 2) who had argued for free will on the ground that Church doctrine required it. Luther argued that man chooses as he will, but his will is controlled by God. All actions would thus seem to be predestined by God, even though Luther wished to preserve freedom in matters not touching on salvation.

(5) Calvin (*q.v.* 5) expressed the doctrine in its strictest sense, while holding that in salvation divine grace renews the will, restoring the human freedom man lost in his original sin.

(6) Melanchthon (*q.v.* 2) held that human regeneration requires the cooperation of man's will. The view was regarded as semi-Pelagian, departing from strict predestination.

(7) At the 1618–19 Synod of Dort, the Dutch Calvinists confirmed the position of Supralapsarianism, *i.e.*, the view that God's decrees of election and reprobation had been ordered before the fall. The doctrine of Infralapsarianism, that these

decrees were ordered after (*infra*) the fall (*lapsus*), was defeated; and the doctrine of Sublapsarianism, that God did not decree the fall, although he foresaw it—a third point at issue—was neither rejected nor confirmed.

(8) Luis de Molina (*q.v.*), a Jesuit, held that since God knows what men will do under various circumstances, including the offering of His grace, God merely decrees the circumstances, and thus knows the result while man retains full freedom, retaining the exercise of decision.

(9) Suarez (*q.v.* 4) developed a doctrine of Congruism in which the grace men possess leads them to yield themselves infallibly to God, while retaining free will.

(10) Jansen (*q.v.* 2) took a strong view of human sin and divine predestination.

(11) It was against the Molinists that Pascal (*q.v.*), finding their viewpoint too libertarian, wrote his *Provincial Letters* defending the dominance of God and His strict predestinate power.

(12) Jonathan Edwards (*q.v.* 3, 4) developed at some length the Lutheran alternative in which man does what he will with a will shaped by God.

PREDICABLE.

From the Latin *praedicare* ("to proclaim or affirm"). The predicable is that which may be affirmed of something.

(1) For Aristotle (*q.v.* 4) the predicables are the kinds of relations which may obtain between a universal term and the subject of which it is predicated. The five relations are those of genus, species, specific difference, property, and contingent accident. It should be noted, however, that Aristotle did not identify "species" as a predicable, although the term entered into his discussion.

(2) Porphyry (*q.v.* 1) diagrammed these relations of predication in what has come to be known as the Tree of Porphyry. It was Porphyry who brought the predicables to five, including "species" among them.

PREDICATE.

In the traditional or subject-predicate logic, that which is affirmed or denied of a subject. The propositions (*q.v.* 1) of this logic are categorical. Letting "S" stand for "subject" and "P" for "predicate" their schema is "S is P." Also *q.v.* Syllogism (1).

PREDICATION.

The act of affirming or denying a predicate of a subject. Where modern logic deals with classes, sets, and relations, the logic of Aristotle (*q.v.* 5) is a logic of predication.

PRE-ESTABLISHED HARMONY.

Leibniz' (*q.v.* 7) solution to the mind-body problem and, more generally, his explanation of all interaction and of the orderliness of the world. Having decided that reality is composed of "windowless" monads, each developing from its own internal power, he found it necessary to explain all forms of interaction on the analogy of two clocks set to keep perfect time with each other. In the same way God, in choosing this world, established a harmony of each monad with all the rest.

PRE-EXISTENCE.

In Christian doctrine one of the alternatives with respect to soul is its preexistence. The doctrine was held by Origen (*q.v.* 3) and before him by Plato (*q.v.* 1). To be contrasted with Creationism (*q.v.*) and Traducianism (*q.v.*).

PREHENSION.

Q.v. Whitehead (13–14).

PREMISE (or PREMISS).

From the Latin *praemissus* ("that which is sent before"), a translation of the Greek *protasis* ("that which is put forward"). In logic, it is from the premises that conclusions are deduced. In the syllogism (*q.v.* 3), Aristotle distinguished between the Major Premise and the Minor Premise which together yield the conclusion.

PRESBYTERIAN CHURCH.

A family of churches, rather than a single church, characterized by a polity in which the highest recognized officer is the "presbyter" or "elder." Historically, the Presbyterian movement derives from John Calvin (*q.v.*) and its doctrine is "Calvinistic."

PRESENT.

That part of time lying between the past and the future.

(1) From Aristotle (*q.v.* 10) to Newton (*q.v.* 3) the present moment was an objective portion of the passage of time.

(2) From Leibniz (*q.v.* 2) through Einstein (*q.v.* 2) to Whitehead (*q.v.* 8), the present moment is relative to the frame of reference of some observer (or awareness).

(3) William James (*q.v.* 2) used the term "specious present" to refer to that span of real duration which we are able to grasp in a single act of awareness, although such a duration always contains also part of the future and part of the past.

(4) In contrast with the above, the present has at times been viewed as a knife-edge, or ideal limit, between the past and the future.

(5) Mead (*q.v.* 4) wrote on the "philosophy of the present," claiming that its uniqueness effectively altered the past as well as the future.

(6) Suzuki (*q.v.* 5), a representative of Zen, identified the Absolute Present, the eternal now, and *satori.*

PRESENTATIONAL IMMEDIACY.
Q.v. Whitehead (24).

PRE-SOCRATICS.
The name commonly given to the early period of Greek philosophy, covering the period from the middle of the 7th to the middle of the 5th century B.C. *Q.v.* Philosophy (31).

PRESUPPOSING.
(1) Collingwood (*q.v.* 2) regarded metaphysics as the study of the absolute presuppositions of a period of time.

(2) Strawson (*q.v.* 2) holds that certain difficulties in Russell's theory of definite descriptions can be avoided by keeping in mind that in referring to an entity, one presupposes, without asserting, existence.

PREVENIENT GRACE.
Q.v. Grace (3).

PRICE, H.H. 1899– .
English philosopher. Educated at Oxford and Cambridge. Taught at Oxford, 1935–59.

Principal writings: *Perception*, 1932; *Hume's Theory of the External World*, 1940; *Thinking and Representation*, 1946; *Thinking and Experience*, 1953; *Belief*, 1969; *Essays in the Philosophy of Religion*; 1972.

(1) Agreeing with Russell (*q.v.* 7–9) that the immediate object of sensation is a sense-datum (*q.v.*), Price nonetheless

rejects Russell's causal theory of perception, emphasizing instead the serial convergence of every family of sense-data on the standard solid. The latter is thus a projection one makes on the basis of sense-data, but it has some of the properties of the real object.

(2) All other sense-data may be regarded as distortions or variations of the standard solid. These variations fit naturally into series leading into the standard solid which is three-dimensional, and which possesses the standard figure and the real volume of the thing perceived. According to Price even visual sense-data can be "bulgy," and not confined to two dimensions.

(3) When reference is made to an object, says Price, one is referring to the appropriate family of sense-data and to the physical object "coincident with" that family. Thus, the physical object is not to be identified even with the standard solid, and Price thus avoids Phenomenalism (*q.v.*), or believes that he has done so.

(4) Concerning concepts, on the other hand, he believes that we can use them without regarding them as objects in the mind. We can think without symbols and when symbols are used, our thought can overflow and go beyond them.

PRICE, RICHARD. 1723–1791.
Welsh philosopher. Born at Tynton. A dissenting minister, he was educated in one of the dissenting academies of London. His pastorates were in and around London. His initial fame came from his writings on financial and political questions, including an influential argument favoring American independence.

Principal writings: *Review of the Principal Questions in Morals*, 1757; *Observations on the American Revolution*, 1776, 1784; *Materialism and Philosophical Necessity* (with Joseph Priestley), 1778.

(1) Opposing Hutcheson's Moral Sense Theory (*q.v.*), Price holds that right and wrong are simple ideas which derive from the understanding. They are simple since, in Lockean terms, they cannot be further disassembled. They derive from the understanding since there is no moral sense. He thus interprets Locke as allowing the possibility of new simple ideas, emerging from reflection, and accepts this as his doctrine.

(2) At the same time, however, there is nothing arbitrary about moral ideas. We derive them necessarily and intuitively from reflection on human actions; and moral approval includes both an act of the understanding and an emotion of the heart. The final end of life is happiness dependent upon rectitude.

(3) The point is that these distinctions finally come from God, and the conformity between our understanding and emotions, is due to the fact that God has so created us. Furthermore, God has given man the power of self-determination, and his soul the properties of unity and immateriality.

PRICHARD, H.A. 1871–1947.

English philosopher. Educated at Oxford. Taught at Oxford. A disciple of Cook Wilson (*q.v.*), Prichard opposed Kant, arguing from the standpoint of Oxford Realism. In ethics he was an intuitionist, holding that we simply know the nature of our duties, and that any attempt to formulate a general theory of duty rests on a mistake.

Principal writings: *Kant's Theory of Knowledge*, 1909; "Does Moral Philosophy Rest on a Mistake?" 1912; "Duty and Ignorance of Fact," 1932.

PRIDE.

The Greek term is *hybris*. Along with concupiscence, pride is the source of sin (*q.v.* 1) in the Christian tradition. Often regarded as a mortal sin, pride implies a lack of dependence on God.

PRIESTLEY, JOSEPH. 1733–1804.

English scientist and philosopher. Born in Fieldhead, Yorkshire. A dissenting minister, he was partly self-educated; for a number of years he attended the dissenting academy at Daventer. He worked in various capacities as pastor, tutor, and librarian, while conducting his scientific experiments in the field of chemistry. Discovering oxygen, and other gases, he prepared the way for Lavoisier. Theologically, he gradually moved to the position of Unitarianism; his support of the French Revolution led to his persecution in England, and finally emigration to America.

Principal philosophical writings: *Hartley's Theory of the Human Mind*, 1775;

Disquisitions Relating to Matter and Spirit, 1777; *Materialism and Philosophical Necessity* (with Richard Price), 1778; *Letters to the Inhabitants of Northumberland*, 1779; *Socrates and Jesus Compared*, 1803.

(1) Adopting Hartley's (*q.v.*) associationist psychology, he argued that its metaphysical correlate is materialism. Viewing matter not as inert but dynamic, he argued that the most reasonable hypothesis is that the brain thinks. Thus, dualism is avoided.

(2) He defended determinism on the ground that it alone is consistent with an ethic rooted in the general happiness principle, although not compatible with praise and blame.

(3) Theology is compatible with materialism, since according to Scripture eternal life begins with the resurrection of the body.

PRIMA FACIE DUTIES.

From the Latin phrase *prima facie* ("first appearance"), a term of law applicable to evidence. *Prima facie* evidence raises a presumption of fact and is taken to establish that fact unless refuted. W.D. Ross (*q.v.* 2) applied the concept to the duties or obligations one senses. One's *prima facie* duties are those he senses and in the order he senses them, although these may change to some extent after reflection. One's responsibility at any moment is to the highest *prima facie* duty relevant to that situation.

PRIMALITIES.

Q.v. Campanella (3)

PRIMAL MAN.

Q.v. Gnosticism (4–5); Manichaeism (2).

PRIMARY QUALITIES.

Q.v. Qualities, Primary and Secondary.

PRIME MATTER.

The utterly formless potentiality introduced by Aristotle (*q.v.* 7). The potentiality of matter requires the actuality of form; and in Aquinas (*q.v.* 5) it is made very clear that if prime matter is at the lower end of the scale of being, pure form, *i.e.*, God, is at the upper end of this scale.

PRIME MOVER.

For Aristotle (*q.v.* 10) the name applied

to God as the first cause of all motion and change. Also q.v. Aquinas (3).

PRIMITIVISM.

The concept of the primitive in man and society has played a number of roles in philosophy.

(1) Rousseau (q.v. 3) pictured the life of the savage as no less undesirable than that of civilized man; but there is a simple community life between the two extremes.

(2) In Marxism (q.v. 1b) the primitive community was regarded as a communal unit.

(3) Lévy-Bruhl (q.v. 1) regarded the primitive as operating on a prelogical level.

(4) Lovejoy (q.v. 2) and Boas investigated the views of primitivism, adopted by civilized societies in times of crisis, namely that the primitive state of affairs was better and that civilization is degeneration.

PRIMORDIAL NATURE OF GOD.

Q.v. Whitehead (10, 16).

PRINCIPIA MATHEMATICA. 3 vols., 1910–13.

The highly influential work of A.N. Whitehead (q.v. 2) and Bertrand Russell (q.v.), demonstrating how mathematics can be constructed on a logical base. The work belongs to, and gave impetus to, the formalist view of mathematics. The discovery of difficulties in the program has prevented universal acceptance of the thesis that mathematics can be so constructed. Some of the difficulties, and their possible treatments, are suggested under Mathematics (B). Whatever may be the case for mathematics, the work gave enormous impetus to the development of symbolic, or formal, logic.

PRINCIPIUM INDIVIDUATIONIS.

Q.v. Individuation, Principle of.

PRINCIPLE.

From the Latin principium, a translation of the Greek arche, ("a beginning"), hence the beginning point.

(1) The early Greek philosophers asked for the principle of all things and found it in a substance from which everything else can be derived. Q.v. Philosophy (31).

(2) Aristotle pointed out that principles may refer to being, generation, or knowledge. In each case the derivation is explained by reference to the relevant principles.

(3) It is in this sense that the principles of identity, contradiction, and excluded middle—also termed the Laws of Thought (q.v.)—are so named. In a sense, ordered thought derives from the principles. Also see Leibniz' Principle of Sufficient Reason (q.v. Leibniz 4).

(4) In a related sense, the primitive propositions of a system, used to derive other propositions, and not themselves proven within the system, are the principles of the system.

(5) Close to the center of the thought of Paul Tillich (q.v. 6) is the Protestant principle, a protection against absolutizing the finite.

(6) Heisenberg (q.v.) referred to the Indeterminacy Principle of quantum mechanics, whereby the position and velocity of particles cannot be precisely and simultaneously determined.

PRINGLE-PATTISON, ANDREW SETH. 1856–1931.

Scottish philosopher. Born in Edinburgh where he studied and eventually taught. A follower of Hegel, he was concerned to see that human individuality was not lost in the Absolute, and that intuitions of value be given a role, along with the principle of coherence, in determining the nature of reality.

Principal writings: Scottish Philosophy, 1855; Hegelianism and Personality, 1887; The Idea of God in the Light of Recent Philosophy, 1917; The Idea of Immortality, 1922; Studies in the Philosophy of Religion, 1930.

PRIOR, A.N.

Q.v. Logic (26); Modal Logic (6).

PRIVATE LANGUAGES.

The possibility of private languages was discussed by Wittgenstein (q.v. 8) in his Philosophical Investigations. Although Wittgenstein decided that there could be no such thing as a private language, because of the absence of a criterion concerning how words are to be used, the thesis has given rise to extensive controversy.

PRIVATION.

From the Latin privatio ("a freeing from or depriving of"), a concept used by

Aristotle (*q.v.* 8) to indicate the lack of a quality—*e.g.*, blindness in a man as the lack of sight—which the thing in question normally would possess.

PROBABILISM.

The doctrine that certainty is unattainable, held by the Skeptics (*q.v.*) including members of the Second Academy. Also *q.v.* Peirce (10) for the related doctrine of Fallibilism.

PROBABILITY.

From the Latin *probare* ("to prove, to approve"). The Latin is a translation of the Greek *eulogon* ("reasonable or sensible"). The term thus refers to the likelihood of the happening of an event, or of the truth of a proposition. Where conclusions follow by necessity in deductive inference, they follow only by probability in induction. Probability theory has been developed into a very sophisticated discipline in modern mathematics.

(1) Among philosophers, "probability" was first discussed by the philosophers of Plato's Academy (*q.v.* 2–3). Taking the position that certainty is unattainable, probability became a central concept. Carneades (*q.v.* 1) advanced a notion of degrees of probability resting on consistency as well as evidence.

(2) Following the skepticism of the Academy, a long hiatus occurred in which the concept of probability dropped from sight. Even when Skepticism reasserted itself, as in the time of Montaigne (*q.v.* 2), the idea of probability was ignored. Montaigne held that the position of the Academy that some judgments are more probable than others is less plausible than the position of Pyrrho (*q.v.*) that all judgments are equally suspect.

(3) The development of the concept of probability came from the mathematicians and scientists—not excluding philosophers who were also mathematicians. In its initial stages the attempt to understand gambling chances was central. Galileo analyzed chances with respect to the throw of dice; and Pascal (*q.v.*) and the mathematician, Fermat, engaged in correspondence over the probabilities of A or B winning in an interrupted game of chance. In the course of the interchange Pascal laid down the two fundamental rules: (a) the probability that both of two

independent events will happen is the product of their separate probabilities; (b) the probability that one or the other of two mutually exclusive events shall happen is the sum of their separate probabilities.

(4) Both mathematicians and non-mathematicians contributed to probability theory: Huygens, in 1657, published a number of proofs concerning mathematical expectation; Johannes Bernoulli in *Ars Conjectandi* (1713) reprinted Huygens' proofs, supplied proofs for problems mentioned by Huygens, and presented what has come to be known as Bernoulli's Theorem. This is a formula according to which, given an initial probability, and a chosen "distance" from that probability, the chances—*e.g.*, throws of the dice—will approach that distance as closely as one pleases as the chances increase. For example, suppose the initial probability is 1/36, the probability of any two sides coming up together in any given roll of two six-sided dice. Suppose, too, that we wish the average of our recorded rolls to be no more than .01 from the initial probability in either direction. The theorem holds that our prospect of reaching that number, or distance, from the initial probability, increases with the number of rolls. D'Alembert (*q.v.* 2) struggled with the conception of probability theory, contributing mostly errors. Bayes' treatment of inverse probability appeared in 1763 (a formula, known as Bayes' Law which seeks to determine initial probabilities on the basis of observed frequencies). Condorcet (*q.v.* 1) attempted to apply these principles to social decision-making.

(5) Laplace (*q.v.* 3) brought together the insights of his predecessors in his 1812 publication, *The Analytic Theory of Probabilities*, creating a discipline from them, while simplifying and interrelating the laws. The discipline, regarded by Laplace as common sense reduced to calculation, followed the rule that the measure of probability—given mutually exclusive possibilities which are equally probable *a priori*—is the ratio of the number of favorable possibilities to the total number of possibilities. The frequency theory of probability grew naturally from these considerations.

(6) Following Laplace, while relating the subject more closely to formal logic,

DeMorgan (*q.v.* 3) held probability to be the degree of belief a rational person ought to grant a given proposition. The probability was to be calculated by the inverse theorem, beginning with consequences and reasoning back to hypotheses.

(7) Jevons (*q.v.* 4) followed DeMorgan in approaching probability as the measure of appropriate belief, using the inverse theorem. Jevons' development of the method revealed its weakness, especially in the establishing of *a priori* probabilities by means of a principle of indifference.

(8) Peirce (*q.v.* 9) adapted the frequency theory to his own ends, regarding probability not as a measure of events, but as a ratio between the true propositions in a given class, and all of the propositions in that class; if the class is infinite one appeals to testing in the long run.

(9) For J. M. Keynes (*q.v.*), following Jevons, probability belongs to a proposition only in relation to other propositions. Probability is a measure of the rationality of believing in the occurrence of a second series of propositions, given the occurrence of a first series.

(10) Richard Von Mises held probability to be the limit of the frequency of an event as the number of its trials approaches infinity. He called the total random sequence of such trials a "collective," and stipulated that the same property with the same limiting value holds of sequences derived from the collective.

(11) Reichenbach (*q.v.* 1) understood probability to be the limit of a relative frequency determined by the "weights" appropriate to the statements under examination.

(12) Carnap (*q.v.* 10) distinguished two types of probability: frequency-probability and confirmation-probability. The former rests on a frequency theory of probability and is appropriate to statistical problems. The latter rests on a confirmation theory of probability, and is appropriate to cases of inductive inference where one's interest is in the probability of the truth of some hypothesis *h*, given evidence *e*.

(13) Braithwaite (*q.v.* 2) modified the "frequency view of probability" by adding a "rejection rule" and a "prudential policy." The former is invoked when relative frequencies depart markedly from the initial probabilities. The latter, based on maximization of the minimum mathematical expectation, is a method for choosing between alternative statistical hypotheses.

(14) Popper (*q.v.* 2) opposes the view that probability is the limit of a frequency, and argues instead that it is the assignment of a propensity to some part of the natural world.

(15) Ramsey (*q.v.*) advanced a subjective theory of probability, turning on degrees of belief.

(16) Non-mathematical philosophers have also employed the term "probability." Berkeley had said that "probability is the guide to life," but the saying remained on the level of aphorism. Cardinal Newman (*q.v.* 6) applied the term "probable" to all instances of "concrete reasoning." In his terminology, however, a judgment could be probable and at the same time certain. G. E. Moore (*q.v.* 2) held it to be more probable that one's hand exists than that the principles of skepticism are true.

Also *q.v.* the applications of probability in Decision Theory.

PROBLEMATIC JUDGMENT.
One of the three modes of judgment distinguished by Kant (*q.v.* 3), that one asserting of a thing that it is possible (or impossible). The other two modes are those of the Assertoric Judgment (*q.v.*) and the Apodeictic Judgment (*q.v.*). The analysis of modality goes back at least to Aristotle. For something of its history *q.v.* Modality. Also *q.v.* Logic (25).

PROCESS PHILOSOPHY.
A term sometimes applied to those philosophies stressing "becoming" rather than "being." Although many philosophies fit within this category, including that of Heraclitus (*q.v.*), the term is usually applied to philosophies such as that of Whitehead (*q.v.* 9) where process is set in contrast to the idea of substance.

PROCLUS. 410–485.
Hellenic philosopher. Born in Constantinople, he studied with Olimpiodorus (*q.v.*) in the Alexandrian School of Neoplatonism, and with Syrianus (*q.v.*) in Athens. He followed Syrianus as head of the School of Athens (*q.v.*), and is said

to have been so fond of his master that he asked to be buried in the same tomb. He attempted to find a system of thought which would accommodate the doctrines of the School of Athens, those of Plotinus (*q.v.*) and Iamblichus (*q.v.*), as well as the systems of Plato and Aristotle. *Q.v.* Neoplatonism.

Principal writings: *Elements of Theology* (T); *Plato's Theology* (T); *Elements of Physics; Ten Doubts Concerning Providence* (T); *Concerning Providence and Fate* (T); *On the Subsistence of Evil* (T); as well as Commentaries on the principal works of Plato.

(1) Attempting to explain the process of emanation by the categories of identity, difference, and return, the first category ("identity") applies primarily to the divine unity, the second ("difference") to the emanations from the One, and the third ("return") from the unity within those emanations which calls them back. The universe is thus held in balance by the interplay of emanation and return.

(2) This explanation led Proclus to a doctrine of *henads*. The doctrine has some resemblance to the monadology of Leibniz (*q.v.* 1), at least in the sense that the One has to contain all diversity within its identity, and the inferior beings—although merely participating in those superior principles from which they are derived—contain in themselves something like a mirroring of the superior reality. The whole hierarchical series, including the One, Being, Life, Intelligence, and Soul is of this reciprocally reflecting type.

(3) The analysis leads Proclus to conclude that the universe is rife with gods, who thus constitute the unity of the whole in relation to the One. Interacting with such a universe, he supported theurgy (*q.v.*), regarding it as a power above all human wisdom.

(4) The soul has an opportunity for ecstatic return to the One on the basis of a faculty which it possesses, which is superior to intelligence.

PRODICUS. c. 460–c. 399 B.C.

Greek philosopher. Born in Ceos. One of the Sophists, Prodicus appears several times in the Socratic Dialogues. Among his interests were the study of grammar, and especially the problems of synonyms, the study of religion, particularly the process whereby parts of the natural world become divinized, and the field of ethics where he professed a pessimism partly countered by a work imperative. Among his writings was a myth of Heracles at the crossroads, choosing arduous virtue over pleasant vice. He is sometimes credited with initiating the argument later used by the Epicureans that death is not to be feared, for when fear is possible one is not dead; and when one is dead, no feelings are possible.

Principal writings: *On Nature; On the Nature of Man; On Propriety of Language; Hours* (including "The Choice of Heracles"); only fragments, references, and summaries remain.

PRODUCT-OBJECTIVISM, ANTI-SUBJECTIVIST.

Q.v. Wahle (2).

PRODUCT-REALISM, AGNOSTIC.

Q.v. Wahle (2).

PROGRESS.

From the Latin *pro* ("forward") and *gradi* ("to step or go"). In philosophy the conception of progress is to be contrasted with the view that the Golden Age was in the past, and with the view that time is eternal recurrence. Of course, in both West and East, views can be cited (*q.v.* Empedocles 3, Ramanuja 4) where the cycle of time includes periods of progress and of regress or decline. But the idea of progress can perhaps best be viewed as a secularized version of the Christian movement toward the apocalypse, and the Kingdom of God.

(1) The secular idea of progress gained prominence among the French *Philosophes* or Encyclopedists (*q.v.*) of the 18th century. Cabanis (*q.v.* 2) preached the idea of progress, ending in a secular utopia. Condorcet (*q.v.* 2, 3) believed in human perfectibility, to be achieved in the tenth stage of civilization, just then dawning. Turgot (*q.v.*) wrote on historical progress and universal history. Voltaire (*q.v.* 2) believed in gradual progress.

(2) Hegel (*q.v.* 3) supported the idea of progress through the dialectical interplay of thesis-antithesis-synthesis. Since the third of these terms represented a qualitative advance over the first two, it can be said that progress occurs through opposition.

(3) According to François Guizot, tolerance is an indispensable condition for progress (*q.v.* Toleration 10).

(4) Comte (*q.v.* 1, 3, 5) formalized the program of the French philosophers in his law of the three stages, where science is viewed as the means to individual development, leading to the scientific age, humanity's historic goal. The social goal is progress combined with order.

(5) Marx (*q.v.* Marxism 1) and his followers employed the Hegelian dialectic to explain how, through class conflict, humanity will progress to a final goal where class distinctions no longer exist.

(6) From all of the above sources, and in addition an application to society of the evolutionary principles of Darwin (*q.v.*) and Spencer (*q.v.*), the idea of progress came to characterize all Western societies. The shock of 20th-century warfare has weakened the belief which, however, still continues.

Also *q.v.* History (C.).

PRO INSIPIENTE.
Q.v. Gaunilo.

PROJECTION.
Q.v. Jung (2, 4–6).

PROLEPSIS.
A Greek term meaning "anticipation." (1) In traditional logic the term referred to the anticipation of an objection, and one's response to it. (2) Among the Stoics (*q.v.* Stoicism 1) the term was used to refer to any one of the principles or "common notions" which the soul contains, whether innately or from common experience.

PROPER NAMES.
Proper names may be confined to such terms as "Socrates," "Plato," "Aristotle," and "Mr. Brown," or extended to all terms which pick out a single individual. In either case, the function of proper names is to refer one to certain objects. They are, then, expected to have denotation.

(1) Some have held that proper names have denotation but no connotation. Among those holding such a view are Plato (*Theaetetus* 201d), J.S. Mill (*Logic* I, 2, sec. 5), and the early Wittgenstein (*Tractatus* 3.203). Among the problems with this view is that if proper names have only denotation, it is not clear how

(except in cases of personal acquaintance) we can be referred from the name to its object.

(2) Others have held that proper names both denote and connote. In this vein Frege (*q.v.* 6–7) taught that proper, along with other, names have both sense and reference when they denote; and when they do not, they may have sense but no reference, *i.e.*, connotation even when denotation is lacking.

(3) Russell agreed with the Wittgenstein of the *Tractatus* that the meaning of a proper name is simply the object for which that name stands; but since what we call proper names refer by means of descriptions, he held that such so-called proper names are really concealed definite descriptions (*q.v.* Russell 4); and that proper names in the "narrow logical sense" are a special class of names which refer to their objects apart from such descriptions.

(4) John Searle ("Proper Names," 1959) argued, on the other hand, that proper names can't refer apart from descriptions. Each proper name has an "identifying description"; and this is the "logical sum" or "inclusive disjunction" of properties commonly attributed to it.

(5) On the view of Frege and Searle the truth values of proper names will sometimes be different for different persons and groups at the same or at different times. Saul A. Kripke (*q.v.* 1–2) expects to overcome this and other difficulties by invoking the term "rigid designator" to designate the object of a proper name in all possible worlds.

PROPERTY.
From the Latin *proprius* ("one's own," "proper"). The term has been used to mark out both what is common to all the members of a class, and that to which a person has a legal title.

(1) In Aristotle (*q.v.* 4) one of five types of attribution. A property is not part of the essence of a thing, and yet it belongs to that thing and it alone. Aristotle gives the example of the capacity to learn grammar as a property of man. Only man has this capacity, and yet it is not, as such, part of the definition of the term "man." Aristotle also tells us that a "property" is convertible.

(2) In the second sense of property,

Locke (*q.v.* 9) speaks of property as a natural right: God gave the world to men in common, and men carved out of the commons by the addition of human labor, the right of property.

(3) Paine (*q.v.* 4) held the earth in its natural state to be the common property of the human race.

(4) Hegel (*q.v.* 12) held property in the Lockean sense to be the first embodiment of human freedom.

(5) Marx (*q.v.* 1) generalized Locke's notion of property in the *Economic and Philosophic Manuscripts*, so that property is regarded as an externalization of man's ideas and purposes, becoming concretized through his activities. He likewise regarded property as the source of divisiveness among men.

PROPHECY.

From the Greek *prophetein* ("the gift of interpreting the will of the gods"). Interpreting the will of the gods sometimes, but by no means always, implied the prediction of future events.

(1) The term is derived from Greek religion, where it was applied to those who interpreted dreams, visions, and enigmatic utterances of the oracles.

(2) Philo Judaeus (*q.v.* 3) defined the true prophet as the one who speaks nothing of his own, but simply repeats what has been given to him in revelation.

(3) All members of the early Church were expected to exhibit the gift of prophecy.

(4) Avicenna (*q.v.* 11), making an Aristotelian interpretation of prophecy, held that the true prophet can receive from the active intelligence at once what an ordinary intellect, in ordinary circumstances, must work out little by little.

(5) Deism (*q.v.*) generally rejected prophecy; for example, *q.v.* Thomas Woolston, and Thomas Chubb.

PROPHYSICAL.

Q.v. Rickert (3).

PROPITIATION.

From the Latin *propitiare* ("to render favorable"). The act of atoning for one's sins, whether through sacrifice, asceticism, or good works. In Christian theology Christ's crucifixion is the supreme atonement or propitiation of man's sins.

PROPORTIONALITY, ANALOGY OF.

Q.v. Analogy (2).

PROPOSITION.

From the Latin *proponere* ("to set forth or propose"). A proposition is, hence, an assertion which proposes or denies something, and is capable of being judged true or false. From Aristotle through Kant, propositions were held to result from judgments (*q.v.*). Such language is no longer usual. Since the same idea may be conveyed by different sentences, one should not identify the proposition with the sentence which is its expression. There is disagreement over the nature of the proposition. Contrasting positions concerning what propositions are may be seen by referring to Boole (*q.v.* 9), Frege (*q.v.*), Church (*q.v.*), and the Theory of Inscriptions (*q.v.*). Our purpose here is merely to cite the basic types of propositions. Among the types of propositions we must distinguish:

(1) Categorical propositions. These propositions include:

(a) Singular propositions: "Socrates is a man." Singular propositions are either predicative (they predicate a property of the subject of the proposition), or impredicative (they deny a property of the subject of the proposition).

(b) Universal Affirmative propositions: "All humans are mortal."

(c) Universal Negative propositions: "No humans are immortal."

(d) Particular Affirmative propositions: "Some lawyers are politicians."

(e) Particular Negative propositions: "Some lawyers are not politicians."

(2) Hypothetical propositions: "If the temperature drops ten degrees more, then the pond will freeze." The "If" clause is called the antecedent, and the "then" clause the consequent.

(3) Disjunctive propositions: "Either it will rain or else the crops will fail." The two clauses are called the disjuncts of the proposition. There is a weak sense of "either-or" to the effect that not both of the disjuncts can be false at the same time. This is the usual sense of "either-or," and this kind of disjunctive is sometimes termed an alternative proposition. That is in fact the kind of disjunction in our example. There is also a strong sense of either-or. And this sense is exemplified

in the disjunction: "Either he was born in Missouri, or he was born in Maine." Not both of these disjuncts can be true at the same time.

For the Categorical Syllogism *q.v.* Syllogism (1–7). For the Hypothetical Syllogism *q.v.* Syllogism (8–10). For the Disjunctive Syllogism *q.v.* Syllogism (11–12).

PROPOSITIONAL ATTITUDES.

Problems raised by statements concerning beliefs, desires, hopes, wishes, and other attitudes have been treated by Quine (*q.v.* 9), Hintikka (*q.v.* 1), Fodor (*q.v.* 2–4), Stich (*q.v.* Psychology 18, and Folk Psychology 2), among others (*q.v.* Quantifying In).

PROPOSITIONAL CALCULUS.

That part of logic concerned with the valid inferences and transformations which can be drawn from the relations of propositions to each other. To be distinguished from the theory of the Syllogism (*q.v.*) where the concern is with the valid inferences which can be drawn from the internal relations of the subjects and predicates of certain kinds of propositions, *i.e.*, those called Categorical. In contemporary logic, the propositional calculus and syllogistic theory are parts of a total system. Syllogism is treated within Quantification Theory (*q.v.*), which has the propositional calculus as its foundation.

A. Paralleling Aristotle's development of the syllogism, the Megarian and Stoic schools of philosophy had anticipated the propositional calculus.

(1) Philo of Megara (*q.v.* 1) was the first to work out the definition of material implication. Of the four possibilities for truth and falsity in the conditional proposition, "if p, then q," Philo held that the conditional is false only when the antecedent is true and the consequent is false. In all other cases it is true (*q.v.* Truth Tables 3). The definition is accepted today. It was worked out independently, however, and only later discovered in Philo.

(2) Chrysippus (*q.v.* 1) had worked out the definitions of Modus Ponens ("if p then q; p; therefore q"); Modus Tollens ("if p then q; not q; therefore not p"); and two forms of the Disjunctive Syllo-

gism ("Not both p and q; p; therefore not q"); and "Either p or q; not p; therefore q"). These definitions likewise became part of the calculus; they had wide currency, and were developed by many different individuals.

B. The valid inferences and transformations of the calculus can be exhibited by allowing the horseshoe "⊃" to stand for material implication ("if-then"), the wedge "∨" to stand for disjunction ("either-or"), the dot "·" to stand for conjunction ("and"), three horizontal bars "≡" to stand for material equivalence ("is equivalent to"), and the tilde "~" to stand for negation ("not"). These signs or connectives will be defined by the appropriate Truth Tables (*q.v.* 1–5). Since these truth-functional connectives, as we shall call them, must connect propositions, we must allow certain letters "p," "q," "r," "s," etc. to stand for propositions. Given the above we can set down the basic argument forms of the calculus.

(3) *Modus Ponens*: $p \supset q$; p; therefore q. "If p then q; p; therefore q."

(4) *Modus Tollens*: $p \supset q$; ~ q; therefore ~ p. "If p then q; not q; therefore not p."

(5) Hypothetical Syllogism: $p \supset q$; $q \supset r$; therefore $p \supset r$. "If p then q; if q then r; therefore, if p then r."

(6) Disjunctive Syllogism: $p \vee q$; ~ p; therefore q. "Either p or q; not p; therefore, q."

[The truth tables of the above four forms are to be found under Truth Tables (6)].

(7) Constructive Dilemma: $(p \supset q) \cdot (r \supset s)$; $p \vee r$; therefore $q \vee s$. "If p then q; and if r then s; but either p or r; therefore either q or s."

(8) Destructive Dilemma:
$(p \supset q) \cdot (r \supset s)$; ~ q ∨ ~ s; therefore ~ p ∨ ~ r. "If p then q; and if r then s; but either not q or not s; therefore either not p or not r."

(9) Simplification: $p \cdot q$; therefore p. "p and q are true; therefore p is true."

(10) Conjunction: p,q; therefore $p \cdot q$. "p and q are true separately; therefore they are true conjointly."

(11) Addition: p; therefore, $p \vee q$. "p is true; therefore the disjunction (p or q) is true."

(12) Composition:
$[(p \supset q) \cdot (p \supset r)] \supset (p \supset q \cdot r)$. "If p

then q; and if p then r; then if p then q and r."

(13) De Morgan's Theorems (*q.v.* De Morgan): ~ (p · q) ≡ (~ p ∨ ~ q). "The negation of (p and q) is equivalent to (not p or not q)." ~ (p ∨ q) ≡ (~ p · ~ q). "The negation of (p or q) is equivalent to (not p and not q)."

(14) Commutation: (p ∨ q) ≡ (q ∨ p). "(p or q) is equivalent to (q or p)." (p · q) ≡ (q · p). "(p and q) is equivalent to (q and p)."

(15) Association: [p ∨ (q ∨ r)] ≡ [(p ∨ q) ∨ r]. "p or (q or r) is equivalent to (p or q) or r." [p · (q · r)] ≡ [(p · q) · r]. "p and (q and r) is equivalent to (p and q) and r."

(16) Distribution: [p · (q ∨ r)] ≡ [(p · q) ∨ (p · r)]. "p and (q or r) is equivalent to (p and q) or (p and r)." [p ∨ (q · r)] ≡ [(p ∨ q) · (p ∨ r)]. "p or (q and r) is equivalent to (p or q) and (p or r)."

(17) Double Negation: p ≡ ~ ~p. "p is equivalent to the negation of not p."

(18) Transposition: (p ⊃ q) ≡ (~ q ⊃ ~ p). "If p then q is equivalent to if not q then not p."

(19) Material Implication: (p ⊃ q) ≡ (~ p ∨ q). "If p then q is equivalent to either not p or q."

[For the truth table of material implication *q.v.* Truth Tables (4)].

(20) Material Equivalence: (p ≡ q) ≡ [(p ⊃ q) · (q ⊃ p)]. "(p is equivalent to q) is equivalent to (if p then q) and (if q then p)." (p ≡ q) ≡ [(p · q) ∨ (~ p · ~ q)]. "(p is equivalent to q) is equivalent to (p and q) or (not p and not q.)"

[For the truth table of the first form of material equivalence, *q.v.* Truth Tables (5). The truth table for the second form can be easily worked out in a similar way.]

(21) Exportation: [(p · q) ⊃ r] ≡ [p ⊃ (q ⊃ r)]. "If (p and q) then r is equivalent to if p then if q then r."

(The second half of the equivalence, [p ⊃ (q ⊃ r)] ⊃ [(p · q) ⊃ r], is sometimes called "Importation.")

(22) Tautology: p ≡ (p ∨ p). "p is true is equivalent to p is true or p is true."

[Truth tables can be worked out for any of the valid forms according to the method used in the entry, Truth Tables (*q.v.*).]

C. It is clear that a number of these forms can be combined into a complex argument. Indeed, in the two forms of the Dilemma (*cf.* 7 and 8 above) material implication, the disjunctive syllogism, and negation have been combined in a single argument. It is also the case that all of us use in our reasoning a great many of these forms. It should be possible, by attention to this list, to gain further clarity concerning the structure of our arguments.

(23) One way of using the calculus is to see whether one's argument in ordinary language has a valid structure. If one can show that one's conclusion follows from the premises by valid steps, then the structure is valid. Let us take an argument in ordinary language and reduce it to its essentials. The argument is: "Either the calculus is useful or a different way of evaluating arguments in ordinary language must be found. If the calculus is useful it will be applicable to ordinary discourse. But ordinary discourse is immensely complicated, and much more subtle than the argument forms presented above. Therefore, the calculus is not really applicable to ordinary discourse, and a different way of evaluating arguments in ordinary language must be found." For the sake of seeing what is involved in this argument we shall use appropriate capital letters to stand for these propositions rather than "p," "q," r," etc. with the following results:

"U" will replace "the calculus is useful."

"D" will replace "a different way of evaluating arguments in ordinary language must be found."

"A" will replace "it will be applicable to ordinary discourse." I suggest that the structure of the argument is the following:

1. U ∨ D
2. U ⊃ A
3. ~ A / therefore, D.

And the question is whether we can derive D from these premises by valid steps. In this case, it is clear that we can. Let us continue the proof with the fourth step.

4. ~ U From 2 and 3 by Modus Tollens
5. D From 1 and 4 by Disjunctive Syllogism

Obviously, the calculus cannot be applied in a mechanical fashion. One might find, for example, that U implies something other than A. The use of the calculus might be mental stimulation, or the revision of ordinary discourse, or something else. In short, looking for the structure of the argument might lead one to a different argument.

In principle, any argument can be diagrammed and tested as we have done; and the section on the calculus in modern introductions to logic will give much additional material. One will not go very far along this path without finding the need to use quantified statements in one's arguments. For a brief discussion of this, *q.v.* Quantification Theory.

PROPOSITIONAL FUNCTION.
Q.v. Function (2).

PROPRIUM.
Q.v. Schleiermacher (3).

PROSOPIC UNION.
Christological doctrine of Nestorius (*q.v.* Nestorianism).

PROSOPON.
Q.v. Sabellius.

PROSYLLOGISM.
A syllogism preliminary to another, its conclusion forming a premise of the syllogism which follows.

PROTAGORAS. 490–c.410 B.C.
Greek philosopher. Born at Abdera in Thrace. According to some sources he was a student of Democritus. The most important of the Sophists, Protagoras was a friend of both Pericles and Euripides and held the respect of Socrates and Plato. Cited as the first to support himself by philosophy, he allegedly received fees up to several thousand dollars per student. It seems that he trained his students to frame arguments on both sides of any question, and he is credited with offering to refute any proposition. He drew up the constitution for the colony at Thurii. Late in life he was exiled from Athens on the charge of atheism.

Principal writings: *On Truth; On the Gods; Antilogic.* He is likewise credited with works on law, grammar, and mathematics. Only fragments of his writings survive.

(1) "Man is the measure of all things; of things that are that they are, and of things that are not that they are not." It

is impossible to determine how Protagoras intended this claim. Plato and Aristotle find a complete relativity of knowledge in Protagoras, so that whatever one perceives to be the case is so, even when the perceptions of different individuals are inconsistent. It is not clear how far such relativity extends but Protagoras did equate truth with workability and health of soul, and regarded the task of education as changing men from a worse to a better condition.

(2) He held that all matter is in a state of flux and, according to Sextus Empiricus, that matter is the sum of the appearances that it has for any and all persons.

(3) On the question of ethics, he argued that whatever seems right and admirable to a city-state is truly right and admirable, so long as the opinion holds.

(4) He presented through myth the picture of social progress occurring by means of the settlement of communities and the development of arts and crafts.

(5) Concerning the gods he said he had "No way of knowing either that they exist or that they do not exist; nor, if they exist, of what form they are."

PROTASIS.
A Greek term meaning "that which is put forward."

(1) In Aristotle's logic, the premise of a syllogism, especially the major premise.

(2) The conditional clause of an "if-then" statement. The second clause is the *apodosis.*

PROTESTANTISM.
The name given to all Christian denominations, sects, or groups rising out of the Reformation. The term "protestant" was applied initially to the German princes who, at the Diet of Speyer in 1529, protested the decision to annul their freedom to manage religious affairs within their territory as they saw fit. Protestant Churches generally agreed that the principle of authority should be the Scriptures rather than the Church or the pope. *Q.v.* Luther (10).

PROTESTANT PRINCIPLE, THE.
Q.v. Tillich (6).

PROTESTANT REFORMATION.

A movement of religious reform in Europe whose leaders span two centuries. Beginning with Wycliffe (*q.v.*), in the 14th century, who first set forth the principles of the Reformation, and with Huss (*q.v.*), in the late 14th and early 15th centuries, who first implemented these principles, the movement extended through the better part of the 16th century. Beginning with Luther's (*q.v.* 1) posting of his 95 Theses in 1517, the Reformation took the center of the European stage. Luther's initiative was continued in the work of Melanchthon (*q.v.*), Zwingli (*q.v.*), Calvin (*q.v.*), and Knox (*q.v.*). The Roman Catholic Church responded with its Counter-Reformation (*q.v.*).

PROTOCOL SENTENCE.

A sentence consisting of an observation report describing directly given experience. Protocol sentences, also called "basic sentences," were regarded by the logical positivists of the Vienna Circle (*q.v.*) as the basis of all science, and of intelligibility in any field. Otto Neurath (*q.v.*) and Carnap (*q.v.*) stressed the importance of protocol sentences. Carnap (*q.v.* 3) argued that protocol sentences can be expressed in the language of physics.

PROTOTHETIC.

Q.v. Leśniewski.

PROUDHON, JOSEPH. 1809–1865.

French philosopher. He believed that philosophy has the responsibility to provide the norms which will make possible a society reorganized on the principles of justice. Among these norms is the ideal of complete toleration. Since, according to his view, any control of one human group over another is unjust, a system of free cooperation among humans must be achieved. This entails voluntary cooperation among the groups to which they belong. In his view, coercive power will not be necessary, and the state as a coercive instrument is intended to disappear. Marx (*q.v.* 4) attacked Proudhon's philosophy.

Principal writings: *What is Property?* (T), 1840; *On the Creation of Order in Humanity*, 1843; *System of Economic Contradictions* (T), 1846; *On Justice in the Revolution and in the Church*, 3 vols., 1852; *The Social Revolu-*tion, 1852; *The Philosophy of Progress*, 1853.

PROVIDENCE.

From the Latin *providere* ("to foresee"). The term refers to the regulative agency of God in the world. A distinction is usually drawn between "general providence" and "special providence."

(1) General providence occurs through the fixed laws of nature. Stoicism (*q.v.*, for example, Epictetus 4) held to the concept of a general providence directing the world.

(2) Christianity added to general providence the idea of a special providence specifically related to each individual being.

PRUDENCE.

From *prudentia*, the Latin translation of the Greek word, *phronesis*.

(1) Socrates (*q.v.* 3) viewed the term as the guarantee of virtue in the equation, "virtue is knowledge."

(2) Prudence, sometimes translated as wisdom, was one of the four Greek cardinal virtues: prudence or wisdom, courage, temperance, and uprightness. Plato (*q.v.* 5c.) explored the interrelations of these terms in the *Republic*, although he used *sophia* (wisdom) in his explication rather than *phronesis*.

(3) Aristotle (*q.v.* 1, 11), however, took account of the distinction of terms, dividing wisdom into two types: speculative wisdom (or *sophia*), and practical wisdom (or *phronesis*). Prudence, or practical wisdom, is a virtue standing between excessive caution and impetuosity.

(4) The Cyrenaics (*q.v.* Cyrenaicism 1) and the Epicureans (*q.v.* Epicurus 10) made prudence one of the chief goals of life.

(5) Thomas Aquinas (*q.v.* 8) followed the analysis of Aristotle, while holding that prudence can be attributed to God, since the ordering of things to their ultimate end is the chief part of prudence.

(6) Hobbes (*q.v.* 5) distinguished—as he said did the Latins generally—between *prudentia* and *sapientia*, the former deriving from experience and the latter from science.

(7) Paley (*q.v.* 1) taught that prudence and virtue, now or in the long run, coincide; and Bentham seems to have followed Paley on the point.

(8) Kant (*q.v.* 6) related prudence to hypothetical imperatives, not the categorical imperative. It is associated with expediency and self-seeking, the practical necessity of an action which is a means to happiness.

(9) Butler (*q.v.* 1) held that reasonable self-love (prudence) and conscience are principles of human nature which it is our manifest obligation to obey.

(10) Sidgwick (*q.v.* 4) believed "prudence" to be an intuitive principle along with "benevolence" and "justice," the three together providing the basis of ethical behavior.

PRUDENTIAL POLICY.
Q.v. Braithwaite (2).

PRZYWARA, ERICH. 1889–1972.
German philosopher. Born in Kattowitz. Taught at the University of Munich. Interested in the relations of philosophy and religion, he took the *Analogia Entis*, or Analogy of Being (*q.v.* Analogy), as his central conception. It allowed him to include in his thought the idea of grades of being, leading to God, and to a view of polarity as the basic law of reality, related to the joint immanence and transcendence of God.

Principal writings: *A Newman Synthesis*, ed., 1931; *Analogia Entis*, 1932; *Polarity* (E), 1933; *An Augustine Synthesis*, ed., 1936; *The Divine Majesty* (T), 1951.

PSELLOS, MICHAEL (THE YOUNGER). 1018–1078.
Byzantine philosopher, probably born in Constantinople. Taught at the University of Constantinople. He served as Secretary of State and Prime Minister of the Byzantine Empire with the honorary title "Prince of Philosophers." A Neoplatonic eclectic philosopher, he argued that Hellenism prepared the way for Christianity. He wrote in many fields, attempting to sum up the knowledge of his day.

Sample writings: *On the Operation of Demons; Common Notions; Brief Solutions to Problems of Physics.*

PSEUDO-DIONYSIUS, THE.
Name given to the unknown author who, at the end of the 4th or at the beginning of the 5th century A.D., used the writings of the Neoplatonist Proclus (*q.v.*)

as the basis of a series of treatises on God and mystical theology. Presented by the author as the work of Dionysius the Areopagite, mentioned in *Acts* 17:34 as one of the converts of the Apostle Paul, the identification was accepted through much of the Middle Ages. Translated into Latin by Erigena (*q.v.*) among others, it was the subject of commentaries by Hugo of Saint Victor (*q.v.*), Robert Grosseteste (*q.v.*), Albertus Magnus (*q.v.*), and Thomas Aquinas (*q.v.*).

Principal writings: *On the Divine Names* (T); *The Mystical Theology* (T); *The Celestial Hierarchy* (T); *The Ecclesiastical Hierarchy* (T).

(1) Positive theology rests on the Holy Scriptures, since all we can know of God is that which God has revealed to us. But even this is subject to the insight of Negative Theology, which demonstrates that man cannot understand the names of God. We need then a Superlative Theology in which we view God as Super-Being, Super-Unity, and Super-Goodness.

(2) But since we still cannot understand what this would mean, we must have recourse at last to a Mystical Theology, which takes advantage of the fact of our supreme ignorance to guide us to the level of supreme knowledge.

(3) The metaphors of light and love are much used in the writings of the Pseudo-Dionysius. There is a divine light, we are told, which bathes all beings; and to allow ourselves to be illuminated by this light is to know that we are linked to our fellow beings by bonds of love, and all of us to the source of this light which we cannot know by reason.

(4) But the light is transmitted to the world (here a typical aspect of Neoplatonism emerges) by means of a celestial hierarchy, as it is transmitted through the world by means of an ecclesiastical hierarchy.

PSEUDO-GROSSETESTE.
The name given to the author of the 13th-century *Summa philosophiae* initially identified with Robert Grosseteste (*q.v.*). While that identification is no longer made, internal evidence suggests that the author is English and Franciscan—or at least Augustinian. The work includes consideration of the history of philosophy, truth, science, matter and form, essence

and existence, the intelligences, the soul, cosmology, and natural philosophy.

PSYCHE.

A Greek term meaning "breath."

(1) In Homer and in Greek life generally the *psyche* was a subtle, breath-like animating principle which left the body at death and continued to exist as a shade or shadow.

(2) In the rites of Dionysus (*q.v.* 2) the *psyche* was for the first time regarded as a principle superior to the body, and imprisoned in it.

(3) In the early Greek philosophers the *psyche* tended to be identified with whatever had been selected as the animating principle of the universe (*q.v.* Greek Philosophy 1–5).

(4) The Pythagoreans held two views of the *psyche*; as a superior principle and as the "harmony" of the body (*q.v.* Pythagoreanism).

(5) Plato (*q.v.* 3) or perhaps Socrates (*q.v.* 5) and Plato, established the doctrine of the *psyche* as immortal (*q.v.*). Since such a conception is usually termed soul, a translation of the Latin *anima*, Plato's conception is treated under Soul (*q.v.* 2–3). And since Aristotle's treatise on the *psyche* or soul is usually given in its Latin translation, *De Anima*, it is customary to speak of Aristotle's doctrine of the soul rather than *psyche* (*q.v.* Soul 4).

(6) The Stoics used the term *pneuma* ("air"), a material and psychical material allowing them a materialistic interpretation of man (*q.v.* Stoicism 1).

PSYCHOANALYSIS.

Q.v. Psychology (10); Freud (4); Jung (9).

PSYCHOLOGISM.

The doctrine that the categories of psychology can be used appropriately in philosophical analysis. The thesis had been advanced by a number of European philosophers in the 19th century, and vigorously denied by others. Descartes held that one should admit into philosophy only clear and distinct ideas. One might pose the issue of psychologism by asking whether one can have logical certainty about the clarity and distinctness of ideas or merely psychological certainty. If one can have only the latter, then Descarte's epistemology reduces to psychologism.

(1) Fries (*q.v.* 1) interpreted Kant's analysis as a reference to human nature, and so to man's psychology and anthropology.

(2) Beneke (*q.v.*) founded metaphysics, ethics, philosophy of religion, and even logic, on psychology.

(3) J.S. Mill (*q.v.* 3) regarded logic as a subdivision of psychology. He regarded the principles of both logic and mathematics as psychologically derived.

(4) Leonard Nelson (*q.v.* 1), a neo-Kantian follower of Fries, set forth a middle way in which psychology might be used in philosophy without falling into psychologism.

(5) Husserl (*q.v.* 1, 2) began his work in an effort to rescue mathematics and logic from psychologism. He later extended his method of "seeing" into essences to metaphysics generally.

(6) Frege (*q.v.*), Russell (*q.v.*), and the movement of Logical Positivism (*q.v.* Vienna Circle) opposed the tendency toward psychologism, especially with respect to logic where they separated validity from any psychological predicates.

PSYCHOLOGY.

From the Greek *psyche* ("breath") and *logos* ("knowledge of"). The term *psyche* (*q.v.*) was used by Greek philosophers to refer to the vital principle in man.

A. The history of the word, "psychology," goes back only to 1590 when Goclenius (*q.v.*) introduced the term to name "the science of the soul."

(1) In the late 16th and 17th centuries the term referred to a deductive elaboration of mental faculties, powers, or functions which stood as a part of special metaphysics, and which has come to be known as Rational Psychology or sometimes, apparently, as Faculty Psychology (*q.v.*).

(2) The distinction between Rational Psychology and Empirical Psychology gradually emerged. Wolff (*q.v.* 3) distinguished the two disciplines in his early 18th-century work.

(3) Empirical psychology became Associationalism or Associational Psychology with the work of Hartley (*q.v.*), Hume (*q.v.* 2, 4, 6), James Mill (*q.v.*), and John Stuart Mill (*q.v.* 1).

(4) Experimental Psychology gained secure footing in the work of Ernst Weber,

Fechner (*q.v.* 1), Helmholtz (*q.v.*), and especially with Wilhelm Wundt (*q.v.* 1). In 1879 Wundt established the first experimental laboratory of psychology; the precedent was quickly followed in scores of university centers both in Europe and in America.

B. As Psychology achieved the status of an independent discipline, those working in the field—while developing experimental methods—divided into a number of schools.

(5) Functional Psychology was inspired by William James (*q.v.* 1–3, 6) and developed by J.R. Angell among others. Mental processes are here treated as adaptations of the biological organism.

(6) Genetic Psychology, describing phases in the development of the mind, was introduced by Ward (*q.v.*).

(7) Structuralism, holding sensations and feelings to be elements in a structured analysis, was introduced by Titchener.

(8) The Behaviorism of Watson (*q.v.*) eliminated all appeals to introspection, interpreting man solely in terms of the data of observation.

(9) Gestalt Psychology, opposing the atomism of the earlier Associational approach, and insisting that the individual person's typical experience is of organized and complex wholes, was introduced by Wertheimer (*q.v.*), Köhler (*q.v.*), and Koffka (*q.v.*).

(10) Freud (*q.v.* 1) introduced Depth Psychology, distinguishing between conscious and unconscious levels of mentality.

(11) Jung (*q.v.*) insisted upon the term Analytic Psychology to characterize his variant of the Freudian approach.

(12) Kurt Lewin (*q.v.*) introduced topological and field theory psychology, featuring the concept of "life space" and the methodology of the "single case."

(13) McDougall (*q.v.*) reintroduced an emphasis on will and purpose in psychological explanations with his system of Hormic Psychology.

C. Given the late development of psychological terminology, there are dangers in attempting to label the psychological positions of philosophers living before the 17th century. To some extent this labeling has occurred, however.

(14) It is supposed that Faculty Psychology had its roots in the analyses of Plato (*q.v.* 3) and Aristotle (*q.v.* 7, 11), and that the psychology of the Middle Ages was largely a faculty psychology. Aristotle is also recognized, however, as the precursor of Functional Psychology; hence, a claim can be made for Aquinas, too, in this regard.

(15) The psychologies of Descartes (*q.v.* 11), Spinoza (*q.v.* 4), and Leibnitz (*q.v.* 14) are often regarded as Rational Psychologies.

(16) Locke (*q.v.* 4) is regarded as the forerunner of Associational Psychology.

D. Other connections between psychology and philosophy are worth mentioning.

(17) The attempt of Brentano (*q.v.* 1) to establish a purely descriptive psychology had influence both on Meinong and upon the discipline of Phenomenology established by Husserl.

(18) In Cognitive Science (*q.v.*) where Folk Psychology (*q.v.*) holds persons to be intensional systems Cognitive Psychology finds them to be nonintensional and perhaps mechanistic. Stephen Stich (*From Folk Psychology to Cognitive Science*, 1983) is a defender of the second view.

PSYCHOPHYSICAL, THE.
Q.v. Ducasse (2).

PSYCHOPLASM.
Q.v. Ward (1).

PTOLEMY, CLAUDIUS. 2nd cent. A.D.
Hellenic scientist and philosopher. Place of his birth uncertain, but he lived in Alexandria and in a general sense belonged to the Aristotelian movement in Alexandria initiated by Andronicus of Rhodes (*q.v.*). His great work in astronomy dealing with all of the planets and 1,022 stars was published around 150 A.D. It held the earth to be a globe in the center of the world system, and that the heavens make a diurnal revolution around an axis passing through the center of the earth. The system was accepted until Copernicus in the 16th century. His philosophy was influenced by Platonism, Stoicism, and neo-Pythagoreanism, as well as by Aristotle.

Principal writings: *Mathematical Composition* (T), 13 vols., also known as the *Almagest; Optics; Mathematical Geography*.

PUEBLA MEETING.
Q.v. Theology of Liberation (4).

PUFENDORF, SAMUEL. 1632–1694.
German jurist and legal philosopher. Born in Chemnitz, Saxony. Educated at Leipzig and Jena. Taught at Heidelberg and the Swedish University of Lund. His first work was composed while imprisoned in Denmark. He served an eight-month sentence due to his connections with the Swedish Ambassador. Later he was named Royal Historian of Sweden, and in 1688 he became Historian and Privy Councillor of Brandenburg.

Principal writings: *The Elements of Universal Law* (T), 1660; *On the Status of the German Empire*, 1667; *On the Law of Nature and Nations* (T), 1672; *On the Duty of Man and Citizen* (T), 1673; *On The Relation Between Church and State* (T), 1687.

(1) Deliberately combining the insights of Grotius and Hobbes, Pufendorf derived a social contract theory of his own. Unlike Hobbes, he argued that the state of nature is that of a feeble and insecure peace which must be superseded by a more rational arrangement. Unlike Grotius (*q.v.* 2), he understood natural law in sociological terms. In partial anticipation of Rousseau, he regarded the state as a moral individual whose will is the sum of the individual wills of its citizens.

(2) With respect to the relation of church and state, he held that the supreme jurisdiction of religious matters rested in the state while ecclesiastical power rested in the church. This power can be transferred to the state by tacit or expressed consent of the church. He likewise supported the collegial approach to church government.

PUNISHMENT.
Q.v. Shang Yang (3); Hegel (14).

PUNISHMENT, CAPITAL.
Held to be inadmissible by Camus (*q.v.* 2).

PURANA.
Q.v. Śastras (3).

PURE EXPERIENCE.
Q.v. Avenarius (1); William James (10).

PURGATORY.
From the Latin *purgare* ("to purify"). Among Roman Catholics a "place" where those who die in God's grace expiate their venal sins or satisfy divine justice for mortal sins which have been remitted (*q.v.* Sin 2). Offerings of prayer and of the Mass are held to aid those in purgatory.

PURIM, FEAST OF.
A Jewish observance celebrated on the 14th of the month Adar (the 12th month of the Jewish religious calendar) to commemorate the deliverance of the Jews of Persia from Haman (*Esther* 9:24).

PURITANISM.
A 16th-century movement within English Protestantism to purify religion of all Roman Catholic forms and influences. A powerful force behind Cromwell's reforms, the Puritans were known as Separatists or non-Separatists depending upon their attitude toward the Anglican Church. One strand of Puritanism gave rise to the Baptist (*q.v.*) movement. In the founding of the New England colonies, Separatists, non-Separatists, and Baptists, were all represented. The Plymouth Bay Colony was made up of moderate Separatists.

PURUṢA (PURUSHA).
From Sanskrit, "man," or "person," but in its developed form the term "soul," "consciousness," "spirituality."

(1) In the *Ṛgveda* (*q.v.*) the term refers to "the first man" from whose dismembered body the four castes (*q.v.*) arose: from his mouth the *Brahmins*, from his arms the *Kshatriyas*, from his thighs the *Vaishyas*, from his feet the *Shudras*.

(2) In the *Upanishads* (*q.v.*) a *purusha/atman* contrast is replaced by a contrast between *Brahman* as the universal self and *atman* as the individual self.

(3) *Purusha* was thus perhaps freed for philosophical use. In any event the philosophy of the schools began to contrast *purusha* with *prakriti* (*q.v.*) as soul and body, as spirit or spirituality and matter. The terms are central to the Sankhya (*q.v.* 1–3) system as well as to Yoga, which takes the Sankhya system as its theoretical counterpart. The act of distinguishing the two principles contributes to the elimination of suffering. *Q.v.* Hinduism (6b).

PURUṢA-NARAYANA (PURUSHA-NARAYANA).
Q.v. Vaiṣnavism (2a).

PURUṢARTHAS (PURUSHARTHAS).
From the Sanskrit *puruṣa* ("man") and

artha ("aim"), thus the "aims of man" or "aims of life." Just as the four *ashramas* (*q.v.*) began as three, so too with the Aims of Life. The three aims in the early expressions of the *Mahabharata* (*q.v.*), the *Ramayana* (*q.v.*) and the *Dharma Sutras* (*q.v. Vedas* 5) are: *dharma* or "right conduct," *artha* or "material success," and *kama* or "pleasure," especially as experienced in sexual love (and having its own detailed manual, the *Kama Sutra, q.v.*). The fourth aim, *moksha* (*q.v.*), "release" or "enlightenment," developed through time, as did the fourth stage of the *ashramas*, the fourth and final *sannyasin* ("renouncer") stage of life.

PURVA MIMAMSA.

Sanskrit term meaning "the early revered thought." The term refers to a school of Indian thought dealing with the earlier portions of the *Vedas*, as *Uttara Mimamsa* (*q.v.*) or Vedanta (*q.v.*) dealt with the later part. One of the six orthodox systems of Indian thought, *Purva Mimamsa* is based on the *Mimamsa Sutra*, composed around 400 B.C. by Jaimini. Turning on the importance of the idea of duty or *Dharma*, and finding its source in the *Vedas*, this system of thought elaborated theory primarily to serve a practical interest. Among its important ideas are the following:

(1) Liberation from rebirth leads in this system to life in heaven, and liberation is tied to the doing of one's duty.

(2) Since the source of information concerning duty is to be found in the *Vedas*, it is necessary that the *Vedas* be not simply individual opinions. Accordingly, the *Vedas* are regarded as eternal. That is to say, there never was a time when they had not been written. The *Vedas*, hence, are without an author; and apparent references to authors are to be understood as references to individuals who explained certain portions of the *Vedas*, but did not compose them. Or such references refer to certain classes of *Brahmins* for whom these passages are particularly relevant.

(3) The eternality of the *Vedas* seems to lead to a theory of language. If the *Vedas* are eternal, so must be the language of the *Vedas*. Hence, the relation between word and meaning is held to be nonconventional: there is a natural and inborn relation between the word and its denotation. Words and their relations are also eternal; they become manifest, they are discovered, not created.

(4) This view of the eternality of language leads to a theory of truth. Whatever statements exist, which have not been proved false, are *ipso facto* true. What needs to be provided is not the truth of a cognition but its falsity.

(5) Along the same line, the *Purva Mimamsa* logicians added to the usual forms of valid knowledge a knowledge by presumption or postulation, and knowledge by absence or negation.

(6) The eternality of the word has a parallel in the working of *Dharma*. The delay between the performance of an act and its fruit means that the working out of *Dharma* requires that the consequence of an act exist as an *Apurva*, or a transcendental potency, or unseen force, until it comes to exist in the world.

(7) For the *Vedas* to be eternal, the world, too, would have to be eternal, and uncreated. *Purva Mimamsa* insists upon this point. The idea of the creation of the world by God is held to be inconsistent, setting up a regress of creators *ad infinitum*; and also, that God as an independent being could have had no motive for creation. Thus, the passages of the *Vedas* which seem to refer to creation must be interpreted as applying to something else, *e.g.*, the importance of sacrifices.

PUTNAM, HILARY. 1926– .

American philosopher. Born in Chicago. Educated at the University of Pennsylvania and U.C.L.A. Has taught at Northwestern, Princeton, M.I.T., and Harvard.

Principal writings: *Philosophy of Logic*, 1971; *Mathematics, Matter, and Method*, 1975; *Mind, Language, and Reality*, 1975; *Meaning and the Moral Sciences*, 1978; *Reason, Truth and History*, 1981; *Realism and Reason*, 1983; *The Many Faces of Realism*, 1987; *Representation and Reality*, 1988; *Renewing Philosophy*, 1992.

(1) Beginning as an empirical (or scientific) realist, Putnam held the existence of the world to be supported by experience just as scientific theory is supported by observational data; and that the "accepted sentences" of scientists "convergently mirror the truth."

(2) His doctrine of realism was linked

to a causal theory of reference, centering both on the "historical" conditions obtaining between the use of a word and its referent, and the presence of underlying traits, a microstructure. What can be said about these matters is extended beyond present experience by "similarity relations." All predicates, then, are given something like the Kripkean (*q.v.*) treatment of proper names.

(3) In this treatment "natural kind" terms (such as matter) function as the proper names of natural kinds, and are understood not only in relation to their historical conditions, but also to their underlying traits. The microstructure of water on earth is H_2O. Suppose a "twin earth" where the analysis of water is XYZ. An informed visitor from Twin Earth to our planet, call it "Earth One", would say: "On Earth One water means H_2O not XYZ." And even had the visit been made before discovery of the chemical composition of water on either earth, when the known traits of water on both were the same (a transparent, drinkable, etc., liquid) the visitor would have been wrong in saying that water had the same meaning on the two earths.

(4) In his period of staunch realism it would have pleased Putnam, one gathers, had Born's interpretation of quantum mechanics been successful; for in that case the reduction of the wave-packet would have been nothing more than a contraction in the state of our own ignorance. Failing this result, Putnam devised a quantum logic for quantum theory in which the distribution rule of classical logic (namely, that $p \cdot (q \vee r)$ is equivalent to $p \cdot q \vee p \cdot r$) is simply dropped. The change was controversial, but not without support.

(5) With the passage of time Putnam has attenuated the sense of the realism he once urged. For one thing we are told that correspondence is triadic, bearing a "certain relation" to the rest of language as well as to "extra-linguistic" facts. For another, we are now told that "the mind and the world jointly make up the mind and the world." Finally, we are told that the empirical world is shaped by what we take to be "rationally acceptable," that is, what fits our "optimal speculative intelligence."

(6) Rationality has at its core one *a*

priori truth: "Not every statement is true." The absolutely inconsistent rule (the AIR) is: Infer every statement from every premise and from every set of premises including the empty set. To accept this is to abandon rationality; to reject it is to believe that not every statement is true (or "Not every statement is both true and false"). There is no "epistemically possible world in which acceptance of the AIR would be fully rational and warranted." Scientific rationality also includes the marks of instrumental efficacity, coherence, comprehensiveness, and functional simplicity.

(7) It is also a part of the more general concept of "human flourishing," so that these are "value facts" as well as physical facts. This is a "practical knowledge" which goes beyond, while supporting, scientific method. It extends into the discussion of ethical principles whose "objectivity" rests upon their width of appeal, rational probity, feasibility, ideality, as well as their "feel" when incorporated into one's life.

(8) At this point Putnam opposes "hard-core metaphysical realism," a position in which truth and "rational acceptability" are independent notions. Metaphysical realism is called both "the God's eye view," and incoherent. He speaks instead for "internal realism," a "human" kind of realism in which use and reference are linked, and truth is "idealized justification." It may be that the realism endorsed in (1) above lies somewhere between metaphysical and internal realism. At least the Peircean (*q.v.* 2) drift toward truth seems no longer stressed.

(9) If metaphysical realism is untenable, so is relativism. Relativism is unintelligible (involving an infinite regress of relativities), without objective justification (by definition). The relativist cannot even refer to "people in other cultures" but only to the concept of such people in his or her mind; for this reason the standards of rationality and truth cannot be culturally (*i.e.*, relativistically) determined. It is Putnam's intention, at least, to stand between the extremes of the two positions.

(10) A functionalist, Putnam believes there is a functional isomorphism between mind and brain, and that psychological properties are functional states,

"metaphysically determined" by physical properties, yet not physical. The distinction allows, so he claims, autonomy in our mental lives.

PYLYSHYN, Z. W.
Q.v. Folk Psychology (2).

PYRRHO. c. 360–270 B.C.
Greek philosopher. Born in Elis. Influenced by Democritus, perhaps through Anaxarchus, and by the Megarian dialectic through Bryson who was the son and disciple of Stilpo, Pyrrho developed his own skeptical philosophy, called Pyrrhonism. Diogenes Laertius (*q.v.*) states that Pyrrho traveled to India with Alexander and there met Indian Gymnosophists whose lives of ascetic solitude he later emulated.

(1) According to his disciple, Timon, Pyrrho's central thesis was that it is impossible to know the nature of anything. Every statement can be countered by its contradictory, with neither more weighty than the other.

(2) Since no assertion is more valid than any other, we must submit to an *epoché*, or suspension of judgment. Since we must suspend judgment even with respect to our ignorance and doubt, we must also preserve *aphasia*, or a noncommital silence, with respect to all things.

(3) In terms of value the human situation suggests that man withdraw into himself, and reflect an attitude of *ataraxia*, or imperturbable serenity and tranquility.

PYRRHONISM.
The school of Skepticism (*q.v.*) deriving from Pyrrho (*q.v.*). Differing from other types of skepticism by the extremity of its views, it likewise represents a disavowal of complex dialectic. Pyrrho had among his followers in ancient times Timon of Phlius (*q.v.*), Aenesidemus of Crete (*q.v.*), Agrippa (*q.v.*), and Sextus Empiricus (*q.v.*). Montaigne (*q.v.* 2) was one of his followers in the 16th century. From the 16th through the 18th centuries a great deal of attention was paid to Pyrrho both on the part of those who were attracted to the position, and on the part of those who sought to demolish it.

PYTHAGORAS. 570–500 B.C.
Greek philosopher. Probably born at Samos. He studied under Pherecydes and other Ionian philosophers. He is thought to have visited Egypt. Saintly in manner, it was reported that he was once seen in two cities at exactly the same time. He established a school in Croton, Italy, with many features of a religious sect, including secret initiation ceremonies, strict vows, vegetarianism, progress through ranks from novitiate to full member, admitting women as well as men, and requiring a communal sharing of goods. The school was destroyed by irate townspeople in a surge of democratic feeling some time in the 5th century B.C. This disaster actually spread the influence of the school as the Pythagoreans re-established themselves in widely separated communities.

A. We shall attempt first to state the insights of the founder, following this with the insights of the school. At least the following ideas would seem to have been the intellectual product of Pythagoras himself:

(1) The end of life lies in gaining a relation to the divine. Belief in God provides a principle of order for human life and for societies, providing a basis for constitutions, laws, and rights.

(2) The way to achieve relation to the divine is through philosophy. Seeking truth, one finds salvation. One decides which of three types of person one is to be: a lover of wisdom, a lover of success, a lover of pleasure; and the first is the superior type.

(3) The way of salvation was related to a doctrine of the transmigration of soul, and philosophy played a role in preparing one to escape from the cycles of reincarnation.

(4) Pythagoras' great discovery concerned the relation between mathematics and the physical world, as exemplified by the relation between arithmetical ratios and the progression of tones produced by lengthening or shortening a vibrating string. This led either to the belief that mathematics holds the key to the explanation of reality, or that number is the essence of reality. Probably Pythagoras held both beliefs.

(5) He believed the earth to be a sphere located in the center of the universe.

B. Beyond these principles there are others some of which may have been the work of Pythagoras and others the work of a number of his followers in the Pythagorean School.

(6) The application of number to the universe comes by means of a list of opposites which plays an important role in Pythagorean thought. The opposites are: limit (*peras*) and unlimited (*apeiron*); odd and even; one and many; right and left; male and female; resting and moving; straight and curved; light and darkness; good and bad; square and oblong.

(7) The list has cosmological-mathematical implications. The "unlimited" is space, the "unlimited" limited once is the unit. It stands also for the point, and hence a possibility for identifying number and reality. One is the point; two the line; three the plane; and four the solid. Hence, by number we have constituted the world. The sum of critical numbers is ten. Ten is therefore the perfect number.

(8) The above ideas have an application in astronomy. The unlimited, once limited, a primal unity, is also the central fire around which all planets and stars revolve. There are ten revolving spheres since the perfection of the heavens requires the perfect number. Moving out from the central fire these are: counter-earth, earth, moon, sun, Mercury, Venus, Mars, Jupiter, Saturn, and the heaven of the fixed stars. All of these, including the sun, shine by reflected light. We do not, as it happens, see the counter-earth, or the central fire, since the earth keeps its inhabited side turned away from these bodies. The central fire is posited as a source of light; and the counter-earth is posited to explain eclipses. It is the shadow of the counter-earth which we see in the sun and moon in moments of eclipse. When we are on the same side of the central fire as the sun we receive its reflected light and it is day. When we are on the side opposite the sun, it is night. The intervals between planets are then identified with the intervals between notes on the musical scale; and it was supposed that a divine music of the spheres, too subtle for human ears, was coming from the ordered planetary scheme in its movement.

(9) In another application, value terms are identified with numbers: *i.e.*, "2" is opinion, "7" is health, "8" is love, justice is a square number, etc.

(10) The lack of complete abstraction in identifying the point with unity is perhaps visible in the distinction between square and oblong (odd and even) numbers, so named by the respective shapes of the orderly rows which the numbered points assume. This suggests some sort of association between unity, point, and pebble, an atomism of number. The highly visual associations used by the Pythagoreans derive, some say, from the practice of setting forth sums by laying out pebbles on a smooth surface.

PYTHAGOREANISM.

The movement of thought initiated by the school of Pythagoras (*q.v.*). The movement centered in the application of number to reality, astronomy as a prime instance of such application, the analysis of harmony, health as a prime instance of harmony, and the development of geometry. A division is usual between the ancient Pythagoreans initially related to the school at Croton, Italy, 6th century B.C. and the neo-Pythagoreans who represent a resurgence of Pythagorean thought in the 1st century B.C.

(1) The ancient Pythagoreans, or more simply, the Pythagoreans, existed in the 6th and 5th centuries B.C. It is not really possible to separate the doctrines of the Pythagorean school from those of its founder, although we have attempted to do so under Pythagoras (*q.v.* 6–10), bringing together some of the more sophisticated Pythagorean ideas as later ideas. With the closing of the school, Pythagoreanism was spread abroad. Among the most notable of the Pythagoreans were Philolaus (*q.v.*), regarded as the systematizer of the school, his student Archytas (*q.v.*), who separated number theory from its initially mystical setting, thus contributing both to its development and that of natural science; Alcmaeon (*q.v.*), who identified the immortality of the soul with circular motion; and Hippasus of Metapontum (*q.v.*). The Pythagorean movement deeply influenced the thought of Plato (*q.v.* 9).

(2) The surge of neo-Pythagoreanism which began in the 1st century B.C. endured through the 2nd century A.D. As the Pythagoreans had influenced Plato, so the neo-Pythagoreans influenced Neoplatonism (*q.v.*). Indeed, the neo-

Pythagorean identification of the divine reality with the One, and all other realities as emanating from the One, exactly fits the Neoplatonic scheme, and is almost certainly responsible for it. Among the important neo-Pythagoreans were Nigidius Figulus (*q.v.*), who combined mysticism and astrology with his Pythagoreanism; Apollonius of Tyana (*q.v.*), who taught Pythagoreanism as a popular philosophy; Moderatus of Gades (*q.v.*), who returned to the emphasis on number theory; Nicomachus of Gerasa (*q.v.*), whose treatise on arithmetic was used in the schools for more than a thousand years and who taught that numbers pre-exist in the mind of God; and Numenius (*q.v.*) of Apamea, sometimes regarded as the founder of Neoplatonism, whose system contains most of the emphases later developed by Plotinus (*q.v.*).

QADARITES.

From the Arabic *qadar* ("power"). An Islamic school of thought which, like the Mutazilites (*q.v.*) adheres to free will. *Q.v.* Islam (6).

"Q" SOURCE.

Q.v. Synoptic Gospels.

QUADRIVIUM.

From the Latin *quatuor* ("four") and *viae* ("ways"). The four advanced studies—arithmetic, geometry, astronomy, and music—following the *Trivium* (*q.v.*) in the medieval curriculum. *Q.v.* Martianus Capella.

QUAESTIONES DISPUTATAE.

Latin for "Disputed Questions." One of the forms of analysis used in Scholastic philosophy. *Q.v.* Disputation.

QUAESTIONES QUODLIBETALES.

Latin for "Selected Questions." One of the forms of analysis developed in the period of Scholasticism, it differed from the *Quaestiones Disputatae* (*q.v.*) in that the auditors chose the question. *Q.v.* Disputation.

QUAKER.

The unofficial, although universally accepted name, given to members of the Society of Friends (*q.v.*). Originally applied in derision, the name seems to have derived from a sermon of George Fox (*q.v.*), the movement's founder, calling upon man to "tremble at the Word of God."

QUALE.

From the Latin *qualis* meaning "of what kind." The term *qualis* was created by Cicero to translate the Greek *poion*. The term, and its plural "*qualia*." are sometimes used in place of the more common term, "quality" and its plural.

QUALISIGN.

Q.v. Peirce (16).

QUALITAS IPSA COGNITIONIS.

Q.v. Gabriel Vásquez.

QUALITIES, PRIMARY AND SECONDARY.

A distinction, going back to the Greeks, between the qualities possessed by things, and qualities produced in us by those things. The primary qualities of things are solidity, extension, figure, motion, rest, and number. The secondary qualities are colors, sounds, tastes, smells, etc.

(1) The distinction between the two types of qualities was first made by the Greek atomists (*q.v.* Democritus 3; Epicurus 4).

(2) After a long period of neglect the distinction reappeared. As the new science developed in the 16th century, Galileo (*q.v.* 3) and Mersenne (*q.v.* 3) found the distinction pertinent to the analysis of bodies and our relation to them.

(3) The precise terminology, "primary qualities," and "secondary qualities," was introduced by the scientist Robert Boyle (*q.v.* 2) and picked up from Boyle by Locke (*q.v.* 6).

(4) Berkeley (*q.v.* 3) called the distinction into question in such a way that from the standpoint of Berkeley's system all qualities became secondary. The consequence was loss of the concept of a material world, and the emergence of Berkeley's philosophy of Immaterialism. *Q.v.* J. J. C. Smart (6).

QUALITY.

From the Latin *qualis* (*q.v.* Quale), a

translation of the Greek *poion*.

(1) One of Aristotle's basic categories, quality is "that by virtue of which a thing is such and such." A quality may be a habit, disposition, capacity, or the form and figure of a thing (*q.v.* Aristotle 6).

(2) In the traditional logic one speaks of the quality of categorical propositions. By this, one means their characteristic of being affirmative or negative (*q.v.* Proposition 1).

(3) Kant (*q.v.* 3) followed both Aristotle and the traditional logic by regarding quality as one of the basic categories while deriving from the characteristic mentioned in (2) above the subcategories of Positive, Negative, and Limited.

(4) For Locke's treatment of the term *q.v.* Primary and Secondary Qualities.

QUANTIFICATION OF THE PREDICATE.

Q.v. Hamilton (1).

QUANTIFICATION THEORY.

In modern logic the method devised for expressing in symbolic form statements of a general nature. Where the Propositional Calculus (*q.v.*) deals with the relations to each other of entire propositions, it is our object here to provide a means for analyzing arguments which require transformations of the internal structure of the propositions making up the argument. The Syllogism (*q.v.*) is one major instance of this type of transformation. There are also asyllogistic inferences of this type; but for the sake of simplicity we shall concern ourselves with showing how syllogistic theory can be built on the foundations of propositional logic by adding to that system certain conventions for the quantification of propositions.

(1) The sample inferences with which we are concerned are those which can be made up of A, E, I, and O propositions (*q.v.* Syllogism 1–4). The conclusion of the syllogism contains one term from each of the two premises, and the term common to these premises (called the Middle Term) has been eliminated. We must have a means for making the valid transformations in these somewhat complex situations.

(2) The quantified proposition is to be understood by means of the Propositional

Function (*q.v.*). The theory of the propositional function tells us that we can analyze propositions into arguments and functions where the subject term of the proposition contains the argument and the predicate term describes the function. If we wished to express in this way the proposition "Socrates is human," the basic syntactical form "Fx" would be filled in by the letters "Hs" where "H" stands for the predicate term "human" and "s" for the subject term "Socrates."

(3) But the type of reasoning with which we are here concerned cannot take place with singular propositions alone. We must be able to express A, E, I, and O propositions with our notation, *i.e.*, "All S is P," "No S is P," "Some S is P," "Some S is not P." Suppose that we wish to express, not the proposition that "Socrates is human," but rather the proposition that "All philosophers are human." It will not do to put down simply "Hp" for that would tell us that some individual, possibly Peter, is human. We must recognize the fact that there is something hypothetical about a universal proposition. We are really saying that if any individual "x" is a philosopher, then that individual is human. We begin, then, by using material implication (*q.v.*), and we write down "Px $\supset$ Hx" to say that "if x is a philosopher, then x is human." To indicate that we range across all of the values of the variable "x," we must add to our statement the sign for universal quantification. Hence, the statement reads "(x) [Px $\supset$ Hx]" that is, "For all x, if x is a philosopher, then x is human." The philosopher, Socrates, is an instance of this universal proposition, or as we say, a value of the variable "x." We instantiate the proposition by writing down "Ps $\supset$ Hs," that is, "If Socrates is a philosopher, then Socrates is human." We shall establish a rule of Universal Instantiation, which allows us to write "Ps $\supset$ Hs," or its equivalent, whenever we have both the quantified universal "(x)" proposition, and "Ps" or an equivalent expression in the premises. Given this rule, and the allowed transformations of the Propositional Calculus, we can validly reach the conclusion "Hs," that is, "Socrates is human," from the premises: "All philosophers are human," and "Socrates is a philosopher."

1. (x) [Px ⊃ Hx]
2. Ps /therefore, Hs
3. Ps ⊃ Hs (From 1 by Universal Instantiation)
4. Hs (From 2 and 3 by Modus Ponens)

(4) When dealing with syllogisms, both of whose premises are universal, we need additional rules. Using a syllogism comparable to one of those discussed in Syllogism (2–3), *i.e.*, "All humans are mortal; all patriarchs are human; therefore, all patriarchs are mortal"—it is obvious that we have in the premises no individual, Socrates, to mention. But we need some sign for an individual since, in removing the brackets, we need to replace "x" with a different symbol. We shall substitute for "x" any arbitrary individual, and we shall designate this individual by "y." In order to get the brackets back after having made the valid transformations, we need to introduce a rule for Universal Generalization. The rule will hold that a proposition concerning an arbitrarily selected individual "y" can be replaced by the appropriate universally quantified proposition. Given this rule, and the one in (3) above, the syllogism can be expressed in symbolic terms as follows:

1. (x) [Hx ⊃ Mx]
2. (x) [Px ⊃ Hx]/therefore,(x) [Px ⊃ Mx]
3. Hy ⊃ My (From 1 by Universal Instantiation)
4. Py ⊃ Hy (From 2 by Universal Instantiation)
5. Py ⊃ My (From 3 and 4 by Hypothetical Syllogism)
6. (x) [Px ⊃ Mx] (From 5 by Universal Generalization)

(5) A syllogism with a universal negative premise yields a similar pattern. Consider the syllogism: "No humans are immortal; all Athenians are human; therefore, no Athenians are immortal." The universal negative proposition, expressed symbolically, is like the universal affirmative proposition with the predicate term negated. The first premise of the syllogism above is thus written: (x) [Hx ⊃ ~ Ix]. The entire syllogism would be worked out as follows:

1. (x) [Hx ⊃ ~ Ix]
2. (x) [Ax ⊃ Hx]/therefore, (x)[Ax ⊃ ~ Ix].
3. Hy ⊃ ~ Iy (From 1 by Universal Instantiation)

4. Ay ⊃ Hy (From 2 by Universal Instantiation)
5. Ay ⊃ ~ Iy (From 3 and 4 by Hypothetical Syllogism)
6. (x) [Ax ⊃ ~ Ix] (From 5 by Universal Generalization)

(6) A syllogism with a particular premise, *i.e.*, "Some Athenians are virtuous," introduces a new problem and requires two additional rules. In Quantification Theory the analysis of the particular premise given above is that there exists at least one Athenian and that Athenian is virtuous. We need a new way of generalizing over this individual or group, however. The most standard convention for this is the use of a backward "E," *i.e.*, an "∃." When we are indicating Existential Generalization, as we shall call it, we write for the above proposition "(∃ x) [Ax · Vx]" and read it as saying, "There is at least one individual x, such that x is an Athenian and x is virtuous." The O proposition, "Some Athenians are not virtuous," would be written (∃ x)[Ax · ~ Vx], *i.e.*, "There is at least one individual x such that x is an Athenian and x is not virtuous." Just as we have rules for Universal Instantiation and Universal Generalization so we must have rules for Existential Instantiation and Existential Generalization.

The new rules and descriptions can be illustrated by proving the syllogism: "No virtuous beings betray a trust; some Athenians are virtuous; therefore, some Athenians will not betray a trust." This syllogism, translated into logical form below, with obvious propositional markers, and transliterated back, reads: "For all x if x is a virtuous being, x will not betray a trust. There is at least one x such that x is an Athenian, and x is virtuous; therefore, there is at least one x such that x is an Athenian, and x will not betray a trust." Once again we are dealing with an unnamed individual or group. We are talking about one or more Athenians, otherwise not identified. And we need a means of designating this person or group. We might employ the "y" which we used for universal syllogisms in (4) and (5) above. But it might be clearer to employ some letter which we have not used before. We shall use "w" for our substitution instance, and the demonstration follows:

1. (x) [Vx ⊃ ~ Bx]
2. (∃ x) [Ax · Vx]
/therefore, (∃ x) [Ax· ~ Bx]
3. Vw ⊃ ~ Bw (From 1 by Universal Instantiation)
4. Aw · Vw (From 2 by Existential Instantiation)
5. Vw (From 4 by Simplification; *q.v.* Propositional Calculus 9)
6. ~ Bw (From 3 and 5 by Modus Ponens)
7. Aw (From 4 by Simplification)
8. Aw· ~ Bw (From 6 and 7 by Conjunction; *q.v.* Propositional Calculus 10)
9. (∃ x) [Ax · ~ Bx] (From 8 by Existential Generalization)

From these few examples it should be clear that patterns of inferences involving quantified propositions can be dealt with by the Propositional Calculus plus rules for the introduction and elimination of quantification.

QUANTIFIER.

The name given to operators "(x)" *i.e.,* "for all x," and "(∃ x)" *i.e.,* "there is an x," in formal logic. By means of these operators and the Propositional Calculus more complex forms of reasoning, including all forms of the syllogism, can be expressed in logical notation. *Q.v.* Frege (3); Quantification Theory.

QUANTIFYING IN.

The principle of substitutivity often fails when either existential or universal quantification is introduced into the middle portions of a sentence. Frege and Quine have both noted this failure in certain non-transparent contexts, called "oblique" by Frege and "opaque" by Quine. The failure often occurs in "being" statements (*q.v.* Quine 9), propositional attitude statements, quotations, and modal statements. An example of the latter is the inference: "9 is necessarily greater than 7; the number of the planets = 9; therefore, the number of the planets is necessarily greater than 7."

(1) Since the conclusion is false and, as Quine has said, concerning statements of identity, one of the terms "may be substituted for the other in any true statement and the result will be true" ("Reference and Modality," 1953, but his discussions of the topic go back into the 1940's, *e.g.,* "Notes on Existence and Necessity," 1943) something is wrong. The

question is what to do when statements like the above fail of "purely referential occurrence."

(2) Arthur Smullyan ("Modality and Description," 1948) and Ruth Barcan Marcus ("Extensionality," 1960) argue that such anomalous results can be handled by separating the scope of the two statements in the premises of the inference, using Russell's (*q.v.* 4) theory of definite descriptions, so that they will not combine in the conclusion.

(3) Quine's (*q.v.* 9) response to this and other suggestions is that only by returning to "Aristotelian essentialism" intensionalising the values of the variables would this move work (an alternative adopted by Plantinga, *q.v.* 4). Rather than this, he would prefer to give up quantified modal logic. David Kaplan, ("Quantifying In," 1969) is among those who embrace essentialism; he even introduces "standard names" which are so "intimately connected with what they name that "they necessarily denote their objects." Kaplan would regard "Nine is necessarily greater than seven" as a quotation, and follows Frege in treating such terms as ambiguous and denoting themselves. On this account one can have quantification within sentences; and the inference of our example simply turns out to be false, as it should.

(4) Dagfinn Follesdal ("Quantification into Causal Contexts," 1965) returns to Frege's decision that names in "oblique" contexts should be taken as referring to their "senses" (*q.v.* Frege 4) rather than to their references. Alonzo Church (*q.v.*) had revived this approach in 1942. When the terms of identity statements are so taken the principle of substitutivity is preserved while the anomalies we have noted are avoided.

(5) Jaakko Hintikka (*q.v.*) has made numerous suggestions with respect to this problem, including the view that Frege's "oblique contexts" were themselves a recognition that failure of the substitutivity of identity can't be handled in first-order logic ("Semantics for Propositional Attitude," 1969). Although feeling we need not be committed to possible worlds even though they are helpful in developing semantical theory, he finds the problem occurring when propositional attitudes "are applied to arbitrary singular

terms." The problem is that such terms "may refer to one and the same individual in the actual world . . . yet fail to refer to the same individual in some other . . . possible world. . . ." His way to a partial answer is through a set of functions F whose members "individuate" what is needed in the "relevant" possible worlds, picking out the appropriate individuals "to serve as values of bound variables."

QUANTITY.
From the Latin *quantitas* ("amount"), a translation of the Greek *poson*.

(1) For Aristotle (*q.v.* 6) one of the basic categories. Quantity in his view is either discrete or continuous; if continuous, it is either a magnitude or a temporal span. Quantity is also further divisible into units of the same kind.

(2) In Scholasticism, and especially in Thomism, quantity is an "extensive accident" of substance; and for Aquinas, in sensible substance one has signate matter ordered to three dimensions (*q.v.* Aquinas 6).

(3) In the traditional logic, by the quantity of a categorical proposition is meant its capacity to be singular, particular, or universal (*q.v.* Proposition 1).

(4) Kant (*q.v.* 3) took quantity to be one of the basic categories, gaining from the propositional characteristics mentioned in (3) above the further categories of unity, plurality, and totality.

Also *q.v.* Matter.

QUANTUM.
From the Latin *quantus* ("how much"). Used in philosophy to refer to a finite and determinate quantity, the term has passed into physics where its reference is to the packets of energy, or quanta, of quantum mechanics.

QUANTUM MECHANICS.
Q.v. Mechanics (2).

QUATERNIO TERMINORUM.
A Latin phrase meaning "four terms." One of the fallacies (*q.v.* 24) of logic, violating the requirement that a syllogism must have three, and only three, terms.

QUATERNITY.
Q.v. Jung (8).

QUESNAL, PASQUIER.
Q.v. Jansenism (10, 14, 16).

QUESNAY, FRANÇOIS.
Q.v. Physiocrats; Encyclopedists.

QUIDDITY.
From the Latin *quidditas* referring to the "whatness" of a thing. The term was introduced in the Latin translations of Avicenna to express Aristotle's distinction of second substance, *i.e.*, what a thing is, in contrast to primary substance, *i.e.*, the individual thing itself. Thus the usual sense of the term is as a synonym for form, nature, or essence.

QUIETISM.
A 17th-century devotional and mystical movement within the Catholic Church, whose leaders included Miguel de Molinos who published his *Spiritual Guide* in 1675, and François Fénelon whose *Explanations of the Maxims of the Saints* appeared in 1697. Molinos was convicted of heresy and sentenced to life imprisonment and Fénelon received a papal censure. The movement held that the path to the discovery of the divine will required one to "sell or kill" one's self-conscious will. One's whole soul may thus be directed to the love of God. Waiting on God, meditation became central. A quietist maxim held that one moment's contemplation is worth a thousand years good works. Jeanne Marie Guyon (*q.v.*) played an important role in the movement.

QUINE, WILLARD VAN ORMAN. 1908–.
American philosopher. Born in Akron, Ohio. Studied at Oberlin College, Oxford University, and Harvard. He has been a professor at Harvard since 1946. Known primarily as a logician relating himself to the programs of Whitehead-Russell *Principia Mathematica* (*q.v.* Whitehead and Russell), his interests extend over many of the basic problems of semantics, epistemology, and metaphysics.

Principal writings: *A System of Logistic*, 1934; *Mathematical Logic*, 1940; *Elementary Logic*, 1941; *Methods of Logic*, 1950; *From a Logical Point of View*, 1953; *Word and Object*, 1960; *Set Theory and Its Logic*, 1963; *Elementary Logic*, rev. ed., 1965; *Selected Logical Papers*, 1966; *The Ways of Pradox*, 1966; *Philosophy of Logic*, 1970; *The*

Roots of Reference, 1974; *The Web of Belief,* (with J.S. Ullian), 1978; *Theories and Things,* 1981; *Quiddities,* 1987; *Pursuit of Truth,* 1990 (rev. ed., 1992).

(1) Unhappy about the unnatural consequences of Russell's simple theory of types (*q.v.*), Quine suggested modifications as early as 1937 and 1940. The substitute theories, known as NF and ML respectively, retained the basic strategy of Russell while reducing the stringency of the restrictions on class membership and class stratification of the original theory. The stratification requirement remains as a classification requirement to be applied when necessary.

(2) Quine's contributions to philosophy almost always begin from a point or problem and lie within the area of semantics. Distinguishing meaning from reference, he calls the former "ideology," treating under this head the analytic-synthetic distinction, synonymy, and similar problems. Under theory of reference, called "ontology," he treats problems of denotation or extension, truth, etc. His claim that "to be is to be the value of a variable" concerns theory of reference, and hence ontology. His point here is, simply, that the sorts of things one recognizes as existing depend upon the values required or allowed by the variables of the language in use, and that there is always a relationship between language and ontic commitments. To speak of what kinds of entities there are is always to speak from the point of view of a given language.

(3) To deal with theory of reference, the use of Quantification (*q.v.*) commits one, initially, to the existence of abstract as well as concrete entities. Preferring desert landscapes, Quine in fact has a preference for Nominalism (*q.v.*). The program of nominalism requires one to show that every formulation referring to an abstract entity can be replaced by others referring only to concrete entities, or individual entities. He grants that it is probably the case that fragments of classical mathematics must be sacrificed for every such replacement. The conclusion would seem to be that either it will turn out the fragments are inessential to science, or else that the tired nominalist will lapse into Conceptualism (*q.v.*), which is better able to express abstract entities.

(4) With respect to meaning, Quine rejects the distinction between analytic and synthetic statements (*q.v.*) on the ground that no one has succeeded in making out a clear ground for the distinction. He points out that the idea of analyticity rests on the idea of synonymy—*i.e.,* if it is analytic that "A bachelor is an unmarried male," this is because "bachelor" and "unmarried male" are synonymous terms. But to say that these terms are cognitively synonymous is to say that our original sentence is analytic. Thus, to invoke synonymy does not save analyticity but demonstrates that the former term faces the same problem as the latter.

(5) Among numerous attempts made by Quine to shore up the concepts of analyticity and synonymy is one which attempts to reduce the concepts to behavioral dispositions of a verbal sort. In this attempt synonymy was interpreted as sameness of stimulus-meaning for an individual or group. Stimulus-meaning was understood as the set of stimuli leading one to give one's assent to a given sentence. Two sentences, then, are stimulus-synonymous when they have a sameness of stimulus meaning. And a sentence is stimulus-analytic if one gives one's assent to it no matter what the stimulus may be. Quine then proposes that the distinctions be tested through a program of radical translation, that is, by the translation of the language of a completely isolated group. But in the test it becomes clear that incompatible translation manuals, fitting all of these dispositions, can be compiled, and that there is an ultimate indeterminacy of translation. Hence, this approach does not succeed in solving the problem.

(6) Quine traces the difficulty in this matter to the Verifiability Criterion (*q.v.*) of meaning which supposes the individual synthetic statement to be the unit of empirical significance. Such statements, when meaningful, are capable of confirmation or "infirmation," and the analytic statement is simply the limiting case, since it is confirmed no matter what else may be the case. Quine holds, against the verification theory, that the unit of empirical significance is not the individual statement but the whole of science. And the difference between "synthetic"

and "analytic" statements is simply the measure of their proximity to the experiential periphery of science, or their remoteness from this periphery. The laws of logic, for example, are so remote from the periphery that they are insulated against the requirement of emendation.

(7) The conceptual scheme of science is, in fact, underdetermined by experience, and contrary experience at the periphery can be handled by many sorts of adjustment within the scheme itself. This is the position that leads Quine to regard himself as a pragmatist. Our situation is like that of rebuilding a ship on an open sea. The changes must take place bit by bit. Factors of convenience and conservatism, simplicity and elegance, or conceptual economy, enter, while the ultimate criterion is the achievement of a pragmatically acceptable conceptual scheme.

(8) Metaphysical systems, to which he sometimes refers as "ontic theories," are simply very general descriptions of the universe and are hence part of the conceptual scheme. Such theories must, of course, be compatible with science, as well as fitting the other criteria mentioned above. Even so, a plurality of such systems is always available. Although Quine would come down hard on the factor of simplicity, and prefer a physicalistic system, it would seem that taste would allow personal differences at this point.

(9) Quine used "quantifying in" to refer to a problem concerning statements containing belief contexts, *i.e.*, phrases governed by such epistemic operators as "knows" and "believes." "There is someone whom Ralph believes to be a spy" would seem to be expressible as "(x) (Ralph believes x to be a spy)." In the expression quantification has invaded the phrase governed by "believes." Contexts into which quantification is allowable are "referentially transparent." Contexts which are not referentially transparent are "referentially opaque." It has been shown by Quine ("Quantifiers and Propositional Attitudes," 1956) that anomalies follow from quantifying in to belief contexts. The quantification given above can be instantiated by proper names ("Ortcutt"), tautologous statements ("The shortest spy is a spy") and even by contradictory statements ("Ralph believes Ortcutt is a spy" and "Ralph believes Ortcutt is not a spy"). In this instance it would appear that quantifying in is not allowable; and that "belief contexts are," as Quine has said, "referentially opaque."

(10) One way of solving the problem of opaque contexts is by making a metaphysical commitment to Aristotelian essentialism so that certain objects will be viewed as carrying the properties of necessity and contingency in themselves and in the true statements made about them. If this is the cost, "So much the worse," he says, "for quantified modal logic."

Also *q.v.* Quantifying In (1, 3).

QUINQUE VIAE.

Latin phrase meaning "five ways." The arguments for God of Thomas Aquinas (*q.v.* 3). For a sixth way *q.v.* Maritain (6).

QUINTILIAN. c. 35–95.

Roman rhetorician. Born in Spain. Known as the Isocrates (*q.v.*) of his time, Quintilian headed the foremost school of oratory in Rome, taking Cicero (*q.v.* 3) as his model. Quintilian urged extensive intellectual cultivation as preparation for rhetoric. At the same time, however, his attention was concentrated on describing the techniques of persuasion. Concerning philosophy, he held only ethics to have any importance, and believed that subject to belong rather to the rhetoricians than to the philosophers.

Principal writings: *The Principles of Oratory; Declamations.*

QUR'AN.

From the Arabic *qara'a* meaning "to read." Hence, the meaning is "the reading" or "the lesson." The sacred book of Islam had its origin in 622 A.D. when, after the migration to Medina, Mohammed (*q.v.*) began to dictate his oracles to a disciple as they were revealed. Part of the contents of the Qur'an derive from the Mecca period (prior to 622); the rest belong to the period from 622 to 632. On Mohammed's death the Qur'an existed in scattered fragments, even though many Muslims knew large sections by heart. The caliph Abu Bekr assigned to Zaid ibn Thabit the task of collecting all of the parts. The copy made by Zaid had no canonicity and other copies had been made. Othman, a later caliph, appointed Zaid and three others to collect all the copies and prepare a text which would be made universally binding. Having done this, all other available codices were destroyed. The result was the Qur'an. The redactors arranged the chapters, or *suras*, in an order discriminated only by length. The longer suras were at the beginning, and the shorter toward the end.

(1) Throughout the Qur'an the speaker is God, although his mediator is an angel. (2) The early Meccan *suras* (identifiable by internal evidence) express great passion, vivid descriptions of the resurrection, the joys of heaven, the torments of hell. (3) The later Meccan and Medina *suras* are less vivid. The faithful are exhorted to battle for the faith, to virtue, to conquer their doubts. There is moral instruction, there are ceremonial, civil, and criminal laws, and outbursts against the Jews. The greatness of God is extolled; idolatry and the deification of human beings (such as Christ) condemned. (4) The Qur'an contains histories, showing how God rewards the righteous and punishes the wicked; there are histories of Joseph, Moses, and Alexander "the Horned." (5) One *sura*, called *alfatiha* ("the opening one") is also called the Lord's Prayer of the Muslims:

"In the name of God, the compassionate compassioner. Praise be to God, the Lord of the worlds, the compassionate compassioner, the sovereign of the day of judgment. Thee do we worship and of Thee do we beg assistance. Direct us in the right way; in the way of those to whom Thou hast been gracious, on whom there is no wrath, and who go not astray."

The original text of the Qur'an is said to be in heaven. It is then literally eternal and uncreated.

R

RABBI.

Hebrew term meaning "my great one." The ordination title for authoritative teachers of Judaism.

RABELAIS, FRANÇOIS.
Q.v. Utopia (9).

RACINE, JOHN.
Q.v. Tragedy (2).

RADHAKRISHNAN, SARVEPALLI. 1888–1975.

Indian philosopher and statesman. Studied at Madras. Taught at Madras, Mysore, Calcutta, Benares, and Oxford. He has served as Ambassador, Vice President, and President of the Republic of India. Seeking the unity of the world's religions and philosophies, his own Vedantic interpretation—taking Shankara (*q.v.*) as his point of departure—led to Idealism as his philosophic position.

Principal writings: *Indian Philosophy*, 2 vols., 1923; *The Philosophy of the Upanishads*, 1924; *An Ideal View of Life*, 1929; *Freedom and Culture*, 1936; *Eastern Religions in Western Thought*, 1939; *Contemporary Indian Philosophy*, 1950; *East and West: Some Reflections*, 1956; *A Source Book in Indian Philosophy* (with C.A. Moore), 1957; *Religion in a Changing World*, 1967.

(1) Indian philosophers, including Shankara, have not equated *Maya* with unreality even though this claim is often made. Instead, the world of ordinary experience is of middling reality, neither unreal nor real, but having its basis in the Absolute.

(2) Not only on this point but, generally, agreement among religions is more striking than difference. The religious seers of all ages testify to a common experience, carrying its own justification. Called a certainty of God, it is a certainty at least that we live ultimately in a spiritual environment which supports truthseeking and realization of the good.

(3) Thus his religion of the spirit includes philosophy. He holds that God is neither completely transcendent nor completely immanent. Philosophers emphasize God's immanent aspect, while in religion the emphasis is on the divine transcendence. The two emphases require each other.

(4) The aim of religious endeavor is the attainment of spiritual insight which brings with it the properties of invincible optimism, ethical universalism, and religious toleration. Such insight is gained through meditation, and developing an ethical life.

(5) But, more specifically, there is much agreement that life perfects itself painfully, and through numerous existences. Its perfection is understood as the achievement of eternal values, a Platonic influence in Radhakrishnan's thought. But its crown is the Hindu religious goal of a divine self-existence.

(6) He urges finally that the divinizing of life is to be an achievement not merely of the isolated individual, but of the race. The ultimate goal is the complete and final release of all.

RADICAL EMPIRICISM.

Q.v. William James (8).

RADICALISM, PHILOSOPHICAL.

Q.v. Philosophical Radicalism.

RADICAL TRANSLATION.

The problem of translation when one does not know the language.

(1) Quine (*q.v.* 5) set the problem with his conclusion concerning the indeterminacy of translation, but not with respect to "stimulus-meanings" (sentences which can be directly related to stimuli presented to sense organs) which are common to all human beings. The indeterminacy for stimulus-meaning is slight. Nor need we suppose that the speakers of the unknown language engage in obvious self-contradictions, but between these extremes the problem of incompatible translations is troublesome.

(2) Davidson (*q.v.* 7–8) believes that such indeterminacy can be managed by Tarski's theory of truth with a great deal of agreement at the lower levels of generality, the theories we construct having been tested through time by the "thin little bits of evidence" of the lower levels.

(3) In addition various authors have advanced qualifying principles to help the situation. One is the "principle of charity" advanced by N.L. Wilson. We are to look for, and accept, whatever interpretation "will maximize truth among the sentences of the corpus" we are translating. This assumes that the beliefs of those who use the unknown language do in general match our own. Davidson says he uses the principle "across the board," and Quine to some extent.

(4) Richard Grandy introduces a "principle of humanity," which puts on trans-

lation the "pragmatic constraint" that we impute to the users of the unknown language. A "pattern of relations among beliefs, desires and the world" which is "as similar to our own as possible."

RADISCHEV, A.N.

Q.v. Russian Philosophy (2).

RAGA.

Sanskrit term signifying the attachments we develop to pleasant things. One of the five kinds of delusive attachment of the Yoga system (*q.v.* Yoga 3).

RAHNER, KARL. 1904– .

German theologian. Born in Freiburg. Studied at Valkenburg (Holland), Freiburg, and Innsbruck. Entered Jesuit order, 1922. Ordained Roman Catholic priest, 1932. Taught at Innsbruck, Munich, and Münster.

Selected writings: *Spirit in the World* (T), 1939; *Hearers of the Word* (T), 1941; *Nature and Grace* (T), 1950; *Theological Investigations* (T), 20 vols., 1954–82; *The Eternal Yes* (T), 1957; *The Church and the Sacraments* (T), 1963; *Faith Today* (T), 1965; *Grace and Freedom* (T), 1968; *Foundation of Christian Faith* (T), 1976.

(1) Rahner initiated his intellectual career with a restudy of the epistemology and metaphysics of Aquinas. His contemporary, Lonergan (*q.v.*), made the same initial move. For both the theme of self-transcendence became central.

(2) Taking becoming seriously, Rahner interpreted evolution as "increase in being," the qualitatively higher emerging from the qualitatively lower. He argued that a transcendent act of God accounts for this increase.

(3) Personal self-transcendence is also the act of God who is present at the "center" of every person's existence, determining that existence, whether accepted or refused by the person (although not thereby compromising human freedom).

(4) Transcendence is also the theme of his "Christology from below" which posits the need for an "absolute bringer of salvation." The irreversible presence of transcendence in history would be signified by the history of a man which is also the history of God. Jesus, the absolute self-communication of God is,

therefore, God himself.

(5) The concept of grace infusing nature is a sub-theme of transcendence. Since divine grace is given freely "annonymous Christianity" is to be found, although not acknowledged, in all religions. Salvation is possible in any religion, and we are allowed to hope that all will be saved.

(6) The human spirit, however, tends to be overwhelmed by the modern world. Human life is experienced as dark and empty, and existence as an incomparable mystery. The key in overcoming the dark mystery lies in accepting oneself fully and completely. In doing so one also accepts "the One who has decided to fill this emptiness . . . with his own infinite fullness," so in accepting oneself one accepts God.

RAJA YOGA.

One of the four basic types of Yoga (*q.v.* 5), Raja Yoga stresses concentration as the path to liberation where the other three stress devotion, knowledge, and physical discipline, respectively.

RAJAS.

Q.v. Hinduism (6b); Sankhya (4–5).

RAMA.

Hindu deity. Along with Krishna (*q.v.*), one of the last two incarnations of Vishnu (*q.v.*). Their followers constitute a considerable portion of the Hindu people and a majority of the Vishnuites (*q.v.* Vaiṣnavism 2a). Rama is the hero of the great epic work, the *Ramayana* (*q.v.* Hinduism 2). In Books Two through Six, apparently the original portion of the work, Rama is described simply as the best of men, a dutiful son, loving husband, and possessor of every virtue. But he succeeds in apparently superhuman undertakings, and so came to be regarded as more than human. In Books One and Seven, regarded as later additions by the scholarly community, his divinity is acknowledged. Since Vishnu, too, had performed miraculous tasks on behalf of men, *e.g.*, destroying demons, there was reason for connecting Rama with Vishnu. The popularity of Rama as an incarnation of Vishnu has continued from the 10th century A.D. to the present.

RAMADAN.

Muslim observance held in the ninth month of the Muslim calendar. Strict fasting is observed from dawn to sunset.

RAMANANDA.

Q.v. Hinduism (5c).

RAMANUJA. 11th cent. A.D.

Indian philosopher. Born in Bautapuri. Originally an adherent of the philosophy of Shankara, Ramanuja fell under the influence of Vaiṣnavism (*q.v.*); and finally became head of a school representing this opinion. Dedicating himself to working out the philosophical basis of the hymns of the Attars, Ramanuja became the philosopher for the *bhakti*, or devotional strand, of Hinduism. Taking Shankara as his opponent, much of his writing was polemical, directed toward refutation of Shankara's philosophy.

Principal writings: *Commentaries on the Vedanta Sutras* (T); *Vedantatattvasara* (T); *Vedarthasangraha* (T).

(1) Convinced that Shankara was illogical in beginning with a world of difference which he at a later stage decreed to be false, Ramanuja insisted that multiplicity must remain a characteristic of reality. At the same time Brahman must retain supremacy as the origin and vital center, or self of all things.

(2) Both objectives are achieved by recognizing the phenomenal world with its components, inanimate matter and individual selves, as constituting the body of Brahman. They are real although their status is subordinate.

(3) Brahman and the individual self are alike in a number of significant ways. In the first place both continue to exist with or without embodiment. In the second place, while souls affect bodies, the reverse is not the case. Hence, Brahman and individual souls remain pure and unaffected. In the case of Brahman this is an absolute requirement. In the case of individual souls the principle is qualified by ignorance, suffering, and the misuse of choice.

(4) For Brahman embodiment or non-embodiment is a matter of vast cosmic cycles. In his gross state Brahman exists as the soul of the world he has caused. In his subtle state, having reabsorbed the world, Brahman exists alone. At this point

apparently even disembodied souls are absorbed in Brahman. These "causal" and "effected" states may be compared to Shankara's "Nirguna Brahman" and "Saguna Brahman" respectively (*q.v.* Śankara 4–5).

(5) The motivation for creation on Brahman's part is a spirit of play (*lila*); to allow Brahman to derive benefit from the world would be to diminish his supremacy. At the same time, Ramanuja makes it clear that all that is is prized by Brahman; hence decisions about values can be derived from Brahman's relation to the world.

(6) And yet, even with his insistence upon diversity, Ramanuja claims Brahman as the sole reality in both the causal and effected states, since all things other than Brahman constitute his body. And it is in this respect that a distinction is drawn to preserve Brahman's immutability. Real difference is allowed in the body of Brahman, but no shadow of turning is to be granted in the self or soul ordering, and indeed calling forth, this body. All change, evil, imperfection, and suffering occurs in the body of Brahman. While in the causal state Brahman decrees, "May I again possess a world body," but this decree, claims Ramanuja, does not imply any change or movement in Brahman's self or soul.

RAMAYANA.

One of the two great epics of Hinduism (*q.v.* 2). Consisting of seven books and 50,000 lines, the *Ramayana* is both older and shorter than its companion, the *Mahabharata* (*q.v.*). Written between the 6th and 4th centuries B.C., the poem tells the story of the birth, youth, marriage, and exile of Prince Rama; the abduction of his wife by a demon and her return; his reign, final years, and death. As a morality tale, the story depicts the victory of Rama over his enemies, both natural and supernatural, through exemplary behavior. Interpolations in the 2nd century B.C. transformed the story into one concerning Rama, the incarnation of Vishnu. On this level the poem becomes devotional literature, telling of the love and protection which Rama-Vishnu provides for those who trust Him.

Q.v. Vaiṣnavism (2b).

RAMIFIED THEORY OF TYPES.

Q.v. Type (4).

RAMOS, SAMUEL.

Q.v. Latin American Philosophy (12).

RAMSEY, FRANK. 1903–1930.

English philosopher. Taught at Cambridge. Influenced by Wittgenstein, Ramsey argued that the Axiom of Reducibility (*q.v.*) was not necessary, since the paradoxes it was introduced to avoid could be avoided by less extreme measures. He proposed a subjective theory of probability turning on an operational test for degree of belief; and regarded general propositions as lacking truth value, standing rather as formulae for drawing further propositions of a certain kind.

Principal writings: *The Foundations of Mathematics* (ed. Braithwaite), 1931.

RAMUS, PETER. 1515–1572.

French philosopher. Born in northern France. Studied at Paris where he later taught. His attacks on Aristotle were so unsettling that his opponents in 1544 procured a royal decree forbidding him to teach philosophy. The decree was canceled in 1547. He became a Protestant in 1561, living in Switzerland and Germany until 1570. He was murdered in the St. Bartholomew's Day Massacre. The logic of Peter Ramus, initially called Dialectic, had considerable vogue, especially in Protestant circles, going through 250 editions, and retaining influence until the end of the 17th century.

Principal writings: *Remarks on Aristotle*, 1543; *The Structure of Dialectic*, 1543; *Dialectic*, 1555, 1556.

(1) Regarding logic as an *ars disserendi*, an art of discourse concerned with the discovery and arrangement of arguments, he contrasted the natural logic of discourse with the artificial logic of the syllogism. Ramus argued that the rules of logic were better learned from Cicero's discussion and practice of persuasion than from Aristotle. Ramus stressed the value of a method of dichotomy, dividing a subject matter into two parts, which was then divided once more, and so on continuously. This method joined his predilection for moving from the general to the particular.

(2) He presented nine locii for argu-

ments: cause, effect, subject, adjunct, opposite, comparative, name, division, and definition.

(3) For major premise, minor premise, and conclusion, Ramus used the terms *axioma*, *assumptio*, and *quaestio*.

(4) A categorical statement is called an *axioma simplex*; a universal statement is an *axioma generale*; a particular statement is an *axioma particulara*; a singular statement, *e.g.*, with a proper name as subject, is an *axioma proprium*.

(5) He made a number of changes in his exposition of the theory of the syllogism, such as interchanging the position of Aristotle's first and second figure. He eliminated the fourth figure, in this sense returning to Aristotle, and followed Valla in attacking the third.

(6) He held that everything merely probable must be removed from science, that the boundaries of the fields of science must be precisely determined, and that exposition should descend from the more general to the less general.

(7) Ethics was to be studied by application of the methodized analysis to biography and history.

Also *q.v.* Logic (13).

RAND, AYN. 1905–1982.

Born Alice Rosenbaum in St. Petersburg, Russia. Russian educated, Rand came to the United States in 1926, becoming a citizen in 1931. After a number of years as a screenwriter, two best-selling novels led her to champion a philosophy she called "Objectivism." Bringing together the four theses that reality is independent of human awareness, truth is reached by reason, the right by an ethics of selfishness, and the good society by a politics of capitalism. Rand believed government should be limited to three functions: (a) the police in protecting against criminals, (b) the military protecting against invasion, (c) courts settling disputes among citizens according to "objective law."

Principal writings: *The Fountainhead*, 1943; *Atlas Shrugged*, 1957; *For the New Intellectual: the Philosophy of Ayn Rand*, 1961; *The Virtue of Selfishness* (with N. Branden), 1964; *Capitalism* (with N. Branden and others), 1966; *The New Left*, 1982; *The Ayn Rand Lexicon: Objectivism from A to Z* (intro. and notes by L. Peikoff,

1984; *The Voice of Reason*, 1989).

RANGE.

For a discussion of the range of sentences, based on state descriptions, *q.v.* Carnap (11).

RANSOM, JOHN CROWE.

Q.v. New Criticism.

RAPOPORT, ANATOL.

Q.v. Philosophy of Science (25); Operationalism.

RASHDALL, HASTINGS. 1858–1924.

English philosopher. Born in London. Educated at Oxford where he later taught.

Principal writings: *The Theory of Good and Evil*, 2 vols., 1907; *Philosophy and Religion*, 1909; *The Problem of Evil*, 1912; *The Moral Argument for Personal Immortality*, 1920.

(1) Calling his ethical position Ideal Utilitarianism to distinguish it from the strict hedonism of Bentham (*q.v.*), Rashdall held the end to be achieved was an ideal containing pleasure and happiness among other components. He regarded the development of character, for instance, as having intrinsic value and forming part of the ideal to be achieved.

(2) His metaphysical position was that of Personal Idealism. Minds exist independently of each other, but matter exists only for mind.

(3) His response to the problem of evil was to regard God as limited in power although he wills the absolute moral idea.

RATIO.

Q.v. Spinoza (5b).

RATIONALISM.

From the Latin *ratio* ("reason"). The principle that reason is to be granted the primary role in explanation. The application of the principle has had many diverse consequences.

(1) Parmenides (*q.v.* 1–3) found it possible on the basis of this principle to identify the rational and the real, describing reality in terms quite foreign to sense experience. Plato (*q.v.* 1), envisioning dialectic as beginning, continuing, and ending in ideas, was likewise basically a Rationalist.

(2) The term is commonly used in the phrase, Continental Rationalists, to refer

to the 17th-century philosophers Descartes (*q.v.* 10), Spinoza (*q.v.* 5b), and Leibniz (*q.v.* 1–12) whose philosophical method—especially in the cases of Descartes and Spinoza—consisted of making a geometry of philosophy.

(3) In the 18th century the philosophers of the Enlightenment (*q.v.*) both in France and Germany were thought of as Rationalists. In this usage, however, the sense of the term has altered to some extent. Here Rationalism means following the new knowledge rather than traditional ways.

(4) In the 19th century, largely due to the influence of Hegel (*q.v.* 1–3), Rationalism came to be associated with philosophical Idealism (*q.v.*). Hegel identified the rational and the real in a manner reminiscent of Parmenides. It was largely among the 19th-century Idealists who succeeded Hegel that the Coherence Theory of Truth (*q.v.* Truth 1, 4 *passim*) prospered. In this theory the marks of systematic unity, rather than mere correspondence to fact, become the test of truth.

(5) In theology the application of the principle has provided additional senses of the term: (a) It has sometimes meant that approach to religious belief where reason replaces faith. (b) At other times it has been equated with Modernism (*q.v.*) in either its Protestant or Catholic forms, the former standing for a critical study of Biblical texts, and the latter a reliance on reason which is excessive and leads to "false doctrine."

RATIONALITY.
Q.v. Rescher (8).

RATIONAL PREFERABILITY.
Q.v. Induction (15).

RATIONAL PSYCHOLOGY.
Q.v. Psychology (2, 15).

RATIONES AETERNAS.
Q.v. St. Augustine (2); *Mundus Intelligibilis* (3).

RATIONES SEMINALES.
The seminal reasons activating the material creation. *Q.v.* Bonaventure (9).

RAUSCHENBUSCH, WALTER.
Q.v. Social Gospel.

RAVAISSON-MOLLIEN, FELIX. 1813–1900.
French philosopher. Born in Namur. Studied with Schelling at Munich, and with Cousin in Paris. Taught at Renne. Later he held several significant educational and cultural posts within the French government. Arguing against the eclecticism of Cousin (*q.v.*), Ravaisson-Mollien supported the spiritualism of Maine de Biran (*q.v.*). His manner of relating space and time to matter and life anticipates Bergson.

Principal writings: *Essay on Aristotle's Metaphysics*, 2 vols., 1837, 1846; *On Habit*, 1838; *Philosophy in France in the Nineteenth Century*, 1867.

RAWLS, JOHN. 1921– .
American philosopher. Born in Baltimore. Educated at Princeton. Has taught at Princeton, Cornell, M.I.T., and Harvard.

Principal writings: *A Theory of Justice*, 1971; *Political Liberalism*, 1993.

(1) Using the social contract doctrine, but separating it from history, Rawls turns it into a hypothetical situation into which one can enter at any time. One chooses from an "original position" (comparable to the state of nature), among alternative contractual relationships with society.

(2) Since one's choice is made behind a "veil of ignorance," it is appropriate to apply the "maximin" rule of game theory: select that strategy whose worst possible outcome is superior to the worst possible outcome of any other strategy.

(3) The rule at once eliminates Utilitarianism as a rational choice, since the maximum social benefit of that alternative is compatible with a benefit below the "social minimum" for some and perhaps then, given the veil of ignorance, for oneself.

(4) The alternative to be chosen, according to Rawls, is the doctrine of justice as "fairness," including two principles: (a) each person has a right to the most extensive basic liberty which is compatible with the same liberty for others; (b) inequalities of wealth are justified to the extent that they work out to the advantage of the disadvantaged; and with the proviso that their reduction or elimination would reduce or eliminate this advantage.

RE, MODALITY DE.
Q.v. Modality (8).

READ, CARVETH. 1848–1931.
English philosopher. Born in Farmouth. Taught in London. A follower of John Stuart Mill in logic, his metaphysical orientation was Idealistic. He adopted the position of Panpsychism as the means of avoiding the traditional mind-body dualism.

Principal writings: *On the Theory of Logic*, 1878; *Logic, Deductive and Inductive*, 1898; *The Metaphysics of Nature*, 1905; *Natural and Social Morals*, 1909; *The Origin of Man and his Superstitions*, 1920.

REAL DEFINITION.
Q.v. Aristotle (4); Genus (2). A definition which states the essence of the thing defined. The possibility of real definitions depends upon things having essences which can be captured in language. The term is to be contrasted with nominal definition. The difference of meaning between the two is a reflection of the differences between Realism (q.v.) and Nominalism (q.v.).

REALE, MIGUEL.
Q.v. Latin American Philosophy (13).

REALISM.
From the Latin *res* meaning "thing." In philosophy the term has had two major references. In the problem of universals (q.v.), Realism is set in contrast to Nominalism. In the problem of the independence of the external world, Realism stands in contrast to Idealism.

A. The first of these two usages has had a long history. The course of the dispute, centered in the Middle Ages, is treated under the topic, Universals. Realism is one of the positions in that dispute. In this connection the doctrine of Realism means that universals have a reality of their own, an extra-mental existence. Positions are often marked out, running from moderate to absolute Realism. The more definite, fixed, and eternal the status of the universals, the more absolute is the Realism.

(1) Plato (q.v. 1 and Universals 2) is usually thought of as an absolute realist, while Aristotle (q.v. 7 and Universals 3) is regarded as a moderate realist. Actually, there is a continuum from the view of Nominalism, *i.e.*, that the universal is only a name, through Conceptualism, *i.e.*, that the universal has existence only in the mind, through Moderate and Absolute Realism.

(2) In the catalogue below we have not distinguished moderate from absolute realists. After Plato and Aristotle, philosophers who held the view of Realism with respect to universals include: Plotinus (q.v. 3 and Universals 4), Porphyry (q.v. 1 and Universals 5), St. Augustine (q.v. 2 and Universals 6), Boethius (q.v. 2 and Universals 7), Erigena (q.v. 1 and Universals 8), Avicenna (q.v. 4–5 and Universals 9), Anselm (q.v. 7 and Universals 10), William of Champeaux (q.v. and Universals 12), possibly Abelard (q.v. 1–3 and Universals 13), Gilbert de la Porrée (q.v. Gilbert of Poitiers and Universals 14), Thomas Aquinas (q.v. 5 and Universals 16), possibly Duns Scotus (q.v. 6 and Universals 17), John Wycliffe (q.v. 1), Hegel (q.v. 6 and Universals 31), F.H. Bradley (q.v. 4 and Universals 34), Bosanquet (q.v. 2 and Universals 34), Blanshard (q.v. and Universals 34), Royce (q.v. 4–7 and Universals 34), Whitehead (q.v. 10 and Universals 36), Russell (q.v. 6 and Universals 37), Moore (q.v. 5 and Universals 38), a number of the representatives of the New Realists such as Holt (q.v. and Universals 39) and Montague (q.v. 1 and Universals 39), and also a number of the Critical Realists, *e.g.*, Santayana (q.v. 2–6 and Universals 39). From Hegel to Royce, the above list consists of Idealists and their view of universals. Furthermore, the New Realists and Critical Realists in opposition to the Idealists, introduce a new sense of Realism treated under (B.) below.

B. In the more recent controversies over Idealism the term has stood for the view that objects of knowledge exist independently of our awareness. Since objects of knowledge include both things and thoughts, in most modern doctrines of Realism this has amounted to the claim that both things and concepts have a real existence. Where concepts are understood to imply the objectivity of universals— and this has often been the case—the second sense of the term is virtually identical with the first.

(3) Recent decades have witnessed a multiplication of the types of philosophical

Realism. Modern science, its initial emphasis on causality and quantitative measure, prepared the way for Representative Realism (*q.v.*). This is the doctrine, quite clearly developed by John Locke (*q.v.* 1–5) that our awareness consists of sense-data of various types which more or less represent the world. For Locke primary qualities, *e.g.*, shapes, represent the world while secondary qualities, *e.g.*, colors, have their basis in the world but do not represent it as such. The view accounts quite adequately for error. We simply misinterpret the sense-data. Since we cannot break out of the circle of sensa, the view does not account so well for truth.

(4) The difficulties of Representative Realism provided at least part of the context leading Berkeley (*q.v.*) to his system of Idealism. One of the 18th-century responses to Berkeley was the Common Sense Realism of Thomas Reid (*q.v.* 1–5). Reid held that the principles of common sense are unquestionably true, and opinions counter to these principles gain their credibility only from the "enchantment of words." These principles relate especially to the existence of the external world, other persons, and questions of this sort.

(5) Idealism (*q.v.*) had its greatest triumph in the 19th century. The neo-Kantian (*q.v.*) response to German Idealism tells part of the story. Certain neo-Kantians, among them Aloys Riehl (*q.v.* 2), referred to themselves as Realists in philosophy.

(6) The early 20th-century movement of New Realism (*q.v.*) initiated the response to British and American Idealism. This form of Idealism had stressed the internal relation of knowledge to its object. A great many philosophers participated directly or indirectly in the movement of New Realism, including G.E. Moore who in fact revived Reid's Common Sense Realism, James, Russell, and the six American New Realists: Holt, Montague, Perry, Pitkin, Spaulding, and Marvin.

(7) Critical Realism (*q.v.*), in turn, formed in opposition to New Realism. In a sense this completes the circle, since Critical Realism, like Representative Realism, recognizes the triad of act of perception, sense-datum, and thing. The

Critical Realists claimed to have overcome the main objections to Representative Realism by beginning with the object, but this seems largely a victory by fiat and the problem of moving from sense-datum to object remains.

(8) An effort to solve the problem by a return at least part way to Idealism was made by E.B. McGilvary (*q.v.*) in his Perspective Realism. McGilvary, who argued for Realism while standing apart from both New and Critical Realism, held that sensation or awareness includes the object from the standpoint of the person sensing. Perspectives, which are something like sets of relations among things, neither exist nor subsist but "intersist." This general approach to the problem was also supported by the Objective Relativism of A.E. Murphy (*q.v.* 1) who discerned in this emphasis a new approach to philosophy.

(9) Lenin (*q.v.* 2) argued for an Epistemological Realism of the most literal sort holding that our mental content must replicate reality outside the mind.

(10) Although both Moore and the Critical Realists claimed to be Common Sense Realists, the most likely heirs to Reid's philosophy are to be found among the Oxford linguistic philosophers who argue for the common-sense view of the world while criticizing the sense-datum theory. Ryle (*q.v.* 3) did so in a general sense, breaking up traditional distinctions, while Austin (*q.v.* 4) worked with special effectiveness against the weaknesses of the sense-datum theory itself.

(11) One must likewise mention the doctrine of Naive Realism (*q.v.*), held by no one, yet widely discussed, that all of the characteristics we sense in objects are truly characteristic of them.

(12) Bergmann (*q.v.* 1) and Chisholm (*q.v.* 3) argue, each in his own way, for Realism against Phenomenalism.

(13) Wilfrid Sellars (*q.v.* 1) gives adherence to a position he calls Scientific Realism.

(14) Dummet (*q.v.* 3–4) works through numerous permutations of realism and antirealism, relating them to the principle of bivalence.

(15) Putnam (*q.v.* 1, 5, 8) discusses empirical or scientific, metaphysical and internal realism, defending the latter.

(16) In the modal realism of David

Lewis (*q.v.* 4) the doctrine is extended to possible worlds.

REALISM, MODAL.
Q.v. David Lewis (4).

REALITY.
From the Latin *realitas*, deriving from *res* ("thing"). The term was introduced into Western philosophy in the 13th century, apparently by Duns Scotus (*q.v.* 1), who used the term as a synonym for "being" (*q.v.*). Indeed, no clear distinction can be drawn between the two terms, nor between these and such terms as "actuality" (*q.v.*) and "existence." Any philosopher's view of "that which is" might be discussed under either "being" or "reality." When a distinction is drawn between what exists and what subsists (*e.g.*, possibilities), the terms "actuality" and "existence" are sometimes identified with the former while "being" and "reality" extend over both what exists and what subsists. The following comments have to do with those who did themselves use the term, "reality."

(1) The Indian philosopher, Nagarjuna, (*q.v.* 9) looked upon reality as beyond intellect, the non-dual Absolute in which all distinctions merge.

(2) Gaudapada (*q.v.* 1, 3) held reality to be Brahman, and Brahman to be the non-dual Absolute; and Shankara (*q.v.* 5–10) developed arguments supporting this position in which Brahman is the sole reality.

(3) Campanella (*q.v.* 3) wrote of a graded reality, embodying perfections in different degrees, and all things possessing the "primalities" of knowledge, power, and love.

(4) Kant (*q.v.* 3) defined the real as that which accords with the material conditions of experience.

(5) Fichte (*q.v.* 2) held that reality was posited by the ego.

(6) Peirce (*q.v.* 12) on the other hand defined reality as that which is believed by the community of inquirers at the end of an ideal series of inquiries.

(7) Bradley (*q.v.* 1–2) held reality to be an Absolute which lies behind experience.

(8) Ostwald (*q.v.* 1), approaching the matter from the side of science, interpreted reality as energy rather than matter.

(9) Freud (*q.v.* 7) used the term "reality principle" to refer to that goal of therapy in which the mature individual is able to forgo illusion in favor of reality.

(10) Royce (*q.v.* 7) viewed reality as a "community of interpretation."

(11) Lossky (*q.v.* 1) regarded reality as an organic whole.

(12) Buber (*q.v.* 3) suggested that the approach to reality is through an "I-Thou" relationship.

(13) Romero (*q.v.* 5) views transcendence as the key to reality.

REALS.
Q.v. Herbart (3b).

REASON.
From the Latin *ratio* ("reckoning"); in Greek there are three terms roughly equivalent in meaning; *phronesis* (*q.v.*), *nous* (*q.v.*), and *logos* (*q.v.*).

(1) Applied to a capacity in man to draw logical conclusions, a long tradition has regarded reason as man's most distinctive faculty. The tradition perhaps began with Plato's differentiation of will, reason, and passion in man (*q.v.* Plato 3). The oldest psychological doctrine, in fact, was a faculty psychology (*q.v.*, and Psychology 1).

(2) Aristotle (*q.v.* 11) made a distinction between active and passive reason, the former a "pure" form of reasoning, and the latter a form of reasoning related to the senses. This distinction was basic to Islamic philosophy (*q.v.*), and prominent throughout the Middle Ages.

(3) In the 1st century B.C. Panaetius (*q.v.* 3) distinguished between the theoretical and the practical reason, giving priority to the latter.

(4) The relation of faith to reason has been widely discussed (*q.v.* Faith). The view of Aquinas (*q.v.* 1) that the two are complementary, but faith has a superior status, is held by many.

(5) Hobbes (*q.v.* 3–4), taking a materialistic approach to reason, described reason as a mechanical computation.

(6) Pascal (*q.v.* 3) drew a distinction between reasons of the mind, and "reasons of the heart" the mind knows not of.

(7) Kant (*q.v.* 11b–c, f), like Panaetius, distinguished between the theoretical and the practical reason. He developed

at length the considerations appropriate to both, including a distinction between the understanding and the reason.

(8) Hegel (*q.v.* 5–6) adopted Kant's distinction between the two, making the development of the ideas of Reason the basis of his deduction of the categories.

(9) Newman (*q.v.* 4–6) distinguished between formal and informal reasoning, and found the latter to be more significant.

(10) Ritschl (*q.v.* 1) made a sharp dichotomy between reason and faith, giving each its own sphere.

(11) Dilthey (*q.v.* 1) developed the concept of the historical reason, extending the Kantian analysis to history.

(12) Peirce (*q.v.* 7, 10) insisted that reason is not possible without will and feeling. The task of reason in his view is to refine belief.

(13) Ortega y Gasset (*q.v.* 1) built his philosophy around the concept of a "vital reason" which is more immediate and more subtle than theoretical or formal reason.

(14) Jaspers (*q.v.* 3) finds *Existenz* an important corollary to reason, relating human beings to reality.

(15) Tillich (*q.v.* 2) distinguished between heteronymous, autonomous, and theonomous reason, finding the last named that which relates one to the depths of being.

REASONS OF THE HEART.
Q.v. Pascal (3).

REBELLION.
The opposition of the individual to the state, as contrasted with revolution. *Q.v.* Max Stirner (3).

REBIRTH.
The general term, referring to a succession of births, of which Reincarnation (*q.v.*) is one basic modification. Reincarnation implies the notion of rebirth while denying the existence of soul. In both doctrines one has the responsibility of coming to terms with one's *Karma* (*q.v.*). This requires that one be born again and again in the conditions to which one's actions have led, until one's *karma* has been used up and release is possible.

RECOLLECTION, DOCTRINE OF.
Q.v. Anamnesis; Plato (1).

RECTIFICATION OF NAMES.
Q.v. Hsün Tzu (4).

RECURSIVE FUNCTION.
Any function containing a hereditary property such that when the value of the function has been determined for one member of a series it is determinable for the next member of the series. Examples of recursive functions are Peano's Postulates for Arithmetic (*q.v.* Peano), and Frege's (*q.v.* 1–2) derivation of arithmetic from logic (also *q.v.* Russell 2). The analysis of recursive functions thus relates to mathematical induction (*q.v.* Induction 10), and has centered in number theory. Church (*q.v.*) identified the property of recursiveness and mechanical calculability, introducing his λ- notation to express it. The so-called Turing machines (*q.v.*) of A.M. Turing likewise approach recursiveness through mechanical calculability.

RECUSANT.
From the Latin *recusare* ("to refuse"). In church history the term is applied to Roman Catholics in England who refused to recognize the authority of the Church of England or attend its services.

REDEMPTION.
From the Latin *redemptio*, from *redimere* ("to buy"). The doctrine that man is ransomed from sin by the divine. It has its most specific form in Christianity.

(1) Most New Testament references come from Paul (*q.v.* 2–3) who elaborated the doctrine of Christ's sacrificial death as a substitute for man in providing satisfaction for the sin of Adam.

(2) Although Paul and the major Christian tradition (*e.g.*, St. Augustine, *q.v.* 12) regarded redemption as selective, Origen (*q.v.* 4) was among those who supported a doctrine of universal redemption made possible by Christ's sacrifice.

(3) Anselm (*q.v.* 6) developed the idea of man's redemption as resting on the proportionality of Christ's Atonement (*q.v.*) to man's sin, making possible man's salvation.

(4) The doctrine of universal redemption is the central doctrine of the modern movement of Universalism (*q.v.* 2).

REDUCIBILITY.

A term similar in meaning to Reductionism (*q.v.*) although used less formally. For example, R.W. Sellars (*q.v.* 3), among others, pointed out that the qualities of life and mind are not reducible to the qualities of inert matter.

REDUCIBILITY, AXIOM OF.

A necessary corrective if one adopts the Ramified Theory of Types (*q.v.* Russell 3). The reason for adopting the ramified theory is to solve paradoxes of self-reference (*q.v.* Paradox 8); but since some self-reference is necessary even in ordinary mathematics, the axiom is a device to reduce the Ramified Theory of Types to the simple theory where necessary.

REDUCTIO AD ABSURDUM.

The Latin phrase, meaning "reduction to absurdity," applies to a method of indirect proof in which one deduces a contradiction from the contradictory of the proposition to be proven. If one wishes to prove P, one supposes not-P (the contradictory of P) to be true. One deduces a contradiction from not-P, say Q and not-Q. Since a proposition which leads to a contradiction cannot be true, not-P is seen to be false. And since the relation between a proposition and its contradictory is such that the falsity of one requires the truth of the other (*q.v.* Square of Opposition), the falsify of not-P requires the truth of P.

REDUCTIO AD IMPOSSIBILE.

Latin phrase meaning "reduction to the impossible." A form of argument which seeks to establish the truth of a proposition by showing that the contradictory of that proposition involves impossible consequences; a form of the *reductio ad absurdum* (*q.v.*).

REDUCTIONISM.

The attempt to reduce one science to another by demonstrating that the key terms of the one are definable in the language of the other, and that the conclusions of the one are derivable from the propositions of the other.

(1) It is claimed by some that in this sense Psychology is reducible to Physiology. (2) It is claimed by others that Biology (*q.v.* 1–3) is reducible to Physics

and Chemistry. The adherents of Organismic Biology (*q.v.*) vigorously dispute the claim. Nagel (*q.v.* 3) has pointed out that in this dispute neither side has succeeded either in demonstrating, or even in clarifying, its contentions.

REDUCTION, PRINCIPLE OF.

Q.v. Pauler (3).

REDUCTIONS, PSYCHOLOGICAL AND EIDETIC.

Q.v. Husserl (6).

REFERENCE, THEORY OF.

An area of contemporary philosophic concern over problems of denotation, or how words and phrases refer.

(1) Meinong (*q.v.* 1) held that non-existent entities, *e.g.*, the golden mountain and the round square, are objects even though they have no being. Otherwise, the phrases "the golden mountain" and "the round square" would lack reference. In Meinong's view the golden mountain is simply an incomplete object and the round square is an impossible object.

(2) Frege (*q.v.* 4–7) avoided this alternative by distinguishing between the sense of a term and its reference. Also *q.v.* Dummet (2).

(3) Russell (*q.v.* 4) accomplished the same end as Frege by means of his theory of definite descriptions. Since he believed all statements about "the so-and-so," where the so-and-so does not exist, are false, there was some urgency in getting rid of definite descriptions. His move was to translate them into a set of other statements which do not have the appearance of referring to anything non-existent.

(4) Strawson (*q.v.* 2) has argued that Russell's move with regard to definite descriptions is more radical than need be. Since definite descriptions are neither true nor false, there is really no issue calling for Russell's theory.

(5) Putnam (*q.v.* 2) linked his doctrine of realism to a causal theory of reference.

REFERENT.

In logic the first term of a relation whose second term is called the "relatum." If A has the relation R to B, A is the referent and B the relatum.

REFLEXIVITY.

The property of those relations in terms of which an entity relates to itself. Since any "x" whatever is identical with itself, "identity" is a reflexive relation. *Q.v.* Logic of Relations (7); Logic (22).

REFORMATION.

The term is used to describe movements seeking to correct abuses in an established order, often by reverting to the principles and customs of an earlier period.

(1) The most notable use of the term is in the phrase "Protestant Reformation," a 16th-century movement whose principal leader was Martin Luther (*q.v.*). Luther's 1517 posting of 95 theses, concerning errors and abuses in the Roman Church, is usually taken as the initial act of the Protestant Reformation. Among the other figures of importance are the humanist, Erasmus (*q.v.*), who initially supported the movement but then withdrew; Melanchthon (*q.v.*), who systematized the new directions struck out by Luther; Calvin (*q.v.*) and Zwingli (*q.v.*), who established the reform in Switzerland, and John Knox (*q.v.*), who carried Calvin's version of Protestantism to Scotland.

(2) The Roman Church's response to the Protestant Reformation came in the "Counter Reformation." The Counter Reformation included the founding of the Society of Jesus by Ignatius Loyola (*q.v.*) and the lengthy deliberations of the Council of Trent which extended from 1545 to 1563.

(3) It is appropriate to speak of periods of reform in philosophy as well. Many Renaissance thinkers set themselves to reform philosophy by eliminating the allegedly arid Scholasticism and Aristotelianism of the medieval period. The British Empiricists (*q.v.*), the French *Philosophes* (*q.v.*), Scotch Common-Sensists (*q.v.*), American Pragmatists (*q.v.*), and especially the Vienna Circle of Logical Positivists (*q.v.*) viewed their mission as that of effecting reform in philosophy by eliminating otiose methods and traditions of philosophizing.

REFORMED CHURCHES.

Q.v. Lutheran and Reformed Churches.

REGENERATION.

From the Latin *regeneratus* ("to have been born again"). In religion a new, spiritual birth. In Christianity the symbolism of baptism is participation in the death, burial, and resurrection of Christ. Also *q.v.* Justification by Faith.

REGULATIVE PRINCIPLE.

A term applied in the Kantian philosophy to the ideas of reason, *i.e.*, God, freedom, and immortality. Theoretically incapable of proof, such ideas nevertheless guide human thought and conduct (*q.v.* Kant 11f). Vaihinger (*q.v.* 1) extended the applicability of the term to all ideas, and in a sense Dewey (*q.v.* 4) did likewise, regarding ideas as instruments for effecting change.

REICHENBACH, HANS. 1891–1953.

German-American philosopher of science. Born in Hamburg. Educated at Berlin, Munich, Göttingen and Erlangen. Taught at the universities of Berlin, Istanbul, and California (Los Angeles). A member of the Berlin group of logical positivists (although he preferred the term "logical empiricist"), Reichenbach contributed especially to probability theory, and the understanding of induction.

Principal writings: *Relativity Theory and A Priori Knowledge*, 1920; *The Axiomatic of Space-Time Relativity Theory*, 1924; *The Philosophy of Space and Time* (T), 1928; *Atom and Cosmos*, 1930; *Theory of Probability* (T), 1935; *Experience and Prediction* (E), 1938; *Philosophic Foundations of Quantum Mechanics* (E), 1944; *Elements of Symbolic Logic* (E), 1947; *The Rise of Scientific Philosophy* (E), 1951; *Nominal Statements and Admissible Operations* (E), 1953; *The Direction of Time* (E), 1956; *Modern Philosophy of Science* (E), 1958.

(1) Reichenbach held that the two-valued logic of truth and falsity should be replaced by an infinite-valued logic based on a relative-frequency view of probability. In this view, a probability statement can always be expressed as the limit of a relative frequency and this limit is assignable through the discovery of the "weight" of the statement in question. Since both general and singular statements can be discussed in terms of their "weights," probability can be assigned in all cases. The "weights" of statements in

ordinary first-level induction are determined by second-level inductions; and, speaking generally, this involves knowledge of inductions in analogous kinds of cases. If one wishes to establish the "weight" of the statement, "Carbon has a melting point," and has no evidence concerning this, inductions concerning the fusibility of other metals can establish the weight by "vertical induction." One would conclude that the weight is high. The weight of the probability of the occurrence of one event rather than another can be determined in the same way: e.g., by asking for the relative frequency with which the documents supporting the two statements are confirmed. If these confirmations occur with a greater relative frequency in the one rather than the other case, the statement with the greater relative frequency has the greater weight.

(2) In keeping with his theory of probability, Reichenbach offered a more open version of the verifiability theory of meaning in which a proposition has meaning if a degree of probability can be determined for it. And he was willing to grant that the propositions of traditional philosophy have some degree of probability.

(3) In criticizing the standard verification theory he used the concept of "surplus meaning." Some propositions, those which are verified indirectly, have meanings in excess of any traceable observable consequences. This is surplus meaning.

(4) He likewise advocated a probability logic which would not be two-valued, recognizing only "true" and "false," but with a range of values extending over all real numbers between "0" and "1."

(5) Identifying "necessity" with nomological statements, "impossibility" becomes the negation of such statements, and "possibility" the denial that either a nomological statement or its negation is applicable.

(6) Using the phrase, "context of discovery," for the actual processes of thinking which lead to a discovery and "context of justification" for the "rational reconstruction" which provides the demonstration presented to the public, Reichenbach held the first to be psychological and of no interest to philosophy. The second involved a logical reconstruction in which one's understanding of the discovery increases as the reconstruction proceeds.

(7) In addition to these methodological considerations, he directed his attention to the philosophical aspects of physics, including relativity theory and quantum mechanics.

REID, THOMAS. 1710–1796.

Scottish philosopher. Born in Strachan. Educated in Aberdeen. He taught first in Aberdeen and then in Glasgow. A Presbyterian minister, he founded the Scottish School of Common Sense Philosophy.

Principal writings: *Inquiry into the Human Mind*, 1764; *On the Intellectual Powers of Man*, 1785; *On the Active Powers of Man*, 1788. (The last two works are often published together under the title, *Essays on the Powers of the Human Mind*.)

(1) Attacking Hume and Berkeley on the basis of their theory of ideas, Reid held that the theory, which makes ideas our sole direct source of knowledge, begins from a wrong principle, and simply dissolves the world. The view Reid was attacking we would today call the representative theory of perception (*q.v.* Perception 3–7). What we need is a different beginning point.

(2) Reid suggested that we begin with a doctrine of "natural signs," in contrast with the conventional signs of ordinary language. Natural signs are the sensations we gain from objects in the world and from other persons. Natural signs lead immediately to their objects, and include a belief in the existence of these objects apart from our perceiving them. Such signs support our belief in the independent reality of objects and of other persons.

(3) Curiously, although utilizing a different principle, Reid found it necessary to retain Locke's distinction between primary and secondary qualities (*q.v.* Locke 6), finding the signs relating to primary qualities clearer and more reliable.

(4) It turns out, however, that the plain descriptions of common sense are to be regarded as more powerful logically than the theories which dissolve these descriptions into ideas or sensations. It is nothing but the "enchantment of words" which leads anyone to prefer the philo-

sophical abstraction to the common sense description which reflects the "constitution of our nature."

(5) What is true in epistemology is likewise the case in ethics. The same dissolution has occurred when ethics is viewed in terms of feelings of approval and disapproval. Ethics is either intuitive or based on self-evident premises or both.

(6) If, finally, one pushes for the explanation of the constitution in us leading to these judgments concerning the external world and ethical truths, the answer is that we are thus created by God. There may be a circle here, however, since Reid argues that we have the same kind of evidence for God that we have for the existence of other persons.

REIFICATION.

From the Latin *res* ("things") and *facere* ("to make"). The fallacy of regarding a mental entity as though it were a thing. Reification, also termed hypostatization, is listed as one of the informal or material fallacies (*q.v.* 7).

REIMARUS, HERMANN S. 1694–1768.

German philosopher. Born in Hamburg. Educated at Jena. Taught at the Gymnasium in Hamburg. A follower of Wolff (*q.v.*), Reimarus wrote popular philosophy, and finally a critique of Christianity from the standpoint of Deism. This latter work, *Apology*, was first published—anonymously and only in part—by Lessing as the "Wolfenbüttel Fragments" after the library where the manuscript was allegedly found.

Principal writings: *On the Noble Truths of Natural Religion*, 1754; *Apology for or Defense of the Rational Worshipper of God*, 1774–7; *Further Unpublished Work from the Wolfenbüttel Fragments*, (ed. Schmidt), 1786.

REINCARNATION.

The doctrine that the soul becomes incarnate in a succession of bodies until by the necessary purification, or the using up of one's *karma* (*q.v.*), final release from the body occurs. A characteristic of Hinduism (*q.v.*), the doctrine has been held in the West by such diverse thinkers as Pythagoras (*q.v.* 3), Plato (*q.v.* 13), Plotinus (*q.v.* 6), Nietzsche (*q.v.* 7), and others. For Buddhism (*q.v.*), which de-

nies the existence of soul, the term "rebirth" (*q.v.*) is more appropriate. In this context it is not a soul but merely certain karmic states which transmigrate. *Q.v. Bardo.*

REISM, ONTOLOGICAL AND SEMANTIC.

Q.v. Kotarbinski (1).

RELATION.

The connection that a thing has, or the reference an idea makes, to other things or ideas. With respect to some relations, *e.g.*, Identity (*q.v.*), that connection or reference is to the thing or idea itself. The concept of relation has had philosophic importance in treatments of categories, logic, and metaphysics.

A. "Relation" has been treated as a category in most of the major listings of philosophic categories.

(1) Aristotle (*q.v.* 6) included relation among his categories having to do with the manner in which substances refer to each other. In addition to numerical relations he recognized the relations of excess to deficiency, knowledge to awareness, actual to potential, active to passive, privation to potential.

(2) For Kant (*q.v.* 3) the categories of relation—deduced from the structure of categorical, hypothetical, and disjunctive propositions—are substance and accident, cause and effect, and community or the reciprocity of action between agent and patient.

(3) All three of the categories of Peirce (*q.v.* 2) are based on the concept of relation: firstness on the monadic relation, secondness on the dyadic relation, thirdness on the triadic relation.

B. Philosophical principles and laws may be construed as relations of various sorts.

(4) The so-called Laws of Thought (*q.v.*), that is, the principles of identity, excluded middle, and contradiction, may be regarded as relations which propositions have to themselves, and their complements.

(5) In the Logic of Relations (*q.v.* 3, 7–17) reflexivity, symmetry, transitivity, and connexity are discussed.

C. In the history of metaphysics the distinction of internal and external relations is among the relational concepts discussed.

(6) Parmenides (*q.v.* 4–7) argued that relations of space, time, and motion are incoherent as usually interpreted, and the introduction of coherency leads to a vision of reality quite unlike the ordinary commonsense view.

(7) William of Ockham (*q.v.* 7) decided that relations do not exist in an ontological sense. This being the case the problem of the relation between God and the world is a pseudo-problem.

(8) Josiah Royce (*q.v.* 5), F.H. Bradley (*q.v.* 1–3), and others, agreeing with Parmenides about the lack of coherent sense in the ordinary interpretations of the relatedness of things, expressed the point by saying that in a proper interpretation all relations are internal. The effect of holding that in "xRy" the relation "R" is internal to "x" and "y," is to make a single entity of "x" and "y." Ultimately, the result is a strongly monistic view of the universe.

(9) William James (*q.v.* 8) found the block universe which resulted from this view of relations to be intolerable, and countered with a pluralistic universe characterized by the presence of external relations.

(10) Among recent thinkers Blanshard (*q.v.* 1) has held to the internality of all relations.

RELATION, MEMBERSHIP.
Q.v. Set Theory (1).

RELATIONS, THE LOGIC OF.
The logic of relations is that part of logic concerned with the expression of relational ideas, where, *e.g.*, some "x" has the relation R to "y." This may be expressed either as "xRy" or "R(x,y)."

(1) A relation holding between two things is termed a binary relation, among three things a ternary relation, among "n" things an n-tuple relation. We shall speak only of binary relations since all of the basic principles of relational logic are present in such relations.

(2) Suppose our relational proposition to be "James is the father of John," *i.e.*, F (James, John). The domain of the relation is James, *i.e.*, the one-member set of all those who have the relation of father to John. The counter-domain of the relation, also called the converse domain, consists of all those who have the converse relation of being fathered by, or being son of, James. In the case of James and John Stuart Mill this is also a one-member set. The field of the relation is the union of its domain and counter-domain. In this case the field of the relation consists of James and John. Of course most relational propositions involve larger sets. If our proposition is "Industrialized nations exploit developing nations," the domain and counter-domain are quite extensive, and the field of this relation may include every nation in the world.

(3) Relations are one-one when the domain and counter-domain are unit sets, one-many when the domain is a unit set and the counter-domain a multiple set, many-many when both domain and counter-domain are multiple.

(4) In (2) above the "union" of domain and counter-domain, *i.e.*, the members belonging to both sets, was mentioned. In the logic of relations the "union" of sets and relations, expressed by "U," figures prominently, as does the "join" or "intersect" of sets and relations, the members two sets or relations have in common. The idea of "join" is expressed by the notation "∩." The union of any two classes, A and B, (A∪B), includes all of the members of A plus all of the members of B. The join of A and B (A∩B) consists of the members common to A and B.

(5) In addition to the foregoing, the logic of relations requires the concept of the universal relation, expressed by "∨," a relation everything has to everything else, and the null relation, "∧," which never holds. Letting "D" stand for domain and "C" for counter-domain, the union of "C" and "D" is universal "(C∪D)= ∨," *i.e.*, it includes every member of the field; while the "join" of "C" and "D," since the two have no members in common, is null "(C∩D)= ∧."

(6) With these concepts and the relevant concepts and operations from the propositional calculus, predicate calculus, and set theory, along with the valid transformations or laws appropriate to relations; it is possible to express and examine patterns of thought which are relational in character.

(7) Among other results, an elaborate analysis of the properties of relations has emerged from the study, including the

following distinctions among relations. A relation is reflexive when any entity "x" bears this relation to itself. Since any "x" will be identical with itself, "identity" is a reflexive relation.

(8) A relation is irreflexive when no entity "x" can bear this relation to itself. Since no "x" can be one's own parent the relation of "being parent of" is irreflexive.

(9) Relations which are neither reflexive nor irreflexive, are called non-reflexive.

(10) A relation is symmetrical when the fact of "x's" having the relation R to "y" entails that "y" will have the relation R to "x." "Being the same size as" is a symmetrical relation.

(11) A relation is asymmetrical when the fact of "x's" having the relation R to "y" entails that "y" cannot have the relation R to "x." "Being older than" is an asymmetrical relation.

(12) Relations which are neither symmetrical nor asymmetrical are termed non-symmetrical.

(13) A relation is transitive when the fact that "x" bears the relation R to "y" and "y" bears R to "z" entails that "x" bears the relation R to "z." "Being greater than" is a transitive relation.

(14) A relation is intransitive when the fact that "x" bears R to "y" and "y" bears R to "z" entails that "x" does not bear the relation R to "z." "Being parent of" is an intransitive relation.

(15) Relations which are neither transitive nor intransitive are termed non-transitive.

(16) Typically, a relation will reflect more than one of these properties. Whitehead and Russell pointed out that serial relations are irreflexive, asymmetrical, and transitive.

(17) They suggested that serial relations likewise have the property of connexity. This is the property such that of any "x" and "y" in a given set, if "x" is not identical to "y" then either "yRx" or "xRy." The relations "greater than" and "less than" have this property in any set of numbers. Others have pointed out a distinction between connexity and strong connectedness. The latter relation holds of any "x" or "y" in a given set, even when "x" and "y" are identical. The relation "less than or equal to" is strongly connected in the set of numbers.

RELATIVE.
   Q.v. Absolute.

RELATIVE FREQUENCY.
   Q.v. Reichenbach (1), Induction (12–15).

RELATIVES, LOGIC OF.
   Peirce's name for the Logic of Relations (*q.v.*). Also *q.v.* Logic (23). According to Peirce, the Logic of Relatives rests on the analysis of relative terms; and relative terms are what remains when one strikes out the subjects in propositions having more than one subject. The relative term, or relative, in "John praises Jill to Jim" is "____ praises ____ to ____."

RELATIVISM.
   The doctrine that no absolutes exist.
   (1) In its epistemological application, the doctrine holds that all truth is relative. This form of the doctrine was apparently held by Protagoras (*q.v.* 1), Pyrrho (*q.v.* 1), and his followers, as well as a wide variety of skeptics (*q.v.* Pyrrhonism, Skepticism).
   (2) Ethical relativism holds that there are no absolute criteria for moral judgments. In addition to many of those mentioned above, Westermarck (*q.v.* 1) holds to ethical relativism, relating the criteria for judgment to individual cultures exhibiting individual differences. The situation ethics (*q.v.*) of Joseph Fletcher holds the morality of an act to be relative to the goodness of the end served by that act. Kohlberg (*q.v.* 3) opposes all forms of ethical relativism.
   (3) For Putnam (*q.v.* 9) the position of relativism is unintelligible, since the standards of rationality and truth cannot be culturally determined.
   Also *q.v.* Jakobson (2).

RELATIVITY, THEORY OR PRINCIPLE OF.
   (1) Renouvier (*q.v.* 1) meant by the principle of relativity that all things are relative to each other, and that hence no absolutes exist. This is the sense, however, usually associated with relativism (*q.v.*).
   (2) By the theory of relativity is meant the special and general theories of Einstein (*q.v.* 2, 3), the former containing the famous $E=MC^2$ formula, the latter dealing with space-time curvature.
   (3) Whitehead (*q.v.* 8) developed an alternate theory of relativity, less opera-

tional in character, and with events having primacy over matter.

RELATUM.
Q.v. Referent.

RELIGATION.
Q.v. Xavier Zubiri.

RELIGION.
From the Latin *religare* ("to bind fast"), typically the term refers to an institution with a recognized body of communicants who gather together regularly for worship, and accept a set of doctrines offering some means of relating the individual to what is taken to be the ultimate nature of reality.

A. The history of religion is coterminous with the history of humanity.

(1) Beginning in animism and sympathetic magic, the high religions have passed through many stages of development. Greek religion (*q.v.*) marks an interesting, transitional stage on the way to high religion. Heraclitus (*q.v.* 7) criticized the Greek popular religions, arguing that since the gods cannot be born or die the common religious accounts purvey a superstition.

(2) The major religions of the world include Christianity (*q.v.*), Judaism (*q.v.*), Islam (*q.v.*), Hinduism (*q.v.*), Buddhism (*q.v.*), Confucianism (*q.v.*), Taoism (*q.v.*), Shinto (*q.v.*), and Zoroastrianism (*q.v.*). Of course, there are subdivisions within each of these religions.

B. A number of typical perspectives have been taken with respect to the subject-matter of religion.

(3) A number of the Christian Apologists (*q.v.*) held that philosophical analysis had no relevance to religious belief. Indeed, Tertullian (*q.v.*) insisted that he believed because it was absurd.

(4) A second attitude, shared by many, is that of Thomas Aquinas (*q.v.* 1) who believed that philosophy had a role in relation to religion, although there are some doctrines which can be established only by faith. Among Renaissance thinkers, Pico della Mirandola (*q.v.* 2) held a similar point of view.

(5) Among the deists who supported natural religion are Tindal (*q.v.* 2), William Wollaston (*q.v.* 1), Thomas Chubb (*q.v.*), Thomas Paine (*q.v.* 5), and Thomas

Jefferson (*q.v.* 7).

(6) Holbach (*q.v.* 6, 7) held that religion, having no certain knowledge, should be replaced by science. His view of Christianity as a superstition fostered by priests has its parallel in the Charvakan claim that religion is adequately explained by the good living afforded priests (*q.v.* Carvaka 5).

(7) Kant (*q.v.* 8) interpreted religion in moral terms, restricting its scope to that of reason alone.

(8) Jefferson (*q.v.* 8) believed that Jesus' pure teachings were obscured by a false background narrative through a conspiracy of priests and kings to control the people. Also *q.v.* Meslier (1).

(9) Herder (*q.v.* 3) was one of the first to find religion intimately related to myth and poetry.

(10) For Hegel (*q.v.* 21) religion is a substitute for philosophy but, among religions, Christianity is the absolute truth in pictorial form.

(11) Schleiermacher (*q.v.* 1–3) on the other hand, related religion to feeling, and in particular to the feeling of dependence.

(12) For Feuerbach (*q.v.* 1) the essence of religion is a projection of human qualities. Comte (*q.v.* 3) and Feuerbach (*q.v.* 2) called for a new religion of humanity.

(13) Kierkegaard (*q.v.* 4) spoke of a universal religion which he distinguished from Christianity; the latter was regarded as superior.

(14) Ritschl (*q.v.*) and Troeltsch (*q.v.*) regarded religion as having an autonomy beyond the power of reason to affect. In fact, the approach they took to religion, *i.e.*, Christianity, was historical; yet in their view Christianity emerges from history as an absolute.

(15) Haeckel (*q.v.* 3) argued for a "monistic religion" with no supernatural overtones.

(16) For Höffding (*q.v.*) religions are distinguished from each other in terms of the differences in the values they enshrine.

(17) Freud (*q.v.* 6) looked upon religion as an illusion and its practice as a participation in mass neurosis.

(18) Durkheim (*q.v.*), continuing the series of contrasts, viewed religion naturalistically, holding its function to be the creation and maintenance of social solidarity.

(19) Santayana (*q.v.* 10) viewed religion as a bridge between magic and science.

(20) Rudolf Otto (*q.v.* 2), in a manner analogous to Ritschl and Troeltsch, gained the concepts he wished to use in philosophy of religion from history. Once gained, he developed them systematically. He did not suppose absoluteness, however, as did his predecessors; he centered his interpretation of religion around the idea of the holy.

(21) Cassirer (*q.v.* 4) regarded religion as a type of communication, essentially metaphorical in nature, in contrast to the type of symbolic thought used in science.

(22) The development of neo-Orthodoxy counted among its members Barth (*q.v.* 1), Brunner (*q.v.* 2), Reinhold Niebuhr (*q.v.* 1), and Richard Niebuhr (*q.v.*). They used reason in a forensic sense to reveal the "demonic" in our common life, leading to the claim that God is "wholly other."

(23) Rising above logic to enlightenment Suzuki (*q.v.* 4–5), representing Zen Buddhism, separates *satori* (*q.v.*) from all of the conventions of religion, providing absolute freedom, even from God. Zen is not philosophy, not religion, but a method for seeing into one's own nature.

(24) Paul Tillich (*q.v.* 1) interpreted God as the ground of being and religion as the object of man's ultimate concern.

(25) Ninian Smart (*q.v.* 2–4) provided a 3 strand analysis of religious doctrine along with a 7-dimensional definition of religion.

C. Philosophy of Religion.

(26) The discipline of Philosophy of Religion is simply philosophical analysis applied to religious data. Some of the above, *e.g.*, Otto, are regarded as philosophers of religion, others as theologians, historians, and sociologists. In addition to the above emphases, philosophers of religion have begun to analyze the language of religion.

(27) Braithwaite (*q.v.* 5) and Hare (*q.v.* 4) agree that religion should be thought of in terms of moral commitment.

RELIGION OF HUMANITY.

Q.v. Comte (3); Feuerbach (2).

RELIGIOUS LIBERTY.

Q.v. Toleration.

REMANENCE.

From the Latin *remanare* ("to remain"). The doctrine of Wycliffe (*q.v.* 1) that in the Eucharist the material bread and wine remain in the sacrament after consecration along with the body and blood of Christ. He propounded the doctrine in opposition to transubstantiation (*q.v.*).

REMINISCENCE, DOCTRINE OF.

From the Greek term *anamnesis* (*q.v.*). Plato's doctrine of knowledge as recollection (*q.v.* Plato 1).

REMONSTRANTS.

From the Latin *remonstrare* ("to demonstrate"). The forty-five Arminian ministers who addressed a remonstrance in 1610 to the States of Holland and Friesland, taking exception to strict Calvinism. Condemned by the Synod of Dort in 1619, they were deprived of their ministries and sentenced to banishment. In 1630 the condemnation was withdrawn. *Q.v.* Arminius; Grotius.

RENAISSANCE.

Originally a French word meaning "rebirth" or "revival." Applied to the period of time in Western Europe running from the 14th through the 16th centuries, the term became current after Michelet in 1855 and Burckhardt in 1860 used the term in titles of historical works on France and Italy, respectively. The period in question came to be regarded as involving a "rebirth of the Greek and Roman spirit," and a "revival" of learning. The major manifestations of the Renaissance were:

(1) The movement of Humanism (*q.v.* 2), dedicated not only to the translation of Greek and Roman sources, but to the human values, or lifestyles, present in them. Petrarch (*q.v.* 1) and Erasmus (*q.v.*) count among the representatives of this movement.

(2) The turning away from the Aristotelian tradition of the Middle Ages. The revival of Platonism, so brilliantly exemplified in the Florentine Academy (*q.v.*), was one consequence of this rejection. In addition, an interest in mysticism was rekindled, including interest in the Cabala (*q.v.*), the Hermetic writings, and alchemy. Nicholas of Cusa (*q.v.*) combined many of these tendencies in his writings.

(3) Renaissance thought likewise contained an openness to the new sciences beginning to form. Giordano Bruno (*q.v.*) and Francis Bacon (*q.v.*) exemplify this openness.

(4) In the sphere of religion the period is characterized by dissatisfaction with the establishment, leading to the Protestant Reformation (*q.v.* Protestantism).

RENAN, ERNEST. 1823–1892.

French religious philosopher. Born in Tréguier, Brittany. Educated at the colleges of Tréguier and St. Nicholas, the Seminar of Issy, and the colleges of St. Sulpice and Stavistas. Taking his degree in philology, he was appointed in 1862 to the chair of Hebrew and Chaldaic languages in the Collège de France. His initial lectures in the post, as well as his *Life of Jesus*, led to his removal from the faculty by the minister of education. He continued his research and writing as a private citizen, late in life being named an administrator of the Collège de France and grand officer of the Legion of Honor. He is best known for his religious writings. He held to a naturalistic position in all his work, regarding Jesus as an "incomparable man."

Principal writings: *Averroës and Averroism*, 1852; *Moral and Critical Essays*, 1859; *The Life of Jesus* (T), 1863; *Recollections of My Youth* (T), 1883; *The Future of Science* (T), 1890; *History of Israel*, 5 vols., 1887–94.

RENOUVIER, CHARLES. 1815–1903.

French philosopher. Born in Montpellier. Calling his philosophy neo-Criticism, Renouvier is regarded as the principal representative of neo-Kantianism (*q.v.* 8) in France. Renouvier, along with many others, accepted Kant's phenomenalism while rejecting the concept of the "thing-in-itself."

Principal writings: *Uchronie: Utopia in History*, 1876; *The Analytic Philosophy of History*, 4 vols., 1895–98; *The New Monadology*, 1899; *History and the Solution of Metaphysical Problems*, 1901; *Personalism*, 1901; *The Dilemmas of Pure Metaphysics*, 1903.

(1) Opposed to all absolutes, to the unconditioned, the infinite, the determined, and the impersonal, he adopted a philosophy stressing the relative (and in the sense of things being relative to each other he spoke of "the principle of relativity"), the conditioned, the finite, and phenomenal, the undetermined and the personal. He supported Comtian positivism (*q.v.* Comte), finding Comte likewise committed to the antimetaphysical side of philosophy.

(2) His opposition to determinism led him to stress the element of chance in the movement of history, and a fondness for what he called *uchronie*. This consisted in imagining at critical junctures of history the occurrence of a slight change which might have led to vast differences in the consequent historic pattern.

(3) Holding liberty to be humanity's fundamental characteristic, he believed that the person acting freely is at the base of history, and the condition for progress. In his later years he saw Personalism (*q.v.*), with its corollaries of individuality as well as liberty, to be the chief hope in the transformation of ethics from an abstract study into a humane social order. He believed, too, that there was an ultimate tension between Personalism, taking its principle from man, and every form of Impersonalism, by which he understood those philosophies taking their principle from anything in the outer world.

(4) He likewise believed there was rational justification for belief in some form of human immortality, and in a finite deity.

RENUNCIATION.
Q.v. Carlyle (1).

REPENTANCE.
From the Latin *poenitere* ("to regret," "to be sorry"). In Christianity one of the stages in regeneration (*q.v.*). It is held to involve abhorrence of one's past life and a disposition for the new birth.

REPETITION.
Q.v. Kierkegaard (6).

REPRESENTAMEN.
That which represents, or stands for, another. *Q.v.* Peirce (16).

REPRESENTATION.
The act or relation of representing.

REPRESENTATIVE REALISM.
Q.v. Representative Theory of Ideas.

REPRESENTATIVES.
Q.v. Searle (2).

REPRESENTATIVE THEORY OF IDEAS.
The view that the mind knows reality only through the mediation of ideas. The theory has been held by Descartes (*q.v* 3, 4), Malebranche (*q.v.* 2), Hobbes (*q.v.* 3), Locke (*q.v.* 1), Berkeley (*q.v.* 1–3), and the Critical Realists (*q.v.*).

REPROBATION.
From the Latin *reprobare* ("to reprove"). In Christianity the state of complete apostasy (*q.v.*) or separation from God. For Calvin the reprobate is predestined to eternal damnation.

REPUBLICANS, JEFFERSONIAN.
Q.v. Federalist Papers (4).

RES.
Latin for "thing." Descartes (*q.v.* 8) distinguished between the *res cogitans* ("thinking thing") and *res extensa* ("extended thing") as the two elements of his mind-body dualism.

RESCHER, NICHOLAS. 1928– .
American philosopher. Born in Hagen, Germany. Naturalized U.S. citizen, 1944. Educated at Queens College and Princeton. Taught at Princeton, Lehigh, and the University of Pittsburgh. At Pittsburgh, founder and editor of the American Philosophical Quarterly; Director of the Center for the Philosophy of Science (1981–). Of his immense corpus of writings we omit the volumes on logic, both Arabic and modern symbolic.
Selected Writings: *The Philosophy of Leibniz*, 1967; *Scientific Explanation*, 1970; *Coherence Theory of Truth*, 1973; *Conceptual Idealism*, 1973; *The Primacy of Practice*, 1973; *A Theory of Possibility*, 1975; *Methodological Pragmatism*, 1976; *Induction*, 1980; *Empirical Inquiry*, 1982; *The Limits of Science*, 1984; *The Strife of Systems*, 1985; *Scientific Realism*, 1987; *Rationalism*, 1988; *Baffling Phenomena*, 1991.
(1) Taking logic as his springboard, Rescher moved into philosophical analysis by puzzling out the relevance of logic for philosophical problems.
(2) The necessity for a conceptual framework in the interpretation of any datum, and so of mental involvement, led him to an "idealistic approach to natu-

ral philosophy," featuring Conceptual Idealism, a Coherence Theory of truth (where coherence means "coherent with the plausible data"), and Methodological Pragmatism (a form of pragmatism in which it is one's methodology which is justified pragmatically). Methodological pragmatism is held to be superior to "thesis pragmatism" since the former avoids the regress of having to justify one thesis beyond another, indefinitely.
(3) Idealism and pragmatism together shape his conclusions. Physical laws are not so much observed in, as imputed to, nature on the basis of inductive method which is itself justified pragmatically.
(4) The laws of logic and the consistency of nature itself turn out to be regulative principles, ordered to our conceptualizing procedures.
(5) Possibilities are likewise imputed to the world. The imputation introduces no "iffiness" to the world; since all possibility is mental, Rescher offers a type of conceptualism with no apparent bridge between mental possibility and nonmental actuality.
(6) The conflict between realism and conceptualism with respect to possibilities is perhaps reduced by another view he has advanced, that of Orientational Pluralism, which presumes the existence of equally eligible alternative orientations on both sides of incompatible philosophical positions.
(7) In any case he has suggested combining plausible versions of realism and idealism with the goal of fruitful collaboration between these positions.
(8) Claiming that Hume (*q.v.* 6) turned reason into the slave of the passions by construing it too narrowly as concern with the means for achieving emotionally held ends, Rescher broadened its applicability to include ends as well as means. Rationality, then, involves the use of appropriate means to achieve appropriate ends, whether the context is belief, action, or evaluation.

RESCRIPT.
From the Latin *rescribere* ("to write"). In the Roman Catholic Church the written answer of the Pope, or sometimes a lesser official, to a question or request, resolving a controversy, providing an interpretation, or granting (or denying) a

favor. A rescript differs from a decretal (*q.v.*) in applying only to the person or situation at issue. Bulls, briefs (less formal than bulls), and Apostolic Letters are all rescripts.

RESEARCH PROGRAMMES.
Q.v. Lakatos (2).

RESEMBLANCE.
One of the basic principles of association (*q.v.* Associationism). By virtue of resemblance one mental object calls up another. Russell (*q.v.* 6) held "resemblance" to be the one universal indispensable to the life of the mind.

RESEMBLANCE DOCTRINE OF IDEAS.
Q.v. Madhva (5); Wittgenstein (5–6); Universals (21, 24–27, 38).

RESIDUES, METHOD OF.
Q.v. Mill, John Stuart (4).

RESPONSIBILITY, MORAL.
The view that one is answerable for one's actions in terms of a moral or ethical criterion. The traditional view is that responsibility implies that humans have free will. The issue involves the alternatives of hard and soft Determinism (*q.v.* 15), as well as indeterminism (*q.v.* Freedom A.)

RES COGNITA.
Q.v. Gabriel Vásquez.

RESPECTFUL SILENCE.
Q.v. Jansenism (12–13).

RES TOTA SIMUL.
Q.v. Time (8).

RESURRECTION.
From the Latin *re* ("again") and *surgere* ("to rise"). The doctrine that the dead shall rise in bodily form. To be distinguished from the idea of Immortality (*q.v.*) which supposes an eventual separation of soul from body.
(1) The doctrine of resurrection gained prominence in the apocalyptic writings. In the day of Jehovah, the dead were to be raised to receive judgment (*q.v.* Apocalypse; Apocrypha).
(2) According to Paul (*q.v.* 3–4, 6) all of the apostles agreed that Christ appeared to them after the resurrection in bodily form. It was Paul's general

doctrine, however, that in the resurrection we shall be clothed with a heavenly body.
(3) The Islamic doctrine of a physical resurrection (*q.v.* Islam 1) combines Zoroastrian and Judeo-Christian influences.
(4) The fourth Lateran Council in 1215 (*q.v.* Christianity 6) affirmed that in the resurrection all men "will rise again with their own bodies which they now bear about with them."
(5) Priestley (*q.v.* 3) makes the interesting point that the resurrection of the body is completely consistent with the philosophy of Materialism.

RETRODICTION.
The inverse of prediction, referring to the process by which one makes an inference into the past on the basis of present knowledge (*q.v.* Explanation 2).

RETRODUCTION.
A synonym for Peirce's process of abduction (*q.v.*), retroduction stands in contrast both to induction and deduction. As N.R. Hanson argues, it is the process of starting from anomalous facts and ending with explanatory hypotheses (*q.v.* Philosophy of Science 28).

REVELATION.
From the Latin *revelare* ("to unveil"). The term usually refers to an unveiling of truths which could not be reached by reason alone. The term stands in contrast to reason much as does its correlative term, "faith" (*q.v.*). The same alternative relations are appropriate and will not be repeated here.
(1) A distinction, however, is sometimes drawn between "natural revelation," derived by reason from nature, and "supernatural revelation," a communication from God by words or signs. The revelation in Scriptures is, of course, held to be of the latter sort.
(2) Ficino (*q.v.* 1) distinguished between natural and special revelation, finding much of the former in the writings of Plato and Plotinus.
(3) Loisy (*q.v.*) argued that there is a continuing revelation in the sacred books of all religions.
(4) Barth (*q.v.* 2) found the "revealed word" in the Bible, and suggested that there is a contradiction between this revelation and the natural results obtained by reason.

(5) For Brunner (*q.v.* 2–3) there is a dialectical relationship between reason and revelation which takes one beyond reason, although it is through revelation that true community is established.

(6) In *Nature, Man, and God*, William Temple (*q.v.*) locates revelation not in the word but in the relation between the divine event and our appreciation of it.

(7) For Tillich (*q.v.* 1) theological questions are asked on the basis of ultimate concern and answered through revelation.

(8) Bonhoeffer (*q.v.* 1), like Temple, uses the event language, speaking of the historical event of the revelation in Jesus Christ.

REVERENCE FOR LIFE.
Q.v. Schweitzer (4).

REVOLT, METAPHYSICAL.
Q.v. Camus (2).

REVOLUTION.
(1) In most versions of the Social Contract Theory (*q.v.*, and Locke 9; Jefferson 2), revolution is the people's right and duty when the state becomes misdirected.

(2) For Marx (*q.v.* 5, and Marxism 1) this right and duty is likewise the inevitable outcome of history.

ṚGVEDA (RIGVEDA).
The most important of that division of the *Vedas* (*q.v.* 1a) called the *Samhitas*. The *Samhitas* are collections of scripture containing hymns and prayers to the Vedic Gods. The *Ṛgveda*, one of four such collections, consists of ten books and was completed before 800 B.C.

RHEMATIC INDEXICAL LEGISIGN.
Q.v. Peirce (16).

RHEMATIC INDEXICAL SINSIGN.
Q.v. Peirce (16).

RHEMATIC SYMBOL.
Q.v. Peirce (16).

RHEME.
Q.v. Austin (2).

RHETIC ACT.
Q.v. Austin (2).

RHETORIC.
From the Greek *rhetor* ("orator"). A discipline, historically related to philosophy, dealing with the principles of persuasion.

(1) The discipline seems to have begun among the Sophists (*q.v.*) whose mission was to prepare youth for public life. The willingness of Sophists to take either side of an argument separated the enterprise from philosophy in the usual sense; Gorgias (*q.v.* 4) is typical in finding rhetoric as the art of persuasion yielding belief but not knowledge.

(2) Isocrates (*q.v.* 1) opposed the rhetoric of the Sophists, viewing the discipline as more technical in nature, with stated rules. He is credited with defining rhetoric as the "science of persuasion."

(3) Aristotle (*q.v.* 14), on the other hand, viewed rhetoric as an art—not an art of persuasion but the art of being able to discern in each case the available means of persuasion. It is the counterpart of dialectic, having the enthymeme (*q.v.*) or popular syllogism as its instrument.

(4) Philodemus of Gadara (*q.v.*) was among those who regarded the basis of rhetoric to be a set of rules drawn from experience and relating to spoken statements characterized by various degrees of probability.

(5) Hermagoras of Temnos built an influential system combining practical rhetoric with Aristotle's philosophical rhetoric.

(6) Cicero (*q.v.* 3) was influenced in part by Hermagoras, emphasizing both philosophical and practical rhetoric. His interest seems to have centered in the former since he defined rhetoric as an art of thought relating to all of the sciences and especially to philosophy. But what he wrote about the techniques of effective speech has had greater influence. He held that the *rhetor* or orator must be a good man who speaks well.

(7) Quintilian (*q.v.*), for example, regarded himself as a follower of Cicero, adhering to the good orator-good man implication and the necessity for prior intellectual cultivation. But his emphasis was on the side of practical rhetoric, stressing its technical rules. His influence, like that of Cicero, extended from the 1st century A.D. through the medieval period, and into the Renaissance.

(8) Hermogenes of Tarsus made a digest of the history of rhetoric and was

a major authority in the schools for a century and a half.

(9) Longinus (*q.v.*) in the 3rd century wrote a volume on the Art of Rhetoric which is more clearly his than the celebrated volume on the sublime.

(10) Other names of importance are those of Aphthonius in the latter half of the 4th century who superseded Hermogenes, and also Aelius Theon.

(11) In the Middle Ages rhetoric was one of three subjects in the *Trivium*. The chief authorities on the subject were Martianus Capella (*q.v.*), Cassiodorus, and Isidorus. These three lived between the 5th and 7th centuries.

(12) The period of the Renaissance witnessed a further shift of orientation. Rhetoric as a discipline provided the means for an attack on the decaying Scholasticism of the day. The appropriate stance was to attack Aristotelianism, calling for a new logic and new linguistic resources. These resources were to be found in rhetoric; the age presented the anomaly that Aristotle's rhetoric was pitted against his logic.

(13) Lorenzo Valla (*q.v.* 3), for example, followed Aristotle in wishing to keep rhetoric and philosophy together, but he called for a linguistic approach more useful in the description of reality.

(14) Juan Luis Vives (*q.v.*) held a view similar to that of Valla, while arguing that the Aristotelian influence in the fields of knowledge had been unfortunate, and that it was time for a reassessment of the disciplines.

(15) Peter Ramus (*q.v.* 1) provided a rhetorical logic, the logic of discourse based more on Cicero's natural logic of persuasion than Aristotle's *Organon*.

(16) In the post-Renaissance philosophical development the importance of rhetoric declined, as well as the sense of its relation to philosophy. George Campbell's *The Philosophy of Rhetoric* (1776) placed logic and rhetoric in the same framework with the purpose of illuminating the understanding, pleasing the imagination, exciting the passions, or influencing the will. In the 19th century Whately (*q.v.*) treated rhetoric as the "art of argumentative composition."

(17) In the contemporary situation, rhetoric began to reappear in philosophic contexts through I.A. Richards' *The Phi-losophy of Rhetoric* (1936), leading to an analysis of language and its functions, and Chaim Perelman's *Rhetoric and Philosophy* (1952). A journal on *Philosophy and Rhetoric* is published in the United States.

RIBOT, THEODULE. 1839–1916.
French psychologist. Born in Brittany. Taught at the Sorbonne and Collège de France. Supporting the development of experimental psychology, Ribot argued for the elimination of all metaphysics from psychology. Eschewing materialism as well as spiritualism, Ribot held at last to an Epiphenomenalism (*q.v.*) of mental processes.

Selected writings: *Contemporary English Psychology* (T), 1870; *Contemporary German Psychology* (T), 1879; *The Psychology of Attention* (T), 1888; *The Psychology of the Emotions* (T), 1896.

RICHARD OF MEDIAVILLA.
Q.v. Richard of Middleton.

RICHARD OF MIDDLETON. fl. late 13th cent.
Scholastic philosopher. A Franciscan, he was probably associated initially with the Oxford resurgence of the order although he taught in Paris, and is also known as Richard of Mediavilla, and is thought by some scholars to be French. An Augustinian influenced by Bonaventure and Peckham, Richard's epistemology remained Thomistic.

Principal writings: *Disputed Questions; Commentary on the Fourth Book of the Sentences; Quodlibeta tria; On the Grades of the Forms.*

RICHARD OF SAINT VICTOR. Late 12th cent.
Scholastic philosopher. A member and eventually Prior of the Abbey of Saint Victor, Richard studied under Hugh of Saint Victor (*q.v.*) and became his disciple. Following Hugh in the analysis of mysticism as consisting of the steps of thought, meditation, and contemplation, Richard emphasized the final stage, involving a "rapture of the mind." In his view of the Trinity he followed Saint Anselm; the influence of Neoplatonism is evident in his work. Dante placed Richard in paradise, regarding him as one of the greatest teachers of the Church.

Principal writings: *On the Trinity; On the Incarnate Word; On the Preparation of the Soul; On the Interior State of Man; On the Grades of Love.*

RICHARDS, I. A. 1893–1979.

British poet and philosopher of literary criticism. Born in Cheshire, England. Educated at Cambridge. Taught at Cambridge and Harvard. Founder of the New Criticism (*q.v.*).

The hinge of Richards' intellectual endeavor may derive from his view that Coleridge's (*q.v.* 4) projective and realist imaginations are only seeming alternatives since "each pressed far enough includes the other." This knowledge should free us to integrate appropriate mythologies, "according to their worth and dignity," into our lives.

Q.v. Aesthetics (33); Metaphor (12); New Criticism; Rhetoric (17).

Principal writings: *The Meaning of Meaning* (with C. K. Ogden), 1923; *Principles of Literary Criticism*, 1924; *Science and Poetry*, 1925; *Practical Criticism*, 1929; *Mencius on the Mind*, 1932; *Basic Rules of Reason*, 1933; *Philosophy of Rhetoric*, 1936; *Coleridge on Imagination*, 1960; *Why So, Socrates?*, 1964; *Plato's Republic* (ed. and trans.), 1966; *Poetries: Their Media and Ends* (ed. T. Eaton), 1974; *Complementarities* (ed. Paul Rosso), 1976;

RICKERT, HEINRICH. 1863–1936.

German philosopher. Born in Danzig. Taught at Freiburg, and then at Heidelberg. At the latter university he succeeded Windelband as head of the Heidelberg School of neo-Kantianism (*q.v.* Neo-Kantianism 4). His own view reflected the influences of Fichte and Hegel as well as Kant.

Principal writings: *The Object of Knowledge*, 1892; *Cultural Science and Natural Science*, 1899; *The Problem of Philosophy of History*, 1905; *Kant as Philosopher of Modern Culture*, 1924; *Predicate Logic and the Problem of Ontology*, 1930; *The Heidelberg Tradition in German Philosophy*, 1931; *Fundamental Problems of Philosophy, Methodology, Ontology, Anthropology*, 1934.

(1) Starting from Windelband's position that an axiological decision lies at the root of every epistemological judgment, that absolute values underlie reality, and that there are great differences between the natural and cultural sciences (*q.v.* Windelband), Rickert elaborated four realms of being to accommodate these distinctions.

(2) The first two of these realms contain objects of knowledge. The first is the realm of sensible objects. This realm provides the subject-matter of science, and is treated as Kant treated the phenomenal world. The second is the realm of cultural objects—history, art, morality, institutions, and the like. We know these objects and make judgments about them, but we don't perceive them. We know them by the mode of *Verstehen*, or understanding. Both of these realms are valuational, the second more richly so than the first. Windelband's distinction of nomothetic and ideographic sciences applies to these two realms (*q.v.* Windelband 2).

(3) The third realm Rickert calls *prophysical*. It is a realm required to ground sensible and cultural objects.

(4) And in the background there is a fourth realm, the metaphysical realm of being related to ultimate questions, and grounding the other three.

RICOEUR, PAUL. 1913– .

French philosopher. Born in Valence. Educated at Rennes and the Sorbonne. Has taught at Strasbourg, Paris-Nanterre, and the University of Chicago.

Selected writings: *The Voluntary and the Involuntary*, 1950 (T as *Freedom and Nature*, 1966); *The Symbolism of Evil* (T), 1960; *On Interpretation: Essay on Freud*, 1965 (T as *Freud and Philosophy*, 1970); *The Conflict of Interpretations* (T), 1969; *The Live Metaphor*, 1975 (T as *The Rule of Metaphor*, 1977); *Hermeneutics and the Human Sciences* (ed. and trans., J. B. Thompson), 1981; *Time and Narrative* (T), 3 vols., 1983, 1984, 1985; *From Text to Action* (T), 1986; *Lectures on Ideology and Utopia* (E), 1986; *Oneself as Another* (T), 1990; *Meanings in Texts and Actions* (ed. D. E. Klemm, W. Schweiker), 1993.

Combining Husserl's phenomenology (*q.v.*) with Heidegger's late exploration of hermeneutics (*q.v.*), Ricoeur's method of interpretation allowed him to fold in ever new material, leading to constant expansion and redescription in his thought.

(2) The primary unit of metaphor is the sentence, within which two terms

have been placed in tension by an impertinent attribution. The tension threatens to violate the linguistic code, but this is prevented by a novel semantic pertinence. In this way metaphor, "shattering and increasing our language," also shatters and increases our sense of reality.

(3) Where metaphor requires the sentence the unifying element of narrative, the plot, requires the text. Other unifying elements, myth and model, likewise require the text. Each text points to a possible world. This is clear in the case of fiction, but true also of myths and models. These synthesizers concern the uses of language in poetry, religion, history, science, politics, and psychoanalysis. These different language-games, as he sometimes calls them, cannot be treated reductively. One simply notes similarities and differences in their redescriptions of reality.

(4) Explanation and understanding are functions of the text, and truth is relative to methodology. One must respect and learn from disciplines practicing interpretation methodically. Fractures are to be observed within and among disciplines aspiring to a total view. Philosophy has the task of arbitrating the absolutist claims of such disciplines.

(5) There is no escape from the hermeneutic circle. Since in interpretation one picks a single reading from a multiplicity of possible readings, and justifies that reading by subjective probability. The circle is not vicious, however, as long as the criteria of validation are selected independently and available intersubjectively.

(6) Meaning and self-understanding are inseparable sides of the same process and the self is episodic, a series of acts of self-reflection mediated through the text. There is "no . . . way from myself to myself except through the round-about way of the appropriation" of signs, works of art, and culture.

(7) Civilization has an "ethico-mythical kernel," consisting of the collection of images and symbols in terms of which society has expressed its relation to reality. We participate in our cultural heritage through reappropriation of this collection.

(8) As between Gadamer's hermeneu-

tics, relating us to the past and Habermas' Critical Theory (*q.v.*), opening us to the future, Ricoeur urges we must reappropriate, and be delivered from, the past, and that even critical theory has a tradition, that of the Enlightenment.

RIDLEY, NICHOLAS. c. 1503–1555.

English Protestant reformer. As Bishop of Rochester and later Bishop of London he pressed for Protestant reforms in the Church of England, *e.g.*, using a plain table for Communion rather than the altar. With the accession of Queen Mary he was arrested, and on October 16, 1555 he was burned at the stake in Oxford along with Latimer (*q.v.*).

RIEHL, ALOYS. 1844–1924.

German philosopher. Born in the Tyrol. Taught at Freiburg, Kiel, Halle, and Berlin. A neo-Kantian who likewise tended toward positivism (*q.v.* Neo-Kantianism 1).

Principal writings: *Philosophical Criticism and its Significance for Positive Science*, 2 vols., 1876, 1887; *On Scientific and Non-Scientific Philosophy*, 1883; *H. von Helmholtz and Kant*, 1904; *Logic and Theory of Knowledge in Contemporary Culture*, 1907.

(1) Unlike some neo-Kantian philosophers (*q.v.* Liebmann), Riehl held the Kantian "thing-in-itself" to be an ineradicable feature of sound philosophy. Even though one cannot experience things directly, they can be inferred from the total conjunct of immediate experience.

(2) Furthermore, he claims that the dualism between mind and body is solved by the position of "philosophical monism," that processes become physical, or psychical depending upon the point of view in which they are regarded (*q.v.* Critical Realism).

(3) The positivistic tone of his philosophy is evident in his rejection of metaphysics. Contrasting scientific with unscientific and non-scientific philosophy, he approved the first, rejected the second as metaphysical, and accepted the third as a practical discipline essential to the realization of human values.

RIGHT.

From the Latin *rectus* ("straight"). The term has numerous involvements with ethics and social philosophy.

(1) The "right" and the "good" are key terms in the study of Ethics (*q.v.* 1–4). The former is sometimes defined as "what ought to exist in its own right," and the latter as "what one ought to do." An ethical theory can be said to be shaped to some extent by the decision as to which concept is dominant in the theory.

(2) Aquinas (*q.v.* 8) related the "right" both to reason and to eternal law, deriving a natural law view of the concept.

(3) Rousseau (*q.v.* 5c) held that rights rest on convention and consent.

(4) According to an important philosophical and juridical tradition, man possesses, in addition to civil rights, certain Natural Rights (*q.v.*), which should be recognized in any system of positive law. Such rights are set forth in the American Declaration of Independence and the American Constitution, the French Declaration of the Rights of Man and the Citizen, and the United Nations Declaration of Human Rights.

(5) Hegel (*q.v.* 9–17) used the phrase "philosophy of right" to describe one segment of his philosophy, that dealing with the development of Objective Spirit. It includes the notions of abstract right and morality coming together in social ethics.

(6) Levinas (*q.v.* 2–3) held that one's rights and duties derive from the ethics of love and justice.

RIGHTEOUSNESS.
From the Latin *rectus* ("straight"). A theological virtue which differs from ethicality in having a transcendent reference. Developed by the prophets of the Old Testament, righteousness involves hating the evil, loving what is good, and living in obedience to the will of God.

RIGID DESIGNATOR.
Q.v. Proper Names (5).

RIN.
Japanese term meaning "companionship." Taken as the basis of ethics by Watsuji Tetsuro (*q.v.*).

RINZAI.
Q.v. Zen Buddhism (4 and B.).

RTA (RITA).
From Sanskrit, "right," "true." Predecessor to the term, *dharma* (*q.v.*), rita stands for the cosmic law providing for both physical and moral order, the gods protect *rita* while also requiring it for their functioning. Embodied in the correct performance of ritual, Vedic tradition held that its incorrect performance would lead to the collapse of cosmic order.

RITSCHL, ALBRECHT. 1822–1889.
German theologian. Born in Berlin. Taught Protestant theology first in Bonn and then in Göttingen. Initially Hegelian, Ritschl later became interested in Kant and Schleiermacher, and is sometimes regarded as a neo-Kantian. His orientation has similarities to those of Harnack (*q.v.*) and Troeltsch (*q.v.*).

Principal philosophical writings: *The Christian Doctrine of Justification and Reconciliation* (T in part), 3 vols., 1870–74; *Schleiermacher's Discourses on Religion*, 1874; *Theology and Metaphysics*, 1881; *Metaphysics and Dogmatics*, 1882.

(1) Sharply distinguishing reason from faith, he held that the latter rests on an autonomous experience. The experience at the basis of faith is a feeling of impotence, and dependence on God. But the most basic point about the matter is that the experience he had in mind was the religious experience of the Christian community. One can interpret this in a systematic theology, but one cannot go behind it. As for philosophy in the traditional sense, he claims it to be too shallow for theology.

(2) The autonomy of the religious experience means that it is not subject to attack by the sciences, which likewise have their own species of autonomy.

ROBERT GROSSETESTE.
Q.v. Grosseteste, Robert.

ROBERT KILWARDBY.
Q.v. Kilwardby, Robert.

ROBERT OF MELUN. 12th cent.
Scholastic philosopher. Studied with Hugh of St. Victor whose influence, along with that of Abelard, is to be found in his work. He taught both on the Continent and in England, late in life holding a position at Oxford. His book of *Sentences* was influential.

Principal writings: *Sentences; Questions on Paul's Epistles.*

ROBLES, OSWALDO.
Q.v. Latin American Philosophy (12).

ROHAULT, JACQUES. 1620–1672.
French physicist and philosopher. A Cartesian, Rohault applied the axiomatic method to both physics and philosophy. Principal writings: *Treatise on Physics*, 1671; *Conversation in Philosophy*, 1671; *Posthumous Works*, 1682.

ROMAGNOSI, GIAN. 1761–1835.
Italian philosopher. Born in Salsomaggiore. Mayor of Trent, 1791–1801, he became professor at Parma in 1802. Influenced by Condillac, he was nonetheless not a sensationalist, since he believed in an internal logical sense. The historicism of Vico likewise exercised influence over his point of view. He regarded man's reality as a product of the civilizing influence of society.
Principal writings: *Genesis of Penal Law*, 1791; *Universal Public Law*, 1805; *Principles of the Science of Natural Law*, 1820.

ROMAN CATHOLICISM.
The central body of Christians, administered from Rome, and claiming continuity from Peter, who is held to be the first head of the Church. The historical development of doctrines is set forth under Christianity (*q.v.*) and Christology (*q.v.*). The Catholicity of the Roman Church was shaken first by the rupture with the Eastern Church which became final in 1054, the Avignon Papacy (*q.v.*) which lasted from 1305 to 1378, and the Protestant Reformation (*q.v.*) which began in the 16th century. Against such obstacles the Roman Church has continued its development, fostering a counter-Reformation (*q.v.*) in the 16th and 17th centuries, and arriving at some of its most distinctive doctrines in the past century. Among these are the doctrine of the Immaculate Conception (*q.v.*) of Mary promulgated by Pius IX in 1854; the Condemnation of Americanism and Modernism in 1894 and 1907, respectively; the 1950 doctrine of the Assumption of the Virgin (*q.v.*), that Mary at her death was "assumed" body and soul into heaven, promulgated by Pius XII. Turning in the direction of religious cooperation, Pope John XXIII created a Secretariat for the Promotion of Christian Unity and, at his behest, the Second Vatican Council (1962–5) called for a common effort toward Christian Unity, holding that both sides have been responsible for past divisions (*q.v.* Ecumenism).

ROMANES, GEORGE. 1848–1904.
British biologist. Born at Kingston, Ontario. Educated at Cambridge. A friend of Charles Darwin, he became one of the principal champions of Darwinian evolution. He quarreled with his fellow Darwinians—*e.g.*, Weismann and A.R. Wallace (*q.v.*)—that their stress on natural selection alone was more narrow than Darwin's own position. He demonstrated that Darwin admitted the probability of an important ancillary role for the doctrine of the inheritance of acquired characteristics. Romanes regarded the world as a "mind-stuff," mental from one aspect and material from another.
Selected writings: *Mental Evolution in Animals*, 1883; *Mental Evolution in Man*, 1888; *An Examination of Weismannianism*, 1892; *Thoughts on Religion*, 1895.

ROMANTICISM.
(1) A movement chiefly in European literature and the arts featuring an emphasis on imagination and emotion rather than reason and formal criteria. Beginning at the close of the 18th century and reaching its peak in the early decades of the 19th century the movement was a revolt against the neo-Classicism of the late 17th and 18th centuries.
(2) In philosophy the movement marked a reaction against the 18th century enlightenment. In a narrow sense the philosophical movement can be viewed as the initial phase of German Idealism, including Schiller (*q.v.*), Fichte (*q.v.*), Schelling (*q.v.*), F. Schlegel (*q.v.*), Goethe (*q.v.* 1–2), Schleiermacher (*q.v.*), and Hegel (*q.v.*). In a broader sense the classification might range back to Rousseau (*q.v.*) with his stress on nature, and forward to Schopenhauer (*q.v.*), and even Nietzsche (*q.v.*). Schlegel (*q.v.* 1) defined Romanticism as the spirit of subjectivity.
(3) Taine (*q.v.*) opposed Romanticism, standing as one of the chief spokesmen for Positivism in the latter half of the 19th century.

ROMERO, ARCHBISHOP OSCAR.
Q.v. Theology of Liberation (3).

ROMERO, FRANCISCO. 1891–1962.
Argentine philosopher. Born in Spain. Professor in the universities of Buenos Aires and La Plata. Influenced by Alejandro Korn, Ortega y Gasset, Dilthey, Scheler, and Hartmann. *Q.v.* Latin American Philosophy (9).

Principal writings: *Logic* (with Pucciarelli), 1938; *A. Korn* (with Vasallo and Aznar), 1940; *Philosophy of the Person*, 1944; *Papers for a Philosophy*, 1945; *Philosophy of Yesterday and Today*, 1947; *Man and Culture*, 1950; *On Philosophy in Ibero-America*, 1952; *Theory of Man* (T), 1952; *Studies in the History of Ideas*, 1953; *What is Philosophy?*, 1953; *The Position of Man*, 1955.

(1) The four levels of reality, in ascending order, are: inorganic, organic, psychic, and spiritual. Man participates in all four.

(2) But man's essential characteristic is intentionality, a characteristic of the psychic level. At the same time, man's proper goal and place is on the spiritual level. Through the projection of intentionality the transition to this level occurs.

(3) The importance of human community lies in the propensity of culture to assist man in the development of spirituality.

(4) The features of spiritual existence include objectivity, unity, universality, liberty, historicity, and transcendence.

(5) The four levels form a single system since each has a degree of transcendence, increasing from the inorganic to the spiritual. Transcendence thus becomes the key to Romero's philosophy, which may be summarized in the claim: to be is to transcend.

RORTY, RICHARD M. 1931– .
Born in New York City. Studied at Chicago and Yale. Has taught at Wellesley, Princeton, and the University of Virginia.

Principal writings: *The Linguistic Turn* (edited and intro.), 1967; *Philosophy and the Mirror of Nature*, 1979; *Consequences of Pragmatism*, 1982; *Contingency, Irony and Solidarity*, 1989; *Essays on Heidegger and Others*, 1991; *Objectivity, Relativism, and Truth*, 1991.

(1) Initially believing progress in philosophy to be possible, or at least that "philosophers *think* they have made progress," Rorty contributed to the ceremonies of analytic philosophy (*q.v.* Identity Theory 3). In 1967, from within the establishment, he chronicled the metaphysical decisions required by the various twists in the linguistic turn taken by Anglo-American philosophy in the 20th century.

(2) His anti-establishment position, fully emergent by 1979, is that both analytic and traditional philosophers believed that their individual approaches to philosophy had achieved final and privileged (although discordant) vocabularies in terms of which philosophy could mirror nature. They are mistaken in this belief which transforms a reasonable human effort to get the hang of things into an unreasonable icon, Philosophy.

(3) Not only does lower-case "philosophy," the "attempt to see how things in the broadest possible sense of the term, hang together, in the broadest possible sense of the term" (Sellars), get off scotfree, so do both pragmatism and other positions which have undergone pragmatic correction. The reason is that such philosophers do not presume to mirror nature. Not only does William James escape censure; so do, for example, Wittgenstein and Heidegger: James as a pragmatist; Wittgenstein as the pragmatic corrective to analytic philosophy; and Heidegger, because he stopped doing "phenomenological ontology" and became interested in the "history of being." In fact, Derrida provides the corrective for the residue of metaphysics still latent even in the later Heidegger. In this instance, sound philosophy may be Heidegger-as-corrected-by-Derrida.

(4) The goal of sound philosophy is edification rather than system. As Rorty redirected his attention, a great deal of European philosophy became relevant to his thinking: the more recent members of the Frankfurt School (*q.v.*), Structuralism (*q.v.*), and Deconstruction (*q.v.*). He adopts the latter's attitude to logocentrism (*q.v.*).

(5) The quality of mind he approves is that of the ironist, who does not presume any finality in the vocabulary to which he or she is drawn. Ironist theorists write about metaphysical theoriz-

ing and in their try for sublimity, face the danger of falling into metaphysics. The safer move is to be an ironist novelist whose goal (beauty) and genre do not suppose a final vocabulary.

(6) Argument is merely a rhetorical device, emphasizing the attractiveness of a new vocabulary. Its game is redescription. This being so, argument and theory should be replaced by narratives whose redescriptions of past vocabularies would utilize the poetic power of self-creation to correlate the present with an imaginative utopian future. The shift would serve to poetize culture, rather than rationalize or scientize it, celebrating not truth but play and metaphor.

(7) Every redescription reflects the final vocabulary of whoever projects it. Rorty recognizes himself as a "liberal ironist." Although liberalism is due for imaginative redescription, liberals now agree in their abhorrence of cruelty, and hope for the future diminution of suffering and humiliation. The narrative is without foundation, of course, and one who thinks otherwise is a "liberal metaphysician." He has also written of progress in terms of increasing human solidarity, in being "one of us" (Sellars again), and trying to expand the "us." In that context he finds nothing amiss in the *focus imaginarius* to which the invented phrases "child of God" and "humanity" point.

(8) Such phrases, however, are to be taken poetically, not essentially. "Essence" and "nature" have no referents. Only non-essentialistic terms, nominalistic and historicist, will do. Life is a web of contingencies, and the self is centerless. There is nothing to it, except what has been socialized into it, and its ability to use language, exchanging beliefs and desires with others.

ROSCELIN. 1050–1120.
Scholastic philosopher. Teacher of Abelard (*q.v.*). Studied at Soissons and Rheims. Taught at Compiègne, Loches, Besançon, Tours. His writings are lost except for a letter to Abelard. St. Anselm (*q.v.* 7) held that for Roscelin the universal was a mere word or *flatus vocis.* Abelard (*q.v.* 1) made a similar interpretation of Roscelin; he argued that since Roscelin believes that only individual

things exist, the idea of a whole consisting of parts is for him a "mere word." And Roscelin seems to have held that since every existent being is individual, were usage to permit we might refer to the three persons of the Trinity as three individual Gods. He was forced to renounce the theological consequences of his position at the Council of Soissons in 1092. The position of Nominalism, that the universal is but a name, derives from the accepted interpretation of Roscelin's point of view. *Q.v.* Universals (1).

ROSENBLUETH, ARTURO.
Q.v. Cybernetics.

ROSENZWEIG, FRANZ.
Q.v. Judaism (20).

ROSICRUCIANISM.
A mystic and esoteric approach to Christianity, combining Eastern and Western motifs. The name is reflected in its symbol, a garland of roses superimposed on a cross. Stressing daily meditation and the strengthening of one's inner spirit, Rosicrucians accept rebirth as a means to the development of their personal destinies, some form of astrological influence, and an interpretation of evolution which includes achieving the goal of personal perfection. Participants in the religion move through a series of stages, from probationary student to initiate of high degree. The headquarters of the movement is in Oceanside, California.
Q.v. Robert Fludd.

ROSMINI-SERBATI, ANTONIO.
1797–1855.
Italian philosopher. Born in Rovereto. Wishing a restoration of the perennial philosophy as a foundation for the Catholic faith, Rosmini attempted in his own day a synthesis like that of the 13th century. The theory of being was central to all of his thought, which he divided into ontology, or universal doctrine of being, theology, or doctrine of absolute being, and cosmology, or doctrine of relative and finite being.

Principal writings: *New Knowledge on the Origin of the Idea,* 1830; *Theodicy* (T), 3 vols., 1845; *Psychology* (T), 2 vols., 1850; *Theosophy,* 5 vols., 1859–74.

ROSS, W.D. 1877–1971.

British philosopher. Born in Thurso, Scotland. Educated at Edinburgh and Oxford. Taught at Oxford from 1900–47. An Aristotelian scholar, and editor of the Oxford edition of Aristotle, he contributed also to the field of ethics.

Principal writing: *Aristotle*, 1923; *The Right and the Good*, 1930; *Foundations of Ethics*, 1939; *Plato's Theory of Ideas*, 1951; *Kant's Ethical Theory*, 1954; *The Development of Aristotle's Thought*, 1958.

(1) An intuitionist in ethics, Ross distinguishes the right from the good, the former pertaining to acts, and the latter to motives.

(2) As a solution to the problem of conflicting obligations—*e.g.*, although one has the duty of telling the truth and the duty of preserving human life, there are situations where one or the other must be sacrificed—Ross advanced the idea of *prima facie* (*q.v.*) duties. Adapting the phrase from the field of law, Ross meant by *prima facie* duty that obligation with a presumptive right to be considered the most important obligation in a given situation. When telling the truth and preserving human life are in conflict, Ross believed the latter to be without question one's *prima facie* duty. As an intuitionist in ethics, Ross believed that man intuitively knows a great deal about the ranking of duties.

ROUGES, ALBERTO.

Q.v. Latin American Philosophy (9).

ROUGIER, LOUIS. 1889– .

French philosopher. Born in Lyon. Taught at Besançon, Annapolis, New York, Montreal, and Caen. An early French supporter of the Vienna Circle of Logical Positivists (*q.v.*), Rougier differed from his confreres in holding that there are many forms of intelligibility and a plurality of languages for expressing them. Both the *a priori* rationalism of Scholasticism and the experimental rationalism of science are intelligible, each in its own way; and the claim of meaninglessness in any case must be within and relative to a chosen language.

Selected writings: *The Paralogisms of Rationalism*, 1920; *The Structure of Deductive Theories*, 1921; *Scholasticism and Thomism*, 1925; *Treatise on Knowledge*, 1955; *Metaphysics and Language*, 1960.

ROUSSEAU, JEAN JACQUES. 1712–1778.

French philosopher. Born in Geneva. Little formal education. France was his adopted home, but he also lived in Italy, England, and Germany. A stormy Romanticist, he was inconstant in all things, alternating between love of city and rural solitude, between Catholicism and Protestantism, and the love of women diverse in charm and status. Highly sentimental, he was capable of both nobility and pettiness. At one time or another he was friend to most of the great men of his time, including Voltaire, D'Alembert, Diderot, Mirabeau, Hume, Gibbon, Boswell, Prince Henry of Russia (the brother of Frederick the Great) and George III. With most of these he promptly quarreled. The most significant European thinker of the 18th century, he is credited with having helped to shape the French Revolution. The turning point of his life came when he entered and won the 1749 essay contest of the Academy of Dijon concerning whether the arts and sciences had purified morals. The essay, published in the following year, brought him instant fame.

Principal writings: *Discourse on the Sciences and the Arts* (T), 1750; *Discourse on the Origin of Inequality among Men* (T), 1755; *Julie or the New Heloise* (T), 1761: *The Social Contract* (T), 1762; *Emile* (T), 1762; *Confessions* (T), 1782; *The Reveries of a Solitary* (T), 1782.

(1) Rousseau begins with the point that men are not naturally equal; but as societies develop from their simple primitive forms into civilizations, the natural inequalities among men are replaced by artificial politically enforced inequalities which have nothing to do with the other. The political inequalities become progressively more extreme, since laws are made by the strong for their own protection. Property rights create a distinction between rich and poor. The courts aggravate the difference between powerful and weak. And the final inequality which civilizations reach, unless the process is interrupted, is the master-slave relationship.

(2) The so-called advance of the arts and the sciences does nothing to alleviate this condition; and has always been paralleled by an increase in depravity and corruption. Indeed, the two are causally

related because in an advanced society virtue has no reward, whereas talent commands all rewards. And since one does not need science, art, sophistication, or position to live morally, better than these is a life which remains in obscurity, guiding itself by instinct, conscience, and "heart."

(3) But if civilization leads to undesirable results, the state of savagery from which man emerged is no better. It is characterized by natural, rather than political, inequalities; but in such a state man has not yet achieved his humanity. Man's savage predecessors communicated by means of cries of fear and joy. There were no abstract ideas. For rationality to be possible language was needed, and its development required thousands of years. The savage lives by instinct, impulse, and appetite. Humanity requires justice, morality, duty, law, and reason.

(4) And yet the development of civilization leads to depravity and corruption. How then is humanity to be possible? Between the states of savagery and civilization there is the simple human community where humanity has been achieved, and corruption lies still ahead. We must find the political constitution which will foster in the modern world the conditions of the simple human community of early times.

(5) In the *Social Contract*, Rousseau worked out the conditions of the appropriate political arrangement which would provide the necessary political reformation of society. It includes the following points:

(a) The object of the necessary political constitution is a form of association which will defend and protect with all the common force the person and goods of each member. It will have to be the case that each person can unite with all, and yet remain as free as he was before. The problem is to achieve this result. (b) We begin, then, with a contract in which each person gives over all his rights to the community. What rights? The rights to all he wants, to follow his inclinations, and act on impulse without reason. (c) In place of his natural rights he receives civil rights, and becomes a citizen of the state. Rousseau stressed the point that rights, like the social contract itself, cannot be established by force, that they rest

on convention and free consent. (d) The transaction in which man becomes a citizen effects a differentiation in his will. He continues to will as an individual; but in addition he is part of the general will; when he wills as an individual it is in support of his individual good. When he wills as a citizen it is in support of the common good. But individuals know only their own opinions about the common good, or what should be the general will. How, starting from this basis, is the common good to be found? Rousseau believes that in their decisions individuals miss the mark of the common good about as much by excess as by deficiency. When they make up their minds individually, and their excesses and deficiencies are allowed to cancel each other out, what remains will be the general will and common good. (e) It is because the general will supports individual willing, and the common good individual goods, that we remain as free as we were before. To oppose the general will is thus irrational; and those in the state who fail to accept the contract may be "forced to be free." Unfortunate though the phrase may be, the conception that freedom must operate within a framework of social agreement is in itself not unreasonable. (f) The result of the agreement is that "public person," called "sovereign" when active, and "state" when passive, a fictive but moral person whose life lies in the union of its members. The sovereign power of the state, which is this general will, cannot be alienated or divided. Finally, there can be no separation of powers; and the officers of the state have a conditional grant of power as an emanation from the general will to which they remain responsible.

(6) If we are to take the "profession of faith of the savoyard vicar" (*Emile*, Book IV) as Rousseau's own position, and this seems to be appropriate, then it can be added that man, living the conditions of the good society, must cultivate his "heart" rather than his reason. Man has an innate ability to grasp the basic truths without reason. Among these truths are the reality of God, freedom, and immortality. Indeed, Rousseau supported a "civic religion" based on such simple truths, and requiring the rejection of intolerance.

(7) The natural goodness of man, uncorrupted by civilization, suggested to Rousseau an approach to education which would be permissive, fitting the nature of the student and following the dictates of the heart; utilitarian in base, eliminating the dross of traditional education; and close to nature, teaching by the natural laws of cause and effect which rule the universe.

ROY, RAM MOHAN.
Q.v. Samaj (1).

ROYCE, JOSIAH. 1855–1916.
American philosopher. Born in Grass Valley, California. He studied first at the University of California (Berkeley), and then at Johns Hopkins University, completing his doctorate in 1878. In addition he studied under Lotze at Göttingen while reading extensively in Schopenhauer, Schelling, Kant and Hegel. He was the chief representative of Idealism in North America between the Civil War and World War I.

Principal writings: *The Religious Aspect of Philosophy*, 1885; *The Spirit of Modern Philosophy*, 1892; *The Conception of God*, 1897; *Studies of Good and Evil*, 1898; *The Conception of Immortality*, 1900; *The World and the Individual*, 2 vols., 1900; *The Philosophy of Loyalty*, 1908; *The Problem of Christianity*, 1913; *Fugitive Essays*, 1920; (ed. J. Loewenberg); *Logical Essays*, 1951 (ed. D.S. Robinson).

(1) The whole of Royce's philosophy is an attempt to show how one can move from the finite and fragmentary character of ordinary experience to an infinite and ordered fullness of experience—God, or the Absolute, or the spirit of the great community. The pattern, first sketched in *The Religious Aspect of Philosophy*, is taken through many permutations in his later writings as he tries to make his argument more decisive. In his initial work he wishes to show that moral obligation and truth are implicit in pessimism and skepticism.

(a) Pessimism is moral despair over the failure to discover an ideal which ought to be accepted by all reasonable persons. But the fact that this failure breeds pessimism is evidence of an inner demand that particular ideals ought to be harmonized. An absolute ideal is hence implicit

in the fact of pessimism. He states the ideal in Kantian terms: "So live as though thine and thy neighbor's life were one to thee." In *The Philosophy of Loyalty*, finding a similar despair over the multiplicity of possible loyalties, he sought the ideal once more in a generality: "Be loyal to loyalty." (b) Skepticism is despair over the fact that we are prone to error. But once again the admission of finite error implies absolute truth. When John and Thomas talk there are six parties to the conversation: the real John and Thomas, their ideas of themselves, and their ideas of each other. When John judges Thomas, it is his idea of Thomas which is the content of his thought. John cannot be in error about his idea of Thomas, since he knows his idea of Thomas so well. Nor can he be in error about the real Thomas, since the real Thomas never becomes part of his thought at all. There must be something wrong here, Royce avers, since John clearly can blunder about the real Thomas. And he concludes that the situation requires "an infinite unity of conscious thought" to whom all of these ideas are present, and concerning which he is their judge. Since error is actual, the infinite judge who is a necessary condition of the possibility of error must likewise be actual.

(2) But if we are part of this infinite unity of thought, how can we exist as individuals? If we remain in "the world of description" it is impossible to see how individuality and totality can go together. But if we move into "the world of appreciation" it is easy to see how this can be. In every instance of love, in all mutual appreciation, humans transcend their individuality and live in unity. Royce argues, in *The Spirit of Modern Philosophy*, that the role of will in allowing us to understand how individuality and infinite unity can be affirmed together shows us that God is not simply an infinite unity of thought, but likewise an attentive and loving total self.

(3) In *The Conception of God* he casts his argument in terms of experience. Here the contrast is between the fragmentary nature of one's experience and some more organized whole of experience in whose unity this fragment finds its "organic place." When we believe that our expe-

rience indicates a reality, the reality indicated must be a more complete experience within which our experience fits. Pushed to the limit, the result is that there is an "Absolute Experience" related to our experience "as an organic whole to its own fragments."

(4) In *The World and the Individual* he was able to find a means of interpreting the external world in the scheme relating the individual and the Absolute. He accomplished this by distinguishing between internal and external meanings. An internal meaning is an intention, as when I mean to do something. An external meaning is an act of reference. Internal meanings demand external objectification, and external meanings demand to be used as fulfillments or satisfactions of our internal meaning. The individual, the world, and God thus coexist in the meaning relation.

(5) In the same work, Royce argues that the temporal implies the eternal. The present moment of one's finite existence has a span lasting from a fraction of a second to several seconds. Any present moment contains both past and future. But just as one can speak of the present moment so one can refer to the present age, or the history of civilization, as a unity. It is in principle possible that to an Eternal Consciousness all of the events of time could be present at once, as a *totum simul*. And if we interpret the world in terms of will, then the entire reality becomes the expression of a single complex Internal Meaning. And just as the internal meaning of one's present moment implies a consciousness, however finite, so the Internal Meaning of the world will imply the Eternal Consciousness which is in principle possible.

(6) In an appendix to volume one of the above book, Royce began his exploration of the same problem in terms of the finite and the infinite. He here presents the idea that the infinite is a self-imaging or self-interpreting structure. Between any two integers of the infinite series of discrete numbers, it is possible to insert a series of fractions, also infinite, which reproduces the structure of the series of integers; between any two fractions the same thing can occur, and so on without end. The map, which includes itself among the things mapped,

implies an infinite series of maps. So, too, the thought which includes itself among the things thought implies an infinite series of thoughts. These series are taken as analogies to the community of finite selves relating to each other, interpreting each other, as part of the infinite. Let the integers represent the series of individual selves, and let them try to relate to each other in communication by way of fractions; thus, an endless community of interpretation will have begun. In working out the idea Royce used Peirce's idea of a triadic process. A interprets B to C in a linkage which is infinite and reflects the basic pattern of the world.

(7) In *The Problem of Christianity* the world has become a single "Community of Interpretation" including all of the social communities of the empirical world. Even physical objects relate to each other in physical communication. And the laws of nature are the forms of this communication. Royce began this conception with Peirce's (*q.v.* 13) community of inquiry, and broadened the framework to make of it a religious community, a community of memory and hope, or faith and redeeming grace. The Great Community is not so much an actuality as a task, that to which we ought to be loyal, and that in which we ought to believe. And God himself is simply the "spirit-of-the-community" and the essence of loyalty.

(8) It is somehow disheartening to find Royce at last interpreting insurance triadically through the insured, the insurer, and the beneficiary; and claiming that the hope of the Great Community in economic terms is the extension of the principle of insurability. Here our 19th-century Idealist and the Yankee trader have somehow become fused, and Absolute Pragmatism, the name by which he called his system in its later stages, has become a kind of practicalism.

ROYER-COLLARD, PIERRE PAUL. 1762–1845.

French philosopher. Born in Sompuis. Self-educated in philosophy. Taught at the Sorbonne, 1811–14, where he also served as dean. He was active in revolutionary councils, represented the moderates in the Convention and, converting to the Monarchist party, from 1815 to 1839 served with considerable distinction as a member of the Chamber of Deputies. At the Sorbonne, Royer-Collard lectured on Thomas Reid and against Condillac, other French ideologists, and British empiricists. He argued that sensation alone would commit one to solipsism; but in perception one has immediate knowledge of the externality of objects. Common sense and reason, the latter characterized by the principles of causality and induction, allow us to form knowledge of the world. In all of this he wished a return to Descartes and the spirit of Port Royal. Victor Cousin (*q.v.*) was among Royer-Collard's students and counts as one of his disciples.

Principal writings: *Philosophical Fragments of Royer-Collard* (ed. S. Schimberg), 1913.

ṚṢABHA (RISHABHA).
Q.v. Vardhamana.

ṚṢI (RISHI).
Probably from the obsolete Sanskrit root, *drs* ("to see"), thus "seer." Presumed authors of the early *Ṛgveda* hymns, which they "heard" the cosmos utter. To ensure efficacious sacrifice, the names of the ancient *rishis* were repeated as part of the sacrificial ritual.

ṚTA (RITA).
Q.v. Rita.

RÜDIGER, ANDREAS. 1673–1731.
German philosopher. Born in Rochlitz, Saxony. Studied at Leipzig and Halle. Taught in turn at both institutions, while carrying on a medical practice at the same time. A student of Christian Thomasius (*q.v.*), he was the teacher of A.F. Hoffman, who was the teacher of Christian August Crusius, the precursor of Kant. The approach to philosophy of the entire group was more subjective than the Wolff-Leibniz school, which they opposed.

Selected writings: *Synthetic Philosophy* (L), 1704; *On the Meaning of True and False* (L), 1709; *Christian Wolff's View of the Nature of the Soul and Andreas Rüdigers Counter-Opinion* (G), 1727.

RUDRA.
The maleficent storm god of the Vedic religion. Rudra brings the destructive aspects of the storm. He likewise inflicts diseases, but also heals them. *Q.v.* Indra.

RULE OF INFERENCE.
The formula or argument form whereby the conclusion follows from a premise or set of premises. A listing of argument forms appropriate to the Propositional Calculus (*q.v.* 3–22) includes *Modus ponens* which is sometimes considered to be the primitive rule of inference, *i.e.*, that rule from which other such rules can be derived.

RULES OF REASONING IN PHILOSOPHY.
Q.v. Newton (4).

RULE UTILITARIANISM.
Q.v. Utilitarianism (12); Brandt (1).

RUPA.
Q.v. Skandhas.

RUSKIN, JOHN.
Q.v. Anthropopathism.

RUSSELL, BERTRAND. 1872–1970.
English philosopher. Born in Ravenscroft in Monmouthshire, West England. In 1890, won a scholarship in mathematics to Trinity College, Cambridge. Fellow of Trinity College, 1859–1901. Lecturer in Philosophy, 1910–16, period in which he developed his mathematical logic (*q.v.* Whitehead 2). Prosecuted and fined in 1916 for a leaflet on conscientious objection; prosecuted and jailed for 6 months in 1918 for a second article. The *Introduction to Mathematical Philosophy* was written at this time. Visited Russia and China. Ran unsuccessfully for Parliament in 1922 and 1923. The first of his lecture tours to the United States was made in 1924. In 1927 he founded a progressive school at Beacon Hill near Petersfield. Upon the outbreak of the Second World War he renounced his pacifism. During the war he held visiting professorships at the University of Chicago and the University of California at City College in New York City (where through trustee prejudice he was held to be unworthy of his teaching post), and at the Barnes Foundation in Philadelphia (from which he was wrongfully dismissed in 1943, as determined by a successful legal action on his part). Returning to England in 1944, Russell's attention was caught up increasingly by social and political matters, participating with Sartre and others in war crime tri-

als against the United States.

Elected a fellow of the Royal Society in 1908, he became the third Earl Russell in 1931. In 1949 he was awarded the Order of Merit, and was made an honorary fellow of the British Academy. In 1952 he received the Nobel Prize in Literature. Married four times, Russell had three children.

Principal writings: *An Essay on the Foundations of Geometry*, 1897; *A Critical Exposition of the Philosophy of Leibniz*, 1900; new ed., 1937; *The Principles of Mathematics*, vol. 1, 1903; new ed., 1938; *Philosophical Essays*, 1910; *Principia Mathematica* (with A.N. *Whitehead*). vol. 1, 1910; vol. 2, 1912; vol. 3 1913; new ed., 1925–27; *The Problems of Philosophy*, 1912; *Our Knowledge of the External World*, 1914; *Principles of Social Reconstruction*, 1916; *Road to Freedom: Socialism, Anarchism and Syndicalism*, 1918; *Mysticism and Logic and Other Essays*, 1918; *Introduction to Mathematical Philosophy*, 1919; *The Analysis of Mind*, 1921; *What I Believe*, 1925; *The Analysis of Matter*, 1927; *An Outline of Philosophy*, 1927; *Sceptical Essays*, 1928; *The Scientific Outlook*, 1931; *Education and the Social Order*, 1932; *Freedom and Organisation*, 1934; *Power: a New Social Analysis*, 1938; *An Inquiry into Meaning and Truth*, 1940; *A History of Western Philosophy*, 1947; *Human Knowledge: Its Scope and Limits*, 1948; *Authority and the Individual*, 1949; *Unpopular Essays*, 1950; *The Impact of Science on Society*, 1951; *New Hopes for a Changing World*, 1952; *Satan in the Suburbs* (fiction), 1953; *Human Society in Ethics and Politics*, 1955; *Logic and Knowledge* (ed. R.C. Marsh), 1956; *Portraits from Memory and Other Essays*, 1956; *My Philosophical Development*, 1959; *Bertrand Russell Speaks his Mind*, 1960; *Fact and Fiction*, 1961; *Essays in Skepticism*, 1962; *The Autobiography of Bertrand Russell, 1872–1914*, 3 vols., 1967.

Three stages are to be noted in Russell's thought. He began as an Idealist; his interest shifted to logic, and he worked valiantly to show that mathematics rests on logic; this objective achieved, he spent the rest of his life experimenting upon basic philosophical problems through the application of the methods of logic. In the course of the experiment it is clear that he believed logic to be capable of untangling most of the problems which have puzzled philosophers through the ages. In addition to the three stages Russell defended what is now called "secular humanism." This theme appeared first in "A Free Man's Worship" (1903), where he argued that since the universe is contingent through and through, life on earth is doomed. Extend the time sufficiently, and the probable misfortunes threatening life, however slight, increase to certainty. Despite their certain extinction, humans must confront the indifferent or hostile universe, continuing to stand for their ideals. Russell's contributions to technical philosophy lie in stages two and three (B. and C., below).

A. (1) Initially influenced by the Idealism of F.H. Bradley, with its corollary sanctions in the thought of Kant and Hegel, Russell quickly made his way to a position of Realism and, along with G.E. Moore, led the anti-Idealistic forces in England. It is almost certain that his rejection of Idealism stemmed from reflection upon the subject-matter of mathematics. (a) The importance of relations for mathematics was at variance with Bradley's view that relations are vicious abstractions. (b) The Idealistic doctrine that what is known is conditioned by the knower contradicts the view that mathematics has some type of objective validity. (c) While both the Idealists and Russell reject the ultimacy of the subject-predicate form of expression, Russell did so not on the grounds of its inconsistency, but of its narrowness. Finding the key to Leibniz' metaphysics in the subject-predicate form of expression, Russell's development was in the direction of discovering a more adequate relational basis for philosophy.

B. The new system of logic, capable of providing the premises of mathematics, was developed in *The Principles of Mathematics* and in *Principia Mathematica*. Since the system and its concepts are applicable to extra-mathematical problems as well as to mathematics, only a wavering line can be drawn between this stage and its successor.

(2) But certainly the definition of number is central to the reduction of mathematics to logic. Impressed with the work of Peano, Russell found a way of defining number in terms of logical expressions in keeping with the five postulates of Peano. The definition arrives

independently at the position of the German mathematician, Frege. In this definition, number results from the grouping of things into classes, so that three is the number of all classes composed of triplets, two is the number of all classes composed of couples, one is the number of all classes with a single member, and zero is the number of all classes without members. The classes of one's, two's, three's, etc., can be identified as similar by making one-one correlations between them; and the cardinal number of each class, i.e., 1, 2, 3, etc., can be defined in strictly logical terms by means of class membership, equality and inequality, and the use of existential quantification. To take the simplest case, "0" would be defined as the class for which it is not the case that there is an "x" such that "x" is a member of "A." With added qualifications one can assert membership in "A" by "x," or "x and y," or "x, y, and z," utilizing nothing more than one needs to define the given number.

(3) The theory of types was advanced by Russell to solve a contradiction he had discovered in the idea of class membership. Most classes are not members of themselves. The class of all pencils is not a pencil, and the class of all objects is not an object. But the class of all countable things would seem to be countable, and the class of all comprehensible things would appear to be comprehensible. Some classes, then, appear to be members of themselves. But is the class of all classes not members of themselves a member of itself, or is it not? If it is a member of itself, then it is not one of those classes which are not members of themselves. But if it is not a member of itself, then it is a member of the classes not members of themselves, and so it is a member of itself after all. There are many other instances of this kind of paradox, including the Cretan who held that all Cretans are liars (q.v. Paradox, B.).

Russell's solution was to hold that no class is a member of itself. A class is on a higher level than its members; the class of which this class is a member is on a still higher level, and so on. If we take the theory of types extensionally the successive levels will be individuals, classes of individuals, classes of classes of individuals, and so on. If we take the theory

intensionally, the successive levels will be individuals, properties of individuals, properties of properties of individuals, and so on. To this point, our discussion has concerned the simplified version of the theory of types. Added complications appear if we venture beyond classes and properties to various kinds of propositional functions. Russell sought to handle these complications in his so-called ramified theory of types. But, inasmuch as the ramified theory carries with it an axiom of reducibility allowing us to translate back into the simplified theory, the latter would seem to be more basic. The value of the theory of types is disputed. Since not all forms of self-reference are objectionable, Russell's mass inoculation may have been a more heroic measure than that required by the incidence of the disease.

(4) The theory of definite descriptions, like the two previous concepts, was developed in his logico-mathematical writings, *Principia Mathematica* and the *Introduction to Mathematical Philosophy.* Russell is seeking a theory which will allow us to refer to nonexistent objects—the present king of France, the golden mountain, the round square—meaningfully without our being tempted to believe they somehow exist. He takes the position that expressions of the form, "the so and so" do not function as names. The strategy is to rewrite the sentences where definite descriptions stand in the subject place in such a way that a "bare particular" is left as subject, and the descriptive phrase becomes a predicate.

Certain conditions must be laid down to allow us to determine the truth or falsity of sentences containing definite descriptions. Given the nature of a definite description: (a) there must be at least one such thing, (b) there must be at most one such thing, (c) the thing in question must be such and such.

"The present king of France is bald" is a false statement under these conditions. We understand the sentence to be saying: (a) there is at least one king of France, (b) there is at most one king of France, and (c) the individual in question is bald. Since the first two conditions are not fulfilled, the statement is false.

"The author of Waverley was Scott" becomes: (a) at least one person wrote

Waverley, (b) at most one person wrote Waverley, (c) it is not the case that anyone both wrote Waverley and was not identical with Scott. And the statement is true. The example can instruct us on the difference between a name and a definite description. One must recognize the difference, since "The author of Waverley was Scott" does not have the same meaning as "Scott was Scott." The description, indeed, is more fundamental than the name. To raise questions of existence or nonexistence with respect to discourse we must in any case substitute descriptions for names. In "The author of Waverley was Scott" as rewritten, the name "Scott" has not disappeared, but it has a subordinate place. And generally the replacement of proper names by definite descriptions removes the plausibility of positing unreal objects as a condition for reference. In Russell's notation "Scott" is replaced by the bare particularity of "$\imath x$) (x wrote Waverley)," the individual x such that x wrote Waverley.

(5) In the same line of development, deciding that the symbols which name classes can be replaced by descriptions, Russell concluded that classes can be defined as incomplete symbols. In Russell's mind this way of viewing classes was compatible with the theory of types and with Cantor's demonstration that there is no highest cardinal number.

C. If we draw the line between the second and third stage here, it should be noted that the ideas of the second stage likewise pertain to the general problems of philosophy, and most of the ideas of the third stage were generated in the second stage.

(6) In The Problems of Philosophy one finds Russell's famous distinction between knowledge by acquaintance and knowledge by description. The first type of knowledge is certain, and forms the basis for the second type which can have only varying degrees of probability. Knowledge by acquaintance extends from one's own sense-data, present and past, to the awareness of one's self, and of universals. Memory is a form of direct knowledge. And some direct knowledge of universals is inevitable. One might be able to dispense with all universals other than the universal of resemblance; but this one is indispensable to the life of

the mind. And having admitted resemblance as a universal, we might as well go on and admit universals of relation and quality, and whatever else may be helpful to us. The view of the self as an item of acquaintance did not remain in Russell's thinking; indeed, it is his usual doctrine that the self is not to be distinguished from the images, thoughts, and feelings of experience.

(7) Similarly, it has been a standard feature of his thought to rely upon a causal theory of perception. In The Problems of Philosophy it is clear that physical objects are instances of knowledge by description, inferred from the sense-data with which we are acquainted. He departs from this standard doctrine in Our Knowledge of the External World and in Mysticism and Logic only to return to the causal theory in later writings. His departure from the standard doctrine is in the direction of a constructionist view of physical objects out of actual and possible sense-data. In this alternative one views a private world from one's own "perspectives," correlating the sense-data of experience with the space of sight and the space of touch. One constructs one's three-dimensional world from this material. But in addition to the perspectives from which the world has been constructed, there are many perspectives now unperceived. Were one's state and position different, some of these perspectives would be part of that experience. The unsensed sense-data of these possible perspectives Russell terms "sensibilia." Apparently, the thought experiment involving sense-data and sensibilia, perceived and unperceived perspectives, was not fruitful. Russell returned to his more usual causal theory of perception.

(8) Still another thought experiment is to be found in Russell's doctrine of logical atomism. The doctrine was Russell's response to Wittgenstein, and was advanced following World War I. The doctrine has a certain harmony with other doctrines we have mentioned, such as the theory of types, definite descriptions, and the distinction between knowledge by acquaintance and knowledge by description. The view is that the world consists of atomic facts, and these can be successfully represented by elementary propositions. An elementary proposition

combines a first level predicate with a logically proper name, and the proper name will stand for a sense-datum. The value of the doctrine lies rather in the impetus it has given to the attempt to construct a language consonant with the world, than in its having succeeded in itself.

(9) Following the lead of William James, Russell developed the doctrine of neutral monism in *The Analysis of Mind*. According to this doctrine the world is neither mental nor material, but composed of some neutral stuff which, organized in keeping with the laws of physics, yields physical objects, and organized according to the laws of psychology, yields minds. Taking our cue from Russell's pronounced interest in sense-data, it would seem reasonable to interpret matter and mind as our constructions out of sense-data, organized according to different rules. Something of this sort seems to obtain and yet it is also possible to hold that our constructions according to different rules parallel a construction in nature. This would seem to be supported by Russell's holding that things organized according to psychological rules engage in "mnemic causation," *i.e.*, an experience at one time produces memory images which can be part of an experience at a later time. At this point he is not speaking of our constructions, but of an aspect of the world organized in a certain manner.

(10) Since he was not attempting to build a system, we should not judge the absence of system in Russell to be a defect. Primarily through his example, philosophical analysis is now characterized by a heightened logical rigor. It is characterized, too, by Russell's elegant sense of solving philosophical problems within the circle of the known and on the basis of a minimal set of assumptions.

RUSSIAN PHILOSOPHY.

The history of Russian philosophy is largely a history of the influence of European philosophy upon Russia. This is the case, of course, even with respect to the philosophy of Marxism. Among philosophers of note the following may be mentioned.

(1) G.S. Skovoroda (1722–1794) is known as the first Russian philosopher.

His thought was Christian in theme with Neoplatonic, mystical, and pantheistic influences.

(2) A.N. Radischev (1749–1802), the leading philosopher of the Russian enlightenment, writing under the influence of Voltaire and Rousseau, criticized the social evils of serfdom, censorship, and autocracy.

(3) M. Bakunin (*q.v.*), who studied in Germany and whose life was spent largely in exile, turned from Hegel to anarchism, calling for violence.

(4) Tolstoy (*q.v.*), moving from literature to an ethically based New Testament Christianity, embraced a religious anarchism, nonviolent in character.

(5) V. Soloviev (*q.v.*) combined Hegel, panpsychism, and pantheism into the vision of a world moving toward a divine humanity.

(6) G.V. Plekhanov (*q.v.*) was a Marxist who approached matter phenomenologically. He was thus regarded as an Idealist, and was criticized by Lenin.

(7) N.O. Lossky (*q.v.*) developed a philosophical system supporting human freedom and the living God.

(8) V.I. Lenin (*q.v.*) was an orthodox Marxist, contributing to the litany of themes an "exact copy" theory of perception and conception. The idea that the world might be exactly copied in awareness was perhaps already present in the view of Engels.

(9) A.A. Bogdanov (*q.v.*) disagreed with both Plekhanov and Lenin, interpreting matter as collective experience, while reinterpreting the dialectic accordingly.

(10) N. Berdyaev (*q.v.*), in exile after 1922, was oriented toward religious philosophy, stressing freedom, creativity, and a mystical relation to the divine.

(11) The philosophy of the Soviet Union, until its dissolution in 1991, was Marxism-Leninism, although with a growing appreciation of other alternatives, including the alternatives within the Russian tradition (*q.v.* Marxism).

RUYSBROECK, JAN VAN. 1293–1381.

Flemish mystic. Born at Ruysbroeck near Brussels. Ordained a priest in 1317 he became Vicar of St. Gudule in Brussels. In 1353, at the age of sixty, Ruysbroeck—along with a few companions—established a religious community in the forest of Soines. He became the prior of the monastery, called Groenendael, near Waterloo and forged a link between the Friends of God and Brothers of the Common Life. Devoting himself to meditation and mystical writing in the tradition of Meister Eckhart (*q.v.*), he argued against the identification of the soul with God through meditation, thus fending off the charge of pantheism made against his predecessor. Still, he was called Doctor *Ecstaticus,* and argued that "The soul finds God in its own depths," tracing its progress from the active life through the inward life, into the contemplative life.

Principal writings: *Adornment of the Spiritual Marriage* (T); *The Sparkling Stone* (T); *The Book of Supreme Truth* (T); *The Spiritual Espousals* (T).

RYLE, GILBERT. 1900–1976.
English philosopher. Educated at Oxford where he also taught. Editor of *Mind* 1948–1971.

Principal writings: *Locke on the Human Understanding,* 1933; *Philosophical Arguments,* 1945; *The Concept of Mind,* 1949; *Dilemmas,* 1954; *A Puzzling Element in the Notion of Thinking,* 1959; *Plato's Progress,* 1966; *Studies in the Philosophy of Thought and Action,* 1968.

(1) Looking upon the task of philosophy as rescuing one from conceptual confusion, the instrument of rescue consists in becoming aware of "systematically misleading expressions" or "category mistakes." One falls into confusion when grammatical similarities and differences are construed to be logical similarities and differences, or more generally when something is taken to belong to one category when it in fact belongs to another.

(2) Such mistakes abound in traditional metaphysics. For example, since one speaks of mental functions as well as bodily functions one might conclude that one is speaking of independent entities of equal weight. Descartes, in fact, falls into this error. It is the dogma of "the Ghost in the machine." Exorcising the dogma rids us of one of the traditional dualisms of philosophy. Ryle's exorcism consists of the strong claim that the mental must be understood entirely in terms of the observable, *i.e.,* in terms of that to which witness can be borne.

(3) Ryle is also interested in the sense datum-object dualism. He works at dissolving this opposition by focussing attention on items of experience less tractable than visual sense-data: *i.e.,* twinges, prickles, flutters, and throbs. The implicit argument is that if, or since, sense-datum theory cannot come to terms with these, it must be given up.

SAADIA BEN JOSEPH AL-FAYYUMI. 882–942.
Jewish philosopher. Born in Fayyum, Egypt. Named to leadership at the School of Sura in Babylon, 928. Translated the Bible into Arabic and compiled the earliest known Hebrew dictionary. He represented the Rabbinite or Talmudic party in a dispute with a party called the Karaites who wished to revert to the written Scriptures as sole Judaic authority. Defending philosophy, he ridiculed the notion that philosophy leads to skepticism. The problem is to find the harmony between philosophy and revealed religion. The Bible should not be discarded, but one might properly attempt to prove by reason the truths which revelation had already given. To that end he argued for the necessity of creation on the ground that the universe is finite. Both past and future have only finite extent. Had past time extended infinitely, it would not be possible to have reached the present. He also argued that the Christian Trinity rests on a misinterpretation of Scripture. *Q.v.* Judaism (6).

Principal writings: *The Book of Beliefs and Opinions* (T); *Refutation of the Unfair Aggressor.*

SABATIER, AUGUSTE. 1839–1901.
French Protestant theologian. Born at Vallon. Educated at Montauban, Tübingen, and Heidelberg. Taught at Strasbourg, the Protestant Theological Faculty of Paris, and the Sorbonne.

Principal writings: *Outlines of a Philosophy of Religion* (T), 1897; *Religion and Modern Culture,* 1897; *The Religions of*

Authority and the Religion of the Spirit (T), 1903; *The Doctrine of Expiation*, 1903.

(1) Working in the tradition of Schleiermacher (*q.v.*), Sabatier substituted for intellectualism an appeal to personal religious experience. The dependence of the finite upon the infinite can be known only in such experience. God is thus "the final reason of everything" and "the scientific explanation of nothing."

(2) Terming his point of view "critical symbolism," Sabatier argued that all dogmas and religious doctrines are attempts to express the infinite, eternal, and invisible reality by means of "sensible images." The effort is never successful, in the sense that symbols cannot replace the experiences they are expected to express. The symbols are thus secondary and transient, useful only so long as they relate to a worshipper's primary experience of the eternal.

SABELLIANISM.

The doctrine of Sabellius (*q.v.*) that Father, Son, and Holy Spirit are the same Being. The name refers loosely to all interpretations of the Godhead which are more unitarian than trinitarian.

SABELLIUS. 3rd cent. A.D.

Christian theologian. Born in Libya, moved to Rome early in the 3rd century. Leader of the Modalist party excommunicated by Calixtus, it was Sabellius' view that the terms "Father," "Son," and "Holy Spirit" applied to one and the same being who was active in three consecutive manifestations—as the Father-Creator, Son-Redeemer, and Spirit-Giver of life. Sabellius' own contribution to the Modalist party was the doctrine of manifestation, or *Prosopon*. The doctrine of the *Prosopon*, placing the Father on the same level as the Son and Holy Spirit, despite the opposition of the Trinitarians, helped to prepare the way for the official doctrine of the Trinity. Sabellius is often, although erroneously, classed with the Patripassionists on the ground that in his view the suffering of the Son must be reflected in the Father.

SACCAS, AMMONIUS.

Q.v. Ammonius Saccas.

SACERDOTALISM.

From the Latin *sacerdos* ("a priest"). Any religious system revolving around the priestly order, or the doctrine that ordination confers special powers and rights.

SACRAMENT.

From the Latin *sacrarer* ("to consecrate"). In Christendom, certain rites of special significance to the believer. The Anglican Catechism defines the term as "an outward and visible sign of an inward and spiritual grace." This form of words is generally accepted, but interpretations vary from one communion to another. The traditional interpretation holds that sacraments have their efficacy through the divine will. In some Protestant interpretations the efficacy depends rather on the will of the communicant.

(1) In Roman Catholicism the sacraments are baptism, confirmation, penance, the eucharist, holy orders, marriage, and unction.

(2) In Protestant communions the two rites most often regarded as sacraments are baptism and communion.

(3) For a view relating the sacraments to the "primordial sacrament" which is Christ, *q.v.* Schillebeeckx (4).

SACRED VOID.

Q.v. Death of God Theologians.

SADDAYATANA.

Sanskrit, "the six senses." *Q.v.* Buddha (2).

SADHARANA.

Q.v. Kautilya (3).

SAGEHOOD.

The goal of life in neo-Confucian philosophy. Mencius (*q.v.*) held that everyone has the capacity to become a Sage. Chou Tun-I (*q.v.* 1) said that the Sage conducts his life according to the mean. The *Doctrine of the Mean* (*q.v.* 4) states that the path to sagehood is through sincerity and a developed nature, allowing one to develop the natures of others. Hsün Tzu (*q.v.* 4) followed Mencius in holding that anyone with sufficient persistence can become a Sage. Ho Yen (*q.v.* 2) said that the Sage is beyond naming. Also *q.v.* Taoism (2).

SAGUNA BRAHMAN.
   Q.v. Śankara (4).

SAINT LOUIS HEGELIANS.
   An Hegelian movement centered in St. Louis, Missouri, which ran its course between 1858 and 1900. A group interested in the study of Hegel, led by Henry C. Brokmeyer and W. T. Harris (*q.v.*), formed in 1858. Initially known as the Kant Club and later as the St. Louis Philosophical Society, the activities of the group led in 1867 to the founding of *The Journal of Speculative Philosophy*. Harris was editor of the journal throughout its twenty-five year existence arranging for the translation and publication of Hegel and other German philosophers. The journal provided a forum for the work of North American philosophers as well, including articles by Emerson, James, Peirce, and Dewey. At one period both the Concord School and an Ohio group were related to the St. Louis Society.

SAINT-SIMON, CLAUDE-HENRI. 1760–1825.
   French philosopher. Born in Paris. A count, he was educated privately. One of his tutors was d'Alembert the Encyclopedist. Active in both the American and French Revolutions, he renounced his title in the latter and participated actively with the Directory. He began to come to public attention through his writings in the Napoleonic era. Regarded as the founder of French socialism, he provided a decisive influence on Auguste Comte (*q.v.*) who was his disciple and collaborator from 1817 to 1824.
   Principal writings: *Introduction to the Scientific Works of the Nineteenth Century*, 1807; *The Reorganization of European Society*, 1814; *Industry*, 1817; *On the Industrial System*, 1821; *The New Christianity*, 1825; *Opinions Literary, Philosophical, and Industrial*, 1825.
   (1) Introducing the terms "positivism" and "positive philosophy" to refer to the scientific approach to the world, along with the ethical, religious, and political implications of this approach, Saint-Simon held this philosophy to be the chief instrument required for bringing the world into a period of harmony.
   (2) Distinguishing between critical epochs and organic epochs, he regarded his time as a critical epoch in which the social "fossilizations" of the Middle Ages were being swept away.
   (3) The organic epoch following this period will be characterized by a pyramid of classes ruled by captains of industry, engineers, artists, and scientists. He suggested that society be administered by a three chamber system: the chamber of invention, made up of artists and engineers who would draw up proposals; the chamber of examination, consisting of scientists, who would evaluate them; the chamber of deputies, consisting of industrialists, who would implement them to the advantage of society.
   (4) Saint-Simon argued as well for a "new Christianity," which he set in contrast to the "degenerate Christianity" of the age. The new Christianity will center on ethics and fraternity—as had primitive Christianity in his view—and be stripped of its present theological and metaphysical dogmas.

SAINT VICTOR, SCHOOL OF. 1108–1789.
   An Augustinian school, located in the suburbs of Paris. Founded by William of Champeaux (*q.v.*), the school endured until the French Revolution, but the high point of its fame was reached during the first century of its existence. Its three most important members were the logician William of Champeaux, and two philosophical-mystical writers on the ascent of the soul, Hugh (*q.v.*) and Richard (*q.v.*) of Saint Victor. In addition, the school attracted such eminent visitors as Peter Lombard (*q.v.*) and Robert of Melun (*q.v.*).

ŚAIVAGAMAS (SHAIVAGAMAS).
   Q.v. Vaiṣnavism (3e).

ŚAIVA (SHAIVA) SIDDHANTINS.
   Q.v. Vaiṣnavism (3b).

ŚAIVISM. (SHAIVISM).
   Q.v. Hinduism (5c); Vaiṣnavism; Śaktism; Śiva.

ŚAKTA (SHAKTA).
   Q.v. Śakti; Vaiṣnavism (4).

ŚAKTA (SHAKTA) SECTS.
   Q.v. Śastras (4).

ŚAKTI (SHAKTI).
   Sanskrit, "power," "might," "energy."

The generative power of the divine in Hinduism. Almost always pictured as the feminine aspect of the divine in contrast to a passive, contemplative masculine aspect, the canonical Shakti is the consort of Shiva. By extension the consorts of all Hindu gods were called their Shaktis. Worshippers of the divinely feminine are Shaktas, that is, worshippers of Shakti. Shakti is worshipped as the Mother Goddess, the Great Mother; as the tender, devoted wife; as the eternal virgin; as the female of illicit love including incest and adultery; and as the bloodthirsty goddess of destruction (*e.g.* Kali, Durga, and Bhavani, goddess of thugs). Worship of the genitals of a living female is said to form part of the Shakta cult. Shakti worship and Tantrism (*q.v.* 3–4) are often identified. The distinction between right and left-hand Shakti is discussed in Vaishnavism (4b) and Tantrism (3–4). *Q.v.* Mahadevi.

ŚAKTISM (SHAKTISM).
Q.v. Vaiṣnavism (4); Śakti.

ŚAKYAMUNI (SHAKYAMUNI).
From Sanskrit, the "holy one" or "sage" of the Shakyas. A term, not of the earliest period, used to refer to Gautama Buddha (*q.v.*). Shakya was the name of the clan from which Buddha came.

SALLUSTIUS THE CYNIC. 5th cent. A.D.
Hellenic philosopher. Born in Syria. Studied in Alexandria and Athens. Influenced both by Cynicism (*q.v.*) and Neoplatonism (*q.v.*), he was equally interested in philosophy and religious mysticism.

SALLUSTIUS THE NEOPLATONIST. 4th cent. A.D.
A member of the school of Pergamum (*q.v.*), he prepared a compendium of doctrines of those related to the school. Principal writings: *On the Gods and the World*.

SALMON, WESLEY C.
Q.v. Induction (13).

SALVATION.
From the Latin *salvare* ("to save"). The Christian term for that state in which man is redeemed, and reconciled to God. The mediator in this event is Jesus Christ, who atones for men's sins (*q.v.* Atonement). There are many interpretations of the nature of salvation. Among them we cite the following:

(1) Origen (*q.v.* 4) held to the view of universal salvation, which he termed the *Apocatastasis*, the final redemption of every soul due to the influence of the Redeemer.

(2) Among the Buddhists the T'ien T'ai (*q.v.* 1) School especially, but not exclusively, believed in universal salvation.

(3) Brunner (*q.v.* 1) holds that while man cannot provide his own salvation he has the power to respond naturally to God's initiative.

SAMADHI.
Sanskrit term meaning "concentration." The eighth and final step in the path of Yogic meditation leading to liberation. *Q.v.* Yoga (4). As *samayaksamadhi* ("right concentration") it is also the eighth step in the eightfold path of Buddhism (*q.v.* Buddha 3).

SAMAJ, BRAHMO AND ARYA.
Two reform movements in 19th century India directed toward "purifying" Hinduism, yet with political consequences.

(1) The *Brahmo Samaj* (Skt., "society of Brahma"). Founded in 1828 by Ram Mohan Roy, the Brahmo Samaj offered a monotheistic version of Hinduism capable of standing up against the Christian missionary work which had begun in India in 1813. The political fact is that only lower-caste *Brahmins*, originally Shudra in origin, were willing to work with the British East India Company. Their willingness to do so brought them wealth and land; but religiously they remained under the control of the upper-caste *Brahmins*. The appearance of Christian missionaries, allowed entry by the ruling British East India Company under religious pressure from England, provided the option of converting to Christianity. The monotheistic Hinduism of the Brahmo Samaj solved their problem. As leaders of the Samaj they were in control of a purified religion, using the import of Christianity as the occasion for strengthening Hinduism. Beginning in Calcutta, the initial impact of the movement was in Bengal. Under a series of powerful leaders, however, its scope became nationwide, extending to

social reform, the founding of colleges, the university education of women, and famine relief. By the turn of the century the Brahmo Samaj had done its work, contributing rationalism to religion, and denying the authority of any sacred book.

(2) The *Arya Samaj* (Skt., "society of honorable ones"), was founded in 1875 by Dayananda Sarasvati, based on the premise that the Vedic hymns alone were sacred and the sole revelation of God. It follows that all religions must turn to the *Vedas* for their inspiration, and that the revealed source of all the sciences is to be found in that body of literature as well. Rejecting Brahmanic control of this Vedic religion, the Samaj was open to women and all castes. The members of this Samaj, too, were active in social reform, established a model college, initiated a program to reconvert Hindus who had become Christians or Muslims, and contributed to the Indian nationalist movement. With a membership exceeding 1,000,000 the Arya Samaj was more successful, at least numerically, than its Brahmo predecessor.

SAMAVEDA.
    Q.v. The *Vedas* (1c).

SAMBHOGAKAYA.
    Q.v. Trikaya (2).

SAMGHA.
    Q.v. Trikaya (3).

SAMHITAS, THE.
    Q.v. Vedas (1); Vaiṣnavism (2b).

SAMJNA.
    Q.v. Skandhas.

SAMSARA.
    From Sanskrit, *sam* ("together") and *sr* ("go," "run," "flow"). The term has come to refer to the "cycle of existence" with its implication of repeated births and deaths, the *Chandogya Upaniṣad* (*q.v. Vedas* 4) relates how those whose *karma* (*q.v.*) requires return become successively sky, air, smoke, mist, cloud, and rain falling to earth, transforming into seeds and plants. Eaten by "men" the plants enter the semen, leading to impregnation, and eventual rebirth. Common to Hinduism, Buddhism, and Jainism, the cycle in which one's *karma* continues to be worked out is often referred to as the Wheel of Becoming (*q.v. Bhavacakra*).

SAMSKARA.
    A Sanskrit term meaning "to put together," "to make perfect."
    (1) In Hinduism the twelve to forty "life cycle" rites of householders, including birth, marriage, investiture with the sacred thread. The death rite is, however, excluded.
    (2) In Buddhism the fourth of the five *skandhas* (*q.v.*), *i.e.*, volitions or dispositions as the elements of consciousness. *Q.v.* Buddha (2, 5).

SÁNCHEZ, FRANCISCO. 1552–1623.
    Portuguese philosopher. Born in Tuy. Educated at Montpellier. Taught at Montpellier and, later, at Toulouse. As was common at the time, his works are in Latin.
    Principal writings: *Oracle of the Comet*, 1578; *Why Nothing Can Be Known*, 1581; *Commentary on Physiognomy*, 1636; *On Divination Through Sleep*, 1636; *On the Length and Brevity of Life*, 1636.
    (1) Opposed to every form of superstition, Sánchez attacked astrological predictions derived from the sighting of the comet of 1577, as well as the interpretation of dreams and the Renaissance antecedents of phrenology.
    (2) His great work, however, was the inquiry into knowledge. His answer to the question implicit in the title of the work is that nothing can be known due to the unreliability of our senses, and the limitless number and changing characters of the objects that exist.
    (3) Scientific inquiry can, however, yield possible conclusions allowing us to come to terms with the ambiguities of experience.

SANCHEZ VAZQUEZ, ADOLFO.
    Q.v. Praxis (14).

SANCTIFICATION.
    From the Latin *sanctus* ("holy") and *ficare* ("to make"). In Christianity the act of God's grace through the Holy Spirit, purifying man's will and alienating him from sin; also, the state of being thus purified.

ŚANKARA (SHANKARA). 788–820.
    Indian philosopher. Born in Kaladi,

South India. His chief biographers arrange for Shankara a divine ancestry, finding him to be an incarnation of the God Shiva, and brought into the world to oppose Buddhism and dualism, establishing the monistic supremacy of Brahman. In fact his position, called Advaita ("non-dualistic") Vedanta, allowed no distinction between the individual self and Brahman. Shankara carried on controversies throughout India, which ended in personal victory for his point of view. He established four seats of religion in the four quarters of India, supervised by his followers.

Principal writings: *Commentaries on the Brahma-Sutras*, the principal *Upanishads*, and, the *Bhagavad-Gita*. Many other writings, both commentaries and independent treatises.

(1) The self is the foundation of experience and knowledge, the starting point of all proof, and itself its own proof, always subject, never object, yet at last not subject to doubt. It is knowledge of the nature of this self which makes liberation, or *moksha* (q.v.), possible.

(2) In fact the self, or *atman*, is undifferentiated consciousness. It is existence, knowledge, and bliss—as such. One can say that the self remains unaffected when the body is destroyed. But there is something curious about the saying, for the self of ordinary experience is a product of *avidya* (q.v.) or a false outlook. The term *maya* (q.v.) is also used. The self of ordinary experience is, indeed, the universal self as individuated by the objects of the phenomenal world.

(3) Equally curious is the status of the phenomenal world; for this world, with its categories of space, time, causality, and empirical individuality, although real from the standpoint of the phenomenal self, is likewise the product of *avidya*.

(4) Along with self and world, Brahman, too, may be viewed from a double stand-point. As the creator and governor of the phenomenal world, Brahman is called Ishvara or *Saguna Brahman* (Brahman with qualities). But as the Absolute Brahman as he really is, he is called *Nirguna Brahman* (Brahman without qualities). Shankara agrees with the *Bṛhadaranyaka Upaniṣad* that it is by eliminating every known specification of anything (*neti neti*, q.v.) that one arrives at the definition of Brahman.

(5) From the standpoint of the highest truth the *atman*, or undifferentiated consciousness, and the *Nirguna Brahman* are identical, and the sole reality. To realize this truth is to attain *moksha*, freedom, self-realization. The goal is attainable only along the path of knowledge, although with the preparatory help of devotion and ethical activity. The relevant knowledge is always part of our nature, of which we have been forgetful.

(6) But how is it that all of us initially take for the reality what is only the appearance? This effect is due to nescience, the fact that we are born into a state of not knowing; and only when nescience is replaced by a state of enlightenment are we able to sense the identity of the self and Brahman as the reality whose appearance seemed a world of individual things.

(7) But nescience is given two interpretations in Shankara's work. His more usual way is to interpret nescience as an error of judgment, and with nothing substantial in the picture. The other way supposes nescience to have as its product, *avidya* or *maya*, i.e., illusion, so that a world of *avidya*, discussed as though it were at least semi-substantial containing modes of time and space, change and process, is sublated through enlightenment. Shankara's position is stronger when nescience is interpreted in the first manner, but he requires the second interpretation, too, since nescience must play a real part in the story as we shall see.

(8) Shankara's more usual analogies picture nescience as instances of mistaken judgment and that alone. No other figure is so often used as the man who mistakes a rope for a snake and runs away in fear. When he has been convinced that the thing he feared is a rope his behavior is markedly different. But the presence, and then the absence, of this erroneous notion have made no difference in the rope itself. He compares the relationship also to the water of a mirage on the salty steppe; to the non-difference between unlimited space, and the parts of space delimited by pots and water jars; and to the phantoms of a dream compared to the waking state.

(9) But he also compares the relationship to an actor playing many roles; and

when thinking of the relation of individual selves to the one highest self, he suggests it is analogous to the case of the snake and its coils. Viewed as a whole the snake is one; viewed from the standpoint of its coils, hood, posture, there is an "element of difference." These analogies cannot be based on mere ignorance, since the actor must involve himself in his role; and since the coils and hood are as real as the whole snake.

(10) It is clear, however, that in Shankara's opinion the two interpretations come to the same thing and that all of the figures can be reduced to error of judgment; and just this is the question on which the viability of the theory depends. One can understand how the rope might seem to be a snake, and Brahman somehow a space-time world of individual things; but this supposes both the reality of Brahman, and the reality of the individual self, as subject to deception. One can understand how an individual self in its commerce with a world of individual things, might be deceived as to its own nature, thinking itself constrained to this world, when in fact its status is superior to that. But then the instrument of deception is the world; so that self-deception would seem to require the reality of both Brahman and the world. There seems to be no way of arguing that both the world and the individual self are illusory.

And in any case, whether nescience is mistaken judgment, or a world of illusion, the same problem arises. If nescience is mistaken judgment, and hence insubstantial, the clearing up of error might leave only Brahman. But the false seeing must surely have been a fact. Whose fact? There are two alternatives. Either the nescience, false seeing, is to be attributed to Brahman, and in this case Brahman is unenlightened—a contradiction in terms—or nescience is to be attributed to something other than Brahman, but on Shankara's theory there is nothing other than Brahman.

(11) If nescience is a world of *maya*, or *avidya*, then one's striving for enlightenment has a locus. One must penetrate the illusion, including the illusion of one's own separate individuality. But the world of illusion needs a locus as much as does one's striving. This locus must either be

a part of Brahman, or something other than Brahman. Again, however, either Brahman is infected with illusion, or there are beings other than Brahman. Since Brahman is reality, and on the theory there is nothing else, neither alternative will hold. For an Indian philosopher who thought such contradictions fatal *q.v.* Ramanuja.

SANKHYA.

One of the six orthodox systems of Indian philosophy (*q.v.*), arising in response to the *Vedas* and the heterodox systems. The system is attributed to Kapila (*q.v.*), who is said to have lived in the 7th century B.C. The philosophy turns on the *Sankhyapravacana-sutra* also attributed, but without evidence, to Kapila. The earliest text on the philosophy is the *Sankhya-Karika* attributed to Ishvara Krishna, 3rd century or 4th century A.D.

(1) Existence is characterized by the basic duality of the knowing subject (*purusa*) and the known object (*prakrti*). By means of these two categories of things all else can be explained. They are, as it were, spirit and matter, soul and body.

(2) There exists a plurality of selves, both in the condition of bondage and of release. Indeed, the entire empirical world with its empirical selves joined to empirical bodies is phenomenal only. The true individual self is free and unembodied, and salvation consists in learning, by means of *purusha*, that this is the case. Bondage consists in the activity of *prakriti* in the empirical individual who lacks this knowledge. The necessary discrimination and release are to be found through virtue and the methods of yoga (*q.v.*).

(3) But although only phenomenal there are elaborate explanations of the development of the common-sense world. For instance, the development of *prakriti* can occur only through the excitation of *purusha*. The two categories cooperate, comparable to a blind man of sure foot carrying on his shoulders a lame man of good vision; and through this cooperation there occurs an evolution of *prakriti* into the phenomenal world.

(4) *Prakriti* is composed of three constituents, called *gunas*: *sattva*—potential consciousness; *rajas*—the source of activity;

tamas—the source of resistance to activity. The three constituents are causally related to pleasure, pain, and indifference respectively.

(5) The evolution of *prakriti* results in the production of (a) *Mahat*, the cosmic base of intelligence; (b) *Buddhi*, intelligence—the substance of all mental process; (c) *Ahankara*, the principle of individuation. (d) From *Ahankara* three lines of development arise: from *sattva* arise the mind, the five organs of perception, and the five instruments of action; from *rajas* arises the energy to empower both the *sattva* and *tamas* developments; from *tamas* arise the five subtle elements from which the gross elements develop. In this evolution the entire phenomenal world comes to be. Its destruction is the dissolution of this world into its original *prakriti*. The phenomenal journey in (2) above is expressed in terms of one's subtle body passing through numerous physical (gross body) careers until liberation is achieved.

(6) The causal doctrine of the system is *satkaryavada*, designed to explain the intelligibility and regularity of change, and to avoid the inconsistency involved in a transition from complete nonexistence to existence.

SAN-LUN.

Q.v. Śunya (6); Kumarajiva; Seng-Chao; Chi-Tsang.

SANNYASIN (SANNYASI).

A Sanskrit term meaning "renouncer." The term refers to the fourth or mendicant stage of the four *ashramas* (*q.v.* 2–3; Hinduism 3d).

SANTAYANA, GEORGE. 1863–1952.

American-European philosopher. Born in Madrid, Spain of a Spanish father and American mother. Educated at Harvard. Taught at Harvard along with William James and Josiah Royce. Upon his father's death in 1912 his inheritance was sufficient to allow him to resign his teaching responsibilities. Moving to the Continent, he made Rome his headquarters, leading a quiet and scholarly life. Poetic by nature, he has expressed himself through poetry and novel, as well as through philosophy.

Principal writings: *Sense of Beauty*, 1896; *Life of Reason*, 5 vols. (analyses of the role of reason in common sense, society, religion, art, and science), 1905–6; *Scepticism and Animal Faith*, 1923; *Realms of Being*, 4 vols. (concerning essence, matter, truth, and spirit), 1927–40; *The Idea of Christ in the Gospels*, 1946; *Dominations and Powers*, 1949.

(1) Developing in his published works a point of view which combines themes germane to the position of the Platonist, materialist, and skeptic, Santayana would seem to be a more likely source for detached poetic insight than for systematic philosophy. And yet a progression of steps can be discerned in this developing thought: Hailing himself as a materialist, "perhaps the only one now living," he nonetheless begins his philosophic quest in skepticism. It is his intention, as it was Descartes', to push the method of doubt as far as possible; but where Descartes thought himself to find certain indubitable truths, Santayana discovers that nothing is indubitable, and that the edge of doubt must be broken, if at all, by faith.

(2) Let one doubt what can be doubted, and both world and self, substance, past, and future disappear in what seems to be a solipsism of the present moment. But it is not even that. Upon inspection it is an intuition of essence accompanied by a suspension of any beliefs about these essences. Looking at this state from outside it could be described as aesthetic in nature. And, indeed, Santayana declares that in the aesthetic suspension of belief one is able to sense and appreciate qualities more intensely. From inside this state, however, there is only the quality, and no evidence that the quality or essence belongs to anyone or thing. And having come to this point no proof of any thing or kind is possible.

(3) But the promptings of one's animal organism require that one believe in whatever is necessary for survival. It is "animal faith" which takes us beyond the sheer entertainment of essence.

(4) Since we are prompted to act, what we must first add to intuition are memory and expectation. Thus we are led to assume both past and future, and the categories of action appear.

(5) If we are to act, then, "substance" must be admitted; and the existence of

substance, made explicit, leads to belief in one's self, other selves, things, and the order of nature.

(6) These admissions in turn imply the realms of being of which matter is declared to be the chief: matter, essence (which we had met in a subintellectual way earlier), spirit, and truth. We can now consider matter to be continuous, primary, and the means whereby work is done. Essences are in this connection the forms and qualities of things, and not really different from matter, but the "logical loci" of matter. Since spirit is generated from matter and the expression of matter, it has no power of its own; it uses the power of the body in carrying out its role of making essences both subsistent and existent. His doctrine of the self is thus sheer Epiphenomenalism (q.v.). And while the nobility of truth, being symbolic, seems to rise far above the realm of matter, still truth is about matter, concerning the standard descriptions of material things.

(7) The interrelations among humans form hierarchies of social organization. Institutions arising from basic human and biological needs make up the "natural society." Those institutions going beyond basic needs providing for matters of individual temperament constitute "free society." Those dealing with religion, art, and science constitute the highest or "ideal society."

(8) Ethics operates in society on three levels: (a) It appears in early society as "pre-rational morality." Framed in aphorisms and carried in pithy sayings, the injunctions of pre-rational morality are characterized by richness and inconsistency. (b) Pre-rational morality, purified, refined, ordered by reason, gives us rational ethics in which life gains its direction from the operation of reason. This is the ideal form for an ethic. It both expresses and shapes the vitality of the society of which it is a part. (c) But rational ethics gives way, as optimism about the world changes to pessimism, to post-natural morality; these are schemes of salvation which look beyond the world, finding goodness not in the world but elsewhere; Santayana makes it clear that post-rational morality is the unfortunate conclusion to the development of value in society.

(9) Holding the sense of beauty to be the sense of pleasure we take in certain of our sense objects, the aesthetic experience differs from other pleasant experiences in that we think of the aesthetic pleasure as a quality belonging to the object; so it is "objectified pleasure" which marks out the beautiful. The creation of art objects is as much a part of the world as religion; and art, like religion, is concerned with the human situation.

(10) Finally, religion stands as the bridge between magic and science. Its origins are primitive and magical; it leads to science and philosophy. In following its career of expressing the life of the spirit, religion generates mythical and poetic symbols while detaching the forms of worship from magic and primitivism. Out of this process, science and philosophy take their rise. Emotionally, Santayana seemed to regard the display of essence present in the forms of religion as more appealing than the forms of either philosophy or science.

(11) The thrust of his philosophic thought would seem to direct us to a way of life stressing kindliness, detachment, contemplation, and gentle irony concerning the shortcomings in one's self, and in the world.

SAPIR, EDWARD.
   Q.v. Language (17).

SARASVATI, DAYANANDA.
   Q.v. Samaj (2).

SARPANITU.
   Q.v. Marduk.

SARTRE, JEAN-PAUL. 1905–1980.
   French philosopher. Born in Paris. Studied at the École Normale Supérieure and the University of Freiburg. A prisoner of war in World War II. He became a member of the Underground during the German occupation of France. Influenced by Husserl and Heidegger, Sartre is the major French Existentialist. He has developed his philosophical ideas by means of novels and plays as well as through didactic essays.
   Principal writings: Novels: *The Roads to Freedom* (T), 4 vols. projected, only 3 published; *Nausea* (T), 1938. Plays: *The Flies* (T), 1946; *No Exit* (T), 1946. Books: *The Transcendence of the Ego* (T), 1936;

Sketch of a Theory of the Emotions (T), 1939; *The Psychology of Imagination* (T), 1940; *Being and Nothingness* (T), 1943; *Existentialism is a Humanism* (T), 1946; *What is Literature?*, 1949; *Critique of Dialectical Reason* (T), 1960; *Situations I–X* (T in part), 1947–75 (English translations of *Situations* under separate titles include *Literary and Philosophical Essays*, 1955; *Between Existentialism and Marxism*, 1975; and *Life/Situations*, 1977); *Notebooks for an Ethics* (T), 1993.

(1) Situating his phenomenological analysis in the human situation, Sartre finds man to be characterized by an awesome degree of freedom. Man is able to choose among alternatives satisfying a given goal, able to choose among the goals which may satisfy and even to choose that individual human nature which is to be satisfied. Hence there is no limitation placed upon man's freedom, and those who argue for psychological determinism, for example, are simply attempting to escape responsibility for their choices.

(2) The formlessness of man's initial situation in the world, thought to be a necessary accompaniment of his radical freedom, is signaled by the axiom—reversing one of the most continuous philosophical traditions—"Existence precedes essence." Both man and the world are merely given; man then invents a nature for himself and a nature for the world. This is the sense to be given to Sartre's statement that man is a "noughting nought." Man negates the nothingness of the world by creating an essence for himself, and a structure for the world.

(3) "God is dead," Sartre reminds us, quoting Nietzsche's Zarathustra. Hence, man can no longer discover in God's will the appropriate values and principles for his life. Since he is free, and since there is no God, he must freely invent his own values, goals, and purposes: Invent the kind of person you want to be, and be it with all your heart! From this standpoint it would seem that active involvement is always good, that the only value-posture with which one might quarrel is the posture of disengagement from life. This does seem to follow and yet it may be an overstatement.

(4) The good and right choice is the authentic choice; and while it is true that

we cannot gain authentic choices from any traditional moralities, or ethical systems, still there is a difference between a decision made in bad faith, and one made soundly. Furthermore, Sartre has said that when we choose, we choose for all men; and this seems to lend a Kantian touch to his ethical point of view.

(5) Some of the same themes can be derived from a very basic distinction which Sartre draws between consciousness and inanimate things; the distinction also leads one to a number of variant conclusions. Sartre distinguishes the *en-soi* from the *pour-soi*. *En-soi* applies to things. A thing exists in-itself. One gains the sense that this means a thing is basically what it is, one thing instead of another, having a definite structure. If this is the case, then the axiom about existence preceding essence can't apply to the world around us. In any case, man is *pour-soi*, not *en-soi*. He is a "for-itself," not an "in-itself." That is, he is a project. He projects himself to distant goals and values. His life is that restless movement to become something he is not, and he defines his own nature. But one project completed, man requires another. The restlessness is endemic; man is always in passage. He defines himself by choice in anxiety, or *Angst*; the anxiety is permanent as well. He is condemned to this as he is condemned to freedom.

(6) From this standpoint an interesting comment is possible concerning God; for the idea of God is a projection which man makes, and must make, being what he is. And also it is necessarily the case that God cannot exist, because the idea of God is a contradiction in terms. How can this be? Man is uncomfortably restless in his *pour-soi* existence, and yearns to be able to combine the life of conscious awareness with the stability of the *en-soi*. He yearns to be a *pour-soi-en-soi*. But exactly that is what he means by God, an awareness which is not a project, and which is not threatened from without. Since, however, the very idea of awareness entails restless transition, an awareness without transition or threat is inconsistent.

(7) Sartre places Nothing alongside Being as a basic category. Our disappointed expectations ("Pierre is not in the café") introduce a sense of "nothingness"

into our experience. At the end of the account it remains unclear whether "nothing" merely refers to a psychological state, or whether Sartre intends for it to have ontological status, *i.e.*, to be the name of something in the world.

(8) Sartre claims to be a Marxist in his social philosophy; but what he says seems not to fit any orthodox version of that position. There is a dialectic at work in the world; but on the human level the dialectic is initiated by the fact of scarcity in the world; and it is carried on in terms of the consequent reactions of human antagonism.

SARVASTIVADA.

One of the four main schools of early Buddhism, along with the Theravada (*q.v.*), the Sautrantika (*q.v.*) and the Vaibhashika. In the Sarvastivada school the doctrine of *anitya* (*q.v.*) was developed into "radical momentariness," the rapid pulsations of reality were conceived to be so infinitesimal in duration that they scarcely existed. They could be truly reported neither in concept nor image. The force of *prapti* ("acquisition," "appropriation"), however, acts within the fluctuating stream of momentary elements to provide a substitute for endurance. *Prapti* is itself momentary but has the capacity to reoccur, uniting the stream of elements, and allowing, *e.g.*, the effects of *karma* to manifest themselves.

ŚASTRAS (SHASTRAS).

From *śastra*, a Sanskrit term meaning "sacred book." The *shastras* are the four classes of Hindu scriptures, consisting of *shruti, smriti, purana,* and *tantra.*

(1) *Shruti* (*śruti*) from Sanskrit *śru* ("to hear"), the body of revealed literature directly "heard" by the ancient seers (*rsis*) and transmitted orally. Included here are the *Vedas* (*q.v.* 1–4), the *Brahmanas*, the *Aranyakas*, and the *Upanishads*. Sometimes the *Bhagavad-Gita* is also included. Those who accept the revelation are *astikas* (*q.v.*) ("believers"); those who do not are *nastikas* (*q.v.*) ("unbelievers").

(2) *Smriti* (*smrti*), from Sanskrit *smr* ("to remember"), the scripture which is recalled, and so a fallible revelation, one of lower order. Included in this group are the *Mahabharata* (*q.v.*) and the *Ramayana* (*q.v.*), the Laws of Manu (*q.v.*) and other

sutras (*q.v. Vedas* 5).

(3) *Purana*, a book of religious poems. The *puranas* are eighteen in number, dating from the 4th century A.D., although containing material from much earlier times. The popular religious sects defined themselves in terms of one or another of the *puranas*, *e.g.*, the Vishnavite religion based on the *Viṣṇu Purana*.

(4) *Tantra*. Magical and mystical writings mostly from the 7th and 8th centuries A.D. The *tantras* are the basis of worship in the Shivite sects, especially the Shakta sects, who worship Kali or Durga as the wife of Shiva. Tantric worship is varied in scope, that of the left-hand Shaktis being orgiastic (*q.v.* Tantrism 4).

SAT.

A Sanskrit term meaning "being, existence, truth, righteousness."

(1) Both Brahman and Vishnu were held to have *sat*; and Brahman was characterized as the embodiment of *sat* ("being"), *chit* ("consciousness") and *ananda* ("bliss").

(2) The feminine form *sati* meant "virtuous woman" and was applied to the now-prohibited practice of wifely self-sacrifice on her husbands funeral pyre (also called *suttee*).

(3) In compound form *satkaryavada* refers to the Sankhya (*q.v.* 6) doctrine that all effects pre-exist in an unmanifest state in their causes.

(4) *Satyagraha* (from *satya*, a form of *sat*, and *graha*, "force") was introduced by Gandhi (*q.v.*) as "truth-force," the positive side of the strategy of non-violence.

SATAN.

A Hebrew term meaning "adversary," "accuser." Unknown to Hebrew thought before the exile, the concept of Satan made its way into post-exilic writings as a result of the influence of Zoroastrianism (*q.v.* Zoroaster). As the opponent of God, Satan came into prominence only with the New Testament writings.

SAT, CHIT, ANANDA.
Q.v. Sat (1); Hinduism (5b).

SATISFACTION.
Q.v. Penance (1).

SATKARYAVADA.
Q.v. Sat (3); Sankhya (6).

SATORI.

Term for "enlightenment." Used within Zen Buddhism (*q.v.* 1–3, 5–6) to refer to the sudden illumination which is the goal of the religious quest, as understood by this tradition. Also, *q.v.* Suzuki (3–5).

SATTVA.

Q.v. Hinduism (6b); Sankhya (4–5).

SATYAGRAHA.

Q.v. Sat (4); Gandhi.

SATYASIDDHI SCHOOL.

Q.v. Śunya (2).

SAUSSURE, FERDINAND DE. 1857–1913.

Swiss linguist. Studied at Berlin and Leipzig. Taught at the École Pratique des Hautes Études, and at Geneva where he delivered the course of lectures resulting in his influential publication.

Principal writing: *Course in General Linguistics* (T), (posthumously from student notes), 1916.

(1) De Saussure established the practice of looking at language both synchronically (in cross-section at a given time), and diachronically (in its temporal flow), as well as distinguishing between *langue* (the structured language) and *parole* (the speech of an individual person).

(2) He argued that the sign consists of two parts, the signifier (*signifiant*), and the signified (*signifié*). A difference in signs is due ultimately to a difference in sound, since spoken language is the archetype. For de Saussure: "Arbitrary and differential are two correlative characteristics," the bond between signifier and signified is arbitrary. It follows, for de Saussure, not only that "the linguistic sign is arbitrary," but also that in language "there are only differences, without positive terms." The point of view of Derrida (*q.v.*) centers on this element of difference.

Q.v. Structuralism (1); Language (14).

SAUTRANTIKA.

One of the four chief schools of Hinayana Buddhism (*q.v.* Buddhism, Theravada). The Sautrantika school holds to an epistemology of indirect realism. External objects are not directly perceived, but inferred from mental copies. Some portions of the school stress the *a priori* elements in knowledge, either holding that thought imposes its form on reality, or that thought and reality correspond like "the two halves of an egg." The school also developed an atomic theory. Cutting more deeply, however, the Sautrantikas in contrast to the Sarvastivadin school viewed the *dharmas* (elements of existence) as point-instants, self-destructing immediately upon occurrence. Thus every point-instant is a creation out of nothing, and causation is replaced by noncausal sequence.

SAVIOR.

From the Latin *salvare* ("to make safe"). Having its origin in the titles of Syrian and Egyptian kings ("Soter") and in the dying and rising gods of the mystery religions, by the 2nd century A.D. the term "savior" began to be applied as the most appropriate name for Christ. It is seldom used in the New Testament (but see I *John* 4:14); and it was used (as "Soter") in Gnosticism (*q.v.* 5).

SAVONAROLA, JEROME. 1452–1498.

Italian monk and martyr. Born at Ferrara. A Dominican whose apocalyptic sermons began to stir Florence in 1490. A number of his prophecies came true, and with the death of Lorenzo de' Medici, Savonarola became the ruler of Florence which he attempted to turn into a theocratic state. Difficulties multiplied, and Savonarola was at last arrested by a Florentine papal court. The charges turned as always on the religious sanction, or "divinity," of his reforming mission. Since, however, that mission finally threatened Pope Alexander VI (formerly Cardinal Borgia) with disposition, the real issue was the relative powers at the disposal of reformer and Pope. With the death of King Charles VIII of France, one of his protectors, and the disaffection of his enemies within Florence the balance tipped against Savonarola. Since repeated tortures failed to produce a suitable confession, a false statement was drawn up by the court, justifying the hanging and burning of the reformer and two of his most loyal followers.

Principal writings: *The Triumph of the Cross*.

SAYING AND THE SAID.

Q.v. Levinas (5).

SCHELER, MAX. 1874–1928.
German philosopher. Born in Munich. Educated at Jena. Taught at Jena, Munich, Cologne, and Frankfort on Main. A disciple of Eucken (*q.v.*), he was influenced by Brentano and, especially, by Husserl. The latter eventually decided that Scheler had improperly gone beyond pure phenomenological description in his work. There are three periods to his thought: a phenomenological period until 1920; from 1920–24, a period of religious philosophy following his conversion to Catholicism; from 1924–28, a metaphysical period characterized by vitalism and pantheism.

Principal writings: *On Resentment and Moral Value Judgments* (T), 1912; *On the Phenomenology and Theory of Sympathy*, 1913; *Formalism in Ethics and the Material Value Ethic* (2 vols.), 1913–16; *On the Eternal in Man* (T), 1921; *Writings on Sociology and the Study of World Views*, 1923–4; *Forms of Knowledge and Society*, 1926; *The Place of Man in the Universe* (T), 1928; *Philosophical World Views* (T), 1929.

(1) Distinguishing three types of knowledge—scientific knowledge of particulars, phenomenological knowledge of essences, and metaphysical knowledge of being itself—Scheler concentrated on the last two types.

(2) Extending phenomenological analysis to the field of values, Scheler sought to overcome the presumed relativity of values. His analysis held that values, no less than percepts and concepts, have objective as well as subjective poles. There is a hierarchy of values ascending from sensory values through life values, spiritual values (aesthetic, ethical, epistemological), to religious values. Values are nontemporal essences possessing an objective validity.

(3) Metaphysical knowledge, combining scientific and phenomenological approaches, takes its rise in philosophical anthropology, or the concept of person. Neither a natural being nor a spiritual entity in the traditional sense, person—understood as the unity of one's concrete and essential being—comprehends and provides the basis and unity for the spiritual and intentional side of our actions. Furthermore, by way of meta-anthropology, the concept of person leads to the concept of God who is one with man in

the latter's most distinctive features. In Scheler's final period God was viewed as identical with the totality of things.

SCHELLING, FRIEDRICH WILHELM JOSEPH. 1775–1854.
German philosopher. Born in Leonberg, Württemberg. Educated at Tübingen where Hegel and Hölderlin were fellow students. He taught at Jena, Würzburg, Munich, Erlangen and Berlin. Known as the philosopher of the Romantic movement, he was friends with Goethe, Schiller, Novalis, Schlegel, and other luminaries of Romanticism. For a time he edited a journal with Hegel who was initially regarded as his disciple.

Principal writings: *On the "I" as Philosophical Principle*, 1795; *Ideas for a Philosophy of Nature*, 1797; *On the World Soul*, 1798; *First Sketch of a System of Nature Philosophy*, 1799; *System of Transcendental Idealism*, 1800; *On the True Idea of Nature Philosophy*, 1801; *Bruno, or on the Divine and Natural Principle of Things*, 1802; *Lectures on the Method of Academic Study*, 1803; *Philosophy and Religion*, 1804; *Of Human Freedom* (T), 1809; *On the Relation of the Plastic Arts to Nature* (T), 1809; *The Ages of the World*, written 1811; *Introduction to Mythology*; *Philosophy of Mythology*; *The Philosophy of Revelation*. The last three volumes were published posthumously in Part II of the *Collected Works*, 1856–58.

(1) Schelling's philosophy developed through five stages: (a) Subjective Idealism. In this stage he is following Fichte's thought. (b) The Philosophy of Nature. In this stage he applies the principles of attraction and repulsion to many philosophical and scientific problems. Nature is viewed as vitalistic, self-creative, and motivated by a dialectical process. (c) Objective or Transcendental Idealism. The Philosophy of Nature is supplemented by an absolute awareness whose development is the revelation of the Absolute in history. His philosophy of art, introduced at this point, finds art to be a unification of subject and object, spirit and nature. Tragedy is viewed as a collision of freedom with necessity, reconciled by the tragic hero's acceptance of punishment, bringing together the real and the ideal. (d) The Philosophy of Identity. The Absolute becomes in this stage

still more important, standing as the identity of all differences. In this stage, Spinoza and Bruno are influential. (e) The Positive Philosophy. In the final phase of his thought he stresses the value of mythology, and recognizes in the contrast between God and universe, and within God himself, the presence of basic polarities. In this stage he follows in part the thought of Jacob Boehme and Neoplatonism. Despite the shifting phases of his thought, much of the content is common throughout.

(2) When Schelling takes the position that nature is alive in all its parts, he must make some disposition of inanimate nature. He decides that inanimate nature can be viewed as a set of slumbering selves. More instructively, perhaps, nature is to be viewed as a series of levels or *Potenzen*, each level repeating the forms achieved on lower levels but within the more exalted novel form of the level in question. The direction of nature's development is thus toward consciousness.

(3) Although he used the principle in a more cosmic sense than his successors, the idea of the unconscious is to be attributed to Schelling. All that comes to conscious expression was first a part of unconscious expression; and our entire body (to say nothing of the rest of nature) is part of this unconscious realm. Schelling believed that artistic creativity was to be explained by a relation between conscious awareness and the unconscious.

(4) Following Fichte's triadic logic of thesis-antithesis-synthesis, which he applied both to nature and history, Schelling found a three-stage development in history: (a) the primitive age was characterized by the predominance of fate; (b) the age of the Romans, still continuing, is characterized by a reaction of the active and voluntary aspect of man to the age of fate; (c) the future will witness the inauguration of the third stage in which a synthesis of the two principles will occur in the balance of life in which the actual and ideal will blend together.

(5) In his philosophy of mythology Schelling holds that myth is to be understood from within, having its own laws, necessity, and reality. Furthermore, he holds that the history of a people is determined by its mythology. An accepted mythology shapes the pure creative potencies of a people. Nature as well as man, however, undergoes a mythological development.

(6) In his final mystical period, the Absolute becomes "primitive will." God evolves through the persons of the Trinity, adding another instance of triadic development.

(7) The source of evil is traced to a desire for existence present in God and all else that antecedes even God, and is a first principle of all existence. Merged indissolubly in God's love, the principle becomes dissociated in men, so that the quality making possible freedom and creativity is also the source of his fall and sin.

(8) Schelling affirms finally, a polarity in God, which does not disturb God's essential unity. It involves a merging of absolute and relative, necessary and contingent, eternal and temporal, potential and actual aspects. At this point God, the "Eternal Contrariety," evolves by means of the opposition between the void of nothingness and the plenitude of being, an opposition internalized in the divine nature itself.

SCHEMA.
Greek term meaning "diagram." In Kant's philosophy (*q.v.* Kant 11c), the term refers to the exercise of the "Transcendental Imagination," bringing sense and understanding together in particular ways to produce various essential concepts. This relationship is "The Schematism of the Pure Understanding." The *schema* of quantity is number; the *schema* of reality is the continuous production of degrees of sensation; the *schema* of substance is permanence in time; the *schema* of causality is "succession of the manifold in time" in so far as subject to rule; the *schema* of reciprocity is "coexistence of the manifold in time" so far as subject to rule.

SCHEMATISM.
Q.v. Schema.

SCHILLEBEECKX, EDWARD. 1914– .
Belgian theologian. Born in Antwerp, Belgium. Educated at the Catholic University of Louvain and Le Saulchoir (Paris). Entered the Dominican Order in 1934; ordained priest in 1941. Has taught at

Louvain and the Catholic University of Nijmegen (Netherlands). Advisor to the Dutch bishops during Vatican Council II.

Principal writings: *The Sacramental Economy of Salvation*, 1951; *Mary, Mother of the Redemption* (T), 1955; *Christ, the Sacrament of the Encounter with God* (T), 1958; *Marriage: Human Reality and Saving Mystery* (T), 1963; *Theological Soundings*, 5 vols. (T), 1964–72 (collections of articles, republished under separate titles); *The Eucharist* (T), 1967; *Jesus: An Experiment in Christology* (T), 1974; *Christ: The Experience of Jesus Christ as Lord* (T), 1979; *Ministry* (T), 1980; *God is New Each Moment* (T), 1982; *The Church with a Human Face* (T), 1985.

(1) Drawn equally to tradition and immediate experience, Schillebeeckx philosophized initially within the Thomistic framework, accepting an interpretation of Aquinas current at Louvain, as one who fused traditional concepts with living experience. The same appreciation is registered by other 20th century Catholic theologians (*q.v.* Theology, 19). Le Saulchoir emphasized a theological return to Biblical and Patristic sources. The combination of these influences shaped Schillebeeckx' approach into the 1960's when his reading in 20th century Continental philosophy (as well as analytic philosophy of language) led him to replace the unitary Thomistic framework with multiple contemporary approaches. At the same time he replaced traditional solutions with his own attempts to overcome intellectual obstacles standing in the way of belief. The new approach created a vast audience for his work while raising questions among the orthodox.

(2) The contrast can be overdrawn. From the start he affirmed the availability of objective knowledge (including religious knowledge) in both Biblical and Patristic sources, and in immediate experience. From the start he asserted the viability of an absolute ethic in both areas. That knowledge appears in new forms and the ethic in new concrete applications was an emergent idea, however, whose full expression was that the traditional faith is subject to reinterpretation in every age while remaining the identical faith, and even though its reinterpretation signals growth in understanding.

(3) A persistent orthodoxy surfaces from within his reinterpretations. He asserts that God is active in both Church and world, and that the promise of salvation is present in both; yet in religions outside of Christianity, only a vague and nameless sense of God is normally possible. A fully developed experience of God is available only in sacramental encounter with Christ.

(4) Similarly double-sided is his view of sacraments, those signs of grace to be understood in terms of the primordial sacrament which is Christ. Sacraments gain their efficacy from Christ's essentially "infallible" promise of salvation. That point is used to explain why the efficacy of the sacrament does not depend on the character of the ministrant (although the fulness of its effect does depend on the attitude of the communicant).

(5) Further, since God's concern is to bring unity, peace, and justice among men, and so is related to every act of true humanity, the Church is merely the instrument of His action, exemplifying more explicitly the implicit divine goals within the human community. The Church is able to play this role, although with constant evangelical purification and reformation, because of its indefectibility. The latter is due to the operative grace of Christ. The Church's indefectibility is offered as a support for papal infallibility.

(6) On the other hand when Schillebeeckx argued that Christians can accept both the historical Jesus and The Christ of faith because the transition from one to the other, although completed in the early Church, had begun in Jesus' own lifetime, he appeared to be treating Jesus' divinity symbolically rather than literally. In 1976 the Congregation of the Doctrine of the Faith (*q.v.* Inquisition) launched an investigation of his Christology. The inquiry lasted through 1979.

(7) Part of his response was that the language of faith points to an "ungraspable" mystery before which all theology is silent, that this mystery cannot be expressed in a clear formula, and that his questioners wanted to hear the dogmatic formulas of the past repeated, a desire which denies the obvious relevance of the hermeneutic task.

(8) In 1980 he published a book on the ministry, arguing that a celibate priest-

hood became part of canon law only in 1139 by virtue of the Second Lateran Council (canons 6 and 7). Since the needs of the Church today call for a relaxation of the rule, Schillebeeckx concluded that "some changes in present canon law" are desirable and "perhaps pastorally urgent." The Congregation questioned his position, beginning its investigation in 1982. In his publication of 1985 he continued to respond to "unfounded criticism" of his position, including that of the *magisterium*.

SCHILLER, F.C.S. 1864–1937.

English philosopher. Born in Schleswig-Holstein. Studied at Oxford. Taught at Cornell, Oxford, and the University of Southern California.

Principal writings: *The Riddles of the Sphinx*, 1891; *Humanism*, 1903; *Studies in Humanism*, 1907; *Formal Logic*, 1912; *Logic for Use*, 1929; *Must Philosophers Disagree?*, 1934; *Our Human Truths*, 1934.

(1) Calling his point of view both humanism and pragmatism, Schiller stressed the extent to which truth and reality are as much a result of human intention and desire as are beauty and goodness. In none of these cases is human construction the sole factor. In particular, while all truth is useful, it does not follow that everything useful is true. Truth is relative both to the evidence and to the purpose of the investigator. It is apparently the latter factor which makes truth changeable and progressive through time.

(2) Logic is an instrument linked to use, usefulness, and value. Its so-called laws are merely postulates fructifying its usefulness. The facts and laws of science have no other basis.

(3) The one fixed point in Schiller's system was the human person. In later years designating himself a Personalist, he believed in human freedom and creativity, and in a finite God struggling alongside men for goodness in a recalcitrant universe.

SCHILLER, FRIEDRICH. 1759–1805.

German poet, dramatist, and philosopher. Born in Marbach. Educated in Stuttgart. An early conflict between medical practice and the writing of drama was resolved in favor of the latter. A friend and collaborator of Goethe. In 1789 he became a professor in the University of Jena. From 1790–96 he studied and wrote philosophy, returning to poetry in the final years of his life.

Principal philosophical writings: *Concerning Grace and Dignity*, 1793; *On the Moral Value of Aesthetic Customs*, 1793; *On the Sublime*, 1793–1801; *The Aesthetic Education of Man in a Series of Letters* (T), 1794–5.

(1) After studying Kant's (*q.v.* 9) *Critique of Judgment* Schiller proposed (especially in letter 15 of 1794–5) three impulses comprising human nature: formal and material impulses, and a play impulse (*spieltrieb*). The first two he carried over from the Kantian dualism of sense and reason. The third he believed to provide a foundation for aesthetics, mediating between, reconciling, allowing a harmony of, the other two, combining form with the life of feeling. Morality differs from aesthetics in that it combines the affective life with something like the necessity of nature, but play is free and spontaneous. It combines with morality to project the ideal of perfection, both for the individual and for humanity in general.

(2) Initially interpreting tragedy as a display of suffering designed to arouse pity, his final view—stemming from Kant—held the point of the representation to be "moral resistance against suffering," thus demonstrating moral freedom. To witness man pitting his free will against the universe inoculates us against "unavoidable fate."

(3) Schiller believed that the world was unknowable, and this fact allowed free conjecture as to its nature. This, indeed, is the locus of human freedom, and is best exemplified by the poets who in fact provide philosophers with their first principles.

SCHISM.

Q.v. Great Schism, The.

SCHIWY, GÜNTHER.

Q.v. Structuralism (7).

SCHLEGEL, AUGUST WILHELM.

Q.v. Tragedy (10).

SCHLEGEL, FRIEDRICH VON. 1772–1829.

German philosopher and litterateur. Born in Hanover. Studied at Göttingen and Leipzig. While a *Privatdozent* at Jena, he became acquainted with and studied the philosophies of Fichte (*q.v.*) and Schelling (*q.v.*). At about the same time he became acquainted with Schleiermacher's (*q.v.*) work, as well as that of Spinoza, Leibniz, and Friedrich Schiller (*q.v.*). All of these influences, converging in Schlegel, enabled him to become the leader of the Romantic movement in Germany.

Principal philosophical writings: *History of the Old and New Literature* (T), 2 vols., 1815; *Philosophy of Life* (T), 1828; *Lectures on the Philosophy of History* (T), 2 vols., 1829; *Philosophy of Language* (T), 1830.

(1) Distinguishing between the spirit of objectivity, where one's personality is dominated by his material, and what one feels impelled to call the spirit of subjectivity (although the phrase seems not to have been used by Schlegel), where the dominating force is the free expression of personality, Schlegel identified the first attitude with the classical period and with the Enlightenment. The second attitude is that of Romanticism where genius is given free rein, dominating the objective material.

(2) Adopting Schelling's view of dialectic as involving finite, infinite, and the synthesis of the two, Schlegel applied the conception to both art and history. In both there is a relation to, and an attempt to express, the Godhead. Human life, too, requires relation to the infinite; and culture remains vital only so long as science and life fuse, as in the Renaissance. When science develops in and as an abstraction separated from life, decadence has occurred.

(3) Distinguishing between tragedy as the art of depiction, the characterization of the whole, and spiritual transfiguration, Schlegel held the last to represent its highest form. In the third type of tragedy the riddle of existence is both posed and settled. The eternal is seen to rise from temporal catastrophe, and the tragic hero is spiritually transfigured. Shakespeare seemed to him to exemplify the second type, and Calderón the third.

SCHLEIERMACHER, FRIEDRICH.
1768–1834.

German philosopher and theologian. Born in Breslau. Educated at Halle. A preacher in Berlin, 1796–1802. He was named professor of theology and philosophy at Halle, and appointed Minister of the Church of the Trinity in Berlin beginning in 1809. In 1810 he began his work as professor of dogmatic theology in the University of Berlin.

Principal writings: *On Religion: Speeches to Its Cultured Despisers* (T), 1799; *On Revelation and Mythology*, 1799; *Soliloquies* (T), 1800; *Outline of a Critique of Previous Ethical Theory*, 1803; *Brief Outline of the Study of Theology* (T), 1811; *Dialectics* (1811), and *Dialectics* (1814/15) with *Introduction to Dialectics* (1833), in *Collected Works*, III, 1835–64; *The Christian Faith* (T), 1821–22; *Hermeneutics*, 1974, (a compendium of materials arranged by Heinz Kimmerle from Schleiermacher sources between 1805 and 1833, including early handwritten notes, rough drafts, the Academy address of 1829, and marginal notes dating from 1832–33).

(1) Religion is the feeling of absolute dependence. It is the dependence of oneself as a finite being upon the infinite. Rather than defining religion in terms of reason or morality, Schleiermacher opts for the importance of feeling which he believes to be the absolute irreducible feature of religion, which constitutes it a sphere of activity independent of any other.

(2) The infinite whole, taken as a set of things, is the world; when taken as a unified whole it is God. Schleiermacher has, thus, a strong component of Pantheism in his system, even though he saw fit to identify himself with St. Augustine and Calvin in his later theological writings.

(3) An individual comes to himself in developing his *proprium*. The *proprium* is that inward differentiation of the individual which expresses his particular place in nature and history, or, to speak more generally, his finite place in the infinite whole. The development of the *proprium* provides an individual identity or life-unity. Ethics, society, and religion are to be understood in terms of individual development, and the relations of individuals.

(4) On miracles Schleiermacher took the position that all causes are natural, but the miracle occurs when God calls forth the sequence of natural causes leading to the miraculous result.

(5) In his *Dialectics* the antithesis of the ideal and the real is associated both with a transcendental philosophy/empirical sciences and a religion/science contrast. The antithesis is overcome dialectically by showing that the "formula for the world is inadequate . . . apart from God," and becomes adequate when it is completed theistically.

(6) The antithesis of the ideal and the real is also an internal/external antithesis. Defining hermeneutics as "the art of avoiding misunderstandings" since misunderstanding follows automatically, Schleirmacher stressed both grammatical, and technical or psychological, interpretation. The latter required identification with the mind-set of the author, a radical principle since his main application of hermeneutics was to Scripture. Beyond scripture, however, his techniques applied to any individual work cast in language and, beyond language, to all human manifestations, including conversations and works of art. Since the psychological aspect of his hermeneutics uses the same ideal/real, internal/external contrast as the dialectics, it is possible that he came to this aspect of his hermeneutics by way of the dialectics.

SCHLICK, MORITZ. 1882–1936.

German-Austrian philosopher. Born in Berlin. Educated at the University of Berlin. Taught at the University of Rostock, Kiel, and Vienna. Initially influenced by Mach, Helmholtz, and Poincaré, his philosophy gained its final shape as a result of the early writings of Wittgenstein and Carnap. Regarded as the founder of the Vienna Circle of Logical Positivists (*q.v.*), Schlick helped bring Carnap to Vienna. His life ended tragically. He was fatally shot by a mentally ill student while on the way to a lecture.

Principal writings: *Space and Time in Contemporary Physics* (T), 1917; *General Theory of Knowledge*, 1918; *Problems of Ethics* (T), 1930; *Philosophy of Nature* (T), 1949; *Aphorisms*, 1962.

(1) It was Schlick who clarified the authentic task of philosophy for logical positivism, holding it to be twofold: (a) an elucidation of the structure of science and the basis of scientific knowledge, now termed an exploration of "the logic of science"; (b) elimination by analysis of the obscurities and equivocations of philosophical language in its traditional usage.

(2) With respect to the first goal, philosophical method involves the application of symbolic logic to scientific concepts. The second goal requires an analysis of the language used by philosophers. In both aspects of philosophical method Schlick used the Verification Theory of Meaning (*q.v.* Verifiability Criterion) in its strong sense.

(3) His philosophical results included the elimination of a number of concepts considered by many to be synthetic *a priori* (*q.v.*)—from mathematical entities to the concept of causality—in effect establishing the point of view that expressions, if meaningful, must be judged to be either analytic or synthetic.

(4) In ethics he believed he had destroyed the idea of absolute value. Regarding value experiences as relative, he found the basic postulate of value in the eudaemonistic injunction to augment one's happiness.

SCHMALKALD ARTICLES.

A summary by Luther (*q.v.* 14) of his teaching, drawn up in 1537. It was regarded by 1580 as an official creed and included by Lutherans in the official collection of confessional materials called the *Book of Concord.*

SCHOLASTICISM.

The intellectual movement comprised of the Schoolmen of medieval Europe. Although fixing bounds to the beginning and end of this, or any, movement is somewhat arbitrary, it can perhaps be specified in terms of its greatest flowering, and this is clearly the period of the great *Summae* or summations of theology and philosophy in the 13th century. A list of those preparing *Summae* would be very lengthy, but among others one may mention Hugo of Saint Victor (*q.v.*), Alexander of Hales (*q.v.*), Peter Lombard (*q.v.*), Robert Grosseteste (*q.v.*), and Thomas Aquinas (*q.v.*). During this period Scholasticism made an immense intellectual effort to investigate and bring into a single system the articles of faith and reason. It was oriented toward the universities, and indeed helped bring them into being. In its most complete expressions it was linked more closely with Aristotelianism than with Platonism; but both philosophies were held by Schoolmen (*q.v.* Medieval Philosophy). The method of the Schoolmen was the method of disputation wherein a problem was divided into its parts, objections were systematically raised and answered, and the appropriate answer to the question finally formed on the basis of performance.

Some would begin the Scholastic period in the 7th century and extend it to the 15th. All agree in finding the movement at its height in the 12th and 13th centuries.

SCHOOL OF ATHENS. c. 380(?)–529. The name given to Plato's Academy after its conversion to Neoplatonism (*q.v.* 8). Especially characteristic of the school was its attempt to reconcile the systems of Plato and Aristotle, while also stressing the systematic features of Neoplatonic thought. Of its many members, mention is made below of four heads of the school, and its final member. The first head known to us is Plutarch of Athens (*q.v.*). He was followed by Syrianus (*q.v.*) The most impressive philosopher of the school, also serving in his time as its head, is Proclus (*q.v.*), a systematic thinker of considerable power. The last head of the school was Damascius (*q.v.*), who argued against the power of reason to comprehend the One, and favored a reliance upon mysticism. Simplicius (*q.v.*), known as the last member of the School of Athens, had connections with the Alexandrian School of Neoplatonism (*q.v.*) as well. The school closed its doors in 529 A.D. after Justin had published an edict forbidding the teaching of philosophy in Athens. The response of Damascius, Simplicius, and other members of the school was to go into exile in Persia.

SCHOPENHAUER, ARTHUR. 1788–1860. German philosopher. Born in Danzig. Studied philosophy at the universities of Göttingen and Berlin. Wolff, Fichte, and Schleiermacher were among his early teachers. Influenced by Goethe's doctrine of colors. In 1820 he lectured at the University of Berlin on his new metaphysics. The lectures met with little success, in part because he set his classes at the same time as the great Hegel to drama-

tize his opposition to Hegelian rationalism. Having inherited a living from his father, he spent the next dozen years traveling through Switzerland and Italy, and living in Munich, Dresden, and Berlin. Finally he settled in Frankfurt in 1833. After 1850 his writing began to attract attention. Kant and Plato were in his view the greatest of the philosophers. But he was also influenced by Buddhism, the first Western philosopher to carry this distinction. His bitter essay "On Women" would seem to reflect his feeling about his mother with whom he broke in 1814 and never saw again.

Principal writings: *On the Fourfold Root of the Principle of Sufficient Reason* (T), 1813; *On Sight and Colors*, 1816; *The World as Will and Idea* (T), 1819 (2nd ed. with a 2nd vol., 1844); *On the Will in Nature* (T), 1836; *The Two Basic Problems of Ethics* (T), 1841; *Parerga and Paralipomena*, 2 vols., 1851.

(1) The representation we have of the world is the result of the application of causality or the principle of sufficient reason to four root areas: the interrelations of our sense impressions, our judgments, our spatial and temporal intuitions, and the motivations of our will. To gain a true representation of the world one must discover how to separate what is primary from what is derivative in the ordinary representation of things.

(2) Through introspection one can discover that one's will is primary over reason and sensation. Given this point it is clear, at least to Schopenhauer, that all else—even one's body—is an expression of, an objectification of, Will. One is called upon to accept the generalization that since man is an instance of reality, what is primary in man is primary in general, and that all that is should be viewed as an expression or objectification of Will.

(3) We can come at this another way. The world as idea is a representation. If in man one's ideas are a representation of one's will, by parity of reasoning the world is a representation of a cosmic Will. Human actions are on one side ideational and phenomenal; on the other side they are volitional and real. It follows that the will in man is blind, when taken by itself, and that the Will in nature is similarly a blind unconscious striving. However strange this may seem, it is one way of

interpreting Kant's separation of the phenomenal order from a noumenal reality, and finding man's ethical will rooted in the noumenal order. Only the adjective "ethical" has been displaced.

(4) The world is a representation of individual things, driven by the Will, characterized by pain and suffering. But there is in the character of the world a sign of release from all of this. Although space and time are the principles of individuation, accounting for the individuality of things, at every level of the hierarchy from unconscious to conscious beings, things divide into genera. These are nothing other than the Platonic Ideas, timelessly characterizing the flux of things. Contemplation of the Ideas is the first step in separating oneself from the domination of one's will, or the Will (finally, the two are one).

(5) The second step lies in aesthetic appreciation. Having located the key to release in contemplation of the Ideas, Schopenhauer commits himself to an ideational view of the aesthetic object. In the aesthetic experience the aesthetic object is freed from its particularity and the knower is freed from his own individuality, and becomes the pure knowing subject. As there is a hierarchy of ideas in the world, so there is a hierarchy of arts, beginning in architecture, passing through sculpture, painting, lyric and tragic poetry, to music. Here we find the highest of the arts. It is a virtual revelation of the Will itself, presenting pain and joy in something like pure abstraction. The separation from the dominion of time and place and circumstance conquers the will through will itself. The victory is, however, only fleeting. Tragic drama simply exemplifies the guiltless, unjust suffering of all existence. Given this universality, Schopenhauer felt it better that the tragic figure be like any one of us, neither hero nor villain.

(6) The final step on the path to liberation comes in the ethics of pessimism. In this step one must overcome the ego which the will has created in its effort to feed and satisfy desire. Compassion for others can break the bonds of ego, when one understands the unity of all beings. When one feels the pain of another with the same intensity with which one feels one's own pain, one has con-

quered pain through pain itself. The move here is renunciation, resignation, and asceticism.

(7) In Schopenhauer's understanding the final step involves a negation of the will to live, which he understands in terms of *nirvana*. In the Buddhist doctrine resignation leads to the escape from individuality through conquering the will to live. This cannot be done through suicide, since that is an action expressing desire. It must occur through the movement into serenity along the path we have sketched.

SCHRÖDER, ERNST. 1841–1902.
German logician and mathematician. Born in Pforzheim. Professor of mathematics in the technical institute of Karlsruhe from 1876 until his death. He systematized and completed the work begun by Boole (*q.v.*) and De Morgan (*q.v.*) in the algebra of logic. His contributions to the algebra of relations have particular importance.

Principal writings: *The Field of Operations of the Logical Calculus*, 1877; *Lectures on the Algebra of Logic* (*Exact Logic*), 4 vols., 1890–1905 (II, 2 ed. E. Müller); *Summary of the Algebra of Logic*, (ed. E. Müller), 2 vols., 1909–10.

SCHRÖDINGER, E.
Q.v. Vienna Circle of Logical Positivists (4).

SCHULZE, GOTTLOB ERNST. 1761–1833.
German philosopher. Born at Heldrungen. Taught at Wittenberg and Göttingen. An opponent of Kant, he argued for the validity of Humean skepticism.
Principal writings: *Aenesidemus*, 1792.

SCHUPPE, WILHELM. 1836–1913.
German philosopher. Born in Brieg. Taught at Griefswald. One of the "Philosophers of Immanence," Schuppe argued that the condition for avoiding solipsism is the doctrine that objects are immanent in consciousness. There is no subject-object duality since the two always form a unity. The consequence is that in some sense we know objects, and even other minds, directly. There are, of course, states of consciousness without objective correlates as there are characters of objects not present in anyone's consciousness. In addition there is an

ideal "general consciousness," having something to do with space and time, which becomes real in individual consciousness.

Principal writings: *Human Thinking*, 1870; *Epistemological Logic*, 1878; *Outline of Epistemology and Logic*, 1894; *The Immanent Philosophy*, 1897; *Solipsism*, 1898.

SCHWEITZER, ALBERT. 1875–1965. German philosopher and theologian. Born in Kayserberg, Alsace. Educated at Strasbourg. A concert organist, interpreter of and authority on Bach, a theologian and New Testament scholar, a philosopher of culture, and a medical missionary who built and served a hospital in Lambaréne, French Equatorial Africa. Schweitzer was a Renaissance man raised to spiritual dimensions.

Principal philosophical and religious writings: *Paul and His Interpreters* (T), 1912; *Christianity and the Religions of the World* (T), 1923; *Civilization and Ethics* (T), 1923; *Philosophy of Culture*, 2 vols. (T), 1923; *Quest of the Historical Jesus* (T), 1926; *The Mysticism of Paul* (T), 1931; *Out of My Life and Thought* (T), 1933; *Indian Thought* (T), 1936.

(1) Regarding culture as a fragile structure contingent upon the constancy of the human will, Schweitzer held that man has an ethical imperative to continue its development.

(2) Man experiences God as Ethical Will within himself, and as impersonal force in nature. The two are identified correctly, in Schweitzer's view, when Ethical Will is taken as God's defining characteristic.

(3) He looked upon Jesus as a historical figure who was convinced that he must introduce the Messianic age, and that the destruction of the world was imminent. Mistaken though Jesus was in these pronouncements, he revealed the nature of God in ethical terms.

(4) Schweitzer believed the basis of ethics to lie in "reverence for life." The phrase occurred to him while traveling in Africa, and stands in his thought in some measure as a final value.

SCIACCA, MICHELE. 1908– . Italian philosopher. Born in Sicily. Educated at the University of Naples. Taught at Naples, Pavia, and Genoa. Influenced by Gentile (*q.v.*). Sciacca's philosophical position is called "Integralism." According to this view, existence is self-generative, positing itself as Act. The self-positing act is termed "objective interiority."

Selected philosophical writings: *The Problem of God and of Religion in Contemporary Philosophy*, 1944; *Italian Thought in the Risorgimento*, 1948; *Objective Interiority*, 1951; *Philosophy Today* (T), 1958; *Death and Immortality*, 1959; *Philosophy and Metaphysics*, 1959; *Freedom and Time*, 1965; *The Tragic Chisciottism of Unamuno*, 1971.

SCIENCE. From the Latin *scientia* ("knowledge"). Of the Greek synonyms (*cf.* 2 below) the most accurate is *episteme*. The nature of science is itself a problem within philosophy, and there are many positions to be considered. At times science has been regarded as a part of philosophy, and at other times as separate from philosophy. It has sometimes been looked upon as a single discipline, and at other times as a plural set of disciplines. There are strong and weak senses of the term, depending upon whether one associates the discipline more closely with unchanging truth, or with changing opinion. Science is sometimes regarded as having to do with reality; by some it is regarded as having to do with phenomena or the appearances of things. The sciences are sometimes divided into deductive and inductive types, or sciences of reason and sciences of fact. At other times they have been regarded as exclusively one or the other of these alternatives. All of the above points are exemplified in the entries which follow. Many of them derive from the areas of epistemology, truth, and philosophy of science, to which reference should also be made.

(1) The goal of the First period of philosophy (*q.v.* 31) was discovery of the basic elements of the universe, a quest which would today be considered scientific. In that period no differentiation was made between science and philosophy. Later, science came to be regarded as a component part of philosophy and, finally, as a set of disciplines altogether separate from philosophy.

(2) Plato (*q.v.* 1), distinguishing between knowledge (*episteme*) and opinion

(*doxa*), treated the former as the subject matter of science in the strict sense. But there are studies preliminary to *episteme*. These studies are sometimes called *mathema* ("lesson" or, in the plural, "mathematics") and at other times *dianoia* ("thought" or "understanding"). The latter term is used by Plato as the third segment in his line of truth. Since such studies are plural, more hypothetical, and less certain than *episteme*, the distinction provided—at an early time—two views of science: the integrated science of *episteme* and the separate studies of *dianoia*. It should also be noted that Plato anticipated Aristotle in separating theoretical from practical science.

(3) Aristotle (*q.v.* 5) regarded science as demonstrated knowledge of the causes of things. It is to be distinguished from Dialectic where the premises are not certain, and from Eristic where the object is to win over an audience. There are theoretical, practical, and productive sciences. Theoretical science is superior to the other two; but the sciences are irreducibly plural, and each is to be understood in its own terms.

(4) There are numerous classifications of the fields of philosophy; it is not our intention to treat such classifications here (for that *q.v.* Philosophy D); but both Stoicism (*q.v.*) and Epicureanism (*q.v.* Epicurus 1) provide classifications of the disciplines in which physics, the study of the natural world, figures as one of the three divisions of philosophy.

(5) During the Middle Ages *scientia* is usually interpreted in the strong sense of science associated with *episteme*, and this is said to be the kind of knowledge God has of the world. The *Trivium* and *Quadrivium*, on the other hand, contained a number of studies qualifying as sciences in the less strict sense.

(6) A somewhat different kind of separation is to be found in Dominic Gundisalvo (*q.v.*). Following a Neoplatonic Arabic version of Aristotelianism, he divided the sciences into human and divine. The former rest on reason and the latter on revelation.

(7) Hugh of St. Victor (*q.v.* 2) distinguished between theoretical, practical, and mechanical sciences, all of which he regarded as ancillary to mystical contemplation.

(8) Averroës (*q.v.* 3), taking "being" as an univocal term, held science to be eternal, dealing with the quiddities of things.

(9) Robert Kilwardby (*q.v.*) likewise distinguished between the sciences treating of divine things and those treating of human things, although he included natural, metaphysical, and mathematical sciences in the former category.

(10) Roger Bacon (*q.v.* 2–3) argued that experimental science, embodying both observation and mathematics, is superior to speculative science. But theology, drawing on internal experience, is superior to both.

(11) William of Ockham (*q.v.* 3) made a distinction between *scientia rationalis*, or rational science, and *scientia realis*, or science of real things.

(12) Francis Bacon (*q.v.* 1, 3–4) stressed the role of induction in science. Inductive method is the path to truth whose other face is utility. The sciences are definitively plural, reflecting human faculties, *e.g.*, natural science derives from reason, and history from memory.

(13) Hobbes (*q.v.* 11) divided the sciences into two types, those deriving from fact and those deriving from reason.

(14) Galileo (*q.v.* 2–3) powerfully exemplified the method sketched out by Roger Bacon, interrelating empirical and formal considerations in such a manner that theories can be confirmed or disconfirmed.

(15) For Descartes (*q.v.* 10) science could have no basis apart from reason, and the method of reason is adaptable to any problem whatever. He associated science with certitude and really agreed with the medieval dictum that true science is identical with God's knowledge.

(16) Newton (*q.v.* 4–5) tended toward a positivistic view of science, claiming that "*hypotheses non fingo*" ("I do not invent hypotheses"). The emphasis lies on discovering the mathematical pattern of the data.

(17) Kant (*q.v.* 1) associated scientific knowledge with synthetic *a priori* judgments, following from principles embedded in human nature. Such judgments relate only to the phenomenal world.

(18) Whewell (*q.v.* 1) stressed the importance of the inductive sciences. He classified the sciences according to their basic concepts; *e.g.*, space, time, number, etc.

(19) Comte (*q.v.* 2) found the sciences to represent a spectrum of decreasing abstractness from mathematics to sociology, in the order of their appearance in the world. His positivism consisted in urging that scientific explanation become dominant in every field of human experience.

(20) J.S. Mill (*q.v.* 2) insisted that all the sciences, even mathematics, are inductive and hence probabilistic.

(21) Spencer (*q.v.* 1) looked on philosophy as the end of knowledge, seeking total unity, and using as its data the partial unities achieved by the separate sciences.

(22) W. Wundt (*q.v.* 1, 5) agreed with Spencer that philosophy had the task of completing the sciences. He regarded the sciences of culture as not reducible to the natural sciences.

(23) Peirce (*q.v.* 13) initiated the pragmatic view of science as the basic mode of inquiry. For Peirce the scientific community, the community of inquirers, is the paradigm of all community.

(24) Dewey (*q.v.* 2) continued the pragmatic view of science as inquiry rising from the problematic situation. Science could thus be regarded as virtually coterminous with rationality.

(25) Windelband (*q.v.* 2) classified the natural sciences as nomothetic and the cultural sciences as idiographic, supporting the view that there are two basic types of science with a real difference of kind between them.

(26) Poincaré (*q.v.* 2) stressed the element of conventionalism (*q.v.*) in science, holding that scientific principles are conventions of various kinds.

(27) Karl Pearson (*q.v.*) argued that science is descriptive but not explanatory.

(28) Duhem (*q.v.* 1) held that it is the object of science to discover the relations holding between appearances. He thus continued the Kantian emphasis with respect to the scope of science.

(29) Cassirer (*q.v.* 4) contrasted scientific with mystical and religious thought. The essence of the former lies in the concept, and of the latter in the use of metaphor. The tendency of the first is outward and of the second inward.

(30) Häberlin regarded the social sciences as primary and the natural sciences as derivative.

(31) The movement of logical positivism held out the prospect of unified science resting on the conventions of a physicalistic language (*q.v.* Neurath; Carnap 3, 6). Opposing the possibility of unified science are all those who deny the thesis of reductionism (*q.v.*), the view that all disciplines can be expressed in the language of physics.

(32) Braithwaite (*q.v.* 1) has presented a complex analysis of scientific explanation in which scientific theories are regarded as partially interpreted calculi with multiple levels of generalization.

(33) Hempel (*q.v.* 1) continues the emphasis of logical positivism, holding the hypothetico-deductive methods of the natural sciences to be valid also for the social sciences.

(34) Quine (*q.v.* 6–7), with affinities for pragmatism, holds that it is science that makes up the largest part of the conceptual scheme appropriate for individual belief. He believes the conceptual scheme of science to be underdetermined by experience. There are always multiple ways of dealing with the evidence which runs counter to a given scientific theory.

(35) Kuhn (*q.v.* 1–2) finds the meanings of scientific theories to be controlled by certain central paradigms which may be displaced only with great difficulty. In his view the scientific community has many of the properties of sectarian religion, including a sense of orthodoxy (normal science), and opposition to heresy (revolutionary science).

(36) For Toulmin (*q.v.* 4) evolutionary biology offers significant analogies to the evolution of scientific theory, including the presence in the latter of accidental variations and natural selection.

(37) Feyerabend (*q.v.*) argues that the progress of science depends more on the multiplication of alternative hypotheses than on the accumulation of facts.

(38) For an alternate view of science, as *Dasein*, and having separate spheres *q.v.* Jaspers (6).

SCIENTIA INTUITIVA.
Q.v. Spinoza (5c).

SCIENTIA MEDIA.
Q.v. Luis de Molina (1).

SCINTILLA CONSCIENTIAE.
Q.v. Synderesis; Conscience (3).

SCOTISM.
The philosophy emerging from the thought of Duns Scotus (*q.v.*). It is an Augustinian type of philosophy (*q.v.* St. Augustine) which was partly shaped by the influence of Aristotle. The Franciscans (*q.v.*) have done most to keep alive the thought of Duns Scotus.

SCOTTI, GIULIO CLEMENT.
Q.v. Egoism (2).

SCOTUS, JOHN DUNS.
Q.v. Duns Scotus, John.

SCOTUS ERIGENA, JOHN.
Q.v. Erigena, John Scotus.

SCRIPTURE.
From the Latin *scriptura* ("writing"). The authoritative, sacred literature of a religion. John Wycliffe (*q.v.* 4) termed Holy Scripture the "charter" of the Christian religion.

SCRIVEN, MICHAEL.
Q.v. Philosophy of Science (28).

SEARLE, JOHN R. 1932– .
American philosopher. Born in Denver, Col. Educated at Wisconsin and Oxford. Teaches at the University of California (Berkeley).
Principal writings: "Proper Names," 1959; *Speech Acts*, 1969; *The Philosophy of Language* (ed.), 1971; *Expression and Meaning*, 1979; *Intentionality*, 1983; *Minds, Brains and Science*, 1984; *The Rediscovery of the Mind*, 1992.
(1) Agreeing with Austin that the basic unit of linguistic communication is the speech act or, more fully, the production of symbol, word, or sentence in the performance of the speech act (rather than the symbol, word, or sentence itself) Searle holds that linguistic communication is characterized by certain kinds of intention.
(2) Confining attention to those speech acts called by Austin "illocutionary acts," Searle uses a taxonomy distinguishing five types of such acts: representatives (committing the speaker to the truth of a representation); directives (attempting to commit the hearer to a course of action); commissives (attempting to commit the speaker to a course of action); expressives (expression of the psycholog-

ical state of the speaker); and declarations (assertions with an intrinsic feature of guaranteed performance).
(3) Searle dismisses problems of mind-body (*q.v.*) dualism by granting two levels of explanation, one on the macro, the other on the micro, level. Mental properties are the macro-level "subjective" effects of micro-level "objective" brain processes. This is no more problematic than in experiencing a macro-level hardness in the table, caused by the micro-level behavior of molecules.
(4) The intentional (*q.v.*) properties of wishing, desiring, believing, etc., on the macro level do not require bridging down to the micro-level in Dennett's (*q.v.* 2–4) manner.
(5) Since there is no macro-level of intentionality in the functioning of computers, machines cannot think, despite the claims of strong AI (*q.v.* Artificial Intelligence 3, 6) advocates. To claim the contrary would be like supposing that the person in the Chinese room who matches the tokens of Chinese characters sent into the room, with English words on the basis of charts also supplied from outside, understands Chinese. The functionary of the Chinese room is preparing responses by mechanical sorting. Computers do likewise.
(6) The belief of freedom (*q.v.* A.) as the capacity to have done otherwise is built into every conscious, intentional action. In fact, however, we are free only in the sense (*q.v.* Freedom B.) of being able to choose what we wish; and such freedom is entirely explicable causally by systems of elements at the micro-physical level. Bereft of radical freedom, we have at most a "psychological libertarianism" compatible with physical determinism.
Also *q.v.* Proper Names (4).

SEBEOK, T.A.
Q.v. Semiotic (13).

SECONDARY QUALITIES.
Q.v. Qualities, Primary and Secondary.

SECOND INTENTION, TERMS OF.
Q.v. William of Ockham (2); Intentionality (1–2).

SECULAR HUMANISM.
Q.v. Russell.

SECULARISM.
From the Latin *saecularis* ("the times," "the age," "the world"). The secular stands in contrast to the sacred, marking an approach to life divorced from the influence of religion, and thus determined by temporal or worldly concerns.

SECUNDUM QUID.
Latin phrase meaning "according to something." It is used in Scholastic terminology as a qualifying phrase. An assertion *secundum quid* is to be taken in a qualified, restricted, or secondary sense. Failure to take an assertion in its properly restricted sense is sometimes called the fallacy of *secundum quid*.

SEELENFÜNKLEIN.
Q.v. Eckhart (3).

SEFIROTH.
Q.v. Cabala (1b).

SEIENDES.
Q.v. Heidegger (5).

SELF.
A term which, in a naturalistic context, often replaces soul (*q.v.*) or psyche (*q.v.*). One way of distinguishing self from soul is to regard the former term as referring to a complex of psychical phenomena, and the latter as referring to an entity separable, and at times separate, from the body.
A. The concept of self, at least in the West, relates to the empirical tradition.
(1) Both Locke (*q.v.* 8) and his French disciple, Condillac (*q.v.* 1), retained a background concept of soul, the former as a "spiritual substance," the latter as the indivisible subject of our perceptions. In the foreground, however, both cite experience as instrumental in the formation of a complex including awareness, sensations, concepts, memory, and affective states deriving from feelings of pleasure and pain. Locke identified this complex with one's "person," coextensive with awareness and memory, and Condillac (*q.v.* 2) generated the complex with his "fictions of the statue."
(2) La Mettrie (*q.v.* 3) considered human beings to be mechanisms, and soul (that is, self) a collection of images.
(3) Failing to discover a self apart from the bundle of perceptions (including feelings) revealed by introspection, Hume (*q.v.* 4) identified the self with its perceptions. This raised the problem of personal identity. Since the perceptions are everchanging, how can one be said to remain the same person through time? In the 20th century Russell (*q.v.* 6) held to a theory of the self much like that of Hume.
(4) William James (*q.v.* 2–3) held a functional view of consciousness, dropping the thought that it is an entity.
(5) In Freud's (*q.v.* 1–4) naturalistic interpretation three features of the psyche are identified—the Id, Ego, and Super-ego. The interrelations of the three are explained in terms of the flow and constraint of libido, the sexual energy of the organism.
(6) Jung (*q.v.* 3–8) offered an archetypal self as the ideal of our developed natures, which we approach through the constituent and competing forces of the ego, persona, shadow, animus or anima, and the *mandalas* of the collective unconscious.
(7) When Skinner (*q.v.* 2) defined self as a "functionally unified system of responses" he was following the functionalism of William James.
(8) Both in hermeneutics (*q.v.*) and deconstruction (*q.v.*), the self is transient and episodic. For Derrida (*q.v.* 10) the self is a function of language. For Ricoeur (*q.v.* 6) the self and the text are cocreators of each other. In his post-structuralist phase Barthes (*q.v.* 10) speaks of the unmasking and dismantling of the "I."
B. Eastern analyses likewise move between the root ideas of self and soul.
(9) The *atman* (*q.v.*) of the *Vedas* is translated as "self" or "soul." As one proceeds through the stages of enlightenment the discovery is made that one's awareness of one's empirical self is illusive, and that one's self is the soul of all things, identical with the eternal Brahman (*q.v.*).
(10) On the conventional level Buddha (*q.v.* 5) analyzed self as an aggregate of physical, mental, and volitional factors (the *skandhas*), always changing and without any underlying nature. So far the analysis sounds like that of Hume. Among the doctrines of Buddhist belief, however, is that of *anatman*, namely, that these factors do not constitute a self and that the idea of self is to be renounced.

SELF-DETERMINATION.
The determination of one's actions by oneself without external compulsion (*q.v.* Freedom C.).

SELF-EVIDENT PROPOSITION.
A proposition whose truth is immediately evident without argument or the presentation of evidence (*q.v.* Truth 15, 17; Tautology).

SELF-INTEREST.
The term occurs in some philosophical analyses of human nature. Also *q.v.* Egoism.

(1) Hobbes (*q.v.* 7) held self-interest to be humanity's sole motivation.

(2) Shaftesbury (*q.v.* 3) regarded self-interest as one of two basic human motives. The other is social interest. According to Shaftesbury, the two can and should work in harmony.

(3) Adam Smith (*q.v.* 2) argued that in following self-interest each person contributes to the general welfare.

(4) Holbach (*q.v.* 4) held that each man is motivated by self-interest, and that this enters into an ethic of pleasure-pain.

(5) Stirner (*q.v.* 1) identified Egoism with the discovery and fulfillment of one's individual nature.

SELF-KNOWLEDGE.
The term appears in philosophy as one of the important human values.

(1) For Socrates (*q.v.* 1) the goal of philosophy is "Know thyself," a famous maxim of the Delphic Oracle. Thales (*q.v.*) is to be credited with its earliest use.

(2) In St. Augustine (*q.v.* 1) self-knowledge is not only the path to happiness, but finally to salvation.

(3) For Hui-neng (*q.v.* Zen Buddhism 3) and Suzuki (*q.v.* Religion 23) the essence of Zen is seeing into one's own nature.

SELF-PRESERVATION.
Telesio (*q.v.* 4) is among those holding self-preservation to be man's basic goal. The basis of the idea is to be discerned in Spinoza's (*q.v.* 4) idea of *conatus* or "striving."

SELF-REALIZATION.
The development of the possibilities of the self. Present in Aristotle's (*q.v.* 11) interpretation of happiness, self-realization as a basic human value is empha-

sized especially by T.H. Green (*q.v.* 2) and other neo-Hegelians.

SELF-REFERENCE.
Q.v. Russell (3).

SELF-RELIANCE.
Q.v. Emerson (2); Thoreau.

SELF-SIMILARITY.
Q.v. Chaos Theory (6).

SELLARS, ROY WOOD. 1880–1973.
American philosopher. Born in Canada. Taught at the University of Michigan from 1905–50. One of the leaders in the movement of Critical Realism (*q.v.*).

Principal writings: *Critical Realism*, 1916; *Essays in Critical Realism* (symposiast), 1920; *Evolutionary Naturalism*, 1922; *The Philosophy of Physical Realism*, 1932.

(1) The appropriate philosophical method begins with the "natural realism" of the "plain man," and strengthens it logically while retaining its essential character, an emphasis on the independence of the object of knowledge. It is with the application of our critical analyses that plain realism becomes "critical" realism.

(2) Along with other critical realists, Sellars holds that our awareness is not of objects but of sense-data or "*sensa.*" Correctly utilized, these guide us toward the object. The likelihood of our arriving at correct interpretations is increased by the fact that the human organism has through evolution arrived at some measure of adjustment to its environment.

(3) There are several levels of being, running from inert matter to life and mind. Each of the levels is physical and based on matter, even though the evolved qualities of life and mind are not reducible to the qualities of inert matter.

SELLARS, WILFRID S. 1912– .
American philosopher. Born in Ann Arbor, Michigan. The son of Roy Wood Sellars. Educated at Michigan, Buffalo, and Oxford. He has taught at Iowa, Minnesota, Yale, and Pittsburgh.

Principal writings: *Science, Perception, and Reality*, 1963; *Philosophical Perspectives*, 1967; *Science and Metaphysics*, 1968; *Essays in Philosophy and its History*, 1974; *Naturalism and Ontology*, 1979; *Pure Pragmatics and Possible Worlds* (ed J. Sicha), 1980.

(1) Holding a position of Scientific Realism, Sellars argues that science deserves the primary role in assessing conceptual frameworks of any kind. This amounts to saying that the real world contains those entities which would be posited by theoretical science in an ideally completed state.

(2) In the absence of that ideal end, each of us must come to terms with two major images of reality, the manifest image and the scientific image. The former is the common-sense personal view of reality, including the reality of persons. The latter is the present scientific view for which the ultimate constituents of the world are imperceptible particles.

(3) Attacking the "myth of the given," Sellars believes that one cannot break out of language and thought, establishing direct cognitive contact with reality. Although he does speak of truth, regarding true perceptual sentences as the correct opening moves in a language game whose function is description, correct closing moves must depend upon something like Peirce's (*q.v.* 12) community of inquirers arriving at the ideal completion of science mentioned in (1) above.

SEMANTICS.

From the Greek *semantikos* ("significant meaning"), from *sema* ("a sign").

A. The term was first used in a technical sense in philology, where it stands for the historical study, empirically oriented, of the changes of meanings in words.

(1) This usage is similar to the sense given to "descriptive semiotic" by Charles Morris (*q.v.* 3; Semiotic 10).

B. In philosophy the term is usually considered to stand alongside Syntactics and Pragmatics as coeval aspects of the study of signs. The study of Semantics in this sense is concerned with the relations between signs and the objects which they designate.

(2) The division of signs into Semantics, Syntactics, and Pragmatics was initiated by Charles Morris (*q.v.* 2). In this respect he has been followed by Carnap (*q.v.* 6) and Tarski (*q.v.* 1). In this context Semantics is understood to deal with problems of truth, denotation, meaning, naming, synonymy, etc. Also *q.v.* Meta-

language (4); Richard Montague (2).

(3) Chwistek (*q.v.*) applied the term "semantics" to the study of logical syntax, which he called "rational meta-mathematics," thus providing an alternate use of the term, identifying it with the more formal aspects of the study of syntactics.

(4) Quine (*q.v.* 2) divides Semantics into two parts: the theory of meaning and the theory of reference. Theory of meaning deals with meaning, synonymy, and analyticity. Theory of reference concerns the problems of naming, truth, and denotation.

C. More recently, the study of linguistics has influenced the philosophical study of Semantics, and even incorporated the study, regarding Semantics as an integral part of linguistics.

(5) Although the Bloomfieldians (*q.v.* Leonard Bloomfield, *Language*, 1933) had separated the problem of meaning from linguistics, thus leaving the field of Semantics to philosophers, the separation did not endure. The *Semantic Analysis* (1960) of Paul Ziff relates very closely to the methods of Zelig Harris, one of Bloomfield's students. (Also *q.v.* Ziff's *Understanding Understanding*, 1972.)

(6) Noam Chomsky (*q.v.* 1, 4) insists that Semantics is an integral part of grammatical analysis, and that the meaning of sentences should be given the same kind of attention as that given their syntactic structures. Involved in this is the distinction between the deep and surface structures of a language.

(7) Among Chomsky's followers, Jerrold Katz and Jerry Fodor (*The Structure of Language*, 1964) agree that the semantic theory of a language is part of its linguistic description. A topical heading claims that "linguistic description minus grammar equals semantics." For them Semantics takes over the explanation of the projection problem, that is, the explanation of how a speaker is able "to produce and understand infinitely many new sentences," where grammar "leaves off." Thus, Semantics deals with the human ability to interpret sentences, along with the properties and relations involved in such interpretation. *Q.v.* Fodor.

D. Currently, discussions include emphases relating to both B. and C. above.

(8) Centering in the "possible worlds"

semantics of such thinkers as Hintikka (*q.v.* 1–2) and Kripke (*q.v.* 1–2), this alternative adds to linguistics the concerns of modal logic (*q.v.*) producing a semantics in which statements of differing modalities will be true in no, some, or all possible worlds. Also, *q.v.* Semiotic.

SEMANTIC THEORY.

Q.v. Davidson (5–7).

SEMI-ARIANISM.

The doctrine that the Son is like, *homoiousian* (*q.v.*) with, the Father; and neither different from (*heteroousian*), as Arianism (*q.v.*) maintained, nor identical (*homoousian*) with the Father as decreed by the Council of Nicaea (*q.v.*).

SEMINAL REASONS.

From the Latin *rationes seminales*, a translation of the Greek *logos spermatikos*. Applied to the active powers of nature and interpreted as forces present in matter through which natural effects occur, the concept had its origin among the Stoics, was adopted by Augustine, and made its way into the doctrines of creation of Bonaventure (*q.v.* 9) and Thomas Aquinas.

SEMIOLOGY.

Q.v. Semiotic (8); Structuralism (1, 5).

SEMIOTIC.

From the Greek *semeiotikos*, (from *semeion* meaning "mark" or "sign") signifying "theory of signs."

(1) The term was used among the Greeks in a variety of ways: among musicians to refer to musical notations; among doctors to refer to signs of disease. Philodemus of Gadara had it refer to probabilistic logic as the "inference of a sign."

(2) In the Middle Ages the *scientia sermocinalis*, or "science of discourse" (from *sermo* meaning "discourse" or "expression"), a virtual translation of the Greek term, viewed logic (*q.v.* 6) as a study of linguistic entities.

(3) Hobbes (*q.v.* 4) stated that names or marks become signs when "disposed and ordered in speech."

(4) From the 16th through the mid-19th centuries physicians employed "semeiotic" and "semeiology" to refer to the symptoms of disease, thus reviving one of the Greek usages.

(5) In his famous *Essay* (4.21.3) Locke (*q.v.*) included both linguistics and logic under "*semeiotike*, or the doctrine of signs."

(6) Lady Victoria Welby (*What is Meaning?*, 1903) used the term "significs," or theory of significations, to refer to the study of the different elements contributing to the meaning of a word.

(7) Peirce (*q.v.* 16), now recognized as founding the modern study of semiotic, used the term frequently from 1865 on, at times spelling it "semeiotic" or "semeotic." He characterized logic "in its general sense" as "semiotic, the quasi-necessary, or formal, doctrine of signs," dividing the subject into pure grammar, logic proper, and pure rhetoric.

(8) De Saussure (*q.v.* 1–2) described the discipline in 1893/94 as Semiology. He distinguished between *signifié* and *signifiant*, between *parole* and *langue*, extending the field to include nonlinguistic modes of communication.

(9) Jakob von Uexküll (*The Organism and the Environment*, 1931) employed the triad of meaning-utilizer, meaning-carrier, and the code which links the other two to extend semiotic to biological processes. Even cells are meaning-utilizers, as are assemblies of cells (plants and animals), of the meaning-carriers in their environment.

(10) Charles Morris (*q.v.* 2) divided semiotic into syntactics, semantics (*q.v.*), and pragmatics. The division, reminiscent of Peirce, is widely accepted, as by Carnap (*q.v.* 7). Morris also distinguished between pure and descriptive semiotic, the former relating to the analysis of signs, and the latter to a study of existent signs.

(11) Structuralism (*q.v.*) can be viewed as the extension of de Saussure's Semiology to areas outside language: Levi-Strauss (*q.v.* 3) to marriage and kinship systems; Althusser to economics; Barthes (*q.v.* 2) whose *Elements of Semiology* applies beyond language to all systems of signs; Foucault (*q.v.*) to social institutions.

(12) Deconstruction (*q.v.*), likewise extends the study of signs beyond linguistics into philosophy, literature, and finally, Derrida (*q.v.* 10) states there is nothing outside the text.

(13) T.A. Sebeok (*Perspectives in Zoosemiotics*, 1972; *The Sign and its Masters*, with E. Brady, 1979) understands *semiosis* to be the principle of organization for all life. He distinguished between endosemiotic sign-processes (occurring internally) and exosemiotic processes (involving the organism and its environment), the boundary between the two virtually disappearing in sleep. Zoosemiotics studies the semiotic processes we share with other animals.

Also, *q.v.* Semantics.

SEMI-PELAGIANISM.

A doctrine widely held in 5th-and 6th-century Gaulist monasteries to the effect that man requires special divine help in overcoming original sin, that this help is available, but that man must take the first step. Condemned in 529 A.D.

SENECA, LUCIUS ANNEUS. 3–65.

Roman philosopher. Born in Córdoba, Spain. Educated by Stoic philosophers. The chief Stoic figure of the imperial period, Seneca—after having reached the position of Quaestor—was banished by Claudius. Recalled after eight years, he was named Praetor and became tutor to the young Nero. When Nero acceded to power Seneca became Consul and was for a number of years one of the most powerful men in Rome. Accused of involvement in a conspiracy against Nero, he committed suicide at his master's order.

Principal writings: *Physical Investigations* (T); *Satire on the Death of Claudius* (T); *Twelve Dialogues* (T); *Letters to Lucilius* (T).

(1) The satire on Claudius is an example of Menippean satire (*q.v.* Menippus of Gadara), mingling prose and verse.

(2) Centering his philosophy on questions of conduct, Seneca added to the popular flavor of his writing by typically addressing a single person in an informal style. His message was the Stoic preachment mixed with overtones having a similarity to Christian morality. We are to follow virtue, distrust the emotions, and overcome evil with good. Since all men are brothers, we are to practice universal benevolence.

SENG-CHAO. 374–414.

Chinese Buddhist philosopher. Studied under Kumarajiva, and helped with his translations. He held to the Middle Doctrine school of Nagarjuna, introduced to China by his teacher. Hence, he represented the Madhyamika school of Mahayana Buddhism, known in China as San-Lun.

Principal writings: *Seng-chao's Treatises* (T).

(1) The ordinary beliefs of men concerning the motion and change of things, and that all things are in flux, are untrue. Things seem to move, but are really at rest. Things seem to go away, but really remain. In fact, they are immutable, and time is illusory.

(2) The nature of things is vacuous; and the nature of nonexistence is not absolutely vacuous, thus existence and nonexistence, things and "not things" have the same meaning and come to the same thing.

(3) What is true of things is true also of the mind. The sage will hence harmonize his mind with the supreme vacuity, and in the midst of the thousand transformations will there sense the way.

SENSATION.

From the Latin *sentire* ("to perceive or feel"). Although usage varies, "sensation" usually is tied more closely to external stimulus than is the term "perception" (*q.v.*).

(1) Democritus (*q.v.* 10) interpreted sensation as the receipt of images of objects.

(2) Aristotle (*q.v.* 2a) interpreted the same phenomenon as the modification of a sensible subject by a substance.

(3) The Cambridge Platonist, John Smith (*q.v.*), held there were "spiritual sensations" which lead one to the truth about God.

(4) For Kant (*q.v.* 11a) a sensation is the content of sensuous intuition grasped by the faculty of sensibility.

(5) Although a long tradition beginning with Parmenides (*q.v.*) has held that sense-experience is illusory, a contrary tradition—sometimes called Sensationalism (*q.v.*)—has held such experience to constitute the sole locus of knowledge. One of these, Mach (*q.v.* 6), regarded the world as consisting of our sensations.

(6) Plekhanov (*q.v.* 3) held a "hieroglyphic theory of sensations." The doctrine is that sensations do not reproduce, but rather symbolize, reality.

(7) Taking the approach of Genetic Psychology, Ward (*q.v.* 1) distinguished three phases in the passage from sensation to idea.

(8) The outcome of sensing has been held by some to be the sense-datum (*q.v.*) or *sensum* (*q.v.*). Others, from James (*q.v.* 11) to Austin (*q.v.* 4), have disputed the claim. Chisholm (*q.v.* 3) substituted for sense-data an adverbial theory of sensing.

(9) Hartshorne (*q.v.* 2) holds sensations to be "feelings of feelings," and thus qualitative at their sources.

SENSATIONALISM.

A term sometimes used in the history of philosophy to designate those who hold that all knowledge has its origin in sensation. The term, when used, differs from the more usual term, "empiricism," simply in the stringency of its interpretation. Hobbes (*q.v.*), Hume (*q.v.*), Condillac (*q.v.*), John Stuart Mill (*q.v.*), and Mach (*q.v.*) are classed among the Sensationalists by those who favor the term.

SENSE.

Q.v. Frege (4, 6–7); Dummet (2).

SENSE AND REFERENCE.

Q.v. Dummet (2).

SENSE-DATUM.

A term referring to that which is immediately given in awareness. The plural is sense-data.

(1) Introduced to philosophy by G.E. Moore (*q.v.* 3–4), the term was adopted by Russell (*q.v.* 6–9) and modified by Broad (*q.v.* 4) into *sensum* (plural *sensa*). R.W. Sellars (*q.v.* 2) and H.H. Price (*q.v.* 1–3) among others, used the concept of sense-data in their analyses of perception.

(2) Those who stress the relevance of sense-data are sometimes referred to as Sense-Datum Theorists, and their view as the Sense-Datum Theory. Among the Sense-Datum Theorists one would include Locke (*q.v.* 1–2, 6) as well as those mentioned above. Also *q.v.* Representative Realism, and Realism (3).

(3) Among those who have argued against the sense-datum theory, one may mention James (*q.v.* 11), Ryle (*q.v.* 2–3), and Austin (*q.v.* 4).

(4) Ayer (*q.v.* 7) regards philosophical analysis as the translation of sentences about material objects into a sense-datum language.

SENSIBILIA.

Q.v. Russell (7); Austin (4).

SENSIBLE FORM.

Q.v. Form (5d).

SENSORIUM.

Latin translation of the Greek *aistheterion*, from *aisthesis* ("perception by the senses").

(1) Both the Greek and Latin terms were used to refer to whatever was regarded as the organ in man where sensations came together in forming the representation of an object.

(2) Newton (*q.v.* 6) referred to space as the "divine sensorium."

SENSUM.

Plural "*sensa.*" Terms referring to the immediately given in awareness. The term was introduced by C.D. Broad (*q.v.* 3). Also *q.v.* Sense-datum; Sellars, R.W. (2).

SENSUS EXTERNUS.

Q.v. Herbert of Cherbury (2c).

SENSUS INTERNUS.

Q.v. Herbert of Cherbury (2b).

SENTENCES.

For the famous *Four Books of Sentences* *q.v.* Peter Lombard.

SEPARATION OF POWERS.

(1) The separation of powers into legislative, executive, and judicial, made concrete in the American Constitution, was recommended by Montaigne (*q.v.*).

(2) Rousseau (*q.v.* 5f), writing in a somewhat different context, held that there was no possible separation of powers, since all power came from the people in a contingent grant to every official.

SERIAL RELATIONS.

Q.v. Logic of Relations (16).

SERMO.

Latin term used by Abelard (*q.v.* 3) to refer to the logical content of a word.

SERVETUS, MICHAEL. 1511–1553.

Spanish theologian. Born in Navarre. Studied at Zaragoza, Toulouse, and Paris. His interest was first in law and then in medicine which he practiced off and on throughout his life. He knew Melanchthon, Luther, and Calvin. The latter attempted in Paris to talk him out of his heresies. Failing in this he connived at Servetus' destruction. First convicted in a Catholic court at Lyons, Servetus escaped, but while passing through Geneva he was recognized and arrested. With Calvin's approval he was convicted of heresy once again and burned at the stake.

Principal writings: *On the Errors of the Trinity* (T), 1531; *On the Trinity* (T), 1532; *The Restitution of Christianity*, 1553.

(1) Departing from the accepted doctrine of the Trinity, Servetus held the Son and Holy Spirit to be not persons but, rather, manifestations of the Father. And the manner in which these manifestations proceed from the Father explains both creation and the pattern of history.

(2) He argued for free will, rejecting the Protestant doctrine of predestination. He opposed Catholic and Protestant alike for using force in matters of conscience. Finally, he rejected the doctrine of immortality, believing rather in the doctrine of the resurrection.

SET THEORY.

The theory of sets was initiated by Cantor (*q.v.* 1–7), and stands at the interface of logic and mathematics. The discipline has moved through many controversies whose locus has been centered in the logical paradoxes (*q.v.* 5–6) concerning sets which are and at the same time are not members of themselves. One solution is that of axiomatic set theory (*q.v.* 9–11 below).

A. The standard elements, characterizing virtually all descriptions of set theory, are the following:

(1) The recognition of a membership relation, "∈," to denote membership in a set. That is to say "∈" is identified with that sense of the verb "to be" which expresses membership in a set or class. When one says "Socrates is a philosopher," the sense is that "Socrates ∈ the set of philosophers."

(2) The recognition of an inclusion relation, often expressed by "⊆," *e.g.*, "philosophers ⊆ human beings," or "The set or class of philosophers is included in the set or class of human beings."

(3) The recognition of an identity relation, "="; *e.g.*, "Sir Walter Scott = the author of Waverley."

(4) The use of negation, often expressed by a slash "/" over a symbol. Thus "∉" means "is not a member of," and "≠" is the sign of inequality.

(5) The recognition of the relation "proper subset," often expressed by "⊂." Set "A" is a proper subset of set "B" when A ⊂ B, and A ≠ B. In fact, since the set of philosophers is not identical to the set of human beings, the sentence in (2) above is more properly written "philosophers ⊂ human beings."

(6) The recognition of the empty set, often expressed by "∧." It is a property of "∧" that, given anything whatever, that thing is not a member of "∧", *i.e.*, (x) [x ∉ ∧].

(7) The use of a symbol, usually "∨," to refer to all of the individuals under discussion, *i.e.*, to all of the subsets of a certain set. The symbol stands for the domain of discourse. In the sentence, "Philosophers are human beings," the domain of discourse consists of all the individuals or subsets making up the set of human beings.

(8) The use of the notions of "union," or "sum" expressed by "∪," and "join," "intersect," or "product," expressed by "∩" (*q.v.* the Logic of Relations 4). "A ∪ B," for example, is the set of all positive integers if "A" is the set of all positive even integers, and if "B" is the set of all positive odd integers. Since all positive integers are either odd or even, "A ∩ B" is in this example the empty set.

B. Given the above, plus the notations and transformations of elementary logic (and notations for "similarity," "precedence," etc.), it is possible to develop axiom systems for the theory of sets.

(9) Zermelo (*q.v.* 1–5) initiated axiomatic set theory, introducing seven axioms—including the Axiom of Choice—from which the theory can be deduced. The paradoxes of sets which are and are not members of themselves are avoided by restricting the admissible sets.

(10) The Lowenheim-Skolem contribution to set theory consists in the proof that if the axioms of set theory are consistent they are also valid, but that set-theoretic relativism is unavoidable, *i.e.*, the notion of sets as absolute in Cantor's

sense must be dropped (*q.v.* Lowenheim-Skolem Proofs).

(11) John Von Neumann avoided the paradoxes of sets which are and are not members of themselves by distinguishing between the kinds of sets which can, and those which cannot, be members of other sets.

(12) Paul Bernays produced an axiomatic set theory which assimilated Von Neumann's approach to that of Zermelo.

SEVEN DEADLY SINS.

Q.v. Sin (1).

THE SEVEN EARLY CHINESE BUDDHIST SCHOOLS. 3rd to 7th cent.

In the century following Buddhism's entry into China it came into close contact with neo-Taoism. As a result there developed seven schools of Buddhism influenced by Taoism, and for several centuries Chinese philosophy was dominated by Buddhism. The schools turned on the doctrines of being and non-being. The first school to be mentioned developed in the north, while all the others were in the south.

(1) Tao-an (312–385) advanced a doctrine of original non-being, which is pure being. Non-being exists behind the myriad things, existed first, and all else is derivative from it. One's mind must find its abode in non-being, understanding the emptiness of the nature of things.

(2) Fa-shen (286–374) represents the variant school of original non-being. First there was non-being, and now there is being. It is only in this sense that being came out of non-being. Although being succeeded non-being, in Fa-shen's version existent things are not empty.

(3) Third, there is the school claiming that matter as it is is empty, since it has no self-nature, existing through external causes and conditions. Chih Tao-lin, (314–366) holds that matter is empty but real, though conditionally so.

(4) Fa-wen, 4th century, taught the non-being of the mind, while recognizing the non-emptiness of the objective sphere of myriad things.

(5) Yü Fa-k'ai, 4th century, held that the consciousness is the function of the spirit. The mind is the basis of a great dream. On awakening to the spirit, we shall be aware of the illusory nature of the dream's content.

(6) Tao-i, 4th and 5th century, held to the illusory nature of all *dharmas* (elements of existence) of worldly truth.

(7) Yü Tao-sui held the absolute truth to be that *dharmas* result from combinations of causes, and as such are worldly truth; but as the causes dissipate the *dharmas* cease to exist.

SEVEN GIFTS OF THE HOLY SPIRIT.

In Scholastic thought, the gifts of wisdom, understanding, counsel, fortitude, knowledge, piety and the fear of the Lord.

SEVERUS. 2nd cent. A.D.

A monistic Platonist whose point of view stressed the world soul as the deity to whom one attributes the totality of what is. There is, however, a hierarchy of realities of different degrees of abstraction between the individual and the divine. The world as divine is thus uncreated, although each particular instance of the world is a result of a creative act.

SEXTUS EMPIRICUS. 2nd and 3rd cents.

Graeco-Roman philosopher. Born in Greece. Lived in Alexandria and Rome. One of the principle sources for our knowledge of Greek philosophy, he is generally regarded as a Skeptical philosopher, although he preferred the adjective "methodical." In the course of defending Pyrrho and the other Skeptics, he gave the positions and arguments of their opponents as well.

Principal writings: *Pyrrhonic Sketches*; *Against the Dogmatists*; *Against the Professors*; *On the Soul* (not extant).

(1) Even though all knowledge must be credited to sense experience, it is impossible to determine when our sense experience is accurate. We are aware of the distortions given to our experience in illusions, dreams, drunkenness, and illness. We are aware, too, of the variability of our experience from one moment to the next. It is impossible for us to eliminate the possibility that distortion occurs also in so-called normal experience.

(2) Furthermore, if we use reason to judge, correct, and validate our sense experience, then we shall need further reason to validate and judge the initial set

of reasons, and this is a vicious regress.

(3) He presented a set of arguments called "tropes." The first trope addresses itself to the syllogism. He argues that the syllogism is circular, since the conclusion is already implicit in the major premise: *i.e.*, "Socrates is mortal" is implicit in the premise, "All men are mortal."

(4) The second trope, concerning causality, argues that if causality is a relation it is subjective; and that there are reasons for denying that the cause precedes, occurs at the same time as, or succeeds the effect.

(5) The third trope concerns God: the impossibility of God's being either finite or infinite (since the former doesn't fit the definition and the latter—*i.e.*, the conception of a being with an infinite number of infinite properties—is inconsistent); and the incompatibility of his perfection in the light of the evil of the world.

SHADOW.

Q.v. Jung (5).

SHAFTESBURY, EARL OF. 1671–1713.

English philosopher. Born in London. Educated privately. Served three years as an elected member of Parliament, retiring for reasons of health. Born as Anthony Ashley Cooper, he succeeded to the earldom of Shaftesbury in 1699, after which he served as a member of the House of Lords. Influenced by the views of Locke, and strongly opposed to those of Hobbes.

Principal writings: *Characteristics of Men, Manners, Opinions, Times*, 3 vols., 1711.

(1) Regarded as the initiator of the Moral Sense theory of ethics, it is Shaftesbury's view that we are able to distinguish right and wrong by a distinctive moral sense which works in us as a special type of feeling-response. The sensing of virtue in actions is comparable to sensing beauty in art, so that the test of a proposed action is whether it contributes to the general harmony of mankind, which he construes as the general welfare.

(2) Beauty is interpreted as a kind of harmony. He mentions the sense of harmony in music and the sense of proportion in architecture.

(3) There is in man a natural sympathy leading to benevolence, social interest, and commitment to the public good. On the basis of this analysis Shaftesbury argues against Hobbes' view (*q.v.* 7) that man's sole motivation is that of self-interest. In the perfection of human nature the two motives—that of self-interest and the social interest—will work together in perfect adjustment.

(4) Since morality has its base in human nature it is not unexpected to find Shaftesbury opposed to the attempt to derive morality from supernatural sanctions. Although the morally odious cannot be religiously respectable, it does not follow either that religion is dependent on morality or morality upon religion. The two are independent, but God—a Being of universal benevolence who implanted in man his moral sense—relates to both areas.

SHAKESPEARE, WILLIAM.

Q.v. Tragedy (2).

SHAMAN.

From the Tunguso-Manchurian word *saman*, "he who knows." Religious leader in many hunting and gathering societies. Although vestiges of shamanism are to be found in many parts of the world, *e.g.*, in the Americas, southeast India, Australia, central Asia, its concentrated expression is to be found among the peoples of northern Asia. The shaman is able to communicate directly with the spirits of the other world and to be assisted by them. His help is needed in all of the transcendent experiences of life. The shaman's communication with the spirits often occurs through possession or wandering ecstasy. In the former case the shaman is possessed by a spirit who speaks through him. In the latter case the spirit of the shaman is thought to leave his body, journeying to the other world.

SHAMANISM.

Any religion centered in the person of the shaman (*q.v.*).

SHANG YANG. 4th cent. B.C.

Chinese philosopher. The Chinese Machiavelli, Shang Yang was motivated to write by the pluralistic power structure of the China of his time. As in the case of Machiavelli, Shang Yang's writings had political consequences. The state of Ch'in began to follow his precepts, and its king in 221 became the "First Emperor" of China. For a generation, it is said, "universal" peace prevailed. Shang Yang was founder of the school known as *Fa Chia*, or the Legalist School (*q.v.*).

Principal writings: *The Book of Lord Shang* (T) may be his although its authenticity is in dispute.

(1) It is the function of the leader to make his people single-minded so that they can be governed more easily.

(2) Ten pursuits in the state militate against such single-mindedness: odes and history, rites and music, virtue and the cultivation thereof, benevolence and integrity, sophistry and intelligence. Debates with high-sounding words are especially to be avoided.

(3) But "punishment produces force, force produces strength, strength produces awe, awe produces virtue, virtue has its origin in punishments." Let the ruler, then, be strong and unbending, and the state will follow, the character of the state following from the character of the monarch.

(4) He must also encourage the appropriate people by offering office and rank; and make his country prosperous through agriculture and war.

SHANKARA.

Q.v. Śankara.

SHAO YUNG. 1011–1077.

Chinese philosopher. He lived in In-Yang. A neo-Confucianist, he received his training from a Taoist. A friend to prominent scholars, officials, and philosophers, he served for a time as keeper of records in the Board of Public Works and as a militia judge.

Principal writings: *Supreme Principles Governing the World* (T in part).

(1) Like neo-Confucianists generally, Shao traces the development of the multiplicity of things from the Great Ultimate through the actions of *Yin* and *Yang*, which are produced by the Great Ultimate without itself engaging in activity.

(2) Unlike the others, he employed the idea of number in his explanation of this development. Every aspect of the universe can be derived by number and is associated with number. In the histori-

cally important *Book of Changes* are 64 hexagrams, and Shao took 4 as the basic number. Thus he needed to educe 16 sets of 4's to reach the critical number of 64 in his philosophy. The scheme gives an appearance of mechanical artificiality, but on the other hand it also stresses development and dynamism, since a progression is sketched, powered by the principles of *Yin* and *Yang* in phases of alternating expansion and contraction.

(3) Shao also formulated a philosophy of history. Combining his theory of numbers with the idea of cycles he presented history as an infinite series of cycles, each cycle extending for 129,800 years and, through *Yin* and *Yang*, having its appropriate periods of growth or expansion, and decay or contraction.

SHAW, GEORGE BERNARD. 1856–1950.

Q.v. Socialism (7).

SHEFFER, H.M. 1883–1964.

American philosopher. Born in Russia. Educated at Harvard where he also taught. He specialized in the foundations of logic and mathematics.

Principal writings: "A Set of Five Independent Postulates for Boolean Algebras," 1913.

(1) Peirce had shown in 1880 how all of the Boolean structure could be expressed by means of a single primitive sign meaning "neither. . . nor." Sheffer rediscovered this insight and provided a stroke function to express it: "a | b" meaning "neither a nor b."

(2) Using the Sheffer stroke function, the postulates for the revised Boolean Algebra become the following:

(a) There are at least two distinct elements.

(b) a | b is an element for all elements a and b.

(c) (a | a) | (a | a) = a for every element a whose combinations here mentioned are also elements.

(d) a | [b | (b | b)] |= a | a for all elements a and b whose combinations here mentioned are also elements.

(e) [a | (b | c)]|[a | (b | c)] = [(b | b) | a] | [(c | c) | a] for all elements a, b, and c whose combinations here mentioned are also elements.

(3) Whitehead and Russell had constructed their logic on two primitive

ideas, negation (*q.v.* 3) and disjunction (*q.v.*). Sheffer demonstrated that p|q (neither p nor q) expresses the meaning of ~ (p∨q); p|p expresses the sense of ~ p; and (p|q)|(p|q) does the same for (p∨q). It follows that the primitive ideas of *Principia Mathematica* (*q.v.*) can be derived from the stroke function, whose single primitive idea Sheffer termed "rejection." It follows, further, that all logic can be developed from the single primitive idea contained in the Sheffer stroke function.

SHEKHINAH.
A Hebrew term meaning "dwelling." The term refers to God's dwelling with, or presence to, the Hebrew people, allowing reference to divine immanence without anthropomorphism. Also reverential substitute for the divine name. Sometimes described as a bright radiance, perhaps from Gen. 40:34.
(1) In the Targums (1st–4th cents. Aramaic translations of the Hebrew Bible), *shekhinah* replaces corporeal manifestations of God: "My *shekhinah* dwells among them" (not "I dwell among them," Nm. 5:3); "You cannot see the face of my *shekhinah*: (not "You cannot see my face . . . ," Ex. 33:20).
(2) In the *Babylonian Talmud* the *shekhinah* is said to have been in the cloud that led the Israelites, and the Tabernacle erected, in the desert; on Mt. Sinai; with Moses throughout his life; resting upon the prophets who spoke by "the holy spirit"; in Solomon's temple; intermittently in the Second Temple; after its destruction, in major synagogues; wherever a quorum of 10 men (a *minyan*) has gathered in prayer; wherever the Jewish people may be (even in exile), and when they are redeemed; finally, everywhere.
(3) In the Zohar (*q.v.* Cabala 2d) the 10th emanation of the *En-sof*, a feminine image which, in conjunction with the 9th emanation, a male image, introduced sexuality into the divine economy.

SHELDON, W.H.
Q.v. Principle of Polarity (4).

SHEN-HSIU. 605–706.
Early leader of Zen Buddhism (*q.v.* 3).

SHESTOV, LEON. 1866–1938.
Russian philosopher. Born in Kiev. Studied at Moscow. Left Russia in 1922,

living first in Berlin and then in Paris. An opponent of rationalism in philosophy, Shestov's view is reminiscent of Kierkegaard.
Principal writings: *Dostoevski and Nietzsche: The Philosophy of Tragedy* (T), 1903; *The Apotheosis of Groundlessness* (T), 1905; *In Job's Balances* (T), 1929; *Athens and Jerusalem* (T), 1936; *Kierkegaard and Existentialist Philosophy* (T), 1939.

SHEVIRAH.
Q.v. Isaac Luria (2–3).

SHIA (SHIITE).
Arabic for "party" or "following." The term was applied to the sects of Islam (*q.v.* 4, 5, 7) for whom Ali was the leader, or Imam, directly following Mohammed. The great majority of Shiites belong to the Twelver *Shia*, adhering to a succession of twelve Imams, the last of whom (the hidden Imam) will one day appear, leading Islam to world domination and a just social order.

SHIN BUDDHISM.
Q.v. Suzuki (2); Mahayana Buddhism (7).

SHINTO.
Japanese transliteration of two ideograms meaning "the way of the gods." The term refers to the set of religious practices, relating to local shrines, and directed to indigenous Japanese deities. The history of Shinto goes back to the 6th century A.D. The religion divides into state Shinto and sectarian Shinto with thousands of shrines, and a membership consisting technically of the entire Japanese population.

SHIVA.
Q.v. Śiva (Shiva).

SHUNYAVADA.
Q.v. Śunyavada (Shunyavada).

SIDGWICK, HENRY. 1838–1900.
English philosopher. Born in Skipton, Yorkshire. Educated at Cambridge where he also taught. One of the founders of the Society for Psychical Research, he is best known for his work in the field of ethics.
Principle writings: *Methods of Ethics*, 1874; *Outline of the History of Ethics*, 1879; *Principles of Political Economy*, 1883; *The*

Scope and Method of Economic Science, 1885; *The Elements of Politics,* 1891; *Practical Ethics,* 1898; *Lectures on the Ethics of Green, Spencer and Martineau* (ed. Jones), 1902; *Philosophy, Its Scope and Relations* (ed. J. Ward), 1902; *The Philosophy of Kant and Other Lectures* (ed. J. Ward), 1905.

(1) Dividing philosophy into theoretical and practical parts, he held the former to concern the unification of scientific knowledge, and the latter to concern the unification of moral knowledge.

(2) Moral knowledge relates to the commonsense world; and analysis of commonsense reveals three approaches to ethics: (a) *Intuitionism,* which holds excellence to be man's goal, building up the notion from the self-evident principles of benevolence, prudence, and justice; (b) *Egoism,* which holds personal happiness to be the goal; (c) *Utilitarianism,* defining man's end as the production of the greater good.

(3) Although the three approaches are in some ways interrelated—the goals of intuitionism and utilitarianism, for example, are harmonious and reinforce each other—they resist incorporation into a single point of view. Were the evidence for theism stronger, such unity would be possible since in that case divine judgment, balancing merit and desert, would bring individual happiness into correlation with excellence and the production of good.

(4) His position, self-styled as Utilitarianism, rejected all attempts to rest Utilitarianism on a strictly empirical base and to define ethical concepts in terms of pleasure. Basing it, instead, on the three self-evident principles named above, his position is sometimes termed Intuitive or Theoretical Utilitarianism.

"SI FALLOR, SUM."

Latin phrase meaning "If I am deceived, I exist." The refutation of skepticism offered by St. Augustine (*q.v.* 4).

SIGER OF BRABANT. c. 1235–c. 1284.

13th-century French philosopher. Taught at the University of Paris. A Scholastic philosopher who interpreted Aristotle according to Averroës, Siger's doctrines that the active intellect is a common principle (ruling out personal immortality), that God does not know the future (so far as it is contingent), and that free will presupposes chance, led to his censure by papal legates and finally to a summons on a charge of heresy. Fleeing France, the record of his life and early death—allegedly by murder or suicide remains obscure.

Principle writings: *On the Intellective Soul; Logical Questions; Natural Questions; On the Eternity of the World; Impossibilities.*

SIGER OF COURTRAI. 14th cent.

Scholastic philosopher. Taught at the University of Paris. A logician, Siger studied fallacies, sophisms, and the modes of signification.

Principal writings: *Fallaciae; Sophismata; A Summa of the Modes of Signification;* as well as a commentary on Aristotle's *Prior Analytics.*

SIGN.

From the Latin *signum* and the Greek *semeion,* originally meaning a verbal signal. The theory of signs is usually called Semiotic (*q.v.*), and is discussed under that heading. We add here only a few items of supplementary material. Also *q.v.* Symbol.

(1) William of Ockham (*q.v.* 4) distinguished between conventional signs, the individual words spoken or written; and natural signs, those whose meanings relate to the effects of objects on us.

(2) This distinction was also used by Reid (*q.v.* 2) who distinguished between natural and artificial signs.

(3) Condillac (*q.v.* 4), divided signs into accidental, natural, and conventional types.

(4) Peirce (*q.v.* 16) divided signs into three basic classes (and many more subclasses): *icons,* which bear their meaning characteristics with them; *indices,* which call attention; and *symbols,* which have an agreed-upon connotation.

(5) Chang Tung-Sun (*q.v.* 3) held to the idea of a progression from sign to symbol.

(6) Langer (*q.v.* 2) distinguished between signs and symbols somewhat in the manner of Peirce but without his division of signs.

SIGNATE MATTER.

Q.v. Aquinas (6); Matter (5).

SIGNIFIANT.
Q.v. de Saussure (2).

SIGNIFICATIO.
Latin word for the meaning or signification of a term. Used by Peter of Spain (q.v. 2) and other Terminist logicians (q.v.) in contrast to the *suppositio* of, or specific individuals signified by, a term.

SIGNIFICATION.
Most often used as synonymous with "meaning," "connotation," or "intension." The signification, connotation, or intension of a term is thus correlative to the term's application, denotation, or extension. Proper names would, then, be without signification. In practice, both proper names and ostensively defined terms are said to signify that to which they refer. Q.v. C.I. Lewis (4b).

SIGNIFICS.
Q.v. Semiotic (6).

SIGNIFIÉ.
Q.v. de Saussure (2).

SIGNIFIER, AND SIGNIFIED.
Q.v. Différance; de Saussure (2); Lacan (5, 6); Barthes (2, 6); Derrida (1, 3, 5); Structuralism (1).

SIGWART, CHRISTOPH. 1830–1904.
German philosopher. Born and educated in Tübingen. Taught at Halle, Blaubeuren, and Tübingen. Regarding logic as a normative discipline charged with discovery of the rules of valid thought, Sigwart approached logic through a study of acts of judgment. Husserl found psychologistic tendencies in this approach.
Principal writings: *Logic* (T), 2 vols., first ed., 1873.

SIKHISM.
A reform movement within Hinduism (q.v. 5c), Sikhism began in India around 1500 A.D. The founder, and first leader or Guru, was Nanak. He was followed by nine other Gurus. The last declared that hereafter the sacred scripture of Sikhism, called *Adi Granth*, would serve as Guru. The religion is strictly monotheistic, rejecting idols and incarnations of the divine, while adhering to reincarnation. In addition to idolatry, the religion rejects caste, wine, tobacco, slander, hypocrisy, and pilgrimages. It requires loyalty, gratitude, philanthropy, justice, impartiality, truth, and honesty. Initially pacifistic, the movement for its own defense began to inculcate military virtues under the tenth Guru, Govind Singh.

SILA.
Q.v. Meditation (6).

SILVA, SEMUEL DA.
Q.v. Costa, Uriel da.

SIMMEL, GEORG. 1858–1918.
German philosopher. Born in Berlin. Taught in Berlin and Strassburg. Initially holding to a relativism in which truth is that which answers to the necessities of the individual or the species, and that each such truth is complete in its own terms, though partial, reflecting a single perspective, Simmel increasingly began to stress elements of permanence and objectivity in man's being. Interpreting life as flux and humans as impatient with their accomplishments, he emphasized the creative life as a necessary step in leading us to an adequate conception of the world (q.v. Neo-Kantianism 7). Regarded as one of the early sociologists, Simmel was interested in the relationship between the individual and culture, the latter consisting of science, history, art, religion, politics, and their institutions.
Principal writings: *Concerning Social Differentiation*, 1890; *Philosophy of Money*, 1900; *Kant*, 1903; *Religion* (T), 1906; *Sociology* (T in part), 1908; *Toward a Philosophy of Art*, 1922.

SIMON, HERBERT.
Q.v. Artificial Intelligence (3).

SIMON MAGUS.
By Christian tradition the founder of Gnosticism, Simon Magus (or Simon the Magician) is identified in *Acts* 8:5–24 as a converted wonder-worker from Samaria who attempted to purchase from the Apostles the gift of the Holy Ghost. Fairly or unfairly, the term "simony" derives from this Scriptural reference.

SIMON OF TOURNAI.
13th-century Scholastic philosopher. Taught at the University of Paris. Influenced by the Pseudo-Dionysius and

Erigena, Simon contrasted this tradition's "belief for the sake of understanding" with Aristotle's "understanding for the sake of belief."

Principal writings: *Sentences; Quaestiones quodlibetales; Summa; Disputations; On Theological Affirmations and Negations.*

SIMPLE CONSTRUCTIVE AND DESTRUCTIVE DILEMMAS.
Q.v. Dilemma.

SIMPLE ENUMERATION.
A term used by Francis Bacon (*q.v.* 2d) to characterize what he believed to be a fallacious inductive approach to knowledge practiced by Aristotle and the Scholastics. Bacon's "simple enumeration" appears to combine the fallacies of "false cause" and "hasty generalization" (*q.v.* Fallacies 12, 16).

SIMPLE LOCATION.
Q.v. Whitehead (6).

SIMPLE NATURES.
Q.v. Nature (7).

SIMPLICITY.
The contemporary equivalent of Ockham's Razor (*q.v.*) is the view held by philosophers of science that simplicity is one of the criteria determining the selection of the primitives or undefined predicates at the base of a conceptual system. Goodman (*q.v.* 3) is among those who have contributed to this discussion.

SIMPLICIUS. fl. 527–565.
Hellenic philosopher. Born in Cilicia. Studied with Ammonius of the Alexandrian School (*q.v.*) as well as with Damascius (*q.v.*) of the School of Athens (*q.v.*). A Neoplatonic philosopher and disciple of Damascus, he went with his teacher into Persian exile when Justin's edict closed the School in 529. An eclectic philosopher, he combined in his thought emphases of both the School of Athens and the Alexandrian School, while attempting to force a reconciliation of the systems of Plato and Aristotle, and assimilating the Stoic philosophy to Neoplatonism.

Principal writings: *Commentary on the Enchiridion of Epictetus; Commentaries* on Aristotle's works on the *Categories, Physics, On the Heavens,* and *On the Soul.*

SIMPLIFICATION.
Q.v. Propositional Calculus (9).

SIMULTANEITY.
Q.v. Einstein (2).

SIN.
From the Latin *peccare.* A religious term, the concept of sin is to be distinguished from that of moral wrong (*q.v.* Ethics). While the latter is committed against men, the former is a transgression against God.

(1) The source of sin in the Christian tradition is held to be *hybris* or pride, and concupiscence or lust. Both attitudes are interpreted as stemming from the failure to recognize the divine authority (*q.v.* St. Augustine 12). In addition to the above, five other sins make up the traditionally accepted list of capital, or deadly, sins. In the listing of Gregory the Great the seven deadly sins are pride, envy, anger, dejection, avarice, gluttony, and lust.

(2) A distinction is made between venial and mortal sins. The former are forgivable, while the latter are not. Mortal sins—idolatry, murder, and adultery—entail the loss of grace, and hence eternal punishment. Through the sacrament of penance, however, grace may be restored to the sinner.

(3) The concept of original sin (*peccatum originis*) entered Christian thought with the formula of the Apostle Paul (*q.v.* 3) that as in Adam all men have sinned, so in Christ they are saved. Origen (*q.v.* 1, 4), in an aberrant view, held this fall to have taken place before the creation of the world. Many views were advanced from different premises. As the orthodox interpretation developed, however, it came to hold that in original sin man lost an original gift of divine grace which "stains" his present natural endowment of rationality and freedom of will. The Protestant reformers, in concentrating on salvation by grace, found it necessary to insist upon a more radical doctrine of man's utter sinfulness (*q.v.* Jonathan Edwards 4).

SINCERITY.
An important Chinese virtue. *Q.v.* Doctrine of the Mean (4); The Great Learning (1); Final Value (3); Wang Yang-Ming (1). Compare Authenticity (*q.v.*).

SIRHAK.
Q.v. Tasan.

SITUATION ETHICS.
The position of Joseph Fletcher (*Situation Ethics*, 1966) that any action may be good or bad depending on the situation. What is wrong in most situations may sometimes be right if the end it serves is sufficiently good. Christian situationism turns on *agápe*, a love characterized by "thankfulness."

ŚIVA (SHIVA).
Sanskrit for "the mild or auspicious one," deriving, however, from the Vedic storm god Rudra ("the howling one," apparently from the sound of storms; alternatively, from the root *rud*, "be red" or "shine," allowing "auspicious" as a derivation). In *The Mahabharata* and *Puranas* the two gods are identified, and in the *Śvetaśvatara Upaniṣad* Rudra-Shiva appears as a monotheistic god. Even as one god Shiva retains the ambivalence of creation and destruction. He destroys Kama, the god of erotic love, with fire from his third eye; cuts off the 5th head of Brahma; inadvertently beheads his own son, Ganesha, then replaces the missing head with that of an elephant with a broken tusk. He is usually presented as an ascetic, living on a mountain in the Himalayas, his body smeared with ashes, his hair matted, wearing animal skins, a cobra, and an image of the crescent moon, accompanied by his wife Parvati and their two sons, the 6-faced Skanda and the elephant-headed Ganesha.
Shiva is the center of worship in the Shaiva sect of Hinduism (*q.v.* 5c and Vaiṣnavism 3). In the Hindu trinity he is the destroyer, while Brahma creates, and Vishnu preserves (*q.v.* Trinity, 17). In this context his wife is Kali, a destroyer goddess, who is worshipped as the terrible mother. Shiva's symbol is the linga or phallus; the bull is associated with his worship. He is also the god of mountains and of the overcoming of death. The contrasting ascriptions given to Shiva as destroyer and redeemer may relate to differences of tradition, the former originating in the north and the latter in the south of India.
Q.v. Vaiṣnavism (1, 3).

ŚIVA (SHIVA) YOGA.
Q.v. Yoga (7).

SKANDHAS.
A Sanskrit term for "heaps." In Buddhism five *skandhas* make up the heap of aggregates constituting a person, or any living being. They are *rupa* (the form or bodily shape factors), *vedana* (the sensation or feeling factors), *samjna* (perceptions, the perceptive factors), *samskara* (volitions, the volitional factor of consciousness), *vijnana* (conceptions, the thought factor of consciousness). The five aggregates are held together only roughly and separate out at death. *Q.v.* Buddha (5).

SKEPTICISM.
From the Greek *skepsis* ("consideration" or "doubt"). The view that reason has no capacity to come to any conclusions at all, or else that reason is capable of nothing beyond very modest results. The more extreme Skeptics are often called Pyrrhonists after Pyrrho (*q.v.*), the founder of the skeptical tradition (also *q.v.* Pyrrhonism). The term "moderate skepticism" is reserved for the less extreme version of the doctrine, and is used to characterize, for example, the members of the Second and Third Academies (*q.v.* Plato's Academy 2–3). The term, "pyrrhonism," is often applied even today to extreme skepticism, although usage is not altogether consistent.
(1) Pyrrho (*q.v.* 2) held that we must suspend all judgment, committing ourselves to a non-committal silence concerning everything.
(2) Less extreme than his teacher, Timon (*q.v.*) answered his opponents with satyric poems.
(3) Arcesilaus (*q.v.*), founder of the Second Academy, continued to moderate the position. A moderate skeptic, he was interested in developing the concept of probability.
(4) Founder of the Third Academy, Carneades (*q.v.*) continued the emphasis on probability while deploying skeptical arguments against, *e.g.*, God and causality in their most powerful form.
(5) Clitomachus (*q.v.*) was Carneades' student and succeeded him as head of the Academy.
(6) Aenesidemus (*q.v.*) revived the

more extreme views of Pyrrho, expressing his grounds for skepticism in ten tropes (*q.v.*).

(7) Cicero (*q.v.* 1) continued the tradition of moderate skepticism, as an eclectic philosopher subject to many influences.

(8) All of the above lived in the four centuries before Christ. In the 2nd and 3rd centuries A.D. other notable skeptics arose. Agrippa (*q.v.*) summarized the grounds for skepticism in five tropes, stressing the absence of a criterion.

(9) In the same period Sextus Empiricus (*q.v.* 2, 3–5) insisted upon the necessity for a criterion of the criterion, and summarized his skeptical arguments in three tropes. Since he reviewed the arguments of his predecessors, Sextus Empiricus' work is the source of most of our knowledge of skepticism.

(10) In the 4th century St. Augustine (*q.v.* 3–4) argued that skepticism is self-defeating since, if one is deceived, then one must exist in order to be deceived; "*Si fallor, sum*," or "If I am deceived, I exist."

(11) In the East, 7th or 8th cent. A.D., Jayarashi (*q.v.*) appeared in southern India as a member of the Lokayata (*q.v.*) school. His analysis of perception and inference led to the conclusion that nothing could be known.

(12) In the West, 15th century, 1000 years after Augustine, Pico della Mirandola (*q.v.*) followed Augustine's approach, using skepticism to lead man to the true religion.

(13) At the start of the 16th century Erasmus (*q.v.* 2) utilized skeptical arguments to support the doctrine of free will. The argument was that since the problem is beyond human determination, one must suspend judgment and follow the doctrines of the Church.

(14) In somewhat the same vein Agrippa von Nettesheim (*q.v.*) argued from the vanity of science to the necessity of faith.

(15) Montaigne (*q.v.* 2, 4), using the motto "What do I know?," returned to a self-conscious Pyrrhonism, suspending judgment on all matters. Yet the return is with a difference. Not only does he praise the simple, natural life, he also utilizes skepticism, as had his immediate predecessors, to make possible the life of faith.

(16) Mersenne (*q.v.* 1) held science to mark a middle way between skepticism and dogmatism, even though science deals only with the phenomenal world.

(17) Descartes (*q.v.* 1–2) took the same position as had St. Augustine, turning the point of skepticism by pushing it to its final limits. The first certainty is "*Cogito, ergo sum*." "I think, therefore I am."

(18) Gassendi (*q.v.* 5) raised the skeptical problem of a criterion for the criterion, applying this to Descartes' equation of truth with clear and distinct ideas.

(19) Pascal (*q.v.* 1–2, 4), influenced by Montaigne, regarded skepticism and dogmatism as the main divisions of philosophy. He held the only valid escape from uncertainty is in abasing one's reason and turning humbly to faith.

(20) Glanvill (*q.v.*) defended both skepticism and witchcraft.

(21) Bayle (*q.v.*) favored skepticism over tradition in the articles of his *Dictionary*; in effect, his destruction of the claims of reason led to the toleration of opposing viewpoints, and the minimal faith of the Enlightenment.

(22) Voltaire (*q.v.* 1) brought into clear focus the standpoint of the Enlightenment, combining skepticism concerning ultimate questions with toleration for alternate positions, and with moral activity intended to reform society.

(23) Hume (*q.v.* 1, 3–4, 7) built skepticism into his philosophical system. Our beliefs rest on probabilities which rest in turn on habit. The more minimal the religious belief, the more reasonable it is. At last it is only the demands of ordinary life which break, at least partially, the hold of skepticism.

(24) Kant (*q.v.* 1) admitted that Hume had roused him from his "dogmatic slumber." From this standpoint the entire Kantian philosophy as well as its neo-Kantian derivatives (*q.v.* neo-Kantianism) can be taken as an effort to answer skeptical arguments over the possibility of knowledge.

(25) Schulze (*q.v.*) was a Humean skeptic who opposed the Kantian philosophy.

(26) Clifford (*q.v.* 1) counselled that one withhold belief unless all evidence pointed in its direction. James (*q.v.* 4) countered this thrust with his doctrine of the "will to believe."

(27) Royce (*q.v.* 1b), somewhat in the manner of St. Augustine and Descartes, held the fact of skepticism to imply the existence of truth. In his language, it implied an "absolute truth."

(28) Santayana (*q.v.* 1–3) held that Descartes' skepticism was not sufficiently thorough-going; and that finally only through "animal faith" can we begin to postulate the existence of a world and of ourselves.

(29) Cavell (*q.v.* 3), following Wittgenstein (*q.v.* 8), thinks of the problem of skepticism as a consequence of insisting upon an inordinately scrupulous criterion for knowledge.

(30) In view of the concern of contemporary philosophy with epistemology, the scope of the skeptical challenge could be broadened to the point that virtually all contemporary philosophy is either skeptical, or concerned with answering the claims of skepticism. The historian of skepticism, Richard Popkin (*The History of Skepticism from Erasmus to Descartes*, 1960), makes some such claim. We have restricted our references to those who have related themselves to some part of the historical tradition of skepticism, or have used the term.

SKINNER, B.F. 1904–1990.
American psychologist. Born in Susquehanna, Penna. Educated at Hamilton College and Harvard. He taught at Minnesota, Indiana, and Harvard.
Principal writings: *The Behavior of Organisms*, 1938; *Walden Two*, 1948; *Science and Human Behavior*, 1953; *Verbal Behavior* (with C.B. Ferster), 1957; *The Analysis of Behavior*, 1961; *Contingencies of Reinforcement*, 1969; *Beyond Freedom and Dignity*, 1971; *About Behaviorism*, 1974; *Reflections on Behaviorism and Society*, 1978; *Upon Further Reflection*, 1987.

(1) Introducing "Operationalism" into psychology, or as he prefers to call it, "Operationism," Skinner continues and extends the tradition of Watsonian behaviorism. From the Skinner box, a learning environment with immediate reinforcement intended for white rats, to his vision of utopia in *Walden Two*, the emphasis is on operant behavior and instrumental conditioning, related to positive and negative reinforcements.

(2) From this perspective, emotion is a change in reflex strength, and the self a "functionally unified system of responses organized around a discriminative stimulus," or a "repertoire of behavior, appropriate to a given set of contingencies."

(3) Although in *Walden Two* these concepts are applied in the context of an isolated utopian community, in *Beyond Freedom and Dignity* they are applied more broadly to the design of culture. Beyond "freedom" and "dignity," concepts which presume the fiction of the "autonomous individual," the need is for explicit, intentional cultural and world design, employing a technology of behavior which will reinforce those who have been induced by their culture to work for its survival.

(4) Claiming that nonoperational explanations in psychology all introduce a *homunculus* (*q.v.*), or little man, into the brain, Skinner argues that it is the task of science to dehomunculize man, and that dehomunculization is not dehumanization.

SKOLEM, THORALF.
Q.v. Lowenheim-Skolem Proofs.

SKOVORODA, G.S.
Q.v. Russian Philosophy (1).

SLAVERY.
Where Aristotle (*q.v.* 12) maintained that those incapable of reasoning, but who understood commands, were natural slaves, Jefferson (*q.v.* 3) held that slavery is contrary to the law of nature.

SMART, J.J.C. 1920– .
Australian philosopher. Born in Cambridge, England. Educated at Glasgow and Oxford. Has taught at the University of Adelaide, La Trobe University, and Australian National University.
Principal writings: "Sensations and Brain Processes," 1959; *An Outline of a System of Utilitarian Ethics*, 1961 (republished with B. Williams' essay, "A Critique of Utilitarianism, as *Utilitarianism: For and Against*, 1973); *Philosophy and Scientific Realism*, 1963; *Between Science and Philosophy*, 1968; *Utilitarianism* (with B. Williams), 1973; *Ethics, Persuasion and Truth*, 1984; *Essays Metaphysical and Moral*, 1987; *Our Place in the Universe*, 1989.

(1) Stressing naturalism (*q.v.*), physicalism (*q.v.*), and extensionalism (*q.v.* Extension 2), Smart helped develop the

Identity Theory (*q.v.* 2) of mental and physical states. His initial identification of sensations with brain states was later extended to all mental phenomena.

(2) The identity theory is explicated in terms of a central-state materialism in which all things mental—pains, thoughts, sensations, after-images—are states of the central nervous system.

(3) Smart supposes that mental states will at first be characterized relationally, followed by scientific identification as "particular" cerebral processes.

(4) Personal identity is replaced by temporal stages exhibiting spatio-temporal continuity. When one reflects on sacrificing an earlier, to a later, stage of one's life, the considerations turn on maximizing utility, and connect with Utilitarianism (*q.v.*), his preferred approach to ethics.

(5) He takes the Utilitarian imperative as doing what will maximize expected utility, *i.e.*, the "sum of the products of the probabilities and the values of the various possible effects" of one's action.

(6) Secondary qualities are disjunctive and idiosyncratic qualities of physical things, and laws of nature are "cosmic coincidences."

(7) The statement of both laws of nature and counterfactuals belongs not to the object language, but to a metalanguage referring to the object language.

(8) Metaphysics is a search for the most plausible theory of the universe, and is continuous with science.

SMART, (RODERICK) NINIAN. 1927–. British philosopher. Born in Scotland. Educated at Oxford. Has taught at the University of Wales (Aberystwyth), University of London, University of Birmingham, University of Lancaster, University of California (Santa Barbara). He has taught in departments of philosophy and departments of religion, establishing at Lancaster the first department of religious studies in Great Britain.

Selected writings: *Reasons and Faiths,* 1958; *Doctrine and Argument in Indian Philosophy,* 1964; *Philosophers and Religious Truth,* 1964; *The Religious Experience,* 1969; *The Concept of Worship,* 1972; *The Phenomenon of Religion,* 1973; *The Phenomenon of Christianity,* 1979; *In Search of Christianity,* 1979; *Beyond Ideology,* 1981; *Worldviews,* 1983; *Concept and Empathy,* 1986; *Religion*

and the Western World, 1987; *Buddhism and Christianity: Rivals and Allies,* 1993; *The World's Religions,* 1989; *Religions of Asia,* 1993.

(1) Philosophy of religion takes as its subject matter the religions of the world, not in order to establish or demolish any religious position or belief, but in order to understand the logic of religious discourse. The philosopher of religion is, therefore, committed to participate in the comparative, *i.e.*, crosscultural, multidisciplinary study of religions.

(2) Smart finds in the religions of the world three widely repeated strands, in different combinations, and with different weightings and priorities: the numinous (*q.v.*) strand, the mystical strand, and the incarnation (*q.v.*) strand. In the numinous strand, God is remote and to be approached through worship. In the mystical strand God is near—in the case of *Atman* (*q.v.*), identical with oneself—and enlightenment requires meditation. In the incarnation strand God incarnate is at hand, taking care of the remoteness problem of the numinous.

(3) Judaism and Islam stress the numinous while accommodating mysticism in a limited manner. The Advaita Vedanta (*q.v.* 2) of Shankara (*q.v.* 5), stressing *Atman*-Brahman identity, is second strand. Third strand incarnate gods are present in Christianity, Hinduism (*e.g.*, the *Avatar, q.v.*), and Mahayana Buddhism (*q.v.* Incarnation 1–3). Christianity is not alone in combining all three strands; but Smart's point is that the meanings of religious concepts shift with different combinations and weightings.

(4) The strand analysis, from 1958, surfaces where relevant in other works, finally (1993a) taking its place in a 7-dimensional "definition" of religion, consisting of: ritual and practice, experience and emotion, narrative and myth, doctrine and philosophy, the ethical and legal, the social and institutional, and their material expressions (this last dimension added to a 6-dimensional scheme of 1983). The dimensional analysis is applied to individual religions, nationalism, Marxism, and scientific humanism.

(5) The schemes are used in various ways, in one case to show that Mao Tse-Tung's version of Marxism fitted contemporary China better than the traditional religious alternatives.

SMITH, ADAM. 1723–1790.
Scottish economist and moral philosopher. Born at Kirkcaldy. Educated at Glasgow and Oxford. Taught at Glasgow for twelve years. This was followed by several years of travel and ten years working on his *The Wealth of Nations*. At last he was named Commissioner of Customs for Scotland, settling in Edinburgh.
Principal writings: *Theory of Moral Sentiments*, 1759; *The Wealth of Nations*, 1776.
(1) A student of Francis Hutcheson, he opposed his teacher's Moral Sense Theory (*q.v.*) of ethics, resting moral sentiment rather on sympathy. Smith argued that through sympathy we "enter into the situations of other men" and share with them in "the passions which those situations have a tendency to excite." Virtue is closely identified with propriety and merit. The former is derived from the accord between the emotions of the principal and the impartial spectator. The latter relates to the accord between the spectator and those affected by the act. Prudence and benevolence likewise enter into the full description of virtue.
(2) Where sympathy motivates ethics, self-interest leads each person to seek his own economic advantage. In seeking this he is "led by an invisible hand" to contribute to the general welfare, "an end which was no part of his intention." The scheme advocates free trade rather than protection; and productive labor is given the key position in his analysis of the creation of wealth.

SMITH, JOHN. c. 1616–1652.
English philosopher. Born at Achurch. Educated at Cambridge where he also taught. One of the Cambridge Platonists (*q.v.*), Smith explored the interrelations of innate ideas and moral goodness. The truth is within us, but only the purified soul is able to grasp it. The path to knowledge is thus identical with that of moral goodness. Rather than attempting to prove theses about God and immortality, it is more appropriate to arouse "spiritual sensations" in a hearer's soul.
Principal writings: *Select Discourses* (ed. John Worthington), 1660.

SMITH, JOSEPH.
Q.v. Latter Day Saints.

SMRTI (SMRITI).
Q.v. Śastras (2).

SMULLYAN, ARTHUR.
Q.v. Quantifying In (2).

SMUTS, JAN CHRISTIAN. 1870–1950.
South African philosopher and statesman. Born in Cape Colony. Educated at Victoria College and Cambridge. He contributed to the formation of the League of Nations, and was for fourteen years (1919–24, 1939–48) Prime Minister of South Africa.
Principal writings: *The League of Nations: A Practical Suggestion*, 1918; *Holism and Evolution*, 1926.
(1) Naming his view the philosophy of Holism, Smuts distinguished a "holistic" factor or tendency in the universe from a mechanical factor. The latter predominates at the bottom of the scale of evolution and the former at the top. The mechanical runs to aggregates which can be subdivided without loss of any quality; the holistic creates "wholes" which cannot be subdivided without qualitative loss. Mind is the supreme embodiment of the holistic factor.
(2) It is his view that evolution has occurred through a series of creative leaps from the physical through the biological and into the mental or spiritual level.

SOCIAL CONTRACT THEORY.
The doctrine that social organization rests on a contract or compact which the people have made among themselves. At times a distinction is made between society and government; and the contract is postulated as the explanation of either one or both. At times the social contract is postulated as an actual historical occurrence. Whether historical or not, a normative sense is usually given to the idea of a social contract; and the doctrine has been often used to argue the people's right to change the conditions which at present obligate them.
(1) The theory is sometimes said to have had its origin in the contention of the Sophists (*q.v.*) that societies exist by convention rather than by nature, or the Stoic distinction between positive and natural law (*q.v.* Stoicism). Explicit statements of a social contract in this period are quite rare. One approximation might

be the view of Socrates (*q.v.*) in the *Crito* that, having accepted the benefits of Athens for so many years, he now has an implicit contract with the city-state which cannot be ignored.

(2) The notion of the social contract is said to have gained strength during the Middle Ages. Thomas Aquinas (*q.v.* 9) supported the concept of natural law. By the early 14th century Marsilius of Padua (*q.v.* 4) and William of Ockham (*q.v.* 16) had argued that the power of the state rests in the people, and that of the Church in general councils.

(3) In the 16th century Juan de Mariana (*q.v.*) held that the state rests on consent, and Richard Hooker (*q.v.* 2), drawing on both Thomas Aquinas and Marsilius of Padua, held—even beyond the latter— that both state and church rest on the consent of the people, a consent which can be revoked.

(4) Grotius (*q.v.* 3) was the first to stress the idea of the social contract as an historical event, determining the framework of government. In his view the contract, once established, could not be revoked by the people.

(5) Hobbes (*q.v.* 8–9) pictures man as entering into a social contract in order to put an end to the inconveniences of the state of nature. In Hobbes' view the most advantageous contract is that one in which men assign their rights to an absolute sovereign. As with Grotius, so with Hobbes, the contract once made is thereafter binding.

(6) Pufendorf (*q.v.* 1) strikes an average between the views of Grotius and Hobbes. His view of natural law was less immutable, more sociological, than that of Grotius. To him the state of nature was less warlike than that of Hobbes, more a state of insecure peace which men strengthen by the social contract. And his conception of the state as a moral individual anticipated Rousseau.

(7) Spinoza (*q.v.* 10) regards the transition from the state of nature to society in terms similar to Hobbes, although the purpose of the state relates to wisdom, and the most advantageous form of government is democracy.

(8) Locke (*q.v.* 9) follows the natural law tradition more closely than Hobbes, thus finding the purpose of the social contract to lie in the implementation of the reason man possesses in the state of nature. Nor is the contract unilateral and irrevocable. There are obligations lying on either side of it; and if the obligations are not fulfilled, men can alter and reconstitute the contract.

(9) Something like the social contract is to be discerned also in the system of Rousseau (*q.v.* 5b). Men give over to the state all of their powers, and receive some of them back with guarantees. In a related sense men gain their humanity as they move into society.

(10) Kant (*q.v.* 10) admired Rousseau, and supported the ideals of the French Revolution. He regarded the social contract not as an historical event, but as an important regulative idea supporting the rule of law.

(11) Thomas Paine (*q.v.* 3) held that the social contract was a compact of individuals with each other, and one generation cannot bind another.

(12) For Jefferson (*q.v.* 2), since the earth belongs to the living, the social contract can be abrogated and reshaped in each generation.

(13) Social contract theory was eclipsed by Utilitarianism in the 18th century. In contemporary thought John Rawls (*q.v.* 1) has reintroduced the social contract as a hypothetical situation involving choice of a contractual relationship with society from an "original position."

(14) Against Rawls, Robert Nozick (*q.v.* 1–2) enshrines porperty relations as central to his view of the state, which he calls libertarian, but which restates the themes of economic liberalism.

SOCIAL DARWINISM.

An application of Darwin's (*q.v.* 5) principle of natural selection, first to the economic order, and by extension to society at large. The claim is that evolution requires one to picture human society as engaged in a competitive struggle whose ruthlessness should not be checked if the fit are to survive.

(1) The phrase, "survival of the fittest," so prominent in the doctrine's late 19th and early 20th century career, came from Darwin's rival, Alfred Wallace (*q.v.*), in 1858, and was featured by Herbert Spencer (*q.v.*) in 1864. John D. Rockefeller and Andrew Carnegie cited the phrase with approval, Carnegie saying that the law

of competition "may be sometimes hard for the individual" but it "insures the survival of the fittest in every department." From his professoriate at Yale, William Graham Sumner (*q.v.* 4) urged "liberty, inequality, survival of the fittest."

(2) Along with natural selection the doctrine assumed Hobbesian (*q.v.* 7) self-interest (also *q.v.* Stirner 1), and the working of Adam Smith's (*q.v.* 2) "invisible hand."

(3) Carnegie, Rockefeller agreeing, blunted the aggressiveness of the doctrine by requiring that those who win out in the economic struggle become philanthropists. In *The Gospel of Wealth* (1901) Carnegie argued that it is the duty of the entrepreneur to amass as much wealth as possible, and then to administer it wisely, acting as trustee for his poorer brethren, "doing for them better than they would or could do for themselves."

SOCIAL ETHICS.

Q.v. Hegel (17).

SOCIAL GOSPEL.

A movement among American Protestant religious leaders in the late 19th and early 20th centuries to shift the focus of Christianity from theology to social relations. Headed by Walter Rauschenbusch (1861–1918), the movement sought to translate the concept of the kingdom of God into operative social principles.

SOCIALISM.

From the Latin *socius* ("comrade"). The term applies to any association, private or public, organized around the principle of group control of property and the production and distribution of wealth. Socialism is usually distinguished from communism (*q.v.*) only in degree.

(1) The term "socialism" was first used, so far as is known, in 1831 in France. It appeared in an anonymous article, attributed to Alexander Vinet, urging that a way be found between "individualism and socialism." Both Pierre Leroux and Louis Reybaud used the term in the 1830's, and both claim, mistakenly it seems, to have introduced it. In fact the term was widely used in this period by the Saint-Simonians to contrast with an individualism held to be false. Saint-Simon (*q.v.*), indeed, is regarded as the

founder of French socialism, and urged a reform of government designed to restore harmony to society.

(2) The term became common in England around 1835 in the meetings of Robert Owen's Association of all Classes of all Nations. Owen (*q.v.* 3–4) called for voluntary communities living, working, and studying together.

(3) Although the French socialist Fourier (*q.v.*) criticized both Saint-Simon and Owen, his system of agricultural phalanges was quite similar to the plan of Owen.

(4) Proudhon (*q.v.*) likewise believed that by cooperative means humanity could progress toward a harmonious social order. He is counted among the anarchists (*q.v.*) for his belief that the state would wither away.

(5) In his 1839 essay on *The Organization of Work*, Louis Blanc coined the slogan, "to each according to his needs, from each according to his abilities." He advocated "social workshops," combining the features of trade unions with a cooperative society; in 1807 he argued, before the French National Assembly for a Ministry of Labor. The proposal was rejected as socialistic.

(6) Marx (*q.v.*) criticized Proudhon for his idealism, and with Engels popularized the term "Utopian Socialism" for all views which adhered to peaceful means—evolution or persuasion—to effect the necessary change. They established a widely accepted distinction between socialism and communism: namely, that the former is a stage through which societies must pass on the way to communism. Communism is thus at the end of history, and socialism is the means to reach this end. Unlike the early socialists, Marxists held that the stage of socialism is also the stage of the dictatorship of the proletariat. Lenin (*q.v.*) held that the Soviet Union was in the stage of socialism. (Also, *q.v.* Marxism.)

(7) Fabian socialism, founded in England in 1884, continued the English emphasis on gradualism. George Bernard Shaw and H.G. Wells were among the well-known members of the Fabian Society.

(8) Socialist parties were organized in European nations, beginning in Germany, (*q.v.* Lassalle) in 1861. In the United

States a Socialist Party was organized in the 1890's. Beginning in 1928 Norman Thomas ran for president six times on the platform of the Socialist Party.

(9) In recent years Michael Harrington (*q.v.* 1–2) has presented an analysis combining the motifs of revolutionary change and gradualism.

SOCIAL PHILOSOPHY.

Centering around the problem of the nature of society and of the state, considering not only how these entities are but how they ought to be ordered, Western political philosophy includes the following alternatives:

(1) Plato (*q.v.* 5) envisioned a republic in which educational success determines one's role in society, even with respect to those who rule; and the just society has the same structure as the just soul, written large.

(2) Where Plato made the developed individual the basic unit of society, Aristotle (*q.v.* 12) regarded the family as that unit. Nor is there a single preferred organization of the state. Instead, monarchy, aristocracy, and polity are the preferred forms of which tyranny, oligarchy, and democracy are the deformations.

(3) Stoicism (*q.v.* 4) developed in theory the idea of the *cosmopolis*, where each individual is regarded as a citizen of the universe, and responsible to the universal law of reason.

(4) St. Augustine (*q.v.* 13) found history to exemplify a struggle between the City of Man and the City of God, one temporal, fallible, and demonic, the other eternal and transcending history.

(5) In the Middle Ages the relations of church and state were subject to considerable reflection, various interpretations of the doctrine of the two swords emerging. Marsilius of Padua (*q.v.*) marks a turning point, holding not only that the state is rightfully supreme in this world, but also that the power of both state and church rests in the people.

(6) Machiavelli (*q.v.*), regarding the purpose of the state to be preservation of its power, sanctioned whatever means may be necessary to reach this end.

(7) Grotius (*q.v.* 2–4) advanced a natural law (*q.v.*) theory of the basis of the state, rooting its precepts in self-evident principles of reason.

(8) Hobbes (*q.v.* 8–10) argued that while governments can be properly structured according to any of Aristotle's three types—monarchies, aristocracies, and democracies—their act of constitution implied a signing away of all individual rights so that the sovereign power is absolute.

(9) Locke (*q.v.* 9) advanced a different kind of social contract whose purpose was to enforce, rather than alienate, individual rights; and which rested on a presumption of man's reasonable nature.

(10) Rousseau (*q.v.* 5) also developed a social contract theory, sharing features of both Hobbes' approach and that of Locke. Distinctive in Rousseau's doctrine is the notion of the general will which rules a properly organized society.

(11) Kant (*q.v.* 6) developed Rousseau's conception in an ethical direction so that the good society became a realm of ends.

(12) For Hegel (*q.v.* 17) the state is the culmination of objective spirit, whose earlier stages are the family, and civil society.

(13) Marx (*q.v.* 5, 7–8) viewed the state in its present form as an instrument of oppression, destined to wither away as class conflicts are resolved. Also *q.v.* Marxism.

(14) For Orthodox Marxism the withering away of the state was a future event to follow an extended period of dictatorial control. The alternative of Anarchism (*q.v.*), with Godwin (*q.v.*), Proudhon (*q.v.*), and Bakunin (*q.v.*) among its representatives, expresses still greater confidence in the viability of a functioning society apart from an organized state.

(15) The social philosophy of Du Bois (*q.v.* 2–6) emphasized democracy, social pluralism, Pan-Africanism, and socialism.

(16) Maritain (*q.v.* 4–5) argued for democracy as the most felicitous means of ordering the state while regarding man's destiny as transcendent over society.

SOCIETY.

Translation of the Latin *societas* from *socio* ("to share or to unite"). The community is an aggregate of persons, or a voluntary association of individuals with common ends. The major philosophical questions here relate to the nature of the state: whether or not it is more than a mere aggregate, and whether or not a distinction should be drawn between state and society.

(1) Plato (*q.v.* 5) seems not to distinguish between the state and society. The state is composed of individuals and no larger unity is mentioned. At the same time the state, as the soul writ large, is more than an aggregate of individuals.

(2) Aristotle (*q.v.* 12) does make a distinction between state and society since his state is composed of societal units, that is, of families.

(3) The distinction is still clearer among the later Stoics (*q.v.* Stoicism 4) where man is regarded not only as a citizen of his city state but of the universe. This latter citizenship appears to function as a society behind the state, providing principles for the latter's organization.

(4) St. Augustine (*q.v.* 13) situated the city of God as above the state and as the appropriate object of man's allegiance. This second city is, however, mainly in opposition to the city of man.

(5) In the medieval period a common doctrine was that of the two swords, a reconciliation of two coexistent societies, one temporal and the other eternal.

(6) In social contract theory (*q.v.*) a distinction is sometimes drawn between the contract establishing the society and that establishing the state.

(7) Hobbes (*q.v.* 8–9) had the contract establish the state. Furthermore, the state is simply the aggregate of its parts in a mechanical sense.

(8) Montesquieu (*q.v.* 1–3) posed his analysis in terms of societies, regarding each society as individual and relative to the conditions which have shaped it.

(9) Rousseau (*q.v.* 1–4) recognized the existence of society prior to the state. He stressed the organic nature of the state, finding in the general will a wisdom not present in its individual citizens.

(10) Hegel (*q.v.* 17) said little about society, but held the state to be an organism to which life, thought, and consciousness "essentially belong." Indeed, Hegel came very close to deifying the national state.

(11) Comte (*q.v.* 4) broadened the analyses to society, holding an organic view of society as more than an aggregate of individuals.

(12) Bosanquet (*q.v.* 2), one of the neo-Hegelians, continued the organismic view

of Hegel. He directed his analysis to the state, although on occasion he used the terms "society" and "community" apparently as synonyms of "state."

(13) Royce (*q.v.* 6–7), likewise an Idealist, and initially Hegelian, applied the organic analysis not to the state, but to the community of interpretation, any group of individuals with common memories and hopes.

(14) Working as a sociologist, Durkheim (*q.v.*) identified the source of social cohesion in the "collective representations" with which all members of a given group identify, allowing them to identify themselves and each other.

(15) Santayana (*q.v.* 7) found a hierarchy of societies leading from "natural" through "free" to "ideal" types.

(16) Spengler (*q.v.* 1) applied the organic analysis to human cultures, a social grouping larger than the state with a typical life-pattern.

(17) Maritain (*q.v.* 4–5) distinguished between the state and society. In his view both have certain obligations to respect nature.

(18) In his *A Study of History* Toynbee (*q.v.*), following Spengler in part, makes an organic analysis of "whole societies," comparing their structural similarities.

(19) Ortega y Gasset (*q.v.* 5) distinguished between society as a form of inauthenticity, and society as a support for the achievement of personal liberty.

(20) Popper (*q.v.* 4) on the other hand attacks the organic view of society, claiming that societies are theoretical constructs, and that only individuals and their relations are subject to analysis.

(21) Parsons (*q.v.* 3), distinguishing in theory between state and society, finds "boundary maintenance" such an important prerequisite of both that the two kinds of collectivity tend to coincide.

SOCIETY OF FRIENDS.
Q.v. Friends, Society of.

SOCINIANISM.
A heterodox religious movement originating from the work of Laelius and Faustus Socinus (*q.v.*). Taking root in Poland due to Faustus, the movement organized in 1556 as the Minor Reformed Church of Poland with a college at Racov and a press disseminating Socinian views

throughout Europe. The most important single document of the movement is the Racovian Catechism of 1605 which circulated widely in the 17th century. The movement returned to the Apostles' Creed, rejecting the trinitarian Nicene version, adhered to the word of Scripture, the humanity of Jesus, the separation of church and state, pacifism, nonresistance, and the selective resurrection of the faithful. In 1638 the center at Racov was broken up. In 1658 the movement was suppressed in Poland. Those who went into exile settled in Transylvania, East Prussia, and Holland, disseminating their views still further. Spreading from Holland into England, Socinianism is regarded as an important influence on the rise of Unitarianism (q.v.).

SOCINUS, LAELIUS (1525–1562) and FAUSTUS (1539–1604).

Italian reformers. Born in Siena. An uncle and nephew whose efforts led to the religious movement known as Socinianism (q.v.). Laelius, coming early under the influence of the evangelical movement in Italy, extended his contacts to Protestant churchmen in Switzerland and Germany visiting, among others, Melanchthon in Wittenberg and Calvin in Geneva. Because of the doubts of several churchmen, including Calvin, about his orthodoxy, Laelius wrote out an acceptable confession of his faith, while reserving the right of further inquiry. Upon his death Faustus carried on his uncle's reforming work. Among Faustus' writings were *Explicatio*, 1562; *On the Authority of Scripture*, 1570; *On Predestination*, 1578; *On the Saviour Jesus Christ*, 1578; *On the Nature of Jesus Christ*, 1584. Much of the philosophical theology is to be found in Otto Fock's *Der Socinianismo*, 1847, containing selected translations into German of Socinus' *Praelectiones theologicae* ("theological lectures"), 1627.

(1) Heterodox in point of view, he believed that Christ was God though by nature entirely human, that His operation affects man alone, that the invocation of Christ in prayer was permissive rather than mandatory, and that baptism applied only to gentile converts to Christianity.

(2) He was called to Transylvania and Poland to help resolve a conflict precisely on the doctrine of invocation, alluded to

above. The controversy had arisen during the twelve years (1559–71) of religious freedom Transylvania had enjoyed under an anti-Trinitarian prince. From this time Poland became the scene of his labors, and the origin of the Socinian movement.

(3) Criticizing the traditional view of God's eternity, the *totum simul* (q.v.), on the ground that it obliterated all temporal distinctions, Socinus held that God's eternity must be everlasting endurance.

(4) Furthermore, he argued that if God knows the future as determinate everything becomes necessary, and nothing is contingent. But God knows things as they are, future necessities as necessary, and future possibilities only as possible, as uncertain. This knowledge is still omniscient, comprising all that there is to know.

SOCIOLOGY.

From the Latin *socio* ("to associate") and *logos* ("knowledge"). The term is taken to refer to a study of the forms, institutions, functions, and interrelations of human groups.

(1) The term was introduced by Comte (q.v. 2, 4) to designate a new science, the most comprehensive of all, dealing with social phenomena. The character he expected of the discipline is suggested by the term, "social physics." his initial name for the subject.

(2) The concern of Marx (q.v. 5, 7) with the role of classes in society, and the relation of economic to cultural matters has resulted in his enshrinement as one of the early figures in the development of sociology.

(3) Herbert Spencer (q.v. 3) treated society as an entity, introducing a qualified organismic analogy into the characterization of its nature. Comte first applied the analogy in question to society; Spengler reinforced it.

(4) Sumner (q.v. 1–2) found "folkways" to be the basic sociological conception. Folkways become mores, gathering sanctions through time.

(5) Pareto (q.v. 2) introduced the terms "residues" and "derivations" to refer to the recurrent and novel elements of society.

(6) Durkheim (q.v.) stressed the role of "social facts" in leading to "collective representations" and a "collective conscience" in society.

(7) Simmel (*q.v.*) explored the relationships between the individual and his culture, viewing human life as ever in flux, giving rise to and being shaped by the artifacts of culture.

(8) Max Weber (*q.v.*) studied society through the construction of "ideal types."

(9) Karl Mannheim (*q.v.*) contributed valuable insights concerning both rationality and ideology.

(10) Ferdinand Tönnies (*q.v.* 1) distinguished between associations and communities, the former resulting from "rational will" and the second from a deeper-lying essential will.

(11) Neurath (*q.v.*) used the positivistic approach of physicalism in his "empirical sociology."

(12) Sorokin (*q.v.* 1) reintroduced an absolute, arguing that societies are shaped in part by their positioning of the "absolute" which they in some form must recognize.

(13) Talcott Parsons (*q.v.* 1) believes sociology's task to be analysis of the institutionalization of patterns of value-orientation.

SOCRATES. 470–400 B.C.
Athenian philosopher. Born in Athens. His father was Sophroniscus, a sculptor; his mother was Phaenarete, a midwife, according to Socrates' own statement. He may have studied under Archelaus (*q.v.*) and he was widely regarded as one of the Sophists. His followers were, however, quick to distinguish between Socrates and the Sophists. He lived through the age of Pericles and the Peloponnesian War. It is probable that he was initially a physical philosopher in the pattern of Anaxagoras (*q.v.*), and possibly the head of a small school. He seems to have been of at least middle class means up to the year 431 when the Peloponnesian War began. The serious nature of this conflict may have led Socrates, then around 40 years of age, to a sense of personal mission for the salvation of Athens. His sense of overpowering commitment may have led him, likewise, to a manner of philosophizing in marked contrast to the Sophists, whom he opposed, and to neglect his own patrimony in the process. The climax of his life was his trial, conviction, and execution by the Athenians.

Principal writings: None, but the early dialogues of Plato (*q.v.*) are thought to be representative of his thought—the *Apology, Crito,* and *Phaedo* covering Socrates' trial, imprisonment, and death.

(1) Among the biographical details in those dialogues are the following: As Plato had Socrates present the matter in the *Apology*, the oracle at Delphi had stated that Socrates was the wisest man in Greece. Not believing the oracle, Socrates set out through questioning his fellow citizens to find one wiser than himself. In posing questions to others he discovered that they believed themselves to possess a wisdom which they did not possess; whereupon Socrates at last was forced to admit that he was indeed the wisest man in Greece. Others knew nothing, not realizing that they knew nothing. Socrates knew that he knew nothing, thus possessing one item of information more than any other Athenian. The mottos of his quest being "Know thyself" and "The unexamined life is not worth living," Socrates characterized his mission in life to be that of a gadfly, causing the lazy steed of Athens to bestir herself, and as a midwife helping others to give birth to their ideas. The process of "midwifery" or "maieutic" has come to be known as the Socratic Method. The mood of irony, called "Socratic irony," is an indispensable part of this method. The mission he felt himself to be fulfilling was not without religious aspects. The inner warning voice which he took to be a sign from God, and which spoke at times when he was on the verge of a mistaken decision, and the heroic calm with which he faced martyrdom, may be cited as evidence in this respect. Nor is this denied by the charge of atheism at his trial: that he had given up the gods of the state and introduced other gods.

The details of his life are to a large extent matter for conjecture. He is supposed to have had a shrewish wife, Xanthippe. In the *Phaedo* his wife brings his two young children to bid him farewell. In addition he had a son who was then in his teens. In the *Apology* and elsewhere, he is represented as penniless; and yet the type of his military service suggests that he possessed property well into his forties at least.

The details of his thought are, likewise, subject to dispute. The difficulty lies in distinguishing between the philosophy of Socrates and that of Plato. This difficulty is called "the Socratic problem." We shall begin with the items widely credited to Socrates, and continue through a spectrum of possibilities with decreasing credibility.

(2) Aristotle grants credit to Socrates for contributing to philosophy "inductive arguments and universal definitions." This comment is reinforced by the character of Plato's earliest dialogues if we think of inductive argument as consisting of an examination of individual cases in order to discover what they have in common, the characteristics under which they are to be classed, *i.e.*, their appropriate definitions. To name three of the very early dialogues, the Euthyphro dealt with the nature of piety, the *Charmides* with temperance, the *Lysis* with friendship. Socrates' typical method in these dialogues was to challenge the use of a word which led to a consideration of cases; and although definitive conclusions are not reached in the dialogues mentioned, Socrates' effort was to detach the appropriate universal definitions from these cases. If we are to accept Book I of the *Republic* as a Socratic dialogue, definitions are to be discredited if they can be reduced to absurdity, or shown to be either vague or inconsistent. One might well, indeed, credit Socrates with a dialogic method having the distinctive form: (a) statement of the question; (b) answer to the question; (c) exploration of objections to the answer; (d) revised answer which evades these objections; (e) exploration of objections to the revised answer. The successful dialogue will have reached its end when the answer stands up against all known objections. Granting just this much allows us to distinguish Socrates from the Sophists for the latters' relativism consisted in large part in utilizing the ambiguities of ordinary language.

(3) Aristotle further credits Socrates with concern for "ethical matters." Such concern, joined to that for conceptual clarity, warrants us in attributing to Socrates the ethical doctrine (also in the early dialogues) that knowledge and virtue are identical. The doctrine has among its consequences the belief that the virtuous can be discovered as a corollary of the increase of knowledge; and that no one does evil knowingly. One doing evil has at that moment, and in that situation, mistaken it for a good. When decisions concern value, individuals choose between real and apparent goods. In this doctrine Socrates means by "good" whatever will lead to one's true happiness. This includes pleasure, certainly, but also virtue.

(4) Granting this much to Socrates, there can be no reason in denying him the further ethical point (which also fits the martyrdom in which his life ended), that it is always better to suffer than to do evil. The absoluteness of this doctrine likewise serves to distinguish the Socratic from the Sophistic point of view, and to reflect the contempt in which he held the masses, believing they could effect neither good nor evil, and that all they did was a result of chance. The argument is that when another aims at doing evil to you, all that person really succeeds in doing is laying down a challenge the facing of which will allow you to develop inner strength. His analogue is the hardship of physical training in which the body becomes stronger. When, however, in response to the attempt of another to do evil, one does evil in return, then the principle of evil is no longer an external condition, but an inner reality, and far from having a challenge, the response to which can increase one's spiritual strength, one has simply weakened one's inner nature by the decision. And since this situation fits every situation of life, it is better always to suffer rather than do evil. This may be the basis of his argument against suicide, since the act would be evil, but suffering whatever pain life may hold is not.

(5) Once this point is granted, an additional one becomes reasonable. If we are able to weaken or strengthen our inner natures in this way, a connection is suggested between ethical activity and the idea of soul. As A.E. Taylor (*q.v.*) pointed out, the Greek notion of soul prior to Socrates is that of Homer, *i.e.*, the ghostly psyche which as a shade of its former self continues to exist in the underworld. But in the post-Socratic world three men influenced by Socrates—Plato, Xenophon, and Isocrates—attribute another notion to Socrates himself: The

center of our beings, and the locus of personality and intelligence, is an immortal soul, the tending and strengthening of which is our chief business in life. On this conception the after-life can be qualitatively richer than life on earth. Clearly, such a conception supports the ethical point as to the value of suffering. It is a contribution to philosophy of such impressive magnitude that it would account for Socrates' reputation. It would help, likewise, in explaining the urgency of his mission.

(6) If we are to credit Socrates with the development of the idea of the immortal soul, then the major theme of the dialogue, *Phaedo*, represented by Plato as occurring on the day of Socrates' death, belongs to Socrates. Certainly the drama of Socrates' death is heightened by the arguments concerning immortality. On the other hand, however, the doctrine of ideas, which tradition has assigned to Plato, is also present in this dialogue. Give this to Socrates, too, and through two-thirds of his career Plato becomes a mere amanuensis for Socrates. That does not seem likely. In this respect we can hold that Socrates framed universal definitions, and in these definitions Plato found absolute ideas. Plato lets it be said in the *Phaedo* that he was not present, hence the possibility of a departure from the conversation as it may have occurred. That absence can relate to the doctrine of immortality, however, as well as to the theory of ideas. The matter thus remains uncertain, and yet, even though we cannot draw the line with certainty, it is the case that Plato's first period of philosophizing, from the early dialogues through the *Republic*, is concerned with setting down Socrates' thought, and drawing out its implications.

SOCRATIC METHOD.
Q.v. Socrates (1).

SOCRATIC SCHOOLS.
The term is used to refer to schools of philosophy shaped by the influence of Socrates. In this sense Plato's Academy (*q.v.*) would qualify as one of the Socratic schools; but the mature Platonic thought is, rather, considered as initiating its own school. Tradition somewhat tenuously looks upon the Cynic, Cyrenaic, and Megarian schools as Socratic. Cynicism is related to Socrates by forging a link between Antisthenes (*q.v.*) and Diogenes (*q.v.*), the founder of the school. Cyrenaicism (*q.v.*) is traced from Aristippus who emphasized the role of pleasure in human life; and Megarianism (*q.v.*) is traced to Socrates through Euclides of Megara (*q.v.*).

SOLGER, K.W.F.
Q.v. Tragedy (14).

SOLIDARITY.
Q.v. Gadamer (6).

SOL INVICTUS.
Latin phrase meaning "the invincible sun." A sun god imported into Rome from the Near East during the Punic wars, in the later years of the Empire he was identified with Mithras (*q.v.* Mithraism) as solar god and lord of the world. The December festival of the god became Christmas in the Christian calendar.

SOLIPSISM.
From the Latin *solus* ("alone") and *ipse* ("self"). The doctrine that the individual human mind has no grounds for believing in anything but itself. The consequence is sometimes drawn that the individual mind coming to that conclusion constitutes all there is of reality. The first claim, taken by itself, may be termed "epistemological solipsism." When the cited consequence is drawn, the view may be called "metaphysical solipsism." The consequence is often drawn as a *reductio ad absurdum* to suggest that the initial claim must be untrue.

(1) Skepticism (*q.v.*), dealing with the problem of knowledge, tends toward the position of epistemological solipsism. St. Augustine (*q.v.* 3–4) and Descartes (*q.v.* 1–2) utilize that form of skepticism as a moment on the way to the establishment of a variety of truths.

(2) Although the issues of Solipsism hover around the pages of Hume and Berkeley, neither was a solipsist in either of our two senses.

(3) In the 17th and 18th centuries the term was sometimes used in a moral sense to signify the position of Egoism (*q.v.*).

(4) Bradley (*q.v.* 5) argued that solipsism

is the consequence if individual experience is not transcended by the Absolute.

(5) Royce (*q.v.* 1b) argued from skepticism to the Absolute, in a sense combining the emphases of St. Augustine, Descartes, and Bradley.

(6) Santayana (*q.v.* 2) made the starting point of thought a "solipsism of the present moment" which can be abrogated only by "animal faith."

(7) In his doctrine of the "egocentric predicament," Perry (*q.v.* 1) argued essentially that the predicament of epistemological solipsism did not justify the leap to metaphysical solipsism.

(8) Wittgenstein (*q.v.* 8) pointed to a way out of both interpretations with his showing that there can be no private language.

SOLOMON BEN ELISHA.
Q.v. Cabala (2c).

SOLOVIEV, VLADIMIR. 1853–1900.
Russian philosopher. Born in Moscow. Educated at Moscow and St. Petersburg. Taught briefly at St. Petersburg.
Principal writings: *The Crisis of Western Philosophy*, 1874; *The Philosophical Principles of Integral Knowledge*, 1877; *Lectures on Godmanhood* (T in part), 1878; *Critique of Abstract Principles*, 1880; *The History and Future of Theocracy*, 1887; *Foundations of Theoretical Philosophy* (T in part), 1897–9; *Stories of the Anti-Christ*, 1900; *Three Conversations* (T), 1900.

(1) He criticized Western rationalism and empiricism, arguing for the validity of internal experience over both the abstractions of rationalism and the external experience of empiricism. In fact, he substituted for the criticized positions a dialectical analysis of culture replete with Hegelian triads.

(2) His vision of the goal of human history developed through time. In an early period he found the unity of humanity in the mystical goal of the "divine Sophia." Still later, he envisioned a universal theocracy, combining Eastern and Western Churches with Judaism, centered in Russia as the "Third Rome." Finally, he conceived of a humanity become divine by the incarnation of Sophia and felt the time of the divine humanity to be at hand.

(3) But even though the specific vision

of Soloviev changed, his conception of reality remained much the same. The notion of the organic remained prominent. At one time he held that humanity was a single organism; later he argued that the Absolute which encloses all is a living organism. The motifs of Panpsychism, Pantheism, and evolution characterized the totality. The dialectic ran from a unity without content, through the contradictions of differentiated evolution to a unity which has risen above the contradictions. The world-view is thus seen to be consistent with the successive visions stated above.

SOMA.
A god of the Vedic religion. Initially an intoxicating beverage of ancient India, Soma by personification became a god.

SOMA SIDDHANTA.
Q.v. Vaiṣnavism (3c).

SOMATISM.
Q.v. Kotarbinski (1).

SOPHIA.
Q.v. Gnosticism (5–6); Soloviev (2).

SOPHISM.
A synonym for "fallacy" (*q.v.* Fallacies) or "apparent refutation." The usage derives from Plato and Aristotle. The latter compiled a list of "sophistical refutations" (*sophistikoi elenchoi*). The term reflects the low opinion Aristotle held of the Sophists (*q.v.*).

SOPHISTS.
From the Greek *sophistes* ("one who professes to make men wise"). Today the term is applied almost exclusively to a remarkable group of teachers in 5th century B.C. Athens. Markedly different in method, interests, and goals from the cosmological speculations of Greek philosophy's initial period, the Sophists centered their interest in language, rhetoric, education, and questions of social philosophy. At least part of the contempt they drew upon themselves came from their transformation of philosophy into a popular, practical, and remunerative subject. The first philosophers to teach for money, the Sophists specialized in training individuals for public responsibilities

Regarded as early rhetoricians, a contrast between nature and convention, and the tendency to probe myth for rational explanations, are present in their writings.

(1) Protagoras (*q.v.* 1, 4) was the most famous of the Sophists, holding to some version of the relativity of knowledge. As with other Sophists he used myth as an explanatory tool.

(2) Prodicus (*q.v.*), sometimes called the "precursor of Socrates," was interested in the problems of synonyms, and the sociology of religion. He is credited with the myth of Heracles.

(3) Hippias (*q.v.*), an encyclopedic philosopher, drew a clear contrast between nature and convention.

(4) Gorgias (*q.v.* 1, 4) defined rhetoric as the art of persuasion. He propounded a famous argument denying existence, knowledge, and the possibility of communication.

(5) Lycophron, one of Gorgias' disciples, suggested elimination of the copula, *i.e.*, the verb "to be," in the interests of clarity.

(6) Thrasymachus (*q.v.*), defining justice as the interest of the stronger, drew a distinction between natural and conventional justice.

(7) Callicles (*q.v.*) makes explicit the superiority of natural to conventional justice. To throw off the conventions of society is to act justly according to nature.

(8) Antiphon likewise distinguished between natural and conventional, holding that the authority of laws is imposed artificially while the authority of nature is intrinsically binding. Aristotle credited him with the view that forms or ideas are conventional, rather than natural, thus providing an anticipatory criticism of Plato (if the rotting wood of a bed were to sprout "the thing that sprouted would be wood but not a bed").

(9) Critias (*q.v.*) offered a sociology of religion (an invention of those in authority), and a view of fear—deriving from threats of punishment by law and religion—as the principal civilizing agent of society.

(10) Cratylus (*q.v.*) held to an extreme form of the Heraclitean doctrine, and believed, it seems, in a natural connection of word and thing.

SOREL, GEORGES. 1847–1922.
French social philosopher. Born in Cherbourg. Educated as an engineer, he followed this profession for 25 years before devoting himself full-time to philosophy. Working as a revisionist within Marxism and regarding himself as the "metaphysician of socialism," he was labelled a "confusionist" by Lenin, and by Croce as a germinal social thinker of the stature of Marx.

Principal writings: *The Decomposition of Marxism*, 1907; *The Illusion of Progress*, 1908; *Reflections on Violence* (T), 1908; The *Dreyfusian Revolution*, 1909; *Materials for a Theory of the Proletariat*, 1919; *Metaphysical Preoccupations of Modern Physics*, 1921; *On the Utility of Pragmatism*, 1921.

(1) Advocating violence as a necessary strategy of social change, Sorel interpreted the term to include all forms of confrontation without compromise. There is a "violence of principles" as well as a violence of physical activity. The justification of violence depends entirely on the justifiability of the cause one serves.

(2) Social movements tend to elaborate myths about the future. Such social myths, representing the aspirations of adherents, are a kind of social will and thus vastly more significant than utopias which represent the intellectual vision of a single person.

(3) He distinguished two basic forms of ethics: an ethic of the producers and that of the consumers. The former is more significant and creative. The bourgeoisie should be replaced because of their decadence and their lack of integrity in handling the tasks of production.

(4) Ultimately, however, any social arrangement is nothing more than a disentropic interlude in the running down of the universe.

SORGE.
Q.v. Heidegger (3).

SORITES.
From the Greek *soreites* ("a heap"). The term derived from a Megarian puzzle or fallacy turning on the vagueness of terms such as "heap." Taking away from a heap one object after another, when is it no longer a heap? In current usage, however, the term "sorites" applies almost exclusively to a syllogistic conclusion derived from an accumulation of premises. The sorites is a complex syllogism

(*q.v.*) or chain of syllogisms with all conclusions save the last suppressed. The sorites gained currency in the Middle Ages, and in any case postdates Aristotle. There are two forms of sorites, called "progressive" and "regressive."

(1) The progressive sorites, wrongly termed Aristotelian, is so ordered that the intermediate premises are major premises, and each intermediate conclusion is a minor premise for the following syllogism. It has the form: all A is B; all C is A; all D is C; all E is D; therefore, all E is A.

(2) In the regressive sorites, also called Goclenian (*q.v.* Goclenius), the intermediate premises are minor premises, and each intermediate conclusion is a major premise for the following syllogism. It has the form: all A is B; all B is C; all C is D; all D is E; therefore, all A is E.

SORLEY, WILLIAM R. 1855–1935.
Scottish philosopher. Born in Selkirk. Educated at Cambridge. Taught at Cambridge. An Idealist opposed to naturalism, Sorley approached metaphysics from the side of ethics, finding value to be the key to reality. Distinguishing between intrinsic and instrumental value, he situated the former in persons and the latter in things. His metaphysical position is ethical theism, featuring a finite God who is the source of values.

Principal writings: *The Ethics of Naturalism*, 1885; *Recent Tendencies in Ethics*, 1904; *Moral Values and the Idea of God*, 1918; *A History of English Philosophy*, 1920.

SOROKIN, PITIRIM. 1889–1968.
Russian sociologist. Born in the village of Touria. Educated at St. Petersburg. Taught at St. Petersburg, Minnesota, and Harvard. The following works were written in English.

Principal writings: *Social Mobility*, 1927; *Social and Cultural Dynamics*, 4 vols., 1937; *Society, Culture, and Personality*, 1947; *Social Philosophies of an Age of Crisis*, 1950; *Sociological Theories of Today*, 1966.

(1) Combining sociology and metaphysics, Sorokin holds that societies are shaped by the nature of their metaphysical posits. Each society has an "absolute." If the absolute is situated in space-time (*e.g.*, as in the modern Western world), society will have a "sensate" mentality;

if situated outside space-time (*e.g.*, India), society will have an "ideational" mentality; if situated both within and beyond (*e.g.*, the medieval period), society will have an "idealistic" mentality.

(2) Paralleling the three forms of mentality, there are three forms of truth: sensory, rational, and spiritual.

(3) A strong tendency toward consistency will be manifest in the law, art, philosophy, science, and religion of any well-defined period of history.

SOSEIN.
Q.v. Meinong (1, 4).

SOTER.
Q.v. Gnosticism (5–6).

SOTO.
Q.v. Zen Buddhism (4).

SOTO, DOMINGO DE. 1494–1560.
Spanish Scholastic philosopher. Born in Segovia. Educated at Alcalá and Paris. Taught at Alcalá and Salamanca. A Dominican, Soto was an important figure in the Council of Trent. He served for a time as confessor to Charles the Fifth.

Principal writings: *Commentaries on the Summulae*, 1529; *On Nature and Grace*, 1547; *On Justice and Law*, 1549; as well as *Commentaries* on Aristotle's logic and physics.

(1) Although Thomistic in the main, Soto followed Duns Scotus in denying the "real distinction" between essence and existence.

(2) His doctrine of nature and grace was Thomistic. Grace is possible because the causes of the terrestrial world are secondary, and are set in motion by God who, nonetheless, bears no responsibility for evil.

(3) Distinguishing natural from positive law in the manner of Thomas Aquinas, he held that positive law emerges from the understanding of the legislator, and thus has a link to the real natures of things which constitute natural law. He is regarded, along with his teacher Vitoria (*q.v.*), as one of those contributing to the developing theory of international law.

SOUL.
An Anglo-Saxon term referring to the

controlling agency, governing center, or vital principle in human beings. The equivalent Greek term is *psyche* or *pneuma* and the Latin term is *anima*. As between soul and psyche, the two terms used in English, there is no fixed pattern of usage; but "soul" is more frequently regarded as superior to or separable from the body than "psyche."

(1) The pre-Socratic conception of psyche (*q.v.* 1–4) derived from the notion of the identity of breath and air, a phenomenon associated with life, joined to a still more primitive conception of soul as a shadow of person surviving the body. Democritus (*q.v.* 9) held to a view of soul atoms diffused through the body, a view which Epicurus (*q.v.* 7), for example, continued. For an Eastern view of soul as an aggregate *q.v.* Buddha (5). Early conceptions of the soul as superior to the body are to be found in the Dionysian religion and among the Pythagoreans (*q.v.* Psyche, 2, 4).

(2) The conception of the soul as superior was brought to fruition in Platonic philosophy (*q.v.* Socrates 5; Plato 3). Regarded not as the shadow of a person, but as one's deepest reality, immortal life could be viewed as more vital than life in relation to the body. Plato treated the soul both as a principle of fixity and under the category of self-motion. He likewise provided the tripartite conception of soul as reason, will, and appetite (*q.v.* Plato 3).

(3) Aristotle (*q.v.* 7, 11) held soul to be the form of the body, while distinguishing in it both rational and irrational aspects, altogether making a tripartite distinction of vegetable, animal, and rational functions.

(4) Strato (*q.v.* 2) held, in a formulation reminiscent of Aristotle, that the soul is the unity of the body.

(5) Tertullian (*q.v.* 5) believed that the soul is passed along in the processes of human generation from a soul-producing "seed." This was the doctrine of Traducianism, one of the alternatives in a theological debate lasting at least until the Protestant Reformation.

(6) Origen (*q.v.* 3) held the soul of man to have pre-existed, its presence in the body now being a sign of its sin and its fall. He regarded the fall of man as due to a misuse of freedom. The doctrine of pre-existence is the second alternative in the theological debate.

(7) St. Augustine (*q.v.* 12) carried on the Platonic conception of soul in a Christian context.

(8) While adhering to the Aristotelian doctrine of tripartite functions, Avicenna (*q.v.* 3, 10) believed the soul, although created at the same time as the body, to be immortal while the body is not.

(9) Bonaventure (*q.v.* 8) held to the doctrine of the immediate creation of the soul by God out of nothing.

(10) Aquinas (*q.v.* 7) continued the Aristotelian tradition, placing it—like Augustine—in a Christian framework.

(11) Pomponazzi (*q.v.* 1), looking for an intermediate position, regarded the soul as absolutely mortal and relatively immortal.

(12) Hobbes (*q.v.* 1) regarded the idea of soul as contradictory, calling for an "immaterial material."

(13) Descartes' (*q.v.* 8–9) dualism of thought and extension led to a system in which minds and bodies are independent of each other, and capable of separate existence, although dependent on God.

(14) Henry More (*q.v.* 1–3), on the other hand, affirmed the idea of soul, arguing that it has extension, "spissitude," and the ability to penetrate matter.

(15) A.E. Taylor (*q.v.* 2) both explicated and defended what he took to be the Socratic view of soul.

(16) Wilhelm Wundt (*q.v.* 2) is among those who have viewed the soul as a process rather than a substance. William James (*q.v.* 3) expressed a similar point of view.

(17) For Gilbert Ryle (*q.v.* 2) the soul is a category mistake, the Cartesian independent entity having the standing of the "ghost in the machine."

SOUL OF THE WORLD.
  Q.v. World Soul.

SOVEREIGNTY.
  From the French *souverain* referring to the "chief" or "supreme" power of the state.

(1) The term is credited to Jean Bodin (*q.v.* 2) who associated it with the power of the French monarch. He believed this power to be indivisible and capable in some

contexts of extending beyond the law.

(2) Once coined, of course, the term was applied to a variety of points of view. One issue concerns whether sovereignty ultimately belongs to the ruler or to the people. Social contract theory (*q.v.* 2–3) was motivated in part by the view that this power belongs to the people. The Middle Ages contains a developing tradition of this alternative. For example, William of Ockham (*q.v.* 16) argued that the people retain a final power of decision over both emperors and popes, and that God's grant of power to any ruler is through the people.

(3) Hobbes (*q.v.* 9) continued Bodin's view, while strengthening the absolute nature of the sovereign's power. He regarded sovereignty as the "artificial soul" of the "artificial man" which is the state.

(4) Rousseau (*q.v.* 5f) supported the contrary position, situating the sovereign power in the general will of the people, a will which emerges only under certain ideal conditions, including the participation of all in decision-making. He held sovereignty to be indivisible and inalienable. He also believed that "sovereign" is applied to a body politic insofar as it is active.

(5) De Maistre (*q.v.*), one of the Traditionalists of the counter-Revolution, reasserted the ultimate sovereignty of God as expressed through pope and king, his earthly representatives.

(6) De Lamennais (*q.v.*), the most extreme of the Traditionalists, held the pope to be the only sovereign being on earth.

SPACE.

Along with time (*q.v.*), one of the ultimate categories of natural philosophy.

(1) Greek philosophy contrasted the plenum and the void. Where Democritus (*q.v.* 2) used the void as his concept of space, that in which atoms move, Parmenides (*q.v.* 6–8) held there could be no empty space, since, as his disciple Zeno of Elea (*q.v.* 2) argued, the concept is contradictory; he therefore interpreted space as a plenum; its fullness, indeed, makes motion impossible.

(2) In the *Timaeus*, Plato (*q.v.* 9) equated space with the "receptacle" in which forms are instantiated, *i.e.*, become individual things, and instances of the universal.

(3) Aristotle (*q.v.* 6) understood space in terms of place, defining the latter as the inner boundary of the containing body.

(4) The Epicureans (*q.v.* Epicurus 3; Lucretius 1) continued the interpretation of space as the void, while the views of Aristotle characterized the Middle Ages.

(5) Descartes (*q.v.* 8a), defining matter as extension, reverted to the notion of the plenum, so interpreted that motion was possible due to the "subtlety" of the matter which fills all space.

(6) Henry More (*q.v.* 4) regarded space as an "obscure representation of the essence of God," apparently initiating the view that it functions as the divine "sensorium."

(7) Spinoza (*q.v.* 6–7) regarded individual spaces as the finite modes of the attribute of extension, one of the infinite attributes of God.

(8) Newton (*q.v.* 3, 6) held to the absoluteness of space, reverting in a sense to the receptacle theory of Plato, while also holding space to be the divine sensorium in which God works his will, and senses the results.

(9) Leibniz (*q.v.* 2) regarded space as relative, deriving from interrelations of the entities making up the universe.

(10) Samuel Clarke (*q.v.* 1), a follower of Newton, regarded space and time as attributes of God.

(11) Berkeley (*q.v.* 5), following Malebranche (*q.v.* 2–3), reduced space to the perception of an idea (ultimately God's).

(12) Kant (*q.v.* 3) signaled a change in analyses of space, regarding it as the *a priori* form of external phenomena.

(13) Einstein (*q.v.* 1–3) developed the concept of the relativity of space, and discovered its curvature. The relativity of space-time means that simultaneity can be established only within a given inertial system, and has no validity for observers in systems moving in relation to the given inertial system.

SPACE-TIME.

A four-dimensional order with four coordinates, three of them spatial and one temporal. Specification of the coordinates precisely locates any physical magnitude whatever.

(1) The initial philosophical use of space-time is to be found in the work of C.L. Morgan (*q.v.* 2) and S. Alexander (*q.v.*

2–3). In this usage, space-time is regarded as the ultimate matrix from which everything else has evolved.

(2) In the work of Minkowski (*q.v.*) the space-time universe is a four-dimensional continuum of events defined by world-lines. The continuum is changeless since the coordinate of time ranges over both the past and the future.

(3) Einstein (*q.v.*) accepted the Minkowski space-time continuum as the basis for his own analysis.

SPARŚA (SPARSHA).
Sanskrit, "contact." *Q.v.* Buddha (2).

SPAULDING, E.G.
Q.v. New Realism (1, 6).

SPECIES.
A Latin term meaning "sort" or "kind." The Greek is *eidos* ("form" or "figure"); the term designates a class standing between the genus and the individuals to which the term refers.

(1) Aristotle (*q.v.* 4) introduced the basic distinctions of species and genus. The species is constituted by adding a "difference" to the genus; the genus is predicated of the species but not conversely. The species term contains more information than the genus term.

(2) Porphyry (*q.v.* 1) regarded "species" as one of the predicables (*q.v.*), a determination Aristotle never made.

(3) The Scholastics followed Porphyry, while developing the basic distinctions of Aristotle. There are three types of species. The "supreme species" has no other species, but only the genus, above it. The "infima species" has no other species, but only individuals, below it. The "subalternate species" has other species both above and below it.

SPECIOUS PRESENT.
Q.v. Present (3, 4).

SPECULATIVE ARGUMENT.
Q.v. Fallacies (19).

SPECULATIVE GRAMMAR.
A term first used in the Middle Ages to refer to philosophical treatments of language. Philosophical analyses of grammar go back, of course, at least to the Sophists (*q.v.*). Between the age of the Sophists and the Middle Ages such analy-

ses were made by Plato, Aristotle, the Stoics (*q.v.*), and Skeptics (*q.v.*), among many others.

(1) So far as is known the term was first used in the early 14th century in a manuscript titled *Grammatica speculativa* or *De Modis significadi.* This analysis of speculative grammar (or modes of signification), originally attributed to Duns Scotus, was in fact the work of Thomas of Erfurt (*q.v.*).

(2) Peirce (*q.v.* 16) used the term to refer to his analysis of the classification of signs. He assumed he was following the usage of Duns Scotus; this claim is unimportant since, in any case, Peirce's treatment, dividing semiotic into Speculative Grammar, Critical Logic, and Speculative Rhetoric, is strikingly original.

SPECULATIVE RHETORIC.
Q.v. Peirce (16).

SPECULATIVE THEISM.
Q.v. Weisse.

SPEECH.
Although an important aspect of human nature, speech has not been subject to much philosophical analysis. Herder (*q.v.* 2) held that speech begins in imitation of the sounds of nature. John Austin (*q.v.* 2), followed by Searle (*q.v.* 1), stress the importance of "speech acts" to philosophical understanding. Derrida (*q.v.* 3) argues for the primacy of speech over writing.

SPENCER, HERBERT. 1820–1903.
English philosopher. Born at Derby. Virtually self-taught. Worked as an engineer and editor. Taking Darwin's principle of evolution as the organizing center of his own life and of philosophy, he applied the principle to one field after another in a series of publications which had a great deal of influence in his own time. In 1864, shortly after Darwin's publication of *The Origin of Species* he used Wallace's (*q.v.*) phrase "the survival of the fittest," perhaps independently of Wallace, to describe the working of the principle of natural selection.

Principal writings: *Social Statics*, 1850; *The Principles of Psychology*, 1855; *Essays on Education*, 1861; *First Principles*, 1862; *Principles of Biology*, 2 vols., 1864–7; *Principles of Sociology*, 3 vols., 1876–96;

Principles of Ethics, 2 vols., 1879–93; *Man Versus the State*, 1884; *Autobiography*, 1904.

(1) Following the empiricism of Hamilton and J.S. Mill, Spencer regarded science as a discovery of laws or regularities in phenomena, each science working a circumscribed area and representing only a partial unity. Philosophy differs from science in terms of scope, its principles being universally applicable; its goal is a total unification of knowledge. From this standpoint the principle of evolution is philosophical, and Spencer proceeded to make this principle—defined as passage from a "relatively indefinite, incoherent homogeneity to a relatively definite, coherent heterogeneity"—the focus of a comprehensive "synthetic" philosophy for the first time resting on the full range of scientific data.

(2) Evolution is thus expressible as a principle of increasing complexity; and Spencer identified "more complex" with "higher." Intelligence emerges from increasing complexity as do sympathy and sociality, these latter characteristics calling forth the state.

(3) In ethics, Spencer was a Utilitarian. His Evolutionary Utilitarianism (*q.v.*) presumes that an adaptation of the code of behavior in the direction of benefit has been going on since societies were formed. All ethical concepts, including those of duty and altruism, are explicable through the categories of long-term benefit or pleasure. He believed that societies, like organisms, have birth-to-death life cycles, but he held that—unlike some organisms—consciousness is present only in the constituent parts of the social organism.

(4) In theological matters Spencer is agnostic, although his concept of the Unknowable, lying behind phenomena, gains some of the aura which in traditional systems gathers around the idea of God.

SPENER, PHILIPP JAKOB. 1635–1705.

German theologian. Born in Rappoltsweiler. Educated at Strassburg. Known as the father of Pietism, Spener—a Lutheran—was instrumental in founding the University of Halle. His program had six emphases: the encouragement of Bible study groups, restoration of the priesthood of all believers, practical Christi-

anity in daily life, the substitution of love for argument in dealing with dissenters and unbelievers, the reform of theological education in the direction of vital personal religion, spirituality in preaching and a return to apostolic simplicity and sincerity.

Principal writings: *Earnest Desires for a Reform of the Evnangelical Church*, 1675.

SPENGLER, OSWALD. 1880–1936.

German philosopher of history. Born in Blankenburg. Educated at Munich, Berlin, and Halle. His initial philosophical influence came from Goethe and Nietzsche.

Principal writings: *The Decline of the West* (T), 2 vols., 1918, 1922.

(1) Championing the position of cultural relativism, Spengler maintained that there is in a strict sense neither universal history nor "humanity." What exist in fact are cultures at various stages of development, each with a life cycle of around 1,000 years. Applying an organic metaphor, Spengler held that each culture passes through the stages of spring, summer, fall, and winter. Each stage has its own characteristics although developed in keeping with the unique life style of the culture it characterizes. Spring is the time of myth and mysticism; summer the time of rebellion against the past, the beginning of philosophy, and the decline of religion; fall is the time of supreme confidence in reason; and winter is characterized by materialism, agnosticism, skepticism, and pragmatism.

(2) On the stages of the organic metaphor, sketched above, Spengler superimposed another distinction characterizing the life cycle of every society: the distinction between the stages of culture and of civilization. In the stage of culture the vital stock of inner possibilities within a society is being realized. This is a stage in which novelty and qualitative richness are added to human life. Civilization, appearing near the end of the organic life cycle, is that stage in which the cultural possibilities have been realized, and are now merely administered in an external fashion. This is a stage in which a state will expand its power over wider areas, controlling the world through technological superiority, and where the quantitative sense of the "colossal" will

have replaced qualitative distinctions.

(3) Spengler distinguished some ten societies, or cultures, the five figuring most prominently in his analysis comprising the Hellenic-Roman, Arabic, Occidental, Russian, and Mayan. In his view Western societies are now in the dead winter of civilization, while the development of Russian society is still in the future.

(4) Replacing the chronological time of universal history with cross-cultural comparisons, Spengler suggested that Nicholas of Cusa, Luther, and Calvin are contemporaries of Dionysus in Hellenic-Roman culture; the Jansenist and English Puritan challenge in Western culture is contemporary with the Islamic challenge to Christianity in Arabic culture; Galileo, Bacon, and Descartes are the pre-Socratics of Western culture; Voltaire and Rousseau are contemporary to Buddha, Socrates, and Al-Kindi in their respective cultures; and Kant and Goethe are the contemporaries of Plato and Aristotle.

(5) In partial contradiction to the sense of the above analysis, Spengler announced the coming of a world empire to be administered by Germany, marking the triumph of skeptical realism over both rationalism and romanticism.

SPEUSSIPPUS. c. 407–339 B.C.

Greek philosopher. Born in Athens. Entered Plato's Academy in 387. A nephew of the great Plato, he is said to have accompanied his master on the third voyage to Syracuse (*q.v.* Plato). He was named by Plato to succeed to the headship of the Academy on the latter's death. He became head of the Academy in 347 and served until his own death in 339, whereupon Xenocrates (*q.v.*) succeeded to the position. It is thought that some of Aristotle's criticisms of Plato are in fact directed against Speusippus who held that the Ideas were numbers, the One is a basic principle which, in conjunction with the divine Reason, produces the Good.

SPINOZA, BARUCH (BENEDICT).
1632–1677.

Jewish philosopher. Born in Amsterdam of Spanish-Portuguese descent. Rabbinical schooling. Banned from the synagogue in 1656 on the charge of athe-

ism and free thought, he devoted himself from the age of 24 to formulating his philosophy. A somewhat uncertain history has it that the ban was formal excommunication calling maledictions down upon him, that he said of the ban, "It compels me to nothing which I should not have done in any case," that he survived attempted assassination by a theology student, that his sister schemed to divert a modest inheritance intended for him (after all, the traditional excommunication ritual asked the lord "to blot out his name from under the sky"), and that his response was to win the case in court and then give the money to his sister. He worked at the trade of lens-grinding only enough to provide himself with the necessities of life. Moving from community to community around the perimeter of Amsterdam as though treasuring isolation, he was a stout defender of freedom of thought and speech. In 1672 he refused a pension from Louis XIV, which was offered on condition of dedicating a work to his Highness. He likewise refused a professorship at the University of Heidelburg, fearing limitations on his thought, speech, and mode of living (*q.v.* Judaism, 16).

Principal writings: *Principles of Cartesian Philosophy* (T), 1663; *Theological-Political Treatise* (T), 1670; *Ethics* (T); *A Political Treatise* (T); *Essay On the Improvement of the Understanding* (T); and the *Short Treatise on God, Man and His Well-Being* (T). The last four books were published posthumously.

Called the God-intoxicated man, Spinoza made his chief contribution to systematic philosophy or metaphysics, working out the implications of Cartesian method when applied to the basic ideas of the "perennial philosophy" of Western Europe. His scheme of ideas in the Ethics can be summarized as follows:

(1) If by substance one means what can exist by itself, there is only one substance, the whole of reality. This emphasis on a single substance is an expression of his famous monism (*q.v.* 1).

(2) If by God we mean "absolutely infinite being," there can be only one God, the whole of reality, and this Being exists necessarily, eternal not temporal, its essence implying its existence. It is its own cause, *causa immanens* and *causa sui*.

An absolutely infinite being will have an infinite number of attributes. Of this infinite number humans know two, thought and extension. The modes of thought and extension apply to the things of this world.

(3) If God and substance mean the same thing, then the goal of inquiry, and the goal of religion, turn out to be identical. The goal of humanity can thus be called either wisdom or "the intellectual love of God." But this identification equally allows us to speak of God or Nature (*Deus sive Natura*) in characterizing the total reality. And nature, then, must be understood in two ways. One of these is as the *Natura naturata* ("nature natured"), that is, as the reality which follows by necessity from the nature of God. The other manner of understanding nature is as the *Natura naturans* ("nature naturing"), that is, God as free cause, as eternal and infinite essence. And the former way of thinking of nature is found within the latter which is its principle and fundament.

(4) Out of the *conatus* or striving central to all living things, a striving to preserve oneself in being, one can derive a rational human psychology. This principal striving, also called affect, is named appetite or desire. According to Spinoza it is the primordial human virtue. From this start other parts of the psychology of affects can be derived. When the desire is satisfied, one experiences happiness; when it is not, one experiences sadness. All other affects, or emotional states, are built out of these three: desire, happiness, and sadness. Love is happiness united to the idea of an external cause. Hate is sadness united to the idea of an external cause. Hope is the representation of something in the future united to happiness. Fear is the representation of some future thing joined to sadness. Good is that which favors the tendency to persevere in being. Evil is that which opposes this tendency.

(5) Through *conatus*, also, one can move toward intellectual salvation. The stages, as Spinoza sees them, are: (a) On the level of imagination, where our intellectual life begins, we combine and fuse images, achieving a mixture of specious and of true universals. Through the power of the mind these can be ordered, and

the foundation of scientific knowledge discovered. In this step one begins to free oneself from the excessive temporality of the flux of images. (b) Hence, one arrives at science, a stage termed *ratio* by Spinoza. Since scientific laws apply to all times and places, the one who is able to lift one's understanding to this plane lives not just in a limited time and place. The understanding, of this person, like the laws of science, extends to all times and places. The individual is thus able to live more broadly and more deeply. Spinoza does not doubt that truth is available to rational beings and that it can be found deductively. The method of working with ideas which he accepted from Descartes and made his own in the *Treatise On the Improvement of the Understanding*, fits the present stage of this thought. The method, geometric or logistic, as it might be termed, begins with the assembling of a number of clear and distinct ideas, which can be regarded as self-evident, their own warranty for truth. Beginning with these necessary ideas, proceeding through deductions from them, one begins to unfold the nature of the real. Since Spinoza believes truth to be its own standard, the true ideas will convict the false ideas of their falsity. As one lives in this pursuit, the pursuit of one's own nature, one transcends the limitations of one's being felt so keenly at the first stage, (c) The human goal is "to live under the aspect of eternity"; or for the value he describes as the "intellectual love of God"; and one is able to achieve this goal in "the third stage of knowledge" (called *scientia intuitiva*). One is to live sensitively, seeing the universal in all the particulars of one's existence. One is to sense the universal qualities in all things around one, and in all the relationships in life, lifting everything to its essential nature. So living, one brings eternity into time, in a sense rises above the duration which characterizes created things, and is able to rise above the need for, and the illusion of believing in, an eternity added to the temporal span of one's life. Immortality hence becomes a quality of life, rather than a quantity of time.

(6) If substance-God-nature is absolutely infinite, it should be characterized by an infinite number of attributes. Spinoza found but two, thought and extension.

Yet he assumed that these two would apply to everything in reality; hence, in a sense are everywhere. He assumes that an infinite number of other qualities likewise characterize the whole of reality.

(7) However it may be with attributes, if there is but one substance, and this is the whole of reality, it is clear that what one ordinarily calls things, including our individual selves, cannot be substances. Spinoza calls them "modes." We are, as it were, modifications of the one substance.

(8) If reality is both thought and thing, everything will have both its reason and its cause. And throughout the universe there will be a parallelism between thought and thing. This means either that for every physical event there is a corresponding mental event or, more likely, that anything whatever can be appropriately interpreted in two ways. As an intelligible whole, each thing has its reason. As an extended plenum each thing has its cause. The result of this manner of viewing the universe leads to a reality which could not have been otherwise, each thing being the result of its causes or its reasons; and a God who could not have been otherwise, whose freedom comes from lack of dependence on any other thing. This has the consequence that miracles are not possible, since God cannot violate the order he has decreed.

(9) Human freedom, similarly, cannot be a freedom to do otherwise; but the freedom of moving toward imperturbability, serenity, independence in one's life. When one asserts that one can do otherwise, or feels capable of doing otherwise, this simply means that one is aware of a will to do a certain thing, while remaining ignorant of the set of causes which determines this will. Is Spinoza's way of blessedness in conflict with his view of a determined universe? If freedom and determinism are incompatible there is such a conflict; however, some will hold freedom and determinism to be compatible.

(10) Believing wisdom to be the goal of life, Spinoza in his political philosophy set the state the task of inculcating wisdom in the lives of its members, thus adding to the rationality of the world. The state comes into being, initially, for Spinoza as for Hobbes, to put an end to the anarchy which threatens human life; but since, unlike Hobbes, Spinoza finds wisdom to be the end of life, all persons must be at liberty to explore and hold the opinions to which they have been led. And thus the appropriate form of government will be democracy, not monarchy. And, short of sedition, the state will make secure the right to disagree.

SPIRIT.

From the Latin *spiritus* ("breath"). Thus, the breath of life. The Greek term is psyche (*q.v.*), and the term stood for the principle of animation, or life. The idea of soul (*q.v.*), also used in this connection, may be restricted to the doctrine, popularized by Plato (*q.v.* 3) that there is a separation of soul and body. Our interest in this entry, however, is the development of an idea of spirit in contradistinction to that of soul.

(1) An early distinction, not typical of later developments, is that of Telesio (*q.v.* 2) where, in addition to soul, the idea of spirit as a subtle matter and the principle of all movement in the universe is introduced.

(2) The idea of spirit in the sense intended occurred in the 19th-century movement of Idealism. Anticipating the movement, however, was Vico (*q.v.* 1) who made history the center of what humans can understand.

(3) Fichte (*q.v.* 5, 8) contributed to this sense of spirit, holding that the end of life is the development of a spiritual order.

(4) Hegel (*q.v.* 4) had the same goal; and in his *Phenomenology of the Spirit* began to trace the lineaments of that development. In his deduction of the categories Hegel (*q.v.* 9, 10, 18) distinguished between objective and absolute spirit.

(5) Dilthey (*q.v.* 1) distinguished the sciences of the spirit, the *Geisteswissenschaften*, from the natural sciences.

(6) Santayana (*q.v.* 6) spoke of a realm of spirit which was a quality of intellectual life supported by the material order.

(7) Croce (*q.v.* 1) presented a "philosophy of the spirit," made up of aesthetics, logic, economics, and ethics.

(8) Klages (*q.v.*) distinguished between soul and spirit, regarding the latter as embodying a false rationality and to be avoided in favor of the creative vital forces within the soul.

(9) For Scheler (*q.v.* 2-3) the spiritual

dimension of persons has its own values and is related to the development of ourselves as persons. Romero (*q.v.* 2) adopted, while developing, Scheler's view of spirit.

(10) For N. Hartmann (*q.v.*) spirit is that dimension of our being able to make contact with an ideal reality, and to discern the nature of values.

SPIRIT OF FINESSE, THE.
Q.v. Pascal (3).

SPIRIT OF GEOMETRY, THE.
Q.v. Pascal (3).

SPIRITO, UGO.
Q.v. Gentile (4); Fascism.

SPIRITUAL BEAUTY.
Q.v. Aquinas (10).

SPIRITUAL SENSATIONS.
Q.v. John Smith.

SPIRITUALISM.
A term with both philosophical and religious associations. Philosophically, the term is sometimes used as a synonym of Idealism (*q.v.*). In religion the term sometimes refers to the indwelling of the Holy Spirit.

(1) In philosophy, a 19th-century French movement of reaction against Comtian Positivism (*q.v.*). The movement was initiated in large part by Victor Cousin (*q.v.*) with Royer-Collard (*q.v.*) as predecessor; Maine de Biran (*q.v.* 1) is also important. Among others, Ravaisson-Mollien (*q.v.*) supported the spiritualism of Maine de Biran as did Galluppi (*q.v.*) in Italy.

(2) The name of a movement, interested in contacting the "spirits of the departed," which began in the United States in 1848, establishing headquarters in Washington, D.C., in 1893.

(3) A 20th-century Italian movement known as Christian Spiritualism, deriving both from Gentile (*q.v.* 4) and from religious existentialism.

SPISSITUDE.
Q.v. Henry More (2).

SPLIT-I, THE.
Q.v. Lacan (4–6).

SPONTANEITY.
From the Latin *sponte* meaning "of free will" or "voluntarily."

(1) The term was first used extensively by Leibniz (*q.v.* 14) who came upon it in a Latin translation of Aristotle's *Nicomachean Ethics*. He understood it to mean that whose principle is in the agent, and related the concept especially to the soul's capacity to make decisions independently of outside circumstances.

(2) The term has had moderate philosophical usage since Leibniz' time, for example Cousin (*q.v.* 2) makes it the basis not only of human freedom, but of the possibility of knowledge.

SPONTANEOUS APPERCEPTION.
Q.v. Cousin (2).

SPRACHFORM.
Q.v. Wilhelm von Humboldt.

SPRANGER, EDWARD. 1882–1963.
German philosopher. Born near Berlin. Taught at Leipzig, Berlin, and Tübingen. Taking as his task the completion, and systematization of the works of Dilthey (*q.v.*), Spranger was led to the development of typologies much in the manner of Max Weber (*q.v.*). Understanding the task of psychology to be a hermeneutic, or explication, of the spirit, Spranger carried out this objective by a study of ideal human types, *i.e.*, of the possible ways of being human. He distinguished the forms of life of theoretical man, economic man, aesthetic man, social man, political man, and religious man. Having isolated pure types, the next step is the development of an applied typology wherein mixed and intermediate forms are studied. For Spranger this was a study of the relations between subjective and objective spirit in terms of Dilthey or Hegel, but with the explicit recognition that spirit also has a normative dimension.

Principal writings: *Forms of Life: A Sketch*, 1914; *Problems of Cultural Morphology*, 1936.

SQUARE OF OPPOSITION.
Q.v. Immediate Inference (1).

ŚRUTI (SHRUTI).
Q.v. Śastras (1).

STACE, W.T. 1886–1967.
American philosopher. Born in London. Educated at Trinity College, Dublin. A

British officer in Ceylon from 1910 to 1932. Stace began his full-time philosophical career at Princeton, teaching there from 1932 to 1955. *Q.v.* Hegel (6).

Principal writings: *The Philosophy of Hegel*, 1924; *The Theory of Knowledge and Existence*, 1932; "The Refutation of Realism," 1934; *The Concept of Morals*, 1937; *Philosophy and the Modern Mind*, 1952; *Time and Eternity*, 1952; *Mysticism and Philosophy*, 1960.

(1) Although solipsism is logically unassailable, commonsense beliefs rest on the assumption of the similarity of human minds, and the possibility of common labor.

(2) On these assumptions, moving from what individuals want and approve, Stace constructs an Utilitarian ethic.

(3) An empiricist, although not a positivist, Stace held that empirical treatment of religion must go beyond logic, recognizing the paradox and mysticism integral to this experience.

STAËL, MADAME DE.
Q.v. Tragedy (9).

STAHL, G.E.
Q.v. Phlogiston Theory.

STALNAKER, ROBERT.
Q.v. Counterfactual Conditionals (4, 6).

STAMMLER, RUDOLF. 1856–1938.
German philosopher. Born in Alsfeld, Hesse. Taught at Marburg, Giessen, Halle, and Berlin. A neo-Kantian of the Marburg School (*q.v.* Neo-Kantianism 2), Stammler applied Kantian thought to the philosophy of law. He held that law is to society what mathematics is to the space-time world, a formal scheme with universal applicability and independence from its subject matter. Only such a conception, in his view, allows one to speak of a just law, and of diverse communities being governed by laws which are common.

Principal writings: *Theory of the Just Law* (T), 1902; *Theory of the Science of Law*, 1911; *Conferences and Essays on Philosophy of Law*, 2 vols., 1925.

STANDARD NAMES.
Q.v. Quantifying In (3).

STANDARD SOLID, THE.
Q.v. H.H. Price (1, 2).

STATE.
From the Latin *status* ("standing" or "position"). A collective entity with territorial boundaries and political organization exercising sovereign power (*q.v.* Sovereignty). The term may have been derived from the feudal "estates of the realm" (clergy, nobles, and commons). The representatives of the estates making up the first legislatures came to be called "states" (*i.e.*, the States-General of Holland). Machiavelli (*q.v.*) used the term to apply to the political entity itself, and that usage is now the accepted one. Some writers make a distinction between state and society (*q.v.*), while others do not. These differences have been discussed under the latter term.

(1) As for the structure of the state, Plato (*q.v.* 5c, f) found its classes to consist of rulers, soldiers, and artisans; and its identifiable permutations to run from aristocracy through timocracy, oligarchy, and democracy, to tyranny.

(2) Aristotle (*q.v.* 12) regarded the state as a creation of nature, since isolated man is not self-sufficient and is thus to be regarded as a part in relation to a whole. Aristotle found monarchy, aristocracy, and polity to be the optimal forms of government whose degenerate forms are tyranny, oligarchy, and democracy.

(3) Hobbes (*q.v.* 8), on the other hand, looked upon the state as an "artificial animal," resulting from the art of man and representing the greatest of human powers, indeed, a "mortal God." It is not, however, organic but merely the aggregate of its parts. He divided governments into monarchy, aristocracy, and democracy.

(4) Rousseau (*q.v.* 5f) regarded the state as a "public person," a "moral person" whose life is to be found in the "union of its members." Less clear is his claim that the body politic is called "state" when it is passive, and "sovereign" when active.

(5) For Kant (*q.v.* 10), who regarded the state as founded on a principle of universal legislation, the final step is a "universal union of states" in a "permanent congress of nations."

(6) Hegel (*q.v.* 17) increased the emphasis on life, thought, and consciousness as characteristics of the state. He even held that the state is to be vener-

ated as the Divine on earth, and the "march of God" in the world. The state thus became in his view a divine, living organism.

(7) Bentham (*q.v.* 5) returned to the Hobbesian concept of the state as an aggregate of individuals. He considered the public interest to be derived from a calculus of the pleasures and pains of individuals.

(8) J.S. Mill (*q.v.* 8), who followed Bentham with modifications, argued for representative government, and a maximum of liberty, as the preferred form of government.

(9) In both Marxism (*q.v.* 1f) and Anarchism (*q.v.*) the "withering away of the state" is expected, by revolution or evolution, depending on the school of thought.

(10) The theory of the Fascist state is associated with the name of Giovanni Gentile (*q.v.*), although his version of Actual Idealism—like the idealism of his master, Hegel—can be viewed either as sacralizing the temporal order or temporalizing the divine. It was not Gentile but one group among his followers, including Ugo Spirito (*q.v.* Gentile 4) who worked out theories of the corporate state.

(11) Parsons (*q.v.* 3) finds "boundary maintenance" an important prerequisite of the state's existence.

STATE DESCRIPTION.

In extensional semantics (*q.v.*) a class comprising, for a given semantical system, every atomic sentence or its negation. A true state description contains all of the true atomic sentences of the system, and the negation of all of the false atomic sentences.

(1) Carnap (*q.v.* 11) was able to define the analytic, synthetic, contradictory, factually true, in terms of state descriptions, along with such logical transformations as implication, equivalence, and disjunction.

(2) Nagel (*q.v.* 2) holds that the state description of quantum mechanics should differ from that of classical mechanics.

STATE OF NATURE.

The initial state of man, according to Social Contract Theory (*q.v.* 4–9), prior to the forming of society. Hobbes (*q.v.* 7) and Spinoza (*q.v.* 10) held the state of

nature to consist of internecine war, while Grotius (*q.v.* 3), Pufendorf (*q.v.* 1), and Locke (*q.v.* 9) found the state of nature both more rational and more peaceful.

STEINER, RUDOLF. 1861–1925.

German philosopher. Born in Hungary. Educated at the Polytechnic Institute of Vienna. Influenced by Goethe, Steiner initially argued for an organic view of the world allowing spiritual freedom. He moved into theosophy, and finally into his own view of Anthroposophy. A mystical system calling for the evolution of spiritual awareness, Anthroposophy developed into a movement with centers in both Europe and the United States.

Principal writings: *Philosophy of Freedom* (T), 1896; *Goethe's World View*, 1897; *Knowledge of the Higher Worlds* (T), 1923; *The Course of my Life* (T), 1925; *The New Art of Education* (T), 1928.

STEPHEN, LESLIE. 1832–1904.

English philosopher. Born in London. Educated at Cambridge. Elected a fellow of Trinity Hall, he took orders in the Church, separating from both within a decade. An agnostic who helped to popularize the term, in his ethics Stephen combined Utilitarianism (*q.v.* 8) with an appreciation of the Darwinian struggle for survival. The motif of survival was dominant in his point of view.

Principal writings: *The Science of Ethics*, 1882; *An Agnostic's Apology*, 1893; *English Utilitarianism*, 3 vols., 1900; *Hobbes*, 1904; *English Thought and Society in the Eighteenth Century*, 2 vols., 1904.

STERN, WILHELM. 1871–1938.

German philosopher and psychologist. Born in Berlin. Taught in Breslau, Hamburg, and at Vassar College. In philosophy he advanced a doctrine of Critical Personalism. While recognizing an irreconcilable difference between "person" and "thing," Stern did not follow the usual line of personalism, generalizing the category of person to the universe. Instead, he turned to psychological investigation and a theory of knowledge similar to Critical Realism (*q.v.*).

Principal philosophical writings: *Person and Thing: System of the Philosophical World-View*, 2 vols., 1906, 1918; *Person and Thing: System of Critical Personalism*, 2 vols., 1923, 1924; *Fundamental Ideas of Personalist Philosophy*, 1918.

STEUCHEN.
Q.v. Philosophia Perennis.

STEVENSON, CHARLES. 1908–1979.
Educated at Yale, Cambridge, and Harvard. Professor of philosophy at the University of Michigan.
Principal writings: *Ethics and Language*, 1944; *Facts and Value*, 1963.

(1) Most ethical theorists in the past have written as though ethical disputes were based on disagreements in belief, when in fact such disputes are based on disagreements in attitude.

(2) Most terms, and all ethical terms, have levels of suggestion, or emotive meaning, in addition to their cognitive meaning. The emotive meaning of a term has a power to produce affective responses in those who hear and use them. What is involved in ethical discourse and discussion is the reinforcing or redirecting of attitudes through the affective power of emotive meaning.

(3) In attempting to redirect attitudes in ethics and elsewhere, "persuasive definitions" are often used. These are definitions which in fact change the cognitive meaning of a term about which, for example, positive attitudes have formed, while using its positive emotive meaning to bring acceptance of the new cognitive meaning.

STEWART, DUGALD. 1753–1828.
Scottish philosopher. Born in Edinburgh. Educated at Edinburgh and Glasgow, he studied under Thomas Reid (*q.v.*), the "common sense" philosopher whose point of view he adopted with minor changes. Questions of one's existence and personal identity, as well as the existence of a world with general laws which operate now, and will continue to do so, belong to "the fundamental laws of human belief." Stewart substituted the foregoing phrase for Reid's locution concerning principles of common sense. Convinced of the objectivity of moral principles, he remained indifferent to the "speculative principles" which explain them.
Principal writings: *Elements of the Philosophy of the Human Mind*, 3 vols., 1792,

1814, 1827; *Philosophical Essays*, 1810; *The Philosophy of the Active and Moral Powers of Man*, 1828.

STHAVIRAVADA.
Sanskrit term meaning "way of the elders." *Q.v.* Buddhism, Theravada.

STICH, STEPHEN.
Q.v. Folk Psychology; Psychology (18).

STILPO. 4th cent. B.C.
Greek philosopher. Born in Megara. A student of disciples of Euclid of Megara (*q.v.*), or of the latter himself, Stilpo urged *apatheia*, or resigned self-control, as the principal virtue of life anticipating and, indeed, shaping Stoicism (*q.v.*). He attacked the Platonic doctrine of Ideas. Zeno of Citium (*q.v.*), the founder of Stoicism, and Bryson, the teacher of the Skeptic Pyrrho (*q.v.*), were among his disciples.

STIMULUS-MEANING.
A concept used by Quine (*q.v.* 5; Radical Translation 1), in an attempt to explicate analyticity and synonymy (*q.v.*) in terms of behavioral dispositions. In addition to the above term he referred to stimulus-analyticity and stimulus-synonymy.

STIPULATIVE DEFINITION.
Q.v. Definition (2).

STIRNER, MAX (born Johann Kasper Schmidt). 1806–1856.
German Philosopher. Born in Bayreuth. Studied at Berlin, Erlangen, and Königsberg. Through Die Freien, an association of young Hegelians, he met Marx and Engels. His point of view, belongs to anarchism rather than to Marxism.
Principal writings: *The Ego and One's Own* (T), 1845; *The History of the Reaction*, 2 vols., 1852.

(1) Believing in the primacy of the will over the reason, as well as in the uniqueness of each individual, Stirner maintained that self-affirmation of the Ego is the supreme law. The end of life is an individualism or Egoism whose only rule is the discovery and fulfillment of one's own will.

(2) He argued that this emphasis on individualism would not increase conflict among men but reduce it, since with-

drawal into one's own uniqueness was a movement opposed to that of wishing to dominate another, and that the "Union of Egoists" could have strength while preserving individual freedom.

(3) The appropriate response to the state is, correspondingly, not revolution, since this submerges one's individuality, but rebellion which is an individual act, rejecting the repressiveness of the state and expressing one's freedom. The object of revolution is to replace one state by a different one; the object of rebellion in relation to the state is simply its collapse.

STÖHR, ADOLF. 1855–1921.

Austrian philosopher. Born in St. Pölten. Educated at Vienna where he also taught. An early student of the philosophy of language, Stöhr warned against linguistic muddles in philosophy. He distinguished three types of metaphysics: pathogonous (deriving from pain and the "suffering heart"); glossogonous (deriving from glossomorphic confusion or the "rolling word"); and theorogonous (deriving from wonder and issuing in imaginative construction). Rejecting the first two types, and with them most traditional metaphysics, he accepted the third, as satisfying an "artistic propensity."

Selected writings: *Outline of a Theory of Names*, 1889; *Psychology: Facts, Problems, and Hypotheses*, 1917; *Ways of Belief*, 1921.

STOICISM.

From the Greek *stoa* ("porch"). A Graeco-Roman School of philosophy founded in 108 B.C. in Athens by Zeno of Citium, and developing its greatest influence in the Roman Empire where at one time it was the dominant intellectual influence. The name of the school derives from the location in Athens where the school first met. The doctrines of the school are diverse but they include the development of a logic (divided into rhetoric and dialectic), physics, and an ethic which likewise involves a theology. Indeed, the Stoics seem to have introduced the division of philosophy into these three disciplines. In many Stoic analyses the three-fold division likewise stands for the three virtues, virtue being defined as the end or perfection of a thing. It is by the ethic that the school is best known, the Stoic resignation or *apathia*, which encourages one to accept one's situation in the world, and to view this as a reflection of the ultimate reason of things. To live according to reason means to simplify one's life. In the theodicy it is assumed that the world reason is in control of the universe, and that when one lives according to one's own reason one is in touch with the universal reason. The concept of nature was the ultimate inclusive category including all things: divine, human, and subhuman. The history of the school is divided into three periods: Ancient Stoicism, Middle Period Stoicism, and the New Stoicism.

(1) Ancient Stoicism begins with the founder, Zeno of Citium (*q.v.*), and includes both Cleanthes (*q.v.*), and Chrysippus (*q.v.*) among many others. In this period the Stoic logic and epistemology were developed (*q.v.* Chrysippus 1), as well as the Stoic physics. Their logic stressed the propositional calculus and derived logical connections from reason itself by a kind of logical necessity. The Stoic epistemology contributed the phrase "common notions" to philosophy. They held that all persons—apparently by virtue of common experience since innateness is not stressed—have a certain basic set of ideas in common. These ideas provide the starting point of knowledge. They are plural in number and come into play in the *synkatathesis*, or acceptance of propositions as true. They relate to many areas, including our knowledge of an external world. The Stoic physics stressed the corporeal nature of things, and held the world to be determined. The determination is, however, an ordering of things according to the universal reason or *logos* which is in control, apparently by virtue of a *pneuma* which animates and controls all matter. Following the Heracliteans (*q.v.* Heraclitus), fire was held to be the central element relating to all other elements, the whole exhibiting a harmonious tension. The ancient Stoics also developed the notion of the world year, a vast cycle of time leading to the periodic destruction and regeneration of the world by fire.

(2) The Middle Period of Stoicism includes Panaetius (*q.v.*) and Posidonius (*q.v.*) the encyclopedist, among others.

The period is characterized by tendencies toward encyclopedism, syncretism, and pantheism.

(3) The New Stoicism coincides with the imperial period of the Roman Empire, and includes among its figures Seneca (q.v.), Epictetus (q.v.), and Marcus Aurelius (q.v.). It is in this period that the ethics of Stoicism was most completely stressed. We have given a sketch of its emphases above, since this was the period that set the image of the Stoic movement. The Stoic emphasis on the control of life by reason led to a widening of the sense of public duty. It also, however, led to the view that it is at times reasonable to take one's own life. In a number of cases, including Seneca himself, public officials among the Stoics committed suicide at the point of real or apparent failure in matters of state.

(4) A final point of considerable importance is the manner in which natural law ideas emerged from the development of the Stoic movement, and operated in the Roman lawyers who were themselves largely Stoic in their training. It was the Stoic vision of the operations of a universal reason in all of the details of world process which made possible the conception of a standard of right beyond the positive law of a given society; this too made possible the conception of all persons living in a *cosmopolis*; one is appropriately cosmopolitan, "people of the cosmos" relating to the cosmos, rather than to a given area only. Doubtless the point of transition was the Roman *jus gentium*, or law of nations, a developing code applying to all communities. But when Ulpian separated the natural law, or *jus naturale*, from the *jus gentium*, and defined it as the "law, which nature has taught all human beings," the Stoic conception is at work. Justinian I accepted the definition.

STORM AND STRESS.
Q.v. Goethe (1); also q.v. *Sturm und Drang*.

STOUT, G.F. 1860–1944.
English philosopher. Born in South Shields. Professor at Cambridge, Aberdeen, Oxford, and St. Andrews.
Principal writings: *Analytic Psychology*, 2 vols., 1896; *A Manual of Psychology*, 1899;

Studies in Philosophy and Psychology, 1930; *Mind and Matter*, 1931; *God and Nature*, 1952.

(1) The representations of thought reflect a "noetic synthesis" such that they contain both sensa and an unbreakable reference to the external world. We are thus not isolated by *sensa*, but have immediate contact with the real world.

(2) With respect to universals he held that they are distributive unities of their respective classes.

(3) As to man, he presented the doctrine of an embodied mind, a single entity with both physical and mental attributes. His view thus combined a monism of substance with a dualism of qualities.

STRAIGHT RULE.
Q.v. Induction (12–15).

STRANGE ATTRACTOR.
Q.v. Chaos Theory (9).

STRATO. 3rd cent. B.C.
Greek philosopher. Born in Lampsacus. A disciple of Theophrastus and member of the Lyceum (q.v.), he followed his master as head of the school, holding this position from around 287 to 269 B.C. Mainly interested in the natural sciences, his work in the areas of physics and medicine exerted influence over the field of scholarship during the Alexandrian period.

(1) Combining the ideas of Aristotle and Democritus, Strato held to a theory of atomism. Unlike Democritean atomism, however, Strato's atoms were infinitely divisible and endowed with the additional qualities of heat and cold.

(2) Adopting a mechanistic view of the world, he held the soul to be the unity of the body, and that psychic processes are grounded in physical processes.

STRAUSS, DAVID F. 1808–1874.
German philosopher and historian of religion. Born at Ludwigsburg. Educated at Blaubeuren, Berlin, and Tübingen. Taught briefly at Tübingen. Under the influence of the Hegelian Left, Strauss regarded Christian mythology as an unconscious human invention, attempting to describe the Absolute in sensible terms. Jesus thus represents an incarnation of the spirit of humanity. Strauss did not regard the accounts of this life in the

gospels as historic but only as a portion of the history of human expression. Christianity is regarded as a preliminary stage of thought which reached its culmination in the philosophy of Hegel (*q.v.*).

Principal writings: *The Life of Jesus* (T), 2 vols., 1835–6; *Christian Dogma*, 2 vols., 1840–1; *The Christ of Belief and the Jesus of History*, 1865.

STRAWSON, P.F. 1919– .

English philosopher. Born in London. Educated at Oxford. Taught at the University College of North Wales, and at Oxford.

Principal writings: "Truth," 1949; "On Referring," 1950; *Introduction to Logical Theory*, 1952; *Individuals*, 1959; *The Bounds of Sense*, 1966; *Logico-linguistic Papers*, 1971; *Freedom and Resentment*, 1974; *Subject and Predicate in Logic and Grammar*, 1974; *Skepticism and Naturalism*, 1985; *Analysis and Metaphysics*, 1992.

(1) Attacking the view that "true" and "false" are descriptive terms, Strawson insists that they are, rather, performative or expressive. To say that a sentence is true is to *express* agreement with the sentence.

(2) Criticizing Russell's theory of definite descriptions (*q.v.* Russell 4), Strawson argues that Russell has confused "referring to" an entity, with "asserting the existence of" that entity. In referring to an entity one presupposes, without asserting, existence. Thus where Russell says of the sentence, "The present king of France is bald," that the sentence is false, there being no king of France, Strawson holds the statement to be neither true nor false since its basic presupposition (that there is a king of France) is false.

(3) Distinguishing M-predicates ("Material body"-predicates) from P-predicates ("Person"-predicates), Strawson develops a descriptive metaphysics rising from study of the uses of these types of terms. He regards material objects to be the basic particulars, since all other particulars must be identified by reference to material objects. He likewise holds "Person" to be more basic than "Mind" or "Body," since "Person" is the more primitive concept, in the sense that both consciousness terms and physical property terms are ascribable to it. In his view, making "Person" the critical and key term enables one to avoid the traditional difficul-

ties of the Mind-Body problem.

(4) Placing himself within the field of analytic philosophy (*q.v.* Philosophy 45), Strawson explored some of the basic concepts "which constitute the framework of our ordinary thought and talk," *e.g.*, body, person, truth, identity, knowledge, sometimes indirectly through consideration of other analytic philosophers' analyses of such concepts.

STRICT IMPLICATION.

Q.v. C.I. Lewis (1); Modal Logic (2); Paradoxes of Strict Implication (Modal Logic 5).

STRIFE.

For Empedocles (*q.v.* 3) a cosmic principle.

STROKE FUNCTION.

Q.v. Sheffer, H.M.

STRONG AI.

Q.v. Artificial Intelligence (3).

STRUCTURALISM.

An interdisciplinary point of view, philosophy, or philosophic movement, achieving prominence in the 1960's. Its central tenet is that all societies and cultures possess a common and invariant structure. Emergent in France as a result of the anthropological writings of Claude Lévi-Strauss, the thrust of Structuralism is away from origins and toward specification of the unchanging structure of relations which—on the hypothesis—all men hold unconsciously and pre-reflectively. Since this structure is likewise manifest in every aspect of society or culture, it is natural that the movement should include specialists not only in anthropology but also in linguistics, literary criticism, history, economics, psychoanalysis, philosophy, and religion. Furthermore, the list of structuralists tends to expand as those in the movement seek their antecedents. Vico, Marx, Freud, Jung, de Saussure, Merleau-Ponty, and Piaget, are among those claimed by structuralists as related to their movement.

(1) Ferdinand de Saussure (*q.v.*) is hailed as the founder of structural linguistics. Distinguishing between signifier and thing signified, de Saussure called for a science of Semiology, dealing with the nature of signs and with their gov-

erning laws. His belief that linguistic laws develop synchronically, *i.e.*, at the same time in different societies, is a key doctrine of the movement.

(2) Lévi-Strauss (*q.v.* 1–3), in examining the structure common to different societies, utilizes in combination the tools of anthropology and linguistics. In the application of his method the basic similarities or identities of apparently different myths and customs in different societies are brought to light. In the course of his analysis man comes to be regarded as a portion of the structure, not "constituted" by the analysis but rather "dissolved" thereby. The shift of emphasis from man to structure is a common feature of structuralist thought.

(3) Jacques Lacan (*q.v.*), founder of the Freudian school of Paris, relates the structuralist concern with language to the unconscious. Not only is it the case for Lacan that language is the tool by which one is able to reach the unconscious, the unconscious is itself "precisely structured" as a language. Lacan questions the importance of human individuality. We must learn how to "de-center" man. Lacan states that man, the apparent subject, does not think. He is, rather (using the passive voice), thought. Man, the "fading subject," should no longer be regarded as central but as one element in the analysis among many others.

(4) Although Louis Althusser (*q.v.*) has been regarded as the philosopher who extended structuralism to the thought of Karl Marx, viewing both history and economics as "engulfed" in structures, his rereading of Marx emphasized the dimensions of ideology in society and reaction against humanistic Marxism.

(5) Among others Roland Barthes (*q.v.*) has applied structural analysis to literary criticism. Regarding different styles of expression or analysis as different "languages," the task of literary criticism becomes one of translation. The literary critic expresses in one of the languages of his own epoch the formal system the author had developed under the conditions of another time. The object is to discern sameness of structure despite linguistic differences. In *S/Z*, however, Barthes declared against structuralism; and from that point on has been regarded by many as part of the movement of Post-

Structuralism (*q.v.*).

(6) Michel Foucault (*q.v.*) applies Structuralism to the field of philosophy. In his view the order of words contains the key to understanding, both in philosophy and elsewhere, and is more important than the order of things. He holds that all theoretical disciplines are charged with the task of eliminating humanism by bringing to light the anonymous system of thought "without a subject" which is present in the language of an epoch.

(7) Günther Schiwy (*Structuralism and Christianity* (T), 1969), is among those relating Structuralism to Christianity. He has attempted to show that the atemporal emphasis of Structuralism has a natural compatibility with the eternalist emphasis of Christianity.

(8) Jonathan Culler (1944–), an American structuralist, finds (in *Structuralist Poetics*, 1975) that to read intelligently is to read in terms of the structural features of the text. The power of such readings suggests that the interpreter is relating somewhat invariant structures of understanding to the structural features selected by the author.

(9) At the present point in its history, at least, Structuralism thus denies the importance of history, stressing rather the importance of system. It minimizes individuality and humanism, emphasizing structure. It finds the differences among societies only apparent, emphasizing their identities. It reduces the emphasis on time, substituting *synchrony*, meaning "occurring together in time" and interpreted as the priority of the state of language to history, for *diachrony*, meaning "successive occurrence in time" and thus emphasis on the historical succession of forms.

(10) The term, "Structuralism," is also used as the name of a school of Psychology (*q.v.* 7) which developed prior to the movement discussed above, and which has no direct relations with it. Structuralism in psychology centers attention on the importance of the structures of psychic phenomena open to introspection, presenting a structural approach to psychological interpretation as preferable to a functional approach.

STRUGGLE FOR EXISTENCE.
Q.v. Darwin (3).

STUMPF, KARL. 1848–1936.

German psychologist and philosopher. Born in Wiesentheid, Bavaria. Educated at Würzburg, Prague, and Munich. A student of Lotze, he was the teacher of Husserl and the psychologist, Wolfgang Köhler (*q.v.*). In philosophy he was an empiricist. One of the founders of psychology as a scientific discipline, his own research related to space, sound, and tone. He believed metaphysics to be valid if construed as a continuation of the sciences.

Selected writings: *On the Psychological Origin of Spatial Representation*, 1873; *Tone Psychology*, 2 vols., 1883, 1890; *Psychology and Theory of Knowledge*, 1891; *Contributions to Acoustics and the Science of Music*, 1898; *The Origin of Music*, 1911; *Theory of Knowledge*, 2 vols., 1939, 1941.

STURM UND DRANG.

A German phrase meaning "storm and stress." A movement in Germany following the principles of Romanticism and opposing the French ideals of Enlightenment. Among its leaders were Herder (*q.v.*), Goethe (*q.v.* 1), Friedrich Schiller (*q.v.*), and others.

SUAREZ, FRANCISCO. 1548–1617.

Spanish Scholastic philosopher. Born in Granada. Educated at Salamanca. Entered the Jesuit order. Taught at Segovia, Valladolid, Alcalá, Salamanca, and Rome. Originally a Thomist, through time he came to discard many of St. Thomas' views. For example he rejected the proof of God on the basis of motion, as well as the reality of the distinction between essence and existence in finite beings (*q.v.* Thomas Aquinas 3a and 6). He is regarded as the most important Scholastic philosopher of the 16th century.

Principal writings: *The Metaphysical Disputations*, 23 vols.

(1) He believed that theology could be aided by philosophical discussion and criticism, and that the two disciplines could appropriately coexist within the higher unity of the Christian faith.

(2) The way in which the two disciplines might cooperate can be seen in Suarez' treatment of arguments for the existence of God. On the one hand he believed that the effects of God's activity in the world provide a clear demonstration of His existence. On the other hand, he held that this demonstration is not one which can be understood by finite minds operating in the created order of things. Hence, a higher perspective is needed, and yet this is somehow beyond finite rationality.

(3) His solution to the problem of individuation, that is, how one is to understand the individual thing, is that the individual is a composite of two distinct kinds of unity, one material and the other formal. Better said, it is a unity of two other unities, these being matter and form. The individuality of the thing is a function of the particular unity of matter and form achieved in a given instance. There are as many "formal unities" as there are individuals.

(4) His doctrine of "Congruism" has been much discussed. His conception here is that with respect to the elect, the grace they possess leads them infallibly to yield themselves to God, and yet this is compatible with, or congruent with, the fact of free will.

SUBALTERNATION.

Q.v. Immediate Inference (1).

SUBCONTRARIETY.

Q.v. Immediate Inference (1).

SUBJECT.

From the Latin *sub* ("under") and *jacere* ("to throw"). As in the case of "object" (*q.v.*), the term "subject" has suffered a dramatic reversal of meaning.

(1) Its initial sense with Aristotle (*q.v.* 5) concerned logic. One spoke of the "subject" and "predicate" of a proposition, that of which something is predicated. What is Subject is also substance (*q.v.* Aristotle 6), that which exists in the world.

(2) Duns Scotus (*q.v.* 2) identified "subjective" and "objective" with the Arabian distinction of first and second intentions. First intentions were subjective, *i.e.*, concrete substances. Second intentions were objective, *i.e.*, things as constituted by mental operations.

(3) Descartes (*q.v.* 7) continued the medieval usage, relating the objective to thought, and the subjective to the things themselves.

(4) Kant (*q.v.* 11d) marks the point where the reversal in meaning occurred.

Holding that "the thing which thinks" is nothing more than a transcendental subject known only "through the thoughts that are its predicates," it is clear that the center of awareness becomes the subject, and the object is forced outside the realm of subjective awareness. This is the meaning of "subject" which has come into general use in the modern world.

SUBJECTIVE IDEALISM.
Q.v. Idealism (1).

SUBJECTIVISM.
A general category including all doctrines stressing the subjective features of experience.

(1) In epistemology, the doctrine that limits knowledge to the mind's awareness of its own states. The doctrine of representative perception (*q.v.*) tends to fit into this category.

(2) In metaphysics, the doctrines of solipsism (*q.v.*) and subjective idealism (*q.v.* Idealism 1).

(3) In aesthetics, the doctrine that aesthetic judgment is nothing more than an expression of individual taste.

(4) "Ethical subjectivism" is the doctrine advanced by Westermarck (*q.v.* 1) to the effect that what ethical judgments assert is that, and no more than that, the person making the judgment has an attitude of approval or disapproval toward the subject in question. On this view no two persons mean the same thing in making the same judgment, since each means, "This is approved (or disapproved) by me." Furthermore, no two persons contradict each other in apparently disagreeing on an ethical judgment. When the contradictory statements, "x is wrong," and "x is right" are properly expanded they read "A approves of x," and "B disapproves of x." But in this form the statements are not contradictory. They merely register the disagreement of A and B. In the same way, no argument or evidence of any kind is relevant to supporting or doubting such judgments.

SUBJECT, THE FADING.
Q.v. Structuralism (3).

SUBJECT-PREDICATE LOGIC.
Aristotle's logic of predication centering in the theory of the Syllogism (*q.v.*).

SUBLAPSARIANISM.
Q.v. Predestination (7).

SUBLIMATION.
Q.v. Nietzsche (3); Freud (4).

SUBLIME, THE.
An aesthetic value usually contrasted with the beautiful.

(1) The notion of the Sublime was introduced to philosophy through a treatise titled *On the Sublime*, mistakenly attributed to Longinus (*q.v.*). In this work by an unknown 1st-century author the sublime is related to the use of language, and rules were given for sublime expression.

(2) Edmund Burke (*q.v.* 1), on the other hand, viewed the sublime as an emotion of delight mixed with terror or pain, and produced by an infinite object.

(3) Kant (*q.v.* 9) followed Burke's lead while eliminating the factor of terror or pain. He regarded the beautiful as that which conforms to our faculties, and the sublime as that which is too vast thus to conform. It somehow extends beyond facile assimilation.

SUBSET, PROPER.
Q.v. Set Theory (5).

SUBSIDIARY, THE.
Q.v. Polanyi (2).

SUBSISTENCE.
From the Latin *subsistere* ("to continue"). Usually contrasted with "existence" as a less complete mode of being, the term has carried a variety of meanings in the history of philosophy.

(1) In Thomism (*q.v.*), Subsistence is a positive perfection relating to essence rather than to existence, and concerning the definitude or termination of a substantial nature, making it distinct from any other. There are two forms of subsistence: an "imperfect" form relating to species and a "perfect" form relating to individual substantial natures (*q.v.* Form 5i).

(2) By way of contrast, Descartes (*q.v.* 8) and the Port Royal Logic (*q.v.* Port Royal) regarded subsistence as the manner of existence of a substance in comparison to that of an accident.

(3) Kant (*q.v.* 3) appears to have taken this position a further step. He held the

substance-accident relation to involve "subsistence" and "inherence" respectively. Accidents inhere in substances, and the latter subsist in their accidents.

(4) Meinong (*q.v.* 1) separated character from existence in his theory of objects, allowing for existence and subsistence, as well as for characters with no being whatever. In chapter nine of *Problems of Philosophy* Russell discussed the first two categories. We say of objects that they exist, he suggested, and of universals that they subsist, *i.e.*, have a timeless being.

(5) Santayana (*q.v.* 6) at times spoke of essences as subsistent, but even their subsistence is regarded as the work of spirit.

(6) Montague (*q.v.* 1) termed his philosophy "subsistential realism," distinguishing between the "merely subsistent" and "existential subsistence." False statements have the former mode of being and true statements the latter.

SUBSTANCE.

From the Latin *sub* ("under") and *stare* ("to stand"), a translation of the Greek term *hypostasis* from *hypo* ("under") and *hitasthai* ("to stand"). The term thus refers to the underlying, supporting substratum of change. But "substance" also contains the idea of the individual subject of change. The Greek terms which best capture this sense are *ousia* and *hypokeimenon*. In turn, however, *ousia* means both "substance" and "essence" and *hypokeimenon* means the "concrete thing," the "substratum," and the "subject." The situation was thus complex at its outset.

(1) Aristotle (*q.v.* 6–7) pointed out that the term "substance" (he used both *ousia* and *hypokeimenon*) can be taken to refer to four different things: the essence, the universal, the genus, and the subject. But since the primary referent of the term is the subject of predication (*q.v.*) which cannot be predicated of anything else, the four meanings can be reduced to two: "first substance" (*ousia prote*), the subject of predication; and "second substance" (*ousia deutera*), *i.e.*, the other references, all of which are general terms capable of representing "first substance" only incompletely.

(2) Medieval speculation on the nature of substance turned on the distinction

between "substance" and "accident." If by "accident" one means that which inheres in something else, whose reason or essence is in something else, then by substance one should mean the subject of accidents which contains its own reason or essence. The factor of being independent of other things in a significant sense thus came to be stressed as one of the distinguishing characteristics of substance. As in Aristotle, first substance (*substantia prima*), the individual subject of predication, was regarded as the primary meaning of the term. Its secondary meaning was second substance (*substantia secunda*) whose analysis centered in the notion of the essence or *quidditas* of first substance. First substance is thus characterized by existence as well as essence, and second substance only by essence. So it was that first substance came to be viewed as existence added to essence (*q.v.* Aquinas 6).

(3) William of Ockham (*q.v.* 9) restricted the reference of the term to first or primary substance alone, thus helping to establish modern usage, while reducing the complexity of the analysis.

(4) Descartes (*q.v.* 8) defined substance, generally, starting from the subject. Any subject containing a "property, quality, or attribute" merits the term "substance." Following the medieval stress on independence, however, he also held substance to be "that which can exist by itself" without the aid of any other thing. On this basis he distinguished between finite and infinite substance, and pointed out that God alone is truly substance.

(5) Spinoza (*q.v.* 1–3, 6–7) simply drew the logical conclusion of Descartes' analysis. If God alone is truly self-existent, then there is but one substance, God himself, and anything else must be simply a mode of that substance.

(6) Leibniz (*q.v.* 1), likewise beginning with the Cartesian self-existent subject, found the ultimate unity of reality to lie in "simple substances" or monads, their self-existence guaranteed by their character as non-extended centers of force.

(7) Locke (*q.v.* 5b) understood substance as the underlying substratum of change. His conception followed the genealogy of the word more closely than any other philosopher. As an empiricist he pointed out that while he could know

the qualities anchored in the substratum, the latter remained a "something I know not what." Similarly, he pointed out that our knowledge extends only to the nominal essence of a thing. Even so he does not doubt that in each case a subject of change and a real essence do exist.

(8) Pushing Locke's point a bit further, Berkeley (*q.v.* 3) denied the existence of material substance while affirming, somewhat unclearly, a substantial soul.

(9) Hume (*q.v.* 1, 4) took the final step in developing the implications of Locke's thought. Armed with the principle that a conception unsupported by any impression is senseless, Locke's "something I know not what" becomes meaningless. Hume was thus led to deny all types of substance—not only the material substance ruled out by Berkeley, but also the spiritual substance the latter had expected to retain.

(10) Kant (*q.v.* 3) regarded both substance and accident as synthetic *a priori* concepts derived from the categorical judgment, *i.e.*, the subject-predicate form of expression. In this context the term refers not to anything in the world, but rather to the manner in which humans order their experience.

(11) The entire movement of Phenomenalism (*q.v.*) is an attempt to construe reality in the absence of the idea of substance. One of their number, Petzoldt (*q.v.*), for example, substituted for substance the idea of a relatively stable complex of sense-qualities.

(12) Santayana (*q.v.* 5) regarded the idea of substance as an ordering element which one posits in order to be able to explicate the further ideas of self and world.

(13) Whitehead (*q.v.* 9) attacked the idea of substance by denying the ultimacy of the subject-predicate mode of expression, and substituting for substance an event ontology.

SUBSTANTIAL FORM.
   Q.v. Form (5a).

SUBSTRATUM.
   Q.v. Substance, especially (7).

SUBSUMPTION.
   From the Latin *sub* ("under") and *sumere* ("to take or include"). In medieval logic the minor premise was called

the "subsumption" of the major premise (the "sumption"). Similarly, individuals are subsumptions of species, species of genera, and facts are subsumptions of the laws which govern them.

SUCCESSION, ORDER OF.
   Leibniz (*q.v.* 2) defined time as the "order of succession" in contrast with space, the "order of coexistence."

SUCHNESS.
   Q.v. Aśvaghoṣa (1, 2, 5); Hsuan-Tsang (1).

ŚUDRAS (SHUDRAS).
   The laboring class of Indian tradition. *Q.v.* Hinduism (4); *Mahabharata* (3); *Laws of Manu* (2).

SUFFERING.
   Identifying "suffering," "ignorance," and "*karma*," Buddha (*q.v.* 2) explained the phenomenon as due to the law of Dependent Origination (*q.v.*).

SUFFICIENT CONDITION.
   Q.v. Necessary and Sufficient Condition; Cause (19).

SUFFICIENT REASON, PRINCIPLE OF.
   In Leibniz (*q.v.* 4) the view that nothing takes place without a reason sufficient to determine why it is as it is and not otherwise. Also *q.v.* Schopenhauer (1).

SUFISM.
   Possibly derived from the Arabic term *suf* meaning "wool." If so the name probably relates to the woolen garments traditionally worn by ascetics. By the eighth century Sufism began to challenge Islamic rationalism. Identified with the Shiite division of the movement, Sufism is a mystical communion seeking union with Allah through love and renunciation. Through time, Sufism became pantheistic (*q.v.*) in tone, and developed the poetry which is the highest achievement of Persian literature. Beginning in the 12th century, Sufism mingled with Hinduism (*q.v.* 5c) in northern India, producing a mystical version of Hinduism.

SUHRAWARDI, SHIHAB. 1155–91.
   Born in Suhraward (N. Iran). Educated at Maragha and Isfahan. Imprisoned as a heretic and executed by starvation or

suffocation by order of the famed Saladin.

Principal writings: In addition to three books rooted in Aristotle (*The Book of Intimations, The Book of Oppositions, The Book of Conversations*), *Theosophy of Illumination* (all four translated into French).

(1) Holding himself to be reuniting the strands of the perennial philosophy whose theoretical aspects had been broken off by the Greeks, Suhrawardi taught that the *philosophia perennis* held reason and intuition together combining doctrine, rite, and spiritual alchemy.

(2) Greek rationalism is exoteric and occidental; the intuitive aspect of philosophy is esoteric and oriental (playing on the similarity between *ishraq*, "illumination," and *mashriq*, the "east"). He believed the occidental side had been carried by the Greek philosophers, including Aristotle, Plato, and the Neoplatonists; and the oriental side by (among others) the Persian priest-kings. The two sides were reunited in Suhrawardi himself.

(3) In fact, Suhrawardi's illuminationism was a development of Ibn Sina's esoteric philosophy (*q.v.* Avicenna 11). It also stems from Persian Zoroastrianism, turning on the symbolic image of light, which plays the role of Greek being as well as form. Each form is now an angel, so the number of angels is innumerable. Each existent thing, called a talisman, has a governing angel (the "lord" of the talisman). The whole scheme moves from God, the "light of lights," to the mere shadow of existence, ready to sink into utter darkness. A successor was Mulla Sadra (*q.v.*).

SUICIDE.

The act of voluntarily taking one's own life. The case enters into discussions of freedom and responsibility. Among the positions held we cite the following examples:

(1) Socrates (*q.v.* 4) offered the mythological argument that man is the property of the gods, and must wait for their decision concerning the termination of his life. This position has been widely held. Socrates' ethical argument, that it is always better to suffer than to do evil, likewise seems applicable to the argument.

(2) The Stoic emphasis on control of life by reason led not only to a wider sense of duty, but also to the view that,

given adequate reason, suicide is appropriate and perhaps required (*q.v.* Stoicism 3). Not only did Seneca (*q.v.*) argue for this position, he put it into practice.

(3) Schopenhauer (*q.v.* 7) opposed suicide on the ground that the act represented desire rather than a renunciation deriving from true discipline. The latter is possible only through art, philosophy, and religion.

(4) Camus (*q.v.* 1) argued that suicide is an inadequate response to the absurdity of life. The more human response is to live through the absurdity in full awareness.

SUMMAE.

From the Latin *summa* ("a compendium"). A form of investigation developed in the 12th century, beginning with the collection of opinions held by Churchmen and philosophers. In the initial stage the *summae* were books of sentences. These led to *summae* dealing with philosophical and theological issues.

(1) Among the *summae* of sentences may be mentioned the *Summa sententiarum* of Hugh of St. Victor (*q.v.*), as well as the *summae* of Peter Lombard (*q.v.*), Alexander of Hales (*q.v.*), and Robert of Melun (*q.v.*).

(2) The work of the 12th-century Abelard (*q.v.*) is transitional, directed toward the conceptual issues which became central to the great *summae* of the 13th century. Among these are the *Summa philosophiae* attributed to Robert Grosseteste (*q.v.* Pseudo-Grosseteste), the *Summa logicae* of Lambert of Auxerre (*q.v.*), the *Summa contra gentiles* and *Summa theologica* of Thomas Aquinas (*q.v.*), and the *Summa modarum significandi* of Siger of Courtrai (*q.v.*).

SUMMUM BONUM.

A Latin term meaning "the highest good." The term has been applied to the ultimate ends of man, or to that which is intrinsically good. The many alternatives offered for the highest good are treated under the heading, Final Value (*q.v.*). The views of a number of authors who used the term are cited here.

(1) Sir Thomas More (*q.v.* 2) identified the term with the greatest amount of pleasure.

(2) Peirce (*q.v.* 11) held that logic, aesthetics, and ethics together produce

the *summum bonum*, that is, the direction which life should take.

(3) For R.B. Perry (*q.v.* 2) the *summum bonum* is greater value inclusiveness.

(4) C.I. Lewis (*q.v.* 5) held the *summum bonum* to be the good life as disclosed by moral or active, cognitive, and aesthetic value experiences.

SUMMUM GENUS.
Q.v. Genus (1).

SUMNER, WILLIAM GRAHAM. 1840–1910.
American sociologist. Born in Paterson, New Jersey. Educated at Yale. In 1863 he began an extensive period of European study. Initially an Episcopalian minister, he taught at Yale beginning in 1872.

Principal writings: *Folkways*, 1907; *Science of Society* (with A.G. Keller), 4 vols., 1927.

(1) Societies are shaped principally by "folkways," patterns of behavior arising spontaneously from the basic needs and interests, including the material interests, of the members of society.

(2) Folkways become "mores," legitimating the structure of society, while gaining reinforcement from religious and political sanctions.

(3) Finally, through the application of reason, "mores" become principles of truth and right. Although initially rising, apart from conscious intention, the attention of reason allows the possibility of change and improvement. The process is, however, long and laborious.

(4) Sumner also supported a version of social Darwinism in which the alternatives were on the one hand, "liberty, inequality, survival of the fittest" and, on the other, "not-liberty, equality, survival of the unfittest." He regarded the economic struggle as a legitimate testing ground for fitness.

SUMPTION.
Q.v. Subsumption.

SUNNI (SUNNITE).
From the Arabic term *sunna* ("behavior," "practice," or "custom"). The term applies to the major division of Islam (*q.v.* 4, 8) which holds the Qur'an, supplemented by *Sunna*, custom or tradition, to be the authority in religious matters. The supplement includes the practices of

Mohammed and the first three caliphs (rejected by their Shia, *q.v.*, rivals), as well as the "consensus of Islam" (agreement among the interpreters of the four schools of Islamic law).

ŚUNYA (SHUNYA).
Also *śunyam*, *śunyata*, different forms of a Sanskrit term signifying the "void," the "empty," the "open," "nothing," "emptiness" (*q.v.*), "openness," "nothingness."

(1) The number of the void is "zero," a transition point between positive and negative. As "0," *Shunya* was carried to the west as Arabic notation, revolutionizing European mathematics. The "emptiness" of zero was simply one application of the *shunya* doctrine, providing the interpretation of all the key concepts of Mahayana Buddhism, *e.g.*, enlightenment, Nirvana, *karma*, the Buddha nature, and bodhisattvahood.

(2) By the second century B.C. a group of *Shunyavadins* ("teachers of emptiness") taught that all distinctions, including that of Nirvana should be viewed as empty. Otherwise, even the striving for enlightenment creates new attachments. The coursing toward enlightenment or bodhisattvahood thus became "non-coursing," and the attainment of enlightenment "non-attainment"; the attitude of emptiness was likewise present in the Satyasiddhi school of Hinayana Buddhism.

(3) In the 2nd century A.D. Nagarjuna (*q.v.*) formalized the doctrine of the Madhyamika (*q.v.*), or Middle Way school with its non-dual approach to the "emptiness of emptiness."

(4) In the 4th or 5th century the nonduality of emptiness was interpreted by the Yogacara (*q.v.*) school to emphasize consciousness as non-dual in its "truly real" form. Leading in this line of interpretation were Asanga (*q.v.*) and Vasubandhu (*q.v.*).

(5) It is worth noting that the Mahayana ethic of compassion for all living things was held to be implied by the attitude of emptiness.

(6) The concern with emptiness was transmitted to Chinese Buddhists on through the Madhyamika and Yogacara schools, the former being the San-Lun school, and the latter as Fa-Hsiang in China and Hosso in Japan. Among the

representatives of San-Lun are Kumarajiva (*q.v.*), Seng-Chao (*q.v.*), and Chi-Tsang (*q.v.*).

(7) Two distinctive schools of emptiness, arising in China in the 6th and 7th centuries were T'ien-T'ai (*q.v.* 4), led by Chih-I (*q.v.*), and Hua-Yen (*q.v.* 4) whose principle figure was Fa-Tsang (*q.v.*).

(8) Finally, Chan or Zen Buddhism (*q.v.*) likewise presents a form of emptiness which is surmounted by going beyond rationality.

ŚUNYAVADA (SHUNYAVADA).

Sanskrit term meaning "teaching of emptiness." Starting from the root term, *śunya* (*q.v.*), the Shunyavadins (*q.v.* *śunya* 2) made the analysis of emptiness which led to the Madhyamika (*q.v.*) school and the doctrines of Nagarjuna (*q.v.*).

SUPERALTERNATION.
Q.v. Immediate Inference (1).

SUPER-EGO.
Q.v. Freud (2).

SUPERLATIVE THEOLOGY.
Q.v. The Pseudo-Dionysius (1).

SUPERMAN.
Q.v. Nietzsche (6).

SUPERNATURALISM.
From the Latin *super* ("above") and *natura* ("nature"). The theological doctrine that the divine is fundamentally different from the temporal order and cannot be approached through its categories, *i.e.*, by means of reason. In this view faith, revelation, and the authority of Scripture take the place of reason.

SUPERVENIENCE.
From the Latin *super* plus *venire* ("to come over"). The concept or doctrine that some second class of properties or predicates supervenes a first class of predicates without being reducible in every sense to the first class. The problem giving rise to the concept is that psychological predicates (mental states) seem not to be reducible in every sense to the physical states which, on most accounts, give rise to them. Physics might "determine" the qualities occurrent in biology or psychology, even if the latter qualities cannot be inferred at this time from the former. Supervenience in properties or qualities might also be traced to supervenience of laws; that is, the laws of chemistry, physiology, and psychology might be said to supervene the laws of physics; the supervenience of quality would then be a result of the supervenience of law.

SUPPLEMENT.
Q.v. Derrida (8).

SUPPOSITIO.
Latin term referring to the specific signification of a sign. The term is important in the Terminist logic of Peter of Spain (*q.v.* 2), as well as in the logic of William of Ockham (*q.v.* 5). Walter Burleigh (*q.v.*) developed the most complete set of distinctions in this regard.

SUPPOSITIO TERMINORUM.
A Latin phrase meaning "substitution of terms." *Q.v.* Logic (6).

SUPPOSITUM INTELLECTUALE.
Q.v. William of Ockham (14).

SUPRALAPSARIANISM.
Q.v. Predestination (7).

SUPREMACY, ACTS OF.
Two acts of Parliament which established the autonomy of the English Church. The first in 1534 declared Henry VIII "supreme head" of the Church of England. The second in 1559 declared Elizabeth "supreme governor" of the realm in all matters.

SURAS.
Q.v. Qur'an.

SURPLUS MEANING.
Q.v. Reichenbach (3).

SURPLUS VALUE.
According to Marx (*q.v.* 7, 11, 12) the difference between the price paid for a product and the price paid labor in its manufacture.

SURVIVAL OF THE FITTEST.
A phrase coined by Herbert Spencer (*q.v.*) to describe the results of the working of Darwin's principle of natural selection (*q.v.* Social Darwinism; Darwin 5; A.R. Wallace; W.G. Sumner 4). Anticipations of the principle are to be found

among the Greek and Roman philosophers: *e.g.*, Lucretius (*q.v.* 6).

SUSO, HENRY. 1295–1366.
German mystic. Born in Überlingen. Educated at Constance and Cologne. At Cologne he met Tauler (*q.v.*) and came under the influence of Meister Eckhart (*q.v.*). A member of the Dominican order and of the Friends of God (*q.v.*), Suso was the poet of the mystical movement. In describing the mystical experience he used the metaphors of Neoplatonism and Eckhart, especially the latter's distinction between Godhead and the Trinity, and his equation of God with nonbeing, while insisting upon his orthodoxy.
Principal writings: *The Little Book of Truth* (T); *The Life of the Servant* (T); *The Little Book of Eternal Wisdom* (T).

SUTRAS.
From *sutra*, the Sanskrit term for "aphorism." An immense body of Indian literature, formed principally between the 6th and 3rd centuries B.C., summarizing the Vedic literature in aphoristic form. The economy of language of the *sutras* invited an additional literature of explanation and interpretation, these commentaries being cast typically in dialogue form. *Q.v. Vedas* (5).

SUTTEE.
Q.v. Sat (2).

SUZUKI, DAISETZ TEITARO. 1870–1966.
Japanese philosopher of religion. Born in Kanazawa, Japan. Studied at Ishikawa College, and Tokyo Imperial University. His interest in Shin Buddhism and Zen Buddhism began with his parents; his mother adhered to the former, his father to the latter. From 1892–97 he practised Zen meditation as a novice in the Engakuji monastery in Kamakura. From 1897–1908 he worked as a translator of Asian classics for Paul Carus and Open Court in La Salle, Illinois. The translation of Ashvaghosha's (*q.v.*) *The Awakening of the Faith in the Mahayana* (1900) was among the translations from this period. He returned to Japan in 1909 after a year in Europe. In Japan he taught at Gakushuin University, Tokyo, Imperial University, and Otani University. He initiated an academic journal, *The Eastern Buddhist*, at Otani. The journal was

published in English. Both before and after World War II Suzuki lectured and taught in Western universities, both the famous British centers, Hawaii, Claremont and among others an extensive stay (1950–57) at Columbia.
Principal writings: *Outlines of Mahayana Buddhism*, 1907 (reprinted 1963 with Alan Watts Introduction); *Self-Power and Other-Power*, 1911 (revised as *Shin Buddhism*, 1970); *Essays in Zen Buddhism*, 3 vols., 1927–34; *Studies in the Lankavatra Sutra* (T and intro.), 1930; *An Introduction to Zen Buddhism* (rev. of vol. I of the *Essays*, 1934; *The Training of the Zen Buddhist Monk*, 1934; *Manual of Zen Buddhism*, 1935; *Zen Buddhism and its Influence on Japanese Culture*, 1938 (rev. ed. and title, *Zen and Japanese Buddhism*, 1958); *Japanese Spirituality*, 1944; *The Essence of Buddhism*, 1947; *Mysticism: Christian and Buddhist*, 1957; *Zen Buddhism and Psychoanalysis* (with Fromm and De Martino), 1960; *Sengai: the Zen Master*, 1971; *What is Zen?*, 1971. In addition, edited compilations selected from these publications (C. Humphries, *Studies in Zen*, 1955; W. Barrett, *Zen Buddhism*, 1956; B. Phillips, *The Essentials of Zen Buddhism*, 1962; E. Conze, *On Indian Mahayana Buddhism*, 1968; C. Humphries, *The Field of Zen*, 1969).

(1) Over a period of more than 60 years Suzuki's writings and lectures aroused the interest of the West in Zen Buddhism. Scholarly opinion has it that his influence was overwhelming in opening West to Zen. Much of Suzuki's work was expository. He presented, with passion, the basic information contained in the entry on Zen (*q.v.*), especially those points held by the Rinzai sect.

(2) Suzuki's depth of conviction and personal experience are scarcely duplicable. As a student of Western thought he was able to draw upon intercultural parallels in explicating Zen. It is said that his studies in Mahayana and Shin Buddhism—one should also add, Christianity—finally, tell one about Zen. It was reported from England that he was among the few who could lift an audience "beyond the limitation of concept," enabling them to share his "living and immediate experience."

(3) He looked upon Zen as the primary means of releasing each individual's personal spiritual vitality. An inner struggle,

involving a long and exacting vigil, is often necessary to reach that point. One's inner pain, he suggested, may resemble boiling oil over a blazing fire before Zen smiles and says, "welcome home."

(4) Quite often, it is only after the exhaustion of one's whole being that *satori*, the awakening of consciousness from the "darkness of blind strivings," comes upon one. The means are meditation (*q.v.*) joined to intuitive understanding (*prajna*, further developed in Intuition 15), utilizing the *koan* (*q.v.*) to pass beyond intellectual distinctions (*vijnana*), related to the obstructiveness of one's ego.

(5) When *satori* comes, it comes suddenly, like water freezing abruptly when it reaches a certain point, or the flashing of a new truth, which is vital, original, thoroughly creative, or the exploding of the shell encasing one's personality. In its happening one reaches the world of "infinity or self or God." He says that infinity is realized in you, your storehouse of creative possibilities is unlocked as your finite self opens to a larger Self, and the serial nature of time gives way to the Absolute Present.

(6) Between the extremes of quietism and aggression is the "passive activity" which transcends opposites by synthesizing them, affirming being in the context of becoming.

SVATANTRIKAS.
Q.v. Madhyamika (3).

ŚVETAMBARAS (SHVETAMBARAS).
Q.v. Jainism (8).

SWEDENBORG, EMANUEL. 1688–1772.
Swedish scientist and religious leader. Born in Stockholm. Educated at Uppsala. In addition to public responsibilities, he published in many areas of science, offering the nebular hypothesis before Kant, and developing theories of light, atomism, crystallography, and activity of the brain. In middle age he turned to psychical and spiritual matters. After a deep religious experience in 1745 "when heaven opened to him," he devoted himself to unlocking the Scriptures, and teaching the doctrines of the "New Church." Although Swedenborg did not envision the latter as a separate denomination, his followers did in fact establish an ecclesiastical organization, the Church of the New Jerusalem, following his doctrines.

Selected writings: *The Principles of Natural Things* (T), 1734; *The Economy of the Animal Kingdom* (T), 1736; *The Hieroglyphic Key* (T), 1741; *On the Love and Wisdom of God* (T), 1745; *The True Christian Religion* (T), 1771.

(1) In his natural philosophy something of Swedenborg's later spiritualism is anticipated. Mathematical points are viewed as connecting the finite with the infinite. Reality is viewed as an organic hierarchy, the series beginning with the mathematical point and rising to God.

(2) Holding to the "co-established harmony" of soul and body, and the division of soul into vegetative, rational, and spiritual degrees, Swedenborg felt that the Fall deprived men of total knowledge by separating the spiritual degree of the soul (the *anima*) from the reason (*mens rationalis*); this knowledge is still locked into us, but is unavailable.

(3) Accepting as his key the doctrine that all terms have natural, spiritual, and divine meanings, he developed a doctrine of correspondence which he used, for example, in the interpretation of Scripture.

(4) He distinguished three "degrees of being" in God: love (the divine level, or, realm of ends), wisdom (the spiritual level, or realm of causes), use (the natural level, or realm of effects). And the trinity in man is love, wisdom, and creative (or useful) life.

(5) He believed that there is a correspondence between the natural and spiritual levels such that the relations of one are mirrored in the other, so that each person lives in both realms at once. Although separated from God by the Fall, one has freedom through one's own will and reason to return by way of the spiritual realm.

(6) He repudiated orthodox interpretations of the Trinity and Atonement, and believed the Judgment had occurred in 1757, along with Christ's Second Coming as a triumph over rebellious spirits.

(7) The Swedenborgian Articles of Faith of the New Church, as elaborated by his followers, are: (a) There is one God in whom there is a divine Trinity; and he is the Lord Jesus Christ. (b) A saving faith is to believe in Him. (c) Evils are to be shunned because they are of

the devil. (d) Good actions are to be done because they are of God. (e) These are to be done by one as though from one-self; but it ought to be believed that they are done from the Lord.

SWIFT, JONATHAN.
Q.v. Utopia (9).

SYADVADA.
Q.v. Jainism (4).

SYLLABI OF ERRORS.
The eighty condemned theses of Pius IX, issued in 1864; and the sixty-five theses (largely against Modernism, *q.v.* 2) of Pius X, issued in 1907.

SYLLOGISM.
From the Greek *syn* ("with," or "togeth-er") and *logizesthai* ("to reckon," "to con-clude by reasoning"). A form of reasoning whereby, given two sentences or propo-sitions, a third follows necessarily from them. In what follows we shall sketch a number of salient points in the theory of the syllogism, not following Aristotle exactly, but rather more the tradition of syllogistic logic which developed from Aristotle's analysis.

A. The categorical syllogism is central to the analysis. In our discussion of it we shall use a language of classes where Aristotle used a language of predication.

(1) The categorical syllogism derives from the interrelations of four kinds of sentences, or propositions: those which are universal and affirmative ("All hu-mans are mortal"); universal and nega-tive ("No humans are immortal"); particular and affirmative ("Some humans are Athenians"); and particular and nega-tive ("Some humans are not Athenians"). The universal affirmative proposition can be pictorially represented as one class within another, the class of humans being situated within the class of mortal beings:

The universal negative proposition can be represented as two classes separated from each other:

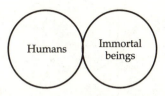

The particular affirmative proposition can be represented as two overlapping classes with at least one common mem-ber in their common area.

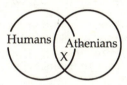

In this usage "X" means that there is at least one item in the part of the dia-gram so marked. The notion of "some" is thus indefinite; and, of course, the assertion that "Some A is B" does not imply that "Some A is not B." That is part of the indefinite nature of the assertion. The particular negative prop-osition can be represented as two over-lapping classes with membership in the indicated area, not within the overlap:

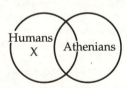

For a different manner of representing these propositions *q.v.* Venn Diagrams.

(2) It becomes clear at once that we must draw certain conclusions, given certain kinds of class relationships. If I assert that "All humans are mortal," and "All patriarchs are human," it is obvi-ous that I must conclude "All patriarchs are mortal."

Indeed it is clear that I cannot believe the former two assertions, and disbelieve the third. Similarly, to hold that "No humans are immortal" and "All Atheni-ans are human," commits one to the be-lief that "No Athenians are immortal."

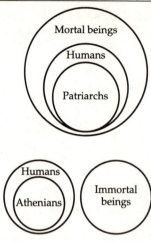

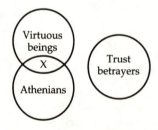

If it is claimed both that "No virtuous beings betray a trust," and that "Some Athenians are virtuous," it follows that "Some Athenians will not betray a trust."

It is not simply that these conclusions follow with a certain degree of probability. They follow necessarily; and this is what is meant by a deductive relationship.

(3) Upon examination of the above it can be seen that the syllogism has certain standard features. It is made up of three statements or propositions. Two of these propositions constitute the premises. The third is deduced from these, and is the conclusion. The subject of the conclusion is to be found in what is called the Minor Premise. The predicate of the conclusion is to be found in what is called the Major Premise.

$$\begin{array}{cc} M & P \end{array}$$
Major Premise: All humans are mortal;
$$\begin{array}{cc} S & M \end{array}$$
Minor Premise: All patriarchs are human;
$$\begin{array}{cc} S & P \end{array}$$
Conclusion: All patriarchs are mortal.

The syllogism is made up of three classes, or terms. One of these, the "middle term," appears in both premises and provides

the bridge allowing the other terms to be related in the conclusion. If in the above syllogism we label the subject, or Minor, term S, the predicate or Major term P, and the middle term M, we gain the following shape for this particular syllogistic inference:

MP
SM
SP

All syllogisms in which the middle term is in the subject of the major premise, and in the predicate of the minor premise are syllogisms in the first figure. Aristotle found three figures. Medieval logicians found four. The additional figures of the syllogism discussed by Aristotle are the second and third figures respectively.

PM   MP
SM   MS
SP   SP

The fourth figure, not discussed by Aristotle, is:

PM
MS
SP

Certain relationships of these terms, but not all, lead to valid syllogisms. One can discover by experimentation which are and which are not valid. Medieval logicians have classified the valid forms; and the list of valid terms can be set forth by joining the convention of the moods of syllogisms to the convention of its figures mentioned above. We shall call the universal affirmative proposition an "A" proposition, and the particular affirmative proposition an "I" proposition (from the first two vowels of the Latin *affirmo*, meaning "to affirm").

We shall call the universal negative proposition an "E" proposition and the particular negative proposition an "O" proposition (from the first two vowels of the Latin *nego*, meaning "to deny"). Turning back to the three instances of syllogisms we had mentioned, if one examines the position of the middle term it will be found that all three are first figure syllogisms. The first instance—

All humans are mortal;

All patriarchs are human;

∴ All patriarchs are mortal

—is in mood AAA (naming in order the major premise, minor premise, and conclusion).

The second syllogism—
No humans are immortal;
All Athenians are human:
∴ No Athenians are immortal
—is in mood EAE.
The third syllogism—
No virtuous beings betray a trust;
Some Athenians are virtuous:
∴ Some Athenians will not betray a trust
—is in mood EIO.
(4) Combining mood and figure it is possible to present a list of the valid syllogisms. We shall set them forth in four figures, although the fourth figure, once called Galenian (*q.v.*), can be reduced to Aristotle's three:

First	Second	Third	Fourth
MP	PM	MP	PM
SM	SM	MS	MS
SP	SP	SP	SP
AAA	AEE	AAI	AAI
AAI	AEO	AII	AEE
AII	AOO	EAO	AEO
EAE	EAE	EIO	IAI
EAO	EAO	IAI	EAO
EIO	EIO	OAO	EIO

The valid moods of the syllogism in each figure were named during the Middle Ages and formed into mnemonic verses so structured that instructions for reducing the syllogism in question to the first figure were included. The names in these verses were the names of girls, and one finds the mood by noticing the vowels in sequence. "Barbara," for example, is the name for AAA, so AAA was often called a syllogism in Barbara. There are a number of somewhat different mnemonic verses dating from the Middle Ages. One of these, without the weakened forms (clearly, if AAA is valid, concluding "All S is P," so is AAI, concluding "Some S is P"), is the following:
"Barbara, Celarent, primae Darii, Ferioque Cesare, Camestres, Festino, Baroco secundae.
Tertia grande sonans recitat: Darapti, Felapton,
Disamis, Datisi, Bocardo, Ferison; quartae
Sunt Bamalip, Calemes, Dimatis, Fesapo. Fresison."
(5) The rules to which every valid

syllogism must conform are:
(a) The middle term must be distributed at least once.
(b) No term may be distributed in the conclusion if it is not distributed in the premises.
(c) If both premises are negative, there is no conclusion.
(d) If one premise is negative, the conclusion must be negative.
(e) If both premises are affirmative, the conclusion must be affirmative.
(6) But when is a term distributed? This returns us to the A,E,I, and O propositions from which we had begun. A term is said to be distributed if a second term refers to the entire extension of the first term.
(a) In the A proposition, "All S is P," reference is made by P to all of S, so S is distributed; reference is made to some only of P, so P is not distributed.
(b) In the E proposition "No S is P," reference is made by P to all of S, and by S to all of P. We know that, examining all the S's we shall find no P, and conversely; hence, both S and P are here distributed.
(c) In the I proposition, "Some S is P," reference is made by S to a part only of P, and by P to a part only of S; hence, neither term is distributed.
(d) In the O proposition, "Some S is not P," reference is made by S to a part only of P, but by P to the whole of S; hence, S is undistributed, but P is distributed. The distribution of the O proposition can best be understood by thinking of the subject term as making the indefinite reference of the I proposition, and the predicate term as making the definite exclusion of the E proposition. Whatever "Some S" may be, it is definitely excluded from P.
Applying this idea of distribution to rules (a) and (b) in (5) above, the validity of any syllogism can be determined.
(7) In common speech, arguments are most often incomplete. They are not fully expressed syllogisms, but incomplete syllogisms, or enthymemes. Enthymemes are called first-order enthymemes if the major premise is missing, second-order enthymemes if the minor premise is missing, third-order enthymemes if the conclusion is missing. Since the three terms of the syllogism are contained in

any two of its propositions, the missing proposition can always be supplied.
First-order enthymeme: "All patriarchs are mortal, because all patriarchs are human." It is clear that the major premise is missing, and that the missing premise is "All humans are mortal."

[All humans are mortal]
All patriarchs are human
∴ All patriarchs are mortal

Second-order enthymeme: "All patriarchs are mortal, because all humans are mortal."
Third-order enthymeme: "All humans are mortal, and all patriarchs are human."

B. Hypothetical Syllogism. This deals with the valid inferences which are possible when employing "if-then" statements, or combinations of "if-then" statements and categorical statements. (For the use of "if-then" statements in the Propositional Calculus q.v. Truth Tables 4–5, 7.)

(8) The straight hypothetical syllogism is in principle much like the categorical syllogism in Barbara (cf. 4 above). A middle clause is eliminated, and the two ends are joined:

If it rains, the streets will be wet.
If the streets are wet, the parade will not be held.
Therefore, if it rains, the parade will not be held.

It is clear that one could continue the process of joining hypothetical statements in this way. The elaboration of such chains is called Sorites (q.v.).

(9) The most common use of hypothetical propositions in inference, however, is Modus Ponens. This is a valid form of inference combining a hypothetical proposition with a categorical proposition which affirms the antecedent, and on the basis of this, affirms the consequent. We may call this: affirming the antecedent.

If it rains, the streets will be wet.
It is raining.
Therefore, the streets will be wet.

(10) Another valid form of inference combining hypothetical and categorical propositions is Modus Tollens. In this inference the consequent of the hypothetical proposition is denied; and on the basis of this denial, the antecedent is also denied. We may call this: denying the consequent.

If a storm is approaching, the barometer will go down.
The barometer is not going down.
Therefore, a storm is not approaching

C. Disjunctive Syllogism. In traditional treatments of the syllogism, a distinction is made between the weaker sense of "either-or" (often called alternative), and a stronger sense (often called disjunctive), q.v. Proposition (3). The Propositional Calculus is built up from the weaker sense of either-or (q.v. Truth Tables 3, 7). In traditional treatments both senses are recognized, and the criteria for validity shift with the sense of either-or under consideration.

(11) We shall call the syllogism employing the weaker sense of either-or an Alternative Syllogism. The weaker sense of either-or tells us that not both of the disjuncts (the "either" clause and the "or" clause) can be false at the same time. In this case, then, the valid move consists of denying one of the disjuncts and affirming the other. We may call this: denying and affirming.

Either it will rain or else the crops will fail.
It does not rain.
Therefore, the crops fail.

You can see that you still have a valid form if you deny the second disjunct, and affirm the first.

(12) We shall call the syllogism employing the stronger sense of either-or a Disjunctive Syllogism. The stronger sense of either-or tells us that not both of the disjuncts can be true at the same time. In this case, then, the valid move consists in affirming either one of the disjuncts, and on the basis of this affirmation, denying the other. We may call this: affirming and denying.

Either he was born in Missouri or he was born in Maine.
He was born in Missouri.
Therefore, he was not born in Maine.

D. The history of logic is treated under the heading, Logic (q.v.). But certain comments on the syllogism are more appropriate here.

(13) Sextus Empiricus (q.v. 3) argued that the syllogism involves circular reasoning.

(14) As was pointed out (cf. 3 above), medieval logicians increased Aristotle's three figures of the syllogism to four.

Peter Ramus (*q.v.* 5) returned in his analysis to the three figures of Aristotle.

(15) J.S. Mill (*q.v.* 2) regarded every syllogism as a *petitio principii*, thus agreeing with Sextus Empiricus.

SYMBOL.

From the Greek *symbolon*. In the history of thought the term has had two very different meanings. In religious thought and practice, symbols are commonly regarded as sensuous representations of a transcendent reality. In systems of logical and scientific thought the term is normally used in the sense of an abstract sign.

(1) In Christian thought, for example, water, bread, and wine, the cross—in certain contexts—are symbols expressive of the religious life.

(2) Christian dogmas and doctrines have also been held to be symbols of the eternal. Sabatier, (*q.v.* 2), for example, has advanced a doctrine of "critical symbolism," stating that symbols are valid to the extent that they relate to the worshipper's primary experience.

(3) For Peirce (*q.v.* 16) the symbol is one of three major classes of signs, the one with an "agreed-upon connotation." Peirce thus used the term in the second of the two senses. In his analysis of signs ordinary nouns and propositions are called Rhematic and Dicent symbols, respectively.

(4) Russell (*q.v.* 5) regarded classes as "incomplete symbols," and replaceable by descriptions.

(5) Urban (*q.v.* 3) distinguished sign from symbol, relating the latter to both art and religion. Certain types of symbols enable us to penetrate reality, and contain some of the character of the thing symbolized.

(6) Cassirer (*q.v.* 1–4) defined man as the "symbolizing" animal. His philosophy of symbolic form covers all uses of signs, from mathematics to religion. He thus used the term "symbol" to include both religious and scientific usages; but scientific concepts are extensive, while those of myth and religion are intensive.

(7) Tillich (*q.v.* 4) used the term "symbol" in the religious sense. In a manner different from other signs, symbols "participate" in the reality to which they point. Furthermore, they have a life—coming into being, developing, and sometimes dying.

(8) Susanne Langer (*q.v.* 3), defining man as the "symbolific animal," draws a distinction between the representational symbols with dictionary meanings and the "unconsummated symbols" of art.

(9) Utilizing Cassirer's approach to symbols in the field of art, Goodman (*q.v.* 5) characterized aesthetic symbols as possessing density, repleteness, exemplification, and both multiple and complex reference.

SYMBOLIC REFERENCE.
Q.v. Whitehead (24).

SYMBOLISM.
Q.v. Lacan (3).

SYMMETRY.

A property of certain relations and matching geometrical elements. A relation is symmetrical when it is reversible, *i.e.*, when xRy ⊃ yRx (*q.v.* Logic of Relations 10). Thus, "If Simon is the brother of Peter, then Peter is the brother of Simon." Two geometrical elements are symmetrical when they manifest a point to point correspondence. Also *q.v.* Logic (22).

SYMPATHY.

Regarded as a natural emotion by Hume (*q.v.* 6) and Adam Smith (*q.v.* 1), both utilized sympathy as fundamental to their systems of ethics.

SYNAGOGUE.

From the Greek *synagoge* ("a bringing together," "an assembly"). Anciently, any local community of Jews; now, an assembly of Jews, or the place of that assembly, coming together for worship. The concept of the synagogue was a new departure in religious history, including worship without idols or visible symbols of the divine, without the propitiation of sacrifice and without priests (since the Rabbi, *q.v.*, is regarded as a teacher).

SYNCATEGOREMATIC TERMS.

From the Greek *syn* ("together") and *categorema* ("predicate"). The derivation may refer to those terms which go together with the predicates or those terms which hold the predicates together; and thus, those terms which cannot be used by themselves but only in conjunction with other terms: e.g., "all," taken alone, has no definite reference to anything, but "all men" has. "All" is syncategorematic and "men" is categorematic. In addition to the quantifiers "all," "some," and "none," included among syncategorematic terms are "not," "if . . . then," "either . . . or," and "both . . . and." The discussion of syncategorematic terms began among the Stoics and came to fruition in the analyses of such thinkers as William of Ockham (q.v. 1–2) and William of Sherwood (q.v.).

SYNCHRONY.

Q.v. Structuralism (9); de Saussure (1); Lacan (5, 6).

SYNCRETISM.

From the Greek synkretizein ("to combine"). A term introduced by Plutarch to characterize the harmonizing efforts of the Neoplatonists. The term refers to the blending of philosophical doctrines from opposing schools, or religious doctrines from different faiths, in an effort to gain a unified point of view. In philosophy the term is usually pejorative, and the mixture of doctrines undistinguished, the common opinion being that superficiality is bound to result from syncretism.

SYNDERESIS.

A term of uncertain etymology originating in the late Patristic period. Its probable origin is the Greek synteresis ("spark of conscience"). This term was introduced by St. Jerome (q.v.) in his explanation of the four living creatures of Ezekiel 1:4–15. Supposing the man, lion, and ox to represent the rational, irascible, and appetitive parts of the soul, he suggests that the fourth creature, an eagle, is the "spark of conscience" which was not extinguished from the breast of Adam when he was driven from paradise. Throughout the medieval period the term, "synderesis," or the Latin for "spark of conscience," scintilla conscientiae, entered into analyses of human nature, including that of Aquinas who considered the "synderesis" a habitus of the first principles of practical reasoning.

SYNDICALISM.

A trade union movement, originating in France, according to which the "syndicates" were to gain control over the means of production by the general strike and direct action. The theory of the movement is usually associated with Georges Sorel (q.v.).

SYNECDOCHE.

Q.v. Metaphor.

SYNECHIOLOGY.

Q.v. Herbart (3).

SYNECHISM.

From the Greek synecheia ("continuity") The doctrine of Peirce (q.v. 5) that continuity is an important feature of the universe, and that both science and philosophy should search for hypotheses embodying this idea.

SYNERGISM.

From the Greek synergein ("to work together"). The doctrine of Melanchthon (q.v. 2) that the Holy Spirit, the word and the human will work together in human regeneration. In the 16th-century disputes the opposing doctrine was "Monergism," which held that the Holy Spirit is the sole agent. The latter doctrine was attributed to Luther; although he did not use the term, his views did run in that direction (q.v. Luther 9).

SYNKATATHESIS.

A Greek term meaning "acceptance." The term was used by the Stoics to signify the assent to, or endorsement of, a proposition as true (q.v. Stoicism 1).

SYNONYMOUS DEFINITION.

Q.v. Definition (3).

SYNONYMY.

From the Greek term synonomia, from syn ("together") and onoma ("name"). The study of identity of meaning, especially as it touches upon the interpretation of analytic statements (q.v.) and the interchangeability of terms.

(1) Carnap (q.v. 9) defined synonymy by "intensional isomorphism" and "intensional structure," but these in turn require the notion of L-equivalence (which is built up from L-truth, i.e., analytic truth).

(2) Quine (*q.v.* 4) argues, against Carnap and others, that no clear characterization of synonymy has yet been discovered, and that the respective characterizations of analyticity and synonymy usually involve each other in a circular manner.

(3) Goodman (*q.v.* 2), interpreting identity of meaning as identity of extension, demonstrated that—taking into account the secondary extensions of terms as well as their primary extensions—no two terms have the same extension, and thus no two terms can have identical meaning. There is, then, no exact synonymy.

SYNOPTIC GOSPELS.

From the Greek *syn* ("together") and *opsis* ("sight," "view"). Thus, the gospels which can be viewed together. The phrase is applied to Matthew, Mark, and Luke, apparently because of their common content. It is now held that this agreement is due to the dependence of Matthew and Luke on Mark, the earliest of the New Testament gospels, as well as upon an unknown source called "Q" (from the German *Quelle*, "source").

SYNSEMANTIC.

Q.v. Brentano (3).

SYNTACTICS.

One of the three major aspects of the general theory of signs, along with Semantics (*q.v.*) and Pragmatics (*q.v.*). Syntactics deals with that aspect of the study concerning the relations of the signs of a language to each other. *Q.v.* Morris, C.W. (2); Metalanguage (4); Carnap (6); Montague, Richard (2).

SYNTHESIS.

A Greek term from *syn* ("together") and *tithenai* ("to place"). The term once designated deductive reasoning, but now stands as the complement of analysis, referring to the joining of separate elements into a whole. It is this meaning which the term bears in synthetic judgment (*q.v.*), synthetic philosophy (*q.v.*), and in the synthesis which in the dialectic follows thesis and antithesis (*q.v.* Fichte 3 and Hegel 4).

SYNTHETIC A PRIORI JUDGMENT, STATEMENT, OR PROPOSITION.

A judgment, statement, or proposition in which the predicate adds content to the subject, and which yet has the necessity of analytic judgments (*q.v.*).

(1) Kant (*q.v.* 1) raised the question, "How are synthetic *a priori* judgments possible?" His answer, in brief, is that they are possible because there are *a priori* categories which humans add to all of their experience.

(2) Kant's analysis has been much discussed. Some have been convinced by his analysis and others have not. As an instance of the viewpoint of logical positivists, the view of Schlick (*q.v.* 3) may be cited that any expression, if meaningful, must be either analytic or synthetic.

SYNTHETIC JUDGMENT, STATEMENT, OR PROPOSITION.

As in the case of analytic judgments (*q.v.*), so the complementary synthetic judgment is sometimes referred to as a synthetic statement or proposition.

(1) The phrase "synthetic judgment" is associated with Kant (*q.v.* 1) who held that in this judgment the predicate is not contained in the subject. It thus lacks the certainty of analytic judgments whose predicates are so contained.

(2) Quine (*q.v.* 6) rejected any rigid distinction between synthetic and analytic statements, holding that of the two the synthetic statement was merely the one closer to the experiential periphery of science.

SYNTHETIC PHILOSOPHY.

The project of Herbert Spencer (*q.v.* 1) to build a philosophical system, drawing upon the whole of scientific knowledge.

SYRIANUS. 5th cent. A.D.

Hellenic philosopher. Member of the Neoplatonic School of Athens (*q.v.*), and a disciple of Plutarch whom he succeeded as head of the school in 432. Emphasizing the importance of Aristotle in understanding Plato, his own version of Neoplatonism (*q.v.*) combined doctrines of Plato and Aristotle with Orphic insights.

Principal writings: *Commentaries* on *Aristotle's Metaphysics, On the Heavens, On Interpretation*, and on Plato's *Timaeus*.

SYSTEM.

From the Greek *syn* ("together") and *stenai* ("to stand up").

(1) The term is sometimes applied to

the characteristic features of the thought of particular individuals and schools, *e.g.*, Plato's system. In this sense the appearance of philosophy as well as science, in the world, is marked by increasing emphasis on system.

(2) In formal terms, by system is meant a set of elements with internal coherence and unity, provided by rules governing their permissible combination and transformation. Any natural language is such a system, as are the artificial, formal languages of logic and mathematics. The basic transformation rules of elementary logic are to be found in the entries, Propositional Calculus (*q.v.*) and Quantification Theory (*q.v.*). Questions of consistency (*q.v.*), completeness (*q.v.*), and decidability (*q.v.*), for systems of logic and mathematics have been carefully considered in the past half-century. Gödell (*q.v.* 1–4) showed the completeness of the system for first-order logic, and its essential incompleteness for every higher-order logic, for the arithmetic of cardinal numbers and other mathematical systems of that or greater complexity.

SYZYGIES.
Q.v. Cabala (1h).

T

TABLES OF INDUCTION.
The tables of Essence and Presence, Absence in Proximity, and Degrees or Comparison, recommended by Francis Bacon (*q.v.* 3) in using inductive method.

TABU.
A Polynesian term signifying a mysterious potency thought to involve danger to oneself or one's group. Among the things believed "tabu" by many primitive groups are those things involving death and blood; thus, corpses, menstruation, the blood at child-birth, warriors after a battle, murderers. In somewhat different classes those transgressing the sexual code, strangers, chiefs, and priests were in various ways "tabu." Depending on the case, rites of purification and

ceremonies warded off the danger, and regularized the relations between individual and group.

TABULA NUDA.
Q.v. Duns Scotus (2).

TABULA RASA.
A Latin term meaning "blank tablet," the concept that the mind begins without innate knowledge, gaining all knowledge from experience.

(1) Bonaventure (*q.v.* 5) held that with respect to ordinary experience our minds begin as blank tablets, although certain ideas, *e.g.*, that of "God," are innate.

(2) Without Bonaventure's qualification, Duns Scotus (*q.v.* 2) held the mind to be a blank tablet apart from experience, although he used the phrase "*tabula nuda.*"

(3) The concept is usually associated, however, with John Locke (*q.v.* 1) who made it the hallmark of his philosophy, vigorously attacking innate ideas.

TACIT KNOWLEDGE.
Q.v. Polanyi (1).

TAGORE, RABINDRANATH. 1861–1941.
Indian poet and philosopher. Born in Calcutta. Educated in London. Founded Visabharati University. His many volumes of poetry were influenced by Bhakti-oriented Bauls of Bengal (*q.v.* Hinduism 5c). His philosophical work was directed toward those central truths which mediate among all positions, or the "one great principle of unity" in everyone. The following books were written in English.

Selected writings: *Sadhana, the Realisation of Life*, 1913; *Personality*, 1917; *Creative Unity*, 1922; *The Religion of Man*, 1931; *Man*, 1937; *Towards Universal Man*, 1961.

TAI CHEN. 1723–1777.
Chinese neo-Confucianist philosopher. Born in Anhui. Taught primary school, 1740–42. In 1762 he obtained the "Recommended Person" degree. In 1773 he was appointed a compiler of the *Four Libraries* by imperial command. The "Presented Scholar" degree was bestowed on him in 1775. He generated the "investigations based on evidence" movement.

Principal writings: *Commentary on the Meaning of Terms in the Book of Mencius.*

(1) An expert in mathematics, astronomy, phonetics, textual criticism, and other fields, Tai Chen—along with other members of the movement—looked back to the Han Dynasty for an interpretation of the Confucian classics supporting this view of investigation. Since principle meant to him "the order of things," the only way of investigating principle is through detailed objective study.

(2) In another sense, principle means feelings that do not err. Desire is to conform to principle, and this happens in a life of balance. Evil occurs when error and obscurity enter into our desires. Through intelligence, what is natural in the sense of "blood and vital force" can be directed toward moral virtue.

T'AI CHI.
Chinese for "the Great Ultimate" (*q.v.*), a basic principle of the universe in Chinese thought.

TAINE, HIPPOLYTE. 1828–1893.
French critic and philosopher. Born in Vouziers. Educated in Paris. Concentrating on philosophy and letters, he applied Positivism and determinism to his analyses of art, history, and society. He thus opposed Romanticism and became, along with Renan (*q.v.*), the spokesman for Positivism in the second half of the 19th century.

Selected writings: *History of English Literature* (T), 1857; *English Positivism*, 1864; *Philosophy of Art* (T), 1865; *Intelligence* (T), 2 vols., 1870.

TALISMAN.
Q.v. Suhrawardi (3).

TALMUD.
From the Hebrew *talmuda* ("instruction"). The body of Jewish civil and canonical law. *Q.v.* Judaism (2b).

TAMAS.
Q.v. Hinduism (6b); Sankhya (4–5).

TAMIL ŚAIVAS (SHAIVAS).
Q.v. Vaiṣnavism (3b).

TAMMUZ.
Q.v. Ishtar.

T'AN SSU-T'UNG. 1865–1898.
Chinese neo-Confucian philosopher. A native of Hunan. Joining in K'ang Yu-Wei's (*q.v.*) program of reform, he promoted the new learning in Hunan. When K'ang went into exile T'an remained, and became a martyr at thirty-three. T'an's teachings represent K'ang's views in a somewhat more developed form.

Principal writings: *The Philosophy of Humanity*.

(1) Following K'ang's association of consciousness, humanity, electricity, and ether, T'an took ether as the first principle of things, a point of universal connection, generation, and harmony. Manifest in the brain as intelligence, and in space as electricity, among humans it is the principle of humanity.

(2) The principle of nature is good; human desires are also good. The denominating of some things as evil is but a name, and not reflected in the world.

(3) Daily renovation of the things of the world occurs through the *Tao*, or Way, renewing the ether.

TANTRAS.
Q.v. Śastras (4); Tantrism.

TANTRISM.
From the Sanskrit *tantra* ("warp" or "loom"). A 19th century term coined by western scholars from texts called *Tantras* to refer to a set of doctrines and practices existing within Hinduism, Buddhism, and Jainism which yet differed from the orthodox doctrines of these religions. The diffusiveness of its existence makes description difficult, but points stand out.

(1) All Tantric groups believe the world to be suffused with divine energy, which may be used to achieve liberation. All share the characteristics of secrecy (the *Tantras* were written obscurely, requiring interpretation), relation to a guru (to provide the interpretation), ceremonies of initiation (which, unlike the *Vedas*, are open to both sexes and all castes), assignment of individual *mantras* by the guru, and the strict discipline of Hatha Yoga (*q.v.* Yoga 5).

(2) The use of *mantras* (*q.v.* 6) and *mandalas* (*q.v.* 1) is also universal; some groups do not go beyond this, stressing the power of such things in image, sound, and letters of the divinity's name. There are many objectives here. One of

them is to call up the god, induce the god or his power to enter one's body, and so to divinize oneself in some manner. Hindu, Buddhist, and Jaina Tantrism share this approach.

(3) Hindu Tantrism is best known, however, for its use of sexual energy in the cause of liberation. In this, it agrees with the practices of Kundalini Yoga (*q.v.* Yoga 10). The background view is that Brahman creates by emancipation, through the opposed aspects of quiescent wisdom (*prajna*) and energy (*śakti*) whose union is the first step in world evolution. This is understood as a sexual union of the god Shiva and the goddess, Shakti, the latter standing for the principle of energy.

(4) This view led in Hinduism to "lefthanded" *Tantra* in which *cakras* or circles were formed of pairs of male and female initiates directed by a male guru and his female consort. Their task was to reenact world-germination. All the males are Shiva, and their partners Shakti. In ritual succession they work their way through the "five elements." The first four are alcohol, meat, fish, and parched grains. These are offered to the god, then consumed by the worshipers. The fifth is sexual union. Here the offering is the male seed, while the Vedic altar is the female sex-organ. As Vedic and Tantric texts are chanted, Shiva and Shakti unite in symbolic world-creation. Since the female deity represents cosmic energy the female tantric, up to this point seated at the left hand of the male (thus the name), becomes the more aggressive partner, mounting from above with the male quiescent. The goal of the exercise is to release energy while remaining in control of mind, breath and, in this instance, semen. The theory is that retention of semen at the point of orgasm forces sexual energy into the 1000-petalled lotus in the crown of the head, leading to liberation. A counterpart phenomenon occurs within the female worshipper. At length the partners are able to rise above the Shiva-Shakti opposition merging into the absolute Brahman.

(5) In popular usage Tantric practices have numerous forms and goals. They are used for healing, where the god of the *mantra* is induced into the affected part of the body (Tantric medicine), to insure material success, in the service of magic, and to divinize one's body in order to gain supernatural powers in this lifetime.

(6) Buddhist Tantrism reversed the Hindu picture, holding the male principle to be active, symbolized as the diamond (Skt., *vajra*), the female principle quiescent, and symbolized as bell (Skt., *ghanta*). From these terms come Vajrayana (*q.v.*) and Diamond Buddhism or "The Diamond Vehicle." The male principle is also compassion (Skt., *karuna*) and the female principle is wisdom (Skt., *prajna*). Resolution of the *karuna-prajna* opposition is effected through the awareness of momentariness and emptiness (Skt., *śunyata*).

(7) The physical partnering is diminished in Buddhist Tantrism, but has not disappeared. The emphasis is on visualization and interiorization of *mantras*, therefore *Mantrayana* (*q.v.* and *Mantra* 4). Even the partnering stage has become *mantra* or *mandala*. The practitioner imagining his partner as goddess of wisdom (*prajna*) whose radiance he draws into his body. The 10th–11th century commentator Naropa, granting that the physical partnering stage goes on, insisted that those of "keen faculty" will omit this stage in favor of the inner *prajna* consort, allowing direct realization of the "body of great bliss."

(8) Tantric Jainism emphasized only *mantra* meditation, adding to ordinary Jainism the Tantric goddess, Padmavati, and Padmavati *mantras*.

(9) Although Tantrism almost certainly began within Hinduism, it became established in all three religions between the 6th and 14th centuries. The basic texts appeared, schools and colleges were founded. When Buddhism disappeared from India (Tantric Buddhism was defunct in India by 1400) Tibet became the undisputed Tantric center. It served as the major storehouse for Tantric literature, and Vajrayana Tantrism was accepted as mainstream Buddhism. *Tantra* also spread to Nepal, Japan, and Indonesia, although never establishing itself in China—some holding that the intricacy of Tantric rites and their sexual symbolism did not appeal to the Chinese mind.

(10) Finally, the terrifying deities of

the Hindu pantheon, and the erotic temple sculptures of southern and southeastern India, are the result of Tantric or Shakti (*q.v.* Śakti) influence: and indeed the two terms are sometimes used interchangeably.

TAO.
    Q.v. Tao-Te Ching (1–3); Hsün Tzu (1); Han Fei Tzu (3); Huai-nan Tzu (1–2); Ho Yen; Chuang Tzu (3); Wang Pi (2).

TAO-AN. 312–385.
    Early Chinese Buddhist philosopher. *Q.v.* Seven Early Chinese Buddhist Schools (1).

TAO-I. 4th and 5th cents. A.D.
    Early Chinese Buddhist philosopher. *Q.v.* Seven Early Chinese Buddhist Schools (6).

TAOISM.
    China's native organized religion. Its scripture is the *Tao Te Ching* (*q.v.*). Its alleged founder, and alleged author of the *Tao Te Ching*, was Lao Tzu (*q.v.*); but the name is probably pseudonymous since it means merely "the old one" or "the old philosopher."
    (1) The underlying motivating source was Chinese mysticism, and the mystic vision as presented in the *Tao Te Ching*. This view held the way of life to be beyond reason ("the *tao* that can be expressed in words is not the eternal *tao*"), but available to one's whole being. One conquers by quietism, letting go, standing in harmony with nature. There are two sets of opposed qualities, the *yin* and *yang* (*q.v.*), which help structure the universe, and must be part of one's personal equation.
    (2) Near the end of the 2nd century B.C. the Taoist mystics organized a church, transforming the *Tao Te Ching* into sacred scripture. The new religion borrowed the name of its scripture and became the Religion of the Way, *Tao chiao*, from which Taoism was derived.
    (3) The *tao* became the means to happiness, wealth, long life. But the intellectual study and understanding of the scripture was possible only for a few. The common people added to its austerities, belief in spirit survival, magic charms for the cure of illness, confes-

sion of sin and absolution on the basis of good works. Taoist intellectuals in the following centuries studied alchemy, seeking a means of immortality, and incidentally adding to their knowledge of human anatomy, chemistry, metallurgy, gunpowder, anaesthetics, pharmaceuticals.
    (4) By the 3rd century A.D., Taoism and Confucianism were chief rivals, with Buddhism more popular among the people and Taoism among the literate ruling classes. Buddhism scored a triumph, while Taoism suffered a partial eclipse, under the Mongols, but the situation was reversed under the Mings.
    (5) Among the important Taoist thinkers are Chuang Tzu (*q.v.* 3) and Huai-nan Tzu (*q.v.* 1).

TAOISTIC CONFUCIANISM.
    Q.v. Yang Hsiung.

TAO-LIN. 314–366.
    Early Chinese Buddhist philosopher. *Q.v.* Seven Early Chinese Buddhist Schools (3).

TAO-TE CHING.
    Chinese phrase signifying "Classic of the Way and its virtue." 6th to 4th cent. B.C. Chinese document of 5,250 characters and 81 chapters serving as scripture for the philosophical and religious movement known as Taoism (*q.v.*). Reputedly the work of Lao Tzu (*q.v.*), said to have been a senior contemporary of Confucius. Probably the work does contain the teaching of Lao Tzu, but the work was both compiled and augmented by his followers. It contains hymns, proverbs, fragments of polemic, and instructional pieces. It is divided into two parts: "Concerning *tao*" and "Concerning *te*," (*i.e.*, "Concerning the Way" and "Concerning virtue"). Showing how to relate oneself to the way or *tao*, a concept with personal, social, and cosmic implications, the *Tao-Te Ching* contains the following ideas:
    (1) Behind all names and ascriptions there is a nameless reality to which we must relate ourselves. This is the *tao*. The named and nameless are associated with the terms, "being" and "nonbeing," although both are ultimately the same.
    (2) The true sage must teach others

how to gain the *tao* without words, since names relate to being, and cannot name the nameless. This may be accomplished by acting through inaction. One gains enlightenment through tranquility, steadfast quietude, complete vacuity.

(3) The *tao* is invisible, inaudible, subtle, formless, infinite, boundless, vague, elusive. When the *tao* declines, the particular goals of humanity and righteousness arise; when knowledge and wisdom appear, so likewise does hypocrisy; when something is wrong with family relations, filial piety appears. One must attain this more complete relation to the *tao* to have everlastingness in life.

(4) This attainment requires that one relate oneself primarily to *yin*, the passive female element in things, rather than to *yang*, the active male element. Thus, remaining receptive, pliant, yielding, submissive, tranquil, spontaneous, and weak, one will be able to master all things. This seems to require an attitude in which one puts oneself in harmony with the pattern, rhythm, and flow of things so that one accomplishes results without effort. The effortless movement of nature adds its power to the life of one who lives by the Way, and such a person becomes an edged tool of the realm.

(5) Indeed, this is the appropriate manner of governing a state. The king should be the chief exemplar of the Way. Of the four great things—the Way, the sky, the earth, and the king—only the king can be admonished and, of the four, only the king can miss the Way. Where the king is blind to the Way, decline and disaster threaten the state. Where the king follows the Way, the people correct themselves, transform themselves, and become prosperous by themselves.

TAPAS.

From *tap*, the Sanskrit term for "heat." Applying initially to the heat of the sun and of the sacrificial fire, it came to denote by extension emotional fervor, primal energy, and ascetic power. The gods both create and destroy by *tapas*. The inner fire of the ascetic is also *tapas*, a force not only capable of burning away personal impurities keeping one from transcendence; but also capable of recreating and reordering the world, or else

dismissing it into irrelevance. *Tapas* is of use in the third *Ashrama* (*q.v.* 2) of Hinduism where personal reordering occurs in Yogic (*q.v.* 4) meditation, in Jainism, Buddhism, and Tantrism, in the *Puranas* (q.v. Śastras 3), and in the epics (*q.v.* Hinduism 2, 3). The *Bhagavad-Gita* distinguishes three types of *tapas*: (1) virtuous (*sattva*), (2) ambitious (*rajas*), (3) perverted (*tamas*) (*q.v.* Hinduism 6b).

TARSKI, ALFRED. 1901–1983.

Polish-American mathematician and logician. Born in Warsaw. Educated at the University of Warsaw where he taught until 1939. Taught at the University of California (Berkeley), 1942–73.

Principal writings: "Contribution to the Axiomatics of Well-Ordered Sets" (P), 1921; "On Finite Sets" (F), 1924; "On Truth Functions According to Russell and Whitehead" (F), 1924; "Fundamental Concepts of the Methodology of the Deductive Sciences" (G), 1930; "Investigations of the Propositional Calculus" (with Łukasiewicz) (G), 1930; "Some Methodological Investigations of the Definability of Concepts" (G), 1935–6; "The Basis of Scientific Semantics" (G), 1936; "The Concept of Truth in Formulated Languages" (G), 1936; *Introduction to Logic and to the Methodology of Deductive Sciences* (T), 1936; "The Semantic Conception of Truth and the Foundations of Semantics" (E), 1944; "On Essential Undecidability" (E), 1949; *Undecidable Theories* (E) (with Mostowski and Robinson), 1953; *Logic, Semantics, Metamathematics* (T), 1956; "From Accessible to Inaccessible Cardinals" (E), 1964; *A Formalization of Set Theory without Variables* (with S. Givant), 1987.

(1) Regarding Semantics as the discipline which studies the expressions of a language and the objects to which such expressions refer, "truth" is viewed as a problem pertinent to this discipline. Viewing "true" as an adjective characterizing sentences, Tarski developed a Correspondence Theory of Truth (*q.v.*) in terms of languages and metalanguages. To avoid paradox (*q.v.*) it is necessary to view the assertion that any given sentence is true or false as a sentence in the metalanguage of the language of the original sentence. Letting "L" stand for language. "M" for metalanguage, "x" for

the name of the original sentence in "L," and "p" for a translation of this sentence into "M," the sentences in "M" asserting truth will read "x is a true sentence if and only if p."

(2) Taken as a criterion of truth, termed "convention T," the sentence in question—referring to sentences in M and L—is itself a part of the metalanguage of M, or the meta-metalanguage of L. The phrase "true sentence" appears without definition and, indeed, Tarski offered a Gödel-type proof that the term must be thus accepted under the pain of further paradox.

(3) The hierarchy of languages necessary in explicating the adjectival concept of "true" and "false" is but one application of the more general point that with respect to any formalized deductive science, the structure of that science must be discussed in a metalanguage which defines the scope of a metascience so that, formally speaking, a hierarchy of metasciences accompanies the hierarchy of languages.

(4) A theory is decidable when the valid sentences of the theory are capable of proof within the theory. Tarski has shown that theories are decidable when the conjuncts of their valid sentences are recursive. Otherwise they are undecidable. A theory is *essentially* undecidable when it is undecidable and when any extension of the theory, using the same constants, is likewise undecidable (*q.v.* Decidability).

Q.v. Davidson (1, 6).

TASAN (HŎNG YAK YONG). 1762–1836.
Korean philosopher. One of a group of Korean thinkers supporting *sirhak* (practical learning) and criticizing the unproductive neo-Confucian tradition of their day. Tasan is regarded as the completer and synthesizer of *sirhak* thought. He served as county magistrate, and as an inspector reporting corruption in local government. Also endured a 17-year exile in a remote village.

Principal writings: *A Guide to Governing the People*, 1818; *A Guide to Administration* and *A Treatise on Ideal Government* (no dates); *Collected Works* (in facsimile), 1883.

(1) Rather than thinking of our physical nature as evil, as had the neo-Confucians against whom Tasan is reacting,

it is neither good nor evil, yet self-cultivation requires that it be brought under control.

(2) It follows that virtue is not innate, and has no ontological status, but is developed in social involvement. *Jen*, ("humanity"), is the fulfillment of moral responsibility, encompassing the three virtues of filial piety, fraternal respect, and compassion.

(3) The three virtues must be extended from the family, and come to reflect the changed attitudes of government leaders.

TATIAN. Late 2nd cent. A.D.
Christian Apologist. Born in Assyria. Educated in Greece. Lived in Rome where he became a follower of Justin Martyr (*q.v.*). The most severe critic of Greek science and philosophy among the Apologists, he also wrote a harmony of the gospels. This book, the *Diatessaron*, which made a single running account of the gospels, threatened for a time to replace the gospels themselves. Later he became a Gnostic of Valentinian persuasion, *q.v.* Gnosticism; Valentinus; Apologists (5).

Principal writings: *An Address to the Greeks*; *Diatessaron* (T); *Perfection According to the Savior* (T).

TATTVA.
Sanskrit term for "category." The term we have translated as "category" in the expositions of, *e.g.*, Jainism and of the Sankhya (*q.v.*) philosophy.

TAT TVAM ASI.
Sanskrit sentence meaning "that art thou." The assertion identifying the *Atman* or inner self, with Brahman, the creator and upholder of all things, is found in the *Chandogya Upaniṣad* (*q.v. Vedas* 4).

TATTVOPAPLAVA.
Q.v. Jayaraśi (5).

TAULER, JOHN. 1300–1361.
German mystic. Born in Strassburg. A Dominican, he was educated in the Dominican Colleges of Strassburg and Cologne. Strongly influenced by Eckhart who taught at Strassburg. He became closely associated with the Friends of God (*q.v.*) through a sojourn in Basel in 1338–39. His sermons are regarded as among the noblest expressions of the German tongue. Following the Neoplatonic line,

he nonetheless believed that the return to God requires self-mortification and the gift of grace.

Principal writings: *Sermons* (T in part), 1498.

TAUTOLOGY.

In logic, a proposition which is true by virtue of its form alone (*q.v.* Propositional Calculus 22). For some, every definition is tautological. In terms of the technique of truth tables (*q.v.*), a tautology is a statement form, all of whose substitution instances are true. One might say, then, that the tautology is necessarily true. Some would hold that while this is so, the truth in question is vacuous.

A. The question can be tested with respect to the laws of thought (*q.v.*). The three laws or principles can be expressed by the following statement forms: The Principle of Contradiction, $\sim (p \cdot \sim p)$; The Principle of Excluded Middle, $p \vee \sim p$; The Principle of Identity, $p \supset p$ and $p \equiv p$.

(1) The Principle of Contradiction, holding that it cannot be the case that "p" and "not-p" are true at the same time is demonstrated by the truth table:

```
p ~ p  (p ·~ p)  ~ (p ·~ p)
T  F     F           T
F  T     F           T
```

The statement of the principle, having only true substitution instances, is tautologous.

(2) The Principle of Excluded Middle, holding of any proposition that it is either true or false, likewise shows itself to have only true substitution instances.

```
p ~ p   p v~ p
T  F      T
F  T      T
```

(3) The same is true of the Principle of Identity which holds that if a proposition is true, then it is true.

```
p  p ⊃ p   p ≡ p
T    T       T
F    T       T
```

B. Added comments on Tautology:

(4) Tillich (*q.v.* 2) regarded all products of the "autonomous" reason as tautologous.

(5) Wittgenstein (*q.v.* 3) divided meaningful propositions into two classes: those which picture facts, and those which express tautologies.

TAYLOR, HARRIET.
Q.v. John Stuart Mill.

TAYLOR, JEREMY. 1613–1667.

English theologian. Born in Cambridge. Educated at Cambridge. Taught at both Cambridge and Oxford. A Churchman and royalist, he forfeited his "livings" during the Cromwellian period. Several times imprisoned, he spent a number of years in Wales and in Ireland, where he died. He is well-known both for his sermons—Emerson called him "the Shakespeare of the divines"—and his plea for toleration. Believing religious truth to be indemonstrable, and theology to be "rather a divine life than a divine knowledge," it is impossible to expect human agreement in this area. And heresy is to be viewed as an error of the will rather than of the understanding. But toleration should not be extended to that which is "against the foundation of faith . . . contrary to good life . . . or destructive to human society, and the public and just interests of bodies politic."

Principal writings: *A Discourse of the Liberty of Prophesying*, 1646; *The Rule and Exercises of Holy Living*, 1650; *The Rule and Exercises of Holy Dying*, 1651; *Twenty-seven Sermons*, 1651; *Twenty-five Sermons*, 1653; *The Real Presence*, 1654; *Unum Necessarium*, 1655.

TAYLOR, NATHANIEL. 1786–1858.

American theologian. Born in New Milford, Conn. Educated at Yale. Minister of the first church of New Haven, he taught theology at Yale. His point of view, called "Taylorism," or the "New Haven Theology," was an effort to defend Calvinism against Arminian (*q.v.*) and Pelagian (*q.v.*) tendencies. But since Taylor distinguished between natural ability and moral inability and claimed that with respect to the right, man "not only can if he will, he can if he won't," he was accused of reflecting the tendencies he opposed. His interpretation of the fall of man was Infralapsarian (*q.v.* Predestination 7).

Principal writings: *Practical Sermons*, 1858; *Essays and Lectures upon Select Topics in Revealed Theology*, 1859; *Lectures on the Moral Government of God*, 2 vols., 1859.

TE.
Chinese term meaning "virtue." In Taoism (*q.v.* Tao-Te Ching), "the abode of *tao*," or *tao* particularized in a thing.

TECHNE.
A Greek term referring to the knowledge and application of principles involved in the production of objects and the accomplishment of specified ends. For Aristotle (*q.v.* 1), where *episteme* implies disinterested knowledge of principles and leads to theoretical science, *techne* implies the application of principles and relates to productive science.

TEICHMÜLLER, GUSTAV. 1832–1888.
German philosopher. Born in Braunschweig. Taught in Göttingen, Basel, and Dorpat. Through a study of the history of philosophy, and especially of classical systems of metaphysics, Teichmüller came to the conclusion that each system was partial, and represented a single perspective of a complex reality. Coining the term "Perspectivism," he argued for the validity of each such point of view.
Principal writings: *Aristotelian Investigations*, 1859–73; *On the Immortality of the Soul*, 1874; *Studies in the History of Ideas*, 1874; *New Studies in the History of Ideas*, 1876–9; *The Real World and the Apparent World*, 1882; *Philosophy of Religion*, 1886.

TEILHARD DE CHARDIN, PIERRE. 1881–1955.
French paleoanthropologist and philosopher. Born in Sarcenat. A Jesuit scientist whose doctrine of evolution extended from the inorganic realm, through the biosphere, and into the "noösphere" (the sphere of mind), Teilhard believed that evolution in the "noösphere" would lead to a world culture and, at the "omega point," to a hyperpersonal consciousness who will be God in history. Due to the opposition of the Church his work was published posthumously.
Principal writings: *The Phenomenon of Man* (T), 1955; *Letters from a Traveller* (T), 1956; *The Realm of the Divine* (T), 1957; *The Future of Man* (T), 1959; *Hymn of the Universe* (T), 1964.

TELEFINALISM.
Q.v. Lecomte Du Noüy.

TELEOLOGICAL ARGUMENT.
From "teleology" (*q.v.*), one of the three basic arguments for God, taking the purpose, order, or design of the universe as premise for the conclusion that God exists. Of the other two arguments, the cosmological (*q.v.*) and ontological (*q.v.*), the former has had intimate involvement with the teleological argument. Indeed, the arguments from motion, contingency, and order have often been regarded as parts of the teleological argument. If one distinguishes between the cosmological and the teleological arguments, motion and contingency fall into the former category, and order into the latter. Given this division, the teleological argument is often called the argument from design or, as Kant preferred, the Physico-Theological argument.
(1) Although the elements of the argument are implicit in the view of Anaxagoras (*q.v.* 3) that mind or *nous* rules the universe, its first statement is to be found in the *Laws*, where Plato (*q.v.* 10) cites the design of nature along with an argument from self-motion.
(2) Aristotle (*q.v.* 8–9) presented a thoroughly teleological universe; indeed, in a sense he invented that conception of the universe. His argument for God is teleological in the first sense mentioned above, since it includes motion and contingency as well as order. Since two of the three components of his argument fit the cosmological argument (*q.v.*), we have treated Aristotle's argument under that heading.
(3) St. Augustine (*q.v.* 5–7) offered a number of arguments including that sense of teleology which combines design and motion.
(4) It is the merit of Thomas Aquinas (*q.v.* 3e) to have separated the elements so long combined in the teleological argument. The separation constituted three of his five arguments. And one of the three was an argument from design. As the arrow is directed by the archer, so the world is directed by an intelligent being.
(5) Telesio (*q.v.* 3) criticized Aristotle's argument from motion but approved the argument from the order of nature.
(6) Newton (*q.v.* 6) likewise invoked an orderer to explain the continuing stability of the structure of the universe.
(7) Leibniz (*q.v.* 8) found an orderer

necessary to explain the harmony of the universe, especially since the monads which constitute that universe are windowless.

(8) Joseph Butler (*q.v.* 2) argued from the presence of providential design in nature to the truth of the Christian faith.

(9) Hume (*q.v.* 7) pointed out that the teleological or design argument, given the nature of the world, could at most prove a finite, imperfect deity.

(10) Kant (*q.v.* 5b), using the term "Physico-Theological" as the name for this argument, asserted that it attempts to pass from the phenomenal to the noumenal, and that it rests on the ontological argument which is not a valid argument.

(11) Paley (*q.v.* 2) provides the clearest instance of the design argument. He was particularly impressed by the structure of living things, and especially by the organ of the eye, in providing premises for his argument.

(12) J.S. Mill (*q.v.* 9) concluded from the design of the universe to the existence of a finite deity.

(13) Darwin (*q.v.* 5) vastly reduced the credibility of arguments from organic structures to the existence of God. It seemed that one could as well argue to the principle of natural selection.

(14) In the 20th century F.R. Tennant (*q.v.* 2) attempted to shore up the teleological argument by citing evidence from a wider range of categories, including the intelligibility and beauty of the universe, while turning attention away from the products of evolution to the process itself.

TELEOLOGICAL ETHICS.

That family of ethical theories which analyze the right in terms of the ends of action. The emphasis is thus on the consequence likely to flow from decision. Since the good is an end to be achieved, teleological ethics may be said to be the approach to ethics which evaluates conduct in terms of its likelihood to produce good. The classical example of teleological ethics is Utilitarianism (*q.v.*) although all approaches, save that of Deontological ethics (*q.v.* Deontology), place some emphasis on the good as an end of action.

TELEOLOGICAL SUSPENSION OF THE ETHICAL.

Q.v. Kierkegaard (4).

TELEOLOGY.

From the Greek *telos* ("end") and *logos* ("discourse" or "doctrine"). The doctrine that ends, final causes, or purposes are to be invoked as principles of explanation. The term was introduced in the 18th century by Christian Wolff (*q.v.* 6).

(1) Although Anaxagoras (*q.v.* 3–4) and Plato (*q.v.* 10) prepared the way for a view of the universe as purposive, it was Aristotle (*q.v.* 8–9) who brought the analysis to completion. Final cause is one of the four causes, and relates—directly or indirectly—to everything in the world.

(2) Teleology retains a role in all theistic conceptions of the universe, and the teleological argument (*q.v.*) is one of the three standard arguments for God.

(3) Furthermore, teleological ethics (*q.v.*) is one of the standard approaches to the problem of right and wrong.

(4) Increasingly, as science has developed, the area of teleological explanation has diminished. Forced out of physics, teleology retained a hold for a time in vitalistic theories of biology (*q.v.* Vitalism). Its presence in psychology has been challenged, less successfully, by Behaviorism (*q.v.*) and Operationalism (*q.v.*).

(5) With respect to biology and psychology, Nagel (*q.v.* 3) regards teleological and non-teleological explanations to be equivalent and interchangeable.

TELESIO, BERNARDINO. 1509–1588.

Italian philosopher. Born in Cosenza. Educated at Padua. An anti-Aristotelian, he founded an academy at Naples stressing empirical methods of investigation. Principal writings: *On the Nature of Things According to Their Principles*, 1586.

(1) Replacing the Aristotelian form-matter analysis with a matter-force approach, Telesio understood matter as extended and observable, and force as expansion and contraction due to heat and cold.

(2) There is no mind-body dichotomy since matter is capable of feeling, and spirit is itself a subtle matter. In addition to these, man has a soul super-added by God.

(3) Since matter is naturally in motion, Aristotle's argument from derived motion to the unmoved mover is fallacious. The argument from design is, however, valid.

(4) He regarded self-preservation as man's fundamental goal and the basis of ethics.

TELOS.
Q.v. Teleology.

TEMPERANCE.
One of the four Greek cardinal virtues. In Plato (*q.v.* 5c) the specific virtue of the artisans.

TEMPLE, WILLIAM. 1881–1944.
English theologian. Archbishop of York and Canterbury. Arguing that God is the supreme value, Temple located revelation in the coincidence between the "divinely guided event" and man's "divinely guided apprehension" of it. The incarnation is the most significant such event.
Principal writings: *Mens Creatrix*, 1917; *Christ the Truth*, 1924; *Nature, Man, and God*, 1934.

TENNANT, FREDERICK R. 1866–1957.
English philosopher-theologian. Educated at Cambridge. Taught at Cambridge.
Principal writings: *The Origin and Propagation of Sin*, 1902; *The Concept of Sin*, 1912; *Miracle and its Philosophical Presuppositions*, 1925; *Philosophical Theology*, 2 vols., 1928, 1930; *Philosophy of the Sciences*, 1932; *The Nature of Belief*, 1943.
(1) Interpreting faith broadly as the volitional element in all knowledge, Tennant found natural theology to be continuous with natural science.
(2) Developing what he took to be a valid form for the teleological argument for God, Tennant stressed the intelligibility of the world, belief that the process of evolution shares something of the nature of a cosmic purpose, the manner in which the inorganic level was preparatory for life and now helps to shelter it, the beauty of nature, and the moral and spiritual life of man. Although no one of these lines of evidence is compelling, he believed that in conjunction they provide grounds for belief in God.
(3) The moral evil of sin and the natural evil of pain are justified respectively as the necessary consequences of human freedom, and necessary concomitants to the conditions allowing the development of personality.

TENOR.
Q.v. Metaphor (12).

TERESA, SAINT. 1515–1582.
Spanish mystic. Born in Avila. An Augustinian, she entered a Carmelite convent where she began the practice of contemplation. With St. John of the Cross (*q.v.*), and against great opposition, she founded the Discalced Carmelites ("Barefoot Carmelites"). Her descriptions of the stages of mysticism, leading to the vision of God, are central to the literature on mysticism.
Principal writings: *Life by Herself* (T), 1562–5; *The Way of Perfection* (T), 1565; *The Interior Castle* (T), 1577.

TERMINATING JUDGMENTS.
Q.v. C.I. Lewis (3).

TERMINIST LOGIC.
A 13th-century movement of logic in which the nature of language was strongly emphasized. The word was treated first as a physical entity, and only secondly as a significant term. Among those in the movement were William of Sherwood (*q.v.*), Lambert of Auxerre (*q.v.*), Nicholas of Paris, and Peter of Spain (*q.v.*).

TERMINUS A QUO, TERMINUS AD QUEM.
Latin terms referring to the point of departure and the point toward which one is leading. In the Cosmological argument (*q.v.*) for God, for example, the *terminus a quo* is the universe and the *terminus ad quem* is God. The terms originated in Scholastic philosophy.

TERTIARIES.
Q.v. Francis of Assisi (1).

TERTIUM NON DATUR.
Q.v. Laws of Thought (2).

TERTIUM QUID.
Latin for a "third something." A Scholastic phrase. After an analysis has concentrated on two points, neither suitable by itself, a search for a *tertium quid*, a third term or point, may be appropriate. Every resolution of the "black or white" fallacy (*q.v.* 15) calls for a third position between the two extremes, and thus a *tertium quid*.

TERTULLIAN. c. 155–c. 222.

Christian Apologist. Born in Carthage. Lived in Rome, working as a lawyer, until his conversion to Christianity in 195. At that time he returned to the North African city of his birth, where he served as Presbyter. The most vigorous and uncompromising of the early Christian Apologists, he in later life adopted Montanism (*q.v.* 2–3) as the interpretation of Christianity most congenial to his views. *Q.v.* Apologists (8).

Principal writings: *To Martyrs; Apology* (T); *Against the Gnostics; Against Marcion; Against Valentinus; Against the Marcionites; Against Praxeas; On the Body of Christ; On the Resurrection of the Body; On the Soul* (T); in addition, a number of Montanist works written between 213 and 222.

(1) "I believe because it is absurd." Tertullian's defense of the faith held to a contradiction between reason and the Christian faith. In this he differed from the strategy of most of the Christian Apologists who emphasized, in greater or lesser degree, a harmony between philosophy and the faith. On Tertullian's view, that the son of God died is to be believed because it is contradictory; and that he rose from the grave has certitude because it is impossible.

(2) The stark nature of the contradiction is explicable because of the extreme limitations of human knowledge. Against the immensity of the divine, this fact renders philosophy not only pointless but pernicious. Hence, his attacks on the entire tradition.

(3) Yet, curiously, his doctrine of the relation of soul and body, and of God and the world, adopts a Stoic materialism where both God and soul are conceived as spiritual matter.

(4) Tertullian was the first to use the Trinitarian formula in which God is viewed as three persons in one substance.

(5) Author of the doctrine of Traducianism, Tertullian held that the soul was produced, or passed along, in conception by a "soul-producing" seed. Thus, it is neither pre-existent nor created at the moment of conception.

TETENS, JOHANN NICOLAUS. 1736–1807.

German philosopher. Born in Tetenbüll. Educated at Rostock and Copenhagen. Taught at Kiel. His analysis of the structure of knowledge anticipated and influenced Kant.

Principal writings: *On General Speculative Philosophy*, 1775; *Philosophical Essays on Human Nature*, 2 vols., 1777.

THALES. 640–546 B.C.

Milesian philosopher. One of the Seven Sages of Greece. Among his scientific exploits is prediction of the eclipse of 585 B.C. Among his engineering achievements is diversion of a river to allow passage for King Croesus and his retinue. He is credited with "Know thyself" and "Nothing in excess." He advocated a federation of the Greek city states, including a central capital.

(1) Everything is contained in water. The universe is hence explicable in terms of this single principle. Aristotle regarded Thales as originating the search for principles of explanation.

(2) All things are full of gods. Apparently this is an attempt to explain the motive power of change in vitalistic terms.

(3) He held that man's soul has a power of self-motion, and the power of initiating motion in other things.

(4) He believed the earth to be a disc, floating on a vast sea of water, like a piece of wood.

THANATOS.

Q.v. Freud (8).

THEISM.

From the Greek *theos* ("God") the term, along with "theist," first appeared in England in the 17th century where it was used in contrast to "atheism" and "atheist." These latter terms, however, had a much earlier origin, going back, in fact, to Plato.

(1) "Deism" and "deist" likewise made their appearance in 17th-century England, but at an earlier date than the *theos*-based terms. For a time, the two pairs of terms were used as synonyms. Eventually, however, the distinction was drawn that in deism (*q.v.*) God is creator but does not relate to His creation. In theism, by contrast God continues to sustain relations to His creation.

(2) Theism is distinguished from Pantheism (*q.v.*) in that for the latter alter-

native God, identified with the world, is wholly immanent. In theism God is both transcendent and immanent.

(3) Hartshorne (*q.v.* 3) has pointed out that in classical theism, *i.e.*, the medieval conception of God as absolute, the feature of divine transcendence is overwhelming in its dominance. In this view, indeed, there is only a one-way relation between God and world, that is, the world is related to God, but God is not related to the world. Hartshorne thus distinguishes between classical theism, stressing the divine absoluteness, and dipolar theism, preserving a balance between immanence and transcendence, absoluteness and relativity, in the conception of God. Also *q.v.* Panentheism.

(4) The views of theists, pantheists, etc., are related to specific thinkers under the heading, God. Some thinkers have used the terminology of the present heading, *e.g.*, John Fiske (*q.v.*) advanced a position of "evolutionary theism," Weisse (*q.v.*) one of "speculative theism," Sorley (*q.v.*) referred to his point of view as "ethical theism," and the view of A.E. Taylor (*q.v.* 3), affirming God's existence on the basis of moral experience, may be called "moral theism."

THEMISTIUS. 317–c. 387.

Born in Paphlagonia, his principal spheres of activity were Rome and Constantinople. An Aristotelian, he held that Plato and Aristotle were in substantial agreement, and that Christianity and Hellenism were two forms of a single universal religion.

Principal writings: *Commentaries and Paraphrases of Aristotle*; *On Virtue*; *Operations and Discourses*.

THEOCRACY.

From the Greek *theokratia* ("the rule of God"), that organization of the state in which the divine commandments are the civil laws, and God Himself is regarded as the sovereign power. Applied to Judaism (*q.v.*) in its early stages, other instances of theocratic states are Florence under Savonarola (*q.v.*), Geneva under Calvin (*q.v.*), and the New England colonies under Puritanism (*q.v.* Calvinism).

THEODICY.

From *theos* ("God") and *dike* ("justice").

A term introduced by Leibniz (*q.v.* 9) to characterize the topic of God's government of the world in relation to the nature of man. The problem is the justification of God's goodness and justice in view of the evil in the world.

THEODORIC (THIERRY) OF CHARTRES. 12th cent. A.D.

Scholastic philosopher. Taught in Paris. The younger brother of Bernard of Chartres (*q.v.*), Theodoric became Chancellor of Chartres in 1142.

Principal writings: *Heptateuch* (a handbook on the seven liberal arts); *On the Six Days' Work*; as well as commentaries on Cicero, Boethius, and Aristotle's *Prior Analytics*.

THEODORUS OF ASINE. 4th cent. A.D.

Neoplatonic philosopher. A student of Porphyry (*q.v.*), heavily influenced by Iamblichus (*q.v.*). He divided the intelligence into trichotomies, following the example of Iamblichus. His commentaries were widely used.

Principal writings: *Commentary on the Timaeus*, as well as on other works of Plato.

THEODORUS, THE ATHEIST. 3rd cent. B.C.

Greek philosopher. A leader of the Cyrenaic school (*q.v.* Cyrenaicism), Theodorus was a disciple of Annikeris (*q.v.*). He broadened the Cyrenaic principle that pleasure was the end of life by holding that the end of life should not be understood as the momentary sensation of pleasure but rather the enduring emotion of joy brought about by the application of practical intelligence. He regarded the happiness produced by wisdom as the greatest good. In religious philosophy he denied not only the gods of Athens but any notion of the divine. For this reason he was exiled from the city. A contributing reason may have been his doctrine, similar to that of Stoicism (*q.v.*), that the world is our fatherland. Theodorus drew from this the conclusion that one ought not to sacrifice oneself for one's city state. It is held that Theodorus' work on the gods was drawn on heavily by Epicurus in his work on that subject.

Principal writings: *On the Gods*.

THEOLOGIA GERMANICA.
Q.v. The German Theology.

THEOLOGICAL UTILITARIANISM.
Q.v. Paley (1); Utilitarianism (4).

THEOLOGY.
From the Greek *theos* ("God") and *logos* ("discourse" or "reason"). As a discipline theology in the West has generally accepted the canons of logic, and reasoning about God is world-wide. In the East, however, the analogue to Western theology contains more figures and traditions moving to their conclusions from premises of non-being rather than being, and stressing contradiction over consistency. In what follows we shall consider theology in Western terms, while broadening its scope to include representative Eastern positions.

(1) *Theologia* was originally viewed as concerned with myth. Hesiod (*q.v.*) and Orpheus were preeminent examples in this sense.

(2) It was Aristotle (*q.v.* 10) who first regarded theology as a discipline, identifying it with first philosophy, the highest of the theoretical sciences, a study which was later termed metaphysics.

(3) The concept of emptiness (*q.v.*), rather than being, became a central concept of Buddhism, beginning in the Hinayana schools, and becoming a dominant characteristic of Mahayana Buddhism.

(4) Philo Judaeus (*q.v.* 2) initiated the concept of negative theology. Due to God's transcendence the only assertions humans can make about Him are negative in form. God is transcendent and one can only say of Him what He is not.

(5) Nagarjuna (*q.v.* 8) moved through 14 contradictions to the affirmation of a non-dual Absolute, in respect to which Buddha can be neither affirmed nor denied.

(6) In the early centuries of Christianity agreements were formulated defining the subject matter of Christian theology. The key work was accomplished by the Christian Apologists (*q.v.*), and especially Justin Martyr (*q.v.*), Irenaeus (*q.v.*), Tertullian (*q.v.*), and Origen (*q.v.*); Athanasius (*q.v.*) and the "homoousian" formula of the Council of Nicaea (*q.v.*); the Cappadocians—Basil (*q.v.*), Gregory Nazianzen

(*q.v.*) and Gregory of Nyssa (*q.v.*)—and St. Augustine (*q.v.*); the decisions of Christology and the Holy Spirit of the synod of Alexandria (362), the Councils of Constantinople (*q.v.*), Ephesus (431), and Chalcedon (*q.v.*).

(7) The task of bringing together key doctrines is not theology as reasoning about God, but as prospecting for an appropriate unity, or orthodoxy, in the doctrines of a living faith. In the East, Buddhism worked to establish orthodoxy through a succession of Buddhist Councils (*q.v.*), as did Christianity (*q.v.*, and Christology) in the West.

(8) The Pseudo-Dionysius (*q.v.* 1–2) distinguished between positive theology (resting on Scripture), negative theology (*cf.* 3 above), and superlative theology (conforming to the Neoplatonic view of God as superlative in all respects). None of these approaches sufficing, a mystical theology is at last recommended.

(9) Boethius (*q.v.* 1) held to a strict definition of theology as reasoning about God. His *On the Trinity* presented theology as a discipline requiring the application of Aristotelian logic to the idea of God. The strict definition helped to shape Scholastic method, and Western theology generally.

(10) In the East Ramanuja (*q.v.*) predated the Protestant Reformation in drawing a set of doctrines from Scripture (the *Vedas*), while finding the basis of belief in *bhakti* (devotion) rather than in knowledge.

(11) Anselm (*q.v.* 6) provided an important analysis of the Atonement; Hugh of St. Victor (*q.v.*), Peter Lombard (*q.v.*), and the fourth Lateran Council (1215) brought to completion the doctrine of the Sacraments. These accomplishments, along with the decisions mentioned in (4) above, provided the framework of Catholic theology.

(12) Maimonides (*q.v.* 2–4) developed the distinction between negative and positive theology, the former separating us from false conceptions and the latter relating, ultimately, to God's effects in the natural world.

(13) The *Summa Theologica* of Thomas Aquinas (*q.v.*) was the culmination of the movement of thought beginning with the Apologists. He brought into an exhaustive statement all of the separate doctrines

alluded to above, their sources including Scripture, Church Councils, and earlier philosophers, especially Aristotle.

(14) A distinction gradually developed between natural and revealed theology. Although Thomas Aquinas distinguished between truths of faith and truths of reason, the two elements work together in his writings, and according to his theory. William of Ockham (*q.v.* 1, 3), on the other hand, held theology to be a discipline resting on revealed truth and independent of both philosophy and science.

(15) Protestant theology, lessening the emphasis on tradition, increasing the emphasis on Scripture, and on faith, found its fullest expression in the systems of Melanchthon (*q.v.*) and Calvin (*q.v.*).

(16) Suarez (*q.v.* 1) believed that theology could be benefited by philosophical criticism, and that the two disciplines could coexist within the "higher unity" of the Christian faith.

(17) The movement of dialectical, or crisis, theology had its origin in the view of Kierkegaard (*q.v.* 4) that a leap of faith was necessary in order to reach the level of Christianity. But the terms belong rather to the writings of Karl Barth (*q.v.*). Emil Brunner (*q.v.* 1) was one of the adherents of this point of view.

(18) Paul Tillich (*q.v.* 1) held the relation of philosophy and theology to be reciprocal, although theology's "method of correlation," answering ultimate questions on the basis of revelation, is beyond the capacity of philosophy.

(19) A number of Catholic theologians (*q.v.* Schillebeeckx 1; Lonergan 1–2; Rahner 1) have benefited from 20th-century interpretations of Thomas Aquinas, making him more relevant to contemporary thought.

(20) In the 1960's the Radical Theology of Altizer and Hamilton made its appearance, containing the "death of God" as its central doctrine (*cf.* Thomas Altizer and William Hamilton, *Radical Theology and the Death of God*, 1966).

(21) Between 1960–85 a social movement called Theology of Liberation (*q.v.*), directed toward the liberation of the oppressed, was very influential in Latin America.

THEOLOGY OF ARISTOTLE.
The title of a work translated from Greek into Arabic in the 9th century A.D. by the Baghdad School (*q.v.*) of translators, and then into Latin. Although passing as the work of Aristotle until the 13th century, the volume in fact comprised books four to six of Plotinus' *Enneads*. The mistaken identification turned Aristotle and his interpreters into Neoplatonists for nearly five centuries (*q.v.* Neoplatonism 12).

THEON OF SMYRNA. 2nd cent. A.D.
Greek philosopher. Associated with the Fourth Academy (*q.v.* Plato's Academy 4) in a period when it and thus he were eclectic, dogmatic, and neo-Pythagorean. He believed that mathematical knowledge formed an essential step in the ascension of the soul to union with God.
Principal writings: *Book of Astronomy*; a book on mathematics and fragments remain.

THEONOMY.
From the Greek *theos* ("God") and *nomos* ("rule or law"). The state of being subject to divine rule or law. Tillich (*q.v.* 2) recommended a "theonomous" reason in contrast to the state of reason as autonomous or heteronomous.

THEOPASCHITES.
From the Greek *theos* ("god") and *paschein* ("to suffer"). A name given to the Monophysites (*q.v.* Monophysitism) around 518 A.D. on the basis of a liturgical response in their service of worship saying "God has been crucified." The response followed from their belief that in Christ the divine and human form a single nature.

THEOPHANY.
From the Greek *theos* ("God") and *phainesthai* ("to appear"). The manifestation of God to humans, especially through incarnation in human form.

THEOPHRASTUS. 360–287 B.C.
Greek philosopher. Born in Eresus. A disciple of Aristotle whom he followed as head of the Lyceum (*q.v.*) in 322, keeping the position until his death. The author of writings in many fields, his work on propositional logic, modal logic, and quantification theory qualifies him as a

key figure in the transition from Aristotelian to Stoic logic (q.v.).

Principal writings: Of his extensive writings in many fields there survive his *Ethical Characters* and *Causes and Descriptions of Plants*; and fragments of his work on meteorology, physics, metaphysics, sensation, and animal physiology.

THEOROGONOUS METAPHYSICS.
Q.v. Adolf Stöhr.

THEORY OF KNOWLEDGE.
Q.v. Epistemology.

THEORY OF MEANING.
Q.v. Davidson (7–9).

THEORY OF TYPES.
Q.v. Type (4); Russell (3).

THEOSOPHY.
From the Greek *theos* ("God") and *sophia* ("wisdom"). Ammonius Saccas coined the term to fit certain systems of thought coming from the Orient, stressing clairvoyance and telepathy. Madame Blavatsky founded the Theosophical Society in 1876; the most notable American leader has been Annie Besant.

THERAVADA BUDDHISM.
One of the four main schools of Hinayana Buddhism. Of the four Theravada (*q.v.* Buddhism, Theravada), the oldest, alone survives. The Pali Canon is the product of this school. The other three shcools, Sarvastivada (*q.v.*), Sautrantika (*q.v.*), and Vaibhashika (*q.v.*) developed from Theravada.

THESES, NINETY-FIVE.
Q.v. Luther (1).

THEURGY.
From the Greek *theos* ("God") and *ergon* ("work"). Hence, a work of God. An occult art, often involving rites and incantations, for controlling divine and beneficent spirits. Theurgy was practiced by the lesser Neoplatonists. Porphyry (*q.v.* 4) was an adherent before meeting Plotinus, writing on the oracles. Proclus (*q.v.* 3) looked upon theurgy as a power above all human wisdom. Iamblichus (*q.v.* 2) wrote on and supported the theurgic mysteries. Maximus (*q.v.*) practiced them with the support of Emperor Julian.

Plotinus opposed them. St. Augustine held them to be motivated by a "criminal curiosity." The medieval church formally rejected theurgy. It revived briefly during the Renaissance.

THIERRY OF CHARTRES.
Q.v. Theodoric of Chartres.

THIRTY-NINE ARTICLES.
Q.v. Thomas Cranmer.

THOMAS À KEMPIS. 1380–1471.
Member of the Brethren of the Common Life. Born in Kempen, Germany. Educated in Gerhard Groote's school in Deventer. Joining the Augustinian order, he was sent to the Convent of Mount St. Agnes at Zwolle, rising to sub-prior. The authorship of the *Imitation of Christ* (*q.v.*), famous devotional handbook once attributed to him, is now in dispute. Among others, Gerhard Groote (*q.v.*) is sometimes regarded as its author.

THOMAS DE VIO.
Q.v. Cajetan.

THOMASIUS, CHRISTIAN. 1655–1728.
German philosopher. Born in Leipzig. Studied at Leipzig. Taught at Leipzig and Halle. He helped to found the latter university, serving as rector. Thomasius combined a faith in the natural reason (leading him to stress natural over revealed law) with a practical attitude toward education (leading to a more "worldly" educational program including university teaching in German rather than in Latin), and a mystical attitude toward first and last things. Thomasius' mysticism was derived from a pietistic religious experience, and was reflected in a vitalistic metaphysics featuring divine illumination as the source of truth, and a divinely created world spirit as the source of animation. The followers of Thomasius, Rüdiger (*q.v.*) among them, were dominant in German universities by 1710. They were eclipsed by followers of Christian Wolff (*q.v.*) by 1730; but under A. F. Hoffman and Christian Crusius (*q.v.*) the way was prepared for Immanuel Kant.

Principal writings: *An Introduction to Philosophy for Courtiers* (L), 1688; *The Principles of Divine Law* (L), 1688; *Confession of One's Doctrines* (L), 1695; *Practical Ethics* (G), 1696; *The Essence of Spirit* (G),

1699; *Basis of the Laws of Nature and of Nations* (L), 1705.

THOMAS, NORMAN.
Q.v. Socialism (8).

THOMAS OF ERFURT. fl. 1325.
Scholastic philosopher. Interested in the philosophy of language, and drawing on a tradition going back to Aristotle, Thomas examined naming, active and passive modes of signification and their relation to modes of understanding and of being.

Principal writings: *Speculative Grammar.*

THOMAS OF YORK.
A 13th-century A.D. English philosopher, educated at Oxford. A disciple of Grosseteste (*q.v.*) and a Franciscan, he denied the eternity of the world. He is known for having developed the first metaphysical *Summa* of the 13th century.

Principal writings: *Sapientiale* or *Metaphysics; The Hand which is Raised Against the Almighty.*

THOMISM.
The philosophy emerging from the thought of Thomas Aquinas (*q.v.*) along with the development of this thought by his followers in later centuries. (1) Recovering by the year 1300 from a condemnation of certain alleged errors in a Parisian judgment of 1277, Thomism continued to grow in influence throughout the 14th century, and into the first part of the 15th. (2) There came a second period of influence in the 16th and 17th centuries. The names of Cardinal Cajetan (*q.v.*) and John of St. Thomas (*q.v.*) belong to this period; and among many others Peter Fonseca (*q.v.*). (3) But the most influential era for Thomism began in the middle of the 19th century and continues to this day. In an encyclical of 1879 Pope Leo XIII called for a return to the traditional philosophy, and directed attention specifically to the philosophy of Thomism. Perhaps the most outstanding of the many neo-Thomists of this era are Etienne Gilson (*q.v.*) and Jacques Maritain (*q.v.*). Also *q.v.* Garrigou-Lagrange, and Joseph Maréchal (1).

THOREAU, HENRY DAVID. 1817–1862.
American naturalist and philosopher. Born in Concord, Mass. Educated at Harvard. Influenced by Emerson (*q.v.* 2) and in a sense his disciple, Thoreau practiced the self-reliance his mentor preached, finding in nature the basis for a life of integrity and spontaneity. He is counted among the New England Transcendentalists, although his commerce was more with nature than with men. With respect to society he upheld the doctrine of "civil disobedience," supporting in government only its right actions, and withholding allegiance from those which are wrong.

Principal writings: "Civil Disobedience," 1849; *Walden, or Life in the Woods,* 1854.

THOUGHT.
In English, the term applies both to the process of mental activity and to its product. The interpretation of either depends upon the position one holds with respect to metaphysics (*q.v.*), universals (*q.v.*), and epistemology (*q.v.*). In general, a list of such interpretations would recapitulate the history of philosophy.

(1) The Platonic approach, from Plato (*q.v.* 1) to Whitehead (*q.v.* 10), holds thought to be an interior dialogue employing abstract forms which are in no sense fictitious, possessing reality in their own right. Plato's line of truth suggests the manner in which, through reflection, the ideas or forms may be derived from images.

(2) The Aristotelian-Thomistic tradition, including even Locke (*q.v.* 4), utilized the idea of abstraction (*q.v.*) to gain general ideas from the phantasms of sense.

(3) The alternative of associationalism (*q.v.* Association of Ideas) discarded abstract ideas, utilizing, instead, congeries of images or sensations related by similarity and contiguity, to allow the sense of a general idea.

(4) When the idea of association is joined to the premises of materialism, one gains views such as those of Hobbes (*q.v.*) where the combining of images is explained in terms of matter and motion. And thought becomes a species of mechanical computation. La Mettrie (*q.v.* 3) explained thought as physical images in the brain correlated to sounds. In this context one also finds the claim that thought is created by the brain. ("The brain secretes thought as the liver secretes

bile.") The consequence may be epiphenomenalism (*q.v.*). Cabanis (*q.v.*), however, regarded thought to be the product of cerebral activity and also held it to exercise some control over that activity.

(5) Through Brentano (*q.v.* 2) and Husserl (*q.v.* 5) the medieval notion of intentionality became central once again as the defining category of thought. Chisholm (*q.v.* 1) is an American representative of this line of development.

THOUGHT-FORCE.
Q.v. Fouillée.

THRASYMACHUS. 5th cent. B.C.
Greek philosopher. Born in Chalcedon. One of the Sophists (*q.v.*) and a teacher of rhetoric, Thrasymachus is featured in Book I of Plato's *Republic* as defender of the claim that justice is "the interest of the stronger." He argues initially that governments and laws are stronger than the individual; and that these interests thus are just. It is clear, then, that justice can derive from convention. On the other hand, his view that individuals prefer injustice suggests that social conventions overlie and only partially control a condition of natural justice deriving from natural strength.

Principal writings: *The Great Art* (only references survive).

THREE-TREATISE SCHOOL.
Q.v. Madhyamika.

TIAMAT.
In Semitic-Babylonian myths the primeval mother, undifferentiated matter, personification of darkness and chaos who, in union with Apsu, gives birth to the gods and to the universe.

TIBETAN BOOK OF THE DEAD.
Q.v. Bardo (3).

T'IEN.
Chinese term meaning "heaven," "the sky," "God," "justice." The term has a broad or narrow meaning, depending on context; it is sometimes understood personally and, at other times, impersonally. Confucius (*q.v.* 6) associated the term both with "heaven" and with the principle of justice. Also *q.v.* Mo Ti, Chuang Tzu, Tao-Te Ching.

T'IEN-T'AI SCHOOL.
Chinese school of Buddhist philosophy traceable to Kumarajiva (*q.v.*) but founded by Chih-I (*q.v.*). Named after the T'ien-T'ai mountain in Chekiang where Chih-I lived and taught. As in all schools of Buddhism, T'ien-T'ai teaches a middle path, but the T'ien-T'ai achieves a typically Chinese synthesis. Deriving its doctrines especially from the *Lotus* scripture and the *Chung Lun*, Chih-I's predecessors, Hui-Wen (550–577) and Hui-Ssu (514–577), contributed to the synthesis.

(1) Beginning with the doctrine that all beings are capable of salvation, and will in fact obtain it, and that the methods of attaining salvation are methods of concentration and insight, it is important to note that the universal possession of Buddhahood is entailed by a view of reality in which all characters interpenetrate so that all things are immanent in each thing. The possibility of Buddhahood anywhere entails its possibility everywhere.

(2) This is caught up in the principle, "The three thousand worlds, immanent in an instant of thought." This multiple immanence exists in the phenomenal world, the realm of temporary truth. In this realm are ten types of manifest being: Buddhas, *Bodhisattvas*, Buddhas-for-themselves, direct disciples of the Buddha, heavenly beings, spirits, human beings, departed beings, beasts, depraved humans. Each of these involves the other, yielding 100 types of phenomenal being. Each of the hundred, further, possesses 10 characteristics: character, nature, substance, energy, activity, cause, condition, effect, retribution, and ultimacy. This yields 1000 types of interrelatedness. Since all of our thousand types relate to living beings, space, and the entities which result from aggregation (matter, sensation, thought, disposition, consciousness), we have in sum three thousand worlds interpenetrating.

(3) All of the above are *dharmas*, that is, elements of existence—real, unreal, or both—and the nature of *dharmas* leads to a doctrine of the three levels of truth. The level of "temporary truth" is the level of differentiated elements of existence, but the *dharmas* are empty, having no character of their own. On a higher level, then, is the "truth of emptiness." This

means that the *dharmas* are not differentiated, as they seem to be, which is the same as saying that reality is not thus differentiated, or that mind is not thus differentiated. This brings us to the final level of truth, the "truth of the mean." Here we find that the *dharmas* exist without differentiation, diversity, change, or destruction. Indeed, they are all the same, and constitute one mind. This is called "true thusness"; and the mind of pure self-nature is also called true thusness.

(4) But although this is the case, the pure mind has the capacity of being contaminated by ignorance (while remaining pure) so that the pure mind remains changeless from infinity, while the unreal characters of the *dharmas* come into and go out of existence.

TIKKUN.
Q.v. Isaac Luria (3–4).

TILLICH, PAUL. 1886–1965.
German theologian. Born in Starzeddel. Educated at Berlin, Tübingen, Halle, and Breslau. Taught at Berlin, Marburg, Dresden, Leipzig, Frankfurt am Main, Union Theological Seminary, Harvard, and the University of Chicago. Ordained in the Evangelical Lutheran Church, he is considered a representative of existentialism in theology. He taught theology and philosophy in the United States from 1933 until his death. Of the volumes set forth below, one, as indicated, is a translation from German. The others were written in English except for the first, third, and tenth which, although first published as books in English, are collections of articles translated from German.

Principal writings: *The Religious Situation*, 1932; *The Interpretation of History* (T), 1936; *The Protestant Era*, 1948; *The Shaking of the Foundations*, 1948; *Systematic Theology*, 3 vols., 1951–63; *The Courage to Be*, 1952; *Love, Power, and Justice*, 1955; *Dynamics of Faith*, 1957; *Theology of Culture*, 1959; *Christianity and the Encounter of the World Religions*, 1963; *Morality and Beyond*, 1963.

(1) Since for Tillich religion is defined as the object of ultimate concern, both philosophy and theology deal with the religious question. Indeed, both disciplines relate to ontological questions about the structure of being, and to axiological questions of ultimate concern. The two are distinguishable in that the philosophical questions and answers tend to be posed and resolved in universal terms. Theological questions tend to be posed in existential terms, and are answered in terms of revelation. There is the slight suggestion that philosophy excels in putting the questions whose answer is the special province of theology. In fact, however, the two disciplines exist side by side, neither in conflict nor with a prospect of synthesis. And theology's "method of correlation" brings together the human or finite perspective and the divine, infinite perspective in a manner not available to philosophy. Among other pairings, the method of correlation gives us individualization and participation dynamics and form, freedom and destiny, being and nonbeing, finite and infinite.

(2) Distinguishing between three forms of reasoning—heteronymous, autonomous, and theonomous—Tillich argued that the last is the most adequate. Heteronomous reason takes its principles from outside itself, and thus is artificial. Autonomous reason takes its principles from within, but thereby reveals itself as vacuous and tautological. Theonomous reason is more deeply based, since it is founded on "Being itself."

(3) "Being itself" is Tillich's name for God, virtually the only non-symbolic or literal term in the lexicon of religion. He likewise describes God as the "power of being," the "ground of being," and "the God beyond the God of theism." Apparently, God as "Being itself" is the answer to the question posed by Schelling. He asked "Why is there not nothing?" And Tillich answered, "Because there is a self-validating concept of existence, Being itself."

(4) Although "Being itself" provides a link between the literal use of terms in philosophy and their symbolic use in religion, the development of the meaning of this term relates to its symbolic use. The basic religious symbols for God are "Lord" and "Father." Symbols differ from other signs in pointing to the ultimate and "participating" in the reality they signify. An effective symbol not only has truth, but it *is* true and using it, we participate in its truth. Symbols also have

lives of their own, become enfeebled, die, and cease to function as vehicles of the ultimate. At this point new symbols are needed.

(5) The approach to the ultimate can also be made through various types of courage which, in a sense, recapitulate stages of culture: the "courage to be as a part," giving way to individuality. the "courage to be oneself," the "courage of despair," as the world turns meaningless; and finally, beyond all traditional formulations, the "courage to accept acceptance."

(6) The ultimacy of religion is protected from the absolutizing tendencies of man by the Protestant principle. This principle forbids the identification of the divine with any human creation whether the creation in question is the biblical writings or the institution of the Church itself.

(7) Tillich's Christology (q.v.) centered on the proclamation of Jesus that the *kairos* (q.v. 3) is fulfilled, and the kingdom of God at hand. In the proclamation is the promise of the "new being" to which repentance leads. Derivative *kairoi* are the existential encounters of groups and individuals with the essential event of history, which he termed the "great *kairos*."

TIME.

From the Latin *tempus* (derived from the Greek *temno*, "to cut off"). The Greek terms for "time" are *chronos* and *aion*.

A. The chief conceptions of time include the following:

(1) In the *Atharvaveda* (q.v. *Vedas* 1) time is regarded as the generator of all things, including Brahman, and will be the source of their destruction.

(2) Heraclitus (q.v. 1) in the West and Buddha (q.v. 6) in the East associated time with both impermanence and flux. Buddha's view led to discussions with respect to momentariness on the part of the Sautrantikas (q.v.) and the Sarvastivadins (q.v.).

(3) Early views of time as cyclical are present in both East and West. For Buddha (q.v. 2) there is a cycle of birth and death with 12 causal links. Heraclitus (q.v. 8) calculates the extent of the world year in terms of which the cycle of existence would come to an end and begin to repeat itself. In Hinduism (q.v. Śankara 4;

Ramanuja 4) such cycles were related to God in his unmanifest and manifest states. For Jainism (q.v. 2) time cycles endlessly through 6 epochs of unimaginable length, in only two of which release is possible. For Shao Yung (q.v. 3) time moved through a repeating cycle of 129,800 years.

(4) Plato (q.v. 9) defined time as the moving image of eternity. Time appears through the agency of the demiurge, embodying forms in the receptacle of space.

(5) Aristotle (q.v. 10) defined time as the numbering of motion with respect to before and after. On the ground that every "now" implies a "before," he concluded that time had no beginning.

(6) Plotinus (q.v. 4) followed Plato, while holding time's reason to be the restless energy of the world soul, intent upon impressing in material form the infinite fullness of being.

(7) St. Augustine (q.v. 12), confessing that he knows what time is only when no one asks, was most aware of its paradoxes. All we really know is that time is present in us, and measured in the mind or soul.

(8) Against Aristotle, Saadia (q.v.) and medieval Schoolmen believed time to have a beginning. Between eternity, the *Res Tota Simul*, and time, the latter posited the *Aevum*, or everlastingness, of heavenly bodies and of angels.

(9) Hobbes (q.v. 5) held that the present has a being in nature, the past in memory, and the future no being at all.

(10) For Spinoza (q.v. 5c) eternity was more basic than time. The latter is an inadequate perception of a limited reality. Reality seen, or conceived, fully, is eternal. Thus, the temporal dimension is in some sense illusory, or partially so.

(11) Newton (q.v. 3) demonstrated, at least to his own satisfaction, that in addition to whatever relativities one may discern in time, there is also an absolute time. Called duration, it flows equably without relation to anything external.

(12) Leibniz (q.v. 2) held time to be the order of successive existence, and relative to the actualization of monads.

(13) Kant (q.v. 3) viewed time as an *a priori* form of the inner sense, an empirically real but transcendentally ideal form of intuition.

(14) William James (*q.v.* 3) viewed past and future as existing in the "specious present." This is not a knife-edge but a "saddleback" with a certain breadth of its own, *i.e.*, a duration.

(15) Bergson (*q.v.* 2, 7) defined time as qualitative change, involving an irreversible becoming, and having its own inner duration. He held that reason "spatializes" time, and that intuition is therefore a more adequate means of apprehending it.

(16) Whitehead (*q.v.* 16–17) thought of time under the category of becoming, the adventure into novelty or, put the other way, the movement from potentiality to actuality of events which thereafter retain an "objective immortality."

(17) Einstein (*q.v.* 2), in relation to Minkowski (*q.v.* 2), made time the fourth dimension of the space-time continuum, the whole stretched out into world-lines with future occurrences as fixed as those in the past.

B. A surprising number of philosophers have argued for the unreality of time.

(18) Parmenides (*q.v.* 4–5) and Zeno of Elea (*q.v.* 6) argued against time, on the grounds that change and motion are unreal.

(19) Bhartrihari, a predecessor of Shankara in an early stage of Vedanta (*q.v.* 1), held time to be a form of *avidya*, or ignorance. Shankara (*q.v.* 3) developed this point of view.

(20) Virtually the same arguments as those of Parmenides were advanced by modern absolute idealists: for example, F.H. Bradley (*q.v.* 3) and J.E. McTaggart (*q.v.* 9). The latter made his argument in terms of an "A" series (past, present, future) and a "B" series (earlier and later). The "B" series is not sufficient to explicate time, while the "A" series is contradictory; thus, we have no reason to deny time's unreality.

(21) Heidegger (*q.v.* 4–5) finds two ways of taking time, depending upon whether one is living authentically or inauthentically. His distinction seems to be parallel to that of Bergson, to which he added the haunting category of Nothingness.

TIMOCRACY.

From the Greek *time* ("honor") and *kratos* ("rule"). Government based on the criterion of honor. One of Plato's five types of government. *Q.v.* Plato (5f).

TIMON OF PHLIUS. c. 320–230 B.C.

Greek philosopher. Born in Phlius, he studied first in Megara under Stilpo (*q.v.*) and then in Elis under Pyrrho (*q.v.*) whose disciple he became. Timon's skepticism gave somewhat more value to appearances, and was thus somewhat less extreme, than the position of Pyrrho. Timon was also known as the Sillographer, or Lampooner, after the satyric poems which in fact embodied his only means of answering opposing points of view. He also wrote comic plays, as well as epic poetry and tragedy.

Principal writings: *Images*; *Lampoons*. Only fragments survive.

TINDAL, MATTHEW. c. 1653–1733.

English jurist. Born at Beer Ferris, Devonshire. Educated at Oxford. Calling himself a Christian deist, his work stirred considerable controversy. One book was condemned by the House of Commons and burned in 1710; his final and most important work went through many editions, and drew over 150 replies.

Principal writings: *Essay of Obedience to the Supreme Powers*, 1694; *Essay on the Power of the Magistrate and the Rights of Mankind in Matters of Religion*, 1697; *The Liberty of the Press*, 1698; *Reasons Against Restraining the Press*, 1704; *The Rights of the Christian Church Asserted*, 1706; *A Defence of the Rights of the Christian Church*, 1709; *Christianity as Old as the Creation*, 1730.

(1) Tindal argued for the supremacy of the state over the church, for "liberty" of the press, toleration for all save atheists, that the magistrate lacks authority to compel conformity, and that persecution of nonconformity violates natural law.

(2) He believed that the true religion must be eternal, universal, simple, and perfect, centering on the simple and universal duties toward God and man, *i.e.*, the practice of morality. This is the religion of nature or reason; and Christianity, if it is the perfect religion, can be nothing other than this and, hence, is as old as the creation.

TITCHENER, E.B.
Q.v. Psychology (7).

TOLAND, JOHN. 1670-1722.
Irish philosopher. Born in Londonderry. Educated at Glasgow, Edinburgh, Leiden, and Oxford. Essentially a pamphleteer, he was for a time under the patronage of the Earl of Shaftesbury and later that of the Earl of Oxford. A victim of the 1720 crash of the speculative scheme known as the South Sea Bubble, he died in poverty. Although regarded as one of the most notable of the deists (*q.v.* Deism), he did not so regard himself, apologizing for his book on Christianity as a "youthful indiscretion." The publication led to a famous controversy between Locke and Stillingfleet.

Principal writings: *Christianity not Mysterious*, 1696; *Life of Milton*, 1698; *Amyntor*, 1699; *Adeisidaemon*, 1709; *Nazarenus*, 1718; *Pantheisticon*, 1720; *Tetradymus*, 1720.

(1) Arguing that the truths of Christianity are neither contrary nor incomprehensible to reason, and that faith requires the confirmation of reason, Toland believed himself to be defending Christianity. The Irish parliament, however, found Toland's view to be an attack rather than a defense and condemned the book in 1696, forcing Toland to flee to England.

(2) He forced the question of canonical writings, referring to "the numerous suppositious pieces under the name of Christ and His apostles," and supplied a list of writings now regarded as apocryphal.

(3) In 1705 Toland coined the term "pantheism" in a discussion of Socinianism (*q.v.*). His final publication had the form of a book of liturgy, containing passages from pagan authors, for pantheistic societies.

TOLEDO, FRANCIS OF. 1533–1596.
Spanish philosopher. Born in Córdoba. Studied at Valencia, Zaragoza, and Salamanca. Taught at Salamanca and Rome. A Jesuit, he was named Cardinal in 1594.

Principal writings: Commentaries on Aristotle's logic, physics, and psychology, as well as on the *Summa Theologica* of Aquinas.

TOLERANCE.
Q.v. Toleration.

TOLERANCE, PRINCIPLE OF.
The principle of Carnap (*q.v.* 5) allowing alternate syntactical strategies.

TOLERATION.
From the Greek *tlenai* ("to bear or endure"). The English term appeared during the religious wars of the 16th century, whose only rational conclusion was that Protestants and Catholics should practice toleration toward (learn to bear or endure) each other. While the negative sense of the term has not disappeared, it has lessened through the years, so that toleration increasingly represents a positive ideal. It now applies to political, as well as to religious, beliefs.

(1) The religious accommodation passed through three stages: *Territorialism*, in which each region recognized and enforced the requirements of one religion, while permitting dissidents to emigrate; *Latitudinarianism*, or Comprehension, in which one religion was recognized as established although the requirements on the populace were deliberately minimal; and *Pax dissidentium* in which complete religious liberty was authorized.

(2) Jeremy Taylor (*q.v.*) developed a theory of toleration on the basis of his own experiences in the time of Cromwell. Arguing that religious truth is indemonstrable, and heresy an error not of the understanding but of the will, Taylor held that diversity of belief is necessary. Toleration is limited, however, by what is in the public interest and the foundations of faith.

(3) Spinoza (*q.v.* 10), finding that the imposition of belief on a people leads to civil strife, argued for toleration with respect to all beliefs, political as well as religious. The state is to provide its citizens the security to hold any opinion not leading to sedition.

(4) John Locke (*q.v.* 10) confined his discussion to religious toleration, opposing persecution and sanctioning religious differences. Toleration is to be extended to all varieties of religious belief and practice. It extends up to but does not include atheism, apparently on the ground that the state itself rests on certain religious sanctions.

(5) Voltaire (*q.v.* 1) expanded the scope of toleration, or latitudinarianism, to every variety of belief, supposedly coin-

ing the credo: "I disapprove of what you say, but will defend to the death your right to say it." Voltaire looked to England as the nation where the freedoms of speech, property, and religion were already guaranteed.

(6) Rousseau (*q.v.* 6) wished to legislate tolerance. The citizens of the state will be required to embrace a simple, latitudinarian religious creed (deistic in content), which includes "the rejection of intolerance."

(7) It is perhaps worth noting that some philosophies encourage toleration merely through the selection of ethical and political criteria neutral to competing interests. The Utilitarianism of Jeremy Bentham (*q.v.* 4–5), using as criterion the greatest happiness of all concerned, is a clear example.

(8) Comte (*q.v.* 5) regarded toleration as essential only in periods of progress when society is unstable. The irruption of Protestantism and the French Revolution mark the end points of such a period. In the feudal period, a time of order and stability, toleration was not relevant due to a massive basis of shared belief. In the coming stage, where science will replace religion, once again there will be a shared agreement, making irrelevant both toleration and liberty of conscience.

(9) J.S. Mill (*q.v.* 8) set the limits of toleration at the point where one individual's liberty threatens that of another; within the area defined by such limits, one's right to think and do what pleases one is unqualified.

(10) Francis Guizot (*History of Civilization in Europe*, 1828) advanced the thesis that tolerance is an essential element in Christianity, and that periods of intolerance are perversions thereof. Tolerance is equidistant from despotism and anarchy, lies between the two, and is fed by both extremes which, by themselves, lead to stagnation. Tolerance is thus an indispensable condition for progress in society.

(11) For Proudhon (*q.v.*) complete toleration is a necessary condition for progress toward the system of voluntary cooperation which is to replace the present coercive state.

(12) John Donoso Cortés (1809–1853), an ultramontanist, attacked both Guizot

and Proudhon in his *Essay on Catholicism, Liberalism, and Socialism*, 1851. In his view, toleration is simply a false ideal. Man is, of course, fallible; but the Church is infallible. Its dogma is the truth. Those who deny it are in error, and error cannot be tolerated.

(13) James Balmes (1810–1843) argued (in *Protestantism Compared with Catholicism*, 4 vols., 1842–4) that partial toleration is appropriate but complete or universal toleration is not. One does not speak of tolerating the truth; hence, the term applies only to situations where the truth is not known. In these situations toleration is to be affirmed.

(14) E.A. Westermarck (*q.v.* 3) found relativism helpful in extending human tolerance.

Also *q.v.* Huguenots.

TOLSTOY, LEO. 1828–1910.

Russian writer and social philosopher. Born in Yasnaya Polyana. Studied at the University of Kazan. After a literary career lasting a quarter of a century Tolstoy experienced a sense of mental crisis from 1876 to 1879. This led to his conversion to an ethically-based New Testament Christianity. He rejected luxury, embraced vegetarianism. He established an experimental school and, influenced by Rousseau, began to write with a social mission. The writings of this period expressed his religious anarchism, and many of them were banned by the government. In 1901 he was excommunicated by the Russian church.

Principal philosophical writings: *A Confession*, 1879–82; *What I Believe*, 1882–4; *What Then Must We Do?* 1882–6; *The Kingdom of God Is Within You*, 1890–3; *The Christian Teaching*, 1894–6; *What Is Art?* 1897–8.

(1) Reporting upon his individual experience, Tolstoy held that the meaning of life depends upon the existence of God, and our relating to God through human fellowship. Furthermore, he believed this to be the common content of all religions.

(2) As a religious anarchist he found all government to be coercive, and involved in criminal conspiracy against the governed. In place of government he stressed the primacy of voluntary associations, collective in nature, and based

on nonviolence. In place of violence he called for moral revolution and, when necessary, passive resistance.

(3) Relating art both to morality and to the communication of emotion, Tolstoy held that art is significant insofar as it communicates the best and highest feelings of humanity. These are precisely the moral and religious feelings which give meaning to human life.

TÖNNIES, FERDINAND. 1855–1936.
German sociologist and philosopher. Born in Schleswig-Holstein. Studied at five German universities, receiving his doctorate from Tübingen. Influenced by Paulsen (*q.v.*) and Wundt (*q.v.*)
Principal writings: *Community and Society* (T), 1887; *Hobbes' Life and Teachings*, 1896; *The Essence of Sociology*, 1907; *Custom* (T), 1909; *Critique of Public Opinion*, 1922; *Sociological Studies and Critiques*, 3 vols., 1925–9.

(1) Distinguishing between natural communities and voluntary associations, Tönnies labeled the first type of group *Gemeinschaft* and the second *Gesellschaft*. Families, friendship groups, and religions are natural communities and *Gemeinschaft* in type. Businesses, universities, and states are *Gesellschaft* in type. The first or natural group is a reflection of man's natural will or *Wesenwille*; the second is a reflection of man's rational will, the *Kurwille*.

(2) Calling attention to elements of will in both custom and public opinion, he argued that the opinion claimed as the public opinion of a total society can be regarded as a group will. Opposition to such an opinion is interpreted as disloyalty.
Also *q.v.* Voluntarism.

TORAH.
From the Hebrew *turath* ("law"). The Mosaic Law consisting of the five books otherwise known as the Pentateuch. *Q.v.* Judaism (2a).

TOSCA, THOMAS VICENTE. 1651–1723.
Spanish philosopher. Born in Valencia. Opposed to Scholastic dogmatism, Tosca followed the atomism of Maignan (*q.v.*) while continuing to adhere to a revised metaphysics of an Aristotelian type.
Principal writings: *Philosophical Compendium; or Logic, Physics, and Metaphysics*, 1721.

TOTEMISM.
From the Ojibwa term *ototeman* ("brother-sister kinship"). A world-view characteristic of primitive societies in which the group regards itself as having blood relationship to a given animal (or plant).

TOTUM SIMUL.
A Latin phrase: *totum* ("the whole," "all") and *simul* ("at the same time"). The phrase is used as a definition of eternity. It was introduced by Boethius (*q.v.* 1), was used throughout the Middle Ages, and in the modern period by such thinkers as Royce (*q.v.* 5).

TOULMIN, STEPHEN. 1922– .
English philosopher. Educated at Cambridge and Oxford. Has taught at Cambridge, Oxford, Melbourne, Leeds, Brandeis, Michigan State, Santa Cruz, Chicago, and Northwestern.
Principal writings: *An Examination of the Place of Reason in Ethics*, 1950; *The Philosophy of Science*, 1953; *The Uses of Argument*, 1958; *Foresight and Understanding*, 1961; *The Discovery of Time* (with J. Goodfield), 1965; *Human Understanding*, 1972; *Wittgenstein's Vienna* (with A. Janik), 1973; *Knowing and Acting*, 1976; *The Return to Cosmology*, 1982; *The Abuse of Casuistry* (with A.R. Jonsen), 1988; *Cosmopolis*, 1990.

(1) Taking a "good reasons" approach to ethics, Toulmin finds that the reasons humans offer for the ethical decisions they make are largely utilitarian; and he offers the negative utilitarian rule that we should follow those moral rules and principles which produce the least amount of avoidable suffering.

(2) His more considered view is, however, that the case study approach of casuistry (*q.v.*) is better suited than any universal rule to the complexities of contemporary ethical problems. It has the advantage of returning ethics from the attempt to become a science to the *phronesis* (*q.v.*) of Aristotle.

(3) Regarding logic as "generalized jurisprudence," a method by which claims of reason may be adjudicated, he turns away from the formal entailments of the logicians to the actual practice of argument in different fields, including science, morality, art criticism, and theology.

(4) An analogy is drawn between science and evolutionary biology, in which the former is viewed as a body of ideas and techniques evolving by variation and selection. The same theoretical move can have merit in dealing with one group of problems, while proving an obstacle in other situations. A variation appearing by chance in one situation may unpredictably acquire great merit in another.

(5) Having worked our way through the modern age, the world is now entering post-modernity. In neither society nor nature is the "Newtonian image of massive power, exerted by sovereign agency through the operation of central force" an appropriate paradigm. Society is now post-national, and the solutions to its problems are likely to be subnational, transnational, multinational. Corresponding shifts are to be expected elsewhere, including the understanding of nature.

TOUSSAINT.
Q.v. Encyclopedists.

TOYNBEE, ARNOLD. 1889–1975.
English philosopher of history. Born in London. Educated at Oxford. Taught at the London School of Economics. Beginning in 1925, he was for forty years director of the Royal Institute of International Affairs.
Principal writings: *A Study of History*, 10 vols., 1934, 1939, 1954; *Civilization on Trial*, 1948; *The World and the West*, 1953; *An Historian's Approach to Religion*, 1956; *Mankind and Mother Earth*, 1976.

(1) Turning his attention from nation-states to "whole" societies, Toynbee has identified twenty-one such social groupings in the history of the world. As in the case of Spengler (*q.v.*), Toynbee applies an organic analysis to these social groupings. They are characterized by cycles of rise and fall which are described in organic terms of birth and death. For Toynbee the cycles are less rigidly determined than for Spengler.

(2) Toynbee finds societies in decline when they fail to respond to the challenges which face them. One recurrent theme in a healthy society is "challenge and response." The response is prepared by the "creative minority" of the society which typically withdraws under the challenge and returns with a response. In a healthy society the creative minority is respected and its response is accepted by the "transmissive majority." A society is in danger when a proletariat appears that feels no identification with the established structure.

TRACE.
Q.v. Derrida (5, 7, 8); *Différance.*

TRADITIONALISM.
An 18th-century theory of history developed by the members of the counter-Revolution in France and Spain. The movement grew out of reflection on the Enlightenment and its culmination in the French Revolution. Carried by Catholic thinkers it called for a return to Church control. The movement is also called Ultramontanism.

(1) Joseph de Maistre (*q.v.*), arguing against the French *Philosophes* and the anarchy of the Revolution, reasserted the foundation of authority in God and, since God cannot be measured by human reason, man's duty of blind obedience.

(2) Louis de Bonald (*q.v.*) took the same line, insisting that the Enlightenment was a mistake, and urging a return to the ordered life, including the supremacy of pope and king, which had preceded it.

(3) Robert de Lamennais (*q.v.*) argued that tradition was the only test for truth, and carried his claims for the papacy to such extremes that his view was condemned by Pope Gregory XVI.

(4) Louis Bautain (*q.v.*) held that faith has precedence over reason, the latter being metaphysically incompetent. The doctrine, called fideism, was condemned in an 1855 decretal.

(5) John Donoso Cortés (1809–53) was the Spanish ultramontanist leader, holding that a secular politics is a contradiction, and that Catholicism is civilization.

TRADUCIANISM.
From the Latin *trans* ("across") and *ducere* ("to lead"). The doctrine, initiated by Tertullian (*q.v.* 5), that souls are passed along in the process of human generation, souls being produced from souls as bodies are produced from bodies. To be contrasted with Creationism (*q.v.*) and Pre-existence (*q.v.*).

TRAGEDY.
From the Greek *tragoedia*, from *tragos* ("he-goat") and *oide* ("song"). The derivation of the term is unclear but probably the reference is to early satyr-like groups of singers, the "chorus of satyrs," dressed in goat-skins related to the cult of Dionysus, their song telling the story of a hero or divinity as part of a commemorative religious observance. Horace suggested that the dramatic form developed from suggested choral competitions where the winner received a goat as his prize. The suggestion, however, carries little weight.

(1) Whatever its origin, by the time of Aristotle the form was ready to become the subject of philosophical analysis. In the *Poetics*, Aristotle (*q.v.* 13) held tragedy to be an imitation of an action by men better than or like us; the action being serious (*i.e.*, passing from happiness to misery by necessity, or at least by probability), complete (*i.e.*, its plot having beginning, middle, and end, and in its best form containing a peripety—or reversal of the situation—and recognition), of a certain magnitude (*i.e.*, usually occurring within the limits of a single day); in language embellished with various kinds of artistic ornament, the several kinds being found in separate parts of the play (*i.e.*, verse in the dialogue and song in the choral parts); in the form of action, not of narrative; the central figure being of heroic dimensions in order that his fall, due to an error of judgment, excite the appropriate emotions of pity and fear; which latter are to effect a catharsis or purgation of emotion in the spectator.

(2) Not all Greek tragedies fitted Aristotle's analysis, and medieval tragedies still less so, these latter centering on the single parameter of the reversal of fortune on the part of a member of the upper classes, and usually teaching a moral lesson. Shakespeare (1564–1616), working on the modern side of the medieval divide, produced tragedies requiring non-Aristotelian analysis. His originality is to be explained not only by the influence upon him of traditional medieval art forms, but by his interest in character—the heightened emphasis on that factor leading to a diminished emphasis on plot. If Shakespeare departed in one way from Aristotelian expectations, French neo-

Classical tragedy—attempting to follow the master—departed from him in another way. The work of Corneille (1606–1684) and Racine (1634–1699) followed a selective interpretation of Aristotle, defining tragedy as the imitation of a serious action preserving the three unities: time, place, and action. Aristotle had insisted upon unity of action, and had commented on a natural unity of time. French neo-Classicism added unity of place and produced a position in which the three unities became a controlling doctrine. 18th-and 19th-century analyses of tragedy thus occurred in a situation altered with respect both to theory and practice.

(3) Voltaire (*q.v.*), although not a strict follower of French neo-Classicism, found Shakespeare's tragedies to be in poor taste, his work "barbarous" when compared to that of Corneille and Racine.

(4) Samuel Johnson (1709–1784) attacked the doctrine of the three unities as unduly restrictive over genius, and defended Shakespeare's intermingling of comedy with tragedy.

(5) Although Kant (*q.v.* 9) did not discuss the nature of tragedy, his aesthetic theory influenced many of those in the modern period who did discuss it. Kant's view of the sublime, as the overpowering yet attractive aspect of the infinite in nature against which we assert our freedom, was very quickly applied to tragedy. The tragic sense was commonly interpreted as an opposition of just this type between the finite and the infinite.

(6) Lessing (*q.v.* 1) reinterpreted Aristotle's doctrine, holding that men are purged in tragedy through "pity with fear," that the tragic figure must be like ourselves and neither above nor below common humanity, that the tragic emotion is our fear of suffering a similar fate, that the viewers must find a "golden mean" of pity and fear transforming their passions into virtuous habits, and that the upshot of tragic drama is the creation of an ideal world leading to the "general effect of good"—*i.e.*, leading to brotherhood and a sense of universal pity.

(7) Goethe (*q.v.* 2) praised Shakespeare, and rejected Aristotle's spectator-theory of catharsis, holding that so far as the spectators are concerned, they will go home and perhaps be "amazed" that they

are no better off for having witnessed the tragic drama. The central point is, rather, expiation and reconciliation of the characters within the drama itself.

(8) Friedrich Schiller (*q.v.* 2) initially followed Lessing's view of tragic drama as a theodicy (*q.v.*), and then shifted somewhat to Kant. He first described tragedy as "poetic imitation" of a complete action showing man in a state of suffering designed to arouse our pity. His final view was that the representation concerned the opposition of fate and freedom, suffering and moral resistance to it, the tragic spectacle serving to inoculate man against his "unavoidable fate."

(9) Madame De Staël (1766–1817) reduced the three unities of neo-Classicism to the single unity of action. Changes of place and time are allowable insofar as they increase the emotion and strengthen the illusion.

(10) August Wilhelm Schlegel (1767–1845) moved to the idea of tragedy from the more general sense of a "tragic mood," deriving from humanity's sense of the transient nature of life and our dependence on unknown powers. The only counter we have for this is a sense of vocation transcending earthly life, and resolving the conflict in an ideal harmony. The infusion of this mood into drama is the essence of tragedy.

(11) Hegel (*q.v.* 19) held that in a literary sense Aristotle's analysis of tragedy is definitive; but in a moral sense tragedy is motivated by a conflict of two great moral forces, both justified and both embodying the divine. The task of the tragic hero is to resolve their conflict, transmuting them into "ethical substance." He found that Greek tragedy exemplified this pattern, but that Shakespearian tragedy did not on the ground that the latter obscured the tragic conflict by introducing contingencies of character. He concluded that Shakespeare's tragedies were inferior to their Greek predecessors and characterized by an "untragic sadness."

(12) Friedrich Von Schlegel (*q.v.* 3) likewise interpreted tragedy through the sublime. He held that in the highest form of tragedy the assertion of man's moral freedom is manifest in such a way that the "eternal" rises from earthly catastrophe and the tragic hero is spiritually transfigured.

(13) In Schelling (*q.v.* 1c), tragedy is to be explained by the struggle between freedom and necessity. The tragic hero is guilty of a crime, but not consciously or deliberately. As the "guiltless guilty" he is to accept punishment freely, thus asserting his freedom, restoring the moral order, and revealing the identity of the real and the ideal.

(14) K.W.F. Solger (1780–1819) found both comedy and tragedy in the conflict between humanity's imperfections and its higher destiny. In both cases the conflict is resolved by irony.

(15) For Schopenhauer (*q.v.* 5) all existence is tragic, revealing guiltless, unjust suffering as the one tragic flaw all humans share in being born. He defended "bourgeois tragedy" without heroes or villains, while recognizing that this sacrificed the "height of fall" in Greek tragedy.

(16) Kierkegaard (*q.v.* 7) regarded the tragic hero as one who renounces himself in order to express the universal, while the man of faith does the converse, renouncing the universal in order to find himself in relation to God.

(17) Nietzsche (*q.v.* 1) regarded the tragic mood to be self-affirmation through suffering. Put otherwise, tragedy affirms the unification of the sundered and opposed Dionysian and Apollonian elements. The elements cannot remain unified in ordinary terms, but only in the self-fulfillment of the extraordinary superman. Tragic emotion is thus not the purging of pity and fear but the superabundant fulfillment of superman.

(18) Unamuno (*q.v.* 2) spoke of "the tragic sense of life," relating this sense to the general problem of faith and reason. According to Unamuno, we thirst for a status in reality which reason cannot support. We live with the tragic sense when we refuse to eliminate either claim, thus living in unresolved and unresolvable tension.

TRANSCENDENT, THE.

From the Latin *transcendere* meaning "to cross a boundary." The term, along with its other forms, "transcendental," "transcendence," and "transcendentalism," has been used in a number of ways, and with a number of distinct interpretations, in the history of philosophy.

(1) A pattern of thought coming out of Pythagoreanism (*q.v.*), influencing Plato (*q.v.* 9), his followers, and the Neoplatonists (*q.v.* Neoplatonism), led to an emphasis on the transcendence of God. Philo Judaeus (*q.v.* 2) gave early expression to this conception. God as transcendent stands in contrast to notions of the divine immanence in, for example, Stoicism (*q.v.*) and Pantheism (*q.v.*)

(2) In Scholastic thought the idea of transcendence was attached to certain terms, called "Transcendentals," which applied to everything and were hence beyond definition by genus and difference (*q.v.* Thomas Aquinas 4). The list of transcendentals varies somewhat. The four most commonly listed are *ens* (being), *unum* (unity), *verum* (truth), and *bonum* (goodness). To these are often added *res* (thing) and *aliquid* (distinction), but these terms seem to have had a later origin than the others. *Pulchrum* (beauty) is sometimes considered one of the transcendentals as well.

(3) Kant (*q.v.* 11) distinguishes a good or legitimate sense of transcendental from a bad or illegitimate sense of the term. In the good sense the term "transcendental" applies to the *a priori* and necessary elements of experience. They go beyond experience in the sense that they are not derived from it empirically. But they do not go beyond experience in the sense of giving us any insight concerning a supra-temporal realm. This is the sense in which he uses the terms "Transcendental Aesthetic" and "Transcendental Logic" (*q.v.* Kant 11e). The attempt to extend beyond experience the concepts which are legitimate within experience is the bad or illegitimate sense of transcendence.

(4) It is precisely the illegitimate sense of transcendental, which came to be featured in most instances where the noun "transcendentalism" was employed. Kant's successors, wishing to move beyond the phenomenalistic use of the term, fostered the notion of the transcendental standpoint as descriptive of reality. And it was this sense of the term that characterized the Transcendental Club of Boston, organized in 1836. The view of Emerson (*q.v.* 6) presumed a special knowledge of the universe derived from intuition. New England Transcendentalism bears the impress of Emerson's views although considerable diversity characterizes the group, including Thoreau (*q.v.*), Channing (*q.v.*), Alcott, Margaret Fuller (*q.v.*), and Theodore Parker (*q.v.*), who are usually classed with Emerson as New England Transcendentalists.

(5) Husserl (*q.v.*) returned to Kant's usage of transcendental, at least for the most part. Both his descriptions of transcendental Idealism and of the transcendental ego (*q.v.* Husserl 4 and 7) seem to be of the approved type.

(6) Ortega y Gasset (*q.v.* 3) held proper transcendence to be the achievement of authenticity.

(7) Romero (*q.v.* 5) identified transcendence and being, utilizing the slogan that "to be is to transcend."

(8) Lonergan (*q.v.* 6) featured self-transcendence both in four levels of awareness, and three forms of conversion.

TRANSCENDENTAL AESTHETIC.
Q.v. Kant (11 e); The Transcendent (3).

TRANSCENDENTAL EGO.
Q.v. Husserl (6–7); The Transcendent (5).

TRANSCENDENTAL IDEALISM.
Q.v. Husserl (4); The Transcendent (5).

TRANSCENDENTALISM, NEW ENGLAND.
Q.v. The Transcendent (4).

TRANSCENDENTAL LOGIC.
Q.v. Kant (11e); The Transcendent (3).

TRANSCENDENTAL PARALOGISMS.
Q.v. Kant (6).

TRANSCENDENTAL SUBJECTIVITY.
Q.v. Husserl (7).

TRANSCENDENTALS, THE.
Q.v. The Transcendent (2); Thomas Aquinas (4).

TRANSFIGURATION.
The divine affirmation of Jesus' divine Sonship as recorded in the Synoptic Gospels, *e.g.*, *Mark* 9:2–8.

TRANSITIVITY.
A logical and mathematical property of transferability such that the relation x has to y and y to x, x must likewise

have to z. *Q.v.* Logic (22); Logic of Relations (13).

TRANSLATION, INDETERMINACY OF.
Q.v. Radical Translation (1); Quine (5).

TRANSMIGRATION OF SOULS.
Q.v. Metempsychosis.

TRANSPARENT CONTEXTS.
Q.v. Quantifying In.

TRANSPOSITION.
Q.v. Propositional Calculus (18).

TRANS-SUBJECTIVITY.
Q.v. Johannes Volkelt.

TRANSUBSTANTIATION.
From the Latin *trans* ("across") and *substantia* ("substance"). The Roman Catholic doctrine that in the Eucharist the bread and wine are converted into the body and blood of Christ. Adopted by the Fourth Lateran Council in 1215, the doctrine was reaffirmed by the Council of Trent (*q.v.*). Wycliffe (*q.v.* 1) claimed that transubstantiation is impossible.

TRANSVALUATION OF VALUES.
Q.v. Nietzsche (5).

TRANSWORLD DEPRAVITY.
Q.v. Plantinga (5).

TRANSWORLD INDIVIDUALITY.
Q.v. David Lewis (4).

TREE OF PORPHYRY.
A manner of illustrating the relations of genus, species, and individuals widely influential throughout the Middle Ages. *Q.v.* Porphyry (1).

TRENDELENBURG, FRIEDRICH A. 1802–1872.
German philosopher. An opponent of Hegel, Trendelenburg urged a return to Aristotle. Kuno Fischer wrote a book, *Anti-Trendelenburg* (1870), opposing him.

TRENT, COUNCIL OF. 1545–1563.
The 19th Ecumenical Council of the Roman Catholic Church. Called to formulate a response to the Protestant Reformation, it anathematized Protestant doctrines, reaffirmed the doctrine of transubstantiation (*q.v.*) and anathematized those who denied it, and established

reforms of religious order and Church finance.

TRIKA ŚAIVISM (SHAIVISM).
Q.v. Vaiṣṇavism (3d).

TRIKAYA.
From the Sanskrit for "triple body," or "three bodies." Three aspects of God in Mahayana Buddhism, derived from three aspects of *dharma* or "doctrine": (1) *Dharmakaya* (Skt., "body of *dharma* or truth"). Initially referring to the body of Buddhist doctrine, it came to designate Buddha himself, presumably because after death Buddha existed in the doctrine (*q.v.* Mahayana Buddhism 5). (2) *Sambhogakaya* (Skt., "body of bliss"). Referring to the pure and glorified state of *dharma*, the term came to designate the Buddhas, continuing to exist in a state of bliss to hear the prayers of worshippers, and to communicate with *bodhisattvas* (*q.v.*). (3) *Nirmanakaya* (Skt., "body of transformation") relates to the manner in which *dharma* operates in the world. Initially designating the *samgha* or "religious order," it came to refer to the manner in which *Buddha* affects the world through multiple appearances.

TRIMURTI.
A Sanskrit term meaning "having three shapes." The Hindu trinity consisting of Brahma, Vishnu, and Shiva. *Q.v.* Hinduism; Trinity (17).

TRINITY, DOCTRINE OF THE.
The view that God is triune.

A. In its usual signification in the West the phrase refers to the traditional Christian doctrine of God. The history of this doctrine is long and involved.

(1) Origen (*q.v.* 2), writing as a Christian in the 3rd century A.D., prior to official determinations, held the Son and Holy Spirit to be subordinate to the Father.

(2) The Neoplatonic trinity, consisting of the One, *Nous*, and World Soul as set forth by Plotinus (*q.v.* 2–4), is based on emanations and was understood to consist of three substances or hypostases (*q.v.*), an anticipation of the language of the Christian doctrine.

(3) Sabellius (*q.v.*) held Father, Son, and Holy Spirit to refer to one and the same being who became manifest successively as Creator, Redeemer, and Giver of Life.

(4) Arius (*q.v.* Arianism) initiated the controversy requiring official action by the Church, when he held the Son to be *homoioiusias* ("of similar nature") to the Father.

(5) The determination of the Council of Nicaea (*q.v.*) followed Athanasius (*q.v.*) in regarding the Son as *homoousias* ("of the same nature") with the Father.

(6) The finally acceptable trinitarian formula, as worked out by the Cappadocians (*q.v.* Gregory of Nyssa and Gregory of Nazianzus) and approved by the council of Constantinople in 381, held that God is one in Being, existing eternally in three hypostases (*q.v.*) or persons, the Father, Son, and Holy Spirit. The equation of hypostasis, which meant "completed substance" in Aristotle's usage, with person is lacking in the Neoplatonic version (*cf.* 2 above).

(7) Augustine (*q.v.* 9) explicated the Christian doctrine of the Trinity as analogous to being, knowledge, and love in man, these three constituting an *imago dei*, or image of God, in man.

(8) Anselm (*q.v.* 5) held the rational mind to be the image of the trinity in man.

(9) Gilbert of Poitiers (*q.v.* 3) drew a distinction between God as pure being and God as triune.

(10) Aquinas (*q.v.* 1) held the widely accepted view that the doctrine of the Trinity is one of the articles of faith and not comprehensible to reason. By the time of Aquinas the doctrine was complete and from this point we shall mention a number of views challenging the orthodox doctrine.

(11) Jacob Boehme (*q.v.*) accepted the doctrine of the Trinity, while deriving it from an *Ungrund*, or primal state, lying behind the universe.

(12) John Milton (*q.v.* 4) reverted to preorthodox interpretations of the Trinity, holding that the Son and Holy Spirit are creatures, created by the one God and thus not of equal status with Him.

(13) Swedenborg (*q.v.* 6) repudiated the orthodox interpretation of the Trinity, while finding many trinities of his own, such as the three degrees of being in God.

(14) Schelling (*q.v.* 6) followed Boehme in regarding the Trinity as having evolved from a primal state.

(15) Feuerbach (*q.v.* 1) reversed the usual image view of the Trinity, denying the existence of, and explaining, God as a projection into infinity of the human faculties of reason, will, and love.

(16) Jung (*q.v.* 8) believed that quaternity rather than trinity is the appropriate religious symbol.

B. Trinitarian interpretations of God developed independently in some other religions.

(17) Within Hinduism there is a trinity (in Sanskrit, *trimurti*) consisting of the Creator God, Brahma; the preserver god Vishnu; and the destroyer god, Shiva. Brahma is a personal creator god and the personalized form of the Brahman which lies behind reality as its impersonal source. The function of Vishnu in preserving the world is not very clear, but the act of devotion itself is part of his power. The destroyer god, Shiva, is associated with sexual energy and the dance, and hence also with the active energy of the universe. But this energy is also sometimes regarded as feminine. Many of his devotees likewise worship his consort under various names, such as Kali (*q.v.*). Kali is also regarded as the terrible mother and worshipped as such in her own right. Since Kali is sometimes pictured as standing with dripping sword, her feet on the prostrate body of Shiva, the third member of the Hindu trinity may sometimes be reasonably interpreted to be the feminine principle of the great and terrible mother.

(18) The trinity of Mahayana Buddhism (*q.v.* 5), on the other hand, consists of the Buddha as the Body of Transformation, Bliss, and *Dharma. Q.v. Trikaya.* Also *q.v.* Tritheism.

TRITHEISM.

From the Greek *tri* ("three") and *theos* ("God"). The doctrine that there are three Gods. The accusation of tritheism has been leveled at certain extreme interpretations of the Trinity. In the 6th century John Philoponus seems to have regarded the three hypostases. of the Trinity as three substances, and in the 11th century Roscelin (*q.v.*) seems to have been pushed to a similar position by his extreme nominalism.

TRIVIUM.

From the Latin *tres* ("three") and *viae* ("ways"). The first three disciplines, namely Grammar, Rhetoric, and Dialectic, of the Seven Liberal Arts. *Q.v.* Quadrivium; Martianus Capella.

TROELTSCH, ERNST. 1865–1923.
German Protestant theologian. Born in Augsburg. Taught at Göttingen, Bonn, Heidelberg, and Berlin. In the last named post he was successor to Dilthey (*q.v.*). Influenced by Schleiermacher as well as Kant, he had relations with a number of neo-Kantian movements including the Heidelberg School (*q.v.* Neo-Kantianism 4). His chief contribution lay in his analysis of the relation between history and the Christian faith. The problem of the analysis lies in avoiding historicism on the one side and theodicy on the other. Troeltsch avoids both extremes by claiming the operation of a dialectic between historical studies and the life of faith. Out of the dialectic emerges the unique deposit of the Christian faith as something absolute and invariable.

Principal philosophical writings: *History and Metaphysics*, 1888; *The Scientific Situation and its Requirements with Respect to Theology*, 1900; *Fundamental Problems of Ethics*, 1902; *The Historical in Kant's Philosophy of Religion*, 1904; *The Social Teaching of the Christian Churches* (T), 1912; *The Dynamic of History according to the Philosophy of History of Positivism*, 1919; *Historical Relativism and its Problems*, 1922.

TROPES.
From the Greek *tropos* meaning "heading." In philosophy, Tropes are the headings under which Greek skeptical philosophers, for the most part those who were followers of Pyrrho (*q.v.*), presented their arguments, that the only rational position is that of suspending judgment. The tropes concerned the unreliability of sense-data, and the circularity and infinite regress involved in argument. Aenesidemus (*q.v.* 2) organized his arguments under ten tropes. Agrippa (*q.v.*) reduced the number to five, while extending their range. Sextus Empiricus (*q.v.* 3–5) presented three tropes, the last concerning an alleged inconsistency in the idea of God.

TRSNA (TRISHNA).
Sanskrit, "craving." *Q.v.* Buddha (2).

TRUCE OF GOD.
From 1027 A.D. until well into the 13th century the Church attempted to enforce two measures designed to limit feudal warfare. The Truce of God outlawed warfare from Thursday evening until Monday morning of each week, from Lent until St. John's Day on June 24, and from the Day of Ascension of the Virgin on August 15 until St. Martin's Day on November 11. The Peace of God held that unarmed ecclesiastics and husbandmen could not participate in warfare under any conditions.

TRUE THUSNESS.
Q.v. Chih-I; T'ien-T'ai School (3).

TRUTH.
From Anglo-Saxon *treowth* ("fidelity"). The Latin term is *veritas* and the Greek is *aletheia*. The putative object of knowledge and goal of inquiry, the term stands in contrast sometimes to "falsity" and at other times to "opinion."

A. Numerous definitions, theories, and criteria of truth have been advanced in the course of the history of philosophy.

(1) The basic theories of truth include the correspondence theory (the true "corresponds" to reality), the coherence theory (the true is the coherent system of ideas), the pragmatic theory (the true is the "workable" or satisfactory solution of a problematic situation), the semantic theory (assertions about truth are in a metalanguage and apply to statements of the base language), the performative theory (the assertion of truth is the performative act of agreeing with a given statement, *q.v.* Performative Utterance).

(2) Criteria of truth are the marks by which we know the truth. "Coherence" and workability" are examples of such criteria. At one time the *Consensus gentium*, or agreement of mankind, was regarded as a criterion for truth. Universal agreement has long since lost standing. A number of additional criteria will be stated in the discussion which follows below.

B. Philosophers concerned themselves with the problem of truth from the very beginning.

(3) Although in its initial stage, as through most of its history, philosophy had proceeded on the basis that there is

an objective truth to be found, this assumption was challenged by the Greek Sophists. Protagoras (*q.v.* 1) held that truth is relative, whether relative to the individual or the species is not clear from his account. But the position of Relativism (*q.v.* 1) has exercised significant influence in the history of philosophy.

(4) Plato (*q.v.* 1, 15) relates both to the correspondence and the coherence theories. He initiated the correspondence theory of truth, although since he stated the principle negatively perhaps his view on correspondence is more properly called a discorrespondence theory of falsity. In any case it is clear from his description of dialectic that truth finally relates to itself alone and only such criteria as coherence and consistency apply to the act of beginning, continuing, and ending in ideas.

(5) Aristotle (*q.v.* 1) provided the definitive expression of the correspondence theory. "To say of what is that it is not, or of what is not that it is, is false, while to say of what is that it is, and of what is not that it is not, is true." It is by the facts of the case, he held, that statements are called true or false.

(6) The Skeptic, Carneades (*q.v.* 1), believed that since truth is simply not available, one should live in a suspension of judgment. For the numerous representatives of this position *q.v.* Pyrrhonism and Skepticism.

(7) Somewhat later than Carneades, the Buddhist philosopher, Nagarjuna (*q.v.* 10), argued that truth has two aspects. One of these is empirical and only an appearance, while the other is absolute and beyond intellect.

(8) Plotinus (*q.v.* 9) argued that truth required an identity between thought and thing. He thus moved beyond correspondence to an identity theory of truth.

(9) For the Indian philosopher, Shankara (*q.v.* 7) truth is obscured by *nescience*.

(10) An intensive discussion occurred in the Middle Ages concerning the doctrine of double truth, presumably held by Averroës (*q.v.* 6). The doctrine claimed that what is true in philosophy might be false in religion, and conversely. Also *q.v.* Averroism.

(11) Aquinas (*q.v.* 4, 6), along with Scholastics generally, continued the cor-

respondence theory, defining truth as the *adequatio rei et intellectus* (the adequation of thought to thing). Two qualifications are, however, necessary. Since truth is a transcendental term applying to all that is, in a sense truth is not a statement of the way things are but simply the things themselves. And since God is His own truth, the ideas in the divine mind are true whether they correspond to anything outside God (*i.e.*, the present state of the world) or not.

(12) Hobbes (*q.v.* 5) regarded truth as the right ordering of names. "True and false," he said, "are attributes of speech not of things." For this reason, he who reasons aright in words can never fall into error.

(13) Although Descartes (*q.v.* 3) accepted the correspondence theory, the most distinctive feature of his view is the belief that the clarity and distinctness of an idea is a sign of its truth.

(14) The concern of Spinoza (*q.v.* 5b) is likewise with the criterion of truth. He argued that truth is its own standard. Just as light reveals both itself and darkness, so "truth is the standard of itself and the false."

(15) Leibniz (*q.v.* 10–11) distinguished between "truths of reason" and "truths of fact." The former rest on the principle of identity, and the latter on the principle of sufficient reason. The former are necessary, and the latter contingent. This is today called the analytic-synthetic distinction.

(16) Locke (*q.v.* 8), continuing the tradition of the correspondence theory though with a hint of the coherence criterion intermixed, also continued Leibniz' distinction of types of truth. Locke distinguished between "truths of words" (resting on the agreement of ideas) and "truths of thought" (resting on the agreement of ideas with things). He insisted too, that truth and falsity relate to propositions rather than to single ideas.

(17) Hume (*q.v.* 5) used different terminology for the analytic-synthetic distinction, separating "matters of fact" from "relations of ideas."

(18) Kant (*q.v.* 1) held truth to relate to judgments and added the synthetic *a priori* judgment to the synthetic-analytic distinction which was developing.

(19) Hegel (*q.v.* 3–5) distinguished be-

tween formal and historical truth. The first relates to mathematics, and the second to concrete existence. He likewise spoke of absolute truth as the final synthesis of universal and individual, abstract and concrete, factors.

(20) Kierkegaard (*q.v.* 1, 4), opposing Hegel, distinguished between truth as subjective appropriation and as objective approximation. Holding that the second approach led to "endless approximation," he supported the first, claiming that in the deeper sense "truth is subjectivity."

(21) Peirce (*q.v.* 13), the founder of Pragmatism, defined truth as the set of beliefs which would be held by the community of inquirers in the long run—after an indefinitely long series of inquiries. The objective counterpart of these beliefs would be the real. Truth, then, is the outcome of inquiry. Since Peirce held inquiry to be self-corrective, it is appropriate to call his view the successful inquiry theory of truth.

(22) The view of William James (*q.v.* 7) is perhaps more commonly regarded as the pragmatic doctrine of truth than is that of Peirce. He regarded truth as whatever puts one into satisfactory relations with the world. Truth is the "expedient in the way of believing as right is the expedient in the way of behaving." It is both changeable and progressive.

(23) F.H. Bradley (*q.v.* 4) held the coherence theory of truth. The inconsistencies of the common sense view of the world drive one, according to his account, to posit an absolute experience, completely individual and at the same time completely universal. Other less universal systems have various degrees of truth, but the Absolute is the Truth.

(24) H.H. Joachim, in *The Nature of Truth* (1906), claimed that coherence is the only feasible criterion of truth, correspondence being in fact an incoherent idea. He, too, emphasized the idea of degrees of truth, pointing out that the parts of a system gain their truth and meaning from their relation to the whole.

(25) Dewey (*q.v.* 3) continued the pragmatic doctrine of truth, relating inquiry to problem-solving. Since the goal of inquiry is a transformed situation rather than abstract truth, Dewey substitutes for such terms as "truth" and "knowledge" the phrase "warranted assertibility."

(26) Santayana (*q.v.* 6) regarded truth as a "standard description" of the features of material things.

(27) F.C.S. Schiller (*q.v.* 1) followed the pragmatic doctrine of truth, agreeing with James concerning its changeable nature.

(28) Although Bertrand Russell (*q.v.* 6–8) changed his mind constantly, engaging in thought experiments both on this and other problems, he held throughout that truth is to be interpreted as a correspondence between a proposition or sentence and a fact. In his phase of logical atomism this correspondence was the principal feature of reality.

(29) G.E. Moore (*q.v.* 5) originally held truth to be, like Good, a simple, unanalyzable property, but later he shifted to a correspondence theory of truth where the correspondence is between a belief and a fact. If the belief is true, there is in the universe a fact to which the belief corresponds. If the belief is false, there is no such fact.

(30) For Jaspers (*q.v.* 7) truth is historical, inseparable from the thinker and his situation.

(31) Wittgenstein (*q.v.* 3, 5) elaborated in his *Tractatus* a correspondence theory of truth with a mirroring relation between atomic sentences and the elementary facts which constitute the world. "Picturing" is less prominent in his later writings but never altogether disappears.

(32) For Heidegger (*q.v.* 8) truth is discovered by the individual in the opening toward the thing made possible by freedom.

(33) Unamuno (*q.v.* 3) denied the idea of objective truth, substituting "true belief." Given that change, it is not surprising to find that for Unamuno the opposite of true belief is not falsity but rather falsehood or "the lie."

(34) Blanshard (*q.v.* 2) is a modern representative of coherence theory. System is the key term. Not only truth but also meaning derive from the relation of a datum to the system of which it is a part.

(35) Tarski (*q.v.* 1–2) offered a semantic doctrine of truth, holding that when one says of a statement that it is true, the saying so is a statement about a statement, and is thus in a metalanguage. Regarding this view as a convention, he called his view of truth "convention T."

(36) Nagel (*q.v.* 8), who follows the pragmatic doctrine of truth in many ways, finds only a verbal difference between saying of a theory that it is satisfactory and saying that it is true.

(37) Strawson (*q.v.* 1) denies the metalinguistic analysis introduced by Tarski, substituting a performative theory of truth. Since, according to Strawson, true and false are not descriptive terms when one says of a statement that it is true, one is merely expressing one's agreement with the statement. Also *q.v.* Austin (3).

(38) Rescher (*q.v.* 2) laid down the requirement that truth be "coherent with the plausible data."

Also *q.v.* Epistemology.

TRUTH-CONDITIONAL THEORY OF MEANING.

Q.v. Davidson (6, 7).

TRUTH TABLES.

Matrices utilized in modern logic to determine the truth value of compound sentences or propositions in terms of the truth or falsity of their constituents.

(1) *Compound sentences contain "truth-functional connectives."* The expression "It is raining, and my motor is running" is composed of two atomic sentences and the conjunction "and." The compound expression is true if and only if both of the parts making up the expression are true. "And" is one of our truth-functional connectives, and is often written as a dot, " · ". It is the sign of conjunction. The truth table for conjunction is easily derived from the meaning of conjunction. The table is derived by exhaustively setting down the truth possibilities of the parts, and so, also, of the whole expression.

(2) *Conjunction.* Clearly, to take our example, we would agree that if it is true that "It is raining" and true that "My motor is running," it is also true that "It is raining and my motor is running."

If it is true that "It is raining" and false that "My motor is running," it is false that "It is raining and my motor is running."

If it is false that "It is raining" and true that "My motor is running," it is false that "It is raining and my motor is running."

If it is false that "It is raining" and false

that "My motor is running," it is false that "It is raining and my motor is running."

Letting p and q stand for the two sentences above (or any substitutes for these sentences), the truth table for conjunction can be set down completely as follows:

p	q	p·q
T	T	T
T	F	F
F	T	F
F	F	F

(3) *Disjunction.* The truth-functional connective, "or," has in English usage both a strong or exclusive, and a weak or inclusive, sense. We are interested in the weak, or inclusive sense, of "or" here because it is more useful. Suppose you were to claim when choosing a vocation that you were going to be either a lawyer or a painter; and suppose that as it turned out, you have become both a lawyer and a painter. Suppose that I now chide you with having made a false statement when you said "I am going to be either a lawyer or a painter." You would not take my chiding seriously, since our ordinary belief about disjunction is that a disjunction is true if either part turns out to be true. (In the exclusive sense of "or" we never have the case where both of the constituent sentences are true.) The possibilities can be set forth as follows:

Lawyer	Painter	Lawyer or Painter
T	T	T
T	F	T
F	T	T
F	F	F

It is now clear that your claim "I am going to be a lawyer or a painter," will be false only if both of the constituent sentences are false.

Generalizing our results, and letting the wedge sign, "∨," stand for the inclusive sense of "or" gives us the truth table for disjunction:

p	q	p∨q
T	T	T
T	F	T
F	T	T
F	F	F

(4) *Material Implication.* We also use an "if-then" connective in discourse: "If it rains, the streets will be wet." The agreed-upon possibilities for "if-then," applied to our compound sentence, and set down in tabular form have the following appearance:

Rain	Wet Streets	If Rain then Wet Streets
T	T	T
T	F	F
F	T	T
F	F	T

The first two lines of the truth table are not surprising in any way. If it is true that it rains, and that the streets are wet, we would expect that the complex "if-then" sentence, resulting from their combination, would also be true. And if the occurrence of rain did not result in wet streets, we would surely believe that the total claim, "If it rains, then the streets will be wet," must be judged to be false. What of the other two lines? How are we to judge the truth or falsity of the sentence, "If it rains, the streets will be wet" when it has not rained but the streets are wet? Clearly, the claim would not be false; but the table tells us the full assertion is in this case true. Since we have not here been given the condition, *i.e.*, rain, common sense would suggest that the full assertion is neither true nor false, but rather undetermined. The last line tells us that if neither the condition occurs, nor its expected consequence, the if-then sentence is also true. Common sense would suggest that the assertion is, in this case, too, undetermined. But truth tables are arranged to have only the values, true and false. If this is a weakness, it is worth reflecting that the important relations for inference are those of the first two lines.

Letting the horseshoe "⊃" stand for "if-then," our truth-table has this appearance:

p	q	p ⊃ q
T	T	T
T	F	F
F	T	T
F	F	T

It will be noted that the kind of implication in question here is called "material implication." It is designedly a weak form of implication, just as the form of disjunction, considered appropriate, was a weak form of disjunction. There exist aspects of material implication, relating to the last two lines of the truth table, which have gained the name, "paradox." The "paradoxes of material implication" are three in number. All three relate to the decision to consider " ⊃ " as a truth-functional connective. This means that any sentences can be substituted for those in our example, and the truth of the whole expression will be determined by the truth of its parts. It does seem odd that we can gain a true if-then statement from constituent statements which are entirely unconnected. It would follow that the following is a true statement: "If zebras have stripes, then there are craters on the moon." This is the first paradoxical consequence and relates to the first line of our truth table. The second paradox relates to the first and the third lines of the table, and can be expressed by saying that a true statement is implied by any statement whatever. An example would be: since it is false that the moon is made of green cheese the following if-then statement is true: "If the moon is made of green cheese, then the earth is a sphere flattened at the poles." The third paradox relates to the third and fourth lines of the truth table, and can be expressed by saying a false statement implies any statement whatever. Hence the following if-then statement is true: "If the moon is made of green cheese, then it is false that the earth is a sphere flattened at the poles." Since the two statements about the moon and earth are contradictory, we must hold that inconsistent statements may be true for the system of material implication.

(5) *Material equivalence* is a truth-functional connective of somewhat greater strength than material implication. Instead of an "if-then" connective, it is an "if-and-only-if—then" connective. One manner of symbolizing material equivalence is by means of the sign "≡". For any two sentences, "p" is materially equivalent to "q" if both "p materially implies q" and "q materially implies p"; expressed otherwise, (p ≡ q) ≡ [(p ⊃ q) · (q ⊃ p)].

The connective can be illustrated by the

following sentence: "If the barometer drops rapidly, this signals a change in the weather." The relationship here is one of equivalence, since if the barometer drops then a change in the weather will occur; and if a change in the weather occurs the barometer will drop.

Barometer Drops	Change in Weather
T	T
T	F
F	T
F	F

Barometer Drops ≡ Change in Weather
T
F
F
T

Substituting "p" and "q" for the above expressions one has the truth table for equivalence:

p	q	p ≡ q
T	T	T
T	F	F
F	T	F
F	F	T

There is an equivalence between two expressions when their truth value varies together. When one is true both are true; when one is false both are false. Of course, material equivalence is given a weak inclusive meaning so that even if there is no connection between p and q they are considered to be equivalent. But since, on the other hand, covariance suggests relationship, even *material* equivalence is a stronger connective than material implication.

(6) *Negation.* A fifth truth-functional sign of importance is negation. Obviously, the negation of a given statement, or the denial of that statement, is provided for in English by the appropriate insertion in that statement of "not," "it is false that . . .," "it is not the case that . . .," or a similar phrase. In logic a sign is needed to express negation, and one widely used sign is the tilde, "~." Since if a given statement is true, its negation will be false; and if the statement is false, its negation will be true, these relations can be expressed in the following manner, letting p stand for any sentence whatever.

p	~ p
T	F
F	T

(7) Combining these connectives in truth tables it is possible to determine the validity of certain steps which we wish to take.

(a) For example, we use a pattern of argument exemplified by: "Either I shall become a lawyer, or I shall become a painter. I have decided not to be a painter, therefore, I shall become a lawyer." This is called a disjunctive syllogism.

The pattern of the argument is "p ∨ q, ~ p, ∴ q." Clearly if, in any case when the two premises are true the conclusion is also true, our pattern will be reliable. We need only look at the truth table to check the validity or reliability of the argument. We need to reproduce the truth table for disjunction and add a row for ~ p. We know by (6) above that ~ p will simply have the values opposite to those of p. Hence, our extended table has the following appearance:

p	q	p ∨ q	~ p
T	T	T	F
T	F	T	F
F	T	T	T
F	F	F	T

Our table covers all of the possibilities. Our question asks if it is the case that whenever "p ∨ q" is true and "~ p" is true, "q" is also true. They are both true in the third line, and in that line "q" is also true. Hence the pattern is reliable. The reader should determine that "p ∨ q, q ∴ ~ p" is not a valid pattern.

(b) A second common pattern is illustrated by, "If it rains, then the streets will be wet. It rains, therefore, the streets are wet." This is called *modus ponens*. It has the form, "p ⊃ q, p, ∴ q." To check this pattern we need only the truth table for material implication. You will note that whenever "p ⊃ q" and "p" are true, "q" is also true.

A variation on this pattern is illustrated by "If it rains, then the streets will be wet. The streets are not wet, therefore, it has not rained." This argument is called *modus tollens*. Its pattern is "p ⊃ q, ~ q, ∴ ~ p." To check this pattern we need to add to our truth table a row for "~ p" (the opposite of "p"), and "~ q" (the opposite of "q"). These rows have been added at the end of the truth table for material implication. You will note that in whatever lines "p ⊃ q" and "~ q" are true, "~ p" is also true.

p	q	p⊃q	~ p	~ q
T	T	T	F	F
T	F	F	F	T
F	T	T	T	F
F	F	T	T	T

The reader should determine that "p ⊃ q, q, ∴ p," and "p ⊃ q, ~ p, ∴ ~ q" do not represent valid patterns.

(c) A third pattern is illustrated by "If it rains then the streets will be wet; if the streets are wet, then driving will be hazardous. Therefore, if it rains, then driving will be hazardous." The example combines two "if-then" sentences, and is known as hypothetical syllogism. Its pattern is, "p ⊃ q, q ⊃ r, ∴ p ⊃ r." The truth table for this pattern will be larger since we have in this case three sentences whose truth values are to be expressed. "It rains," "the streets will be wet," and "driving will be hazardous." Let these sentences be represented by "p," "q," and "r." Our truth table will have three initial rows. To set down all of the alternatives eight lines will be required. Using the appropriate initial rows and the definition of material implication we may set down the appropriate truth values for "p ⊃ q," "q ⊃ r," and "p ⊃ r." The completed table will have the following appearance:

p	q	r	p⊃q	q⊃r	p⊃r
T	T	T	T	T	T
T	T	F	T	F	F
T	F	T	F	T	T
T	F	F	F	T	F
F	T	T	T	T	T
F	T	F	T	F	T
F	F	T	T	T	T
F	F	F	T	T	T

The pattern is reliable, we now know, if the conclusion is true in any case where the premises are true. When "p ⊃ q" and "q ⊃ r" are true, is "p ⊃ r" also true? There are four different lines on which "p ⊃ q" and "q ⊃ r" are true. In every

case "p ⊃ r" is true. Hence, the pattern is valid.

Other patterns can be tested by truth tables following this procedure. Under the heading "Propositional Calculus" methods of using these and other patterns in arguments is discussed.

TRUTH VALUE.
Q.v. Frege (7); Truth Tables.

TSCHIRNHAUSEN (TSCHIRNHAUS), EHRENFRIED W. 1651–1708.
German scientist and philosopher. Born in Kiesslingswalde. Educated at Görlitz and Leiden. Acquainted with Cartesian philosophy from his university days, Tschirnhausen maintained contact with Spinoza, Leibniz, and Huygens. His method of invention leading to "real knowledge," combined empiricism with the deductive methods of Descartes and Spinoza.
Principal writings: Medicina Mentis or *The Art of Inventing General Precepts,* 1687.

T-SENTENCE.
Q.v. Davidson (6, 7).

TSIMTSUM.
Q.v. Isaac Luria (1).

TSONGKAPA.
Q.v. Lamaism (4).

TSOU YEN. 305–240 B.C.
Chinese philosopher credited with formalizing the *Yin Yang* philosophy. *Q.v. Yin* and *Yang* (2); *Yin Yang* Philosophy.

TUNG CHUNG-SHU. 179–104 B.C.
Chinese philosopher. Taught at the National University. Even as a student he devoted himself to the *Spring and Autumn Annals,* a Confucian classic. He was twice named top scholar of China. By royal command he appeared before Emperor Wu to answer questions of importance to the emperor. A *Yin Yang* Confucianist, he was chiefly responsible for having Confucianism recognized as state doctrine by Emperor Wu in 136 B.C. The exclusive supremacy thus gained for the Confucian philosophy lasted until 1905. The "ruler as standard" doctrine (*cf.* 2 below) may explain the official enthusiasm for the Confucian philosophy.
Principal writings: Luxuriant Gems of the Spring and Autumn Annals (T in part).

(1) Human nature has in it the seeds of goodness. It is potentially good and needs to be developed. Humanity thus belongs to man's nature; and this nature is an instance of *Yang*. Man's feelings are potentially evil, and need to be controlled. Greed, etc., thus belong to man's feelings, and these feelings are an instance of *Yin*. The *Yin* of feeling may be avoided if one's feelings are controlled by the *Yang* of human nature.

(2) The ruler, father, and husband are superior to the ruled, son, and wife, and are instances of *Yang* in relation to *Yin*. Since *Yang* is superior to *Yin*, ruler, father, and husband are in fact the standard of the ruled, the son, and the wife. But the ruler must first receive the mandate of heaven, an expression of the natural cosmic forces of *Yin* and *Yang*. As these forces were interpreted by Confucian scholars, the final standard of correctness rested with them. Many have suggested that the "ruler as standard" doctrine is the key to understanding how Confucianism became the official Chinese philosophy.

(3) Goodness is higher than human nature, and the sage is higher than goodness. Hence, man requires education and training to achieve goodness. In achieving goodness, one employs the principles of humanity in relation to others, loving them and not oneself, and the principles of righteousness to rectify the self, correcting oneself, and not others. But these principles require wisdom also since, *e.g.*, to love without wisdom is to love without discrimination. And wisdom requires humanity, for wisdom without humanity means knowledge not translated into action.

(4) Utilizing a sequence of the five elements—wood, fire, earth, metal, water— he draws many correspondences between man and nature, which suggest in general that man is a microcosm of the macrocosm, and that number can be applied to all things.

TURGENEV, IVAN.
Q.v. Nihilism.

TURGOT, A.R.J. 1727–1781.
French economist and political philosopher. Born in Paris. Educated at the Sorbonne. A physiocrat in the line of Quesnay and Gournay, recognized by the *Philosophes*, (*q.v.*), and a contributor to the *Encyclopédie*. Turgot was appointed Comptroller-General of France in 1774. In this post he attempted a reform of French finances. Although his measures met with initial success, jealousies at court forced his resignation. His view that commerce and industry should be free from control influenced Adam Smith. His philosophical views, in keeping with the spirit of the *Philosophes*, stressed religious toleration and a belief in progress rooted in the growth of knowledge.

Principal writings: *On the Historical Progress of the Human Mind* (T), 1749; *On Universal History* (T), 1750; *Letters to a Grand Vicar on Toleration*, 1753–4; *Reflections on the Formation and Distribution of Riches* (T), 1766.

TURING, A.M.
Q.v. Artificial Intelligence (1); Cybernetics; Recursive Function; Turing Machine.

TURING MACHINE.
A term deriving from A.M. Turing's proposal ("Computing Machinery and Intelligence," 1950) that a computer which could provide satisfactory and sustained answers to human questions, in an appropriately controlled experiment, would have to be regarded as having the attribute of thought. The term "Turing Machine," is useful in discussions of artificial intelligence (*q.v.*), distinguishing the advocates of strong A.I., who presume that appropriately programmed digital computers would be Turing machines, from their opponents who argue that the Turing machine proposal is a contradiction.

TU-SHUN.
Q.v. Hua-Yen School.

TWARDOWSKI, KAZIMIERZ. 1866–1938.
Austrian-Polish philosopher. Born in Vienna. Educated at Vienna. Taught at Vienna briefly, and at Lvov from 1895 until 1930. A disciple of Brentano, Twardowski is regarded as the most influential figure in Polish philosophy. He is credited with establishing the School of Lvov, of which the Warsaw School—with Łukasiewicz (*q.v.*), Leśniewski, and Kotarbinski—may be regarded as an extension.

Principal writings: *A Theory of the Content and Object of Representation*, 1894; *Representations and Concepts*, 1898; *On*

Relative Truths, 1900; Fundamental Concepts of Didactic and Logic, 1901; On Psychological Method, 1910.

TWICE-BORN.
Q.v. Aśramas (2); Hinduism (4); William James (5).

TWICE DIVIDED LINE.
Q.v. Plato (1).

TWIN EARTH.
Q.v. Putnam (3).

TWOFOLD TRUTH.
Q.v. Double Truth, Doctrine of.

TWO SWORDS, DOCTRINE OF THE.
Q.v. Divine Right of Kings.

TYCHISM.
From the Greek tyche ("chance" or "fortune"). The term was introduced as a formal philosophical concept by Charles Peirce (q.v. 4) who held chance to be an objective feature of the universe.

TYLOR, E.B.
Q.v. Animism (1); Myth (9).

TYNDALE, WILLIAM.
Q.v. Bible.

TYNDALL, JOHN. 1820–1893.
British physicist and philosopher. Born in Ireland. Educated at the University of Marburg. From 1853 on he was professor of natural philosophy at the Royal Institution as a colleague of Faraday. A longtime friend of T.H. Huxley, his philosophic importance lies in his helping to influence the public mind to accept the freedom of scientific inquiry. He supported the theory of evolution and opposed religious dogma.
Principal writings: Fragments of Science, 2 vols., 1915.

TYPE.
From the Latin typus and the Greek typos, meaning "impression, image, or model." The term seems to have been derived from something like the contrast between a seal and its imprint.
(1) Perception was explained by both Stoics and Epicureans as the imprint of object types upon sensory awareness. For Plato and Aristotle the term was applied to schematic representations or summary images.

(2) In logic the relation between token and type is roughly that of the meaning of a word to its written or spoken instances.
(3) Max Weber (q.v.) utilized the concept of "ideal types" as constants in sociological analysis. Edward Spranger (q.v.) and others followed him in that regard.
(4) Bertrand Russell (q.v. 3) invented the "theory of types" to solve certain logical and semantical paradoxes. Russell's paradox concerns the distinction between classes which are, and classes which are not, members of themselves (q.v. Paradox). The class of all classes not members of themselves turns out both to be and not to be a member of itself. Russell decided that no class could be a member of itself. The class is thus of a higher type than its members. In the assertion "Socrates is human," the predicate is thus of a higher type than the subject. In the simple theory of types, the initial type level is that of individuals followed by properties of individuals, properties of properties, etc. The simple theory of types solved the logical paradoxes in question, but did not touch certain semantical paradoxes, such as the Grelling paradox (q.v. Paradox 4). Russell and Whitehead set themselves to solve the second type of paradox by a ramified theory of types. In the ramified theory attention is given not only to the elements of the simple theory but also to the hierarchy of orders—first order functions, second order functions, third order functions, etc., each function quantifying over a lower type. Violations of the ramified theory of types were called "vicious circle fallacies" by Russell and Whitehead. An alternative to the theory of types was set forth by Zermelo (q.v. 3) in what is known as Axiomatic Set Theory (q.v. Set Theory 9–11). Quine (q.v. 1) seeks the best of both worlds through a stratification requirement for certain kinds of sentences, those which—unstratified—would lead to paradox.

TYRANNY.
From the Greek tyrannos ("lord"). A form of government based on absolute rule, the decisions of the ruler serving as law and constitution.
(1) For Plato (q.v. 5f) tyranny was the most degenerate of the five forms of government he distinguished.
(2) For Aristotle (q.v. 12) tyranny was

the degenerate form of monarchy, the latter being one of the three acceptable types of government.

UBIQUITY.
From the Latin *ubique* ("everywhere"). In theology, applied to God's existence as a synonym for "omnipresence" (*q.v.*). In Christology, Luther argued for the ubiquity of Christ at each enactment of the Lord's Supper.

UCHRONIE.
A Greek term coined by Renouvier (*q.v.* 2) meaning "out of time." Used by Renouvier to refer to what did not happen in history, thus emphasizing its accidental character.

UDAYANA ACARYA.
Q.v. God (45).

UEXKÜLL, JAKOB VON.
Q.v. Semiotic (9).

ULRICH, ENGELBERT. 1248–1278.
Scholastic philosopher. Studied under Albertus Magnus (*q.v.*). Taught at Paris. A Dominican, he served five years as Provincial of the German division of his order. Principal writings: *On the Highest Good*.

ULTIMATE SITUATIONS.
Q.v. Jaspers (7).

ULTIMATE, THE GREAT.
Q.v. Chou Tun-I (1).

ULTRAMONTANISM.
The doctrine that the entire social and historical order is subject to the authority of the Roman Catholic Church. The doctrine is not, without qualification, acceptable to the Church. *Q.v.* Traditionalism; Lamennais.

UMA.
Q.v. Vaiṣṇavism (3c).

UMWELT.
Q.v. Husserl (8).

UNAMUNO, MIGUEL DE. 1864–1936.
Spanish philosopher. Born in Bilbao. Educated at Madrid. Taught at Salamanca, where he was rector in 1901, 1931, and 1934–6. Exiled from 1924 until 1930, he was a deputy in the Cortes, 1931–33, and under house arrest the last year of his life. His difficulties derived from a fierce sense of independence and a dislike of dictatorship. Influenced by Kierkegaard, he is often counted among the existentialists.

Selected writings: *On Purism*, 1895; *Peace in War*, 1897; *Love and Pedagogy*, 1902; *Life of Don Quixote* (T), 1905; *Against This and That*, 1912; *The Tragic Sense of Life* (T), 1913; *Mist* (T), 1914; *Essays*, 7 vols., 1916–18; *Abel Sánchez* (T), 1917; *The Agony of Christianity* (T), 1931; *Saint Emanuel the Good* (T in part), 1933.

(1) Centering his attention not on abstract humanity, nor the equally abstract philosophical conception of man as a thinking being, but on the concrete individual man of flesh and bone ("*carne y hueso*"), Unamuno finds the latter hungering and thirsting desperately for immortality. The man of flesh and bone hungers for a survival of body as well as soul, and indeed the very body of his present life.

(2) Since there is no basis in reason to support this concern it must rest on faith, but faith is simply hope that death does not mean annihilation. Man thus lives in a tension of faith and reason, and his life is characterized by agony, passion, and struggle. This tension is the "tragic sense of life."

(3) Unamuno's movement away from abstraction and falsely announced objectivity led him to a conception of the Word, not as *logos* (an abstraction) but as the intimate expression of the man of flesh and bone. This also led him to deny objective truth (another abstraction) in favor of true belief, so that the opposite of truth is simply the lie. And even though this direction of thought does not solve the tragic sense of life, it can lead us to translate systems of philosophy into the situations of their authors and to seek the philosophy of a country not alone in its philosophies, but also in the religious and literary expressions of its people.

UNCERTAINTY RELATIONS.
Q.v. Werner Heisenberg.

UNCONDITIONED, THE.
Q.v. William Hamilton (4).

UNCONSCIOUS, THE.
The doctrine that a portion of human mental processes or memories exists below the threshold of consciousness.

(1) Plato (*q.v.* 1) in fact anticipated the view with his doctrine of recollection in which all knowing is recalling, the trauma of birth blocking the way to this portion of the psyche.

(2) The doctrine of *petites perceptions* in Leibniz (*q.v.* 14) anticipated the unconscious in a different manner. For Leibniz the body is receiving a continual flood of perceptions. We have but a dim awareness of much of this content due to the faintness of the perceptions.

(3) Schelling (*q.v.* 3) introduced a doctrine of the unconscious, explaining artistic creation in its terms.

(4) Schopenhauer (*q.v.* 3) found man's driving force in a "blind will," and thus in a portion of one's nature not open to one's awareness.

(5) Eduard von Hartmann (*q.v.* 1) developed a "philosophy of the unconscious" on the basis of Schopenhauer's work. Finding the key to human development in the unconscious, he posited a gradation of levels from the unconscious to conscious awareness.

(6) The doctrine came to fruition in the system of Sigmund Freud (*q.v.* 3) who regarded the unconscious as once conscious content, now repressed, yet still actively conditioning our conscious awareness.

(7) For Jung (*q.v.* 1–7) the unconscious is collective, containing archetypes which pervade all human experience.

(8) Lacan (*q.v.* 1, 4–6; Structuralism 3) holds language to be the tool by which one reaches the unconscious, for the latter has its own structure and this is reflected in language.

(9) According to Lévi-Strauss (*q.v.* 1) the unconscious contains the original of society's structure.

UNCTION.
Q.v. Sacrament (1); Extreme Unction.

UNDISTRIBUTED MIDDLE TERM.
One of the fallacies of structure (*q.v.* Fallacies 23), the fallacy of undistributed middle term misapplies the doctrine of the syllogism (*q.v.* 3), failing to connect the middle term with the major and minor terms of the syllogism.

UNGRUND.
A German term meaning "groundless." The term has been of use in Western mystical thought.

(1) Jacob Boehme (*q.v.* 1) apparently introduced the term. For him it referred to the Abyss which is also God, lying behind the world as its source and explanation.

(2) In Berdyaev (*q.v.* 1) the term signifies the "nothingness" from which freedom comes.

UNIFIED FIELD THEORY.
Q.v. Einstein (4).

UNIFIED SCIENCE.
Q.v. Vienna Circle of Logical Positivists (6); Neurath.

UNIFORMITY OF NATURE, PRINCIPLE OF THE.
The principle of induction (*q.v.*) that similar occurrences follow from similar conditions.

(1) The principle was first enunciated by William of Ockham (*q.v.* 11, 13) as essential to empirical investigation. For Ockham the principle required an order of nature established by God.

(2) Hume (*q.v.* 3) found the principle to be involved in circularity, and thus indefensible."

(3) John Stuart Mill (*q.v.* 5) argued that the principle is itself inductive, and that every successful causal induction helps to confirm it.

UNIGENITUS.
Q.v. Jansenism (14–15).

UNIO MYSTICA.
A Latin term meaning "mystical union." The term is applied to the mystical experience in which the soul of man is said to enter into union with God.

UNION.
Q.v. Logic of Relations (4).

UNION OF EGOISTS.
Q.v. Max Stirner (2).

UNITARIANISM.
The religious doctrine that God is one, and that Jesus is to be regarded as human and not as a supernatural being. In a general sense many of the doctrines opposing Trinitarianism (q.v.) may be assimilated to Unitarianism, i.e., Arianism (q.v.), Adoptionism (q.v.), Monarchianism (q.v.), etc. As a movement Unitarianism began in the 16th and 17th centuries. The term "unitarius" was first used in 1569 in Transylvania, and adopted by the churches in 1633. The term "unitarian" appeared first in England in 1682. A good deal of anti-Trinitarian discussion arose as a result of the Protestant Reformation. Unitarianism thus developed independently in separated areas at about the same time. Socinianism (q.v.) was often a factor in its development.
(1) The Hungarian Unitarian Churches separated from the Reformed Church in 1568, becoming one of four recognized religions. Developing in isolation, this group did not make contact with English and American Unitarians until 1821.
(2) Between 1548 and 1612 many English anti-Trinitarians were condemned to burn. Some saved themselves by recanting. Ten were executed. In 1705 Emlyn, who regarded himself as a Unitarian preacher, established a London congregation. In 1825 the British and Foreign Unitarian Association was formed.
(3) In America by the middle of the 18th century, Harvard College was the center of a Unitarian movement. King's Chapel, Boston, transformed itself into a Unitarian Church in 1782, and by the beginning of the 19th century virtually all of the ministers of Boston were Unitarian. One of these, William Ellery Channing (q.v.), became the coordinator of the movement. In 1825 the American Unitarian Association was formed.

UNIT CLASS.
A class having a single member.

UNITED BRETHREN IN CHRIST.
An American religious denomination of Arminian (q.v.) theology, established in 1800. Its national offices are in Dayton, Ohio.

UNITED CHURCH OF CHRIST.
Q.v. Congregationalism.

UNITIES, THE THREE.
Q.v. Tragedy (2).

UNITY.
From the Latin unitas ("one"). Thus the character of being one thing, event, idea, society, or whatever.
(1) The Pythagorean school (q.v. Pythagoras 6–7) held the One and the Many to be ultimate categories, and the number one, representing the point, to be the ultimate constituent of all things.
(2) Plato (q.v. 1, 6) regarded the One as a basic philosophical principle, interpenetrating with beauty, truth, and the good.
(3) In the Metaphysics Aristotle held that unity and being (q.v.) are strictly correlative and have the same number of meanings.
(4) Plotinus (q.v. 1, 2) made the idea of unity central to his system, finding the "One" an adequate name for God whose power holds the world together, and a key to the meaning of "beauty."
(5) "Transcendental unity" is a Scholastic term reflecting the correlativity of unity and being. In Aquinas (q.v. 4, 10) unity is one of the transcendentals, characterizing everything that is. It is to be found, for example, in every instance of beauty in the form of integritas or perfection. Also q.v. The Transcendent (2).
(6) For Kant (q.v. 3) unity is one of the categories of quantity contributed to experience by the human mind. The unity of human awareness contributes unity to all of one's cognitions by means of the "transcendental unity of apperception" (q.v. Kant 11d).
(7) French neo-Classicism enshrined the three unities of time, place, and action as defining characteristics of tragedy (q.v. 2). Q.v. One.

UNIVERSAL CHARACTERISTIC.
Q.v. Leibniz (11–13).

UNIVERSAL CLASS.
In that part of logic called the algebra of classes, the concept of that class in the universe of discourse to which everything belongs. Boole (q.v. 5) symbolizes this class by "1." Among the ways the universal

class is used in Boolean algebra is to express the complement of a class. The complement of a class "x" is written as "1-x." Another symbol for the universal class is "V." Also *q.v.* Null Class.

UNIVERSALE ANTE REM, IN RE, POST REM.
Q.v. Universals (16).

UNIVERSALISM.
The doctrine that all men will be saved.
(1) Origen (*q.v.* 4) was an early advocate of the doctrine, which he called *apocatastasis.*
(2) The modern movement arose in England in the 18th century and spread to the colonies, becoming a separate denomination. Hosea Ballou argued for the doctrine in his *Treatise of the Atonement*, 1805.

UNIVERSAL QUANTIFIER.
The notation used in Universal Generalization and Universal Instantiation (*q.v.* Quantification Theory 4 and 3, respectively).

UNIVERSAL RELATION.
In the algebra of relations, that relation everything has to everything else. The symbol used is often "V̌" or "V̇" or "V." *Q.v.* Universal Class; Null Relation; Logic of Relations (5).

UNIVERSALS.
From the Latin term *universalis* meaning "that which pertains to all." The Greek term usually employed by Plato was *eidos* or "idea." Aristotle's term was *to katholon* which has about the same meaning as the Latin term given above. The term "universal" is related to the concepts of species, genus, and class. It stands in contrast to the terms "particular" and "individual." The problem of universals arises when one asks about the status in reality, or the ontological status, of universals. An intense debate over universals took place during the Middle Ages (*cf.* 10–20 below). The terms *Nominalism* (*q.v.*), *Realism* (*q.v.*), and *Conceptualism* (*q.v.*) were used in, and as a result of, that debate. For the Realist the universal has some kind of reality outside the mind. For the Conceptualist the universal has reality only within the mind. For the Nominalist the universal is noth-

ing but a name, and has reality neither within nor outside the mind. In fact, however, these distinctions exist along a continuous spectrum, and the distinction is sometimes so fine between Nominalist and Conceptualist, or between Conceptualist and Moderate Realist, that the distinctions are not very useful, nor is there anything approaching complete agreement on the classification of various individual philosophers. In what follows we shall use these distinctions where appropriate, as well as a theory of resemblances, departing from them as the situation demands. The materials for the medieval debate, and subsequent reflection on the problem of universals, were prepared during the period of Greek philosophy.
(1) Socrates (*q.v.* 2) set the stage for the discussion by pressing his colleagues for the "common nature" or universal definition of any given set of things. A question as to the status of the common nature and universal definition emerged from the Socratic quest.
(2) Plato (*q.v.* 1) held that such common natures or "ideas" required their own reality; and that they are in fact the exemplars according to which individuals or instances in the world are created. In the language of the medieval dispute, Plato is a realist. He believed in the extramental reality of universals. Further, since the Ideas or universals depend upon nothing in the world, having their own eternal realm, he is an absolute realist, and his view is one of Absolute Realism.
(3) Aristotle (*q.v.* 7), finding difficulty with the absoluteness of Plato's conception, lent moderation to it by holding that the Ideas do not exist by themselves, but as the elements of form in sensible things, complementing a second element of matter. Matter and form together constitute the individual sensible substance. Since Aristotle believed in the reality of universals, but not in their absolute reality, he is regarded as a moderate realist.
(4) Plotinus (*q.v.* 3) and the Neoplatonists generally (*q.v.* Neoplatonism), developed the Platonic notion of a realm of ideas, called by Plotinus the *Nous* or Intelligence. Thus, they are to be classed as absolute realists.
(5) Porphyry (*q.v.*), however, treated of genus and species in Aristotle's manner,

while insisting that solution of the question of the status of these entities was beyond man's power.

(6) It was a Christianized version of the Neoplatonic alternative which St. Augustine (*q.v.* 2) employed in supporting the Absolute Realism of Plato. He gave the eternal ideas an eternal home by placing them in the mind of God.

(7) Boethius (*q.v.* 2) is credited with sparking the medieval dispute over universals. He follows Porphyry in claiming not to decide between the views of Plato and Aristotle, but in fact his analysis follows the Moderate Realism of Aristotle.

(8) Erigena (*q.v.* 1), along with many early medievals, held an Absolute Realism of ideas in the Platonic sense.

(9) Avicenna (*q.v.* 4–5), the great Islamic interpreter of Aristotle, followed his master's doctrine while modifying it to hold that our own mental operation gives the universal no more than potential existence. In order to grasp it actually we must make contact with the active intellect, an intermediary between ourselves and God.

(10) Anselm (*q.v.* 7) followed the Platonic-Augustinian line, adhering to the reality of abstract, intelligible objects both in sensible things and in the mind of God. Anselm participated in the dispute over universals, attacking the position of Roscelin.

(11) Roscelin (*q.v.*), whose writings are lost, is taken to be the founder of Nominalism. Both Anselm and Abelard report that for Roscelin the universal was a mere *flatus vocis* or "mere word."

(12) William of Champeaux (*q.v.*), Roscelin's student, reacted to his teacher's doctrine by swinging to the opposite extreme of an absolute realism. He first held the extreme position, according to Abelard, that the same essential nature is present in every member of the species (*q.v.* Anselm 6), and then moderated the view to hold that the individual members of the species are the same, not essentially but "indifferently."

(13) Abelard (*q.v.* 1–3) studied under both Roscelin and William of Champeaux, and sought a middle way between the two positions. The position he reached is called by some Conceptualism. Others regard Abelard as a moderate realist. The universal exists, he says, in the

mind; it also exists in things but not as conceived.

(14) Gilbert de La Porrée (*q.v.* 2) was a realist, finding forms both in things and in the mind of God. He seems to have held that, although the form is individual in each thing, we find by comparison a likeness in the members of any species or genus.

(15) Hugh of Saint Victor (*q.v.*) essentially followed Abelard, utilizing a doctrine of abstraction and holding that universals do not exist as such in reality.

(16) Thomas Aquinas (*q.v.* 5) adopted the position of Moderate Realism which he found in Abelard and in John of Salisbury, while retaining some of the emphases of St. Augustine. The consequence was a view wherein one spoke of the universal in three connections: (a) the *universale ante rem*, (before the thing), exists in the mind of God (although not as a plurality); (b) the *universale in re*, (in the thing), is the concrete individual essence of the individual thing, numerically distinct but alike in all members of a given species; (c) the *universale post rem*, (after the thing), is the abstract universal concept in the mind.

(17) Duns Scotus (*q.v.* 2, 6) added to the discussion of universals his notion of a "formal distinction," less than a real distinction and more than a virtual distinction. With respect to universals he taught that there is a formal distinction between the *haecceitas*, or individual essence, of Socrates, and the universal, "human nature." Hence, universals are founded in things, but are not in things.

(18) Peter of Aureol (*q.v.*) was a predecessor to Ockham not only with respect to Nominalism, but also in the general tone of his philosophy.

(19) William of Ockham (*q.v.* 6) is regarded as a nominalist, holding that universals are simply general names. Certainly Ockham attacked all forms of realism. He held that there are no universal things corresponding to universal terms. Whatever exists is individual; and anything predicable of many things is of its nature in the mind. Since there are no exemplars of creation in the divine mind, the similarities which we discern among things are only so from the perspective of human nature.

(20) Durando of Saint Pourcain (*q.v.*) may also be counted among the nominalists of the period.

(21) In 13th-century India a Vedantan philosopher, Madhva (*q.v.* 5), had substituted a resemblance doctrine for the theory of universals. A similar doctrine arose somewhat later in the West (*cf.* 25–28, 40 below).

(22) John Wycliffe (*q.v.* 1) moved from an Augustinian to a realist theory of universals.

(23) John Major (*q.v.*) led a Scottish revival of Ockham's Nominalism in the last half of the 15th and the first half of the 16th centuries.

(24) Thomas Hobbes (*q.v.* 3–5), utilizing a materialistic ontology, built concepts from the sounds of language without invoking any type of generality. He explained the operations of the mind in terms of sense and decaying sense. His scheme is clearly nominalistic.

(25) John Locke (*q.v.* 4), asserting the reality of abstract ideas while holding that only individual things exist in nature, may be taken as a representative of Conceptualism in the late 17th and early 18th centuries. There are other tendencies in his thought, one of them nominalistic. His emphasis on the principles of association really initiated that tradition.

(26) Berkeley (*q.v.* 2) denied the existence of abstract ideas. This would seem to separate him from both Realism and Conceptualism in the usual sense. When he emphasizes the Lockian suggestion that names may relate to groups of particular ideas he expresses nominalistic tendencies. But his usual emphasis, also derived from Locke, that particular ideas may be taken to stand for groups of things, hovers somewhere between Nominalism and Conceptualism.

(27) Hume (*q.v.* 2), holding that particular ideas become general by having general terms affixed to them, is operating—at least in this portion of his view—within the framework of Nominalism.

(28) Condillac (*q.v.* 2–4), although a follower of Locke, stressed the principles of association so completely that these principles, attached to names, allow him a nominalistic framework for his thought. In the principles of association of the last four philosophers, the foundation of a resemblance theory is present which be-

came central finally in the thought of Wittgenstein (*cf.* 40 below).

(29) Thomas Reid (*q.v.* 2), a contemporary of Condillac, argued against the theory of ideas in the British empiricists, substituting signs for ideas, and distinguishing between natural and conventional signs in the manner of Ockham. This return to William of Ockham suggests that Reid be classed with the nominalists, although—if one is to think of Kant (*cf.* 30 below) as a conceptualist—it is true that Reid's principles of common sense bear a striking resemblance to Kant's categories and general approach. Perhaps, as in the case of Berkeley, he may be said to be between Nominalism and Conceptualism.

(30) Kant (*q.v.* 3 and 11f) speaks of ideas of the understanding and ideas of reason. Both sets of ideas originate in the mind and have universality. Since we can make no judgment about things-in-themselves, Kant would seem to fit the framework of Conceptualism.

(31) Hegel (*q.v.* 6) returns to the position of realism, although with a distinction between the abstract universals of the understanding and the "concrete universals" which play a role in the dialectical process in the world. His essentialism, no less than that of his idealistic successors, identifies the rational and the real.

(32) John Stuart Mill (*q.v.* 1, 10) continued the emphasis on principles of association so congenial to the British empirical tradition. He did, however, also support the view that universals are real in an intensional sense. At the same time, since his interpretation of the external world tended to be phenomenalistic, it would appear that he is most appropriately placed as a conceptualist.

(33) W.E. Johnson (*q.v.* 4) substituted the terms "determinable" and "determinant" for "universal" and "particular."

(34) F.H. Bradley (*q.v.* 4) is one of the many idealists whose realism with respect to universals follows the pattern of Hegelian "concrete universals." Bosanquet (*q.v.* 2) and Blanshard (*q.v.* 1) are other examples. Royce (*q.v.* 7) is in the same tradition, although construing the entire world as a community of interpretation.

(35) G.F. Stout (*q.v.* 2) returns to the assumption of abstract universals, interpreting

them to be distributive unities of classes.

(36) Whitehead (*q.v.* 10) returns to Platonic realism. All that is, whether thought or thing, gains its definiteness from combinations of what Whitehead calls "eternal objects." These have their own reality, outside the mind and outside the actual world, although constitutive of that world.

(37) Russell (*q.v.* 6) argued that in order to explain classes we are forced to admit the universal of resemblance; and having admitted the existence of one universal we might as well admit as many others as we find convenient.

(38) G.E. Moore (*q.v.* 5) held universals to be either relations, relational properties, or non-natural properties such as numbers and colors.

(39) Some, but by no means all, of the representatives of New Realism (*q.v.*) and Critical Realism (*q.v.*) featured essences or universals in their systems. Among the former (in addition to Russell) were Holt (*q.v.*), Nunn, Spaulding, and Montague (*q.v.* 1). Among the latter were Drake, Rogers, Santayana (*q.v.* 2–6), and Strong.

(40) Wittgenstein (*q.v.* 5–6) finally brings to fruition the theory of resemblances. In place of universals one looks for "family resemblances," carrying them as far as may be appropriate in a given case.

(41) Nelson Goodman (*q.v.* 1) provides an instance of a contemporary nominalist. For him, since only individual things are recognized, classes are understood extensionally and exist always as the result of construction.

(42) Quine (*q.v.* 3) has committed himself to the nominalist program of attempting to demonstrate that all references to abstract entities can be replaced by references to concrete entities. If the attempt fails, as he believes it may, then Conceptualism becomes the most attractive alternative.

(43) Using his own terminology, Chomsky (*q.v.* 6) distinguishes between substantive and formal universals.

UNIVERSE.

From the Latin *unus* ("one") and *versus* ("turned into"). The Greek is *to olon* ("the whole").

(1) By physical universe is meant all that exists in the whole of time and space. It is the *summa rerum*, the *universae res*.

The single universe is thus compatible with the conception, held by the Epicureans among others, of a plurality of worlds.

(2) In 1846 De Morgan (*q.v.* 1) introduced the phrase "universe of discourse" to refer to the totality of ideas, elements, or classes relevant to a given argument. The universe of discourse may be the physical world, the number system, the world of mythology, or any other system.

(3) In Indian philosophy, *e.g.*, Nagarjuna (*q.v.* 5), the universe is sometimes held to be unreal.

UNIVOCITY.

From the Latin *unus* ("one") and *vocare* ("to call"). A word has univocity, or is univocal, if it carries the same meaning in its several uses. Cajetan (*q.v.* 1) used the term in contrast to analogy (*q.v.*) and equivocation (*q.v.*). In contemporary discussions synonymy (*q.v.*) has replaced the older term.

UNKNOWABLE, THE.

A concept of Herbert Spencer (*q.v.* 4) referring to the ultimate principles of explanation, lying beyond human reach. Also consider an apparent anticipation of the point in Friedrich Schiller (*q.v.* 3).

UNLIMITED COMMUNITY.

Q.v. Peirce (13–14).

UNMOVED MOVER.

For Aristotle (*q.v.* 10) the name applied to God as the first cause of all motion and change, yet not itself involved in motion or change. He held that logic required, in addition to moved movers, the concept of an unmoved mover.

UNTOUCHABLES.

Q.v. Harijans.

UPADANA.

Sanskrit, "grasping." *Q.v.* Buddha (2).

UPANISHADS, THE.

The basic philosophical texts of Hinduism. *Q.v.* The *Vedas* (4).

UPEKṢA (UPEKSHA).

From Sanskrit, "equanimity." One of the Four Immeasurable Attitudes of Mahayana Buddhism (*q.v.* 4).

UPPSALA SCHOOL OF PHILOSOPHY.
Q.v. Hägerström.

URBAN, WILBUR M. 1873–1952.
American philosopher. Born in Mt. Joy, Pennsylvania. Educated at Princeton, Leipzig. Taught at Trinity, Dartmouth, and Yale.

Principal writings: *Valuation*, 1909; *The Intelligible World*, 1929; *Language of Reality*, 1929; *Beyond Realism and Idealism*, 1949; *Humanity and Deity*, 1951.

(1) Developing an idealistic philosophy with a "realistic direction," Urban hoped to bring together fact and value, idealism and naturalism, thus providing an instance of the *philosophia perennis*, or perennial philosophy, in the manner of Plato, Aristotle, and the Scholastic philosophy of the medieval period.

(2) Among those introducing the term Axiology for theory of value, he held that values are objective and part of an intelligible world lying behind existence.

(3) He found symbols to differ from signs in that symbols share to some extent the characters of their objects as well as the character of human awareness. He divided symbols into extrinsic or arbitrary, intrinsic or descriptive, and penetrative—the last type serving as a vehicle of the human effort to make contact with reality.

(4) He held that some insights cannot be translated into literal language, and that therefore metaphor can convey truth. In particular, metaphysical concepts are essentially metaphorical and untranslatable into literal speech.

URFORM.
Q.v. Lask.

URINTUITION.
Q.v. Brouwer (1).

URPFLANZE.
Q.v. Goethe (3).

USE-MENTION DISTINCTION.
The term arose in relation to the development of metalanguages (*q.v.*). Russell's theory of types (*q.v.* Russell 3) was a principal source. A sign is mentioned when it appears in single quotes. Otherwise, it is being used in the sentence. When using the sign "man," one might say that man is a rational animal.

If one mentions the sign "man," one might say that "man" is a three letter word. Although the term is of recent origin, medieval logicians made the same distinction, calling the former *suppositio formalis* and the latter *suppositio materialis* (*q.v.* Walter Burleigh 2).

UTILITARIAN CALCULUS.
The principle in Utilitarian ethics by which the right act is determined. It is a calculation of the greatest pleasure or least pain to all concerned. For an elaboration of various aspects of the principle *q.v.* Jeremy Bentham (1–4); John Stuart Mill (7–8); Ethics (18, 21–23, 25); Utilitarianism.

UTILITARIANISM.
The doctrine that the principle of greatest utility should be the criterion in ethical matters, and that the criterion is to be applied to the consequences flowing from ethical decisions. The principle is often expressed as the greatest happiness, or the greatest good, for the greatest number. A distinction is often made between Act and Rule Utilitarianism, depending upon whether the criterion is applied to individual acts or to rules. Utilitarians, generally, seem to have had in mind individual actions; but since rules grow from acts, there is no clear line separating Act from Rule Utilitarianism. Those who use the distinction tend to agree that Bentham (*q.v.* 5 below) is an act Utilitarian, J. S. Mill (*q.v.* 7 below) an act-type Utilitarian, intermediate between act and rule, and Brandt (*q.v.* 12 below) an ideal rule Utilitarian.

(1) Cumberland (*q.v.* 3), who preceded the Utilitarians, made his criterion of ethics "the greatest good of the universe of rational beings," and Wollaston (*q.v.* 2) spoke of a "moral arithmetic" of pleasures and pains.

(2) Hutcheson (*q.v.* 4), although not regarded as an Utilitarian, introduced the phrase "greatest happiness for the greatest number" to test the rightness of an action.

(3) John Gay (*q.v.*) likewise employed the happiness principle, deriving it from the will of God.

(4) Hume (*q.v.* 6), like Cumberland and Hutcheson a forerunner of Utilitarianism, followed the latter on many points of ethical theory. Hume did not use the

"greatest happiness" phrase, but did introduce the principle of utility as the basis of ethical theory.

(5) The doctrine of Utilitarianism came into its own in the early 19th-century English movement known as "philosophical radicalism." The movement was active in promoting the English reform bills of the 1830's. Founder of the group of philosophical radicals, known also as the English Utilitarians, was Jeremy Bentham (*q.v.*), who introduced the term, "Utilitarianism," in 1781. Supporting the position of psychological hedonism, Bentham interpreted "greatest good" as meaning the greatest sum of pleasure or the least amount of pain.

(6) Likewise associated with the philosophical radicals or English Utilitarians were James Mill (*q.v.*), who followed Bentham closely, and William Godwin (*q.v.* 3), who held the "general happiness" principle and believed it to be incompatible with self-interest.

(7) John Stuart Mill (*q.v.*), son of James Mill, modified the original principle of distinguishing between higher and lower pleasures. The criterion thus became the greatest sum of "higher pleasures" for the greatest number.

(8) A "theological Utilitarianism" was developed by William Paley (*q.v.* 1), interpreting Christian ethics in utilitarian terms while adding theological sanctions.

(9) A new phase in the developing doctrine was introduced by the Theoretical or Intuitive Utilitarianism of Sidgwick (*q.v.* 4). Departing from hedonism, he based his Utilitarianism on self-evident principles.

(10) A view of Evolutionary Utilitarianism was advanced by Herbert Spencer (*q.v.* 3) and Leslie Stephen.

(11) Hastings Rashdall (*q.v.* 1) named his doctrine "Ideal Utilitarianism," on the ground that other elements, along with pleasure, make up the ideal good.

(12) Brandt's (*q.v.*) ideal rule Utilitarianism maximizes utility in terms of an ideal moral code relativized to a given society.

(13) J.J.C. Smart (*q.v.* 4, 5) centers the Utilitarian calculus on "expected utility."

UTILITY.

From the Latin *utilis* ("useful"). In the philosophic tradition a property of those things which have value not in themselves but as a means to some end.

(1) Spinoza (*q.v.* 4) related the useful to that which conserves one's being, the basic principle of his rational psychology. He thus distinguished between that which allows one to adapt to one's environment, either socially or physically, and the truly useful which conduces to the development of one's reason.

(2) David Hume (*q.v.* 6) introduced the term into ethics as the basic criterion of ethical value.

(3) Croce (*q.v.* 4) found it to be the governing idea of the sphere of economics, one of the four areas making up Croce's "philosophy of the spirit." In economics the term has often been regarded as interchangeable with the concept of "demand."

UTOPIA.

From the Greek *ou* ("not") plus *topos* ("a place"). The term was coined by Thomas More in 1516 as the name for his ideal society, and used by Rabelais after 1534 as the name for an ideal island. It has been used by philosophers, social thinkers, and novelists to refer to any ideal, unrealizable social structure. In what follows we shall classify utopias according to the division suggested above, while recognizing the inevitability of overlap among the classes.

A. The term has been used of philosophers in reference to their ideal social structures.

(1) It has often been applied to Plato's (*q.v.* 5) vision, both to the Atlantis legend of the *Timaeus* and the structured society of the *Republic*, that aristocracy utilizing the educational system to determine one's place in society, including a determination on merit of those who are to rule.

(2) Thomas More's (*q.v.* 1) *Utopia* combined the major emphases of Plato's *Republic* with Epicureanism and the idea of Christian providence.

(3) Francis Bacon (*q.v.* 5) projected the ideals of a scientific society in *The New Atlantis*. Regarding science as the key to universal happiness, he called for a college of experimental science where scientific studies were to take place under state guidance and control.

(4) In his *City of the Sun* Campanella

(*q.v.* 4), like many others, followed Plato's lead in the *Republic*. The scheme was modified in a number of ways; for example, Campanella's philosopher-kings were also priests.

(5) Mandeville (*q.v.* 1, 3) in *The Fable of the Bees* argued against organizing society on "other-regarding" principles. A society of altruists would have no motivating force. His hypothetical society thus turned out to be non-utopian, demonstrating that private vices are public benefits.

(6) There is a strongly normative, even utopian, motive in all of the writings of Rousseau (*q.v.*), from *The Discourse on Inequality* through the educational philosophy of Émile. His goal throughout is a new vision of society.

B. Although all utopias are social it is perhaps possible to distinguish between those whose authors' intent is more decidedly social and practical rather than philosophical.

(7) In this category we include Plutarch of Chaeronea's idealized description of Sparta in the *Lives* (*i.e.*, in the section on Lycurgus); James Harrington's *Oceana* (1656), regarding property as the basis of power and calling for an executive of limited duration; Etienne Cabet's *Voyage in Icaria* (1840), presenting the views of Robert Owen; William Morris in *News From Nowhere* (1891), setting forth his socialist position; and B.F. Skinner (*q.v.* 1, 3) approaching the possibility of a utopia from the stand point of a social scientist in *Walden Two* (1948).

(8) The views of such thinkers as Proudhon (*q.v.*), Saint Simon (*q.v.*), Charles Fourier (*q.v.*), and Robert Owen (*q.v.*) were dubbed "Utopian Socialism" by Marx and Engels who regarded their own position as "Scientific Socialism" (*q.v.* Socialism 6).

C. (9) Among literary utopias one would include that part of Rabelais' *Gargantua and Pantagruel* (1534–52) where Pantagruel journeys to the island of Utopia; book four of Swift's *Gulliver's Travels* (1726) where the ideal kingdom of the Houyhnhnms is described; Samuel Johnson's *Rasselas, Prince of Abyssinia* (1754); Bulwer Lytton's *The Coming Race* (1871); Samuel Butler's *Erewhon* (1872), and *Erewhon Revisited* (1901); Edward Bellamy's *Looking Backward* (1887); H.G.

Wells' *Anticipations* (1901), *A Modern Utopia* (1904), and *New Worlds for Old* (1908). Among negative utopias are Aldous Huxley's *Brave New World* (1932) and George Orwell's *Animal Farm* (1945) and *Nineteen Eighty-Four* (1949).

UTOPIAN SOCIALISM.
Q.v. Socialism (6).

UTRAQUISTS.
Q.v. John Huss.

UTTARA MIMAMSA.
A Sanskrit term literally meaning "the later revered thought" and referring to a school of Indian thought dealing with the latter portion of the *Vedas* (*q.v.*). The school is better known as Vedanta (*q.v.*), meaning "end of the *Vedas*."

VACASPATI.
Q.v. Vedanta (2).

VAGUENESS.
A word or term is said to be vague, or to have the property, "vagueness," when there are borderline cases and uncertainty concerning whether or not the term applies to these cases. *Q.v.* Ambiguity.

VAIBHAṢIKA (VAIBHASHIKA).
One of the four chief philosophical schools of Hinayana Buddhism (*q.v.*), standing for the epistemology of direct realism.

VAIHINGER, HANS. 1852–1933.
German philosopher. Born in Tübingen. Professor of philosophy at the University of Halle, beginning in 1884. In addition to his writings, he aided the development of philosophical thought, particularly that of Kant, through the establishment of the journals *Kantstudien* in 1896, and *Kant-Gesellschaft* in 1904. A journal dedicated to his own philosophy of "As if" was the *Annalen der Philosophie*, initiated by Vaihinger and Schmidt in 1919.

Principal writings: *Commentary on Kant's Critique of Pure Reason*, 2 vols., 1881, 1892; *The Philosophy of As If* (T), 1911.

(1) Taking his cue from the Kantian analysis of the regulative nature of ideas, Vaihinger developed a system which he called Idealistic Positivism, but which is more commonly known as Fictionalism, or simply the "philosophy of 'As if'" (in German *"die philosophie des Als Ob."*).

(2) The point of view is that on both biological and pragmatic grounds, *i.e.*, for purposes of adaptation and usefulness, many of our most important ideas are mental constructions, which we do not know to fit the facts. We hold them because of the aid they give us in dealing with a problematic reality. And this is the case in mathematics, science, philosophy, law, religion, and economics. We hold concepts "as if" they were true; examples include both atomic theory and the idea of God.

(3) Vaihinger's solution is merely to become aware of the fictive nature of the ideas which guide us. This may make possible going beyond adaptation and utility to the recognition of nonfictive realities.

VAILATI, GIOVANNI. 1863–1909.
Italian philosopher. Born in Crema. Educated at Turin. Taught at Turin. Interested in Peirce, Vailati viewed philosophy as analysis, leading perhaps to clarification but not adding to knowledge. Principal writings: *Writings*, 1911; *Pragmatism* (ed. Papini), 1911.

VAIŚEṢIKA (VAISHESHIKA).
From the Sanskrit *viśeṣa* ("difference" or "particularity"). *Vaisheshika* is one of the six systems of Indian philosophy to arise in the period following the Vedic age. Paired with Nyaya (*q.v.*), for which it provides the metaphysics, the Vaisheshika system was regarded as unique in recognizing the role of "difference" among its categories, and holding that basic differences made possible the composition of the universe. The *Vaiśeṣika Sutras* were composed by Kanada probably sometime after 300 A.D., although expert opinion is divided on the matter. Among the basic ideas of the sutras and system are the following:
(1) The categories of experience (and

of being) are: substance, quality (*guna*), activity, universality, particularity (*viśeṣa*), inherence, and negation (or absence). The last category was added by Kanada's successors.

(2) Nine substances are distinguished: earth, water, fire, air, ether, space, time, soul, and mind.

(3) Sensible things are composed of invisible atoms, eternal in nature, and bearing one of four characteristics: earth, water, fire, or air.

(4) Souls are also eternal, pervading bodies for a time. Each soul has its individual characteristic, and this is true even after the soul has been freed from its body.

(5) God is not a feature of the system although there is a supersensible force (*adṛṣṭa*), generated by Vedic observance; which is behind the phenomena of nature, and related to the merits and demerits pertaining to *moksha* and *karma*.

(6) In practice the Nyaya (*q.v.* 3–4) idea of God is accepted, and identified with Ishvara, an eternal soul endowed with superhuman qualities, including omniscience.

VAIṢNAVA (VAISHNAVA) ALVARS.
Q.v. Vaiṣnavism (2b, 3b).

VAIṢNAVISM, ŚAIVISM, ŚAKTISM (VAISHNAVISM, SHAIVISM, SHAKTISM).
The three major Hindu cults (*q.v.* Hinduism 5c) which became powerful in post-Vedic times, centered on the gods Vishnu, Shiva, and the goddess Shakti, respectively.

(1) Vishnu (*q.v.*) and Shiva are two of the gods in the Hindu trinity (*trimurti, q.v.*) which emerged in the late Vedic period. The third was Brahma; but Brahma faded in public esteem so that no cult centers around his name, and only one prominent shrine (Pushkar). Vishnu and Shiva, on the other hand, became major gods. During the Vedic period, the cults centering on Vishnu and Shiva were of minor importance; but as the *Vedas* declined in power (8th to 6th cents., B.C.), the two cults came into their own.

(2) Among the pre-Vedic cults leading to Vaishnavism, *Bhakti* (*q.v.*) was the most significant. Vaishnavism emerged with force by way of cultic fusion. We shall

consider first this process, and then its literature.

(a) By the 4th century the cult of Vasudeva had merged with the cult of Krishna (both coming from the deification of tribal heroes), the god becoming Vasudeva-Krishna. The Vasudeva-Krishna cult then absorbed the Gopala-Krishna cult. One early Vaishnava sect, the Pancaratrins, worshipped Narayana, whom they claimed as their founder, and who became Purusha-Narayana before (probably) separating into the paired gods, Arjuna (suggesting an earlier Arjuna sect) and Krishna. Another early Vaishnava sect, the Bhagavatas, worshipped Vasudeva-Krishna as an incarnation of Vishnu. Alongside Krishna, the cult of Rama (*q.v.*) (probably also a deified hero) worshipped Rama as an incarnation of Vishnu. The process continued and, as Vishnu gained in power, the number of incarnations (*avataras*) increased to ten.

(b) Many of the names occurring in (a) above are to be found in the great Hindu epics; and the sacred literature of Vaishnavism includes the *Mahabharata* (*q.v.*) with its sub-epic of the *Bhagavad-Gita* (*q.v.*) and *Narayaniya*, as well as the *Ramayana* (*q.v.*) ("the romance of Rama"). The sect's working scriptures, however, are the Vaishnava *Samhitas* ("collections," the name borrowed from the Vedic, *q.v.* 1, *Samhitas*). The *bhakti* or devotional tradition developed through the Alvars of southern India, and was furthered by Ramanuja (*q.v.*), Ramananda, Kabir, and others (*q.v.* Hinduism 5c).

(3) Shaivism celebrates the god Shiva (*q.v.*), whose ambivalence extended to positive and negative aspects, not only in himself but in most of the goddesses taken alternatively to be his consorts. For one thing, where Vishnu always supported the projects of the gods, Shiva at times opposed the gods on behalf of the demons. Although Shiva was said to be both benevolent and frightful, both creator and destroyer, providing in his role as dancer the eternal rhythms sustaining the universe, his most traditional polarity was between asceticism and eroticism. Married to the beautiful Parvati, to fit his mood, she too was viewed as alternating between austerity and lust. Their union was taken by Shaivites as the prototype of human marriage, providing a manner of combining the obligations of asceticism with the sexual requirements of the householder state. The sects of Shaivism retain this ambivalence, and add others. The four principal sects, mentioned in the early history of Shaivism, are the Pashupatas, the Kalamukhas, the Shaiva Siddhantins, and the Kapalikas.

(a) The first two are now extinct but gave rise to the Lingayats (or Virashaivas) who reject temple worship, sacrifice, pilgrimages, the caste system, and child marriage, while encouraging the equality of the sexes and the right of widows to remarry. The devotees also carry at all times a *linga* (phallic symbol), in a small tube fastened to the arm or neck. Twice daily the *linga* is "worshipped." Death is regarded as reabsorption into the *linga*.

(b) The Shaiva Siddhantins are monotheistic (as also were the Pashupatas and Kalamukhas), combining *bhakti* ("devotion") and grace in attaining salvation. The cult emerged from the Tamil devotional movement of southern India, the devotional poems of whose 63 Nyanars (poet saints) remain a prominent feature of Shaiva worship. Along with the Vaishnava Alvars (2b above) the Tamil Shaivas contributed the *bhakti* element to Hinduism.

(c) The *Kapalikas* (from Skt., *kapala*, "skull") are defined by their ascetics who carry a skull as begging bowl, emulating Shiva's 12-year wandering penance. In a fit of anger Shiva had cut off one of the five heads of Brahma, but found that the skull had stuck to his hand, and remained so for 12 years, finally falling off in Banaras, the holy city of Shiva. The Kapalikas reenact the penance (known as the Great Vow), their hair matted and bodies smeared with ashes. It is widely presumed that Tantrism (*q.v.*) plays a role in Kapalikan worship. The Kapalikan doctrine is called *Soma Siddhanta*, the doctrine (*siddhanta*) of Shiva in union with his wife, Uma (*Sa-Uma*).

(d) In addition to these are many Kashmir-related sects: Krama Shaivism, a neo-Kapalika sect in which the goddess, Kali, and her emanations (other goddesses) are worshipped in sequence (*krama*) leaping to ecstasy and liberation;

Trika Shaivism (also Kali-related) in which a triad of goddesses, one beneficent and two wild and terrifying, as well as eight mother goddesses, are invoked and placated through offerings of blood, flesh, wine, and sexual fluids. The Shakti (q.v. and Tantrism 3–4) sexual congress is likewise practised in order to reveal the blissful consciousness of the true self. Finally, Kashmir Shaivism contains the school of Pratya-Bhijna (Skt., "recognition") for which Shiva is the sole reality "shining forth" as the many-faceted universe. When this forgotten truth is recognized, cosmic bliss is at once experienced, and may become a permanent state, even in this life.

(e) The basic scriptures of Shaivism are called Śaivagamas (from śaiva and agamas, "traditions"), to be distinguished from the Nigamas ("established doctrines") of the Vedas.

(4) Shaktism is named for shakti (q.v.) (Skt., for "energy"), considered here to be the female consort of Shiva. The interpretation is that Shiva stands for the male (passive energy) and Shakti for the female (active energy). The worshippers are called shaktas and, as in the case of Shaivism the scriptures are recognized as agamas, although called Tantras (Skt., "web" or "loom"). The sect has two aspects.

(a) In one the macrocosmic Shakti is related to the mother goddesses of Shaivism, over 1,000 in number, all of them regarded as manifestations of Shakti. Some are beneficent; others are terrifying, among them Kali, Durga, Bhavani (the goddess of thugs) and Shitali (the goddess of smallpox).

(b) In the other the microcosmic Shakti, standing for the sexual energy of the individual, is addressed, to the end of releasing this energy and turning it to spiritual account. We shall use the terminology of "right-handed" and "left-handed" shakti, although these accepted terms apparently derive from an error in translation. Vamacara, often translated as "left-handed path" comes from vama ("women" or the "sexual urge") and acara ("ritual practice"); the term thus describes the object of the sect in a very direct manner. In Right-handed Shakti bhakti and the general techniques of Yoga are employed. In Left-handed Shakti ritual

sex is the means for arousing the serpent energy of Kundalini (q.v. Yoga 10), coiled at the base of the spine, whose energy is to be directed upward toward the head. The method is further described in Tantrism (q.v. 3–4) with which this aspect of Shaktism is often identified.

VAIŚYAS (VAISHYAS).
The commercial class of Indian tradition. Q.v. Aśramas (2); Hinduism (4); Mahabharata (3); Laws of Manu (2).

VAJRAYANA.
Q.v. Lamaism (5); Tantrism (6, 9).

VALENTINUS. c. 100–165.
Gnostic teacher. Born in Alexandria where he taught until 135 A.D. Moved to Rome where he continued his teaching until 160 A.D. Died in Cyprus. Developed a complex system out of Gnostic, Platonic, Stoic, and Christian elements. In agreement with other Gnostics, Valentinus' system turned on a dualism of good and evil in the universe, and the manner in which man can purify himself, triumphing over the evil, material principle. Valentinus' originality lies in his reading of the drama of the universe. The Father or Abyss unites with the feminine principle of Silence. The result of the union is the appearance of Nous (Mind) and Aletheia (Truth). These principles form the first tetrad. Through further union within the tetrad an octad is generated. And from this are generated the essential forces of the universe, the Aeons constituting a Pleroma or Fullness of Being. The Aeons include the Word, Life, the Primal Man, the Church, Sophia or Wisdom, and the Purifier or Christ. The return to the spiritual—i.e., the rescue from matter—is initiated by the desire of Sophia to learn the nature of the Primal Father. When the work of the Purifier, who takes upon himself the task of redemption, is completed, all those capable of spirituality will have ascended to the Pleroma and the material world will be destroyed in an immense conflagration.

VALIDATION.
Q.v. Feigl (3).

VALIDITY.
From the Latin validitas ("strength"). A concept of logic characteristic of sound

arguments. Validity must be carefully distinguished from truth.

(1) In ordinary deductive logic, validity is semantical. It is a property of those arguments whose conclusions follow necessarily from their premises (*q.v.* Syllogism 3–5, Venn Diagrams 6). Given true premises and a valid argument, the argument's conclusion is necessarily true. Given false premises and a valid argument, the conclusion may or may not be true.

(2) In the Propositional Calculus (*q.v.*) validity is a property of those argument forms, the truth tables (*q.v.* 6) of whose combinations yield the value "true" on every line without exception. Validity is thus distinguishable from "consistency" which requires the value "true" only on some line or other, and "inconsistency" where the value "false" appears on every line. If an argument form is valid, the negation of that form will be inconsistent.

(3) In all formal or logistic systems, including the propositional calculus, validity is syntactical. That is, it is a property rather than of the system than of individual arguments. The argument forms of logistic systems, also known as "truth functional schema," are valid when true under every interpretation of the *Wffs*, or "well-formed formulas" of the system. This may be seen in the case of the propositional calculus by noting that "p, q, r" etc. are place-markers for any significant sentence.

(4) Peirce (*q.v.* 8–9) extended the notion of validity to inductive and abductive arguments. In the latter cases it is not truth, but a tendency toward the truth, which is at issue.

VALLABHA.

Q.v. Vedanta (4).

VALLA, LORENZO. 1405–1457.

Italian philosopher. Born and educated in Rome. Taught rhetoric at the University of Pavia. In 1435 he became private secretary to King Alfonso of Aragon. While serving Alfonso he published a document revealing the spurious nature of the Donation of Constantine (*q.v.*). In his later years Valla became an apostolic secretary in Rome under Pope Nicholas V.

Principal writings: *On Pleasure*, 1431; *The Donation of Constantine* (T), 1440; *On Free Will* (T); *On the Elegance of the Latin Language*, 1471; *Dialectic*, 1497; plus edited works of his writings on religion.

(1) Regarded as one of the most important humanists of the Italian Renaissance, Valla's analysis of pleasure is typical of his posture; the work provides expositions of both Stoicism and Epicureanism. The conclusion is that the principles of the latter, though valid, are to be deferred in Christian piety to the next world.

(2) His position on free will and divine foreknowledge appears to sacrifice the former to preserve the latter; and Luther (*q.v.* 9), taking the same position, cites Valla as a predecessor.

(3) As a professional rhetorician Valla followed Aristotle, Cicero, and Quintilian, insisting with Aristotle and Cicero on the importance of the relation of rhetoric and philosophy. At the same time he held Aristotle's logic and metaphysics to be barbarous linguistically, and called for a linguistic approach, and thus a rhetoric, more appropriate to the description of reality.

(4) His opposition to Aristotle also turned on the manner in which Aristotle had been used to integrate the realms of knowledge and faith, *i.e.*, Scholasticism. He viewed with the same distaste the Renaissance attempts to revive other ancient philosophies (*e.g.* Stoicism) to serve this purpose.

VALUE.

From the Latin *valere* ("to be strong," "to be worth"). The concept of value both complements, and stands in contrast to, the concept of fact. One merely recognizes the latter, but must select out the former. For anything, attitude, ideal, purpose, or goal to be of value, it must be the object of a preference, or of a judgment of importance. In the history of philosophy a number of suggested classifications of value has emerged. We shall treat those distinctions here. Second, many philosophers have argued that some given value is the end of life. That aspect of value is treated under the heading "Value, Final" (*q.v.*). Third, numerous theories have been advanced concerning the nature of value. Such theories are discussed under the heading "Value Theory" (*q.v.*).

(1) Plato (*q.v.* 14) distinguished between instrumental, intermediate, and

intrinsic values. Regarding the first as means values and the last as end values, intermediate values were held to have both characteristics. The instrumental-intrinsic contrast is sometimes termed an extrinsic-intrinsic contrast.

(2) Sorley (*q.v.*) was among the many who followed Plato in distinguishing between instrumental and intrinsic values. He held the former to relate to things, and the latter to persons.

(3) Dewey (*q.v.* 4) with his concept of the means-end continuum, held all values to be of the intermediate, extrinsic-intrinsic type.

(4) R.B. Perry (*q.v.* 3) classified value into eight types, which he sometimes called realms of value. They are: moral, aesthetic, scientific, religious, economic, political, legal, and customary.

(5) Alejandro Korn (*q.v.* 5) distinguished nine types of value: economic, instinctive, erotic, vital, social, religious, ethical, logical, and aesthetic. Each type has its own value polarity. The polarities of the first two for example, are "useful-useless" and "agreeable-disagreeable." Each also has its own system. The systems for the first two are Utilitarianism and Hedonism.

(6) Scheler (*q.v.* 2) found a hierarchy of value-types, consisting of sensory, life, spiritual and religious values in ascending order.

(7) C.I. Lewis (*q.v.* 5) distinguished five types of value, consisting of utility, instrumental, inherent, intrinsic, and contributory.

(8) G.H. Von Wright (*q.v.* 2), regarding values as forms of goodness, distinguished the following types: instrumental, technical, utilitarian, hedonic, and welfare.

VALUE, FINAL.

That value, or set of values, at which all humans do or should aim. While some philosophers believe there is no such value or set of values, more philosophers than can be mentioned have advanced specific values as candidates to perform this function.

(1) Aristotle (*q.v.* 11), for example, held happiness, or *eudaemonia*, to be the value all men seek. He believed, however, that the components of happiness differ for different types of individual, while in every case development of one's ration-

al capacities is to be included in the self-fulfillment of happiness. Whether due to the influence of Aristotle, or some other cause, happiness is the most widely accepted candidate for final value. Thomas Aquinas (*q.v.* 7–8) accepted Aristotle's analysis, while supplying a transcendental extension of the meaning of the term. Almost at random, additional adherents of the view may be mentioned: *e.g.*, Wollaston (*q.v.*) in the 17th century and Schlick (*q.v.* 4) in the 20th. In addition it should be noted in passing that many of those who argue for some other value, state that it is the surest path to happiness.

(2) "Pleasure" was suggested as the final value at least as early as Aristippus (*q.v.*), founder of the Cyrenaic School (*q.v.*) and a predecessor of Aristotle. It is not entirely clear, however, that pleasure is to replace happiness. He suggested, rather, that pleasure provides the chief means of gaining happiness. Epicurus (*q.v.* 10), likewise, held happiness to be the end; but the latter's chief constituent is *ataraxia*, or pleasure enjoyed in tranquility, a state of being first recommended by Democritus (*q.v.* 11). Pyrrho (*q.v.* 3) held *ataraxia* to be the final value, as did Lucretius (*q.v.* 9) somewhat later. In the 15th century Lorenzo Valla (*q.v.* 1) held to a Christian hedonism. In recent centuries pleasure has been regarded as the chief value of human life by such thinkers as Jeremy Bentham (*q.v.* 1), James Mill (*q.v.*), John Stuart Mill (*q.v.* 7), and Sigmund Freud (*q.v.* 7).

(3) The Confucian tradition (*q.v.* Confucius 2–5) underlined a plurality of values with *jen* or "humanity" and *li* or "propriety" central. The tradition endured for millennia. All neo-Confucianists stressed the same values, although with modifications. Ch'eng Hao (*q.v.* 3), for example, added to the above values an emphasis on sincerity (*q.v.*).

(4) Also the Taoistic concept of the *tao*—adaptability to context, flexibility, moving with the times, and inaction (*wu wei*) can be taken to stand for a complex final value (*q.v.* Tao-Te Ching 3).

(5) The movement of Stoicism stressed *apathia* or tranquility of mind (*q.v.* Marcus Aurelius 1; Epictetus 1–2) as the final value to be sought. Panaetius (*q.v.* 2) substituted "peace of mind" for *apathia*.

(6) *Agápe*, or selfless love, was held by

the Christian community to be the chief value of human life. C.S. Peirce (*q.v.* 13) advanced a doctrine of "Agapism" to the effect that *agápe* would gradually increase in importance in all human relations.

(7) Theodorus the Atheist (*q.v.*), one of the later leaders of the Cyrenaic School, held the end of life to be the enduring emotion of joy brought about by the application of practical intelligence.

(8) Among other candidates for final value, Petrarch (*q.v.* 1) and Cheng I (*q.v.* 3) stressed self-cultivation, Telesio (*q.v.* 4) suggested self-preservation, and Geulincx (*q.v.* 3), in a choice reminiscent of Stoicism, argued for "resigned optimism" as final value.

(9) Spinoza (*q.v.* 5c, 10) argued for the importance of wisdom as the central value of human life, an extension of Socrates' (*q.v.* 1) and St. Augustine's (*q.v.* 1) value of self-knowledge (*q.v.*). Apparently, however, wisdom does not replace but is the surest means to a continuing happiness.

(10) Schopenhauer (*q.v.* 6) urged "renunciation" as the finally appropriate value.

(11) Other analyses have emphasized social values as central. Comte (*q.v.* 5), for example, stressed order and progress, and some modification of Comte's view appeared in Latin American adaptations of positivism.

(12) Self-realization (*q.v.*) or self-fulfillment as life's final value became popular with the neo-Hegelians. In fact, Aristotle's eudaemonistic view contained a large amount of self-realization. T.H. Green (*q.v.* 2–3) emphasized self-realization, likewise interpreted as the drive for "human perfection." Stirner's (*q.v.* 1) emphasis on "individuality" is a closely related concept. Also *q.v.* Ferguson, and Friedrich Schiller (1).

(13) Nietzsche (*q.v.* 3) held the "will to power" to be man's most basic drive and this will, sublimated into diverse forms of value, is also man's final goal.

(14) Royce (*q.v.* 1a) regarded loyalty as life's absolute ideal and as the criterion for ethics.

(15) For Albert Schweitzer (*q.v.* 4) "reverence for life" was held to be both life's final value and the key to ethics.

(16) William Temple (*q.v.*) argued that, quite simply, God is to be recognized as the supreme value.

(17) For Ortega y Gasset (*q.v.* 3) and Jean-Paul Sartre (*q.v.* 3) authenticity is the final value. At least for the latter, values are human inventions.

(18) Camus (*q.v.* 2) suggested that human solidarity has paramount importance, and is thus somewhat akin to a final value.

VALUE THEORY.

The designation, along with Axiology, for the field of philosophy investigating the nature of value and valuation. Although a good deal of work has been done in this field, the results are less satisfying than in most areas of philosophy, and the theories less penetrating. In general, value theories can be divided into those which relate value to "interest" and those which suppose values to be in some sense objective and known by intuition. But there are other distinctions which extend the framework of the above division. Depending upon the theory, values have been viewed as cognitive or noncognitive, absolute or relative, objective or subjective, natural or non-natural, essentialistic or existentialistic, and justifiable or nonjustifiable.

(1) In one early approach, that of the Pythagoreans, value was identified with number. For example, "7" was health and justice a square number (*q.v.* Pythagoras 9). In another (*q.v.* Heraclitus 4) it was claimed that value is generated in conflict.

(2) For Plato (*q.v.* 1) values were essences, known by intuition, and apparently involved in some sort of hierarchic realm. In the modern period of growing interest in Axiology, W.M. Urban (*q.v.* 2) followed Plato, holding values to be objective features of an intelligible world while both Max Scheler (*q.v.* 2) and Nicolai Hartmann (*q.v.* 5) argued specifically that values are hierarchical, nontemporal essences. Also *cf.* the Heidelberg School (6 below).

(3) Aristotle (*q.v.* 11) seems to have held that values are not essences but, rather, that they are defined by human interest. The interest theory of value was developed by Perry (*q.v.* 2) who defined value as "any object of any interest." Among many others Christian Ehrenfels (*q.v.*) held a similar view.

(4) That value-theory rests on intuition

was initiated somewhat unclearly by Sidgwick (*q.v.* 2), developed and defended by G.E. Moore (*q.v.* 6), and held by W.D. Ross (*q.v.* 1).

(5) Nietzsche (*q.v.* 5), holding to the need for a "transvaluation of values," seems to have regarded values both as constructed and yet subject to judgments of better and worse. They rise in situations of resentment and power, but are capable of creative transformation.

(6) The Heidelberg School of neo-Kantianism (*q.v.* Neo-Kantianism 4) believed values to be objective, universally valid, underlying existence, and the key to epistemology. One of their members, Münsterberg (*q.v.*), found the absolute system of values to rest upon a Fichtean act of absolute will.

(7) Meinong (*q.v.* 4) understood value to emerge as the affective human response to the world through four types of value-feelings. C.I. Lewis (*q.v.* 4) held a similar view, finding value in a moral, cognitive, or aesthetic response to the given.

(8) Dewey (*q.v.* 5–6) is regarded as a naturalist in value theory, believing that values are discovered in experience (in the same sense C.I. Lewis, *q.v.* 5, too, deserves the label). But Dewey stressed valuation rather than values, finding the key to the latter in the human processes of "prizing" and "apprizing." Both means and ends are subject to evaluation, and the two form a continuous process.

(9) Moritz Schlick (*q.v.* 4) held that values are relative and that indeed his positivistic analysis had destroyed the idea of absolute value.

(10) Sartre (*q.v.* 3–5) argued that values are inventions of humans in an existential situation. They are not essences and are not rationally justifiable.

(11) Charles Stevenson (*q.v.* 1–2) is among those who find only emotive meaning in value terms, while R.M. Hare (*q.v.* 1) holds that although such terms have both descriptive and evaluative meanings, the latter are primary.

VANAPRASTHA.
From Sanskrit, "forest-dweller." *Q.v.* Aśramas (2); Hinduism (3c).

VAN FRAASSEN, BASS C. 1941– .
North American philosopher of science.

Born in the Netherlands. Educated at Alberta and Pittsburgh. Has taught at Yale, Toronto, Southern California, and Princeton.

Principal writings: *An Introduction to the Philosophy of Time and Space*, 1969; *Formal Semantics and Logic*, 1971; *Derivation and Counter Example* (with Lambert, 1972); *Contemporary Research in the Philosophy and Foundations of Quantum Theory*, 1973; *The Scientific Image*, 1980; *Current Issues in Quantum Logic* (joint ed.), 1981; *Laws and Symmetry*, 1989.

(1) Approaching science as an anti-realist in which explanation is contrastive (why questions require multiple alternatives. It is not just "why P?" but "why P rather than some contrasting fact Q?") and empiricism is "constructive" (theory acceptance requires no more than empirical adequacy), scientific theories "need not to be true to be good."

(2) From this perspective the observable is theory-independent. Limitation to the "actual and observable" forces theories about modality into the philosophy of language, and one is delivered from metaphysics.

(3) In a "gentle polemic" he proposes a reluctant conversion to scientific realism in which the theoretical entities "discussed by our best available scientific theories" are accepted as literally true. Since the conversion also requires accepting an ontic version of Aquinas' five arguments for God the point would seem to be that scientific realists are closet theologians.

VAN HELMONTS, THE.
Q.v. Helmont.

VANINI, GIULIO. c. 1584–1619.
Italian philosopher. Born in Taurisano. Studied at Naples and Padua. A Carmelite, Vanini was heterodox, believing in the probable eternity of the world and the mortality of the soul. He believed God to be immanent in nature, ruling a deterministic universe.

Principal writings: *Amphitheater of Eternal Providence*, 1615; *Dialogues on Nature*, 4 vols., 1616.

VARDHAMANA (MAHAVIRA). 599–527 B.C.
Indian philosopher and religious leader.

A leader of the Jains (*q.v.* Jainism), Vard-hamana systematized the doctrines of the movement in terms of his understanding of the traditional founders, Rishabha, Ajitanatha, and Arishtanemi. All three of these men are mentioned in the *Yajur Veda*, a document central to Jainism.

VARELA, FELIX.
Q.v. Latin American Philosophy (1).

VARIABLE.
From the Latin *varius* ("various"). In mathematics, a quantity which can take a succession of values. In logic, an indeterminate conception capable of taking a succession of values. In both cases the value chosen will make a determinate expression of the mathematical or propositional Function (*q.v.*). The variable is typically represented by a letter, for example, "x." All of the instances which may replace "x" make up the "range" of the variable."

(1) The distinction between "free" and "bound," or "real" and "apparent," variables is that in the former case, given certain values, "x" will be true and, given other values, "x" will be false. If "x" is a bound variable, the truth of the expression does not depend on the choice of the value selected for "x." Another way of expressing the distinction is to say that in the case of the "free" variable the meaning of the expression depends on the meaning of the value selected for "x." The meaning of the bound variable is not thus dependent upon a given substitution instance. In "x is a politician," "x" is a free variable. In "x is a man⊃x is human," "x" is a bound variable.

(2) The distinction between independent and dependent variables may be exemplified by "y=f(x)." Since "y" is a function of "x," it is "y" that is the dependent variable and "x" is the independent variable. *Q.v.* Function (1).
Also *q.v.* Frege (3).

VARIATIONS, CONCOMITANT.
Q.v. J.S. Mill (4d).

VARISCO, BERNARDINO. 1850–1933.
Italian philosopher. Born at Chiari. Taught at Rome. Initially a positivist he became, through Gentile's influence, a metaphysician idealistic and panpsychic in tone, supporting the idea of a deity

who limits Himself for the sake of creative participation alongside man. Principal writings: *Science and Opinion*, 1901; *The Great Problems* (T), 1910; *Know Thyself* (T), 1912; *Summary of Philosophy*, 1928; *From Man to God*, 1939.

VARNA.
Sanskrit, "color." *Q.v.* Caste.

VARNAŚRAMADHARMA (VARNASHRAMADHARMA).
Q.v. Dharma (2).

VARONA, ENRIQUE JOSÉ.
Q.v. Latin American Philosophy (6).

VARRO, MARCUS TERENTIUS. 116–c. 27 B.C.
Roman philosopher. Born in Reate. Friend and aide to both Pompey and Caeser, he was involved in the latter's project to collect Greek and Latin literature. Philosophically, Varro was a disciple of Antiochus of Ascalon (*q.v.*), an eclectic mingling the dogmatism of the Fourth Academy (*q.v.* Plato's Academy 4) with the Stoic doctrine of soul, Panaetius' (*q.v.*) theology, and the influence of Posidonius (*q.v.*). He is mentioned by his contemporary, Cicero. Principal writings: *Menippean Satires; On the Latin Language; On Country Life*.

VARUNA.
Once chief among the Vedic divinities, Varuna was the sky god guaranteeing cosmic order.

VASCONCELOS, JOSÉ. 1882–1959.
Mexican philosopher. Born in Oaxaca. Professor in the Universidad Nácional. Rector of the university, Secretary of Education, 1921–3. Beginning with an aesthetic analysis of rhythm in Pythagoras, Vasconcelos developed a Plotinian interpretation of reality in which the concept of aesthetic unity is viewed as the principal metaphysical category. Joining this concept to that of an evolving universe, beauty becomes the end of evolution and its highest state. *Q.v.* Latin American Philosophy (12). Principal writings: *Pythagoras, a Theory of Rhythm*, 1916; *Aesthetic Monism*, 1918; *The Cosmic Race*, 1925; *Indology: an Interpretation of Spanish-American Culture*, 1927; *Treatise on Metaphysics*, 1929; *Ethics*, 1932;

Spanish-American Culture, 1934; Aesthetics, 1936; Scientifc Realism, 1943; Organic Logic, 1945.

VÁSQUEZ, GABRIEL. 1549–1604.

Spanish neo-Scholastic. Born at Villaescusa del Haro. Educated at Belmonte del Tajo and Alcalá. A member of the Society of Jesus, he taught at Madrid, Alcalá, and Rome. His views were shaped by Thomas, Cajetan, and Scotus. He drew a distinction between the qualitas ipsa cognitionis or the quality of a conception, and the res cognita or thing known, which may have prepared the way for the split between idea and reality characterizing modern philosophy. Among his arguments for God was a moral argument anticipating Kant.

Principal writings: Metaphysical Disputations, 1617.

VASSALLO, ANGEL.

Q.v. Latin American Philosophy (9).

VASUBANDHU. 4th or 5th cent. A.D.

Indian philosopher. Younger brother of Asanga (q.v.), founder of Yogachara (the Way of Yoga). Initially a Vaibhashikan (q.v.) of the Sarvastivadan (q.v.) order, Vasubandhu was eventually converted by his brother to Yogachara. Thereafter, he wrote many books in support of this version of Mahayana Buddhism, and was known as the systematizer of the Yogachara school his brother founded. He was also skilled in debate, winning many contests against rival schools, often before royalty.

Principal writings: Vijnaptimatratasiddhi ("the treatise in twenty stanzas on cognitions-only") (T); The Thirty Verses on the Mind-only Doctrine (T); Vadhavidhi ("method for argumentation") (T); Vadavidhana; Vadakausala; Abhidharma Kośa.

(1) Supporting the view of the school that only pure consciousness exists, Vasubandhu turns to defending the position against its opponents. To the arguments that external objects must exist because such objects have spatial and temporal determination, because there is common agreement as to these determinations, and because fruitful activity is possible, Vasubandhu answers that in dreams and in hell one has these four things and yet the objects of perception

in these situations do not exist.

(2) To the objection that if there is no difference between the states of dreaming and waking, then when we are awake we should know that external objects do not exist, just as we know that dream objects do not exist. Vasubandhu replies that we can realize the unreality of external objects only by transcending vikalpa (mental forms of our own construction), and the subject-object duality they represent. In doing this we go beyond intellect to Buddha-hood.

(3) In the Vadhavidhi Vasubandhu defined perception as the knowledge caused by an object, and inference as knowledge of an object through its "mark." He advanced beyond Nyaya (q.v.) logic by reducing the syllogism to a three-membered argument, similar to that of Aristotle. He also reduced the number of logical fallacies to three: arguments which are not justified, those not sufficiently certain, and those involving self-contradiction. In all of these cases there is a failure of "logical pervasion" or "invariable concomitance" in the terms or their relations. In the West this would be called a failure of distribution (q.v.) in the related terms.

VASUDEVA.

Q.v. Kṛṣna; Vaiṣnavism (2).

VASUDEVA-KṚṢNA (KRISHNA).

Q.v. Vaiṣnavism (2a).

VATICAN COUNCIL I. 1869–70.

The 20th ecumenical council of the Roman Catholic Church, called by Pope Pius IX, at which the doctrine of papal infallibility was promulgated.

VATICAN COUNCIL II. 1962–65.

The 21st ecumenical council of the Roman Catholic Church. Announced by Pope John XXIII in 1959, and convened in 1962, the meetings of the council generated a sense of renewal and openness to change within the Church. Q.v. Theology of Liberation (2).

VATSYAYANA.

The name of the compiler of the Kama Sutra (q.v.), and the developer of Nyaya (q.v.), very likely two different people.

VAUVENARGUES, LUC DE CLAPIERS. 1715–1747.
French philosopher. Born in Aix-en-Provence. Essentially a moralist, he held that man is motivated by self-interest, but that such motivation has room within it for the interests of others, and need not be identical to self-love.
Principal writings: *Introduction to the Knowledge of the Human Spirit*, 1746.

VAZ FERREIRA, CARLOS.
Q.v. Latin American Philosophy (11).

VEBLEN, THORSTEIN. 1857–1929.
American economist. Born in Manitowoc County, Wisconsin. Educated at Carleton College, Yale, and Cornell. Taught at Chicago, Stanford, Missouri, and the New School. Influenced by Darwin and Marx, Veblen made his mark as a social critic of American institutions.
Principal writings: *Theory of the Leisure Class*, 1899; *The Theory of Business Enterprise*, 1904; *The Instinct of Workmanship*, 1914; *Imperial Germany and the Industrial Revolution*, 1915; *The Higher Learning in America*, 1918; *The Place of Science in Modern Civilization*, 1919; *The Engineers and the Price System*, 1921; *Absentee Ownership*, 1923.
(1) Arguing the goal of the pecuniary interest in modern capitalism to be "conspicuous consumption" and "conspicuous waste," Veblen drew a distinction between the instinct for workmanship which pertains to the artisan, the legitimate value of industrial technology and planning, and the lack of value in the pecuniary manipulations of the owners of industry. It is the latter who set the style, as it were, for conspicuous consumption and waste.
(2) He found the power of imperial Germany to derive from a marriage of the techniques of the Industrial Revolution and the feudal-militaristic structure congenial to business. He likewise argued that the American universities, to their detriment, are under the control of businessmen.
(3) He drew a contrast between business and industry. The tendency of the latter is always toward production, while that of the former—having a "marketable right to get something for nothing"—tends to sabotage production in the in-

terests of scarcity. His solution was a soviet of technicians taking control of the economy.

VEDANA.
Sanskrit, "feeling." *Q.v.* Buddha (2); *Skandhas.*

VEDANTA.
From the Sanskrit *veda* ("knowledge") and *anta* ("end"). One of the six philosophical systems of India, arising after the period of the *Vedas,* and in response to the heterodox systems. As a school of thought its concern is with the later portions of the Vedic scriptures. The *Vedanta Sutra,* composed by Badarayana (between 500 and 200 B.C.), is also known as *Uttara Mimamsa,* and forms a companion piece to the *Purva Mimamsa.* The former treats the religious and philosophical themes of the later portions of the *Vedas,* as the latter deals with the earlier portions. The 555 sutras of the *Vedanta Sutra* are also known as the *Brahma Sutra* and the *Sariraka Sutra,* treating as it does, the doctrines of Brahman and the unconditioned self. The chief interpretations of Vedanta are three:
(1) The 7th century Bhartrihari in his *Vakyapadiya* argued that *brahman* is derived from the "word" which is quintessentially the *Veda* itself, that the power of *brahman* allowing multiplicity and change is time, and that time is a form of *avidya,* or ignorance.
(2) The most widely admired and accepted view, Advaita Vedanta, is that of Shankara (*q.v.*); in this non-dual interpretation Brahman is the sole reality, the world is an appearance, and Brahman and *Atman* are identical. Shankara's position was influenced by Gaudapada (*q.v.*) who, in turn, shows Buddhist influence of the Shunyavada (*q.v. Sunya* 2), Vijnavada variety. The Shankara line was continued, with modifications by many followers. Vacaspati (*fl.* 841), writing a commentary on Shankara's commentary, produced his own school of Advaita Vedanta.
(3) The interpretation of Ramanuja (*q.v.*) admits the reality of God, selves, and world, although the two latter exist only as the body of God, who has two forms. Ramanuja utilized the *Upanishads* in support of Vaishnavism (*q.v.*).
(4) Among the schools of Vaishnava

Vedanta, in addition to Ramanuja, were schools shaped by Nimbarka (fl. mid-14th cent.), whom Ramanuja influenced, that of Madhva (q.v.) whose dualism is less ultimate than that of the Sankhya system with which his view is frequently linked, and that of Vallabha (1479–1531) for whom Brahman pervades the whole world but is untouched by it.

THE VEDAS.

Sanskrit term meaning "knowledge." The *Vedas*, its oldest material dating from 1100 B.C., whose initial works constitute the earliest extant literature of humanity, are an ancient Indian collection of hymns, rituals, regulations for religious sacrifices, and philosophical essays. The *Vedas* are customarily divided in the following manner.

(1) There are the *Samhitas*. These are hymns addressed to gods and goddesses, and were used in the Vedic sacrifices. These early *Vedas* find in the living human being something immaterial which is understood in one of four ways: as *jiva* (Skt., "living being") applying to the functional personality distinguishing us from each other and conceived to exist after death; as *manas* (Skt., "mind"), the source of awareness including the sense of being alive; as *asu* (Skt., "breath of life"), the vital force enlivening inert matter and the source of animation in human beings; as *paramatman* (Skt., "universal soul"), the source of all existence. The fourth conception contains in germ the identity of *Atman* and Brahman. There are four collections of *Samhitas*: the *Ṛg, Sama, Yajur*, and *Atharva*—one for each of the four main priests of the sacrifice: (a) The *Ṛgveda* is the oldest and most important, numbering more than 1,000 priestly hymns, arranged in 10 books, to be addressed to the gods during the sacrifices, which featured the offering of *soma* to the gods (a fermented beverage from a "deified" plant), and tossing *ghi* (a clarified butter), representing Agni (the fire god) into the sacred fire. (b) The *Yajurveda* consists of liturgical verse to be chanted during the sacrifices. The verses are mostly from, and so repeat, the *Ṛgveda*. (c) The verses of the *Samaveda* are called *samani* ("melodies"), and the third part of the collection consists of "songbooks" with notes attached to the verses to guide the chanting. (d) The *Atharvaveda* consists of 750 hymns, some in the form of blessings, some in the form of curses, many addressed to Brahma as a personification of the ritual.

(2) The *Brahmanas* ("statements on Brahman") (ca. 900–500 B.C.), unlike the verses of (1a-d) above, were set down in connected prose sentences, the earliest Indo-European prose. The ritual and sacrifices are described in detail and commented upon. Although the subject matter is the magical power of ritual in the *Vedas*, they should probably be thought of as intermediate between the magic of the early period and the insight of the *Upanishads* that *Atman* and Brahman are identical.

(3) Added on to the *Brahmanas* are the *Aranyakas*. These interpret the meaning of the Vedic sacrifices. Composed in forest retreats, or perhaps to be studied in such retreats because of their aura of secrecy and danger. Since the material seems to have had its origin in the world of warriors whose nomadic existence was often in the wilds, wilderness, war, and esoteric vision became linked; and vision turned into philosophic thought.

(4) The *Upanishads*, virtually all of them dating from the 8th to the 4th centuries B.C., emerged from the *Aranyakas* so gradually that late *Aranyaka* and early *Upanishad* are indistinguishable. Later *Upanishads*, however, embody the height of Vedic philosophy while the *Aranyakas* do not. The teachings of the *Upanishads* are generally referred to as the *Vedanta* which means "the end of the *Vedas*," both chronologically and teleologically. There are over 200 *Upanishads*, although the more important are 14 in number, *i.e.*, *Isa, Kena, Katha, Praśna, Mundaka, Mandukya, Taittiriya, Aitareya, Chandogya, Bṛhadaranyaka, Śvetaśvatara, Kauṣitaki, Mahanarayana*, and the *Maitri*. Many of the older *Upanishads* can be dated in the 8th and 7th centuries B.C. Providing the basic source of Indian philosophical doctrine among the *astikas* or "orthodox," the *Upanishads* are, in a general sense, philosophically neutral among competing interpretations. And yet, of course, all of the themes of Indian philosophy are sounded in its pages: (a) The identification of one's being with the *Atman*, or inner self, which can be discovered

through contemplation. (b) The reality of Brahman, the Absolute, source and controller of all things. The *Bṛhadaranyaka Upaniṣad* states that *neti neti* or "not this, not this," is the only suitable description of Brahman who remains "the truth of truth." (c) The ultimate identity between *Atman*, the self within, and Brahman. "*Ayam atma brahma*" ("This self is Brahman") announces the *Bṛhadaranyaka Upaniṣad*. (d) Our ignorance of this identity which it is the purpose of meditation further to reveal, and the identification of ignorance with the illusory, or quasi-illusory, nature of the commonsense world. (e) The three paths to enlightenment: faith, works, and knowledge. (f) The state of the unreleased self, controlled by *Karma*, and the state of final release. Competing interpretations merely provide systems, uniting these ideas, and imposing a common perspective.

(5) The *Sutras* form a late stage of Vedic literature, expressing in aphoristic form the essential requirements of the Vedic religion. The *sutras* deal with priestly matters, domestic rites, social duties, philosophy, magic, astronomy, etc. The *Dharma Sutras* deal with the questions of one's social duties. The *Laws of Manu* is the chief of the *Dharma Sutras*, and of ancient Hindu codes.

VEHICLE.
Q.v. Metaphor (12).

VENDIDAD.
One of the five parts of the *Avesta*, sacred scriptures of Zoroastrianism (*q.v.* 4).

VENN, JOHN. 1834–1923.
British logician. Born in Hull. Studied at Cambridge University. Professor of philosophy at Cambridge beginning in 1862. President of his college from 1903 until his death. Although devoting himself largely to inductive logic, he is known today for the so-called Venn Diagrams (*q.v.*), which exhibit deductive class relationships.

Principal writings: *Logic of Chance*, 1866 (3rd ed. 1888); *Some of the Characteristics of Belief*, 1870; *Symbolic Logic*, 1881 (2nd ed., 1894); *The Principles of Empirical or Inductive Logic*, 1889 (2nd ed., 1907).

(1) In the *Logic of Chance*, Venn pro-

vided the first careful statement of the frequency theory of probability (*q.v.*). (2) The book on symbolic logic is a survey of previous work done in this field. It called attention to the long neglected work of Frege (*q.v.*). (3) The work on inductive logic relies largely, although not uncritically, on the writings of Hamilton and Mill (*q.v.*).

VENN DIAGRAMS.
A more powerful way of representing class relationships than the Euler diagrams (*q.v.* Euler), this type of diagrammatic representation allows one to check the validity of syllogistic inferences by means of three overlapping circles, standing for the terms of the syllogism. The method was developed by John Venn (*q.v.*).

(1) The universal affirmative statement, *e.g.*, "All humans are mortal," appears in the diagram, as:

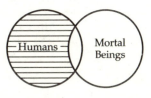

The crossed-out area is considered nonexistent so that the diagram tells us that no humans exist outside the class of mortal beings; hence all the humans there are, if any, fit within this class.

(2) The universal negative statement, *e.g.*, "No dogs are cats," requires us to cross out the overlapping area of our two classes:

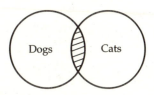

The diagram tells us that no elements exist in the overlapping area common to the two classes.

(3) The partial affirmative statement is diagrammed by placing an x in the appropriate area, meaning that there exists at least one member in this area, *e.g.*, "Some humans are intelligent."

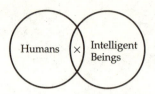

(4) The partial negative statement is also diagrammed by the appropriate placing of an "x," *e.g.*, "Some humans are not intelligent."

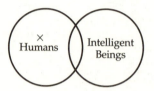

The diagram tells us that there exists at least one member of the class of humans outside the class of intelligent beings.

(5) The addition of a third overlapping circle in the following manner will allow us to check the validity of any syllogistic inference:

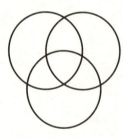

(6) A syllogism will be valid if, when we have diagrammed the two premises, the conclusion likewise appears, already diagrammed. And if the conclusion does not so appear, the inference is not valid.

Suppose the syllogism, "All humans are mortal; all patriarchs are humans; therefore, all patriarchs are mortal." We diagram the premises:

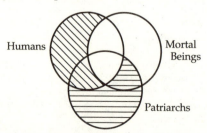

Upon examining the diagram it is clear that the conclusion, "All patriarchs are mortal," has been diagrammed by the joint action of the premises; *i.e.*, every portion of the class of patriarchs lying outside the class of mortal beings has been crossed out. All the patriarchs which exist are within the class of mortal beings.

Suppose the syllogism, "No humans are immortal; all Athenians are humans; therefore, no Athenians are immortal."

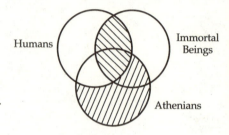

Once again it is clear that in diagramming the premises we have diagrammed the conclusion.

(7) It may be instructive to see that the conclusion does not follow diagrammatically from an invalid inference. Let our example of an obviously invalid inference be: "All dogs are mammals; all cats are mammals: therefore, all cats are dogs."

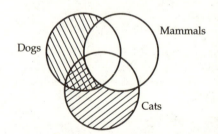

If the conclusion were now present in the diagram, there would be no clear area of the class "cats" lying outside the class "dogs." But this inference is invalid; the conclusion did not appear when we diagrammed the premises.

(8) All syllogisms have at least one universal premise, either affirmative or negative. When we turn to syllogisms in which one premise is universal, and the other particular or partial, we must accept two conventions in order to be able to complete our diagrams: (a) We must always diagram the universal premise

before we diagram the particular premise. (b) If, after we have diagrammed the universal premise, the "x" for the particular premise can be placed in either of two areas, it must be placed on the line between them.

Let us consider the syllogism, "No virtuous beings betray a trust; some Athenians are virtuous; therefore, some Athenians will not betray a trust."

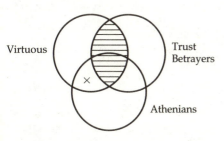

Diagramming the premises has given us the conclusion.

Similarly with the syllogism, "All bachelors are unmarried; some redheaded men are bachelors; therefore, some redheaded men are unmarried."

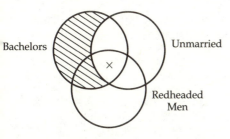

The conclusion appears when the premises are diagrammed.

There are cases, however, where the conclusion does not appear; and these inferences are not valid. "All congressmen are patriotic; some resident aliens are patriotic; therefore, some resident aliens are congressmen."

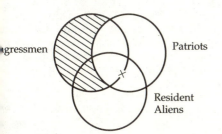

In this instance, even after we had diagrammed the universal premise, there were two areas in each of which the "x" representing the particular premise might appear. There being no unambiguous directive for the placing of the "x," our convention calls upon us to place it on the line between the two areas. Hence, the conclusion does not follow, and the syllogism is not valid.

VERA CAUSA.
Q.v. Causa.

VERIFIABILITY CRITERION.

A criterion of meaning derived from a theory of meaning elaborated initially in the Vienna Circle of Logical Positivists (*q.v.*). The verifiability of a sentence or proposition is regarded as a necessary condition of its having meaning. Unverifiable sentences or propositions are regarded as nonsense. The object of the criterion is to purify philosophy by eliminating meaningless assertions, such as those which they believed to abound in the field of metaphysics. Two general forms of the criterion emerged. The stronger form spoke simply of "verifiability," the weaker form insisted merely on "verifiability in principle."

(1) Schlick (*q.v.* 2) used the verifiability criterion in its strong sense. Concepts to be meaningful must be supported by operational evidence.

(2) Reichenbach (*q.v.* 2) utilized a weaker sense, suggesting that a proposition has meaning if a degree of probability can be determined for it.

(3) Carnap (*q.v.* 6) moved from the verifiability principle to the suggestion that a language be constructed which would disallow empty assertions. In place of "verifiability," however, he preferred to use the term "testability" or "confirmability."

(4) Popper (*q.v.* 1) shifted from the original position, holding "falsifiability" to be a more appropriate criterion than "verifiability."

(5) Ayer (*q.v.* 3–4), who did much to popularize the verifiability criterion in the English-speaking world, held the strong version in the first edition of *Language, Truth and Logic* (1936), and its weaker analogue in the preface to the 1946 revised edition of the same work.

(6) Quine (*q.v.* 6) opposes the criterion, arguing that the theory behind it supposes the individual synthetic statement to be the basic unit of meaning. It is his claim that this supposition is in error.

(7) Dummet (*q.v.* 5) links "verificationism" with holism in his discussions of theory of meaning.

VERIFICATION, DOCTRINE OF.
Q.v. Verifiability Criterion.

VERMUTUNGSEVIDENZ.
Q.v. Meinong (3).

VERSTEHEN.
From the German ("to understand").

(1) Dilthey (*q.v.* 2) found the type of thinking appropriate to the *Geisteswissenschaften* (*q.v.*), or sciences of the spirit, to be *Das Verstehen*, a noun formed from the active verb *verstehen*. *Das Verstehen* suggests greater participation on our part than does the normal substantive, *Das Verstand*. Dilthey finds empathy playing a role in the more individual experience of reality common to the *Geisteswissenschaften*, both in the humanities and in the social sciences.

(2) Rickert (*q.v.* 2) and Max Weber (*q.v.*) have followed, while expanding on, Dilthey's analysis. Rickert added valuation, and Weber "ideal types."

(3) For Heidegger (*q.v.* 5 and *passim*), every text is grounded in the question of the meaning of being (*sein*). For this reason hermeneutics and ontology come to the same point, which one discovers through the self-clarification of *Verstehen*. Beginning with *Dasein*, the process moves through *Seiendes* (individual beings) to their grounding in *Sein*. At the stage of *seiendes*, *verstehen* becomes an appreciation of the possibilities leading to authentic existence.

VESTAL VIRGINS.
Priestesses of a Roman cult, derived from Vesta—chief of the Roman household divinities and related to the hearthfire. While the organized cult lasted, 6–36 A.D., the Vestal Virgins were granted royal prerogatives.

VIA EMINENTIAE.
Latin phrase meaning "the way of eminence." In Maimonides (*q.v.* 3–4) and in Aquinas (*q.v.* 2), the positive way to the discovery of God.

VIA NEGATIONIS.
Latin phrase meaning "the negative way." In Maimonides (*q.v.* 2) and in Aquinas (*q.v.* 2), the negative way to the discovery of God. In this method, God's otherness from the universe means that he can be approached by negating the world; the negation of these characteristics allows us to gain some understanding of the divine nature.

VICENTE DE BEAUVAIS. c. 1190–c. 1264.
A member of the Dominican order and encyclopedist.

Principal writings: *Speculum triplex* (*Speculum doctrinale; Speculum historiale; Speculum naturale*); *On Institutions.*

(1) Although the completed encyclopedia, influential until the 17th century, was in four parts and titled *Speculum quadruplex* (four-part mirror), Vicente was author of no more than the first three parts.

(2) He seems to have been the first to use in conjunction the two phrases: *natura naturans* (nature naturing), the creative principle or God; and *natura naturata* (nature natured), the effect of God's creative act.

VICIOUS CIRCLE.
From the Latin *circulus vitiosus.*

(1) Applied to arguments, the term refers to the fallacy of *petitio principii* (*q.v.*) or arguing in a circle (*circulus in probando*), *i.e.*, assuming in the premises the conclusion one is expected to prove. The Greek term is *diallelus*. Also *q.v.* Fallacies (20).

(2) As applied to definitions, a vicious circle has occurred (*circulus in definiendo*) when the *definiens* of A is B, and that of B is A once again. The Greek term is *diallelon.*

(3) The phrase "vicious circle fallacy" is used by Russell and Whitehead for violations of their ramified theory of types (*q.v.* Type 4), and by Hermann Weyl for impredicative definitions (*q.v.* Paradox 8).

VICO, GIOVANNI BATISTA. 1668–1744.
Italian philosopher. Born in Naples. Taught at Naples. Vico introduced into philosophy the appreciation of history. He was a vigorous opponent of 17th-century rationalism and, especially, of Cartesianism.

Principal writings: *On the Method of the Studies of Our Time*, 1709; *On the Most*

Ancient Knowledge of the Italians, 1710; *Universal Right*, 3 vols., 1720–22; *Principles of a New Science* (T), 1725; 2nd rev. ed., 1730; 3rd rev. ed., 1744.

(1) Man understands only what he makes. Thus, the center of man's reality must be history. This he has made. God as the creator of the world also understands nature; but the Cartesian criterion of clear and distinct ideas in regard to nature cannot be considered a sign of man's having the truth.

(2) "Everything is history," but not all is disorder and caprice in history. There are historical laws controlling the larger movements of history. Each society moves from the age of gods through the age of heroes into the age of man. The style of society changes from theocratic to heroic to rational. The creations of a society reflect the age in which it finds itself. In the first two ages of mankind the typical form of expression is mythological. Myth gives expression to the history of the group as present in its customs. At the end of the cycle, by means of an unavoidable crisis and the destruction of the nation involved, a new age of the gods emerges and the cycle repeats itself.

(3) As Vico saw it, behind the rise and fall of nations there is an eternal ideal history, a Platonic relating of time to eternity, and through all of this there is the working of divine providence.

VICTORINES.

Q.v. Saint Victor, School of.

VIENNA CIRCLE OF LOGICAL POSITIVISTS.

A reform movement in philosophy centering in the University of Vienna in the 1920's and 1930's. The movement was directed toward the achievement of a scientific philosophy, and the elimination of pseudo-propositions, including the propositions of metaphysics.

(1) Vienna was an appropriate location for this movement for many reasons. A chair in the Philosophy of the Inductive Sciences had been established at the university in 1895 in the name of Ernst Mach (*q.v.*) who is, in fact, regarded as the spiritual father of the circle. But Vienna had also been the locus of many other anti-speculative intellectuals including

Bolzano (*q.v.*), Brentano (*q.v.*), Marty (*q.v.*), Meinong (*q.v.*), Höfler (*q.v.*), and of the conventionalism of Poincaré (*q.v.*) and Duhem (*q.v.*).

(2) By 1910 there was a group at Vienna impressed with the importance of Mach, while hopeful of complementing his work with that of Poincaré, Duhem, Schröder (*q.v.*), Hilbert (*q.v.*), Boltzmann and Einstein (*q.v.*). This group included Philipp Frank, Otto Neurath (*q.v.*), and Hans Hahn.

(3) By 1920 the group had become interested in the work of Wittgenstein (*q.v.*) as well as in the *Principia Mathematica* of Russell and Whitehead.

(4) In 1922, Moritz Schlick (*q.v.* 1) was named to the Mach chair of philosophy. At about the same time Carnap (*q.v.*) arrived at the university and the circle was complete, including—in addition to the foregoing—Herbert Feigl (*q.v.*), Kurt Gödel (*q.v.*), R. von Mises, and E. Schrödinger. A series of informal Thursday meetings with Schlick, attended by both philosophers and scientists, lent continuity to the group.

(5) Related to the circle were the Berlin group formed by Hans Reichenbach (*q.v.*), the Warsaw Circle of logicians including Tarski (*q.v.*), Łukasiewicz (*q.v.*), Kotarbinski (*q.v.*), and separate individuals such as Rougier (*q.v.*) in France.

(6) In 1929 the circle published a position paper titled *Wissenschaftliche Weltanschauung. Der Wiener Kreis* (Scientific World-view. The Vienna Circle). An international congress on scientific philosophy was held the same year. From 1930–39 the journal *Erkenntnis* was published as the organ of the group. The *Journal of Unified Science* was begun in 1939, and the *International Encyclopedia of Unified Science*, edited by Neurath, Carnap, and Charles Morris (*q.v.*), began its program of monograph publication. The latter was the organ of the Institute for the Unity of Science, established in 1936 in the Hague and later transferred to Boston with Philipp Frank.

(7) The group dispersed due to a number of factors: the assassination of Schlick in 1936; the Nazi *Anschluss*, and the war of 1939. Many members of the group, as well as its close associates, moved to the United States in this period. Rudolf Carnap went to Chicago,

Herbert Feigl to Minnesota, Philipp Frank to Harvard, Hans Reichenbach to U.C.L.A., Alfred Tarski to Berkeley, and Kurt Gödel to Princeton.

VIJNANA.

A Sanskrit term initially (in the early *Upanishads*) denoting both understanding and wisdom. Through time its meaning shifted to refer primarily to "perception," as over against *Jnana* (*q.v.*) which appropriated the two senses of understanding, especially in Buddhist thought. Among its applications is its role as a stream of perceptions in the five *skandhas* (*q.v.*), and the third member in the chain of Dependent Origination (*q.v.*). For Asanga (*q.v.*) the term is used to refer to a store of "seeds" of all natures, entering into awareness. *Q.v.* Buddha (2); Suzuki (4).

VIKALPA.

Q.v. Vasubandhu (2).

VINDICATION.

Q.v. Feigl (3).

VIOLENCE.

Q.v. Sorel (1).

VIRGIN MARY.

Q.v. Assumption of the Blessed Virgin Mary.

VIRTUE.

From the Latin *virtus* ("manliness"), paralleling the Greek term *arete* ("excellence"). Although the initial sense of the term included the meanings of "strength," "courage," and "excellence," an ethical signification quickly arose, and has remained central. In recent discussion "virtue" and "vice" have been largely replaced: in the singular by "good" and "evil," "right" and "wrong"; and in the plural by "values" and "disvalues."

(1) Socrates (*q.v.* 3) began the discussion by identifying virtue with knowledge, and holding that one could not know the good without likewise willing it.

(2) Plato (*q.v.* 5c) contributed an extensive and subtle analysis of four virtues: wisdom, courage, temperance, and justice.

(3) Aristotle (*q.v.* 11) made the distinction between intellectual and moral virtues, relating the former to the theoretical life and the latter to the practical life. Moral virtue, in his view, requires the

development of habits leading to the choice of the mean between extremes in conduct.

(4) Paul, the Apostle (*q.v.* 7), contributed the values of faith, hope, and charity or love as central to the Christian life. These were later termed the theological virtues.

(5) The Stoics treated the idea of virtue in a number of ways, at times identifying it with the divisions of philosophy, at times distinguishing between theoretical and practical virtue (*q.v.* Stoicism), and at times specifying individual virtues. Marcus Aurelius (*q.v.* 3) believed justice to be the foundation of all other virtues. He also held that justice is its own reward and the main source of human gratification. In each of these alternatives virtue is closely related to nature.

(6) It was St. Ambrose (*c.* 340–397) who introduced the term "cardinal virtues" after reading of Plato's classification in the writings of Cicero.

(7) St. Augustine (*q.v.* 12) retained the cardinal virtues of Plato while insisting that love is the fundamental source of all virtue.

(8) Throughout the Middle Ages Christian moralists spoke of the "seven virtues," adding to the cardinal virtues the "theological virtues" of faith, hope, and charity or love (*q.v.* Aquinas 8).

(9) Hobbes (*q.v.* 8) believed that the moral virtues were founded in the desire for peace, which is a law of nature. He cited "justice, gratitude, modesty, equity, mercy" as being so founded, along with "the rest of the laws of nature." Perhaps inconsistently, he also viewed the moral virtues as "inconstant names" changing with each speaker.

(10) Geulincx (*q.v.* 3) held the cardinal virtues to be diligence, obedience, justice, and humility.

(11) Spinoza (*q.v.* 4–5) returned partway to the initial meaning of virtue, regarding man's primordial virtue to be the effort to conserve one's being; the development of that virtue requires one to live in conformity with reason.

(12) Locke (*q.v.* 9) held that virtue and vice are the approbation or dislike, the praise or blame, of individual societies.

(13) Malebranche (*q.v.* 5) regarded the love of order as the basis of all moral virtue.

(14) Montesquieu (*q.v.* 8) looked upon the love of law and country as the defining characteristic of political virtue, from which in turn all other virtues can be derived.

(15) Voltaire (*q.v.* 2) looked upon virtue in social, rather than personal, terms, having to do with the good of others.

(16) Rousseau (*q.v.* 7), along with a number of other 18th-century thinkers, reverted to one of the basic Stoic positions, where virtue is identified with following nature.

(17) Virtue for Kant (*q.v.* 7–8) related to those duties which are "firmly settled" in our characters. It concerned not happiness, but our worthiness to be happy. It is its own end and reward, although God's task, in one sense, is that of making commensurate, if not in this life then in another, human virtue and human happiness.

Also *q.v.* Ethics.

VISCHER, FREDERICK T. 1807–1887.
German philosopher. Born in Ludwigsburg. Educated at Tübingen. Taught at Tübingen, Zurich, and Stuttgart. Specializing in aesthetics, his basic work in the field is Hegelian, defining beauty as "the ideal in the form of limited appearance," and deriving, *e.g.*, the beautiful, comic, and sublime in dialectical fashion. In later life he treated the Hegelian ideal of wholeness as an unattainable ideal, and his aesthetic analysis became more empirical.

Principal writings: *Aesthetics or the Science of Beauty*, 6 vols., 1847–58; *On the Relation Between Content and Form in Art*, 1858; *The Beautiful and Art* (ed. R. Vischer), 1898.

VIŚEṢA (VISHESHA).
Q.v. Vaiśeṣika (1).

VIS INSITA.
Latin term meaning "the innate force of matter." *Q.v.* Newton (2).

VIṢNU (VISHNU).
Hindu God. Center of worship in the great Vaishnava or Vishnuite sect of Hinduism (*q.v.* 5c). In the Hindu *trimurti*, or trinity, Vishnu is the preserver where Brahma creates and Shiva destroys. In the *Vedas* initially a relatively unimportant sun god, his importance increased to the point where he is said to have had many incarnations, among them Krishna (*q.v.*), Rama (*q.v.*), and Buddha (*q.v.*). The sect can count many famous men among its leaders: *e.g.*, Ramanuja (*q.v.*) and Ramananda (*q.v.*). *Bhakti*, or devotion, is the defining characteristic of the Vaishnava sect. Also *q.v.* Trinity (17); Vaiṣnavism (1–2).

VIṢNUISM (VISHNUISM).
Hindu sect. *Q.v.* Vaiṣnavism (1–2); Viṣnu; Hinduism (5c).

VISPERED.
One of the five parts of the *Avesta*, sacred scriptures of Zoroastrianism (*q.v.* 4).

VITALISM.
The name given to that interpretation of biological phenomena (*q.v.* Biology 1–3) which assumes the presence of some force or principle within the organism not reducible to the categories of physics and chemistry. In the case of Hans Driesch (*q.v.*) the vital force is said to be a directing and supporting Entelechy (*q.v.*). Many philosophers have held that this reduction cannot be made, among them Antoine Cournot (*q.v.* 4).

VITORIA, FRANCISCO DE. c. 1492–1546.
Spanish philosopher. Born in Vitoria. Educated in Burgos and Paris. Taught at Salamanca. A member of the Dominican order, he is recognized both as an important theorist of the Counter-Reformation, and as the founder of international law.

Principal writings: *Theological Lectures* (T), 1528–40; *Commentaries on the "Secunda Secundae" of Saint Thomas*, 1557.

(1) Since every nation has the right to existence and independence, it is proper to act in support of that right. A war waged in support of that right, a defensive war, is therefore just. In addition, a nation has a right to intervene when a weaker nation is attacked by a stronger, or when a nation has fallen under the sway of a domestic tyrant.

(2) With respect to Spanish rule in the "Indies," he held that a nation incapable of self-rule may be ruled by another until the capacity for self-rule has been developed. The conditions for trusteeship include humane treatment of the subject peoples.

(3) He believed that an international

community of nations, consisting of all the nations of the world, Christian and non-Christian, is in existence and is governed by international law. The *Jus Gentium* is a blend of natural law, positive law, and the treaties they have made among themselves. Part of this international law is that all nations have juridical equality.

VIVES, JUAN LUIS. 1492–1540.
Spanish philosopher. Born in Valencia. Educated at the University of Paris. Taught at Louvain. In 1523 he visited Oxford University and was made Doctor of Laws. One of the Renaissance humanists, Vives was a close friend of Erasmus. As a humanist he stressed the utility of the arts, seeking their revitalization and reform, and, as a rhetorician, the subordination of rhetoric to philosophy. Anti-Aristotelian in that he felt a false Aristotelianism had descended upon all the disciplines, his philosophy was eclectic, drawing on Aristotle, Plato, and the Stoics as well as more recent influences.
Principal writings: *Against the Pseudo-Dialecticians*, 1520; *On the Truth of the Christian Faith*, 1528; *On the Causes of Corruption in the Arts*, 1531; *On Education* (T), 1531; *On the Soul and Life*, 1538.

VOCATION.
From the Latin *vocare* ("to call").
(1) The term derives from the Christian tradition. Men are "called" to be saints and they are "called" to the position in life which is theirs.
(2) Fichte (*q.v.* 7) used the term more broadly, holding that our human vocation is to build an ethical world culture.
(3) Ortega (*q.v.* 3) treated vocation in more personal terms as that vital program in pursuit of which one becomes his authentic self.

VOID.
Q.v. Democritus (1–2); Epicurus (3); Gassendi (4). For Eastern concepts of the void, *q.v.* the thinkers and schools listed under *Śunya* and Emptiness.

VOLKELT, JOHANNES. 1848–1930.
German philosopher. Born in Lipnik, Galicia. Taught at Leipzig. Beginning as an Hegelian, he became a neo-Kantian. His thesis that reality is the self-realiza-

tion of absolute value is strikingly similar to the thesis of the Heidelberg School of neo-Kantianism (*q.v.* neo-Kantianism 4).
Principal writings: *Kant's Theory of Knowledge Analyzed into its Basic Principles*, 1879; *A System of Aesthetics*, 3 vols., 1905, 1910, 1914; *Certainty and Truth*, 1918; *Phenomenology and the Metaphysics of Time*, 1925; *The Problem of Individuality*, 1928.

VOLONTÉ GÉNÉRALE.
Q.v. The General Will.

VOLSKI, STANISLAW. 1880–c.1936.
Russian philosopher. Educated at Moscow. Developing a philosophy of struggle in which good is identified with all that increases struggle, and evil with all that diminishes it, Volski held socialism to be "freedom of struggle," and regarded the "friend-enemies" with whom one struggles for life and death as most essential and precious to oneself.
Principal writings: *The Philosophy of Struggle*, 1909; *The Social Revolution in the West and in Russia*, 1917.

VOLTAIRE, FRANÇOIS MARIE AROUET DE. 1694–1778.
French philosopher. Born in Paris. Educated at Louis-le-Grand. A prominent writer and social critic, he was associated with the 18th-century *Philosophes*. He was imprisoned twice for his beliefs, spent three years in England, and many years outside France, first in Lorraine and then in Geneva in semi-exile. At the end of his life he returned to Paris where he was warmly greeted by the people in an astonishing series of triumphs. Those who knew him best said of him that work was necessary for his very existence. It was his practice to work 18 to 20 hours per day, writing often in bed, taking no regular hours for food or sleep. In one of the rare departures from his usual urbanity Voltaire attacked the crudities of Shakespearian tragedy defending, against its formlessness, the purity of French neo-Classicism.
Principal writings: *Philosophical Letters* (T), 1734: *Elements of Newton's Philosophy*, 1738; *Essay on the Customs and Spirit of the Nations*, 1756; *Candide* (T), 1759; *Treatise on Toleration* (T), 1763 *Philosophical Dictionary* (T), 1764; *The Philosophy of History* (T), 1766.

(1) Born to an age in which the spread of knowledge was highly cherished by the educated both for itself, and for its results, Voltaire lived an urbane, skeptical, humanitarian and literary existence characterized by passionate dedication both to his work, and to the cause of humanity, as he understood it. He fought the battle against intolerance of every variety, having allegedly coined the famous credo of the latitudinarian: "I don't believe a word you say, but I'll defend to the death your right to say it." Too skeptical to adhere to any systematic philosophy, or to provide one, his ideas sometimes shifting, he believed the most satisfactory approach to the world to result from a combination of skepticism concerning ultimate questions, and moral activity in behalf of humanity.

(2) Ethics rests on self-love and justice. Self-love, or self-preservation, as one's exclusive motive is bad. But there is a natural sense of justice deriving from a love of order which humans naturally possess. It defines virtue and has to do with the good of others. History is a battle between these two forces, qualified by the influence of climate, government, and religion. History moves by means of the embodiment of ideas. Ideas, hence, change the world. And, generally, progress does occur, even though it does not occur inevitably.

(3) Evidences of design convinced Voltaire that a Supreme Being does exist as creator and governor of the natural and moral worlds. He found convincing both the argument by analogy which proceeds from the order of a watch to the order of nature, and the first cause argument which rests on the denial of an infinite series of causes. But he found it impossible for man to know God's nature, or whether God is just, unjust, cruel, or kind. His position was, in general, deistic; and God assumes a deistic role as cause of a universe controlled by law, and not requiring intervention.

(4) With respect to human nature, the position consistent with such a universe, and a position held by Voltaire, is that freedom in the sense of willing without a cause is a contradiction in terms. Our will is determined by the laws of the universe, and causes which have played upon the individual; but individuals are free so long as they can carry out their wishes. Humans have the "power of doing what they choose." They do not have the power of "election without reason, without any other motive than that of free will."

(5) Concerning one's fate it is just not possible to know if the soul is immortal or mortal. It is possible to know that there are evils in the world of sufficient magnitude that they must affect our understanding of our position in the world. The Lisbon earthquake of 1775 was one such evil, and led Voltaire to write *Candide*, in parody of Leibniz' claim that ours is "the best of all possible worlds." On the contrary, it seemed to Voltaire that either man is born guilty and God is punishing him, or God is indifferent to his creatures. And he tended to find the latter the more plausible explanation.

Also *q.v.* Meslier (1).

VOLUNTARISM.

From the Latin *voluntas* ("will"). The term was introduced by F. Tönnies in 1883 in a study of Spinoza. Tönnies was concerned to contrast then-current doctrines with the intellectualism of 17th-century rationalism. Quickly adopted by others, *e.g.*, Wundt and Paulsen (*cf.* below), voluntarism is the doctrine that the will has primacy over the intellect. It stands in contrast to intellectualism or rationalism, and has been advanced as a metaphysical, psychological, ethical, epistemological, and theological doctrine by different thinkers at different times.

(1) St. Augustine (*q.v.* 11–12), combining Greek intellectualism with the Christian emphasis on faith and love, made the latter primary, thus increasing the importance of the will (both human and divine) in all of the areas cited above.

(2) Avicebron (*q.v.* 3), an 11th-century Jewish philosopher, held the divine will, proceeding from God, to be the creator and sustainer of the world.

(3) Duns Scotus (*q.v.* 11–13) emphasized the divine will as the source and sanction of morality, and the primacy of the human will as the explanation of human freedom.

(4) William of Ockham (*q.v.* 6, 13–15) explained the similarities in things, the contingency characterizing the order of nature as well as the order of grace, and

the moral law by the action of the divine will. As with Scotus, the primacy of man's will guarantees man's freedom.

(5) Thomas Hobbes (*q.v.* 6–7), explaining human behavior in terms of desire and aversion, may be taken as an instance of psychological voluntarism.

(6) Even Descartes (*q.v.* 7), an avowed rationalist, explained error as occurring in those cases where the will becomes dominant, outrunning human reason. He likewise saw human freedom as deriving from the will.

(7) Hume (*q.v.* 6) may be regarded as a voluntarist in his psychological and ethical position. Regarding reason as the slave of the passions, both ethics and political theory stem from the emotive side of life.

(8) Although Kant's (*q.v.* 11) major reputation rests on the achievements of his *Critique of Pure Reason*, his initial program was designed to show the primacy of the practical reason; and certainly for Kant ethical judgment depends upon the moral will. He was at the very least an ethical voluntarist, and his general program encouraged other philosophers to develop his general stance.

(9) Fichte (*q.v.* 1), for example, strengthened the Kantian emphasis on the practical reason. In his idealism of the moral will all philosophical decisions are made in terms of the will's requirements.

(10) Maine de Biran (*q.v.* 1) stressed psychological voluntarism in his philosophy of Spiritualism.

(11) Schopenhauer (*q.v.* 2–4), starting from Kant, ended with a view in which the will, although "blind," is the dominant feature of the universe, including in its dominion both human reason and sensation.

(12) Max Stirner (*q.v.* 1) is likewise among those who hold to the primacy of the will over the reason.

(13) Wilhelm Wundt (*q.v.* 1, 5) held spirit to be the fundament of matter, the psychic to be more basic than the physical, and the sciences of spirit and culture to be irreducible to natural science.

(14) William James (*q.v.* 8–10) brought together the emphases of Renouvier (*q.v.*), likewise considered a voluntarist, and a psychology similar to but developed beyond the associationalism of Bain (*q.v.*), presenting a philosophy which is volun-

taristic psychologically, ethically, and metaphysically.

(15) Paulsen (*q.v.*) held to a voluntarism in which man's will is the force of the universe become conscious.

(16) The voluntarism of Bergson (*q.v.* 4–5), stressing human freedom, the primacy of intuition, regarding matter as effete spirit, and finding an *élan vital* as the source of the dynamism of the world is at once metaphysical, epistemological, psychological, and ethical.

VON MISES, RICHARD.
Q.v. Probability (10); Vienna Circle or Logical Positivists (4).

VON NEUMANN, JOHN.
Q.v. Set Theory (11).

VRANICKI, PREDRAG.
Q.v. Praxis (7, 10).

VULGATE.
The generic name given to Latin translations of the Bible and more particularly to the translation of Jerome dating from the 4th century. Jerome's translation received the official sanction of the Roman Church; it was the first book produced from movable type, and the basis of Wycliffe's English translation.

WAHLE, RICHARD. 1857–1935.
Austrian philosopher-psychologist. Born and educated in Vienna. Taught at Vienna and Czernowitz.

Principal writings: *The Whole of Philosophy and its End,* 1894; *On the Mechanism of the Spiritual Life,* 1906; *The Tragi-Comedy of Wisdom,* 1915; *Cheerful Catalogue of the Few Philosophical Truths,* 1934.

(1) Developing the positivism and empirio-criticism of Mach (*q.v.*) and Avenarius (*q.v.*), Wahle arrived at a "philosophy of occurrences" in which the "given" is made up of neutral, self-dependent images and ideas.

(2) He believed that his epistemological position—"antisubjectivist product-objectivism" or "agnostic product-realism"

—allowed him to avoid dualisms of the subject-object or materialist-idealist type.

WAISMANN, FRIEDRICH. 1896–1959.
Austrian-English philosopher. Born in Vienna. Educated at Vienna and Cambridge. Taught at Cambridge. Assistant to Schlick in Vienna. He moved to Cambridge to study with Wittgenstein. Beginning as a logical positivist committed to mathematical rigor and formalism under Wittgenstein, Waismann changed to the view that linguistic methods held more promise in dealing with the problems of philosophy. Like Wittgenstein, he believed that philosophy has to do with the clarification of thought. His later writings were in English.
Principal writings: *Introduction to Mathematical Thinking* (T), 1936; *The Principles of Linguistic Philosophy* (ed. R. Harré), 1965; *How I See Philosophy* (ed. R. Harré), 1968.

WALLACE, ALFRED R. 1823–1913.
English naturalist. Born at Usk (Monmouthshire). Self-educated. He spent four years on the Amazon and eight in the Malay Archipelago observing and collecting plant and animal life. In February, 1858, there suddenly "flashed" before his mind the "idea of the survival of the fittest." Writing out the hypothesis, he sent it to Darwin (*q.v.*) who generously had it read, along with an abstract of his own views, at a meeting of the Linnaean Society in July, 1858. Thereafter, Wallace was second only to Darwin in championing the theory of natural selection.
Principal writings: *Contributions to the Theory of Natural Selection*, 1871; *Darwinism*, 1889; *Man's Place in the Universe*, 1903; *The World of Life*, 1910.

WALTZ, DAVID.
Q.v. Artificial Intelligence (4).

WANG CH'UNG. c. 27–100.
Chinese philosopher. Regarded as one of the three geniuses of his age. Although his metaphysics is Taoistic, Wang Ch'ung is usually not identified with any school, or is regarded as a member of the Miscellaneous School. In fact the dominant Confucian philosophy had sunk into a superstition which he devoted his energies to combat. The result was a natu-

ralistic philosophy. Against the reading of portents he insisted that fortune and misfortune are due to chance, prodigies occur spontaneously, the world has no teleology, heaven takes no action, and humans do not become ghosts after death.
Principal writings: *The Balanced Inquiries* (T in part).
(1) To be intelligent, wise, and good is to have an unimpaired organism. Humanity, righteousness, propriety, wisdom, and faithfulness—the five constant virtues—relate to heart, liver, stomach, lungs, and kidneys. When these become diseased the virtues become enfeebled. At death they have nothing to which to attach.
(2) Death is like the extinction of a fire. The vital force is gone, and only the body remains. One need not, then, fear the dead.
(3) Nor is it possible for us by obedience to influence heaven, any more than it would be possible for a cricket by obedience to alter the crack in which it hides.
(4) The truth is that nature operates spontaneously, giving forth and distributing a material force, but without either purpose or intelligence.

WANG FU-CHIH. 1619–1692.
A Chinese materialistic philosopher, native of Hunan, he lived at the time the Manchus were breaking up the Ming Dynasty. Having passed the civil service examination, and receiving his first degree in 1642, he raised an army to fight the Manchus who were invading his native province of Hunan. Defeated, he retired at 33, devoting the next 40 years to his writings. Forgotten for centuries, many of his writings were published only in the middle of the 19th century. His philosophy is similar to that of Chang Tsai (*q.v.*), whose successor he may be said to be.
Principal writings: *Surviving Works of Wang Fu-Chih.*
(1) Rejecting both rationalistic and idealistic neo-Confucianism, Wang assimilated principle to material force, as its order or arrangement. Consequently, other abstractions, such as the great ultimate, and the principle of nature, must also be interpreted in terms of force. Taoist non-being also disappears; he dismisses the notion on logical grounds; and

"the world consists only of concrete things," but every concrete thing has its principle within it.

(2) The universe is a continuous process of production and reproduction containing an intermingling of the elements of *Yin* and *Yang*, renewing the force and principle of the universe, resulting in progress.

WANG PI. 225–249.

Chinese philosopher. A neo-Taoist, Wang Pi served as minister in the Wei government. Substituting "principle" for "destiny" this philosopher anticipated the neo-Confucianists (*q.v.* Chinese Philosophy 7). He introduced the concept of original non-being as transcending all distinctions, the unity underlying all phenomena, and in accord with principle.

Principal writings: *Commentaries on the Book of Changes* and the *Lao Tzu* (T in part).

(1) Behind all distinctions, descriptions, and modes of being, is the original non-being. This is the pure being and original substance. All being originated from non-being.

(2) Once originated, the *Tao* develops, controls, and completes all things with due regard to their substance and function.

(3) But the sage must discern that the unity in all this multiplicity is due to their common relation to non-being. In relating oneself to absolute tranquility and vacuity, heaven and earth are revealed.

WANG YANG-MING. 1472–1529.

Chinese philosopher. Born in Chekiang. In 1492 he gained the "Recommended Person" degree and in 1499 the "Presented Scholar" degree. He occupied numerous administrative posts commendably, one of which involved the establishment of schools. A neo-Confucian, his influence became dominant in China during his lifetime and for 150 years thereafter. Posthumously he was awarded the titles of Marquis, and Wench'eng (Completion of Culture). In 1584 he was offered sacrifice in the Confucian temple by imperial decree.

Principal writings: *Inquiry on the Great Learning* (T); *Instructions for Practical Living* (T).

(1) Opposing Chu Hsi's (*q.v.*) view that the "investigation of things" is primary,

Wang Yang-Ming held that principle exists within the mind and that therefore development of the sincerity of the will should precede the investigation of things.

(2) He held that every man has an innate knowledge of the good, and that knowledge is the beginning of action, or action the completion of knowledge. In any event he insisted upon the unity of knowledge and action.

(3) The unity between the mind of man and the whole of nature is so exact that either without the other is vacuous: "Before you look at these flowers, they and your mind are in the state of silent vacancy. As you come to look at them their colors at once show up clearly."

WARD, JAMES. 1843–1925.

English philosopher and psychologist. Born at Hull in Yorkshire; educated at Cambridge where he also taught.

Principle writings: *The Relation of Physiology to Psychology*, 1875; *Naturalism and Agnosticism*, 2 vols., 1899; *The Realm of Ends*, 1911; *Psychological Principles*, 1918; *A Study of Kant*, 1922; *Essays in Philosophy* (ed. Sorley and Stout), 1927.

(1) Adopting a genetic approach to psychology (in contrast with associationalism), Ward offered the concept of a "psychoplasm"—a presentational continuum within which presentations take place—distinguishing three phases in the process from sensation to idea: (a) a sensory stage involving the differentiation, retention, and assimilation of presentations; (b) an integrative stage where sensations become percepts; (c) the emergence of a derivative continuum of images complete with "memory threads" and "ideational tissue."

(2) Dividing mental experience into three types—cognitive, affective, and conative—Ward held that we have only an inferred knowledge of ourselves as subject, our feelings, and our acts of attention.

(3) His general orientation was to a theistic Idealism resting on a panpsychic and pluralistic view of the world.

WAR, JUST.

Q.v. Vitoria (1).

WARRANTED ASSERTIBILITY.
Q.v. Dewey (3).

WARREN, AUSTIN.
Q.v. New Criticism.

WARSAW CIRCLE.
A group of philosophers centered in Warsaw and Lvov, similar to the Vienna Circle of Logical Positivists (*q.v.*) and sustaining relations with the latter group. Many of the members of the group were disciples of Kazimierz Twardowski (*q.v.*). Among those in the group may be counted Łukasiewicz (*q.v.*), Leśniewski (*q.v.*), Zawirski (1882–1948), Tarski (*q.v.*), Chwistek (*q.v.*), and Kotarbinski (*q.v.*).

WATSON, J.B. 1878–1958.
American psychologist. Born in Greenville, South Carolina. Educated at the University of Chicago. Taught at Johns Hopkins. The founder of Behavioral Psychology, Watson rejected all introspection, restricting psychological data to the direct results of observation and laboratory experiment. Consciousness, purpose, and the concept of mind were ruled out by his behavioristic method.
Principal writings: *Behavior*, 1914; *Psychology from the Standpoint of a Behaviorist*, 1919; *Behaviorism*, 1924; *The Ways of Behaviorism*, 1928.

WATSUJI TETSURO. 1889–1960.
Japanese philosopher. Born in Himeji. Taught at Kyoto. Although influenced by Husserl and Heidegger, his major contribution was a system of ethics, or *rinri*, based on the companionship (*rin*) of man to man, family, and society.
Principal writings: *Ethics As Anthropology*, 1931; *History of Japanese Ethical Thought*, 1952.

WAVE MECHANICS.
Q.v. Mechanics (2).

WAYLAND, FRANCIS. 1796–1865.
American philosopher. Born in New York City. Educated at Union College and Andover Theological Seminary. A Baptist minister, he served as president of Brown University for twenty-eight years. Basically a member of the Scottish School of Common-Sense Realism, his ethics was deontological (*q.v.* Deontology) rather than Utilitarian (*q.v.*).

Principal writings: *Elements of Moral Science*, 1835; *Elements of Intellectual Philosophy*, 1854.

WEALTH, GOSPEL OF.
Q.v. Social Darwinism (3).

WEBER, ALFRED. 1868–1958.
German sociologist. Born in Erfurt. The younger brother of Max Weber. Studied in Berlin and Prague. Taught at Heidelberg. Distinguishing the "civilization process" from the "culture process," he regarded the former as cumulative and continuous, while the latter is sporadic, discontinuous, and unpredictable. Not subject to analysis in terms of causal law, culture derives from man's "immanent transcendence."
Principal writings: *Principles of Culture-Sociology* (T), 1920–1; *Cultural History as Culture-Sociology*, 1935; *The Tragic and History*, 1943.

WEBER, ERNST.
Q.v. Fechner (1); Psychology (4); Weber-Fechner Law.

WEBER-FECHNER LAW.
A psychophysical law (S = C log R) according to which the intensity of sensation (S) is equal to the logarithm of its stimulus (R) given a constant (C). Deriving from work of E.H. Weber (1795–1878) and Gustav Fechner (*q.v.* 1), the law formalizes the experienced fact that stimuli and sensations do not increase and decrease in simple direct proportionality, but rather in the complex manner expressed above.

WEBER, MAX. 1864–1920.
German sociologist. Born in Erfurt. The older brother of Alfred Weber. Taught in Berlin, Freiburg, Heidelberg, and Munich. Sustaining relations to the Heidelberg School as well as other movements of neo-Kantianism (*q.v.* Neo-Kantianism 4, 6), Weber held that the object of sociological study is the discovery of essences within history. He called these rational constructions of the historian, *ideal types*. Though constructions, they are not falsifications, and provide an important key to the understanding of a given period. An *ideal type* is a type of person shaped in a certain manner due to the influences of social organization

and historical conditioning. Weber did his work in the sociology of religion, and was interested in the relations between religion and the economic and social conditions playing upon it. Along with Dilthey and Rickert, he applied the concept of Verstehen (*q.v.*) to the social sciences. He believed that *verstehen* should be linked to causal explanation in order to reduce its tendency to subjective bias.

Principal writings: *Capitalism and the Protestant Ethic* (T), 1904–5; *The Economic Ethic of the World Religions*, 1915; *Economy and Society* (T), 1922; translated selections from his writings are included in *From Max Weber: Essays in Sociology* (trans. Gerth and Mills), 1946; and *On the Methodology of the Social Sciences* (trans. Shils and Finch), 1949.

WEIGEL, VALENTIN. 1533–1588.
German mystic. Born in Grossenhain. A Lutheran minister, Weigel was influenced by Sebastian Franck, Paracelsus (*q.v.*), and the Friends of God (*q.v.*). His writings distinguished between inauthentic and authentic knowledge. The former is based on sense-perception and the latter on internal reflection which provides knowledge of self, world, and God. The latter alternative involves mystical illumination and the action of God on the human soul. Some of his writings were in German, and others in Latin.

Principal writings: *The Two Useful Treatises* (G), 1570; *The Little Book of the Beatific Life* (L), 1571; *Apology* (G), 1572; *The Basic Commentary on Faith* (G), 1576; *On the Life of Christ* (G), 1578; *Dialogue on Christianity* (L), 1584.

WEIL, SIMONE. 1909–1943.
French philosopher-mystic. Born in Paris. Educated at École Normale Supérieure in Paris. Concerned with the conflict between the sacred expectations of the person and the mechanical necessities of the universe and indeed, of modern industry, Weil finds her answer in "decreation," the systematic relinquishment of individuality in mystic experience.

Principal writings: *Gravity and Grace* (T), 1946; *The Need for Roots* (T), 1949; *Waiting for God* (T), 1950; *Letter to a Priest* (T), 1951; *Notebooks*, 3 vols., (2 in trans.), 1951–6; *Pre-Christian Intuitions* (T in part), 1951; *Oppression and Liberty* (T), 1955; *On Sci-*ence, *Necessity and the Love of God* (T), 1968

WEISS, PAUL. 1901– .
American philosopher. Born in New York City. Educated at City College and Harvard. Taught at Bryn Mawr, Yale, and Catholic University. Founder of the Metaphysical Society of America and the *Review of Metaphysics*. A metaphysician in the grand style, it is Weiss' central insight that reality consists of four modes of being whose interrelations provide the structure and function of the cosmos. The modes—actuality, ideality, existence, and God—cannot be collapsed into each other either ontologically or in interpretation. Inadequate philosophies tend to concentrate on one or another mode; but adequacy requires the exploration of each of the modes as well as their interplay and togetherness. In social philosophy the same design is evident. Everything is said in relation to everything else, and nothing that needs to be said is left unsaid.

Principal writings: *Nature of Systems* 1929; *The Collected Papers of Charles Peirce* 6 vols., (ed. with C. Hartshorne), 1931–5; *Reality*, 1938; *Nature and Man*, 1947; *Man's Freedom*, 1950; *Philosophy in Process* 11 vols., 1955–89; *Modes of Being*, 1958; *Our Public Life*, 1959; *Nine Basic Arts* 1961; *The World of Art*, 1961; *Religion and Art*, 1963; *The God We Seek*, 1964; *Sport; a Philosophic Inquiry*, 1969; *Beyond All Appearances*, 1974; *Cinematics*, 1975; *First Considerations*, 1977; *You, I, and the Others*, 1980; *Privacy*, 1983; *Toward a Perfected State*, 1986; *Creative Ventures*, 1992.

WEISSE, CHRISTIAN H. 1801–1866.
German philosopher. Born and educated in Leipzig. Taught at Leipzig. Initially Hegelian, he became disenchanted with the pantheism and abstract intellectualism of that philosophy, and with Fichte' son (Immanuel Hermann Fichte, 1796–1879) constructed a system called "speculative theism." The point of the system was to avoid identifying God with the Absolute. Revelation and history were allowed a role in philosophical thinking about the divine. Man was viewed as a free, finite person whose center is the infinite Person of God.

Principal writings: *The Idea of the Divine*, 1833; *Main Features of Metaphysics*

1835; *Dogmatic Philosophy, or the Philosophy of Christianity*, 3 vols., 1855–62; *Psychology and Doctrine of Immortality*, 1869.

WELBY, LADY V.
   Q.v. Semiotic (6).

WELLEK, RENÉ.
   Q.v. New Criticism.

WELLS, H.G.
   Q.v. Utopia (9); Socialism (7).

WELTANSCHAUNG.
   From the German, meaning "world view."
   (1) Dilthey (*q.v.* 5), finding world-views (*Weltanschaungen*) to be a composite of factual beliefs, value-judgments, and ultimate goals, established a *Weltanschaungslehre* (teaching or doctrine about world-views). Each world-view makes thought, feeling, or will basic to its system and develops the appropriate categories to express its interpretation of life.
   (2) Mannheim (*q.v.*) distinguished between partial and total ideology, equating the latter with the *Weltanschaung* of an age or of a concrete historico-social group.

WERTHEIMER, MAX. 1880–1943.
   Czechoslovakian psychologist. Born in Prague. Taught at Frankfurt, Berlin, and later in the United States. Along with Koffka (*q.v.*) and Köhler (*q.v.*), the founder of Gestalt Psychology. The three worked together at Frankfurt, and collaboration with Köhler continued at Berlin, Wertheimer was led by his studies of the perception of movement to the view that we directly experience complex structures.
   Principal writings: *Three Essays on Gestalt Theory*, 1925; *Productive Thinking* (E), 1945.

WESENWILLE.
   Q.v. Ferdinand Tönnies (1).

WESLEY, CHARLES. 1707–1788.
   English religious leader. Born at Epworth Rectory. Educated at Oxford. Along with his brother John (*q.v.*), the founder of Methodism (*q.v.*). Although John became the dominant figure of the movement, Oxford Methodism began when Charles by his own account "awoke out of his lethargy" and persuaded oth-

ers to begin to take more seriously the religious life, holding weekly meetings of self-examination. As his brother became the organizer of the movement, Charles became its hymnodist, writing some 6,500 hymns in all, "the great hymn-writer of all ages."

WESLEY, JOHN. 1703–1791.
   English religious leader. Born in Epworth. Educated at Oxford. Along with his brother, Charles (*q.v.*), the founder of Methodism (*q.v.*), he quickly became its central figure. Although John had participated in the Holy Club at Oxford, where Methodism began, and had formed a religious society in Georgia in 1736, it was the reading of Luther's *Preface to the Epistle to the Romans*, in a 1738 London meeting in Aldersgate Street which led him to trust in "Christ alone" for salvation, and he received in that moment "the faith whereby alone we are saved." As a consequence, his preaching gained a new authority, and his life merged with the history of Methodism. Working initially in London and Bristol, in 1747 he made the first of 47 journeys to Ireland. In 1751 he made the first of 22 visits to Scotland. Throughout his life he was perfecting the Methodist organization, and presiding over a growing movement kept harmonious by the force of his personality.
   Principal writings: *Memoirs of John Wesley*, 3 vols., 1791; *Sermons* (4 vols.): *Doctrine of Original Sin, Appeals to Men of Reason and Religion, Plain Account of Christian Perfection, Plain Account of the People Called Methodists*, all in his *Works*, 14 vols., 1829–31; *Journal of John Wesley*, 8 vols., 1909–16.

WESTERMARCK, EDWARD A. 1862–1939.
   Finnish philosopher. Born in Helsinki. Educated at the University of Helsinki. Taught at London, Helsinki, and Abo. Influenced by J.S. Mill and Spencer, Westermarck dedicated himself to careful historical studies of morality and of the institution of marriage. His books were written in English.
   Principal writings: *The Origin and Development of the Moral Ideas*, 2 vols., 1906–8; *Ethical Relativity*, 1932; *Christianity and Morals*, 1939.
   (1) Arguing against ethical objectivity

in all of its forms from intuitionism to Kantian formalism, Westermarck proposed ethical relativism or ethical subjectivism as the basis of ethics. Ethical judgments in his view derive from attitudes of approval and disapproval, and rest on human emotions. Such judgments gain a rational appearance, even the appearance of being objective truths, by means of an "objectivizing" tendency in humans, which becomes solidified in custom.

(2) He observed that while the good derives from attitudes of approval, the right develops from attitudes of disapproval.

(3) Religiously, he adopted the position of agnosticism, and found Christianity harmful in moral terms. He believed relativism, however, helpful in the sense of extending human tolerance.

WESTMINSTER ASSEMBLY.
Q.v. Westminster Confession.

WESTMINSTER CONFESSION.
A confession of faith, summarizing Christian doctrine in thirty-three chapters, completed in 1646 by an assembly of Churchmen created by the Puritan Long Parliament and named the Westminster Assembly. Receiving the partial approval of Parliament in 1648, it has been widely accepted among Protestants.

WEYL, HERMANN. 1885–1955.
German-American scientist and philosopher. Born in Elmshorn, Germany. Educated at Munich and Göttingen. Taught at Göttingen and Princeton. Making contributions to both geometry and relativity theory, Weyl's philosophical interest was in philosophy of mathematics and philosophy of science.
Principal writings: *The Continuum*, 1918; *Space, Time, Matter* (T), 1918; *Philosophy of Mathematics and Natural Science* (T), 1927; *Theory of Groups and Quantum Mechanics* (T), 1928; *Symmetry* (T), 1952.

WFF.
Acronym for "well-formed formula." A well-formed formula is one which conforms to the requirements of the system of which it is a part (*q.v.* Validity 3).

WHATELY, RICHARD. 1787–1863.
English philosopher. Educated at Oxford. Taught at Oxford. Was named Archbishop of Dublin. Regarded by De Morgan as the "restorer" of logical study in England, he provided a standard treatment of induction and deduction. He viewed rhetoric as the "art of argumentative composition."
Principal writings: *Historic Doubts Relative to Napoleon Bonaparte*, 1819; *Elements of Logic*, 1826; *Elements of Rhetoric*, 1828.

WHEWELL, WILLIAM. 1794–1866.
English philosopher. Born in Lancaster. Professor of philosophy at Cambridge.
Principal writings: *History of the Inductive Sciences*, 3 vols., 1837; *The Philosophy of the Inductive Sciences*, 2 vols., 1840.
(1) Interested in the methods of the inductive sciences, he suggested the importance of "colligation" in the ordering of scientific data—*i.e.*, finding the conception which allows one to see the facts as connected. Since "colligation" assimilates induction to the hypothetico-deductive method, Whewell—despite his attention to induction—is rather more on the side of a rationalistic than inductivistic philosophy of science.
(2) Introducing the phrase "consilience of inductions," he used it to refer to that concurrence of inductions from disparate areas which allows one to discern their "rule and reason," thus gaining a unification of thought not sensed before.
(3) He held that numbers, space, time, cause, etc., were "fundamental ideas" serving as the basis of axioms in the sciences, and whose negation was inconceivable to us. He traced such ideas finally to the mind of God.

WHICHCOTE, BENJAMIN. 1609–1683.
English philosopher. Born at Whichcote Hall, Stoke, Shropshire. Educated at Cambridge. Taught at Cambridge, where he also served for a time as provost of King's College and Vice-Chancellor of the university. Consulted by Cromwell during the period of the Commonwealth, in the Restoration of 1660 he lost his Cambridge position. A liberal Churchman, he believed in the objective nature of right and wrong even in relation to God. Whichcote is regarded as the founder of the Cambridge Platonists.
Principal writings: *Several Discourses* (ed. Jeffrey), 1701; *Moral and Religious Aphorisms* (ed. Jeffrey), 1703; *On the True*

Nature of Peace in the Kingdom or Church of Christ, 1717.

WHITEFIELD, GEORGE. 1714–1770.
English religious leader. Born in Gloucester. Educated at Oxford, where he made contact with the Methodism (*q.v.*) of the Wesleys. Working within the context of this religion initially, he eventually became an independent, his powerful preaching stirring enthusiasm both in Great Britain and America.

WHITEHEAD, ALFRED NORTH. 1861–1947.
British philosopher. Born at Ramsgate, Isle of Thanet, East Kent, England. Studied mathematics at Trinity College, Cambridge, beginning in 1880. Subsequently elected a Fellow in mathematics. He was made a Fellow of the Royal Society in 1903. From 1910 until 1924 he held the chair of Applied Mathematics at the Imperial College of Science in South Kensington. From 1924 until 1947 he served as professor of philosophy at Harvard University. His collaboration with Russell on the logical foundations of mathematics occurred during the Cambridge period. The London years saw the development of his interest in philosophy of science. While at Harvard, he elaborated his metaphysical system. In 1945 he was awarded the Order of Merit.

Principal writings: *A Treatise of Universal Algebra, with Applications,* 1898; *Principia Mathematica* (with Russell), 3 vols., 1910, 1912, 1913 (2nd ed., 1925–27); *An Enquiry Concerning the Principles of Natural Knowledge,* 1919; *The Concept of Nature,* 1920; *The Principle of Relativity,* 1922; *Religion in the Making,* 1926; *Science and the Modern World,* 1926; *Symbolism, Its Meaning and Effect,* 1928; *The Aims of Education, and other Essays,* 1929; *The Function of Reason,* 1929; *Process and Reality, an Essay in Cosmology,* 1929; *Adventures of Ideas,* 1933; *Nature and Life,* 1934; *Modes of Thought,* 1938; *Essays in Science and Philosophy,* 1947.

Whitehead brought to philosophy a tremendous breadth of interest, an impressive knowledge of mathematics, physics, and other sciences, as well as a sensitive appreciation for the varied aspects of human culture. He is a philosopher of flux and change, and a phi-

losopher of continuity as well. He took his starting point from the sciences, but for him science was merely one of the resources of philosophy, along with aesthetics, history, religious experience, and the deliveries of common sense. He produced the most impressive metaphysical statement of the 20th century. It is appropriate to consider his contributions under the three heads of logic and mathematics, philosophy of science, and metaphysics.

A. Logic and Mathematics.
(1) In his work on universal algebra Whitehead presented general formal descriptions of addition and multiplication. It was this work which gained him admission to the Royal Society.

(2) As the result of a decade of collaboration with his brilliant student, Bertrand Russell, *Principia Mathematica* was published. This work found a basis for mathematics in logic, and vastly extended the latter's scope. Each part of the work was gone over by each of the collaborators. One suspects that Whitehead's head was in the work but not his heart. At least, it is true that many of the problems solved in the *Principia* were Russell's problems; it is also the case that the volume on geometry—closer to Whitehead's interests than some of the subject matter of the study—was never published. One suspects that the lure of metaphysical speculation was already at work in Whitehead.

B. Philosophy of Science.
(3) Certainly Whitehead moved relatively quickly into the area of philosophy of science. His program in regard to natural philosophy, or philosophy of science, was to deduce scientific concepts from the simplest elements of our perceptual knowledge. Put otherwise, the object of the analysis is nature, and by nature Whitehead means the world as presented to our awareness. And although he speaks of *percipient events,* meaning the relevant bodily states of observers, individual minds are regarded as outside nature, and so outside the scope of philosophy of science. Value, too, is excluded from the study. Philosophy of science, or natural philosophy, is therefore vastly different from metaphysics, which must include such considerations. It will not be surprising to discover, then,

a number of modifications and specifications as his interest in metaphysics increased.

(4) The ultimate fact for sense-awareness is an event. Events are the most concrete facts of nature. They pass and are gone. They are extended in space and time. They are included in other events, and include others in themselves. It would thus seem that there is no end to the complexity of nature. (But see point 9 below where the epochal theory of time requires him to give up the compact divisibility of events.)

(5) In contrast to events, *objects* recur. This means that objects characterize events. Objects are abstractions and enter experience through intellectual recognition. One must distinguish sense objects (*e.g.*, shades of color), perceptual objects (veridical or delusive), physical objects (veridical perceptual objects), and scientific objects (*e.g.*, electrons, atoms, molecules). In Whitehead's language, objects are ingredient in, or they "ingress into," events. (Compare this with point 10 below where *eternal objects* represent a further specification of the idea.)

Objects are, however, never merely in a single place at a single time. Each object has a complex ingression so that it is in some sense ingredient throughout nature.

(6) When one accepts simple location for physical and scientific objects, one has mistaken an abstraction for a concrete element of nature. One has thus committed the *fallacy of misplaced concreteness*. All instances of confusing the abstract and the concrete, supposing an abstract element to be concrete, are instances of this fallacy. Whitehead particularly opposed the habit of mind which dismissed the non-recurring events in favor of the recurring abstract objects ingredient in those events.

(7) Events occur, and objects relate to each, other, in a four-dimensional space-time manifold, termed the *extensive continuum*. The geometric properties of this field are defined by the *method of extensive abstraction*. Points, lines, planes, and other geometrical elements, are ideal limits of converging classes of appropriate kinds. For example, squares and circles converge to a point, while rectangles converge to a line segment. These routes of approximation toward an ideal limit (compare the notion of limit in differen-

tial calculus) involve time as well as space. Indeed, the character of space is dependent upon the character of time, and the routes of approximation of geometrical elements are fixed by the intersections of alternate time-systems. The ultimate elements of the space-time manifold are event-particles. An event-particle is an instantaneous point-flash, a point-event, or a point of instantaneous space, as much an instant of time as a point of space. Geometrical elements can thus be described as the loci of the complete sets of event-particles covered by appropriately intersecting moments of different time-systems. (In the metaphysical studies, the method of extensive abstraction is revised; events and event-particles are replaced by regions; *cf.* point 12 below.)

(8) Whitehead's theory of relativity differed from that of Einstein by means of its grounding in philosophical realism rather than operationalism. They differ, too, with respect to the importance of events. Where Einstein derived events from the intersections of particles of matter, Whitehead derived matter from events as one of their contingent characteristics. Finally, where Einstein sought a unified field theory, Whitehead stressed the atomicity of nature as well as its continuity. In a unified field Whitehead felt that knowledge would be impossible for finite minds with only partial perception of the world.

C. Metaphysics.

(9) In his metaphysical period Whitehead utilized "imaginative generalization" to develop a "categoreal" scheme applicable to all experience. The scheme includes a Category of the Ultimate (creativity or becoming), 8 Categories of Existence, and 27 Categories of Explanation. One of the most important Categories of Existence is that of the Actual Occasion, or Actual Entity, replacing the traditional category of substance, actual occasions are the final real things of which the world is composed. They replace the events of the philosophy of science, but where events are indefinitely divisible, the actual occasions are thoroughly atomic. God fits this classification, and so does the most trivial puff of existence.

(10) Eternal Objects, likewise among the Categories of Existence, are the forms

of definiteness we observe in experience. They divide into "objective species," *e.g.*, geometric entities and relationships; and "subjective species": colors, emotions, intensities, pleasures, pains. Eternal objects characterize actual occasions. It is complex eternal objects which provide the characteristics which define an object for us. Eternal objects play the role of universals in those philosophies which give universals a real status in the world. Eternal objects are where they are relevant. They are part of the potentiality of the *extensive continuum*, as well as being part of the *primordial nature* of God. For Whitehead the predicates of propositions refer to eternal objects.

(11) The *extensive continuum* gains in importance as Whitehead develops the metaphysical aspect of his thought. It expresses a new emphasis on potentiality, as the source of continuity. The extensive continuum includes both temporal and spatial extension. It thus comprehends qualitative creative advance, as well as spatial division and aggregation. Actual occasions thus atomize the continuum, while also adding to it.

(12) The *method of extensive abstraction* is modified in the metaphysics. It is now developed in terms of the connection of regions, and these regions are potentialities of the extensive continuum. They are extensive standpoints of the real potentiality for actualization which is the extensive continuum. Instead of the earlier language the geometrical elements are derived through the convergence to simplicity of oval, or ovate, regions. This represents an adjustment from description of the method in terms of events to a description in terms of regions.

(13) Each actual occasion is related, positively or negatively, to the entire antecedent universe. This relating, or taking account of, the universe is called *prehension*. When an actual occasion prehends positively, what is prehended becomes part of its own constitution, characterizing it in an appropriate manner. In addition to *positive prehensions* there are *negative prehensions*. The solidarity of the world demands that elimination from influence is itself an influence. In this sense each actual occasion reflects the universe from its own standpoint.

(14) Through prehensions, connections become established among actual occasions. Such facts of togetherness are termed *nexūs*. The singular form is *nexus*. In addition to positive and negative prehensions, there are physical and conceptual prehensions. A *physical prehension* is the prehension by one actual occasion of another actual occasion. A *conceptual prehension* is the prehension by an actual occasion of an eternal object.

(15) The fact that actual occasions may take account of things physically or conceptually requires that the extensive continuum contain both physical and conceptual possibilities. A distinction present in all actual occasions and societies of actual occasions is the distinction of the physical from the mental pole. Emphasis on the former yields physical continuity; emphasis on the latter yields novelty.

(16) But the eternal objects of the extensive continuum would not by themselves permit a constant venture into novelty. In addition, then, to the extensive continuum, Whitehead posits the *primordial nature of God*. This nature of God accounts for the fact that the world never runs out of possibility. There is a grading of possibilities beyond possibilities allowing creative advance as selected groups of possibilities are actualized. Whitehead speaks of a primordial valuation of possibilities to account for this feature of the world.

(17) Not only is there adventure into novelty, however; there is also a retention of the novelties achieved as the contingent future becomes the actual present and the immortal past. And since this retention apparently does not occur in the ordinary processes of coming to be and perishing through time, Whitehead posits the *consequent nature of God* to provide for such retention.

(18) He has thus presented us with a dipolar view of God, providing the foundation for process, and conserving its results by retention of the past in the divine immediacy. The supreme being, for Whitehead, is beyond challenge by any other being, yet is in process in the sense that all of the happenings of the world become part of his nature. Far from being impassive, God suffers and rejoices with the world.

(19) It might be thought that to posit

an entity to account for the features mentioned above is an *ad hoc* procedure. But from Whitehead's standpoint it is merely an application of the *ontological principle*: actual entities are the only reasons. To search for a reason is to search for an actual entity.

(20) There is an emphasis on feeling in Whitehead. One has to say that each actual occasion is seeking its own satisfaction. This is, of course, on a level below consciousness, yet physical happenings on any level are not antithetical to consciousness. Consciousness itself is simply a more specialized form of satisfaction. It would seem that there is an urge in the universe toward greater intensity of feeling, and that God is the ultimate source of this desire.

(21) In any event it is in societies of actual occasions that increasing structure is possible, leading finally to the goal of increased intensity of feeling. In its simplest sense, a society is simply a *nexus* of actual occasions with a complex eternal object as its defining characteristic. This characteristic is inherited by later members of the society from earlier members, and thus the relative permanence of a characteristic is ensured.

(22) Causal laws are simply the defining characteristics of the most widely spread societies of a given cosmic epoch. Such laws are not immutable. They might well change from one cosmic epoch to another.

(23) Each society has a wider background which, together with the given society, constitutes a more inclusive society. Structured societies include subordinate societies and subordinate *nexūs* with definite patterns of interrelation. It is in such societies that intensified satisfaction is possible. Inorganic societies stress the physical pole. Living societies require inorganic societies at their base, and are thus able to increase the stress on conceptual prehensions and the mental pole. *Personal order societies* have purely temporal and serial order. Examples are enduring objects and persons. Both human beings and electrons, protons, and photons share this class. Corpuscular societies are societies made up of strands of enduring objects. Any material object is an instance of a corpuscular society. Human beings are both corpuscular

and personal order societies with inorganic societies at their base. The shelter provided by this complex structure allows increased intensity of feeling, and increased emphasis on conceptual prehensions.

(24) Human beings perceive in two modes; *causal efficacy* and *presentational immediacy*. The former mode stresses time, while the latter stresses space. I am perceiving in the mode of causal efficacy when I sense the manner in which the immediate past exerts a shaping influence on my present awareness. I am perceiving in the mode of presentational immediacy when I sense a region, spread out and characterized by contrasting eternal objects. The more basic of these two modes of perception is that of causal efficacy, since data about the world must come to me in that mode. It was Hume's misfortune not to sense the distinction of the two modes, and thus to interpret the world almost solely in terms of presentational immediacy. The two modes are combined in a particularized perception, such as the perception of a "grey stone." The word "stone" refers to feelings of causal efficacy in the immediate past, and the immediate future, while "grey" refers to a quality or eternal object projected onto a region. This combination of the two modes Whitehead calls *symbolic reference*.

(25) Stressing feeling, dynamic movement, and creative advance, Whitehead abjured all mechanical models, avoiding the standard mind-body dualism, as well as others, through his *philosophy of organism*.

WHITMAN, WALT.
Q.v. Personalism.

WHORF, BENJAMIN LEE.
Q.v. Language (21).

WIEMAN, H.N. 1884–1975.
American theologian. Born in Richhill, Mo. Educated at Jena and Harvard. Taught at Occidental College, Chicago, Houston, and Southern Illinois. Holding to the operation in the world of a fourfold creative event which inevitably results in "creative good," Wieman viewed the subevents as consisting of: an emerging awareness of qualitative meaning, integration of the emergent meaning with

earlier meanings, a consequent expansion of one's appreciable world, and a deepening of community. He identified the creative event not merely with the work of God, but with God as such.

Principal writings: *Religious Experience and Scientific Method*, 1926; *The Source of Human Good*, 1946; *Man's Ultimate Commitment*, 1958.

WIENER, NORBERT.
Q.v. Cybernetics.

WILL.
An Anglo-Saxon term equivalent to the Latin *voluntas* and the Greek *boulema*. The term refers to a potency, faculty, or force in man involved in decision-making. The view that the will is dominant over the reason is termed "voluntarism" (*q.v.*). The view that reason is determinative over will is termed "intellectualism," or simply "rationalism" (*q.v.*). In addition there are views providing a balance between reason and will.

(1) In the tripartite doctrine of the soul advanced by Plato (*q.v.* 3) and by Aristotle (*q.v.* 11), the will stands between the reason and the appetites. For both, the will was regarded as more closely related to the former than the latter. It is the function of the reason to control the will, and man is obliged to build good habits allowing such control.

(2) Aquinas (*q.v.* 7) followed the same line, defining the will as "rational appetite" (*appetitus intellectualis*), influenced by and influencing the reason.

(3) For Hobbes (*q.v.* 6) will is identified with the appetites. Indeed, Hobbes regarded will as the final link in the chain of appetites leading to action: "The last appetite or aversion immediately adhering to the action."

(4) Descartes (*q.v.* 7) regarded the power of the will as almost limitless in comparison to the limitations within which the reason must work. For Descartes it is the power of the will that makes possible human freedom. The tendency to regard will as an entity may have given rise to the view of will as a faculty.

(5) In contrast to Descartes, Spinoza (*q.v.* 4) identified the will with *conatus*, a striving to persevere in being that is characteristic of all living things. This in effect pluralized the will into individual volitions. In addition, since for Spinoza volitions are merely the affirmations or negations of ideas, the two are intimately related and almost identical.

(6) Kant (*q.v.* 6) likewise came close to identifying will and reason. He held that the faculty of the will can operate without taking account of "desires and inclinations," and as determinative of voluntary acts it is the "practical reason" itself.

(7) Freud (*q.v.* 1–2) returned to something like the tripartite soul of the Greeks, finding its elements to be Id, Ego, and Super-Ego. Roughly speaking the Ego, mediating between the constraints of the Super-Ego and the passions of the Id, represents the volitional function.

WILL TO BELIEVE.
A concept of William James (*q.v.* 4) to the effect that we can believe beyond the evidence in cases where our options are forced, living, and momentous.

WILL TO POWER.
Q.v. Nietzsche (3).

WILLIAM OF AUVERGNE. c. 1180-1249.
French philosopher and theologian. Born in Aurillac. Teacher of theology at the University of Paris, and Bishop of Paris beginning in 1228.

Principal writings: *On the Immortality of the Soul*; *On the Soul*; *On the Trinity*; *On the Universe*.

(1) Standing for the Platonic-Augustinian tradition in theology, he showed signs of Neoplatonic influence, including that of Avicebron (*q.v.*).

(2) He stood opposed to the Aristotelian tradition, including the writings of Maimonides, and still more especially the tradition of Averroism (*q.v.*) whose doctrines of the eternity of the world and the absence of personal immortality were particularly abhorrent to him.

(3) His practical solution to the opposition of the two traditions was to admit that the Aristotelian-Arabic tradition was true of the material world, while the Platonic Augustinian tradition was true of the intelligible world, providing the appropriate responses to ultimate questions.

WILLIAM OF AUXERRE. Early 13th cent.
French Scholastic. Born in Auxerre. Taught at Paris. Named by Pope Gregory

IX to a commission concerned with a study of the works of Aristotle, William typically incorporated in his work Aristotelian ideas along with the more traditional Augustinian and Neoplatonic elements. On the other hand he accepted the ontological proof of Anselm.

Principal writings: *Summa on Four Books of Sentences; The Golden Summa; Commentary on the Anticlaudianus.*

WILLIAM OF CHAMPEAUX. 1070–1120.
Scholastic philosopher. Disciple of Anselm, and student of Roscelin, he was teacher of Abelard. Bishop of Châlons-sur-Marne from 1113 until his death. A teacher of logic at the Cathedral School of Paris, he founded the house and school of St. Victor in 1108. Although his teacher, Roscelin (*q.v.*), was opposed to Realism with respect to the problem of universals (*q.v.*), William's initial position was an extreme form of Realism, the identity theory of universals. According to this view the individual members of a species have the same essential nature; hence, their individual differences are not substantial but accidental. Abelard (*q.v.* 2) criticized this position on the grounds that if it were true the same substance would exist in more than one place at the same time; and that, since God is substance, all things are identical and Pantheism is true. In response to these criticisms William shifted to an indifference theory of universals. The individual members of a species, he now held, are not the same essentially, but they are the same indifferently. This meant that the essences of the individual members of a species are similar, and this similarity provides the basis for the concept of the species which applies indifferently to all of its members. Principal writings: *Sentences.*

WILLIAM OF CONCHES. 1080–1145.
French philosopher. Born in Conches. Studied under Bernard (*q.v.*) of Chartres. Taught at Chartres and, perhaps, in Paris. Interested in the created universe, he brought into his writings most of the science of his day, interpreting the Christian Trinity in Platonic terms. He was attacked for this and for following Abelard.

Principal writings: *Philosophy of the World; Dragmaticon Philosophiae; Commen-tary on Boethius' "Consolation of Philosophy"*; as well as glosses on writings of Plato and Macrobius.

WILLIAM OF MOERBEKE. 1215–1286.
Belgian philosopher. Born in Moerbeke. A Dominican, his translations of Aristotle were encouraged by Aquinas. Although other translations had preceded his, the accuracy of William's work allowed a much better picture of Aristotle's thought. His translation of Proclus made it possible to disentangle Aristotle from Neoplatonism. The *Book of Causes*, associated with Aristotle for centuries, was seen to be an extract from Proclus' *Elements of Theology*. In his own thought there were Neoplatonic elements, including Proclus' doctrine of light as an emanation from God.

Principal writings: Translations of most of the works of Aristotle, the works of Proclus, and many commentaries.

WILLIAM OF OCKHAM. c. 1290–1349.
English Scholastic philosopher. Born in Ockham, Surrey. Oxford educated and a member of the Franciscan order, he lectured and prepared a commentary on Peter Lombard's *Book of Sentences* as part of his Master's work. The lectures had a great effect; and in 1323 the former chancellor of Oxford charged Ockham before the papal court with adhering to heretical doctrines, and called attention to 56 suspect propositions from the Oxford commentary. William was summoned to Avignon and the examination, which required several years, was concluding without result when a second issue arose. Pope John XXII challenged the Franciscan doctrine of apostolic poverty. Since Ockham opposed the pope on the issue he fled Avignon, accepting the protection of Emperor Louis of Bavaria. Excommunicated, Ockham settled in Munich and proceeded to attack the pope, claiming that Pope John had forfeited his right to the papal office. After John's death he continued his campaign against other Avignon popes until the last years of his life. It is thought that his death came in an epidemic of the black plague. An opponent of Duns Scotus (*q.v.*), Ockham is regarded as the major figure of the Nominalist (*q.v.*) or Terminist (*q.v.*) movement.

Principal writings: *Golden Exposition of the Ancient Art; Exposition of Eight Books of the Physics; Summa of All Logic; Summulae in the Books of the Physics; Quodlibeta septem; Tractatus de sacramento altaris* (T); *Treatise on Predestination and God's Foreknowledge of the Contingent Future; Dialogue Between Teacher and Disciple; On Four Books of the Sentences; De Imperatorum et pontificium potestate; A Brief Statement on Papal Power; Exposition of Porphyry's Book on Predication.*

(1) Ockham makes an important distinction between *categorematic* and *syncategorematic* terms. Terms which refer to reality are *categorematic*, while terms which refer to *categorematic* terms are *syncategorematic*. Most common nouns are *categorematic*, while words such as "not," "all," and "some" are *syncategorematic*.

(2) Terms that refer to things are called terms of *first intention*. Terms referring to terms of first intention are called terms of *second intention*. In one sense the syncategorematic terms mentioned above are second intentional; but, as Ockham wishes to use the distinction, categorematic terms and syncategorematic terms, functioning together, refer to things. "All men are mortal" is thus first intentional. But when we use terms such as "genus," "species," and "difference" we are using terms of second intention. Propositions utilizing such terms refer not to the world but to terms of first intention.

(3) On the basis of the distinction just mentioned, Ockham divides the sciences into two types. *Scientia rationalis,* or rational science, is second intentional. Logic is a science of this type. *Scientia realis* is first intentional. Physics is an example of a science of real things.

(4) We must, further, distinguish between absolute and connotative, conventional and natural signs. *Absolute signs* are univocal, as "man" stands absolutely for man, while "just," a *connotative sign,* stands primarily for a quality and secondarily for the subject of that quality. *Conventional signs* are the individual words, spoken or written, which we use in conveying our thought. *Natural signs* are signs considered in terms of their meanings. Any sign whose meaning is constituted by the effect the object of that sign has had upon us, is a natural sign;

trees, chairs, houses, etc., are examples.

(5) Taken by themselves natural signs have meaning. Put together in sentences, they gain an added feature, which Ockham follows Peter of Spain (*q.v.*) in calling *suppositio. Suppositio* is the capacity of signs to designate particular things or groups of things. When the sign stands for a specific individual, *e.g.,* "the man is my neighbor," we have an instance of *suppositio personalis.* When the sign stands for a whole class, *e.g.,* "man is rational," we have an instance of the natural sign in its simple form; he calls this *suppositio simplex.* When the sign refers to itself, *e.g.,* " 'Man' is a noun," we have a case of *suppositio materialis.*

(6) The point of Ockham's Nominalism (*q.v.*) is that names or signs of the kinds discussed can perform all of the functions of naming without requiring universals in any sense. He says very clearly that extra-mental reality is composed of individual substances and individual qualities. Substances do not have essences or quiddities. To be sure, they have similarities; and while these similarities may be properly attributed to God's will, there is no point in relating them to a class of eternal divine ideas. From these similarities, through natural signs, reference can be made to groups of things. The only general feature here is the act of the understanding itself.

(7) Just as there are not universals in things, so there are not relations in things. There are not even relations of similarity or causality behind general concepts. There exist simply the resemblances and regularities out of which these concepts are constructed. Ockham argues that the universe becomes too complex if one supposes relations to be in things. A single change occurs anywhere and, on the doctrine that relations are real, every relation in the universe must change. One consequence of the denial of relations is that Ockham is able to dismiss the traditional doctrine of the relations which obtain between God and the world: *i.e.,* that the creature has a real relation to God, but that the relation of God to creatures is mental only.

(8) The principle of economy underlying Ockham's denial of relations or universals to things is the *Principle of Parsimony,* although it has come to be

known as Ockham's razor. A number of statements of the principle are given: e.g., "What can be done with fewer is done in vain with more"; or "Multiplicity is not to be assumed without necessity." The second of these statements is fairly close to the most common form of the principle, i.e., "*Entia non sunt multiplicanda praeter necessitatem,*" or "Entities are not to be multiplied beyond necessity," although its exact statement is not to be found in Ockham's works.

(9) His use of the principle was constant. Against those who held to the analogy of being, Ockham argued that the concept of being is univocal, predicable of God and of creatures in the same sense, even though the two may not be either substantially or accidentally alike. He understands the term "substance" in the sense of Aristotle's primary substance, i.e., the individual subject of qualities, so that corporeal substance is the individual subject of sensible qualities. He views matter not as pure potentiality (q.v. Aristotle 7), but as body with spatially distinguishable parts. He views form as the structure of the material parts. He finds efficient cause to be the most useful of Aristotle's causes, and thinks final cause a metaphor. He finds no compelling reason to accept the existence of the active intellect; it is not needed to explain the formation of universal concepts; but in this case he says that he accepts it on the authority of the saints and the philosophers. The effort to achieve simplification led him in the direction of a positivistic approach.

(10) With respect to knowledge the initial category is that of intuitive knowledge, *notitia intuitiva*, referring to acts of immediate awareness leading to evident judgments of contingent fact. Such contingent propositions concern the existence or nonexistence of a given thing, or the presence or absence of a given quality. We know the world and our own acts intuitively, and such knowledge carries its own guarantee.

(11) From such intuitive knowledge we gain general propositions. He distinguishes between two kinds of general propositions. One kind is *per se nota*, i.e., evident by the meaning of the terms. The second kind is *nota per experientiam*, i.e., evident by experience. There are premises

in logic, mathematics, and in the natural sciences to fit the first kind of proposition. But in the natural sciences most propositions are of the second kind. General propositions of the second sort require a principle of induction which rests, at length, on the assumption of a common course of nature. And such a view of nature requires the idea of God.

(12) The approach to God is finally through revealed theology. Highly critical of the traditional arguments for God, he finds one argument stronger than the rest. This is an argument from the conservation of a thing in being to its conserver. The argument reasons to an actual conserver and, hence, if one posits an infinite series of conservers, one will be committed to an actual infinity of the impossible sort. The argument is therefore valid. But even in this case we cannot know that this conserver is the Supreme Being we refer to as God.

(13) Accepting the reality of God, Ockham holds that God has established an order of nature and an order of grace. We learn of the order of nature through experience, using the postulate of the uniformity of nature as the basis of the inductions appropriate to this type of investigation. And we learn of the order of grace through revelation. Both of these orders are contingent. They could be otherwise were God to will differently. Viewing the matter in this way Ockham is able to preserve the omnipotence and unqualified freedom of God, protect theology from philosophical contamination, establish the independence of theology and the sciences from each other, while making them both radically dependent upon the will of God.

(14) He holds that intellect and will in man are not distinct faculties, and that man is a *suppositum intellectuale*, that is, a complete rational being, incapable of inhering in anything and not supported by anything. This suggests that man has the power of freedom; and, indeed, Ockham believes that man can indifferently and contingently produce effects. He can cause them or not cause them, everything else remaining the same except the willed decision. Even after reason has reached a given conclusion, the will is free to will it or not; and this power even extends to willing or not

willing happiness as one's final end or goal. Believing so strongly in man's freedom he has to hold that future events are contingent. At the same time he cannot avoid the belief that God knows the future contingent events resulting from our choices. But he confesses that it is impossible to understand or to explain how this can be the case.

(15) The emphasis on the will applies to God as well as to man, and is made the basis of Ockham's ethics. The moral law is that which is commanded or prohibited by the will of God. The only limitation on this will is that God cannot will a contradiction. Evil consists in doing one thing when one is under obligation to do the opposite. Although finally the right can be known only through knowledge of God's decrees, Ockham seems to have believed that following "right reason" and conscience provides a reliable index to those decrees.

(16) Since all men are born free, in matters of political and religious governance they have the right to choose their rulers if they so desire. This applies to popes as well as to emperors. God's grant of power to rulers is through the people. With respect to the Church, he supported the establishment of a General Council, consisting of representatives from provincial synods elected by the members of individual parishes, monasteries, and other religious institutions.

WILLIAM OF SHERWOOD. c. 1210–1270.
English philosopher. Studied and taught at Oxford. A prominent logician, and one of the founders of the terminist logic (*q.v.*), William almost certainly taught in Paris and from that vantage point influenced Peter of Spain (*q.v.*), Lambert of Auxerre (*q.v.*), Albertus Magnus (*q.v.*), and Thomas Aquinas (*q.v.*). Among other properties of terms he dealt with *significatio* (*q.v.*) and *suppositio* (*q.v.*). Making the distinction between categorematic and syncategorematic terms (*q.v.*), under the latter he analyzed terms such as "every," "except," "only," "is," "not," "if," "or," and "necessary."
Principal writings: *Introduction to Logic; Syncategoremata; On the Insolubles; Obligations; Petitiones contrarium.*

WILSON, COOK. 1849–1915.
English philosopher. Born in Nottingham. Educated at Oxford. Initially an Idealist he became, in opposition to F.H. Bradley (*q.v.*), the leader of Oxford realism, holding knowledge to contain a simple, indefinable apprehension of the real. Other Oxford realists include H.A. Prichard (*q.v.*), H.W. Joseph, and W.D. Ross (*q.v.*).
Principal writings: *Statement and Inference*, 1926.

WILSON, N.L.
Q.v. Radical Translation (3).

WIMSATT, W.K.
Q.v. New Criticism.

WINCH, PETER.
Q.v. Forms of Life.

WINDELBAND, WILHELM. 1848–1915.
German philosopher. Born in Potsdam. Taught in Zürich, Freiburg, Strassburg, and Heidelberg. An eminent historian of philosophy, he was the first leader of the Heidelberg School of neo-Kantianism (*q.v.* Neo-Kantianism 4).
Principal writings: *The History of Modern Philosophy* (T), 2 vols., 1878, 1880; *Manual of the History of Philosophy* (T), 1892; *History and Science*, 1894; *On Free Will*, 1904.

(1) Maintaining that problems of epistemology rest on judgments of axiology, Windelband expected to be able to overcome relativism by reference to values of universal validity. He thought, indeed, that the concept of the "thing-in-itself" could be given up without any loss if a system of such values is accepted.

(2) Classifying the natural sciences as *nomothetic* ("based on law"), and the cultural sciences as *ideographic* ("based on the particular individual"), he held that the former seek the law governing the individual case, and the latter seek the form of the individual.

(3) It was his view that each of the cultural sciences related to a sphere of human culture and that a particular set of absolute values underlay each one. In a more general sense, this is also true of the natural sciences.

WISDOM.
An Anglo-Saxon term, comparable in

meaning to the Greek *sophia*. *Sophia* initially referred to the practical arts, only gradually assuming the significations given below.

(1) Plato (*q.v.* 5c) viewed wisdom as one of the four chief, or cardinal, virtues (*q.v.*). It concerned "knowledge of the whole." The path to wisdom required both scientific knowledge and practical experience.

(2) Aristotle (*q.v.* 1, 11) distinguished between speculative and practical wisdom, *i.e.*, between *sophia* and *phronesis*. The latter term is also, and usually, translated as "prudence." While practical wisdom relates to the conduct of life, speculative wisdom—requiring the elements of intuitive reason and rigorous knowledge of first causes and principles—is best exemplified by that highest branch of speculative science known as "theology," "first philosophy," or "metaphysics."

(3) *Phronesis*, or practical wisdom, was the type of wisdom stressed by the Cyrenaics, Epicureans, and Stoics (*q.v.* Prudence 4; Stoicism).

(4) Thomas Aquinas (*q.v.* 1) followed Aristotle's distinction between speculative and practical wisdom, while finding speculative wisdom not in metaphysics but rather in sacred doctrine or revealed theology.

(5) Nicholas of Cusa (*q.v.* 1) defined wisdom as "learned ignorance."

(6) Spinoza (*q.v.* 5, 10) distinguished between *ratio* or reason, interpreted as knowledge of scientific law, and *scientia intuitiva* or intuitive knowledge, where one "sees" the universal in all the particulars of existence. Wisdom is identified with the latter and interpreted as living "under the aspect of eternity."

(7) In Madhyamika (*q.v.* 1) Buddhism wisdom involves going beyond knowledge to emptiness (*śunyata*).

WISDOM, JOHN. 1904– .
English philosopher. Born in London. Educated at Cambridge. Taught at Saint Andrews in Scotland, Cambridge, and the University of Oregon. Influenced by Wittgenstein and Moore, he concerned himself a great deal with the nature of philosophy. His basic conception is that it is a second level discipline concerned with the gaining of "clearer insight" into the "ultimate structure" of facts. The

method may be reductive, where the "x" of one's ostensible discussion is replaced by a "y" which illuminates the discussion, taking it to a more satisfactory level. Properly done, one would have shown that the "x" is a logical construction, appropriately replaceable by "y." The dramatic statement that "philosophy is the disease of which philosophy is the cure" reflects Wisdom's belief that the reduction may, likewise, have therapeutic value and has points of comparison to psychoanalysis. The method was applied at length to the problem of other minds.

Principal writings: *Interpretation and Analysis*, 1931; *Problems of Mind and Matter*, 1934; *Other Minds*, 1952; *Philosophy and Psycho-Analysis*, 1953; *Paradox and Discovery*, 1965; *Logical Constructions*, 1969; *Wisdom, Twelve Essays* (ed. R. Bambrough), 1974; *Philosophy and Its Place in Our Culture*, 1975.

WITELO. c. 1230–c. 1275.
Born in Legnica, Silesia (now Poland). Studied at Papua. Influenced by William of Moerbeke, to whom he dedicated his study of light. Combining optical studies with a Neoplatonic doctrine, he held that light emanates from God through intelligible substances into the inferior world.

Principal writings: *Perspective*.

WITHDRAWAL AND RETURN.
Q.v. Toynbee (2).

WITTGENSTEIN, LUDWIG. 1889–1951.
Austrian philosopher. Born in Vienna. Studied engineering in Berlin and Manchester. Through mathematical engineering he was led to the work of Frege and Russell on mathematical logic. He worked with Russell at Cambridge in 1912–13, exercising considerable influence over the latter (*q.v.* Russell 8). He served with the Austrian army during World War I, undergoing deep mystical experience at the front possibly as a result of reading Tolstoy. He became a prisoner of war in Italy. The *Tractatus Logico-Philosophicus* was published in Germany in 1921 and in London in 1922. As a result of the mystical experience mentioned above, he gave away an inherited fortune and became an elementary schoolmaster in

Austria. He did, however, maintain relations with Schlick and Waismann of the Vienna Circle of Logical Positivists (*q.v.*). In 1929 he returned to Cambridge permanently, having revisited it in 1925, and accepted the chair of philosophy formerly held by G.E. Moore. In 1947 he resigned his Cambridge chair. His health deteriorated, and he died of cancer in 1951.

Principal writings: *Tractatus Logico-Philosophicus*, 1921 (second ed. with changes, 1933; new trans., 1961); "Logical Form," Aris. Soc. Supplement, vol. IX, 1929, pp. 162–171; *Philosophical Investigations*, (trans. Anscombe), 1953; *Philosophical Remarks on the Foundations of Mathematics* (ed. von Wright, Rhees, Anscombe), 1956; *Preliminary Studies for the "Philosophical Investigations" (The Blue and Brown Books)*, 1958; *Lectures and Conversations on Aesthetics, Psychology, and Religious Belief* (notes of Smythies, Rhees, Taylor), 1966; *Zettel* (ed. Anscombe, von Wright), 1967.

The writings of Wittgenstein divide into two parts, marking very different ways of doing philosophy.

A. The *Tractatus* was written between 1914 and 1918. It exercised influence over the development of logical positivism.

(1) The world, in this view, is made up of elementary facts. These seem to be independent of each other. They are the subject matter of empirical science.

(2) It is the primary purpose of language to state facts. It does this by picturing. When a fact is pictured there is a structural similarity between the language used and what is pictured. A secondary purpose of language is to state tautologies. Tautologies are true but empty. They tell us nothing but their use is necessary. The operations of both logic and mathematics are series of tautologies. Given any two propositions "p" and "q" the general form of tautology is exemplified by "If p then p and if q then q" (*q.v.* Tautology).

(3) Any proposition which fails either to picture a fact, or to express a tautology, is nonsense. Statements of both metaphysics and ethics fall into this category.

(4) Even the *Tractatus* is nonsense, since it is an instance of a kind of metaphysics. It is, however, useful nonsense inasmuch as its lesson, once learned, will make it unnecessary for the learner to be concerned with philosophy, having risen above the temptation to talk nonsense.

B. Much of the above was later rejected. Wittgenstein's mature philosophy has exercised a strong influence over the analytic movement in philosophy. This stage of his philosophical development is recorded in *The Blue and Brown Books* of 1933–35, and the *Philosophical Investigations* which continues the record of his thought from the mid-thirties until his death.

(5) Wittgenstein's new approach to philosophy was signaled by a new approach to language. In place of thinking of language as having a single purpose, Wittgenstein came to view it as serving many purposes, each of these defining a language game. Language games include that "picturing" of facts which had occupied him in his earlier thought, but extend beyond this to prayer and praise, cursing, requesting, and ceremonial greeting. There is simply no point in attempting to reduce the endless kinds of language games to a single pattern. Each must be understood in its own terms.

(6) As one comes to understand the language game being played in a given situation, one is doing philosophy by overcoming philosophical perplexity, concerning the use to which language is being put. Rather than supposing that words stand for the same thing in the same way in each instance of usage, or that there are features common to every language game, one will expect nothing more than "family resemblances" among a number of instances of usage.

(7) The method of coming to terms with our own puzzlement was worked out with some precision in Wittgenstein's practice. (a) One selects a set of concepts which may cause difficulty, leading us to make paradoxical statements with respect to them. (b) One examines repeated instances of the normal use of these concepts in an effort to banish the philosophical puzzlement. (c) One reveals the nature of the language games being played in the instances of usage by inventing new language games for purposes of comparison. (d) When we see that everything is open to view, and there is nothing further to explain, it is a sign that, with respect to the concepts in question, we

have overcome our intellectual bewitchment.

(8) Raising the more general question as to whether a private language might be possible, Wittgenstein decided it was not possible on the grounds that language implies some agreement, which he calls a "form of life," concerning the use of words. In a private language this condition cannot be satisfied; it would lack a criterion of use. The problem of the criterion assumes importance not only with respect to private language, but also with respect to unobservable mental states, solipsism, and skepticism.

(9) The remarks on the foundations of mathematics approach the subject as a language game.

(10) On aesthetics, Wittgenstein takes correctness as the central concept instead of beauty. Ultimately, it seems that the right explanation is the one the individual accepts.

(11) *Zettel* is concerned with language games of sense impressions, visual images, mental images, fancies, hallucinations, and after-images.

WOLFF, CHRISTIAN. 1679–1754.

German philosopher. Born in Breslau. Educated at Jena and Leipzig. Taught at Halle and Marburg. Influenced by Leibniz whom he knew personally, and by the Cartesian method which he sought to emulate in philosophy while retaining the framework of the Scholastic tradition, Wolff elaborated a philosophy which he believed to follow rigorously from the principles of contradiction and sufficient reason (*q.v.* Leibniz 4). He wrote in opposition to Thomasius (*q.v.*), the leader of Pietism; and since Halle was the headquarters of the Pietistic movement, Wolff very soon was the object of a concerted attack which led to his expulsion from Halle by King Frederick William in 1723. He moved to the University of Marburg where he remained until 1740, when he was recalled to Halle by Frederick the Great, successor to Frederick William. His return was triumphal and he was named chancellor of the university in 1743. Wolff had many followers, not only in Germany, but also in France, Italy, and Spain. His most notable follower was Immanuel Kant. His earlier writings were in German, but from 1728 on he wrote in Latin,

hoping to reach an international audience. Principal writings: *Rational Philosophy or Logic*, 1728; *General Cosmology*, 1731; *Empirical Psychology*, 1732; *Rational Psychology*, 1734; *Natural Theology*, 2 vols., 1736–7; *Practical Philosophy*, 1738–9; *Elements of Universal Mathematics*, 1740–6; *Law of Nature*, 8 vols., 1740–8; *Economics*, 1750; *Law of Nations*, 1750; *Moral Philosophy or Ethics*, 1750–3.

(1) Defining philosophy as the science of the possible and viewing it as embracing the whole of human knowledge, Wolff subdivided the discipline into the following parts: (a) Theoretical philosophy, consisting of formal and material logic, and metaphysics. The latter is divided, in turn, into general metaphysics or ontology on the one hand, and special metaphysics on the other hand, consisting of theology, cosmology, and rational psychology. (b) Practical philosophy, which subdivides into ethics, economics, and politics. (c) Criteriology or Theory of Knowledge.

(2) Defining ontology as the science of being in general, and "first philosophy" as its synonym, he held the method and the discipline to be deductive, its organon the principles of noncontradiction and sufficient reason, and its goal a system of necessary truths.

(3) Distinguishing between rational and empirical psychology, he understood the former to consist of a metaphysical analysis of the soul, and the latter to refer to a study of its powers as revealed to one's inner sense.

(4) He differentiated between postulates and axioms, regarding the former to consist of indemonstrable, practical, and particular propositions; and the latter to consist of propositions which are indemonstrable, theoretical, and universal.

(5) His own views, filling in these divisions, are not very notable. Ontology is to provide a base for cosmology which is concerned with what can be known *a priori* about the nature and laws of moving bodies. Here he retained part of the Leibnizian monadology. The ultimate elements of reality are extensionless points of force, but they do not mirror the universe. Wolff adhered to a spiritual-material dualism, and to mechanism. In natural theology he relied on the cosmological and ontological arguments.

He rested political philosophy and natural law on ethics, defining good as what increases, and evil as what diminishes, human perfection.

(6) Much of Wolff's importance relates to his introduction of philosophical terminology. It was he who popularized the term "ontology," and who introduced the use of the term "cosmology" as a philosophical discipline separated from ontology. He introduced the terms "monism" and "teleology," applied the term "dualism" to the mind-matter opposition, and invented the word "*Begriff*" to stand for "concept" in German.

WOLLASTON, WILLIAM. 1659–1724.

English philosopher. Born at Coton-Clanford. Educated at Cambridge. A Deist, he was influenced by Samuel Clarke.

Principal writings: *The Religion of Nature Delineated*, 1722; *On The Design of the Book of Ecclesiastes*, 1724.

(1) Identifying natural religion with both morality and reason, Wollaston argued that religion is "the pursuit of happiness by the practice of truth and reason." Happiness is defined as a justly desirable end at which every rational being ought to aim.

(2) Right and wrong are determined, in his view—anticipating Bentham (*q.v.*)—by a "moral arithmetic" of pleasures and pains. In addition, however, ethical judgments relate to truth: moral good is the practical affirmation of a true proposition, and moral evil is its denial.

(3) In epistemology he was a rationalist. The deliverances of the senses are subordinate and subject to reason. Where reason is unavailable, one follows probability. But the important religious truths, such as the existence of God (first cause argument) and immortality based on desert, can be established by reason.

WOODBRIDGE, F.J.E. 1867–1940.

American philosopher. Born in Canada. Taught first at the University of Minnesota; beginning in 1902 he was professor of philosophy at Columbia University.

Principal writings: *The Realm of Mind*; *An Essay in Metaphysics*, 1926; *The Son of Apollo, Themes of Plato*, 1929; *Nature and Mind*, 1937; *An Essay on Nature*, 1940.

(1) Recognizing the influence of Aris-

totle, Spinoza, and Locke upon his thought, guiding him to a structuralistic metaphysics, he found in Santayana an influence opposing any transcendentalism, and leading him to a view of the organic interdependence of the forms of nature.

(2) The confluence of these sources led Woodbridge to a position of naturalism in philosophy, oriented toward the scientific community, and yet opposed to reductionism.

WOODGER, J.H. 1894–1981.

English biologist. Born in Great Yarmouth, Norfolk. Educated at University of London. Taught at University of London. Interested in adding to the rigor of theory construction in biology, Woodger applied to his discipline the techniques of contemporary philosophy, especially those in logic.

Principal writings: *Biological Principles*, 1929; *The Axiomatic Method in Biology*, 1937; *The Technique of Theory Construction*, 1939; *Biology and Language*, 1952; *Physics, Psychology, and Medicine*, 1956.

(1) In *Biological Principles* he developed his view of Organismic Biology, suggesting that the structure of organisms approximates a hierarchical organization of levels from O-level to some level number *n*. O-level for any given organism will consist of elementary particles, 1-level of molecules, 2-level of cells, etc. Depending upon the level of one's analysis, it is appropriate to say that the organism consists entirely of elementary particles, entirely of molecules, or entirely of cells, etc. Each level of organization has laws appropriate to that level. The laws of physics, appropriate to O-level, will not contain the entire explanation of the behavior of 1-level and 2-level constituents. Indeed, the explanation of the behavior of 1-level entities will have to take into account the patterns of organization of, *e.g.*, both O-level and 2-level entities.

(2) Adapting the logical calculus of *Principia Mathematica* to biology through the addition of ten "biological constants" and set theory to the evolutionary portion of biology, he explored at length the possibilities of formalizing the basis of the discipline.

WOOLSTON, THOMAS. 1669–1731.

English Deist. Born at Northampton. Educated at Cambridge. Taking orders in the Church of England, he remained a Cambridge fellow until 1720. Convicted of blasphemy in 1729, he died in prison. Essentially a pamphleteer, Woolston argued that Origen's allegorical interpretation of Scripture should be followed. The consequence, in his view, is that both prophecy and miracle are to be rejected if taken in a literal sense, including prophecies concerning the Messiah and the miracle of the Resurrection. They are to be interpreted allegorically as types of "spiritual things." Attacking the established priesthood, he defended religious toleration and freedom of thought.

Principal writings: *The Old Apology for the Truth of the Christian Religion*, 1705; *Four Free-Gifts to the Clergy*, 1723–4; *The Moderator Between an Infidel and an Apostate*, 1725; *A Discourse on the Miracles of Our Savior*, 1727.

WORD, THE.

From the Greek *Logos* (*q.v.*). Unamuno (*q.v.*3) regarded the Word as the intimate expression of the man of flesh and bone; while Heidegger (*q.v.* 8) found the Word present in all discourse and capable of revelatory disclosures of Being.

WORDSWORTH, WILLIAM.

Q.v. Epiphany (4).

WORLD-LINES.

Q.v. Minkowski (1, 2).

WORLD SOUL.

A conception of the divine as extended in space and including the world as its internal environment.

(1) For Plato (*q.v.* 9) the world soul represents a lesser God, as "divine as a changing thing can be," who is self-moved and the principle of animation in all other things.

(2) The view of the Stoics held many similarities to Plato's doctrine of the world soul. One difference is that the Stoics held a materialistic conception of soul. Given this difference it should be noted that Cleanthes (*q.v.* 2) identified the world with God, and Chrysippus (*q.v.* 5), starting from the presumption that soul is material, viewed God as a material, thinking being extending through-

out the universe and identical with it.

(3) Among some Platonists as well, *e.g.*, Severus (*q.v.*), the world soul assumed the role of the ultimate deity.

(4) In Plotinus (*q.v.* 4), who in his own way systematized the Platonic themes, the world soul is an emanation from God, the One, by way of the *Nous* or intelligible world, and contains the physical world as its body.

(5) Among Eastern philosophers Ramanuja (*q.v.* 4) holds Brahman to be the world soul when he is in his gross state.

(6) There are approximations to the concept of world soul in those who emphasize the microcosm-macrocosm analogy (*q.v.* Macrocosm), in Panpsychism (*q.v.*), and, of course, in many versions of Pantheism (*q.v.*).

WORLD-VIEW.

Q.v. Weltanschaung. For world-making *q.v.* Goodman (5).

WORLD YEAR.

Q.v. Heraclitus (8); Stoicism (1). Similar cyclical views of time (*q.v.* 3) were propounded by Eastern thinkers.

WORMS, DIET AND EDICT OF. 1521.

The Diet of Worms was a meeting of the estates of the German empire called by Charles V to consider the case of Martin Luther. Meeting in the town of Worms, it issued an edict denouncing Luther's views.

WORRINGER, W.

Q.v. Empathy.

WRIGHT, CHAUNCEY. 1830–1875.

American philosopher. Born in Northampton, Mass. Educated at Harvard. An occasional lecturer at Harvard. A proponent of evolution, his view of natural selection attracted Darwin's attention and was reprinted in England with the latter's support. Interested in the problem of self-consciousness, he tried to show how that quality developed from more elementary conscious processes common to animal life. Wright's influence was dominant in the Harvard Metaphysical Club; thus the evolutionary emphasis present in American pragmatism is to be explained by his influence on Peirce (*q.v.* 5), James (*q.v.*), and Holmes.

Principal writings: *Philosophical Discussions* (ed. Norton), 1877; *Letters* (ed. Thayer), 1878; *Philosophical Writings*, (ed. Madden), 1958.

WRIGHT, GEORGE H. VON. 1916–.
Finnish philosopher. Born in Helsinki. Educated at the University of Helsinki. Taught at Helsingfors 1946–61; Academy of Finland (Research professor 1961–86); in addition, numerous visiting appointments. The works which follow were written in English.
Principal writings: *The Logical Problem of Induction*, 1941; *An Essay in Modal Logic*, 1951; *A Treatise on Induction and Probability*, 1951; *Logical Studies*, 1957; *The Logic of Preference*, 1963; *Norm and Action*, 1963; *The Varieties of Goodness*, 1963; *An Essay in Deontic Logic*, 1968; *Time, Change and Contradiction*, 1969; *Explanation and Understanding*, 1971; *Causality and Determinism*, 1974; *Freedom and Determination*, 1980; *Wittgenstein*, 1982; *Philosophical Logic*, 1983; *Practical Reason*, 1983; *Truth, Knowledge, and Modality*, 1984; *The Tree of Knowledge and Other Essays*, 1993. Edited, with others, much of the Wittgenstein corpus.
(1) In Deontic Logic, Von Wright has worked out ways in which deontic operators, indicating obligation or permissibility, can be restricted to sentences which describe actions, thus avoiding the problems of actions which are not sentences and sentences which do not describe actions.
(2) Among the varieties of goodness, von Wright distinguishes instrumental, technical, utilitarian, hedonic, welfare, and moral types, standing respectively for the goodness of an instrument, of a technique, of something useful, of something pleasant, or something good for humankind. In his view, moral goodness is a subclass of utilitarian goodness.
Also *q.v.* Value (8).
(3) Distinguishing between causation in nature and in human action, von Wright also distinguishes two kinds of determinism: predetermination, allowing predictability and related to the first type of causation; and post-determination, yielding "intelligibility" and related to the second type.
Q.v. Modal Logic (6).

WRONSKI, JOSEPH. 1775–1853.
Polish-French philosopher. Born in Poland, but a resident of France, Wronski attempted to give philosophic expression to a messianic interpretation of history leading to world federation.
Principal writings: *Messianic Metapolitics* (F), 1839; *Messianism or the Absolute Reform of Human Knowledge* (F), 3 vols., 1847; *Absolute Philosophy of History* (F), 2 vols., 1852; *Progressive Development and Final End of Humanity* (F), 1861.

WUNDT, MAX. 1879–1963.
German philosopher. Born in Leipzig. Son of Wilhelm Wundt (*q.v.*). Taught in Marburg, Jena, and Tübingen. Beginning with studies of Greek philosophy, specifically in the area of ethics, he moved through a Kantian period, ending with a dialectical system closer to that of Hegel. For all that, he is regarded as a neo-Kantian, influencing both Paulsen (*q.v.*) and Adickes (*q.v.*). His final system is one which distinguishes pure being from ordinary being. The former is beyond our reach, but the latter implies the former, and there is a dialectical relation between the two forms of being which is at the same time the relation between finite and infinite, time and eternity.
Principal writings: *The History of Greek Ethics*, 2 vols., 1908, 1911; *Kant as Metaphysician*, 1924; *History of Metaphysics*, 1931; *Christian Wolff and the German Enlightenment*, 1941; *Hegel's Logic and Modern Physics*, 1949; *Investigations of Aristotle's Metaphysics*, 1953.

WUNDT, WILHELM. 1832–1900.
German philosopher. Born in Neokarau (Baden). Professor of physiology in Heidelberg; then professor of philosophy in Leipzig. It was in Leipzig that, in 1879, he established the first experimental laboratory of psychology, thus initiating psychology as an independent discipline. He strongly influenced Friedrich Paulsen (*q.v.*), H. Münsterberg (*q.v.*), and many others.
Principal writings: *The Influence of Philosophy on the Empirical Sciences*, 1876; *Logic*, 1880–83; *Ethics*, 1886; *System of Philosophy*, 1889; *The Sensible and the Supersensible World*, 1914; as well as many works on physiology.
(1) Wundt countered the positivism of

his day by recognizing the nonreducibility of the sciences of culture and the spirit, while viewing psychology as an experimental science open to the data of both external and internal experience.

(2) Rather than viewing the soul as a substance, it was for Wundt an ensemble of psychical processes.

(3) He regarded logic as a theory of the forms of synthetic thought, lying at the base of all the sciences, and especially of the methodology of the sciences.

(4) Ethics had a strong normative component for Wundt, resting on *a priori* knowledge of absolute values. It begins with a descriptive examination of customs from a psychological standpoint. But the history of different groups merely reflects the evolution and development of absolute values.

(5) Metaphysics rests on the special sciences, but extends them into a coherent and complete image of existence. In his own version of this extension, Wundt holds that with respect to the mind and body, or the psychic and the physical, the former have primacy over the latter. Soul or spirit is, then, the fundament of matter, and God as the supreme will is simply the most general synthesis of particular wills, and the ground of an evolution which includes physical as well as psychical processes.

WU WEI.

A Chinese term meaning "inaction" or "taking no unnatural action." A central term in the history of Taoism, the concept is stressed in the *Tao-Te-Ching* (*q.v.* 1–2). It is found in Taoist leaders such as Chuang Tzu (*q.v.* 3) and Huai-nan Tzu (*q.v.* 1).

WYCLIFFE, JOHN. c. 1320–1384.

English Scholastic philosopher and religious reformer. Born at Ipreswel, near Richmond, Yorkshire. Educated and taught at Oxford. Wycliffe's is the interesting case of an academic figure, called the last important "Oxford scholastic," whose abstruse philosophizing gradually led to a reform position in practice, the religious reform which later burst upon the world as the Protestant Reformation. Since Wycliffe's reform was in the national interest, he was protected from the Church by the nation no less than by his university. If Wycliffe thus escaped condemnation, all proceedings against him proving ineffectual, it was not the case with his followers. In particular, Wycliffe's doctrines, which had found a home in Bohemia, carried back by the scholars who accompanied Queen Anne of Bohemia to England on the occasion of her marriage to Richard II, became implanted in the university curriculum of that country. It was John Huss (*q.v.*) of Bohemia who, a half century after Wycliffe, speaking with the latter's voice, created a national Protestant religion and who was seized by the Church, condemned, and burned.

Principal writings: *Summa of Being; The Limits of Dominion; On Civil Dominion; Summa theologiae; On the Euchartst; Trialogue; Opus evangelicum; On the Office of the King; Sermons*; and the translation of the *Vulgate* into English.

(1) Adopting, as an Augustinian, the realist position on universals as existing prior to things (*ante rem*) in the mind of God, Wycliffe viewed their embodiment as implying a stability inconsistent with the idea of transubstantiation. For Wycliffe, every created thing or being is the same as its idea. Transubstantiation, in holding that bread and wine change into the body and blood of Christ, calls for annihilation of the universals of bread and wine, and this is impossible. Wycliffe's own view, called "remanence," and holding that the bread and wine remain in the sacrament along with the body and blood of Christ, anticipated the consubstantiation introduced by Luther (*q.v.* 13).

(2) All dominion derives from the dominion of God over all things. Any grant of temporal dominion is in the nature of a fief, conditional upon due service to the Supreme Overlord. The service expected by God is righteousness and its works. Furthermore, since the Church is not expected to be concerned about temporal matters, and since it is sinful for the clergy to have property, it is lawful for statesmen to deprive the clergy of goods whose possession they have in any case forfeited by unrighteousness.

(3) The king is God's vicar on earth. In his "palpable dignity" toward the world, the king is superior to the priest

and provides the latter his jurisdiction. The priest is superior to the king only in terms of the former's "impalpable dignity" toward God.

(4) Regarding Holy Scripture as the "charter" of the Christian religion Wycliffe, aided by friends, was responsible for the translation of the Vulgate (*q.v.*) into English. He likewise sent out across the country his own group of secular priests, itinerant preachers charged with religious instruction, anticipating by four centuries the methods of the Wesleys (*q.v.*).

XENOCRATES. 396–314 B.C.

Greek philosopher. Born in Athens. Studied in Plato's Academy. Like Speusippus (*q.v.*) he is said to have accompanied Plato on his third visit to Syracuse. Named to head the Academy in 339 after Speusippus' death, he discharged this responsibility for twenty-five years. Aristotle's criticisms of Plato are thought to be directed largely against Xenocrates and his predecessor, Speusippus.

(1) He contributed to philosophy a number of tripartite classifications, the most useful of which have been his division of epistemological objects into knowledge, opinion, and perception; and his division of the fields of knowledge into logic or dialectic, physics, and ethics.

(2) Following the Pythagoreans in their number theory, he believed all numbers to be generated from the One and the dyad. The numbers are at the same time ideas, and the One is the divinity which infuses all reality.

(3) He held the stars to be divine, and the terrestrial elements to contain demons both good and bad.

XENOPHANES. 570–c. 470 B.C.

Greek philosopher. Born in Colophon. Exiled from his home, probably by a Persian victory, tradition has it that he was a wandering minstrel for 67 years, serving as a social critic through his songs; impatient of the false values, luxuries, and sloth of the citizens. He criticized Homer and Hesiod for attributing vice and crime to the gods.

(1) Holding that there is no certain knowledge about the gods or any other matter, Xenophanes pointed out that men create gods in their own image, just as animals would make them like themselves had they the ability to draw.

(2) But this is not appropriate, since God does not move from place to place; nor has He sense organs nor any physical form. He is unmoving, changeless, all-perceiving, homogeneous, and ruler of all. Apparently He is the unity of the whole universe, and its ruling spirit.

(3) If the view also requires an identity of God and nature, this would lead to the further conclusion that change and movement in the universe are somehow and to some extent an illusion. He would then stand as a forerunner of the Eleatics (*q.v.*), and tradition so places him.

XENOPHON. c. 430–c. 355 B.C.

Greek writer and moralist. Born in Athens. An active participant in civic life, Xenophon was one of the young Athenians who felt friendship for Socrates. After the latter's death, Xenophon, although not himself a philosopher, answered the charges that Socrates was guilty of impiety and corrupting the youth. The charges had been made at the trial and were repeated later by Polycrates. Xenophon replied to the charges in his *Memorabilia* by picturing Socrates as a teacher of virtue and practical knowledge who exerted a beneficial influence on all who knew him. Socratic irony and subtlety are missing, probably due to limitations in Xenophon's understanding. In another dialogue, the *Symposium*, Socrates praises nobility of spirit and contrasts heavenly to earthly love.

Principal writings: *Anabasis* (T); *Apology* (T); *Memorabilia or Reflections of Socrates* (T); *Household Management* (T); *Symposium* (T); *Education of Cyrus* (T); *Hellenica* (T).

XIRAU, JOAQUIN. 1895–1946.

Spanish philosopher. Born in Figueras. Educated at Barcelona. Taught at Barcelona and the National University of Mexico. Influenced by Ortega y Gasset, Xirau attempted to solve the problems of being and value by taking neither subject nor object, but rather the subject-object relationship, as ultimate.

Principal writings: *The Meaning of Truth*, 1927; *Love and World*, 1940; *The Philosophy of Husserl*, 1941; *The Passing and the Eternal*, 1942.

YAHWEH.
The name of the God of Israel, originally written "YHWH," without the vowels, as a sign of reverence.

YAJURVEDA.
One of the four *Vedas* (*q.v.* 1b) of early Hinduism, the *Yajurveda* is highly ritualistic in character.

YAMAZAKI ANSAI. 1618–1682.
Japanese philosopher. A Confucian of the Chu Hsi (*q.v.*) school, Yamazaki developed a Confucian Shintoism (*q.v.*), leading to increasing interest in Shinto studies.

Principal writings: *Collected Commentaries on Chu Hsi's Regulations for the School of the White Deer Cave.*

YANG CHU. c. 440–360 B.C.
Chinese philosopher. A representative of Taoism (*q.v.*), he nonetheless supported a hedonistic and egoistic point of view, allegedly holding that he would not pluck out a single hair were it to benefit the entire world. Strongly attacked by Mencius (*q.v.*).

YANG HSIUNG. 53 B.C.–18 A.D.
Chinese Taoistic, Confucianist philosopher, of the Han period.

Principal writings: *Model Sayings; Classic of the Supremely Profound Principle.*

(1) Human nature is a mixture of good and evil. If the good is cultivated, man will become good. If the evil is cultivated, man will become evil. Hence man must study hard and practice earnestly to fulfill the Way.

(2) Although Yang Hsiung, following Confucius, held that questions about the

existence of immortal beings are fruitless, and to be replaced by questions on loyalty and filial piety, still he held to the existence of a Supremely Profound Principle as the operative power behind *yin* and *yang*, responsible for the origin of material force, originating the various species, and determining the course of events in the world.

YASNA.
One of the five parts of the *Avesta*, sacred scriptures of Zoroastrianism (*q.v.* 4).

YEHUDA HA-LEVI.
Q.v. Ha-Levi.

YEW YÜAN. 1635–1704.
Chinese neo-Confucian philosopher. A native of Chih-Li. A poor man, he was first devoted to the idealism of Wang Yang-Ming, and then to the rationalism of Chu Hsi. Became director of an academy in 1696, where he put his educational theories into practice.

Principal writings: *Preservation of Human Nature; Corrections of Wrong Interpretations of the Four Books; Classified Conversations of Chu Hsi.*

(1) Turning back to the ideas of Confucius and Mencius, Yew Yüan stressed practical experience over book learning, and the solution of practical problems over meditation. Knowledge and action form a unity. His school had four emphases: classics and history, literary matters, military craft, and practical arts.

(2) He advocated return to a system of agriculture allegedly followed in ancient times, in which eight families would constitute a unit, each having its own plot of land, and jointly cultivate for the government a ninth plot of similar size.

(3) Identifying principle and material force, he found the origin of evil neither in human nature nor in physical nature, but in agitation, obscuration, and bad influence.

YIN AND YANG.
Chinese terms appearing in Chinese thought from remote times, standing for two opposed and yet complementary principles of the universe. *Yin* stands for the feminine, negative, passive, weak,

and destructive element. *Yang* is the masculine, positive, active, constructive element. All that happens is said to be a product of these two elements.

(1) One of the most important sources for the ideas of *yin* and *yang* is the *Tao-Te Ching* (*q.v.* 4), chief scripture of Taoism (*q.v.*). In this context the two elements are related to the finding of the *tao*, or way, in life.

(2) Another source is the *Yin Yang Philosophy* (*q.v.*), combining *yin* and *yang*, the two principles, with the concept of the "rotation of dominance" of the "five agents"—metal, wood, water, fire, and earth. The combination of the two sets of ideas yields a cyclical view of history. Tsou Yen (*q.v.*) in the 3rd century B.C. is regarded as the chief thinker of the school, although little is known about him and his writings are lost.

(3) Chuang Tzu (*q.v.* 4) taught that from non-being the One originated, dividing into *yin* and *yang* and producing all other things.

(4) Tung Chung Shu (*q.v.* 2) related the principles of *yin* and *yang* to the "Ruler as standard" doctrine of his *Yin Yang* Confucianism.

(5) Huai-Nan Tzu (*q.v.* 2) used *yin* and *yang* to explain the seasons, sun, moon, stars, planets, and the elements.

(6) Shao Yung (*q.v.* 1–3), a neo-Confucianist, traced *yin* and *yang* to the Great Ultimate. He applied the principles to astronomy, cosmology, and philosophy of history.

(7) Chang Tsai (*q.v.* 1) held the principles of *yin* and *yang* to be aspects of material force, his basic category.

(8) Chou Tun-I (*q.v.* 1) regarded *yin* and *yang* as the basic, productive principles of the universe.

(9) Chu Hsi (*q.v.* 3) identified *yin* and *yang* with the principles of the one and the many.

Also *q.v.* Yang Hsiung (2); Wang Fu-Chih (2).

YIN YANG PHILOSOPHY.

A Chinese doctrine, not the product of a school of philosophy or of a particular distinguished philosopher (although Tsou Yen, 305–240 B.C., is given credit for it), but a natural development which has influenced most Chinese philosophers, and many aspects of Chinese life. The

doctrine runs so far back into Chinese history that its origins are obscure. The following ideas are relevant:

(1) Reality is in constant change, and this change is to be explained by the interaction of two primal elements, forces, or principles: *yin*, the female principle, negative, passive, weak, yielding; and *yang*, the male principle, positive, active, strong, assertive. The respective force of these principles in objects and events determines their character. But the *yin-yang* opposition does not carry the entire burden of explanation. These principles work in conjunction with another set of principles.

(2) The five elements—metal, wood, water, fire, earth—provide a matrix for the working of *yin* and *yang*. But in nature and in history there is a succession in which these elements are dominant in turn. Thus the idea of cycles in nature and history, and a cyclical philosophy of history, are introduced. And man and nature are joined in a single scheme of explanation.

(3) The notion of fives was elaborated into other areas. There are the five activities: appearance, speech, seeing, hearing, thinking. The five parts of time: year, month, day, zodiacal distinctions, and the calendric calculations. The five blessings: longevity, wealth, health, virtue, and an end crowning life. In addition there are the five directions, the five musical notes, five sense organs, five metals, five virtues, five feelings, and five social relations.

YOGA.

A Sanskrit term meaning both "yoke" and "union." Thus, a practical means of discipline leading to union of the individual self and the universal soul. The term may also derive from the root *yuj* ("to contemplate").

(1) Although there are anticipations or parallels of Yoga in the Yogachara (*q.v.*) School of Mahayana Buddhism, the School of Yoga is one of the six orthodox schools of Indian philosophy, respecting the Vedic scriptures. Patanjali (*q.v.*) is regarded as the founder.

(2) Yoga is really the applied side of the Sankhya school, another of the orthodox systems. Indeed, Sankhya (*q.v.* 2) is said to have elaborated the theory while

Yoga established the practice leading to the same end. Yoga differs from most varieties of the Sankhya system by being theistic.

(3) The concept of *citta* has importance in the yoga system. *Citta* is a kind of mind-stuff in terms of which the human ego is built. Both *citta* and the ego have an ultimate unreality. The ego is a result of (a) *Avidya*, confusing the non-eternal with the eternal; (b) *Asmita*, identifying self with body and mind: (c) *Raga*, building attachments to pleasant things; (d) *Dvesha*, developing antipathies to fear of death; (e) *Abhinivesha*, persistent attachment to multiplicity. Freedom from *citta*, on the other hand, destroys the ego and reveals the self.

(4) *Ashtangayoga* develops an eightfold path leading to liberation. The eight steps include: (a) *yama* or negative ethical preparation. This requires the five vows of Jainism: abstention from injury (*ahimsa*), falsehood, stealing, passion, and avarice; (b) *niyama* or positive ethical preparation. This includes internal and external purification, austerity (*tapas*), study, and devotion to God; (c) *asana* or posture as a means of assisting the act of meditation; (d) *pranayama* or breath control as an aid in concentrating the mind; (e) *pratyahara* or control of the senses, checking their outward tendencies and concentrating them internally; (f) *dharana* or fixing the mind on the object of meditation; (g) *dhyana* or the undisturbed flowing meditation itself; (h) *samadhi* or complete, absorbed concentration. In conscious concentration, one of the two types, one is aware of the object of meditation. In supraconscious concentration, the meditator and the object of meditation completely fuse, and there is no awareness of the object of the meditation.

(5) Of the many types of yoga, differentiated by the elements which are stressed, four are usually considered basic: (a) *Raja Yoga* stresses concentration. The yoga of Patanjali belongs to this type. (b) *Bhakti* yoga stresses devotion as the path to liberation. (c) *Jnana* yoga stresses knowledge as the path leading to enlightenment. (d) *Hatha* yoga stresses posture, physical discipline of the body, as the basic means of reaching the goal, while including all of the emphases made in (4) above. In addition to these four,

many other types and combinations of types have been practiced.

(6) Advocating the *Asparsha* yoga view of the Advaita Vedantin, Gaudapada (*q.v.*) emphasizes "uncontaminated meditation," and requires that one remain aloof from contact with all living things. Regarded as extremely difficult, it is held that success in the endeavor leads at once to identification with Brahman.

(7) *Shiva* yoga differs from Raja yoga only in the relation of the former to Shiva, the lord of sleep. The discipline, then, includes knowledge of Shiva, devotion to Shiva, contemplation of Shiva, observance of the austerities connected with Shiva, and ritual worship of Shiva.

(8) The *Bhagavad-Gita* speaks of *karma* yoga, a method of seeking release through acting according to one's duty.

(9) *Mantra* yoga seeks self-control by means of the secret power of sounds. The rhythmic repetition of the sound, "om," the sacred "syllable of obeisance," or of other more complex formulae devised by seers of old with alleged knowledge of the power of sounds, is expected to result in enlightenment, release of vital energy, and strengthening of mental awareness. The *mantras* are often related to the beads of a special rosary. The *mantras* of the various deities, properly employed, lead to the dissolving of the mind into the deity represented.

(10) In *Kundalini* yoga it is held that the human being consists of a self or soul, a gross body, and a subtle body. The subtle body is identified with immense energy resources trapped within one's being, and the point of the yogic discipline is to release this energy under the control of mental awareness. This is held to be the same thing as achieving the pure self, and making a breakthrough to the universal consciousness. The basic coiled energy, called *kundalini*, relates to certain centers of the body, and to certain arteries along which the vital energy may be induced to rise toward the highest center at the crown of the head (called the "lotus of a thousand petals"). Other centers of importance are at the base of the spinal column, in the sexual organs, in the region of the navel, in the region of the heart, in the region of the throat, and between the brows.

(11) *Laya* yoga, assuming a male-

female, person-nature dualism and taking the six centers and the "lotus of a thousand petals" as its framework, identifies the crown of the head with the male principle and person, and the root center at the base of the spine with the female principle and nature. The task is to awaken and release the feminine, natural energy, leading it from center to center to the crown of the head of the person. The final goal is merging with the supreme person. Some of the practices of Hatha yoga are employed. In addition there is an emphasis upon listening for the inner sound from each of the centers, leading to the appearance of the light of the self.

(12) The term "integral yoga" is used by the Advaita Vedantin, Sri Aurobindo (*q.v.* 3), to designate the process of personal transformation onto the spiritual plane.

Also *q.v.* Aesthetics (1).

YOGACARA (YOGACHARA).
Sanskrit term meaning "the way of Yoga." *Q.v.* Asanga; Vasubandhu; Consciousness (1); *Śunya* (4).

YOUNG, BRIGHAM.
Q.v. Latter Day Saints.

YÜ FA-K'AI. 4th cent. A.D.
Chinese Buddhist philosopher. *Q.v.* Seven Early Chinese Buddhist Schools (5).

YÜ TAO-SUI.
Chinese Buddhist philosopher. *Q.v.* Seven Early Chinese Buddhist Schools (7).

Z

ZABARELLA, JACOPO. 1533–1589.
Italian philosopher. Born in Padua. Taught at Padua. An outstanding Renaissance Aristotelian, Zabarella made liberal use of Averroës interpretations of the master. Alexandrine interpretations likewise exerted an influence. In logic, he distinguished between compositive and resolutive methods, the former beginning with premises and reasoning to a conclusion; the latter beginning with

the conclusion, or desired end, and reasoning back to the premises necessary to achieve the intended result. Zabarella's views on the structure of science led to controversy with his Paduan colleagues, Piccolomini and Petrella. His works are in Latin.

Principal writings: *Logic*, 1587; *On the Nature of Things*, 1589; *The Order of Doctrine*, 1589; *Physics*, 1601; *Defense Against the Objections of Piccolomini on the Order of Doctrine*, 1606; and commentaries on a number of the works of Aristotle.

ZARATHUSTRA.
The uncorrupted version of the name, Zoroaster (*q.v.*), founder of Zoroastrianism (*q.v.*), the one time national religion of Iran. Also, the central character of Nietzsche's philosophical poem, *Thus Spake Zarathustra* (*q.v.* Nietzsche).

ZAWIRSKI.
Q.v. Warsaw Circle.

ZAZEN.
The term for meditation in Zen Buddhism (*q.v.* 8).

ZEA, LEOPOLDO.
Q.v. Latin American Philosophy (12).

ZELLER, EDUARD. 1814–1908.
German philosopher. Born in Kleinbottwar. Educated at Tübingen where he first taught. Later he held posts at Berne, Marburg, Heidelberg, and Berlin. Influenced by Hegel, but later saw a need to return to the epistemological basis of Kant.

Principal writings: *Greek Philosophy*, 3 vols., 1844, 1846, 1852; *Lectures and Discussions*, 1865; *Compendium of the History of Greek Philosophy*, 1883.

(1) Following the Hegelian idea in which the history of philosophy shows a development of the human spirit, Zeller produced important work in the history of Greek philosophy.

(2) Regarding theory of knowledge as the fundamental philosophical discipline, and calling for a return to this discipline which, he said, implies a return to Kant, Zeller counts among the neo-Kantians of the second half of the 19th century. Having taught at both Marburg and Heidelberg, he can perhaps be considered as belonging to both schools although we

have treated him in a more general way as precursor to the neo-Kantian schools (*q.v.* Neo-Kantianism 1).

ZEN BUDDHISM.

Called *Zen* in Japan, *Ch'an* in China (both terms signifying "meditation"), a form of religion which developed out of, and in reaction to, Hinayana and Mahayana Buddhism, while remaining a form of the latter.

A. The history of the movement includes its origin in India, rise to prominence in China, and transfer to Japan where it flourishes.

(1) Although originating in India, Zen became visible only in China, having been introduced by Bodhidharma (460–534) who by tradition taught the *Lankavatara Sutra* (concerning the entry of the Buddha into Lanka). Evidence that the development of Zen in China was influenced by Taoism is seen in the presence of the word "tao" in Zen writings as an equivalent to *dharma* or "Buddha-nature, and in locating the goal of understanding beyond language."

(2) The movement gained its present focus with Hung-jen (601–674) who taught the *Chin-kang ching* or *Diamond Scripture*, emphasizing not ultimate reality but the human mind.

(3) Following Hung-jen, the movement divided into two schools: a northern school led by Shen-hsiu (605–706), stressing gradual enlightenment; and a southern school led by Hui-neng (638–713), stressing sudden enlightenment. The position may be suggested by the story of Hui-neng's accession to power. An itinerant seller of firewood, Hui-neng was attracted to the monastery where the fifth patriarch (Hung-jen) was instructing his disciples. For eight months he worked in the stables. When the reigning patriarch, near death, decided to pick as his successor the one who wrote the best verse summarizing the teaching of Zen, the favorite candidate inscribed his verse on the wall outside the master's hall:

The body is like unto the Bodhi-tree,
The mind is the stand of a bright
  mirror.
Carefully we cleanse it hour by hour
Lest dust should fall upon it.

Hui-neng saw the verse, felt something

wrong with it, and had a corrective verse placed beside the other:

Neither is there Bodhi-tree,
Nor has the bright mirror any stand.
Since Buddha is forever clear and pure
Whereon can the dust fall?

The patriarch sensed Hui-neng's comprehension of Zen and appointed him successor. In his first declaration Hui-neng identified Zen with "seeing into one's own nature."

(4) Energizing powerfully in China until the 13th century, Zen found a home in Japan in 1191 when Eisai (1141–1215) brought it from China. The Rinzai sect of Zen Buddhism developed from Eisai's school. This school featured sudden enlightenment and extensive use of the *koan* (*q.v.* 7 below). The Soto sect, a rival to Rinzai, was established by Dogen (1200–53) who stressed the gradual attainment of enlightenment and such extensive use of *zazen* (Japanese for "sitting cross-legged in meditation") that he called his method "*zazen* only." Although the Soto sect has a larger number of adherents, both sects remain influential today.

B. Of the tenets set forth in this section Rinzai stresses (7) while Soto stresses (8). Soto rejects (7) and Rinzai uses (8) to focus attention on one's *koan*.

(5) For Zen Buddhism generally *Nirvana* and *Samsara* are identical. One's usual life and the *Tao* are self-same. The Buddha-nature is in everyone, so that all can become Buddhas; and the Buddha-mind is everywhere, so that anything can occasion its realization. Enlightenment can hence be gained in the midst of ordinary living. The difference between a Buddha and an ordinary person is that one realizes it while the other does not. How, then, is the realization to be gained?

(6) Enlightenment, or *satori*, is so near to us and so obvious that it is ordinarily overlooked. It involves a return to one's original nature, and one's original relations with the world of nature. But it cannot be found through rigorous asceticism as such, and it cannot be found conceptually. It was thus necessary to find ways to move the seeker beyond conceptual formulations to the "nonattachment" of one's original nature, characterized by "absence of characters" and absence of thought.

(7) Just this is the point of the *koan*, a problem designed to baffle one's ordinary intellectual apprehension, forcing a new orientation of awareness: "A sound is made by the clapping of hands. What is the sound of one hand?" "Whenever there is any question, one's mind is confused. What is wrong? Kill! Kill!" "What is the Buddha nature? Three pounds of flax." *Koans* are not nonsense, strictly speaking, but problems set in all seriousness for disciples at different levels in their struggles for enlightenment. The *koan* poses a dilemma capable of arresting the mind, of calling up analogies; but the point is to pass beyond this symbolic formulation, to move through the *koan*, emerging on its other side with a unity of mind and spirit one had not possessed before. A cuff on the side of the head administered at the proper time by the master, a tweaked nose in answer to a question, a beating with a stick, likewise serve as *koans*. When a *koan* is solved, typically a flash of enlightenment comes. In successive cases, enlightenment remains with the individual for longer periods of time. Finally, when *satori* is achieved, the enlightenment is in full flood, every vestige of doubt is swept away, and the world is seen in all of its incredible beauty. One then has become "a Buddha in this very body."

(8) Meditation, called *zazen*, is employed for the purpose of encouraging *satori*. For Dogen, the founder of Soto, *zazen*, which provides inner peace, is ultimately equivalent to *satori*. For Rinzai it allows the individual mental quiescence, conserving psychic energy, and concentrating attention on the struggle with one's *koan*.

(9) Zen has had a powerful influence on Chinese and Japanese culture, especially the latter, and is reflected in the simplicity of its architecture and the subtlety of its paintings.
Q.v. Suzuki.

ZEND-AVESTA.
Q.v. Avesta.

ZENO OF CITIUM. c. 335–264 B.C.
Greek philosopher. Born in Cyprus. A disciple of the Cynic philosopher Crates (*q.v.*), of the Megarian Stilpo (*q.v.*), and of the Academic philosophers Xenocrates

(*q.v.*) and Polemon (*q.v.*). Zeno is regarded as the founder of the Stoic school of philosophy (*q.v.* Stoicism) whose views were refined and unified by Zeno's students, among them Cleanthes (*q.v.*) and Chrysippus (*q.v.*). Zeno's own orientation was toward Cynicism (*q.v.*).

Principal writings: *On the Republic; On the Life According to Nature; On Human Nature; On Love; Exhortation.* Only fragments remain.

ZENO OF ELEA. 490–430 B.C.
Greek philosopher. A disciple of Parmenides (*q.v.*) and one of the most prominent Eleatic philosophers, he is known for his skillful defense of the Parmenidean doctrines. Regarded by Aristotle as the inventor of dialectic, Zeno supported Parmenides' view of reality as changeless being by developing paradoxes of space, time, motion, and change which he believed to be implicit in the commonsense conception of the world.

Principal writings: Fragments remain of his book which contain the paradoxes set forth below.

(1) If one grain of millet is dropped it falls noiselessly to the ground; and so, too, with any number of grains taken singly; but if a bushel of millet is poured out it falls with a great noise. Yet it is paradoxical that 10,000 instances of noiselessness should produce any noise at all.

(2) Space is a contradictory notion and reality is indivisible, for the opposite claim leads to absurdity. Suppose that reality is divisible. It will be composed either of a finite or of an infinite number of parts. Reality could have a finite number of parts only if the magnitude of the parts disappeared in a finite number of divisions; but this would lose the finite space with which we began, since a finite number of parts without magnitude cannot produce a magnitude. If, on the other hand, reality has an infinite number of parts, the parts will have magnitude or else they will not. If they do not have magnitude, once again we have lost the space with which we began. If they do have magnitude, and we have an infinite number of them, we can construct a space as much larger than the initial space as we please. Hence, we must give up the idea of space, and of a divisible reality.

(3) Any line, *e.g.*, "xy," is either divisible or indivisible. If divisible, it is divisible either into a finite number or an infinite number of parts. These will either have or lack magnitude. If the line is divisible into a finite number of parts lacking magnitude, we cannot reconstitute the line. If divisible into an infinite number of parts lacking magnitude, the same result follows. And if the line is divisible into an infinite number of parts, and each part has magnitude, we can constitute a line as much longer than the original as we please. Hence, lines are not divisible.

(4) The flying arrow cannot be flying, for if the arrow is moving it must either be moving in a place where it is, or in a place where it is not. It cannot be moving in a place where it is, or it would not be there; and it cannot be moving in a place where it is not, for it is not there.

(5) Achilles, running swiftly, cannot catch the tortoise, crawling slowly, for in order to do so he would have to reach the end of an infinite series, and an infinite series has no end. If Achilles is, at the start, 100 yards behind the tortoise and covers the 100 yards while the tortoise is crawling ten, then while Achilles is running the remaining ten yards the tortoise is crawling one, and while Achilles is covering one yard the tortoise is crawling 1/10; so that, while Achilles approaches infinitely closely, he can never reach the slowly crawling tortoise. Nor can he do so even by increasing his speed, so long as the tortoise remains in motion. The conclusion, then, holds that the commonsense world is fraught with contradiction.

(6) Time, likewise, is contradictory. Let us suppose three rows of bodies. one row ("A") at rest, and the other two ("B" and "C") moving in opposite directions. Beginning from the positions indicated in figure one, by the time they are in the same part of the course (figure two), the B's will have passed twice as many C's as A's. (Consider the matter from the standpoint of the B on the right by way of illustration.) Hence, it would take twice as long to pass the A's as it takes to pass the C's; but it takes B and C exactly the same time to reach the position of A. Hence, double the time is equal to the half.

```
A A A A          A A A A
B B B B          B B B B
    C C C C      C C C C
(Fig. one)       (Fig. two)
```

For similar Eastern views *q.v.* Hui Shih, Nagarjuna, Seng-chao (1).

ZENO'S PARADOXES.
Q.v. Zeno of Elea.

ZERMELO, ERNST. 1871–1953.
German mathematician. Born in Berlin. Studied at Göttingen. Taught at Zurich beginning in 1910.

Principal writings: "A Proof That Every Set Can Be Well Ordered" (T), 1904; "Investigations on the Foundations of Set Theory" (T), 1908; "On Finite Sets and the Principle of Complete Induction" (F), 1909; "On Number Limits and the Range of Sets" (G), 1930.

(1) Beginning from a small number of primitive relations and seven axioms, Zermelo demonstrated that set theory could be organized into a deductive system. He thus initiated what is known as "Axiomatic Set Theory."

(2) His seven axioms deal with the equality of sets, their conjunction, comprehension, union, subsets, infinite sets, and the Axiom of Choice.

(3) Since the project of developing an Axiomatic Set Theory rejects the principle of unrestricted set existence, it avoids the paradoxes which led Russell to the theory of types (*q.v.*) and restores consistency to the foundations of mathematics. The paradoxes about sets which are and are not members of themselves are called indifferently the Zermelo Paradox or the Russell Paradox (*q.v.* Paradox 5).

(4) Sets may be either finite or infinite (*q.v.* Cantor 1–7), and ordered or not ordered. Well-ordered sets have the properties of comparability and inductivity. While there is no difficulty in proving that finite, ordered sets are well-ordered, infinite sets present a special problem. Well-ordering is proven for such sets by the introduction of a special axiom.

(5) This is the famous seventh axiom, called by Zermelo the Axiom of Choice.

This axiom posits an operation whereby the well-ordered selection set which one needs is created. It holds that, given any family of sets, no matter how large, including infinite sets, it is possible to choose simultaneously an element from each subset, constructing a set containing just those elements. Had the infinite set in question consisted of shoes, to use Russell's example, we could have created a selection set by comprehension from the third axiom; that is, from the infinite set of shoes we could create the selection set of all left shoes. But if one is confronted by an infinite set of stockings, the axiom of comprehension is not applicable, and we must invoke a special means of establishing the selection set which is needed. For Zermelo and the majority of set theorists who have followed him this means is the Axiom of Choice.

ZETETIC.
From the Greek *zetesis* ("art of inquiry"). Hence, one who engages in inquiry or the act itself. The term came to be applied to the followers of Pyrrho (*q.v.*), and thus came to refer to the skeptical doctrine itself and to those who held it.

ZIEGLER, THEOBALD. 1846–1918.
German philosopher. Taught at Strassburg. Interested in philosophy of education and philosophy of religion, Ziegler first regarded feeling as the basis of religious belief. Later he expanded the role of feeling, viewing it as the basic psychological process in man from which both reason and will are derivative.
Principal writings: *Feeling*, 1893; *Faith and Knowledge*, 1899; *Men and Problems*, 1914.

ZIEHEN, THEODOR. 1862–1950.
German psychologist-philosopher. Born in Frankfurt am Main. Taught at Utrecht, Halle, and Berlin. He defended a "neutralist" doctrine of epistemology in which the *gignomene* or "given" is the sole reality. Interpreted according to causal laws, the *gignomene* is viewed in quantitative, physiological terms. Interpreted according to the parallel laws of mental life, the *gignomene* is qualitative. The laws of logic are to be found in both interpretations and are thus likewise based on the *gignomene*.
Principal writings: *Psycho-physiological*

Theory of Knowledge, 1898; *On the General Relations Between Mental and Spiritual Life*, 1902; *Theory of Knowledge on a Psycho-physiological and Physical Basis*, 1913; *Theory of Knowledge*, 2 vols., 1934, 1939.

ZIFF, PAUL. 1922– .
American philosopher. Born in New York City. Educated at Cornell. Taught at the University of Michigan, Harvard, University of Pennsylvania, University of Wisconsin, University of Illinois, University of North Carolina.
Principal writings: *Semantic Analysis*, 1960; *Philosophic Turnings*, 1966; *Understanding Understanding*, 1972; *Antiaesthetics*, 1984; *Epistemic Analysis*, 1984.
(1) Led to the study of language by the difficulty of making sense in philosophy, Ziff believed that a rigorous semantic theory is required to avoid "philosophical rubbish," and considered his work in semantic analysis an informal introduction to that theory. Major flaws, pointed out in the positions of the icons of philosophy, support his contention.
(2) Apart from his essays in aesthetics (containing an intrinsic value definition of "good work of art"), his constant preoccupation concerned doing philosophy in an appropriate manner.
Q.v. Semantics (5).

ZINZENDORF, COUNT NICOLAUS LUDWIG VON. 1700–1760.
German religious leader. Born in Dresden. Educated at Halle and Wittenberg. As a Lutheran, Zinzendorf's original goal was to stimulate vital religious experience within the Lutheran church. When a group of refugees from Bohemia arrived at his Berthelsdorf estate, Zinzendorf found himself in charge of a movement which gained its own identity as the Moravian Church or the Moravian Brethren. The original settlement, called Herrnhut ("the Lord's tabernacle"), spread out into colonies in Germany, Denmark, Russia, England, Holland, the Baltic states, and North America. It was contact with the Moravian Brethren which led John Wesley (*q.v.*) to the doctrine of justification by faith.

ZIONISM.
From the Hebrew *tsiyon* ("Jerusalem"). The name given to the movement for the

return of Jews to the promised land for the purpose of establishing a national state in Palestine. Originally associated with the doctrine of the Messiah, Zionism became a modern movement beginning in the second half of the 19th century and continuing into the 20th through the writings of Heinrich Graetz, Leo Pinsker, Theodor Herzl, and Chaim Weizmann. The 1927 Balfour Declaration by the English government sanctioned the Herzl program, and the Second World War gave it impetus.

ZOHAR.

From the Hebrew, meaning "splendor" or "brightness." A Jewish mystical work reputedly deriving from the 2nd century A.D., which formed one of the central documents of the Cabala (*q.v.* 2d). In the form of a commentary on the Pentateuch, esoteric interpretations of Scripture combine with mysticism, magic, and astrology. The book was compiled, and probably in large part created, by Moses de Leon in the 13th century.

ZOOSEMIOTICS.

Q.v. Semiotic (13).

ZOROASTER.

The name is a corrupt Greek form of the Iranian "Zarathustra." His date is a matter for conjecture, but he probably lived some time after 1000 B.C. He was founder of the Zoroastrian religion, which endured until crushed by the persecutions following the Islamic invasion of 636 A.D. It is likely that Zoroaster emerged from the school of the Magi in Media, that he began to preach his purified religion in Media with little success, that he wandered into the east of Iran where he gained important followers. According to the *Gathas*—that part of the *Avesta*, or sacred scriptures of Zoroastrianism, claiming to contain the words of the prophet—Zoroaster gained the backing of King Vishtaspa in east Iran. Having converted the king and his court, Zoroaster gained a strong base, allowing the successful growth of the new religion. The religion of Zoroaster became the national religion of Iran and spread throughout the Near East. The dualistic system of Zoroaster represents a purification of the Aryan-Indian folk religions, and contains the following emphases:

(1) At the beginning there were two powerful, creative spirits, one good and the other evil. The good spirit is Ahura Mazda, or Ormazd. The evil spirit is Ahriman, or Angra Mainyu. Ahura Mazda is the creative force expressed in light, life, law, order, truth, and all that is pure and good. Ahriman expresses himself in darkness, filth, death, and evil.

(2) Ahura Mazda has around him a group of helpers, the "immortal holy ones," who do his bidding. They seem to be the embodiment of ethical ideas, such as the good, truth, power, authority, perfection, and immortality. The evil spirit, too, has hosts of helpers.

(3) The history of the world is the scene of the struggle between these two forces. Although they are at present in balance, Ahura Mazda will at length triumph over the evil spirit. When he does, the kingdom of heaven will be at hand. A judgment will occur, leading to the plunging of the wicked, and their leader Ahriman, into the abyss, forever destroying the power of evil. The righteous will then live forever in the one undivided kingdom of Ahura Mazda in eternal fellowship with each other, with Ahura Mazda, and his angels.

(4) But there is also a judgment which comes to each man at the end of his life. The fate of a man after death is a strict consequence of his life on earth. While he lives, every deed, every word, and every thought of every man is recorded in the book of life. At the end an accounting is made. It is said that after death man passes to the accountant's bridge. If he has a balance of good over evil, he is able to cross the bridge into paradise. If evil outweighs the good, he loses his footing and falls forthwith into hell. If the good and the evil are in balance, he goes into an intermediate stage of existence, and his fate is not determined until the final judgment.

(5) In both kinds of judgment it is clear that man is central to the world drama. Man is the creation of Ahura Mazda, but was created with free will. He can render service to Ahura Mazda by doing good, or service to Ahriman by doing evil. But due to man's blindness and ignorance he is easily led astray; thus the victory of Ahura Mazda has been delayed. In this circumstance Ahura Mazda determined

to send a prophet to lead men to salvation. The prophet was Zoroaster.

(6) Zoroaster felt within himself the call to help deliver mankind. He experienced many visions, and he felt that he was in direct communication with God and the archangels. According to the record he was tempted by ·Ahriman, but withstood the temptation. His coming, he felt, was Ahura Mazda's final appeal to mankind. He believed that the end of the present dispensation of time was not far distant, and that he and his followers might well see the dawn of the new age when the power of the evil one would be broken.

ZOROASTRIANISM.

The religion of Zoroaster (*q.v.*), and the religion of all of Persia prior to the conversion of the Persians to Islam (*q.v.*). Zoroastrianism flourished in Persia during the first millennium B.C.

(1) After Zoroaster's death a priesthood arose, organizing the doctrines and ceremonies, performing the rites of purification, and codifying the scriptures. Old gods were admitted to the ritual, and new gods added. The *fravashi*, or guardian angels of the faithful, appeared. These are protecting spirits who accompany a devotee of the religion everywhere. The center of worship was the holy fire on the altar. The day of judgment was pushed off until 3000 years after the death of the founder.

(2) Under the Sasanides, Zoroastrianism was recognized as the state church, and the head of the church was second in power only to the king.

(3) Manichaeism (*q.v.*) is the best-known sect to have split off from the parent stock.

(4) The scriptures of Zoroastrianism, known as the *Avesta*, were destroyed by Alexander in the 4th century B.C. Further losses were suffered in the Islamic book burnings of the 7th century A.D. Out of the remnants the present scriptures were pieced together, consisting of five parts: the *Yasna*—the chief liturgical work including the *Gathas* or hymns ascribed to Zoroaster himself; the *Vispered*—a supplementary ritual; the *Yashta*—hymns to angels and lesser divinities; the *Vendidad*—an account of creation along with homiletic material (according to the tradition only this work has survived in full); and the *Khorda Avesta*, a collection of short prayers for the use of worshipper as well as priest.

(5) The Parsis of India were Zoroastrians who migrated eastward to escape Alexander and the Gabars of Persia. Present-day Parseism (*q.v.*) in India continues to recognize Zoroaster as its prophet, uses the *Avesta* as its scriptures, and maintains the old practices, while having rejected the evil spirit, Ahriman, in favor of monotheism.

ZUBIRI, XAVIER. 1898– .

Spanish philosopher. Born in San Sebastian. Educated at Rome, Madrid, and Freiburg. Taught at Madrid and Barcelona. Oriented toward existentialism, Zubiri invented the concept of "religation" to replace Heidegger's (*q.v.* 1, 4) concept of one's being hurled (*geworfen*) into the world. According to Zubiri's doctrine we come into the world with a sense of obligation to find the task we must fulfill. The sense of religation is ultimately our bond to the divine. Zubiri looked upon philosophy and science as two complementary and interdependent approaches to a single reality.

Principal writings: *Essay on a Phenomenological Theory of Judgment*, 1923; *Nature, History, God*, 1944; *Philosophical Studies: On Essence*, 1962; *Five Lessons of Philosophy*, 1963.

ZUHANDENE.

Q.v. Heidegger (5).

ZWINGLI, HULDREICH. 1484–1531.

Swiss religious leader. Born at Wildhaus, St. Gall. Educated at Vienna and Basel. Taught at Basel. Ordained a priest in 1506, he was generally humanistic in outlook and a correspondent both of Erasmus (*q.v.*) and of Pico della Mirandola (*q.v.*). Gradually, Zwingli moved to a view of the Bible as a sufficient revelation of God. His 1519 sermons on the New Testament attacked the abuses of the Roman Church, marking the beginning of the Protestant Reformation in Zurich. Believing in democratic government but not in the separation of church and state, he relied on the Swiss cantons, winning a number over to his point of view. The opposition of the "Forest cantons," however, led to war and to Zwingli's death in battle. Zwingli differed with Luther on the interpretation of the Lord's Supper, holding it to be a remembrance of the sacrifice Christ made once and for all. Zwingli's doctrines are present in th（ Sixty-Seven Articles he produced i） response to the criticism of the pope, an（ in the First Helvetic Confession produce（ by his disciples (*q.v.* Helvetic Confessions）